# MARIJUANA LAW, POLICY, AND AUTHORITY

## *Editorial Advisors*

**Rachel E. Barkow**
*Segal Family Professor of Regulatory Law and Policy*
*Faculty Director, Center on the Administration of Criminal Law*
*New York University School of Law*

**Erwin Chemerinsky**
*Dean and Distinguished Professor of Law*
*Raymond Pryke Professor of First Amendment Law*
*University of California, Irvine School of Law*

**Richard A. Epstein**
*Laurence A. Tisch Professor of Law*
*New York University School of Law*
*Peter and Kirsten Bedford Senior Fellow*
*The Hoover Institution*
*Senior Lecturer in Law*
*The University of Chicago*

**Ronald J. Gilson**
*Charles J. Meyers Professor of Law and Business*
*Stanford University*
*Marc and Eva Stern Professor of Law and Business*
*Columbia Law School*

**James E. Krier**
*Earl Warren DeLano Professor of Law*
*The University of Michigan Law School*

**Tracey L. Meares**
*Walton Hale Hamilton Professor of Law*
*Yale Law School*

**Richard K. Neumann, Jr.**
*Professor of Law*
*Maurice A. Deane School of Law at Hofstra University*

**Robert H. Sitkoff**
*John L. Gray Professor of Law*
*Harvard Law School*

**David Alan Sklansky**
*Stanley Morrison Professor of Law*
*Faculty Co-Director, Stanford Criminal Justice Center*
*Stanford Law School*

ASPEN CASEBOOK SERIES

# MARIJUANA LAW, POLICY, AND AUTHORITY

**ROBERT A. MIKOS**
*Professor of Law*
*Vanderbilt University Law School*

Copyright © 2017 Aspen Publishing. All Rights Reserved.

No part of this publication may be reproduced or transmitted in any form or by any means, electronic or mechanical, including photocopy, recording, or utilized by any information storage or retrieval system, without written permission from the publisher. For information about permissions or to request permissions online, visit us at www.AspenPublishing.com.

To contact Customer Service, e-mail customer.service@aspenpublishing.com, call 1-800-950-5259, or mail correspondence to:

Aspen Publishing
Attn: Order Department
PO Box 990
Frederick, MD 21705

Printed in the United States of America.

4 5 6 7 8 9 0

ISBN 978-1-4548-5942-0

**Library of Congress Cataloging-in-Publication Data**

Names: Mikos, Robert A., author.
Title: Marijuana law, policy, and authority / Robert A. Mikos, Professor of
  Law, Vanderbilt University Law School.
Description: Frederick, MD: Aspen Publishing, 2017. | Series: Aspen casebook series
Identifiers: LCCN 2017007279 | ISBN 9781454859420
Subjects: LCSH: Marijuana—Law and legislation—United States. | LCGFT: Casebooks.
Classification: LCC KF3891.M2 .M55 2017 | DDC 345.7302/77—dc23
LC record available at https://lccn.loc.gov/2017007279

# About Aspen Publishing

Aspen Publishing is a leading provider of educational content and digital learning solutions to law schools in the U.S. and around the world. Aspen provides best-in-class solutions for legal education through authoritative textbooks, written by renowned authors, and breakthrough products such as Connected eBooks, Connected Quizzing, and PracticePerfect.

The Aspen Casebook Series (famously known among law faculty and students as the "red and black" casebooks) encompasses hundreds of highly regarded textbooks in more than eighty disciplines, from large enrollment courses, such as Torts and Contracts to emerging electives such as Sustainability and the Law of Policing. Study aids such as the *Examples & Explanations* and the *Emanuel Law Outlines* series, both highly popular collections, help law students master complex subject matter.

**Major products, programs, and initiatives include:**

- **Connected eBooks** are enhanced digital textbooks and study aids that come with a suite of online content and learning tools designed to maximize student success. Designed in collaboration with hundreds of faculty and students, the Connected eBook is a significant leap forward in the legal education learning tools available to students.

- **Connected Quizzing** is an easy-to-use formative assessment tool that tests law students' understanding and provides timely feedback to improve learning outcomes. Delivered through CasebookConnect.com, the learning platform already used by students to access their Aspen casebooks, Connected Quizzing is simple to implement and integrates seamlessly with law school course curricula.

- **PracticePerfect** is a visually engaging, interactive study aid to explain commonly encountered legal doctrines through easy-to-understand animated videos, illustrative examples, and numerous practice questions. Developed by a team of experts, PracticePerfect is the ideal study companion for today's law students.

- The **Aspen Learning Library** enables law schools to provide their students with access to the most popular study aids on the market across all of their courses. Available through an annual subscription, the online library consists of study aids in e-book, audio, and video formats with full text search, note-taking, and highlighting capabilities.

- Aspen's **Digital Bookshelf** is an institutional-level online education bookshelf, consolidating everything students and professors need to ensure success. This program ensures that every student has access to affordable course materials from day one.

- **Leading Edge** is a community centered on thinking differently about legal education and putting those thoughts into actionable strategies. At the core of the program is the Leading Edge Conference, an annual gathering of legal education thought leaders looking to pool ideas and identify promising directions of exploration.

*Dedication*

*for Mom and for Cindy, Charlotte, and Henry*

# Summary of Contents

| | |
|---|---|
| *Contents* | xi |
| *Preface* | xxvii |
| *Acknowledgments* | xxix |

## PART I
## INTRODUCTORY MATERIALS — 1

**CHAPTER 1**
Introduction — 3

**CHAPTER 2**
What Is Marijuana? — 17

## PART II
## MARIJUANA USERS — 33

**CHAPTER 3**
The Regulation of Marijuana Users in Prohibition Regimes — 35

**CHAPTER 4**
The Regulation of Marijuana Users in Legalization Regimes — 99

**CHAPTER 5**
Policy Toward Marijuana Users — 195

**CHAPTER 6**
Authority over Marijuana Users — 253

## PART III
## MARIJUANA SUPPLIERS — 301

**CHAPTER 7**
The Regulation of Marijuana Suppliers in Prohibition Regimes — 303

**CHAPTER 8**
The Regulation of Marijuana Suppliers in Legalization Regimes — 413

**CHAPTER 9**
Policy Toward Marijuana Suppliers — 483

**CHAPTER 10**
Authority over Marijuana Suppliers — 527

## PART IV
# THIRD PARTIES  569

### CHAPTER 11
### The Regulation of Third Parties  571

### CHAPTER 12
### The Law, Policy, and Authority Issues Confronting Professionals  601

### CHAPTER 13
### The Law, Policy, and Authority Issues Confronting Businesses  645

### CHAPTER 14
### The Law, Policy, and Authority Issues Confronting Government Officials  697

*Table of Cases*  735
*Index*  741

# Contents

*Preface*     xxvii
*Acknowledgments*     xxix

## PART I
## INTRODUCTORY MATERIALS     1

### CHAPTER 1
### Introduction     3

    A. Why Care About Marijuana Law and Policy?     4
    B. Using This Book     7
       1. The Topics Covered in the Book     7
       2. The Organization of the Book     9
       3. The Features of the Book     13

### CHAPTER 2
### What Is Marijuana?     17

    A. What Is Marijuana?     17
          Notes and Questions     20
    B. Controversies over the Legal Definition of Marijuana     21
       1. Is It Still Marijuana if It Does Not Contain THC?     21
          *New Hampshire Hemp Council, Inc. v. Marshall*     22
          Notes and Questions     25
       2. Is Cannabis Indica Covered by the Definition of Marijuana?     27
          *United States v. Honneus*     28
          Notes and Questions     29
       3. Is Synthetic Marijuana (K2, Spice, etc.) Considered (or Treated Like) Marijuana?     29
          Notes and Questions     31

## PART II
# MARIJUANA USERS     33

### CHAPTER 3
## The Regulation of Marijuana Users in Prohibition Regimes     35

- A. What Is Simple Possession?     35
  - Notes and Questions     36
  - 1. Culpable Knowledge     37
    - a. Proof of Knowledge     38
      - *Ervin v. Virginia*     38
      - Notes and Questions     45
    - b. Presumptions Regarding Knowledge     45
      - *Missouri v. Bell*     45
      - Notes and Questions     46
    - c. Knowledge of the Substance's Nature     47
      - (i) Proof of Knowledge About a Substance's Nature     48
        - *Missouri v. Paul*     48
        - Notes and Questions     50
      - (ii) Knowledge of the Law     51
        - *Iowa v. Heinrichs*     52
        - Notes and Questions     54
  - 2. Control     54
    - *Regan v. Wyoming*     54
    - Notes and Questions     57
    - a. Control and Ownership     57
      - *Oregon v. Fries*     57
      - *Iowa v. Bash*     60
      - Notes and Questions     61
    - b. Duration of Control     62
    - c. Proof of Control     63
      - (i) Exclusive Access     63
        - *In Re R.L.H.*     64
        - Notes and Questions     65
      - (ii) Non-exclusive Access     66
        - *Iowa v. Cashen*     66
        - Notes and Questions     68
        - *Iowa v. Henderson*     69
        - Notes and Questions     71
      - (iii) Joint Possession     72
        - *Folk v. Maryland*     72
        - Notes and Questions     74

|  |  |  |
|---|---|---|
| 3. | Marijuana | 75 |
|  | Notes and Questions | 75 |
| 4. | Defenses | 77 |
|  | a. Necessity | 77 |
|  | *United States v. Randall* | 77 |
|  | Notes and Questions | 80 |
|  | *United States v. Oakland Cannabis Buyers' Coop.* | 80 |
|  | Notes and Questions | 82 |
|  | b. Innocent Possession | 83 |
|  | Notes and Questions | 84 |
|  | c. Unwitting Possession | 84 |
|  | *City of Kennewick v. Day* | 85 |
|  | Notes and Questions | 87 |
| B. What Are the Sanctions for Simple Possession? | | 87 |
| 1. | Criminal Sanctions | 87 |
|  | *North Carolina v. Mitchell* | 89 |
|  | Notes and Questions | 91 |
| 2. | Civil Sanctions | 92 |
|  | *United States v. One Clipper Bow Ketch Nisku* | 93 |
|  | Notes and Questions | 95 |
|  | *Illinois ex rel Neal v. Ryan* | 95 |
|  | Notes and Questions | 96 |
| 3. | Sanctions Under Decriminalization | 96 |
| 4. | Actual Versus Authorized Sanctions | 97 |
|  | Notes and Questions | 98 |

## CHAPTER 4
## The Regulation of Marijuana Users in Legalization Regimes   99

|  |  |  |
|---|---|---|
| A. Who Is Allowed to Possess and Use Marijuana? | | 100 |
| 1. | Medical Marijuana Regimes | 100 |
|  | a. Qualifying Condition | 101 |
|  | *Washington v. Fry* | 101 |
|  | Notes and Questions | 105 |
|  | *California v. Spark* | 106 |
|  | Notes and Questions | 109 |
|  | b. Recommendation | 110 |
|  | *Washington v. Shepherd* | 111 |
|  | Notes and Questions | 113 |
|  | c. Registration | 116 |
|  | Notes and Questions | 117 |

|  |  |
|---|---|
| d. Other Limitations on Eligibility | 119 |
| (i) Residency | 119 |
| (ii) Age | 119 |
| (iii) Criminal History | 120 |
| Notes and Questions | 121 |
| 2. The Special Case of CBD States | 123 |
| Notes and Questions | 124 |
| 3. Recreational Marijuana States | 124 |
| Notes and Questions | 125 |
| B. What Limitations Are Imposed on the Possession and Use of Marijuana? | 125 |
| 1. Quantity | 126 |
| Notes and Questions | 127 |
| 2. Purpose | 129 |
| Notes and Questions | 130 |
| 3. Type | 131 |
| Notes and Questions | 131 |
| 4. Place | 133 |
| a. Public | 133 |
| *New York v. Jackson* | 134 |
| Notes and Questions | 139 |
| b. Schools | 141 |
| Notes and Questions | 142 |
| 5. Driving Under the Influence | 143 |
| a. DUI-Impaired | 143 |
| *Pennsylvania v. Hutchins* | 144 |
| *United States v. Davis* | 146 |
| Notes and Questions | 149 |
| b. DUI-Per Se | 149 |
| (i) What Is Marijuana for Purposes of DUI-per se Laws? | 150 |
| *Arizona ex rel. Montgomery v. Harris* | 150 |
| Notes and Questions | 154 |
| (ii) Proof of the Presence of Marijuana | 154 |
| *Illinois v. McPeak* | 155 |
| Notes and Questions | 156 |
| 6. Other, Forgotten(?) Crimes | 157 |
| *California v. Young* | 157 |
| Notes and Questions | 159 |
| C. Legal Protections | 161 |
| 1. Search | 161 |
| a. Recreational Marijuana States | 162 |
| *Alaska v. Crocker* | 162 |
| Notes and Questions | 166 |

|   |   |
|---|---|
| b. Decriminalization States | 166 |
| *Oregon v. Smalley* | 166 |
| *Massachusetts v. Cruz* | 168 |
| Notes and Questions | 170 |
| c. Medical Marijuana States | 172 |
| *Washington v. Fry* | 172 |
| Notes and Questions | 177 |
| 2. Prosecution | 178 |
| a. Immunity and Affirmative Defenses | 179 |
| *Michigan v. Hartwick* | 180 |
| Notes and Questions | 187 |
| b. The Necessity Defense | 189 |
| *Washington v. Kurtz* | 189 |
| Notes and Questions | 193 |

## CHAPTER 5
## Policy Toward Marijuana Users — 195

|   |   |
|---|---|
| A. What Are Marijuana's Benefits? | 195 |
| 1. Medical Benefits | 196 |
| a. The DEA's Position on Marijuana's Medical Benefits | 196 |
| *Department of Health and Human Services*, Basis for the Recommendation for Maintaining Marijuana in Schedule I of the Controlled Substances Act | 197 |
| Notes and Questions | 200 |
| b. The States' Positions on Marijuana's Medical Benefits | 203 |
| Notes and Questions | 206 |
| 2. Recreational Benefits | 210 |
| *Douglas Husak*, For Drug Legalization | 210 |
| Notes and Questions | 212 |
| B. What Are Marijuana's Harms? | 213 |
| 1. The Harms of Marijuana Use | 214 |
| *Department of Health and Human Services*, Basis for the Recommendation for Maintaining Marijuana in Schedule I of the Controlled Substances Act, (cont'd) | 214 |
| Notes and Questions | 218 |
| 2. Which Harms Should Inform Policy? | 222 |
| *Ravin v. Alaska* | 223 |
| Notes and Questions | 225 |
| C. How Do Policymakers Influence Marijuana Use (or Its Harms)? | 227 |
| 1. Law's Impact on Overall Use | 227 |
| a. Legal Sanctions | 227 |
| Notes and Questions | 229 |

|  |  |
|---|---|
| b. Marijuana Prices | 230 |
| Notes and Questions | 231 |
| c. Transaction Costs | 231 |
| Notes and Questions | 232 |
| d. Individual Attitudes Toward Marijuana | 232 |
| (i) Media Campaigns | 233 |
| Notes and Questions | 234 |
| (ii) Signaling Through Law | 235 |
| Notes and Questions | 236 |
| e. Social Norms | 236 |
| Notes and Questions | 238 |
| f. Review | 239 |
| Notes and Questions | 239 |
| 2. Law's Impact on Unapproved Use | 239 |
| Notes and Questions | 240 |
| 3. Driving Harms and DUI | 241 |
| *Andrea Roth*, The Uneasy Case for Marijuana as Chemical Impairment Under a Science-Based Jurisprudence of Dangerousness | 243 |
| Notes and Questions | 244 |
| D. What Are the Costs of Different Regulatory Approaches? | 245 |
| 1. Fiscal Costs | 245 |
| Notes and Questions | 246 |
| 2. Liberty Costs | 247 |
| a. Prohibition Regimes | 248 |
| *American Civil Liberties Union*, The War on Marijuana in Black and White | 248 |
| Notes and Questions | 249 |
| b. Legalization Regimes | 249 |
| Notes and Questions | 250 |

## CHAPTER 6
## Authority over Marijuana Users

|  | 253 |
|---|---|
| A. What Is the Scope of the Federal Government's Authority over Marijuana Possession and Use? | 253 |
| 1. Federalism Constraints | 253 |
| *Gonzales v. Raich* | 254 |
| Notes and Questions | 265 |
| 2. Due Process Constraints | 266 |
| *Raich v. Gonzales* | 266 |
| Notes and Questions | 270 |
| B. How Is Authority Allocated *Within* the Federal Government? | 272 |
| 1. The Executive Branch's Scheduling Authority | 272 |
| 2. Limits Imposed by Treaty Obligations | 274 |

|   |   |   |
|---|---|---|
| 3. | The Criteria for Re-Scheduling | 275 |
| 4. | The Role of the DEA and FDA | 275 |
|   | Notes and Questions | 276 |

C. What Authority Do the States Have over Marijuana Possession and Use? 277
   1. Preemption Constraints 278
      *Robert A. Mikos*, On the Limits of Supremacy: Medical Marijuana and the States' Overlooked Power to Legalize Federal Crime 278
      Notes and Questions 282
   2. Right to Travel Constraints 283
     a. Denying Non-residents the Benefits of State Law 283
       *Brannon Denning*, One Toke over the (State) Line: Constitutional Limits on "Pot Tourism" Restrictions 284
       Notes and Questions 287
     b. Refusing to Apply Other States' Laws 288
       Notes and Questions 289
     c. Regulating Residents' Out-of-State Conduct 289
       Notes and Questions 289
D. How Is Authority Allocated *Within* the States? 290
   1. Ballot Initiatives 291
      *Michael Vitiello*, Why the Initiative Process Is the Wrong Way to Go: Lessons We Should Have Learned from Proposition 215 291
      Notes and Questions 293
   2. Localism 295
     a. Local Regulations that Are Stricter than State Regulations 295
       *City of North Charleston v. Harper* 295
       Notes and Questions 297
     b. Local Regulations that Are More Permissive than State Regulations 297
       *Joslin v. Fourteenth District Judge* 298
       Notes and Questions 298
       *Ruggles v. Yagong* 299
       Notes and Questions 300

## PART III
# MARIJUANA SUPPLIERS     301

### CHAPTER 7
## The Regulation of Marijuana Suppliers in Prohibition Regimes     303

A. What Are Marijuana Supply Offenses? 304
   1. Manufacture 304
      Notes and Questions 304
     a. Manufacture of Hash Oil 305
       *Utah v. Horsley* 305
       Notes and Questions 306

|   |   |   |   |
|---|---|---|---|
| | b. Manufacture for Personal Use | | 308 |
| |    *Massachusetts v. Palmer* | | 308 |
| |    Notes and Questions | | 312 |
| | c. Proof of Manufacturing | | 313 |
| |    *Idaho v. Vinton* | | 313 |
| |    Notes and Questions | | 315 |
| 2. | Distribute | | 315 |
| | a. Commercial Purpose | | 316 |
| |    *Meek v. Mississippi* | | 316 |
| |    Notes and Questions | | 318 |
| |    *Massachusetts v. Jackson* | | 318 |
| |    Notes and Questions | | 320 |
| | b. Distribution Between Joint Possessors | | 323 |
| |    *United States v. Swiderski* | | 324 |
| |    Notes and Questions | | 326 |
| 3. | Possession with Intent to Distribute or to Manufacture | | 327 |
| | Notes and Questions | | 327 |
| | a. Proof of Intent to Distribute | | 328 |
| |    *United States v. Glenn* | | 328 |
| |    *North Carolina v. Wilkins* | | 329 |
| |    Notes and Questions | | 330 |
| | b. Proof of *Defendant's* Intent | | 331 |
| |    *Louisiana v. Kelly* | | 332 |
| |    Notes and Questions | | 334 |
| | c. Intent to Distribute the Marijuana in Possession | | 334 |
| |    Notes and Questions | | 334 |
| 4. | Attempts | | 335 |
| | *Lewis v. Virginia* | | 335 |
| | Notes and Questions | | 337 |
| 5. | Review and Double Jeopardy Issues | | 338 |
| | Notes and Questions | | 340 |
| 6. | Defenses | | 341 |
| | a. Entrapment | | 341 |
| |    (i)  The Conventional Entrapment Defense | | 341 |
| |    (ii)  Entrapment by Estoppel and DOJ Enforcement Guidelines | | 343 |
| |        *United States v. Washington* | | 343 |
| |        Notes and Questions | | 349 |
| |        *Deputy Attorney General James M. Cole*, Guidance Regarding Marijuana Enforcement | | 349 |
| |        Notes and Questions | | 352 |
| | b. Congressional Spending Limitations | | 353 |
| |    *United States v. McIntosh* | | 353 |
| |    Notes and Questions | | 357 |

|   |   |   | c. Jury Nullification | 358 |
|---|---|---|---|---|
|   |   |   | *United States v. Rosenthal* | 358 |
|   |   |   | Notes and Questions | 361 |
| B. | What Are the Criminal Sanctions for Supplying Marijuana? | | | 362 |
|   | 1. | Calculating Sentences | | 362 |
|   |   | Notes and Questions | | 366 |
|   | 2. | Measuring Quantity | | 367 |
|   |   | a. THC Content | | 367 |
|   |   | b. Weight of Material That Is Not Marijuana | | 367 |
|   |   | c. Weight of Marijuana Plants | | 368 |
|   |   | Notes and Questions | | 369 |
|   |   | d. What Is a "Plant"? | | 371 |
|   |   | e. Aggregating Quantities | | 371 |
|   |   | f. Knowledge of Quantity | | 372 |
|   | 3. | Sentencing for "Fake" Marijuana | | 373 |
|   |   | *Conner v. Indiana* | | 374 |
|   |   | Notes and Questions | | 375 |
|   | 4. | Aggravated Circumstances | | 375 |
|   |   | Notes and Questions | | 377 |
|   | 5. | What Sentences Are Actually Imposed? | | 378 |
|   |   | Notes and Questions | | 379 |
| C. | What Are the Civil Sanctions for Supplying Marijuana? | | | 379 |
|   | 1. | Forfeiture | | 379 |
|   |   | a. Property Subject to Seizure | | 379 |
|   |   | Notes and Questions | | 380 |
|   |   | b. Forfeiture Procedures | | 381 |
|   |   | (i) Criminal Forfeiture | | 381 |
|   |   | Notes and Questions | | 381 |
|   |   | (ii) Civil Forfeiture | | 382 |
|   |   | *United States v. $61,200.00 in U.S. Currency, More or Less* | | 383 |
|   |   | Notes and Questions | | 386 |
|   |   | c. Defenses to Forfeiture Actions | | 386 |
|   |   | (i) The Eighth Amendment | | 387 |
|   |   | *United States v. Levesque* | | 387 |
|   |   | Notes and Questions | | 389 |
|   |   | (ii) The Innocent Owner Defense | | 389 |
|   |   | *von Hofe v. United States* | | 390 |
|   |   | Notes and Questions | | 392 |
|   |   | d. The Appeal of Civil Forfeiture | | 394 |
|   |   | *United States v. Real Property and Improvements Located at 1840 Embarcadero, Oakland, California* | | 394 |
|   |   | Notes and Questions | | 395 |

|   |   |   |
|---|---|---|
| 2. Taxes | | 396 |
| a. Special Marijuana Taxes | | 396 |
| b. Section 280E | | 397 |
| *Benjamin M. Leff*, Tax Planning for Marijuana Dealers | | 397 |
| Notes and Questions | | 399 |
| 3. RICO | | 400 |
| *Robert A. Mikos*, A Critical Appraisal of the Department of Justice's New Approach to Medical Marijuana | | 400 |
| *Safe Streets Alliance v. Alternative Holistic Healing, LLC* | | 403 |
| Notes and Questions | | 405 |
| 4. Trademark (and Other Intellectual Property) | | 406 |
| *In re Morgan Brown* | | 407 |
| Notes and Questions | | 409 |

## CHAPTER 8
## The Regulation of Marijuana Suppliers in Legalization Regimes — 413

A. Personal Supply — 413
  1. May Users Cultivate Their Own Marijuana? — 413
    Notes and Questions — 416
  2. What Limits Are Imposed on User Cultivation? — 416
    Notes and Questions — 417
  3. May Users Grow Collectively? — 418
    *California v. Colvin* — 418
    Notes and Questions — 421
  4. May Lawful Users Distribute Marijuana to Other Lawful Users? — 424
    *Michigan v. McQueen* — 425
    Notes and Questions — 429
  5. May Anyone Assist Patients with the Cultivation and Handling of Marijuana? — 429
    a. Who May Serve as a Caregiver? — 431
      *California v. Mentch* — 432
      Notes and Questions — 436
    b. What Limits Are Imposed on Caregivers? — 437
      (i) Number of Patients — 437
        *Washington v. Shupe* — 438
        Notes and Questions — 439
      (ii) Compensation — 440
        Notes and Questions — 440
  6. What Legal Protections Do Users and Caregivers Enjoy as Suppliers? — 440
B. Commercial Supply — 443
  1. Who Is Allowed to Produce and Sell Marijuana Commercially? — 444
    Notes and Questions — 444

|  |  |  |  |  |
|---|---|---|---|---|
|  |  | a. The Number of Licenses | 445 |
|  |  | Notes and Questions | 445 |
|  |  | b. Who Can Get a License? | 446 |
|  |  | Notes and Questions | 447 |
|  |  | c. The Role of Criminal History | 447 |
|  |  | Notes and Questions | 450 |
|  |  | d. The Role of Residency | 451 |
|  |  | Notes and Questions | 452 |
|  |  | e. Other Criteria | 452 |
|  |  | (i) Non-profit Status | 452 |
|  |  | Notes and Questions | 453 |
|  |  | (ii) Geography | 453 |
|  |  | Notes and Questions | 454 |
|  | 2. | What Regulations Do States Impose on Commercial Licensees? | 455 |
|  |  | a. Vertical Integration | 455 |
|  |  | Notes and Questions | 456 |
|  |  | b. Product Testing, Labeling, and Packaging | 456 |
|  |  | (i) Testing | 456 |
|  |  | Notes and Comments | 458 |
|  |  | (ii) Labeling and Packaging | 458 |
|  |  | Notes and Questions | 461 |
|  |  | c. Sales | 462 |
|  |  | Notes and Questions | 463 |
|  |  | d. Advertising | 464 |
|  |  | Notes and Questions | 465 |
|  |  | e. Reporting | 466 |
|  |  | Notes and Questions | 467 |
|  | 3. | How Are Licensees Disciplined? | 468 |
|  |  | a. Investigations | 468 |
|  |  | Notes and Questions | 469 |
|  |  | b. Disciplinary Process | 472 |
|  |  | Notes and Questions | 474 |
|  |  | c. Licensing Sanctions | 475 |
|  |  | Notes and Questions | 477 |
| C. | Government Supply |  | 478 |
|  | Notes and Questions |  | 479 |
| D. | Summary |  | 480 |
|  | Notes and Questions |  | 481 |

## CHAPTER 9
## Policy Toward Marijuana Suppliers — 483

| | | | |
|---|---|---|---|
| A. | How Does the Regulation of Supply Impact Use? | 483 |
|  | 1. Supply Prohibitions and Marijuana Consumption | 484 |
|  |  a. Prohibition, Prices, and Consumption | 484 |
|  |   Notes and Questions | 486 |

|   |   |   |   |   |
|---|---|---|---|---|
| | | b. The Magnitude of Prohibition's Impact on Price and Consumption | | 486 |
| | | *Jonathan Caulkins, Beau Kilmer, and Mark A.R. Kleiman,* Marijuana Legalization: What Everyone Needs to Know | | 487 |
| | | Notes and Questions | | 488 |
| | 2. Legalized Supply and Marijuana Use | | | 489 |
| | | a. Marijuana Taxes | | 489 |
| | | Notes and Questions | | 491 |
| | | (i) Designing a Tax | | 491 |
| | | | *Jonathan P. Caulkins et al.,* Considering Marijuana Legalization: Insights for Vermont and Other Jurisdictions | 491 |
| | | | Notes and Questions | 494 |
| | | (ii) Evasion | | 495 |
| | | | *Robert A. Mikos,* State Taxation of Marijuana Distribution and Other Federal Crimes | 495 |
| | | | Notes and Questions | 498 |
| | | b. Product Packaging and Labeling Requirements | | 499 |
| | | Notes and Questions | | 500 |
| | | c. Marijuana Advertising Restrictions | | 501 |
| | | (i) Do Advertising Restrictions Violate the First Amendment? | | 501 |
| | | | *Alex Kreit,* What Will Federal Marijuana Reform Look Like? | 501 |
| | | | Notes and Questions | 503 |
| | | (ii) Alternatives to Restricting Advertising | | 504 |
| | | | *Blue Ribbon Commission on Marijuana Policy,* Pathways Report: Policy Options for Regulating Marijuana in California | 504 |
| | | | Notes and Questions | 505 |
| | | d. Regulations Affecting Industry Structure | | 507 |
| | | (i) Banning Commercial Supply | | 507 |
| | | | *Montana Cannabis Indus. Ass'n v. Montana* | 507 |
| | | | Notes and Questions | 510 |
| | | (ii) Licensing Rules Restricting Industry Concentration | | 512 |
| | | | Notes and Questions | 512 |
| | | (iii) Government-Owned and -Operated Marijuana Suppliers | | 515 |
| | | | *Jonathan P. Caulkins et al.,* Considering Marijuana Legalization: Insights for Vermont and Other Jurisdictions (cont'd) | 515 |
| | | | Notes and Questions | 517 |
| B. Regulatory Costs | | | | 517 |
| | 1. Fiscal Costs | | | 518 |
| | | Notes and Questions | | 520 |
| | 2. Liberty Costs | | | 520 |
| | | (i) Minority Participation in the Legal Marijuana Industry | | 521 |
| | | | *Amanda Chicago Lewis,* How Black People Are Being Shut Out of America's Weed Boom | 521 |

|  |  |
|---|---|
| Notes and Questions | 522 |
| (ii) How Can States Boost Minority Participation in the Legal Marijuana Industry? | 522 |
| *The Attorney General of Maryland, Office of Counsel to the General Assembly*, Letter to Delegate Chris West, March 13, 2015 | 523 |
| Notes and Questions | 524 |

## CHAPTER 10
## Authority over Marijuana Suppliers — 527

| | |
|---|---|
| A. Can the President Stop Enforcing the Federal Marijuana Ban? | 527 |
| Sam Kamin, Prosecutorial Discretion in the Context of Immigration and Marijuana Law Reform: The Search for a Limiting Principle | 528 |
| Notes and Questions | 531 |
| B. Are State Licensing Laws and Similar Regulations Preempted by the Federal CSA? | 533 |
|    1. An Introduction to Preemption | 533 |
|       Robert A. Mikos, Preemption Under the Controlled Substances Act | 533 |
|    2. The State Suit Against Amendment 64 | 535 |
|       *States of Nebraska and Oklahoma v. State of Colorado*, Complaint | 535 |
|       Notes and Questions | 544 |
| C. May Local Governments Ban State-Approved Production and Distribution of Marijuana? | 550 |
|    1. Introduction to Local Authority | 550 |
|       Robert A. Mikos, Marijuana Localism | 550 |
|       Notes and Questions | 552 |
|    2. Why Have Courts Reached Different Conclusions Regarding Local Authority to Regulate Marijuana Supply? | 553 |
|      a. The View that Local Bans Are Permitted | 553 |
|        *City of Riverside v. Inland Empire Patients Health & Wellness Ctr., Inc.* | 553 |
|        Notes and Questions | 558 |
|      b. The View that Local Bans Are Preempted | 558 |
|        *Ter Beek v. City of Wyoming* | 558 |
|        Notes and Questions | 560 |
| D. Who *Should* Regulate the Supply of Marijuana? | 560 |
|    Robert A. Mikos, Marijuana Localism (cont'd) | 561 |
|    Notes and Questions | 568 |

## PART IV
# THIRD PARTIES 569

### CHAPTER 11
## The Regulation of Third Parties 571

- A. Aiding and Abetting 571
  - *Washington v. Gladstone* 573
  - Notes and Questions 575
- B. Conspiracy 577
  - *Massachusetts v. Camerano* 578
  - Notes and Questions 581
- C. Financial Crimes 584
  1. Money Laundering 587
     a. Knowledge (and Willful Ignorance) 589
        - *United States v. Campbell* 589
        - Notes and Questions 593
     b. Designed to Conceal 593
        - *United States v. Corchado-Peralta* 593
        - Notes and Questions 597
  2. Use of Criminal Proceeds 597
     - Notes and Questions 598

### CHAPTER 12
## The Law, Policy, and Authority Issues Confronting Professionals 601

- A. Physicians 601
  1. May Physicians Be Sanctioned for Recommending Marijuana? 602
     - *Conant v. Walters* 602
     - Notes and Questions 607
  2. What Must Physicians Do to Make Valid Recommendations? 610
     - Notes and Questions 614
  3. Are Physicians Willing and Able to Recommend Marijuana? 616
     - Notes and Questions 618
  4. Are Some Physicians Too Willing to Recommend Marijuana? 618
     - *Colorado Office of The State Auditor,* Medical Marijuana Regulatory System, Part II (June 2013) 619
     - Notes and Questions 624
- B. Attorneys 626
  1. What Services May Attorneys Provide to Marijuana Users and Suppliers? 626
     a. The Restrictive Interpretation of Rule 1.2 627
        - *Ohio Supreme Court, Board of Professional Conduct,* Ethical Implications for Lawyers under Ohio's Medical Marijuana Law 627
        - Notes and Questions 629

   b. The Permissive Interpretation of Rule 1.2   631
    *New York State Bar Association Committee on Professional Ethics*, Counseling Clients in Illegal Conduct; Medical Marijuana Law   631
    Notes and Questions   634
  2. May Attorneys Use or Supply Marijuana?   635
   Notes and Questions   637
  3. Can Federal Courts Punish Attorneys for Assisting Marijuana Users and Suppliers?   638
   *Eli Wald et al.*, Representing Clients in the Marijuana Industry: Navigating State and Federal Rules   639
   Notes and Questions   644

## CHAPTER 13
## The Law, Policy, and Authority Issues Confronting Businesses   645

 A. Contracting Parties, Generally   645
  1. Will Courts Enforce Contracts with Marijuana Suppliers?   645
   *Hammer v. Today's Health Care II, Co.*   646
   Notes and Questions   648
   *Green Earth Wellness Ctr., LLC v. Atain Specialty Ins. Co.*   649
   Notes and Questions   651
  2. What Are the Consequences If Contracts Are Unenforceable?   652
   *Luke Scheuer*, Are "Legal" Marijuana Contracts "Illegal"?   652
   Notes and Questions   654
 B. Landlords   655
  1. May Landlords Rent Property to Tenants Who Use or Supply Marijuana on It?   655
   Notes and Questions   656
  2. Can Landlords Ever Be Sanctioned for *Refusing* to Rent to Marijuana Users?   659
   Notes and Questions   660
 C. Employers   662
  1. Are Employers Ever Required to Accommodate an Employee's Marijuana Use?   662
   a. Express Duty to Accommodate   662
    Notes and Questions   663
   b. Implied Duty to Accommodate   665
    *Ross v. RagingWire Telecommunications, Inc.*   665
    Notes and Questions   671
  2. Is a State-Imposed Duty to Accommodate Marijuana Use Preempted by Federal Law?   672
   *Emerald Steel Fabricators, Inc. v. Bureau of Labor and Industries*   673
   Notes and Questions   678

| | |
|---|---|
| D. Banks | 681 |
|    1. May Banks Do Business with the Marijuana Industry? | 681 |
|       *Julie Andersen Hill*, Banks, Marijuana, and Federalism | 681 |
|    2. *Should* Banks Be Allowed to Do Business with the Marijuana Industry? | 687 |
|       Notes and Questions | 688 |
|    3. Who Ultimately Decides the Marijuana Banking Question | 689 |
|       *Julie Andersen Hill*, Banks, Marijuana, and Federalism (cont'd) | 690 |
|       Notes and Questions | 694 |

## CHAPTER 14
## The Law, Policy, and Authority Issues Confronting Government Officials    697

| | |
|---|---|
| A. Could State Officials Be Criminally Prosecuted Under the Federal CSA? | 697 |
|    1. . . . for Growing and Selling Marijuana? | 698 |
|       *United States v. Rosenthal* | 699 |
|       Notes and Questions | 701 |
|    2. . . . for Returning Marijuana? | 704 |
|       *Office of the Attorney General, State of Michigan* | 705 |
|       *The City of Garden Grove v. Kha* | 706 |
|       Notes and Questions | 708 |
| B. Could State Officials Be Held Civilly Liable? | 710 |
|    *County of Butte v. Superior Court* | 711 |
|    Notes and Questions | 714 |
| C. Can State Officials Stop the Federal Government from Accessing Information They Collect About Marijuana Users/Suppliers? | 716 |
|    *United States v. Michigan Department of Community Health* | 716 |
|    Notes and Questions | 720 |
| D. Could State Agencies Lose Federal Funding because of State Reforms? | 722 |
|    1. Schools | 723 |
|       a. Higher Education | 723 |
|          Notes and Questions | 724 |
|       b. Primary Schools (K-12) | 725 |
|          *Colorado Legislative Council*, Student Medical Marijuana Use at School | 725 |
|          Notes and Questions | 726 |
|    2. Public Housing | 727 |
|       *Helen R. Kanovsky*, Medical Use of Marijuana and Reasonable Accommodation in Federal Public and Assisted Housing | 727 |
|       Notes and Questions | 731 |
| *Table of Cases* | 735 |
| *Index* | 741 |

# Preface

This is a first-of-its-kind textbook that explores the fascinating legal issues that surround marijuana users, their suppliers, and the sundry third parties (physicians, employers, investors, etc.) who deal with them. It surveys the competing approaches jurisdictions have adopted toward regulating marijuana, the policies behind those approaches, and the power that various federal, state, and local government actors have to pursue each of them. Chapter 1 provides more details about the content and features of the book and how it can be used in the classroom or as a reference work. It also explains why marijuana law and policy is such a worthwhile area of study, even for people who never intend to work in this field.

Although marijuana can be a divisive subject, the book strives to take an evenhanded approach to all of the issues it covers. It fully explores the different sides to the controversies surrounding marijuana law and policy, not to persuade the reader that any one position is necessarily correct, but to foster lively discussion and hone the reader's ability to think more critically about issues in the field. Through this evenhanded approach, I hope the book will help improve our discourse and decision-making concerning marijuana policy, wherever that may lead us.

If you have any feedback on the book, or if you are interested in teaching about any aspect of marijuana law and policy, I would be happy to hear from you.

Robert A. Mikos
March 2017
Nashville, Tennessee
robert.mikos@vanderbilt.edu

# Acknowledgments

Needless to say, writing a book about an emerging field of law—especially a dynamic one that is frought with conflicts—was no easy task. I could not have finished the book—indeed, I might not have even started it—without heaps of encouragement and help from many other people.

Throughout this project, my wonderful colleagues and students at Vanderbilt offered me their generous support and assistance—not to mention a few good-natured ribbings (e.g., "Will the book include rolling paper?"). I owe a special debt of gratitude to Owen Jones, who encouraged me to undertake this project in the first instance. Owen, Suzanna Sherry, Chris Slobogin, and Kevin Stack also offered sage advice on how to make the textbook accessible and engaging, and my Dean, Chris Guthrie, assisted my efforts to teach and write in this new field. Thank you as well to the many students who have taken my Marijuana Law and Policy classes at Vanderbilt: their enthusiasm for the subject has fueled my own. And thank you to my very capable research assistants Emily Burns, Sara Morgan, Aaron Rothbaum, and Rachel Johnston: their diligent research and analyses helped me to make sense of many developments in the law.

The book also benefited greatly from the perspectives of keen minds outside of Vanderbilt. I am especially grateful to the eight scholars who reviewed several draft chapters of the book and generously shared their insights, advice, and perspectives with me. I hope they agree the book is much improved as a result of their input! So thank you to Doug Berman, Jonathan Caulkins, Beau Kilmer, Rob MacCoun, Mark Osbeck, David S. Schwartz, Frank Snyder, and Jay Wexler. I am also grateful for insights gleaned from countless conversations with a host of other scholars, government officials, and practioners, including Phil Alma, Doug Greene, John Hudak, Sam Kamin, Alex Kreit, Shabnam Malek, Pat Oglesby, and Fred Yarger, among many others.

My publisher, Aspen Publishing, has been a generous sponsor. I am particularly grateful to David Herzig at Aspen Publishing, who was an early and enthusiastic backer of the project. I am also thankful for the team of developers and editors at The Froebe Group who helped bring the book to fruition—and especially Kathy Langone, Geoff Lokke, and Nick Walther. They not only provided thoughtful advice and feedback, but also exhibited patience with me as I continued to tinker with the book . . . Thank you!

Most importantly, I want to thank my family. Cindy provided unwavering and extraordinary support, especially during crunch time (which lasted a *long* time). And Charlotte and Henry often let Daddy work a few extra minutes after they got up . . . at 5AM. The book is done. Yes, Daddy can come out and play now.

## Acknowledgments

Lastly, I want to thank the many scholars, practitioners, and judges whose writings and other works have enriched my understanding of the topics discussed in the book, including the following who granted permission to include portions of their works in the book:

*Books and Articles*

American Bar Association, Model Rules of Professional Conduct, Rule 1.2(d), cmts. 9, 10, 12; Rule 8.4, cmts. 2, 7. Copyright © 2012 by the American Bar Association. Reproduced by permission. All rights reserved.

Blue Ribbon Commission on Marijuana Policy, Pathways Report: Policy Options for Regulating Marijuana in California (July 22, 2015). Courtesy of the Office of Lieutenant Governor Gavin Newsom and American Civil Liberties Union of California.

Caulkins, Jonathan P., Beau Kilmer, and Mark A. R. Kleiman. Marijuana Legalization: What Everyone Needs to Know? Copyright © 2016 by Oxford University Press. Reproduced by permission. All rights reserved.

Caulkins, Jonathan P., Beau Kilmer, Mark A. R. Kleiman, Robert J. MacCoun, Gregory Midgette, Pat Oglesby, and Peter H. Reuter. Considering Marijuana Legalization: Insights for Vermont and Other Jurisdictions. Copyright © 2015 by the RAND Corporation. Reproduced by permission. All rights reserved.

Hill, Julie Andersen, Banks, Marijuana, and Federalism, 65 Case Western Reserve Law Review 597 (2015). Copyright © 2015 by Julie Andersen Hill. Reproduced by permission. All rights reserved.

Lewis, Amanda Chicago. How Black People Are Being Shut Out of America's Weed Boom. BuzzFeed. Copyright © 2016 by BuzzFeed, Inc. Reproduced by permission. All rights reserved.

Wald, Eli, Eric Liebman, and Amanda Bertrand, Representing Clients in the Marijuana Industry: Navigating State and Federal Rules, 44 Colorado Lawyer 61 (2015). Copyright © 2015 by the Colorado Bar Association. Reproduced by permission. All rights reserved.

*Photographs and Images*

100% Pure Evil Botanical Incense. Courtesy of the United States Drug Enforcement Administration, El Paso Division.

1962 Plymouth Valiant V-200 Signet. Courtesy of sv1ambo / Wikimedia Commons.

Become a Burrito Taster poster. Courtesy of Above the Influence / Office of National Drug Control Policy.

Cannabis flower. Copyright © 2016 by Dale A. Clark / Stock Pot Images. Reproduced by permission. All rights reserved.

Cannabis patient identification card. Copyright © 2012 by Jeff Chiu / AP Images. Reproduced by permission. All rights reserved.

Cannabis, 1.5 grams. Copyright © 2016 by the RAND Drug Policy Research Center. Reproduced by permission. All rights reserved.

Chocolate brownie. Courtesy of Wikimedia Commons.

Colorado retail marijuana license. Copyright © 2014 by Rick Wilking / Reuters / Alamy Stock Photo. Reproduced by permission. All rights reserved.

## Acknowledgments

Colorado THC symbol. Courtesy of Colorado Department of Revenue, Marijuana Enforcement Division.

Dried oregano. Copyright © 2016 by Mirabile / Shutterstock. Reproduced by permission. All rights reserved.

Electronic cigarette. Copyright © 2016 by Tibanna79 / Shutterstock. Reproduced by permission. All rights reserved.

Harborside Health Center in Oakland, CA. Copyright © 2010 by John Patriquin / Portland Press Herald via Getty Images. Reproduced by permission. All rights reserved.

Joint in ashtray. Copyright © 2016 by Samantha Geballe / Stock Pot Images. Reproduced by permission. All rights reserved.

Ketch *Naga Lee*. Courtesy of Jean-Pierre Bazard / Wikimedia Commons.

Leafly strains. Copyright © 2017 by Leafly Holdings, Inc. Reproduced by permission. All rights reserved.

Loose marijuana. Courtesy of the United States Drug Enforcement Administration.

Map of licensed marijuana stores, downtown Denver, CO. Courtesy of Alan Kikuchi Design.

Medicinal cannabis dispensary. Copyright © 2016 by Mark Rutherford / Stock Pot Images. Reproduced by permission. All rights reserved.

Marijuana chocolate bar. Courtesy of Colorado Department of Revenue, Marijuana Enforcement Division.

Medical marijuana and cannabis accessories. Copyright © 2015 by Lew Robertson / Stock Pot Images. Reproduced by permission. All rights reserved.

Medical marijuana chocolate brownie. Copyright © 2016 by Mike Ledray / Shutterstock. Reproduced by permission. All rights reserved.

Medical marijuana shop in Venice Beach, Los Angeles, CA. Courtesy of Adam Jones / Flickr.

Nebraska drug tax stamp. Courtesy of marijuanastamps.com.

New Hampshire State Liquor Store. Courtesy of Peter Dutton / Flickr.

RFID tags on marijuana plants. Copyright © 2014 by Blaine Harrington III / Alamy Stock Photo. Reproduced by permission. All rights reserved.

Rootless marijuana cutting. Copyright © 2012 by Ben Holmes / CSD Centennial Seeds. Reproduced by permission. All rights reserved.

Snuff rolling, ashtray and cigar. Copyright © 2016 by Calamardebien / Dreamstime. Reproduced by permission. All rights reserved.

Vape pen at the Cannabis World Congress and Business Exposition. Copyright © 2016 by Nancy Kaszerman / ZUMA Wire / Alamy Live News. Reproduced by permission. All rights reserved.

# MARIJUANA LAW, POLICY, AND AUTHORITY

# PART I

# INTRODUCTORY MATERIALS

# CHAPTER 1

# Introduction

Following nearly two decades of regulatory reform in the states, marijuana law and policy has emerged as a robust and fascinating field of study. Abandoning the strict prohibitions that dominated the previous seven decades, and that are still in effect at the federal level, more than forty states have legalized marijuana in at least some circumstances. **Figure 1.1** displays the proliferation of state reforms from 1996 to 2016.

The chart depicts the running tally of states that have legalized (1) both the recreational and medical use of marijuana; (2) only the medical use of marijuana; and (3) only the medical use of cannabidiol (CBD), one of the chemicals found in marijuana.

The reforms have sparked lively debates about the content of marijuana regulations, the wisdom of competing regulatory approaches, and the authority of different government actors to choose among them. Who may use and supply marijuana under state law? Does legalization increase use of the drug? Could the President legalize marijuana without the passage of new congressional legislation? May the states legalize the drug while Congress forbids it? Even so, are state licensing requirements and similar regulations

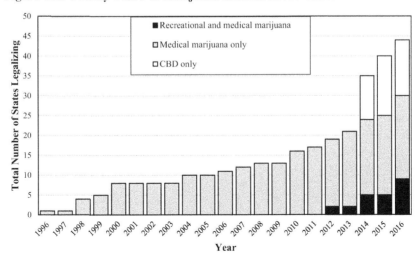

Figure 1.1. Twenty Years of Marijuana Reform in the States

preempted by federal law? These are a just a few of the intriguing questions that are now being confronted in this field.

The standard law school curriculum—and even courses devoted to drug law and policy—do not begin to prepare one for such questions. This first-of-its-kind textbook in Marijuana Law, Policy, and Authority is intended to fill this gap. It guides students, teachers, and practitioners alike through the competing approaches to regulating marijuana, the policies behind those approaches, and the power of various federal, state, and local government actors to pursue them. Importantly, the book takes an evenhanded approach to these often divisive issues. It fully explores the different sides of the many controversies surrounding marijuana law and policy, not to persuade the reader that any one position is necessarily correct, but to foster lively discussion and hone the reader's ability to think more critically about issues in the field.

The sections below provide further introduction to this burgeoning field and to the content, organization, and features of the book.

## A. WHY CARE ABOUT MARIJUANA LAW AND POLICY?

Given that you opened this book, you probably already have some inkling of why the subject matters. But because marijuana law and policy has undergone major upheavals of late, this section highlights a few reasons why this field has become so interesting and worthwhile of study.

First, and most obvious, the laws and policies governing marijuana affect a huge segment of the population. Marijuana is one of the most widely used substances in the United States. More than 44 percent of Americans aged 12 or older have tried marijuana sometime during their lives, and more than 22 million Americans are considered *regular* (i.e., past-month) users of the drug. Substance Abuse and Mental Health Services Administration, *Results from the 2014 National Survey on Drug Use and Health: Detailed Tables*, tbl. 1.12B, https://perma.cc/LH4J-723T. In fact, more people use marijuana than use *all other illicit substances combined*. *Id.* (estimating that 8.7 million people regularly use illicit drugs like heroin or abuse licit drugs like opioid painkillers).

The demand for marijuana has also attracted a large number of people willing to grow and distribute the drug, both licitly (at least at the state level) and illicitly. For example, as of September 2016, more than 600 vendors had obtained a license from the state of Colorado to sell medical and/or recreational marijuana. Colorado Dep't of Revenue, *MED Licensed Facilities*, https://perma.cc/BP55-F7JL. These licensees sold nearly $1 *billion* dollars' worth of marijuana in 2015 alone. Ricardo Baca, *Colorado marijuana sales skyrocket to more than $996 million in 2015*, The Cannabist (Feb. 9, 2016).

Figure 1.2. Map of Licensed Marijuana Stores in Downtown Denver, Colorado

But users and their suppliers are not the only ones who are affected by the laws and policies governing marijuana. A broad array of third parties who interact with users and suppliers—including physicians, lawyers, banks, schools, universities, landlords, insurers, investors, and employers, among others—are increasingly being drawn into the ambit of this field. For example, physicians are being asked to recommend marijuana to patients, a necessary step for those patients to obtain the legal protections created by state medical marijuana laws. Firms are being asked to accommodate their employees' medical use of marijuana, much as they accommodate their use of other state-approved drugs. Banks are being asked to provide loans and payment services to licensed marijuana growers and distributors, just as they do for other types of businesses. Even if these third parties never participate directly in the marijuana market itself, they are nonetheless affected by the laws and policies governing the drug.

The need for informed legal advice for all of these parties—users, suppliers, and various third parties—should be abundantly clear. Marijuana is one of the most highly regulated substances in the United States, and the laws governing users, suppliers, and third parties are incredibly complex, even in (and sometimes *especially* in) states that have legalized the drug. In prohibition regimes, questions abound concerning whether sharing a joint with a friend constitutes "distribution" of the drug (and thus is subject to harsh criminal sanctions), whether DOJ enforcement guidelines provide a defense in federal marijuana prosecutions, and whether suppliers are liable in civil Racketeer Influenced and Corrupt Organizations (RICO) lawsuits, among many other matters. Though prohibition has faded in popularity, these questions have not lost their relevance. To cite just two telling statistics: police made more than 700,000 arrests for marijuana-related offenses in 2014, Fed. Bureau of Investigation, *2014 Crime in the United States*, and there are roughly 12,000 people now serving time in *federal* prisons due principally to a conviction for a marijuana offense, Bureau of Justice Statistics, *Drug Offenders in Federal Prison: Estimates of Characteristics Based on Linked Data* (Oct. 2015).

Even in jurisdictions that have legalized marijuana, the drug remains subject to a litany of regulatory restrictions. Colorado, for example, has passed more than 150 pages of civil regulations governing just the retail distribution of marijuana. See Colorado Dep't of Revenue, Marijuana Enforcement Division, *Retail Marijuana Code*, https://perma.cc/4F6H-6EM3. Among many other things, Colorado's regulations require marijuana suppliers to apply for a special license from the state; maintain detailed records of inventory; install advanced security systems; submit to 24/7 web-based video monitoring; test, package, and label products in a particular way; and verify customer eligibility to purchase marijuana. The many firms that are supplying marijuana in Colorado and elsewhere need legal advice to help them comply with these and other regulations (not to mention federal prohibitions), akin to the advice regularly provided to firms in other highly regulated industries, like energy, alcohol, gaming, and pharmaceuticals.

Indeed, the need for informed legal advice is perhaps even more acute in this field as compared to others because of questions surrounding the enforceability of many of the aforementioned regulations. Conflicts among the policies pursued by different government actors have sparked challenges to federal, state, and local marijuana regulations and have exacerbated the confusion over the legal risks and obligations faced by marijuana users, their suppliers, and various third parties. Does Congress have the constitutional power to ban the simple possession and use of marijuana? May the DOJ suspend its enforcement of the congressional ban? Do the states have the authority to legalize possession and use of a drug that Congress strictly forbids? Even so, may they license private firms to produce and distribute the drug? May local governments ban distribution of the drug if their state allows it? May a state legislature repeal or amend a marijuana ballot initiative passed by the people of a state? Are contracts with marijuana distributors enforceable?

Not surprisingly, the legal market is already responding to the demand for advice in this field. Lawyers have developed boutique firms and practice groups dedicated to serving the market, including Vincente-Sederberg (which bills itself as the Marijuana Law Firm) and Harris-Bricken's Canna Law Group, among others. Enterprising lawyers have even founded the National Cannabis Bar Association. State bar associations have begun to issue special guidelines addressing the ethical issues that confront the growing number of lawyers practicing in the field. And a growing number of law schools are now offering courses on or related to marijuana law and policy.

Of course, marijuana law and policy also impacts other stakeholders in society besides lawyers and the people they represent. For one thing, marijuana affects the public health, for good or ill. In large part, the reforms depicted in **Figure 1.1** above reflect the belief that there is a "beneficial use for marijuana in treating or alleviating the pain or other symptoms associated with certain debilitating medical conditions." N.J. Code 24:6I-2(a) (establishing New Jersey's medical marijuana program). Outright prohibitions, by contrast, reflect the belief that marijuana is harmful to users and others, say, because it impairs driving, and the belief that the drug lacks any medical utility that might redeem it. *E.g.*, Dep't of Health and Human Services, *Basis for the Recommendation for Maintaining Marijuana in Schedule I of the Controlled Substances Act*, 81 Fed. Reg. 53690 (Aug. 12, 2016) (recommending against rescheduling marijuana under the federal Controlled Substances Act).

How marijuana is regulated also has a significant impact on public finances. By some estimates, circa 2010, prohibition regimes were spending between $1.2 billion and $6 billion combined (annually) enforcing their bans on marijuana. American Civil Liberties Union, *The War on Marijuana in Black and White*, 68-77 (2013) (surveying estimates). In contrast, some jurisdictions have reportedly turned marijuana into a net revenue *generator* for public budgets, by legalizing and taxing distribution of the drug. As an example, Colorado collected $103 million in taxes and fees from its licensed marijuana vendors in 2015. Colorado Dep't of Revenue, *Marijuana Tax Data*, https://www.colorado.gov/pacific/revenue/colorado-marijuana-tax-data. The possible impacts on public health and on public finance give citizens more reasons to care about this subject, even if they never plan to participate in the marijuana market themselves.

Given all of the reasons to care about marijuana law and policy, policymakers face a host of questions about how they should regulate the drug: Is marijuana beneficial? What are its harms? Which of those benefits and harms should inform policy decisions? Should marijuana be banned or allowed, and if allowed, for whom? How can jurisdictions prevent diversion of the drug to non-approved uses? How do different policies affect the use of marijuana and any harms associated with such use? What are the costs of competing approaches to regulating marijuana?

These are not idle or purely academic questions. In contrast to many other policy domains characterized by gridlock, marijuana law and policy is dynamic. **Figure 1.1** above captures just a small slice of the changes (big and small) that have been adopted in this domain in recent years, changes that have been fueled at least in part by growing public support for regulatory reform. *E.g.*, Pew Research Center, *6 Facts About Marijuana*, https://perma.cc/6DKN-UT47 (Apr. 14, 2015). In light of the interest the field is attracting, policymakers need to know what other jurisdictions are doing, how those regulations are performing, and what options they have the power to pursue. In other words, policymakers need informed advice, just like the people who are affected by their policies do.

A final reason why marijuana law and policy matters is that it may hold lessons for other fields as well. Marijuana law has been at the center of cutting-edge legal controversies over the President's duty to enforce the laws, the courts' obligation to apply the literal language of statutes and referenda, and the ability of private litigants to challenge state laws as preempted, among other issues. How courts and policymakers choose to resolve these controversies could have far-reaching ramifications. In fact, marijuana law can be used as a focal example to explore a host of important legal topics that are relevant for lawyers (and others) working in a range of fields and industries. Indeed, marijuana law provides a terrific vehicle for this purpose—after all, it takes little effort to explain marijuana or to get people interested in the subject.

## B. USING THIS BOOK

The book is designed to guide readers through the multifaceted legal and policy issues now confronting lawyers, lawmakers, judges, scholars, and students working in this emerging field. It gives readers an in-depth understanding of and ability to critically evaluate:

- the different ways of controlling the use and supply of marijuana and other substances
- the disagreements over whether marijuana use and similar behaviors should be controlled and how best to do so
- the complex battles between (and within) federal, state, and local governments for control over public policy domains, including (but hardly limited to) marijuana policy
- the interrelationship among law, policy, and authority

Although the book is written in a style that is familiar to law students and is thus well-suited for the law school classroom or as a desk reference for lawyers, it is designed to be accessible to non-law audiences as well. The book provides the non-lawyer or non-law student enough background to enable them to examine even the trickiest legal subjects. It is thus suitable for undergraduate and graduate courses across a variety of non-law disciplines, and, of course, for the reader pursuing the topic on her own.

The sections below discuss in more detail the topics covered by the book, the organization of its chapters, and its key design features.

### 1. The Topics Covered in the Book

The book explores three broad interrelated topics: the law, policy, and governmental authority surrounding marijuana. This section briefly explains the scope of each topic and the connections among them.

**The Substantive Law.** Several chapters of the book are devoted to surveying the competing approaches to regulating marijuana-related activities. These chapters detail the legal restrictions jurisdictions impose on marijuana users, suppliers, and third parties, and the legal consequences of violating those restrictions.

The substantive law chapters divide jurisdictions into two basic categories: prohibition regimes and legalization regimes. Prohibition regimes are those that ban outright the possession, manufacture, and distribution of marijuana (and related activities); they include regimes that have decriminalized marijuana—i.e., those that have reduced the sanctions for but do not yet allow the possession of marijuana. Legalization regimes, by contrast, are those that explicitly permit at least some people to possess, manufacture, and/or distribute marijuana for medical or other purposes without sanction. Sorting jurisdictions into these two broad categories makes the discussion of the law more manageable, but the book also highlights key differences among the jurisdictions within each of these categories, such as the differences among the three types of legalization regimes depicted in **Figure 1.1** above.

**Policy.** The book also explores the policies behind the competing regulatory approaches surveyed in the substantive law chapters. The policy chapters explore the *objectives* behind different substantive rules and the beliefs (both factual and philosophical) that animate those objectives. In other words, what are lawmakers trying to accomplish and why? The policy chapters also compare the *outcomes* produced by different regulatory regimes. In other words, how well do regulations achieve their objectives and what is sacrificed by pursuing those regulations? The discussions of policy objectives and outcomes enable readers to critically evaluate and more fully comprehend the laws governing marijuana.

**Authority.** Regulatory power in the United States is diffused both across and within different levels of government. The federal government and the states both wield some authority in this field, and a variety of officials within each level of government—from members of Congress to the deputies of a local township—have influenced how that power has been exercised. But they do not always agree about how marijuana should be regulated. Indeed, their divergent views have generated extensive litigation and debate over who has the authority to determine marijuana policy, as noted in Section A above.

The chapters devoted to authority issues guide readers through these power disputes. The chapters discuss key legal doctrines in federalism, separation of powers, localism, and individual rights that illuminate how courts resolve these controversies. Just as importantly, however, these chapters also discuss the practical (i.e., de facto) power these same actors wield over marijuana policy. Developments in this field over the last twenty years have demonstrated the need to consider both de jure (i.e., formal) and de facto power over marijuana.

Although each of these three topics is fascinating and significant in its own right, it is also important to recognize the connections among them—a theme emphasized throughout the book. Indeed, one would be hard-pressed to grasp many of the nuances in marijuana law, policy, or authority without having some understanding of each of the other topics.

Consider just one simple example to illustrate the connections among the topics. All states that have legalized marijuana for medical purposes now require prospective users to obtain a physician's "recommendation" to use the drug. The recommendation requirement and what it entails are essentially *substantive law* issues: To satisfy the requirement, for example, a physician must usually diagnose her patient with a designated condition, stipulate with some degree of confidence that marijuana would improve the patient's outlook, and submit forms to a state health agency attesting to these findings. The rationale for imposing the recommendation requirement is more of a *policy* issue: The requirement helps states limit access to marijuana. In theory, the recommendation ensures that only people who are using marijuana for *bona fide* medical purposes are shielded from criminal and civil sanctions under state law. But the reason why states require a "recommendation" as opposed to a "prescription"—a more familiar and well-tested requirement the states use to limit access to other controlled substances—stems from limitations on state and federal *authority*. The federal Drug Enforcement Agency (DEA) has threatened to punish physicians who prescribe marijuana, and the states cannot block the DEA from imposing those sanctions. But the DEA arguably cannot punish physicians for merely recommending marijuana, because a recommendation, unlike a prescription, is considered protected speech under the First Amendment (at least in the eyes of one important court). The states designed their recommendation requirement to exploit this limitation on the DEA's power and thereby defuse the threat posed by the agency's control over physician prescriptions. This example helps to illustrate the linkages among law, policy, and authority in this field. By highlighting such linkages, the book imparts a much richer and deeper understanding of marijuana law and policy.

## 2. The Organization of the Book

The heart of the book is divided into three parts (II-IV).[1] Each part explores the law, policy, and authority issues surrounding one distinct set of regulated parties: marijuana users, their suppliers, or the third parties who interact with users and suppliers. The paragraphs below highlight some of the specific topics covered in each part and the rationale behind discussing the three parties separately.

**Part II.** Part II, which includes Chapters 3-6, explores the law, policy, and authority issues that are most relevant to marijuana users. Chapter 3 begins by examining the law governing users in prohibition regimes. It elaborates on the elements of the key prohibition directed at users in such regimes, namely, bans on the simple possession of marijuana; the defenses users might raise against possession charges (e.g., the defense of necessity); and the criminal and civil sanctions that commonly attach to simple possession offenses. Chapter 4 then surveys the laws governing users in legalization regimes, including medical marijuana states, recreational marijuana states, and CBD states. It explores who is allowed to use marijuana in each type of jurisdiction, the restrictions such jurisdictions commonly impose on lawful marijuana users (e.g., bans on driving under the influence), and the different levels of protection jurisdictions provide against search, arrest, prosecution, and other government-imposed sanctions for marijuana possession or use.

---

1. Part I of the book includes this introductory chapter as well as the next chapter on the definition of marijuana.

Chapter 5 turns to the policy issues raised by the use of marijuana and the regulation of marijuana users. It explores the medical/scientific debates over the harms and benefits of marijuana use, as well as the more philosophical debates over which of those harms and benefits should motivate government policy. Using social science theory and evidence, the chapter then discusses the impact of different user regulations on marijuana use and harms, as well as the comparative costs of those regulations.

Finally, Chapter 6 explores the authority of different government actors to influence the regulation of marijuana users. It first examines the federal government's authority to regulate marijuana use and possession, focusing on the limits of Congress's enumerated powers as well as the potential protections given users by the Due Process Clause of the United States Constitution. It then examines the states' power over marijuana users, focusing on their ability to *legalize* marijuana for purposes of state law, i.e., to remove the sanctions *they* previously imposed on the possession (etc.) of marijuana. The chapter also examines how authority is allocated within the federal and state governments. At the federal level, the chapter focuses on the executive branch's delegated authority to reschedule drugs under the federal Controlled Substances Act (CSA). For the states, the chapter focuses on the ability of citizens and local governments to influence state policy toward marijuana users.

**Part III.** Part III focuses on the law, policy, and authority issues surrounding marijuana *suppliers,* i.e., those who grow or distribute marijuana. Chapter 7 details the elements of and criminal sanctions imposed for key marijuana trafficking crimes in prohibition regimes, including the manufacture of marijuana, distribution of marijuana, and possession with the intent to distribute marijuana. It also explores the viability of various legal defenses, including ones based on recent Department of Justice (DOJ) enforcement guidelines and congressional budget legislation. Chapter 7 then discusses the additional costs marijuana suppliers face stemming from civil forfeiture actions, special tax impositions, private RICO suits, and the inability to register trademarks at the federal level.

In a similar fashion, Chapter 8 details the regulation of marijuana suppliers in legalization regimes. The chapter details who is allowed to grow or distribute marijuana (e.g., users, their caregivers, licensed commercial firms, etc.) and the myriad restrictions states place on the cultivation and distribution of marijuana, like those imposed by the Colorado Retail Marijuana Code noted above in Section A. Chapter 8 also details how legalization regimes supervise and discipline commercial suppliers.

Chapter 9 explores key policy issues surrounding marijuana suppliers. It builds on the discussion in Chapter 5 by exploring how various regulations directed at these *suppliers* are expected to affect marijuana *use*. The chapter also discusses the comparative costs of different supply regulations, including the net fiscal impact of state reforms.

Chapter 10 completes the discussion of marijuana suppliers by examining the authority different government actors wield over them. The chapter begins by discussing the constitutionality of DOJ memoranda that discourage enforcement of the congressional marijuana ban against state-licensed marijuana suppliers. The chapter then examines the limits imposed on state authority over marijuana suppliers. It looks beyond the states' power to legalize the use and supply of marijuana (covered in Chapter 6) and instead focuses on their power to *regulate* those same activities, i.e., to impose restrictions and conditions (like licensing and labeling requirements) on the production and distribution of marijuana. To that end, it explores whether any of the state regulations detailed in Chapter 8 are preempted by federal law. The chapter concludes by examining the power of local governments to resist state reforms, and in particular, to ban the local production or distribution of marijuana after a state has legalized those activities.

**Part IV.** Part IV focuses on the law, policy, and authority issues surrounding third parties who commonly interact with marijuana users and suppliers, including professionals (like physicians and lawyers), businesses (like banks and employers), and state officials (like school administrators and police officers). Chapter 11 begins by surveying the regulations that potentially apply to all such third parties, including aiding and abetting, conspiracy, and money laundering offenses. Given the heterogeneity of third parties, however, the remaining chapters in Part IV each focus on one specific type of third party and the law, policy, and authority issues confronting it.

Chapter 12 covers the unique law, policy, and authority issues confronting professionals. It first examines the issues surrounding physicians. For example, it explores whether physicians may be sanctioned for recommending marijuana to their patients and how states have regulated physician recommendation practices. The chapter next examines the issues surrounding attorneys. For example, it asks what sorts of legal services attorneys may provide to clients regarding marijuana activities that are still prohibited at the federal level.

Chapter 13 then addresses the key law, policy, and authority issues confronting businesses that deal with marijuana users and suppliers. Transacting with marijuana users and suppliers raises a host of thorny questions addressed by the chapter: Will courts enforce contracts between marijuana suppliers and other businesses? If those contracts are not enforceable in court, how can businesses protect their reliance interests? Do some types of contracts expose businesses to legal sanctions? For example, could a landlord be criminally prosecuted for leasing property for a marijuana storefront? Can banks handle the proceeds of marijuana sales? May employers terminate employees for using marijuana? Who decides these questions?

Lastly, Chapter 14 covers the law, policy, and authority issues surrounding government officials. State officials have been caught in the crossfire of marijuana law and policy. While the federal government continues to criminalize the possession, manufacture, and distribution of marijuana, state lawmakers have ordered state officials to implement more permissive policies toward the same activities. Marijuana reforms thus raise challenging questions concerning the rights and duties of these state officials. Could state officials be prosecuted under the federal CSA for implementing state reforms? Could they be held civilly liable if they *refuse* to implement such reforms? May state officials prevent federal law enforcement agents from obtaining sensitive information the states gather from marijuana users and suppliers? Will state agencies lose federal funding by pursuing a softer approach toward marijuana? Chapter 14 addresses these and related questions.

The book's discussion of three basic topics surrounding each of three regulated parties results in a three by three organizational structure, depicted in **Figure 1.3** below. **Figure 1.3** highlights where some key issues are discussed regarding each topic and regulated party.

Figure 1.3. The Organization of the Book and Some Selected Topics

|  | **Users (II)** | **Suppliers (III)** | **Third Parties (IV)** |
|---|---|---|---|
| **Law** | Possession; necessity; physician recommendation; registration; qualifying condition; open use/use in public; DUI impaired; DUI-per se; search; probable cause; immunity; affirmative defense | Manufacture; distribution; possession with intent; sentencing; DOJ enforcement memoranda; budget restrictions; forfeiture; Section 280E; civil RICO; trademarks; personal cultivation; licensing; advertising restrictions; labeling and packaging laws; marijuana taxes | Conspiracy; aiding and abetting; money laundering; crack house statute; rules of professional conduct; DEA prescription authority; employment and housing discrimination; Section 885(d) immunity |
| **Policy** | CSA scheduling; medical benefits; recreational benefits; physical harms; the harm principle; law's impact on usage; fiscal costs; racial disparities | Diversion; law's impact on price; tax collections; industry concentration; racial disparities in licensing | Access to physicians, lawyers, and banking services; recommendation mills |
| **Authority** | Congress's enumerated powers; DEA scheduling authority; anti-commandeering rule; Due Process | Preemption; private preemption suits; Take Care Clause; the local option | Preemption; contract enforcement; First Amendment; federal grant conditions |

This three-by-three organizational structure serves two main purposes. First, it helps to emphasize that the issues surrounding the three regulated parties, while often similar, are by no means identical. Nearly all jurisdictions, for example, impose far less onerous regulatory restrictions on marijuana users than they do on marijuana suppliers. In some jurisdictions, marijuana use (or possession) may be lawful or at least decriminalized, while marijuana cultivation or distribution remain subject to criminal prohibitions and correspondingly harsh sanctions. To be sure, one could cover all of the substantive law, policy, or authority issues surrounding all three parties at one time. The structure of the book even makes this possible; e.g., the instructor or reader could regroup the chapters around a particular topic rather than a particular party. But doing so could be overwhelming; consider that the book devotes nearly 300 pages just to the substantive laws governing marijuana. Interspersing discussions of law, policy, and authority adds some variety to the subject and thereby helps to keep each topic more engaging.

Second, the organization enables the book to gradually introduce more complexity into each of the topics. The book starts with marijuana users in large part because the rules, policies, and authority issues surrounding them are relatively straightforward. It then introduces the more complicated rules, policies, and authority issues that apply to suppliers, and, finally, those that apply to third parties. There is, of course, some inescapable overlap in the topics across the three groups. However, the book is careful to discuss a common issue only once, and to refer the reader to that discussion any time it becomes relevant elsewhere in the book.

While following the suggested order of topics has advantages, the book's structure allows the instructor (or reader) to easily and seamlessly customize the ordering of topics or to focus on a specific topic or regulated party of interest. For example, the instructor who is particulary interested in the health law issues surrounding marijuana might focus on the laws defining who may use marijuana for medical use (Chapter 4), the debates over marijuana's health harms and benefits (Chapter 5), the DEA's authority to reschedule marijuana (Chapter 6), and the laws governing physicians who recommend the drug to their patients (Chapter 12). Likewise, the instructor who is particularly interested in the business law issues surrounding marijuana might focus on the unique federal tax, trademark, contracting, and banking risks faced by such businesses (Chapters 7 and 13), the sundry regulations legalization states have imposed on them (Chapter 8), and the preemption challenges directed at those (and local) regulations (Chapter 10). Along these lines, the Teacher's Manual provides suggestions for customizing a syllabus to meet the needs of a particular course of study.

## 3. The Features of the Book

The book includes several distinctive features that are designed to explain, to provoke critical thinking about, and to facilitate discussions of each of the topics outlined above. This section briefly describes those features.

**Text.** The book includes a substantial amount of original text. The text clearly introduces each of the issues covered, providing the background needed for the reader to understand and evaluate the materials—a critical feature for a relatively new subject, especially one implicating a diverse array of legal doctrines and topics. The text also provides summaries of the laws and it highlights key discrepancies in the regulations adopted by different jurisdictions. The text and structure of the book also help to explain the relationships among topics—i.e., how all of the pieces of this complex puzzle fit together.

**Excerpts from Primary Sources.** The book also includes excerpts from a variety of primary materials, including cases, statutes, regulations, government reports, memoranda, lawsuits, and secondary scholarship. There is no shortage of potential materials in this field; the difficult part is figuring out the ones on which the time-strapped instructor or reader should focus. To that end, I reviewed *several thousand* sources as I was writing this book. Each source that is included was chosen because it provides an illuminating discussion or treatment of a particular topic—whether or not I agree with it. (Note, however, that the omission of a source is not meant to suggest that it is unimportant or unhelpful—there is simply far too little space to fit everything I would have wanted to include in the book.) I trimmed each excerpt down to a manageable size to focus on key points of interest and to save the reader time, but the companion website (described below) contains links to full versions of many of them.

**Notes and Questions.** Following most excerpts and many sections of text, you will find a Notes and Questions section. The Notes and Questions sections include questions about the excerpt or text, further details on the topic at hand and related subjects, and Problems (discussed below). These materials are important but generally less essential than the main excerpt or text they follow. Putting these materials into a separate section enables instructors and readers to probe certain issues more fully as they choose, without having to spend time on issues that may be of less import or relevance to them.

**Website.** The law governing marijuana is constantly evolving and research in the field is growing at a fast clip. Nonetheless, the materials excerpted in the book were chosen to stand the test of time; i.e., their discussions of particular issues should remain enlightening and relevant, notwithstanding changes to the law. However, the book also has a companion website to help keep the reader abreast of important developments in the field. The website also provides supplemental materials, such as links to sources excerpted in the book and additional cases and statutes from different jurisdictions that can be used to focus on the laws of a particular state, if so desired.

**Problems.** Another valuable feature of the book are the more than 100 Problems interspersed throughout every chapter. Each Problem is carefully and clearly constructed to facilitate critical thinking about and provoke thoughtful discussion of the issues raised in the text and excerpts. Some Problems are based on real-life cases and events; those Problems typically include citations to and even quotes from the inspirational materials. Here are some examples of Problems, taken from different chapters in the book:

**Problem 4.15:** While driving her car, Camilla is stopped for speeding. In the course of inspecting Camilla's license and car registration, the officer detects the faint smell of unburnt marijuana emanating from Camilla's car. Does the smell of the marijuana alone give the officer probable cause to search the car? How, if at all, does your answer change if the state has: prohibited possession outright, decriminalized possession, legalized possession for certain medical uses, or legalized possession by adults of up to one ounce irrespective of the purposes for which it will be used?

**Problem 5.1:** Suppose you meet a genie with magical powers. The genie makes you the following offer: at your command, she will make all of the marijuana (plants included) in the world instantly disappear forever. There is no catch, and you believe she could do it. Would you give the command? Why, why not?

**Problem 8.16:** Delilah is the owner of a licensed Retail Marijuana Store in Small Town, Colorado. Seventy-five percent of the population of Small Town is 21 years old or older. In early December, Delilah runs a small advertisement for her store in the local paper. The ad has a picture of Santa Claus stuffing marijuana into a stocking with the name "Mrs. Claus" on it. Does the ad violate the Colorado Retail Marijuana Code advertising restrictions? *Cf.* Beer Institute, Advertising and Marketing Code § 3(b) (June 2015).

**Problem 10.6**: In 2016, the City of Oakland, California, adopted the Dispensary Equity Permit Program, under which the City will award at least 50 percent of its marijuana business licenses to applicants who meet the following criteria:

    A. Criteria. Applicant must have at least one member who meets all of the following criteria:
        1. Be an Oakland resident who:
            a. Resides for at least two (2) years prior to the date of application in Oakland Police Department Beats 26Y, 30X, 30Y, 31Z, 32Y, and 34X; or those individuals who, within the last ten (10) years, have been previously incarcerated for a marijuana-related offense as a result of a conviction arising out of Oakland, California;
            b. Maintains not less than a fifty percent (50%) ownership in the Dispensary applicant entity, partnership, limited liability corporation, collective, corporation, worker cooperative or other recognized ownership entity; and
        2. Prior marijuana or cannabis conviction shall not be a bar to equity ownership.

Oakland Mun. Code 5.80.045 (2016). Is the Dispensary Equity Permit Program constitutional? *See generally* Brian T. Fitzpatrick, *Can Michigan Universities Use Proxies for Race After the Ban on Racial Preferences?*, 133 Mich. J. Race & L. 277 (2007).

**Problem 12.11**: Andy is an attorney who is licensed to practice in a recreational marijuana state. Camila tells Andy that she wants to launch a retail marijuana store. Under the state's marijuana law, Camila must first apply for a retail marijuana license from the state. Camila has no legal training. She asks Andy for help in completing the license application, which is 13 pages long and includes many questions for which a legal background would be helpful. If Andy completes the application on behalf of Camila, would he be in violation of Rule 1.2(d) of the Model Rules of Professional Conduct? Suppose Camila completes the application herself, but she asks Andy for help in deciphering the meaning of certain questions on the application (e.g., "Has any interest or share in the profits of the sale of Marijuana been pledged or hypothecated as security for a debt or deposited as a security for the performance of an act or to secure the performance of a contract?"). Can Andy answer Camila's questions under Rule 1.2(d)?

**Problem 13.1**: Ivan is an investor who loaned $500,000 to Oma. Oma is the owner of The Dude Ranch, a state-licensed medical marijuana dispensary. Pursuant to the terms of the loan agreement, Oma was supposed to use the funds "to grow and sell marijuana through The Dude Ranch, to the extent permitted by state law." In return, Oma would pay Ivan 12 percent interest annually over 30 years, with the principal due at the end of the loan term. However, Oma instead used the $500,000 to buy a house for herself. She has

15

refused to pay Ivan any of the interest due on the loan, and she has refused to refund any of the loan principal. Ivan has sued Oma in state court for breach of contract. Will the court enforce the contract? If so, what remedy will it award?

**Teacher's Manual.** The Teacher's Manual helps instructors to design and prepare to teach their own courses on this subject. Among other things, the Manual offers explanatory notes about topics and materials (e.g., why a particular case was included in the book, etc.), suggestions for additional classroom exercises, and thoughts about questions posed in the text and Problems. The Manual also provides sample syllabi to help instructors design their course around different credit requirements, themes, and so on.

\* \* \*

I hope this brief Introduction inspires you to read on. And as you read on, I hope the book enlightens your views on this important subject—whatever they might be—just as writing the book challenged, informed, and refined my own views.

So, without further ado, let's get going!

# CHAPTER 2

# What Is Marijuana?

This chapter provides some basic background information on the subject of the book: marijuana. It is designed to enable readers to better understand the law and policy issues discussed throughout the remaining chapters.

The book uses the term marijuana to describe both the Cannabis plant and the drugs made from that plant. Section A describes the Cannabis plant and the chemicals it produces, called cannabinoids. These chemicals are responsible for the harms and benefits many people associate with marijuana use, as discussed in Chapter 5. Section A also describes the different ways in which marijuana is now consumed. Section B then discusses how jurisdictions have defined marijuana for purposes of their laws. It also explores three controversies that have been sparked by those definitions, such as whether drugs (or other products) made from the Cannabis plant are still considered marijuana if they do not contain intoxicating cannabinoids.

## A. WHAT IS MARIJUANA?

For purposes of this book, marijuana refers both to the Cannabis plant and to the drugs made from the Cannabis plant. As discussed below in Section B, this definition mirrors the legal definition of marijuana employed by most jurisdictions. The reader should note that many individuals and even some jurisdictions use a different spelling ("marihuana") or a different term (e.g., "cannabis," weed, etc.) to describe the Cannabis plant and the drugs made therefrom. The choice of terminology has even stirred up some controversy. *See* Alfonso Serrano, *Weed all about it: The origins of the word 'marijuana'*, Al Jazeera America (Dec. 14, 2013), https://perma.cc/52EY-RU5E (discussing possible motivations behind early adoption of the term marijuana in the United States). This book does not seek to take sides in this controversy; rather, it uses the term "marijuana" simply because it remains the most commonly employed of the possible terms in the United States.

The Cannabis plant is an annual flowering herb with a distinctive fan leaf pattern, as shown in **Figure 2.1**.

The plant produces chemical compounds, called cannabinoids, that effect the body and (in some cases) the mind. The most well-known cannabinoid is delta-9-tetrahydrocannabinol (THC). THC is intoxicating (some say "psychoactive"). It produces the high that many people experience when using marijuana. The substance has been blamed for many of the harms—and credited with many of the benefits—associated with marijuana use. (These harms and benefits are discussed in greater detail in Chapter 5.) In recent years, a second cannabinoid, Cannabidiol (CBD), has received increasing attention because some claim it has beneficial properties without producing the high (or other alleged harms) associated with THC. There are dozens of other cannabinoids found in the Cannabis plant, but because they have attracted far less attention than THC and CBD, the book will not discuss them further.

Figure 2.1. Cannabis Plant

The quantity and assortment of cannabinoids found in a given Cannabis plant depends largely on the plant's genetics. Cannabis sativa L.—the plant's species—includes three main subspecies or varieties (there is disagreement in the field about taxonomy): sativa, indica, and ruderalis. However, breeders have produced a staggering array of distinct plant strains from these three varieties, catalogued under names like purple kush, Acapulco gold, and sour diesel.

Each of these strains purportedly produces a distinct effect, stemming from its unique blend and concentration of different cannabinoids. For example, some strains, bred mostly for recreational use, contain as much as 30 percent THC by dry weight, whereas other strains grown for CBD or industrial hemp (discussed more below) contain less than 1 percent THC. *See* Brian Handwerk, *Heavy Metals and Fungus*, Smithsonian.com (Mar. 23, 2015) (describing results of tests on marijuana in Colorado). To assist consumers, some states now require vendors to label marijuana products with their cannabinoid profiles. (These requirements are discussed in Chapter 8.) And at least one company has developed a web-based catalog listing the characteristics of nearly 2,000 strains now available on the market. *See* https://www.leafly.com/explore. A chart depicting just a small sampling of those strains is shown in **Figure 2.2**.

The most notable cannabinoid, THC, is concentrated in the flowering buds and leaves of the Cannabis plant. The unfertilized buds (sinsemilla) of the female plant, which need to be isolated by growers to prevent pollination, contain the highest concentrations of THC. However, very little, if any, THC is found in the mature stalks and seeds of the Cannabis plant. What is more, these parts of the plant can be used to make a variety of ordinary products, like textiles, foodstuffs, and cosmetics. For both of these reasons, as discussed below, these parts of the Cannabis plant are commonly excluded from the legal definition of marijuana.

The drugs produced from the Cannabis plant can be consumed in four main ways, as explained in this excerpt from the Drug Policy Alliance:

> Inhalation is the fastest method of delivery to the consumer. Most consumers prefer using marijuana this way. When a consumer inhales marijuana, the majority of cannabinoids enter the body through the lungs where they are passed along directly into the consumer's blood stream. The effect is almost instantaneous. . . .

Figure 2.2. A Chart Depicting Some of the Marijuana Strains Found on Leafly.com

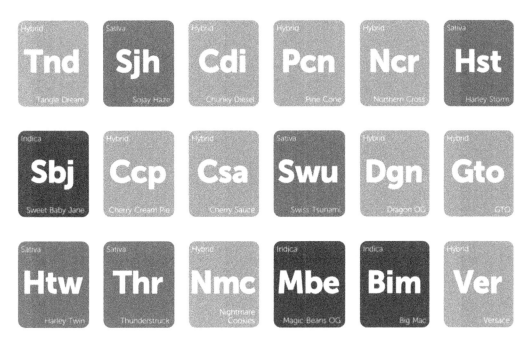

There are two ways to inhale marijuana, smoking and vaporizing. Smoking marijuana involves burning the flowers and inhaling the active components of the plant that are released. Vaporization acts in the same way, but the plant is not burned, rather it is heated to a temperature at which the active ingredients in the plant are released as vapor that is inhaled by the consumer . . .

. . .

Marijuana can also be ingested orally. This can be in the form of edibles, tinctures, capsules or oils. The onset for oral ingestion is slower and the effects are stronger and last longer than with inhalation. People who consume marijuana orally usually report feeling the effects within thirty minutes to one hour or longer, with peak effects around the two hour mark and total duration of effects ranging as long as six hours. This is because, during the process of digestion, the cannabinoids undergo a chemical transformation that makes them stronger. Also, when ingesting orally, none of the product is lost by sticking to the pipe or rolling paper. . . .

Marijuana can also enter the blood stream when placed under the tongue and held in the mouth [the sublingual method]; within the mouth there are a large number of blood vessels which can absorb cannabinoids. Common examples of these type of products include dissolvable strips, sublingual sprays, or medicated lozenges or tinctures. Sativex, the one clinically approved, cannabinoid medication that includes the entire spectrum of natural cannabinoids, is delivered as a sublingual spray. The time of onset for this method of

Figure 2.3. Some of the Ways Marijuana Can Be Consumed

consumption is similar to those seen in general oral consumption, however, some studies have reported an earlier onset.

. . .

A final way to consume marijuana is through topical applications. These come in the form of lotions, salves, bath salts and oils that are applied to the skin. The skin has a relatively complex absorption process that is based on a chemical's ability to dissolve in H20. . . . While not widely studied, there is research that shows that topical application of cannabinoids has an onset of action within minutes locally (i.e. creams and balms applied to a joint), with duration of these effects lasting one to two hours. . . . [T]he topical application of marijuana does not allow a significant amount of cannabinoids to reach the brain and therefore is unlikely to cause any intoxication.

Drug Policy Alliance, *How Marijuana is Consumed*, https://perma.cc/XHL7-5ST9. **Figure 2.3** displays some of the forms marijuana can take, reflecting these four methods of consumption.

## Notes and Questions

1. Although smoking remains the most popular method of consumption, other methods are increasing in popularity. For data on the popularity of different forms of consumption, see Colorado Department of Public Health & Environment, *Marijuana Use in Colorado* (2014), https://perma.cc/BF76-BQUV and Beau Kilmer et al., RAND Drug Policy Research Center, *Before the Grand Opening: Measuring Washington State's Marijuana Market* (2013).

2. For more information on the botany of the Cannabis plant, see Robert C. Clark & Mark D. Merlin, *Cannabis: Evolution and Ethnobotany* (U.C. Berkeley, 2013).

## B. CONTROVERSIES OVER THE LEGAL DEFINITION OF MARIJUANA

Jurisdictions commonly define "marijuana" to include the drugs made from the Cannabis plant, as well as parts of the Cannabis plant itself. The definition employed by the federal Controlled Substances Act (CSA) is representative:

> The term "marihuana" means all parts of the plant Cannabis sativa L., whether growing or not; the seeds thereof; the resin extracted from any part of such plant; and every compound, manufacture, salt, derivative, mixture, or preparation of such plant, its seeds or resin. Such term does not include the mature stalks of such plant, fiber produced from such stalks, oil or cake made from the seeds of such plant, any other compound, manufacture, salt, derivative, mixture, or preparation of such mature stalks (except the resin extracted therefrom), fiber, oil, or cake, or the sterilized seed of such plant which is incapable of germination.

21 U.S.C. § 802(16). Many states employ a similar definition, *e.g.*, Mass. Gen. Laws Ch. 94c § 1, although, as discussed in the materials below, some have narrowed (or even broadened) their definitions.

Because marijuana is tightly controlled, the definition that is given to the term helps determine whether individuals are allowed to possess, manufacture, or distribute a given Cannabis plant or any number of products made therefrom. Not surprisingly, then, the definition of marijuana has spawned several controversies, discussed in the sections below.

### 1. Is It Still Marijuana If It Does Not Contain THC?

As noted above, THC is blamed for most of the harms associated (rightly or wrongly) with marijuana use. But not all Cannabis plants produce usable quantities of THC. So, does the law distinguish among plants based on their THC content? In other words, is a Cannabis plant—or a product produced from the plant—still considered "marijuana" under the law if it contains no (or little) THC?

The question has arisen most often regarding industrial hemp. Industrial hemp is a strain of the Cannabis plant, but it produces little THC. Its stalks and seeds are used to manufacture a variety of non-controversial products, including

> foods and beverages, cosmetics and personal care products, and nutritional supplements, as well as fabrics and textiles, yarns and spun fibers, paper, construction and insulation materials, and other manufactured goods. Hemp can be grown as a fiber, seed, or other dual-purpose crop. Some estimate that the global market for hemp consists of more than 25,000 products. Precise data are not available on the size of the U.S. market for hemp-based products, but current industry estimates report annual sales at more than $580 million annually.

Renée Johnson, Congressional Research Service, *Hemp as an Agricultural Commodity* (Feb. 2, 2015), https://perma.cc/T55W-THUA.

The possession and distribution of many hemp-based products and the parts of the hemp plant used to produce them are legal in the United States because those items fall outside the legal definition of marijuana. *See* 21 U.S.C. § 802(16) (excluding the "mature stalks of such plant, fiber produced from such stalks, oil or cake made from the seeds of such plant, any other compound, manufacture, salt, derivative, mixture, or preparation of such mature stalk" from the definition of "marihuana"). But because one cannot grow the parts of the hemp plant that are excluded from the legal definition of marijuana without also growing the parts that are included in that definition—i.e., the plant's leaves, flowers, and germinating seeds, farmers in the United States are effectively barred from cultivating the hemp plant domestically. As a result, hemp products and the stalks and seeds used to produce them must be imported from one of the 30 or so other countries that allow the commercial cultivation of industrial hemp. *See* Johnson, *Hemp as an Agricultural Commodity, supra*.

Seeing lost opportunity in the hemp market, some farmers in the United States have argued that the definition of marijuana found in statutes like the CSA should be interpreted narrowly to include only Cannabis plants that produce usable quantities of THC, an interpretation that would exclude industrial hemp plants. In the following case, the court discusses the arguments both for and against such a limitation.

## *New Hampshire Hemp Council, Inc. v. Marshall*
### 203 F.3d 1 (1st Cir. 1999)

BOUDIN, J.

This case, which involves the definition of marijuana as used in federal criminal statutes, has its origin in a defeated legislative proposal in New Hampshire. In 1998, Derek Owen, a member of the New Hampshire state legislature, co-sponsored a bill to legalize and regulate the cultivation of "industrial hemp." The connection between the criminal statutes and Owen's bill is that both the drug commonly known as marijuana and various industrial products (*e.g.*, rope) derive from different portions of the plant popularly called the hemp plant and designated *Cannabis sativa* in the Linnaean system of botanical classification.

In general, the drug is derived from the flowers or leaves of the plant while the fibers used for rope and other industrial products are taken from the stalk. Cannabis sativa plants grown for industrial products generally are derived from different strains and are cultivated and mature differently from those intended for the marijuana drug. All contain THC (a short-hand reference to tetrahydrocannabinol), the ingredient that gives marijuana its psychoactive or euphoric properties; but those plants grown for drug use contain a higher concentration of THC than those grown for most industrial products. Owen's bill limited its definition of "industrial hemp" to those cannabis sativa plants containing a THC concentration of 1 percent or less.

Several witnesses testified on Owen's bill before a New Hampshire house subcommittee. One witness, George Festa, appeared on behalf of the U.S. Drug Enforcement Administration ("DEA"). He testified that regardless of intended "industrial" use, the DEA views the cultivation of cannabis sativa plants as the manufacture of marijuana and therefore illegal under federal law (absent federal licensing). Although Owen's bill was thereafter recommended for passage by the house committee, it was defeated on a relatively close vote (175 to 164) in the full house on February 6, 1998.

On April 30, 1998, Owen and the New Hampshire Hemp Council brought the present action in the federal district court in New Hampshire against the DEA Administrator. Owen, who farms in New Hampshire, said that he and the Hemp Council wanted to cultivate cannabis sativa plants to produce fiber and other industrial products but were deterred by the DEA's position. The complaint sought a declaration that in defining "marijuana," Congress had not criminalized the growth of "non-psychoactive" (i.e., low-THC) cannabis sativa as well as an injunction to prevent the DEA from prosecuting producers.

[The district court rejected the complaint and Owen and the Hemp Council appealed.]

. . .

For purposes of the federal criminal statutes, "marijuana" is defined—not by the DEA but by Congress—as follows:

> [*A]ll parts of the plant Cannabis sativa L.,* whether growing or not; the seeds thereof; the resin extracted from any part of such plant; and every compound, manufacture, salt, derivative, mixture, or preparation of such plant, its seeds or resin. *Such term does not include the mature stalks of such plant, fiber produced from such stalks,* oil or cake made from the seeds of such plant, any other compound, manufacture, salt, derivative, mixture, or preparation of such mature stalks (except the resin extracted therefrom), fiber, oil, or cake, or the sterilized seed of such plant which is incapable of germination.

21 U.S.C. § 802(16)(emphasis added).

Owen's own complaint concedes that the industrial products at issue are produced from plants of the "species" cannabis sativa; strictly speaking, "cannabis" is the genus and "sativa" is the species, . . . and the "L." in the statute simply refers to Linnaeus' system of botanical classification. . . . Owen's own expert admitted . . . that the plant from which the industrial products are derived is cannabis sativa. The literature to which Owen cites . . . says the same thing. In short, on a literal reading of the statute, the plant—which is what Owen proposes to grow—is within the statute's ban.

Statutory language is the starting point in statutory interpretation . . . , and, . . . it is the ending point unless there is a sound reason for departure. . . . Here, nothing in Owen's complaint or arguments warrants a narrower reading, nor have somewhat similar arguments persuaded the several other circuits in which they have been advanced, in attempts to carve out various exceptions for cannabis sativa plants with low THC levels. We take Owen's key arguments one by one.

Owen's main argument is that plants produced for industrial products contain very little of the psychoactive substance THC. However, the low THC content is far from conclusive. . . . It may be that at some stage the plant destined for industrial products is useless to supply enough THC for psychoactive effects. But problems of detection and enforcement easily justify a ban broader than the psychoactive variety of the plant. Owen's own expert testified . . . that young cannabis sativa plants with varying psychoactive properties are visually indistinguishable. And the statute does not distinguish among varieties of cannabis sativa.

Owen's best argument stems from legislative history. The present definition of marijuana was first employed in the Marihuana Tax Act of 1937. . . . There, the basic definition covered all cannabis sativa plants whether intended for industrial use or drug production, . . . but the statute effectively distinguished between them by taxing them differently. All producers of cannabis sativa and certain legitimate users (*e.g.*, doctors) were subject to a small tax, ($1 per year), . . . but no tax was applied to transfers of the mature stalk of the plant, which is useful only for industrial use, . . . and which was specifically excluded from the definition of "marijuana[]" under the Marihuana Tax Act. . . .

By contrast, to discourage "illicit" uses, an extremely high tax ($100) applied to *each* transfer of other parts of the plant to anyone who had not registered with the government and paid his own occupational tax. . . . And while the scheme permitted producers and legitimate customers to register (*e.g.*, doctors, researchers), . . . it made no explicit provision for registration by most consumers (except to exempt entirely patients receiving marijuana by medical prescription . . .). Transfers that did not comply were made criminal. . . .

In 1970 Congress adopted the Controlled Substances Act, . . . codified at 21 U.S.C. § 801 et seq. . . . , repealing the 1937 tax statute, . . . but carrying forward its definition of marijuana into the present criminal ban on production, sale and possession. . . . While in 1937 Congress had indicated in legislative history that production for industrial uses would be protected (primarily by a relatively low tax), . . . we can find no indication that Congress in 1970 gave any thought to how its new statutory scheme would affect such production.

Given the 1937 intent to protect industrial uses and the carrying forward of the definition, Owen colorably argues that the 1970 statute should also be read to protect production for industrial uses by interpolating his distinction between psychoactive and non-psychoactive strains of cannabis sativa. The difficulty is that Congress' main vehicle for protecting industrial-use plant production in 1937 was not its basic definition of "marijuana," which included plants ultimately destined for industrial use; it was the complex scheme of differential tax rates and other requirements for transfers. That is the regime that was drastically modified in 1970 in favor of a broad criminal ban (subject only to federal licensing), a ban which read literally embraces production of cannabis sativa plants regardless of use.

The possibility remains that Congress would not have adopted the 1970 statute in its present form if it had been aware of the effect on cultivation of plants for industrial uses. But that is only a *possibility* and not a basis for reading the new statute contrary to its literal language . . . at least absent a clear indication that Congress intended to protect plant production for industrial use as it existed under the prior tax statute. Nor, given Congress' enlargement of drug crimes and penalties in recent years, would one bank on its adoption of an exception strongly opposed by the DEA as constituting a threatened loophole in the ban on illegal drugs.

Owen hints at one other argument that cries out to be addressed. In a number of cases, the courts have extended the 1970 statute—arguably beyond its literal language—to embrace not only the sativa species of cannabis but what may (or may not) be several other cannabis species. The courts found that these plants can provide the same level of THC as cannabis sativa grown for drug use, expressed doubts that they are (or at least were regarded by Congress as) species distinct from sativa, and felt confident that Congress did not mean to distinguish among related major THC agents. . . .

If plants arguably beyond the literal language of the statute are condemned because of their THC content, this gives Owen some basis for contending that plants within the literal language should be excluded based on their (comparative) lack of THC content. But the symmetry is misleading. Reading the statute to cover other possible species rests (as just noted) on a number of grounds—not just THC content. By contrast, where cannabis sativa plants are grown for industrial use, the statute's coverage is supported alike by literal language, enforcement concerns and the broad application of the definition under the 1937 tax statute.

Despite the myth that Congress intends every result entailed by its statutes, new laws are often like jigsaw puzzles whose pieces do not quite fit; some have to be squeezed into place and there may be gaps in the pattern. But in this instance, on the issue of whether the statute includes all cannabis sativa plants, the considerations favor a literal reading of the statute and preclude Owen's construction.

## Notes and Questions

1. Interpreting the language of the CSA, the *New Hampshire Hemp Council* court finds that the hemp plant is "marijuana" regardless of THC content. Should Congress have lumped the hemp plant into the definition of marijuana? Does the fact that hemp plants are "visually indistinguishable" from other Cannabis plants containing higher levels of THC provide a convincing reason for treating hemp the same as, say, sour diesel, agent orange, or other, more potent strains of the Cannabis plant? *See Kentucky v. Harrelson*, 14 S.W.3d 541, 550 (Ky. 2000) (Cooper, J., concurring) ("I disagree with the proposition that the mere fact that hemp resembles marijuana provides a rational basis for criminalizing the possession of hemp. If that were true, the legislature could criminalize the possession of sugar because it resembles powder cocaine.").

2. In 2015, New Hampshire joined at least 27 other states that have expressly excluded industrial hemp from the definition of marijuana under state law. National Conference of State Legislatures, *State Industrial Hemp Statutes* (Aug. 19, 2016), https://perma.cc/FQ3N-B3V2. California's definition is illustrative:

> 'Marijuana' means all parts of the plant Cannabis sativa L., whether growing or not; the seeds of that plant; the resin extracted from any part of the plant; and every compound, manufacture, salt, derivative, mixture, or preparation of the plant, its seeds or resin. *It does not include industrial hemp*, . . . except where the plant is cultivated or processed for purposes not expressly allowed for by . . . the Food and Agricultural Code.

Cal. Health & Safety Code § 11018 (emphasis added). California limits the quantity of THC that may be included in "industrial hemp":

> "Industrial hemp" means a fiber or oilseed crop, or both, that is limited to nonpsychoactive types of the plant Cannabis sativa L. and the seed produced therefrom, having no more than three-tenths of 1 percent tetrahydrocannabinol (THC) contained in the dried flowering tops, and that is cultivated and processed exclusively for the purpose of producing the mature stalks of the plant, fiber produced from the stalks, oil or cake made from the seeds of the plant, or any other compound, manufacture, salt, derivative, mixture, or preparation of the mature stalks, except the resin or flowering tops extracted therefrom, fiber, oil, or cake, or the sterilized seed, or any component of the seed, of the plant that is incapable of germination.

*Id.* at § 11018.5.

Members of Congress have proposed similar legislation that would expressly exclude industrial hemp from the definition of marijuana under federal law. *See* Industrial Hemp Farming Act of 2015, https://perma.cc/KYL6-GN45 (excluding industrial hemp with less than 0.3 percent THC concentration from definition of marijuana). And Congress has already passed more limited legislation that permits universities and state departments of agriculture to grow industrial hemp for research purposes, as long as certain requirements are met. *See* 7 U.S.C. § 5940.

3. Now consider the flip side of the issue discussed in *New Hampshire Hemp Council*. Namely, what happens if a product contains THC, but is made from a part of the Cannabis plant that is *excluded* from the definition of marijuana (like the mature stalks of the plant)? The CSA actually lists "Tetrahydrocannabinols" and any "material, compound, mixture, or preparation" containing the same as a separate Schedule I controlled substance, subject to the same stringent regulations applicable to marijuana. 21 U.S.C. § 812(c)(17). In 2003, the DEA interpreted the statutory language as covering both natural and synthetic versions of THC, including natural THC found in any part of the Cannabis plant:

> [For purposes of the CSA, Tetrahydrocannabinols means] tetrahydrocannabinols naturally contained in a plant of the genus Cannabis (cannabis plant), as well as synthetic equivalents of the substances contained in the cannabis plant, or in the resinous extractives of such plant, and/or synthetic substances, derivatives, and their isomers with similar chemical structure and pharmacological activity to those substances contained in the plant. . . .

21 C.F.R. § 1308.11(d).

However, the DEA's interpretation of THC was successfully challenged in *Hemp Industries Association v. Drug Enforcement Agency*, 357 F.3d 1012 (9th Cir. 2004). The case arose when the DEA tried to block the Appellant's importation and distribution of food and cosmetics made from the stalks, seeds, and oil of the Cannabis plant because they contained trace amounts of natural THC. The *Hemp Industries Association* court held that

> [T]he definition of THC under the CSA includes only synthetic THC. . . . As we noted in [*Hemp Industries Assoc. v. DEA*, 333 F.3d 1082 (9th Cir. 2003)], with a more elaborate explanation than we will provide here:
>
>> Notably, if naturally-occurring THC were covered under THC, there would be no need to have a separate category for marijuana, which obviously contains naturally-occurring THC. Yet Congress maintained marijuana as a separate category. . . .
>
> . . .
>
> The non-psychoactive hemp in Appellants' products is derived from the "mature stalks" or is "oil and cake made from the seeds" of the *Cannabis* plant, and therefore fits within the plainly stated exception to the CSA definition of marijuana [found in 21 U.S.C. § 802(16)].
>
> Congress was aware of the presence of trace amounts of psychoactive agents (later identified as THC) in the resin of non-psychoactive hemp when it passed the 1937 "Marihuana Tax Act," and when it adopted the Tax Act marijuana definition in the CSA. As a result, when Congress excluded from the definition of marijuana "mature stalks of such plant, fiber . . . , [and] oil or cake made from the seeds," it also made an exception to the exception, and included "resin extracted from" the excepted parts of the plant in the definition of marijuana, despite the stalks and seeds exception. 21 U.S.C. § 802(16). Congress knew what it was doing, and its intent to exclude non-psychoactive hemp from regulation is entirely clear. The DEA's Final Rules are inconsistent with the unambiguous meaning of the CSA definitions of marijuana and THC, and the DEA did not use the appropriate scheduling procedures to add non-psychoactive hemp to the list of controlled substances.

357 F.3d at 1017-18.

4. Is CBD extracted from the flowers or leaves of the Cannabis plant also covered by the definition of marijuana discussed above? Yes, according to the DEA: "CBD derived from the cannabis plant is controlled under Schedule I of the CSA because it is a naturally occurring constituent of marijuana." Statement of Joseph T. Rannazzisi, Deputy Assistant Administrator, Drug Enforcement Administration, Before the Caucus on International Narcotics Control, United States Senate, June 24, 2015.

5. The relationship between THC and the legal definition of marijuana also arises in contexts not involving hemp, as illustrated by the following Problems:

Problem 2.1: The police stop Andy for speeding. During the course of the traffic stop, Andy consents to a search of his vehicle. In the car's ashtray, the police find "a metal cleaning rod with burned marijuana residue on it." Andy admits the rod is his, but he argues, and the police agree, that the burnt residue would no longer produce a high for anyone who dared to consume it. Is the substance on the cleaning rod nonetheless considered "marijuana" under the law? *See North Dakota v. Peterson*, 799 N.W.2d 67 (N.D. 2011) (discussing whether the unusable residue of burned marijuana is nonetheless covered by the state's definition of "marijuana").

Problem 2.2: Camila smokes marijuana at a friend's house and then walks home. On her way, she is stopped by the police. Camila consents to a blood test, which reveals the presence of THC in her system. Is the THC found in Camila's body still considered "marijuana"? *Compare* South Dakota C.L. § 22-42-1(1) (defining "controlled drug or substance" to include the "altered state of a drug or substance listed in Schedules I through IV *absorbed into the human body*") (emphasis added) *with Cronan v. Georgia*, 511 S.E.2d 899, 901 (Ga. App. 1999) (holding that "the presence of THC [in the body] 'without the morphological features' of the marijuana plant . . . [is] excluded from the definition of 'marijuana' under [state law]"). What would the *Hemp Industries Association* court say?

## 2. Is Cannabis Indica Covered by the Definition of Marijuana?

In the scientific community, there is some disagreement concerning the classification of Cannabis plants, and in particular, whether all Cannabis plants are members of a single species. The disagreement has legal significance because the CSA's definition of marijuana mentions by name only one species: "Cannabis sativa L." Nonetheless, federal courts have uniformly held that the CSA's reference to Cannabis sativa L. encompasses *all* Cannabis plants, including Cannabis sativa, Cannabis indica, and Cannabis ruderalis. The following case discusses the issue.

Part I. Introductory Materials

## *United States v. Honneus*
508 F.2d 566 (1st Cir. 1974)

CAMPBELL, J.:

[The defendant, Geoffrey Honneus, was convicted of several crimes stemming from his purchase and subsequent importation of large quantities of a substance alleged to be marijuana.]

Honneus has persistently insisted that the Government never proved him guilty of dealing in "Cannabis sativa L." ...

Honneus sought to introduce testimony by Dr. Richard Schultes, [Professor of Natural Sciences and Director, Botanical Museum, Harvard University,] that the Cannabis plant is a genus having three species, sativa, indica, and ruderalis, and that both sativa and indica presently grow in Jamaica. As the Government recovered no marihuana for analysis, there was no proof that the type or types of Cannabis Honneus purchased in Jamaica and later shipped to the United States were not indica rather than sativa.

Dr. Schultes testified during a voir dire that the disputed nomenclature could be traced back to Linnaeus' famous eighteenth century botanical compendium which listed under the genus Cannabis only a single species, sativa. A generation later, Lamarck named a Cannabis specimen collected in India, "indica", and in the 1920's Russian botanists published in their native country a study naming a third variant "ruderalis." Noneth[e]less, according to Dr. Schultes, the "usually accepted view" (which he himself "echoed") until a few years ago was that there was only one species of Cannabis. Now, after more study, Dr. Schultes believes there are three. ...

The district court, ruling in a Memorandum and Order that Congress meant to include any and all marihuana-producing Cannabis in specifying "Cannabis sativa L.", excluded Dr. Schultes' testimony and denied Honneus' motions for acquittal and for jury instructions. Courts in three circuits have similarly held, based upon the statutory history of the 1970 Act's predecessor, the marihuana Tax Act of 1937, ... from which the definition of marihuana was taken. ... In testimony on the Marihuana Tax Bill before the House Committee on Ways and Means, Commissioner of Narcotics [Harry] Anslinger in 1937 stated that "Cannabis indica, or marihuana, has as its parent the plant known as Cannabis sativa". The Commissioner went on to say,

> "It's popularly known in India as Cannabis indica; in America, as Cannabis American; in Mexico as Cannabis Mexicana, or marihuana.
> 'It is all the same drug, and is known in different countries by different names. It is scientifically known as Cannabis sativa. ..."

575 Hearings on H.R. 6385 before the Comm. on Ways & Means, 75th Cong., 1st Sess. at 37-38 (1937).

Dr. Lyster Dewey, a botanist formerly in charge of the Agriculture Department's fibre division, also testified that there was "only one species known as hemp." *Id.* at 55. Honneus argues that this certainty as to only one species is misleading, that others concerned with the 1937 Act were much less clear that sativa included other types if there were any others. There is indeed evidence of confusion over terminology, but none that Congress meant to exclude from regulation any type of the plant producing the hallucinogenic material popularly known in this country as "marihuana". ... Appellant's suggestion that sativa was selected because of an intention to deal only with the type most commonly grown in America is not borne out by the legislative record. Such an approach would have amounted to exemption of material from easily procurable plants having the same properties as the ones regulated. . . . We are persuaded that Congress adopted "Cannabis sativa L." believing it to be the term that scientists used to embrace all marihuana-producing Cannabis; the other named sorts were not seen as separate Cannabis species. Linnaeus had listed but the one species, and appellant's own expert concedes that until recently the monotypic view has been the "usually accepted" one. This is not to try to refute Dr. Schultes' present view. The issue is not whether marihuana is monotypic or polytypic but what Congress meant when it used the term "Cannabis sativa L.". We hold that the district court's [ru]ling and exclusion of Dr. Schultes' testimony were correct.

## Notes and Questions

1. Is it possible to reconcile the decision in *New Hampshire Hemp Council*, which emphasizes the literal language of the CSA, with the decision in *Honneus*, which appears to emphasize instead the purposes of the statute? Why, why not?

### 3. Is Synthetic Marijuana (K2, Spice, etc.) Considered (or Treated Like) Marijuana?

A similar issue has arisen from the proliferation of *synthetic* cannabinoids (or cannabinoid receptor agonists), in essence, human-made chemicals that mimic some of the effects produced by natural marijuana:

> Synthetic cannabinoids refer to a growing number of man-made mind-altering chemicals that are either sprayed on dried, shredded plant material so they can be smoked (herbal incense) or sold as liquids to be vaporized and inhaled in e-cigarettes and other devices (liquid incense).
>
> These chemicals are called cannabinoids because they are related to chemicals found in the marijuana plant. Because of this similarity, synthetic cannabinoids are sometimes misleadingly called "synthetic marijuana" (or "fake weed"), and they are often marketed as "safe," legal alternatives to that drug. In fact, they may affect the brain much more powerfully than marijuana; their actual effects can be unpredictable and, in some cases, severe or even life-threatening.
>
> Synthetic cannabinoids are included in a group of drugs called "new psychoactive substances" (NPS). NPS are unregulated psychoactive (mind-altering) substances that have become newly available on the market and are intended to copy the effects of illegal drugs. Some of these substances may have been around for years but have reentered the market in altered chemical forms or due to renewed popularity.
>
> Manufacturers sell these herbal incense products in colorful foil packages and sell similar liquid incense products, like other e-cigarette fluids, in plastic bottles. They market these products under a wide variety of specific brand names; in past years, K2 and Spice were common. Hundreds of other brand names now exist, such as Joker, Black Mamba, Kush, and Kronic.
>
> For several years, synthetic cannabinoid mixtures have been easy to buy in drug paraphernalia shops, novelty stores, gas stations, and through the Internet. Because the chemicals used in them have a high potential for abuse and no medical benefit, authorities

> have made it illegal to sell, buy, or possess some of these chemicals. However, manufacturers try to sidestep these laws by changing the chemical formulas in their mixtures.
>
> Easy access and the belief that synthetic cannabinoid products are "natural" and therefore harmless have likely contributed to their use among young people. Another reason for their use is that standard drug tests cannot easily detect many of the chemicals used in these products.

National Institute on Drug Abuse, DrugFacts: Synthetic Cannabinoids (Nov. 2015), https://perma.cc/A5HS-6GTY.

The emergence of these synthetic cannabinoids poses a challenge for regulators. While these drugs generate the same (if not greater) harms as those attributed to natural marijuana,[1] they generally do not fall under the standard definition of marijuana or that of THC. These synthetic cannabinoids are, after all, human-made, and are thus not the "resin extracted from any part of [the Cannabis] plant," or a "compound, manufacture, salt, derivative, mixture, or preparation of such plant." 21 U.S.C. § 802(16). *But see* Utah Code § 58-37-2(aa) (defining marijuana to include "[a]ny synthetic equivalents of the substances contained in the plant cannabis sativa or any other species of the genus cannabis which are chemically indistinguishable and pharmacologically active"). And while the CSA and similar laws also cover *synthetic* THC, see 21 C.F.R. § 1308.11(d), many synthetic cannabinoids are (by design) chemically distinct from THC, meaning they are not necessarily "synthetic equivalents" of the natural substance. See Bridgit O. Crews, American Association of Clinical Chemistry, *Synthetic Cannabinoids* (Feb. 1, 2013) (describing three distinct categories of synthetic cannabinoids), https://perma.cc/YLU3-V4SR.

Regulators have pursued two basic approaches to ensuring that synthetic cannabinoids are subject to regulations like those governing marijuana and natural THC. The ex post approach seeks to add synthetic cannabinoids to the schedules of controlled drugs whenever these designer drugs hit the market. In 2011, for example, the DEA added five specific synthetic cannabinoids to Schedule I under the CSA (the same schedule as marijuana and THC). Drug Enforcement Administration, *Schedules of Controlled Substances: Temporary Placement of Five Synthetic Cannabinoids Into Schedule I*, 76 Fed. Reg. 11075 (Mar. 1, 2011). (The DEA's scheduling authority is discussed in Chapter 6.)

However, it is difficult for regulators to keep pace with chemists seeking to circumvent regulatory controls. In 2012 alone, for example, scientists identified 51 *new* synthetic cannabinoids. White House, ONDCP, *Synthetic Drugs (a.k.a. K2, Spice, Bath Salts, etc.)*, https://perma.cc/HL66-QSQS. As one commentator has concluded, "the sheer number of synthetic cannabinoids available renders the control of [a small number of] unique compounds moot." Timothy P. Stackhouse, Note, *Regulators in Wackyland: Capturing the Last of the Designer Drugs*, 54 Ariz. L. Rev. 1105, 1118 (2012).

The second, ex ante, approach, uses broader, more flexible terminology to define controlled substances. The hope is that such terminology will cover all substances already in existence as well as any substances yet to be discovered that prove similar to marijuana or THC. Congress pursued this approach in both the Controlled Substance Analogue

---

1. Marijuana's perceived harms are discussed in Chapter 5. It is worth noting that many people who deem natural marijuana to be safe nonetheless view synthetic cannabinoids as dangerous.

Enforcement Act of 1986 (Analogue Act) and the Synthetic Drug Abuse Prevention Act of 2012 (Synthetic Act). The Analogue Act defines a "controlled substance analog" as a substance:

> (i) the chemical structure of which is substantially similar to the chemical structure of a controlled substance in schedule I or II;
> (ii) which has a stimulant, depressant, or hallucinogenic effect on the central nervous system that is substantially similar to or greater than the stimulant, depressant, or hallucinogenic effect on the central nervous system of a controlled substance in schedule I or II; or
> (iii) with respect to a particular person, which such person represents or intends to have a stimulant, depressant, or hallucinogenic effect on the central nervous system that is substantially similar to or greater than the stimulant, depressant, or hallucinogenic effect on the central nervous system of a controlled substance in schedule I or II.

21 U.S.C. § 802(32)(A). It further provides that a "controlled substance analogue shall, to the extent intended for human consumption, be treated, for the purposes of any Federal law as a controlled substance in schedule I." 21 U.S.C. § 813. The later adopted Synthetic Act was more specifically targeted at synthetic cannabinoids. It places "any material, compound, mixture, or preparation which contains any quantity of cannabimimetic agents" on Schedule I, unless it has been listed on another Schedule or otherwise exempted. 21 U.S.C. § 812(c), Schedule I (d)(1). To simplify somewhat, it further defines "cannabimimetic agents" as "any substance that is a cannabinoid receptor type 1 (CB1 receptor) agonist," *id.* at (d)(2), that is, any substance that acts on the same cells (CB1 receptors) as the cannabinoids found in marijuana.

## Notes and Questions

1. For a more detailed description of state and federal efforts to define and regulate synthetic cannabinoids, see Stackhouse, Note, *supra*, at 1114-31.

2. Even though (as noted above) many people deem synthetic cannabinoids to be more dangerous than natural marijuana, the DEA and FDA have approved two synthetic cannabinoids (synthetic D9-THC and nabilone) for medical use in the United States. Chapter 5 discusses the approval of these substances and the implications for debates over natural marijuana.

3. One potential problem raised by the broad language (e.g., "substantially similar") used in statutes like the Analogue Act is that such language fails to give individuals adequate notice that a particular substance has been regulated. *See* Stackhouse, *supra*, at 1115 (discussing vagueness challenges to synthetic cannabinoid statutes). Chapter 3 discusses these vagueness concerns in more detail.

4. How should regulators respond to the development of designer drugs, including synthetic cannabinoids? Which approach—ex post or ex ante—do you prefer? Is there any other way to fill gaps in the law's coverage of substances that are similar to those found in marijuana?

# PART II

# MARIJUANA USERS

CHAPTER 3

# The Regulation of Marijuana Users in Prohibition Regimes

How governments treat marijuana users is at the crux of many debates over marijuana policy. Many commentators claim, for example, that prohibition regimes treat marijuana offenders, and especially marijuana *users*, far too harshly. But to evaluate such claims, it is necessary to understand the particulars of the laws governing marijuana users, as well as how those laws are being enforced. To that end, this chapter examines the regulation of marijuana users in prohibition regimes. (In similar fashion, the next chapter examines the regulation of users in legalization regimes.)

The chapter focuses on the chief prohibition directed at marijuana users: the offense of *simple possession* of marijuana.[1] For example, the federal Controlled Substances Act declares that:

> It shall be unlawful for any person knowingly or intentionally to *possess* a controlled substance unless such substance was obtained directly, or pursuant to a valid prescription or order, from a practitioner, while acting in the course of his professional practice. . . .

21 U.S.C. § 844(a) (emphasis added). Section A begins by discussing the three core elements of the possession offense. It also discusses three prominent legal defenses that have been raised to fend off otherwise successful prosecutions for simple possession of marijuana. Section B then discusses the range of criminal and civil sanctions that jurisdictions threaten to impose for the simple possession of marijuana, as well as the sanctions they actually impose.

## A. WHAT IS SIMPLE POSSESSION?

Possession seems like a simple concept at first, but possession doctrine has struggled to accommodate the almost infinite variety of cases to which it has been applied. No one doubts that someone caught alone with a marijuana joint in his hand "possesses" the drug. But what if the joint was found in his coat pocket? What if the joint was found wedged

---

1. There are, of course, other prohibitions directed at marijuana users, including bans on driving under the influence of marijuana and bans on the public consumption of marijuana. Those prohibitions are discussed in Chapter 4 below.

between the seats of a car in which he was one of several passengers? What if it was found in plain sight on a table in a shared hotel room? What if no joint was found at all, but marijuana was detected in the individual's bloodstream?

While courts and legislatures have devised a battery of tests to address situations like these, these tests have generated much confusion and criticism. *See, e.g., United States v. Holland,* 445 F.2d 701, 704-05 (D.C. Cir. 1971) (Tamm, J., concurring) ("The rhetorical legerdemain ... [regarding possession] invokes abstractions which appear more designed to achieve a particular result in an individual case than to stabilize and formalize a workable index of objective standards."); Charles Whitebread & Ronald Stevens, *Constructive Possession in Narcotics Cases: To Have and Have Not,* 58 Va. L. Rev. 751, 752 (1972) ("[T]he various tests that the courts have formulated to [determine whether a defendant possessed a drug] have failed to provide meaningful response, clouded judicial decision-making with conclusory labels, and created a morass of confusion and inconsistency."). Nevertheless, it is possible to identify and describe in abstract terms three core elements comprising the offense of simple possession of marijuana. Namely, the government must prove:

(1) that defendant was aware of the presence of marijuana and of its nature (culpable knowledge); and
(2) that defendant had the ability and desire to control the substance (control); and
(3) that it was, in fact, marijuana (marijuana).

There is no more to it. The government need not show what the defendant intended to do with the marijuana. For this reason, the offense is commonly called *simple* possession. Chapter 7 considers the offense of possession with the intent to distribute marijuana, a more serious charge reserved for drug suppliers that does require proof of an additional mens rea (state of mind) element.

The sections below discuss the legal definitions of each of the three elements in turn, including important variations across jurisdictions. Equal in importance to the abstract definitions of these elements are the rules jurisdictions have developed regarding the quantum of evidence that is required to satisfy each of them. These rules help define the strength of the inferences that juries and trial judges are allowed to draw from known facts. For example, when marijuana is found on the person of the defendant—say, in her coat pocket—courts generally allow the fact finder to presume that the defendant was aware of and desired to control the contraband. But when marijuana is found in a common area—say, a crowded hotel room—courts generally demand additional evidence of a defendant's knowledge and control of the marijuana in order to sustain a conviction. Hence, the sections below also discuss key rules regarding the proof required to establish each element.

## Notes and Questions

1. Why do jurisdictions prohibit the *possession* of marijuana (and other drugs), as opposed to the *use* of the drug? For one thing, possession serves as a proxy for use. After all, anyone who possesses marijuana is likely to use (or distribute) it someday. *See* Markus D. Dubber, *Policing Possession: The War on Crime and the End of Criminal Law,* 91 J. Crim. L. & Criminology 829, 907 (2001) ("One way of thinking of possession

offenses is to view them as criminalized presumptions of some other offense. In criminalizing possession, the legislature really criminalizes import, manufacture, purchase. Or forward looking, the legislature really criminalizes use, sale, or export."). But targeting this proxy *in lieu* of (or in addition to) use itself has some practical advantages. As Ronald Stevens and the late Professor Charles Whitebread observed,

> Criminalization of possession allows the police to arrest and convict an individual before he can use the proscribed object. Moreover, possession statutes provide a pragmatic means of facilitating law enforcement. In the drug area, for example, it is easier to show possession than to prove use, distribution, or sale.

*Constructive Possession in Narcotics Cases: To Have and Have Not*, 58 Va. L. Rev. 751, 753-54 (1972).

2. Understanding possession doctrine is critically important for anyone interested in marijuana law and policy. For one thing, possession is the most common offense involving marijuana (and other drugs). Between 2001 and 2010, there were more than 7 million arrests involving marijuana possession, compared to a (still rather large) 1 million arrests involving marijuana trafficking. *E.g.*, American Civil Liberties Union, *The War on Marijuana in Black and White* 4 (2013). Indeed, marijuana possession is one of the most common of *all* offenses in the nation's criminal justice system. *E.g.*, Federal Bureau of Investigation, *Crime in the United States*, 2014 (reporting that arrests for marijuana possession accounted for more than 5 percent of *all* arrests in the United States in 2014). Even though the number of arrests of marijuana users is sure to decline as marijuana law reforms continue to proliferate, possession doctrine will continue to play an important role in marijuana law and policy throughout the country.[2] After all, legalization regimes continue to proscribe possession by at least *some* persons, such as recreational users (in regimes that permit only medical use) or minors. And as noted above, possession doctrine also plays a role in the laws governing marijuana suppliers.

## 1. Culpable Knowledge

In nearly all jurisdictions, the crime of possession requires culpable knowledge. The mens rea (state of mind) requirement is explicit in most statutes. For example, 21 U.S.C. section 844(a) makes it unlawful "*knowingly* or *intentionally* to possess" marijuana (emphases added).[3] A very small minority of jurisdictions have eliminated the culpable knowledge requirement. *See Washington v. Cleppe*, 635 P.2d 435 (Wash. 1981) (en banc) (recognizing that Washington legislature's excision of "knowingly or intentionally" language from Uniform Controlled Substances Act created a strict liability offense of possession); *City of Kennewick v. Day*, 11 P.3d 304 (Wash. 2000) (en banc) (holding that local ordinance making it "unlawful for any person to possess marijuana" created a strict

---

[2]. Possession remains an important concept in other areas of law as well, as jurisdictions ban possession of a wide variety of contraband apart from marijuana, including other drugs, obscenity, tools commonly used to commit burglary, stolen property, counterfeit goods, and firearms, among many other things. *See* Dubber, *Policing Possession*, *supra*.

[3]. Mens rea is such a bedrock principle of American criminal law that some courts have read a "knowledge" requirement into statutes that do not explicitly include one.

liability offense of possession). But even those jurisdictions that have eliminated the culpable knowledge requirement generally give defendants the chance to raise an "unwitting possession" defense, as discussed below in Section A.4.c.

For the offense of possession, culpable knowledge entails awareness of two distinct facts. In particular, the defendant must be aware of the *presence* of a substance and must also be aware that the substance is marijuana, or at least an illicit drug of some sort.

### a. Proof of Knowledge

It is unusual to have direct proof of a defendant's culpable knowledge, such as an admission by the defendant. Instead, a defendant's knowledge usually must be established circumstantially, *McFadden v. United States*, 135 S. Ct. 2298, 2304, n.1 (2015), through facts such as defendant's nervous behavior, *New York v. Van Vorst*, 118 A.D.3d 1035 (N.Y. App. 2014), her prior convictions for a marijuana offense, *Iowa v. Henderson*, 696 N.W.2d 5, 11 (Iowa 2005), or her prior use of marijuana, *Washington v. Weiss*, 438 P.2d 610 (Wash. 1968).

The following case provides a detailed discussion of several different types of evidence that governments might use to establish culpable knowledge. It also illuminates the disagreements that can arise over interpreting such evidence.

### *Ervin v. Virginia*
704 S.E.2d 135 (Va. App. 2011)

BEALES, J.:

[Samuel Ervin was convicted of possession of marijuana with intent to distribute. He appealed, claiming, inter alia, that there was insufficient evidence that he had guilty knowledge of the marijuana found in his car.]

On February 29, 2008, at 8:20 p.m., Portsmouth Officers O'Brien and Rad stopped a vehicle being driven by appellant after the officers observed a traffic violation. Appellant was the sole occupant of the vehicle. Neither officer observed him make any furtive movements during their observations of him. However, as the officers approached the vehicle, "a strong odor of marijuana" was discernible through the car's open windows. . . .

. . . The officers then searched the vehicle both for the source of the strong odor of marijuana and for the vehicle's registration. Using the key that was in the vehicle's ignition, Officer Rad unlocked the glove compartment. The officers immediately observed two Ziploc bags inside the glove compartment. One of the Ziploc bags held ten knotted plastic bag corners ("baggie corners") containing marijuana, and the other Ziploc bag held thirteen baggie corners containing marijuana. No smoking devices or drug paraphernalia were found inside the vehicle or in appellant's possession.

The vehicle belonged to Tiffany Killabrew, the mother of appellant's daughter. It was Killabrew's "secondary car," which she loaned to various people, including appellant, her brother, and her sister. Killabrew testified that appellant borrowed the vehicle sometime between 6:00 and 7:00 p.m. on February 29, 2008. . . .

Appellant testified in his own defense, denying ownership of the marijuana. When asked on cross-examination whether he was familiar with the smell of marijuana, appellant initially replied, "Maybe." When asked to clarify his answer, appellant then

testified, "No, not really. Usually you can smell like—no, not really. I'm not even going to claim that. Not really." . . .
. . .

Appellant does not appear to contest the trial court's finding that the marijuana recovered from the glove compartment was subject to his dominion and control.[5] However, he argues that the Commonwealth failed to prove beyond a reasonable doubt that he had the requisite guilty knowledge of this marijuana. . . .

### . . . FACTORS INDICATIVE OF GUILTY KNOWLEDGE

[M]ere occupancy and proximity, although factors to be considered among the totality of the circumstances, are insufficient *standing alone* to prove a defendant's guilty knowledge of illegal drugs. . . .

Here, . . . the evidence at trial *did* present other facts and circumstances permitting the trial court to draw the conclusion that appellant was aware of the presence and character of the marijuana in the glove compartment—and these facts and circumstances may be considered *in addition to* appellant's occupancy of the vehicle and proximity to the marijuana. Based on the combined force of these concurrent and related circumstances, the trial court's finding that appellant had guilty knowledge of the marijuana in the glove compartment was not plainly wrong or unsupported by the evidence.

### . . . THE STRONG ODOR OF MARIJUANA

A defendant's knowledge of the presence and character of a drug may be shown by evidence of the acts, statements, or conduct of the accused, . . . as well as by "other facts or circumstances" tending to demonstrate the accused's guilty knowledge of the drug . . . .

Here, appellant was driving a vehicle that smelled strongly of marijuana—the very same illegal drug discovered in the vehicle's glove compartment. This odor, which was readily discernible to both officers as marijuana when they approached appellant's vehicle, would certainly have been apparent to appellant as he sat in the vehicle. The strong and distinctive odor of the drug provided a significant indication to anyone inside (or even near) the vehicle that marijuana was located within the vehicle. . . .

Based on the officers' testimony, the trial court found that the strong marijuana odor emanating from the vehicle was from marijuana that had been smoked. . . .

The trial court not *only* found that the officers smelled *already* smoked marijuana, it *also* found that the marijuana had been *recently* smoked by appellant or someone in the car with him. The trial court's finding, which was certainly not unreasonable given the officers' testimony concerning the strength and obviousness of the marijuana odor as they approached the vehicle, is entitled to deference during appellate review for sufficiency of the evidence. . . .

Furthermore, Killabrew's testimony established that appellant took possession of the vehicle between 6:00 and 7:00 p.m., approximately two hours before the traffic stop.

---

5. The key to the vehicle, which appellant used to engage the ignition, was also capable of unlocking the glove compartment where the marijuana was found. "'The law is well established that possession of the means to exercise dominion [and] control over an item gives the possessor dominion [and] control over the item [itself].'" . . .

Thus, the trial court's inference that the marijuana detected by the officers must have been smoked—either by appellant or by someone else in appellant's presence—while appellant was in possession of the vehicle was "reasonable and justified" based on the strength of the odor. . . . Therefore, the officers' detection of the strong odor of recently burnt marijuana certainly does not undermine the trial court's conclusion that appellant was aware of the "fresh" marijuana in the glove compartment.[8] . . . Nothing in this record suggests any other means, in the approximately two hours that appellant had possessed the car, of creating such a strong odor of marijuana that people could readily identify the odor before actually reaching the vehicle.

. . . [T]he strong odor of marijuana from within the vehicle . . . tends "to show or allow [ ] the trial court to reasonably infer" that appellant was aware of the marijuana in the glove compartment. . . . Several additional facts and circumstances in the record here further support the trial court's finding that appellant was aware of the presence and character of the marijuana discovered in the glove compartment. . . .

### . . . APPELLANT'S SOLE POSSESSION OF THE VEHICLE AND HIS POSSESSION OF THE KEY TO THE GLOVE COMPARTMENT

Appellant was in *sole* possession of the vehicle at the time the marijuana was found. . . . Appellant also possessed the key to the vehicle and its glove compartment and, therefore, was the *sole* person at that time with means to access the glove compartment containing the marijuana. The trial court, acting as factfinder in this case, was permitted to consider these facts as circumstances further indicating appellant's guilty knowledge of the marijuana found in the glove compartment. . . .

. . .

### . . . APPELLANT'S APPARENT RELUCTANCE TO ACCESS THE GLOVE COMPARTMENT

The officers' testimony reflects that appellant did not attempt to retrieve the vehicle's registration from the glove compartment—where, of course, the officers eventually found the marijuana—despite the glove compartment's obvious utility as "a customary place" to find a vehicle's registration. . . . Indeed, when asked to produce a vehicle's registration, suspects routinely access a vehicle's glove compartment . . . , even in instances, like here, where the vehicle is not actually owned by the suspect. . . .

Here, however, despite being asked by the officers to produce both the registration and his driver's license, appellant readily provided the officers with only his driver's license, which was suspended. He did not even attempt to retrieve the vehicle's registration from the glove compartment. This evidence suggests that appellant was reluctant to access, in the officers' presence, the glove compartment where the drugs were located. . . . .

Based on this apparent reluctance to open the glove compartment, where the vehicle's registration would customarily be located, . . . a rational factfinder could infer that appellant knew, if he opened the glove compartment, the officers would immediately

---

8. It is axiomatic that burnt marijuana must originate as unburnt marijuana. Therefore, the fact that the Ziploc bags of unburnt marijuana did not contain the same number of baggie corners (ten in one and thirteen in the other) supports the trial court's inference that someone had recently smoked this marijuana inside the vehicle. In addition, no other source for the marijuana odor was found in the vehicle.

observe the illegal substance. Again, considered in isolation this fact perhaps would not provide sufficient evidence on appeal to support the factfinder's determination that appellant was aware of the character and nature of the substance in the glove compartment. However, considered together with all the evidence presented at trial, this fact adds to the mounting collection of circumstances that support the trial court's finding of guilt.

### . . . APPELLANT'S SELF-SERVING TESTIMONY

The trial court obviously rejected appellant's testimony that the marijuana did not belong to him. This rejected claim of innocence, when viewed in the light most favorable to the Commonwealth, as we must since it was the prevailing party below, "'must be interpreted . . . as [a] mere fabrication [ ] to conceal his guilt.'" The trial court also clearly rejected appellant's equivocal and ultimately self-serving testimony that he would not recognize the smell of marijuana . . .

This Court, following the precedent of the United States Supreme Court, has recognized a "general principle of evidence law that the factfinder is entitled to consider a party's dishonesty about a material fact as 'affirmative evidence of guilt.'" . . . Here, given the strong odor of marijuana emanating from the vehicle and the circumstantial nature of this case, appellant's ability to recognize the smell of marijuana certainly concerned a relevant and material fact. The trial court, therefore, was permitted to assign appropriate weight to appellant's equivocal testimony that perhaps he could, and then that he could not, recognize the smell of marijuana. Again, this evidence is not an isolated factor in this case, but instead is further support for the trial court's determination that, based on the totality of the circumstances, appellant was aware of the presence of the marijuana in the glove compartment.

### . . . ABANDONMENT OF VALUABLE CONTRABAND

Although appellant asserts that the evidence failed to exclude the possibility that the marijuana baggies belonged to someone else and that he was simply unaware of the presence of drugs in the glove compartment, the Commonwealth "is not required to prove that there is no possibility that someone else may have planted, discarded, abandoned or placed the contraband where the contraband is discovered." . . . A factfinder is permitted to infer that "drugs are a commodity of significant value, unlikely to be abandoned or carelessly left in an area." . . .

Here, it is uncontested that the key to the vehicle's ignition also unlocked the glove compartment. The glove compartment's lock provided little security—given several people were known to use the vehicle. Thus, the person who put the marijuana in the glove compartment did so knowing that anyone who drove the vehicle would have the ability to open the locked glove compartment—for any reason—and would then see the marijuana, which was readily observable the moment the glove compartment was opened since it was then in plain view as it was not hidden by anything in the glove compartment. Any other driver of the vehicle, therefore, could easily take that marijuana from the glove compartment.[15]

---

15. Killabrew regularly permitted appellant to use the vehicle, and appellant admitted that he used the car when he needed to run errands. This regular use of the vehicle is very different than a situation where a person leases a rental car or where a person unwittingly drives a friend's car on an irregular or one-time basis.

Under these circumstances, the trial court was entitled to find it highly unlikely that someone else simply left the marijuana—which had a street value of over $200—in the glove compartment of the car. This inference is another factor supporting the trial court's finding that appellant possessed the marijuana with knowledge of its nature and character . . .

. . . Consequently, based on the combined effect of all of the facts and circumstances presented at trial, which were far more significant than appellant's mere occupancy of the vehicle in which drugs were found and proximity to those drugs, . . . we cannot say that the trial judge here was not a rational factfinder—just as we cannot say that *no* rational factfinder in this Commonwealth could have found beyond a reasonable doubt that appellant constructively possessed this marijuana with knowledge of its nature and character. . . .

[The court also upheld the trial court's verdict that appellant possessed the marijuana with the intent to distribute it (a crime discussed in Chapter 7), based on the testimony of a police expert concerning the packaging and quantity of marijuana found in the glove compartment.]

ALSTON, J., dissenting:
. . . I respectfully disagree with the majority's portrayal of each of [the facts used to prove defendant's knowledge] . . . and the legal significance the majority awards to them.

### . . . THE ODOR OF BURNT MARIJUANA

First, the majority places great emphasis on the smell of marijuana emanating from the vehicle. The evidence established that when the officers approached the driver's side of the vehicle, they smelled a strong odor of marijuana coming from the car. As the majority notes, the trial judge interpreted the evidence as suggesting the odor was that of marijuana that had been smoked, *i.e.* burnt marijuana. . . . The trial court stated, "Either [appellant] had been smoking [marijuana] or he had recently just had someone in the car who was smoking it." There was no evidence that the odor detected by the officers was coming from appellant's person, that appellant appeared intoxicated, that appellant showed any physical signs of having recently used marijuana, or that appellant possessed any drugs or drug paraphernalia on his person. Moreover, no matches, smoking devices, or remnants of previously smoked marijuana were apparently found in the car.

The record does not show that the odor was that of fresh marijuana, which might indicate that appellant had at least reason to suspect the vehicle contained fresh marijuana.[17] The majority dismisses the importance of the distinction between the smell of fresh marijuana and the smell of burnt marijuana. . . . However, the majority gives no reason why the trial court could reasonably infer, based on the smell of *burnt* marijuana, that appellant was aware of *fresh* marijuana in the glove compartment. . . .

The majority also relies upon the trial court's finding that the officers smelled marijuana that had been *recently* smoked by appellant or someone in the car with him and that

---

17. The majority notes, "It is axiomatic that burnt marijuana must originate as unburnt marijuana." . . . While that may be true, the Commonwealth had the burden to prove appellant was aware of this *particular* marijuana. The existence of an odor does not necessarily establish who is responsible for the odor. In any event, the constructive possession of marijuana odor is not a crime in our Commonwealth. . . .

appellant had taken possession of the vehicle approximately two hours before the traffic stop. . . . . Even if the trial court was entitled to conclude, based on the officers' testimony about the strength of the smell of the marijuana, that it had been "recently" smoked,[19] this does not necessarily support the holding that appellant was aware of the character and nature of the marijuana in the glove compartment. Appellant took possession of the vehicle only two hours before the traffic stop. Marijuana could have been smoked in the car hours before appellant took possession of the vehicle and still resulted in a strong odor of marijuana suggesting it was "recently" smoked in the car. . . .

[T]he distinctive odor of a drug is not, by itself, sufficient circumstantial evidence to establish a defendant's knowledge of the character and presence of the drug. Although the majority cites additional factors that purportedly constitute circumstantial evidence of appellant's knowledge of the presence and character of the marijuana, their primary reliance on the odor of the drug in the car effectively affirms the conviction of appellant on the basis of possession of the *odor* of marijuana. Even more problematically, the smell of burnt marijuana is simply not indicative of the presence of fresh marijuana. Thus, the presence of the distinctive odor of burnt marijuana is not sufficient to establish appellant's knowledge of the fresh marijuana in the glove compartment.

### . . . APPELLANT'S SOLE POSSESSION OF THE VEHICLE AND HIS POSSESSION OF THE KEY TO THE GLOVE COMPARTMENT

Next, the majority notes that appellant was the sole person with means to access the glove compartment containing the marijuana. . . . While this establishes appellant's dominion and control over the vehicle and the items located therein, . . . this fact does not prove appellant's knowledge about the nature and character of those items. . . . In this case, the key that unlocked the glove compartment was the same key that was necessary to operate the vehicle. Put simply, the fact that appellant possessed that key does not logically lead to the inference, beyond a reasonable doubt, that appellant knew the glove compartment's contents.

### . . . APPELLANT'S "RELUCTANCE" TO ACCESS THE GLOVE COMPARTMENT

Further, the majority notes that appellant did not attempt to produce the vehicle's registration and cites this failure as evidence that appellant was aware of the marijuana in the glove compartment. . . . However, there is no evidence to suggest appellant refused to produce the registration or that he refused to look in the vehicle's glove compartment. Rather, appellant's testimony, corroborated by the arresting officers, was that when the officers approached the vehicle, appellant explained that he did not have the vehicle's registration because the car did not belong to him. Notably, the officers asked appellant

---

19. I note that there was no evidence in the record concerning the length of time that the smell of marijuana would linger after it is smoked, nor that appellant's person or clothing smelled of marijuana, that appellant was intoxicated, or that any matches, smoking devices, or remnants of previously smoked marijuana were found in the car. Furthermore, the majority states that "the fact that the Ziploc bags of unburnt marijuana did not contain the same number of baggie corners (ten in one and thirteen in the other) supports the trial court's inference that someone had recently smoked this marijuana inside the vehicle." . . . The difference in the number of Ziploc baggies does not suggest that marijuana had been smoked in the vehicle at all, let alone *recently* smoked in the vehicle. The majority's statement on this point rests upon an assumption that each Ziploc bag began with an equal number of baggie corners, a fact we have no reason to assume.

for "*his* driver's license and registration," rather than simply "*the* registration" for the vehicle. Thus, appellant's statement that the vehicle did not belong to him was responsive to the officers' request; appellant was simply anticipating the officers' reason for requesting the registration and advising the officers that the registration would show he was not the owner of the vehicle. . . .

Although appellant did not access the glove compartment here, there was no prevailing legal justification for the trial court to infer that he had knowledge of the glove compartment's contents. Where a fact "is equally susceptible of two interpretations one of which is consistent with the innocence of the accused, [the trier of fact] cannot arbitrarily adopt that interpretation which incriminates him." . . . In fact, the Commonwealth presented no evidence to suggest appellant made any motion toward the glove compartment as police stopped the vehicle, or that appellant engaged in any other behavior that would indicate he knew there were drugs in the locked glove compartment. There was no evidence that appellant appeared nervous, and in fact, the officers testified that appellant was entirely cooperative throughout the stop. I cannot reach the conclusion that these facts somehow support appellant's culpability in this instance.

### . . . "ABANDONMENT" OF VALUABLE CONTRABAND

The majority also notes, "'drugs are a commodity of significant value, unlikely to be abandoned or carelessly left in an area.'" . . . However, in the instant case, there is no indication that the marijuana was "abandoned or carelessly left." On the contrary, the fact that the drugs were secured in a locked glove compartment could suggest the drugs' owner attempted to secure and hide the marijuana from the view of others. Thus, this factor does not support a finding that appellant knew the nature and character of the marijuana found in the car.

### . . . APPELLANT'S "SELF-SERVING" TESTIMONY

Finally, the majority relies upon appellant's "equivocal" testimony that he would not recognize the smell of marijuana. . . .

[The majority suggests] that the trial court was entitled to consider appellant's dishonesty as affirmative evidence of guilt.

However, appellant's initial statement that he may be familiar with the smell of marijuana followed by the statement "No, not really" does not amount to a change in statements, first suggesting that he is familiar with the smell of marijuana and then stating that he is not. "Maybe" is defined as both "perhaps" and "uncertainty." *Merriam-Webster's Collegiate Dictionary* 767 (Frederick C. Mish et al. eds., 11th ed. 2005). Thus, appellant's initial answer could have conveyed appellant's *uncertainty* about his own knowledge of the smell of marijuana, not a statement that "perhaps he could" recognize the smell of marijuana. . . .

Furthermore, even assuming the trial judge correctly determined appellant was familiar with the smell of marijuana based on appellant's equivocal testimony, there was no evidence presented by the Commonwealth suggesting appellant's familiarity with that smell proved that he had smoked marijuana in the vehicle, or knew the vehicle contained fresh marijuana *at the time he occupied the vehicle.*

. . .

[Other] factors connecting appellant to the marijuana found in the glove compartment in the car are not present in this case. Although appellant was in the car, he was not the owner of the car. Personal items belonging to appellant were not found in the glove compartment with the marijuana. Appellant made no furtive gestures suggesting he was aware of the presence of the marijuana. . . .

Given the facts of this case, I would conclude the evidence is at best in equipoise. "If, after [the court resolves all conflicts in the evidence], the evidence of guilt or innocence remains anywhere near equipoise—that is, the facts are 'equally susceptible to two or more constructions'—then reasonable doubt exists as a matter of law." . . . In this case, it is equally likely that someone else used marijuana in the car or used marijuana prior to getting in the car, at some time prior to the traffic stop. This is especially true given Killabrew's testimony that she lent the car to several people on a regular basis. . . . Because Killabrew either did not or could not fall on the sword of criminal responsibility in this matter does not require that appellant must therefore assume criminal responsibility. . . .

Thus, I would conclude that as a matter of law, the evidence is insufficient to find appellant guilty of possession of marijuana. . . .

## Notes and Questions

1. Do you agree with court's ruling? Consider each of the factors on which the court bases its decision: Do you agree more with the majority's or the dissent's assessment thereof? Based on the totality of the circumstances, was there enough evidence for a rational jury to conclude beyond a reasonable doubt that the defendant knew there was marijuana in the glove compartment?

### b. Presumptions Regarding Knowledge

In the vast majority of jurisdictions, courts allow juries to presume that a defendant had culpable knowledge based solely on the fact the a prohibited substance was found on the defendant's person or somewhere to which the defendant had exclusive access. The following case discusses the use of presumptions that help the government satisfy the knowledge element.

### *Missouri v. Bell*
719 S.W.2d 763 (Mo. 1986)

BILLINGS, J.

On October 21, 1984, David Andrews, a guard at the Missouri Training Center for Men at Moberly, a correctional institution, conducted a general search of inmates, including defendant [Tessie Bell]. Andrews testified that he found a "marijuana joint" and a small packet containing marijuana in defendant's left rear pocket. Chemical analysis confirmed that the substance in the packet was marijuana. Defendant testified that another inmate had given him the packet to deliver to a third inmate and that he did not know what was in the packet until Andrews opened it. The jury found the defendant guilty of . . . [possession of marijuana in a correctional institution], and the trial court sentenced him to a term of five years imprisonment, to run consecutively to a term that defendant was then serving.

Defendant first contends that there was not sufficient evidence to support the verdict against him because the state failed to prove that he "knowingly" possessed a controlled substance. . . . There is no direct evidence regarding defendant's knowledge that he possessed marijuana other than his testimony that he was unaware of the contents of the packet taken from him. Knowledge, however, may also be shown by circumstantial evidence. . . . A prima facie case of knowing possession of a controlled substance is made out by the prosecution showing the defendant's possession of the substance. . . . A defense that defendant was not aware of the controlled substance in his possession merely creates a conflict in the evidence, the resolution of which is for the jury. . . . Thus, the state's uncontradicted evidence showing defendant's possession of a packet containing marijuana constituted substantial evidence from which a jury could rationally have determined that defendant knowingly possessed the marijuana. . . .

WELLIVER, J., dissenting:

The majority allows a jury to convict a defendant after the prosecution has produced evidence of only two of the three required elements of the offense. Heretofore, we have required that the prosecution prove each and every element of the offense, by either direct or circumstantial evidence . . . The majority now holds that a showing of one element, possession, creates a prima facie case for another element, knowledge. The defendant is no longer innocent until proven guilty, but, now he must prove his lack of knowledge and his innocence.

## Notes and Questions

1. Under *Bell* and similar cases, the jury may convict a defendant based solely on finding that the defendant had exclusive access to the area where the marijuana was found. The presumption, however, may be rebutted by the defendant. Nonetheless, is the presumption sound? To test your intuitions, check the contents of your backpack, purse, coat pocket, etc. Were you surprised by anything you found? Are you now more or less inclined to support the presumption?

2. Is the dissent correct in suggesting that the presumption of knowledge transforms simple possession into a strict liability crime (i.e., one for which no knowledge is required)? Consider the following Problem:

**Problem 3.1**: Andy gave Benjamin a small wrapped box for Benjamin's birthday. Benjamin sets the wrapped box on the front passenger seat of his car as he drives home. Along the way, a police officer stops Benjamin for speeding. The officer looks through Benjamin's window and asks "What's in the box?" Benjamin says "I don't know. It's a present I got from my friend, but my birthday isn't until next week." The officer says "Go ahead and open it. I won't tell." Benjamin opens the box and finds a bag of marijuana inside. The

officer charges Benjamin with simple possession of marijuana. Under *Bell*, would a jury be allowed to convict Benjamin of possession? Even so, would a jury necessarily do so? In any event, should Benjamin bear the burden of rebutting the presumption?

3. Virginia is a rare jurisdiction that does not allow a jury to presume knowledge of contraband based solely on the defendant's exclusive access to it. Va. Code Ann. § 18.2-250 ("Upon the prosecution of a person for a violation of this section, ownership or occupancy of premises or vehicle upon or in which a controlled substance was found shall not create a presumption that such person either knowingly or intentionally possessed such controlled substance."). *See also Ervin, supra*, at 154 (Alston, J., dissenting) (recognizing that under Virginia law, "the fact that appellant possessed [the key to the glove compartment] does not logically lead to the inference, beyond a reasonable doubt, that appellant knew the glove compartment's contents").

4. Should the presumption of knowledge apply when the quantity of marijuana possessed is minute? *See* Seth Davidson, Note, *Criminal Liability for Possession of Nonusable Amounts of Controlled Substances*, 77 Colum. L. Rev. 596 (1977) (discussing the relationship between quantity and knowledge). Consider the following Problem:

**Problem 3.2:** Andy was stopped by police. During a search, the police found a few "minute particles" of marijuana leaves mixed among the lint and debris in Andy's jacket pocket. The particles weighed less than 20 milligrams. May a jury presume that Andy knew the marijuana was there? *Compare Ohio v. Dempsey*, 259 N.E.2d 745 (Ohio 1970) ("Common experience does not tend to indicate that one knows what is in the linty debris of his pockets. It is just as likely, if not more so, that one has no idea what is hidden there."), *with Minnesota v. Siirila*, 193 N.W.2d 467 (Minn. 1971) ("[T]he inference is permissible that, marijuana having been found in a jacket shown to belong to defendant and to have been worn by him, whatever was in the jacket was there with his knowledge.").

### c. Knowledge of the Substance's Nature

As noted above, the government needs to prove not only that the defendant was aware that she possessed a substance but also that she was aware of the *nature* of that substance. As the Supreme Court has explained, the government can satisfy this burden in two distinct ways:

> . . . [The] knowledge requirement [under the CSA] may be met by showing that the defendant knew he possessed a substance listed on the schedules, even if he did not know which substance it was. Take, for example, a defendant whose role in a larger drug organization is to distribute a white powder to customers. The defendant may know that the white powder is listed on the schedules even if he does not know precisely what substance it is. And if so, he would be guilty of knowingly distributing "a controlled substance."

> The knowledge requirement may also be met by showing that the defendant knew the identity of the substance he possessed. Take, for example, a defendant who knows he is distributing heroin but does not know that heroin is listed on the schedules . . . Because ignorance of the law is typically no defense to criminal prosecution, . . . this defendant would also be guilty of knowingly distributing "a controlled substance."

*McFadden*, 135 S. Ct. at 2304.

### *(i) Proof of Knowledge About a Substance's Nature*

In many cases, the same evidence can be used to prove both awareness of the presence of a substance and awareness of its identity. In *Ervin*, for example, the pungent smell of marijuana was used to establish both that defendant must have known *something* was in the car but also that defendant must have known that something was marijuana.

But recognizing that a substance is *marijuana* necessarily requires having some basic knowledge about the drug's physical properties: its look, smell, and so on. Even if it is safe to assume that most people are familiar with the physical properties of conventional marijuana products like joints, marijuana can be consumed in a variety of forms, as discussed in Chapter 2. Some products, like vape pens and edibles, lack the distinctive smell and look of more traditional forms of marijuana. How is the government supposed to demonstrate that someone caught with a marijuana lollipop or vape pen actually knew it contained prohibited marijuana? In the following case, the court is confronted by a similar question stemming from a prosecution for possession of *synthetic* marijuana.

## *Missouri v. Paul*
### 436 S.W.3d 713 (Mo. App. 2014)

HARDWICK, J.

On November 22, 2011, Chief Glen Garton and Officer Dennis Banks of the Lathrop police department, went to Paul's residence in connection with an unrelated matter. Chief Garton knocked on the door of Paul's residence and identified himself. Paul opened the door and invited the officers in. While inside, Chief Garton observed what appeared to be the burnt end of a marijuana cigarette in an ashtray on Paul's kitchen table. Chief Garton seized the cigarette, which was later determined by laboratory analysis to contain .03 grams of synthetic cannabinoid.

The State subsequently charged Paul with the class A misdemeanor of possession of a controlled substance . . . , alleging that . . . ["]the defendant possessed a synthetic cannabinoid (synthetic marijuana), . . . knowing of its presence and nature." Following a bench trial, . . . the court [found] Paul guilty of possession of a controlled substance and sentence[ed] her to forty-eight hours in jail. Paul appeals. . . .

. . .

. . . In 2011, the statutory definition of "controlled substance" was amended to include "synthetic cannabinoids." . . . "To sustain a conviction for possession of a controlled substance, the State must prove the following two elements: (1) conscious and intentional possession of the substance, either actual or constructive; and (2) awareness of the presence and nature of the substance." . . .

Here, Paul does not dispute that she had possession of the controlled substance, nor does she dispute that she was aware of such possession. Rather, Paul argues that she "lacked the knowledge of the *nature* of the drug found in her home." The crux of Paul's argument is that she "had no knowledge of the presence of an *illegal* substance in her home." (Emphasis added). She notes that the possession of synthetic marijuana did not become illegal until August 28, 2011. . . .

Paul presented testimony at trial that she hosted a "card party" at her home on November 17, 2011. When Paul left her party briefly "for a beer run," her guests called her and asked if they could burn "K2" or "Mr. Happy"—both brand names for synthetic marijuana. One of Paul's guests had purchased the "Mr. Happy" at a gas station. Paul testified that she instructed her guests to wait until she got home because she was not familiar with the product.

When Paul returned home, she inspected the package. Paul testified that the substance's label warned that its contents were "not for human consumption," and that the label stated "probably three times" that its contents were "one hundred percent legal." After reading the "Mr. Happy" package, Paul allowed the cigarette to be burned in the ashtray "like . . . incense." Paul testified that no one actually smoked the substance.

The flaw in Paul's argument is that the State was not required to prove that she knew the subject substance was illegal. The Narcotic Drug Act previously defined "possessing a controlled substance" as occurring when "a person, with the knowledge of the presence and illegal nature of a substance, has actual or constructive possession of the substance." § 195.010(33), RSMo 1997. The Act, however, has since been amended to delete the word "illegal" from the definition of possession. § 195.010(34). Thus, while the State is required to prove that the defendant had knowledge of the general character of the substance—"i.e., that the substance was a drug of some sort, and not just baking power"—the State is not required to prove that the defendant knew the substance was illicit. . . . Consequently, Paul's arguments that she believed the substance was legal must fail because a defendant's knowledge of the illegal status of a substance is irrelevant in a prosecution for possession of a controlled substance.

In addition to her arguments regarding her ignorance of the illegality of the substance, Paul asserts that "she genuinely believed the cigarette contained a form of incense." To the extent Paul is arguing that there was insufficient evidence to prove that she had knowledge of the substance's general character, that argument also fails. While there was testimony at trial supporting Paul's position, when properly viewing the record in the light most favorable to the verdict, the evidence is sufficient to prove beyond a reasonable doubt that Paul had knowledge of the general nature of the substance found in her kitchen. When Chief Garton found the substance in Paul's home, it was in an ashtray and was rolled up in a paper in a manner commonly used to smoke marijuana. Additionally, Paul testified that the "Mr. Happy" package referred to its contents as "hash"—a common slang term for marijuana and the short form of "hashish," which is the resin extract of the cannabis plant. . . . Finally, the substance's label made multiple statements regarding its legality. Based on this evidence, the circuit court could reasonably infer that Paul was not under the impression that the "Mr. Happy" product was simply incense and that she was aware of the substance's drug-like nature. . . .

Part II. Marijuana Users

## Notes and Questions

1. Take a look at each pair of photos below. Only one of the pictures in each pair depicts marijuana. Can you spot which one?

Pair 1

Pair 2

Pair 3

Pair 4

2. Compare the definitions of knowledge under Missouri law (see *Paul*) and federal law (see *McFadden*). How, if at all, do they differ? The synthetic marijuana Paul possessed is also a controlled substance under federal law. See Chapter 2, *supra*. Did Paul have culpable knowledge under the federal CSA?

3. Consider the following Problem:

<u>Problem 3.3</u>: Camila is caught with a small bag of hashish and charged with possession of marijuana. She admits that the bag is hers, but she insists "I thought it was heroin!" Assuming Camila is telling the truth, is she guilty of possession of marijuana? Does the *Paul* court provide a clue? *See also McFadden*, 135 S. Ct. at 2304 (discussing the knowledge requirement and transferred intent under the federal Controlled Substance Act).

*(ii) Knowledge of the Law*

What happens if a defendant knows that she is dealing with marijuana, but mistakenly (albeit genuinely) believes that possession of marijuana is not illegal? The following Problem illustrates this scenario:

<u>Problem 3.4</u>: Delilah is caught with a small bag of hashish and is charged with possession of marijuana. She admits the bag is hers, but she insists "I thought marijuana was legal!" Assuming Delilah is telling the truth about her beliefs, is she guilty of possession of marijuana? What would the *Paul* court say?

"[I]gnorance of the law is typically no defense to criminal prosecution." *McFadden*, 135 S. Ct. at 2304. Nonetheless, under the Due Process Clause of the federal constitution (and many state analogs), "a criminal statute must give fair warning of the conduct that it makes a crime. . . ." *Bouie v. City of Columbia*, 378 U.S. 347, 350 (1964). And it is possible for a statute to be so vague that it fails to give ordinary people adequate notice that some conduct is illegal. The following case discusses the Due Process notice requirement in the context of another prosecution for possession of synthetic marijuana.

## *Iowa v. Heinrichs*
845 N.W.2d 450 (Iowa App. 2013)

Tabor, J.

While patrolling . . . Waterloo police noticed a silver Kia with expired plates; Heinrichs was a passenger in the Kia. The stopping officer noticed an odor of marijuana coming from the car. After asking Heinrichs to step out of the car, the officer asked him if he "had anything on him." Heinrichs said he had a pipe for smoking "incense." The officer also found Henrichs in possession of a small black foil bag labeled "100% Pure Evil" that said it was "not for human consumption." Heinrichs later identified the substance as "K-2" and told the officer he bought it over the counter at the New Star liquor store.

The officers arrested Heinrichs for possessing [synthetic marijuana]. . . . The court found him guilty. . . .

. . .

Section 124.204(4)(u) [of the Iowa Code] reads as follows:

> Tetrahydrocannabinols, except as otherwise provided by rules of the board for medicinal purposes, meaning tetrahydrocannabinols naturally contained in a plant of the genus Cannabis (Cannabis plant) as well as synthetic equivalents of the substances contained in the Cannabis plant, or in the resinous extractives of such plant, and synthetic substances, derivatives, and their isomers with similar chemical structure and pharmacological activity to those substances contained in the plant, such as the following:
> (1) 1 cis or trans tetrahydrocannabinol, and their optical isomers.
> (2) 6 cis or trans tetrahydrocannabinol, and their optical isomers.
> (3) 3, 4 cis or trans tetrahydrocannabinol, and their optical isomers. (Since nomenclature of these substances is not internationally standardized, compounds of these structures, regardless of numerical designation of atomic positions covered.)

Heinrichs argues he was denied due process because section 124.204(4)(u) is overly vague [under the Due Process Clauses of the federal and state constitutions]. The void-for-vagueness doctrine has three foundations:

> First, a statute cannot be so vague that it does not give persons of ordinary understanding fair notice that certain conduct is prohibited. Second, due process requires that statutes provide those clothed with authority sufficient guidance to prevent the exercise of power in an arbitrary or discriminatory fashion. Third, a statute cannot sweep so broadly as to prohibit substantial amounts of constitutionally-protected activities, such as speech protected under the First Amendment. . . .

Because Heinrich argues the statute is vague as applied to him, only the first two foundations are at issue. . . .

In assessing whether a statute is void for vagueness, we presume constitutionality and give the statute any reasonable construction to uphold it. . . . It is incumbent on Heinrichs to "negate every reasonable basis to sustain" the provision. . . .

According to the lab analysis, Heinrichs possessed a "potent synthetic cannabinoid." He nevertheless contends a reasonable person could not have known it was contraband. He argues section 124.204(4)(u) . . . "does not define the criminal offense with sufficient definiteness that ordinary people could understand what conduct is prohibited." He complains: "[O]ne needs an advance degree in chemistry to understand what substances are illegal." Heinrichs also emphasizes: "Nowhere in schedules I through V of division II is 'K-2', '100% Pure Evil botanical potpourri' [] listed as a controlled substance." He asserts an ordinary person's confusion would be compounded by the fact that "K-2" was being sold over the counter at . . . retail locations.

As an initial point, we decline to find the schedule of controlled substances is constitutionally defective because it uses scientific terms that are obscure to persons of ordinary intelligence lacking in specialized knowledge. "The use of scientific or technical terminology or terms of art common in a regulated field does not automatically render a statute unconstitutionally vague." . . . We likewise reject Heinrichs's assertion the state legislature needed to specifically name the substance in the code to avoid a vagueness challenge. "The fact that a type of contraband may have various nicknames on the street does not render a statute punishing possession of that contraband invalid simply because it fails to list all of the then current nicknames."

The harder question is whether the catch-all language of section 124.204(4)(u) adequately notified Heinrichs that possession [of K-2] was illegal. That code section includes tetrahydrocannabinols, meaning the compounds naturally contained in Cannabis plants, as well as "synthetic equivalents of the substances contained in the Cannabis plant, or in the resinous extractives of such plant, and synthetic substances, derivatives, and their isomers with similar chemical structure and pharmacological activity to those substances contained in the plant. . . ." Iowa Code § 124.204(4)(u). . . .

We will not find a statute to be unconstitutionally vague if the meaning of the words used can be "fairly ascertained by reference to similar statutes, other judicial determinations, reference to the common law, to the dictionary, or if the words themselves have a common and generally accepted meaning." . . .

Here, we look to the dictionary definitions of the critical terms in section 124.204(4)(u). "Cannabis" is defined as "any of preparations (as marijuana or hashish) or chemicals (as THC) that are derived from hemp and are psychoactive." *Cannabis Definition*, Merriam-Webster, http://www.merriam-webster.com/dictionary/cannabis (last visited Aug. 30, 2013). "Synthetic" means "produced artificially". *Synthetic Definition*, Merriam-Webster, http:// www.merriam-webster.com/dictionary/synthetic (last visited Aug. 30, 2013). "Equivalent" is defined as "corresponding or virtually identical especially in effect or function". *Equivalent Definition*, Merriam-Webster, http://www. merriam-webster.com/dictionary/equivalent (last visited Aug. 30, 2013). We find the terminology used in section 124.204(4)(u) would provide persons of ordinary understanding the ability to ascertain what substances were prohibited. . . .

. . .

. . . Whatever doubts exist about the applicability of section 124.204 to those who may innocently purchase the substance over the counter at a retail store, Heinrichs's conduct falls squarely within the statute's intent to prohibit the possession of hallucinogenic substances. The packaging warned the substance was "not for human consumption," yet Heinrich was using a pipe to smoke it.[4] . . .

---

4. Commentators have concluded "a conspicuous 'not for human consumption' label has in many ways become code for 'this product is a drug.'" Timothy P. Stackhouse, 54 Ariz. L. Rev. 1105, 1131 (2012).

## Notes and Questions

1. Do you agree with the *Heinrichs* court? Is the ordinary citizen on notice that a package like the one pictured in **Figure 3.1** contains contraband and that possession of it is a crime?

Figure 3.1. Synthetic Marijuana

### 2. Control

Control constitutes the most difficult element to parse and to prove. Like culpable knowledge, the control element requires the government to demonstrate two things, namely:

(1) that defendant had the *power* to control (i.e., dispose of) marijuana, and
(2) that defendant had the *desire* to do so (another mens rea element).

The following case provides a useful introduction to the element of control and some of the legal controversies that surround it.

### *Regan v. Wyoming*
350 P.3d 702 (Wyo. 2015)

DAVIS, J.:

... Regan and his roommate Shayne Trujillo drove from Denver to Gillette[, Wyoming].... Officer Troy Cyr [of the Gillette Police Department], pulled them over after they stopped at a yield sign because there was no traffic on the roadway to yield to, and because the officer could not tell whether the vehicle had a rear license plate. Regan was the driver and owner. When Officer Cyr approached his window, he immediately smelled raw marijuana and requested that a drug dog be dispatched. Officer Vos arrived on the scene.... He also smelled marijuana ... [and] his dog ... alerted at the front passenger door, signaling that it had detected the odor of a controlled substance in the car.

Officer Vos then directed Trujillo to get out of the car, looked inside, and saw two glass jars containing what he recognized as marijuana on the passenger floorboard. After further inspection of the vehicle's interior, he discovered a plastic grocery bag, Ziploc sandwich bags, and a large white plastic bin in the passenger and cargo portions of the vehicle. Each contained clumps of a green leafy substance that he recognized as marijuana. The total weight of the marijuana was approximately one and a half pounds. Vos also found paraphernalia commonly associated with the sale of marijuana and $1,000 in cash in the glove box.

The officers arrested Regan and Trujillo . . . Regan voluntarily consented to an interview. . . . [Regan told the officers that w]hile still in Denver, Regan saw Trujillo load marijuana into his vehicle. He . . . expressly rejected Trujillo's offer to join in Trujillo's plan to make money distributing marijuana because "it wasn't worth the risk."

When they arrived in Gillette, Trujillo directed Regan to three different locations, and at each one Trujillo got out of the car and delivered marijuana. Regan remained in the vehicle at each stop. He gave the interviewing officer detailed descriptions of each location and the amount of marijuana Trujillo delivered at each stop. . . . Regan admitted that a quarter-ounce of the marijuana found in the car was his, but maintained that the rest of the marijuana in the vehicle belonged solely to Trujillo.

Trujillo testified at Regan's trial and corroborated Regan's claim. He confirmed his admission to officers that over a pound of marijuana in the car belonged exclusively to him, and that no one else had anything to do with it. . . . .

The jury found Regan guilty of felony possession of marijuana. . . . He was sentenced to . . . five years of supervised probation and a $5,000 fine. . . . [Regan then appealed his conviction.]

Wyo. Stat. Ann. § 35-7-1031(c)(iii) makes it a felony "for any person knowingly or intentionally to possess [more than three ounces of] a controlled substance [in plant form.]" Wyo. Stat. Ann. § 35-7-1031(c)(i), (iii). . . . [Inter alia,] Regan argues . . . that the State failed to prove that he "possessed" enough marijuana to support a felony conviction. . . .

. . . The parties disagree as to whether the State proved . . . that Regan exercised the requisite dominion and control over a sufficient quantity of the marijuana to support a felony conviction.

Our case law defines the terms "dominion and control" in a somewhat vague and circular manner, reciting the requirement that the accused must have the "requisite control" without offering much guidance as to the proof required to establish it. . . . Wyoming's Criminal Pattern Jury Instruction regarding constructive possession provides in part that "[a] person who, although is not in actual possession, knowingly has both the power and the intention, at a given time, to exercise dominion or control over a thing either directly or through another person or persons, is in constructive possession of it." . . .

We therefore focus specifically on the requirement that the accused must have "both the power and the intention" to control the substance. . . .

We have said "if a defendant is sufficiently associated with the persons having physical custody so that he is able, without difficulty to cause the drug to be produced for a customer, he can also be found by a jury to have dominion and control over the drug, and therefore, possession." . . . Something akin to that sort of power was what the Court of Appeals for the Tenth Circuit characterized in U*nited States v. King*, when it said "what matters is whether the defendant has an 'appreciable ability' (i.e. the power) to exercise dominion or control over the contraband." *United States v. King*, 632 F.3d 646, 652 (10th Cir. 2011) (citing *United States v. Al-Rekabi*, 454 F.3d 1113, 1118 (10th Cir. 2006)). In *Al-Rekabi*, the court even more helpfully addressed what is meant by the "power to control" by discussing constructive possession as evincing "an appreciable ability to guide the destiny of the contraband." *Al-Rekabi*, 454 F.3d at 1118.

However, this is only one element of constructive possession. Even if we assume that a jury could reasonably find beyond a reasonable doubt that Regan could have controlled the marijuana because it was in his vehicle and he could have driven away with it while Trujillo was making deliveries, the State also had to show that Regan intended to control the marijuana. . . .

. . . Our precedent allows an inference of constructive possession when the accused has exclusive possession over the premises where drugs are found. . . . The State seems to rely on this principle by emphasizing that Regan "actually owned and drove the car containing the marijuana" and that "he knew that the marijuana was present in the car that he owned and was driving."

However, this Court has also noted that, "if possession is not shown to be exclusive, there must be other evidence to warrant such inference." . . .

. . .

The evidence in this case shows that Regan and Trujillo drove from Denver to Gillette where Trujillo directed Regan to his requested stops. To show that Regan had "complete access to the marijuana," the State emphasizes that "[w]hile Trujillo was inside three different homes, Regan stayed in his car." However, that evidence does not prove that he intended to access the marijuana. It only shows that Regan waited for his passenger to return, and that he did not actually do anything which might support a conclusion that he intended to control the drugs. "Mere presence in a vehicle belonging to another where contraband is discovered does not amount to possession of a controlled substance." . . .

. . . Regan did not initiate the illegal activity. Trujillo directed Regan to specific locations at which he delivered the marijuana and collected money himself. Regan did not get out of the vehicle. There was no evidence indicating that Regan arranged any of the interactions, took any part in any negotiations, or made any attempt at all to associate himself with or influence the destiny of the marijuana. In fact, . . . Regan told [the officers] that he refused to become involved in the transactions "because it wasn't worth the risk[.]" Regan's complete and purposeful noninvolvement in these activities does nothing to meet the State's burden to prove that he had the intent and power to exercise dominion and control over the drugs.

We therefore conclude that the evidence presented was insufficient, even when viewed in the light most favorable to the State and after giving it the benefit of all favorable inferences, to support a conviction of felony possession of marijuana. We note that Regan was not charged with being an accessory before the fact (aiding and abetting) to the distribution of marijuana, or with conspiracy to distribute, which the evidence might have supported. . . .

## Notes and Questions

1. Oftentimes, the same action(s) may violate more than one criminal prohibition, allowing the government to choose the charge(s) it will bring against a defendant. Because the elements of these prohibitions (may) differ, the choice of charges can be crucial. After all, if the government lacks the evidence needed to prevail on one charge (as in *Regan*), it might nonetheless prevail on another charge where such evidence (say, of control) is not required. In *Regan*, was possession the best charge to pursue? The court hints that the government could have instead charged Regan with aiding and abetting or conspiracy, without having to prove that Regan controlled the marijuana. The distinct elements of these offenses are covered in Chapter 11.

### a. Control and Ownership

What happens if someone holds marijuana *but does not own* the drug? Does the individual nonetheless *control* the marijuana? The following cases appear to espouse competing views of the relationship between control and ownership.

### Oregon v. Fries
185 P.3d 453 (Or. 2008) (en banc)

KISTLER, J.

One evening, defendant's friend Albritton called defendant[, Thomas Fries,] and told him that he (Albritton) was being evicted. Albritton asked defendant if he would help him move his marijuana plants to his new home. Because Albritton had a medical marijuana card, defendant understood (and we assume for purposes of review) that Albritton lawfully possessed the marijuana plants. Defendant went to Albritton's new home, picked him up, and drove Albritton to his former home to pick up the marijuana plants. Albritton's former home was in an upstairs apartment, on the top floor. Defendant and Albritton went into the back bedroom of the apartment. Albritton pointed out the plants and said, "This is what I really needed help moving." According to defendant, there were three or four marijuana plants in "one long, big-type thing," which defendant moved from Albritton's apartment to defendant's Jeep.

Defendant loaded the plants and some of Albritton's other belongings into the back of his Jeep. Albritton got in the front passenger seat of the Jeep, and defendant started driving to Albritton's new home. As they were driving, a police car began following them. Defendant pulled into a driveway. The officer drove past, circled around, and later observed defendant driving on a different street. The officer followed defendant's Jeep as defendant turned onto another street and then pulled into another driveway. Defendant and Albritton remained in the Jeep. The officer approached them and spoke with them briefly. When asked why "they were being so evasive tonight, [defendant] said, 'We didn't want to get stopped and have to answer any questions about the marijuana.'" The officer then arrested defendant and Albritton.

The state charged defendant with possessing marijuana. At the end of defendant's trial, he argued that there was no evidence from which a reasonable trier of fact could find that he had possessed the marijuana plants. Specifically, he contended that, because the evidence showed only that he moved the plants under Albritton's direction, he did not "possess" them. The trial court denied defendant's motion for a judgment of acquittal and, sitting as the trier of fact, found defendant guilty. The court found initially that defendant knew that the plants were marijuana. It then found that defendant "actually physically possessed [the marijuana plants] because he moved [them] from Point A to Point B, knowing . . . what it was." The trial court explained that, although the medical marijuana statutes permit designated caregivers to possess medical marijuana, defendant was not Albritton's designated caregiver. The court concluded:

> "Is it fair? Perhaps not. In the overall scheme of things, he was someone helping his buddy. And perhaps it's unfair that [defendant] didn't have legal permission to have that particular controlled substance. But there's actually no doubt in my mind that he knowingly possessed that controlled substance, the growing marijuana."

The court accordingly found defendant guilty of possessing marijuana and sentenced him to 18 months probation, conditioned on serving five days in jail and paying a $500 fine and costs. . . . [Defendant appealed.]

. . . ORS 475.840(3) makes it unlawful for "any person knowingly . . . to possess a controlled substance." ORS 161.015(9) in turn provides that "'[p]ossess' means to have physical possession or otherwise to exercise dominion or control over property." As the text of that definition makes clear, a person may possess property in one of two ways. He or she may "have physical possession" of the property, which customarily is referred to as actual possession. . . . Alternatively, even if a person does not have actual possession of the property, he or she may have constructive possession of it if the person "otherwise . . . exercise[s] dominion or control over [the] property."

Because the trial court found that defendant actually possessed the marijuana plants, we begin with the first part of the statutory definition. The legislature used the infinitive phrase "to have physical possession" to define actual possession. We note . . . that the definition of actual possession is somewhat circular. . . . That said, the definition contains some clues that aid our analysis. The dictionary defines possession as meaning,

> 1 a: the act or condition of having in or taking into one's control or holding at one's disposal . . . b: actual physical control or occupancy of property by one who holds for himself and not as a servant of another without regard to his ownership and who has legal rights to assert interests in the property against all others having no better right than himself. . . .

Webster's Third New Int'l Dictionary 1770 (unabridged ed. 2002). The dictionary thus distinguishes possession from ownership and defines possession to mean, at its core, "control." "Physical" is an adjective that defines the type of control necessary to establish actual possession. In this context, physical means "of or relating to the body." *Id.* at 1706. As a general rule, "to have physical possession" of property means to have bodily or physical control of it.

. . .

Defendant argues that the definition of constructive possession in the second part of ORS 161.015(9) demonstrates that a person who holds property at another's direction does not actually possess it. Defendant's argument runs as follows. He notes that ORS 161.015(9) provides that "'[p]ossess' means to have physical possession or otherwise to exercise dominion or control over property." Defendant argues that, in order to prove sufficient dominion or control to establish constructive possession, the state must offer evidence of "sovereignty, supremacy, power or authority" over property. He then contends that, in using the word "otherwise," the legislature manifested its intent that actual possession requires proof of the same type of "dominion or control" that constructive possession does. From that premise, defendant concludes that a person who holds property at another's direction does not exercise sufficient sovereignty, supremacy, power, or authority over the property to constitute actual possession.

One problem with defendant's argument is that it gives too little weight to the legislature's use of the word "otherwise." "Otherwise" means "in a different way or manner." Webster's at 1598. As used in ORS 161.015(9), "otherwise" signals that the state may prove "possession" either by showing physical control or by showing dominion or control "in a different way or manner." To be sure, as defendant argues, actual and constructive possession share a common element—control. But the legislature's use of the word "otherwise" makes clear that actual and constructive possession contemplate different types of proof. The former requires proof of physical control. The latter contemplates proof of other attributes of dominion or control. . . . The fact that a person holds property at another's direction does not necessarily mean that he or she does not actually possess it.

The statutory context leads to the same conclusion. The legislature has established a number of exceptions to the general prohibition against possessing controlled substances. Among other things, a "common . . . carrier . . . or an employee thereof" may "lawfully possess controlled substances" if the possession occurs "in the usual course of business or employment." ORS 475.125(3)(b). Similarly, an "agent or employee of any registered manufacturer, distributor or dispenser of any controlled substance" may "lawfully possess controlled substances" if the "agent or employee is acting in the usual course of business or employment." ORS 475.125(3)(a).

If defendant were correct that "possess" does not include persons who handle or transport controlled substances at another's direction, then there would have been no need for the legislature to provide that common carriers or agents lawfully may possess controlled substances in certain circumstances. Common carriers and agents ordinarily act at another's direction. . . . We should not read the definition of "possess" in a way that would render those exemptions largely redundant. . . .

Considering the text and context of ORS 161.015(9), we conclude that the statutory phrase "to have physical possession" means what it says: to have physical control. That said, we recognize that some physical contacts with property may be too transient or fleeting to say that a person has established physical "control" over the property and that, when the duration of the physical contact is minimal, the circumstances surrounding the contact can bear on the question whether the defendant exercised sufficient physical control to find actual possession. . . .

. . . On this record, a reasonable trier of fact could find that defendant carried Albritton's marijuana plants out of the back bedroom of Albritton's apartment, took them down the stairs, loaded the plants in the back of defendant's Jeep, and drove the Jeep for several minutes before the police stopped him. This was not a fleeting, momentary, or unintentional physical touching, or so a reasonable trier of fact could find. . . . Rather, defendant's acts were part of an extended effort to move the marijuana plants from one location to another location. . . .

. . . [N]either the definition of possession nor the statutes criminalizing possession of controlled substances contain a categorical exception for persons who possess controlled substances at another person's direction. . . .

## *Iowa v. Bash*
670 N.W.2d 135 (Iowa 2003)

LAVORATO, J.:

On January 17, 2001, six Spirit Lake[, Iowa,] police officers executed a search warrant at an apartment shared by the defendant, [Patricia Bash,] her husband Kevin, and her three sons. The search warrant indicated that the officers were looking for, among other things, controlled substances and a safety deposit box.

. . .

One of the officers read the search warrant to the defendant whereupon, according to the officer, the defendant said she could "show [him] where the stuff is." The officer testified that he believed the defendant was referring to "[a]ny illegal drugs or contraband that may be in the residence." After reading the defendant her Miranda rights, the officer followed the defendant into the master bedroom and she told him, "it's on his nightstand in a cardboard box, that it's Kevin's stuff, that his bong . . . was sitting on the floor next to the bed."

The defendant's version was somewhat different from the officer's testimony. She testified she heard officers talking about a lock box they were looking for in the residence. When officers asked her if there was "anything in the house they should know about," she responded, "If there is anything here, it would be on Kevin's side of the bed." She pointed towards his nightstand which was on the left side of the bed. . . .

On Kevin's nightstand the officers found a cardboard box bearing the word "Friscos." Inside the box, they found a green plant material later identified as 1.37 grams of marijuana. The defendant testified she did not know what was in the box until after the officers opened it. However, she admitted that she knew there had been marijuana in the house, in the box, in the past.

. . .

[The jury found the defendant guilty of possession of marijuana, and she was given a 30-day suspended sentence and fined $325. The defendant appealed, claiming the government's proof of her control of the marijuana was legally insufficient.]

At the time of this incident, it is undisputed that the premises were shared by the defendant, her husband, and their children. Under these circumstances, knowledge of the presence of the marijuana and the authority or right to maintain control of it, that is, constructive possession, could not be inferred by the jury from the defendant's joint control of the premises, but had to be established by other proof. . . . [*Iowa v. Webb*, 648 N.W.2d 72, 79 (Iowa 2014)] Such proof could include incriminating statements made by the defendant, incriminating actions of the defendant upon the police's discovery of the controlled substance among or near the defendant's personal belongings, the defendant's fingerprints on the packages containing the controlled substance, and any other circumstances linking the defendant to the controlled substance. *Id.*

. . . [To establish the defendant's] authority or right to maintain control of the marijuana . . . the State relies heavily on the following testimony from the defendant:

Q. Now, could you have—was there any legal reason that would prevent you from taking that box and disposing of it? A. It wasn't mine.
Q. I understand that. But is there—it's proper that you generally regard it as your husband's? A. Correct.
Q. But you shared that apartment with him? A. Correct.
Q. Now, is there any legal reason why you could not have picked up that box and taken it and removed it from the house. A. It was not mine.
Q. . . . Could you have taken the contents of that box and flushed it down the toilet? A. No. It was not mine.
Q. Okay. Physically, would you have been able to do that? A. Physically, yes.

The State argues that the defendant's admission that she could physically have flushed the marijuana down the toilet is proof that she had the authority or right to maintain control of the marijuana. This position is at odds with what we said in [*State v. Atkinson*, 620 N.W.2d 1 (Iowa 2000)]:

> While it seems anomalous to look at a defendant's "right" to control illegal drugs in order to establish possession, that concept basically distinguishes a defendant's *raw physical ability* to exercise control over contraband simply because of the defendant's proximity to it and the type of rights that can be considered constructive possession.
> . . . (emphasis added).

Thus, the authority or right to maintain control includes something more than the "raw physical ability" to exercise control over the controlled substance. The defendant must have some proprietary interest or an immediate right to control or reduce the controlled substance to the defendant's possession. . . . No such proof was produced here. The State seems to concede, as it must, that the box containing marijuana was located on the husband's side of the bed with his personal effects. Additionally, there was no evidence that the defendant shared any ownership of the box or the marijuana in it or had any right to control either item.

Accordingly, we conclude the State failed to prove the defendant had dominion and control over the marijuana and thus failed to prove constructive possession of it. . . .

## Notes and Questions

1. The *Fries* court suggests that ownership is *not* a prerequisite to control, yet the *Bash* court suggests that a defendant "must have some *proprietary* interest or an immediate right to control" marijuana (emphasis added). Is it possible to reconcile the two decisions? If not, which approach would you follow? In other words, should ownership be a prerequisite to establishing control (and thus possession) of marijuana? If so, how would the government establish ownership?

2. Consider the following Problem based on *Fries*:

<u>Problem 3.5</u>: Albritton asks his friend Thomas Fries, "May I stash my cannabis plants at your place for a day or so while I move all of my other belongings into my new apartment?" Thomas responds "Sure. You can put them in my

bedroom." Albritton himself later carries his plants into Thomas's house and lays them down in the corner of Thomas's bedroom. Thomas stays at home doing chores while Albritton moves his other belongings. While Albritton is away, however, the police knock on Thomas's door (he's an unlucky fellow). Thomas consents to a search of his house, and the police discover the plants in his bedroom. The police arrest Thomas for possession of marijuana. How would the *Fries* court decide the case? How would the *Bash* court decide the case?

### b. Duration of Control

What if someone holds marijuana for only a fleeting moment? Would the individual thereby acquire control over the drug? The *Fries* court hinted that "some physical contacts with property may be too transient or fleeting to say that a person has established physical 'control' over the property." *Fries, supra. See also Moreau v. State*, 588 P.2d 275, 286 (Alaska 1978) (holding that possession is not established by "a passing control, fleeting and shadowy in nature") (citation omitted). But not all states agree. *E.g., Florida v. Eckroth*, 238 So. 2d 75, 77 (Fla. 1970) (holding that "possession and control . . . need not be . . . of great duration"); *Massachusetts v. Harvard*, 253 N.E.2d 346, 349 (Mass. 1969) (same). In *Eckroth*, the court suggested that a durational requirement would undermine the purpose of the state's prohibition, "which is to prohibit or limit the use of drugs which are destructive to the user and detrimental to the public generally." 238 So. 2d at 78. And in *Harvard*, the court suggested that a "standard based on duration would be exceedingly difficult to apply." 253 N.E.2d at 349.

Should fleeting possession suffice to establish criminal liability? If not, how would you define "fleeting possession"? To test your intuitions, consider the following Problems:

**Problem 3.6:** Delilah is at a party. She sits in a circle formed by several people. Someone passes her a marijuana joint. She takes a quick puff, then passes it on to the person seated to her left. She does not handle the marijuana again. Is Delilah guilty of simple possession? *See Eckroth*, 238 So. 2d at 77.

**Problem 3.7:** Delilah is a passenger in a car driven by Andy. Andy says "I could really use a hit." Delilah says "I know somebody, pull into that parking lot over there." As soon as Andy parks the car, Samuel approaches the passenger side. Delilah rolls down her window and asks Samuel, "could you sell a bit of weed to my friend here?" Samuel agrees, hands a small bag of marijuana to Delilah, who quickly passes it on to Andy. Is Delilah guilty of possession? *See Harvard*, 253 N.E.2d at 349. Is she perhaps guilty of any other offense based on these facts? *See* Chapter 11 (discussing aiding and abetting and conspiracy liability).

**Problem 3.8**: Delilah is driving her car, when her friend Samuel flags her down. She talks to Samuel for 30 to 40 seconds, and agrees to buy some marijuana from him. However, when a nearby police car turns on its lights, Samuel drops a paper bag into Delilah's car and runs away. Delilah quickly throws the bag out the passenger side window. The police stop her car and retrieve the bag, which contains several small plastic bags of marijuana. Is Delilah guilty of possession? *Turner v. Arkansas*, 749 S.W.2d 339 (Ark. Ct. App. 1988) (en banc). Would it be more apt to say she is guilty of a different crime? *See* Chapter 7 (discussing attempts).

### c. *Proof of Control*

The circumstances surrounding where marijuana is found dictate what sort of proof may be needed to show that a defendant controlled the drug. Courts divide cases into two basic factual scenarios:

(1) marijuana is found in area to which defendant had exclusive access, or
(2) marijuana is found in area to which defendant shared access with another person(s).

In general, courts hold that the first scenario raises a permissible (albeit rebuttable) presumption that a defendant had knowledge of and control over the marijuana. In the second scenario, however, the government must offer some additional proof of a defendant's knowledge and control. The Mississippi Supreme Court aptly states the general rule:

> [O]ne in possession of premises upon which contraband is found is presumed to be in constructive possession of the articles, but the presumption is rebuttable. . . . [W]here contraband is found upon premises not in the exclusive control and possession of the accused, additional incriminating facts must connect the accused with the contraband.

*Powell v. Mississippi*, 355 So. 2d 1378, 1379 (Miss. 1978).

#### (i) *Exclusive Access*

The easiest case for the government to establish a defendant's control over (and knowledge of) marijuana is one in which the marijuana was found on the defendant's person or in some other area to which the defendant had exclusive access. In *Gimble v. State*, 18 A.3d 955 (Md. App. 2011), for example, the court allowed a jury to presume that the defendant had knowledge of and control over marijuana in a backpack that had been ejected from a car that the defendant was driving alone when the car crashed. The court reasoned that "[t]he jurors in this case reasonably could infer that the backpack (and its contents) were inside the sedan before it crashed and that the appellant, as the driver and sole occupant of the sedan, knew that the contraband was in the sedan. They further reasonably could infer from the fact that the appellant was driving the vehicle that contained the contraband that he was exercising dominion or control over the contraband." *Id.* at 964.

Most courts have limited the strength of the inference that juries can make when marijuana is found *in* the defendant's person rather than *on* it. As a North Carolina appeals court has noted, "the majority of courts that have confronted this issue have held that a positive drug test alone cannot support a conviction for possession." *North Carolina v. Harris*, 632 S.E.2d 534, 537 (N.C. App. 2006). The following case discusses the issue and the rationale behind the majority rule.

## *In re R.L.H.*
### 116 P.3d 791 (Mont. 2005)

WARNER, J.:

[R.L.H. is a juvenile female who was placed on probation for assault in April 2002. In September 2002, R.L.H. was found to have violated the terms of her probation for using and possessing marijuana, and she was placed in a shelter. On December 19, 2002, R.L.H.'s urine tested positive for methamphetamines, opiates, and marijuana. At a probation hearing on January 2, 2003, R.L.H. admitted to using methamphetamines, and she was ordered to undergo drug treatment. The drug treatment facility diagnosed R.L.H. with alcohol and cannabis dependency and methamphetamine abuse. When she ran away from the facility before completing her treatment program, the state moved to place R.L.H. in a more secure youth detention facility. To do so, however, the state had to prove that R.L.H. had committed a crime while on probation. Based on the December 2002 positive urine test and her January 2003 admission to using methamphetamine, a jury convicted her of possession of methamphetamines, possession of opiates, and possession of marijuana. R.L.H. was committed by the court to a youth detention facility, and she appealed.]

Whether constructive possession can be proved by a positive urinalysis is an issue of first impression in Montana.

R.L.H. argues that she was not in "possession" of dangerous drugs because once the drugs were in her system, she did not have dominion or control over them. . . .

In the alternative, R.L.H. argues that if this Court concludes that the presence of an illegal substance in a person's blood or urine constitutes circumstantial evidence of prior possession, such circumstance is not sufficient to prove guilt beyond a reasonable doubt in criminal proceedings because it is impossible to determine from a urinalysis or blood test when or how the substance entered the body and whether it was taken knowingly. . . .

We do conclude that once a substance is ingested and then assimilated into the bloodstream, the person who ingested it does cease to exercise dominion and control over the substance. . . . However, like many of those jurisdictions which have addressed this issue, we also conclude that the presence of an illegal substance in the body constitutes circumstantial evidence of prior possession of that substance. The theory is that in order to have ingested the drug the person had to have possessed it, if even for a short period of time. . . . We also agree with those courts that have reached the logical conclusion that loss or destruction of evidence by ingestion prior to arrest should not be allowed to automatically defeat a possession charge. . . .

In Montana, to constitute an offense, the possession of a dangerous drug must be knowing[]. Sections 45-9-102; 45-2-103(1), MCA. In order to prove that the possession of a dangerous drug is with knowledge, it is necessary for the state to present evidence that the person charged with the offense was aware that they possessed the dangerous drug, or that such person was aware of a high probability that such substance is a dangerous drug. Section 45-2-101(34), MCA. Further, to establish criminal possession of a dangerous drug, the state must present evidence that such possession was voluntary. Section 45-2-202, MCA. Based on Montana's statutory definitions we conclude that while the presence of a dangerous drug in one's body constitutes a circumstance that indicates prior possession of that substance, it is insufficient, standing alone, to sustain a conviction for possession of dangerous drugs. This is so because without more than proof that a person had a dangerous drug in their system, there is no evidence to establish that such drug was knowingly and voluntarily ingested. . . .

We conclude that the presence of a controlled substance in a person's blood or urine constitutes sufficient circumstantial evidence to prove prior possession beyond a reasonable doubt only when accompanied by other corroborating evidence of knowing and voluntary possession, such as an admission of drug use. . . .

[R.L.H.'s earlier admission to using methamphetamine], presented to the jury at trial, provides direct evidence that R.L.H. knowingly and voluntarily possessed the dangerous drug methamphetamine, as charged. Thus, the State presented sufficient direct evidence to corroborate the circumstantial evidence of the urinalysis test which was positive for methamphetamine.

However, as the State concedes, R.L.H. made no admission that she used opiates or marijuana. Thus, there was no corroborating evidence to support the urinalysis test which was positive for these substances. The determination that R.L.H. committed the offenses of felony possession of opiates and misdemeanor possession of marijuana must be reversed and the charges dismissed. . . .

## Notes and Questions

1. Why is a positive drug test not enough by itself to establish control (and/or knowledge) of a drug? The *R.L.H.* court cites two possible rationales. One is that a defendant no longer has control over any substance that has already been ingested and detected by a test. However, as the court notes, the test results could still help prove *prior* possession of the drug. The second rationale is that a positive drug test does not necessarily prove that a defendant ever knew she was consuming marijuana or did so voluntarily, i.e., that she had the requisite desire to control the drug. A New Mexico appeals court has elaborated on this rationale:

> [I]t is quite possible that a defendant may have involuntarily ingested the drugs either through coercion, deception, or second-hand smoke. Accordingly, without some corroborating proof of knowledge and intent, . . . a positive drug test alone does not prove a defendant's knowledge of the drug or intent to possess it. . . . Moreover, we believe the State's argument ["that knowledge and intent can be properly inferred from the positive drug test"] impermissibly shifts the burden of proof to Defendants. In our view, it would be difficult if not impossible for a defendant to present credible evidence that he or she ingested drugs unknowingly.

*New Mexico v. McCoy*, 864 P.2d 307, 312-13 (N.M. Ct. App. 1993), *reversed on other grounds by New Mexico v. Hodge*, 882 P.2d 1 (N.M. 1994).

2. Do you think a positive drug test should be sufficient to prove beyond a reasonable doubt that a defendant knowingly possessed marijuana at some earlier point in time? Along these lines, consider the following Problem:

Problem 3.9: Compare the following two scenarios:

(1) The police detect a THC metabolite in Delilah's urine sample
(2) The police find a small bag of marijuana in Delilah's jacket pocket

Does one of these scenarios give rise to a stronger inference of Delilah's knowledge of and desire to control a quantity of marijuana? Does *R.L.H.* suggest that Delilah has *less* control over what goes into her body than what goes into her jacket pocket? Why not require Delilah to explain the positive drug test to the jury? Conversely, why not require the prosecutor to produce additional evidence that Delilah actually knew about and desired to control the marijuana found in her pocket?

3. In *R.L.H*, was there any other evidence (besides the drug test results) that R.L.H. had knowingly and voluntarily ingested (and had thus possessed) marijuana?

4. Would the *R.L.H.* court have reached a different result if Montana had defined marijuana to include the "altered state of a drug or substance listed in Schedules I through IV *absorbed into the human body*"? S.D.C.L. § 22-42-1 (1) (emphasis added). (The definition of marijuana is discussed in Chapter 2.) South Dakota added this language in 2001, apparently in response to cases suggesting that a positive drug test was not enough to sustain a conviction for possession of drugs. *See South Dakota v. Schroeder*, 674 N.W.2d 827 (S.D. 2004) (holding that the quoted statutory language "'permit[s] a defendant to be convicted of 'unauthorized possession' of a controlled drug or substance when the only . . . evidence is from the ingested or absorbed unauthorized [substance in] the defendant's body'").

*(ii) Non-exclusive Access*

More difficult for the government are the cases where marijuana is found in an area to which the defendant had non-exclusive access, such as a shared apartment or a crowded car. In these cases, the government must offer some additional proof, apart from access, that ties the marijuana to the defendant. The following cases discuss the sufficiency of evidence tying a defendant to marijuana found in a common area.

## *Iowa v. Cashen*
666 N.W.2d 566 (Iowa 2003)

STREIT, J.:

Ross Cashen was convicted of possession of marijuana. Cashen was a back seat passenger in a car that was stopped for a traffic violation. There were six people in the car, four of whom were sitting in the back seat. Cashen was sitting next to a window with his girlfriend sitting on his lap. . . .

After receiving Cashen's consent to a search, the officer found a lighter and Zig-Zag cigarette rolling papers on him. Another officer searched Cashen's girlfriend and found cigarette rolling papers and a small baggie of marijuana seeds in her pants pocket.

The driver consented to a search of the car. The officers found a baggie of marijuana wedged in the rear seat on the side where Cashen and his girlfriend had been seated. The baggie was stuck in the crack between the back and the bottom of the rear seat. Cashen twice denied any knowledge of the pot. At the jail, Cashen asked an officer if anyone had "fessed up" to owning the marijuana. The officer said no and asked if Cashen thought someone should claim ownership. Cashen said his girlfriend owned the marijuana. While at the jail, the girlfriend admitted the marijuana was hers.

The State charged Cashen with possession of marijuana. A jury found Cashen guilty. . . . Cashen appealed claiming there was insufficient evidence to support the conviction because the State failed to prove he had constructive possession of the marijuana. . . .

. . .

To prove possession the State must establish by proof: (1) the accused exercised dominion and control over the contraband; (2) the accused had knowledge of the contraband's presence; and (3) the accused had knowledge the material was a narcotic. . . .

Cashen, along with five other people, was present in the vehicle in which the drugs were found. This fact does not permit an inference of possession because (1) Cashen was not in exclusive possession of the premises—the car, and (2) Cashen did not have exclusive access to the place where the drugs were found—the back seat. The State was required to introduce other evidence that proved Cashen's actual knowledge of the drugs and his authority or right to maintain control of them.

When the police officer searched Cashen, he found cigarette rolling paper and a lighter. It could be argued Cashen's possession of the rolling papers and lighter shows he had the equipment necessary to use marijuana and he intended to use such drugs if the opportunity presented itself. It is argued that the fact Cashen had rolling papers on his person may suggest he knew the drugs were present. For this fact alone to give rise to a finding of constructive possession, we would have to make the inferential leap that Cashen had some degree of control and dominion over the drugs. Zig-Zag papers, at most, show Cashen had possession of marijuana in the past and intended to do so again in the future. However, we cannot infer from this fact alone Cashen had authority or the ability to exercise unfettered influence over these drugs.

Another, and perhaps stronger, factor tending to show Cashen knew the marijuana was in the car is the two statements he made to the police regarding the identity of the rightful owner. At the scene, the officers told Cashen he was under arrest for possession of marijuana. Cashen said he knew nothing about the marijuana. Again at the jail, he denied having any knowledge of the drugs. At the police station, Cashen asked if anyone had "fessed up" to its ownership. Responding that no one had claimed ownership, the police officer asked Cashen if he thought someone should. Cashen said the marijuana belonged to his girlfriend. Viewing these facts in the light most favorable to the State, we conclude the statements, at most, show Cashen had knowledge of the presence of the marijuana. Even assuming the State offered substantial evidence to prove Cashen's knowledge, the State still failed to prove the second element of the offense, i.e., Cashen had dominion and control over the marijuana.

There is only one relevant fact to this element of the prosecution. Cashen's closeness to the drugs was the only evidence offered by the State relevant to the question of control and dominion. As we have already concluded, however, Cashen's proximity to the drugs, though pertinent, is not enough to show control and dominion. Cashen sat in the back seat of the car with his girlfriend seated on his lap with her back to the window. The police officer found the baggie of marijuana lodged in the rear seat on the side where Cashen had been sitting. At trial, the officer testified the baggie, in relation to Cashen, was just behind him and off to the left of his hip.

Just as proximity to the drugs should not be used to infer knowledge, it is insufficient to prove control and dominion. In [*State v. Atkinson*, 620 N.W.2d 1 (Iowa 2000)], we quoted with approval an Arkansas case discussing certain factors to consider when examining cases where

> contraband is found in a vehicle occupied by more than one person . . . : (1) was the contraband in plain view, (2) was it with defendant's personal effects, (3) was it found on the same side of the car seat as the defendant or immediately next to him, (4) was the defendant the owner of the vehicle, and (5) was there suspicious activity by the defendant.

*Atkinson*, 620 N.W.2d at 4. . . . In this case, Cashen was not the owner of the car. The drugs were not in plain view. The marijuana was not found with Cashen's personal effects. After the police found the marijuana, it cannot fairly be said that Cashen's actions were of an incriminating nature. Cashen did not behave suspiciously when the car was stopped for the traffic violation. There is no evidence to suggest Cashen made any suspicious or furtive movements in an effort to conceal the drugs from the officers once the car was pulled over. An officer also testified Cashen did not smell of marijuana. There was no evidence of how long the marijuana had been in the vehicle. The State did not offer evidence showing Cashen's fingerprints on the baggie. No witness testified that the marijuana belonged to Cashen. In fact, his girlfriend claimed ownership. There was no evidence showing Cashen had control and dominion of the drugs with the ability to access them. . . .

The only fact relevant to Cashen's alleged control and dominion over the drugs was his proximity to the marijuana. Simply because a person can reach out and grasp something does not mean he or she has control or dominion over the object. A defendant's mere proximity to contraband is insufficient to support a finding of constructive possession. We do not presume possession where the defendant does not own the car and a finding of constructive possession cannot rest on mere proximity. . . . Cashen was a passenger in a car crammed with six passengers, four of whom were seated in the back seat. The other three passengers riding in the back seat were just as close to the drugs as was Cashen. Because Cashen was not in exclusive possession of the premises, but shared the vehicle with five other people, and because he did not have exclusive access to the place where the drugs were located, the State was required to prove facts *other* than mere proximity to show his dominion and control of the drugs. Regardless of one's suspicions, this evidence was insufficient as a matter of law to show that Cashen had control and dominion over the marijuana. . . .

## Notes and Questions

1. Surely the marijuana belonged to *someone*. But under the *Cashen* court's reasoning, could the government have successfully prosecuted any of the car's occupants? If so, whom? If not, are you troubled by this result?

2. What is the relationship between knowledge and desire? Many courts suggest that knowledge of the presence of marijuana is a necessary prerequisite to harboring any desire to control the drug. *E.g.*, *North Carolina v. Harris*, 632 S.E.2d 534 (N.C. App. 2006) ("Necessarily, power and intent to control the controlled substance can exist only when one is aware of its presence."). But knowledge alone is normally not *sufficient* to

establish such a desire. *See Cashen, supra* ("Even assuming the State offered substantial evidence to prove Cashen's knowledge, the State still failed to prove the second element of the offense, i.e., Cashen had dominion and control over the marijuana.").

3. Can you imagine a scenario in which a defendant had control over something but lacked the culpable knowledge? Consider the following Problem:

**Problem 3.10:** Andy is lurking at a bus stop. He sees a stranger lay a backpack on a bench while the stranger bends down to tie his shoes. Andy quickly grabs the stranger's backpack and runs. The stranger yells at Andy, which catches the attention of a nearby police officer. Andy is stopped by the officer one block away. When questioned, Andy insists the backpack is his and consents to a search of it. The officer discovers a bag containing three ounces of marijuana inside of the backpack. Can Andy be charged with simple possession of marijuana?

---

In the next case, the same court finds the evidence sufficient to sustain a conviction for simple possession.

## *Iowa v. Henderson*
696 N.W.2d 5 (Iowa 2005)

TERNUS, J.:

The defendant, Argilee Henderson, appeals from a judgment of conviction after a jury found she was guilty of possession of marijuana and possession of methamphetamine. . . .

. . .

. . . On August 22, 2002, Woodbury County Deputy Robert Aspleaf served a writ of removal and possession at Henderson's apartment. (Henderson was the only person on the lease.) The writ required Aspleaf to remove the defendant and her possessions from the apartment and place the landlord in possession of the premises. Aspleaf was accompanied by the landlord and three helpers brought by the landlord.

When this group arrived at Henderson's apartment, the deputy knocked loudly several times, but no one answered. The landlord's master key did not work because the door had been locked from the inside. Consequently, a helper forcibly kicked the door open, revealing the defendant standing on the other side of the doorway. Over profanity-laced protests from Henderson, the landlord and his helpers began to pack up Henderson's belongings. The deputy attempted to calm her down, but the defendant's agitation escalated to the point where she pushed one of the men who was packing her electronic components. Upon being informed she was under arrest, Henderson retreated to the only bedroom in the apartment and slammed the door shut. The deputy followed her and placed her under arrest for interference with official acts.

After other officers arrived to take Henderson to the police station, the deputy began to look at the items in the apartment to determine whether there was anything that should not be set out on the curb, for example, knives, weapons, or pornographic materials.

During this process he discovered the following contraband: (1) on top of the refrigerator in the kitchen, a clear plastic bag containing what appeared to be marijuana; (2) on the coffee table in the living room, a homemade "pot pipe", an ashtray with pieces of a blunt in it, and two clear plastic bags, one with a yellowish residue and one with remnants of plant material in it; (3) in the bedroom between the mattresses, a small silver tube of the type used to smoke methamphetamine; (4) in the same bedroom on the headboard, a similar, but larger-diameter, tube with burn marks on the ends, a homemade pipe or smoking device for marijuana made of tinfoil with burn residue, and a clear plastic bag containing what appeared to be methamphetamine; and (5) in an end table in the same bedroom, two bags containing what appeared to be marijuana, a forceps commonly used to smoke marijuana, a small piece of tinfoil commonly used to smoke methamphetamine with burn marks on it, and two outside barrels of ink pens that could be used to snort methamphetamine. The substance found on the refrigerator and the substance found on the headboard were tested and confirmed to be marijuana and methamphetamine, respectively. These items provided the basis for Henderson's prosecution for two counts of possession of a controlled substance. . . .

Deputy Aspleaf testified at trial that another woman was present in the apartment during these events, Lisa Williams. Williams was cooperative and did not attempt to obstruct the eviction process. She told the deputy that she had only been staying at the apartment for a few days after having a fight with her mother. When the deputy asked her if any of the drugs they found were hers, Williams stated they were not.

The deputy also testified that both Henderson and Williams had prior convictions for possession of marijuana. Henderson had been convicted of this offense in 1998, and Williams' conviction was in 1991.

In addressing the sufficiency of this evidence, we first examine the State's burden of proof: "Unlawful possession of a controlled substance requires proof that the defendant: (1) exercised dominion and control over the contraband, (2) had knowledge of its presence, and (3) had knowledge that the material was a controlled substance." *State v. Bash*, 670 N.W.2d 135, 137 (Iowa 2003). Henderson challenges the sufficiency of the State's proof on the first element: her dominion and control over the marijuana and the methamphetamine.

Because the contraband was not found on the defendant's person, the State sought to prove Henderson's constructive possession of the illegal substances. . . . "Constructive possession occurs when the defendant has knowledge of the presence of the controlled substance and has the authority or right to maintain control of it." *Id.* "The existence of constructive possession turns on the peculiar facts of each case." *State v. Webb*, 648 N.W.2d 72, 79 (Iowa 2002).

Notwithstanding the fact-specific inquiry on this element, inferences are often used to prove constructive possession. . . . One such inference of dominion and control arises when the premises on which the illegal substances are found are in the exclusive possession of the accused. *State v. McDowell*, 622 N.W.2d 305, 308 (Iowa 2001). That inference is of no assistance to the State here, however, because at the time of this incident, the premises were shared by Henderson and Williams. See *Bash*, 670 N.W.2d at 138. . . . Under these circumstances, the defendant's authority or right to maintain control of the drugs must be established by proof in addition to the fact that the drugs were found in the defendant's apartment. See *Bash*, 670 N.W.2d at 138; *Webb*, 648 N.W.2d at 77, 79. We think the record contains such proof.

There was no suggestion in the evidence that the contraband found in Henderson's apartment belonged to anyone other than Henderson or Williams. We think the jury could have concluded from the very disparate reactions of these individuals to the presence of the deputy on August 22, 2002 that the drugs belonged to Henderson. When the deputy's party entered Henderson's apartment, they were greeted by Henderson's defiant opposition to their presence. She swore at them and insisted that she would move her own belongings. She yelled at them to leave and physically interfered with their efforts to pack her property. Eventually, she retreated to the bedroom, specifically to the side of the bed where the methamphetamine was found. In contrast, Williams cooperated with the persons moving the defendant's personal belongings and even carried some of Henderson's clothes to Henderson's car.

Henderson's conduct implied guilty knowledge; Williams' conduct did not. . . . Certainly one could also explain the defendant's response to the situation by the fact that she was the object of a forcible eviction from her residence. On the other hand, Williams' obliging manner was not consistent with one who had something to hide. Moreover, Williams denied the drugs were hers.

Other facts also support a finding that the drugs belonged to Henderson. Illegal substances were found throughout the apartment, together with multiple items of drug paraphernalia, some of which showed signs of use. Although some of these items were in plain view, some were in drawers, or in the case of a pipe used to smoke methamphetamine, between the mattresses. The quantity of drugs and drug paraphernalia in the premises, their widespread disbursement throughout the apartment, and their location in places that would not ordinarily be used by a guest suggest that these items did not belong to a temporary visitor, but rather to the person residing there.

## Notes and Questions

1. Are the facts of *Henderson* distinguishable from the facts of *Cashen*?

2. How much evidence should the government have to offer in order to establish a defendant's control over marijuana found in a common area? Consider the following Problem:

Problem 3.11: Following up on a complaint about an illegally parked car, Police Officer Pasha knocks at the door of a house. An occupant lets her in, and, when Pasha asks where she can find the driver of the car, the occupant points her to an upstairs bedroom. Pasha knocks on the bedroom door, and someone tells her to "come on in." Pasha opens the door and immediately notices smoke and smells burning marijuana. The room is small. Three bongs and three clear plastic bags containing marijuana are on the floor. Delilah is sitting on the floor about one foot from one of the bags and one of the bongs. Two other persons are seated on a couch, and a fourth person is seated on the bed. Pasha asks them, "What are you doing?" and Delilah responds "We're having a party!" Pasha arrests the four occupants of the bedroom and the man who let her into the house. A subsequent search discovers a fourth bag of

marijuana tucked into the couch and drug paraphernalia in other rooms of the house. Pasha never saw Delilah touch the marijuana or paraphernalia, and she does not find any marijuana or paraphernalia on Delilah's person or her personal property. Delilah is not a resident of the house, which is rented by two of the other people Pasha found in the bedroom. Is there enough evidence to demonstrate that Delilah had control over any of the marijuana found in the house? See *Illinois v. Schmalz*, 740 N.E.2d 775 (Ill. 2000).

*(iii) Joint Possession*

In cases involving non-exclusive access to marijuana, the government may be able to proceed on a theory of joint possession (pun unavoidable). Joint possession is commonly noted but rarely discussed at any length. It arguably stands for the proposition that more than one person can be found guilty of possessing the same marijuana, in the same way that more than one person may own the same house, car, bank account, and so on. The decision in the following case rests on the application of the theory of joint possession.

## *Folk v. Maryland*
275 A.2d 184 (Md. App. 1971)

MOYLAN, J.:

[Lillie Mae Folk was adjudged to be a delinquent child based on a trial judge's finding that she had unlawfully possessed marijuana. She appealed, claiming insufficient evidence to support her possession of the drug beyond a reasonable doubt.]

Beginning sometime at approximately 9:15 p. m. on the evening of April 7, 1970, Corporal Carl R. Harbaugh of the Maryland State Police, operating in civilian clothing and in an unmarked vehicle, undertook the surveillance of a red Valiant automobile on the western outskirts of the city of Frederick. Some fifteen to twenty minutes later Corporal Harbaugh and another State Trooper who had joined him approached the red Valiant as it was parked on a secluded, overgrown and abandoned baseball diamond just beyond the western fringe of the city. The lights were off, the motor was off and the windows were tightly shut. As Corporal Harbaugh approached the driver's side, the left front window was suddenly rolled down and Corporal Harbaugh, whose expertise in narcotic investigation was well-established, detected the strong odor of marihuana coming from the closed car. All of the occupants were ordered out of the automobile and placed under arrest. One of the occupants, exiting on the right-

Figure 3.2. Example of a 1962 Plymouth Valiant

hand side of the vehicle, attempted to throw an object into the surrounding grass and underbrush. That object was immediately recovered and determined to be a small black plastic container which contained . . . marihuana.

The appellant was one of the six occupants of the automobile. The evidence did not establish that she was ever in direct physical possession of the contraband marihuana. The evidence was clear, however, that some person or persons in that automobile were in possession of the contraband marihuana.

It is well-settled that the proscribed possession of marihuana or of narcotic drugs under the Maryland law need not be sole possession. "(T)here may be joint possession and joint control in several persons. . . ."

Nor is it necessary, in order to be found in joint possession of a contraband drug, that the appellant have a "full partnership" in the contraband. It is enough that she controlled so much of it as would be necessary to permit her to take a puff upon a marihuana cigarette. . . .

In the case at bar, the proximity between the appellant and the marihuana could not be closer, short of direct proof that the appellant herself was in exclusive physical possession of the marihuana. She was one of six occupants in a Valiant automobile and was, therefore, whatever her position in the car, literally within arm's length of every other occupant of that automobile. The marihuana cigarette being smoked was, at any point in time, within direct physical possession of one of those occupants. Proximity could not be more clearly established.

Nor would there be, under the circumstances of this case, any difficulty in drawing a reasonable inference that the marihuana was within the view, or otherwise within the knowledge, of the appellant. In a darkened car in a dark field, the glow from a lighted cigarette is clearly visible within that maximum radius of four to five feet between the glow and the viewer. Knowledge of the presence of marihuana would be imparted even more emphatically by the sense of smell, in a situation where the cloud of smoke and the peculiar pungent odor filled the interior of a tightly-closed automobile. Neither would the inference be unreasonable that some conversation transpired among the six persons huddled there in the dark dealing with what the cigarette and the fumes were all about. It would, indeed, be unreasonable not to infer knowledge of the marihuana on the part of the appellant.

There was, furthermore, before the fact-finder in this case the presence of abundant circumstances from which a reasonable inference could be drawn that the appellant was participating with the five other occupants of the car in the mutual use and enjoyment of the marihuana. Six persons drove in an automobile to a lonely and secluded field that had once been a baseball diamond but was now overgrown. They there turned off the motor and the lights of the automobile. Whatever their mission, it was one where seclusion from public view was at a premium. The progress of three men and three women to a lonely field after dark, taken alone, might give rise to several reasonable hypotheses, but each of those hypotheses must then be tested against the other known data. The failure of the group to disperse two-by-two to different corners of the field, the absence of any evidence of contraceptives and the absence of any evidence of even partial disrobing would serve to negate a possible initial hypothesis that the mission was sexual in nature. The absence of alcoholic beverages of any sort would serve to negate a possible initial hypothesis that the mission was for the consumption of alcoholic beverages. Nor was there any evidence, whatsoever, to suggest that a picnic or a campfire was the mission of the party. Every

Part II. Marijuana Users

item of additional evidentiary data strongly supports the hypothesis, however, that the common mission of the group was the inhalation of marihuana.

Shortly before the group left the parking lot of a shopping center in the western part of Frederick, the driver of the automobile was observed to go to the trunk and to bring out a roll of paper towels. It is common knowledge that marihuana cigarettes are not commercially manufactured and prepackaged. The illicit consumer obtains marihuana leaves on the black market and must then proceed to "roll his own." It would not be an unreasonable inference that the paper towels may have been serving that office on the night of April 7. Corporal Harbaugh also observed that what appeared to be a cigarette was lighted on the back seat of the car and was then passed to the front seat. It is common knowledge that in the marihuana smoking culture a common cigarette is passed communally from one smoker to another in the fashion of an Indian pipe of peace, rather than each smoker hoarding a personal cigarette unto himself. There was further evidence that when Corporal Harbaugh approached the Valiant automobile in the deserted field, the windows were tightly closed and the interior was full of the marihuana smoke. It is also common knowledge that in the marihuana-smoking culture even the smoke which has been exhaled is not permitted to go to waste but is reinhaled and reinhaled again by all of the common participants as long as it pervades the surrounding atmosphere. Ventilation is purposefully discouraged just so that the smoke will continue to pervade the atmosphere. Corporal Harbaugh personally detected, as the windows of the automobile were rolled down upon his approach, the strong odor of marihuana. Upon exiting the vehicle, one of the male occupants, Robert Rippeon, was observed to throw something into the field. It turned out to be a small black plastic container, containing what chemical analysis proved to be marihuana.

The appellant did not offer any evidence to explain her presence in the deserted field in the darkened automobile wherein marihuana was being smoked.

. . . The trial judge inferred, from all of the circumstances, that the appellant went to the deserted field on the night of April 7 with five other persons for the purpose of participating with the others in the mutual use and enjoyment of marihuana and that she was so participating at the moment of her arrest. We cannot say that he was clearly wrong. . . .

. . .

## Notes and Questions

1. Do you agree with the *Folk* court? Was there sufficient evidence to demonstrate beyond a reasonable doubt that the defendant and the other five occupants of the car exercised joint possession over the marijuana? Or was the court merely speculating? Could the government have proceeded on a theory of joint possession in *Cashen, supra*, as well? Are the two cases (*Folk* and *Cashen*) distinguishable?

2. If the government attempts to prosecute more than one defendant for possession of the same marijuana, should it be required to establish a *conspiracy to possess* marijuana? We will discuss conspiracy in more detail in Chapter 11. For now, suffice to say that the essence of conspiracy is an agreement among two (or more) persons. Was there evidence of an agreement to possess marijuana in *Folk* (or *Cashen*)?

## 3. Marijuana

Finally, the government must prove that what the defendant possessed was, in fact, marijuana. (Chapter 2 discussed the legal definition of marijuana.) This element is called an attendant circumstance; it is an additional fact that helps define the crime of possession.

Just as they do for the other elements of simple possession, courts allow governments to utilize many types of evidence to establish that the substance possessed by the defendant was marijuana. The testimony of scientists who have performed laboratory tests on the substance will suffice, although this is an expensive mode of proof and some state crime labs refuse to test for marijuana in simple possession cases. Similarly, the testimony of law enforcement officers who have observed the substance will suffice, so long as they have sufficient experience or training from which to form an expert opinion. *Compare Massachusetts v. MacDonald*, 945 N.E.2d 260 (Mass. 2011) (testimony of police officer with 20 years' experience in narcotics squad handling thousands of investigations was sufficient), *with Illinois v. Park*, 363 N.E.2d 884 (Ill. App. 1977) (testimony of police officer with only 3.5 years of experience and unproven track record of identifying marijuana in prior cases was insufficient). Even the testimony of experienced marijuana users who have inspected (or consumed!) the substance involved in the offense may be sufficient. *Compare United States v. Durham*, 464 F.3d 976 (9th Cir. 2006) (testimony of witness who had extensive experience using marijuana, including with the defendant, sufficient to identify residue in water pipe as marijuana), *with Montana v. Burwell*, 313 P.3d 119 (Mont. 2013) (testimony of past marijuana user who claimed she got marijuana from defendant was not sufficient to identify substance as marijuana).

Much of the evidence used to demonstrate the defendant's knowledge, such as visual or olfactory inspection, appears equally adequate to demonstrate the identity of the substance, at least when the substance is in a familiar form. But as noted above and in Chapter 2, new forms of marijuana (edibles, vape pens, and so on) are becoming increasingly popular. These new forms not only challenge long-standing assumptions about what defendants know, they might also challenge beliefs about what law enforcement experts know.

### Notes and Questions

1. Consider the following Problem:

Problem 3.12: The state of Nebraska has charged Andy with simple possession of marijuana. The state alleges that a one-inch gummy bear found in a medicine vial in Andy's car as it was crossing over from Colorado is laced with marijuana. Andy admits that he knew the gummy bear was in his car; he also admits that he very much desired to eat the gummy bear. But Andy denies that the gummy bear contains marijuana. What evidence could the state use to meet its burden of proving beyond a reasonable doubt that the gummy bear contains marijuana?

2. What if the substance does not, in fact, contain marijuana? Consider the following Problem:

**Problem 3.13:** Michael has an ax to grind with his co-worker, Toby. He decides to frame Toby for marijuana possession in the hopes it will get Toby fired. But Michael has never even seen marijuana. He goes to a nearby warehouse and approaches a surly man he assumes to be a drug dealer, offering the man $500 cash for marijuana. The man says "okay, let me get my stash." The man reaches into his lunchbox and hands Michael a Ziploc bag containing a green leafy substance. Michael gives the man $500 and gets back in his car. On his way back to the office, Michael is stopped by the police for speeding. The officer spies the baggie on the front passenger seat. Michael immediately confesses to what he has done. The police charge him with possession of marijuana. But tests demonstrate that the green leafy substance in the bag is actually basil (part of a Caprese salad) and not marijuana. (Based on Episode 508, "Frame Toby," of *The Office*.) Is Michael guilty of possession of marijuana? Is there another *drug* crime that might better fit this case? *See Lucas v. State*, 771 S.E.2d 142 (Ga. App. 2015) (holding in prosecution for attempted possession of marijuana that government was not required to prove substance defendant stole from trunk of car was actually marijuana, given that defendant and his co-defendants "told friends of their plan to get 'pounds of weed'" by stealing from a suspected drug dealer's car).

3. While most jurisdictions permit a conviction to be based on any amount of marijuana, no matter how small, *see, e.g., Eckroth*, 238 So. 2d at 76 (holding that "the quantity possessed is immaterial"), a minority of states require the government to show that the defendant possessed a *usable quantity* of the drug. Texas, for example, specifies that "a person commits an offense if the person knowingly or intentionally possesses a *usable* quantity of marihuana." V.T.C.A. §481.121(a) (emphasis added). Nonetheless, even very small amounts may be considered usable quantities in these jurisdictions. *See Andreade v. Texas*, 662 S.W.2d 446 (Tex. App. 1983) ("[T]here must be possessed an amount sufficient to be applied to the use commonly made thereof which is to smoke it in cigarettes. . . . The amount of marihuana involved here, 0.38 grams, was already in 'cigarette' form, the use commonly made thereof, and was sufficient to establish that it was a 'useable quantity' of marihuana, even in the absence of any direct testimony."); *Buntion v. Texas*, 476 S.W.2d 317 (Tex. App. 1972) (holding that (apparently) used cigarette stubs containing total of 0.10 gram of marijuana was sufficient).

The usable quantity requirement is arguably designed to serve two broad purposes: (1) because "prohibition of possession is designed to control the future use or sale of a drug, the legislature could not have intended to criminalize possession of trace amounts which fail to pose this danger to society"; and, as discussed above, (2) "where the amount is a mere trace, the necessary mens rea cannot be inferred." Davidson, Note, *supra*, at 622.

## 4. Defenses

Even if the government satisfies its burden on each of the abovementioned elements, most jurisdictions allow a defendant to raise certain defenses to the crime of simple possession. This section considers three defenses that seem most applicable to users of marijuana. (Chapter 7 discusses additional defenses that are arguably more relevant for supply offenses, including defenses based on internal DOJ enforcement guidelines and budget restrictions imposed by Congress.)

### a. Necessity

Necessity is a long-standing defense to a wide range of criminal offenses. *United States v. Randall* appears to be the first case to successfully raise the defense against a marijuana possession charge. The case discusses the elements of the defense and why the court found it applicable to a charge of possession of marijuana.

### *United States v. Randall*
D.C. Crim. No. 65923-75 (D.C. Super. Ct. Nov. 24, 1976)

WASHINGTON, J.:

[The police charged defendant with simple possession of marijuana in violation of the laws of the District of Columbia. The defendant admitted that he possessed the marijuana.]

Defendant nonetheless sought to exonerate himself through the presentation of evidence tending to show that his possession of the marijuana was the result of medical necessity.... [D]efendant testified that he had begun experiencing visual difficulties as an undergraduate in the late 1960's. In 1972 a local ophthalmologist, Dr. Benjamin Fine, diagnosed defendant's condition as glaucoma, a disease of the eye characterized by the excessive accumulation of fluid causing increased intraocular pressure, distorted vision and ultimately, blindness. Dr. Fine treated defendant with an array of conventional drugs, which stabilized the intraocular pressure when first introduced but became increasingly ineffective as defendant's tolerance increased. By 1974, defendant's intraocular pressure could no longer be controlled by these medicines, and the disease had progressed to the point where defendant had suffered the complete loss of sight in his right eye and considerable impairment of vision in the left.

Despite the ineffectiveness of traditional treatments, defendant during this period nonetheless achieved some relief through the inhalation of marijuana smoke. Fearing the legal consequences, defendant did not inform Dr. Fine of his discovery, but after his arrest defendant participated in an experimental program being conducted by ophthalmologist Dr. Robert Hepler under the auspices of the United States Government. Dr. Hepler testified that his examination of the defendant revealed that treatment with conventional medications was ineffective, and also that surgery, while offering some hope of preserving the vision which remained to defendant, also carried significant risks of immediate blindness. The results of the experimental program indicated that the ingestion of marijuana smoke had a beneficial effect on defendant's condition, normalizing intraocular pressure and lessening visual distortions.

. . .

## I. DOES THE COMMON LAW RECOGNIZE THE DEFENSE OF NECESSITY IN CRIMINAL CASES? IF SO, WHAT ARE ITS PARAMETERS?

... While a consensus has not been reached concerning the specific contours of the defense, there is substantial unanimity in the belief that ... a defense [of necessity] exists. ...

Necessity is the conscious, rational act of one who is not guided by his own free will. It arises from a determination by the individual that any reasonable man in his situation would find the personal consequences of violating the law less severe than the consequences of compliance. While the act itself is voluntary in the sense that the actor consciously decides to do it, the decision is dictated by the absence of an acceptable alternative. Unlike compulsion or duress, necessity arises from the press of events rather than through the imposition on the actor of the will of another person.

...

... [The defense is based on] the belief that punishment should not be visited upon one who did not act of his own free will. Penalizing one who acted rationally to avoid a greater harm will serve neither to rehabilitate the offender not to deter others from acting similarly when presented with similar circumstances. This point is implicitly recognized by the three traditional limitations on the applicability of the necessity defense. The defense will not shield an actor from criminal responsibility if:

(1) The duress or circumstance has been brought about by the actor himself;
(2) The same objective could have been accomplished by a less offensive alternative which was available to the actor; or
(3) The evil sought to be averted was less heinous than that performed to avoid it.

...

## II. HAS NECESSITY BEEN ESTABLISHED IN THE INSTANT CASE?

In the case at bar, defendant alleges that he is suffering from glaucoma, an incurable eye disease which results inevitably in loss of sight. While conventional medications and surgery offer little hope of improvement, defendant contends that the inhalation of marijuana smoke has a beneficial effect on his condition, relieving the symptoms and retarding the progress of the disease. Defendant therefore asserts that he should not be visited with the criminal consequences of possession of the proscribed narcotic marijuana. The Court finds upon these facts that the defendant has established the basic elements of the traditional necessity defense. It remains to consider whether he is barred from asserting it by one of the limitations.

A brief consideration reveals that of the three limitations, only the third poses any threat to this defendant's use of this defense. While the exact cause of defendant's glaucoma is unknown, neither the government nor any of the expert witnesses has suggested that the defendant is in any way responsible for his condition. Similarly, no alternative course of action would have secured the desired result through a less illegal channel. ...

The question of whether the evil avoided by the defendant's action is less than the evil inherent in his act is more difficult. It requires a balancing of the interests of the defendant against those of the government. While defendant's wish to preserve his sight is too obvious to necessitate further comment, the government's interests require a more detailed examination.

...

Medical evidence suggests that the prohibition [on marijuana] is not well founded. . . . [T]here is no conclusive scientific evidence of any harm attendant upon the use of marijuana. . . . [R]esearch has failed to establish any substantial physical or mental impairment caused by marijuana. Reports of chromosome damage, reduced immunity to disease, and psychosis are unconfirmed: actual evidence is to the contrary. Furthermore, unlike the so-called hard drugs, marijuana does not generally appear to be physically addictive or to cause the user to develop a tolerance, requiring more and more of the drug for the same effects. . . . [A report by the Department of Health, Education, and Welfare] also notes the possibility of valid medical uses for this drug. Both the [Report of the National Commission on Marihuana and Drug Abuse] and HEW found the current penalties too harsh in view of the relatively inoffensive character of the drug, and recommended decriminalization. . . .

The right of an individual to protect his body has been weighed by several courts against the interest of the government in guarding the health and morals of the general public. Most importantly, the Supreme Court addressed this question in *Roe v. Wade*, 410 U.S. 113 (1973) and *Doe v. Bolton*, 410 U.S. 179 (1978), cases which attacked the constitutionality of state statutes restricting abortions. In an opinion which stressed the fundamental nature of the right of an individual to preserve and control her body, the Court held that abortion cannot constitutionally be denied a woman under certain circumstances. These decisions recognize first that a woman may at any stage end a pregnancy which threatens her own existence, her right to life being more significant than that of the fetus, however close to term. The opinions go on to affirm the prerogative of a woman during the first three months of pregnancy to terminate it for any reason whatsoever, establishing that she may control her body at the expense of the life of a fetus less than four months old. The significance of these decisions to the instant case lies in the revelation of how far reaching is the right of an individual to preserve his health and bodily integrity.

. . .

Under these circumstances, the Court finds that this defendant does not fall within the third limitation to the necessity defense. The evil he sought to avert, blindness, is greater than that he performed to accomplish it, growing marijuana in his residence in violation of the District of Columbia Code. While blindness was shown by competent medical testimony to be the otherwise inevitable result of defendant's disease, no adverse effects from the smoking of marijuana have been demonstrated. . . . In any event, it is unlikely that such slight, speculative and indemonstrable harm could be considered more important than defendant's right to sight.

. . .

Finally, it is appropriate here to discuss the burden of proof where the necessity defense is raised. . . . In general, an accused who raises any of the so-called affirmative defenses bears to some extent the risk of nonpersuasion. . . . Where the defense is actually an attempt to negate an element of the crime, for example, it must be proven beyond a reasonable doubt that the facts alleged by the defendant are not to be believed. Where defendant interposes a justification defense such as duress, necessity, or self-defense, on the other hand, a less stringent requirement, such as the preponderance standard, is employed. . . .

. . .

Since the defense [of necessity] does not attempt to disprove any element of the government's case, it should be classified as an affirmative defense which the accused bears the burden of establishing. In addition, the necessity defense . . . is one uniquely within the knowledge of the defendant. Placing the burden of persuasion on the defendant does not conflict with the presumption of innocence, since necessity of its nature arises only in cases where the defendant admits committing the prohibited act. Thus, a defendant who seeks to avail himself of the necessity defense should be required to prove it by a preponderance of the evidence. The defendant in the instant case has earned this evidentiary burden.

## Notes and Questions

1. Under the *Randall* court's reasoning, which of the following conditions would give rise to a cognizable necessity defense to marijuana possession charges:

(1) Wasting syndrome associated with HIV/AIDS
(2) Nausea associated the chemotherapy treatments
(3) Abdominal pain associated with Crohn's disease
(4) Stress associated with the death of a loved one

Put differently, how is a court supposed to judge the third element of the necessity defense, namely, whether the defendant's gain from using marijuana is greater than the harm such use imposes on society?

Not all courts have embraced the necessity defense. In the following case, the United States Supreme Court held the defense inapplicable to marijuana prosecutions brought under *federal* law.

### *United States v. Oakland Cannabis Buyers' Coop.*
532 U.S. 483 (2001)

THOMAS, J.:

[After California voters enacted the Compassionate Use Act (CUA) to "[t]o ensure that seriously ill Californians have the right to obtain and use marijuana for medical purposes," the Oakland Cannabis Cooperative was formed to supply the needs of qualifying patients.[4] The United States sued to enjoin the Cooperative from manufacturing and distributing marijuana. The Cooperative sought to raise a necessity defense, claiming that "any distributions were medically necessary" because marijuana "is the only drug . . . that can alleviate the severe pain and other debilitating symptoms of the Cooperative's patients."]

The Controlled Substances Act provides that, "[e]xcept as authorized by this subchapter, it shall be unlawful for any person knowingly or intentionally . . . to manufacture, distribute, or dispense, or possess with intent to manufacture, distribute, or dispense,

---

4. Author's note: The details of medical marijuana laws like the CUA are discussed in Chapters 4, 8, and 12, *infra*.

a controlled substance." 21 U.S.C. §841(a)(1). The subchapter, in turn, establishes exceptions. For marijuana (and other drugs that have been classified as "schedule I" controlled substances), there is but one express exception, and it is available only for Government-approved research projects, §823(f). Not conducting such a project, the Cooperative cannot, and indeed does not, claim this statutory exemption.

The Cooperative contends, however, that notwithstanding the apparently absolute language of §841(a), the statute is subject to additional, implied exceptions, one of which is medical necessity. According to the Cooperative, because necessity was a defense at common law, medical necessity should be read into the Controlled Substances Act. We disagree.

As an initial matter, we note that it is an open question whether federal courts ever have authority to recognize a necessity defense not provided by statute. A necessity defense "traditionally covered the situation where physical forces beyond the actor's control rendered illegal conduct the lesser of two evils." *United States v. Bailey*, 444 U.S. 394, 410 . . . (1980). Even at common law, the defense of necessity was somewhat controversial. . . . And under our constitutional system, in which federal crimes are defined by statute rather than by common law . . . it is especially so. As we have stated: "Whether, as a policy matter, an exemption should be created is a question for legislative judgment, not judicial inference." . . . Nonetheless, we recognize that this Court has discussed the possibility of a necessity defense without altogether rejecting it. . . .

We need not decide, however, whether necessity can ever be a defense when the federal statute does not expressly provide for it. In this case, to resolve the question presented, we need only recognize that a medical necessity exception for marijuana is at odds with the terms of the Controlled Substances Act. The statute, to be sure, does not explicitly abrogate the defense. But its provisions leave no doubt that the defense is unavailable.

Under any conception of legal necessity, one principle is clear: The defense cannot succeed when the legislature itself has made a "determination of values." 1 W. LaFave & A. Scott, Substantive Criminal Law §5.4, p. 629 (1986). In the case of the Controlled Substances Act, the statute reflects a determination that marijuana has no medical benefits worthy of an exception (outside the confines of a Government-approved research project). Whereas some other drugs can be dispensed and prescribed for medical use, . . . the same is not true for marijuana. Indeed, for purposes of the Controlled Substances Act, marijuana has "no currently accepted medical use" at all. §812.

The structure of the Act supports this conclusion. The statute divides drugs into five schedules, depending in part on whether the particular drug has a currently accepted medical use. The Act then imposes restrictions on the manufacture and distribution of the substance according to the schedule in which it has been placed. Schedule I is the most restrictive schedule. The Attorney General can include a drug in schedule I only if the drug "has no currently accepted medical use in treatment in the United States," "has a high potential for abuse," and has "a lack of accepted safety for use . . . under medical supervision." §§812(b)(1)(A)-(C). Under the statute, the Attorney General could not put marijuana into schedule I if marijuana had any accepted medical use. . . .

It is clear from the text of the Act that Congress has made a determination that marijuana has no medical benefits worthy of an exception. The statute expressly contemplates that many drugs "have a useful and legitimate medical purpose and are necessary to maintain the health and general welfare of the American people," §801(1), but it includes no exception at all for any medical use of marijuana. Unwilling to view this omission as an accident, and unable in any event to override a legislative determination manifest in a statute, we reject the Cooperative's argument. . . .

For these reasons, we hold that medical necessity is not a defense to manufacturing and distributing marijuana.[7] . . .

STEVENS, J., concurring in the judgment:

Lest the Court's narrow holding be lost in its broad dicta, let me restate it here: "[W]e hold that medical necessity is not a defense to *manufacturing* and *distributing* marijuana.". . .

Congress' classification of marijuana as a schedule I controlled substance—that is, one that cannot be distributed outside of approved research projects . . .—makes it clear that "the Controlled Substances Act cannot bear a medical necessity defense to distributions of marijuana.". . .[1]

[T]he Court reaches beyond its holding, and beyond the facts of the case, by suggesting that the defense of necessity is unavailable for anyone under the Controlled Substances Act. . . . Because necessity was raised in this case as a defense to distribution, the Court need not venture an opinion on whether the defense is available to anyone other than distributors. Most notably, whether the defense might be available to a seriously ill patient for whom there is no alternative means of avoiding starvation or extraordinary suffering is a difficult issue that is not presented here. . . .

## Notes and Questions

1. Why does the *Oakland Cannabis* court reach a different conclusion than the *Randall* court regarding the availability of the necessity defense?

2. The *Oakland Cannabis* court suggested that it would be impossible for any defendant to satisfy the rigors of a medical necessity defense, in light of Congress's judgment that marijuana has no medical utility. Might the Court nonetheless find the defense available in a prosecution for simple possession of marijuana, as Justice Stevens suggested? Is there any statutory basis for making such a distinction?

---

7. Lest there be any confusion, we clarify that nothing in our analysis, or the statute, suggests that a distinction should be drawn between the prohibitions on manufacturing and distributing and the other prohibitions in the Controlled Substances Act. Furthermore, the very point of our holding is that there is no medical necessity exception to the prohibitions at issue, even when the patient is "seriously ill" and lacks alternative avenues for relief. Indeed, it is the Cooperative's argument that its patients are "seriously ill," . . . and lacking "alternatives." . . . We reject the argument that these factors warrant a medical necessity exception. . . .

1. In any event, respondents do not fit the paradigm of a defendant who may assert necessity. The defense "traditionally covered the situation where physical forces beyond the actor's control rendered illegal conduct the lesser of two evils." . . . Respondents, on the other hand, have not been forced to confront a choice of evils—violating federal law by distributing marijuana to seriously ill patients or letting those individuals suffer—but have thrust that choice upon themselves by electing to become distributors for such patients. Of course, respondents also cannot claim necessity based upon the choice of evils facing seriously ill patients, as that is not the same choice respondents face.

### b. Innocent Possession

**Problem 3.14**: Peter, who is principal of a high school, searches a student's locker and finds a small stash of marijuana. Peter takes the marijuana and puts it in his own locker for safekeeping until he can confront the student and inform her parents. Tipped off by a friend of the student, the police later conduct their own search of Peter's locker and find the marijuana stored therein. Is Peter guilty of marijuana possession?

On its face, the case against Peter appears to satisfy all of the elements for simple possession: Peter knew it was marijuana, for he had no other reason to seize it, and he had the ability and desire to control it, as manifested by his placing it in his own locker. But holding someone like Peter criminally liable for simple possession seems grossly unjust, if his motive is to be believed. To address this situation, some courts have recognized an "innocent possession" defense. The Kentucky Supreme Court discusses the defense in *Kentucky v. Adkins*, 331 S.W.3d 260, 263-64 (Ky. 2011):

> As courts in several sister states which have addressed the "innocent possession" defense have noted, it is easy to imagine numerous circumstances in which a person might take possession of a controlled substance without any unlawful intent. . . . A parent confiscating drugs from his or her child, a teacher finding drugs in his or her classroom, a daughter picking up a prescription for her bedridden parent, a homeowner finding medicine left behind by a guest, all could be, deemed illegal possessors under strictly construed possession statutes. Moreover, if the teacher transferred the drugs to his or her principal, or the homeowner gave the drugs to the guest's spouse who came by to pick them up, the teacher and homeowner could be deemed guilty of trafficking as well. We are confident that the General Assembly did not intend to criminalize the possession or transfer of controlled substances in circumstances such as these, and it is for that reason, among others, that our statutes prohibiting possession and trafficking all require that the possession or trafficking be "knowing and unlawful." . . . [T]hese statutes implicitly recognize an innocent possession or innocent trafficking defense, and whenever the evidence reasonably supports such a defense—where there is evidence that the possession was incidental and lasted no longer than reasonably necessary to permit a return to the owner, a surrender to authorities, or other suitable disposal—the instructions should reflect it.

In *United States v. Teemer*, 394 F.3d 59 (1st Cir. 2005), however, the court expressed a more skeptical view of the innocent possession defense. A jury convicted the defendant, Kenya Teemer, of unlawful possession of a firearm (an AK-47). On appeal, the defendant argued that the trial court should have given the jury the following instruction regarding innocent possession:

> The evidence may tend to show that the Defendant was touching the firearm merely to move it out of his way. You are instructed that if a person has possession of a firearm under certain circumstances which indicate that he did not have the intent to do the acts which constitute the possession of a firearm, that person would not be guilty of the offense charged. If the actual possession of the firearm by the Defendant was fleeting without the intent to exercise control, then this defense is applicable. . . . If you find beyond a reasonable doubt that the Defendant did not have the specific intent to have a possessory interest in the firearm and that he did have a "transitory" possession of the firearm, then you must find him not guilty.

The appeals court rejected the defendant's request, finding that "If a jury wished to acquit in such a situation, it could do so; but why should it be told that it had to?" *Teemer*, 394 F.3d at 64. The court explained:

> Neither the language of the felon-in-possession statute, nor its evident purpose, encourage the court to develop defenses that leave much room for benign transitory possession. The statute bans possession outright without regard to how great a danger exists of misuse in the particular case. . . .
>
> In this case, the instruction [actually used] did not say that merely to touch the AK-47 constituted a crime. The instruction said that "possession" required the defendant to "exercise authority, dominion, or control"—giving the jury latitude to employ its judgment and to conclude that moving the weapon did not constitute possession. The closing argument for the defense pressed just such an argument, but the conviction is no surprise: riding around in a car with an AK-47 is a risky business for an ex-felon.
>
> . . .
>
> Relying upon the jury is reasonable, for common sense is the touchstone in situations of innocent contact, and the occasions that might warrant leniency are myriad and hard to cabin in advance. Assuming that Teemer moved the gun to sit down and did nothing else (i.e., had never carried it into the house or ridden with it deliberately in reach), we think that the jury was still entitled—but not required—to conclude that he had broken the law. . . .
>
> No record exists in this circuit of abusive indictments for innocent contact, let alone convictions, that would warrant an effort to craft a general limitation. And, so long as judges leave juries the kind of latitude that the trial judge sensibly did in this case, it is unlikely that juries will be foolish enough to convict in cases [involving innocent contact]. If the worst happens, the courts are competent to deal with such cases individually or in gross when they arrive.

*Id.* at 64-65.

## Notes and Questions

1. The *Teemer* court suggests that police, prosecutors, judges, and juries can be trusted to prevent the parade of horribles that has inspired the innocent possession defense. Do you agree? The *Teemer* court also suggests that it would be impossible to craft a defense that would address every possible scenario. What do you think? Should we rely on the good sense of police, prosecutors, judges, and juries to ensure that someone like Peter in **Problem 3.14** does not get charged, prosecuted, and convicted? What about requiring governments to prove an intent to use the marijuana (or other contraband) as an additional element of the offense of simple possession?

### c. Unwitting Possession

As noted above, a few jurisdictions have made simple possession of marijuana a strict liability offense. The elimination of the culpable knowledge element arguably increases the risk of unjust prosecutions. For this reason, some courts have recognized an "unwitting possession" defense similar to the "innocent possession" defense discussed above.

Although Washington has since legalized possession of marijuana by adults, the state's earlier experience creating an unwitting possession defense remains instructive. The Washington Supreme Court first recognized the defense in *Washington v. Cleppe*, 635 P.2d 435 (Wash. 1981) (en banc), a prosecution for simple possession of marijuana brought under Washington's (now defunct) strict liability statute. The court further elaborated on the rationale for the defense in the following case.

## *City of Kennewick v. Day*
11 P.3d 304 (Wash. 2000) (en banc)

MADSEN, J.:

Doug R. Day was convicted by a Benton County District Court jury of possession of marijuana and possession of drug paraphernalia. At trial, Day asserted the defense of "unwitting possession."

On November 4, 1996, Day was stopped for investigation of driving under the influence after maneuvering his truck around a police barrier set up to facilitate an accident investigation. The officer who stopped Day immediately suspected he was intoxicated. Day claimed he had not been drinking, but was unwilling to take a field sobriety test or a portable "BAC DataMaster" test. Day was arrested and his truck was searched.

In the center armrest console, between the front seats, the officer found a small amount of marijuana and a marijuana pipe. Day immediately claimed the items were not his, that he had never seen them before, and that he had just picked up his truck from a repair shop. Day's postarrest BAC reading was .04, so he was only charged with negligent driving in the first degree. . . . The arresting officer also cited Day for possession of marijuana under 40 grams and possession of drug paraphernalia under the Kennewick Municipal Code.

. . . With respect to the drug-related charges, Day asserted the defense of "unwitting possession," . . . claiming he was unaware that the marijuana and marijuana pipe were in his car prior to the officer finding them. In support of his defense, Day offered the testimony of Don Simmonson. Simmonson, the owner of an auto repair shop, testified that Day's vehicle had been in his shop undergoing major modifications for approximately four months up until a "couple" of days prior to Day's arrest. . . . He also testified that one of the employees who worked on Day's vehicle was fired for suspected drug use outside of work, and Simmonson recounted a prior incident in which a customer complained about finding drug paraphernalia in a car after it was picked up from his shop. Defense counsel proceeded to ask Simmonson if he was aware of Day's reputation in the community for sobriety, as to both drugs and alcohol. The court sustained the prosecutor's objection to this question.

The trial court excluded Day's proffered character evidence stating that "[i]t's not an issue of character, it's an issue of conduct and past conduct is not necessarily admissible to show present conduct." . . . The trial judge also noted that Day "doesn't have to smoke [marijuana] to be in possession or use it to be in possession." . . .

The jury acquitted Day of negligent driving, but found him guilty of possession of marijuana and possession of drug paraphernalia. . . . Day petitioned this Court for review and review was granted, limited to the issue of whether the trial court erroneously precluded Day from presenting evidence of his reputation for sobriety from drugs and alcohol. . . .

The second charge against Day was for possession of marijuana. KMC 9.32.020(1) provides:

> It is unlawful for any person to possess marijuana, unless the same was obtained directly from, or pursuant to, a valid prescription or order from a medical practitioner while acting in the course of medical practice, or except as otherwise authorized by the laws of the State of Washington. . . .

This provision is similar to . . . the state controlled substance possession statute. Under the State provision, we have held that "[t]he State is not required to prove either knowledge or intent to possess, nor knowledge as to the nature of the substance[.]" . . . Simply put, possession is a strict liability crime. . . . Thus, the City's argument that "use" is not relevant to "possession" is persuasive when applied to the possession of marijuana charge.

In a typical strict liability case, in which no affirmative defenses are available, character evidence is irrelevant. . . .

Day does not contest this point. Instead, he argues that when the defense of "unwitting possession" is raised, a defendant should be permitted to introduce character evidence that is "pertinent" or "relevant" to this defense. . . . This is true, argues Day, even if it is not relevant to whether a technical violation of the underlying law has occurred. . . . According to Day, the evidence of a character trait is "pertinent" if it makes it more or less probable that an affirmative defense should be accepted. . . .

The unwitting possession defense is unique to Washington and North Dakota. . . . This Court adopted the defense to "ameliorate[ ] the harshness of the almost strict criminal liability our law imposes for unauthorized possession of a controlled substance. If the defendant can affirmatively establish that his 'possession' was unwitting, then he had no possession for which the law will convict["] . . . [*Washington v. Cleppe*, 635 P.2d 435 (1981).] This defense is supported by one of two alternative showings: (1) that the defendant did not know he was in possession of the controlled substance, . . . or (2) that the defendant did not know the nature of the substance he possessed. . . . In both cases the defendant bears the burden of proving this defense by a preponderance of the evidence. . . .

When the defense of unwitting possession is raised, the defendant's knowledge is directly relevant to the defense of unwitting possession. Accordingly, the universe of relevant evidence expands. . . . For example, if a defendant claims to be unaware that a particular substance is controlled, the defendant's knowledge as to the nature of the substance is relevant (e.g., being able to distinguish marijuana from oregano). . . . If a defendant claims to have been unaware he or she possessed the substance itself (e.g., someone placed it in my car), the defendant's intent to possess the controlled substance is relevant. . . .

Character evidence may assist a defendant in meeting his or her burden of proving by a preponderance of the evidence a lack of knowledge under the unwitting possession defense. For instance, if a defendant claims to have believed a bag of marijuana was oregano, evidence that the defendant has the reputation for not using drugs lends support to this contention. It is more likely that a defendant who does not use drugs (by reputation at least) would be unable to identify marijuana. Similarly, if a defendant claims to have been unaware of the presence of a controlled substance at all, the defendant's nonuse of drugs lends support to this claim. A person who does not use drugs (by reputation) is less likely to possess drugs. In this case, Day asserted the defense of unwitting possession, claiming he was unaware that the marijuana and marijuana pipe were inside his vehicle. His knowledge was thus at issue, and his reputation for sobriety from drugs and alcohol was a "pertinent" trait of character under [the rules of evidence]. . . .

Day's reputation for sobriety from drugs and alcohol is "pertinent" to the charge of possession of drug paraphernalia because "intent to use" is an element of the offense. Further, Day's reputation for sobriety from drugs and alcohol is "pertinent" to the charge of simple possession because he raised the defense of unwitting possession. Day presented evidence tending to establish that the marijuana and marijuana pipe were placed in his truck while it was being repaired. Defendant's presentation of third party testimony regarding his reputation for abstention from the use of drugs was important to his defense.

. . . Accordingly, we reverse and remand for a new trial.

TALMADGE, J., concurring:

I . . . understand this Court's oft-expressed antipathy toward strict liability crimes, even where the Legislature's intent to create a strict liability crime is clear. . . . Despite the creation of strict liability crimes by state and local legislative action, we have imported an intent element into drug possession crimes by our adoption of the unwitting possession defense. . . . This is judicial legislation in its most direct form. . . .

## Notes and Questions

1. Each of the defenses just discussed was created by judicial decision. Should courts have the power to create new defenses to legislatively defined crimes? Would you limit this power in any way?

2. Short of abandoning prohibition, how (if at all) would you revise the laws governing the possession and use of marijuana in prohibition regimes?

## B. WHAT ARE THE SANCTIONS FOR SIMPLE POSSESSION?

This section explores the criminal and civil sanctions that prohibition regimes authorize for simple possession of marijuana. It also discusses the criminal sanctions that are actually imposed in practice.

### 1. Criminal Sanctions

Many jurisdictions criminalize the simple possession of marijuana, although their numbers are dwindling. The penalties for a criminal conviction of simple possession of marijuana under federal law are specified in 21 U.S.C. section 844(a):

> . . . Any person who violates this subsection may be sentenced to a term of imprisonment of not more than 1 year, and shall be fined a minimum of $1,000, or both, except that if he commits such offense after a prior conviction under this subchapter . . . he shall be sentenced to a term of imprisonment for not less than 15

days but not more than 2 years, and shall be fined a minimum of $2,500, except, further, that if he commits such offense after two or more prior convictions under this subchapter . . . he shall be sentenced to a term of imprisonment for not less than 90 days but not more than 3 years, and shall be fined a minimum of $5,000. . . . Further, upon conviction, a person who violates this subsection shall be fined the reasonable costs of the investigation and prosecution of the offense . . . except that this sentence shall not apply and a fine under this section need not be imposed if the court determines . . . that the defendant lacks the ability to pay.

The federal sentencing guidelines also play a role in determining sanctions for possession under federal law. For example, United States Sentencing Guidelines section 2D2.1 specifies a base offense level of 4 for simple possession of marijuana, which translates into a suggested sentence of zero to six months imprisonment for defendants with all but the most egregious of criminal histories. (Chapter 7 discusses the Guidelines at greater length.)

Some states authorize harsher sanctions for simple possession. At the sternest end of the spectrum, Florida treats simple possession of marijuana as a third-degree felony carrying a prison term of up to five years, though it treats simple possession of 20 grams or less of marijuana as a first-degree misdemeanor punishable by up to one year imprisonment. Fla. Stat. Ann. § 893.13(6)(a) & (b).

Like Florida, many states grade and punish simple possession cases according to the quantity and type of marijuana involved in the offense. North Carolina's punishment scheme is illustrative:

> . . . [A person who possesses marijuana] shall be guilty of a Class 3 misdemeanor, but any sentence of imprisonment imposed must be suspended and the judge may not require at the time of sentencing that the defendant serve a period of imprisonment as a special condition of probation. If the quantity of the controlled substance exceeds one-half of an ounce (avoirdupois[5]) of marijuana, 7 grams of a synthetic cannabinoid or any mixture containing such substance, or one-twentieth of an ounce (avoirdupois) of the extracted resin of marijuana, commonly known as hashish, the violation shall be punishable as a Class 1 misdemeanor. If the quantity of the controlled substance exceeds one and one-half ounces (avoirdupois) of marijuana, 21 grams of a synthetic cannabinoid or any mixture containing such substance, or three-twentieths of an ounce (avoirdupois) of the extracted resin of marijuana, commonly known as hashish, or if the controlled substance consists of any quantity of synthetic tetrahydrocannabinols or tetrahydrocannabinols isolated from the resin of marijuana, the violation shall be punishable as a Class I felony.

N.C.G.S.A. § 90-95(4). The difference in the punishment for different quantities of possessed marijuana can be fairly dramatic. Under North Carolina law, a Class 3 misdemeanor is punished with 30 days' imprisonment or less, or a fine, N.C.G.S.A. § 14-3(a)(3), though the state prohibition expressly declares that imprisonment shall *not* be imposed for this offense. In comparison, a Class 1 misdemeanor carries a penalty of up to one year's imprisonment. *Id.* at § 14-3(a)(1). A Class I felony is punishable by 3 to 12 months' imprisonment, depending on prior record, as well as a fine. N.C.G.S.A.

---

5. Author's note: Avoirdupois is simply a fancy word for a measuring system in which a pound is sixteen ounces.

§ 15A-1340.17. Under the state's sentencing guidelines, the presumptive sentencing range is 4 to 6 months' imprisonment for the most serious possession offense committed by someone with a clean criminal history. *Id.*

In states like North Carolina, quantity is considered an additional element of the offense. This means that the government bears the burden of proving beyond a reasonable doubt not only that the substance possessed was marijuana but also that the quantity possessed met the minimum specified by the statutory offense charged. The following case discusses the issue.

## *North Carolina v. Mitchell*
442 S.E.2d 24 (N.C. 1994)

Exum, C.J.:

On 6 September 1989, at about 9:30 p.m., defendant and Bob Kennedy drove to Jimmy's Pic-Up Store . . . in a black vehicle. Kennedy is disabled and he compensates defendant for transporting him to various places. Defendant entered the convenience store alone. Defendant and the clerk were the only individuals in the store. Defendant selected several items for purchase and approached the clerk.

The clerk, Iris Williams, was an off-duty Bunn police officer[, who testified that] . . . Defendant had two bags of what appeared to be marijuana in his shirt pocket. She inquired of the bags, and defendant identified them as containing marijuana. She requested the bags, and he gave them to her. She then identified herself as a police officer and proceeded to call the police, at which time the defendant left without his marijuana.

Defendant testified that he did not enter the store with marijuana. According to defendant, the bags were on the counter when he approached Williams and Williams asked him to hand the bags to her. Defendant then left the store when Williams called the police. . . .

Kennedy corroborated defendant's version. He testified that he saw no marijuana in defendant's pocket and that he would have noticed if defendant had marijuana in his pocket. . . .

. . .

[Defendant was convicted of felonious possession of marijuana (more than 1.5 ounces). He appealed.]

. . .

In order for the State to convict defendant under [N.C.G.S. § 90-95(d)(4)] of a crime more serious than simple possession, it must prove that the marijuana which defendant possessed weighed more than one-half ounce to convict of the general misdemeanor and more than one and one-half ounces to convict of the felony. . . .

. . . [T]he State, in order to prove the element of weight of the marijuana in question, must either offer evidence of its actual, measured weight or demonstrate that the quantity of marijuana itself is so large as to permit a reasonable inference that its weight satisfied this element. In other words, to prove defendant guilty of more than simple possession and to prove misdemeanor possession, the State must offer evidence that the measured weight of the marijuana exceeded one-half ounce or show that the quantity of marijuana was so large that it could be reasonably inferred that its weight exceeded one-half ounce. To prove felony possession the State must offer evidence that the measured weight of the marijuana exceeded one and one-half ounces or show that the quantity of marijuana was so large that it could be reasonably inferred that its weight exceeded one and one-half ounces.

Here the State introduced into evidence only the two bags of marijuana seized by the store clerk, State's Exhibits Nos. 1 and 2, together with the clerk's testimony that she observed the bags sticking out of defendant's shirt pocket by approximately four inches. There was no evidence as to the measured weight of the marijuana.

. . .

The issue before us then becomes whether the record supports the proposition that the quantity of the marijuana itself, as introduced into evidence and described by the testimony, is so large as to permit a reasonable inference that it weighed more than one-half or more than one and one-half ounces. We think in this case the record does not support that proposition.

First, the description of the quantity of marijuana introduced is quite sparse. The record shows simply that it was contained in two rolled bags which were observed to be in defendant's shirt and protruding from the pocket by about four inches. The record contains no description of the actual size of the bags, the extent to which they were "rolled" nor the extent to which the bags were filled with the marijuana. Were the bags full, half full or a quarter full? How large were the bags? The record does not say. The trial court found that the quantity of marijuana was sufficient to permit the jury reasonably to infer that it weighed more than one and one-half ounces; but there is nothing in the record before us to support that finding. The marijuana was not brought forward on appeal, and we have not been able to see it for ourselves.

The State contends that the jury's ability to handle and observe the two bags is sufficient to prove that its weight exceeds one and one-half ounces. The State relies on the principle that, "whatever the jury may learn through the ear from descriptions given by witnesses, they may learn directly through the eye from the objects described." . . . The State contends that the jurors could rely on their own personal knowledge and experience which they have acquired in everyday life, as well as an opportunity to observe the evidence at trial, in order to determine for themselves whether the marijuana exceeded one and one-half ounces in weight.

When determining whether an element exists, the jury may rely on its common sense and the knowledge it has acquired through everyday experiences. . . . Thus, the jury may, based on its observations of the defendant, assess whether the defendant is older than twelve. . . . The jury's ability to determine the existence of a fact in issue based on its in-court observations, however, is not without limitation. The jury may not find the existence of a fact based solely on its in-court observations where the jury does not possess the requisite knowledge or expertise necessary to infer the fact from the evidence as reflected in the record.

Applying the foregoing, we conclude that the State failed to meet its burden of producing substantial evidence that the defendant possessed more than one-half ounce of marijuana. . . . The jury saw the two bags of marijuana, which would fit in a shirt pocket. Williams also testified that she saw "two bags sticking up approximately four inches out of his pocket." A juror's finding that the amount of marijuana as reflected by this record exceeds one-half ounce is unreliable. Unlike age, the weight of a given quantity of marijuana is not a matter of general knowledge and experience. Every adult has had experience dealing with and estimating the age of others. Human characteristics associated with various ages are matters of common knowledge. The same cannot be said regarding the weight of various quantities of marijuana. This is a matter familiar only to those who regularly use or deal in the substance, who are engaged in enforcing the laws against it, or who have developed an acute ability to assess the weight of objects down to the ounce. The average juror does not fall into any of these categories. As Judge Johnson noted below:

> While jurors may and do rely on their five senses and their life experience in deciding the facts from the evidence placed before them, I would not place a defendant in jeopardy of a felony conviction based on the jury's perception of the total weight of dried vegetable material contained in two small plastic bags-material with which the jurors presumably have little or no experience, either in handling generally or in the weighing of it. Most people, in fact, do not have experience dealing in ounces of anything, much less a substance with the specific density and bulk of marijuana.

Since the record does not reflect that the State produced sufficient evidence that the marijuana exceeded one and one-half ounces, the conviction for possession of more than one and one-half ounces of marijuana is reversed. The case is remanded to the Court of Appeals for further remand to the trial court for resentencing as if defendant had been convicted of simple possession of marijuana.

## Notes and Questions

Figure 3.3. How Much Marijuana is Pictured?

1. Why punish simple possession of larger quantities of marijuana more severely? Does the distinction reflect an assumption that the individual who possesses larger amounts is really a supplier rather than a user? If that is so, why not require the government to prove possession with the intent to distribute (a crime discussed in Chapter 7)? Do statutes that impose harsher sentences for *simple* possession of larger quantities of marijuana blur the distinction between use and supply offenses?

2. As the *Mitchell* court notes, when the government fails to prove the quantity involved in the offense, the defendant is sentenced for a class 3 misdemeanor carrying no term of incarceration. *See* N.C.G.S.A. § 90-95(4).

3. What sort of evidence might be used to gauge quantity reliably? Do you think you can accurately estimate the quantity of marijuana based on sight alone? Look at the picture in **Figure 3.3**. How much marijuana is shown?

(1) ¼ gram
(2) 1.5 grams
(3) 28.5 grams (i.e., 1 ounce)
(4) 1 kilogram

*See* Beau Kilmer et al., *Before the Grand Opening: Measuring Washington State's Marijuana Market in the Last Year Before Legalized Commercial Sales*, App. A (2013) (reporting results of web-based survey using picture in **Figure 3.3** to help users estimate daily use quantities).

## 2. Civil Sanctions

In addition to the criminal sanctions just discussed, individuals who possess marijuana also face a variety of civil sanctions. These sanctions include the loss of certain public benefits, like student financial aid, e.g., 20 U.S.C. § 1091(r)(1) (denying federal student financial aid for one year following first conviction for simple possession of any drug), and federally subsidized public housing, 24 C.F.R. § 966.4(l)(5) (enabling public housing authority to terminate lease based on tenant's drug use) (discussed in Chapter 14), the loss of employment for failing a drug test (discussed in Chapter 13), and forfeiture of the drug and some related property, 21 U.S.C. § 881(a).

Civil forfeiture is perhaps the most onerous of these sanctions. The federal CSA provides that the "following shall be subject to forfeiture to the United States and no property right shall exist in them":

> (1) All controlled substances which have been manufactured, distributed, dispensed, or acquired in violation of this subchapter.
>
> (2) All raw materials, products, and equipment of any kind which are used, or intended for use, in manufacturing, compounding, processing, delivering, importing, or exporting any controlled substance . . . in violation of this subchapter.
>
> (3) All property which is used, or intended for use, as a container for property described in paragraph . . . [(1) or (2)].
>
> (4) All conveyances, including aircraft, vehicles, or vessels, which are used, or are intended for use, to transport, or in any manner to facilitate the transportation, sale, receipt, possession, or concealment of property described in paragraph . . . [(1) or (2)].
>
> (5) All books, records, and research, including formulas, microfilm, tapes, and data which are used, or intended for use, in violation of this subchapter.
>
> (6) All moneys, negotiable instruments, securities, or other things of value furnished or intended to be furnished by any person in exchange for a controlled substance . . . in violation of this subchapter, all proceeds traceable to such an exchange, and all moneys, negotiable instruments, and securities used or intended to be used to facilitate any violation of this subchapter. . . .
>
> (8) All controlled substances which have been possessed in violation of this subchapter. . . .
>
> (10) Any drug paraphernalia (as defined in . . . the Mail Order Drug Paraphernalia Control Act).
>
> (11) Any firearm . . . used or intended to be used to facilitate the transportation, sale, receipt, possession, or concealment of property described in paragraph (1) or (2) and any proceeds traceable to such property.

21 U.S.C. § 881(a). Although most of these assets are forfeitable only when connected to a drug *supply* offense (as discussed in Chapter 7), some valuable assets may be seized in connection to simple possession offenses as well, as the following case illustrates.

## United States v. One Clipper Bow Ketch NISKU
548 F.2d 8 (1st Cir. 1977)

GIGNOUX, J.:

In this action the United States seeks the forfeiture of a $25,000 ketch, the NISKU, alleging that it was used to transport and conceal contraband substances, including a quantity of marihuana and cocaine. . . . Claimant, Ralph Washington, a resident of Arizona, purchased the NISKU in December 1973 in Marblehead, Massachusetts, and returned to Arizona, leaving one Jose Giner to attend to the fitting out of the boat for a planned two-year cruise around the world. Giner was to serve as captain and teach Washington and several others, who had no boating experience, to sail. With the exception of two visits of a few days each, one to close the deal on the purchase of the NISKU and one to see her put into the water for the first time, Washington remained in Arizona until a few days before they were to set off on the cruise. The NISKU set sail from Marblehead early on May 21, 1974, and, with Washington at the helm, ran aground on a sandbar near Plymouth harbor around 10 A.M. Later that evening, the Plymouth harbormaster, accompanied by an agent of the Drug Enforcement Agency (DEA), came out to the NISKU. According to the testimony of the DEA agent, contradicted by Washington, Washington and others on the boat were smoking a marihuana cigarette. The harbormaster said that he would return later to lead the NISKU into the harbor. After the tide had freed the boat from the sandbar, it proceeded to the dock in the harbor. At 5:00 A.M. the next morning, DEA agents, pursuant to a search warrant, boarded the NISKU and found approximately three-quarters of a pound of marihuana in the area of the vessel where Giner slept. The NISKU was seized and the crew arrested.[2]

Figure 3.4. A Ketch Like the NISKU

In the district court proceedings on the government's forfeiture complaint, . . . the court found that there was marihuana on board the NISKU and that Washington knew it was there. Forfeiture was ordered.

Claimant's principal argument is that the forfeiture statutes ought not to be interpreted to apply to this case: that the statutes should be construed to require forfeiture only where a vessel has been used in illegal drug trafficking, not where a quantity of illicit drugs for personal consumption has been found in a vessel. If we had discretion in the matter, we might find claimant's proposed distinction appealing, for it cannot be denied that drug trafficking is at the core of the conduct at which the forfeiture statutes are directed, and the justification for imposing forfeiture in cases involving solely possession of contraband for personal use is far less apparent. However, the statutory language

---

2. Washington was charged with illegal possession of controlled substances . . . but the criminal charge was voluntarily dismissed by the government.

belies the argument that the forfeiture provisions are limited to commercial trafficking. . . .

The relevant statutes are 21 U.S.C. § 881, which provides, in pertinent part:

> The following shall be subject to forfeiture to the United States and no property right shall exist in them:
>
> (4) All conveyances, including aircraft, vehicles, or vessels, which are used, or are intended for use, to transport, or in any manner to facilitate the transportation, sale, receipt, possession, or concealment of (controlled substances).

and 49 U.S.C. §§ 781, 782, which provide, in pertinent part:

> § 781. (a) It shall be unlawful (1) to transport, carry, or convey any contraband article in, upon, or by means of any vessel, vehicle, or aircraft; (2) to conceal or possess any contraband article in or upon any vessel, vehicle, or aircraft, or upon the person of anyone in or upon any vessel, vehicle, or aircraft; or (3) to use any vessel, vehicle, or aircraft to facilitate the transportation, carriage, conveyance, concealment, receipt, possession, purchase, sale, barter, exchange, or giving away of any contraband article.
>
> § 782. Any vessel, vehicle, or aircraft which has been or is being used in violation of section 781 of this title, or in, upon, or by means of which any violation of said section has taken or is taking place, shall be seized and forfeited. . . .

The language of these statutes furnishes no support for the distinction urged by claimant. By the express terms of 21 U.S.C. § 881, a vessel is to be forfeited if used "to transport" controlled substances. The plain meaning of "to transport" is simply to carry or convey from one place to another. The statute is silent as to the purpose for which the transportation is undertaken, and we cannot read such a limitation into the words used. 49 U.S.C. §§ 781, 782 even more clearly foreclose the interpretation urged by claimant. In addition to a clause similar to that in 21 U.S.C. § 881 requiring forfeiture of any vessel, vehicle or aircraft used "to transport, carry, or convey" contraband, 49 U.S.C. §§ 781, 782 provide for forfeiture where contraband is "conceal(ed)" or "possess(ed)" in or upon any vessel, or upon the person of anyone in or upon a vessel. Given such unambiguous language, we cannot feel free to limit the application of the statutes to commercial trafficking. . . . While it is true that Congress' expressed concern was with trafficking, . . . this does not preclude the possibility that other conduct was also intended to fall within the statutes. In any event, "there is no need to refer to the legislative history where the statutory language is clear." . . .

Although there are state court decisions construing similar forfeiture statutes as claimant urges, . . . the federal courts have consistently rejected the position claimant advocates. . . . These cases have all held that the sweeping statutory language clearly requires forfeiture where any contraband has been physically present in the conveyance.

The evidence amply supports the finding of the district court that the NISKU was used, with claimant's knowledge, to transport marihuana, and therefore the judgment of forfeiture was proper. The result is harsh, but that alone does not warrant the court's refusal to enforce the statutes. . . . Congress has provided a means for ameliorating the harshness of these statutes the Attorney General may return the property if he finds "such mitigating circumstances as to justify the remission" of the forfeiture, 19 U.S.C. § 1618; 28 C.F.R. § 9 and we must assume that this was intended to be the sole mechanism for affording leniency. . . .

## Notes and Questions

1. Was forfeiture an excessive sanction for the crime involved (possession of ¾ pound of marijuana) in *NISKU*? Should the court have refused to order forfeiture? Did it have any choice?

2. Which of the assets listed in 21 U.S.C. section 881(a) can be seized in relation to a simple possession offense?

---

Some state courts have attempted to rein in their own versions of civil forfeiture statutes.

### *Illinois ex rel. Neal v. Ryan*
672 N.E.2d 47 (Ill. App. 1996)

McCuskey, J.:

[Edmund Ryan was stopped by police because his truck was missing a rear license plate. During the course of the traffic stop, the police discovered marijuana in a duffel bag seized from Ryan's person. The state brought felony drug charges against Ryan and also sought forfeiture of his truck pursuant to the state's Cannabis Control Act, which subjects to forfeiture "all conveyances, including aircraft, vehicles or vessels, which are used, or intended for use, to transport, or in any manner to facilitate the transportation, sale, receipt, possession, or concealment" of marijuana. 720 Ill. Comp. Stat. Ann. 550/12 (West 1994). The trial court found the forfeiture statute inapplicable to Ryan's offense, and the state appealed.]

The [Illinois] supreme court has pointed out that the key word in [a related Forfeiture Act] is "facilitate," which means "to make easier or less difficult." . . .

. . .

. . . [W]e hold that the trial court in the instant case was correct in denying the complaint for forfeiture based on its conclusion that Ryan's truck was not used to facilitate the possession of cannabis. The contraband in question was secreted in a duffel bag which the trial court found was seized from Ryan's person. The fact Ryan was in the truck some time prior to the seizure does not give rise to a conclusion that the truck made it easier for Ryan to possess the cannabis. We find that the use of the vehicle was completely incidental to the possession of the cannabis. . . . Ryan's possession of the cannabis would have been no more difficult had he "been walking, taking a bus, or riding a motorcycle." . . .

. . .

In determining what "transportation" means under the forfeiture provisions of [the Cannabis Control Act], the State urges us to look only to federal case law for guidance in reaching our decision. We decline to do so. . . .

We are mindful of the general rule of law that forfeitures are not favored and that forfeiture statutes must be strictly construed in favor of the property owner. . . .

. . . The trial court determined that Ryan took the drugs from his residence and was returning home with the drugs at the conclusion of his work day. The trial court also determined that the cannabis was possessed solely for the personal use of either Ryan or his wife. The record is undisputed that Ryan was not possessing the cannabis for sale or delivery to another person.

Based upon our review of applicable Illinois law, we conclude that the General Assembly did not intend for the transportation language of the Cannabis Control Act to be interpreted so as to forfeit motor vehicles in those cases where: (1) the trial court has found that the claimant merely possessed a small amount of cannabis which was solely for personal use and not intended to be sold or delivered to another person; and (2) where the use of the vehicle was completely incidental to the possession of the controlled substance.

## Notes and Questions

1. Do you agree with the *Ryan* court's interpretation of Illinois forfeiture law? Why does the "used . . . to transport" language of the law cover only transportation for delivery or sale to another person and not transportation for personal use? In any event, if Ryan was transporting the marijuana at least in part for *his wife's use*, why was this requirement not met?

## 3. Sanctions Under Decriminalization

Even though they continue to ban simple possession of marijuana, many states—and to a limited extent, *the federal government*—have decriminalized simple possession, at least when small quantities are involved. In these jurisdictions, simple possession is now considered only a civil offense, akin to many traffic violations. In lieu of the criminal penalties and civil forfeiture sanctions discussed above, decriminalization regimes generally impose only small fines for simple possession of marijuana.

Illinois' decriminalization regime is illustrative. While it remains "unlawful for any person knowingly to possess cannabis" in Illinois, legislation adopted in 2016 specifies that a possession violation involving "not more than 10 grams of any substance containing cannabis" constitutes a "civil law violation punishable by a minimum fine of $100 and a maximum fine of $200." Ill. Comp. Stat. Ann. 550/4 (West 2016). Possession of more than 10 grams remains a criminal offense, and it is graded and punished according to the quantity involved. For example, the possession of 10-30 grams is considered a Class B misdemeanor, punishable with up to 6 months imprisonment and a fine of up to $1,500. *Id.* at 5/5-4.5-60.

Interestingly, a seldom noticed provision of federal law likewise *authorizes* (but does not require) federal prosecutors to treat simple possession of marijuana as a civil offense triggering a potentially harsh fine but no prison term:

> (a) In general
> Any individual who knowingly possesses a controlled substance . . . in violation of section 844 of this title in an amount that . . . is a personal use amount shall be liable to the United States for a civil penalty in an amount not to exceed $10,000 for each such violation.
> . . .
> (c) Prior conviction
> A civil penalty may not be assessed under this section if the individual previously was convicted of a Federal or State offense relating to a controlled substance.
> (d) Limitation on number of assessments

A civil penalty may not be assessed on an individual under this section on more than two separate occasions.

21 U.S.C. §844a.

## 4. Actual Versus Authorized Sanctions

Even when the law threatens harsh sanctions for possession offenses, how commonly are those sanctions actually imposed on users? The availability of prison sentences for marijuana use has sparked some controversy. Some commentators have claimed that state and federal governments have actually incarcerated thousands of people merely for possessing marijuana for their own use and not for trafficking the drug. *E.g.*, Ryan S. King & Marc Mauer, *The War on Marijuana: The Transformation of the War on Drugs in the 1990s*, 3 Harm Reduction J. tbl. 5 (2006) (estimating prisons hold 6,600 low-level marijuana offenders); ACLU, *The War on Marijuana in Black and White* 8 (2013) (estimating 20,000 people incarcerated solely for marijuana possession).

The Office of National Drug Control Policy, however, has criticized estimates (like those above), claiming they grossly overstate the number of marijuana users who are incarcerated as such:

> The idea that our nation's prisons are overflowing with otherwise law abiding people convicted for nothing more than simple possession of marijuana is treated by many as conventional wisdom.
>
> But this, in fact, is a myth—an illusion conjured and aggressively perpetuated by drug advocacy groups seeking to relax or abolish America's marijuana laws. In reality, the vast majority of inmates in state and federal prison for marijuana have been found guilty of much more than simple possession. Some were convicted for drug trafficking, some for marijuana possession along with one or more other offenses. And many of those serving time for marijuana pled down to possession in order to avoid prosecution on much more serious charges.
>
> In 1997, the year for which the most recent data are available, just 1.6 percent of the state inmate population were held for offenses involving *only* marijuana, and less than one percent of all state prisoners (0.7 percent) were incarcerated with marijuana *possession* as the only charge, according to the U.S. Department of Justice's Bureau of Justice Statistics (BJS). An even smaller fraction of state prisoners in 1997 who were convicted just for marijuana possession were firsttime offenders (0.3 percent).
>
> The numbers on the federal level tell a similar story. Out of all drug defendants sentenced in federal court for marijuana crimes in 2001, the overwhelming majority were convicted for trafficking, according to the U.S. Sentencing Commission. Only 2.3 percent—186 people—received sentences for simple possession, and of the 174 for whom sentencing information is known, just 63 actually served time behind bars.
>
> . . .
>
> Seldom does anyone in this country go to prison for nothing more than smoking pot.

Office of National Drug Control Policy, *Who's Really in Prison for Marijuana?* 9 (2005). *See also* United States Sentencing Commission, Weighing the Charges: Simple Possession of Drugs in the Federal Criminal Justice System tbl. 7 (2016) (providing detailed information on the sentences imposed for marijuana simple possession offenses in the federal system in 2013).

## Notes and Questions

1. Do you think it is commonplace for people to be incarcerated only for possessing marijuana for their own use? How should we judge the severity of the sanctions imposed on marijuana users: by the sanctions that are *authorized* by the law, or by the sanctions that are usually meted out?

2. Is incarceration necessarily the most important sanction users face? Consider the following rejoinder to the ONDCP:

> While not all of those individuals arrested are eventually sentenced to long terms in jail, the fact remains that the repercussions of a marijuana arrest alone are significant—including (but not limited to):
>
> - probation and mandatory drug testing;
> - loss of driving privileges;
> - loss of federal college aid;
> - asset forfeiture;
> - revocation of professional driver's license;
> - loss of certain welfare benefits such as food stamps;
> - removal from public housing;
> - loss of child custody; and
> - loss of employment.
>
> In other words, whether or not marijuana offenders ultimately serve time in jail, the fact is that hundreds of thousands of otherwise law-abiding citizens are having their lives needlessly destroyed each year for nothing more than smoking marijuana.

NORML, *Your Government Is Lying to You (Again) About Marijuana* (undated), https://perma.cc/X4TU-TDC4.

But how commonly are these *other* sanctions actually imposed on marijuana *users*? Consider the denial of federal student financial aid under 20 U.S.C. section 1091(r)(1). On the one hand, roughly 25,000 people were denied financial aid in fiscal year 2004-2005 due to a prior drug conviction. See Robert A. Mikos, *Enforcing State Law in Congress's Shadow,* 90 Cornell L. Rev. 1411, 1471 (2005). On the other hand, this figure includes denials for *all* drug offenses, i.e., not just marijuana and not just *possession* offenses. What is more, eligibility is restored one year after the date of a first possession offense (later for subsequent offenses), or immediately after completion of a drug treatment program. See 20 U.S.C. § 1091(r)(2).

3. What *should* be the sanction for simple possession of marijuana in prohibition states?

# CHAPTER 4

# The Regulation of Marijuana Users in Legalization Regimes

Beginning with the passage of Proposition 215 (the Compassionate Use Act) in California in 1996, a growing number of states have eschewed the strict prohibitions discussed in Chapter 3, opting instead to allow at least some people to possess and use marijuana.[1]

The first reforms were all limited to the medical use of marijuana. For example, California's Proposition 215 provides that the state's laws banning the simple possession and cultivation of marijuana (since repealed by Proposition 64) "shall not apply to a patient, or to a patient's primary caregiver, who possesses or cultivates marijuana for the personal medical purposes of the patient upon the written or oral recommendation or approval of a physician." Cal. Health & Safety Code § 11362.5(d). In the ensuing decades, more than half of the states have adopted similar measures. Even more traditionally conservative states have adopted reforms, albeit more limited in scope. For example, Alabama's Carly's law, passed in 2014, provides "an affirmative and complete defense" to a prosecution for simple possession of marijuana for defendants who have "a debilitating epileptic condition" and who have "used or possessed cannabidiol (CBD) pursuant to a prescription authorized by the [University of Alabama, Birmingham]. . . ." Ala. Code § 13A-12-214.2.

But more recently, several states have expanded their reforms to legalize recreational marijuana as well. In 2012, for example, Colorado voters passed Amendment 64, which provides, in relevant part:

> (3) Personal use of marijuana. Notwithstanding any other provision of law, the following acts are not unlawful and shall not be an offense under Colorado law or the law of any locality within Colorado or be a basis for seizure or forfeiture of assets under Colorado law for persons twenty-one years of age or older:
>
> (a) Possessing, using, displaying, purchasing, or transporting marijuana accessories or one ounce or less of marijuana.

Colo. Const. art. XVIII, § 16(3). (**Figure 1.1** in Chapter 1 displays the number of states that pursued each of these reforms from 1996 to 2016.)

---

1. Some states also allow users to grow marijuana for their own consumption. The rules governing personal cultivation are covered in Chapter 8.

Part II. Marijuana Users

This chapter begins our discussion of these proliferating reforms. It focuses on three key substantive questions the reforms seek to answer regarding marijuana users: (A) who is allowed to possess and use marijuana; (B) what limitations are placed on their use; and (C) what legal protections they enjoy. (Later chapters discuss the reforms governing marijuana suppliers and third parties, such as physicians.) The sections below address these questions and explore the differences both across and within the broad types of reform outlined above (i.e., medical marijuana states, recreational marijuana states, and CBD states).

## A. WHO IS ALLOWED TO POSSESS AND USE MARIJUANA?

This section discusses the criteria that states commonly employ to limit eligibility to use and possess marijuana. Because medical, CBD, and recreational states use different criteria, this section discusses each group of states separately.

### 1. Medical Marijuana Regimes

Medical marijuana states impose a similar set of requirements on individuals who wish to possess and use marijuana. To become a qualified patient, an individual normally must:

(1) obtain a diagnosis with a qualifying condition (all states); and
(2) obtain a physician's recommendation to use marijuana (all states); and
(3) register with a state agency (most states)
(4) be a state resident (some states)

Under Washington law, for example, "Qualifying patients with terminal or debilitating medical conditions who, in the judgment of their health care professionals, may benefit from the medical use of marijuana, shall not be arrested, prosecuted, or subject to other criminal sanctions or civil consequences under state law based solely on their medical use of marijuana, notwithstanding any other provision of law." Wash. Rev. Code Ann. § 69.51A.005(a). The state's medical marijuana law defines "Qualifying patient" as a person who:

> (i) Is a patient of a health care professional
> (ii) Has been diagnosed by that health care professional as having a terminal or debilitating medical condition;
> (iii) Is a resident of the state of Washington at the time of such diagnosis;
> (iv) Has been advised by that health care professional about the risks and benefits of the medical use of marijuana
> (v) Has been advised by that health care professional that they may benefit from the medical use of marijuana
> (vi)(A) Has an authorization from his or her health care professional; or (B) Beginning July 1, 2016, has been entered into the medical marijuana authorization database and has been provided a recognition card; and
> (vii) Is otherwise in compliance with the terms and conditions established in this chapter.

Wash. Rev. Code Ann. § 69.51A.010(4). The following sections discuss each of the primary requirements in turn.

### a. Qualifying Condition

Medical marijuana states limit access to those individuals who have been diagnosed with a condition that state policymakers believe would benefit from the use of marijuana. This book refers to such conditions as "qualifying conditions," although states employ sundry terms to the same effect (e.g., "debilitating medical condition").

Most medical marijuana states have created lists of specific qualifying conditions that are covered by their statutes. New Jersey's medical marijuana law provides an illustrative example. Under the statute, the state defines qualifying condition ("debilitating medical condition") as

> (1) one of the following conditions, if resistant to conventional medical therapy: seizure disorder, including epilepsy; intractable skeletal muscular spasticity; or glaucoma;
> 
> (2) one of the following conditions, if severe or chronic pain, severe nausea or vomiting, cachexia, or wasting syndrome results from the condition or treatment thereof: positive status for human immunodeficiency virus; acquired immune deficiency syndrome; or cancer;
> 
> (3) amyotrophic lateral sclerosis, multiple sclerosis, terminal cancer, muscular dystrophy, or inflammatory bowel disease, including Crohn's disease;
> 
> (4) terminal illness, if the physician has determined a prognosis of less than 12 months of life; or
> 
> (5) any other medical condition or its treatment that is approved by the department by regulation.

N.J. Stat. Ann. 24:6I-3. In states that enumerate qualifying conditions via statute or regulation, only patients who have been diagnosed with one of the specifically enumerated conditions may claim the protections afforded by the state's medical marijuana law. (Chapter 5 discusses in more detail the types of conditions that states have included in their medical marijuana laws and the procedures for adding new conditions to their lists.)

*Washington v. Fry* discusses the qualifying condition requirement in detail.

## *Washington v. Fry*
228 P.3d 1 (Wash. 2010)

JOHNSON, J.:

Two police officers were informed of a marijuana growing operation at the residence of Jason and Tina Fry. When the officers approached the home, the smell of burning marijuana was apparent. Jason Fry did not consent to a search, and Tina Fry presented a document purporting to be authorization for medical marijuana. The officers obtained a telephonic search warrant, entered the Frys' home, and seized over two pounds of marijuana. . . .

[Jason Fry was charged with possession of marijuana. The judge denied his motion to suppress the marijuana as evidence and refused to allow Fry to present a medical marijuana defense at trial because Fry did not have a qualifying condition. Fry appealed both rulings. The court's opinion discussing the legality of the search is excerpted in Section C.1 below.]

The intent of the medical marijuana statute was that "[q]ualifying patients *with terminal or debilitating illnesses* who, in the judgment of their physicians, would benefit from the medical use of marijuana, shall not be found guilty of a crime under state law for their possession and limited use of marijuana." Former RCW 69.51A.005 (emphasis added).

A "qualifying patient" is a person who:

> (a) Is a patient of a physician licensed under chapter 18.71 or 18.57 RCW;
> (b) Has been diagnosed by that physician as having a terminal or debilitating medical condition;
> (c) Is a resident of the state of Washington at the time of such diagnosis;
> (d) Has been advised by that physician about the risks and benefits of the medical use of marijuana; and
> (e) Has been advised by that physician that they may benefit from the medical use of marijuana.

Former RCW 69.51A.010(3) (1999). The State argues Fry is not a qualifying patient under the Act because Fry has not been diagnosed as having a terminal or debilitating medical condition under former RCW 69.51A.010(3)(b). Fry's doctor listed "severe anxiety, rage, & depression related to childhood" as the debilitating medical condition qualifying Fry to use medical marijuana. . . . These conditions did not qualify under I-692 as enacted.

In 2007, after the search and seizure in this case, the legislature revised the medical marijuana statute to include additional terminal or debilitating medical conditions that would qualify under the Act. RCW 69.51A.010(4). Fry's conditions of severe anxiety and rage are not included in the list of qualifying conditions, even as amended. In 2004, the State of Washington Department of Health Medical Quality Assurance Commission issued a final order denying a petition to include depression and severe anxiety in the list of "terminal or debilitating medical conditions" under RCW 69.51A.010(4). Final Order on Pet., *In re Condrey*, No. 04-08-A-2002MD (Wash. Med. Quality Assurance Comm'n Nov. 19, 2004).

Fry did not actually have a terminal or debilitating medical condition as provided in the Act. The stated intent of the statute was to allow a qualifying patient with a terminal or debilitating illness to be found not guilty of marijuana possession under certain circumstances. Former RCW 69.51A.005. ("The people of Washington state find that . . . [q]ualifying patients with terminal or debilitating illnesses . . . shall not be found guilty. . . ."). Conversely, the intent was not to excuse a marijuana user without a terminal or debilitating illness from criminal liability. Former RCW 69.51A.005.

In the only case we have decided under the Act, an otherwise qualifying patient received authorization to use medical marijuana from a doctor in California. [*Washington v. Tracy*, 147 P.3d 559 (Wash. 2006).] This court interpreted the provision in the Act defining qualifying doctors as "those licensed under Washington law" to require a doctor formally licensed in Washington. . . . The majority opinion concluded that "[s]ince Tracy was not a patient of a qualifying doctor, she is not entitled to assert the defense." The court stated unequivocally that "[o]nly qualifying patients are entitled to the defense under the act." . . .

This court declined to extend the defense to Tracy, who was not in compliance with the statute because the doctor was not authorized to issue the medical marijuana authorization. Similarly, we will not extend the statute to permit an individual without a qualifying illness to claim its benefits.

In order to avail himself of the compassionate use defense, Fry must qualify under the Act. Fry does not have one of the listed debilitating conditions, and therefore does not qualify. We affirm the Court of Appeals decision to not permit Fry to claim the compassionate use defense. . . .

CHAMBERS, J., concurring:

As a compassionate gesture, the people of this state, by initiative, allowed patients afflicted with medical conditions that might be eased by marijuana to use it under limited circumstances. Generally, whether a patient has a medical condition that qualifies under the Washington State Medical Use of Marijuana Act (the act), ch. 69.51A RCW, is a question of fact, not law. I disagree with the lead opinion's holding that as a matter of law Jason Fry did not have a qualifying condition under the act simply because the words used by Fry's doctor in issuing the authorization may have been inartful. The lead opinion approves the trial court's pretrial application of the law to the facts, its weighing of the evidence, and its decision as a matter of law that the compassionate use of marijuana defense was unavailable to Fry. In my view, a defendant in Fry's position should have the opportunity to offer evidence that he in fact had a qualifying condition and that his doctor issued the medical marijuana authorization for that condition. . . .

Fry was smoking marijuana. Two Stevens County police officers smelled marijuana burning as they approached Fry's house. When questioned, Fry acknowledged the use of marijuana, and his wife, Tina, produced a form entitled "Documentation of Medical Authorization to Possess Marijuana for Medical Purposes in Washington State" issued by Fry's physician, Dr. Thomas Orvald. Clerk's Papers (CP) at 67, 20. The authorization stated that Dr. Orvald was treating Fry for "a terminal illness or debilitating condition as defined in RCW 6951A.010." CP at 20. On a separate page under a section marked "Documentation of debilitating medical condition from previous healthcare provider," Dr. Orvald wrote, "severe anxiety, rage, & depression related to childhood." Under the "subjective" section of his own notes detailing Fry's background Dr. Orvald wrote, "Severe anxiety!!! Can't function." CP at 22. The authorization also included notes from Dr. Orvald's physical examination of Fry where he noted a scar behind Fry's right ear and on his chin from being injured by a horse. These notes also reflect that Fry suffered from neck and lower back pain. In the comments section Dr. Orvald wrote: "Pt has found use of medical cannabis allows him to function [with] self control of anger, rage, & depression. Pt has been kicked in head 3 times by horse." . . .

There seems to be no question that Fry's physician was qualified, that he advised Fry of the risks and benefits of medical marijuana use, and that Fry was a resident of the state of Washington. Further, Fry possessed what would appear to be a valid authorization as defined by the statute. The issue before us is whether Fry could have had a qualified condition. The statute defines "Terminal or Debilitating Medical Condition" in the disjunctive. One permissible condition is intractable pain, meaning pain unrelieved by standard medical treatments and medications. Former RCW 69.51A.010(4)(b). It may be that Fry's doctor prescribed medical marijuana for chronic pain related to his head or neck injury. Or the authorization may have been to alleviate nausea, vomiting, or appetite loss caused by his severe anxiety and depression. In my opinion, whether Fry was suffering from any of these symptoms can only be determined after a factual inquiry. Without allowing Fry to present a defense, we cannot know whether a fact finder would conclude that Fry had symptoms that would qualify him under the terms defined under the statute. It is the role of the jury to apply the law to facts presented at a trial. . . .

Procedurally, the trial court struck Fry's medical use of marijuana defense upon the prosecutor's motion in limine, because anxiety was listed in the authorization and the court found as a matter of law that it was not a qualifying condition. Despite the signed authorization from Fry's physician that in his medical opinion "the potential benefits of the medical use of marijuana would likely outweigh the health risks for this patient" and that Fry had "a terminal illness or debilitating condition as defined in RCW 69.51A.010," . . . the lead opinion nevertheless affirms the conclusion of the trial judge that Fry did not have a debilitating condition as a matter of law. In my view, Dr. Orvald's authorization was sufficient to satisfy the threshold showing required of Fry that he was a qualified person under the act. It was not the proper role of the trial judge to review the doctor's records and conclude as a matter of law that Fry did not have a qualifying condition. There is nothing in the act that requires the debilitating condition be listed or described in the authorization, and surely the voters did not intend that whether a person is guilty of a felony should turn on a physician's choice of words when filling out an authorization. . . . Whether Fry had a qualifying condition under the act was a question of fact, not law.

The lead opinion uses our decision in Tracy to bolster its holding that Fry was not entitled to raise a defense. However, in Tracy, the issue was much different. In Tracy, the doctor was not authorized to issue the medical marijuana authorization. . . . Our decision was controlled by the fact that a qualifying patient under the statute is one who has been diagnosed by a Washington-licensed physician and Tracy had been diagnosed only by a California physician not licensed in Washington. . . . Tracy presented a clear question of law, a question of statutory interpretation: could a physician not licensed in Washington satisfy the statutory condition of being diagnosed by a Washington licensed physician as required by former RCW 69.51A.010(3)(a)? We did not mean to imply that the issue of whether a person is a qualified person under the statute is always a question of law to be determined by the court.

When a defendant is charged with a violation of state law involving marijuana, he may assert that he intends to raise a medical marijuana defense under chapter 69.51A RCW. The State may make a motion to preclude the defendant from asserting the defense, arguing that the requirements of the statute have not been met. But in my view, if the defendant is able to present a written authorization from a Washington-licensed physician stating that the defendant has a qualifying condition, then he should be allowed to move forward with the defense. Whether a defendant can meet the burden of proving by a preponderance of the evidence that he in fact has a qualifying condition will of course depend on what is presented at trial to the trier of fact.

Although I conclude that the trial court erred by determining from the authorization alone that Fry did not have a qualifying condition and therefore was not a qualifying patient, I would affirm on alternative grounds. A trial judge has an additional role as a gatekeeper to ensure that there is sufficient evidence to permit any affirmative defense to proceed to trial. An opponent has the right to challenge any claimed defense. Here the prosecutor made a motion in limine to strike Fry's medical marijuana defense, arguing that Fry did not have a qualifying condition and that Fry had well more than a 60 day supply of marijuana. Although Fry was prepared to offer the testimony of a doctor and a botanist on the issue of the quantity of marijuana necessary for a 60 day supply, counsel conceded that Fry did not have a "qualifying condition" under the act. While the trial court erroneously, in my view, concluded as a matter of law that Fry was not a "qualified person" under the act, when the State moved in limine to exclude the defense Fry failed to offer additional supporting evidence that he had a qualifying condition. Based on Fry's concession and failure to provide any additional evidence to support the medical use of marijuana defense I would affirm.

## Notes and Questions

1. Barring the concession made by Fry's counsel, should he have been allowed to present a medical marijuana defense to the jury? Did he present any evidence that he had been diagnosed with a qualifying condition, or is the concurring judge merely speculating? Was it enough that Fry's physician recited the words of the statute—"a terminal illness or debilitating condition"—on his authorization (i.e., recommendation) form? *See Washington v. Constantine*, 652, 330 P.3d 226, 234 (Wash. App. 2014) (Korsmo, J., dissenting) ("In a properly presented case, the defense would offer medical evidence that the patient was diagnosed *with a particular condition*.") (emphasis added).

2. To curb abuse of their medical marijuana laws, some states impose an additional exhaustion requirement for certain qualifying conditions, like chronic pain, that are difficult for physicians (and the state) to corroborate. Thus, some states consider chronic pain a qualifying condition only when the patient has already attempted (unsuccessfully) other, more conventional treatments. *E.g.*, Rev. Code Wash. 69.51A.010(6)(d) (defining "terminal or debilitating medical condition" to include "[i]ntractable pain, limited for the purpose of this chapter to mean pain unrelieved by standard medical treatments and medications").

Does it make sense to require a patient to try all "standard medical treatments" before turning to marijuana? What if such treatments involve the use of powerful opioid painkillers? If so, does the exhaustion requirement run counter to the common advice that patients should use opioid painkillers only as a last resort? *See* Federation of State Medical Boards, Model Policy on the Use of Opioid Analgesics in the Treatment of Chronic Pain 11, July 2013, https://perma.cc/A8WX-24T8 ("Generally, safer alternative treatments should be considered before initiating opioid therapy for chronic, non-malignant pain."). Consider the following Problem:

<u>Problem 4.1</u>: Andy's physician has diagnosed him with degenerative disc disease, which has caused chronic pain. The physician initially prescribed Percocet, a combination of acetaminophen and oxycodone, a powerful opioid painkiller. The Percocet eliminated Andy's pain, but it also made him nauseous. When Andy complained about the side effects and expressed some concern over becoming addicted to Percocet, his physician recommended that he use marijuana instead because he believes it has the same benefits but with less serious side effects. Does Andy have a qualifying condition, as defined by Washington law? *See Washington v. Dalton*, 162 Wash. App. 1062 (2011 unreported) (no, because Percocet relieved his pain).

---

A handful of states empower physicians to authorize patients to use marijuana for medical purposes, even when they have not been diagnosed with an enumerated qualifying condition. California has adopted the most open-ended approach. Proposition 215 lists several specific conditions for which marijuana may be used as a treatment, but it also allows physicians to recommend the drug for conditions not specifically listed in the initiative. The relevant portion of the initiative provides that:

> seriously ill Californians have the right to obtain and use marijuana for medical purposes where that medical use is deemed appropriate and has been recommended by a physician

who has determined that the person's health would benefit from the use of marijuana in the treatment of cancer, anorexia, AIDS, chronic pain, spasticity, glaucoma, arthritis, migraine, or *any other illness for which marijuana provides relief.*

Cal. Health & Safety Code § 11362.5 (emphasis added).[2]

In states that allow a physician to determine whether a patient is authorized to use marijuana, is the physician's determination subject to review? *California v. Spark* addresses the question.

## *California v. Spark*
16 Cal. Rptr. 3d 840 (Cal. App. 2004)

ARDAIZ, J.

[A jury found appellant guilty of cultivating marijuana in violation of California Health & Safety Code § 11358. He raised a defense based on Section 11362.5 of the Compassionate Use Act, which states that "Section 11358, relating to the cultivation of marijuana, shall not apply to a patient, or to a patient's primary caregiver, who possesses or cultivates marijuana for the personal medical purposes of the patient upon the written or oral recommendation or approval of a physician." The jury had been instructed that one of the elements of a defense under Section 11362.5 was that the defendant "was seriously ill." The jury rejected the defense and found the appellant guilty; he was sentenced to six months in the county jail and three years' probation. On appeal, the appellant claimed, inter alia, that the jury had been erroneously instructed on the medical marijuana defense.]

On October 10, 2001, the Kern County sheriff received an anonymous tip about marijuana growing in the backyard of Zelma Spark's trailer home in Inyokern. Two sheriff's deputies went to the home on the night of October 25 and saw a marijuana plant growing in the backyard area. The plant was about six feet tall.

The deputies went to the front door and contacted Ms. Spark. She told them her son, appellant Noel Spark, had been given permission to grow marijuana. The deputies searched the backyard and found two more marijuana plants. One of the plants was about three feet tall and was in full bloom; the other was a recently harvested stalk. The officers seized all three plants from the backyard. The plants belonged to Ms. Spark's son, appellant Noel Spark, who was living with his mother at the time.

The next day, appellant telephoned the police and said he had stayed in his mother's home for three or four weeks but now lived in San Bernardino County. He admitted the marijuana plants seized from his mother's home were his, and he said he took lengths to keep the plants hidden. He also said he smoked about a half-ounce of marijuana per week. Appellant claimed that he smoked marijuana for pain and that he had obtained a marijuana prescription from Dr. William Eidelman. . . .

Appellant called to the stand Dr. William Eidelman. On May 8, 2001, appellant consulted Dr. Eidelman about medicinal marijuana. Appellant complained he had suffered from chronic back pain for about 10 years. Dr. Eidelman conducted an examination and

---

2. In 2003, the California legislature passed the Medical Marijuana Program (MMP), which provided additional legal protections to qualifying patients who suffered from specific "serious medical conditions" enumerated in the MMP. Cal. Health & Safety Code § 11362.5(h).

determined appellant suffered from back pain. He gave appellant a letter approving the use of medicinal marijuana pursuant to Proposition 215. At trial, Dr. Eidelman opined appellant was in fact a seriously ill patient who qualified for medicinal marijuana to treat his pain.

On cross-examination, Dr. Eidelman acknowledged he was no longer licensed to practice medicine at the time of the trial. His license had been suspended for giving medicinal marijuana recommendations to four undercover police officers.

Dr. Eidelman also acknowledged that, when he examined appellant in May 2001, he did not review any of appellant's medical records before making his recommendation for marijuana use. The doctor used only his hands and his eyes when examining appellant. Dr. Eidelman's medical practice consisted only of himself—he had no receptionist or nurse. He did not accept insurance and usually only accepted cash payment. He did not arrange to have appellant return for a follow-up consultation.

Appellant also called to the stand Dr. David Bearman. On June 7, 2002—well after appellant's arrest—Dr. Bearman saw appellant to determine if he met the criteria for a recommendation for medicinal marijuana under Proposition 215. After giving appellant a physical examination and reviewing some of appellant's medical records, Dr. Bearman concluded appellant suffered from chronic back pain. Dr. Bearman considered appellant's condition to be serious, qualifying for medicinal marijuana.

Appellant took the stand on his own behalf. He said he was growing the three marijuana plants seized from his mother's yard solely for medicinal use to control back pain. He also said he had suffered from back pain for over 10 years.

Appellant claimed Dr. Eidelman recommended marijuana for treatment and gave him the letter only after the doctor examined him and concluded that appellant suffered from serious, chronic back pain. Only then did appellant begin cultivating marijuana. He claimed he had never grown marijuana prior to the doctor's recommendation. He also said he provided the police with Dr. Eidelman's recommendation after the police seized the plants. Appellant also said Dr. Bearman later examined him and also found his back condition was a serious illness warranting the use of medicinal marijuana. . . .

[In rebuttal, the prosecution sought to discredit Dr. Eidelman.] The San Bernardino County police [had] received information that Dr. Eidelman would sell a medicinal marijuana recommendation "for $250 with no medical condition needed." Police Detective Michael Wirz conducted an undercover operation to investigate the matter. On October 10, 2001, he telephoned Dr. Eidelman to arrange a meeting. Dr. Eidelman told the detective a recommendation would cost $250 to be paid in cash only.

The detective went to Dr. Eidelman's office that same day. He told the doctor he had no medical condition but wanted to buy a marijuana recommendation to keep the police away while he grew his own marijuana. With no further questions, Dr. Eidelman printed a written recommendation. The doctor handed over the certificate and said he needed to list some illness for his records. Detective Wirz again said he smoked marijuana because he liked it, because it made him happy, and because it helped him sleep. Dr. Eidelman then said he would list the detective as suffering from depression for purposes of the recommendation.

The detective then handed Dr. Eidelman $250 in cash. At no time did Dr. Eidelman ask anything about medical history or conduct any kind of examination.

Santa Monica Police Detective Joan Rosario also conducted an undercover investigation of Dr. Eidelman's practice. On August 1, 2001, she telephoned Dr. Eidelman. He said she could come to his office to buy a marijuana prescription letter for $250 in cash. She went to Dr. Eidelman's office that same day and said she was there to purchase a marijuana prescription. Again, Dr. Eidelman conducted no examination and took no medical history. Again, he simply gave her a recommendation letter and took $250 in return. Again, the detective never complained of any actual illness but simply said she was unable to sleep and suffered from headaches without marijuana. . . .

The Compassionate Use Act of 1996, approved by the electorate in November of that year, states:

> (b)(1) The people of the State of California hereby find and declare that the purposes of the Compassionate Use Act of 1996 are as follows:
> (A) To ensure that seriously ill Californians have the right to obtain and use marijuana for medical purposes where that medical use is deemed appropriate and has been recommended by a physician who has determined that the person's health would benefit from the use of marijuana in the treatment of cancer, anorexia, AIDS, chronic pain, spasticity, glaucoma, arthritis, migraine, or any other illness for which marijuana provides relief.
> (B) To ensure that patients and their primary caregivers who obtain and use marijuana for medical purposes upon the recommendation of a physician are not subject to criminal prosecution or sanction. . . .
> . . .
> (d) Section 11357, relating to the possession of marijuana, and Section 11358, relating to the cultivation of marijuana, shall not apply to a patient, or to a patient's primary caregiver, who possesses or cultivates marijuana for the personal medical purposes of the patient upon the written or oral recommendation or approval of a physician. . . .

The instruction given by the court, over appellant's objection, to the jury on appellant's compassionate use defense was as follows:

> . . .
> The defense of compassionate use is only available to a defendant who proves all of the facts necessary to establish the elements of the defense, namely:
> 1. The defendant was seriously ill and suffered from a medical condition where the use of marijuana as a treatment was medically appropriate;
> 2. The defendant's use of marijuana was recommended by a physician who had determined orally or in writing that the defendant's health would benefit from the use of marijuana in the treatment of cancer, anorexia, AIDS, chronic pain, spasticity, glaucoma, arthritis, migraine, or any other illness for which marijuana promotes relief; and
> 3. The amount of marijuana possessed or cultivated was reasonably related to the defendant's then current medical needs.

Appellant contends that the essence of the Compassionate Use Act defense is set forth in subdivision (d) of section 11362.5 (that he "cultivates marijuana for the personal medical purposes of the patient upon the written or oral recommendation or approval of a physician") and does not include a requirement that he present evidence that he was "seriously ill." As we shall explain, we agree with appellant. . . .

First, the only reference to "seriously ill" is in the prefatory, or purpose, statement of the act. It is omitted from the heart of the act, that provision set forth in section 11362.5, subdivision (d). . . .

Second, although the prefatory language of subdivision (b)(1)(A) of section 11362.5 contains a reference to "seriously ill Californians," that subdivision also contains a list of specified illnesses or conditions for which the medical use of marijuana might be "deemed appropriate" and "recommended by a physician who has determined that the person's health would benefit from the use of marijuana in . . . treatment." (*Ibid.*) The list ends with a catchall phrase "or any other illness for which marijuana provides relief." (*Ibid.*)

. . . [W]e conclude that the voters of California did not intend to limit the compassionate use defense to those patients deemed by a jury to be "seriously ill." As is evidenced by the entirety of the language of subdivision (b)(1)(A) and the language of subdivision (d) of section 11362.5, the question of whether the medical use of marijuana is appropriate for a patient's illness is a determination to be made by a physician. A physician's determination on this medical issue is not to be second-guessed by jurors who might not deem the patient's condition to be sufficiently "serious." Our conclusion is further buttressed by subdivision (b)(1)(B) of the statute, which points outs that another purpose of the Compassionate Use Act of 1996 was "[t]o ensure that patients and their primary caregivers who obtain and use marijuana for medical purposes upon the recommendation of a physician are not subject to criminal prosecution or sanction." (§ 11362.5, subd. (b)(1)(B).)

. . . The instructional error in this case was clearly prejudicial. The evidence that appellant cultivated the marijuana plants was undisputed. Appellant's defense was entirely based upon the Compassionate Use Act. The prosecutor argued to the jury: "Their case rest [*sic*] upon the believability of the Defendant. Someone that says he is seriously ill, yet has no medical records for 12 to 13 years. Someone that has not been to a doctor for 12 to 13 years. He is unbelievable and their case rest upon his believability." Defense counsel, on the other hand, argued to the jury that appellant was indeed seriously ill: "Now, the Prosecution argues his condition is not serious but do not present any evidence. . . . Did you see any medical testimony from the prosecution? No. They said Mr. Spark's condition was not serious. Why would that be? Why would they not find a doctor? They should be able to find a doctor if his condition is not serious. They should find a doctor that says that. I would argue his condition was serious and they cannot find a doctor that would say it was not serious." Indeed, respondent does not even attempt to persuade us that if there was error, the error was not prejudicial. . . .

The judgment is reversed.

## Notes and Questions

1. As a matter of policy, do you agree with the court's ruling? Should a physician's determination as to a patient's eligibility be unreviewable? Consider the following Problem:

<u>Problem 4.2</u>: Andy is a reporter with the Los Angeles Tribune. Recently, he has been having trouble meeting his deadlines. His physician has diagnosed him with "writer's block" and has suggested to Andy that his condition might be improved if he were to use marijuana. After buying five ounces of marijuana

(the amount his physician suggested to get Andy started), Andy is arrested by the police and charged with simple possession. Andy asserts a medical marijuana defense and moves to dismiss the charges against him. Does he have a qualifying condition for purposes of California's Proposition 215? What if the physician had instead diagnosed Andy with a case of "dragon bite"?

2. As the *Spark* court notes, Proposition 215 makes reference to "seriously ill Californians," but it does not actually make being "seriously ill" a requirement for invoking the legal protections afforded by the Proposition. Why do you think this language was included in the measure if not to limit access to its protections?

### b. Recommendation

In addition to requiring a qualifying diagnosis, every state also requires patients to obtain a physician's recommendation to use marijuana. The recommendation is sometimes referred to as a physician's "certification" or "authorization" or "valid documentation." But for reasons discussed in Chapter 12, it is *NOT* a prescription, even though many commentators mistakenly refer to it as such. So what, exactly, does a recommendation entail?

In every state, a recommendation requires a physician[3] to determine that marijuana would—with some specified degree of confidence—benefit the patient's medical condition. However, the precise degree of confidence that the physician must have about the medical benefits of marijuana use appears to vary from state to state.

In some states, the physician must find that the patient "would benefit" or "is likely" to benefit from the use of marijuana. *E.g.*, Cal. Health & Safety Code § 11362.5 (recommendation means a physician's "determin[ation] that the person's health *would benefit* from the use of marijuana in the treatment of cancer, anorexia, AIDS, chronic pain, spasticity, glaucoma, arthritis, migraine, or any other illness for which marijuana provides relief") (emphasis added); Mich. Comp. Laws Ann. § 333.26423(m) ("'Written certification' means a document signed by a physician, stating all of the following: (1) The patient's debilitating medical condition. (2) The physician has completed a full assessment of the patient's medical history and current medical condition, including a relevant, in-person, medical evaluation. (3) In the physician's professional opinion, the patient *is likely to receive therapeutic or palliative benefit* from the medical use of marihuana to treat or alleviate the patient's debilitating medical condition or symptoms associated with the debilitating medical condition.") (emphasis added).

In other states, by contrast, the physician need only find that the patient "might" or "may benefit" from the drug. *E.g.*, Alaska Stat. Ann. § 17.37.010(1) (recommendation means a statement signed by the patient's physician "(A) stating that the physician

---

3. Some states allow other licensed health care professionals to make the recommendation and/or diagnosis, but for ease of exposition, the book refers to the requirement as a physician recommendation.

personally examined the patient and that the examination took place in the context of a bona fide physician-patient relationship and setting out the date the examination occurred; (B) stating that the patient has been diagnosed with a debilitating medical condition; and (C) stating that the physician has considered other approved medications and treatments that might provide relief, that are reasonably available to the patient, and that can be tolerated by the patient, and that the physician has concluded that the patient *might benefit* from the medical use of marijuana") (emphasis added); Wash. Rev. Code Ann. §69.51A.010(7)(a) ("[A]uthorization" means: (i) A statement signed and dated by a qualifying patient's health care professional written on tamper-resistant paper, which states that, in the health care professional's professional opinion, the patient *may benefit* from the medical use of marijuana.") (emphasis added).

The *Shepherd* case below, involving a previous formulation of the requirement used by Washington state ("the potential benefits . . . *would likely* outweigh the health risks") suggests the choice of statutory language *does* matter, at least in some cases. The case concerns a prosecution against a designated caregiver charged with growing and possessing marijuana on behalf of a patient (topics covered in Chapters 7 and 8), but the analysis is equally relevant for simple possession cases brought against a patient instead.

## *Washington v. Shepherd*
41 P.3d 1235 (Wash. App. 2002)

SWEENEY, J.

This is the first time a court has had to interpret and apply Washington Initiative Measure No. 692, . . . the Medical Use of Marijuana Act (the Act). The State charged Arthur C. Shepherd with manufacturing marijuana, although the State and Mr. Shepherd ultimately stipulated to the substitution of a reduced charge, felony possession of marijuana. Mr. Shepherd presented evidence that he was a primary caregiver pursuant to the Act and that he provided marijuana to a "qualifying patient," again as defined by the Act.

The question here is whether the showing he made is sufficient under the Act to satisfy the Act's requirements for an affirmative defense to his charge. Specifically, whether a physician's statement that "the potential benefits of the medical use of marijuana *may* outweigh the health risks for this patient" is sufficient to satisfy the "valid documentation" requirement of the Act that "the potential benefits of the medical use of marijuana *would likely* outweigh the health risks for a particular qualifying patient[.]" RCW 69.51A.010(5)(a) (emphasis added). We conclude that it does not. . . . We therefore affirm the conviction.

Washington voters passed Initiative Measure No. 692 on November 3, 1998. . . . Mr. Shepherd . . . tried to comply with that Act and grow marijuana for his friend, John Wilson. As part of this process, Mr. Wilson designated Mr. Shepherd as his primary caregiver. . . .

Mr. Wilson suffers from a variety of conditions including bipolar disorder and a debilitating spine condition. The spine condition also disables him from growing and maintaining his own marijuana supply.... [Mr. Shepherd has supplied marijuana to Mr. Wilson,] which is the source of Mr. Shepherd's current legal difficulties.

Mr. Wilson is treated by Dr. Gregg Sharp. He provided Mr. Wilson with an "Authorization to Possess Marijuana for Medical Purposes in Washington State" [which stated]:

> I have diagnosed and am treating the above named patient for a terminal illness or debilitating condition as defined in RCW 69.51A.010 (should the conditions be listed, a check list? I think not as it may be seen as violating physician-patient confidentiality).
>
> I have advised the above named patient about the potential risks and benefits of the medical use of marijuana. I have assessed the above named patient's medical history and medical condition. It is my medical opinion that the potential benefits of the medical use of marijuana may outweigh the health risks for this patient.

... A number of government agencies work together on joint marijuana eradication in northern Stevens County. As part of that program, they spotted Mr. Shepherd's marijuana grow. Police first seized 15 marijuana plants from Mr. Shepherd. Mr. Shepherd sued to recover the plants. He presented documentation from Dr. Sharp to support Mr. Wilson's need for the marijuana and Mr. Wilson's statement that Mr. Shepherd was the primary caregiver. Judge Larry Kristianson refused to return the plants. He concluded that the statement by Mr. Wilson's doctor was inadequate because it failed to set out the specific nature of Mr. Wilson's medical condition. . . .

Following Judge Kristianson's determination and armed with the same documentation, Mr. Shepherd repeatedly went to both the Stevens County sheriff and the prosecuting attorney and declared that he was growing medical marijuana. Later the sheriff's office seized another 20 to 31 plants from Mr. Shepherd's property. . . .

The State charged Mr. Shepherd by amended complaint with felony possession of marijuana. He waived his right to a jury trial.... [The trial judge found that Mr. Shepherd had exceeded the quantity limits (60-day supply) imposed by state law.]

Judge Baker also concluded that Dr. Sharp's statement of need was inadequate because it only specified that Mr. Wilson "*may* benefit from the medical use of marijuana"..., whereas the statute requires a statement from the doctor that "the potential benefits of the medical use of marijuana *would likely outweigh* the health risks," RCW 69.51A.010(5)(a) (emphasis added).

## THE MEDICAL USE OF MARIJUANA ACT

In 1998, the citizens of Washington enacted the Medical Use of Marijuana Act by way of Initiative Measure No. 692. RCW 69.51A.005. . . . The purpose of the Act is to allow patients with terminal or debilitating illnesses to use marijuana when authorized by their treating physician. . . . The Act also protects people who supply marijuana to such patients: "Persons who act as primary caregivers to such patients shall also not be found guilty of a crime under state law for assisting with the medical use of marijuana[.]" RCW 69.51A.005. . . .

## BURDEN OF PROOF

Mr. Shepherd is required to show only by a preponderance of evidence that he has met the requirements of the Medical Use of Marijuana Act for affirmatively defending this criminal prosecution. . . . That means considering all the evidence the proposition asserted must be more probably true than not true. . . .

## VALID DOCUMENTATION

The trial court found, and we agree, that Mr. Wilson satisfies the requirements of a "qualifying patient." RCW 69.51A.010(3). That is, someone who has been diagnosed with a debilitating medical condition, has been advised of the risks and benefits of the use of marijuana, and has been advised by the physician that he or she may benefit from the medical use of marijuana.

But the Act requires more. It also requires "valid documentation" to prove the affirmative defense. RCW 69.51A.040(4)(c). And the Act is very specific in the elements required for valid documentation. It requires (1) a statement, (2) signed by a qualifying patient's physician (or a copy of the qualifying patient's pertinent medical records) which states, (3) that in the physician's professional opinion, (4) the potential benefits of the medical use of marijuana *would likely outweigh* the health risks for a particular qualifying patient. RCW 69.51A.010(5)(a). It is not enough, as Dr. Sharp did here, to simply say that the potential benefits of the medical use of marijuana *may* outweigh the health risks for a particular patient.

The required proof is tantamount to the level of certainty required of expert opinions in courts. And a well-developed body of law in this state sets out the requirements for admission of professional opinions when the expert must express an opinion on a "more likely than not" basis. Expert testimony should express "'a reasonable probability rather than mere conjecture or speculation.'" . . . For example, medical opinion testimony that an accident caused a physical condition must be based on a more probable than not, or more likely than not, causal relationship. . . . Likewise in the criminal case, expert testimony on a person's mental status is not admissible unless the expert's opinion is based on reasonable medical certainty, which is the equivalent of more likely than not. . . . There are legal consequences that attach to these scientific opinions. And therefore a level of medical certainty is required.

Here, the required medical opinion is that one scientific consideration (the "potential benefits of the medical use of marijuana") outweighs another scientific consideration ("the health risks for a particular qualifying patient"). RCW 69.51A.010(5)(a). The statute requires a stronger showing on necessity than simply "may."

## Notes and Questions

1. Is the court splitting hairs? Is it being too formalistic? How do you think patients and physicians would respond to the ruling?

2. Postscript on *Shepherd*. In 2007, the Washington legislature amended the state's medical marijuana statute to lower the standard, such that a physician need only determine that the "medical use of marijuana *may benefit* a particular qualifying patient." 2007 Wash. Legis. Serv. Ch. 371 §4 (S.S.B. 6032) (emphasis added), codified as Rev. Code Wash. 69.51A.010. In 2015, the legislature removed the standard from the statute and defined authorization instead by reference to a form developed by the state department of health. That form, however, continues to employ the "may benefit" standard. Washington State Department of Health, Washington State Medical Marijuana Authorization Form, https://perma.cc/STB7-PUER.

3. To test your intuitions about the sufficiency of statements made by physicians, consider whether the individuals in the following Problems have satisfied the recommendation requirement:

**Problem 4.3:** Benjamin has been charged with simple possession of marijuana in a medical marijuana state. He raises a medical marijuana defense, and the state uses the same standard ("would likely benefit") followed by *Shepherd*. As part of his defense, Benjamin submits the written statement of his doctor, which states that the "patient should be able to use marijuana for appetite stimulation. He has tried Marinol, but it is not effective for him & he has lost weight." Is the statement sufficient? *Compare Shepherd*, 41 P.3d 1235, *with Washington v. Otis*, 213 P.3d 613, 618 (Wash. App. 2009) (holding that "'valid documentation' merely requires a written statement that generally conveys a physician's professional opinion that the benefits of the medical use of marijuana outweigh the risks for a particular patient, without requiring the physician to [use] the specific language in the statute").

**Problem 4.4:** Camila has been charged with simple possession of marijuana in a medical marijuana state, and she raises a medical marijuana defense. As part of her defense, Camila testifies that she visited her physician and asked him about using marijuana for her migraines, and he replied orally that it "might help, go ahead." Sufficient? *Compare* Mich. Comp. Laws Ann. § 333.26423(m) (requiring "*written* certification" signed by physician) (emphasis added) (stating majority rule) *with* Cal. Health & Safety Code section 11362.5(d) (requiring "written or *oral* recommendation or approval of a physician") (emphasis added); *California v. Jones*, 4 Cal. Rptr. 3d 916 (Cal. App. 2003) (defendant's testimony that physician had told him that marijuana "might help, go ahead" is sufficient to establish medical marijuana defense).

4. Some state medical marijuana programs have been criticized for making it too easy for individuals to obtain a physician's recommendation and thereby evade state prohibitions on the non-medical use of marijuana. The problem of recommendation mills and the steps states have taken to address them are discussed at length in Chapter 12.

5. When must a patient obtain the necessary qualifying diagnosis and recommendation? The following Problem sets up the issue:

**Problem 4.5:** The police search Delilah's car and find marijuana. They arrest Delilah for simple possession of marijuana. The next day, Delilah visits her physician. The physician diagnoses Delilah with a qualifying condition (severe pain) and states that her condition would "certainly benefit" from the use of marijuana. Do you think Delilah has satisfied the diagnosis and recommendation requirements?

The dominant rule is that a patient must obtain the qualifying diagnosis and recommendation *before* taking possession of or using marijuana. *E.g., Montana v. Stoner*, 285 P.3d 402 (Mont. 2012) ("The purpose of the registry identification card under the MMA was to limit the possession and use of marijuana to qualified individuals for specific debilitating conditions, not—as the District Court observed—to be acquired by a person as a 'get-out-of-jail-free' card *after* getting busted.") (emphasis added); *California v. Rigo*, 81 Cal. Rptr. 2d 624 (Cal. App. 1999) (recommendation obtained 3.5 months after arrest is not timely, barring exigent circumstances).

The courts have based the timeliness requirement on both statutory language and the gatekeeping function served by the qualifying diagnosis and recommendation. The Michigan Supreme Court has explained:

> [The immunity provided by section 8(a)(1) of the Michigan Medical Marijuana Act requires, in relevant part, that a physician "has stated that . . . the patient is likely to receive therapeutic or palliative benefit from the medical use of marihuana. . . ." Mich. Comp. L. § 333.26428.]
>
> [T]he term "has stated" is in the present perfect tense, which "indicates action that was started in the past and has recently been completed or is continuing up to the present time." . . . [T]he term "has stated" indicates that the physician's statement must have been made sometime before a defendant filed the motion to dismiss under § 8 but not necessarily before commission of the offense.
>
> Other language of § 8(a)(1), however, indicates that the statement must in fact have been made even before the patient began using marijuana for the defense to apply. Reading the term "has stated" in conjunction with the language in the same sentence "is likely to receive [benefit from the medical use of marijuana]" indicates a future event that will occur after the physician's statement. Stated differently, § 8(a)(1) contemplates that a patient will not start using marijuana for medical purposes until after the physician has provided a statement of approval. It necessarily follows that any marijuana use before the physician's statement was not for medical purposes. . . .
>
> This interpretation makes sense in light of the laws criminalizing possession, manufacture, and delivery of marijuana and the fact that the MMMA allows such charges to be dismissed under certain circumstances. A reasonable inference to be drawn from the MMMA's provisions allowing the medical use of marijuana is that § 8 is intended to protect those individuals who believe they have a genuine medical need for marijuana that has been recognized by a physician, but for whatever reason have not obtained a registry card. It would be illogical to extend this protection to individuals who have not obtained a physician's recognition of their medical need because the MMMA provides no protections to such individuals. An after-the-fact exception to criminal liability would encourage individuals to engage in self-medication or criminal activity on the basis of the possibility that if prosecuted they could then obtain a doctor's approval postoffense and avoid criminal charges. Because the MMMA was not intended to legitimize illegal marijuana use, it makes sense to require that a defendant obtain a physician's statement authorizing the medical use of marijuana before the defendant actually uses marijuana for that purpose.

*Michigan v. Kolanek*, 817 N.W. 2d 528, 542-44 (Mich. 2012).

6. Now consider this variation on **Problem 4.5**:

**Problem 4.6:** The police search Andy's car and find marijuana. They arrest Andy for simple possession of marijuana. He immediately shows the police a recommendation from his physician that was issued one week earlier. He also shows them a separate document from the same physician, issued three years ago, indicating that he has diagnosed Andy with severe pain stemming from a (then) recent hip surgery. Has Andy satisfied the recommendation and diagnosis requirements?

In most states, patients must periodically renew their diagnoses and recommendations to maintain their eligibility to use medical marijuana. *See, e.g.,* Or. Rev. Stat. § 475.319 (limiting medical marijuana defense to person who "[w]as diagnosed with a debilitating medical condition within 12 months of the date on which the person was arrested and was advised by the person's attending physician that the medical use of marijuana may mitigate the symptoms or effects of that debilitating medical condition"); *Oregon v. Luster,* 350 P.3d 574 (Or. App. 2015) (rejecting defense based on diagnosis and recommendation made more than 12 months prior to arrest).

In California, recommendations and diagnoses do not expire, at least for purposes of the Compassionate Use Act. *California v. Windus,* 81 Cal. Rptr. 3d 227, 231 (Cal. App. 4th 2008) (finding defendant could present medical defense based on three-year old recommendation because "nothing in the [CUA] . . . requires a patient to periodically renew a doctor's recommendation regarding medical marijuana use"). However, patients must provide "updated written documentation" of their medical conditions annually to take advantage of the additional legal protections afforded by the state's Medical Marijuana Program Act (MMP). Cal. Health & Safety Code § 11362.76(a)(2)(A).

Why do states impose a renewal requirement? Should states instead follow California and permit a patient to use marijuana indefinitely once a physician has made the qualifying diagnosis and recommendation? Does it depend on the type of condition?

### c. Registration

In the vast majority of medical marijuana states, a patient must also register with a state health agency in order to obtain the protections of the state's medical marijuana law. *See* Conn. Gen. Stat. Ann. § 21a-408a(a) ("A qualifying patient shall register with the Department of Consumer Protection . . . prior to engaging in the palliative use of marijuana. A qualifying patient who has a valid registration certificate from the Department of Consumer Protection . . . and complies with the requirements of [Connecticut law] . . . , shall not be subject to arrest or prosecution, penalized in any manner. . . ."). Even when states do not require registration, they usually grant patients additional legal benefits for voluntarily registering. *See, e.g., Michigan v. Kolanek,* 817 N.W.2d 258 (Mich. 2012) (discussing the benefits of voluntary registration under Michigan law). These legal benefits and protections are discussed in Section C below.

To register, patients must complete a registration application form, supply copies of supporting documentation (e.g., a physician's recommendation), and pay a fee. To see a registration form with instructions, following the link for one of these states:

Chapter 4. The Regulation of Marijuana Users in Legalization Regimes

- California, https://perma.cc/9G3X-YRX5
- Colorado, https://perma.cc/U5S9-W8AC
- Rhode Island, https://perma.cc/E2N9-4MV2

If everything is in order, the state agency will add the patient to its registry and provide the patient with a registration identification card. The card looks something like the one pictured in **Figure 4.1**:

Figure 4.1. A Registry Card

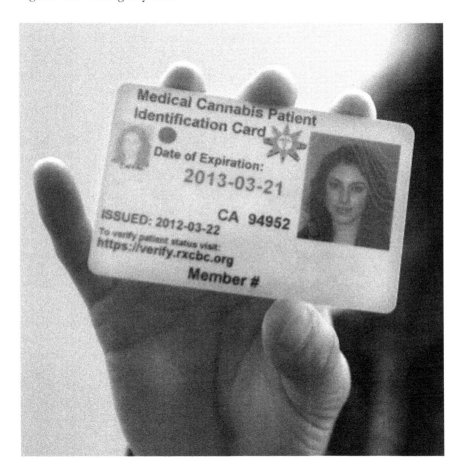

## Notes and Questions

1. Must qualified patients carry their registration card with them at all times? Consider the following Problem:

<u>Problem 4.7</u>: Andy has successfully registered with his state's medical marijuana program. He plans to spend the following week working at a friend's cabin upstate. Andy packed his clothes and one ounce of marijuana to take with him. On his drive

to the cabin, Andy is stopped for a traffic violation. The police notice the marijuana in the back seat of the car. Andy explains that he is a registered medical marijuana patient, but discovers that he left his card at home. May the police arrest Andy for possession of marijuana? May the state prosecute him? The law on this point (even within some states) is not entirely clear. *Compare Michigan v. Hartwick*, 870 N.W.2d 37, 51 (Mich. 2015) (holding that patient is entitled to assert immunity under state medical marijuana law only "if *all conduct* underlying [the] charge *occurred during a time when the qualifying patient . . . possessed* a valid registry identification card") (emphases added), *with Michigan v. Nicholson*, 822 N.W.2d 284, 289 (Mich. App. 2012) (holding that patient who is arrested without a registration card could still assert immunity from prosecution if she later produces the card for the court).

2. Even assuming that possession of a registry card is required to assert immunity, what does it mean *to possess* the card? For example, could someone like Andy in **Problem 4.7** argue that he was in constructive possession of his card, even if he was not carrying it on his person at the time he was arrested? After all, he would be in constructive possession of any *marijuana* he left back at home, as discussed in Chapter 3. In *Nicholson, supra*, the court refused to apply constructive possession principles to the registry card requirement, reasoning that:

> provid[ing] immunity to any person who merely makes the claim that they have a valid registry identification card, but is unable to display it, is unworkable because it would eviscerate the ability to enforce the prohibition against the unlawful possession of marijuana with respect to anyone who simply makes a representation of entitlement to immunity without any proof of that status. If only constructive possession of a registry identification card is required, police officers would have no ability to evaluate the legitimacy of a claim of immunity made by individuals in possession of marijuana.

822 N.W.2d at 289, n.6. Do you agree? In this regard, consider that states have adopted confidentiality rules that generally bar the police from accessing medical marijuana registries, except for purposes of verifying whether a given card is valid. *E.g.*, Mich. Comp. L. § 333.26246(h) ("(2) The department [of health] shall maintain a confidential list of the persons to whom the department has issued registry identification cards. Except as provided in subdivisions (3) and (4), individual names and other identifying information on the list are confidential and are exempt from disclosure. . . . (3) The department shall verify to law enforcement personnel whether a registry identification card is valid, without disclosing more information than is reasonably necessary to verify the authenticity of the registry identification card. (4) A person, including an employee, contractor, or official of the department or another state agency or local unit of government, who discloses confidential information in violation of this act is guilty of a misdemeanor, punishable by imprisonment for not more than 6 months, or a fine of not more than $1, 000.00, or both. . . ."). Do such confidentiality rules justify the requirement to carry a registration card at all times when one is in possession of marijuana?

### d. Other Limitations on Eligibility

States restrict eligibility for the protections afforded by medical marijuana laws based on other criteria as well, including residency, age, and the criminal history of prospective users.

#### (i) Residency

Some states explicitly limit participation in medical marijuana programs to in-state residents. *E.g.*, Minn. Stat. Ann. § 152.22 ("'Patient' means a Minnesota resident . . ."); Nev. Rev. Stat. § 453A.210(b) (requiring "[p]roof . . . that the person is a resident of this State" in order to register for the state's medical marijuana program). Even in states that do not explicitly require residency, some courts have found their state programs to impose such a requirement. In *Michigan v. Jones*, for example, the court held that a non-Michigan resident could not seek the protections of the Michigan Medical Marijuana Act:

> The MMMA does not directly address residency. However, § 4(j) of the act does contain a provision allowing a "visiting qualifying patient" to use medical marijuana in conformance with the MMMA while visiting the state of Michigan. A "visiting qualifying patient" is defined by the act to be "a patient who is not a resident of this state or who has been a resident of this state for less than 30 days." MCL 333.26423(l). Moreover, MCL 333.26422 lists several other states that do not penalize the medical use of marijuana, and notes that "Michigan joins in this effort for the health and welfare of *its citizens*." (Emphasis added.) In light of the reference to Michigan citizens, and the provisions regarding a visiting qualifying patient in the MMMA, we agree with the trial court that Michigan residency is a prerequisite to the issuance and valid possession of a registry identification card. If the MMMA were read not to require Michigan residency, there would be no reason to specifically refer to Michigan citizens or to include a provision regarding medical use of marijuana by visitors to Michigan. . . . Thus, we affirm the trial court's conclusion that Michigan residency is a prerequisite to valid possession of a registry identification card.

837 N.W.2d 7, 14-15 (Mich. App. 2013).

As the *Jones* court mentions, however, some states (including Michigan) grant reciprocity to non-residents who have successfully registered in their home states. *E.g.*, Mich. Comp. Laws Ann. § 333.26424(j) ("A registry identification card, or its equivalent, that is issued under the laws of another state . . . that allows the medical use of marihuana by a visiting qualifying patient . . . shall have the same force and effect as a registry identification card issued by the [Michigan health] department."); Ariz. Rev. Stat. § 36-2804.03 (same, except that "a visiting qualifying patient is not authorized to obtain marijuana from a nonprofit medical marijuana dispensary"). As of July 2016, 7 out of 26 states (including D.C.) recognized out-of-state registration cards for purposes of their own medical marijuana laws. *See* Marijuana Policy Project, Key Aspects of State and D.C. Medical Marijuana Laws (July 24, 2016), available at https://www.mpp.org/issues/medical-marijuana/state-by-state-medical-marijuana-laws/key-aspects-of-state-and-d-c-medical-marijuana-laws/.

Chapter 6 discusses some possible constitutional issues with residency-based requirements.

#### (ii) Age

All medical marijuana states now appear to allow minors to use marijuana for medical purposes. These states, however, generally require underage patients (or their parents) to jump through additional hoops, including obtaining parental consent and the recommendation of a second physician, in order to take advantage of the state's medical marijuana law. For example, in Michigan, a minor may use medical marijuana if

> (1) The qualifying patient's physician has explained the potential risks and benefits of the medical use of marihuana to the qualifying patient and to his or her parent or legal guardian;
> (2) The qualifying patient's parent or legal guardian submits a written certification from 2 physicians; and
> (3) The qualifying patient's parent or legal guardian consents in writing to:
>    (A) Allow the qualifying patient's medical use of marihuana;
>    (B) Serve as the qualifying patient's primary caregiver; and
>    (C) Control the acquisition of the marihuana, the dosage, and the frequency of the medical use of marihuana by the qualifying patient.

Mich. Comp. Laws § 333.26426; § 6(a)(7)(b).

What do you think of medical marijuana use by minors? Should it be allowed? What additional requirements, if any, would you impose?

*(iii) Criminal History*

States also restrict access to medical marijuana by members of the criminal justice population, including individuals who are incarcerated, on parole or probation, and those who have prior convictions for certain types of drug offenses.

To begin, nearly every state bars the possession and use of marijuana by those who are currently incarcerated. *See, e.g.*, Conn. Gen. Stat. Ann. § 21a-408 (West 2015) ("'Qualifying patient' does not include an inmate confined in a correctional institution or facility under the supervision of the Department of Correction[.]"); Minn. R. 4770.4009 (providing that registration of any prisoner "must be suspended for the term of the incarceration"). California is the rare state that tolerates medical use of marijuana inside of its prisons. It allows—but does not require—individual correctional facilities to accommodate medical use of marijuana by prisoners, so long as such use "will not engender the health or safety of other prisoners or the security of the facility." Cal. Health & Safety Code § 11362.785(a), (b).

Some, but not all, states bar possession and use of marijuana by probationers and parolees. On the one hand, Washington has explicitly barred possession and use of marijuana by individuals on probation and other forms of supervised release. Rev. Code Wash. § 69.51A.010(19)(b) ("'Qualifying patient' does not include a person who is actively being supervised for a criminal conviction by a corrections agency or department that has determined that the terms of this chapter are inconsistent with and contrary to his or her supervision and all related processes and procedures related to that supervision."). And one Colorado appellate court has suggested that a condition imposed on every probation in that state—"that defendant not commit another offense"—likewise effectively bars all probationers from using or possessing marijuana as long as *federal* law continues to proscribe those activities. *Colorado v. Watkins*, 282 P.3d 500 (Colo. App. 2012). On the other hand, Arizona and Montana appear to grant probationers the same access to marijuana as all other residents, reasoning that revocation of probation is an impermissible sanction under their medical marijuana laws. *Reed-Kaliher v. Hoggatt*, 347 P.3d 136, 140 (Ariz. 2015) ("[A]ny probation term that threatens to revoke probation for medical marijuana use that complies with the terms of [Arizona Medical Marijuana Act] is unenforceable and illegal under AMMA."); *Montana v. Nelson*, 195 P.3d 826, 833 (Mont. 2008) ("[T]he [Montana Medical Marijuana Act] states unequivocally that a qualified patient . . . 'may not be arrested, prosecuted, or penalized in any manner or be denied any right or privilege . . . for the medical use of marijuana.'... The MMA simply does not give sentencing judges the authority to limit the privilege of medical use of marijuana while under state supervision.").[4]

The remaining states that have addressed the issue, including California, appear to grant courts discretion to decide, on a case by case basis, whether or not a defendant should be allowed to possess or use marijuana while on probation or parole. *See, e.g.,* Cal. Health & Safety Code § 11362.795 (establishing procedure through which probationers may petition court to allow medical marijuana use); *California v. Leal*, 210 Cal. App. 4th 829 (Cal. App. 2012) (holding that voters who passed the Compassionate Use Act did not mean "to abrogate a court's longstanding authority... to prohibit lawful behavior, as now represented by CUA-approved use of marijuana"). In such states, the sentencing court need only find that a restriction on conduct that is not itself criminal "is reasonably related to the crime of which the defendant was convicted or to future criminality." *California v. Lent*, 541 P.2d 545, 548 (Cal. 1975).

A handful of states also bar felony drug offenders from possessing or using medical marijuana, even after they have completed their sentences. For example, Rhode Island excludes anyone who is "convicted of; placed on probation; ... pleads nolo contendere; or whose case is deferred ... for any felony offense under [the] 'Rhode Island Controlled Substances Act' ... or a similar offense from any other jurisdiction" from enjoying the protections of the state's medical marijuana law. R.I. Gen. Laws § 21-28.6-9(c) (2015). *See also* Ill. Admin. Code tit. 77, § 946.220 (barring anyone convicted of a felony drug offense from receiving the protections of the state's medical marijuana law, but making an exception for individuals convicted of the "possession, cultivation, transfer, or delivery of a reasonable amount of marijuana for medical use").

## Notes and Questions

1. What purpose is served by temporarily (or even permanently) barring convicted drug felons from using or possessing marijuana for medical purposes? Do you think such a ban is fair? Necessary?

2. Now consider the following Problems. Do the probation conditions imposed therein reasonably relate to the crime of conviction or to future criminality?

Problem 4.8: During a routine traffic stop, the police discovered two pounds of marijuana in Andy's car. Andy claimed the marijuana was for his personal medical use. Although the government conceded that Andy was a bona fide medical marijuana patient, it proffered evidence that he had planned to sell the marijuana in violation of state law. A jury convicted Andy of possession with the intent to distribute marijuana, and the court sentenced him to two years' probation and barred him from possessing or using marijuana during that time. Is the court's prohibition on the *possession* or *use* of marijuana during probation sufficiently related to Andy's crime of conviction, namely, the possession *with the intent to distribute* marijuana? Why, why not? Might the prohibition instead be upheld as a

---

4. The *Nelson* court acknowledged that "just as a sentencing court may impose a condition that prohibits a defendant from *abusing* lawfully-obtained prescription drugs, so may a court prohibit a defendant from *abusing* medical marijuana." 195 P.3d at 833 (emphasis added).

reasonable means of preventing Andy from engaging in criminal activity *in the future*? If so, what sort of criminal activity? *See California v. Brooks*, 107 Cal. Rptr. 501, 504 (Cal. App. 2010).

**Problem 4.9**: Benjamin pled guilty to possession of a concealed firearm. During his sentencing hearing, Benjamin testified that he regularly used marijuana pursuant to his physician's recommendation to treat migraine headaches. The court sentenced Benjamin to two years' probation and barred him from possessing or using marijuana during that time. At the sentencing hearing, the judge explained that:

> "A handgun like this is good for one thing, and that's shooting somebody. So if he's in a situation where he needs to have a gun to shoot somebody, he's got real problems going on in his life, and smoking dope isn't helping him. That's the bottom line. So I'm willing—I mean, he has a really, almost no criminal history. He's a young man. Obviously, he's got potential, but he keeps smoking dope and carrying firearms, and he's going to have a lot of problems in this life, if he lives very long."

Why do you think the judge imposed the prohibition on possessing and using marijuana? Does the prohibition relate to Benjamin's crime of conviction, namely, the possession of a concealed firearm? How, exactly? Is the prohibition likely to reduce the chances that Benjamin will offend again in the future *See California v. Moret*, 180 Cal. App. 4th 839 (Cal. App. 2009); *California v. Leal*, 210 Cal. App. 4th 829 (Cal. App. 2012).

**Problem 4.10**: Same facts as **Problem 4.9**. But at the sentencing hearing, the court also remarked that "medical marijuana is a sham. It's not really medicine. I don't believe it." Does the court's additional statement regarding marijuana change your view of the validity of the probation condition? In other words, is this scenario distinguishable from **Problem 4.9**? Why, why not? *See California v. Hughes*, 136 Cal Rptr. 3d 538, 544 (Cal. App. 2012).

**Problem 4.11**: Same facts as **Problem 4.9**. But instead of barring Benjamin from possessing or using marijuana, the judge orders him to "obey all laws, both state *and federal*." *Compare Watkins*, 282 P.3d 500, 505 (Colo. App. 2012) ("In light of the purposes of probation, one of which is to 'ensure that the defendant will lead a law-abiding life,' the prohibition . . . is a reasonable restriction on defendant's freedom, even to the extent that it prohibits violations of federal law."), *with Reed-Kaliher v. Hoggatt*, 347 P.3d 136, 141 (Ariz. 2015) ("Federal law does not require our courts to enforce federal law, and Arizona law does not permit them to do so in contravention of AMMA."), *Montana v. Nelson*, 195 P.3d 826, 834 (Mont. 2008) ("[W]hile the District Court may require Nelson to obey all federal laws as a condition of his deferred

sentenced, it must allow an exception with respect to those federal laws which would criminalize the use of medical marijuana in accordance the MMA."), *and California v. Tilehkooh*, 113 Cal. App. 4th 1433, 1447 (Cal. App. 2003) ("California courts do not enforce the federal marijuana possession laws when defendants prosecuted for marijuana possession have a qualified immunity under [the CUA]. Similarly, California courts should not enforce federal marijuana law for probationers who qualify for the immunity. . . .").

## 2. The Special Case of CBD States

As of 2016, at least fourteen states have legalized the possession and use of cannabidiol (CBD), a non-psychoactive cannabinoid found in marijuana. Although these CBD laws are motivated by the desire to unlock the medical benefits of marijuana, they are much more restrictive than the medical marijuana laws discussed above. Alabama passed the first CBD law in the nation in 2014. Its law has served as a template for other CBD laws and provides, in relevant part:

> (b) As used in this section, the following words shall have the following meanings: . . .
> (2) CANNABIDIOL (CBD). A (nonpsychoactive) cannabinoid found in the plant Cannabis sativa L. or any other preparation thereof that is essentially free from plant material, and has a THC level of no more than 3 percent. . . .
> (3) DEBILITATING EPILEPTIC CONDITION. Epilepsy or other neurological disorder, or the treatment of epilepsy or other neurological disorder that, as diagnosed by a board-certified neurologist under the employment or authority of the [Department of Neurology at the University of Alabama at Birmingham (UAB)] . . . produces serious, debilitating, or life-threatening seizures. . . .
> (c) In a prosecution for the unlawful possession of marijuana under the laws of this state, it is an affirmative and complete defense to the prosecution that the defendant has a debilitating epileptic condition and used or possessed cannabidiol (CBD) pursuant to a prescription authorized by the UAB Department. . . .
> . . .
> (f) . . . Health care practitioners of the UAB . . . shall be the sole authorized source of any prescription for the use of cannabidiol (CBD), and shall be the sole authorized source to use cannabidiol (CBD) in or as a part of the treatment of a person diagnosed with a debilitating epileptic condition. A health care practitioner of the UAB Department shall have the sole authority to determine the use or amount of cannabidiol (CBD), if any, in the treatment of an individual diagnosed with a debilitating epileptic condition. . . .
> . . .
> (j) Pursuant to the filing requirements of . . . the Alabama Rules of Criminal Procedure, the defendant shall produce a valid prescription, certification of a debilitating epileptic condition, and the name of the prescribing health care professional authorized by the UAB Department. . . .
> . . .
> (l) Nothing in this section shall be construed to allow or accommodate the prescription, testing, medical use, or possession of any other form of Cannabis other than that defined in this section.

Ala. Code § 13A-12-214.2.

## Notes and Questions

1. In what ways do CBD laws like Alabama's differ from the medical marijuana laws discussed above? Do they constitute meaningful reforms? For the textbook author's take on these questions, see Robert A. Mikos, Did Alabama Just Legalize Medical Marijuana? Marijuana Law, Policy, and Reform Blog (Mar. 21, 2014) (discussing the differences between CBD laws and medical marijuana laws), https://perma.cc/2G5P-FD6E.

### 3. Recreational Marijuana States

As of 2016, eight states and the District of Columbia have legalized marijuana for recreational purposes. These states impose comparatively few restrictions on who may possess and use the drug. Colorado's Amendment 64, for example, provides that:

> Notwithstanding any other provision of law, the following acts are not unlawful and shall not be an offense under Colorado law or the law of any locality within Colorado or be a basis for seizure or forfeiture of assets under Colorado law for persons twenty-one years of age or older:
>
> (a) Possessing, using, displaying, purchasing, or transporting marijuana accessories or one ounce or less of marijuana.
>
> (b) Possessing, growing, processing, or transporting no more than six marijuana plants, with three or fewer being mature, flowering plants, and possession of the marijuana produced by the plants on the premises where the plants were grown, provided that the growing takes place in an enclosed, locked space, is not conducted openly or publicly, and is not made available for sale.
>
> (c) Transfer of one ounce or less of marijuana without remuneration to a person who is twenty-one years of age or older.
>
> (d) Consumption of marijuana, provided that nothing in this section shall permit consumption that is conducted openly and publicly or in a manner that endangers others.
>
> (e) Assisting another person who is twenty-one years of age or older in any of the acts described in paragraphs (a) through (d) of this subsection.

Colo. Const. art. XVIII, § 16(3).

In many respects, these recreational marijuana states have modeled their laws on laws governing alcohol. As they do with alcohol, all states impose a minimum age of 21 years on who may buy, possess, or use marijuana for recreational (or other non-medical) purposes. *E.g., id.*; Wash. Rev. Code § 69.50.4013(3)(a) ("The possession, by a person twenty-one years of age or older, of useable marijuana . . . in amounts that do not exceed those set forth in RCW 69.50.360(3) is not a violation of this section . . . or any other provision of Washington state law."). The possession of marijuana by minors is still prohibited and remains a criminal offense in at least some of these states. For example, Oregon law treats simple possession by a minor as a violation carrying a presumptive fine of $650 if it involves one ounce or less and a class A misdemeanor carrying a maximum sentence of one year's incarceration if it involves eight ounces or more of the drug. Or. Rev. Stat. §§ 161.615, 475.864(3)(4).

Apart from the minimum age requirement, recreational marijuana states impose no special limitations on who may possess or use the drug, although these states (like medical marijuana states) do impose several restrictions on *how* and *where* the drug may be used (discussed below in Section B).

## Notes and Questions

1. What happens to medical marijuana laws after a state legalizes recreational marijuana? To date, every state that has legalized recreational marijuana had previously legalized medical marijuana. The time lag between the adoption of a medical marijuana law and the adoption of a recreational marijuana law has ranged from as few as 4 years (D.C. and Massachusetts) to as many as 20 years (California). Marijuana's status as an approved drug for both medical and recreational use raises an important question for lawmakers: Does legalizing recreational marijuana eliminate the need for special rules to govern medical marijuana? In other words, is there any reason to maintain the relatively strict and burdensome regulations that apply only to qualified medical marijuana users? After all, why would patients bother to jump through the hoops of diagnosis, recommendation, and registration, if they could more easily obtain the drug through the recreational market?

To answer these questions, it is important to recognize that many states have bestowed special legal benefits that only apply to *medical* marijuana. These benefits include higher quantity limits (discussed below); unique exemptions from restrictions on marijuana use (e.g., in schools) (discussed below); exemptions from marijuana taxes (discussed in Chapter 9); and protections from various forms of private discrimination, such as employment discrimination (discussed in Chapter 13). What is more, there is a small population of qualified patients who would not be allowed to possess the drug for recreational purposes, including minors and potentially some people in the corrections population.

2. Can you think of any other substance that has both *approved* medical and recreational uses? Is marijuana unique in this regard?

## B. WHAT LIMITATIONS ARE IMPOSED ON THE POSSESSION AND USE OF MARIJUANA?

Even though many states now allow certain individuals to possess and use marijuana, they continue to restrict some activities involving possession and use of the drug, such as driving under the influence of marijuana. The restrictions on marijuana use are commonly enumerated by state reforms. For example, section 7 of Michigan's Medical Marijuana Act provides that

> (b) This act shall not permit any person to do any of the following:
> (1) Undertake any task under the influence of marihuana, when doing so would constitute negligence or professional malpractice.
> (2) Possess marihuana, or otherwise engage in the medical use of marihuana:
> (A) in a school bus;
> (B) on the grounds of any preschool or primary or secondary school; or
> (C) in any correctional facility.
> (3) Smoke marihuana:
> (A) on any form of public transportation; or
> (B) in any public place.
> (4) Operate, navigate, or be in actual physical control of any motor vehicle, aircraft, or motorboat while under the influence of marihuana.

(5) Use marihuana if that person does not have a serious or debilitating medical condition.

Mich. Comp. Laws Ann. § 333.26427. The following sections discuss the most common restrictions imposed by both medical and recreational marijuana states.

## 1. Quantity

All states limit the quantity of usable marijuana that an individual may lawfully possess (or purchase) at any one time. (Several states also allow individuals to grow marijuana for their own consumption. The limits on the number of plants one may possess and grow at any one time are covered in more detail in Chapter 8.)

In most medical marijuana states, the amount of marijuana that a qualified patient may possess is limited expressly via statute. The limits vary considerably from one state to the next. At opposite ends of the spectrum, Alaska allows qualified patients to possess up to 1 ounce of marijuana, whereas Oregon allows them to possess up to 24 ounces. Ak. Stat. § 17.37.040(a)(4); Or. Rev. Stat. § 475.320 (1)(a). Most states fall somewhere between those two extremes. See Marijuana Policy Project, Key Aspects of State and D.C. Medical Marijuana Laws, https://www.mpp.org/issues/medical-marijuana/state-by-state-medical-marijuana-laws/key-aspects-of-state-and-d-c-medical-marijuana-laws/ (surveying quantity limitations).

In some states, these statutes only create *presumptive* limits. Patients may possess more if their physicians determine it is necessary. *E.g.*, 105 Mass. Code Regs. 725.010(I) ("A certifying physician may determine and certify that a qualifying patient requires an amount of marijuana exceeding ten ounces as a 60-day supply and shall document the amount and the rationale in the medical record and in the written certification. For that qualifying patient, that amount of marijuana constitutes a 60-day supply.").

A few states do not impose specific limitations (presumptive or otherwise), but instead permit physicians to determine how much marijuana their patients may possess in a given period of time. *E.g.*, N.Y. Pub. Health Law § 3362(1)(a) (McKinney) ("[T]the marihuana that may be possessed by a certified patient shall not exceed a thirty day supply of the dosage as determined by the practitioner, consistent with any guidance and regulations issued by the commissioner, provided that during the last seven days of any thirty day period, the certified patient may also possess up to such amount for the next thirty day period[.]").

California's quantity rules are unique. California's Compassionate Use Act (CUA) is silent about the quantities that patients may possess. In 2003, however, the California legislature attempted to impose a presumptive limit of 8 ounces, as part of its Medical Marijuana Program (MMP) reforms. The limits were only presumptive because local governments could raise them, and physicians could still recommend higher doses. Cal. Health & Safety Code § 11362.77.

However, the California Supreme Court later held that the presumptive limit conflicted with the CUA and was thus unenforceable. *California v. Kelly*, 222 P.3d 186, 209-10 (Cal. 2010). (The *Kelly* court's decision regarding the legislature's authority to amend popular ballot initiatives is discussed in Chapter 6.) As a result, for purposes of the CUA, patients "are not subject to any specific limits and do not require a physician's recommendation in order to exceed any such limits; instead they may possess an amount of medical marijuana reasonably necessary for their . . . personal medical needs." *Id.* at 209. To take advantage of the added legal protections available only under the MMP, however, patients do need to abide the quantity limits imposed by that statute. *Id.* at 214.

The limits states impose on possession of recreational marijuana are generally (much) lower than those they apply to medical marijuana. Some recreational marijuana states have also begun to adjust the limits for the different ways marijuana is consumed (smoked, ingested, etc.), reflecting differences in the potencies of different forms of marijuana (as discussed in Chapter 2). **Table 4.1** summarizes the quantity limits for the five jurisdictions that had legalized recreational marijuana as of July 2016. The limits adopted by the four jurisdictions that legalized recreational marijuana in the fall 2016 elections are similar.

Table 4.1. Quantity Limits in a Sampling of Recreational Marijuana States[5]

| State | Possession limits |
|---|---|
| Alaska | 1 oz. of marijuana (4 oz. in home) <br> 6 marijuana plants |
| Colorado | 1 oz. of marijuana <br> 6 marijuana plants |
| District of Columbia | 2 oz. of marijuana <br> 6 marijuana plants |
| Oregon | 8 oz. of usable marijuana (1 oz. in public) <br> 1 oz. marijuana extracts <br> 16 oz. of marijuana-infused solids <br> 72 oz. of marijuana-infused liquids <br> 4 marijuana plants |
| Washington | 1 oz. of usable marijuana <br> 7 grams of marijuana concentrate <br> 16 oz. of marijuana-infused solids <br> 72 oz. of marijuana-infused liquids |

## Notes and Questions

1. Are quantity limitations necessary in medical marijuana states? In recreational marijuana states? What purpose(s) do they serve? What do you think would happen if they were abolished?

2. Does it make sense for a state to set strict or even presumptive limits by statute for medical marijuana patients, given the wide range of conditions for which marijuana may be recommended and the various forms in which it may be consumed? *See, e.g., California v. Windus*, 81 Cal. Rptr. 3d 227, 233 (Cal. App. 4th 2008) (noting patient

---

5. The quantity rules can be found in Alaska Stat. § 17.38.020(1)-(2) (outside home); *Noy v. Alaska*, 83 P.3d 538, 543 (Alaska Ct. App. 2003) (in home); Colo. Const. Art. XVIII, § 16(3); D.C. Code Ann. § 48-904.01(a)(1)(A) (West); Or. Rev. Stat. § 475.864(6); Rev. Code. Wash. § 69.50.360(3).

Part II. Marijuana Users

claims that "eating [marijuana] requires four to eight times the amount of marijuana than that needed when smoking it").

3. In medical marijuana states, how are physicians supposed to determine the correct dosage for any given patient? Chapter 12 discusses the practical difficulties physicians now face in meeting their obligations to patients and the state.

4. How is marijuana to be measured for purposes of determining compliance with quantity limitations? Chapter 7 discusses the measurement issues that arise in the analogous context of criminal sentencing.

5. In medical marijuana states, what are the consequences if a qualified patient exceeds the relevant quantity limits? Consider the following Problem.

**Problem 4.12:** Camila is a qualified patient, but she possessed a total of 3 ounces of marijuana, which is more than the 2.5-ounce maximum permitted by state law. She acknowledges that she was using the extra half-ounce for purely recreational purposes. Under state law, possession of one ounce or less of marijuana is considered a civil infraction, whereas possession of more than one ounce is considered a misdemeanor. May Camila assert a medical marijuana defense with respect to the 2.5 ounces she was allowed to possess? *Compare Arizona v. Fields*, 304 P.3d 1088, 1092 (Ariz. App. 2d 2013) ("*None* of a cardholder's marijuana use or possession is protected by the AMMA if he or she fails to abide by the enumerated conditions", including quantity limitations.") (emphasis added), *with California v. Trippet*, 66 Cal. Rptr. 2d 559, 570 (Cal. App. 1997) (permitting defendant who claimed to use marijuana for both medical and religious reasons to assert a partial defense to possession charges). What do you think? Should qualified patients be allowed to assert a partial defense when they violate conditions imposed on marijuana possession and use?

6. What are the consequences if someone exceeds the quantity limits in a recreational marijuana state? **Table 4.2** details the penalties under Colorado law for possession of more than one ounce of marijuana.

Table 4.2. Penalties for Exceeding Possession Limits in Colorado[6]

| Quantity | Offense grade | Penalty range |
|---|---|---|
| ≤ 2 oz. | Petty offense | Maximum $100 fine |
| ≤ 6 oz. | Level 2 drug misdemeanor | 0-12 months' imprisonment and $50-$750 fine |
| ≤ 12 oz. (3 oz. concentrate) | Level 1 drug misdemeanor | 6-18 months' imprisonment and up to $5,000 fine |
| > 12 oz. (3 oz. concentrate) | Level 4 drug felony | 6-12 months' imprisonment (presumptive), and up to $100,000 fine |

---

6. *See* Colo. Rev. Stat. §§ 18-18-406, 18-1.3-501.

## 2. Purpose

All medical marijuana states limit patients to using marijuana solely for *medical* purposes. Typically, this means that a patient may use marijuana only to alleviate his/her qualifying condition or the symptoms associated therewith. *See, e.g.,* Mich. Comp. L. § 333.26423(f). Notwithstanding the name this textbook gives them, recreational marijuana states allow adults to use the drug for *any* purpose they deem fit, medical, recreational, religious, or otherwise.

Determining whether a patient has used (or will use) marijuana for a medical purpose could prove challenging. To address this evidentiary issue, some states have created a rebuttable presumption that a patient uses marijuana for medical purposes as long as he/she satisfies the other requirements imposed by state medical marijuana laws (e.g., registration). Under Michigan's Medical Marijuana Act, for example,

> (d) There shall be a presumption that a qualifying patient or primary caregiver is engaged in the medical use of marihuana in accordance with this act if the qualifying patient or primary caregiver:
> (1) is in possession of a registry identification card; and
> (2) is in possession of an amount of marihuana that does not exceed the amount allowed under this act. The presumption [that one is engaged in the medical use of marihuana] may be rebutted by evidence that conduct related to marihuana was not for the purpose of alleviating the qualifying patient's debilitating medical condition or symptoms associated with the debilitating medical condition, in accordance with this act.

Mich. Comp. L. § 333.26423. *See also* Minn. Stat. Ann. § 152.32(1) (West) (same).

*Michigan v. Hartwick*, 870 N.W.2d 37 (Mich. 2015), provides a rare discussion of the purpose limitation and the evidentiary rules surrounding it. In the case, the police arrested one of the defendants, Tuttle, for selling marijuana to another individual, Lalonde, in violation of the Michigan Medical Marijuana Act (MMMA). The police then searched Tuttle's home and found marijuana plants and a small quantity of dried marijuana. Based on the sale to Lalonde, the state charged Tuttle with distribution of marijuana. But it also charged Tuttle with the possession and manufacture of the marijuana and plants found at Tuttle's home. Against these latter charges, Tuttle sought to invoke immunity from prosecution under the Michigan Medical Marijuana Act (MMMA) (immunity is discussed below in Section C.2). Tuttle was a registered qualifying patient and a registered caregiver for at least one other patient under the MMMA, and he arguably possessed no more marijuana than was allowed by the MMMA. However, the prosecution claimed that Tuttle's sale of *some* of his marijuana to Lalonde rebutted the presumption of medical use for *all* of Tuttle's marijuana-related activities, including marijuana he might have been growing/possessing for his own medical use. The court rejected the prosecution's claim:

> Tuttle argues that unprotected marijuana-related conduct may only rebut the presumption as to otherwise protected conduct if a nexus exists between the unprotected conduct and the protected conduct. . . .
>
> . . .
>
> It is clear, as Tuttle concedes, that conduct violating the MMMA directly rebuts the presumption of medical use when a defendant's charges are based on that specific conduct. . . . It is not clear, however, that conduct violating the MMMA would also rebut the presumption of medical use related to other charges against the defendant when the

illicit conduct does not form the basis of charges. . . . While the statutory language is neither compelling nor expressly direct, we nonetheless conclude that the statutory text lends support for Tuttle's proposition.

Use of the permissive "may," [Mich. Comp. L. § 333.26423(d) (presumption "may be rebutted"),] in conjunction with the trial court's general gatekeeping responsibility to admit only relevant evidence, leads us to conclude that to rebut the presumption of medical use the prosecution's rebuttal evidence must be relevant, such that the illicit conduct would allow the fact-finder to conclude that the otherwise MMMA-compliant conduct was not for the medical use of marijuana. In other words, the illicit conduct and the otherwise MMMA-compliant conduct must have a nexus to one another in order to rebut the . . . presumption [of medical use]. . . .

Further, Tuttle's view not only has statutory support, but also comports with how generally a presumption should be rebutted. Only relevant evidence that allows the fact-finder to conclude that the underlying conduct was not for "medical use" may rebut the . . . presumption. A wholly unrelated transaction—i.e., a transaction with no nexus, and therefore no relevance, to the conduct resulting in the charged offense—does not assist the fact-finder in determining whether the defendant actually was engaged in the medical use of marijuana during the charged offense. Conduct unrelated to the charged offense is irrelevant and does not rebut the presumption of medical use.

Therefore, . . . the prosecution may rebut the presumption of medical use for each claim of immunity. Improper conduct related to one charged offense may not be imputed to another charged offense unless the prosecution can establish a nexus between the improper conduct and the otherwise MMMA-compliant conduct. The trial court must ultimately determine whether a defendant has established by a preponderance of the evidence that he or she was engaged in the medical use of marijuana. The defendant may do so by establishing this powerful presumption of medical use. If the presumption of medical use has been rebutted, however, the defendant may still prove through other evidence that, with regard to the underlying conduct that resulted in the charged offense and for which the defendant claims immunity, the defendant was engaged in the medical use of marijuana. . . .

*Id.* at 54-55.

## Notes and Questions

1. Does the presumption make the medical purpose requirement superfluous? After all, how are the police supposed to rebut the presumption? Consider the following Problem:

**Problem 4.13:** On the drive home from a Phish concert, the car in which Delilah was riding was stopped for speeding. Delilah consented to a search of her backpack, which contained about ½ ounce of usable marijuana. When questioned, Delilah acknowledged that she had also smoked one marijuana joint at home before the concert. However, Delilah is a registered qualified patient who suffers from chronic back pain, and she showed the officer her registry identification card. Is Delilah entitled to the presumption of medical use for her possession of the ½ ounce of marijuana in her backpack, the joint she smoked earlier, or both? Could the state successfully rebut the presumption for either (or both)? What if Delilah had shared the joint with her friends—none of whom is a qualified patient—before the concert?

## 3. Type

Some states also limit the type or form of marijuana that individuals may possess and consume. (The forms marijuana takes and the methods used to consume it are discussed in Chapter 2.) Not surprisingly, CBD states are the most restrictive in this regard. In these states, the only type of marijuana patients may possess and consume is CBD, usually in oil form, and then, only if it contains very little THC. *E.g.*, Ala. Code § 13A-12-214.2(b)(2) (patient may possess CBD that "has a THC level of no more than 3 percent"); Iowa Code Ann. § 124D.6 (West) ("The defenses afforded a patient . . . apply . . . only if the quantity of cannabidiol *oil* possessed by the patient does not exceed thirty-two ounces.") (emphasis added).

By contrast, all recreational marijuana and most medical marijuana states allow qualified individuals to possess and use marijuana in whatever form they choose. *See, e.g., California v. Mulcrevy*, 182 Cal. Rptr. 3d 176 (Cal. App. 2014) (holding that CUA implicitly adopted pre-existing definition of marijuana, which includes all parts of the plant and concentrated cannabis oil). However, a few medical marijuana states continue to ban possession of certain forms of the drug, including, most notably, smokable marijuana. In New York state, for example, the products approved for the medical marijuana market are limited to:

> (1) liquid or oil preparations for metered oromucosal or sublingual administration or administration per tube;
> (2) metered liquid or oil preparations for vaporization;
> (3) capsules for oral administration; or
> (4) any additional form and route of administration approved by the commissioner. *Smoking is not an approved route of administration.*
> (5) approved medical marihuana products may not be incorporated into edible food products by the registered organization [i.e., a medical marijuana dispensary], unless approved by the commissioner.

N.Y. Comp. Codes R. & Regs. tit. 10, § 1004.11(g) (emphasis added).

## Notes and Questions

1. Attempts to limit the types of marijuana individuals may consume have generated some delicious legal disputes. In *Michigan v. Carruthers*, 837 N.W.2d 16 (Mich. App. 2013), for example, the court had to decide whether patients and caregivers are allowed to possess THC infused *brownies* under the Michigan Medical Marijuana Act (MMMA). Section 4 of the MMMA grants immunity for possession only of "*usable* marihuana." Mich. Comp. L. 333.26424(a) & (b)(1) (emphasis added). The statute defines "usable marihuana" as the "dried leaves and flowers of the marihuana plant, and any mixture or preparation thereof, but . . . not . . . the seeds, stalks, and roots of the plant." *Id.* at 26423(k). The *Carruthers* court concluded that the brownies the defendant in the case possessed (and sought to distribute) did not satisfy this definition even though they contained marijuana and were otherwise usable (in the practical sense of the term):

> The prosecution offered into evidence the testimony of the forensic chemist who analyzed the brownies in this case. The chemist testified that there was no detectable plantlike material in the brownies, but they contained THC. . . . The chemist also testified that THC extraction techniques involve extracting THC from the resin of the marijuana plant. . . .

... [D]efendant acknowledged that THC was extracted from marijuana and infused into the brownies. Defendant's counsel also stated that the brownies were "not made of ... ground up marijuana" but were instead made with cannabutter containing THC extract. ...

... By excluding resin from the definition of "usable marihuana," as contrasted with the definition of "marihuana," and defining "usable marihuana" to mean only "the dried leaves and flowers of the marihuana plant, and any mixture or preparation *thereof*," Mich. Comp. L. 333.26423(k) (emphasis added), the drafters clearly expressed their intent *not* to include resin, or a mixture or preparation of resin, within the definition of "usable marihuana." They therefore expressed their intent not to include a mixture or preparation of an *extract* of resin. Consequently, an edible product made with THC extracted from resin is excluded from the definition of "usable marihuana." Rather, under the plain language of the MMMA, the only "mixture or preparation" that falls within the definition of "usable marihuana" is a mixture or preparation of "the dried leaves and flowers of the marihuana plant. ..." *Id.*

Nor are we persuaded by the ... argument that usable marijuana merely constitutes marijuana that is "usable" and that a brownie containing THC extracted from the resin of a marijuana plant is usable marijuana because it is marijuana that is "usable" simply by virtue of its ingestion. That argument requires a circularity of reasoning that would read into the drafters' definition of "usable marihuana" a component (resin) that the drafters expressly excluded. Moreover, it ignores the fact that the term "usable marihuana" is not simply a combination of the words "usable" and "marihuana"; rather, it is a term of art specifically defined by the MMMA. We are not at liberty to ignore that definition in favor of our own. ... The drafters' definition of the term "usable marihuana" clearly was not intended to encompass all marijuana that theoretically is "usable," in the colloquial meaning of the term, by virtue of its ability to be ingested. Rather, as a term of art, it is designed to identify a subset of marijuana that may be possessed in allowed quantities for purposes of an immunity analysis under §4 of the MMMA. ...

In defining the parameters of legal medical-marijuana use, the drafters of the MMMA adopted a definition of "usable marihuana" that we believe comports with the voters' desire to allow limited "medical use" of marijuana and yet not to allow the unfettered use of marijuana generally. ... Given the heightened potency of the THC extract, as compared with "the dried leaves and flowers," ... this definition of "usable marihuana" ... strikes us as a sound and reasoned mechanism to promote the "health and welfare of [Michigan] citizens[]." ...

Our interpretation also does not preclude the medical use of marijuana by ingestion of edible products; to the contrary, that use is authorized by the MMMA, within the statutory limitations, provided that the edible product is a "mixture or preparation" of "the dried leaves and flowers of the marihuana plant," rather than of the more potent THC that is extracted from marijuana resin. Mich. Comp. L. 333.26423(k). ...

...

For the reasons stated, ... [the] brownies [defendant possessed] did not constitute "usable marihuana." ... The parties agree, however, as do we, that the brownies did constitute "marihuana" under that term's statutory definition. Possession of THC extracted from marijuana is possession of marijuana. ... By possessing edible products that were not usable marijuana under the MMMA, but indisputably were marijuana, he failed to meet the requirements for §4 immunity.

*Carruthers*, 837 N.W.2d at 21-27.

2. Do you think the limitations on the forms of marijuana qualified patients may consume are reasonable? What is the purpose behind such limitations?

3. The defendant in *Carruthers* had been convicted by a jury and sentenced to three years' probation with 33 days in jail. However, in a portion of its decision not excerpted here, the appeals court vacated the defendant's conviction and remanded for a new hearing. It found that the defendant should have been allowed to assert an affirmative defense under a different provision of the MMMA (section 8), even though he did not satisfy the more demanding criteria for immunity applicable under section 4. In pertinent part, the court noted that section 8 "does not refer to 'usable marihuana,' but instead states that a patient or primary caregiver, or both, 'may assert the medical purpose for using marihuana as a defense to any prosecution involving marihuana.' Mich. Comp. L. 333.26428(a)." *Carruthers*, 837 N.W.2d at 29. Section C below discusses the different types of legal protections medical marijuana states now afford users, including the differences between affirmative defenses and immunities.

## 4. Place

All jurisdictions that have legalized marijuana use continue to bar the use and sometimes even possession of the drug in certain places, such as near public parks and schools. The Connecticut medical marijuana statute below provides a representative formulation of these place restrictions. It provides that state law does not permit the use of marijuana:

> (A) in a motor bus or a school bus or in any other moving vehicle, (B) in the workplace, (C) on any school grounds or any public or private school, dormitory, college or university property, unless such college or university is participating in a research program and such use is pursuant to the terms of the research program, (D) in any public place, or (E) in the presence of a person under the age of eighteen, unless such person is a qualifying patient or research program subject. For the purposes of this subdivision, (i) "presence" means within the direct line of sight of the palliative use of marijuana or exposure to second-hand marijuana smoke, or both; (ii) "public place" means any area that is used or held out for use by the public whether owned or operated by public or private interests. . . .

Conn. Gen. Stat. Ann. §21a-408a (West) (2016).

### a. Public

Perhaps the most widely adopted place restriction bars the use and/or possession of marijuana in public. These bans have two distinct formulations. One formulation bans the *public use* of marijuana. For example, Colorado's Amendment 64, which legalizes recreational use of marijuana, provides that:

> (I) . . . a person who openly and publicly displays, consumes, or uses two ounces or less of marijuana commits a drug petty offense and, upon conviction thereof, shall be punished by a fine of up to one hundred dollars and up to twenty-four hours of community service.
>
> (II) Open and public display, consumption, or use of more than two ounces of marijuana or any amount of marijuana concentrate is deemed possession thereof, [a level 2 drug misdemeanor—level 4 drug felony, depending on quantity,] and violations shall be punished [by imprisonment of 0-12 months and a fine of $50 to $100,000].

Colo. Rev. Stat. 18-18-406(5)(b). A second formulation instead bans the open use of marijuana *in a public place*. For example, Michigan's medical marijuana law provides that it "does not permit any person to . . . [p]osess marihuana, or otherwise engage in the medical use of marihuana . . . [i]n any public place." Mich. Comp. L. 333.26427 (2016).

What sort of actions do these bans prohibit? The following case examines the application of a state ban that incorporates both formulations of the offense.

## *New York v. Jackson*
967 N.E.2d 1160 (N.Y. Ct. App. 2012)

GRAFFEO, J.

While operating his vehicle on a public street in Brooklyn, defendant committed a traffic infraction that was witnessed by a police officer. When the officer pulled him over and approached his vehicle, she detected a strong odor of marihuana and saw defendant holding a ziplock bag of marihuana in his hand. Other items of contraband were subsequently discovered as a consequence of the motor vehicle stop, including more than a dozen bags of marihuana. Defendant was ultimately charged with one count of criminal possession of marihuana in the fifth degree, two counts of unlawful possession of marihuana and other offenses. He pleaded guilty to criminal possession of marihuana in the fifth degree in satisfaction of all the charges and was sentenced to five days in jail.

Despite the guilty plea, defendant appealed his conviction . . . , arguing that . . . because he was in a private vehicle, he was not in a public place when he was found in possession of marihuana. He further asserted that the police officer's allegation that he was holding the marihuana in his hand exposed to public view was too conclusory to satisfy that element of the offense. . . .

. . .

[In 1977, the New York Legislature] . . . restructured marihuana possession offenses with the intent to reduce criminal culpability for the possession of a small quantity of marihuana for personal use in a private place (such as in the home), making such conduct a violation when it had previously been a misdemeanor. . . . However, the Legislature did not alter its view that the possession or use of marihuana in public constituted a crime. Toward that end, [New York Penal Law § 221.10] was enacted creating the misdemeanor offense of criminal possession of marihuana in the fifth degree. Under the subsection at issue in this case, "[a] person is guilty of criminal possession of marihuana in the fifth degree when he knowingly and unlawfully possesses . . . marihuana in a public place, as defined in section 240.00 of this chapter, and such marihuana is burning or open to public view." . . .

### PUBLIC PLACE

When the Legislature made possession in a "public place" an element of criminal possession of marihuana in the fifth degree, . . . it incorporated by reference a preexisting definition of the phrase from article 240, a separate Penal Law article relating to a broad range of offenses against public order. Under Penal Law § 240.00(1), a "public place" is "a place to which the public or a substantial group of persons has access, and includes, but is not limited to, highways, transportation facilities, schools, places of amusement, parks, playgrounds, and hallways, lobbies and other portions of apartment houses and hotels not constituting rooms or apartments designed for actual residence."

In this case, where defendant was found in possession of marihuana during a motor vehicle stop on a public street, the People alleged that defendant was in a "public place" because he was on a "highway"—a location that the Legislature specifically designated as a public place in Penal Law § 240.00(1).

Defendant does not dispute that a public street is a highway within the meaning of Penal Law § 240.00(1). Rather, he contends that he was not in a public place because he was situated inside his vehicle when the officer observed marihuana in his hand. Thus, defendant characterizes the issue as whether the interior of a car used for personal transportation is a "public place." Although defendant acknowledges that a pedestrian walking on a public street would be in a "public place," under his rationale a location would change from a public street to a private place if a person is in a private vehicle. We disagree.

With one exception, Penal Law § 240.00(1) defines a "public place" in terms of fixed physical locations—highways, schools, parks and the like—declaring these spaces to be public no matter whether a person is standing still or moving through them and regardless of the particular means of locomotion in use, if any. Thus, though certainly relevant to the second issue we address (the "open to public view" element), for purposes of the Penal Law § 240.00(1) definition of "public place," the fact that defendant was in his personal automobile does not alter the fact that he was on a highway—and was therefore in a public place—when he was seen in possession of marihuana. . . .

. . . [D]efendant notes that [section 240.00(1)] also incorporates "transportation facilities" which are defined to include not only certain physical spaces (e.g. airports and train stations) but also vehicles used for public passenger transportation, such as "aircraft, watercraft, railroad cars, buses" and the like. . . . By referencing certain types of public transit in the definition of "public place," defendant argues that the Legislature must have intended to exclude privately-owned automobiles used exclusively for personal transportation, intending such vehicles to be private. Again, the question is not whether a person's automobile is "public" or "private" but whether defendant was in a public place when he was in his car on the street. The People do not argue that a privately-owned vehicle used exclusively for personal transportation is a "public place" akin to a subway train or public bus. Rather, a driver of a personal automobile will be in a public place only when the vehicle is in a location that qualifies under the statute as a public place. In contrast, by defining certain vehicles used for public transportation—such as a bus—as themselves constituting "public places," the Legislature made the location of those vehicles at the time of the crime irrelevant; they are "public places" whether they are being driven on a highway or are parked in a private parking lot. The Legislature's decision to broadly incorporate public transit vehicles within the definition of "public place" regardless of their location in no way undermines our conclusion that a person is in a public place when located on a highway even if he or she is inside a personal automobile.

In fact, the contrary view of the statute propounded by defendant and the dissent would distinguish unfairly between those prosecuted for less serious violations and those subject to misdemeanor convictions. For example, under their rationale, because the "public place" element would be lacking, a person smoking marihuana while sitting in a parked personal vehicle on a public street with the windows open, readily observable to anyone passing by, would be guilty of nothing more than a violation (the same offense that would apply were the person at home)—while a person standing just outside the vehicle in the same location engaged in the same behavior would be guilty of misdemeanor possession under Penal Law § 221.10(1). This would be true even though both hypothetical parties would have engaged in conduct that impacted the public in precisely the same manner. Although acknowledging that the marihuana possession offenses were restructured to reduce penalties for private marihuana possession or use in some circumstances, the dissent and defendant would extend the 1977 reforms well beyond the private conduct the Legislature intended to address, encompassing behavior that can fairly be described as occurring in public.

Moreover, given that the Penal Law § 240.00(1) definition of "public place" applies to a wide variety of crimes, many involving conduct bearing little similarity to the marihuana possession offense to which defendant pleaded guilty, it would be imprudent to give the phrase the restricted reading urged by defendant and the dissent. A holding that a person in a private vehicle can never be in a public place could have a far-reaching impact on the scope of other offenses—leading to results likely never intended by the Legislature. For example, under Penal Law § 240.62, entitled "[p]lacing a false bomb or hazardous substance in the first degree," it is a class D felony to position in a "public place any device or object that by its design, construction, content or characteristics appears to be . . . a bomb, destructive device, explosive or hazardous substance, but is, in fact, an inoperative facsimile or imitation of such a bomb." Were we to conclude that the interior of a private automobile is not a "public place" under the Penal Law § 240.00(1) definition, then a person that put a convincing—though fake—bomb on the passenger seat of a private vehicle and parked it on the street in front of a government building would not be guilty of this offense, despite the significant public disruption, fear and even chaos that would likely ensue when the device was observed by the police or a passing civilian. Similarly, were we to conclude that a highway is not a public place as long as an individual remains inside a private vehicle, then someone who engaged in harassment by slowly traveling alongside a pedestrian walking on a secluded public street, thereby placing that person in reasonable fear of physical injury, might avoid prosecution for harassment in the first degree (Penal Law § 240.25). Under the theory suggested by defendant and the dissent, by electing to follow the victim in an automobile rather than on foot, the offender would have negated the "public place" element of that offense. Considered in this broader light, we are unpersuaded that the Legislature could have intended the definition of "public place" to have the narrow meaning they ascribe to it.

. . .

## OPEN TO PUBLIC VIEW

Next, defendant contends that even if he was in a public place, [the allegations against him failed to demonstrate that the marijuana was "open to public view"]. . . .

. . . [T]he "open to public view" element . . . is not defined either in Penal Law § 221.10(1) or elsewhere. But in keeping with the policy underlying the 1977 restructuring of marihuana possession offenses, it is evident that the Legislature included this requirement to limit the criminal culpability of a party that possesses a small quantity of marihuana in a public place but does so in a manner that conceals the drug. In many respects, this element speaks more directly to the legislative concern for personal privacy—whether an individual is in a private automobile or elsewhere—than the "public place" element. That marihuana must be "open to public view" (or burning) to support prosecution under Penal Law § 221.10(1) ensures that a pedestrian walking on a public street carrying an inconsequential amount of marihuana secreted in a bag or pocket would not be subject to misdemeanor prosecution. When considered in the context of this case, it is this element that recognizes that, although a vehicle may be located in a public place, this does not mean that its occupants and owners have relinquished privacy interests in items concealed inside. Thus, it is the "open to public view" requirement—rather than the "public place" provision—that addresses the concern expressed by the dissent that personal automobiles are, in some respects, private in the sense that certain areas within the interior of an automobile are hidden from view. . . .

. . . Although not a model of specificity, we conclude that the allegations [against the defendant were legally sufficient to satisfy this element] . . . Here, the accusatory instrument[7] alleges that, upon approaching the vehicle, the officer "smelled a strong odor of marihuana emanating from inside the . . . vehicle" and "observed the defendant holding a quantity of marihuana in [his] hand, open to public view." Additional allegations—in which the officer explains the basis for her conclusion that the substance was marihuana . . . indicate that the contraband was in a ziplock bag. Although the officer did not describe the precise location of defendant's hand, since she was standing outside the vehicle when she saw the substance in the ziplock bag, these allegations support the inference that any other member of the public could also have seen the marihuana from the same vantage point—meaning that the marihuana was in an unconcealed area of the vehicle that would have been visible to a passerby or other motorist. Indeed, the statute does not require that a member of the public (other than a law enforcement officer) have actually seen the contraband—it requires only that the substance have been "open" or unconcealed in a manner rendering it susceptible to such viewing. The allegations were therefore sufficient to supply a jurisdictionally adequate accusatory instrument. . . .

LIPPMAN, C.J., dissenting:

Thirty-five years ago, recognizing the dangers to society and individuals inherent in overcriminalization, the Legislature amended the Penal Law to lessen the burden on an already overtaxed justice system by decriminalizing private possession of small amounts of marihuana. The majority's conclusion that a private car on a highway is a "public place" under Penal Law § 240.00(1) and § 221.10(1) is not only contrary to the plain meaning of the statutory language, but also fails to accord sufficient weight to the broader legislative intent. The purpose of the subject Penal Law amendments was to decrease the penalty for nonviolent private conduct that does not pose a threat to public safety, while making clear that such behavior was still illegal and not to be condoned or encouraged. For these reasons, I respectfully dissent.

---

7. Author's note: An accusatory instrument is an information, indictment, complaint, or similar document charging a person with a criminal offense. *See* N.Y. Penal Law § 100 (defining accusatory instruments).

A public place is defined in the statute as "a place to which the public or a substantial group of persons has access" (Penal Law § 240.00[1]). The idea that the public or a substantial group of persons has access to the interior of a private car, whether traveling or parked, such that drivers and all passengers in private cars on public roads are in a "public place," contravenes the plain meaning of the statute's words. The majority claims that defendant's "situation is no different than if he were riding a bicycle on a highway," . . . but a car, unlike a bicycle which is clearly open and exposed to public access, is an enclosed private space. Based on the definition in the statute, the interior of a private car is a private place whether it is on a highway or in a privately owned driveway. . . .

Criminal statutes must be interpreted in terms of their plain meaning. . . . The majority broadens the scope of the statute beyond what the words of that provision reasonably convey. It is important to keep in mind that the underlying offense in this case is a low-level possessory violation, which under certain specific circumstances (namely when occurring in public)—and *only* under those circumstances—is transformed into a crime. The majority, in elevating a violation to a misdemeanor crime, without justification, has failed to adhere to the plain meaning of the statute. . . .

The majority's decision runs afoul of . . . fundamental principles [of due process notice] and conflicts with the reasonable interpretation of the statute as written. Certainly, the Legislature *could have* included all motor vehicles within the definition of a "public place." Had the Legislature intended such meaning, it would have used language to that effect, and indeed it has done just that in another context (*see* Penal Law § 240.37[1] [prohibiting "(l)oitering for the purpose of engaging in a prostitution offense," and defining a "public place" as "any street, sidewalk, bridge, alley or alleyway, plaza, park, driveway, parking lot or transportation facility or the doorways and entrance ways to any building which fronts on any of the aforesaid places, *or a motor vehicle in or on any such place*"] [emphasis added]). If the Legislature desired to include private cars in the definition of "public place" prescribed by Penal Law § 240.00(1), it seems rather odd that it did not include them in much the same way it did in Penal Law § 240.37(1). The Legislature's choice lends itself to only one logical conclusion—that it deliberately excluded private cars from the meaning of "public place" in this particular statute while reserving and exercising the right to classify such vehicles as public places in other contexts. This choice is entirely rational and it is not for this Court to determine whether it represents an unwise policy decision. . . .

Not every unlawful act is also criminal, and in decriminalizing certain conduct, the Legislature recognized a need to provide for "more lenient treatment of marihuana offenses, as opposed to those involving other drugs." . . . This distinction is more than a mere difference in wording and it is a significant one. It reflects the view that when people are needlessly "arrested and prosecuted for simply possessing marihuana," lives are ruined, and police and judicial resources are wasted. . . . The Legislature determined that decriminalization was necessary in order to conserve public resources and avoid the "staggering" costs to society caused by prosecution of possession of small amounts of marihuana, and that it was important that people who possess inconsequential amounts of the substance for personal, private use would no longer have to live in fear of criminal penalties. . . . These changes made it extremely important for courts to properly distinguish between criminal possession and noncriminal (but unlawful) possession in order to avoid the adverse consequences of overcharging, including the stigmatization arising from a misdemeanor conviction resulting in a permanent criminal record.

In making the distinction between conduct that amounts to a violation and criminal behavior, the Legislature identified two key factors. In order for possession to qualify as a violation, warranting only a fine of up to $100, the amount possessed must be small (under 25 grams) and the possession must occur somewhere that is not designated as a "public place" within the meaning of Penal Law § 240.00. Here, these requirements were met.

Contrary to the majority's contention, it is expanding the scope of Penal Law § 240.00(1) to include private vehicles that may lead to absurd results. For example, a person in possession of a small quantity of marihuana while parked on a public street adjacent to his home would be guilty of a crime whereas if he moved the car by a matter of feet to his driveway, he would be responsible only for a violation; a recreational vehicle parked at an otherwise empty rest stop or a privately owned car on an isolated road would be deemed "public places" for purposes of Penal Law § 221.10(1).

Because the possession did not occur in a "public place," there is no need to reach the "public view" element of the crime. . . .

## Notes and Questions

1. Jurisdictions commonly treat these offenses (however formulated) as an aggravated form of simple possession/use, subject to more severe penalties than simple possession in other places. For example, New York normally classifies the simple possession of marijuana as a civil violation punishable by a fine of not more than $100, N.Y. Penal Law § 221.05 (McKinney), but it classifies open (or burning) possession in a public place as a class B misdemeanor, *id.* at § 221.10, which is punishable by up to three months in jail, *id.* at § 70.15(2).

2. Do you agree with the majority or the dissent in *Jackson*? If you think the legislature probably did not mean to punish Jackson's offense as a crime (as opposed to a civil violation), who should correct the result? The court? Or the legislature? How, if at all, would you rewrite New York's statute?

3. As the *Jackson* court notes, the crime of public possession in New York requires both that the defendant *openly* possess (or burn) marijuana *and* that the defendant do so in a place *open to the public*. Do both elements serve a useful function? Along these lines, consider the following Problem:

Problem 4.14: Suppose that Andy does one of the following:

(1) smokes a marijuana joint in plain view on the front porch of his house
(2) vapes marijuana discretely in a public

Does (1) violate a ban on public use? Does (2) violate a ban on use in a public place? Does one of these actions seem more likely to cause harm than the other? If so, which one?

4. Scenarios like the one posed by **Problem 4.14** have vexed some policymakers. Most notably, Colorado's Amendment 64 Implementation Task Force, which was formed to work out some of the details of Colorado's marijuana legalization initiative, could not agree on how to define "open and public . . . consumption." As recounted by two members of the Task Force:

> Defining "open and public consumption" of marijuana, which is expressly prohibited by the plain language of Amendment 64, has proven to be one of the most contentious issues in the new law. The Governor's Task Force could not reach consensus on this issue after hours of debate. A common hypothetical posed was the burning of a joint in a backyard or on a front porch. Since one's front porch is private property but viewable from the curb, and a burning joint can certainly be smelled from afar, it was unclear if such conduct constituted open and public use. . . .
>
> There is also confusion about when a gathering is private enough for "consumption" to occur. Most would agree, on the one hand, that a group of friends aged twenty-one and above gathered in a private home can smoke or otherwise consume marijuana without violating the law. On the other hand, most would also agree that public facilities such as bars and restaurants are off limits. However, there is a wide gray space in between these two extremes. For example, does an otherwise public facility that charges a "membership fee" for admission to an evening of marijuana consumption create a space private enough to pass legal muster? What about a private club with initiation fees and monthly dues?
>
> The confusion about what is not "open and public" has prompted a clamoring for marijuana social clubs—public locations run for the exclusive purpose of providing a controlled environment in which to consume marijuana and socialize with like-minded consumers. There are advantages to licensing such establishments. For example, under the new law, tourists visiting Colorado for mountain sports can legally purchase and possess . . . marijuana, but unless they stay at a pot-friendly hotel, they cannot consume the product. A mountain town social club dedicated to marijuana would solve that problem. However, social clubs have yet to be authorized by state authorities, as they bring with them myriad issues related to local zoning, public health, nuisance complaints, and drugged driving. Only a few establishments have conducted a risk assessment and opened their doors as private clubs, including one with local government approval.
>
> A central challenge of crafting rules in this area is distinguishing between burning cannabis and consuming an edible cannabis product. While an argument could be made that smoking a joint on a front porch clearly visible from a public sidewalk constitutes open and public consumption, it would be difficult also to conclude that a group of friends inconspicuously eating candies or cake infused with marijuana on that same porch would be engaged in open and public consumption. And because Colorado law makes no distinction between smoking tobacco and smoking marijuana when prohibiting both in public places, smoking marijuana is generally proscribed in all indoor facilities open to the public. But could an infused edible product be enjoyed in a public gathering place—from a bar or restaurant to a sports stadium or public park—if its consumers give no notice that it contains cannabis?

David Blake & Jack Finlaw, *Marijuana Legalization in Colorado: Learned Lessons*, 8 Harv. L. & Pol'y Rev. 359, 374-75 (2014).

5. As Blake and Finlaw note in the excerpt, some entrepreneurs have created members-only clubs that (arguably) are not open to the public and thus, not subject to bans on public consumption of marijuana. *See* Paresh Dave, *Colorado Pot Law Bans Smoking in*

*Public*, L.A. Times, May 14, 2014 (discussing clubs and ticketed events). The Clubs include Studio A64 in Colorado Springs, https://perma.cc/V74U-37KC, and the Lazy Lion in Colorado Springs, https://perma.cc/PGM2-WAV6. Are these members-only clubs violating the law? What if the only requirement for membership is to pay a small fee at the door?

6. In the fall 2016 elections, Denver voters passed a new ordinance (Initiative 300) that permits the public use of marijuana in some businesses, such as bars and restaurants. The measure states, in relevant part:

> [T]he City and County of Denver . . . may permit a business or a person with evidence of support of an eligible neighborhood association or business improvement district to allow the consumption of marijuana ("cannabis") in a designated consumption area; such associations or districts may set forth conditions on the operation of a designated consumption area, including permitting or restricting concurrent uses, consumptions, or services offered, if any; the designated consumption area is limited to those over the age of twenty-one, must comply with the Colorado Clean Indoor Air Act, may overlap with any other type of business or licensed premise, and cannot be located within 1000 feet of a school; a designated consumption area that is located outside cannot be visible from a public right-of-way or a place where children congregate. . . .

Denver, Colo., Code of Ord., Tit. II, ch. 6, Art. VI (2016), at https://perma.cc/F6AK-US4K (providing full text of measure). *See also* Ricardo Baca, *Initiative 300: Everything You Need to Know About Denver's Social Cannabis Use Measure*, Denver Post, Nov. 8, 2016 (discussing Initiative 300). What do you think of the Denver measure? Is it consistent with the provisions of Colorado's Amendment 64 governing public use?

7. Notably, three of the four new state recreational marijuana measures adopted in the fall 2016 election all permit the public consumption of marijuana in certain establishments, so long as those establishments obtain the approval of local authorities. Cal. Health & Safety Code § 11362.3(a)(1) (2016) (permitting consumption in licensed marijuana businesses); Me. Stat. tit. 7, § 2452(5)(B) (2016) (permitting consumption in marijuana social clubs); Mass. Gen. Laws Ann. ch. 94G, § 7(a)(1) (2016) (permitting consumption in marijuana establishments). These measures arguably signal a growing receptivity toward allowing limited public use of marijuana (or use of marijuana in public places) as part of state marijuana reforms. Do you think jurisdictions should ban public use/use in public places? Why, why not? Chapter 5 considers some of the policy arguments for and against such bans.

### b. Schools

Until recently, every state banned the possession and consumption of marijuana on school grounds, including both K-12 schools and universities. No exception was made for students who were otherwise permitted to use the drug for medical purposes. The Connecticut statute quoted at the start of Section B.4 provides an example.

In 2015, however, Maine and New Jersey became the first states to allow the use of medical marijuana in K-12 schools. For example, New Jersey's legislation provides:

> a. A board of education or chief school administrator of a nonpublic school shall develop a policy authorizing parents, guardians, and primary caregivers to administer medical

marijuana to a student while the student is on school grounds, aboard a school bus, or attending a school-sponsored event.

    b. A policy adopted pursuant to subsection a. of this section shall, at a minimum:

        (1) require that the student be authorized to engage in the medical use of marijuana pursuant to [New Jersey's Compassionate Use Medical Marijuana Act (NJCUMM)] and that the parent, guardian, or primary caregiver be authorized to assist the student with the medical use of marijuana . . . ;

        (2) establish protocols for verifying the registration status and ongoing authorization pursuant to [NJCUMM] . . . concerning the medical use of marijuana for the student and the parent, guardian, or primary caregiver;

        (3) expressly authorize parents, guardians, and primary caregivers of students who have been authorized for the medical use of marijuana to administer medical marijuana to the student while the student is on school grounds, aboard a school bus, or attending a school-sponsored event;

        (4) identify locations on school grounds where medical marijuana may be administered; and

        (5) prohibit the administration of medical marijuana to a student by smoking or other form of inhalation while the student is on school grounds, aboard a school bus, or attending a school-sponsored event.

    c. Medical marijuana may be administered to a student while the student is on school grounds, aboard a school bus, or attending school-sponsored events, provided that such administration is consistent with the requirements of the policy adopted pursuant to this section.

N.J. AB 4587 (2015), codified at N.J. Rev. Stat. § 18A:40-12.22. For background on the legislation, see Susan K. Livio, *N.J. School 1st in Nation to Allow Medical Marijuana for Students*, NJ.com, Nov. 12, 2015, https://perma.cc/8AFQ-9QHR.

## Notes and Questions

1. By contrast, no state bans outright the use or possession of other legal medications in schools, including psychotropic drugs like Adderall. Authorities do, however, tightly regulate how some drugs are used, both to prevent diversion to illegal uses and also to protect the safety of legitimate users. Thus, among other things, many jurisdictions specify how certain medications are to be delivered, stored, and administered in schools. *See, e.g.*, 14 Del. Admin. Code 817. Should medical marijuana states allow qualified patients to possess and use marijuana on school grounds, at least on terms similar to those that apply to other drugs?

2. What about recreational marijuana on college campuses? It appears that no college yet formally permits of-age students to possess and use recreational marijuana on campus. *See* Eliza Gray, *How Colleges are Dealing with Legal Pot*, Time.com, Feb. 19, 2015, https://perma.cc/88JH-BBQC?type=image. Many colleges do, however, permit of-age students to use *alcohol* on campus. *See* K.M. Lenk et al., *Alcohol Policies and Practices among Four-Year Colleges in the U.S.: Prevalence and Patterns*, 73 J. Stud. Alcohol & Drugs, 361 (2012). Should states treat the use and possession of recreational marijuana the same way they treat the use and possession of alcohol? Why, why not?

3. The materials in Chapter 14 suggest that federal law may be at least partly responsible for the states' reluctance to allow marijuana (medical or otherwise) on school grounds.

## 5. Driving Under the Influence

Marijuana's potential impact on traffic accidents and related harms is one of the chief concerns now surrounding marijuana reforms. This section considers how the states have reacted to this concern. (Chapter 5 discusses in more detail marijuana's impact on driving harms and the impact that the regulations discussed below have had on this harm.)

Every state has prohibited driving under the influence of marijuana (DUI-impaired). A sizable contingent of states has also prohibited driving with marijuana (or some metabolite thereof) in the body, regardless of whether the driver was impaired (DUI-per se). This section discusses the elements of these DUI offenses and the legal issues that have arisen under them.

### a. DUI-Impaired

All states have made it a criminal offense to

(1) drive a motor vehicle (or be in actual physical control thereof)
(2) while under the influence of marijuana

For purposes of the offense, the latter element (being "under the influence") connotes something more than having consumed the drug, though that is obviously a prerequisite. It connotes being *impaired* by the drug. In *Webb v. Georgia*, for example, the defendant had been convicted of driving while under the influence of marijuana. At trial, the government demonstrated that the defendant had been driving 60 mph in a 50 mph zone and had, at some prior point, consumed marijuana (the defendant's urine had tested positive for the drug and the police discovered a small baggie of marijuana and a partially smoked marijuana cigarette in the defendant's car). But the appeals court nonetheless reversed the defendant's conviction because the government had failed to produce enough evidence that the defendant's driving had been *impaired* by marijuana. The only evidence the prosecution had offered for impairment was the fact that the defendant had been driving ten miles per hour over the speed limit. The court held that this evidence, standing alone, was insufficient to meet the government's burden on the second element. It emphasized that "the mere fact that a defendant has ingested marijuana is not sufficient to support a conviction [for driving while under the influence of a drug].... The State is required to present some other form of evidence showing the defendant was impaired." 476 S.E.2d 781, 783 (Ga. App. 1996).

The degree of impairment required for a conviction varies across the states. In some jurisdictions, the government must demonstrate that the marijuana rendered the defendant "incapable of driving safely." 23 Vt. Stat. §1201 ("a person shall not operate.... any vehicle on a highway ... when the person is under the influence of [marijuana] ... to a degree which renders the person incapable of driving safely").

In a small number of jurisdictions, however, the government need only show that the defendant was slightly impaired. For example, Arizona provides that "[i]t is unlawful for a person to drive or be in actual physical control of a vehicle . . . [w]hile under the influence of intoxicating liquor, any drug, a vapor releasing substance containing a toxic substance or any combination [thereof] . . . if the person is impaired *to the slightest degree.*" Ariz. Rev. Stat. § 28-1381(A)(1) (emphasis added).

There are many types of evidence that the government may use to demonstrate that a defendant both consumed marijuana and was impaired thereby, including blood or urine tests, field sobriety tests, the defendant's demeanor, the smell of burnt marijuana in the defendant's car or on the defendant's person, the presence of marijuana or marijuana paraphernalia in the car or on the defendant's person, and the defendant's admission of marijuana use. In *Oregon v. Beck,* for example, the court upheld the defendant's conviction for DUI marijuana, based on evidence that the defendant's poor driving (he had crossed a median divider), admission to using marijuana the previous evening, and performance on a field sobriety test (his eyelids and legs trembled, his pupils were dilated, and the taste buds on the back of his tongue were raised, which is a sign of recent usage). 292 P.3d 653, 67-68 (Or. App. 2012).

Although blood or urine tests may help the government make its case, courts have held that the government is not required to perform such tests in order to demonstrate that a defendant had ingested or was impaired by marijuana (or other drugs). *E.g., Richardson v. Georgia,* 682 S.E.2d 684, 685 (Ga. App. 2009) ("[The appellant] has cited to no authority, and we are aware of none, that requires the State to present the results from scientific testing of a driver's blood or urine in order to prove the specific type of drug allegedly ingested by the defendant so that the State may obtain a conviction for DUI less safe. . . .").

The following cases explore the sufficiency of different types of evidence in meeting the government's burden of demonstrating impairment.

## *Pennsylvania v. Hutchins*
42 A.3d 302 (Pa. App. 2012)

OLSON, J:

[The appellant, Corey Adam Hutchins, was convicted of various offenses, including driving under the influence of a controlled substance. On appeal, he challenged the sufficiency of the evidence supporting his conviction for DUI. The court recited the facts as recorded by the trial court:]

> On September 19, 2009, at approximately 4[:00] p.m., Christopher White was traveling eastbound on Jonestown Road, a two-lane road, when Appellant's car, a 1999 Dodge Stratus turned in front of his vehicle. [Appellant was driving his car. His three young daughters were also in the vehicle.] Appellant's vehicle was making a left turn in front of White's vehicle on Old Jonestown Road. White testified that at this particular section of Old Jonestown Road there are no hills or slopes in the road. Rather, the location where the accident occurred was flat. On the date in question, there were no adverse weather conditions, such as rain or sleet, and there were no problems with lighting because it was a sunny day. White was traveling approximately forty-five (45) miles per hour, the posted speed limit, before the accident occurred. The force of impact was enough to deploy the airbags in his vehicle, and White's car was totaled.

Trooper David Mays was dispatched to assist with the accident. Trooper Mays testified that he arrived at the scene in a matter of a couple of minutes. Upon arriving at the scene, Trooper Mays observed a two-car crash along the roadway. . . . As Trooper Mays searched Appellant's vehicle for registration and insurance information, he smelled an odor of [ ] marijuana. He found a Camel cigarette case in the left driver's side door pocket that contained marijuana.

The Commonwealth also presented testimony of Trooper Nathan Trate. He testified that he arrived on the scene of the accident at approximately 4:20 p.m. . . . At the scene, Appellant admitted that the accident was his fault because he was "distracted" and thought that he could make the turn. Trooper Trate testified that Appellant's demeanor was "unusually calm" or "flat line" after the accident. After being asked whether he had consumed alcohol, Appellant stated that he had not, but he admitted to smoking marijuana earlier in the day.

. . . Trooper Trate believed that in his opinion, based on his experience and training, the Appellant was under the influence of marijuana and that this had an impairing effect on his ability to drive. To come to that conclusion, Trooper Trate considered Appellant's "unusually calm" demeanor after the accident; furthermore, he did not see another reason why the Appellant would turn in front of a car on a straight roadway. Trooper Trate also noted that the Appellant's pupils seemed "constricted" and considered Appellant's statement that "he had a lot of things on his mind" before the accident.

In addition, Trooper Trate explained that the effects of marijuana on the body include a "lack of depth perception, fatigue [and an] inability to concentrate." Furthermore, he revealed that marijuana is a depressant which slows the body down, including one's reaction time.[ ] No standard field sobriety tests were performed because Appellant left the scene to accompany his daughters to the hospital before Trooper Trate was able to conduct the tests. At the hospital, Trooper Trate placed Appellant under arrest. The Appellant then admitted to smoking a half of a bowl [of marijuana] hours earlier in the day.

The parties stipulated that the substance found in Appellant's car was determined to be [.63 grams of] marijuana. . . .

Appellant consented to a blood draw. The toxicology report prepared by Good Samaritan Hospital indicated that Appellant had no alcohol in his blood. The Appellant's blood sample contained 43 ng/ml of carboxy acid [a metabolite of the marijuana plant].

. . .

On September 14, 2010, a jury convicted Appellant of the aforementioned crimes. . . .

Appellant's first issue challenges the sufficiency of the evidence for his conviction under 75 Pa. C.S.A. § 3802(d)(2) [which states that "an individual may not drive, operate or be in actual physical control of the movement of a vehicle" if the individual "is under the influence of a drug . . . to a degree which impairs the individual's ability to safely drive."] . . .

. . .

According to Appellant, the blood test result showing the presence of metabolites in his blood stream, without any expert explanation[, (the government provided none)], fails to establish that he was under the influence of a controlled substance at the time of the accident. . . . Moreover, Appellant argues that the only other evidence establishing intoxication is his admission that he had smoked marijuana earlier in the day. . . . Appellant contends that his admission, by itself, is insufficient to establish that his use of marijuana prevented him from safely operating his vehicle on the occasion in question. . . .

We agree with Appellant that, under the circumstances of this matter, any reliance upon the result of Appellant's blood test for purposes of establishing causation . . . required expert testimony. Specifically, the result of Appellant's blood test showed the presence of carboxy acid metabolite in Appellant's system. . . . That metabolite is a waste product of marijuana, not evidence of active marijuana. . . . What the discovery of carboxy acid in Appellant's blood stream reveals as far as Appellant's ability to safely drive that afternoon is not an issue within the knowledge of an ordinary layman. . . . Indeed, absent expert explanation, Appellant's blood test result tells us only that Appellant ingested marijuana in the past; the test result, without expert explanation, fails to establish that Appellant was under the influence of marijuana at the time of the accident. . . .

However, . . . we disagree with Appellant that the only other evidence against him is his confession to having smoked marijuana earlier in the day. . . .

To the contrary, the Commonwealth presented evidence that upon arriving at the scene of the accident, Trooper Trate observed that, despite the fact that Appellant's three daughters were injured (one bleeding profusely), covered in glass, and crying, Appellant was unusually calm in his demeanor. . . . Appellant's reaction caused Trooper Trate, who is trained to detect the effects of controlled substances on the body, to suspect that Appellant was under the influence. . . . Trooper Trate inquired as to whether Appellant was intoxicated, to which Appellant confessed that he had not been drinking, but that he had smoked marijuana earlier in the day. . . . However, before Trooper Trate could inquire further or perform any field sobriety tests, Appellant left the scene, accompanying his daughters to the hospital. Later, at the hospital, Appellant confessed to having smoked half a bowl of marijuana at approximately noon that day.

In the meantime, Trooper Mays remained with the vehicles involved in the accident, and entered Appellant's vehicle to obtain the registration and insurance information for that vehicle. Upon entry of the vehicle, Trooper Mays, who is trained to detect the smell of marijuana, smelled marijuana and discovered raw marijuana in the driver's side door. Finally, all evidence presented regarding the accident, including Appellant's own confession, indicates that the accident was Appellant's fault in that Appellant turned directly into on-coming traffic.

Considering the totality of the above circumstances, viewed in the light most favorable to the Commonwealth, we hold that there was sufficient evidence to establish that the accident was caused as a result of Appellant's inability to safely operate his vehicle due to the influence of marijuana. Therefore, we hold that, even without the consideration of Appellant's blood test result, the evidence was sufficient to establish Appellant's conviction under Subsection 3802(d)(2).

## *United States v. Davis*
261 F. Supp. 2d 343 (D. Md. 2003)

Day, Magistrate J.:

Clifton Davis ("Defendant") is charged with [inter alia] . . . Driving Under the Influence of Alcohol and/or Drugs in violation of 36 C.F.R. 4.23(a)(1). . . .

### I. FINDINGS OF FACT.

At approximately 8:00 p.m. on July 27, 2002, . . . Officer Gary E. Hatch [of the United States Park Police] . . . was alerted by another motorist that a vehicle was being operated erratically on the [Baltimore-Washington] Parkway. Shortly thereafter, Officer Hatch heard a crashing sound and observed a black sports utility vehicle make contact with construction barrels on the right shoulder of the Parkway.... The black vehicle, later identified as Defendant's 2001 Isuzu Rodeo, moved off to the right shoulder and then swerved back into the far-right travel lane after having hit three to four barrels. Officer Hatch... began pursuing Defendant... [who] was traveling at approximately 65 miles per hour. Defendant was observed swerving onto the right shoulder of the Parkway and returning to the far right traveling lane several times. After Officer Hatch noticed Defendant's pattern of doing so, the Officer activated his emergency equipment (i.e., roof rack lights, flashing headlights, and siren).

Defendant increased his speed to approximately 75 to 80 miles per hour, occasionally encountering slower-moving vehicles, getting "right on top of them and then had to slam his breaks on to avoid striking them." Defendant, while breaking [sic], would repeatedly swerve as if losing control of his vehicle before correcting. Defendant also changed lanes a number of times to take an open lane and increased his speed when no other vehicle was directly in front of him. Officer Hatch changed lanes as Defendant did until the Officer finally took the center lane when he saw that Defendant was quickly approaching a commercial truck. Defendant approached the commercial truck and applied his brakes to avoid hitting it, causing his own vehicle to slide sideways. Defendant then attempted to move to the left lane, where Officer Hatch was driving, causing the Officer to swerve to avoid a collision with Defendant. Officer Hatch pursued Defendant in this manner... [for] a span of approximately 6 to 7 miles.

Sergeant William E. Hayes of the Maryland State Police entered the Parkway... [,] activated his vehicle's emergency equipment and positioned his vehicle in front of Defendant in an effort to slow Defendant's speed. At that point, by Sergeant Hayes' estimate, Defendant was traveling at 75 to 80 miles per hour. Sergeant Hayes remained in front of Defendant's vehicle, changing lanes each time Defendant changed lanes—approximately 4 to 5 times—eventually slowing him down to a stop after approximately 1 mile....

Once Defendant's vehicle was stopped, Officer Hatch and Sergeant Hayes approached Defendant's vehicle with their weapons drawn. Both Defendant and his passenger were non-responsive and appeared disoriented. When asked to show their hands, neither occupant of the vehicle responded with more than a "blank" stare. Officer Hatch reached into the vehicle and across Defendant's lap to unlatch Defendant's seatbelt, then physically removed Defendant from the vehicle. The passenger was removed from the vehicle in the same manner. According to Sergeant Hayes, Defendant was not combative in any way.

Defendant was taken to the United States Park Police station... for processing. Defendant continued to appear disoriented and confused about where he was and the reason why he was there. Defendant was asked for his name and home address, but did not appear able to provide that information. Officer Hatch considered performing field sobriety tests, but given Defendant's apparent inability to communicate, the Officer opted not to conduct such testing. Defendant was then taken to [the hospital] where blood samples were taken for screening. Officer Hatch escorted Defendant to... detention. Officer Hatch testified that it was at that time, approximately three hours after initially encountering Defendant, that Defendant began to speak normally and appeared coherent.

## II. CONCLUSIONS OF LAW

... The Court finds Defendant not guilty driving under the influence of alcohol and/or drugs in violation of 36 C.F.R. § 4.23(a)(1).

The Code of Federal Regulations prohibits "[o]perating or being in actual physical control of a motor vehicle" while "under the influence of alcohol, or a drug, or drugs, or any combination thereof, to a degree that renders the operator incapable of safe operation." 36 C.F.R. § 4.23(a)(1) (2003). The Government bears the burden of proving ... that (1) Defendant was operating or was in actual physical control of a vehicle, (2) that Defendant was under the influence of alcohol, or a drug, or drugs, or any combination thereof, and (3) to a degree of intoxication that rendered Defendant incapable of safe operation. ... Clearly, Defendant was operating his vehicle, however, the Government failed to carry its burden with regard to the final two elements of this offense.

The Government bears the burden of proving that a defendant is under the influence of a substance and what the substance actually is at the time of the conduct in question. The Government's burden is a high one. This Court cannot convict Defendant given the exculpatory results of chemical blood analysis performed here. The Government does not and cannot assert that the chemical analysis performed in the instant case revealed the presence of alcohol in Defendant's blood. Nor is there any other evidence of the consumption of alcohol by Defendant. Further, the results of the chemical analysis ruled out the presence of PCP, LSD, or some other hallucinogenic drug. The only evidence presented regarding the presence of any drug in Defendant's system was that marijuana was present in an unspecified concentration.

Defendant admitted to having used marijuana in the two weeks prior to July 27, 2002 but denied having used marijuana on the day in question. Officer Hatch's search of Defendant's person and vehicle upon arrest did not reveal any drugs or drug paraphernalia. The support for the Government's claim that Defendant was inebriated were his "glassy eyes" and his prolonged appearance that seemed to convey an absence of knowledge of what was going on, coupled with bad driving. Defendant did not appear to be alert and oriented in any fashion. The Government offered no evidence that the amount of marijuana affected Defendant to the extent of rendering him incoherent or disoriented. The Government failed to provide any evidence that Defendant's driving was affected by alcohol, or a drug, or drugs, or any combination thereof, to a degree that rendered the operator incapable of safe operation.

...

There are other explanations for a person to become disoriented or catatonic other than drug and/or alcohol use. Officer Hatch recalled asking Defendant whether he suffered from a medical condition that contributed to his behavior and testified in court that from his training and experience it is possible for some medical conditions to cause a person to act the way Defendant acted. Defendant could have suffered from a medical condition or may have fallen under the spell of vehicle fumes. While direct evidence of voluntary intoxication may be difficult to adduce, the Government must do more to support a conviction than claim that Defendant's version of events is merely a collection of self-serving denials while simultaneously ignoring the fact that there was no significant evidence of the presence of alcohol and/or drug use. The Government's evidence is simply not enough to prove Defendant's guilt beyond a reasonable doubt.

## Notes and Questions

1. Was the evidence sufficient to convict the defendant in *Hutchins* of DUI-impaired? Can you think of a reason (other than marijuana) why someone like the defendant might have been distracted when making the left turn? How about *Davis*? Do you agree with the judge's conclusion that there was insufficient evidence to show beyond a reasonable doubt that the defendant was under the influence of some drug at the time of the offense? Is it possible to reconcile the two decisions?

### b. DUI-Per Se

Beginning with Arizona in the 1990s, several states have added a separate per se offense for driving with drugs (including marijuana) in the driver's body. The Department of Transportation, NHTSA, Drug Per Se Laws: A Review of Their Use in the States (2010) (surveying per se DUI laws in the states). This new offense supplements the core DUI offense just discussed. In other words, a defendant may be charged with either the core driving while impaired offense, or the per se offense, or (perhaps) even both. For example, Arizona makes it a crime to "drive or be in actual physical control of a vehicle"

> 1. While under the influence of intoxicating liquor, any drug, a vapor releasing substance containing a toxic substance or any combination of liquor, drugs or vapor releasing substances if the person is impaired to the slightest degree.
> . . .
> 3. While there is any drug defined in Section 13-3401[, which includes marijuana,] or its metabolite in the person's body.

A.R.S. § 28-1381(A).

The DUI-per se offense simplifies the government's burden of demonstrating a violation. Under the per se approach, the government need only show that the defendant

(1) was driving a motor vehicle (or in actual physical control thereof), and
(2) had a requisite quantum of marijuana or marijuana metabolites in his or her system at the time

As with the DUI-impaired offense, there is some variation in the second element of the DUI-per se offense. Namely, some jurisdictions employ a zero tolerance approach, meaning that *any* amount of marijuana in the body constitutes an offense. The Arizona statute quoted above, for example, makes it a crime to drive with "any drug" prohibited by the state "or its metabolite in the person's body." *See also* Mich. Stat. 257.625 (making it a crime to operate a vehicle "if the person has in his or her body any amount of a controlled substance listed in schedule 1" of the state's drug law). However, other jurisdictions have set the threshold above zero, normally between 2 and 5 nanograms of cannabinoids or metabolites per milliliter of blood (and higher amounts for urine). For example, Nevada provides that

> It is unlawful for any person to drive or be in actual physical control of a vehicle on a highway or on premises to which the public has access with an amount of a prohibited substance in his or her blood or urine that is equal to or greater than [10 nanograms per milliliter of marijuana in urine or 2 nanograms per milliliter in blood; or 15 nanograms per milliliter of marijuana metabolites in urine or 5 nanograms per milliliter of same in blood]

N.R.S. 484C.110(3). (As discussed in Chapter 5, doubts have been raised concerning the reliability of predicting impairment based on specific quantities of marijuana or metabolites found in blood or urine tests.)

In most of these states, once the government establishes the requisite presence of marijuana, it need not demonstrate any impairment therefrom. In Colorado, however, establishing the presence of marijuana merely creates a permissible inference of impairment. The Colorado law provides that if the "driver's blood contained five nanograms or more of delta 9-tetrahydrocannabinol per milliliter in whole blood, as shown by analysis of the defendant's blood, such fact gives rise to a *permissible inference* that the defendant was under the influence of one or more drugs." Col. Stat. 42-4-1301(6)(IV) (emphasis added). This means that a jury will not necessarily convict a defendant based solely on the fact that she had the requisite quantum of marijuana metabolite in her blood while driving, though it would be allowed to do so.

*(i) What Is Marijuana for Purposes of DUI-Per Se Laws?*

There is also some variation across the states in terms of what is considered "marijuana" for purposes of DUI-per se law. Namely, some states appear leery of applying their DUI-per se prohibitions to marijuana metabolites like 11-carboxy-tetrahydrocannabinol that might be found in the blood or urine of a driver. *See, e.g., People v. Feezel*, 783 N.W.2d 67 (Mich. 2010) (holding that 11-carboxy-tetrahydrocannabinol is not a controlled substance or its derivative under Michigan law, and hence, positive test for 11-carboxy-THC was not enough to establish violation of per se drugged driving law). Marijuana metabolites are basically the waste product produced after the body has consumed (i.e., metabolized) marijuana's psychoactive ingredient (THC). As compared to THC, these metabolites are easier to detect: they stay in the body for longer periods of time and may pass through to the urine (THC is only found in the blood).

In the following case, the court discusses the different marijuana metabolites that may be found in the body and why one state's DUI-per se law does not cover them all.

## *Arizona ex rel. Montgomery v. Harris*
322 P.3d 160 (Ariz. 2014)

BRUTINEL, J.

Police stopped a vehicle driven by Hrach Shilgevorkyan for speeding and making unsafe lane changes. Suspecting that he was impaired, officers administered field sobriety tests. After participating in the tests, Shilgevorkyan admitted that he had smoked some "weed" the night before and voluntarily submitted to a blood test that revealed [Carboxy-Tetrahydrocannabinol ("Carboxy-THC"), a non-impairing metabolite of marijuana] . . . in his blood.

The State charged Shilgevorkyan with two counts of driving under the influence. Count one alleged a violation of A.R.S. § 28-1381(A)(1) ("the (A)(1) charge"), which prohibits a person from driving a vehicle in Arizona "[w]hile under the influence of . . . any drug . . . if the person is impaired to the slightest degree." Count two alleged a violation of A.R.S. § 28-1381(A)(3) ("the (A)(3) charge"), which prohibits driving a vehicle "[w]hile there is any drug defined in § 13-3401 or its metabolite in the person's body."

Shilgevorkyan moved to dismiss the (A)(3) charge, arguing that the blood test revealed neither the presence of THC nor "its metabolite" Hydroxy-Tetrahydrocannabinol

("Hydroxy-THC"). At an evidentiary hearing, the State presented expert witness testimony that: (1) marijuana has "many, many metabolites," (2) Hydroxy-THC and Carboxy-THC are the two major marijuana metabolites, (3) although it is possible to test for Hydroxy-THC in the blood, the Arizona Department of Public Safety chooses not to do so because Hydroxy-THC does not "exist in the blood for very long" and is quickly converted to Carboxy-THC, (4) Carboxy-THC is inactive and does not cause impairment, and (5) Carboxy-THC can remain in a person's body for as many as twenty-eight to thirty days after the ingestion of marijuana.

[The trial court granted Shilgevorkyan's motion to dismiss the (A)(3) charge and the State appealed.]

. . .

The term "metabolite" is not defined by statute. . . . A standard medical dictionary defines metabolite as "[a]ny product of metabolism." Taber's Cyclopedic Medical Dictionary 1349 (20th ed. 2005). It defines metabolism in pertinent part, as "the sum of all physical and chemical changes that take place within an organism." *Id.* These definitions comport with the State's expert's testimony, which defined "metabolite" as "any chemical compound that is produced during the process of metabolism, the breakdown process of getting rid of a drug or substance."

Shilgevorkyan argues that the meaning of "its metabolite" in § 28-1381(A)(3) is clear. He asserts that because the statute uses the possessive singular, it prohibits only Hydroxy-THC, the initial product of the metabolism of THC. Labeling Hydroxy-THC the "primary" metabolite, he contends the statute does not include the products of the further breakdown of Hydroxy-THC into subsequent or "secondary" metabolites such as Carboxy-THC. He further argues that interpreting "metabolite" in the plural expands the statutory definition to include a "secondary non-psychoactive metabolite . . . [that] does not cause impairment," which is inconsistent with the legislature's intent to criminalize driving under the influence of an intoxicating substance. The State, on the other hand, argues we should construe "metabolite" in the plural in accordance with A.R.S. § 1-214(B), which generally provides that statutory "[w]ords in the singular . . . include the plural. . . ."

. . .

Because the term "its metabolite" is reasonably susceptible to differing interpretations, the statute is ambiguous and we cannot determine from the term alone whether the legislature intended to penalize the presence of any byproduct, including Carboxy-THC, in a driver's blood. . . .

. . . When a statute's meaning cannot be discerned from its language alone, "we attempt to determine legislative intent by interpreting the statute as a whole, and consider 'the statute's context, subject matter, historical background, effects and consequences, and spirit and purpose.'" . . . Furthermore, we consider a statute "in light of its place in the statutory scheme[]." . . .

The State's interpretation that "its metabolite" includes any byproduct of a drug listed in § 13-3401 found in a driver's system leads to absurd results. . . .

Most notably, this interpretation would create criminal liability regardless of how long the metabolite remains in the driver's system or whether it has any impairing effect. For example, at oral argument the State acknowledged that, under its reading of the statute, if a metabolite could be detected five years after ingesting a proscribed drug, a driver who tested positive for trace elements of a non-impairing substance could be prosecuted.

Additionally, this interpretation would criminalize otherwise legal conduct. In 2010, Arizona voters passed the Arizona Medical Marijuana Act ("AMMA"), legalizing marijuana for medicinal purposes. 163 A.R.S. § 36-2801 et seq. Despite the legality of such use, and because § 28-1381(A)(3) does not require the State to prove that the marijuana was illegally ingested, prosecutors can charge legal users under the (A)(3) provision. Because Carboxy-THC can remain in the body for as many as twenty-eight to thirty days after ingestion, the State's position suggests that a medical-marijuana user could face prosecution for driving any time nearly a month after they had legally ingested marijuana. Such a prohibition would apply even when the driver had no impairing substance in his or her body and notwithstanding the State's ability to test both for THC, the primary substance that causes impairment, and Hydroxy-THC, the metabolite capable of causing impairment. . . .

. . . Section 28-1381(A)(3)'s placement within the statutory scheme also demonstrates a legislative intent to prevent and punish impaired driving, not simply driving while having a non-impairing metabolite in one's system. The "its metabolite" language appears in the "Driving Under the Influence" section of Arizona's statutes. . . . And the statute's title begins "Driving or actual physical control *while under the influence.* . . ." A.R.S. § 28-1381 (emphasis added). . . .

This legislative intent is further evidenced by A.R.S. § 28-1381(A)(2), which provides that "[i]t is unlawful for a person to drive or be in actual physical control of a vehicle . . . [i]f the person has an alcohol concentration of 0.08 or more within two hours of driving or being in actual physical control of the vehicle. . . ." Neither the (A)(2) nor (A)(3) charge requires that the State prove impairment. The (A)(2) charge creates a per se threshold at which a driver is presumed to be under the influence. . . .

Similarly, in enacting the (A)(3) charge, the legislature sought to proscribe driving by those who could be impaired from the presence of illegal drugs in their body. However, unlike alcohol, there is no generally applicable concentration that can be identified as an indicator of impairment for illegal drugs. . . . The (A)(3) charge establishes that a driver who tests positive for any amount of an impairing drug is legally and irrefutably presumed to be under the influence. Although the legislature could rationally choose to penalize the presence of any amount of an impairing metabolite, we do not believe that the legislature contemplated penalizing the presence of a metabolite that is not impairing.

. . .

Because the legislature intended to prevent impaired driving, we hold that the "metabolite" reference in § 28-1381(A)(3) is limited to any of a proscribed substance's metabolites that are capable of causing impairment. Accordingly, marijuana users violate § 28-1381(A)(1) if they drive while "impaired to the slightest degree," and, regardless of impairment, violate (A)(3) if they are discovered with any amount of THC or an impairing metabolite in their body. Drivers cannot be convicted of the (A)(3) offense based merely on the presence of a non-impairing metabolite that may reflect the prior usage of marijuana. . . .

The record establishes that Carboxy-THC, the only metabolite found in Shilgevorkyan's blood, does not cause impairment. Accordingly, we . . . affirm the trial court's dismissal of the (A)(3) charge.

Justice Timmer, dissenting:

Arizona is one of at least seven states that combats drugged driving with a zero-tolerance, per se ban on driving with any controlled substance or its metabolite in the body. . . . One of these states, Delaware, explicitly excludes inactive metabolites from its per se ban. Del. Code Ann. tit. 21, § 4177(c)(10) (West 2014). The Majority aligns Arizona with Delaware by construing A.R.S. § 28-1381(A)(3) in a manner that contradicts its plain meaning. I respectfully dissent.

The Majority holds that § 28-1381(A)(3) is ambiguous because the phrase "its metabolite" can mean all of a proscribed drug's metabolites, some of its metabolites, or only those that can cause impairment. . . . But "metabolite" has an accepted meaning, . . . and nothing in the language of § 28-1381 suggests that the legislature intended to exclude certain types of metabolites from the statutory prohibition. Because § 28-1381(A)(3) "admits of only one meaning," it is not ambiguous. . . .

I also disagree with the Majority that the legislature must have intended something different from what it plainly stated in § 28-1381(A)(3) because imposing a flat ban on driving with any metabolite of an illegal drug in the body is absurd. . . . The legislature reasonably could have concluded that a zero-tolerance provision would most effectively enhance detection and prosecution of drugged driving.

First, the difficulty of detecting drug impairment justifies a flat ban. . . . For example, an expert witness in this case testified that Hydroxy-THC converts quickly to Carboxy-THC, which is why law enforcement typically does not test blood for Hydroxy-THC. Thus, a driver with Carboxy-THC in the blood at the time of testing may or may not have had Hydroxy-THC in the blood while driving. The flat ban ensures that a driver who had an impairing substance in the body while driving is prosecuted even though that substance may have quickly metabolized into a non-impairing substance.

Second, the flat ban permits law enforcement to detect drugged driving by testing urine as well as blood. "[W]hile a urine test detecting metabolites does not conclusively establish the presence of the active proscribed parent drug in the bloodstream, neither does it rule it out, because the metabolite and the active parent will often be present in the body simultaneously." . . . Imposing a flat ban on driving with a metabolite of a controlled substance in the body enhances law enforcement's ability to detect drugged driving. . . .

The Majority contends that a flat ban is absurd because it permits prosecution if the non-impairing metabolite in the driver's body derives from ingesting . . . medically authorized marijuana. . . . [But the] scenario described by the Majority would unquestionably trigger constitutional scrutiny that might invalidate § 28-1381(A)(3) as applied in particular circumstances. . . . And § 28-1381(A)(3) might not apply if the detected metabolites—active or inactive—emanated from medically authorized marijuana use. See A.R.S. § 28-1381(D) ("A person using a drug as prescribed by a medical practitioner . . . is not guilty of violating subsection A, paragraph 3 of this section."). This case does not present either situation.

I share some of the Majority's concerns about imposing a zero-tolerance, per se ban on driving with the presence of non-impairing metabolites in the body. But because § 28-1381(A)(3) clearly and unambiguously reflects that the legislature intended this result, it is not appropriate to employ secondary canons of statutory construction to find a different meaning. Any constitutional challenges to this provision should be addressed on a case-by-case basis.

## Notes and Questions

1. Do you agree with the majority's decision? Is it absurd to criminalize driving with the non-impairing metabolites of an impairing drug in one's body? If the majority's assessment is correct, is it any less absurd to criminalize driving with minute quantities of an impairing drug (or metabolite) in one's body?

2. Do you think per se DUI laws like Arizona's strike an appropriate balance between security and liberty? Are such bans even necessary to protect public safety? The *Harris* court briefly mentions that the state originally charged Shilgevorkyan under both section (A)(3) and section (A)(1), which bans driving while impaired *to the slightest degree*. Do you think the state could have prevailed on the (A)(1) charge? Is the added burden on the government of pursuing that charge (discussed earlier) too high? Does the DUI-impaired offense fail to adequately address the driving harms of marijuana use?

3. One of the key issues surrounding DUI-per se laws is whether they should apply to lawful marijuana users (e.g., qualified patients), an issue that simply did not exist when these laws first came into vogue. The problem identified by the *Harris* court is that DUI–per se laws could effectively prohibit lawful medical marijuana users from ever driving, given the length of time some marijuana metabolites remain in the body.

To address this concern, many medical marijuana states have adopted specific provisions of law designed to shield lawful medical marijuana users from DUI-per se laws (though not DUI-impaired laws). Indeed, even Arizona has such a shield, although *not* the one cited by the dissent in *Harris*. That provision, a part of Arizona's DUI law, provides that a "person using a drug *prescribed* by a medical practitioner ... is not guilty of violating [(A)(3)]." A.R.S. §28-1381(D) (emphasis added). As the Arizona Supreme Court later held, section 28-1381(D) does not protect medical marijuana users because they do not have a *prescription* for marijuana, as opposed to a recommendation. *Dobson v. McClennen*, 361 P.3d 374, 392-93 (Ariz. 2015). Nonetheless, the *Dobson* Court found that another provision of state law, passed as part of the state's medical marijuana law, gave medical marijuana users an affirmative defense to DUI-per se charges. *Dobson v. McClennen*, 361 P.3d 374, 392-393 (Ariz. 2015) (discussing Ariz. Rev. Stat. section 36-2802(D) ("[A] registered qualifying patient shall not be considered to be under the influence of marijuana *solely because of the presence of metabolites* or components of marijuana that appear in insufficient concentration to cause impairment.")) (emphasis added). Other states have adopted similar provisions. *E.g.*, 625 Ill. Comp. S. 5/11-501(a)(6) (specifying that state's DUI-per se law "does not apply to the lawful consumption of cannabis by a qualifying patient ... unless that person is impaired by the use of cannabis"). *See also Michigan v. Koon*, 832 N.W.2d 724 (Mich. 2013) (holding that medical marijuana law supersedes state's DUI-per se law, so that qualified patients are liable only under state's DUI-impaired law).

### (ii) Proof of the Presence of Marijuana

How is the government supposed to prove that a defendant had marijuana in her system? Although the government is not required to perform a blood or urine test on the defendant, as noted above, obtaining a conviction under a DUI-per se law may be difficult without one, as the following case demonstrates.

## *Illinois v. McPeak*
927 N.E.2d 312 (Ill. App. 2010)

JORGENSEN, J.

[The defendant, Samuel McPeak, was charged under Illinois' DUI-per se law, which bars a person from operating a vehicle while "there is any amount of a drug, substance, or compound in the person's breath, blood, or urine resulting from the unlawful use or consumption of cannabis." Ill. Comp. Stat. Ann. 5/11-501(a)(6).]

... [A] bench trial was held on stipulated facts. Those facts included that [in the course of a traffic stop, Officer Steve] Howell smelled burnt cannabis "about Mr. McPeak's person" and that McPeak admitted that "about an hour ago" he had "taken two hits out of a hitter box." McPeak also stipulated that, after he was arrested, Howell located in the vehicle a smoking pipe that contained a burnt substance that smelled like cannabis and that later field-tested positive for cannabis. ... The court found McPeak guilty and sentenced him to 18 months of court supervision and assessed various fines, fees, and costs. ...

[On appeal,] McPeak contends that the evidence was insufficient to convict him of DUI, because there was no evidence of the presence of cannabis in his breath, blood, or urine as required by section 11-501(a)(6). ...

Two cases are helpful when considering McPeak's argument. In [*People v. Allen*, 873 N.E.2d 30 (Ill. App. 3d 2007),] the defendant was arrested under section 11-501(a)(6) after the arresting officer noticed an odor of burnt cannabis on the defendant's breath and the defendant's pupils seemed dilated. However, the officer was precluded from testifying that he believed the dilated pupils meant that the defendant had consumed cannabis. The defendant told the officer that he had smoked cannabis the night before. There was nothing unusual about how the defendant walked, his speech was clear, and there was no drug paraphernalia or residue located inside the defendant's vehicle. The defendant was convicted of DUI, and the [court] reversed based on insufficient evidence, stating:

> "The statute does not criminalize having breath that smells like burnt cannabis. Furthermore, even though the trial court found the officer's testimony credible regarding defendant's admission of smoking cannabis the night before his arrest, the State put on no evidence that there would have been 'any amount' of the illegal drug in defendant's breath, urine, or blood at the time of defendant's arrest as a result of smoking cannabis the night before." ...

[*Id.*]

In comparison, in *People v. Briseno*, ... [799 N.E.2d 359 (Ill. App. 1st 2003)], also involving section 11-501(a)(6), the defendant told the arresting officer that he smoked cannabis "in his vehicle, just before driving it." The officer smelled cannabis on the defendant's breath, the defendant's motor skills were slower than average, and the defendant had trouble performing field sobriety tests. Under those circumstances, the [court] determined that there was sufficient evidence of DUI. ...

Unlike in *Briseno*, where the defendant's admission was that he smoked cannabis "in his vehicle" and "just before driving," where an odor of cannabis was on the defendant's breath, and where the defendant showed signs of impairment, here there was a lack of evidence that McPeak had cannabis in his breath, blood, or urine when he was driving. ... McPeak admitted to smoking "two hits" of cannabis "about an hour ago" but there was no evidence whether consuming that amount of cannabis would result in any cannabis being left in his breath, blood, or urine an hour later. Also, there was no evidence that McPeak was impaired and no evidence of any odor of cannabis on McPeak's breath, as opposed to his "person."

. . . We believe that evidence of the odor of cannabis on the breath of a defendant could provide circumstantial evidence that the defendant has cannabis in his breath. . . . [However], in McPeak's case there was no such evidence. The evidence was that Howell smelled burnt cannabis about McPeak's person, something that does not address whether McPeak had cannabis in his breath, blood, or urine at that time. Thus, based on the lack of evidence that there was cannabis in McPeak's breath, blood, or urine when he was driving, we reverse.

. . . [Likewise,] evidence of the presence of open alcohol (or, here, drug paraphernalia) may be circumstantial evidence that the defendant has recently consumed the substance at issue. . . . But here, there is no dispute that McPeak consumed cannabis about an hour before the stop. Instead, the issue is whether there was sufficient evidence that any of that cannabis remained in his breath, blood, or urine when he drove. Unlike each case cited by the State, which provided additional evidence of the presence of alcohol in the defendant's body while he was driving, notably evidence of impairment and the odor of alcohol on the defendant's breath, here the State provided no evidence that cannabis remained in McPeak's breath, blood, or urine while he was driving.

## Notes and Questions

1. Apart from offering the results of a blood or urine test, what else could the government have done to satisfy its evidentiary burden in *McPeak*?

2. Blood or urine tests can obviously help the government build its case, but must a driver submit to them? All states appear to have some form of implied consent law that allows the police to obtain a blood or urine sample from a driver. A driver's refusal to submit a sample can lead to the suspension of driving privileges and may give rise to an inference that the driver was intoxicated. Georgia law illustrates:

> Georgia law requires you to submit to state administered chemical tests of your blood, breath, urine, or other bodily substances for the purpose of determining if you are under the influence of alcohol or drugs. If you refuse this testing, your Georgia driver's license or privilege to drive on the highways of this state will be suspended for a minimum period of one year. Your refusal to submit to the required testing may be offered into evidence against you at trial.

Ga. Code Ann. §40-5-67.1 (West). However, the government's power to require such tests is not without limit. *See Birchfield v. North Dakota*, 136 S. Ct. 2160, 2185 (2016) ("Our prior opinions have referred approvingly to the general concept of implied-consent laws that impose civil penalties and evidentiary consequences on motorists who refuse to comply [with testing requirements]. . . . It is another matter, however, for a State not only to insist upon an intrusive blood test, but also to impose criminal penalties on the refusal to submit to such a test. There must be a limit to the consequences to which motorists may be deemed to have consented by virtue of a decision to drive on public roads.").

## 6. Other, Forgotten(?) Crimes

Lawful marijuana users might also be ensnared by a variety of less-well-known prohibitions that were added during the heyday of marijuana prohibition (e.g., bans on the transportation of marijuana), but that have not always been addressed in reforms. California's experience with such prohibitions following the passage of Proposition 215 is illustrative and provides lessons for other states considering their own marijuana law reforms. The following materials discuss the legal issues the state confronted in trying to reconcile its medical marijuana reforms with sundry pre-existing prohibitions implicating marijuana users.

### *California v. Young*
111 Cal. Rptr. 2d 726 (Cal. App. 3d 2001)

SIMS, J.

On November 6, 1999, California Highway Patrol Officer Rick LaGroue was on patrol . . . on State Route 36. . . . He noticed a green car with Oregon plates travelling in the opposite direction. The car abruptly went off the right shoulder of the road and then jerked back onto the road.

Officer LaGroue made a U-turn to investigate. By the time he caught up with the car, it had pulled over on the shoulder. Officer LaGroue went up to speak with the driver. Defendant was the sole occupant of the car. Defendant told the officer he lived in Paynes Creek[, California]. . . .

While the officer was conducting a routine records check on the defendant, the defendant took off his straw hat and dropped it on a small blue gift bag on the passenger side floorboard of his car. The officer asked defendant if he had any drugs in the car. Defendant told him he had marijuana in the blue gift bag he then handed it to the officer. The gift bag contained a baggie of marijuana marked "Awesome Shake Bud," a black tin container, some cigarette rolling papers, a rolling device, matches, and 16 burnt marijuana ends (roaches). The black tin contained a smoking pipe, 21 hand rolled marijuana cigarettes, another roach, and a small sandwich baggie containing marijuana marked "Maggie."

The officer searched the car and found another clear gallon-sized baggie containing marijuana marked "Rhonda Flower" with a "121" crossed out with a "113" next to it. The officer also found a second gallon-sized baggie containing seven smaller bags of marijuana marked with the words "Star-76." All told, the officer recovered 135.3 grams (about 4.74 ounces) of marijuana.

Defendant handed Officer LaGroue a document entitled "California Compassionate Use Act of 1996, Health & Safety Code § 11362.5, Physician's Statement." That document stated: "James W. Young . . . is under my medical care and supervision for treatment of the serious medical condition(s): Traumatic Arthritis Major Dep [*sic*] Recurrent. . . . I have discussed the medical risks and benefits of cannabis use with him/her as an appropriate treatment. I recommend and approve his/her use of cannabis with the following limitations/conditions: No more than ten plants." The document was signed by Dr. Tod H. Mikuriya.

[The state charged defendant with the transportation of marijuana, a felony drug trafficking offense under California law:

> Except as otherwise provided by this section or as authorized by law, every person who transports, imports into this state, sells, furnishes, administers, or gives away, or offers to transport, import into this state, sell, furnish, administer, or give away, or attempts to import into this state or transport any marijuana shall be punished by imprisonment . . . for a period of two, three or four years.

Cal. Pen. Code § 13360(a). Defendant claimed that he believed transportation of marijuana was lawful under the Compassionate Use Act. The trial court refused to instruct the jury on this claim.[8] He was convicted by a jury and sentenced to four years in prison. In upholding the jury's verdict, the appeals court discussed the ongoing validity of the state's ban on transportation following passed of the CUA.]

. . .

In 1996, the voters of this state enacted the Compassionate Use Act "[t]o ensure that seriously ill Californians have the right to obtain and use marijuana for medical purposes. . . ." (§ 11362.5, subd. (b)(1)(A).) Subdivision (d) of the Compassionate Use Act provides: "Section 11357, relating to the possession of marijuana, and Section 11358, relating to the cultivation of marijuana, shall not apply to a patient, or to a patient's primary caregiver, who possesses or cultivates marijuana for the personal medical purposes of the patient upon the written or oral recommendation or approval of a physician."

In *People v. Trippet*[, 66 Cal. Rptr. 2d 559 (Cal. App. 1st 1997), the court] examined whether the Compassionate Use Act provided the defendant with a defense to charges she transported marijuana. The court stated, "the statute specifically identifies only two penal provisions (out of five) from article 2 of division 10 of the [Health and Safety] Code, section 11357, dealing with possession, and section 11358, dealing with cultivation, etc. It would have been a simple matter for the drafters to have included a reference to section 11360 within subdivision (d) of section 11362.5. Thus, that subdivision could just as easily have read: 'Sections 11357, 11358 and 11360 shall not apply to a patient . . . who possesses, cultivates, or transports marijuana for the personal medical purposes of the patient' but it doesn't. We may not infer exceptions to our criminal laws when legislation spells out the chosen exceptions with such precision and specificity." The court went on, "Not only is there no evidence of any 'contrary' intent here, indeed the voters were expressly told by the Legislative Analyst that the proposed law 'does not change other legal prohibitions on marijuana. . . .' [Citation.] This symmetry between legal principle and evidence of the voters' intent compels the conclusion that, as a general matter, Proposition 215 does not exempt the transportation of marijuana allegedly used or to be used for medical purposes from prosecution under section 11360." . . . [*Id.*]

Despite the plain language of the statute, the *Trippet* court stated, "practical realities dictate that there be *some* leeway in applying section 11360 in cases where a Proposition 215 defense is asserted to companion charges. The results might otherwise be absurd. For example, the voters could not have intended that a dying cancer patient's 'primary caregiver' could be subject to criminal sanctions for carrying otherwise legally cultivated and possessed marijuana down a hallway to the patient's room. Our holding does not, therefore, mean that *all* transportation of marijuana is without any defense under the new law.

---

8. Author's note: Defendant styled his claim as a mistake of fact defense, but as the appeals court correctly noted, it amounted to a non-cognizable mistake of law defense. For a discussion of the difference between these two defenses, see Chapter 3, *supra*.

But so stating is a far cry from agreeing that transportation of two pounds of marijuana in a car by one who claims to suffer from migraine headaches is, even assuming the necessary medical approval, ipso facto permissible, as appellant would have it. The test should be whether the quantity transported and the method, timing and distance of the transportation are reasonably related to the patient's current medical needs. If so, we conclude there should and can be an implied defense to a section 11360 charge; otherwise, there is not." . . . [*Id.*] The *Trippet* court remanded the case so that the defendant could attempt to prove that he met this test. . . .

. . . The Compassionate Use Act does not provide a defense to the transportation of marijuana in the circumstances presented here. The statute on its face exempts only possession and cultivation from criminal sanctions for qualifying patients. . . . It does not exempt transportation as defined in section 11360. "Absent ambiguity, we presume that the voters intend the meaning apparent on the face of an initiative measure [citation] and the court may not add to the statute or rewrite it to conform to an assumed intent that is not apparent in its language." . . .

We need not decide whether we agree with the *Trippet* court that incidental transportation of marijuana from the garden to a qualifying patient may implicitly fall within the safe haven created by the Compassionate Use Act. This case does not involve the movement of marijuana from a plant legally cultivated in a garden to a seriously ill cancer patient but rather the transportation of marijuana in a vehicle. That kind of transportation is not made lawful by the Compassionate Use Act.

## Notes and Questions

1. Does the decision in *Young* make sense? Do you think the drafters of Proposition 215, or those who voted on the measure, ever considered the transportation issue? If not, do you think the court should try to "fix" the oversight by recognizing an exception to the plain language of section 13360? If so, what would that exception look like? If you think the court should not recognize any exception to the statute, would anything stop a prosecutor from charging a caregiver for carrying marijuana across a hallway to a seriously ill qualified patient (the scenario that bothered the *Trippet* court)? Do you think the prosecution in *Young* doubted that the defendant was a legitimate medical marijuana patient? If so, why not charge him with simple possession of the drug?

2. In 2003, the California legislature addressed the specific issue raised by *Young* in the Medical Marijuana Program Act (MMP). In relevant part, the MMP provides:

> (a) Subject to the requirements of this article, the individuals specified in subdivision (b) shall not be subject, on that sole basis, to criminal liability under Section 11357, 11358, 11359, 11360, 11366 [maintaining property for distributing or using marijuana], 11366.5 [renting property to store, manufacture, or distribute marijuana], or 11570 [nuisances]. . . .
> 
> (b) Subdivision (a) shall apply to all of the following:
> 
> (1) A qualified patient or a person with an identification card who transports or processes marijuana for his or her own personal medical use.
> 
> (2) A designated primary caregiver who transports, processes, administers, delivers, or gives away marijuana for medical purposes, in amounts not exceeding those established in subdivision (a) of Section 11362.77, only to the qualified patient of the primary

caregiver, or to the person with an identification card who has designated the individual as a primary caregiver.

Cal. Health & Safety Code § 11362.765 (2004).

However, the MMP did not specifically address *another* provision of California law, found in the state Vehicle Code, that prohibits the simple possession of not more than one ounce of marijuana while driving a motor vehicle. Cal. Vehicle Code § 23222. Nonetheless, in *City of Garden Grove v. Kha*, 157 Cal. App. 4th 355 (Cal. App. 2007), a different California appeals court found that the MMP shielded qualified patients from charges under section 23222, even though that provision was not specifically mentioned in the MMP:

> Although the CUA speaks only to the possession and cultivation of marijuana (§ 11362.5, subd. (d) [referencing §§ 11357 and 11358]), the MMP is more broadly intended to protect a qualified patient "who transports . . . marijuana for his or her own personal medical use." (§ 11362.765, subd. (b)(1) . . . [T]he record indicates Kha is such a patient. However, the only transportation statute referenced in the MMP is section 11360. . . .
>
> The MMP does not mention Vehicle Code section 23222, subdivision (b), the law with which Kha was charged. . . . Obviously, a violation of this provision also constitutes a violation of section 11360, subdivision (b). The Vehicle Code provision is simply a more specific statute covering the act of driving, as opposed to other methods of transportation.
>
> We are therefore impelled to the conclusion it would be illogical to find the MMP covers one provision, but not the other. Such a result would lead to the absurd consequence of permitting a defendant who drives with a large amount of marijuana to invoke the MMP . . . , while excluding drivers who transport the small amount covered by the Vehicle Code section. We cannot construe the law to permit such a clearly unintended and patently nonsensical result. . . .
>
> There is an additional, even more fundamental reason why qualified patients who are charged with violating Vehicle Code section 23222, subdivision (b) should be included within the ambit of the state's medical marijuana laws. As Kha notes, that section prohibits driving with marijuana, "[e]xcept as authorized by law." (Veh. Code, § 23222, subd. (b).) Since the MMP allows the transportation of medical marijuana, . . . the MMP effectively authorizes the conduct described in Vehicle Code section 23222, subdivision (b), when, as here, the conduct at issue is the transportation of a small amount of medical marijuana for personal use—conduct "authorized by law."

*Id.* at 375-76. Is it possible to reconcile *Young* and *Kha*? Why does the *Kha* court hold that the MMP covers an unmentioned provision (section 23222), while the *Young* court holds that the CUA does not (section 13360)?

3. How would you recommend that state lawmakers address the issue raised by *Young* and *Kha*? Is there a way to anticipate and address all of the possible legal charges that might be brought against individuals who possess and use marijuana when contemplating reforms? One Tennessee legislator has proposed medical marijuana legislation that would exempt qualified patients from prosecution for several specifically enumerated offenses, such as the possession of marijuana, as well as "[a]ny other criminal offense in which the possession, delivery, or production of marijuana or cannabis or the possession or delivery of drug paraphernalia is an element of the offense." S.B. 1248 § 68-1-2608 (2015). Would this provision have shielded the patients in *Young* and *Kha* from criminal charges? Do you think reform legislation should include such a catch-all provision? Why, why not?

## C. LEGAL PROTECTIONS

The states have adopted elaborate rules to delineate who may possess and use marijuana (discussed above). So what is the payoff to following the rules? Put differently, what rights do state laws confer on law-abiding marijuana possessors in criminal investigations? This is one of the most important, complicated, and (unfortunately) neglected questions surrounding state marijuana reforms.

This section begins to explore the legal protections states have created. It focuses on rights and remedies in the criminal justice system. Rights and remedies in the civil justice system, including rights against other private parties, such as employers and landlords, are covered in Part IV of the book.

Every state has adopted some legal protections for individuals who are permitted to possess and use marijuana. For example, the Arizona Medical Marijuana Act (AMMA) provides, in relevant part:

> A registered qualifying patient or registered designated caregiver is not subject to arrest, prosecution or penalty in any manner, or denial of any right or privilege, including any civil penalty or disciplinary action by a court or occupational or professional licensing board or bureau:1. For the registered qualifying patient's medical use of marijuana pursuant to this chapter, if the registered qualifying patient does not possess more than the allowable amount of marijuana. . . .

Ariz. Rev. Stat. Ann. § 36-2811 (B).

As the materials below will demonstrate, however, the rights of marijuana users vary considerably across the states, both in terms of their scope and the ease of successfully invoking them. The differences become evident when examining rights at each of the most important stages of a criminal investigation. Section C.1 discusses the protections states afford marijuana users against police investigations, focusing on searches. Section C.2 then discusses the protections states afford marijuana users against criminal prosecutions.

### 1. Search

> The right of the people to be secure in their persons, houses, papers, and effects, against unreasonable searches and seizures, shall not be violated, and no Warrants shall issue, but upon probable cause, supported by Oath or affirmation, and particularly describing the place to be searched, and the persons or things to be seized.

U.S. Const. amend. IV.

To understand how (if at all) state reforms shield marijuana users from police searches, it is necessary have at least a rudimentary understanding of the Fourth Amendment and probable cause. Under the Fourth Amendment to the United States Constitution, the police need probable cause to conduct a search. (The police also need probable cause to make an arrest, but to simplify discussion—and because it is the focus of the caselaw—this section will focus on probable cause to conduct a search.)

To satisfy the probable cause standard, the police must have enough facts to convince a reasonable person to believe there is evidence of a crime—or in some states, a civil offense (as discussed below)—in the area to be searched. Normally, the police must demonstrate probable cause to a judge before conducting the search—this is called the warrant requirement; however, the same probable cause standard applies regardless of whether a warrant is required.

The adequacy of the government's cause for conducting a given search has important ramifications for the use of any evidence that is discovered in course of the search. If the police had probable cause at the time of the search, they may use any evidence they discovered in a subsequent prosecution against the suspect. But if the police lacked probable cause to conduct the search in the first instance, any evidence they discovered will normally be considered tainted and thus inadmissible in a criminal prosecution. *Mapp v. Ohio*, 367 U.S. 643 (1961).

With this background in mind, consider the following Problem:

**Problem 4.15:** While driving his car, Benjamin is stopped for speeding. In the course of inspecting Benjamin's license and car registration, the officer detects the faint smell of unburnt marijuana emanating from Benjamin's car. Does the smell of the marijuana alone give the officer probable cause to search the car?

Not surprisingly, the answer to the question in the Problem will depend to a large extent on the scope of the state's marijuana prohibition. When marijuana is strictly prohibited—as it was until recently in all states—facts that suggest an individual possesses marijuana, such as the drug's distinctive odor, would normally be sufficient to establish probable cause to conduct a search of the area where the marijuana might be found. *See, e.g., Washington v. Olson*, 869 P.2d 110, 115 (Wash. App. 1994) ("When an officer who is trained and experienced in marijuana detection actually detects the odor of marijuana, this by itself provides sufficient evidence to constitute probable cause justifying a search."). But when some people are allowed to possess (grow, etc.) marijuana, it may change the probable cause calculus.

### a. Recreational Marijuana States

The change in the probable cause calculus is most dramatic and consistent in states that allow adults to possess and use marijuana recreationally. After all, if a state no longer bans the possession of marijuana (at least by adults), then the simple fact that an individual possesses marijuana, by itself, no longer reasonably suggests that the individual has violated the law. The following case discusses the issue.

### *Alaska v. Crocker*
97 P.3d 93 (Alaska Ct. App. 2004)

MANNHEIMER, J.:

Leo Richardson Crocker Jr. was charged with fourth-degree controlled substance misconduct after the police executed a search warrant at his home and found marijuana plants, harvested marijuana, and marijuana-growing equipment. The superior court later concluded that the search warrant for Crocker's home should not have been issued. The superior court therefore suppressed all of this evidence and dismissed the charges against Crocker. The State now appeals the superior court's decision.

Our main task in this appeal is to clarify what the State must prove in order to obtain a warrant to enter and search a person's home for evidence of marijuana possession. The issue arises because not all marijuana possession is illegal. In *Ravin v. State*, [537 P.2d 494 (Alaska 1975),] the Alaska Supreme Court held that the privacy provision of our state constitution (Article I, Section 22) protects an adult's right to possess a limited amount of marijuana in their home for personal use.[9] And recently, in *Noy v. State*, [83 P.3d 538 (Alaska App. 2003), *on rehearing*, 83 P.3d 545 (Alaska App. 2003),] we held (based on *Ravin*) that Alaska's marijuana statutes must be construed to allow possession by adults of any amount less than four ounces of marijuana in the home for personal use.

For the reasons explained in this opinion, we hold that a judicial officer should not issue a warrant to search a person's home for evidence of marijuana possession unless the State's warrant application establishes probable cause to believe that the person's possession of marijuana exceeds the scope of the possession that is constitutionally protected under *Ravin*. And, because the State's warrant application in Crocker's case fails to meet this test, we conclude that the superior court properly suppressed the evidence against Crocker. . . .

Under . . . [Alaska Stat. 12.35.020], a judicial officer is empowered to issue a warrant authorizing the police to enter a premises and search for specified property . . . [only if the government can show] probable cause to believe that the property being sought is connected in one of these ways to the commission (or intended commission) of a crime. . . .

Not all marijuana possession is a crime in Alaska. Under *Ravin* and *Noy*, an adult may possess any amount of marijuana less than four ounces in their home, if their possession is for personal use. Thus, it would seem that a court should not issue a search warrant based on an allegation of marijuana possession unless the State establishes probable cause to believe that the type of marijuana possession at issue in the case is something other than the type of possession protected under *Ravin*. (For instance, a court might properly issue a search warrant if the State establishes probable cause to believe that the marijuana is possessed for commercial purposes, or that the amount of marijuana is four ounces or more.)

But the State disputes this conclusion. . . . [T]he State argues that *Ravin* . . . established an affirmative defense—the defense of personal use—that can be raised by people who are charged with marijuana possession. Based on this interpretation of *Ravin*, the State argues that all possession of marijuana continues to be crime in Alaska—and, thus, a judicial officer can lawfully issue a search warrant for evidence of marijuana possession so long as the State establishes probable cause to believe that the premises to be searched contains *any* marijuana. . . .

We addressed and rejected this same argument in our opinion on rehearing in *Noy*:

> *Ravin* did not create an affirmative defense that defendants might raise, on a case-by-case basis, when they were prosecuted for possessing marijuana in their home for personal use. . . . T]he Alaska Supreme Court has repeatedly and consistently characterized the *Ravin* decision as announcing a constitutional limitation on the government's authority to enact legislation prohibiting the possession of marijuana in the privacy of one's home.

---

9. Author's note: The *Ravin* decision is discussed in Chapters 5 and 6.

Accordingly, we reject the State's suggestion that *Ravin* left Alaska's marijuana statutes intact but created an affirmative defense to be litigated in each individual case.

[83 P.3d at 547-48.] . . .

The State further argues that if search warrant applications must establish probable cause to believe that the marijuana possession at issue in that case falls outside of the marijuana possession protected by *Ravin*, this would be tantamount to "a presumption that all marijuana possessed in a home is for purely personal use." But this "presumption" of non-criminality is built into the search and seizure clause of the Alaska Constitution and the statutory law governing the issuance of search warrants.

Before a search warrant can lawfully issue, the government must establish probable cause to believe that the evidence being sought is connected to a crime. This same rule governs search warrants for all controlled substances, not just marijuana.

Every day, people obtain controlled substances legally through a doctor's prescription. For instance, several prescription painkillers contain codeine, which is a Schedule IA controlled substance [under Alaska law]. Our state constitution protects people from government intrusion into their homes unless the government affirmatively establishes a valid reason for the intrusion. Thus, even though the police may have firm information that a person currently possesses codeine in their home, a judicial officer should not issue a warrant that authorizes the police to enter the person's home and search the person's cupboards and drawers for evidence of this codeine possession unless the police also present the magistrate with some affirmative reason to believe that the codeine was obtained illegally or that (having been obtained lawfully) it is being distributed illegally.

The same rule applies to marijuana possession. . . . [N]o search warrant can issue for evidence of marijuana possession unless the State affirmatively establishes probable cause to believe that the type of marijuana possession at issue in that case is something other than the type of possession protected under *Ravin*.

As the State correctly points out, the question is one of probable cause, not ultimate proof. Thus, the search warrant application need not negate every other reasonable, exculpatory explanation of the observed facts. But the search warrant application can not rely solely on the fact that someone is in possession of marijuana. The warrant application must provide an affirmative reason to conclude that the possession is illegal or that the marijuana otherwise constitutes evidence of a crime.

. . .

Under the law advocated by the State . . . (that is, if possession of any amount of marijuana in one's home constituted adequate grounds for the issuance of a search warrant), Alaska citizens would have the constitutional right to possess marijuana for personal use in their homes, but they would exercise this right at their peril—because their possession of marijuana would subject them to thorough-going police searches of their homes. If this were the law, the Alaska Constitution's protection of the right of privacy in one's home—the cornerstone of the *Ravin* decision—would be eviscerated. . . .

. . .

. . . [The warrant application alleged that when the officers launched their investigation on the basis of an anonymous tip, they] smelled "a strong odor of growing marijuana" when they stood at [Crocker's] front door. . . .

The State asserts that the strength of the smell (including the fact that the officers could detect the odor while standing outside the house) tends to show that the amount of marijuana inside the house must have exceeded the amount protected by *Ravin* and *Noy*. But the search warrant application contains no assertion that the strength of the smell gave the officers any indication of the amount of marijuana that might be growing in the house.

Moreover, we can not simply assume that there is a direct proportionality between the strength of the odor and the amount of marijuana giving rise to that odor. . . .

There may or may not be a correlation between the strength of the odor of growing marijuana and the amount of marijuana being grown. But the search warrant application in the present case makes no assertion concerning such a potential correlation, and we will not assume such a correlation in the absence of evidence.

Moreover, even if such a correlation exists, the officer in this case merely asserted that the odor was "strong." There was nothing to indicate whether an odor of this unexplained degree of strength provided a reasonable basis for concluding that the amount of marijuana in the house exceeded the amount protected under *Ravin* and *Noy*.

The State also argues that the amount of electricity usage at the . . . residence provided probable cause to believe that the amount of marijuana inside the house exceeded the amount of marijuana protected under *Ravin* and *Noy*.

After receiving the tip from their "confidential source" that marijuana was being grown at the . . . residence, the police—employing unspecified means—conducted a "check" of the utility usage at the residence. They discovered that, over the preceding thirteen months, the average electricity usage at [the] home was 56.6 kilowatt hours per day. The officer who applied for the search warrant asserted that, "[b]ased on [his] training and experience, the [electricity] consumption . . . [was] higher than average for a home of [its] size."

One of the boilerplate paragraphs of the search warrant application contains an assertion that, according to the Homer Electric Association, "prospective customers should expect an average monthly [electricity] consumption of approximately 22 [kilowatt-hours] per day with natural gas heating, and 27 to 31 [kilowatt-hours] per day with electric heat." However, the search warrant application does not describe [Crocker's] house (other than identifying its address). The magistrate had no way of knowing whether [the] house was of average size or was smaller or larger than average. Thus, the magistrate had no way of knowing whether one would reasonably expect [Crocker's] electricity usage to fall within, below, or above the average range for all of the Homer Electric Association's customers.

Indeed, when the officer who applied for the search warrant made his assertion about the "higher than average" electricity usage at [the] residence, he did not rely on the estimate given by the Homer Electric Association. Rather, the officer relied on his "training and experience." But the officer did not explain what training or experience he might have received that would allow him to offer an informed opinion concerning the typical or average electricity usage for homes of various sizes.

And although the officer asserted that the electricity usage at [Crocker's] home was "higher than average" for a house its size, the officer did not say how much higher than average this usage was. When an "average" amount of electricity usage has been identified for a particular type or size of house, this means that many (conceivably, up to half) of those houses will have electricity usage that is *higher* than average. Thus, even if we credit the officer's assertion that the . . . residence was using more electricity than average for a house its size, this unelaborated assertion did not significantly bolster the assertion that

[Crocker's] house was the site of marijuana cultivation. Much less did this "higher than average" electricity usage establish probable cause to believe that the amount of marijuana being cultivated in the house exceeded the amount protected under *Ravin* and *Noy*.

For these reasons, . . . the search warrant should not have been issued, and the superior court correctly suppressed the evidence obtained under the authority of that warrant.

## Notes and Questions

1. Do you agree with the *Crocker* decision? Why, why not?
2. What could the police have done to establish probable cause to conduct a lawful search of Crocker's residence?

### b. Decriminalization States

The probable cause analysis is somewhat more complicated in states that have decriminalized but not legalized the simple possession of marijuana. In these states, marijuana is still contraband and the possession of it remains a *civil* offense. But not all states grant the police authority to conduct searches based on suspicion that someone has committed a civil offense, as the following cases demonstrate.

### *Oregon v. Smalley*
225 P.3d 884 (Or. App. 2009)

SCHUMAN, J.:

Medford Police Officer Jewell conducted a lawful traffic stop of a pickup truck in which defendant was a passenger. During the course of that stop, Jewell obtained the driver's consent to search the truck. Upon opening the driver's-side door, Jewell noticed the odor of marijuana. When he lifted the seat forward, the odor became stronger. Behind the seat, he found a backpack. As he got closer to the backpack, the odor of marijuana became still stronger; according to his testimony, it was "obvious" to him that the backpack contained "a large amount of marijuana." He opened the backpack, and, indeed, it contained a large amount of marijuana—approximately 62 ounces. After the driver denied owning the backpack, defendant admitted that it was his.

Defendant was charged with unlawful manufacture of marijuana, ORS 475.856, and unlawful possession of marijuana, ORS 475.864. Before trial, he moved to suppress the evidence obtained as a result of the warrantless search of his backpack. . . . The trial court . . . granted defendant's motion [on the grounds that the police had failed to obtain a warrant], and ordered that the evidence be suppressed. . . .

On appeal, the state . . . [argued] that the search was lawful under the automobile exception [to the warrant requirement]. Defendant argues, in response, that "the state failed to demonstrate . . . that [the officer] had probable cause to believe that evidence of a *criminal offense* (as opposed to a violation) would be found." (Emphasis in original.) According to defendant, because possession of less than one ounce of marijuana is not a criminal offense, *see* ORS 475.864(3), the state needed to prove that the officer had probable cause to believe that defendant's backpack contained more than that amount, which, defendant asserts, it failed to do. . . .

We conclude that the court erred in suppressing the evidence.

"[W]arrantless . . . searches . . . are *per se* unreasonable unless falling within one of the few specifically established and well-delineated exceptions to the warrant requirement." . . . One such exception is the automobile exception, under which

> "probable cause to believe that a lawfully stopped automobile which was mobile at the time of the stop contains contraband or crime evidence justifies an immediate warrantless search of the entire automobile for the object of the search, despite the absence of any additional exigent circumstances."

[*Oregon v. Brown*, 721 P.2d 1357 (Or. 1986).] . . .

In those circumstances, the police may search any area of the vehicle or any container within the vehicle in which they have probable cause to believe that the contraband or crime evidence may be found. . . . The state need not articulate particular circumstances demonstrating the impracticality of obtaining a warrant; rather, exigency is presumed. . . .

[In this case], the automobile exception applied. . . . [T]o establish that exception, the state must show (1) that the truck was mobile at the time that Jewell stopped it and (2) that probable cause existed for the search of the backpack—that is, that Jewell subjectively and reasonably believed that defendant's backpack contained contraband or crime evidence. Defendant does not dispute that the truck was mobile at the time that it was stopped by police. And Jewell's testimony—that he "noticed the odor of marijuana"; that the odor "[got] stronger" as he got closer to the backpack; that it was "obvious to [him] that there[ ] [was] a large amount of marijuana in [it]" because the odor "permeat[ed] out of [it]"; that the odor had been "pretty strong," "probably about a six or seven" on a scale of one to 10; and that, based on his training and experience, which included "the opportunity to seize various amounts of marijuana," he had been able to "tell that there was a significant amount"—is more than sufficient to establish that he believed that defendant's backpack would contain at least some amount of contraband and that his belief was reasonable.

According to defendant, that objectively reasonable belief was not enough; rather, the officer had to believe that the backpack contained more than an ounce of marijuana, because possessing an amount smaller than that is not a crime. Without probable cause to believe that evidence of a *crime* would be found, no search was justified. . . .

According to defendant, . . . first, the automobile exception requires probable cause to believe that a crime, not a mere violation, has occurred, and second, that a strong odor cannot by itself form the basis for an objectively reasonable belief that an automobile contains more than an ounce of marijuana. Additional evidence is necessary, defendant contends, and, in the present case, there is nothing beyond odor.

We reject defendant's argument. . . . [T]his court has never directly confronted the question whether the automobile exception encompasses situations in which an officer has probable cause to believe a violation, as opposed to a crime, has occurred. . . . However, the [Oregon] Supreme Court in [Oregon v.] *Brown* specified that "probable cause to believe that a lawfully stopped automobile which was mobile at the time of the stop contains *contraband or crime evidence* justifies an immediate warrantless search of the entire automobile." . . . 721 P.2d 1357 [(Or. 1986)] (emphasis added). By using the phrase, "contraband or crime evidence," the court signaled its understanding that the two things were not identical and that probable cause to believe in the presence of either could justify an automobile search. . . .

Defendant does not argue that marijuana becomes contraband only in quantities of more than an ounce, and we know of no authority for that proposition. Indeed, both the legal and common definitions of "contraband" indicate that the term encompasses anything that the law prohibits possessing. *Black's Law Dictionary* defines "contraband" as "[g]oods that are unlawful to import, export, produce, or possess." *Id.* at 365 (9th ed. 2009); *see also Webster's Third New Int'l Dictionary* 494 (unabridged ed. 2002) ("goods or merchandise the importation, exportation, or sometimes possession of which is forbidden"). Marijuana falls within these definitions regardless of its quantity.

---

In the next case, the Massachusetts Supreme Judicial Court breaks with *Smalley* and holds that, following decriminalization of simple possession of the drug, the odor of marijuana, standing alone, no longer supplies probable cause to conduct a search.

The case arose when police spotted a car parked in front of a fire hydrant in a high-crime Boston neighborhood. While approaching the car, the officers detected the "faint odor" of burnt marijuana coming from inside. Based on the "odor of marijuana and just the way they were acting," the police ordered the driver and his passenger, defendant Benjamin Cruz, to exit the vehicle. As the defendant got out of the car, one of the officers asked him if he had "anything on his person," to which defendant replied that he had "a little rock for myself." The officer reached into defendant's pocket and seized four grams of crack cocaine.

The defendant was charged with several offenses related to the crack cocaine, including possession of the drug in a school zone. Prior to trial, however, he moved to suppress the crack cocaine evidence, and the judge granted his motion. The judge found that the police lacked a valid reason for ordering the defendant to exit the vehicle in the first instance. The state appealed, claiming, inter alia, that the police had probable cause to search the car, and that the exit order was necessary to facilitate that search. (The state (unsuccessfully) offered other grounds for issuing the exit order, but because they fall beyond the scope of this book, the court's discussion of them is excluded here.)

## *Massachusetts v. Cruz*
945 N.E.2d 899 (Mass. 2011)

IRELAND, J.:

Although we have held in the past that the odor of marijuana alone provides probable cause to believe criminal activity is underway, we now reconsider our jurisprudence in light of the change to our laws. On November 4, 2008, voters approved [an initiative, later codified as] . . . "An Act establishing a sensible State marihuana policy." This act changed the status of the possession of one ounce or less of marijuana from a criminal to a civil offense. It became effective on December 4, 2008. Our analysis must give effect to the clear intent of the people of the Commonwealth in accord with art. 14 of the Massachusetts Declaration of Rights and the Fourth Amendment to the United States Constitution. . . .

. . .

... We have held that the odor of burnt marijuana is sufficient to believe that there is contraband in the car. ... As the Commonwealth appears to argue, it follows then, that if the police have probable cause to believe that contraband, i.e., any amount of marijuana, exists in the car, the police may then validly conduct a warrantless search [pursuant to the automobile exception to the warrant requirement] (and order any passengers out of the car to facilitate that search).

At least one court has adopted this reasoning. In *State v. Smalley*, 233 Or. App. 263, 265, 270-71, 225 P.3d 844 (2010), the Court of Appeals of Oregon determined that, despite the decriminalization of marijuana in small amounts for personal use, when an officer has probable cause, based on the odor of burnt marijuana, to believe that a validly stopped automobile contains any quantity of marijuana, a warrantless search is justified based on the likely presence of contraband. ...

We are not persuaded by this reasoning. The standard used to determine the validity of a warrantless search is the same as that used by a magistrate considering the application for a search warrant. ... In Massachusetts, search warrants are issued by magistrates "authorized to issue [them] in criminal cases." G.L. c. 276, § 2B. Moreover, this court concluded more than 150 years ago:

> "Search warrants were ... confined to cases of public prosecutions, *instituted and pursued for the suppression of crime or the detection and punishment of criminals*. ... The principles upon which the legality of such warrants could be defended, and the use and purpose to which, by the common law, they were restricted, were well known to the framers of our constitution. ... Having this knowledge, it cannot be doubted that by the adoption of the 14th article of the Declaration of Rights it was intended strictly and carefully to limit, restrain and regulate the granting and issuing of warrants of that character to the general class of cases, in and to the furtherance of the objects of which they had before been recognized and allowed as justifiable and lawful processes, and certainly not so to vary, extend and enlarge the purposes for and occasions on which they might be used. ..." (Emphasis added.)

*Robinson v. Richardson*, 79 Mass. 454, 13 Gray 454, 456-57 (1859).

Here, no facts were articulated to support probable cause to believe that a *criminal* amount of contraband was present in the car.[10] We conclude, therefore, that in this set of circumstances a magistrate would not, and could not, issue a search warrant.[31] ...

---

10. Author's note: In another portion of the decision, the court had already ruled that:

> The stop's location [in a high-crime neighborhood], ... cannot justify reasonable suspicion to believe a person is involved in criminal activity. ... Further, the officers knew that the defendant lived on ... the very street on which the encounter occurred. Surely the officers could not find it suspicious that the defendant was spending time on his own street. Moreover, the defendant's nervous demeanor cannot be the grounding factor on which to base suspicion of criminal activity. ... It is common, and not necessarily indicative of criminality, to appear nervous during even a mundane encounter with police, even though, as a passenger, the consequence of receiving a citation is not personal. Here, ... a myriad number of innocent reasons other than hiding criminal contraband may more readily explain why a nineteen year old man would appear nervous while being addressed by a police officer.

945 N.E.2d at 904.

31. We note that in other jurisdictions a search warrant could, potentially, issue. See *United States v. Pugh*, 223 F. Supp. 2d 325, 330 (D. Me. 2002), citing *State v. Barclay*, 398 A.2d 794, 797 (Me. 1979) ("Under Maine law, marijuana, even in an amount that would only give rise to a civil violation, can be the legitimate

Because the standard for obtaining a search warrant to search the car could not be met, we conclude that it was unreasonable for the police to order the defendant out of the car in order to facilitate a warrantless search of the car for criminal contraband under the automobile exception.

Our conclusion is in accord with our oft-repeated principle of proportionality. . . . In these circumstances, without probable cause that a crime is being committed, we cannot condone such an intrusive measure as a warrantless search. . . . It also is supported by the intent of the ballot initiative, which was, in part, to free up the police for more serious criminal pursuits than the civil infraction of low-quantity marijuana possession. . . . It is unreasonable for the police to spend time conducting warrantless searches for contraband when no specific facts suggest criminality.

. . . Because the exit order issued to the defendant cannot be justified on [the grounds discussed above], the . . . seizure of the crack cocaine . . . must be suppressed [under the fruit of the poisonous tree doctrine]. . . .

## Notes and Questions

1. Why do the Oregon and Massachusetts courts disagree about the impact that decriminalization has on the probable cause inquiry? Do you think the police should be allowed to search an individual based on a reasonable belief that the individual has committed a civil offense, as opposed to a crime?

2. In *Cruz*, even if the smell of burnt marijuana did not give the police probable cause to believe the defendant possessed criminal quantities of marijuana, could it have given them probable cause to believe that defendant was engaged in *another* crime—namely, driving under the influence of marijuana? In an omitted portion of the opinion excerpted above, the *Cruz* majority rejected this argument, noting that the officers who conducted the search "could not recall whether the engine was running" and the record did not reveal "how long the vehicle had been parked." *Cruz*, 945 N.E.2d at 908, n.17. Under these circumstances, the court concluded that the police did not have probable cause to believe that the driver—let alone the defendant, who was a passenger in the car—had committed a DUI offense at the time the officers approached the vehicle. *Id.*

3. At the time both *Smalley* and *Cruz* were decided, the possession of more than one ounce of marijuana was still considered a criminal offense in both Oregon and Massachusetts. Although the *Smalley* court based its decision on other grounds, it noted the state's alternative argument that the odor of marijuana emanating from the defendant's backpack was so strong that it allowed Officer Jewell to reasonably believe the defendant possessed a criminal quantity of marijuana (i.e., more than one ounce). The *Cruz* and *Crocker* courts noted the argument as well, but both found it unnecessary to address. What do you think about this argument? In other words, do you think it is reasonable to estimate the quantity of marijuana to be found in an area based on the strength of the smell of the drug?

---

object of a search warrant. . . ."). In contrast, the Commonwealth has cited no law in Massachusetts permitting a search warrant to issue solely based on probable cause that a civil violation has been committed.

After *Cruz* was decided, the Massachusetts Supreme Judicial Court addressed and rejected the claim that the police can normally make reliable inferences about quantity based on smell:

> Massachusetts cases since 2008 . . . have recognized the dubious value of judgments about the occurrence of criminal activity based on the smell of burnt marijuana alone, given that such a smell points only to the presence of some marijuana, not necessarily a criminal amount. . . . . Although the odor of unburnt, rather than burnt, marijuana could be more consistent with the presence of larger quantities, . . . it does not follow that such an odor reliably predicts the presence of a criminal amount of the substance, that is, more than one ounce, as would be necessary to constitute probable cause.
>
> The officers in this case detected what they described as a "strong" or "very strong" smell of unburnt marijuana. However, such characterizations of odors as strong or weak are inherently subjective; what one person believes to be a powerful scent may fail to register as potently for another. See Doty, Wudarski, Marshall, & Hastings, Marijuana Odor Perception: Studies Modeled from Probable Cause Cases, 28 Law & Hum. Behav. 223, 232 (2004) (identifying traits such as gender and age that may influence ability to smell). Moreover, the strength of the odor perceived likely will depend on a range of other factors, such as ambient temperature, the presence of other fragrant substances, and the pungency of the specific strain of marijuana present. . . . [*Id.* at 231-32]. As a subjective and variable measure, the strength of a smell is thus at best a dubious means for reliably detecting the presence of a criminal amount of marijuana.
>
> Although it is possible that training may overcome the deficiencies inherent in smell as a gauge of the weight of marijuana present, see . . . [*id.* at 232], there is no evidence that the officers here had undergone specialized training that, if effective, would allow them reliably to discern, by odor, not only the presence and identity of a controlled substance, but also its weight. Indeed, in somewhat related cases that turn on the sense of smell, such as those involving canine alerts and canine tracking evidence, we have required that a sufficient foundation be laid as to the canine's ability before the evidence may be admitted at trial.
>
> In sum, we are not confident, at least on this record, that a human nose can discern reliably the presence of a criminal amount of marijuana, as distinct from an amount subject only to a civil fine. In the absence of reliability, "a neutral magistrate would not issue a search warrant, and therefore a warrantless search is not justified based solely on the smell of marijuana," whether burnt or unburnt.

*Massachusetts v. Overmyer*, 11 N.E.3d 1054, 1058-60 (Mass. 2014). Do you agree with the *Overmyer* court? Can you imagine any set of facts under which a police officer might reasonably believe that a suspect possesses more than one ounce of marijuana, based solely on the smell of the drug?

4. The *Overmyer* court based its decision, in part, on a fascinating study of human ability to detect the odor of marijuana. *See* Richard L. Doty et al., *Marijuana Odor Perception: Studies Modeled from Probable Cause Cases*, 28 Law & Human Behavior 223 (2004). The authors of the study conducted a set of experiments designed to test scientifically the sniff-based evidence commonly used to make probable cause determinations in marijuana cases. In one of the experiments (Experiment 1) that is most relevant here, the authors placed a garbage bag containing either marijuana or newspapers into the trunk of a car, then asked each of nine subjects to sniff the interior of the car and indicate whether they smelled marijuana. The authors repeated this trial

twelve times for each subject, alternating between the bag containing marijuana and the control. Even though they were familiar with the smell of marijuana, the subjects could not accurately detect its presence in the trunk of the car. Indeed, the authors report that "the number of false positives (9.26%; 5 of 54 trials) was essentially the same as the number of correct positives (12.96%; 7 of 54 trials)," and that there was no statistically meaningful difference between the two. *Id.* at 226. Does the Doty et al. study support the result in *Overmyer*? Might it have even broader ramifications? For example, might the study be used to challenge the widely held notion that the smell of marijuana, standing alone, is enough to establish probable cause in prohibition regimes?

### c. Medical Marijuana States

Medical marijuana laws are typically much narrower in scope than recreational marijuana laws, in the sense they allow a comparatively small subset of the state's population to possess and use marijuana. In medical marijuana states, does the fact that someone possesses marijuana, standing alone, still provide probable cause to believe that a crime has been committed? The majority and dissenting opinions in *Washington v. Fry* highlight the competing positions states have taken on the issue. (The *Fry* court's decision regarding qualifying conditions was excerpted above in Section A.1.a.)

## *Washington v. Fry*
228 P.3d 1 (Wash. 2010)

JOHNSON, J.:

On December 20, 2004, Stevens County Sheriff Sergeant Dan Anderson and Deputy Bill Bitton (officers) went to the residence of Jason and Tina Fry. The officers had received information there was a marijuana growing operation there.

The officers walked up to the front porch and smelled the scent of burning marijuana. Jason Fry opened the door, at which time the officers noticed a much stronger odor of marijuana. Fry told the officers he had a legal prescription for marijuana and told the officers to leave absent a search warrant. Tina Fry gave the officers documents entitled "medical marijuana authorization." The authorization listed Fry's qualifying condition as "severe anxiety, rage, & depression related to childhood." . . .

The officers obtained a telephonic search warrant and found several containers with marijuana, growing marijuana plants, growing equipment, paraphernalia, and scales in the Frys' home. The marijuana was found to weigh 911 grams (more than 2 pounds).

Prior to trial, Fry made a motion to suppress the evidence seized by the officers pursuant to the search warrant. The motion also indicated Fry would assert the affirmative defense of medical marijuana authorization (compassionate use defense) pursuant to former RCW 69.51A.040 (1999).

After hearing arguments, the superior court judge denied Fry's motion to suppress. The court concluded the officers demonstrated probable cause to search the Frys' home based on the strong odor of marijuana and other facts described in the telephonic affidavit. The court also concluded that Fry did not qualify for the compassionate use defense because he did not have a qualifying condition.[1]

After a stipulated facts bench trial, Fry was convicted of possession of more than 40 grams of marijuana. The court sentenced him to 30 days of total confinement, converted to 240 hours of community service. [This appeal followed.] . . .

Fry argues the marijuana evidence seized by the officers should have been suppressed. . . .

. . .

There is no contention that the facts, including the information and smell of marijuana, do not support a finding of probable cause to search the Frys' residence. However, Fry contends the probable cause was negated once he produced the authorization. Although there was a later dispute over the validity of the authorization, there is no indication in the record that the officers or the magistrate questioned the validity at the time the search warrant was issued. Nevertheless, the officers' search and arrest were supported by probable cause, and a claimed authorization form does not negate probable cause. . . .

By passing Initiative 692 (I-692), the people of Washington intended that

> [q]ualifying patients with terminal or debilitating illnesses who, in the judgment of their physicians, would benefit from the medical use of marijuana, shall not be found guilty of a crime under state law for their possession and limited use of marijuana.

Former RCW 69.51A.005 (1999). Additionally,

> [i]f *charged with a violation* of state law relating to marijuana, any qualifying patient who is engaged in the medical use of marijuana, or any designated primary caregiver who assists a qualifying patient in the medical use of marijuana, *will be deemed to have established an affirmative defense to such charges* by proof of his or her compliance with the requirements provided in this chapter. Any person meeting the requirements appropriate to his or her status under this chapter shall be considered to have engaged in activities permitted by this chapter and shall not be penalized in any manner, or denied any right or privilege, for such actions.

Former RCW 69.51A.040(1) (emphasis added). Based on I-692 and the derivative statute, we have recognized that Washington voters created a compassionate use defense against marijuana charges. . . . An affirmative defense admits the defendant committed a criminal act but pleads an excuse for doing so. . . . The defendant must prove an affirmative defense by a preponderance of the evidence. . . . An affirmative defense does not negate any elements of the charged crime. . . .

Possession of marijuana, even in small amounts, is still a crime in the state of Washington. *See* RCW 69.50.4014. A police officer would have probable cause to believe Fry committed a crime when the officer smelled marijuana emanating from the Frys' residence. Fry presented the officer with documentation purporting to authorize his use of marijuana. Nevertheless, the authorization only created a potential affirmative defense that would excuse the criminal act. The authorization does not, however, result in making the act of possessing and using marijuana noncriminal or negate any elements

---

1. Because the court found Fry was not a "qualifying patient," it declined to reach the State's other arguments. The State also argued Fry would not qualify because the amount of marijuana in his possession, over 2 pounds, exceeded the 60-day supply the statute allowed. . . .

of the charged offense. Therefore, based on the information of a marijuana growing operation and the strong odor of marijuana when the officers approached the Frys' home, a reasonable inference was established that criminal activity was taking place in the Frys' residence. Therefore, the officers had probable cause and the search warrant was properly obtained.

This conclusion is supported by *McBride v. Walla Walla County*, . . . 990 P.2d 967 (Wash. App. 1999). In *McBride*, a police officer arrested McBride for hitting his son. The officer had substantial facts and information to indicate McBride acted in self-defense. Nevertheless, the officer arrested McBride as mandated by the domestic violence section in former RCW 10.31.100(2)(b) (1996).

Like the compassionate use defense, self-defense is an affirmative defense. . . . McBride argued it was the officer's duty to evaluate the self-defense claim and determine whether it negated the existence of probable cause to arrest him. . . . The court concluded, "[t]he officer is not judge or jury; he does not decide if the legal standard for self-defense is met." *Id.* . . . The court determined the affirmative defense "did not vitiate probable cause." *Id.*

Fry attempts to distinguish *McBride*. He notes that the officers in that case were required to arrest an individual involved in a domestic violence dispute. There was no statutory requirement compelling the officers to search Fry's residence and seize the marijuana. However, probable cause is not created or negated by statutory mandate to search or arrest (or lack thereof). In most cases, including the one before us, officers have discretion as to whether they will conduct a search or make an arrest once they have probable cause. However, this discretion has no impact on whether probable cause exists.

Under the Act, a person "charged with a violation of state law relating to marijuana . . . will be deemed to have established an affirmative defense to such charges by proof of his or her compliance with the requirements provided in this chapter." Former RCW 69.51A.040(1). One of the requirements is that a qualifying patient "[p]resent his or her valid documentation to any law enforcement official who questions the patient regarding his or her medical use of marijuana" (presentment requirement). Former RCW 69.51A.040(2)(c).

. . . It is argued that if the presentment requirement is to have meaning, presentation of a patient's authorization must establish lawful possession of marijuana, and thereby the absence of criminal activity that would provide probable cause for a search or seizure.

The presentment requirement must be read in context. . . . One of the other requirements [of the state's medical marijuana law] mandates that . . . [an] individual "[p]ossess no more marijuana than is necessary for the patient's personal, medical use, not exceeding the amount necessary for a sixty-day supply." Former RCW 69.51A.040(2)(b). It would be impossible to ascertain whether an individual possesses an excessive amount of marijuana without a search.

Instead, the presentment requirement facilitates an officer's decision of whether to use his or her discretion and seize the marijuana and/or arrest the possessor. Once the officer has searched the individual and established that the individual is possessing marijuana in compliance with the Act (i.e., appropriate documentation, limited supply, etc.) the officer would then have sufficient facts to determine whether an arrest is warranted. This view is supported by the 2007 amendment to RCW 69.51A.040. The current version reads, "[i]f a law enforcement officer determines that marijuana is being possessed lawfully under the medical marijuana law, the officer may document the amount of marijuana, take a representative sample that is large enough to test, but not seize the marijuana." RCW 69.51A.040(1). It is difficult to imagine how a law enforcement officer, having been presented with a medical marijuana authorization, would be able to determine that the marijuana is otherwise being lawfully possessed (and take a sample) without some kind of search.

I-692 did not legalize marijuana, but rather provided an authorized user with an affirmative defense if the user shows compliance with the requirements for medical marijuana possession. *See* former RCW 69.51A.005, .040. As an affirmative defense, the compassionate use defense does not eliminate probable cause where a trained officer detects the odor of marijuana. A doctor's authorization does not indicate that the presenter is totally complying with the Act; e.g., the amounts may be excessive. An affirmative defense does not per se legalize an activity and does not negate probable cause that a crime has been committed. We therefore affirm the Court of Appeals on this issue.

SANDERS, J., dissenting:

Former RCW 69.51A.040(1) (1999) provides, "Any person meeting the requirements appropriate to his or her status under this chapter shall be considered to have engaged in activities permitted by this chapter and *shall not be penalized in any manner, or denied any right or privilege, for such actions.*" (Emphasis added.) Under our state constitution we have a right to be free from searches and other invasions of privacy, absent authority of law. Const. art. I, § 7. This authority of law comes in the form of a warrant, which requires probable cause to believe a person is involved in criminal activity and a search will uncover evidence of that criminal activity. . . .

Here, police officers smelled burnt marijuana at Jason Fry's residence and therefore initially had probable cause to believe Fry was involved in *criminal* activity stemming from the possession of marijuana.[1] However, Fry produced documentation to the officers demonstrating he met the requirements of former RCW 69.51A.040(2) permitting him *legally* to possess marijuana. This documentation alleviated any probable cause to believe Fry was engaged in *criminal* activity based upon the smell of burnt marijuana. As the lead opinion recognizes, there is no indication the officers questioned the validity of the documentation at the time the search warrant was issued. . . . Nevertheless the officers conducted the search, invading Fry's home and his private affairs in violation of article I, section 7 and former RCW 69.51A.040(1).

The lead opinion reads the Washington state medical use of marijuana act to provide only an affirmative defense. Majority at 4 (quoting RCW 69.51A.005 (1999); .040(1)). Even so this ignores the protections of the second sentence of former RCW 69.51A.040(1): "Any person meeting the requirements appropriate to *his or her status* under this chapter *shall be considered* to have engaged in activities permitted by this

---

1. The officers were informed of a marijuana-growing operation at Fry's residence, but the State has provided no additional details regarding that information. The probable cause justifying the search warrant was based entirely on the officers' smelling burnt marijuana. . . . There is no argument here that additional grounds existed to provide probable cause absent the smell.

chapter and shall not be penalized in any manner, or denied any right or privilege, for such actions." (Emphases added.) Fry's wife provided documentation to the officers to show Fry's "status" under the chapter—the status of a "qualifying patient." See former RCW 69.51A.010(3) (1999). As a facially "qualifying patient" Fry should have been "considered to have engaged in activities permitted by this chapter"—a presumption that a qualifying patient is acting in accordance with the chapter. See former RCW 69.51A.040(1). The only basis for probable cause was the smell of burnt marijuana. That evidence is consistent with activities permitted for qualifying patients under the chapter.

The requirement under former RCW 69.51A.040(2)(c) supports this reading of the second sentence of former RCW 69.51A.040(1). That provision requires a person asserting compliance with the act to "[p]resent his or her valid documentation to any law enforcement official who questions the patient or provider regarding his or her medical use of marijuana." Doing so provides officers with the basis to determine whether a person meets the requirements for a "qualifying patient" and thus invokes the presumption. Conversely, if former RCW 69.51A.040(1) provides only an affirmative defense after one is charged with a crime, as the majority asserts, the requirement to provide valid documentation to the officer serves no purpose as the officer has no reason to view the documentation relevant only to establishing an affirmative defense in court. Therefore with or without the required documents the individual is still arrested and jailed.

The lead opinion clings to the notion that an officer must conduct a search, even when an individual produces documentation of his status, because the search is the only way for the officer to confirm the individual does not possess more than a 60-day supply of marijuana. See majority at 5-6 (quoting former RCW 69.51A.040(2)(b)). But this ignores the fact that the officers here did not have probable cause to believe Fry possessed more than a 60-day supply; thus a search on this basis is unconstitutional. Whereas former RCW 69.51A.040(1) provides a reason for an officer to confirm an individual's status and former RCW 69.51A.040(2)(c) provides the means to do it, nothing in the act suspends constitutional privacy rights (nor could a statute trump the constitution in any event) permitting officers to confirm that all criteria in the act are met by searches not supported by probable cause.

Ultimately the lead opinion's interpretation of the act provides an absurd form of protection to qualifying patients. When an officer smells burnt marijuana coming from the home of an individual with a terminal or debilitating illness who benefits from marijuana use, the individual must provide his documentation to the officer to show he is a "qualifying patient." Yet according to the lead opinion, he is still subject to a search of his home and to an arrest. Certainly, at the individual's trial, he can assert the affirmative defense of the lead opinion's neutered version of the Washington state medical use of marijuana act; however this does not cure the unconstitutional search. Upon release he can return home once again, exhausted and in pain, and use marijuana again to alleviate his pain. However, following another knock on his door from an officer smelling burnt marijuana, the individual is again subject to interrogation, home search, and arrest. I do not find the mercy of the people of Washington for individuals with terminal or debilitating illnesses to be so fickle.

The trial court erred by not suppressing the fruits of a search that was based upon a warrant lacking probable cause. . . .

## Notes and Questions

1. The majority and dissenting opinions in *Fry* illustrate two competing approaches to search and arrest practices in medical marijuana states. The approach espoused by the *Fry* dissent appears to impose an affirmative duty on the police to investigate whether marijuana possession is lawful before conducting a search (or making an arrest) in any given case. E.g., *Massachusetts v. Canning*, 28 N.E.3d 1156, 1165 (2015) (holding that a "search warrant affidavit setting out facts that simply establish probable cause to believe the owner is growing marijuana on the property in question, without more, is insufficient to establish probable cause to believe that the suspected cultivation is a crime," in light of state medical marijuana law allowing some qualifying patients to cultivate marijuana). In contrast, the approach espoused by the *Fry* majority appears to leave search and arrest practices largely unchanged by medical marijuana laws. The police may search and arrest an individual based solely on the reasonable belief that the individual possesses marijuana. E.g., *Arizona v. Sisco*, 373 P.3d 549, 554 (Ariz. 2016) ("AMMA makes marijuana legal in only limited circumstances. Possession of any amount of marijuana by persons other than a registered qualifying patient . . . is still unlawful, and even those subject to AMMA must strictly comply with its provisions to trigger its protections and immunities. . . . A reasonable officer is therefore justified in concluding that [the] sight or smell [of marijuana] is indicative of criminal activity, and thus probable cause exists."). In other words, the police have no duty to investigate whether or not the individual's behavior comports with the state's medical marijuana law. See *California v. Mower*, 49 P.3d 1067, 1074 (Cal. 2002) (holding that the CUA "does not grant any immunity from arrest, and certainly no immunity that would require reversal of a conviction because of any alleged failure on the part of law enforcement officers to conduct an adequate investigation prior to arrest").

Which approach strikes a better balance between the rights of qualified patients and ongoing concerns about use of marijuana for non-medical purposes? On the one hand, does an affirmative duty to investigate unduly burden the ability of officers to enforce state marijuana laws, including prohibitions on recreational marijuana? What if only 1 out of every 10 people who use (grow, etc.) marijuana in a state were allowed to do so under the state's medical marijuana laws? On the other hand, does subjecting all marijuana users to searches based on presence of marijuana unduly burden the rights of qualified medical marijuana users?

2. Does the law's treatment of other items that are sometimes—but not always—possessed lawfully shed light on the prior question? For example, in *Crocker, supra*, the court suggests that the police may not search and arrest someone who possesses a prescription drug (like codeine) that is lawful for some—but not all—to possess, absent some indication that the possessor is breaking the law. Similarly, in *Canning*, 28 N.E.3d at 1164, the court noted that the police may not search and arrest someone who possesses a firearm, absent some indication that the possessor lacked a license (or was committing some other crime). Should the same logic apply to marijuana? Can you think of reasons to treat marijuana differently?

3. Even when they have no affirmative duty to investigate, may the police ignore evidence suggesting that a suspect's marijuana possession comports with the state's medical marijuana law? It is generally accepted that the police must consider *all* available

evidence, including exculpatory evidence, when making probable cause determinations. The court's statement in *Michigan v. Brown* is instructive:

> While we decline . . . to impose an affirmative duty on the police to obtain information pertaining to a person's noncompliance with the [Michigan Medical Marijuana Act] MMMA before seeking a search warrant for marijuana, if the police do have clear and uncontroverted evidence that a person is in full compliance with the MMMA, this evidence must be included as part of the affidavit because such a situation would not justify the issuance of a warrant.

825 N.W.2d 91, 95 n.5 (Mich. App. 2012). *See also Mower*, 49 P.3d at 1073 ("Probable cause depends on all of the surrounding facts . . . , including those that reveal a person's status as a qualified patient or primary caregiver under [the CUA]."). Now consider the following Problems that test this proposition.

**Problem 4.16**: The police conducted a flyover of Camila's house, where they observed "at least three marijuana plants" in the backyard. Based on this information, the police obtained a warrant to search Camila's home. Before the police could execute the warrant, however, Camila showed them what appeared to be a qualifying diagnosis and physician's recommendation to use marijuana. State law allows qualified patients to possess up to three marijuana plants and eight ounces of usable marijuana. May the police proceed to conduct their search of Camila's home? *See California v. Fisher*, 117 Cal. Rptr. 2d 838 (Cal. App. 3d 2002).

**Problem 4.17**: Delilah was seated in the driver's seat of her car, which was parked at a gas station. A police officer approached the car on foot and smelled marijuana. When asked, Delilah acknowledged she had been smoking marijuana just before the officer arrived, and she showed him a bag containing less than one ounce of the drug. Delilah also told the officer "I have a medical marijuana card," but the officer refused to look at it and told her "We don't think much of that stuff in this county." State law permits qualified patients to possess up to eight ounces of marijuana. May the officer search Delilah's car for (more) marijuana? *See California v. Strasburg*, 56 Cal. Rptr. 3d 306 (Cal. App. 1st 2007). Would it make a difference if the state had a per se DUI offense?

## 2. Prosecution

Apart from being searched, qualified patients might also be prosecuted for simple possession of marijuana if their states continue to classify possession as a criminal offense in some circumstances. The following Problem illustrates this scenario:

**Problem 4.18**: While conducting a consensual search of Andy's residence, the police find a bag containing one ounce of marijuana in his dresser drawer. Andy openly acknowledges that the marijuana belongs to him, but he insists he

has scrupulously complied with the state's medical marijuana law. Nonetheless, the district attorney charges Andy with simple possession. What can Andy do to challenge the prosecution?

### a. Immunity and Affirmative Defenses

Every medical marijuana state has provided its qualified patients some form of protection against prosecution for simple possession and related charges. To simplify somewhat, this protection may be labeled either: (1) immunity from prosecution, or, (2) an affirmative defense in a criminal prosecution. Although both are designed to shield qualified patients from criminal sanctions that are levied against other marijuana users, immunity is more defendant-friendly, largely because it makes it easier for defendants to have charges dismissed *before* trial.

The Michigan Medical Marijuana Act (MMMA) grants both immunity and an affirmative defense and thus provides a useful vehicle for exploring and comparing the procedures surrounding each. The relevant portions of the MMMA provide:

> Section 4: [Immunity]
>
> (a) A qualifying patient who has been issued and possesses a registry identification card shall not be subject to arrest, prosecution, or penalty in any manner, or denied any right or privilege, including but not limited to civil penalty or disciplinary action by a business or occupational or professional licensing board or bureau, for the medical use of marihuana in accordance with this act, provided that the qualifying patient possesses an amount of marihuana that does not exceed 2.5 ounces of usable marihuana, and, . . . 12 marihuana plants kept in an enclosed, locked facility. Any incidental amount of seeds, stalks, and unusable roots shall also be allowed under state law and shall not be included in this amount. The privilege from arrest under this subsection applies only if the qualifying patient presents both his or her registry identification card and a valid driver license or government-issued identification card that bears a photographic image of the qualifying patient.
>
> . . .
>
> (f) Any marihuana, marihuana paraphernalia, or licit property that is possessed, owned, or used in connection with the medical use of marihuana, as allowed under this act, or acts incidental to such use, shall not be seized or forfeited.
>
> Section 8: Affirmative Defense and Dismissal for Medical Marihuana
>
> (a) Except as provided in [Mich. Comp. L. 333.26427(b)[11]], a patient and a patient's primary caregiver, if any, may assert the medical purpose for using marihuana as a defense to any prosecution involving marihuana, and this defense shall be presumed valid where the evidence shows that:
>
> (1) A physician has stated that, in the physician's professional opinion, after having completed a full assessment of the patient's medical history and current medical condition made in the course of a bona fide physician-patient relationship, the patient is likely to receive therapeutic or palliative benefit from the medical use of marihuana to treat or alleviate the patient's serious or debilitating medical condition or symptoms of the patient's serious or debilitating medical condition;

---

11. Author's note: The exceptions include those discussed above in Section B, such as possessing marijuana on school grounds or driving while under the influence of marijuana.

(2) The patient and the patient's primary caregiver, if any, were collectively in possession of a quantity of marihuana that was not more than was reasonably necessary to ensure the uninterrupted availability of marihuana for the purpose of treating or alleviating the patient's serious or debilitating medical condition or symptoms of the patient's serious or debilitating medical condition; and

(3) The patient and the patient's primary caregiver, if any, were engaged in the acquisition, possession, cultivation, manufacture, use, delivery, transfer, or transportation of marihuana or paraphernalia relating to the use of marihuana to treat or alleviate the patient's serious or debilitating medical condition or symptoms of the patient's serious or debilitating medical condition.

(b) A person may assert the medical purpose for using marihuana in a motion to dismiss, and the charges shall be dismissed following an evidentiary hearing where the person shows the elements listed in subsection (a). . . .

Mich. Comp. L. 333.26424, 28.

The Michigan Supreme Court describes both section 4 immunity and the section 8 affirmative defense in the following case. The excerpt focuses on the procedural and substantive differences between immunity and the affirmative defense. Because the facts of the case are largely irrelevant to this description, they are omitted here.

## *Michigan v. Hartwick*
870 N.W.2d 37 (Mich. 2015)

ZAHRA, J.:

The possession, manufacture, and delivery of marijuana are punishable criminal offenses under Michigan law. Under the MMMA, though, "[t]he medical use of marihuana is allowed under state law to the extent that it is carried out in accordance with the provisions of th[e] act." The MMMA grants to persons in compliance with its provisions either immunity from, or an affirmative defense to, those marijuana-related violations of state law. In the cases before us, we must resolve questions surrounding the § 4 grant of immunity and the § 8 affirmative defense. . . .

### . . . SECTION 4 IMMUNITY

Section 4 grants broad immunity from criminal prosecution and civil penalties to "qualifying patient[s]" and "primary caregiver[s]." Subsection (a) specifically grants immunity to qualifying patients and states in relevant part:

(a) A qualifying patient who has been issued and possesses a registry identification card shall not be subject to arrest, prosecution, or penalty in any manner . . . for the medical use of marihuana in accordance with this act, provided that the qualifying patient possesses an amount of marihuana that does not exceed 2.5 ounces of usable marihuana, and, if the qualifying patient has not specified . . . a primary caregiver . . . , 12 marihuana plants kept in an enclosed, locked facility.

. . .

#### 1. Procedural Aspects of § 4

We begin our analysis of the procedural aspects of § 4 with the rather unremarkable proposition that entitlement to immunity under § 4 is a question of law. Immunity is a unique creature in the law and is distinguishable from other traditional criminal defenses. A successful claim of immunity excuses an alleged offender for engaging in otherwise illegal conduct, regardless of the sufficiency of proofs in the underlying case. This is consistent with the way claims of immunity are handled in other areas of law. Moreover, the parties agree that §4 immunity should be determined as a matter of law. There is no indication that the voters who enacted the MMMA intended to treat §4 immunity differently than other claims of immunity.

Our decision in [*People v. Kolanek*, 817 N.W.2d 528 (Mich. 2012),] supports this conclusion. There we explained that §4 "'grants qualifying patient[s]' who hold 'registry identification card[s]' broad immunity *from* criminal prosecution, civil penalties, and disciplinary actions." A registered qualifying patient, however, "who do[es] not qualify for immunity under §4, as well as unregistered persons, are entitled to assert *in* a criminal prosecution the affirmative defense . . . under §8. . . ." By contrasting the broad grant of immunity in §4 "*from* prosecution" with the affirmative defense in §8 "*in* a criminal prosecution," we implied that the decision regarding entitlement to immunity must be made before trial. By its very nature, immunity must be decided by the trial court as a matter of law, and in pretrial proceedings, in order to establish immunity *from* prosecution.

Deciding these questions of law necessarily involves resolving factual disputes. To determine whether a defendant is entitled to the §4 grant of immunity, the trial court must make factual determinations, including whether the defendant has a valid registry identification card and whether he or she complied with the volume, storage, and medical use limitations. The expediency of having the trial court resolve factual questions surrounding §4 underscores the purpose of granting immunity *from* prosecution.

Other matters routinely conducted in pretrial contexts, such as entrapment hearings, call for the trial court to act as both the finder of fact and arbiter of law. Like entrapment, §4 immunity "is not a defense that negates an essential element of the charged crime. Instead, it presents facts that are collateral to the crime that justify barring the defendant's prosecution." We therefore conclude that the trial court must resolve factual disputes for the purpose of determining §4 immunity.

Of course, the trial court's determinations are not without review. Questions of law are reviewed de novo by appellate courts. A trial court's factual findings are subject to appellate review under the clearly erroneous standard:

> Findings of fact by the trial court may not be set aside unless clearly erroneous. In the application of this principle, regard shall be given to the special opportunity of the trial court to judge the credibility of the witnesses who appeared before it.

. . . .

### 2. Substantive Aspects of §4

Section 4 provides a broad grant of immunity from criminal prosecution and civil penalties to registered qualifying patients and connected primary caregivers. . . . [T]he statute leaves much to be desired regarding the proper implementation of this grant of immunity. . . .

#### a. Burden of Proof

The MMMA is silent regarding the burden of proof necessary for a defendant to be entitled to immunity under §4. When statutes are silent as to the burden of proof, "we are free to assign it as we see fit, as long as we do not transgress the constitutional requirement that we not place on the defendant the burden of persuasion to negate an element of the crime." . . .

Assigning the burden of proof involves two distinct legal concepts. The first, the burden of production, requires a party to produce some evidence of that party's propositions of fact. The second, the burden of persuasion, requires a party to convince the trier of fact that those propositions of fact are true. The prosecution has the burden of proving every element of a charged crime beyond a reasonable doubt. This rule of law exists in part to ensure that "there is a presumption of innocence in favor of the accused . . . and its enforcement lies at the foundation of the administration of our criminal law." . . . To place the burden on a criminal defendant to negate a specific element of a crime would clearly run afoul of this axiomatic, elementary, and undoubted principle of law.

A defendant invoking §4 immunity, however, does so without regard to any presumption of innocence. The defendant does not dispute any element of the underlying charge when claiming immunity. Indeed, the defendant may even admit to otherwise unlawful conduct and yet still be entitled to §4 immunity. When claiming §4 immunity, the defendant places himself in an offensive position, affirmatively arguing entitlement to §4 immunity without regard to his or her underlying guilt or innocence of the crime charged. In [a prior case], we determined that the accusatorial nature of a defendant's request for a defense of entrapment, without regard to his or her guilt or innocence of the underlying criminal charge, required the burden of proof by a preponderance of the evidence to be allocated to the defendant. The accusatorial nature of an entrapment defense and the offensive nature of immunity are similar because in both the defendant posits an affirmative argument, rather than defending a particular charge. We now follow this well-established rule of criminal procedure and assign to the defendant the burden of proving §4 immunity by a preponderance of the evidence.

### b. Elements Required to Establish Immunity

A defendant may claim entitlement to immunity for any or all charged offenses. Once a claim of immunity is made, the trial court must conduct an evidentiary hearing to factually determine whether, for each claim of immunity, the defendant has proved each element required for immunity. These elements consist of whether, at the time of the charged offense, the defendant:

(1) was issued and possessed a valid registry identification card,
(2) complied with the requisite volume limitations of §4(a) and §4(b),
(3) stored any marijuana plants in an enclosed, locked facility, and
(4) was engaged in the medical use of marijuana.

The court must examine the first element of immunity—possession of a valid registry identification card—on a charge-by-charge basis. In most cases, satisfying the first element will be an all-or-nothing proposition. A qualifying patient or primary caregiver who does not have a valid registry identification card is not entitled to immunity because the first element required for immunity cannot be satisfied. Conversely, a qualifying patient or primary caregiver satisfies the first element of immunity if he or she possessed a valid registry identification card at all times relevant to the charged offenses. . . . A qualifying patient or primary caregiver can only satisfy the first element of immunity for any charge if all conduct underlying that charge occurred during a time when the qualifying patient or primary caregiver possessed a valid registry identification card.

Generally, the second and third elements of immunity are also all-or-nothing propositions. The second element—the volume limitations of § 4(a) and § 4(b)—requires that the qualifying patient or primary caregiver be in possession of no more than a specified amount of usable marijuana and a specified number of marijuana plants. When a primary caregiver is connected with one or more qualifying patients, the amount of usable marijuana and the number of plants is calculated in the aggregate—2.5 ounces of usable marijuana and 12 marijuana plants for each qualifying patient, including the caregiver if he or she is also a registered qualifying patient acting as his or her own caregiver.[54] When a qualifying patient cultivates his or her own marijuana for medical use and is not connected with a caregiver, the patient is limited to 2.5 ounces of usable marijuana and 12 marijuana plants. A qualifying patient or primary caregiver in possession of more marijuana than allowed under § 4(a) and § 4(b) at the time of the charged offense cannot satisfy the second element of immunity.

The third element of § 4 immunity requires all marijuana plants possessed by a qualifying patient or primary caregiver to be kept in an enclosed, locked facility. Thus, a qualifying patient or primary caregiver whose marijuana plants are not kept in an enclosed, locked facility at the time of the charged offense cannot satisfy the third element and cannot receive immunity for the charged offense.

The fourth element conditions immunity on the "medical use" of marijuana, as defined in § 3(f). Unlike elements two and three, the fourth element does not depend on the defendant's aggregate conduct. Instead, this element depends on whether the conduct forming the basis of each particular criminal charge involved "the acquisition, possession, cultivation, manufacture, use, internal possession, delivery, transfer, or transportation of marihuana or paraphernalia relating to the administration of marihuana to treat or alleviate a registered qualifying patient's debilitating medical condition or symptoms associated with the debilitating medical condition." Whether a qualifying patient or primary caregiver was engaged in the medical use of marijuana must be determined on a charge-by-charge basis.

While the qualifying patient or primary caregiver retains the burden of proving this fourth and last element of immunity, § 4(d) of the MMMA creates a rebuttable presumption of medical use when the qualifying patient or primary caregiver . . . establish[es] the first two elements of § 4 immunity.

### c. Rebutting the Presumption

The presumption of the medical use of marijuana is a powerful tool for a defendant in asserting § 4 immunity. But this presumption is rebuttable. . . .

According to § 4(d)(2), the presumption of the medical use of marijuana may be rebutted by examining "conduct related to marihuana. . . ." While the statute does not

---

54. For example, a registered qualifying patient who is his or her own caregiver and the caregiver to five other qualifying patients is allowed to possess up to 72 marijuana plants and up to 15 ounces of usable marijuana. If that individual actually possessed 73 marijuana plants or 16 ounces of usable marijuana and was charged with multiple marijuana-related offenses, the individual could not satisfy the second element of immunity under § 4 for any of the charged offenses because the individual possessed marijuana in excess of the volume limitations in § 4(a) and § 4(b).

specifically state whose marijuana-related conduct may be used, when read in context it is clear that it refers to the defendant's conduct. Stated differently, in § 4(d), only the defendant's conduct may be considered to rebut the presumption of the medical use of marijuana. This interpretation is consistent with the purpose of § 4, which is to provide immunity from prosecution to a defendant who abides by certain restrictions. . . .[12]

### . . . Section 8 Defense

Section 8(a) of the MMMA provides any patient or primary caregiver—regardless of registration with the state—with the ability to assert an affirmative defense to a marijuana-related offense. The affirmative defense "shall be presumed valid where the evidence shows":

> (1) A physician has stated that, in the physician's professional opinion, after having completed a full assessment of the patient's medical history and current medical condition made in the course of a bona fide physician-patient relationship, the patient is likely to receive therapeutic or palliative benefit from the medical use of marihuana to treat or alleviate the patient's serious or debilitating medical condition or symptoms of the patient's serious or debilitating medical condition;
>
> (2) The patient and the patient's primary caregiver, if any, were collectively in possession of a quantity of marihuana that was not more than was reasonably necessary to ensure the uninterrupted availability of marihuana for the purpose of treating or alleviating the patient's serious or debilitating medical condition or symptoms of the patient's serious or debilitating medical condition; and
>
> (3) The patient and the patient's primary caregiver, if any, were engaged in the acquisition, possession, cultivation, manufacture, use, delivery, transfer, or transportation of marihuana or paraphernalia relating to the use of marihuana to treat or alleviate the patient's serious or debilitating medical condition or symptoms of the patient's serious or debilitating medical condition.

In *Kolanek*, we determined that if a defendant establishes these elements and no question of fact exists regarding these elements, then the defendant is entitled to dismissal of the criminal charges. We also clarified that if questions of fact exist, then "dismissal of the charges is not appropriate and the defense must be submitted to the jury." Additionally, if a defendant has not presented prima facie evidence of each element of § 8 by "present[ing] evidence from which a reasonable jury could conclude that the defendant satisfied the elements of the § 8 affirmative defense, . . . then the circuit court must deny the motion to dismiss the charges," and "the defendant is not permitted to present the § 8 defense to the jury."

A defendant seeking to assert the MMMA's statutory affirmative defense must present prima facie evidence for each element of § 8(a).[69] Overcoming this initial hurdle of presenting prima facie evidence of each element is not an easy task. The elements of § 8 are clearly more onerous than the elements of § 4. The statutory scheme of the MMMA is

---

12. Author's note: The court's discussion of the presumption is discussed in greater detail in Section B.2, *supra*.

69. . . . In *Kolanek*, we did not determine the standard by which a defendant must establish a § 8 defense. We now clarify that well-established rules of criminal procedure require a defendant to prove the affirmative defense by a preponderance of evidence. . . . Thus, when the § 8 affirmative defense is submitted to a fact-finder, the defendant's burden of proof is to establish the elements of § 8(a) by a preponderance of the evidence.

designed to benefit those who properly register and are meticulous in their adherence to the law. Presumably, a properly registered defendant facing criminal charges would invoke immunity under § 4. However, a § 8 defense may be pursued by any defendant, regardless of registration status. With this background, we consider each element of the § 8 affirmative defense.

### 1. Section 8(a)(1): The Imprimatur of the Physician-Patient Relationship

Section 8(a)(1) requires a physician to determine the patient's suitability for the medical use of marijuana . . .

This provision may be reduced to three elements:

(1) The existence of a bona fide physician-patient relationship,
(2) in which the physician completes a full assessment of the patient's medical history and current medical condition, and
(3) from which results the physician's professional opinion that the patient has a debilitating medical condition and will likely benefit from the medical use of marijuana to treat the debilitating medical condition.

Each of these elements must be proved in order to establish the imprimatur of the physician-patient relationship required under § 8(a)(1) of the MMMA. [Defendants] Hartwick and Tuttle argue that the registry identification card establishes these three elements. We do not find merit in this position.

As part of the process for obtaining a registry identification card, an applicant must submit, among other materials, a "written certification." At the time of the offenses at issue,[72] the MMMA defined a written certification as:

[A] document signed by a physician, stating the patient's debilitating medical condition and stating that, in the physician's professional opinion, the patient is likely to receive therapeutic or palliative benefit from the medical use of marihuana to treat or alleviate the patient's debilitating medical condition or symptoms associated with the debilitating medical condition. [former MCL 333.26423(l)]

. . .

Comparing the definition of "written certification" with the elements of § 8(a)(1), a registry identification card satisfies the third element (the patient has a debilitating medical condition and would likely benefit from the medical use of marijuana). A registry identification card, however, does not establish the second element (a physician has completed a full assessment of the patient's medical history and current medical condition). The second element must be established through medical records or other evidence submitted to show that the physician actually completed a full assessment of the patient's medical history and current medical condition before concluding that the patient is likely to benefit from the medical use of marijuana and before the patient engages in the medical use of marijuana. Additionally, the physician certification leaves unsatisfied the first element of § 8(a)(1) (the existence of a bona fide physician-patient relationship).

---

72. In 2012, the Legislature garnered sufficient votes to satisfy the three-fourths super majority required to amend a voter-enacted initiative and amended the MMMA to include the additional requirement that the physician conducted a full, in-person assessment of the patient. . . .

### 2. Section 8(a)(2): The Quantity of Marijuana

[Section 8(a)(2) imposes limits on the quantity of marijuana a patient or primary caregiver may possess.] . . .

The critical phrase . . . is "reasonably necessary to ensure uninterrupted availability of marihuana [for treatment]. . . ." Hartwick and Tuttle maintain that a registry identification card establishes a presumption that any amount of marijuana possessed by a defendant is a reasonable amount of marijuana under the MMMA. In the alternative, they argue that a valid registry identification card, coupled with compliance with the volume limitations in § 4, establishes a presumption that the amount of marijuana possessed is reasonable. Again, we do not find support for the defendants' position in the text of the MMMA.

The issuance of a registry identification card or compliance with the volume limitations in § 4 does not show that an individual possesses only a "reasonably necessary" amount of marijuana "to ensure uninterrupted availability" for the purposes of § 8(a)(2). A registry identification card simply qualifies a patient for the medical use of marijuana. It does not guarantee that an individual will always possess only the amount of marijuana allowed under the MMMA.

Further, nothing in the MMMA supports the notion that the quantity limits found in the immunity provision of § 4 should be judicially imposed on the affirmative defense provision of § 8. Sections 4 and 8 feature contrasting statutory language intended to serve two very different purposes. Section 4 creates a specific volume limitation applicable to those seeking immunity. In contrast, § 8 leaves open the volume limitation to that which is "reasonably necessary." The MMMA could have specified a specific volume limitation in § 8, but it did not. In the absence of such an express limitation, we will not judicially assign to § 8 the volume limitation in § 4 to create a presumption of compliance with § 8(a)(2). . . .

A patient seeking to assert a § 8 affirmative defense may have to testify about whether a specific amount of marijuana alleviated the debilitating medical condition and if not, what adjustments were made to the consumption rate and the amount of marijuana consumed to determine an appropriate quantity. Once the patient establishes the amount of usable marijuana needed to treat the patient's debilitating medical condition, determining whether the patient possessed "a quantity of marihuana that was not more than was reasonably necessary to ensure [its] uninterrupted availability" also depends on how the patient obtains marijuana and the reliability of this source. . . .

### 3. Section 8(A)(3): The Use of Marijuana for a Medical Purpose

. . . [Section] 8(a)(3) requires a patient and primary caregiver to show that any marijuana use complied with a very similar "medical use" requirement found in § 4, and defined in § 3. . . .

The slight variance between the definition of "medical use" in § 4 and medical use as it appears in § 8 can be attributed to the fact that only registered qualifying patients and registered primary caregivers may engage in the "medical use" of marijuana, as indicated by use of the term in § 4. Those patients and primary caregivers who are not registered may still be entitled to § 8 protections if they can show that their use of marijuana was for a medical purpose—to treat or alleviate a serious or debilitating medical condition or its symptoms. Hartwick and Tuttle again argue that a registry identification card alone, or a registry identification card coupled with compliance with either the volume limitations of § 4(a) and (4)(b) or § 8(a)(2), satisfies § 8(a)(3). Once again, defendants seek to attribute greater significance to the registry identification card than that which is expressly provided in the MMMA. . . .

A registry identification card merely qualifies a patient for the medical use of marijuana. It does not establish that at the time of the charged offense, the defendant was actually engaged in the protected use of marijuana. Section 8(a)(3) requires that both the patient's and the primary caregiver's use of marijuana be for a medical purpose, and that their conduct be described by the language in § 8(a)(3). Thus, patients must present prima facie evidence regarding their use of marijuana for a medical purpose regardless whether they possess a registry identification card. . . .

## Notes and Questions

1. Although *Hartwick* holds that judges alone decide whether defendants are entitled to immunity from criminal prosecution, not all states give judges exclusive authority to decide all questions concerning immunity. For example, even though Arizona gives judges the power to decide whether a defendant's claims establish immunity from prosecution, it gives juries the power to resolve any factual disputes surrounding those claims. *E.g., Arizona v. Liwski*, 2015 WL 5090356, at *2 (Ariz. Ct. App. Aug. 28, 2015) ("[I]f there are disputed facts related to immunity, such facts must be resolved by the jury before the trial court determines if immunity has been established."); *Arizona v. Fields*, 304 P.3d 1088, 1092 (Ariz. App. 2d 2013) ("Whether . . . immunity exists is a question of law for the trial court. . . . 'If the existence of immunity turns on disputed factual issues, the jury determines the facts and the court then determines whether those facts are sufficient to establish immunity.'"). Who do you think should decide whether (or not) a defendant is entitled to legal protection (immunity or a defense) under a state's medical marijuana law? What are the implications—for prosecutors and defendants—of assigning authority to a judge versus a jury?

2. In nearly all states, the defendant bears the burden of persuading the relevant decisionmaker (judge or jury) by a preponderance of the evidence that all of the elements of immunity or the affirmative defense have been satisfied. *See Hartwick, supra; Fry, supra; Arizona v. Cheatham*, 237 Ariz. 502 (Ariz. App. 2015). As the *Hartwick* court notes, however, some states have created evidentiary presumptions that ease the defendant's burden.

3. The California Supreme Court has created a (very) unique set of protections for qualified patients under the state's Compassionate Use Act (CUA). While the CUA "does not grant any immunity from arrest", it does "grant a defendant a limited immunity from prosecution" that would enable a defendant to have charges dismissed after arrest but before trial. *California v. Mower*, 49 P.3d 1067, 1074-75 (Cal. 2002). In particular, a defendant may make a motion to set aside an indictment by demonstrating that "in light of the evidence presented to the grand jury or the magistrate, he or she was indicted or committed 'without reasonable or probable cause' to believe that he or she was guilty of

possession or cultivation of marijuana in view of his or her status as a qualified patient...." *Id.* at 1076. The CUA also allows a patient to raise a defense at trial, should a motion to dismiss prove unsuccessful. Because the defense is based on facts "peculiarly within the defendant's knowledge"—namely, that she was a qualifying patient, possessed marijuana for medical purposes, and did so on the recommendation of a physician, the defendant bears the burden of proof regarding the facts underlying the defense. *Id.* at 1079. However, because those same facts also relate to the defendant's guilt or innocence, namely, whether her possession was "unlawful," the defendant need only raise a reasonable doubt as to their existence in order to prevail at trial. *Id.* at 1083.

Does the *Mower* decision make it too easy for defendants to prevail on the medical marijuana defense? Should defendants be required to prove by a preponderance of the evidence that they have satisfied the criteria of the CUA? Along these lines, consider the following Problem:

**Problem 4.19:** The state charges Camila with simple possession of 7 ounces of marijuana. At trial, Camila gave the following testimony:

*Defense attorney*: Camila, is the marijuana yours?

*Camila*: Yes, the marijuana is mine. But I'm only using it for medical purposes. You see, I've had chronic pain ever since I suffered a bike accident a decade ago. I've seen some doctors about the pain. Less than a year ago I saw one who told me that marijuana would help, and that it would be a lot safer than the prescription painkillers I'd been using before.

*Defense attorney*: What is the name of this doctor? Did he write down his recommendation?

*Camila*: I'm sorry, but I won't tell you his name. I know that sounds fishy, but the doctor was very reluctant to talk about marijuana. He only did so because he was so worried I might get hooked on the opioids I had been taking. He told me that talking about marijuana could get him into a lot of legal trouble with the feds.

Has Camila raised a reasonable doubt about the CUA? Has she established her compliance by a preponderance of the evidence?

4. When the California legislature added the Medical Marijuana Program Act (MMP) in 2003, it provided immunity for qualifying patients who voluntarily register with a county health department:

> No person or designated primary caregiver in possession of a valid identification card shall be subject to arrest for possession, transportation, delivery, or cultivation of medical marijuana in an amount established pursuant to this article, unless there is reasonable cause to believe that the information contained in the card is false or falsified, the card has been obtained by means of fraud, or the person is otherwise in violation of the provisions of this article.

Cal. Health & Safety Code § 11362.71(e). Assuming that the immunity afforded by the MMP operates similarly to that granted by Michigan and other states, what are the advantages (if any) of invoking MMP immunity as opposed to making the motion to set aside created by the *Mower* court?

### b. The Necessity Defense

May a defendant fall back on the necessity defense (discussed in Chapter 3), if she fails to meet all of the requirements of immunity or the affirmative defense? Most states that have addressed the question have found that the adoption of a specific medical marijuana statute abrogates the generic necessity defense for marijuana charges. *E.g., Oregon v. Miles*, 104 P.3d 604 (Or. App. 2005) ("[I]f marijuana manufacture was necessary to address defendant's chronic pain and nausea, . . . defendant had legal means of obtaining that relief under the [Oregon Medical Marijuana Act (OMMA)]. Defendant failed to present evidence of an inability to follow the legal course of action—compliance with the OMMA—or that there was an 'emergency requiring immediate extra-legal action.'") (citation omitted); *Noy v. Alaska*, 83 P.3d 538, 544 (Alaska App. 2003) (because Alaska's medical marijuana law "specifically addresses this issue . . . and defines a separate affirmative defense of medical necessity to possess marijuana . . . [defendant's] claim of necessity was . . . governed by the specific [medical marijuana law] . . . rather than by the general necessity statute"); *California v. Galambos*, 128 Cal. Rptr. 2d 844 (Cal. App. 3d 2002) (finding that common law necessity defense must give way to voters' choice of a narrower medical marijuana law).

These courts have rejected the necessity defense for the reasons given by the dissent in *Washington v. Kurtz*, a case in which the Washington Supreme Court holds that the defense *is* still available notwithstanding the state's adoption of a specific medical marijuana statute.

## *Washington v. Kurtz*
178 309 P.3d 472 (Wash. 2013)

Madsen, C.J.:

In 2010, police executed a search warrant on petitioner William Kurtz's home and found marijuana and marijuana plants. The State charged Kurtz with manufacturing and possession of marijuana. . . .

The jury found Kurtz guilty and he appealed. . . .

Kurtz contends the trial court erred by not allowing him to present a common law medical necessity defense for his marijuana use. Specifically, he argues that the necessity defense was not . . . superseded by the [Washington State Medical Use of Marijuana Act]. . . .

[The court first noted that Washington courts had previously recognized a medical necessity defense to marijuana possession charges "in very limited circumstances," notwithstanding the state legislature's classification of marijuana as a Schedule I controlled substance. Under the test adopted by the state courts, defendants had to demonstrate: (1) that they reasonably believed their use of marijuana was necessary to minimize the effects of their conditions; (2) the benefits derived from their use of marijuana were no greater than the harms sought to be prevented by the state marijuana ban; and (3) no other drug was as effective in minimizing the effects of their conditions. *See, e.g., Washington v. Diana*, 604 P.2d 1312 (Wash. App. 3d 1979). The Washington Supreme Court then turned to the issue whether the passage of the Act in 1998 or subsequent legislative amendments had abrogated this common law necessity defense.]

In general, Washington is governed by common law to the extent it is not inconsistent with constitutional, federal, or state law. . . . "However, we are hesitant to recognize an abrogation or derogation from the common law absent clear evidence of the legislature's intent to deviate from the common law." . . . When "the provisions of a later statute are so inconsistent with and repugnant to the prior common law that both cannot simultaneously be in force, the statute will be deemed to abrogate the common law." . . .

The Act contains no language expressing a legislative intent to abrogate the common law. To the contrary, a 2011 amendment to chapter 69.51A RCW added that "[n]othing in this chapter establishes the medical necessity or medical appropriateness of cannabis for treating terminal or debilitating medical conditions as defined in RCW 69.51A.010," suggesting the legislature did not intend to supplant or abrogate the common law. RCW 69.51A.005(3). In explaining the purpose of the Act the legislature stated that "[h]umanitarian compassion necessitates that the decision to use cannabis by patients with terminal or debilitating medical conditions is a personal, individual decision, based upon their health care professional's professional medical judgment and discretion." RCW 69.51A.005(1)(b). To hold that this Act limits existing defenses for medical necessity would undermine the legislature's humanitarian goals.

The State argues, however, that because the legislature spoke directly to the purpose of the common law necessity defense, it intended to abrogate the common law. The State relies on two United States Supreme Court cases for this rule of construction. . . . The federal common law analysis proceeds on the principle that Congress, not federal courts, is to articulate the standards to be applied as a matter of federal law. . . . In contrast, common law is not a rarity among the states and is often developed through the courts, as was the case with medical necessity for marijuana. . . . Indeed, Washington has several statutory provisions addressing the authority of common law. . . . Because the federal and state schemes differ, federal cases are unhelpful. . . .

The State also contends that each element of the medical necessity defense is addressed by the Act and establishes inconsistencies between the two. As to the requirement that a defendant provide medical testimony to support his belief that use of marijuana was medically necessary, the State notes that the Act similarly requires a defendant to obtain authorization for use from a qualifying physician. As to the balancing of harms requirement, the state contends this element is met by the Act's limitation on the quantity of marijuana that a patient may possess. Responding to the final requirement, that no drug is as effective at treatment, the State notes an individual under the Act is not required to show there are no other drugs as effective. While some of these elements are indeed similar to the common law defense, they are not identical and are not clearly inconsistent. For example, the fact that the Act does not require proof that no other drug is as effective simply means the Act is broader in that respect. Other elements in the Act may overlap with the common law defense, but are not identical nor "so inconsistent with and repugnant to the prior common law that both cannot simultaneously be in force." . . .

The State points to other aspects of the Act that it views as "obvious inconsistencies." . . . For example, the State hypothesizes that an individual who obtains authorization by an unqualified physician would not satisfy the Act but will be able to assert the common law defense. The State also posits that an individual who possesses a certain amount of marijuana may not have a defense under the Act but would under the common law. While correct, these examples do not show inconsistencies, but rather demonstrate that the common law may apply more broadly in some circumstances.

The State also asserts that the statutory language and initiative make it clear that the Act was intended to replace the common law defense with an affirmative defense for certain individuals with terminal or debilitating illnesses. . . . [However], the Act is not so broad as to cover every situation of marijuana use that might arise. . . .

Moreover, in 2011 the legislature amended the Act making qualifying marijuana use a legal use, not simply an affirmative defense. RCW 69.51A.040. A necessity defense arises only when an individual acts contrary to law. Under RCW 69.51A.005(2)(a), a qualifying patient "shall not be arrested, prosecuted, or subject to other criminal actions or civil consequences under state law based solely on their medical use of cannabis, notwithstanding any other provision of law." One who meets the specific requirements expressed by the legislature may not be charged with committing a crime and has no need for the necessity defense. Only where one's conduct falls outside of the legal conduct of the Act, would a medical necessity defense be necessary. The 2011 amendment legalizing qualifying marijuana use strongly suggests that the Act was not intended to abrogate or supplant the common law necessity defense. . . .

The State argues, though, that even if the necessity defense is theoretically available, Kurtz could not rely on the defense because the Act provides a legal avenue for his marijuana use. . . .

The United States Supreme Court . . . addressed necessity and duress defenses and noted that "[u]nder any definition of these defenses one principle remains constant: if there was a reasonable, legal alternative to violating the law, 'a chance both to refuse to do the criminal act and also to avoid the threatened harm,' the defenses will fail." [*United States v. Bailey*, 444 U.S. 394 (1980)]. . . . Thus, implicit in the marijuana necessity defense is whether an individual has a viable legal alternative to the illegal use of marijuana. In other words, the mere existence of the Act does not foreclose a medical necessity defense, but it can be a factor in weighing whether there was a viable legal alternative to a violation of the controlled substances law. . . .

Here, the trial court did not consider whether the evidence supported a necessity defense . . . , including whether Kurtz had a viable legal alternative. Instead, the record suggests that the trial court denied the common law defense concluding it was unavailable . . . and denied the statutory defense because Kurtz did not obtain timely medical authorizations. Accordingly, we reverse . . . and remand to the trial court to determine whether Kurtz presented sufficient evidence to support a medical necessity defense, including whether compliance with the Act was a viable legal alternative for Kurtz. If the evidence supports the necessity defense, Kurtz is entitled to a new trial.

Owens, J., dissenting:

While I sympathize with William Kurtz's unfortunate situation, I am compelled to dissent because the common law defense of necessity is predicated on a lack of legal alternatives. Washington voters have provided a comprehensive statutory scheme for the use of medical marijuana, enacted by initiative in 1998. Because individuals in this state have a legal way of using medical marijuana, the previously articulated common law defense of medical necessity for marijuana use is no longer appropriate. Therefore, I respectfully dissent.

. . .

When the Court of Appeals created the medical necessity defense for marijuana use in 1979, there was no provision for legal medical use of marijuana to treat the defendant's multiple sclerosis. [*Diana*, 604 P.2d 1302.] . . . Accordingly, the Court of Appeals created a three-part medical necessity defense, including a requirement that defendants present evidence that there was no legal alternative to using marijuana illegally to treat their symptoms. *Id.* . . . Specifically, defendants had to show that no legal drug was as effective as marijuana in minimizing the effects of their disease. *Id.* Defendants that made such a showing could assert the medical necessity defense because they had no legal alternative to use marijuana for medical purposes.

But in 1998, the people of this state passed Initiative Measure 692 (the Washington State Medical Use of Marijuana Act, chapter 69.51A RCW), which provided a legal alternative for individuals to use marijuana for medical purposes. Consequently, the crucial underpinning to the necessity defense—the lack of legal alternatives—no longer existed for medical marijuana use. This change is particularly evidenced by *Diana*'s requirement that defendants show that no legal drug was as effective as marijuana in minimizing the effects of their disease. Logically, I do not see how Kurtz can show that no legal drug is as effective as marijuana when marijuana itself is now allowed for medical purposes. The specific necessity defense designed by the Court of Appeals for medical marijuana use has become moot by its own terms.

. . .

Of course the overall common law necessity defense continues to protect defendants who are forced to violate the law to avert a greater harm. But the narrow medical necessity defense developed in *Diana* specifically for individuals with a medical need to use marijuana no longer makes sense in a state that specifically provides a legal method for the medical use of marijuana. I would hold that a defendant wishing to assert a necessity defense would have to prove the broader elements that have developed over hundreds of years—including the lack of legal alternatives—not the narrow medical necessity test developed in a context that no longer exists. In Kurtz's case, the record shows that he was later able to obtain appropriate authorization to legally use medical marijuana for his serious condition. He had a legal alternative to violating the law and thus does not qualify for the necessity defense.

. . .

Furthermore, I find no way to avoid the conclusion that the Medical Use of Marijuana Act abrogated the common law defense. A statute abrogates the common law when "'the provisions of a . . . statute are so inconsistent with and repugnant to the prior common law that both cannot simultaneously be in force.'" . . . In this case, the Medical Use of Marijuana Act created a defense to charges of use or possession of marijuana if the defendant can show that he or she was using the marijuana for medical purposes—the exact issue addressed by the common law defense. Because the Medical Use of Marijuana Act addresses the very concern addressed by the common law, the two cannot coexist. The Medical Use of Marijuana Act sets out a comprehensive structure for the defense, including the qualifying conditions or diseases, the amount of marijuana allowed, and documentation of a physician's recommendation. As a result of these detailed requirements, the statutory defense is much narrower than the common law defense. The common law did not require any communication with a physician nor did it place a limit on the amount of marijuana at issue. Therefore, the provisions of the Medical Use of Marijuana Act's defense are so inconsistent with the prior common law that both cannot simultaneously be in force. It does not make sense that the state would create a significantly narrower and more detailed statutory defense if it did not mean to replace the broader common law defense.

Moreover, allowing the common law defense to coexist with the statutory defense would frustrate the purpose of the Medical Use of Marijuana Act. When determining whether a statute is exclusive, this court has repeatedly indicated that it must strive to uphold the purpose of the statute. . . . . In passing the Medical Use of Marijuana Act voters set up a structure to allow medical marijuana, but they specifically limited the defense to individuals using medical marijuana under a doctor's supervision. If the court were to uphold the broader common law defense without the requirement of a doctor's supervision, the court would frustrate the purpose of the voters that specifically added that requirement for the medical use of marijuana.

## Notes and Questions

1. What do you think? Should courts continue to recognize a common law necessity defense for marijuana when their states have adopted medical marijuana legislation? Does the defense undermine the design of a state medical marijuana system? Consider the following Problems. In which, if any, would you recognize a medical necessity defense? Would your answer be different if the state had never adopted a medical marijuana law?

Problem 4.20: Andy suffers from PTSD linked to his military service in Afghanistan. Although Andy lives in a state with a medical marijuana law, the state does not recognize PTSD as a qualifying condition. Since being diagnosed with PTSD three years ago, Andy has tried a handful of medications and therapies, but they have not fully resolved his symptoms. He continues to suffer from mild depression, occasional memory loss, and irritability at work and at home. In a recent visit, Andy asked his doctor whether marijuana might help him. She told Andy, "It's not legal for your condition here, but a few other states do allow people to use marijuana for PTSD. I suppose it might help your symptoms." Following the visit, Andy bought one ounce of marijuana from a friend. On his way home, however, he was stopped for speeding. He promptly told the officer he had one ounce of marijuana, and the officer proceeded to charge Andy with simple possession of the drug.

Problem 4.21: Benjamin has not worked regularly for nearly three years and has no health insurance. He does occasional odd jobs, but otherwise gets by with help from his parents and friends. Eighteen months ago, Benjamin was diagnosed with Crohn's disease, which his state medical marijuana program recognizes as a qualifying condition. At the time, his physician recommended marijuana to treat his symptoms. Benjamin subsequently registered with the state medical marijuana program. He has continued to use marijuana ever since, but his registration, recommendation, and diagnosis expired five months ago. Benjamin says he does not want to pay another $100 to renew his registration, or $150 to visit his physician for another diagnosis and recommendation. While driving to a friend's house, Benjamin was pulled over for speeding. He promptly told the officer that he had one ounce of marijuana, and he showed him his expired registration card. But the officer proceeded to charge him with possession of marijuana.

**Problem 4.22**: Camila lives in a state that recently adopted a law allowing residents who suffer from severe intractable epilepsy to use CBD. Camila has been diagnosed with wasting syndrome associated with AIDS. On the recommendation of her physician, she has been using marijuana to restore her appetite. So far, she believes the treatment has helped her. However, last week, on her way home from buying one ounce of marijuana from a black market dealer, Camila was stopped for speeding. She promptly told the officer she had one ounce of marijuana, and the officer proceeded to charge Camila with simple possession of the drug.

2. Chapter 14 discusses the availability of legal remedies against law enforcement agents for wrongful search, arrest, seizure, or prosecution.

# CHAPTER 5

# Policy Toward Marijuana Users

This chapter delves into the policy arguments behind the regulations of marijuana possession and use surveyed in Chapters 3 and 4. What are the benefits of marijuana use? What are the harms? What impact does the law have on use? What are the costs of regulating marijuana possession and use? The chapter addresses these and related questions. Importantly, it does not aim to persuade the reader; rather, the chapter is designed to enable the reader to better understand why policymakers have come to such different conclusions about how marijuana possession and use should be regulated. To that end, the chapter draws on materials from diverse fields, including the natural and social sciences, law, and philosophy.

The chapter proceeds as follows. Sections A and B discuss the objectives that policymakers have pursued through regulating marijuana use. These sections examine the medical-scientific debates over the benefits and harms of marijuana use, as well as the more philosophical debates over which of those benefits and harms should motivate government policy. Sections C and D then discuss the competing means policymakers have chosen to pursue their policy objectives. These sections examine the relative impact that competing regulatory approaches have on marijuana use and related harms, and the comparative costs of those approaches.

## A. WHAT ARE MARIJUANA'S BENEFITS?

Problem 5.1: Suppose you meet a genie with magical powers. The genie makes you the following offer: at your command, she will make all of the marijuana (plants included) in the world instantly disappear forever. There is no catch, and you believe she could do it. Would you give the command? Why, why not?

Your response to the genie's offer likely reflects your opinions of marijuana use. But is marijuana use good or bad for society? And how do we decide? This section focuses on marijuana's benefits. It examines the scientific debates over whether marijuana has medical utility and the more philosophical debates over whether recreational enjoyment of the drug should command equal respect under the law. Section B will then discuss similar debates over marijuana's harms.

## 1. Medical Benefits

Much of the debate over marijuana policy has focused on whether marijuana has any medical benefits. The CSA makes the existence of medical benefits one of the most important criteria for scheduling drugs. *See* 21 U.S.C. §§ 811(c) & 812(b). If a drug has "no currently accepted medical use in treatment in the United States" it is placed on Schedule I (assuming other criteria are met).[1] *Id.* at § 812(b)(1). Such a drug may not be possessed except in approved research studies. By contrast, if a drug has a "currently accepted medical use," it is placed on one of the lower schedules (II-V), depending on its abuse and dependence potential (roughly speaking, its harms), and it may be used for medical treatment. *Id.* at § 812(b)(2). It is thus safe to say that whether a drug has medical utility drives federal policy toward the drug.

But medical utility also plays a key role in shaping state policy toward marijuana. After all, medical marijuana states have approved only those uses of the drug they have deemed to be medically beneficial. California's Compassionate Use Act, for example, declares that its purpose is "[t]o ensure that seriously ill Californians have the right to obtain and use marijuana for *medical* purposes," while also insisting that "[n]othing in this section shall be construed to supersede legislation prohibiting persons from engaging in conduct that endangers others, nor to condone the diversion of marijuana for *nonmedical* purposes." Cal. Health & Safety Code § 11362.5 (b) (emphases added). Even states that have legalized marijuana for non-medical purposes continue to grant medical users some special privileges. *See* Chapter 4.

Notwithstanding their shared belief that medical benefits should drive policy, however, federal and state policymakers clearly disagree about whether marijuana ever generates such benefits. The next two sections explore the disagreement and its causes.

### a. The DEA's Position on Marijuana's Medical Benefits

For its part, the federal government remains unconvinced that marijuana has any medical utility. The DEA has denied several petitions to reschedule marijuana, all because the agency has concluded that the drug has no "acceptable medical use," per the CSA's scheduling criteria. As discussed further in Chapter 6 below, the DEA is required to defer to the Department of Health and Human Services' (HHS) medical/scientific evaluation of the drug when making its scheduling decisions. The excerpt below describes HHS's medical/scientific evaluation of marijuana's medical benefits, completed in response to a rescheduling petition filed by the Governors of Rhode Island and Washington in December 2011. Governors of Rhode Island and Washington, *Rulemaking Petition to Reclassify Cannabis for Medical use from a Schedule I Controlled Substance to a Schedule II* (Nov. 30, 2011) [Governors' Petition]. The excerpt explains the standards the federal

---

[1]. The CSA also requires that a substance have a high potential for abuse and lack protocols for safe use to be placed on Schedule I. 21 U.S.C. § 812(b)(1). But because all of the other Schedules (II-V) require a currently accepted medical use, the DEA has argued that Schedule I is the correct place for any drug lacking medical utility, regardless of the severity of its abuse or dependence potential. For a discussion of the DEA's argument and the confusion surrounding the CSA's scheduling criteria, see Alex Kreit, *Controlled Substances, Uncontrolled Law*, 6 Alb. Gov't L. Rev. 332 (2013).

government uses to assess the medical utility of a drug and why HHS believes those standards have not yet been satisfied for marijuana.

## *Department of Health and Human Services*, Basis for the Recommendation for Maintaining Marijuana in Schedule I of the Controlled Substances Act
81 Fed. Reg. 53690 (Aug. 12, 2016)

On November 30, 2011, Governors Lincoln D. Chafee of Rhode Island and Christine O. Gregoire of Washington submitted a petition to the Drug Enforcement Administration (DEA) requesting that proceeding be initiated to repeal the rules and regulations that place marijuana 4 in Schedule I of the Controlled Substances Act (CSA). The petition contends that cannabis has an accepted medical use in the United States, is safe for use under medical supervision, and has a relatively low abuse potential compared to other Schedule II drugs. The petition requests that marijuana and "related items" be rescheduled in Schedule II of the CSA. In June 2013, the DEA Administrator requested that the U.S. Department of Health and Human Services (HHS) provide a scientific and medical evaluation of the available information and a scheduling recommendation for marijuana, in accordance with the provisions of 21 U.S.C. 811(b).

. . .

State-level public initiatives, including laws and referenda in support of the medical use of marijuana, have generated interest in the medical community and the need for high quality clinical investigation as well as comprehensive safety and effectiveness data. . . .

. . .

In general, a drug may have a "currently accepted medical use" in treatment in the United States if the drug meets a five-part test. Established case law (Alliance for Cannabis Therapeutics v. DEA, 15 F.3d 1131, 1135 (D.C. Cir. 1994)) upheld the Administrator of the DEA's application of the five-part test to determine whether a drug has a "currently accepted medical use." The following describes the five elements that characterize "currently accepted medical use" for a drug:

    i. the drug's chemistry must be known and reproducible.

"The substance's chemistry must be scientifically established to permit it to be reproduced into dosages which can be standardized . . ."

    ii. there must be adequate safety studies.

"There must be adequate pharmacological and toxicological studies, done by all methods reasonably applicable, on the basis of which it could fairly and responsibly be concluded, by experts qualified by scientific training and experience to evaluate the safety and effectiveness of drugs, that the substance is safe for treating a specific, recognized disorder."

    iii. there must be adequate and well-controlled studies proving efficacy.

"There must be adequate, well-controlled, well-designed, well-conducted, and well-documented studies, including clinical investigations, by experts qualified by scientific training and experience to evaluate the safety and effectiveness of drugs, on the basis of which it could be fairly and responsibly concluded by such experts that the substance will have the intended effect in treating a specific, recognized disorder."

    iv. the drug must be accepted by qualified experts.

"The drug has a New Drug Application (NDA) approved by the Food and Drug Administration, pursuant to the Food, Drug and Cosmetic Act, 21 U.S.C. 355. Or, a consensus of the national community of experts, qualified by scientific training and experience to evaluate the safety and effectiveness of drugs, accepts the safety and effectiveness of the substance for use in treating a specific, recognized disorder. A material conflict of opinion among experts precludes a finding of consensus." and

v. the scientific evidence must be widely available.

"In the absence of NDA approval, information concerning the chemistry, pharmacology, toxicology, and effectiveness of the substance must be reported, published, or otherwise widely available, in sufficient detail to permit experts, qualified by scientific training and experience to evaluate the safety and effectiveness of drugs, to fairly and responsibly conclude the substance is safe and effective for use in treating a specific, recognized disorder."

Marijuana does not meet any of the five elements necessary for a drug to have a "currently accepted medical use."

Firstly, the chemistry of marijuana, as defined in the petition, is not reproducible in terms of creating a standardized dose. The petition defines marijuana as including all Cannabis cultivated strains. Different marijuana samples derived from various cultivated strains may have very different chemical constituents including delta9-THC and other cannabinoids.... As a consequence, marijuana products from different strains will have different safety, biological, pharmacological, and toxicological profiles. Thus, when considering all Cannabis strains together, because of the varying chemical constituents, reproducing consistent standardized doses is not possible. Additionally, smoking marijuana currently has not been shown to allow delivery of consistent and reproducible doses.

However, if a specific Cannabis strain is grown and processed under strictly controlled conditions, the plant chemistry may be kept consistent enough to produce reproducible and standardized doses.

As to the second and third criteria; there are neither adequate safety studies nor adequate and well-controlled studies proving marijuana's efficacy. To support the petitioners' assertion that marijuana has accepted medical use, the petitioners cite the American Medical Association's (AMA) 2009 report entitled "Use of Cannabis for Medicinal Purposes." The petitioners claim the AMA report is evidence the AMA accepts marijuana's safety and efficacy. However, the 2009 AMA report clarifies that the report "should not be viewed as an endorsement of state-based medical cannabis programs, the legalization of marijuana, or that scientific evidence on the therapeutic use of cannabis meets the same and current standards for a prescription drug product."

Currently, no published studies conducted with marijuana meet the criteria of an adequate and well-controlled efficacy study.... In order to assess this element, [the Food and Drug Administration (FDA)] conducted a review of clinical studies published and available in the public domain before February, 2013. Studies were identified through a search of PubMed for articles published from inception to February 2013, for randomized controlled trials using marijuana to assess marijuana's efficacy in any therapeutic indication.

Additionally, the review included studies identified through a search of bibliographic references in relevant systematic reviews and identified studies presenting original research in any language. Selected studies needed to be placebo-controlled and double-blinded. Additionally, studies needed to encompass administered marijuana plant material. There was no requirement for any specific route of administration, nor any age limits on study subjects. Studies were excluded that used placebo marijuana supplemented by the addition of specific amounts of THC or other cannabinoids. Additionally, studies administering marijuana plant extracts were excluded.

The PubMed search yielded a total of 566 abstracts of scientific articles.... [O]nly 11 studies met all the criteria for selection.... These 11 studies were published between 1974 and 2013.... The identified studies examine the effects of smoked and vaporized marijuana for the indications of chronic neuropathic pain, spasticity related to Multiple Sclerosis (MS), appetite stimulation in human immunodeficiency virus (HIV) patients, glaucoma, and asthma....

The 11 identified studies were individually evaluated to determine if they successfully meet accepted scientific standards. Specifically, they were evaluated on study design including subject selection criteria, sample size, blinding techniques, dosing paradigms, outcome measures, and the statistical analysis of the results.... The review found that all 11 studies that examined effects of inhaled marijuana do not currently prove efficacy of marijuana in any therapeutic indication based on a number of limitations in their study design; however, they may be considered proof of concept studies. Proof of concept studies provide preliminary evidence on a proposed hypothesis involving a drug's effect. For drugs under development, the effect often relates to a short-term clinical outcome being investigated. Proof of concept studies often serve as the link between preclinical studies and dose ranging clinical studies. Thus, proof of concept studies generally are not sufficient to prove efficacy of a drug because they provide only preliminary information about the effects of a drug.

In addition to the lack of published adequate and well-controlled efficacy studies proving efficacy, the criteria for adequate safety studies has also not been met.... "No drug can be considered safe in the abstract. Safety has meaning only when judged against the intended use of the drug, its known effectiveness, its known and potential risks, the severity of the illness to be treated, and the availability of alternative remedies" (57 FR 10504). When determining whether a drug product is safe and effective for any indication, FDA performs an extensive risk-benefit analysis to determine whether the risks posed by the drug product's side effects are outweighed by the drug product's potential benefits for a particular indication. Thus, contrary to the petitioner's assertion that marijuana has accepted safety, in the absence of an accepted therapeutic indication which can be weighed against marijuana's risks, marijuana does not satisfy the element for having adequate safety studies such that experts may conclude that it is safe for treating a specific, recognized disorder.

The fourth of the five elements for determining "currently accepted medical use" requires that the national community of experts, qualified by scientific training and experience to evaluate the safety and effectiveness of drugs, accepts the safety and effectiveness of the substance for use in treating a specific, recognized disorder. A material conflict of opinion among experts precludes a finding of consensus. Medical practitioners who are not experts in evaluating drugs are not qualified to determine whether a drug is generally recognized as safe and effective or meets NDA requirements....

There is no evidence that there is a consensus among qualified experts that marijuana is safe and effective for use in treating a specific, recognized disorder. As discussed above, there are not adequate scientific studies that show marijuana is safe and effective in treating a specific, recognized disorder. In addition, there is no evidence that a consensus of qualified experts have accepted the safety and effectiveness of marijuana for use in treating a specific, recognized disorder. Although medical practitioners are not qualified by scientific training and experience to evaluate the safety and effectiveness of drugs, we also note that the AMA's report, entitled "Use of Cannabis for Medicinal Purposes," does not accept that marijuana currently has accepted medical use. Furthermore, based on the above definition of a "qualified expert," who is an individual qualified by scientific training and experience to evaluate the safety and effectiveness of a drug, state-level medical marijuana laws do not provide evidence of a consensus among qualified experts that marijuana is safe and effective for use in treating a specific, recognized disorder.

As to the fifth part of the test, which requires that information concerning the chemistry, pharmacology, toxicology, and effectiveness of marijuana to be reported in sufficient detail, the scientific evidence regarding all of these aspects is not available in sufficient detail to allow adequate scientific scrutiny. Specifically, the scientific evidence regarding marijuana's chemistry in terms of a specific Cannabis strain that could produce standardized and reproducible doses is not currently available.

. . . In conclusion, to date, research on marijuana's medical use has not progressed to the point where marijuana is considered to have a "currently accepted medical use" or a "currently accepted medical use with severe restrictions."

## Notes and Questions

1. What do you think of the HHS recommendation, and in particular, the standards the agency employs for deciding whether a drug has a currently accepted medical use? Are the agency's standards too demanding? What standards would you use? What evidence would you consider when assessing marijuana's (or any other drug's) medical utility? Would you give any weight to anecdotes, for example, the testimony of individuals who have tried marijuana and claim that it has improved their medical conditions? What about the opinions of practicing physicians? The passage of state medical marijuana laws?

2. Is it possible to satisfy the agency's standards, given the difficulty of researching marijuana's medical effects? The agency demands large scale, "adequate, well-controlled, well-designed, well-conducted, and well-documented studies" to demonstrate medical utility, but completing such studies on marijuana poses some unique challenges. Part of the difficulty stems from the drug itself. Well-controlled studies typically keep subjects in the dark (i.e., blind) about whether they have been given the drug being studied or a placebo (the control group). As the DEA Administrator explained in denying a previous petition to reschedule marijuana, 57 Fed. Reg. 10499, 10502 (1992), "[p]atients have a tendency to respond to drugs as they believe is expected of them." But it can be difficult to keep subjects in the dark when administering marijuana, at least when it contains a psychoactive substance like THC. See Food and Drug Administration, *The Medical Application of Marijuana: A Review of Published Clinical Studies* (Mar. 2015), in 81 Fed. Reg. 53688, 53724 ("[E]ven under the most rigorous experimental conditions, blinding can be difficult in studies with smoked marijuana because the rapid onset of psychoactive effects readily distinguishes active from placebo marijuana."). For similar reasons, subjects who are administered THC might report feeling better, even if their medical conditions have not improved. 57 Fed. Reg. at 10502 (noting that "any mind-altering drug that produces euphoria can make a sick person think he feels better"). Another difficulty stems from the fact that not all marijuana is created alike. As discussed in Chapter 2 and noted in the excerpt above, different plants contain different combinations and concentrations of different cannabinoids, making it

difficult for researchers to maintain consistency both within and across studies and to isolate what is causing any medical benefits they might observe.

But some of the difficulty surrounding research on marijuana also appears to have stemmed from federal regulations of the drug itself. Scientists face a number of barriers to conducting research on all Schedule I substances, but the barriers to research on marijuana may be more pronounced. *See* John Hudak & Grace Wallack, *Ending the U.S. Government's War on Medical Marijuana Research* (Brookings Oct. 2015). For one thing, for nearly 50 years the federal government has maintained a monopoly on the production of all marijuana used in research studies in the United States. *Id.* at 6, n.14. The monopoly is operated by the University of Mississippi under a contract with NIDA and the DEA. *Id.* The monopoly produces only limited varieties of marijuana, and until recently, produced only a limited quantity of the drug (roughly 20 kg annually). *Id.* at 5. In the past, the DEA has refused requests by other institutions to produce marijuana for research, *id.* at 10, although in 2016 the agency announced a "new policy that is designed to increase the number of entities registered under the Controlled Substances Act (CSA) to grow (manufacture) marijuana to supply legitimate researchers in the United States." Drug Enforcement Agency, *Applications to Become Registered Under the Controlled Substances Act to Manufacture Marijuana to Supply Researchers in the United States*, 81 Fed. Reg. 53846 (Aug. 12, 2016). Apart from limiting the supply of research grade marijuana, the federal government also imposes other requirements that increase the cost and difficulty of conducting large-scale research studies to test the efficacy of marijuana (and other Schedule I drugs). *See* Hudak & Wallack, *supra*, at 10. *See also* Peter J. Cohen, *Medical Marijuana: The Conflict Between Scientific Evidence and Political Ideology*, 2009 Utah L. Rev. 35, 77-81 (discussing examples of past research projects that were allegedly stymied by federal regulations).

3. Should the DEA (further) relax restrictions on marijuana research? Professor Alex Kreit has previously criticized the regulatory barriers to marijuana research:

> . . . The CSA appears to take the position that Schedule I substances should be hard to study in part because they do not have a currently accepted medical use. This might make sense if Schedule I substances were limited to those that had been thoroughly vetted and found not to have medical value. But many substances are barely investigated at all before being placed into Schedule I. In some cases, the studies that do exist indicate the substance may potentially have medical uses. By design, the CSA makes it incredibly difficult to research these substances. This is a serious and underappreciated flaw in the CSA. It is hard to rationalize blocking research into a substance we know has potential as a medicine, particularly in comparison to new, unscheduled drugs. . . .
>
> According to the CSA, strict research controls are needed to "adequately safeguard against diversion" of Schedule I drugs. This rationale seems premised on the existence of a world in which it is nearly impossible to obtain Schedule I substances—a world where breaking into research laboratories or manufacturing facilities would pose a real risk of letting otherwise unobtainable drugs out into the public. But this is not the world we live in. Widely abused Schedule I substances like marijuana, cocaine, or heroin are relatively easy to find and buy on the black market . . . .
>
> Guarding against diversion from Schedule I research may be a reasonable goal in the abstract, but in the context of the market for illegal drugs that exists today, it is hard to make sense of . . . .
>
> One could also argue that the Schedule I drugs are unusually dangerous substances and so the CSA must significantly limit research into them in order to help protect would-be test

subjects. The trouble with this rationale is that substances are placed into Schedule I because of their lack of accepted medical use and potential for abuse and dependency, not because they have particularly dangerous side effects. There is thus little reason to think that a Schedule I substance would be riskier to study than a pharmaceutical substance going through the FDA approval process. To be sure, the potential for addiction of Schedule I substances is a legitimate concern, but Food, Drug, and Cosmetics Act regulations on medical research into non-Scheduled substances already accounts for even more significant risks, like the possibility that the substance being researched may increase the risk of cancer.

In sum, strict research restrictions for Schedule I substances provide few tangible benefits at a significant cost. . . .

*Controlled Substances, Uncontrolled Law*, *supra*, at 356-357. Do you agree with Kreit's criticisms? If so, would you relax the controls for other Schedule I substances as well?

4. As noted in Chapter 2, the DEA and FDA have approved two *synthetic* cannabinoids for medical use. Dronabinol (brand name Marinol) is a Schedule III drug containing synthetic delta-9-tetrahydrocannbinol. The drug is taken orally in capsule form. It is indicated for (i.e., approved for treatment of) boosting appetite in AIDS patients and for combatting the nausea associated with cancer chemotherapy in patients who fail to respond to other medications. Food and Drug Admin., New Drug Application 18-651: Marinol (2004), https://perma.cc/45RA-VHFB. Nabilone (brand name Cesamet) is a Schedule II drug containing a synthetic cannabinoid that resembles THC. It is also taken orally in capsule form. Like Dronabinol, it has been approved for the treatment of nausea associated with cancer chemotherapy. Food and Drug Admin., New Drug Application 18-677: Cesamet (2006), https://perma.cc/69M3-RS57.

The approval of synthetic cannabinoids raises (at least) two questions. On the one hand, how can federal agencies conclude that botanical marijuana lacks a currently accepted medical use when they have previously approved for medical use synthetic versions of one of the key substances found in marijuana? For criticisms of the agency's treatment of botanical versus synthetic cannabinoids, see Governors' Petition, Exh. B, at 12 (arguing that "it is inconsistent that [natural] cannabis, with 15 percent THC, remains a Schedule I drug, while dronabinol, at 100 percent THC, is Schedule III"). HHS has provided the following rationale for distinguishing Marinol:

> Major differences in formulation, availability, and usage between marijuana and the drug product, Marinol, contribute to their differing abuse potentials.
>
> [It has been] estimated that delta9-THC by smoking is 2.6 to 3 times more potent than delta9-THC ingested orally. The intense psychoactive drug effect achieved, rapidly by smoking is generally considered to produce the effect desired by the abuser. This effect explains why abusers often prefer to administer certain drugs by inhalation, intravenously, or intranasally rather than orally. . . . Thus, the delayed onset and longer duration of action for Marinol may be contributing factors limiting the abuse or appeal of Marinol as a drug of abuse relative to marijuana.

*HHS Recommendation*, *supra*, at 53694. Is this answer responsive to the point raised by the Governors' Petition?

On the other hand, if dronabinol and nabilone *are* similar to botanical marijuana, why does anyone need to use botanical marijuana? Consider this explanation:

> Many of the undesired psychoactive effects of cannabis are due to THC, which is among the reasons that dronabinol is not a suitable alternative (because dronabinol is 100 percent

THC as opposed to natural cannabis which is only 15 percent THC). However newer medicinal strains of cannabis are lower in THC and higher in the non-psychoactive, more therapeutic cannabinoids, such as CBD, and CBN. These compounds further improved the efficacy of cannabis.

*Governors' Petition, supra,* at Exh. B p. 10. Is this explanation persuasive?

### b. The States' Positions on Marijuana's Medical Benefits

While the federal government insists there is no demonstrated medical benefit from marijuana, medical marijuana states (and CBD states) are convinced that marijuana has at least some beneficial medical applications. *E.g.*, N.J. C24:6I-2 ("(a) Modern medical research has discovered a beneficial use for marijuana in treating or alleviating the pain or other symptoms associated with certain debilitating medical conditions . . ."). Indeed, the belief that marijuana has medical benefits is the most common reason people cite for supporting legalization of the drug, as displayed in **Figure 5.1**:

Figure 5.1. Reasons Why People Support Legalization*

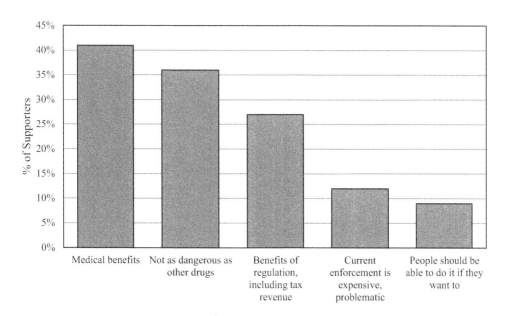

More than half of the states have acted on this belief and approved marijuana to treat a broad range of medical conditions or their symptoms. **Figure 5.2** lists a sample of the conditions for which marijuana may be used as a treatment and the percentage of medical marijuana states where it is so allowed.

---

* Pew Research Center Poll (poll conducted Mar. 26-29, 2015) (question asked of the 53 percent of respondents who supported outright legalization). Note that total exceeds 100 percent because respondents were allowed to provide more than one answer.

Part II. Marijuana Users

Figure 5.2. Qualifying Conditions in Medical Marijuana States*

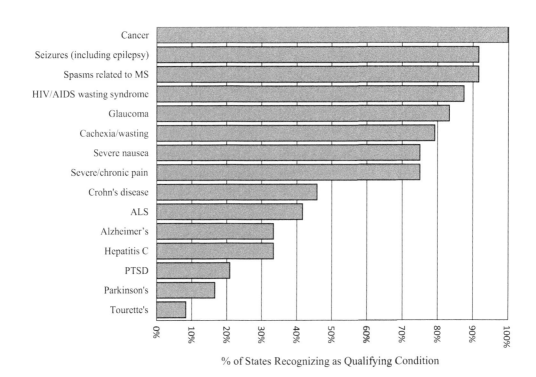

% of States Recognizing as Qualifying Condition

A state's initial list of qualifying conditions is usually created by the legislation or initiative establishing the state's medical marijuana program. The same political process may also be used to add new qualifying conditions later, but most states also allow conditions to be added via a separate administrative process. A handful of states permit additions to be made *only* via the political process. *E.g.*, MT 50-46-302(2)(k) (defining qualifying condition to include "any other medical condition or treatment for a medical condition *approved by the legislature*") (emphasis added); Washington State Department of Health, *Medical Marijuana: Petitions to Add Qualifying Conditions*, https://perma.cc/6AAD-4WW5 (explaining that as of July 24, 2015, new conditions can be added only through legislation or initiative).

The administrative process varies somewhat from state to state, both in terms of the standards employed and the composition of the administrative body that makes the decision. The Colorado regulations below illustrate the process followed by some states:

> D. The department [of Public Health and Environment] shall accept physician or patient petitions to add debilitating medical conditions . . . , and shall follow the following procedures in reviewing such petitions.

---

* Data as of July 31, 2015, in 24 medical marijuana states.

1. . . . Upon receipt of a petition, the executive director . . . shall review the information submitted in support of the petition and shall also conduct a search of the medical literature for peer-reviewed published literature of randomized controlled trials or well-designed observational studies in humans concerning the use of marijuana for the condition that is the subject of the petition using PUBMED, the official search program for the National Library of Medicine and the National Institutes of Health, and the Cochrane Central Register of Controlled Trials.

2. . . . The department shall deny a petition to add a debilitating medical condition within (180) days of receipt of such petition without any hearing of the board in all of the following circumstances:

    a. If there are no peer-reviewed published studies of randomized controlled studies nor well-designed observational studies showing efficacy in humans for use of medical marijuana for the condition that is the subject of the petition;

    b. If there are peer-reviewed published studies of randomized controlled trials or well-designed observational studies showing efficacy in humans for the condition that is the subject of the petition, and if there are studies that show harm, other than harm associated with smoking such as obstructive lung disease or lung cancer, and there are alternative, conventional treatments available for the condition;

    c. If the petition seeks the addition of an underlying condition for which the associated symptoms that are already listed as debilitating medical conditions for which the use of medical marijuana is allowed, such as severe pain, are the reason for which medical marijuana is requested, rather than for improvement of the underlying condition; or

    d. If a majority of the ad hoc medical advisory panel recommends denial of the petition in accord with paragraph (3) of this section D.

3. Medical marijuana scientific advisory council. [Author's note: The council is made up of the chief medical officer of the state health department, along with 6-13 members appointed by department's executive director, who must include physicians from designated specialties, an epidemiologist, and a medical marijuana advocate. *See* Colo. Rev. Stat. § 25-1.5-106.5(3).]

    . . .

    b. The medical marijuana scientific advisory panel council will review petitions to add debilitating medical conditions if the conditions for denial set forth in paragraphs (2)(a),(b) and (c) of this section D are not met. . . .

    c. The council shall review the petition information presented to the department and any further medical research related to the condition requested, and make recommendations to the executive director, or his or her designee, regarding the petition.

    d. Within (120) days of receipt of a petition to add a debilitating medical condition, the department shall petition the board for a rulemaking hearing to consider adding the condition to the list of debilitating medical conditions if the council recommends approval of the petition to add the condition.

4. Final agency action. The following actions are final agency actions, subject to judicial review . . .

    a. Department denials of petitions to add debilitating medical conditions.

    b. Board of health denials of rules proposed by the department to add a condition to the list of debilitating medical conditions for the medical marijuana program.

5 Colo. Code Reg. 1006-2:6.

## Notes and Questions

1. What evidence exists to suggest that marijuana is an effective treatment for the specific conditions listed in **Figure 5.2**? Systematic reviews of the scientific literature can help to answer the question. Such reviews gather and evaluate the quality of all of the studies that have been conducted on a particular research question. The reviews then reliably summarize the overall state of scientific knowledge on the question. For recent reviews of studies on marijuana's health benefits (and harms), see Adam J. Gordon et al., *Medical Consequences of Marijuana Use: A Review of Current Literature*, 15 Curr. Psychiatry Rep. 419 (2013), Wayne Hall, *What Has Research over the Past Two Decades Revealed About the Adverse Health Effects of Recreational Cannabis Use?*, 110 Addiction 19 (2014); Nora D. Volkow et al., *Adverse Health Effects of Marijuana Use*, 370 New England J. Medicine 2219 (2014); Penny F. Whiting et al., *Cannabinoids for Medical Use: A Systematic Review and Meta-Analysis*, 313 J. Am. Med. Ass'n 2456 (2015); National Academies of Science, Engineering, and Medicine, Cannabinoids: The Current State of Evidence and Recommendations for Research (2017), https://www.nap.edu/read/24625/chapter/1#ii.

The Cochrane Collaboration, a network of independent researchers, has published several reviews of studies examining marijuana's medical utility. These Cochrane Reviews are generally well-regarded in the health research community. **Table 5.1** provides the conclusions of all of the Cochrane Reviews published as of August 2016 that have examined the efficacy of marijuana as a treatment for a specific medical condition. Based on these conclusions, do you think there is sufficient evidence to approve marijuana as a treatment for any of the conditions that were the subject of a Cochrane Review? Are the states basing their decisions on science? Or politics? *See* Cohen, *Medical Marijuana: The Conflict, supra*, at 101 (suggesting that "in part due to perceived governmental obstinacy . . . advocates of marijuana have rejected the role of scientific evidence and replaced it with political action"); Alicia Wallace, *How PTSD Became the Most Divisive Medical Pot Issue of 2016*, The Cannabist (July 26, 2016) ("The politics are far outpacing the research.") (quoting Dr. Samuel Wilkinson regarding the addition of PTSD as a qualifying condition).

Table 5.1. Cochrane Reviews of Marijuana Research

| Condition | Conclusion | Source |
|---|---|---|
| **AIDS/HIV** | "The use of cannabis (marijuana), its active ingredient or synthetic forms such as dronabinol has been advocated in patients with HIV/AIDS, in order to improve the appetite, promote weight gain and lift mood. Dronabinol has been registered for the treatment of AIDS-associated anorexia in some countries. However, the evidence for positive effects in patients with HIV/AIDS is limited, and | Elizabeth E. Lutge et al., *The Medical Use of Cannabis for Reducing Morbidity and Mortality in Patients with HIV/AIDS* (Apr. 30, 2013), http://onlinelibrary.wiley.com/doi/10.1002/14651858.CD005175.pub3/full (review of 7 randomized/quasi-randomized control trials) |

| Condition | Conclusion | Source |
|---|---|---|
| | some of that which exists may be subject to the effects of bias. Those studies that have been performed have included small numbers of participants and have focused on short-term effects. Longer-term data, and data showing a benefit in terms of survival, are lacking. There are insufficient data available at present to justify wide-ranging changes to the current regulatory status of cannabis or synthetic cannabinoids." | |
| **Ataxia** | "Across the studies, cannabis was well tolerated. Common side effects were mild dizziness, intoxication and drowsiness. . . . [However, t]he conclusion derived from all three studies was that cannabis based medicine resulted in no significant improvement in tremor." | Roger J. Mills et al., *Treatment for Ataxia in Multiple Sclerosis* (Jan. 24, 2007), http://onlinelibrary.wiley.com/doi/10.1002/14651858.CD005029.pub2/full (review of 3 randomized control trials) |
| **Cancer chemotherapy** | "[F]ewer people who received cannabis-based medicines experienced nausea and vomiting than people who received placebo . . . The proportion of people who experienced nausea and vomiting who received cannabis-based medicines was similar to conventional anti-nausea medicines. However, more people experienced side effects such as 'feeling high', dizziness, sedation (feeling relaxed or sleepy) and dysphoria (feeling uneasy or dissatisfied) and left the study due to the side effects with cannabis-based medicines, compared with either placebo or other anti-nausea medicines. In trials where people received cannabis-based medicines and conventional medicines in turn, overall people preferred the cannabis-based medicines. . . . | Lesley A. Smith et al., *Cannabinoids for Nausea and Vomiting in Adults with Cancer Receiving Chemotherapy* (Nov. 12, 2015), http://onlinelibrary.wiley.com/doi/10.1002/14651858.CD009464.pub2/full (review of 23 randomized control trials) |

Part II. Marijuana Users

| Condition | Conclusion | Source |
|---|---|---|
| | The trials were of generally of low to moderate quality and reflected chemotherapy treatments and anti-sickness medicines that were around in the 1980s and 1990s. Also, the results from combining studies on the whole were of low quality. This means that we are not very confident in our ability to say how well the anti-sickness medicines worked, and further research reflecting modern treatment approaches is likely to have an important impact on the results. Cannabis-based medicines may be useful for treating chemotherapy-induced nausea and vomiting that responds poorly to commonly used anti-sickness medicines." | |
| **Dementia** | "Laboratory studies have indicated that cannabinoids may regulate some of the processes that lead to neurodegeneration. This suggests that cannabinoids could be useful in the treatment of neurodegenerative dementias such as Alzheimer's disease. So far, only one small randomized controlled trial has assessed the efficacy of cannabinoids in the treatment of dementia. This study had poorly presented results and did not provide sufficient data to draw any useful conclusions." | Sarada Krishnan et al., Cannabinoids for the Treatment of Dementia (Apr. 15, 2009), http://onlinelibrary.wiley.com/doi/10.1002/14651858.CD007204.pub2/full (review of 1 randomized control trial) |
| **Epilepsy** | "No reliable conclusions can be drawn at present regarding the efficacy of cannabinoids as a treatment for epilepsy. The dose of 200 to 300 mg daily of cannabidiol was safely administered to small numbers of patients generally for short periods of time, and so the safety of long term cannabidiol treatment cannot be reliably assessed." | D. Gloss & B. Vickrey, Cannabinoids for Epilepsy (Mar. 5, 2014), http://onlinelibrary.wiley.com/doi/10.1002/14651858.CD009270.pub3/full (review of 4 randomized control trials) |

| Condition | Conclusion | Source |
|---|---|---|
| **Tourette's Syndrome** | "Cannabinoid medication might be useful in the treatment of the symptoms in patients with Tourette's syndrome. At the present time only two relevant studies have been conducted. Both studies used tetrahydrocannabinol ($\delta$9THC). In both studies $\delta$9THC was associated with tic reduction. However the sample size was small [28 participants total] and a large number of multiple comparisons were made. . . . There is not enough evidence to support the use of cannabinoids in treating tics and obsessive compulsive behaviour in people with Tourette's syndrome." | Adrienne Curtis et al., Cannabinoids for Tourette's Syndrome (Oct. 7, 2009), http://onlinelibrary.wiley.com/doi/10.1002/14651858.CD006565.pub2/abstract (review of 2 randomized control trials) |

2. Why is there so much variation across state medical marijuana laws? After all, if marijuana is a beneficial treatment for PTSD in one state, why haven't all of the other medical marijuana states approved it as well? Does the variation undermine the claim that some conditions (say, those recognized by the fewest states) could genuinely benefit from the use of marijuana?

3. How does Colorado's administrative process compare to the administrative process used by the federal government for scheduling marijuana? What does the state require in order to approve marijuana as a treatment for a medical condition?

4. Which process *should* states use to recognize qualifying conditions: the initiative process, the legislative process, or the administrative process (and if so, which one)?

5. What is the downside to approving marijuana as a treatment for a medical condition, if there is little (or no) scientific evidence to suggest the drug will actually improve the condition? For one thing, marijuana could potentially harm the user's health, as discussed in Section B. But the DEA Administrator has also suggested a second reason for caution in approving marijuana as a medical treatment:

> Sick men, women and children can be fooled by these claims and experiment with the drug. Instead of being helped, they risk serious side effects. If they neglect their regular medicines while trying marijuana, the damage could be irreversible. It is a cruel hoax to offer false hope to desperately ill people.

57 Fed. Reg. at 10503. What do you think? Should states demand more evidence when approving marijuana for use as a medical treatment? If so, how much more?

## 2. Recreational Benefits

All jurisdictions accept that marijuana's *medical* benefits should inform how they regulate the drug, even if they disagree about the existence of such benefits. But what about the *recreational* benefits of marijuana use? Should recreational enjoyment "count" as a benefit when policymakers consider how to regulate marijuana possession and use? The following excerpt argues that policymakers should recognize the recreational value of drugs like marijuana.

### *Douglas Husak*, For Drug Legalization
The Legalization of Drugs (Douglas Husak & Peter de Marneffe, eds. 2005)

. . . If drug use has absolutely no value, we need a less weighty reason before we allow it to be criminalized. But if drug use has some value, we should demand a better reason to criminalize it. . . . Therefore, a full evaluation of the injustice of punishing drug users depends on whether we should attach any value to the use of drugs for recreational purposes. Is there some good that is brought about by recreational drug use? . . .

In a free society, we typically allow consumers themselves to judge whether the activities in which they engage are worthwhile. If we choose to spend millions of dollars on hula hoops, pet rocks, or the latest fashion craze, it is not the job of government (or anyone else) to tell us we may not do so—much less to punish us if we disagree. In the absence of fraud or duress, sane adults should be permitted to find value in whatever they want—unless there are good reasons to prevent them from doing so. . . . The fact that tens of millions of Americans choose to use illicit drugs each year may be all the evidence of value we should require.

When consumers are granted this freedom, we must be prepared to accept that some will elect to engage in activities that seem strange and unusual to many of us. Individuals often care passionately about pursuits that appear to be trivial and meaningless to others. Any number of examples could be given; I will mention only one. Most of us are acquainted with fanatical sports fans. They follow their favorite team around the country. Every victory fills them with pride and glee; every loss is an occasion for gloom and despair. Notice how difficult it would be for fans to defend that passion if they were called upon to do so. After all, none of their friends or relatives is a member of the team; they do not know any players personally. They have no financial stake in the prosperity of the team. They might admit that they would feel just as devoted to a different team if they had been born in some other city. Yet there is not much in life they care about more deeply than the success of their favorite team.

Fortunately, our fanatical fans need *not* defend their passion. The state does not tell them that their preferred activity is unimportant. Any philosopher who reported that he could find no value in this activity would be told by the fan to mind his own business. We do not demand that those who enjoy such pursuits must explain why they attach so much meaning to them. We allow people the liberty to act according to their own preferences, however odd they may seem to the rest of us. This willingness is the central mark of a free society. Of course, I do not mean to suggest that we have an unlimited freedom to find value in *any* activity. Surely it *is* the business of the state when someone claims to find value in child abuse or murder. These crimes are concerns of the state because a just society protects the rights of persons who are victimized by them. The sports fan, however, need not harm or violate the rights of anyone.

The difficulty of defending the value of an activity is especially acute when it is purely recreational—pursued for pleasure, euphoria, satisfaction, or some other positive psychological state. If I find a given activity to be enjoyable. I am typically at a loss to explain my reaction to someone who disagrees with me. This is certainly true of taste in foods. Suppose that I love the flavor of anchovies. How can I possibly hope to persuade someone who detests this food to share my preference? Clearly, the whole endeavor is bizarre. Why should we have to defend the value of the fun and enjoyment we experience when we engage in an activity we like? Many moral philosophers have claimed that pleasure is intrinsically valuable. In fact, some have gone so far as to say that pleasure and the absence of pain are the *only* things that are intrinsically valuable. We should not be made to feel shallow and superficial when we admit that our only reason for doing something is that we find it to be pleasant and enjoyable.

Nor should we be apologetic or embarrassed if the particular activity we find to be pleasant and enjoyable involves the use of a *drug*. Invariably, the decision to use illicit drugs for recreational purposes is attributed to peer pressure, boredom, alienation, immaturity, compulsion, ignorance, depression, or some other pathological condition. Even tolerant, liberal abstainers tend to believe that users of illicit drugs need treatment. But empirical support for these preconceptions is dubious; some surveys find that adolescents who have high sel[f]-esteem are more likely to use licit drugs than those whose self-confidence is low. In any event, no one proposes comparable pathological explanations about the popularity of *licit* drugs. Punishment or mandatory treatment is never recommended for wine connoisseurs. As is so much else about prohibition, attitudes about why people use drugs are extraordinarily selective. In fact, people have exactly the same reasons to use licit and illicit drugs. After all, no known societies—except perhaps that of Eskimos—refrain from using drugs for recreational purposes. . . .

. . .

Why is the value of recreational drug use so difficult to comprehend and acknowledge? We should recognize a widespread psychological tendency to devalue activities that we ourselves do not like. People who love to ski can appreciate the exhilaration of those who share their passion. Others may be baffled to understand why anyone would bother to make the effort. This psychological tendency is pervasive in our attitudes about drugs—both licit and illicit. If we loathe the smell of cigars, we cannot fathom how anyone could possibly enjoy them. In our more thoughtful moments, however, we realize that tastes differ, and that our own preferences give us no reason to limit the freedom of those who disagree with us.

To this point, I have called attention to the peculiarity of demanding that drug users defend their preference. We do not impose comparable requirements on those who watch soap operas or patronize amusement parks. But we cannot expect to satisfy those who make this demand by telling them to mind their own business. We all know that recreation is valuable, despite the curious and indefensible exception that is made when illicit drugs provide the source of the positive psychological state we seek. If we agree, we must be willing to allow people to undertake some risks when engaged in recreational activities. We sympathize with those who use dangerous drugs to treat a medical condition—a condition that qualifies as a disease or illness. Evidently, however, no hazard is worth risking when that same drug is used simply to gain pleasure or euphoria.

Our refusal to tolerate any level of risk when drug use is recreational is very hard to defend. After all, no drug is without risks and side effects. According to 1998 estimates, prescription drugs cause about 100,000 fatalities each year in the United States—even when these drugs are used exactly as prescribed. This figure far exceeds the most pessimistic estimates of deaths caused by illicit drugs. Why do we tolerate these staggering levels of risk? The answer can only be the value we attach to health. When a drug used for recreational purposes gives rise to relatively minor risks—as with the dehydration associated with ecstasy—the state responds by increasing the severity of criminal penalties. Why do we not allow these lesser risks? Again, the answer can only be the lack of value we attach to recreation. The key to understanding our present drug policy, then, is to realize that the use of recreational drugs is regarded as having so little value that it fails to justify even the smallest risks. This is why our drug policy places medical and recreational use in entirely different categories.

Notice that we allow people to take enormous risks when they engage in recreational activities that do *not* involve the use of drugs. Consider the risks of skydiving, skiing, or scuba diving. These recreational activities are dangerous—more dangerous than any widely used illicit drug. Still, we do not require individuals to have a very good reason, such as the need to cure a disease or illness, before we allow these risks to be taken. Why not? The answer is that we attach value to these activities. More precisely, we are willing to allow people to decide for themselves whether they value these activities. Even when we do not fathom why anyone would jump out of an airplane with a parachute simply for the thrill, we defer to the judgments of those who disagree with us about whether such activities are worth the danger. Sometimes we even admire people who undertake enormous risks in recreational activities such as mountain climbing. We write books and make movies about their courage. Why, then, are medical reasons required before we allow people to undertake the lesser risks inherent in drug use? Why do we punish people for the risks they take by using illicit drugs recreationally, when virtually no other dangerous recreational activity is punished? I have no good answers to these important questions, which lie at the heart of our drug policy.

. . .

If I am correct, recreational drug use has positive value. I have tried not to exaggerate the extent of this value. I have not relied on grand claims that portray drugs as the key to personal fulfillment or spiritual enlightenment. Most of the value of recreational drug use consists in simple fun and euphoria—goods that should require no elaborate defense. More specifically, the ability to alter mood in desired ways at given times and places can increase control over life and add to its enjoyment. Our assessment of the injustice of prohibition is incomplete unless we take the value of illicit drug use into account. When this value is added to the inquiry, the injustice of punishing recreational users of illicit drugs becomes even more apparent.

## Notes and Questions

1. Is recreation any less legitimate—or important—than treatment of a medical condition? When deciding how to regulate marijuana, should policymakers place any value on the pleasure marijuana gives users? What about other drugs, like heroin or LSD?

2. What is the federal government's view of the recreational "benefits" of marijuana use? In a portion of its marijuana scheduling recommendation excerpted below, HHS acknowledged that marijuana use is "pleasurable to many humans." *Recommendation*, 81 Fed. Reg. at 53693. It also lists several seemingly positive subjective effects associated

with marijuana use, including "Increased merriment . . . and even exhilaration at high doses," "Disinhibition, relaxation, increased sociability, and talkativeness," "Enhanced sensory perception, which can generate an increased appreciation of music, art and touch," and "Heightened imagination which can lead to a subjective sense of increased creativity." *Id.* at 53693-94. However, rather than viewing these effects as evidence of marijuana's *benefits*, the agency instead considers them evidence of marijuana's *harms*, because they demonstrate the drug's high potential for *abuse* (another criterion for placement on Schedule I). Does the agency's reasoning (or the CSA's criteria) make sense? Along these lines, consider the following Problem:

> <u>Problem 5.2</u>: Suppose that Congress repealed the language of 21 U.S.C. section 802(6), which exempts alcoholic beverages and tobacco from the provisions of the CSA. Following the repeal, on what schedule would alcohol and tobacco be placed?

3. Is it even possible to distinguish recreational from medical use? In another portion of his book essay advocating for liberalization of drug laws, Douglas Husak addresses the definitional quandary:

> When *are* drugs used medically? The most popular drugs can be used to illustrate the difficulty of answering this question. Consider caffeine—and try to decide when it is used medically, as opposed to when it is used recreationally. Why do people drink caffeine? Why do people typically prefer regular coffee, and why do they occasionally choose coffee that is decaffeinated? The obvious answer is that people tend to use caffeine when they want to attain a given psychological state—when they want to become more alert, awake, or energetic. Should we categorize this purpose as recreational? Perhaps—although I think that the question is hard. Suppose a student drinks coffee in the morning to combat drowsiness. Is this use medical or recreational? Fortunately, we do not *need* to answer this question. Caffeine is among those drugs permitted either for medical or for recreational purposes. But the distinction between recreational and medical use becomes important when we consider other drugs as examples. Suppose the student substitutes amphetamines for caffeine. Is this use recreational or medical? We have asked the same question as before, but here it is crucial, since state policy differs depending on how we answer it. If his use is recreational, he is a criminal; if his use is medical, he is not. How do we decide which answer is correct?

Husak, *For Drug Legalization, supra*, at 19. Can you distinguish between medicinal and recreational (or other) uses of drugs like marijuana? How, exactly?

4. Why do you think medical benefits have gotten most of the attention in debates over marijuana policy? Is it simply path dependence, i.e., the CSA demands examining the drug through the lens of medicine? Is there a political explanation? In other words, are medical benefits simply more politically palatable than recreational benefits?

## B. WHAT ARE MARIJUANA'S HARMS?

Judgments about marijuana's health *harms* also loom large in marijuana policy debates. After all, if marijuana were harmless, there would be little reason to restrict its use, whether or not the drug has any demonstrable benefits (medical or otherwise).

But what are the harms attributable to marijuana use? And should the government attempt to address all of these harms? The following sections address these questions.

## 1. The Harms of Marijuana Use

The federal government has long maintained that marijuana is a harmful drug. The CSA does not make "harm" a scheduling criteria as such. But two scheduling criteria, namely, whether a drug has a potential for abuse and whether it is safe for medical use, 21 U.S.C. §812(b), are clearly harm-related. And in making scheduling decisions, the DEA is required to consider several factors that likewise reflect the harms of marijuana use, including: (1) the drug's potential for abuse; (2) its pharmacological effects; (3) its risks to public health; and (4) its dependence liability. 21 U.S.C. §811(c).[2]

But what, exactly, are the harms attributable to marijuana use? The HHS's latest scheduling recommendation provides a window into the federal government's position on harms. The agency's findings regarding marijuana's harms are excerpted below (its findings regarding marijuana's benefits were excerpted above). The excerpt is organized around four of the factors the agency is required to consider when making scheduling determinations. 21 U.S.C. §811(c). (The remaining four factors are excluded here either because HHS's discussion of them largely repeats its discussion of the four included factors or because the factors are not related to marijuana's harms.)

### *Department of Health and Human Services*, Basis for the Recommendation for Maintaining Marijuana in Schedule I of the Controlled Substances Act, (cont'd)
81 Fed. Reg. 53690 (Aug. 12, 2016)

#### 1. ITS ACTUAL OR RELATIVE POTENTIAL FOR ABUSE

Under the first factor the Secretary must consider marijuana's actual or relative potential for abuse. The CSA does not define the term "abuse." However, the CSA's legislative history suggests the following in determining whether a particular drug or substance has a potential for abuse:

. . .

a. There is evidence that individuals are taking the drug or drugs containing such a substance in amounts sufficient to create a hazard to their health or to the safety of other individuals or to the community.

Evidence shows that some individuals are taking marijuana in amounts sufficient to create a hazard to their health and to the safety of other individuals and the community. . . . [M]arijuana is the most commonly used illicit drug among Americans aged 12 years and older, with an estimated 18.9 million Americans having used marijuana

---

2. The relationship between the CSA's scheduling criteria and the factors the DEA is required to consider in its scheduling decisions is muddled. For an insightful discussion of the confusion created by the statutory scheme, see Kreit, *Controlled Substances, supra*.

within the month prior to the 2012 [National Survey on Drug Use and Health (NSDUH)]. Compared to 2004, when an estimated 14.6 million individuals reported using marijuana within the month prior to the study, the estimated rates in 2012 show an increase of approximately 4.3 million individuals. The 2013 Monitoring the Future (MTF) survey of 8th, 10th, and 12th grade students also indicates that marijuana is the most widely used illicit substance in this age group. Specifically, current month use was at 7.0 percent of 8th graders, 18.0 percent of 10th, graders and 22.7 percent of 12th graders.

Additionally, the 2011 Treatment Episode Data Set (TEDS) reported that primary marijuana abuse accounted for 18.1 percent of non-private substance-abuse treatment facility admissions, with 24.3 percent of those admitted reporting daily use. However, of these admissions for primary marijuana abuse, the criminal justice system referred 51.6 percent to treatment. [The Substance Abuse and Mental Health Services Administration's (SAMHSA's)] Drug Abuse Warning Network (DAWN) was a national probability survey of U.S. hospitals with emergency departments (EDs) and was designed to obtain information on ED visits in which marijuana was mentioned, accounting for 36.4 percent of illicit drug related ED visits. . . .

A number of risks can occur with both acute and chronic use of marijuana. . . .

b. There is a significant diversion of the drug or drugs containing such a substance from legitimate drug channels.

There is a lack of evidence of significant diversion of marijuana from legitimate drug channels, but this is likely due to the fact that marijuana is more widely available from illicit sources rather than through legitimate channels. . . .

. . .

c. Individuals are taking the drug or drugs containing such a substance on their own initiative rather than on the basis of medical advice from a practitioner licensed by law to administer such drugs in the course of his professional practice.

Because the FDA has not approved [a New Drug Application (NDA)] or [Biologics License Application (BLA)] for a marijuana drug product for any therapeutic indication, the only way an individual can take marijuana on the basis of medical advice through legitimate channels at the federal level is by participating in research under an [Investigational New Drug (IND)] application. That said, numerous states and the District of Columbia have passed state-level medical marijuana laws allowing for individuals to use marijuana under certain circumstances. However, data are not yet available to determine the number of individuals using marijuana under these state-level medical marijuana laws. Regardless, . . . 18.9 million American adults currently use marijuana. . . . Based on the large number of individuals reporting current use of marijuana and the lack of an FDA-approved drug product in the United States, one can assume that it is likely that the majority of individuals using marijuana do so on their own initiative rather than on the basis of medical advice from a licensed practitioner.

. . .

## 2. SCIENTIFIC EVIDENCE OF ITS PHARMACOLOGICAL EFFECTS, IF KNOWN

Under the second factor, the Secretary must consider the scientific evidence of marijuana's pharmacological effects. Abundant scientific data are available on the neurochemistry, toxicology, and pharmacology of marijuana. . . .

## Psychoactive Effects

Below is a list of the common subjective responses to cannabinoids.... [T]hese responses to marijuana are pleasurable to many humans and are often associated with drug-seeking and drug-taking.

(1) Disinhibition, relaxation, increased sociability, and talkativeness.
(2) Increased merriment and appetite, and even exhilaration at high doses.
(3) Enhanced sensory perception, which can generate an increased appreciation of music, art, and touch.
(4) Heightened imagination, which can lead to a subjective sense of increased creativity.
(5) Initial dizziness, nausea, tachycardia, facial flushing, dry mouth, and tremor.
(6) Disorganized thinking, inability to converse logically, time distortions, and short-term memory impairment.
(7) Ataxia and impaired judgment, which can impede driving ability or lead to an increase in risk-tasking behavior.
(8) Illusions, delusions, and hallucinations that intensify with higher doses.
(9) Emotional lability, incongruity of affect, dysphoria, agitation, paranoia, confusion, drowsiness, and panic attacks, which are more common in inexperienced or high-dosed users.

. . .

## Behavioral Impairment

Marijuana induces various psychoactive effects that can lead to behavioral impairment. Marijuana's acute effects can significantly interfere with a person's ability to learn in the classroom or to operate motor vehicles.... [For example,] administration of 3.95 percent delta9-THC in a smoked marijuana cigarette ... increased the latency in a task of simulated vehicle braking at a rate comparable to an increase in stopping distance of five feet at 60 mph ...

. . .

A number of factors may influence marijuana's behavioral effects including the duration of use (chronic or short term), frequency of use (daily, weekly, or occasionally), and amount of use (heavy or moderate). ...

The effects of chronic marijuana use do not seem to persist after more than 1 to 3 months of abstinence. After 3 months of abstinence, any deficits observed in IQ, immediate memory, delayed memory, and information-processing speeds following heavy marijuana use compared to pre-drug use scores were no longer apparent ...

Another aspect that may be a critical factor in the intensity and persistence of impairment resulting from chronic marijuana use is the age of first use. Individuals with a diagnosis of marijuana misuse or dependence who were seeking treatment for substance use, who initiated marijuana use before the age of 15 years, showed deficits in performance on tasks assessing sustained attention, impulse control, and general executive functioning compared to non-using controls. These deficits were not seen in individuals who initiated marijuana use after the age of 15 years. ...

### Behavioral Effects of Prenatal Exposure

Studies with children at different stages of development are used to examine the impact of prenatal marijuana exposure on performance in a series of cognitive tasks. However, many pregnant women who reported marijuana use were more likely to also report use of alcohol, tobacco, and cocaine. . . . Thus, with potential exposure to multiple drugs, it is difficult to determine the specific impact of prenatal marijuana exposure. . . .

### Association of Marijuana Use With Psychosis

. . .

Extensive research has been conducted to investigate whether exposure to marijuana is associated with the development of schizophrenia or other psychoses. Although many studies are small and inferential, other studies in the literature use hundreds to thousands of subjects. At present, the available data do not suggest a causative link between marijuana use and the development of psychosis. . . . Numerous large, longitudinal studies show that subjects who used marijuana do not have a greater incidence of psychotic diagnoses compared to those who do not use marijuana.

. . .

### Cardiovascular and Autonomic Effects

Single smoked or oral doses of delta9-THC produce tachycardia and may increase blood pressure. . . . Some evidence associates the tachycardia produced by delta9-THC with excitation of the sympathetic and depression of the parasympathetic nervous systems. . . . During chronic marijuana ingestion, a tolerance to tachycardia develops. . . .

However, prolonged delta9-THC ingestion produces bradycardia and hypotension. . . .

Marijuana smoking by individuals, particularly those with some degree of coronary artery or cerebrovascular disease, poses risks such as increased cardiac work, catecholamines and carboxyhemoglobin, myocardial infarction, and postural hypotension. . . .

### Respiratory Effects

After acute exposure to marijuana, transient bronchodilation is the most typical respiratory effect. . . . [O]ccasional use of marijuana is not associated with decreased pulmonary function. However, some preliminary evidence suggests that heavy marijuana use may be associated with negative pulmonary effects. . . . Long-term use of marijuana can lead to chronic cough and increased sputum, as well as an increased frequency of chronic bronchitis and pharyngitis. In addition, pulmonary function tests reveal that large-airway obstruction can occur with chronic marijuana smoking, as can cellular inflammatory histopathological abnormalities in bronchial epithelium. . . .

Evidence regarding marijuana smoking leading to cancer is inconsistent, as some studies suggest a positive correlation while others do not. . . .

. . .

### 6. WHAT, IF ANY, RISK THERE IS TO THE PUBLIC HEALTH

[Many of the risks to public health are discussed under other factors.]
. . .

. . . Overall, research does not support a direct causal relationship between regular marijuana use and other illicit drug use. The studies examining the gateway hypothesis are limited. . . .

Little evidence supports the hypothesis that initiation of marijuana use leads to an abuse disorder with other illicit substances. . . .
. . .

### 7. ITS PSYCHIC OR PHYSIOLOGIC DEPENDENCE LIABILITY

Psychic or psychological dependence has been shown in response to marijuana's psychoactive effects. Psychoactive responses to marijuana are pleasurable to many humans and are associated with drug-seeking and drug-taking . . . 2012 NSDUH statistics that show that of individuals years 12 or older who used marijuana in the past month, an estimated 40.3 percent used marijuana on 20 or more days within the past month. This equates to approximately 7.6 million individuals aged 12 or older who used marijuana on a daily or almost daily basis. Additionally, the 2013 MTF data report the prevalence of daily marijuana use, defined as use on 20 or more days within the past 30 days, in 8th, 10th, and 12th graders is 1.1 percent, 4.0 percent, and 6.5 percent, respectively.
. . .

Discontinuation of heavy, chronic marijuana use has been shown to lead to physical dependence and withdrawal symptoms. . . . In heavy, chronic marijuana users, the most commonly reported withdrawal symptoms are sleep difficulties, decreased appetite or weight loss, irritability, anger, anxiety or nervousness, and restlessness. Some less commonly reported withdrawal symptoms are depressed mood, sweating, shakiness, physical discomfort, and chills. . . . The occurrence of marijuana withdrawal symptoms in light or non-daily marijuana users has not been established.

## Notes and Questions

1. Make a list of the possible harmful effects of marijuana use discussed by HHS. How confident is the agency that marijuana causes each harm? How significant is each harm? Do you agree that each of the harms discussed by the agency (e.g., recreational use) is, in fact, a "harm"? Ultimately, do you think the harms HHS attributes to marijuana use justify prohibitions on the possession and use of the drug?

2. The DEA has noted a steady rise in the potency of marijuana, as measured by THC content. From 1995 to 2015, for example, the THC content of marijuana seized by the agency rose from 3.96 percent to 11.16 percent. *See* Drug Enforcement Administration, *Denial of Petition to Initiate Proceedings to Reschedule Marijuana*, 81 Fed. Reg. 53688, 53745 (Aug. 12, 2016). Is the increase in potency cause for alarm? In other words, are the harms of marijuana correlated with THC content? Even the DEA is cautious on this point. *Id.* at 53758 ("Additional studies are needed to clarify the impact of greater potency, but one study shows that higher levels of D9-THC in the body are associated with greater psychoactive effects . . . which can be correlated with higher abuse potential.").

3. As discussed in Chapter 2, federal (and most state) law defines marijuana to include all chemicals extracted from the buds and leaves (and other parts) of the Cannabis plant. But are any of the harms the HHS associates with marijuana use attributable to *CBD*? In its recommendation, HHS repeatedly mentioned the effects of THC, but the agency had comparatively little to say about the effects (good or bad) of CBD. In one section, it remarked that "[t]he pharmacological actions of CBD have not been fully studied in humans." HHS, *Recommendation, supra* at 53692. However, the Director of the National Institute on Drug Abuse has testified that "[t]he different pharmacological properties of CBD give it a different safety profile from THC. A review of 25 studies on the safety and efficacy of CBD did not identify significant side effects across a wide range of dosages. . . ." *Barriers to Cannabidiol Research: Hearing Before the Senate Caucus on International Narcotics Control*, 114th Cong. (2015) (statement of Nora D. Volkow, Director, National Institute on Drug Abuse), https://perma.cc/L38J-NDF4. If there are as yet no demonstrated harms stemming from CBD use, should CBD be treated as a Schedule I controlled substance? More generally, how should a government regulate a substance for which neither the benefits nor the harms have been thoroughly studied?

4. Neither HHS nor the DEA suggests that marijuana use causes crime. This is notable because sensationalized accounts of marijuana-induced violence (reefer madness) may have motivated passage of marijuana bans in the early 1900s. Richard J. Bonnie & Charles H. Whitebread, Jr., *The Forbidden Fruit and the Tree of Knowledge: An Inquiry Into the Legal History of American Marijuana Prohibition*, 56 Va. L. Rev. 971, 1012-16 (1970). Although studies have demonstrated a *correlation* between marijuana use and crime, the evidence that marijuana actually *causes* crime is very thin. *E.g.*, Jonathan P. Caulkins et al., Considering Marijuana Legalization: Insights for Vermont and Other Jurisdictions 41-42 (Rand 2015) (noting that while "[t]here is a long-established positive correlation between marijuana and crime. . . . rigorous examinations using techniques that enable causal interpretation of results are rare . . . [and] never completely eliminate the possibility that [some] . . . unobserved factor is causing the statistical association").

5. Is marijuana a gateway drug? Marijuana's relationship to the use of other substances has figured prominently debates over marijuana policy. HHS discusses (and largely dismisses) the gateway hypothesis in its scheduling recommendation above. But what is the relationship between use of marijuana and the use of other substances, and why is it important for marijuana policy? Jonathan Caulkins and his co-authors discuss:

> . . . [E]ven if . . . a catalog of direct effects [of marijuana use] were both exact and exhaustive, it could still be a terribly incomplete and misleading basis for a benefit-cost analysis because legalization's indirect effects, via changes in the use of other substances, could well outweigh the importance of the marijuana-related outcomes themselves. . . . Unfortunately, the uncertainty about these indirect effects is, in many instances, even greater than the uncertainty about legalization's effect on marijuana related outcomes. . . .
>
> This story of indirect effects mediated through other substances is easiest to tell, and most often raised, in terms of alcohol. Suppose that legalization led to a doubling of marijuana consumption of all sorts, including not only a doubling of controlled recreational use but also a doubling of compulsive abuse and dependence. One might well view this as a net bad because of all of the marijuana-related harms discussed above.
>
> However, the total social cost associated with alcohol abuse is very much larger than all costs and outcomes related directly to marijuana use. So if the doubling of marijuana use

came about because all these new marijuana users switched from drinking alcohol, that could be a net win from a public-health perspective, particularly if these people would otherwise have been binge drinking. . . . Indeed, . . . even a 10-percent reduction in alcohol abuse accompanying the doubling in marijuana use could be a net win for society.

Alas, that story of increased marijuana use being a substitute for alcohol use is not the only possibility. It is also possible for two consumer goods to be complements, such that, when market conditions change in ways that promote greater use (and abuse) of one, that might lead to greater—not lesser—use (and abuse) of the other.

If marijuana and alcohol proved to be complements, and legalization led to any sizable increase in alcohol use and abuse, then legalization would be a net loss. Even if all marijuana related costs magically disappeared, that could not offset the harm caused by a 10-percent increase in alcohol-related problems.

. . .

The descriptive statistics concerning overlap in use are clear. Marijuana users are much more likely than are nonusers to drink and to abuse alcohol. For example, current marijuana users are five times as likely as nonusers to meet DSM-IV criteria for alcohol abuse or dependence (26 percent versus 5 percent). . . .

. . .

. . . [C]orrelation need not, however, imply causality. Alcohol use might cause marijuana use, not the other way round. Or there could be third variables—such as coming from a broken home or having a risk-taking personality—that lead people to consume more intoxicants generally, including both alcohol and marijuana. . . . [S]ome scientific literature makes a serious attempt to tease out these complicated overlapping causal pathways, but, unfortunately, that literature is inconclusive.

Nor is alcohol the only substance with which there could be important interactions. Consider the one substance that could cause even greater social harms than alcohol— namely, tobacco. The overlap between marijuana and tobacco use is at least as strong as the overlap between marijuana and alcohol use. Past-month marijuana users are three times as likely as nonusers to smoke cigarettes (59 percent versus 19 percent), a ratio that rises to 6:1 for those under the age of 21 (53 percent to 9 percent). . . .

Suppose that legalizing marijuana caused even a 1-percent increase in tobacco smoking. Because tobacco kills well over 400,000 people in the United States every year, then, in that hypothetical, legalizing marijuana might—in the long run—cause 4,000 additional premature deaths per year, an outcome that could outweigh any plausible benefits of marijuana legalization.

. . .

Legalization could also affect the use and abuse of other illegal drugs. Long ago, there was great concern that trying marijuana could be a gateway that caused users to go seek stronger and stronger highs. Those fears arose from the combination of conditional probabilities (children who use marijuana are much more likely to progress to harder drugs) and sequential order (marijuana usually predates use of harder drugs). But those facts together do not imply causality. Various observers . . . have shown that the same patterns could emerge if third variables (e.g., broken homes, risk-seeking personalities) cause use of both marijuana and hard drugs, and marijuana gets used first simply because it becomes available to children first.

But showing that the data do not imply that a causal version of the gateway hypothesis holds is not the same as showing that there is no causal effect. Third variables could account for some but not all of the correlation. Furthermore, the connection need not be purely biochemical. For example, use of marijuana could lead teens to spend more time with others who use marijuana (birds of feather flock together or, more formally, homophily), and those marijuana-using peers might have more-positive attitudes toward use of other drugs or know how to obtain those other drugs. Likewise, marijuana use might lead the individual to self-identify and to be identified by others (labeling) as being the sort of person who uses drugs of all kinds. And so on. So there could be a causal path from greater marijuana use to use of hard drugs that is social or psychological, even if there is no biochemical link. Hence, although confidence in the old-fashioned version of the gateway hypothesis went beyond the empirical evidence, confidence in the irrelevance of the gateway hypothesis might be equally naïve.

Marijuana could also be both a complement and a substitute for other drugs but on different time scales—e.g., they might be substitutes in the short run and complements in the long run. Or marijuana might also be a complement for some drugs but a substitute for others.

. . .

One can be slightly more definitive when considering each substance or category of substances one at a time. Table 3.1 captures the gist of this complicated literature in the simplest possible terms, distinguishing along just two dimensions: (1) size of the literature underpinning the estimates and (2) degree of consensus among those studies.

Table 3.1 Summary of Literature on the Extent to Which Marijuana Is a Substitute for or Complement with Other Drugs

| Substance | Studies | Agreement Among Studies | Finding |
|---|---|---|---|
| Alcohol | Many | No consensus | Unknown |
| Tobacco | Many | High consensus | Complementarity |
| Prescription opioids | Few | Consensus | Substitution |
| Illegal drugs | Few | No consensus | Unknown |

For alcohol and for the other illegal drugs, the existing literature is ambiguous, with some studies pointing in one direction and others pointing in the opposite direction. For opioids, there is consistency, but perhaps only because there are so few studies. The one substance for which the literature provides clearer indication is the interaction with tobacco use, for which there is considerable evidence and it tilts strongly toward complementarity (i.e., greater marijuana use would be expected to lead to greater tobacco use). Complementarity can arise with respect to initiation (marijuana initiation often predates tobacco initiation, creating the possibility of a reverse gateway), concurrent use (some users think that nicotine enhances the marijuana high), or cessation (marijuana use predicts lower success rates when trying to quit tobacco use).

Caulkins et al., Considering Marijuana Legalization, *supra*, at 43-47. What do you think? How should marijuana's relationship with the use of other drugs affect regulation of the possession and use of marijuana?

6. Do states that have legalized marijuana necessarily disagree with the federal government's assessment of marijuana's harms, just as they disagree with its assessment of marijuana's benefits? Some states, of course, reject the federal government's *definition* of harms. For example, unlike the federal government, recreational marijuana states do not

equate all recreational marijuana use with abuse of the drug. But putting aside such philosophical objections, does HHS's recommendation reflect consensus regarding marijuana's negative impact on health? For reviews of the scientific literature on marijuana's harms, see Gordon et al., *Medical Consequences of Marijuana Use, supra*; Hall, *What Has Research over the Last Two Decades Revealed, supra*; Volkow et al., *Adverse Health Effects of Marijuana Use, supra*; and National Academies of Science, Engineering, and Medicine, Cannabinoids: The Current State of Evidence and Recommendations for Research, *supra*.

7. How do marijuana's harms compare to those of other substances? Many policy advocates and analysts point out that marijuana is less harmful than other substances on Schedule I, like LSD and heroin, and less harmful even than some legal substances, like alcohol or tobacco. *E.g.*, Caulkins et al., Considering Marijuana Legalization, *supra*, at 43 (suggesting that "the total social cost associated with alcohol abuse is very much larger than all costs and outcomes related directly to marijuana use"); *id.* at 44 (suggesting that tobacco is a "substance that could cause even greater social harms than alcohol"). The general public seems to share this view. In one poll, for example, 69 percent of respondents indicated that they believed marijuana is safer than alcohol. Pew Research Center Poll (poll conducted Mar. 25-29, 2015). And as shown in **Figure 5.1** above, marijuana's comparative safety was the second most common reason (behind marijuana's medical benefits) people gave for supporting legalization of the drug.

But should comparative safety matter? In its latest scheduling decision, the DEA noted that "Congress established only one schedule, schedule I, for drugs of abuse with 'no currently accepted medical use in treatment in the United States.' . . . Thus, any attempt to compare the relative abuse potential of schedule I substance to that of a substance in another schedule is inconsequential since a schedule I substance must remain in schedule I until it has been found to have a currently accepted medical use in treatment in the United States." *Denial of Petition, supra*, at 53747. Are you satisfied by the DEA's response? Should the DEA be required to consider *comparative* safety when scheduling a drug like marijuana? For example, even if alcohol, tobacco, LSD, heroin, etc. are more harmful than marijuana, does that suggest that governments should necessarily relax their restrictions on marijuana? Why, why not?

8. The HHS and many of the reviews cited above find that marijuana use is more harmful for some types of users than others, for example, minors, chronic users (i.e., those who use frequently), and heavy users (i.e., those who use large quantities). What are the implications for policy? Is there a way to prevent more harmful use of marijuana without necessarily restricting or prohibiting less harmful use?

## 2. Which Harms Should Inform Policy?

Problem 5.3: Suppose that you are a policymaker deciding whether to regulate a new drug called Xanadu. Xanadu is consumed just before bedtime. It produces a sense of euphoria during sleep, which users recall (pleasantly) after waking up. Xanadu only works on adults—i.e., it produces no effect on minors. It is non-addictive, and the sought-after effect can only be experienced

by a user once every 30 days. Although Xanadu is appealing to many users, it has one well-known side effect: upon taking a dose (of any size), there is a 1 in 10 million risk that the user will die instantly (albeit painlessly) in their sleep. Does this risk justify restricting the possession and use of Xanadu? Does it justify prohibiting the drug outright? What if the risk of death were higher (say, 1 in 10,000)?

Some policymakers believe that the harms attributable to marijuana use cannot justify government restrictions insofar as they are borne by users of the drug. This limitation on government power is known as the *harm principle*. It is derived from John Stuart Mill's canonical philosophical work, which outlines Mill's views of the proper objectives of government policy:

> The object of this Essay is to assert one very simple principle, as entitled to govern absolutely the dealings of society with the individual in the way of compulsion and control, whether the means used be physical force in the form of legal penalties, or the moral coercion of public opinion. That principle is, that the sole end for which mankind are warranted, individually or collectively, in interfering with the liberty of action of any of their number, is self-protection. That the only purpose for which power can be rightfully exercised over any member of a civilised community, against his will, is to prevent harm to others. His own good, either physical or moral, is not a sufficient warrant. . . . In the part which merely concerns himself, his independence is, of right, absolute. Over himself, over his own body and mind, the individual is sovereign.

J. S. Mill, *On Liberty and Considerations on Representative Government* 8-9 (1946).

The harm principle has surfaced in debates over marijuana policy, both in the United States and elsewhere. In the following case, the Alaska Supreme Court discusses the application of the harm principle to the state's ban on simple possession and use of marijuana.

## *Ravin v. Alaska*
### 537 P.2d 494 (Alaska 1975)

RABINOWITZ, C.J.:

. . . [W]e conclude that citizens of the State of Alaska have a basic right to privacy in their homes under Alaska's constitution. This right to privacy would encompass the possession and ingestion of substances such as marijuana in a purely personal, non-commercial context in the home unless the state can meet its substantial burden and show that proscription of possession of marijuana in the home is supportable by achievement of a legitimate state interest.

. . .

The justifications offered by the State to uphold [the state ban on simple possession] are generally that marijuana is a psychoactive drug; that it is not a harmless substance; that heavy use has concomitant risk; that it is capable of precipitating a psychotic reaction in at least individuals who are predisposed towards such reaction; and that its use adversely affects the user's ability to operate an automobile. The State relies upon a number of medical researchers who have raised questions as to the substance's effect on the body's immune system, on chromosomal structure, and on the functioning of the brain. On the other hand, in almost every instance of reports of potential danger arising from marijuana use, reports can be found reaching contradictory results. It appears that there is no firm evidence that marijuana, as presently used in this country, is generally a danger to the user or to others. But neither is there conclusive evidence to the effect that it is harmless. The one significant risk in use of marijuana which we do find established to a reasonable degree of certainty is the effect of marijuana intoxication on driving. . . .

Possibly implicit in the State's catalogue of possible dangers of marijuana use is the assumption that the State has the authority to protect the individual from his own folly, that is, that the State can control activities which present to harm to anyone except those enjoying them. Although some courts have found the 'public interest' to be broad enough to justify protecting the individual against himself, most have found inherent limitations on the police power of the state. An apposite example is the litigation regarding the constitutionality of laws requiring motorcyclists to wear helmets. Most of the courts addressing the issue, including this one, have resolved it by finding a connection between the helmet requirement and the safety of other motorists, but a significant number of courts have explicitly rejected such restrictive measures as beyond the police power of the state because they do not benefit the public. . . .

We glean from these cases the general proposition that the authority of the state to exert control over the individual extends only to activities of the individual which affect others or the public at large as it relates to matters of public health or safety, or to provide for the general welfare. We believe this tenet to be basic to a free society. The state cannot impose its own notions of morality, propriety, or fashion on individuals when the public has no legitimate interest in the affairs of those individuals. The right of the individual to do as he pleases is not absolute, of course: it can be made to yield when it begins to infringe on the rights and welfare of others.

Further, the authority of the state to control the activities of its citizens is not limited to activities which have a present and immediate impact on the public health or welfare. It is conceivable, for example, that a drug could so seriously develop in its user a withdrawal or amotivational syndrome, that widespread use of the drug could significantly debilitate the fabric of our society. Faced with a substantial possibility of such a result, the state could take measures to combat the possibility. The state is under no obligation to allow otherwise 'private' activity which will result in numbers of people becoming public charges or otherwise burdening the public welfare. But we do not find that such a situation exists today regarding marijuana. It appears that effects of marijuana on the individual are not serious enough to justify widespread concern, at least as compared with the far more dangerous effects of alcohol, barbiturates and amphetamines. . . .

. . .

But one way in which use of marijuana most clearly does affect the general public is in regard to its effect on driving. All of which brings us to the opposite (from the home) end of the scale of the right to privacy in the context of ingestion or possession of marijuana, namely, when the individual is operating a motor vehicle. Recent research has produced increasing evidence of significant impairment of the driving ability of persons under the influence of cannabis. Distortion of time perception, impairment of psychomotor function, and increased selectivity in attentiveness to surroundings apparently can combine to lower driver ability. In this regard, Ravin points out that marijuana usually produces passivity and inactivity, in contrast to alcohol, which increases aggressiveness and is likely to result in overconfidence in one's driving ability. Although a person under the influence of marijuana may be less likely to attempt to drive than a person under the influence of alcohol, there exists the potential for serious harm to the health and safety of the general public.

In view of the foregoing, we believe that at present, the need for control of drivers under the influence of marijuana and the existing doubts as to the safety of marijuana, demonstrate a sufficient justification for the prohibition found in [Alaska law] as an exercise of the state's police power for the public welfare. Given the evidence of the effect of marijuana on driving an individual's right to possess or ingest marijuana while driving would be subject to the prohibition provided for [in Alaska law]. However, given the relative insignificance of marijuana consumption as a health problem in our society at present, we do not believe that the potential harm generated by drivers under the influence of marijuana, standing alone, creates a close and substantial relationship between the public welfare and control of ingestion of marijuana or possession of it in the home for personal use. Thus we conclude that no adequate justification for the state's intrusion into the citizen's right to privacy by its prohibition of possession of marijuana by an adult for personal consumption in the home has been shown. The privacy of the individual's home cannot be breached absent a persuasive showing of a close and substantial relationship of the intrusion to a legitimate governmental interest. Here, mere scientific doubts will not suffice. The state must demonstrate a need based on proof that the public health or welfare will in fact suffer if the controls are not applied.

The state has a legitimate concern with avoiding the spread of marijuana use to adolescents who may not be equipped with the maturity to handle the experience prudently, as well as a legitimate concern with the problem of driving under the influence of marijuana. Yet these interests are insufficient to justify intrusions into the rights of adults in the privacy of their own homes. Further, neither the federal or Alaska constitution affords protection for the buying or selling of marijuana, nor absolute protection for its use or possession in public. Possession at home of amounts of marijuana indicative of intent to sell rather than possession for personal use is likewise unprotected.

In view of our holding that possession of marijuana by adults at home for personal use is constitutionally protected, we wish to make clear that we do not mean to condone the use of marijuana. The experts who testified below, including petitioner's witnesses, were unanimously opposed to the use of any psychoactive drugs. We agree completely. It is the responsibility of every individual to consider carefully the ramifications for himself and for those around him of using such substances. With the freedom which our society offers to each of us to order our lives as we see fit goes the duty to live responsibly, for our own sakes and for society's. This result can best be achieved, we believe, without the use of psychoactive substances.

## Notes and Questions

1. Regardless of whether you think any state or the national constitution employs the harm principle as a limit on government power, *should* policymakers follow it when deciding how to regulate marijuana? In other words, do you think that protecting people from themselves constitutes a legitimate policy objective?

2. *Ravin* may be the only judicial decision that has explicitly used the harm principle to limit the regulation of marijuana possession and use. In *R. v. Malmo-Levine* and *R. v. Caine*, the Canadian Supreme Court rejected a similar harm principle–based challenge to Canada's ban on the possession of marijuana:

> Contrary to the appellants' assertion, we do not think there is a consensus that the harm principle is the sole justification for criminal prohibition. . . . No doubt, . . . the *presence* of harm to others may justify legislative action under the criminal law power. However, we do not think that the *absence* of proven harm creates the unqualified barrier to legislative action that the appellants suggest. On the contrary, the state may sometimes be justified in criminalizing conduct that is either not harmful (in the sense contemplated by the harm principle), or that causes harm only to the accused.
>
> . . .
>
> Several instances of crimes that do not cause harm to others are found in the [Canadian] *Criminal Code*. . . . Bestiality . . . and cruelty to animals . . . are examples of crimes that rest on their offensiveness to deeply held social values rather than on Mill's "harm principle."
>
> A duel fought by consenting adults is an example of a crime where the victim is no less culpable than the perpetrator, and there is no harm that is not consented to, but the prohibition . . . is nevertheless integral to our ideas of civilized society . . . In none of these instances of consenting adults does the criminal law conform to Mill's expression of the harm principle that "[o]ver himself, over his own body and mind, the individual is sovereign." . . .

2003 S.C.R. 571, 634-636. Can you distinguish the bans cited by the Canadian court from the ban on simple possession of marijuana? What would be the broader ramifications of adopting the harm principle as a limit on government policy?

3. Do you agree with the *Ravin* court's application of the harm principle? The case was decided in 1975. Is the court's analysis now outdated? Are the harms to others associated with marijuana significant enough to justify prohibiting use by all?

4. The harm principle does recognize some exceptions, in other words, some situations in which the government does have a legitimate interest in stopping individuals from harming themselves. The exceptions typically involve vulnerable individuals who cannot be trusted to make reasoned decisions about drug use, etc., for themselves, including children, addicts, and the already impaired. See Mill, *supra*, at 9 ("[T]this doctrine is meant to apply to human beings in the maturity of their faculties. . . . Those who are still in a state to require being taken care of by others, must be protected against their own actions as well as against external injury."). The principle also permits the government to try to *persuade*—rather than coerce—reasoning adults not to harm themselves. Does the fear that children or other vulnerable individuals might use marijuana justify a criminal prohibition against possession and use of the drug among the entire population? Why, why not?

5. For the fascinating history of Alaska's response to *Ravin*, see *Noy v. Alaska*, 83 P.3d 538, 541-542 (Alaska App. Ct. 2003). In 2014, of course, the state's voters passed an initiative that went beyond *Ravin* to legalize the simple possession of up to one ounce of marijuana even outside the home. Alaska Stat. § 17.38.020(1)-(2).

# C. HOW DO POLICYMAKERS INFLUENCE MARIJUANA USE (OR ITS HARMS)?

Of course, policymakers need to decide not only what objectives to pursue, but also how best to pursue them. Does outright prohibition reduce overall use of marijuana? Do lesser restrictions, like those surveyed in Chapter 4, help curb unapproved (and presumably more harmful) use of the drug? Do per se DUI laws lessen the driving harms associated with marijuana? This section explores these and related questions.

Section 1 outlines a framework for thinking about whether (and how) law can curb the overall use of marijuana. Section 2 then examines law's ability to distinguish between approved and unapproved use of marijuana. Finally, Section 3 explores law's ability to curb the harms associated with use, such as accidents caused by impaired drivers.

## 1. Law's Impact on Overall Use

<u>Problem 5.4</u>: Suppose you are a policymaker who believes that marijuana use should be curbed as much as possible. No genie is offering to make the drug disappear. How would you attempt to curb its use?

The demand for marijuana is influenced by many factors, including the legal risks associated with marijuana use and possession, the price and availability of the drug, individual beliefs about the drug's harms and benefits, and the social norms surrounding use of the drug. *E.g.*, Robert MacCoun & Peter Reuter, Drug War Heresies, 72-94 (2001) (discussing determinants of demand for drugs and law's influence on them). Lawmakers might be able to influence each of these factors in order to suppress the demand for marijuana. This section outlines a framework similar to one employed by MacCoun and Reuter, *supra*, for gauging law's influence over marijuana consumption. It identifies and discusses five distinct ways the law could potentially influence the demand for marijuana.

### a. Legal Sanctions

Most directly, governments can suppress demand for marijuana by threatening to impose legal sanctions on those who possess and use the drug. For the rational consumer, these sanctions raise the true cost of possessing and using marijuana. The magnitude of this added cost is a function of both the magnitude of the legal sanction (S) and the probability the sanction will actually be imposed (p) on the user—i.e., the probability the consumer would be caught and punished for simple possession. Economists refer to this as the *expected* legal sanction (i.e., the expected sanction, S * p) associated with marijuana possession. See Gary Becker, *Crime and Punishment: An Economic Approach*, 76 J. Pol. Econ. 169 (1968).

Deterrence theory predicts that the higher the expected legal sanction for marijuana possession is, the lower the demand for the drug will be. This prediction is illustrated by the two hypothetical demand curves in **Figure 5.3**. (**Figure 5.3** also shows a hypothetical supply curve. We will revisit this curve in Chapter 9; for now, just focus on the demand curves.)

Figure 5.3: Hypothetical Demand and Supply Curves for Marijuana

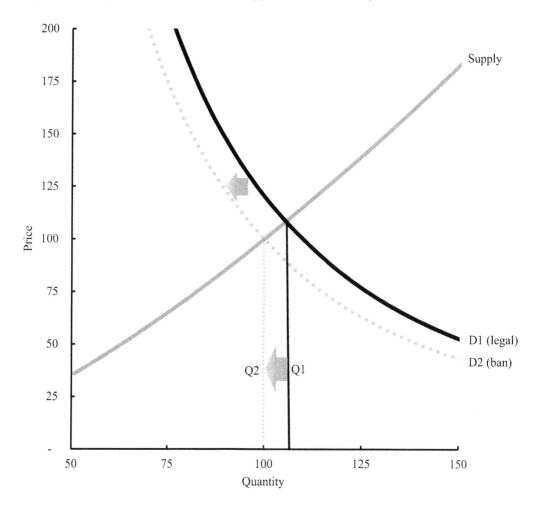

The demand curves (D1 and D2) show the total quantity of marijuana (x-axis) that all consumers in society would buy at different market prices (y-axis) under two different legal regimes: D1 models a regime in which possession and use are *legal*—i.e., there are no legal sanctions imposed on these activities; and D2 models a regime in which possession and use of marijuana are *banned*—i.e., there is an expected legal sanction (S * p) associated with these activities. The graph places D2 to the left of D1, reflecting the theory that legal sanctions suppress demand. The idea is that consumers will buy less marijuana at any given market price if they also have to "pay" the expected legal sanction imposed by prohibition. The point at which each demand curve intersects the supply curve indicates the total quantity of marijuana that is consumed under each legal regime. In **Figure 5.3**, the total quantity consumed is less under prohibition (Q2) than under legalization (Q1), again reflecting the theory that legal sanctions suppress demand.

## Notes and Questions

1. What *is* the expected legal sanction for possessing marijuana? Chapter 4 discussed the legal sanctions (S) that are authorized for simple possession of marijuana in different prohibition regimes, including forfeiture, fines, and even incarceration. The probability (p) that a marijuana user will actually incur any of these sanctions, however, is generally quite low. Namely, researchers estimate that, on average, the probability that a marijuana user will be arrested over the course of a year ranges between 0.8 percent and 3.2 percent. *See* Beau Kilmer, *Do Cannabis Possession Laws Influence Cannabis Use?*, at 130, in Cannabis 2002 Report (2002) (estimating that average user faced 2.8 to 3.2 percent yearly probability of arrest from 1995 to 1999); Holly Nguyen & Peter Reuter, *How Risky is Marijuana Possession? Considering the Role of Age, Race, and Gender*, 58 Crime & Delinq. 879, 887 (2012) (estimating that average user faced 0.8 to 1.9 percent yearly probability of arrest from 1982 to 2008). Furthermore, not all users who are arrested are necessarily *punished*. For example, the ACLU estimates that only about 27 percent of those who are arrested for marijuana possession are convicted and punished. ACLU, The War on Marijuana in Black and White, 71-75 (2013).

2. Now consider the following Problem:

**Problem 5.5:** Doug is an occasional marijuana user. He buys about an eighth of his favorite strain from an acquaintance every month for $40. Absent the threat of legal sanction, Doug would be willing to pay up to $50 for each eighth (that is his reservation price). But Doug lives in a jurisdiction that prohibits the simple possession of marijuana. Violations of the ban trigger a mandatory fine of $250. Assume there are no other consequences that stem from arrest and punishment and no escalating penalties for repeat offenders. Based on these facts, and assuming that Doug is risk neutral, what is the yearly probability of arrest it would take to deter Doug from buying marijuana? How does this compare to the actual rates of arrest facing marijuana users estimated by Kilmer and by Nguyen & Reuter above?

3. Might a ban on marijuana deter use even if the probability of enforcement (p) is low or zero? The textbook author has explained:

> Some people refrain from behavior because they feel morally obliged to obey a legal prohibition. In this sense, people are prone to obey law not because they think it is in their self-interest (narrowly defined) to do so, but because it is the right, the moral thing to do; it is what people *should* do, even when they disagree with the law. In his seminal work on obedience to law, Tom Tyler found that "[c]itizens who view legal authority as legitimate are generally more likely to comply with the law." [Tom Tyler, Why People Obey the Law 62 (1990).] Tyler explains that "citizens may comply with the law because they view the legal authority they are dealing with as having a legitimate right to dictate their behavior; this represents an acceptance by people of the need to bring their behavior into line with the dictates of an external authority." [*Id.* at 25.]
>
> Nonetheless, in spite of the generalized obligation to obey law that many people feel, the obligation to obey the federal marijuana ban is probably quite weak, for two main reasons.

First, violations of the ban are commonplace, thus undermining its moral influence. When everyone knows a law is not being observed, the moral obligation to obey that law dissolves and compliance suffers. As Dan Kahan explains "Most individuals regard compliance with law to be morally appropriate. But most also loathe being taken advantage of. The latter sensibility can easily subvert the former if individuals perceive that those around them are routinely violating a particular law. When others refuse to reciprocate, submission to a burdensome legal duty is likely to feel more servile than moral." [Dan M. Kahan, Social Influence, Social Meaning, and Deterrence, 83 Va. L. Rev. 349, 358 (1997).]

Congress's ban may have lost its moral influence because so many people flout it, and federal authorities have done little thus far to punish them. In other words, the lack of enforcement of the federal ban may have undermined not only the deterrent effect of the ban's sanctions, but also the deterrent effect of the generalized moral obligation to obey the law.

Second, people may feel relieved of the obligation to obey the federal ban because state law permits marijuana use. It is, of course, possible to obey both state and federal law by not using marijuana at all, but citizens may dismiss the obligation to obey federal law when they deem the state—and not Congress—as having the "legitimate right to dictate their behavior" regarding marijuana use. Congress's perceived right to dictate behavior may be even weaker in the nine states where medical marijuana laws were passed by voter referenda. In such states, people may see themselves collectively as having the exclusive right to dictate marijuana policy, in which case the federal ban will command very little moral authority.

Mikos, *On the Limits of Supremacy*, at 1472-74. What do you think? Do people feel morally obliged to obey strict marijuana laws today? Why, why not?

4. One key assumption of deterrence theory is that individuals know the likely consequences (S * p) of flouting the law. But do people even know the law governing marijuana possession? Analyzing responses to surveys asking individuals to identify the penalties for possession of marijuana, Robert MacCoun and his co-authors concluded that while "[p]eople are not oblivious to their marijuana laws . . . the average citizen's awareness is pretty tenuous." Robert MacCoun et al., *Do Citizens Know Whether Their State Has Decriminalized Marijuana? Assessing the Perceptual Component of Deterrence Theory*, 5 Rev. L. & Econ. 347 (2009). What are the implications for marijuana policy if citizens have only limited awareness of the law?

5. Some research suggests that some individuals are more responsive to the threat of legal sanctions than are others. See, e.g., Kenneth W. Clements, *More on the Economic Determinants of Consumption*, in Economics and Marijuana: Consumption, Pricing, and Legalisation, at 173 tbl. 4.17 (Kenneth W. Clements & Xueyan Zhao, eds. 2009); MacCoun et al., *Do Citizens Know, supra*, at 350. Who do you think is *most* responsive to the threat of legal sanctions? Who is *least* responsive? What are the implications for marijuana policy?

### b. Marijuana Prices

Demand for marijuana—like that of most other goods—is also sensitive to its price. Simply put, most consumers would buy less marijuana as the price of the drug rises. The drop in demand reflects the tradeoff that buying marijuana entails. Namely, as the price of marijuana rises (at least as compared to other goods), consumers must devote a larger portion of their incomes to acquire the drug.

The *price elasticity of demand* is the technical phrase economists use to describe how much the demand for marijuana changes in response to changes in the price of the drug. It is calculated as *(% change in quantity demanded)/(% change in price)*. Of course, calculating the price elasticity of marijuana is trickier than calculating the price elasticity of a fully legalized good, like ice cream. But researchers generally estimate that the price elasticity of demand for marijuana falls between -0.3 and -0.5. In other words, the demand for marijuana would fall 3 to 5 percent in response to a 10 percent increase in the price of the drug. For detailed discussions of these estimates and the methods used to generate them, see Clements, *More on the Economic Determinants of Consumption, supra,* and Rosalie Liccardo Pacula & Russell Lundberg, *Why Changes in Price Matter When Thinking About Marijuana Policy: A Review of the Literature on the Elasticity of Demand*, 35 Pub. H. Rev. 1 (2014). (The upward slope of the demand curves in **Figure 5.3** reflects a price elasticity of demand of -0.5.)

## Notes and Questions

1. Studies also suggest that some individuals are more price sensitive than others. *See* Clements, *supra*, at 176 tbl. 4.19; Pacula & Lundberg, *supra*, at 13. Who do you think is *most* responsive to changes in the price of marijuana? Who do you think is *least* responsive? Again, what are the implications for marijuana policy?

2. The law's ability to influence the price of marijuana stems primarily from regulations imposed on *suppliers* rather than those imposed on users. The idea is that supply-side regulations—sanctions, taxes, licenses, and so on—increase the cost of manufacturing and distributing marijuana, and suppliers, in turn, pass these costs on to consumers in the form of higher prices. Put another way, these measures are supposed to shift the supply curve in **Figure 5.3** to the left. The effects of supply regulations on the supply curve are discussed in Chapter 9.

### c. Transaction Costs

In a similar way, demand for marijuana is sensitive to the transaction costs that consumers must incur when buying the drug. These transaction costs include the time, effort, and money consumers spend searching for marijuana, consummating purchases, and enforcing the terms of their bargains. The idea is that consumers consider such costs—alongside expected legal sanctions and market prices—when deciding whether or not to purchase marijuana and will purchase less marijuana the higher these transaction costs are.

Lawmakers can increase transaction costs in several ways. For example, prohibiting marijuana possession might make it harder for prospective buyers to search for the drug (e.g., by posting a "pot wanted" ad on Craigslist). Likewise, prohibiting marijuana trafficking might reduce the number of people willing to supply marijuana, disrupt their inventory, or drive them underground where they are harder for buyers (and not just the police) to locate. Even jurisdictions that permit the sale of marijuana might limit the number, hours, and location of suppliers through licensing and zoning regulations, again increasing the costs of acquiring the drug. (Such regulations are discussed in Chapter 8.)

Return to **Figure 5.3** above. Like laws that sanction marijuana possession and use, regulations that increase buyer transaction costs are expected to shift the demand curve to the left.

## Notes and Questions

1. What are all of the transaction costs associated with buying marijuana? How large of a role do these costs play in suppressing demand for marijuana? How much does government policy affect these transaction costs? To answer this last question, consider the following Problem:

Problem 5.6: Delilah is looking to buy a small amount of marijuana for herself. Suppose she lives in one of the following five cities:

(1) Atlanta
(2) Denver
(3) Philadelphia
(4) San Francisco

In which of these cities would Delilah have the easiest time buying marijuana? In which of them would she have the most difficult time? How much higher would the transaction costs be in the latter city as compared to the former?

### d. Individual Attitudes Toward Marijuana

Individual attitudes toward marijuana use also exert a strong influence on demand for the drug. Naturally, to the extent individuals have positive attitudes toward marijuana use—that is, they deem it pleasurable or healthful—they are likely to demand more of the drug. Conversely, to the extent they have negative attitudes toward marijuana use—that is, they deem it unpleasant or dangerous—individuals are likely to demand less of it. Indeed, studies suggest that attitudes toward marijuana are one of the key determinants of the rate of marijuana use. *E.g.*, J.G. Bachman et al., *Explaining Recent Increases in Students' Marijuana Use: Impacts of Perceived Risks and Disapproval, 1976 through 1996*, 88 Am. J. Pub. Health 887, 890 (1998) ("[A]ttitudes about specific drugs—disapproval of use and perceptions of risk of harmfulness—are among the most important determinants of actual use."); Yvonne M. Terry-McElrath et al., *Saying No to Marijuana: Why American Youth Report Quitting or Abstaining*, 69 J. Stud. Alcohol Drugs 796, 798 tbl. 1 (2008) (reporting that attitudes about the harms and benefits of marijuana use were the most commonly cited reasons for quitting or not using marijuana among high school seniors).

These individual attitudes toward marijuana are not set in stone. Indeed, attitudes toward the drug have changed markedly over time. **Figure 5.4** displays the views of high-school seniors toward marijuana use from 1991 to 2015, along with trends in their past-year use:

Figure 5.4. Attitudes Toward Marijuana Use among High School Seniors, 1991-2015*

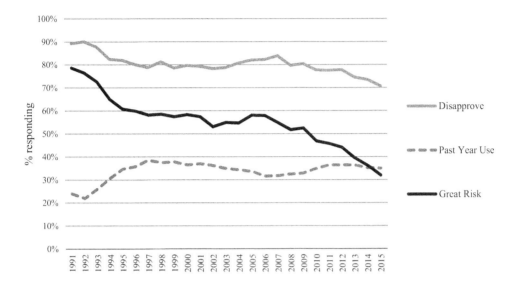

**Figure 5.4** shows a sharp drop in the percentage of high school seniors who deem regular marijuana use to carry "great risk," from 79 percent in 1991 to 32 percent in 2015. Over the same time period, high school seniors have also become less disapproving of the drug. The portion expressing disapproval of regular use of marijuana dropped from 89 percent to 71 percent. (We will return to this finding below in the discussion of social norms.) All the while, marijuana use among high school seniors appears to have increased. In 1991, 24 percent of high school seniors reported that they had used the drug in the prior year, whereas in 2015, 35 percent indicated they had done so.

But even assuming the survey accurately captures attitudes toward marijuana use, do policymakers exert any influence over these attitudes? In other words, can policymakers persuade people to think that marijuana use is bad (or good), and thereby reduce (or increase) their desire to use the drug? There are at least two means by which policymakers have attempted to shape attitudes toward marijuana, discussed in the following sections.

*(i) Media Campaigns*

First, policymakers have invested large sums in media campaigns intended in part to shape attitudes toward marijuana and thereby persuade people not to use the drug. The most notable of these efforts was the National Youth Anti-Drug Media Campaign run by the federal Office of National Drug Control Policy (ONDCP). From 1998 to 2011,

---

* Source: L.D. Johnston et al., *Monitoring the Future National Survey Results on Drug Use, 1975-2015: Overview, Key Findings on Adolescent Drug Use* (2016).

Congress invested more than $2 billion in the campaign, one of the primary goals of which was to discourage youth from using marijuana. 21 U.S.C. § 708(j)(2).

Figure 5.5: An Anti-Marijuana Ad

The ONDCP emphasized different messages throughout its campaign. But many of its ads emphasized the negative consequences of marijuana use. One television ad from 2002, for example, famously depicted the terrible consequences that could follow from teen marijuana use. In the ad, two teenagers (Bob and Frank) are using marijuana and chatting when Bob finds a gun in a desk. Frank asks, "Cool, is it loaded?," and immediately after Bob retorts "Nah," the gun goes off. The ad cuts to a screen warning that "Marijuana can distort your sense of reality." Another print ad from 2008, pictured in **Figure 5.5**, more humorously warned of the damage marijuana use can do to one's career prospects.

But do government media campaigns actually reduce marijuana use? The social science evidence is, again, mixed. Different studies have found that different campaigns either (1) reduced marijuana use; (2) failed to reduce marijuana use; or (3) even—counterproductively—*increased* marijuana use. For a review of 19 studies examining the effects of different anti-drug media campaigns (including ONDCP's), see Elias Allara et al., *Are Mass-Media Campaigns Effective in Preventing Drug Use? A Cochrane Systematic Review and Meta-analyses*, 5 Brit. Med. J. Open (2015).

For its part, Congress appears to have been swayed by the skeptics. It pulled funding for the ONDCP media campaign in 2011, following an earlier review by the ONDCP's own contractor finding that the first few years of the ONDCP campaign had failed to reduce marijuana use among youth and might have even increased the prevalence of use among some youth. *See* General Accountability Office, ONDCP Media Campaign: Contractor's National Evaluation Did Not Find That the Youth Anti-Drug Media Campaign Was Effective in Reducing Youth Drug Use (2006).

## Notes and Questions

1. Notwithstanding the uncertainty of the efficacy of media campaigns, even some states that have legalized marijuana have invested in them to discourage youth marijuana use. *See* Dan Frosch, *Colorado "Lab Rat" Campaign Warns Teens of Pot Use*, Wall St. J. Oct. 5, 2014 (describing Colorado's media campaign to warn teens about the dangers of marijuana use).

2. Does the message matter? Campaigns have emphasized a number of different messages, which may help to explain why studies have reached such different conclusions about their efficacy. Watch some of the marijuana ads linked below:

- Partnership for Drug Free Kids Above the Influence campaign: https://www.youtube.com/user/abovetheinfluence
- Australia "Stoner Sloth" campaign: https://www.youtube.com/watch?v=7rHm8GbTHyE
- Colorado's "Don't Be a Lab Rat" campaign: https://vimeo.com/dontbealabrat
- Colorado's "What's Next" campaign (which replaced Lab Rat in 2015): http://protectwhatsnext.com/

Do you find any of these ads persuasive? Why, why not?

3. Might the *messenger* matter as well? The textbook author explains:

> The reason the federal government's campaign is not shaping preferences may be that citizens simply do not trust the messenger. Not surprisingly, the persuasiveness of any campaign may depend as much on its source as on its content. Imagine, for example, Cheech Marin trying to convince students not to use drugs, or one-time General Motors' Hummer division trying to convince Americans that global warming is a hoax. The government's ability to shape citizens' preferences hinges in large part on lawmakers' credibility and trustworthiness. And as a general matter, the public does not trust federal authorities very much, particularly compared to their state counterparts. When it comes to drug policy in particular, the public seems to harbor doubts about the motive behind certain federal drug policies. One common concern is that the federal marijuana ban is not premised on science but is instead motivated by the financial interests of large drug manufacturers, which could lose billions in drug sales if an ordinary plant were to displace some of their patented medicines, or so the story goes. Whether such beliefs are correct is beside the point; what matters is simply that as long as the federal government suffers a trust deficit, it will have a difficult time nudging people's beliefs in the direction federal lawmakers deem desirable.
>
> State lawmakers, by contrast, arguably have more influence over public beliefs and preferences. Owing to a variety of factors, citizens on average deem state and local governments far more trustworthy than the national government. Consequently, state lawmakers may have an advantage vis-á-vis their federal counterparts when it comes to manipulating citizens' views of marijuana use or other behaviors. . . .

Mikos, *On the Limits, supra*, at 1470. What do you think? Do you think the same ad might have a different effect depending on who sponsors it? If so, who would be the *most* convincing sponsor? Who would be the *least*?

*(ii) Signaling Through Law*

Policymakers might also shape attitudes in a second, more indirect way as well. Namely, prohibiting marijuana might make use of the drug seem more dangerous and depraved, whereas legalizing marijuana might make use of the drug seem more efficacious and safe. Indeed, one of the chief objections raised against state marijuana reforms has been that they send the wrong signal to youths concerning the harms of marijuana use and might thereby soften their attitudes toward the drug and increase their demand for it. In testimony before Congress, for example, then federal drug czar General Barry McCaffrey warned that "[r]eferenda that tell our children that marijuana is a 'medicine' send them the wrong signal about the dangers of illegal drugs—increasing the likelihood that more children will turn to drugs." *Medical Marijuana Referenda in America: Hearing Before the Subcomm. on Crime of the H. Comm. on the Judiciary*, 105th Cong. (1997).

## Notes and Questions

1. For research examining the impact of regulations on attitudes toward marijuana, see Richard A. Miech et al., *Trends in Use of Marijuana and Attitudes Toward Marijuana Among Youth Before and After Decriminalization: The Case of California 2007-2013*, 26 Int'l J. Drug Pol'y 336, 341 (2015) (finding that "[a]fter decriminalization [in 2010] youth attitudes toward marijuana . . . became significantly more permissive among California 12th graders as compared to their peers in the rest of the U.S., as predicted by the signaling hypothesis").

2. Are your views of the safety of an activity or product ever influenced by whether (or not) some government has banned it? Can you think of activities or products you thought were *more* dangerous because of a government ban? Likewise, can you think of activities or products you thought were *less* dangerous than you might have otherwise because the government permitted them?

### e. Social Norms

One final influence on marijuana use stems from social norms. Social norms are non-legal rules and precepts (e.g., "don't cheat on your spouse") that define what constitute appropriate behavior and beliefs within a given community—a nation, state, city, neighborhood, workplace, religious congregation, and so on. Such norms are backed by a variety of non-legal sanctions (e.g., shame), giving these norms a potentially powerful influence over behavior. Social norms regarding the propriety of marijuana use could either make such use less likely (if one's community disapproves of the drug), or more likely (if one's community approves of it). Indeed, studies suggest that social norms exert a powerful influence on marijuana use, especially among youths. *E.g.*, Christine Arazan et al., *The Effect of Marijuana Legalization on Anticipated Use: A Test of Deterrence Theory*, 4 Int'l J. of Crim. & Soc. 181, 184 (2015) (discussing literature and concluding that "peer influence is one of the most well-documented risk factors for marijuana use among adolescents").

Just like attitudes, social norms toward marijuana can shift over time. **Figure 5.4** above shows how one measure of these norms—the percentage of high-school students who disapprove of its regular use—has shifted. It appears that social norms toward marijuana use have softened somewhat from 1991 to 2015, from 89 percent disapproval to 71 percent, though not quite as much as individual attitudes toward the drug.

But what can policymakers do about norms? The relationship between law and norms is complicated, as the textbook author explains:

> On one view of the legislative process, lawmakers can shape social norms by manipulating whether society condemns or condones a given behavior, similarly to the way they can shape personal beliefs about that behavior. Norms, of course, put added pressure on group members to behave a particular way (in addition to the pressure exerted

by their own personal preferences). Indeed, because of this pressure to conform, norms may influence the behavior even of those outlier members who remain unconvinced by the government's message (i.e., members whose personal beliefs do not comport with the norm).

. . .

On another view of the legislative process, norms are entrenched; lawmakers must take norms as they find them, meaning they cannot necessarily control whether society condemns or condones any given behavior. This, in effect, makes norms a double-edged sword. Nonetheless, even if they cannot necessarily change the content of norms, lawmakers can augment or diminish the influence of a norm on behavior by educating citizens about the content and potency of that norm.

The passage of a new law may help reduce citizens' uncertainty about norms, particularly when they are in flux. The basic idea is that citizens demand laws that comport with community norms, and lawmakers, subject to constraints such as majority rule, respond by supplying such laws. Hence, the passage of a law banning marijuana use suggests the existence of a similar social norm condemning marijuana use—i.e., it educates citizens about the content and potency of community norms concerning marijuana.

In turn, clarifying the content and potency of norms—particularly new or evolving norms—can change people's behavior. To illustrate, suppose X is considering smoking marijuana to treat his glaucoma but is uncertain whether society now condemns use of marijuana for such purposes. As Robert Scott explains in a different example, the passage of a law regulating marijuana use provides X Bayesian information concerning what his fellow citizens now think about it. [*See* Robert E. Scott, *The Limits of Behavioral Theories of Law and Social Norms*, 86 Va. L. Rev. 1603, 1614-16 (2000).] The law thus helps X more accurately determine the expected social sanction, if any, for using marijuana. For example, the passage of a law proscribing marijuana signals society's disapproval of it. It informs X that he should expect to incur a cost apart from legal sanctions for smoking marijuana. On account of this cost, X might refrain from using marijuana, despite the absence of formal legal sanctions and even though X feels he might benefit from marijuana use.

In the case of marijuana, of course, state and federal laws send conflicting signals about the social acceptability of using the drug as medicine. The CSA strongly suggests societal disapproval, but permissive state laws suggest societal tolerance—and possibly even approval—of medical use of the drug. If citizens take their cues from federal law, Congress may have far more de facto impact on marijuana use than previous Sections have suggested. Conversely, if citizens take their cues from state law, Congress's influence in this domain is even weaker than previously noted.

When it comes to educating citizens about norms, state laws generally give citizens more current and relevant information, and as a result are more likely to shape their choices than are federal laws. For one thing, state laws typically convey more up-to-date information about current social norms. The main reason is that states employ comparatively majoritarian-friendly lawmaking processes, such as referenda, that make updating state laws to keep up with changes in societal views much easier. To be sure, passage of a congressional law regulating an activity signals something about how the nation feels about that activity when the law is passed. Indeed, because it takes supermajority support to push any measure through Congress, laws that do emerge from the national process usually signal a strong national consensus and norm. But because federal laws are so resistant to change, the signal broadcast by the passage of federal law fades quickly with time.

The CSA illustrates the point. The federal ban on medical use of marijuana was adopted nearly forty years ago, when Congress placed marijuana on Schedule I of the CSA.

Whatever society's views were circa 1970, they have since changed: the strict marijuana ban is out of sync with current social norms. Society no longer condemns the use of marijuana for medical purposes (assuming it ever did). On the contrary, opinion polls consistently show more than 70 percent of the American public now approves of the use of marijuana for medical conditions. But given the enormous challenge of changing any congressional law, the resilience of the now seemingly passé federal ban is hardly surprising. It would take an even more dramatic shift in public opinion to formally undo it.

By contrast, state medical marijuana laws have all been enacted more recently than the federal ban, starting with California in 1996 and continuing through Michigan in 2008. These state laws have been supported by large and growing majorities. Support for the most recently enacted measure—Michigan's Proposition 1—topped 63 percent. The passage of thirteen state laws, many by wide margins, signals that society is more likely to support than to censure medical use of marijuana. Thus, there is no social sanction for using marijuana for medical purposes, or at least no consensus to condemn such behavior, in these states.

In addition to being more current, state laws also convey more accurate information about *local* norms. This is important because norms held by local society exert far more influence on one's behavior than do norms held by distant strangers. After all, we interact more—and care more about our standing—with neighbors, co-workers, close family, and fellow worshipers than we do with people who live far away. Thus, for example, the passage of California's Compassionate Use Act in 1996 may have signaled the emergence of a new, more permissive norm governing the medical use of marijuana in that state. This event may have been enough to foster use of the drug in California, even if drug norms elsewhere had not yet changed.

In short, even if they cannot shield people from federal legal sanctions or change federal law in the short term, states *can* make people feel secure from social sanctions by credibly signaling public approval of once taboo conduct. In this way, states wield another powerful influence on private behavior, an influence that is not necessarily subject to congressional preemption. What is more, by signaling societal approval of marijuana use, states may even hamstring Congress's already limited ability to impose legal sanctions on those who violate the federal ban. For example, jurors may be unwilling to convict people who use marijuana for medical purposes (or the people who help them) if they know that local society generally approves of medical marijuana. In fact, in order to avoid sympathetic juries, the DEA has been attacking medical marijuana suppliers primarily by using civil injunctions and civil sanctions such as forfeiture, which are tactics that do not require jury participation.

Mikos, *On the Limits*, supra, 1475-79.

## Notes and Questions

1. How do you think social norms regarding marijuana use have changed over the last decade? Think of the people you know best: Would they act any differently toward you if they knew you used marijuana? Would you act any differently toward them if you knew they used marijuana?

2. Do you think the law has changed social norms regarding marijuana use? Or has the law changed in response to shifts in social norms (and/or attitudes)?

## f. Review

Given all of the above, how much does the law actually influence demand? In other words, how big of a shift in demand would follow from a change in the laws governing possession and use? While it seems reasonable to suppose that D2 falls *somewhere* to the left of D1 on **Figure 5.3**, just *how far* to the left is a hotly debated point.

Many studies have attempted to gauge the overall effects of changes to the law governing marijuana possession, including decriminalization and legalization. Unfortunately, however, it is enormously difficult to isolate the impact of specific changes to the law. Among other reasons, many factors influence use, and it is challenging to control for them all; different types of users (the young, heavy users, etc.) may respond differently to changes in the law; and legal reforms vary considerably across the states (as discussed in Chapter 4), complicating the task of making interjurisdictional comparisons. Not surprisingly, then, the results of studies have been mixed. Some studies have found that user sanctions reduce use, while others have failed to find such an effect. For reviews of studies and discussions of possible explanations for the mixed results, see, e.g., Kilmer, *Do Cannabis Possession Laws Influence Cannabis Use?*, supra, at 120-26; MacCoun et al., *Do Citizens Know*, supra, at 348-51; Rosalie L. Pacula & Eric L. Sevigny, *Marijuana Liberalization Policies: Why We Can't Learn Much from Policy Still in Motion*, 33 J. Pol'y Analysis & Mgmt. 212, 212-14 (2014).

## Notes and Questions

1. How should lawmakers proceed in the face of uncertainty about policy effects? If policy analysts cannot confidently predict the effect of a proposed change to marijuana law (or gauge the impact of an existing marijuana law), how should lawmakers decide what laws to adopt?

## 2. Law's Impact on Unapproved Use

Of course, many jurisdictions do not want to curb *all* use of marijuana. As discussed in Section A above, many states deem some marijuana use to be beneficial. Nonetheless, as explained in Chapter 4, even jurisdictions that allow some people to possess and use marijuana continue to ban others (e.g., minors) from doing so. But can jurisdictions prevent unapproved use once they allow some people to possess and use marijuana?

Most of the regulations discussed in Chapter 4 are designed at least in part to prevent the diversion of legal marijuana into unapproved uses. Consider the mandatory registration requirement imposed by most medical marijuana states. Under this requirement, qualifying patients must successfully register with a state health agency *before* they are permitted to possess and use marijuana. As the textbook author has explained, "[c]ompulsory registration systems help state law enforcement agents quickly, cheaply, and accurately determine who may legally possess marijuana." Robert A. Mikos, *Can States Keep Secrets from the Federal Government?* 161 U. Pa. L. Rev. 103, 132 (2012). "To determine whether someone who asserts a medical marijuana defense actually meets the eligibility requirements under state law, state police need only call a registry hotline—the determination has already been made by a civil regulatory agency." *Id.* at n.127. By contrast, in a no-registration state, "police must determine for themselves whether a suspect is eligible to use marijuana for medical purposes. The cost of making such determinations in the context of a criminal investigation is comparatively high, making it expensive for police to pursue criminal charges against suspects who claim a medical need for the drug, even when their claim seems disingenuous." *Id.* at 132-33.

But does registration—or any of the other requirements imposed on users by reform states—actually prevent diversion to unapproved uses? It is early and the jury is still out. Rosalie Pacula and her co-authors found "inconsistent evidence regarding the effect of . . . registration requirements on recreational marijuana use, which appears to depend on the data set, subpopulation, and specific margin of use." Rosalie L. Pacula et al., *Assessing the Effects of Medical Marijuana Laws on Marijuana Use: The Devil is in the Details,* 34 J. Pol'y Analysis & Mgmt. 7, 29 (2014). Other studies have found evidence that recreational users are obtaining marijuana from registered medical marijuana patients. *E.g.,* Stacy Salomonsen-Sautel et al., *Medical Marijuana Use Among Adolescents in Substance Abuse Treatment,* 51 J. Am. Acad. Child Adolesc. Psychiatry 694 (2012) (finding that 74 percent of 164 adolescents in substance abuse program had obtained marijuana from a medical marijuana patient); Christian Thurstone et al., *Medical Marijuana Diversion and Associated Problems in Adolescent Substance Treatment,* 118 Drug Alcohol Depend. 489 (2011) (finding that 49 percent of 80 adolescents in substance abuse program had obtained marijuana from registered medical marijuana user); Abraham M. Nussbaum et al., *Use and Diversion of Medical Marijuana Among Adults Admitted to Inpatient Psychiatry,* 41 Am. J. Drug Alcohol Abuse 166 (2015) (reporting results of survey of 623 psychiatric patients finding that "the use of diverted medical marijuana was quite common, with almost a quarter of respondents reporting that someone with a medical marijuana card had shared or sold marijuana to them"). Chapter 9 explores diversion of marijuana supplies in more detail.

## Notes and Questions

1. Do you think registration (or anything else reform states have tried) reduces unapproved use? If you think that outright prohibition has little or no deterrent effect on use, is there any hope that these requirements—which amount to narrower prohibitions—can be effective? Why, why not?

2. Registration provides states with a treasure trove of information about who is using medical marijuana and for which qualifying conditions. Many states make this data publicly available (in aggregate form) for researchers. For example, Colorado's Health Department reports that there were 109,922 registered patients in Colorado as of November 2015. The number and percentage of those patients reporting certain qualifying conditions is displayed in **Table 5.2**.

Table 5.2: A Snapshot of Colorado's Registered Patients in 2015*

| Qualifying Condition | Number of patients reporting | Percentage of registered patients** |
|---|---|---|
| Cachexia | 965 | 0.9% |
| Cancer | 3,926 | 3.6% |
| Glaucoma | 1,290 | 1.2% |
| HIV/AIDS | 612 | 0.6% |
| Muscle Spasms | 21,526 | 19.6% |
| Seizures | 2,585 | 2.4% |
| Severe Nausea | 12,599 | 11.5% |
| Severe Pain | 102,121 | 92.9% |

## 3. Driving Harms and DUI

Most policymakers appear to agree that marijuana use impairs driving and contributes to driving accidents. Although they disagree about the precise magnitude of this harm, policymakers have sought to combat it both through broad prohibitions on the possession and use of marijuana and through narrower prohibitions on driving under the influence of marijuana. But is it necessary—or even helpful—to prohibit possession and use of marijuana in order to curb the drug's driving-related harms? Or can jurisdictions curb driving harms solely by prohibiting impaired driving? In any event, how should jurisdictions define impaired driving?

Consider the first question. Notwithstanding consensus that marijuana use increases the risk of crashes to at least some degree, the impact of legalizing marijuana use on crashes is less clear. *Compare* D. Mark Anderson et al., *Medical Marijuana Laws, Traffic Fatalities, and Alcohol Consumption*, 56 J.L. & Econ. 333 (2013) (finding that legalization of medical marijuana is associated with an 8 to 11 percent reduction in traffic fatalities), *with* Brian C. Tefft et al., *Prevalence of Marijuana Involvement in Fatal Crashes: Washington, 2010-2014* (AAA Foundation for Traffic Safety, 2016) (finding that fatal crashes involving drivers who had recently used marijuana doubled following legalization of recreational marijuana in Washington).

The uncertainty stems in large part from marijuana's as-yet uncertain relationship to the consumption of other impairing substances, like alcohol. *See supra*, Section B.1. If

---

\* Colorado Department of Public Health & Environment, Medical Marijuana Registry Program Statistics, Nov. 2015, https://perma.cc/H66T-4ZGD.

\*\* Total does not add to 100 percent because some patients report more than one condition.

marijuana is a substitute for alcohol—i.e., the increase in marijuana use is offset by a decrease in alcohol use—legalization might result in fewer crashes, as long as DUI-marijuana is safer than DUI-alcohol (as is commonly thought). Anderson et al., *Medical Marijuana Laws, supra*, at 335. And even if the crash risks associated with the two substances were equal, marijuana legalization could still reduce traffic harms, at least so long as jurisdictions continue to ban use of marijuana in bars and restaurants. Anderson and his co-authors explain:

> Alcohol is often consumed in restaurants and bars, while many states prohibit the use of medical marijuana in public. If marijuana consumption typically takes place at home or other private locations, then legalization could reduce traffic fatalities simply because marijuana users are less likely to drive while impaired.

*Id.*

Now consider the second question. Is there a way for jurisdictions to combat DUI-marijuana short of prohibiting possession and use of the drug? Policing DUI-marijuana poses unique challenges for law enforcement agents, especially as compared to DUI-alcohol. Demonstrating that marijuana use *caused* a driver's impairment—a necessary element of the traditional DUI-impaired offense—poses perhaps the most daunting of these challenges. As of yet, there is no simple test akin to the breathalyzer used to demonstrate impairment from alcohol that police can use to demonstrate impairment from marijuana. (Chapter 4 discusses the types of proof police now use to establish impairment.)

The practical challenges are part of the reason why some jurisdictions have adopted per se bans on driving with a minimum level of THC in one's system. A report from the National Highway Traffic Safety Administration explains:

> In most . . . per se States, the compelling argument for adoption of the drug per se statute was that, prior to the laws, a driver was far less likely to be prosecuted for impaired driving if he/she were under the influence of an illegal substance than if he/she were under the influence of a legal substance (alcohol). This dilemma existed because there was a per se level for alcohol but no practical or legal way to establish an impairment-linked per se level for controlled substances. The per se approach creates an important legal distinction between having to prove a nexus between the observed driver impairment and drug use (causal relationship) and simply demonstrating observed impaired-driving behavior was associated with specified concentrations of drug/metabolite in the individual's body while operating the motor vehicle.

The Department of Transportation, NHTSA, Drug Per Se Laws: A Review of Their Use in the States 5 (2010). As discussed in Chapter 4, the per se offense relieves the government of the burden of demonstrating that a driver was actually impaired by marijuana. Instead, the government need only show that the driver had a requisite quantum of marijuana (or its metabolites) in his/her system.

But do these per se laws accurately predict dangerousness? In other words, does the presence of a specified quantum of marijuana or marijuana metabolites in one's body reliably demonstrate that someone was a more dangerous driver? In the following excerpt, Professor Andrea Roth argues that per se laws lack a scientific foundation and thus do a poor job of addressing any driving harms that might be associated with marijuana use.

## Andrea Roth, The Uneasy Case for Marijuana as Chemical Impairment Under a Science-Based Jurisprudence of Dangerousness
103 Cal. L. Rev. 841 (2015)

In 1931, Prohibition was on its last legs, . . . [t]he specter of drunk driving had begun to invade the nation's psyche, and law enforcement and health officials scrambled to address the issue by urging states to criminalize driving "while impaired" by or "driving under the influence" of (DUI) alcohol, which jurors were told meant driving unsafely as a result of the effects of alcohol. But jurors did not always believe uncorroborated police testimony about a suspect's drunkenness. Moreover, the medical community was concerned that much of the dangerous impairment causing fatal crashes did not manifest in obvious drunkenness, and might not even be capable of detection through means other than difficult-to-perform blood tests. The criminal law, as an instrument of protecting the nation from a burgeoning public health crisis, was failing.

Help would arrive in the form of the "Drunk-O-Meter," a balloon-like device that could measure a motorist's blood-alcohol concentration (BAC) simply by capturing one's breath. On New Year's Eve 1938, in the streets of Indianapolis, the Drunk-O-Meter made its public debut, and the jurisprudence of dangerousness undergirding drunk driving laws entered the scientific age. Not only could the Drunk-O-Meter offer corroboration of police testimony of DUI, it also allowed researchers, through experiments and studies of crashes, to explore the relationship between particular BACs and a driver's level of impairment. The machine could do so because of the uniquely predictable and uniform properties of ethyl alcohol, which allowed scientists to easily infer proximity of use, precise level of alcohol intoxication in the brain, and level of driver impairment from one's BAC. Still, this initial wave of experimentation lacked the scientific rigor typical of epidemiological research of public health problems.

Luckily for drunk driving jurisprudence, the country's first "traffic czar" in the late 1960s, the bow-tie-wearing "workaholic government bureaucrat" William Haddon Jr., was an epidemiologist. Haddon transformed the science of alcohol and traffic safety by explaining the need to test BACs of drivers in single-car fatal crashes, conduct case-control studies comparing BACs of fatal crash victims with those of randomly stopped drivers in similar circumstances, and conduct realistic on-road and simulated BAC-specific driver impairment studies. Bathed in the scientific ethos Haddon established, researchers conducted meticulous studies with thousands of motorists that showed precise increased relative crash risks at precise BACs. For example, these studies revealed a precipitous rise in crash risk at .10 and .15 percent BAC, and a lesser but still troubling increased relative crash risk at .08 percent. At the prodding of federal officials, states would eventually adopt these BACs as presumptive proof of impairment, and later—after DUI enforcement took a punitive, law-and-order turn in the 1980s—would redefine the very crime of DUI in terms of BAC.

. . .

Unfortunately, Haddon's lessons appear to be lost on policymakers attempting to resolve the next perceived public health crisis being addressed through the criminal law: drugged driving. As the marijuana legalization movement advances, states face a jurisprudential dilemma. Before legalization, a number of states had passed "zero-tolerance" laws banning driving with *any* amount of any *illicit* drug in one's system. These laws were justified under a jurisprudence of prohibition; the state could legitimately criminalize driving under the influence because it considered the drug use itself morally blameworthy. But in those states that have wholly or partially legalized marijuana, prohibition is no longer a good fit as a theory of punishment. Voters have instead chosen to treat marijuana like alcohol.

In line with marijuana legalization advocates' own analogies to alcohol, law enforcement and policymakers in several states have reasoned that the way to criminalize DUI marijuana is simply to import the DUI alcohol model. But to these officials, who are often not aware of the history of DUI alcohol science, adopting the DUI alcohol model has meant simply choosing some numerical definition of chemical impairment by marijuana as analogous as possible to alcohol's .08 percent. Six states have done just that, by picking thresholds such as one, two, or five nanograms per milliliter of tetrahydrocannabinol (THC)—the main psychoactive compound in marijuana—in the blood, and redefining the crime of DUI as driving with a THC level over that threshold. These officials have made their case by invoking the DUI alcohol analogy and, in a political twist, legalization advocates have themselves acquiesced as a means of winning over hesitant voters and law enforcement groups in their fight for legalization. . . .

Remarkably, a surge of new criminal laws, to be enforced on the nation's highways, has been unleashed without their sponsors ever having to articulate a legitimate theory of punishment. Haddon's established framework of BAC-specific single-car crash studies, BAC-specific case-control studies, and realistic and BAC-specific impairment studies bears no resemblance to the rushed and unscientific process that produced per se DUI marijuana laws. The well-acknowledged truth is that there is no known relationship between THC blood levels and increased relative crash risk documented by single-crash or classic case-control studies, and no known relationship between a driver's THC blood level and his level of driving impairment. To the extent single-car and case-control crash studies do exist, they suggest, if anything, that drivers with only THC in their blood are not causing a disproportionate number of fatal crashes.

In short, once Haddon's established scientific framework for defining dangerous impairment is understood as a mandatory hurdle for any legitimate chemical impairment law, the illegitimacy of per se DUI marijuana laws under a jurisprudence of dangerousness becomes painfully obvious. Scientific validity is not a light switch that policymakers can turn on and off when convenient; it is the very premise of any legitimate chemical impairment law, like alcohol's .08 percent, that criminalizes having a measurable amount of a drug in one's body while performing a potentially dangerous activity. Acknowledging the illegitimacy of this new wave of DUI marijuana laws is critical to any future attempt to use science as a jurisprudential tool in addressing drugged driving. . . .

## Notes and Questions

1. Roth argues that the lack of science demonstrating a link between impairment and the presence of a given quantity of THC or THC metabolites in the body undermines the rationale behind DUI-per se laws—namely, that the presence of those substances demonstrates dangerousness. But might the per se approach still make sense in regimes that prohibit marijuana possession and use? Roth appears to think so, suggesting that under a jurisprudence of prohibition, "the state could legitimately criminalize driving under the

influence [per se] because it considered the drug use itself morally blameworthy." *Supra*. Do you agree? Is there a legitimate penological justification for per se bans in jurisdictions that prohibit possession and use of marijuana? If so, would prohibition jurisdictions likewise have a legitimate penological justification for banning walking or sitting while having any marijuana in one's system? After all, why do prohibition jurisdictions make DUI-per se marijuana a separate offense—often punishable by higher sanctions than possession itself—unless driving with some quantum of marijuana in one's body is more *dangerous*? To put it another way, if simply having some quantum of marijuana (or its metabolites) in one's body does not necessarily make one more dangerous, is there any reason (any legitimate penological justification) for any regime to adopt a DUI-per se law for marijuana? *See Love v. Georgia*, 517 S.E.2d 53, 57 (Ga. 1999) (finding state per se DUI-marijuana law irrational because it applied only to unlawfully used marijuana).

2. What do you think? How should jurisdictions combat the driving harms associated with marijuana:

(1) Banning (or restricting) marijuana possession and use in general
(2) Banning (or restricting) marijuana possession and use outside of the home
(3) Banning DUI-impaired
(4) Banning DUI-per se
(5) Some combination of the above

Can you think of any other measures jurisdictions might adopt to combat driving harms associated with marijuana use?

## D. WHAT ARE THE COSTS OF DIFFERENT REGULATORY APPROACHES?

Problem 5.7: Suppose you are a policymaker who wants to curb the use of marijuana. Suppose you also believe that you have the ability to do so—e.g., that regulations you adopt (including prohibitions) would help curb marijuana use. How much would you be willing to spend to stop one individual from using the drug? What sort of enforcement tactics would you authorize to that end?

All regulations of marijuana possession and use have some costs associated with them. Determining what is the "best" regulatory approach necessarily requires consideration of these costs. To that end, this section discusses the costs associated with different policies governing marijuana possession and use. Broadly speaking, these costs fall into two categories: 1) fiscal costs, i.e., the monies spent on enforcing the law; and 2) liberty costs, i.e., the degree of personal freedom sacrificed by the law and its enforcement.

### 1. Fiscal Costs

All of the existing approaches to regulating marijuana possession and use require *some* government expenditure on regulation and enforcement. In prohibition regimes, these expenditures include the monies spent to catch, prosecute, and punish individuals who possess marijuana. By some estimates, the nation spent somewhere between $1.2 billion and $6.0 billion in 2010 (before many states had adopted reforms) enforcing criminal prohibitions on marijuana possession. *See* American Civil Liberties Union, The War on Marijuana in Black and White, 68-77 (2013) (surveying estimates).

The ACLU has provided what it terms a conservative estimate of the average cost of arresting, convicting, and punishing a single marijuana possessor. Its cost estimates are detailed in **Table 5.3**:

Table 5.3 Cost of a Marijuana Possession Conviction*

| Category | Cost (2010 dollars) |
| --- | --- |
| Arrest (police) | $750 |
| Adjudication | $400 |
| Punishment** | $672 |
| **Total** | **$1,822** |

## Notes and Questions

1. Do you think the per case cost estimated by the ACLU is too high, too low, or just about right? What about fines collected and assets seized, both of which might help to offset some of the costs of enforcement? For another estimate of the costs of handing individual marijuana cases that includes such offsets, see Caulkins et al., Considering Marijuana Legalization, *supra* at 23-26.

2. Would legalization reduce total criminal justice expenditures or simply redirect those expenditures? If the latter, how are law enforcement officials likely to use the resources once devoted to enforcing marijuana prohibition? How *should* they use those resources?

3. Assuming that legal sanctions suppress demand for marijuana, do they do so efficiently? Consider the following Problem.

**Problem 5.8:** There are currently roughly 20 million regular (i.e., monthly) marijuana users in the United States, making up about 6.25 percent of the total population (320 million). Suppose that regular users currently face a 3 percent probability of arrest and a 33 percent probability of conviction and punishment after arrest, or a combined 1 percent probability of facing *both* arrest and punishment. *See supra*, Section C.1.a. Now, suppose that

---

\* Taken from ACLU, The War on Marijuana, *supra*, at 71-75. Note that the ACLU estimates that only about 27 percent of marijuana possession arrests result in conviction and punishment. *Id.*

\*\* This assumes an average sentence of 5.5 days in jail and 74.5 days on supervised release. *Id.* at 73-74.

increasing the combined probability of arrest and punishment by 10 percent (e.g., from 1 to 11 percent) would reduce the probability of past month use by 3 percent (e.g., from 6.25 to 3.25 percent of the population). *See* Matthew C. Farrelly et al., *The Joint Demand for Cigarettes and Marijuana: Evidence from the National Household Surveys on Drug Abuse*, 20 J. Health Econ. 51, 61 (2001) (estimating the impact of arrest rate on past-month use among youths). Assuming a $1,000 net cost per arrest and an additional $500 cost for punishment per case (when applicable), and assuming that legal sanctions do not affect use in any other way (e.g., by changing attitudes), how much would it cost to reduce the number of regular users in the United States to 10.4 million (or 3.25 percent of the population), solely by increasing enforcement of user prohibitions? Do you think the cost would be worthwhile? Might there be a more efficient means of reducing use?

4. Might strict enforcement of marijuana laws help police prevent other, potentially more serious, crimes as well? In a fascinating study using data on more than 2 million stops conducted by the New York City Police Department between 2004 and 2008, including more than 50,000 stops on suspicion of marijuana possession, Amanda Geller and Jeffrey Fagan tested and rejected this hypothesis:

> Marijuana stops . . . lead to weapon seizures in only approximately one-half of 1 percent of stops. If marijuana enforcement is designed to stop more serious crime by catching criminals 'on their day off' . . . , it is quite inefficient.

Amanda Geller & Jeffrey Fagan, *Pot as Pretext: Marijuana, Race, and the New Disorder in New York City Street Policing*, 7 J. Emp. Leg. S. 591, 618 (2010).

5. Legalization regimes, of course, must bear some regulatory and enforcement costs, too. To some extent, these regimes continue to spend money catching, prosecuting, and punishing actions by marijuana users that have not been legalized—e.g., possession by youths, possession by recreational users (in medical marijuana states), DUI-marijuana, possession of amounts that exceed quantity limits, and possession and use in prohibited places. *See* Letter from Colorado Chiefs of Police to Gov. Hickenlooper, Mar. 3, 2014 (requesting additional funds to cover enforcement costs, including costs of DUI-marijuana enforcement), https://perma.cc/HQA7-TSFL. How do the costs of regulating marijuana possession and use compare across jurisdictions with different regulatory approaches? In particular, how do the costs compare among: (1) recreational states; (2) medical marijuana states; (3) decriminalization states; and (4) criminal prohibition states?

## 2. Liberty Costs

In addition to incurring the fiscal costs just discussed, all regulations also curtail personal liberty to some degree. The sections below examine these costs in prohibition and legalization regimes.

### a. Prohibition Regimes

Prohibition regimes, of course, necessarily exact the highest toll on personal liberty. In such regimes, all individuals who wish to use marijuana are denied the right to do so by law. And if these individuals flout prohibition, they might be arrested and possibly even incarcerated for their crimes. Indeed, even individuals who do not possess or use marijuana might lose some of their personal liberty in prohibition regimes. After all, they might be stopped, searched, and questioned by the police based on reasonable (albeit erroneous) suspicion that they too possess marijuana.

The toll exacted by prohibition, however, is not evenly distributed, raising additional and distinct concerns about equal justice. Many studies have shown that minorities—and especially blacks—are much more likely to be arrested for marijuana possession than are whites, even controlling for any differences in rates of use. *E.g.*, ACLU, The War on Marijuana, *supra*, at 4 (estimating that a black marijuana user is 3.73 times more likely than white user to be arrested for possession); Nguyen & Reuter, *How Risky Is Marijuana Possession?*, *supra*, at 895 (estimating that in 2008, a black juvenile marijuana user was 1.5 times more likely to be arrested than was a white juvenile user, but that a black adult user was 3 times more likely to be arrested than a white adult user). The following excerpt suggests that these racial disparities bolster the case for repealing criminal prohibitions on the possession of marijuana.

## *American Civil Liberties Union*, The War on Marijuana in Black and White (2013)

The War on Marijuana has largely been a war on people of color. Despite the fact that marijuana is used at comparable rates by whites and Blacks, state and local governments have aggressively enforced marijuana laws selectively against Black people and communities. In 2010, the Black arrest rate for marijuana possession was 716 per 100,000, while the white arrest rate was 192 per 100,000. Stated another way, a Black person was 3.73 times more likely to be arrested for marijuana possession than a white person—a disparity that increased 32.7% between 2001 and 2010. . . .

In the states with the worst disparities, Blacks were on average over six times more likely to be arrested for marijuana possession than whites. In the worst offending counties across the country, Blacks were over 10, 15, even 30 times more likely to be arrested than white residents in the same county. These glaring racial disparities in marijuana arrests are not a northern or southern phenomenon, nor a rural or urban phenomenon, but rather a national one. The racial disparities are as staggering in the Midwest as in the Northeast, in large counties as in small, on city streets as on country roads, in counties with high median family incomes as in counties with low median family incomes. They exist regardless of whether Blacks make up 50% or 5% of a county's overall population. The racial disparities in marijuana arrest rates are ubiquitous; the differences can be found only in their degrees of severity.

Thus, while the criminal justice system casts a wide net over marijuana use and possession by Blacks, it has turned a comparatively blind eye to the same conduct occurring at the same rates in many white communities. Just as with the larger drug war, the War on Marijuana has, quite simply, served as a vehicle for police to target communities of color.

. . .

The most effective way to eliminate arrests for marijuana use and possession, the racial disparities among such arrests, and the Fourth Amendment violations that often accompany such arrests, is to legalize marijuana. For instance, in Washington, Blacks were almost three times more likely to be arrested for marijuana possession as whites, and the Black/white racial disparity in marijuana possession arrests increased by 42% between 2001 and 2010. By passing Initiative 502, which legalized possession of marijuana for people 21 years or older and thus ended arrests of adults for possession, Washington has also ended such racial disparities with respect to marijuana possession arrests of people 21 years or older.

## Notes and Questions

1. Would legalizing marijuana eliminate racial disparities in arrest rates, even for marijuana possession, as the ACLU suggests? *See* Mike Males, *Are Young People and African Americans Better Off Under Marijuana Reform?*, YouthFacts (Mar. 2016), https://perma.cc/8KL7-QUFP (reporting preliminary analysis showing that while total arrests for marijuana had fallen substantially, "reforms have not reduced racial disparities in arrest rates"). And even if legalizing marijuana does eliminate the racial disparities among arrests for marijuana possession, will it necessarily reduce racial disparities in the criminal justice system? In other words, might disparities simply reappear as police turn their attention to other crimes? *See generally* Dorothy E. Roberts, *Social Meaning of Order-Maintenance Policing*, 89 J. Crim. L. & Criminology 775 (1999) (noting that racial disparities appear in arrest rates for other types of low-level offenses as well, like loitering and vagrancy).

2. Is there any way for governments to reduce or eliminate racial disparities in enforcement of marijuana laws without repealing prohibition? *E.g.*, Robert J. Smith, *Reducing Racially Disparate Policing Outcomes: Is Implicit Bias Training the Answer?*, 37 U. Haw. L. Rev. 295, 310 (2015) (advocating implicit bias training for police, but noting that decriminalization of marijuana possession may "do more to remedy racially disparate outcomes than we could ever expect a reduction in implicit racial biases to achieve").

### b. Legalization Regimes

Legalization regimes are more tolerant of marijuana use than are prohibition regimes and thus exact a lower toll on personal liberty. But such jurisdictions still restrict personal liberty. For example, medical marijuana regimes do not allow people to use marijuana for non-medical purposes. What is more, as discussed in Chapter 4, individuals must take several steps, such as obtaining a physician's recommendation, before using the drug, and even then, they may still be subject to arrest and prosecution for simple possession of marijuana.

Do the regulations imposed by legalization regimes limit personal liberty too much? Consider one limit that has been imposed by nearly all legalization states (including recreational states) to date: the ban on use of marijuana in public places. (As discussed in Chapter 4, a few jurisdictions recently voted to permit the use of marijuana in designated public places.) Is even this restriction too much of an imposition on personal liberty? Consider this argument:

> Recreational marijuana use has been legal in Seattle since 2012, but I still felt like I was getting away with something when I walked into a dispensary there this fall. There was a bouncer waiting behind a roped-off entryway on the otherwise quiet Capitol Hill side street. . . . The staff inside was friendly, but sampling the product was strictly prohibited. In fact, there was almost nowhere to legally smoke what they were selling—not the sidewalk outside, not at the park a few blocks away, and definitely not in the patio smoking section at the neighborhood bar. The only safe place was at home—or the home of the friends I was staying with.
>
> At such moments, it's easy to think marijuana legalization in Seattle is largely a technicality, more of a theoretical freedom that leaves plenty of potential for smokers to run afoul of the law. In Washington state, marijuana is governed under the same laws that prohibit public consumption of alcohol. "If you're smoking in plain public view, you're subject to a ticket," Seattle City Attorney Pete Holmes warned in late 2012, just as Initiative 502—the legalization measure—was going in to effect. . . .
>
> . . .
>
> Laws against public consumption of intoxicants like marijuana or alcohol have done little to prevent anyone from consuming them in public. Instead, they've helped create a toxic anxiety about always being watched, leaving some small part of your brain on alert for cops, cameras, or tattle-minded neighbors, all of which quietly sour our shared spaces instead of securing them. . . .
>
> Marijuana's long prohibition seems to be nearing its end, but what's come from it so far feels as eerily controlled and haphazardly punitive as what's followed the repeal of alcohol's prohibition—a reminder that many American freedoms are easier to brag about than put into practice.

Michael Thomsen, *Legalizing Weed Isn't Enough*, Slate.com, Dec. 28, 2015, https://perma.cc/R6BQ-QSYV.

## Notes and Questions

1. Should states and localities permit the consumption of marijuana in public places, like bars and restaurants? What is the rationale behind such bans anyway? Do they curb marijuana's harms, like the accidents associated with DUI-marijuana? Does consumption in public simply bother other citizens? *See* Pew Research Center Poll (poll conducted Mar. 25-29, 2015) (reporting that 62 percent of Americans would be bothered if someone smoked marijuana in public, even if marijuana were legal), https://perma.cc/6DKN-UT47. Is the harm (however defined) of use in public enough to justify the restriction on liberty?

2. Are any of the other regulations imposed by medical and recreational marijuana states and discussed in Chapter 4 excessive restrictions of personal liberty? Ultimately, how do we measure the sacrifice of personal liberty against the potential benefits of legal restrictions, such as improvements in health and road safety? Requiring regulations to satisfy the harm principle discussed in Section B.2, *supra*, is one possible approach. One assumption underlying the harm principle is that individuals know best what is in their own best interests. After all, lawmakers may easily misjudge the costs and benefits to the individual of activity. But the same logic does not hold when the activity harms *other people*. If individuals do not internalize the full costs of the activity, government regulation

may be needed to curb it. For further elaboration on the harm principle and its relationship to efficiency, see Jim Leitzel, Regulating Vice 19-20 (2008). Which of the regulations considered in Chapter 4 would satisfy the harm principle? In other words, which of those regulations address harms to others, rather than harms to the users of marijuana?

Along these lines, consider the following Problem:

<u>Problem 5.9</u>: You work for a lawmaker who is deciding whether to support several proposed regulations on marijuana possession and use. The lawmaker is a fan of J.S. Mill and asks you which of the following regulations are consistent with the harm principle:

(1) Ban on possession of marijuana
(2) Ban on possession of marijuana for non-medical purposes
(3) Requirement that all marijuana users obtain a physician's diagnosis and recommendation before using the drug
(4) Ban on possession of more than one ounce of marijuana
(5) Ban on possession and use of marijuana by individuals under 21 years old, 25 years old, etc.
(6) Ban on possession of marijuana within 500 feet of a school, 1,000 feet, 5,000 feet, etc.
(7) Ban on DUI-impaired and/or DUI-per se
(8) Ban on marijuana use in public bars and restaurants

What do you tell the lawmaker?

3. Congress did not explicitly make the costs—or the efficacy—of regulations a criterion for scheduling drugs under the CSA. Should it have? In other words, should the DEA be required to consider the cost and effectiveness of prohibition (or regulatory alternatives) when deciding how to schedule marijuana or other drugs?

4. Ultimately, how should governments regulate the possession and use of marijuana?

# CHAPTER 6

# Authority over Marijuana Users

As demonstrated by the previous chapters, there are several competing approaches to regulating marijuana possession and use, ranging from outright prohibition to legalization for all adult use. But who gets to decide how to regulate the possession and use of marijuana? This is one of the most important and complicated questions surrounding marijuana law and policy. Indeed, it is impossible to fully understand the choices that have been made—or those that *could* be made going forward—without first understanding the limits on the authority of different government actors to pursue the policies of their choice.

This chapter examines the authority of different government actors to shape marijuana policy toward users. Section A discusses the scope of the federal government's power over marijuana possession and use. It examines both the federalism- and individual rights-based constraints the Constitution imposes on that power. Section B then discusses how the federal government's power is allocated across the branches of government, focusing on the executive branch's authority to re-schedule marijuana under the CSA. Section C follows by exploring the states' authority over marijuana possession and use. It examines the limits imposed on that power by the federal CSA and the Constitution. Finally, Section D explores the division of power within individual states, including the power of citizens to enact reforms directly via ballot initiatives and the power of local governments to break ranks with state policies toward marijuana use and possession.

## A. WHAT IS THE SCOPE OF THE FEDERAL GOVERNMENT'S AUTHORITY OVER MARIJUANA POSSESSION AND USE?

This Section discusses the scope of the federal government's authority to regulate the simple possession and use of marijuana. Section 1 discusses the federalism-based constraints on that authority, while Section 2 discusses the constraints imposed by the Due Process Clause of the Constitution.

### 1. Federalism Constraints

One of the distinguishing features of our federal system of government is that Congress's powers are limited to those enumerated in the Constitution. *E.g.*, Erwin Chemerinsky, Constitutional Law: Principles and Policies 240 (5th ed. 2015) ("A basic principle of

American Government is that Congress may act only if there is express or implied authority to act in the Constitution; states, however, may act unless the Constitution prohibits the action."). In other words, Congress may not regulate activities, like the possession and use of marijuana, unless the Constitution has affirmatively empowered it to do so. (The states' authority, by contrast, is not so limited; they possess the so-called police power to regulate the health, safety, and morals of the population, subject only to the constraints imposed by the Constitution and by congressional override in cases of preemption.)

For present purposes, the most relevant of Congress's enumerated powers is the power to "regulate Commerce . . . among the several States." U.S. Const. Art. I, cl. 8. What sorts of marijuana-related activities can Congress regulate under the Commerce Clause? In particular, may it regulate even the non-commercial intrastate possession and cultivation of marijuana? The Supreme Court addressed this question in the following case, one of its most notable federalism decisions of the last few decades.

## *Gonzales v. Raich*
545 U.S. 1 (2005)

STEVENS, J.:

California is one of at least nine States that authorize the use of marijuana for medicinal purposes. The question presented in this case is whether the power vested in Congress by Article I, §8, of the Constitution "[t]o make all Laws which shall be necessary and proper for carrying into Execution" its authority to "regulate Commerce with foreign Nations, and among the several States" includes the power to prohibit the local cultivation and use of marijuana in compliance with California law.

I

. . .

Respondents Angel Raich and Diane Monson are California residents who suffer from a variety of serious medical conditions and have sought to avail themselves of medical marijuana pursuant to the terms of the [California] Compassionate Use Act. They are being treated by licensed, board-certified family practitioners, who have concluded, after prescribing a host of conventional medicines to treat respondents' conditions and to alleviate their associated symptoms, that marijuana is the only drug available that provides effective treatment. Both women have been using marijuana as a medication for several years pursuant to their doctors' recommendation, and both rely heavily on cannabis to function on a daily basis. Indeed, Raich's physician believes that forgoing cannabis treatments would certainly cause Raich excruciating pain and could very well prove fatal.

Respondent Monson cultivates her own marijuana, and ingests the drug in a variety of ways including smoking and using a vaporizer. Respondent Raich, by contrast, is unable to cultivate her own, and thus relies on two caregivers, litigating as "John Does," to provide her with locally grown marijuana at no charge. . . .

On August 15, 2002, county deputy sheriffs and agents from the federal Drug Enforcement Administration (DEA) came to Monson's home. After a thorough investigation, the county officials concluded that her use of marijuana was entirely lawful as a matter of California law. Nevertheless, after a 3-hour standoff, the federal agents seized and destroyed all six of her cannabis plants.

Respondents thereafter brought this action against the Attorney General of the United States and the head of the DEA seeking injunctive and declaratory relief prohibiting the enforcement of the federal Controlled Substances Act (CSA), [21 U.S.C. § 801 et seq.], to the extent it prevents them from possessing, obtaining, or manufacturing cannabis for their personal medical use. . . . [Among other things, r]espondents claimed that enforcing the CSA against them would violate the Commerce Clause. . . .

. . .

. . . The case is made difficult by respondents' strong arguments that they will suffer irreparable harm because, despite a congressional finding to the contrary, marijuana does have valid therapeutic purposes. The question before us, however, is not whether it is wise to enforce the statute in these circumstances; rather, it is whether Congress' power to regulate interstate markets for medicinal substances encompasses the portions of those markets that are supplied with drugs produced and consumed locally. Well-settled law controls our answer. The CSA is a valid exercise of federal power, even as applied to the troubling facts of this case. . . .

II

. . .

. . . The main objectives of the CSA were to conquer drug abuse and to control the legitimate and illegitimate traffic in controlled substances. Congress was particularly concerned with the need to prevent the diversion of drugs from legitimate to illicit channels.

To effectuate these goals, Congress devised a closed regulatory system making it unlawful to manufacture, distribute, dispense, or possess any controlled substance except in a manner authorized by the CSA. 21 U.S.C. §§ 841(a)(1), 844(a). The CSA categorizes all controlled substances into five schedules. § 812. The drugs are grouped together based on their accepted medical uses, the potential for abuse, and their psychological and physical effects on the body. §§ 811, 812. Each schedule is associated with a distinct set of controls regarding the manufacture, distribution, and use of the substances listed therein. . . . The CSA and its implementing regulations set forth strict requirements regarding registration, labeling and packaging, production quotas, drug security, and recordkeeping. . . .

In enacting the CSA, Congress classified marijuana as a Schedule I drug. . . . This preliminary classification was based, in part, on the recommendation of the Assistant Secretary of HEW "that marihuana be retained within schedule I at least until the completion of certain studies now underway." Schedule I drugs are categorized as such because of their high potential for abuse, lack of any accepted medical use, and absence of any accepted safety for use in medically supervised treatment. § 812(b)(1). These three factors, in varying gradations, are also used to categorize drugs in the other four schedules. For example, Schedule II substances also have a high potential for abuse which may lead to severe psychological or physical dependence, but unlike Schedule I drugs, they have a currently accepted medical use. § 812(b)(2). By classifying marijuana as a Schedule I drug, as opposed to listing it on a lesser schedule, the manufacture, distribution, or possession of marijuana became a criminal offense, with the sole exception being use of the drug as part of a Food and Drug Administration preapproved research study. . . .

The CSA provides for the periodic updating of schedules and delegates authority to the Attorney General, after consultation with the Secretary of Health and Human Services, to add, remove, or transfer substances to, from, or between schedules. §811. Despite considerable efforts to reschedule marijuana, it remains a Schedule I drug.

### III

Respondents in this case do not dispute that passage of the CSA . . . was well within Congress' commerce power. . . . Nor do they contend that any provision or section of the CSA amounts to an unconstitutional exercise of congressional authority. Rather, respondents' challenge is actually quite limited; they argue that the CSA's categorical prohibition of the manufacture and possession of marijuana as applied to the intrastate manufacture and possession of marijuana for medical purposes pursuant to California law exceeds Congress' authority under the Commerce Clause.

. . .

Cases . . . have identified three general categories of regulation in which Congress is authorized to engage under its commerce power. First, Congress can regulate the channels of interstate commerce. . . . Second, Congress has authority to regulate and protect the instrumentalities of interstate commerce, and persons or things in interstate commerce. . . . Third, Congress has the power to regulate activities that substantially affect interstate commerce. . . . Only the third category is implicated in the case at hand.

Our case law firmly establishes Congress' power to regulate purely local activities that are part of an economic "class of activities" that have a substantial effect on interstate commerce. . . . [*Wickard v. Filburn*, 317 U.S. 111, 128-29 (1942).] As we stated in *Wickard*, "even if appellee's activity be local and though it may not be regarded as commerce, it may still, whatever its nature, be reached by Congress if it exerts a substantial economic effect on interstate commerce." . . . We have never required Congress to legislate with scientific exactitude. When Congress decides that the "'total incidence'" of a practice poses a threat to a national market, it may regulate the entire class. . . . In this vein, we have reiterated that when "'a general regulatory statute bears a substantial relation to commerce, the *de minimis* character of individual instances arising under that statute is of no consequence.'" . . . .

Our decision in *Wickard* . . . is of particular relevance. In *Wickard*, we upheld the application of regulations promulgated under the Agricultural Adjustment Act of 1938, . . . which were designed to control the volume of wheat moving in interstate and foreign commerce in order to avoid surpluses and consequent abnormally low prices. The regulations established an allotment of 11.1 acres for Filburn's 1941 wheat crop, but he sowed 23 acres, intending to use the excess by consuming it on his own farm. Filburn argued that even though we had sustained Congress' power to regulate the production of goods for commerce, that power did not authorize "federal regulation [of] production not intended in any part for commerce but wholly for consumption on the farm." . . . Justice Jackson's opinion for a unanimous Court rejected this submission. He wrote:

> "The effect of the statute before us is to restrict the amount which may be produced for market and the extent as well to which one may forestall resort to the market by producing to meet his own needs. That appellee's own contribution to the demand for wheat may be trivial by itself is not enough to remove him from the scope of federal regulation where, as

here, his contribution, taken together with that of many others similarly situated, is far from trivial." . . .

*Wickard* thus establishes that Congress can regulate purely intrastate activity that is not itself "commercial," in that it is not produced for sale, if it concludes that failure to regulate that class of activity would undercut the regulation of the interstate market in that commodity.

The similarities between this case and *Wickard* are striking. Like the farmer in *Wickard*, respondents are cultivating, for home consumption, a fungible commodity for which there is an established, albeit illegal, interstate market. Just as the Agricultural Adjustment Act was designed "to control the volume [of wheat] moving in interstate and foreign commerce in order to avoid surpluses . . ." and consequently control the market price, . . . a primary purpose of the CSA is to control the supply and demand of controlled substances in both lawful and unlawful drug markets. . . . In *Wickard*, we had no difficulty concluding that Congress had a rational basis for believing that, when viewed in the aggregate, leaving home-consumed wheat outside the regulatory scheme would have a substantial influence on price and market conditions. Here too, Congress had a rational basis for concluding that leaving home-consumed marijuana outside federal control would similarly affect price and market conditions.

More concretely, one concern prompting inclusion of wheat grown for home consumption in the 1938 Act was that rising market prices could draw such wheat into the interstate market, resulting in lower market prices. *Wickard*, 317 U.S., at 128. . . . The parallel concern making it appropriate to include marijuana grown for home consumption in the CSA is the likelihood that the high demand in the interstate market will draw such marijuana into that market. While the diversion of homegrown wheat tended to frustrate the federal interest in stabilizing prices by regulating the volume of commercial transactions in the interstate market, the diversion of homegrown marijuana tends to frustrate the federal interest in eliminating commercial transactions in the interstate market in their entirety. In both cases, the regulation is squarely within Congress' commerce power because production of the commodity meant for home consumption, be it wheat or marijuana, has a substantial effect on supply and demand in the national market for that commodity.[29]

. . .

In assessing the scope of Congress' authority under the Commerce Clause, we stress that the task before us is a modest one. We need not determine whether respondents' activities, taken in the aggregate, substantially affect interstate commerce in fact, but only whether a "rational basis" exists for so concluding. . . . Given the enforcement difficulties that attend distinguishing between marijuana cultivated locally and marijuana grown elsewhere, . . . and concerns about diversion into illicit channels, we have no difficulty concluding that Congress had a rational basis for believing that failure to regulate the intrastate manufacture and possession of marijuana would leave a gaping hole in the CSA. Thus, as in *Wickard*, when it enacted comprehensive legislation to regulate

---

29. To be sure, the wheat market is a lawful market that Congress sought to protect and stabilize, whereas the marijuana market is an unlawful market that Congress sought to eradicate. This difference, however, is of no constitutional import. It has long been settled that Congress' power to regulate commerce includes the power to prohibit commerce in a particular commodity. . . .

the interstate market in a fungible commodity, Congress was acting well within its authority to "make all Laws which shall be necessary and proper" to "regulate Commerce . . . among the several States." U.S. Const., Art. I, § 8. That the regulation ensnares some purely intrastate activity is of no moment. As we have done many times before, we refuse to excise individual components of that larger scheme.

### IV

To support their contrary submission, respondents rely heavily on two of our more recent Commerce Clause cases. In their myopic focus, they overlook the larger context of modern-era Commerce Clause jurisprudence preserved by those cases. Moreover, even in the narrow prism of respondents' creation, they read those cases far too broadly.

Those two cases, of course, are [*United States v. Lopez*, 514 U.S. 549 (1995),] . . . and [*United States v.*] *Morrison*, 529 U.S. 598 [(2000)]. . . .

At issue in *Lopez* . . . was the validity of the Gun-Free School Zones Act of 1990, which was a brief, single-subject statute making it a crime for an individual to possess a gun in a school zone. . . . 18 U.S.C. § 922(q)(1)(A). The Act did not regulate any economic activity and did not contain any requirement that the possession of a gun have any connection to past interstate activity or a predictable impact on future commercial activity. Distinguishing our earlier cases holding that comprehensive regulatory statutes may be validly applied to local conduct that does not, when viewed in isolation, have a significant impact on interstate commerce, we held the statute invalid. We explained:

> "Section 922(q) is a criminal statute that by its terms has nothing to do with 'commerce' or any sort of economic enterprise, however broadly one might define those terms. Section 922(q) is not an essential part of a larger regulation of economic activity, in which the regulatory scheme could be undercut unless the intrastate activity were regulated. It cannot, therefore, be sustained under our cases upholding regulations of activities that arise out of or are connected with a commercial transaction, which viewed in the aggregate, substantially affects interstate commerce." 514 U.S., at 561. . . .

The statutory scheme that the Government is defending in this litigation is at the opposite end of the regulatory spectrum. As explained above, the CSA . . . was a lengthy and detailed statute creating a comprehensive framework for regulating the production, distribution, and possession of five classes of "controlled substances." . . .

. . . Our opinion in *Lopez* casts no doubt on the validity of such a program.

Nor does this Court's holding in *Morrison*. . . . The Violence Against Women Act of 1994, . . . created a federal civil remedy for the victims of gender-motivated crimes of violence. 42 U.S.C. § 13981. The remedy was enforceable in both state and federal courts, and generally depended on proof of the violation of a state law. Despite congressional findings that such crimes had an adverse impact on interstate commerce, we held the statute unconstitutional because, like the statute in *Lopez*, it did not regulate economic activity. We concluded that "the noneconomic, criminal nature of the conduct at issue was central to our decision" in *Lopez*, and that our prior cases had identified a clear pattern of analysis: "'Where economic activity substantially affects interstate commerce, legislation regulating that activity will be sustained.'" *Morrison*, 529 U.S., at 610. . . .

Unlike those at issue in *Lopez* and *Morrison*, the activities regulated by the CSA are quintessentially economic. "Economics" refers to "the production, distribution, and consumption of commodities." Webster's Third New International Dictionary 720 (1966).

The CSA is a statute that regulates the production, distribution, and consumption of commodities for which there is an established, and lucrative, interstate market. Prohibiting the intrastate possession or manufacture of an article of commerce is a rational (and commonly utilized) means of regulating commerce in that product. . . . Because the CSA is a statute that directly regulates economic, commercial activity, our opinion in *Morrison* casts no doubt on its constitutionality.

. . . We have no difficulty concluding that Congress acted rationally in determining that none of the characteristics [of "the intrastate, noncommercial cultivation, possession and use of marijuana for personal medical purposes on the advice of a physician and in accordance with state law"], whether viewed individually or in the aggregate, compelled an exemption from the CSA; rather, [this] class of activities . . . was an essential part of the larger regulatory scheme.

First, the fact that marijuana is used "for personal medical purposes on the advice of a physician" cannot itself serve as a distinguishing factor. . . . The CSA designates marijuana as contraband for *any* purpose; in fact, by characterizing marijuana as a Schedule I drug, Congress expressly found that the drug has no acceptable medical uses. Moreover, the CSA is a comprehensive regulatory regime specifically designed to regulate which controlled substances can be utilized for medicinal purposes, and in what manner. Indeed, most of the substances classified in the CSA "have a useful and legitimate medical purpose." 21 U.S.C. § 801(1). Thus, even if respondents are correct that marijuana does have accepted medical uses and thus should be redesignated as a lesser schedule drug, the CSA would still impose controls beyond what is required by California law. The CSA requires manufacturers, physicians, pharmacies, and other handlers of controlled substances to comply with statutory and regulatory provisions mandating registration with the DEA, compliance with specific production quotas, security controls to guard against diversion, recordkeeping and reporting obligations, and prescription requirements. . . . Furthermore, the dispensing of new drugs, even when doctors approve their use, must await federal approval. . . . Accordingly, the mere fact that marijuana—like virtually every other controlled substance regulated by the CSA—is used for medicinal purposes cannot possibly serve to distinguish it from the core activities regulated by the CSA.

. . . More fundamentally, if, as the principal dissent contends, the personal cultivation, possession, and use of marijuana for medicinal purposes is beyond the "'outer limits' of Congress' Commerce Clause authority," . . . (opinion of O'Connor, J.), it must also be true that such personal use of marijuana (or any other homegrown drug) for recreational purposes is also beyond those "'outer limits,'" whether or not a State elects to authorize or even regulate such use. . . . That is, the dissenters' rationale logically extends to place *any* federal regulation (including quality, prescription, or quantity controls) of *any* locally cultivated and possessed controlled substance for *any* purpose beyond the "'outer limits'" of Congress' Commerce Clause authority. One need not have a degree in economics to understand why a nationwide exemption for the vast quantity of marijuana (or other drugs) locally cultivated for personal use (which presumably would include use by friends, neighbors, and family members) may have a substantial impact on the interstate market for this extraordinarily popular substance. The congressional judgment that an exemption for such a significant segment of the total market would undermine the orderly enforcement of the entire regulatory scheme is entitled to a strong presumption of validity. . . .

Second, limiting the activity to marijuana possession and cultivation "in accordance with state law" cannot serve to place respondents' activities beyond congressional reach. The Supremacy Clause unambiguously provides that if there is any conflict between federal and state law, federal law shall prevail. It is beyond peradventure that federal power over commerce is "'superior to that of the States to provide for the welfare or necessities of their inhabitants,'" however legitimate or dire those necessities may be. . . .

Respondents acknowledge this proposition, but nonetheless contend that their activities were not "an essential part of a larger regulatory scheme" because they had been "isolated by the State of California, and [are] policed by the State of California," and thus remain "entirely separated from the market." . . . The dissenters fall prey to similar reasoning. . . . The notion that California law has surgically excised a discrete activity that is hermetically sealed off from the larger interstate marijuana market is a dubious proposition, and, more importantly, one that Congress could have rationally rejected.

Indeed, that the California exemptions will have a significant impact on both the supply and demand sides of the market for marijuana is not just "plausible" as the principal dissent concedes, . . . it is readily apparent. The exemption for physicians provides them with an economic incentive to grant their patients permission to use the drug. In contrast to most prescriptions for legal drugs, which limit the dosage and duration of the usage, under California law the doctor's permission to recommend marijuana use is open-ended. The authority to grant permission whenever the doctor determines that a patient is afflicted with "any other illness for which marijuana provides relief," Cal. Health & Safety Code Ann. § 11362.5(b)(1)(A) . . . , is broad enough to allow even the most scrupulous doctor to conclude that some recreational uses would be therapeutic. And our cases have taught us that there are some unscrupulous physicians who overprescribe when it is sufficiently profitable to do so.

The exemption for cultivation by patients and caregivers can only increase the supply of marijuana in the California market. The likelihood that all such production will promptly terminate when patients recover or will precisely match the patients' medical needs during their convalescence seems remote; whereas the danger that excesses will satisfy some of the admittedly enormous demand for recreational use seems obvious. Moreover, that the national and international narcotics trade has thrived in the face of vigorous criminal enforcement efforts suggests that no small number of unscrupulous people will make use of the California exemptions to serve their commercial ends whenever it is feasible to do so. Taking into account the fact that California is only one of at least nine States to have authorized the medical use of marijuana . . . Congress could have rationally concluded that the aggregate impact on the national market of all the transactions exempted from federal supervision is unquestionably substantial.

. . .

V

Respondents also raise a substantive due process claim . . . [, but because the claim was] not reached by the Court of Appeals . . . [we do not address it]. We do note, however, the presence of another avenue of relief. As the Solicitor General confirmed during oral argument, the statute authorizes procedures for the reclassification of Schedule I drugs. But perhaps even more important than these legal avenues is the democratic process, in which the voices of voters allied with these respondents may one day be heard in the halls of Congress. Under the present state of the law, however, the judgment of the Court of Appeals must be vacated. The case is remanded for further proceedings consistent with this opinion. . . .

SCALIA, J., concurring in the judgment:

I agree with the Court's holding that the Controlled Substances Act (CSA) may validly be applied to respondents' cultivation, distribution, and possession of marijuana for personal, medicinal use. I write separately because my understanding of the doctrinal foundation on which that holding rests is, if not inconsistent with that of the Court, at least more nuanced.

. . .

. . . [A]ctivities that substantially affect interstate commerce are not themselves part of interstate commerce, and thus the power to regulate them cannot come from the Commerce Clause alone. Rather, . . . Congress's regulatory authority over intrastate activities that are not themselves part of interstate commerce (including activities that have a substantial effect on interstate commerce) derives from the Necessary and Proper Clause. . . . And the . . . authority to enact laws necessary and proper for the regulation of interstate commerce is not limited to laws governing intrastate activities that substantially affect interstate commerce. Where necessary to make a regulation of interstate commerce effective, Congress may regulate even those intrastate activities that do not themselves substantially affect interstate commerce.

. . .

. . . Unlike the power to regulate activities that have a substantial effect on interstate commerce, the power to enact laws enabling effective regulation of interstate commerce can only be exercised in conjunction with congressional regulation of an interstate market, and it extends only to those measures necessary to make the interstate regulation effective. As *Lopez* itself states, and the Court affirms today, Congress may regulate noneconomic intrastate activities only where the failure to do so "could . . . undercut" its regulation of interstate commerce. . . .

. . .

The application of these principles to the case before us is straightforward. In the CSA, Congress has undertaken to extinguish the interstate market in Schedule I controlled substances, including marijuana. The Commerce Clause unquestionably permits this. The power to regulate interstate commerce "extends not only to those regulations which aid, foster and protect the commerce, but embraces those which prohibit it." . . . To effectuate its objective, Congress has prohibited almost all intrastate activities related to Schedule I substances—both economic activities (manufacture, distribution, possession with the intent to distribute) and noneconomic activities (simple possession). See 21 U.S.C. §§ 841(a), 844(a). That simple possession is a noneconomic activity is immaterial to whether it can be prohibited as a necessary part of a larger regulation. Rather, Congress's authority to enact all of these prohibitions of intrastate controlled-substance activities depends only upon whether they are appropriate means of achieving the legitimate end of eradicating Schedule I substances from interstate commerce.

By this measure, I think the regulation must be sustained. Not only is it impossible to distinguish "controlled substances manufactured and distributed intrastate" from "controlled substances manufactured and distributed interstate," but it hardly makes sense to speak in such terms. Drugs like marijuana are fungible commodities. As the Court explains, marijuana that is grown at home and possessed for personal use is never more than an instant from the interstate market—and this is so whether or not the possession is for medicinal use or lawful use under the laws of a particular State. . . . Congress need not accept on faith that state law will be effective in maintaining a strict division between a lawful market for "medical" marijuana and the more general marijuana market. . . . "To impose on [Congress] the necessity of resorting to means which it cannot control, which another government may furnish or withhold, would render its course precarious, the result of its measures uncertain, and create a dependence on other governments, which might disappoint its most important designs, and is incompatible with the language of the constitution." . . .

. . . The Court has repeatedly recognized that, if authorized by the commerce power, Congress may regulate private endeavors "even when [that regulation] may pre-empt express state-law determinations contrary to the result which has commended itself to the collective wisdom of Congress." . . .

O'CONNOR, J., dissenting:

We enforce the "outer limits" of Congress' Commerce Clause authority not for their own sake, but to protect historic spheres of state sovereignty from excessive federal encroachment and thereby to maintain the distribution of power fundamental to our federalist system of government. . . . One of federalism's chief virtues, of course, is that it promotes innovation by allowing for the possibility that "a single courageous State may, if its citizens choose, serve as a laboratory; and try novel social and economic experiments without risk to the rest of the country." . . .

This case exemplifies the role of States as laboratories. The States' core police powers have always included authority to define criminal law and to protect the health, safety, and welfare of their citizens. . . . Exercising those powers, California . . . has come to its own conclusion about the difficult and sensitive question of whether marijuana should be available to relieve severe pain and suffering. Today the Court sanctions an application of the federal Controlled Substances Act that extinguishes that experiment, without any proof that the personal cultivation, possession, and use of marijuana for medicinal purposes, if economic activity in the first place, has a substantial effect on interstate commerce and is therefore an appropriate subject of federal regulation. . . .

. . . Today's decision suggests that the federal regulation of local activity is immune to Commerce Clause challenge because Congress chose to act with an ambitious, all-encompassing statute, rather than piecemeal. In my view, allowing Congress to set the terms of the constitutional debate in this way, *i.e.*, by packaging regulation of local activity in broader schemes, is tantamount to removing meaningful limits on the Commerce Clause.
. . .

The hard work for courts . . . is to identify objective markers for confining the analysis in Commerce Clause cases. . . . I agree with the Court that we must look beyond respondents' own activities. Otherwise, individual litigants could always exempt themselves from Commerce Clause regulation merely by pointing to the obvious—that their personal activities do not have a substantial effect on interstate commerce. . . . The task is to identify a mode of analysis that allows Congress to regulate more than nothing (by declining to reduce each case to its litigants) and less than everything (by declining to let Congress set the terms of analysis)....

A number of objective markers are available to confine the scope of constitutional review here. Both federal and state legislation—including the CSA itself, the California Compassionate Use Act, and other state medical marijuana legislation—recognize that medical and nonmedical (*i.e.*, recreational) uses of drugs are realistically distinct and can be segregated, and regulate them differently. ... Respondents challenge only the application of the CSA to medicinal use of marijuana. ... California, like other States, has drawn on its reserved powers to distinguish the regulation of medicinal marijuana. To ascertain whether Congress' encroachment is constitutionally justified in this case, then, I would focus here on the personal cultivation, possession, and use of marijuana for medicinal purposes.

. . .

Having thus defined the relevant conduct, we must determine whether, under our precedents, the conduct is economic and, in the aggregate, substantially affects interstate commerce. Even if intrastate cultivation and possession of marijuana for one's own medicinal use can properly be characterized as economic, and I question whether it can, it has not been shown that such activity substantially affects interstate commerce. Similarly, it is neither self-evident nor demonstrated that regulating such activity is necessary to the interstate drug control scheme.

The Court's definition of economic activity is breathtaking. ... [and] threatens to sweep all of productive human activity into federal regulatory reach.

. . . It will not do to say that Congress may regulate noncommercial activity simply because it may have an effect on the demand for commercial goods, or because the noncommercial endeavor can, in some sense, substitute for commercial activity. Most commercial goods or services have some sort of privately producible analogue. Home care substitutes for daycare. Charades games substitute for movie tickets. Backyard or windowsill gardening substitutes for going to the supermarket. To draw the line wherever private activity affects the demand for market goods is to draw no line at all, and to declare everything economic....

In *Lopez* and *Morrison*, we suggested that economic activity usually relates directly to commercial activity. ... The homegrown cultivation and personal possession and use of marijuana for medicinal purposes has no apparent commercial character. Everyone agrees that the marijuana at issue in this case was never in the stream of commerce, and neither were the supplies for growing it. (Marijuana is highly unusual among the substances subject to the CSA in that it can be cultivated without any materials that have traveled in interstate commerce.) *Lopez* makes clear that possession is not itself commercial activity. ... And respondents have not come into possession by means of any commercial transaction; they have simply grown, in their own homes, marijuana for their own use, without acquiring, buying, selling, or bartering a thing of value....

. . .

Even assuming that economic activity is at issue in this case, the Government has made no showing in fact that the possession and use of homegrown marijuana for medical purposes, in California or elsewhere, has a substantial effect on interstate commerce. Similarly, the Government has not shown that regulating such activity is necessary to an interstate regulatory scheme....

That is why characterizing this as a case about the Necessary and Proper Clause does not change the analysis significantly. Congress must exercise its authority under the Necessary and Proper Clause in a manner consistent with . . . the notion of enumerated powers. . . . Accordingly, something more than mere assertion is required when Congress purports to have power over local activity whose connection to an interstate market is not self-evident. Otherwise, the Necessary and Proper Clause will always be a back door for unconstitutional federal regulation. . . .

There is simply no evidence that homegrown medicinal marijuana users constitute, in the aggregate, a sizable enough class to have a discernable, let alone substantial, impact on the national illicit drug market—or otherwise to threaten the CSA regime. . . .

. . .

. . . Because here California, like other States, has carved out a limited class of activity for distinct regulation, the inadequacy of the CSA's findings is especially glaring. The California Compassionate Use Act exempts from other state drug laws patients and their caregivers "who posses[s] or cultivat[e] marijuana for the *personal* medical purposes of the patient upon the written or oral recommendation or approval of a physician" to treat a list of serious medical conditions. Cal. Health & Safety Code Ann. §§ 11362.5(d), 11362.7(h) . . . (emphasis added). *Compare ibid. with, e.g.,* § 11357(b) . . . (criminalizing marijuana possession in excess of 28.5 grams); § 11358 (criminalizing marijuana cultivation). The Act specifies that it should not be construed to supersede legislation prohibiting persons from engaging in acts dangerous to others, or to condone the diversion of marijuana for nonmedical purposes. § 11362.5(b)(2). . . . To promote the Act's operation and to facilitate law enforcement, California recently enacted an identification card system for qualified patients. §§ 11362.7-11362.83. We generally assume States enforce their laws, . . . and have no reason to think otherwise here.

The Government has not overcome empirical doubt that the number of Californians engaged in personal cultivation, possession, and use of medical marijuana, or the amount of marijuana they produce, is enough to threaten the federal regime. Nor has it shown that Compassionate Use Act marijuana users have been or are realistically likely to be responsible for the drug's seeping into the market in a significant way. The Government does cite one estimate that there were over 100,000 Compassionate Use Act users in California in 2004, . . . but does not explain, in terms of proportions, what their presence means for the national illicit drug market. . . . It also provides anecdotal evidence about the CSA's enforcement. . . . The Court also offers some arguments about the effect of the Compassionate Use Act on the national market. It says that the California statute might be vulnerable to exploitation by unscrupulous physicians, that Compassionate Use Act patients may overproduce, and that the history of the narcotics trade shows the difficulty of cordoning off any drug use from the rest of the market. These arguments are plausible; if borne out in fact they could justify prosecuting Compassionate Use Act patients under the federal CSA. But, without substantiation, they add little to the CSA's conclusory statements about diversion, essentiality, and market effect. Piling assertion upon assertion does not, in my view, satisfy the substantiality test of *Lopez* and *Morrison*.

. . .

Relying on Congress' abstract assertions, the Court has endorsed making it a federal crime to grow small amounts of marijuana in one's own home for one's own medicinal use. This overreaching stifles an express choice by some States, concerned for the lives and liberties of their people, to regulate medical marijuana differently. If I were a California citizen, I would not have voted for the medical marijuana ballot initiative; if I were a California legislator I would not have supported the Compassionate Use Act. But whatever the wisdom of California's experiment with medical marijuana, the federalism principles that have driven our Commerce Clause cases require that room for experiment be protected in this case. For these reasons I dissent.

## Notes and Questions

1. How does the *Raich* Court distinguish the federal prohibition on simple possession of marijuana from the federal prohibition on simple possession of firearms that was invalidated in *Lopez*? In light of *Raich*, can you think of *any* marijuana-related activity that Congress would be unable to regulate under the Commerce Clause?

2. What does it mean to "regulate" the possession, distribution, and production of marijuana, for purposes of the Commerce Clause? Does an outright ban on these activities count as a regulation thereof? Both the majority (in footnote 29) and Justice Scalia intone that "[i]t has long been settled that Congress' power to regulate commerce includes the power to prohibit commerce in a particular commodity." But for the argument that this settled view is unfounded, see Barry Friedman & Genevieve Lakier, *"To Regulate," Not "To Prohibit": Limiting the Commerce Power*, 2013 Sup. Ct. Rev. 255, 320 ("Congress's power 'to regulate' interstate commerce does not include the power to prohibit commerce in products or services that the states themselves, or some of them, do not want to prohibit. This interpretation of the Commerce Clause is supported by history, and by the structure and theory of the Constitution.").

3. Putting aside the doctrinal question, *should* Congress have the authority to regulate the possession and use of marijuana? The *Raich* majority suggested that some marijuana ostensibly grown for medical consumption in California could be diverted into the interstate drug market, imposing costs on other states that continue to ban the drug. (These costs are referred to as "externalities" and are discussed again in Chapter 10.) Are you convinced? In other words, even assuming that Congress should be allowed to control the interstate market for marijuana, does it need to control intrastate possession of the drug to effectively control that market? Per Justice O'Connor's dissent, should Congress be required to make a stronger demonstration of this need? If so, what evidence would you require?

4. Both Justice O'Connor and Justice Thomas, in a dissent not excerpted above, suggested that California was regulating medical marijuana effectively, and had thus defused the concerns over diversion. *E.g., Raich*, 545 U.S. at 62-63 (Thomas, J., dissenting) ("California strictly controls the cultivation and possession of marijuana for medical purposes."). Based on what you have learned about California's medical marijuana laws, do you agree with the dissenters' assessment? In any event, are state laws relevant to the task of defining Congress's enumerated powers? Both the majority and Justice Scalia insist that "state action cannot circumscribe Congress's plenary commerce power," 545 U.S. at 29, "even if [state] controls . . . are 'effective,'" *id.* at 29, n.38. As an abstract matter, do you agree? For the argument that courts should consider state law when assessing whether congressional regulation is necessary, see William Baude, *State Regulation and the Necessary and Proper Clause*, 65 Case W. Res. L. Rev. 513, 514 (2015)

("Congress's power to reach purely in-state conduct is premised on the possibility of interstate spillovers. If a state legalizes and regulates a drug in a way that minimizes the risk of spillovers into the interstate black market, the federal drug laws should be forbidden to apply within that state.") and Ernest A. Young, *Just Blowing Smoke? Politics, Doctrine, and the Federalist Revival After* Gonzales v. Raich, 2005 Sup. Ct. Rev. 1, 35 (2005) ("Doctrinally, recognition of the existence and capacity of state governments can and should occur through the 'necessary and proper' analysis. . . . Federal action may well be necessary when failure to act would leave a regulatory void; it may well be less necessary when state regulation is taken into account.").

5. The *Raich* Court suggests that the respondents might find relief in "the democratic process, in which the voices of voters allied with these respondents may one day be heard in the halls of Congress." How likely is Congress to heed calls for reform? Given the apparent popularity of some reforms, why has Congress not amended the CSA already? *See* Robert A. Mikos, *Medical Marijuana and the Political Safeguards of Federalism*, 89 Denv. U. L. Rev. 997, 1001-02 (2012) (arguing that "the same forces that originally failed to block adoption of the federal marijuana ban," including bicameralism and the Senate filibuster, "now work to entrench it"). Do you think the President is any more receptive to calls for marijuana law reform? David S. Schwartz, *Presidential Politics as a Safeguard of Federalism: The Case of Marijuana Legalization*, 62 Buff. L. Rev. 599, 602 (2014) ("[P]residential electoral politics can be far more sensitive to state regulatory autonomy interests than the courts and perhaps even than Congress."). Even so, what can the President do without new congressional action? (Section B below focuses on this question.)

## 2. Due Process Constraints

Even when a congressional statute is authorized by one of Congress's enumerated powers, it may still be invalidated in whole or part if it violates some individual right protected by the Constitution, such as the right to Free Speech protected by the First Amendment. But do individuals ever have a federal constitutional right to marijuana, one that would restrict Congress's authority to regulate their possession and use of the drug?

The respondents in *Raich* claimed such a right, although for procedural reasons, the Supreme Court did not need to address the claim in its decision above. On remand from the Court's ruling in *Raich*, however, the Ninth Circuit addressed the rights claim.[1]

### *Raich v. Gonzales*
500 F.3d 850 (9th Cir. 2007)

Pregerson, J.:

Appellant Angel McClary Raich is a Californian who uses marijuana for medical treatment. Raich has been diagnosed with more than ten serious medical conditions, including

---

1. The *Raich II* court provides a useful background on rights jurisprudence, but for more background on these issues, see Chemerinsky, Constitutional Law: Principles and Policies, *supra*.

an inoperable brain tumor, a seizure disorder, life-threatening weight loss, nausea, and several chronic pain disorders. Raich's doctor, Dr. Frank Henry Lucido, testified that he had explored virtually every legal treatment alternative, and that all were either ineffective or resulted in intolerable side effects. Dr. Lucido provided a list of thirty-five medications that were unworkable because of their side effects.

Marijuana, on the other hand, has proven to be of great medical value for Raich. Raich has been using marijuana as a medication for nearly eight years, every two waking hours of every day. Dr. Lucido states that, for Raich, foregoing marijuana treatment may be fatal. As the district court put it, "[t]raditional medicine has utterly failed [Raich]." *Raich v. Ashcroft*, 248 F. Supp. 2d 918, 921 (N.D. Cal. 2003).

. . .

This action arose in response to a law enforcement raid on the home of another medical marijuana user, former plaintiff-appellant Diane Monson [who withdrew from the case]. . . .

Fearing raids in the future and the prospect of being deprived of [her] medicinal marijuana, Raich . . . sued the United States Attorney General and the Administrator of the DEA in federal district court on October 9, 2002. The suit sought declaratory and injunctive relief. Specifically, [Raich] argued [inter alia] . . . that the Controlled Substances Act unconstitutionally infringed [her] fundamental rights protected by the Fifth and Ninth Amendments. . . .

. . .

Although the Fifth Amendment's Due Process Clause states only that "[n]o person shall . . . be deprived of life, liberty, or property, without due process of law," *see* U.S. Const. amend. V, it unquestionably provides substantive protections for certain unenumerated fundamental rights. "The Due Process Clause guarantees more than fair process, and the 'liberty' it protects includes more than the absence of physical restraint." *Washington v. Glucksberg*, 521 U.S. 702 . . . (1997). . . .

In *Glucksberg*, the Supreme Court set forth the two elements of the substantive due process analysis.

> First, we have regularly observed that the Due Process Clause specially protects those fundamental rights and liberties which are, objectively, "deeply rooted in this Nation's history and tradition," and "implicit in the concept of ordered liberty," such that "neither liberty nor justice would exist if they were sacrificed." Second, we have required in substantive-due-process cases a "careful description" of the asserted fundamental liberty interest.

*Glucksberg*, 521 U.S. at 720-21. . . .

The Supreme Court has a long history of recognizing unenumerated fundamental rights as protected by substantive due process, even before the term evolved into its modern usage. See, e.g., *Roe v. Wade*, 410 U.S. 113 . . . (1973) [(to have an abortion)]; *Eisenstadt v. Baird*, 405 U.S. 438 . . . (1972) (to use contraception); *Griswold*, 381 U.S. 479 . . . (to use contraception, to marital privacy); *Loving v. Virginia*, 388 U.S. 1, 87 . . . (1967) (to marry); *Rochin v. California*, 342 U.S. 165 . . . (1952) (to preserve bodily integrity); *Skinner v. Oklahoma ex rel. Williamson*, 316 U.S. 535 . . . (1942) (to have children); *Pierce v. Society of Sisters*, 268 U.S. 510 . . . (1925) (to direct the education and upbringing of one's children). . . . But the Court has cautioned against the doctrine's expansion. *See Glucksberg*, 521 U.S. at 720 . . . (stating that the Court must restrain the expansion of substantive due process "because guideposts for responsible decisionmaking in this uncharted area are scarce and open-ended" and because judicial extension of constitutional protection for an asserted substantive due process right "place[s] the matter outside the arena of public debate and legislative action" . . . ). . . .

Bearing that rubric in mind, we consider Raich's substantive due process claim. In the present case, it is helpful to begin with the second step—the description of the asserted fundamental right—before determining whether the right is deeply rooted in this nation's history and traditions and implicit in the concept of ordered liberty.

. . .

*Glucksberg* instructs courts to adopt a narrow definition of the interest at stake. . . .

*Glucksberg* involved a substantive due process challenge to Washington state's ban on assisted suicide. . . . The Court in *Glucksberg* rejected the suggestion that the interest at stake was the "right to die" or "the right to choose a humane, dignified death," and instead held that the narrow question before the Court was "whether the 'liberty' specially protected by the Due Process Clause includes a right to commit suicide which itself includes a right to assistance in doing so." . . .

. . .

Raich asserts that she has a fundamental right to "mak[e] life-shaping medical decisions that are necessary to preserve the integrity of her body, avoid intolerable physical pain, and preserve her life." We note that Raich's carefully crafted interest comprises several fundamental rights that have been recognized at least in part by the Supreme Court. . . .

Yet, Raich's careful statement does not narrowly and accurately reflect the right that she seeks to vindicate. Conspicuously missing from Raich's asserted fundamental right is its centerpiece: that she seeks the right to use *marijuana* to preserve bodily integrity, avoid pain, and preserve her life. . . .

Accordingly, the question becomes whether the liberty interest specially protected by the Due Process Clause embraces a right to make a life-shaping decision on a physician's advice to use medical marijuana to preserve bodily integrity, avoid intolerable pain, and preserve life, when all other prescribed medications and remedies have failed.

. . .

We turn to whether the asserted right is "deeply rooted in this Nation's history and tradition," and "implicit in the concept of ordered liberty," such that "neither liberty nor justice would exist if they were sacrificed." *Glucksberg*, 521 U.S. at 720-21 . . .

It is beyond dispute that marijuana has a long history of use—medically and otherwise—in this country. Marijuana was not regulated under federal law until Congress passed the Marihuana Tax Act of 1937, . . . and marijuana was not prohibited under federal law until Congress passed the Controlled Substances Act in 1970. . . . There is considerable evidence that efforts to regulate marijuana use in the early-twentieth century targeted recreational use, but permitted medical use. *See* Richard J. Bonnie & Charles H. Whitebread, *The Forbidden Fruit and the Tree of Knowledge: An Inquiry into the Legal History of American Marijuana Prohibition*, 56 Va. L. Rev. 971, 1010, 1027, 1167 (1970) (noting that all twenty-two states that had prohibited marijuana by the 1930s created exceptions for medical purposes). By 1965, although possession of marijuana was a crime in all fifty states, almost all states had created exceptions for "persons for whom the drug had been prescribed or to whom it had been given by an authorized medical person." *Leary v. United States*, 395 U.S. 6, 16-17 . . . (1969).

The history of medical marijuana use in this country took an about-face with the passage of the Controlled Substances Act in 1970. Congress placed marijuana on Schedule I of the Controlled Substances Act, taking it outside of the realm of all uses, including medical, under federal law. As the Supreme Court noted in *Gonzales v. Raich*, ... no state permitted medical marijuana usage until California's Compassionate Use Act of 1996. Thus, from 1970 to 1996, the possession or use of marijuana—medically or otherwise—was proscribed under state and federal law.[14]

Raich argues that the last ten years have been characterized by an emerging awareness of marijuana's medical value. She contends that the rising number of states that have passed laws that permit medical use of marijuana or recognize its therapeutic value is additional evidence that the right is fundamental. Raich avers that the asserted right in this case should be protected on the "emerging awareness" model that the Supreme Court used in *Lawrence v. Texas*, [539 U.S. 558, 571 (2003)].

The *Lawrence* Court noted that, when the Court had decided *Bowers v. Hardwick*, 478 U.S. 186 ... (1986), [upholding a state ban on sodomy,] "[twenty-four] States and the District of Columbia had sodomy laws." *Lawrence*, 539 U.S. at 572. ... By the time a similar challenge to sodomy laws arose in *Lawrence* in 2004, only thirteen states had maintained their sodomy laws, and there was a noted "pattern of nonenforcement." ... The Court observed that "times can blind us to certain truths and later generations can see that laws once thought necessary and proper in fact serve only to oppress." *Id.* at 579. ...

Though the *Lawrence* framework might certainly apply to the instant case, the use of medical marijuana has not obtained the degree of recognition today that private sexual conduct had obtained by 2004 in *Lawrence*. Since 1996, ten states other than California have passed laws decriminalizing in varying degrees the use, possession, manufacture, and distribution of marijuana for the seriously ill. ... Other states have passed resolutions recognizing that marijuana may have therapeutic value, and yet others have permitted limited use through closely monitored experimental treatment programs.

We agree with Raich that medical and conventional wisdom that recognizes the use of marijuana for medical purposes is gaining traction in the law as well. But that legal recognition has not yet reached the point where a conclusion can be drawn that the right to use medical marijuana is "fundamental" and "implicit in the concept of ordered liberty." See *Glucksberg*, 521 U.S. at 720-21. ... For the time being, this issue remains in "the arena of public debate and legislative action." ...

As stated above, Justice Anthony Kennedy told us that "times can blind us to certain truths and later generations can see that laws once thought necessary and proper in fact serve only to oppress." *Lawrence*, 539 U.S. at 579. ... For now, federal law is blind to the wisdom of a future day when the right to use medical marijuana to alleviate excruciating pain may be deemed fundamental. Although that day has not yet dawned, considering that during the last ten years eleven states have legalized the use of medical marijuana, that day may be upon us sooner than expected. Until that day arrives, federal law does not recognize a fundamental right to use medical marijuana prescribed by a licensed physician to alleviate excruciating pain and human suffering. ...

---

14. The mere enactment of a law, state or federal, that prohibits certain behavior does not necessarily mean that the behavior is not deeply rooted in this country's history and traditions. It is noteworthy, however, that over twenty-five years went by before any state enacted a law to protect the alleged right.

## Notes and Questions

1. Is *Raich II* now outdated? As the Ninth Circuit notes, courts look to prevailing legal practices to help define unenumerated due process rights. At the time *Raich II* was decided, only 11 states had allowed people to use marijuana pursuant to a physician's recommendation, leading the Ninth Circuit to conclude that it was not deeply rooted in nation's history. But as of 2016, at least 28 states (and D.C.) had done so. Has the situation changed enough to revisit the court's decision? If so, what, exactly, would a right to use marijuana entail? In other words, what would be the contours of that right? How would the courts answer that question, given the differences among state laws discussed in Chapter 4?

2. The *Raich II* court found that there is no *fundamental* due process right to use marijuana for medical purposes. As a result, it did not subject Congress's ban on marijuana to strict scrutiny—the most demanding level of scrutiny that is applied only to regulations that implicate core liberties. Under strict scrutiny, the government must demonstrate that a challenged regulation is the only way to pursue a substantial government interest.

Nonetheless, all government regulations must be rational, even if they do not burden fundamental rights. Under the rational basis test, the government must show that a challenged regulation is reasonably related to a legitimate government interest. Although not without teeth, this test is far easier for the government to satisfy than is the strict scrutiny test. Many individuals have claimed the federal marijuana ban is irrational, but the courts have uniformly rejected these challenges.

In one recent case, a federal district court did take the unusual step of holding extensive hearings on the merits of the federal government's decision to place marijuana on Schedule I, but the court—like all of the courts before it—ultimately concluded that placement on Schedule I was, at a minimum, rational. *United States v. Pickard,* 100 F. Supp. 3d 981, 1005-09 (E.D. Cal. 2015). The court's decision provides a useful description of the rational basis test and the difficulty of mounting a successful challenge under it:

> Under the deferential standard of rational basis review, as long as there is some conceivable reason for the challenged classification of marijuana, the CSA should be upheld. Such a classification comes before the court "bearing a strong presumption of validity," and the challenger must "negative every conceivable basis which might support it...." *F.C.C. v. Beach Commc'ns, Inc.,* 508 U.S. 307, 314-15 ... (1993).... The asserted rationale may rest on "rational speculation unsupported by evidence or empirical data." *Id.* at 315.... The law may be overinclusive, underinclusive, illogical, and unscientific and yet pass constitutional muster. In addition, under rational basis review, the government "has no obligation to produce evidence to sustain the rationality of a statutory classification." [*Heller v. Doe by Doe,* 509 U.S. 312, 320 (1993).] ...
> 
> In light of the foregoing, the question before the court is a narrow one: whether Congress acted rationally in classifying marijuana as a Schedule I substance in light of the record created before this court. To ask that question in this case, under rational basis review, is to answer it....
> 
> Defendants, here, have not met their "heavy burden of proving the irrationality of the Schedule I classification of marijuana," [*United States v. Fogarty,* 692 F.2d 542, 547 (8th Cir. 1982)], because they have not negated "every conceivable basis which might support it," *F.C.C.,* 508 U.S. at 315.... Even though the medical landscape related to marijuana clearly has changed and is changing, "[w]hen Congress undertakes to act in areas fraught

with medical and scientific uncertainties, legislative options must be especially broad and courts should be cautious not to rewrite legislation, even assuming, arguendo, that judges with more direct exposure to the problem might make wiser choices." See *Marshall v. United States*, 414 U.S. 417, 427 . . . (1974). In view of the principled disagreements among reputable scientists and practitioners regarding the potential benefits and detrimental effects of marijuana, this court cannot say that its placement on Schedule I is so arbitrary or unreasonable as to render it unconstitutional. Congress still could rationally choose one side of the debate over the other.

After careful consideration, the court joins the chorus of other courts considering the same question, and concludes as have they that—assuming the record created here is reflective of the best information currently available regarding marijuana—the issues raised by the defense are policy issues for Congress to revisit if it chooses. . . .

What would it take to convince a court that banning marijuana is irrational and thus unconstitutional?

3. Although *Raich II* continues to reflect the majority view, some courts have found that state and foreign constitutions protect an individual's right to use marijuana under some circumstances. In the United States, the Alaska Supreme Court has held that the right to privacy protected by the Alaska constitution protects an individual's right to possess and use marijuana (medically or not) in the home. *Ravin v. Alaska*, 537 P.2d 494 (Alaska 1975). In relevant part, the *Ravin* court held:

> [C]itizens of the State of Alaska have a basic right to privacy in their homes under Alaska's constitution. This right to privacy would encompass the possession and ingestion of substances such as marijuana in a purely personal, non-commercial context in the home unless the state can meet its substantial burden and show that proscription of possession of marijuana in the home is supportable by achievement of a legitimate state interest. . . .
>
> [However,] no adequate justification for the state's intrusion into the citizen's right to privacy by its prohibition of possession of marijuana by an adult for personal consumption in the home has been shown.

*Id.* at 504-11. The *Ravin* decision is discussed in more detail above in Chapter 5.

The Canadian courts have found that the Canadian Charter of Rights and Freedoms guarantees an individual's right to use marijuana for medical purposes. See *R. v. Parker*, 146 C.C.C. (3d) 193 (Ont. Ct. App. 2000) (reasoning that "forcing [an individual] to choose between his health and imprisonment violates his right to liberty and security of the person"). See also *R. v. Smith*, 2015 SCC 34 (acknowledging that "a blanket prohibition on medical access to marihuana infringes the Canadian Charter of Rights and Freedoms"). And in Mexico, the Mexican Supreme Court recently ruled that individuals have a human right to grow and possess marijuana for personal use (medical or otherwise), although, for the present time, the Court's ruling applies only to a handful of petitioners. See Dudley Althaus, *Mexico's Supreme Court Rules in Favor of Personal Marijuana Use*, Wall St. J., Nov. 4, 2015.

Should courts recognize a federal constitutional right to possess and use marijuana, and in what circumstances? Would recognition of such a right be consistent with federalism values, given that the right would limit the power of the states and not just Congress? What would be the practical difference between judicial recognition of a right to possess and use marijuana and congressional repeal or amendment of the CSA?

# B. HOW IS AUTHORITY ALLOCATED *WITHIN* THE FEDERAL GOVERNMENT?

In light of *Raich* and *Raich II*, it appears that the federal government writ large has the power to regulate the possession and use of marijuana. But this begs another question: Who within the federal government decides how to exercise this power?

Just as the Constitution allocates power between the federal government and the states, it also allocates power among the three branches of the federal government. In simplistic terms, Congress wields the legislative power—the power to make laws. The President wields the executive power—the power to enforce or to implement those laws. And the courts wield the judicial power—the power to interpret and to apply the laws.

When it comes to marijuana, Congress has the power to decide whether (and under what conditions) the possession and use of the drug shall be legal. Indeed, Congress created the CSA's elaborate scheduling system, and it placed marijuana on Schedule I in the first place—a decision that effectively banned possession and use (as well as manufacture and distribution) of the drug under federal law. And Congress, of course, is free to change its mind. In other words, Congress could pass new legislation to reschedule marijuana or even exempt the drug from the CSA's scheduling system altogether, an approach it took for alcohol and tobacco. *See* 21 U.S.C. § 802(6) (specifying that "controlled substance" does "not include distilled spirits, wine, malt beverages, or tobacco").

But the executive branch also has authority to shape the federal government's marijuana policy.[2] This section discusses one source of that authority: the power Congress has expressly delegated to the executive branch to reschedule drugs like marijuana under the CSA. Chapter 10 will discuss a second, more controversial source of influence the executive branch wields over federal marijuana policy: its de facto control over the enforcement of federal laws governing marijuana.

## 1. The Executive Branch's Scheduling Authority

In the CSA, Congress explicitly delegated to the Attorney General the power to reschedule and even de-schedule drugs like marijuana and to thereby change the rules that govern such drugs under federal law. In relevant part, 21 U.S.C. section 811 provides:

> (a) Rules and regulations of Attorney General; hearing
> The Attorney General shall apply the provisions of this subchapter to the controlled substances listed in the schedules established by section 812 of this title and to any other drug or other substance added to such schedules under this subchapter. Except as provided in subsections (d) and (e) of this section, the Attorney General may by rule—
> > (1) add to such a schedule or transfer between such schedules any drug or other substance if he—

---

2. As revealed in many of the cases already discussed, the federal (and state) courts also wield some influence over marijuana policy. In cases like *Oakland Cannabis*, *Raich*, and *Raich II*, for example, the federal courts have been called on to interpret the CSA and to determine whether the application of the statute comports with the Constitution. But because many of the controversies surrounding judicial review of federal (and state) marijuana laws were already covered in Chapters 3 and 4, the role of the judicial branch of government is not discussed separately in this chapter.

(A) finds that such drug or other substance has a potential for abuse, and

(B) makes with respect to such drug or other substance the findings prescribed by subsection (b) of section 812 of this title for the schedule in which such drug is to be placed; or

(2) remove any drug or other substance from the schedules if he finds that the drug or other substance does not meet the requirements for inclusion in any schedule.

Rules of the Attorney General under this subsection shall be made on the record after opportunity for a hearing pursuant to the rulemaking procedures prescribed by [the Administrative Procedure Act]. Proceedings for the issuance, amendment, or repeal of such rules may be initiated by the Attorney General (1) on his own motion, (2) at the request of the Secretary, or (3) on the petition of any interested party.

(b) Evaluation of drugs and other substances

The Attorney General shall, before initiating proceedings under subsection (a) of this section to control a drug or other substance or to remove a drug or other substance entirely from the schedules, and after gathering the necessary data, request from the Secretary [of the Department of Health and Human Services] a scientific and medical evaluation, and his recommendations, as to whether such drug or other substance should be so controlled or removed as a controlled substance. In making such evaluation and recommendations, the Secretary shall consider the factors listed in paragraphs (2), (3), (6), (7), and (8) of subsection (c) of this section and any scientific or medical considerations involved in paragraphs (1), (4), and (5) of such subsection. The recommendations of the Secretary shall include recommendations with respect to the appropriate schedule, if any, under which such drug or other substance should be listed. The evaluation and the recommendations of the Secretary shall be made in writing and submitted to the Attorney General within a reasonable time. The recommendations of the Secretary to the Attorney General shall be binding on the Attorney General as to such scientific and medical matters, and if the Secretary recommends that a drug or other substance not be controlled, the Attorney General shall not control the drug or other substance. If the Attorney General determines that these facts and all other relevant data constitute substantial evidence of potential for abuse such as to warrant control or substantial evidence that the drug or other substance should be removed entirely from the schedules, he shall initiate proceedings for control or removal, as the case may be, under subsection (a) of this section.

(c) Factors determinative of control or removal from schedules

In making any finding under subsection (a) of this section or under subsection (b) of section 812 of this title, the Attorney General shall consider the following factors with respect to each drug or other substance proposed to be controlled or removed from the schedules:

(1) Its actual or relative potential for abuse.

(2) Scientific evidence of its pharmacological effect, if known.

(3) The state of current scientific knowledge regarding the drug or other substance.

(4) Its history and current pattern of abuse.

(5) The scope, duration, and significance of abuse.

(6) What, if any, risk there is to the public health.

(7) Its psychic or physiological dependence liability.

(8) Whether the substance is an immediate precursor of a substance already controlled under this subchapter.

(d) International treaties, conventions, and protocols requiring control; procedures respecting changes in drug schedules of Convention on Psychotropic Substances

(1) If control is required by United States obligations under international treaties, conventions, or protocols in effect on October 27, 1970, the Attorney General shall issue an order controlling such drug under the schedule he deems most appropriate

to carry out such obligations, without regard to the findings required by subsection (a) of this section or section 812(b) of this title and without regard to the procedures prescribed by subsections (a) and (b) of this section.

. . .

(e) Immediate precursors

The Attorney General may, without regard to the findings required by subsection (a) of this section or section 812(b) of this title and without regard to the procedures prescribed by subsections (a) and (b) of this section, place an immediate precursor in the same schedule in which the controlled substance of which it is an immediate precursor is placed or in any other schedule with a higher numerical designation. If the Attorney General designates a substance as an immediate precursor and places it in a schedule, other substances shall not be placed in a schedule solely because they are its precursors.

21 U.S.C. § 811. The Attorney General has delegated its authority to the Administrator of the Drug Enforcement Administration (DEA), 28 C.F.R. § 0.100(b), and the Secretary of Health and Human Services has delegated its authority to the Food and Drug Administration (FDA) and the National Institute on Drug Abuse (NIDA).

Since the CSA was passed in 1970, there have been several petitions filed by interested parties asking the DEA to re-schedule or even de-schedule marijuana. However, none of them has proven successful. (The DEA's latest decision is discussed in more detail above in Chapter 5.) While the DEA's response to past petitions has engendered criticisms, *see, e.g.*, Drug Policy Alliance, *The DEA: Four Decades of Impeding and Rejecting Science* (undated), https://perma.cc/6R97-74F8 (discussing history of past petitions), challenges to those responses have also illuminated several important constraints on the DEA's scheduling authority, discussed in the Problems and sections that follow.

## 2. Limits Imposed by Treaty Obligations

**Problem 6.1:** In response to a petition to reschedule marijuana, the Administrator of the DEA requests the FDA's scientific and medical evaluation of the drug. The FDA reviews the relevant evidence and provides a lengthy response, concluding that marijuana has a currently accepted medical use in treating the nausea associated with chemotherapy and only a low potential for abuse. Based on these findings, the FDA recommends moving marijuana to Schedule IV. After reviewing the evidence for herself, the DEA Administrator agrees with the FDA's findings and recommendation. May the Administrator move marijuana to Schedule IV?

By the express terms of the CSA, the DEA's authority to reschedule marijuana is limited by United States' treaty obligations. 21 U.S.C. § 811(d). The DEA has argued, successfully, that the Single Convention on Narcotic Drugs, which the United States ratified in 1967, precludes the agency from moving all but the leaves and seeds of the Cannabis plant below Schedule II.[3] *Nat'l Org. for Reform of Marijuana Laws (NORML) v. Drug*

---

3. The requirements for marijuana (cannabis) are found in Article 28 of the Convention, which can be found at https://perma.cc/9H54-GYSQ.

*Enforcement Admin.*, 559 F.2d 735, 757 (D.C. Cir. 1977) (describing the limitations on the DEA's scheduling authority stemming from treaty obligations).

## 3. The Criteria for Re-scheduling

<u>Problem 6.2</u>: In response to a petition to reschedule marijuana, the Administrator of the DEA requests the FDA's scientific and medical evaluation of the drug. The FDA reviews the relevant evidence and provides a lengthy response, concluding that marijuana lacks a currently accepted medical use and has a high potential for abuse, and thus, belongs on Schedule I. After reviewing the evidence herself, the Administrator agrees with the scientific and medical assessment made by the FDA. Nonetheless, the Administrator, who is a professed libertarian and believes government should not interfere with an individual's decision to use drugs unless such use harms non-consenting third parties, staunchly opposes outright prohibition. Putting aside the treaty limitations just discussed, may the Attorney General re-schedule or even de-schedule marijuana?

Even within the scheduling range permitted by treaty obligations, the CSA further circumscribes the DEA's authority by specifying the criteria by which the agency must make its scheduling decisions. 21 U.S.C. §811(a) & (c) and §812(b). These criteria are largely medical and scientific in nature, including judgments about a drug's abuse potential and its medical benefits. (The criteria are discussed in more detail above in Chapter 5.) Importantly, the agency may not place a drug on a schedule unless all of the applicable criteria have been met (or a treaty requires it). For example, after concluding that marijuana had a high potential for abuse, no currently accepted medical use, and was not safe even under medical supervision, the DEA insisted that it had no choice but to keep marijuana on Schedule I: "The statutory mandate of 21 U.S.C. §812(b) is dispositive. Congress established only one schedule, schedule I, for drugs of abuse with 'no currently accepted medical use in treatment in the United States' and 'lack of accepted safety for use under medical supervision.'" *Denial of Petition to Initiate Proceedings to Reschedule Marijuana*, 81 Fed. Reg. 53688, 53688 (Aug. 12, 2016).

The CSA itself also specifies to a large extent how a drug shall be regulated once it has been scheduled. As the Supreme Court observed in *Gonzales v. Raich*, "[t]he CSA requires manufacturers, physicians, pharmacies, and other handlers of controlled substances to comply with statutory and regulatory provisions mandating registration with the DEA, compliance with specific production quotas, security controls to guard against diversion, recordkeeping and reporting obligations, and prescription requirements." 541 U.S. at 27.

## 4. The Role of the DEA and FDA

<u>Problem 6.3</u>: Same facts as **Problem 6.1** above, only now, the FDA concludes that while marijuana has an accepted medical use, the drug's abuse potential is high and thus it warrants placement on Schedule II (rather than IV). After

reviewing the evidence herself, the Administrator disagrees with the FDA's recommendation because she remains unconvinced that the drug has an accepted medical use. May the Administrator refuse to move marijuana to Schedule II? What if the judgments of each agency were flipped?

Apart from the substantive criteria just noted, the CSA also specifies the procedures the DEA must follow in responding to any petition to reschedule marijuana. At the outset, the CSA requires the DEA to seek the opinion of the HHS (via FDA) concerning the statute's medical and scientific scheduling criteria. *See* 21 U.S.C. §811(b). It also requires the DEA Administrator to defer to the FDA's medical and scientific judgments. *Id.* The DEA may also consult the opinions of other sources, including law enforcement agencies, in evaluating the other scheduling criteria. After gathering input, the DEA must determine whether the "facts and all other relevant data constitute *substantial evidence* of potential for abuse such as to warrant control or *substantial evidence* that the drug or other substance should be removed entirely from the schedules." 21 U.S.C. §811(b) (emphases added).

If requested by a party, the DEA Administrator must hold hearings to be presided over by an Administrative Law Judge (ALJ). Upon the conclusion of these hearings, the ALJ will issue proposed findings of fact, conclusions of law, and recommendations regarding scheduling. 21 CFR §1316.65. The ALJ's recommendations, however, may be rejected by the DEA Administrator. Indeed, in proceedings arising from the very first petition to reschedule marijuana, the DEA Administrator overruled an ALJ's recommendation to move marijuana from Schedule I to Schedule II, arguing that the ALJ had misinterpreted and misapplied the CSA's scheduling criteria. *Alliance for Cannabis Therapeutics v. Drug Enforcement Admin.*, 930 F.2d 936, 938 (D.C. Cir. 1991) (discussing Administrator's rationale for rejecting ALJ recommendation). The Administrator's final decision may be appealed, but the courts apply a very deferential standard of review on appeal. A federal court explained the standard in upholding the DEA's decision rejecting one recent rescheduling petition:

> On the merits, the question before the court is not whether marijuana could have some medical benefits. Rather, the limited question that we address is whether the DEA's decision declining to initiate proceedings to reschedule marijuana under the CSA was arbitrary and capricious. These questions are not coterminous. "The scope of review under the 'arbitrary and capricious' standard is narrow and a court is not to substitute its judgment for that of the agency."

*Americans for Safe Access v. Drug Enforcement Admin.*, 706 F.3d 438, 440 (D.C. Cir. 2013).

## Notes and Questions

1. Why did Congress empower the DEA to revise Congress's original scheduling decisions? Who should be responsible for deciding how to regulate marijuana at the federal level—an agency (and if so, which one) or Congress?

2. If you are dissatisfied with the federal government's handling of marijuana, do you think the DEA has the legal authority to redress your concerns? Along these lines, consider two final Problems:

**Problem 6.4:** Camila suffers from nausea caused by chemotherapy treatments. Her oncologist has recommended that she use marijuana to treat the nausea, but Camila is reluctant to do so because she lives in a state (Missouri) that bans the possession and use of marijuana. Suppose the DEA Administrator issues a valid rule moving marijuana from Schedule I to Schedule II. Following the rule announcement, would Camila be allowed to possess and use marijuana as a matter of *state* law? See Alex Kreit, *Beyond the Prohibition Debate: Thoughts on Federal Drug Laws in an Age of State Reforms*, 13 Chap. L. Rev. 555, 562 (2010) (discussing likely impact federal rescheduling would have on state prohibition).

**Problem 6.5:** Benjamin has been diagnosed with a qualifying condition under California law and has obtained a physician's recommendation to use marijuana. As in the prior Problem, suppose the DEA Administrator issues a valid rule moving marijuana from Schedule I to Schedule II. Without taking any further action, may Benjamin lawfully possess marijuana under federal law? See 21 U.S.C § 829 (specifying requirements for obtaining Schedule II drugs under federal law); *see also Gonzales v. Raich*, 545 U.S. at 27 (comparing regulatory controls imposed by the federal CSA and California's Proposition 215); Kevin A. Sabet, *Much Ado About Nothing: Why Rescheduling Won't Solve Advocates' Medical Marijuana Problem*, 58 Wayne L. Rev. 81, 101 (2012) (discussing likely impact federal rescheduling would have on access to marijuana).

## C. WHAT AUTHORITY DO THE STATES HAVE OVER MARIJUANA POSSESSION AND USE?

Given that Congress's strict marijuana ban has survived multiple constitutional challenges, it is hardly surprising that many people have questioned the states' power to chart a different approach. *E.g.*, Nebraska & Oklahoma v. Colorado, No. 220144 ORG, 6 (U.S. docketed Dec. 18, 2014) (seeking declaration that Amendment 64 conflicts with federal law and is therefore void); Zachary Bolitho, Op-Ed, *The Case Against Colorado's Pot Law*, L.A. Times, June 25, 2015 (arguing that "the CSA preempts Colorado's marijuana law").[4]

---

[4]. The suit brought by Nebraska and Oklahoma to block Colorado's marijuana laws is discussed (along with similar lawsuits) in Chapter 10.

Justice O'Connor's famous warning in *Raich* is representative of the skepticism: "California . . . has come to its own conclusion about the difficult and sensitive question of whether marijuana should be available to relieve severe pain and suffering. Today the Court sanctions an application of the federal Controlled Substances Act that *extinguishes that experiment*. . . ." 545 U.S. at 43 (O'Connor, J., dissenting) (emphasis added).

However, neither the *Raich* decision in 2005 nor Congress's refusal to repeal or amend its marijuana ban have stopped the states from pushing forward with their own reforms. Indeed, as discussed above and in Chapter 1, more states have adopted medical marijuana reforms in the eleven years *since Raich* was decided than had done so in the ten years prior to the case, and some states have pursued even broader reforms in those intervening years. Were the doubters wrong, and if so, why? In any event, does the passage of these state reforms matter, in a practical sense? What are the real limits to state authority?

This section examines the authority of the states to break ranks with federal marijuana policy. It focuses on the states' power to *legalize* activities, like the possession and use of marijuana, which the federal government forbids. Later chapters will build on this discussion to examine in more depth the states' power to *regulate* such activities.

### 1. Preemption Constraints

The Supremacy Clause of the United States Constitution provides that,

> This Constitution, and the laws of the United States which shall be made in pursuance thereof; and all treaties made, or which shall be made, under the authority of the United States, shall be the supreme law of the land; and the judges in every state shall be bound thereby, anything in the Constitution or laws of any State to the contrary notwithstanding.

U.S. Const. art. VI. In a nutshell, the Supremacy Clause ordains that federal law is supreme and trumps state law when the two conflict (at least if Congress so desires).

In light of the Supremacy Clause, do the states have the authority to legalize marijuana—a drug that Congress has forbidden outright? The following excerpt explores the question and highlights a limit imposed on federal supremacy.

### *Robert A. Mikos*, On the Limits of Supremacy: Medical Marijuana and the States' Overlooked Power to Legalize Federal Crime
62 Vand. L. Rev. 1421 (2009)

It is taken for granted in federalism discourse that if Congress possesses the authority to regulate an activity, its laws reign supreme and trump conflicting state regulations on the same subject. When Congress legalizes a private activity that has been banned by the states, the application of the Supremacy Clause is relatively straightforward: barring contrary congressional intent, such state laws are unenforceable and, hence, largely immaterial in the sense they do not affect private decisions regarding whether to engage in the activity.

When Congress bans some activity that has been legalized by the states, however, both the legal status and practical import of state law are far less obvious. Contrary to conventional wisdom, state laws legalizing conduct banned by Congress remain in force and, in many instances, may even constitute the de facto governing law of the land. The survival and success of these state laws are the result of previously overlooked constraints on Congress's preemption authority under the Supremacy Clause as well as practical constraints on its enforcement power. Using medical marijuana as a case study, this Article closely examines the states' underappreciated power to legalize activity that Congress bans.

. . .

Congress's preemption power is, of course, expansive. It is hornbook law that Congress may preempt any state law that obstructs, contradicts, impedes, or conflicts with federal law. Indeed, it is commonly assumed that when Congress possesses the constitutional authority to regulate an activity, it may preempt any state law governing that same activity . . .

Though expansive, Congress's preemption power is not, in fact, coextensive with its substantive powers, such as its authority to regulate interstate commerce. The preemption power is constrained by the Supreme Court's anti-commandeering rule. That rule stipulates that Congress may not command state legislatures to enact laws nor order state officials to administer them.[100] To be sure, the rule does not limit Congress's substantive powers but rather only the means by which Congress may pursue them. For example, Congress may designate the sites for new radioactive waste dumps, though it may not order state legislatures to do so, and it may require background checks for gun purchases, though it may not order state law enforcement officials to conduct them. All the same, the anti-commandeering rule constrains Congress's power to preempt state law in at least one increasingly important circumstance—namely, when state law simply permits private conduct to occur—because preemption of such a law would be tantamount to commandeering.

To see why, it is necessary to examine carefully the boundary between commandeering and preemption. Legal scholars suggest that boundary depends on a crucial distinction between action and inaction. Commandeering compels state *action*, whereas preemption, by contrast, compels *inaction*. Congressional laws blocking state action (preemption) are permissible, whereas congressional laws requiring state action (commandeering) are not.

Obviously, drawing the boundary between commandeering and preemption based on an action/inaction distinction requires a clear definition of positive action. Matt Adler and Seth Kreimer are to my knowledge the only scholars to have proposed such a definition for use in this circumstance. Employing a definition widely used in philosophy, Adler and Kreimer suggest positive action connotes physical movement, and inaction connotes immobility.[102] As it sounds, this definition of action is very broad: it encompasses literally *any* physical movement by state officials—e.g., when state legislators "open their mouths or raise their hands to vote 'yea'" on legislation; or when state law enforcement agents "raise their pens, or touch their fingers to computer keyboards, so as to issue arrest warrants, subpoenas, indictments, and so on."

---

100. Printz v. United States, 521 U.S. 898, 935 (1995); New York v. United States, 505 U.S. 144, 188 (1992).

102. Matthew D. Adler & Seth F. Kreimer, *The New Etiquette of Federalism: New York, Printz, and Yeskey*, 1998 Sup. Ct. Rev. 71, at 92, 93.

The trouble with this broad definition of action is that it generates arbitrary results in an important subset of cases—namely, anytime a state must take one action (e.g., repeal a law) in order to stop taking another (e.g., impose sanctions under that law). To illustrate, suppose California currently has a law on the books imposing a minimum one-year prison term for simple possession of marijuana. Clearly, the imposition of the sanction entails positive action by the state: state agents must investigate, arrest, charge, prosecute, convict, and imprison offenders—all, presumably, positive actions. Congress could not, of course, compel California to enact this law. But suppose California is now considering repealing the law. If positive action entails any physical movement by state officials, then repealing an old law is indistinguishable from passing a new one; after all, both require positive action by state officials. Legislators must say "aye" to pass the measure, the Governor must sign the bill, and so on. It follows that if Congress can block any positive action, it could seemingly bar California from repealing its law even though it could not compel California to adopt the law in the first instance. The result is arbitrary, and I doubt anyone, including Adler and Kreimer, thinks it accurately predicts how the Court would actually rule. Unfortunately, however, nothing in the unadorned action/inaction framework and expansive definition of action enables a court to avoid the result.

If not all positive actions by the states are preemptable, we must figure out how to distinguish the actions that are preemptable from the ones that are not. I suggest we can do that by asking whether the state action in question constitutes a departure from, or a return to, the proverbial state of nature. In the state of nature, many private forces shape human behavior: endowments, preferences, norms, and so on. Critically, however, government has no distinct influence on behavior. Government departs from the state of nature when it engages in some action, broadly defined, that makes a given behavior occur more or less frequently than it would *if we were to consider only the private and social forces shaping that behavior*. For example, imposing a fine of $100 (or awarding a subsidy of $100) for doing X would decrease (or increase) the incidence of X as compared to the state of nature. It is the state of nature—and not action/inaction, per se—that defines the boundary between permissible preemption and impermissible commandeering. Namely, Congress may drive states into—or prevent states from departing from—this state of nature (preemption), but Congress may not drive them out of—or prevent them from returning to—the state of nature (commandeering).

Using the state-of-nature benchmark to shield some state action from congressional preemption closes an arbitrary loophole in the action/inaction framework while also closely adhering to longstanding Supreme Court jurisprudence. First, by examining the consequences of positive action and not just its presence or absence, the state-of-nature benchmark avoids the arbitrary result illustrated above. Congress could not stop California from repealing its sanctioning law under the benchmark even though repeal of that law clearly entails some positive action, for the repeal merely restores the state of nature in California—no direct state government influence on possession of marijuana. Second, the state-of-nature benchmark tracks an important and often overlooked feature of the Court's preemption jurisprudence. Namely, the Court has never held that Congress could block states from merely allowing some private behavior to occur, even if that behavior is forbidden by Congress. To be sure, the Court has found myriad state laws preempted, but only when the states have punished or subsidized (broadly defined) behavior Congress sought to foster or deter—i.e., only when states departed from the state of nature. Even field preemption, the ultimate exercise of preemption power, only restores states to the state of nature; it does not require them to depart from it.

Time and again, legal authorities have failed to distinguish between state laws that punish (or subsidize) behavior and those that merely tolerate it. This oversight has generated confusion and mistaken conclusions about state medical marijuana laws and other state legislation. I propose the state-of-nature benchmark as an interpretive guide that more accurately and completely captures the distinction between commandeering and preemption than does the unadorned action/inaction framework. It is intended as a positive synopsis of Supreme Court precedent and not necessarily a normative defense of it. Though not a panacea, the state-of-nature benchmark should lessen the confusion that has emerged and generate more consistent results across cases.

. . .

The core of all state medical marijuana programs are the state laws that exempt the possession, cultivation, and distribution of marijuana for medical purposes from state-imposed legal sanctions. In enacting such laws, the states have clearly taken positive action, broadly defined. In substance, however, these exemptions merely restore the state of nature that existed until the early 1900s when marijuana bans were first adopted. The states are doing no more than turning a blind eye to conduct Congress forbids; by exempting that conduct from state imposed punishment, they do not require or necessarily even facilitate it in the relevant sense (i.e., against the state-of-nature baseline).

So understood, the exemptions *cannot* be preempted. A congressional statute purporting do so . . . would be unconstitutional. In effect, Congress would be ordering the state legislatures to re-criminalize medical marijuana—to depart from the state of nature. Just as Congress cannot order states to criminalize behavior in the first instance, it cannot order states to maintain or restore criminal prohibitions.

In fact, the suggestion that state exemptions are or even could be preempted has troubling implications, given that the states commonly treat many drug cases more leniently than does the federal government, even outside the context of medical marijuana. State law enforcement agents drop cases federal authorities would probably prosecute if they had the resources. They expunge drug convictions that trigger federal supplemental sanctions. And they punish offenders less severely than would federal sentencing authorities. None of these decisions by the states has been declared preempted, and for good reason. A ruling any other way would force states to criminalize drugs Congress has banned, adopt mandatory prosecution policies, raise sanctions, revise sentencing laws, and shift resources toward marijuana cases—effectively treading on whatever values the anti-commandeering rule seeks to promote. Under the CSA, states remain free to proscribe or not to proscribe the same drugs that Congress bans and to punish violations more or less sternly than does Congress.

To be sure, private conduct has unquestionably changed as a result of the passage of the state exemptions. . . . Citizens almost certainly use marijuana for medical purposes more frequently now than they did when states punished the conduct. But this change in behavior has resulted not because the states have *departed* from the state of nature, but because the states have (albeit only partially) *restored* it, by removing an obstacle not found in the state of nature—namely, the threat of state-imposed punishment for the possession, use, and cultivation of marijuana for medical purposes. It seems safe to suppose that in the state of nature, marijuana use would be rampant. Thus, in lifting their sanctions, the states have not taken positive action that can be preempted, a point that is easy to see once that action is judged against the appropriate baseline, which is the state of nature rather than the status quo (or the unadorned action/inaction paradigm).

. . .

In sum, Congress may not preempt the exemptions at the core of state medical marijuana laws. The exemptions merely restore the proverbial state of nature. To be sure, marijuana use has increased following passage of these laws, but the increase is not a result of anything the states have done. Rather, it is a result of what the states stopped doing: punishing medical use of the drug. Arguments that the CSA already does preempt—or that Congress even could preempt—state exemptions are mistaken. Properly understood, this is commandeering, not preemption.

## Notes and Questions

1. Apart from removing state sanctions, might state reforms undermine the federal ban on marijuana use and possession in a more subtle way? Consider the following Problem:

> Problem 6.6: Andy lives in Colorado. All of his life he has believed that marijuana is a very dangerous drug. As a result, he has abstained from using it. Following passage of Amendment 64, however, he begins to question those fears, thinking "if the state has legalized this drug, it must not be that harmful." Soon thereafter, Andy tries marijuana and becomes a casual user. Is Amendment 64 (and reforms like it) preemptable because of the "signal" it sends about the harms (and benefits) of marijuana use? Why, why not? See Mikos, *On the Limits of Supremacy, supra,* at 1454-55 (discussing this scenario and how the courts would likely address the anti-commandeering and First Amendment issues raised thereby).

For a discussion of law's potential impact on attitudes toward marijuana, see Chapter 5.

2. Even though states can legalize marijuana for purposes of their own legal codes, they cannot block enforcement of the *federal* marijuana ban—a fact that many states have acknowledged in their marijuana reforms. *E.g.*, Mass. Gen. Laws Ann. ch. 94C App., § 1-7 ("Nothing in this law . . . purports to give immunity under federal law . . . [or] poses an obstacle to federal enforcement of federal law."). But if the states cannot preclude enforcement of the federal ban, do state reforms *matter*? Another section of the article excerpted above addresses this question:

> . . . Though the CSA certainly threatens harsh sanctions, the federal government does not have the resources to impose them frequently enough to make a meaningful impact on proscribed behavior.

To begin, the federal law enforcement apparatus is small. The federal government employs 105,000 law enforcement agents, only about 4,400 of whom work for the DEA, the lead federal agency on drug crimes. The remainder work for dozens of departments—FBI, ICE, ATF, and so on—and spend only a fraction of their time handling drug crimes. All told, federal agents made 154,000 arrests in 2007—30,000 for all drug offenses, including 7,276 for marijuana. These figures amount to only 1 percent of all criminal arrests, 1.6 percent of all drug arrests, and less than 1 percent of all marijuana arrests made in the United States that year. Compared to the number of federal law enforcement agents, the number of potential targets in the war on marijuana is enormous. More than 14.4 million people regularly use marijuana in the United States every year, including 4 million who live in states that legalize medical use . . . [including] perhaps 400,000 or so, do so legally under state law pursuant to medical exemptions. . . .

. . .

Given limited resources and a huge number of targets, the current expected sanction for medical marijuana users is quite low. Suppose that only 5 percent of all marijuana offenders are currently discovered by law enforcement (state and federal combined). Of that figure, only 1 percent of offenders are handled by federal law enforcement. Assuming no cooperation between the sovereigns, only 0.05 percent—or roughly 1 in 2,000—of medical marijuana users would be uncovered by federal authorities following current practices. Hence, even if nominal federal sanctions are set very high (as they currently are), the expected legal sanction remains quite low. For example, a fine of $100,000 results in an expected sanction of only $50 ($100,000 * 0.0005), a price many people would be willing to pay for access to marijuana—especially considering that many deem it a life-changing medicine.

Robert A. Mikos, *On the Limits of Supremacy*, supra, 1463-68.

3. Just as the anti-commandeering rule bars Congress from ordering state *legislators* to pass laws, including state laws banning the possession of marijuana, it also bars Congress from ordering state *executive officials* from enforcing federal law, including the federal marijuana ban. *Printz v. United States*, 521 U.S. 898, 936 (1997) ("The Federal Government may neither issue directives requiring the States to address particular problems, nor command the State's officers . . . to administer or enforce a federal regulatory program."). Chapter 14 discusses the latter application of the anti-commandeering rule, including whether it bars the federal government from demanding that state executive officials turn over information they have gathered concerning violations federal law.

## 2. Right to Travel Constraints

Section A.2 above discussed the limits that Due Process imposes on the ability of governments (both federal *and* state) to regulate marijuana possession and use. This section discusses additional limitations imposed on state regulation by the constitutional right to travel. *Saenz v. Roe*, 526 U.S. 489 (1999) (discussing the right to travel).

### a. Denying Non-residents the Benefits of State Law

First, may a state deny non-residents the same legal benefits it accords its own residents under state law? This question arises when an individual travels to another state and seeks to take advantage of the destination state's more permissive marijuana laws. As noted in Chapter 4, several states appear to discriminate against non-residents when regulating the possession, use, or purchase of marijuana. For example, some states do not allow non-residents to possess or use medical marijuana even when they allow their own residents to do so, see Chapter 4, *supra*, and for a time, Colorado limited the quantity of marijuana state-licensed vendors could sell to non-residents (1/4 ounce) as compared to residents (1 ounce). The following excerpt analyzes whether discrimination against non-residents, like that found in Colorado's since repealed sales restriction, violates the constitutional right to travel.

## *Brannon Denning*, One Toke over the (State) Line: Constitutional Limits on "Pot Tourism" Restrictions
66 Fla. L. Rev. 2279 (2014)

Colorado's law makes a distinction on its face between residents and nonresidents seeking to purchase marijuana, thus implicating the Privileges and Immunities Clause and the [Dormant Commerce Clause Doctrine (DCCD)], which both generally prohibit discrimination against nonresidents and interstate commerce.

. . .

Because the Colorado law "poses the question whether [Colorado] can deny out-of-state citizens a benefit that it has conferred on its own citizens," the Privileges and Immunities Clause of Article IV, Section Two of the Constitution would seem the most appropriate ground for a constitutional challenge. . . . [T]he Privileges and Immunities Clause of Article IV reads: "The citizens of each state shall be entitled to all privileges and immunities of citizens in the several states." The Founders intended the Clause—described by Alexander Hamilton as "the basis of the Union"—to promote political union by prohibiting state discrimination against outsiders that might provoke retaliation and disrupt that union. As interpreted by the Court today, the Clause prohibits state discrimination against nonresidents unless there is a "substantial reason" for the discrimination and the discrimination itself is "substantially related" to the reason for the discriminatory treatment. The Privileges and Immunities Clause, however, guarantees only "fundamental rights" such as the right to earn a living on terms of substantial equality as residents and the right to receive medical care available to residents.

Predicting what a court (or the Court) would do with a Privileges and Immunities Clause challenge to a law limiting the amount of pot nonresidents could buy, as compared to residents, certainly involves guesswork. The Court has never clearly stated what rights are fundamental and trigger the protection of the Clause; neither has the Court been clear about what counts as a substantial reason for differential treatment; nor about how tight the means–ends fit must be to satisfy the substantially-related prong. However, several reasons exist for courts to give some latitude to a state seeking to curb pot tourism by restricting the amount of marijuana nonresidents may obtain at each dispensary visit.

. . .

The threshold difficulty with bringing a successful Privileges and Immunities Clause claim against a nonresident purchase limit would be proving that buying pot in a state where it is legal is a fundamental right. In *Baldwin v. Fish & Game Commission* [436 U.S. 371 (1978)], the Court rejected a Privileges and Immunities Clause challenge to a Montana law charging out-of-state hunters more for elk hunting permits. Elk hunting, the

Court reasoned, was mere recreation and not a fundamental privilege or immunity guaranteed by Article IV. The *Baldwin* Court, though, neither defined the class of fundamental rights that the Clause protected, nor articulated the criteria for the future evaluation of fundamental rights claims.

The recent *McBurney v. Young* [133 S. Ct. 1709 (2013)] decision shored up *Baldwin* by reaffirming that the privileges and immunities protected by the Clause must be fundamental, and clarifying that the Clause "does not mean . . . that 'state citizenship or residency may never be used by a State to distinguish among persons.'" *McBurney* involved a challenge to Virginia's Freedom of Information Act (FOIA), which makes public records available for inspection or copying, but only to citizens of the state. The petitioners were nonresidents whose requests for information under Virginia's FOIA were denied because they were not Virginia citizens; the petitioners claimed the citizens-only provision violated the Privileges and Immunities Clause and the DCCD.

The petitioners—one seeking records from the state regarding a child support matter, the other requesting real estate tax records on behalf of clients—argued that the citizens-only provision implicated four fundamental rights. These included "the opportunity to pursue a common calling, the ability to own and transfer property, access to the . . . courts, and access to public information." The Court unanimously held that the Virginia law did not infringe the first three and that the fourth was not a fundamental privilege or immunity.

In dispatching the claim that the provision infringed "the right to access public information," the Court concluded that no such broad right was a fundamental right under the Clause. It reaffirmed the Court's prior holdings that "there is no constitutional right to obtain all the information provided by FOIA laws." The Court also looked to history, noting that early cases "do not support the proposition that a broad-based right to access public information was widely recognized in the early Republic." The Court observed that "FOIA laws are of relatively recent vintage" and that however useful they might be, "[t]here is no contention that the Nation's unity foundered in their absence, or that it is suffering now because of the citizens-only FOIA provisions that several States have enacted."

The holdings of *Baldwin* and *McBurney* would almost certainly doom any Privileges and Immunities Clause claim related to nonmedical marijuana use. First, purchasing marijuana for recreational use is, like elk hunting, *recreational*—not the sort of activity essential to the maintenance of the Union. In fact, far from causing friction between states, which the Clause was meant to prevent, Colorado's law seeks to ameliorate any friction by reducing the incentives for nonresidents to purchase pot in Colorado and import it into states where it is still illegal. Second, *McBurney* also seems to stand for the proposition that the fundamental-right inquiry is, in part, a historical one. If access to public records does not qualify because FOIA laws are of "relatively recent vintage," arguments that equal access to legal marijuana is a fundamental right seem almost frivolous.

. . .

On the other hand, at least some out-of-state purchasers might seek marijuana for medicinal purposes and might seek equal access under *Doe v. Bolton* [410 U.S. 179 (1973)]. In *Doe*, the Court invalidated provisions of a Georgia law restricting nonresidents from obtaining abortions in that state. For the Court, Justice Blackmun wrote that:

> Just as the Privileges and Immunities Clause . . . protects persons who enter other States to ply their trade . . . so must it protect persons who enter Georgia seeking the

medical services that are available there. . . . A contrary holding would mean that a State could limit to its own residents the general medical care available within its borders.

. . .

In any event, it is hardly a stretch to argue that access to needed medical care in another state, no less than the right to earn a living or ply a trade there, is the sort of fundamental right the Clause was intended to secure. . . . [However], marijuana remains a Schedule I drug under the Controlled Substances Act (CSA), meaning that the federal government does not acknowledge it as having any acceptable medical use. . . . Conceivably, the absence of any recognized medical use for marijuana under the CSA would bar a nonresident's Privileges and Immunities Clause challenge even for medicinal purposes.

. . .

The difficulties with a Privileges and Immunities Clause claim do not end with an answer to the question of whether the right of nonresidents to obtain pot on the same terms as residents is fundamental. Article IV, Section Two does not guarantee absolute equality in all fundamental rights; rather, the Court has said that nonresidents are guaranteed the right to *substantial* equality with residents. The test is whether there is a substantial reason for discrimination and whether the discrimination bears a substantial relationship to the end the state is pursuing. As the Court put it, "classifications based on the fact of non-citizenship" are unconstitutional under the Clause, "unless there is something to indicate that non-citizens constitute a *peculiar source of evil* at which the statute is aimed." In deciding whether there is a sufficiently established relationship between the harm the state is trying to prevent and noncitizens, "the Court has considered the availability of less restrictive means." In practice, this test has been difficult to satisfy, though, the Court's recent *McBurney* decision offers additional support for Colorado's law.

The *McBurney* Court held that Virginia's FOIA did not infringe three fundamental rights guaranteed by the Privileges and Immunities Clause—"the opportunity to pursue a common calling, the ability to own and transfer property, [and] access to the [] courts." The Virginia law did not infringe the right to ply a trade or business because, according to the Court, it "has struck laws down as violating the privilege of pursuing a common calling only when those laws were enacted for the protectionist purpose of burdening out-of-state citizens." The petitioner did not "allege—and has offered no proof—that the challenged provision of the Virginia FOIA was enacted in order to provide a competitive economic advantage for Virginia citizens." Virginia law, moreover, did not prevent noncitizens from obtaining "title documents and mortgage records . . . necessary to the transfer of property." Further, the state and its subdivisions generally made real estate tax assessment records, sought by one of the petitioners, available online rendering a FOIA request unnecessary.

The other petitioner, who sought agency records relevant to a child-support dispute with his ex-wife, claimed the citizens-only provision burdened his access to public proceedings. The Court noted that he was able to obtain almost all the information sought under the state FOIA by using another Virginia statute. The Court held that the Privileges and Immunities Clause "does not require States to erase any distinction between citizens and noncitizens that might conceivably give state citizens some detectable litigation advantage."

Interestingly, the Court in *McBurney* treated the lack of any lurking protectionist purpose and the availability of functional alternatives as dispositive. The Court did not inquire further into the substantialness of the reasons for the differential treatment nor did it assess the means-ends fit between the citizens-only restriction and whatever end Virginia was pursuing. This bodes well for Colorado's law, especially if a court were to conclude that the purchase of marijuana for medicinal purposes was a fundamental right under *Doe*.

Unlike other laws successfully challenged under the Privileges and Immunities Clause, Colorado did not design the purchase limits for nonresidents to enrich in-state residents at the expense of those from out-of-state, or to hoard a resource to keep prices artificially depressed for instate consumers. The task force mentioned three reasons for differentiating between in-state and out-of-state residents: (1) preventing diversion of legal marijuana to the black market; (2) reducing federal scrutiny; and (3) respecting the policy choices of neighboring states. These reasons—coupled with the lack of any explicit (or covert) protectionist motive—ought to qualify as substantial. Under *McBurney*, the lack of any protectionist motive might be sufficient to end the inquiry.

Assuming a reviewing court applied the rest of the test, could . . . Colorado's law survive scrutiny? Specifically, would purchase amount restrictions bear a substantial relationship to the reasons given for differentiating between residents and nonresidents in the first place? And would those reasons themselves qualify as "substantial"?

. . . Here again, Colorado could make a strong case. The state would argue that the goal of the law was not to discriminate against nonresidents qua nonresidents. Rather, it was to prevent nonresidents from buying legal marijuana in Colorado and transporting it in interstate commerce—a federal crime—back to their state of residence where it may be illegal to possess marijuana for recreational or even medical use. If the federal government found pot tourists overly eager to return home with souvenirs of their travels, it might feel pressure to take a more proactive enforcement role than it is currently inclined to take. Further pressure on the federal government could come from neighboring states whose policy choices are being undermined by their proximity to Colorado. From Colorado's perspective then, nonresidents—at least nonresidents currently living in states where marijuana is illegal, which is most everywhere—*are* a "peculiar source of evil" because they are likely the very purchasers who would carry pot out of the state and draw unwanted attention to Colorado's permissive regime.

In addition, Colorado's law does not bar nonresidents from obtaining marijuana; it simply potentially requires nonresidents to engage in more transactions than residents to obtain the same desired quantity. In a similar fashion, Virginia made it marginally more difficult for nonresidents to obtain certain public records by restricting its FOIA to citizens, but alternate sources of information existed that the Court determined were sufficient. Colorado might argue that nonresidents' ability to obtain the same quantity by visiting multiple retail establishments means that despite appearances, its law does not really discriminate at all, or only discriminates incidentally, much like Virginia's citizen-only FOIA provision.

## Notes and Questions

1. Denning argues that Colorado's discriminatory limits on sales to non-residents do *not* violate the federal constitution. Do you agree? What if the state criminalized all sales to non-residents (as well as possession by non-residents)? At least one court has upheld a state's refusal to extend to non-residents the legal benefits created under its medical marijuana program. In *Oregon v. Berringer*, an Oregon appeals court rejected a California

resident's claim that Oregon had violated his right to travel by denying him the same right to possess medical marijuana the state had afforded its own residents:

> [E]ven if Oregon law made access to medical marijuana more difficult for nonresidents, that would not violate defendant's right to travel. As the Supreme Court has explained:
>
>> "Some distinctions between residents and nonresidents merely reflect the fact that this is a Nation composed of individual States, and are permitted; other distinctions are prohibited because they hinder the formation, the purpose, or the development of a single Union of those States. Only with respect to those 'privileges' and 'immunities' bearing upon the vitality of the Nation as a single entity must the State treat all citizens, resident and nonresident, equally."
>
> *Baldwin*, 436 U.S. at 383. Although access to publicly funded medical care . . . and abortion services . . . have been held to fall into the latter category, we conclude that access to a particular form of treatment—in this case, access to a particular drug—is not a privilege "bearing upon the vitality of the Nation as a single entity."

229 P.3d 615, 619-21 (Or. App. Ct. 2010).

2. What would happen if the federal government were to move marijuana to another schedule under the CSA, based in part on a finding that the drug has a currently accepted medical use in the United States? Assuming they are allowed to do so now, would the states still be allowed to prevent outsiders from taking full advantage of their medical marijuana laws?

### b. Refusing to Apply Other States' Laws

Second, may a state refuse to recognize legal benefits created under another state's marijuana laws? This question arises when an individual travels to another state that imposes *tighter* restrictions on the possession and use of marijuana than does her home state. The following Problem illustrates this scenario:

**Problem 6.7**: Andy is a resident of Colorado. He is a registered qualified patient under Colorado's medical marijuana laws. Andy drives to Nebraska to visit his friend, Nina. He brings with him ¼ ounce of marijuana, the bare minimum he needs to treat his medical condition on his trip. In Nebraska, he is stopped for speeding and searched. The police find the marijuana and charge Andy with simple possession of marijuana. Andy explains that his actions are in strict compliance with Colorado law. May Nebraska nonetheless punish him?

In confronting a similar scenario, a Kansas appellate court explained why a state is not necessarily required to accommodate behaviors that are lawful elsewhere:

> As a resident of Colorado, [Troy James] Cooper lawfully obtained medical marijuana there. Cooper came to Kansas with his medical marijuana and intended to stay here for several weeks visiting family and friends before returning to Colorado. A law enforcement officer stopped Cooper in Ellsworth County and found him to have the prescribed medical marijuana. The State charged Cooper with simple possession of marijuana, a misdemeanor, in violation of [Kansas law] . . . The district court acquitted Cooper on the grounds the prosecution contravened protections afforded him under the Privileges or Immunities

Clause of the Fourteenth Amendment and impermissibly interfered with his constitutional right to interstate travel. [The appeals court reversed.] . . .

The Privilege or Immunities Clause of the Fourteenth Amendment does not bar the enforcement of Kansas criminal statutes prohibiting possession of marijuana against someone traveling through or staying temporarily in this state even though that individual possesses the marijuana in conformity with another state's law allowing its use and possession for medical purposes. In those circumstances, the right to lawfully possess the marijuana rests on state law and, therefore, is outside the scope of the Clause.

*Kansas v. Cooper*, 301 P.3d 331, 332-34 (Kan. App. 2013).

## Notes and Questions

1. Do you agree with the result in *Cooper*? Should a state be required to accommodate behaviors by visitors that would be lawful elsewhere? Even if not, does the *Cooper* court provide a satisfying rationale for its decision?

### c. Regulating Residents' Out-of-State Conduct

Third, may a state regulate the possession and use of marijuana by its residents when those behaviors occur in another state? Like the first question posed above, this question arises when an individual travels to another state to take advantage of the destination state's more permissive laws. This time, however, the issue involves an attempt by the traveler's *home* state to regulate her behavior in the destination state:

Problem 6.8: Nina is a resident of Nebraska, which strictly forbids the possession and use of marijuana. Nina drives across the border into Colorado to visit her friend, Andy. While there, she buys ¼ ounce of marijuana (legally) and consumes it at Andy's house. The next day, Nina returns to Nebraska and openly talks about her marijuana use. May Nebraska punish Nina for possessing and using marijuana elsewhere, or for traveling across state lines to circumvent Nebraska law? *Compare* Seth F. Kreimer, *The Law of Choice and Choice of Law: Abortion, the Right to Travel, and Extraterritorial Regulation in American Federalism*, 67 N.Y.U. L. Rev. 451, 464 (1992) ("The Constitution was framed on the premise that each state's sovereignty over activities within its boundaries excluded the sovereignty of other states."), *with* Mark D. Rosen, *"Hard" or "Soft" Pluralism?: Positive, Normative, and Institutional Considerations of States' Extraterritorial Powers*, 51 St. Louis U. L.J. 713, 714 (2007) ("[C]ontrary to many people's strong intuitions, states in our country's federal union generally do have the power to regulate their citizens' out-of-state activities.").

## Notes and Questions

1. Should states be allowed to regulate marijuana possession by residents outside of their borders? Kreimer and Rosen provide contrasting views of the desirability of extraterritorial regulation. According to Kreimer,

> [T]he American Constitution as reformulated after the Civil War contemplates a national citizenship which gives to each of its members the right to travel to other states where, on a basis of equality with local residents, they can take advantage of the economic, cultural and moral options permitted there. The effort of any political subdivision of the nation to coerce its citizens into abjuring the opportunities offered by its neighbors is an affront not only to the federal system, but to the rights that the citizens hold as members of the nation itself.

Kreimer, *The Law of Choice, supra,* at 462. In response, Rosen argues:

> A state's power to regulate its citizens' out-of-state activities is important to secure political heterogeneity across states. A federal system in which states did not have extraterritorial powers over their traveling citizens would systematically favor more permissive laws, undermine the states' ability to pursue paternalistic and norm-shaping goals, undercut the states' powers to protect third-party interests, and limit the extent of experimentation across subfederal polities that otherwise could occur. It is thus desirable that the Constitution is not interpreted as flatly foreclosing on extraterritorial regulation, contrary to the views of many courts and noted commentators.

Mark D. Rosen, *Extraterritoriality and Political Heterogeneity in American Federalism,* 150 U. Pa. L. Rev. 855, 964 (2002). Who do you think has the better of the argument? Should citizens be allowed to evade the restrictions imposed by home state laws by traveling to other states? If so, would this undermine the ability of states to pursue distinct approaches to regulating marijuana (and other subjects), as Rosen claims?

2. Even if they may not prohibit actions that take place outside of their borders, might there still be a way for states to regulate the extra-territorial *use* of marijuana? Consider the following Problem:

**Problem 6.9:** Samuel flies to Colorado, where he buys a small quantity of marijuana. He consumes all of it in his Denver hotel room. Samuel then returns to his home state of South Dakota. Upon his return, Samuel consents to a blood test, which reveals the presence of THC metabolites in his system. May South Dakota prosecute Samuel for simple possession of marijuana? See South Dakota C.L. §22-42-1(1) (discussed in Chapter 2). Is this scenario distinguishable from the one in **Problem 6.8** above?

## D. HOW IS AUTHORITY ALLOCATED *WITHIN* THE STATES?

The states arguably have some power to set their own marijuana policies, even when those policies diverge from federal policy. But who decides how the states will exercise this power?

Just as there are different actors who can influence marijuana policy within the federal government, there are different actors who can influence marijuana policy within each state. In some respects, the division of power within the states resembles the division within the federal government. For example, many state health departments have been delegated the power to add new qualifying conditions to state medical marijuana laws, similar to the way the DEA has been given the power to re-schedule marijuana. *E.g.*, Code Del. Regs. 4470-6.0 (2015) (authorizing individuals to petition the Delaware Department of Health to add medical conditions to the qualifying list); Ill. Admin. Code tit. 77, § 946.30 (similar). Chapter 5 discusses this state administrative process in more detail.

But in some important respects, the division of power within the states differs markedly from the separation of powers in the federal government. This section focuses on two unique features of the state polity that further complicate the allocation of authority over marijuana policy within the states: (1) ballot initiatives; and (2) localism.

## 1. Ballot Initiatives

In at least 21 states and the District of Columbia, citizens can pass statutes directly via the initiative process. Philip L. Dubois & Floyd Feeney, Lawmaking by Initiative: Issues, Options and Comparisons 27-28 (Agathanon Press, New York) (1998) (providing a helpful survey of the rules governing direct democracy across the states). This form of direct democracy is not available under the national Constitution, which makes Congress the sole legislative body for the federal government.

In many states, the people have taken the lead in reforming state marijuana policy by passing voter initiatives. Indeed, nearly half (14 of 29) of the state medical marijuana laws that were adopted through 2016—and seven out of eight of those adopted between 1996 and 2003—were adopted via ballot initiative. And all nine of the jurisdictions that have legalized recreational marijuana through 2016 have done so via ballot initiative. Why have so many states—and especially the early movers—adopted marijuana reforms via the initiative process, rather than through their state legislatures? And should voters directly decide how their states regulate marijuana?

Direct democracy was introduced in the 1800s in large part to address some of the shortcomings of representative democracy, including the perceived unresponsiveness of state legislatures. Dubois & Feeney, Lawmaking by Initiative, *supra*, at 16-17 (discussing history of movement). Despite its populist appeal, however, direct democracy has also provoked many criticisms. *Id.* at 18-22. The following excerpt takes a skeptical view toward the use of ballot initiatives to reform marijuana laws.

## *Michael Vitiello*, Why the Initiative Process Is the Wrong Way to Go: Lessons We Should Have Learned from Proposition 215
### 43 McGeorge L. Rev. 63 (2012)

A stranger to our legal system would have a hard time understanding the laws governing marijuana use in California. That is so not just because of our federal system, but also because Proposition 215 has helped to create chaos. . . .

California came close to enacting medical marijuana legislation. First in 1994, and then again in 1995, the legislature passed laws aimed at getting marijuana to seriously ill patients. For example, AB 1529 would have authorized medical use of marijuana for only four medical conditions: AIDS, glaucoma, cancer and multiple sclerosis. Governor

Wilson vetoed both bills at a time when a large majority of Californians favored medical use of marijuana.

. . . [H]is veto opened the door for Proposition 215. And it turned out to be a Trojan horse.

Supporters of Proposition 215 included many believers in the medicinal value of marijuana. But among its drafters and vocal supporters were many long-time advocates for legalizing marijuana. Many of them saw the medical marijuana movement as a vehicle to achieve their broader goal of full legalization. Or so many of us thought when we read the broad language in the initiative. Dennis Peron, one of the co-authors of Proposition 215 and a supporter of legalization, was remarkably forthcoming in discussing his intentional use of broad language in the proposition: "Peron added potentially expansive language to Proposition 215 not included in AB 1529. His hope was to assure support from both those interested in medical use of marijuana and from those in favor of the unrestricted legalization of marijuana."

Not surprisingly, the well-funded campaign emphasized that the initiative would allow the compassionate use of marijuana for those who are "seriously and terminally ill." Unlike AB 1529, the proposition was not carefully tailored to limit marijuana to such patients. The initiative contained a number of open-ended terms. The broadest language relates to serious conditions for which a physician may recommend marijuana. After listing such conditions ("cancer, anorexia, AIDS, chronic pain, spasticity, glaucoma, arthritis, migraine"), the initiative concluded that marijuana may be recommended for "any other illness for which marijuana provides relief."

The underfunded opposition campaign pointed out that the catchall phrase could include "stress, headaches, backaches, upset stomach or other minor ailments," as well as anxiety and menstrual cramps. That was not merely the rhetoric of the initiative's opponents. As one proprietor of a cannabis club said in response to a question whether marijuana would make anyone feel better, "Now you're getting the point."

The initiative contained other drafting problems. For example, it did not explain where a qualifying patient could get marijuana; it failed to unambiguously define several important terms, including who qualified as a "primary caregiver"; and it did not provide a defense to a number of marijuana offenses, including transporting marijuana. But this catchall phrase created the possibility for virtually anyone who could pay for a doctor's visit to come within the law's protections.

Not surprisingly, courts and the legislature have been left to clean up the problems created by the initiative. . . .

. . . [S]o what is wrong with the initiative process? . . . I see three major problems in the wake of Proposition 215.

My first concern is that the law lacks legitimacy. Insofar as we have de facto legalization of marijuana, it came about without an honest debate. Instead, it resulted from manipulation of the initiative process.

My second concern is that the initiative process has limited the legislature's ability to reform the law in light of experience with its enforcement. Proposition 215 has created many problems for city planners and law enforcement agencies. But the legislature cannot reform the initiative if the legislation is inconsistent with the initiative.

My third concern is that Proposition 215 has created chaos for fifteen years. That uncertainty has significant human costs, with some individuals acting in good faith and ending up running afoul of the law. Uncertainty is also economically inefficient. . . .

## Notes and Questions

1. What do you think of Vitiello's criticisms of Proposition 215 (a measure examined in depth in Chapter 4)? Are the problems Vitiello sees in Proposition 215 endemic in all ballot initiatives? The Michigan Supreme Court has levied similar criticisms against marijuana reforms adopted via the initiative process in that state. At the outset of its opinion in *Michigan v. Hartwick*, 870 N.W.2d 37 (Mich. 2015), a case discussed in Chapter 4, the court remarked that:

> In 2008, the voters of Michigan passed into law a ballot initiative now codified as the Michigan Medical Marihuana Act (MMMA), MCL 333.26421 *et seq*. Unlike the procedures for the editing and drafting of bills proposed through the Legislature, the electorate—those who enacted this law at the ballot box—need not review the proposed law for content, meaning, readability, or consistency.

In a footnote, the court described the procedures used by the state legislature to draft proposed legislation:

> Members of the Legislature generally request that the Legislative Council, a bipartisan, bicameral body of legislators established in Article 4, § 15 of the 1963 Constitution of Michigan, see that bills to be proposed in their respective chambers are drafted. . . . The council oversees the Legislative Service Bureau. . . . The bureau has a director and staff, and maintains a legislative reference library containing material which may be of use in connection with drafting and editing proposed legislation. . . . At the request of the members of the Legislature, the bureau drafts "bills and resolutions or amendments to, or substitutes for, bills and resolutions; draft[s] conference committee reports; and examine[s], check[s], and compare[s] pending bills with other pending bills and existing laws to avoid so far as possible contrary or conflicting provisions." . . . In sum, the Legislature has a staff of experienced attorneys who work with the various legislators to develop and revise any manner of laws. After a bill is drafted and supported, the chambers of the Legislature may refer it to conference committees for additional review by legislators and the public. The Governor also has an opportunity to review bills before signing them into law. This extensive drafting process works to clarify language, limit confusion and mistakes, and in a general sense, ensure that enacted laws have a modicum of readability and consistency.

*Id.* at 41 n.3.

The court then noted several problems that it attributed to the procedures used to draft initiatives:

> . . . The lack of procedural scrutiny in the initiative process leaves the process susceptible to the creation of inconsistent or unclear laws that may be difficult to interpret and harmonize. The MMMA is such a law. While the MMMA has been the law in Michigan for just under seven years, this Court has been called on to give meaning to the MMMA in nine different cases. The many inconsistencies in the law have caused confusion for medical marijuana caregivers and patients, law enforcement, attorneys, and judges, and have consumed valuable public and private resources to interpret and apply it.

*Id.* at 41-42.

2. States with an initiative process do have rules and procedures that are designed to ensure that voters are "able to reach an intelligent and informed decision for or against" proposed initiatives and "understand[] the consequences" of their votes. *Rose v. Martin*,

500 S.W.3d 148, 152 (Ark. 2016). For example, Arkansas law provides that the description of a proposed initiative that appears on a ballot must provide "an impartial summary" of the initiative and "must give the voters a fair understanding of the issues presented and the scope and significance of the proposed changes in the law." *Id.* at 151. *See also id.* at 154 (holding that Arkansas Medical Marijuana Amendment of 2016, which was later approved by voters, met this standard). Do such rules and procedures adequately ensure that voters understand initiatives? Do they also address the drafting concerns raised by the *Hartwick* Court, *supra*?

3. Imagine that states did not have a ballot initiative process. What sort of marijuana laws would they have today? Would the marijuana reform movement still have gotten off the ground? Would California still have pursued reforms? What would those reforms have looked like? It is worth noting that California's legislature *did* pass a medical marijuana law *in 1994*—i.e., two years before Proposition 215. The law would have moved marijuana to Schedule II under state law, but it was vetoed by then Governor Pete Wilson, who cited concerns over the conflict with federal law as the basis for his decision. Veto Letter from Governor Pete Wilson to California State Senate (Sept. 30, 1994) (returning Senate Bill 1364 without his signature).

4. Part of the concern over initiatives (noted by Vitiello) is that they can be comparatively difficult to amend, making it more likely that flawed rules adopted via the initiative process will become entrenched features of state policy. In California, for example, the state legislature passed the Medical Marijuana Program Act (MMP) in 2003 in part to combat perceived abuses of the CUA. Among other things, the MMP imposed new limits on the quantity of marijuana that qualified patients were allowed to possess. However, in *California v. Kelly*, 222 P.3d 186 (Cal. 2010), the California Supreme Court invalidated those limits. It found that the MMP unconstitutionally *amended* Proposition 215, which, under court precedent, allowed patients to possess "*any amount of marijuana reasonably necessary*" for their current medical conditions. *Id.* at 209-10. The court noted that the California Constitution permitted the legislature to amend or repeal initiatives only when the affected initiative permits it—something Proposition 215 did not do. *Id.* (discussing Cal. Const. art. II, sec. 10(c)).

5. Although California's limits on amending ballot initiatives are relatively strict, the *Kelly* court noted that several other states impose at least some constraints on their legislatures' power to amend initiatives:

> Currently, 21 state constitutions allow the electorate to adopt statutes by initiative measure. . . . Of those jurisdictions, 12 place no limitation whatsoever upon the authority of the legislature to repeal or amend an initiative statute. In those states, an initiative statute is treated just like any other statute, and may be repealed or amended at any time. . . .
>
> Eight of the remaining nine states that allow voters to adopt statutes by initiative measure place various limitations upon the authority of the legislature to act in response to an initiative statute. Two of these jurisdictions allow *amendment* by the legislature at any time, but impose a moratorium on legislative *repeal* until two years after adoption of the initiative statute. Three states place a two- to seven-year moratorium on repeal or amendment; and yet some of these same jurisdictions allow amendment by a two-thirds vote during the moratorium period, and by a simple majority thereafter. Three other states allow amendment at any time by a supermajority vote of the legislature, and one of those

states . . . additionally requires that the amending legislation "further[s] the purposes" of the original initiative measure.

222 P.3d at 200-01. Should state legislatures have the power to amend ballot initiatives? Would you impose any constraints on such power? In light of California's experience and its relatively tight restrictions on legislative authority, who do you think should draft marijuana policy in California: the legislature or the people?

## 2. Localism

Local governments can also shape marijuana policy within a state. The materials in this section explore in greater depth local authority over marijuana possession and use. Chapter 10 will explore local authority over marijuana supply.

Most states appear to allow local governments to adopt their own regulations governing marijuana possession and consumption, *provided*, however, that these local regulations do not *conflict* with state law. But what constitutes a conflict with state law?

### a. Local Regulations that Are Stricter than State Regulations

Consider, first, local regulations that are *stricter* than state regulations. Generally—though not without exception—such local measures have been deemed to conflict with state law and thus held preempted. Indeed, no state that has legalized medical or recreational marijuana permits local governments to ban simple possession of the drug in circumstances where state law permits it. Robert A. Mikos, *Marijuana Localism*, 65 Case W. Res. L. Rev. 719, 723 (2015). Some state marijuana reforms make this limitation on local power very clear. For example, Amendment 64 in Colorado explicitly states that it "shall not be an offense under Colorado law *or the law of any locality within Colorado*" for anyone 21 years of age or older to possess one ounce or less of marijuana. Colo. Const. art. XVIII, § 16(3)(a) (emphasis added).

Even in states that continue to prohibit marijuana, however, local governments may be foreclosed from increasing the penalty imposed for simple possession of marijuana. The following case examines the tension between local measures that increase the penalties for simple possession that is forbidden by state law.

### *City of North Charleston v. Harper*
410 S.E.2d 569 (S.C. 1991)

HARWELL, J.:

Clarence B. Harper (Harper) was arrested for simple possession of marijuana in contravention of North Charleston City Code § 13-3. City Code § 13-3 provides for a mandatory thirty day sentence for those found guilty under the ordinance.

. . . He was found guilty and sentenced to thirty days in jail. On appeal [Harper argues, inter alia,] . . . that the mandatory thirty day sentence in City Code § 13-3 offended Article VIII, § 14 of the South Carolina Constitution . . . [and] that City Code § 13-3 conflicted with state law that grants municipal judges discretion in imposing punishment and suspending sentences. . . .

S.C. Code Ann. § 44-53-370(c) and (d) (1976) provides:

> It shall be unlawful for any person knowingly or intentionally to possess a controlled substance. . . . [A]ny person who violates this subsection with respect to twenty-eight grams or one ounce or less of marijuana or ten grams or less of hashish shall be deemed guilty of a misdemeanor and, upon conviction, shall be subject to imprisonment for a term not to exceed thirty days or a fine of not less than one hundred dollars nor more than two hundred dollars. . . . (emphasis added)

City Code § 13-3 provides:

> It shall be unlawful for any person to knowingly be in actual or constructive possession of less than twenty-eight (28) grams or one ounce of marijuana or ten (10) grams of hashish. Anyone convicted of violating this section shall be deemed guilty of a misdemeanor and shall be sentenced to thirty (30) days in jail. . . . (emphasis added)

The City of North Charleston (City) argues that both the state statute and the city ordinance prohibit the same conduct, and that City Code § 13-3 merely imposes the maximum punishment allowed under state law, and thus does not usurp state law. We disagree.

Article VIII of the South Carolina Constitution deals generally with the creation of local government. Article VIII, § 14 limits the powers local governments may be granted by state law by providing that, among other things, local governments may not attempt to set aside state "criminal laws and the penalties and sanctions in the transgression thereof. . . ." The question is whether City Code § 13-3, in denying offenders under the ordinance the possibility of paying a fine after being found guilty of simple possession of marijuana, sets aside a criminal penalty established by state law. We hold that it does.

The legislature has provided parameters within which local governments may enact ordinances dealing with the criminal offense of simple possession of marijuana. This legislation occupies the field as far as penalties for this offense are concerned. Local governments may not enact ordinances that impose greater or lesser penalties than those established by these parameters. City Code § 13-3 exceeds the parameters established under state law by denying offenders the opportunity to pay a fine and thus avoid a jail sentence. The City has attempted to set aside a penalty the legislature has found to be appropriate to punish persons guilty of simple possession. Accordingly, we hold City Code § 13-3 violates the strictures of Article VIII, § 14 of the South Carolina Constitution.

. . .

The City next argues that state law establishes only the outer parameters of municipal court sentencing jurisdiction, and that a municipal judge's discretion may be limited by an ordinance establishing the substantive offense and punishment. We disagree.

Local governments derive their police powers from the state. S.C. Const. art. VIII, §§ 7, 9. The state has granted local governments broad powers to enact ordinances "respecting any subject as shall appear to them necessary and proper for the security, general welfare and convenience of such municipalities." S.C. Code Ann. § 5-7-30 (1976). This is in recognition that more stringent regulation often is needed in cities than in the state as a whole. . . . However, the grant of power is given to local governments with the proviso that the local law not conflict with state law. . . . A city ordinance conflicts with state law when its conditions, express or implied, are inconsistent or irreconcilable with the state law. . . . Where there is a conflict between a state statute and a city ordinance, the ordinance is void. . . .

A municipal judge possesses the power to "suspend sentences imposed by him upon such terms and conditions as he deems proper, including, without limitation, restitution or public service employment." S.C. Code Ann. § 14-25-75 (Supp. 1990). A municipal judge may impose fines or imprisonment, or both, not exceeding two hundred dollars or thirty days. S.C. Code Ann. § 14-25-65 (Supp. 1990). These statutes allow municipal judges a great degree of discretion to impose appropriate punishment and to suspend sentences.

Municipal judges' discretionary authority has been given pursuant to state law. The City has attempted to circumvent this grant of authority by enacting an ordinance which by its terms deprives municipal judges of discretionary authority. Power granted pursuant to state law can be restricted only by state law. A local government may not forbid what the legislature expressly has licensed, authorized, or required. . . . Consequently, we hold that City Code § 13-3 conflicts with state law and therefore is void.

## Notes and Questions

1. Should local governments be allowed to prohibit marijuana possession, even when their state allows it? What is the rationale for limiting local authority? The dissent in *City of Niles v. Howard*, 466 N.E.2d 539 (Ohio 1984), suggests one answer. The case arose when the City of Niles, Ohio, prosecuted Jeff Howard for simple possession of 46 grams of marijuana under a City ordinance. The ordinance made simple possession a first degree misdemeanor, punishable by up to six months in jail and a fine of up to $1,000. Howard claimed the ordinance was unconstitutional, because Ohio state law at that time treated simple possession of marijuana as a minor misdemeanor, punishable by a fine of no more than $100 and no jail term or criminal record. Although the Ohio Supreme Court upheld the Niles ordinance, the dissent questioned the fairness of local measures that increase penalties for state crimes:

> Municipalities are now granted the authority to convert any minor misdemeanor into a misdemeanor in the first degree; and, as a result, uniformity in the application of criminal laws and penalties in Ohio will be diminished. Individuals traveling on our highways under the belief that their conduct is not punishable by imprisonment will suddenly find themselves inside the boundaries of a municipality, like Niles, where their conduct is punishable by six months in jail. Having no notice of the "recriminalization" of their activities upon entering the city limits, certain of these individuals undoubtedly will be arrested and convicted under these municipal ordinances. These individuals will face imprisonment, be burdened with a criminal record, and potentially suffer from a loss of employment or even a destroyed career, while their counterparts outside the city limits merely will receive a citation and no more than a $100 fine. This scenario technically may not "qualify" as a deprivation of either due process or equal protection, but it clearly is highly inequitable. . . .

*Id.* at 543 (Sweeney, J., dissenting). Are you convinced?

### b. Local Regulations that Are More Permissive than State Regulations

Many local governments have instead pursued marijuana policies that are *less strict* than those adopted at the state level. See *Local Marijuana on the Ballot*, https://perma.cc/UT7Q-RBT2 (surveying local marijuana measures). These measures do not repeal or amend state prohibitions, but some do attempt to hinder the enforcement thereof, generating controversy that is explored in the cases and materials below.

## *Joslin v. Fourteenth District Judge*
255 N.W.2d 782 (Mich. App. 1977)

RILEY, J.:

... [O]n August 1, 1974, an assistant prosecutor in Washtenaw County, acting on the request of an Ypsilanti police officer, authorized prosecution of defendants Joslin and Christante for violation of Michigan's Controlled Substances Act, ... warrants were issued charging possession of marijuana with intent to deliver, a felony carrying a maximum penalty of 4 years imprisonment and $2,000 fine. . . .

On September 19, 1974, defendants filed motions before the district court to dismiss the charges on the ground that the instant prosecution contravened Ypsilanti City Ordinance No. 437 [which states, in relevant part:

> (a) No person shall possess, control, use, give away, or sell marijuana or cannabis . . .
> (b) Any violation of this section shall be subject to a sentence of up to FIVE DOLLARS ($5), including judgment fees and costs, and no probation or any other punitive or rehabilitative measure shall be imposed . . .
> (d) No Ypsilanti police officer, or his or her agent, shall complain of the possession, control, use, giving away, or sale of marijuana or cannabis to any other authority except the Ypsilanti City Attorney, and the City Attorney shall not refer any said complaint to any other authority for prosecution. . . .]

[D]efendants argued that the Ypsilanti police officer who had filed the complaint in this matter had violated section (d) of the ordinance by taking the case to the Washtenaw County Prosecutor rather than to the Ypsilanti City Attorney as the ordinance requires.
. . .
. . . The prosecutor charges that section (d) of the ordinance impermissibly restrains Ypsilanti police officers from enforcing state law. We agree.

By its terms, section (d) purports to prevent the Ypsilanti police from complaining to anyone but the city attorney about marijuana violations. The law is clear, however, that municipal police are authorized to enforce state law. M.C.L.A. § 764.15; M.S.A. § 28.874 ("Any peace officer may, without a warrant, arrest a person (a) For the commission of any felony or misdemeanor committed in his presence; (or) (b) When such person has committed a felony although not in the presence of the officer"). . . . The power of a city to enact ordinances "relating to its municipal concerns, property and government, (is) subject to the constitution and law." Const. 1963, Art. VII, § 22. Accordingly, to the extent section (d) limits the authority of city police to enforce state law, we hold it void. . . .

## Notes and Questions

1. What if a local measure merely repealed any local restrictions on marijuana, but did not attempt to hinder enforcement of state law? In 2014, for example, voters in Berkley, Michigan, passed an initiative stating that "Nothing in the [City] Code of Ordinances shall apply to the use, possession or transfer of less than 1 ounce of marijuana, on private property not used by the public, or transportation of less than 1 ounce of marijuana,

by a person who has attained the age of 21 years." November-Election—Marijuana Charter Amendment, Nov. 7, 2014, https://perma.cc/7CD8-5LG7. In response to questions from residents, the City Manager informed them that "If determined to be in violation of state law, you will be subject to prosecution. The City Charter amendment only precludes enforcement of City ordinance, but does not affect state law or its enforcement." Is the Berkley measure preempted by state law? Even if not, does it serve any purpose, if it does not change state law or the enforcement thereof?

---

The next case considers the validity of a similar type of local measure that does not bar enforcement of marijuana prohibition altogether, but instead instructs local officials to make it their lowest law enforcement priority.

## *Ruggles v. Yagong*
### 353 P.3d 953 (Haw. 2015)

McKenna, J.:

At issue in this appeal is whether Article 16 of Chapter 14 of the Hawai'i County Code, entitled "Lowest Law Enforcement Priority of Cannabis" ("LLEP"), is preempted in its entirety by state law. . . .

[The LLEP provides, in relevant part:]

> "Lowest Law Enforcement Priority" means a priority such that all law enforcement activities related to all offenses other than the possession or cultivation of cannabis for adult personal use shall be a higher priority than all law enforcement activities related to the adult personal use of cannabis. The Lowest Law Enforcement Priority regarding possession or cultivation of cannabis shall apply to any single case involving twenty four or fewer cannabis plants at any stage of maturity or the equivalent in dried cannabis, where the cannabis was intended for adult personal use.
> 
> . . .
> 
> (a) The cultivation, possession and use for adult personal use of cannabis shall be the Lowest Law Enforcement Priority for law enforcement agencies in the county.
> 
> (b) The council, the police commissioner, the chief of police and all associated law enforcement staff, deputies, officers and any attorney prosecuting on behalf of the county shall make law enforcement activity relating to cannabis offenses, where the cannabis was intended for adult personal use, their Lowest Law Enforcement Priority. Law enforcement activities relating to cannabis offenses include but are not limited to the prosecution of cannabis offenses involving only the adult personal use of cannabis.
> 
> . . .
> 
> (a) Neither the council, nor the police commissioner, nor the chief of police, nor any attorneys prosecuting on behalf of the county, nor any associated law enforcement staff, deputies, or officers shall spend or authorize the expenditure of any public funds for the investigation, arrest, or prosecution of any person, nor for the search or seizure of any property in a manner inconsistent with the Lowest Law Enforcement Priority . . .

. . . The Plaintiffs[, a group of concerned citizens brought suit, alleging, inter alia] . . . the prosecutors and police violated the LLEP by "continu[ing] to prosecute cannabis cases where the amount processed or grown is less than 24 plants or the dried equivalent of 24 ounces. . . ."

. . .

[T]he Plaintiff's argue that "there is no conflict between the Ordinance and Hawai'i Revised Statutes. . . ." We disagree and affirm the [court of appeal's] clear holding that "the LLEP conflicts with, and is thus preempted by state law governing the investigation and prosecution of alleged violations of the Hawai'i Penal Code concerning the adult personal use of cannabis," [including state statutes banning the possession of marijuana]. . . .

. . . [T]he LLEP also conflicts with state law requiring the state attorney general and county prosecuting attorney to investigate and prosecute violations of the statewide Penal Code. HRS § 28-2.5(b) (2009) delineates the investigative powers of the attorney general and county prosecuting attorneys when conducting criminal investigations. Pursuant to HRS § 28-2 (2009), the attorney general "shall be vigilant and active in detecting offenders against the laws of the State, and shall prosecute the same with diligence." HRS § 26-7 (2009) does state that "unless otherwise provided by law, [the department of the attorney general shall] prosecute cases involving violations of state laws. . . ." The phrase as "otherwise provided by law" does not, however, countenance laws such as the LLEP. Rather, it recognizes that, although "the attorney general, as the chief legal officer for the State," has "the ultimate responsibility for enforcing penal laws of statewide application," "[t]he public prosecutor . . . has been delegated the primary authority and responsibility for initiating and conducting criminal prosecutions within his county jurisdiction." . . . Thus, although the county prosecutor has been delegated primary prosecutorial duties, under Hawai'i County Charter § 9-3(a)(2) (2010), the duties of the prosecuting attorney for the County of Hawai'i include "[p]rosecut[ing] offenses against the laws of the State under the authority of the attorney general of the State." Therefore, county laws such as the LLEP cannot usurp the attorney general's duty, delegated to the prosecuting attorney, to prosecute violations of the statewide penal code.

## Notes and Questions

1. The states' influence over marijuana policy stems in part from their entitlement to refuse to help the federal government enforce policies with which they disagree (as discussed above in Section C.1). But do localities wield the same control over their own law enforcement resources? Both the *Joslin* and *Ruggles* courts suggest that localities may *not* refuse to enforce state marijuana policy, a difference that seemingly constrains their influence over marijuana policy.

2. Should local governments be allowed to opt out of state marijuana prohibitions? Do the concerns over diversion and externalities discussed in *Raich* justify limiting local power over marijuana possession and use? Chapter 10 revisits this question when considering local authority to regulate the supply of marijuana.

# PART III

# MARIJUANA SUPPLIERS

CHAPTER 7

# The Regulation of Marijuana Suppliers in Prohibition Regimes

This chapter explores how prohibition regimes regulate the supply of marijuana. Although there is some variation, prohibition regimes generally define supply to include three basic activities: (1) the manufacture of marijuana; (2) the distribution of marijuana; and (3) the possession of marijuana with the intent to manufacture or distribute it.[1] Under federal law, for example, it is "unlawful for any person knowingly or intentionally . . . to manufacture, distribute, or dispense, or possess with intent to manufacture, distribute, or dispense, a controlled substance." 21 U.S.C. § 841(a).

Importantly, prohibition regimes generally punish these actions much more severely than they punish actions (like simple possession) that are associated with the use of marijuana. Under federal law, for example, the maximum penalty for distributing one ounce of marijuana is five years' imprisonment, *id.* at § 841(b)(1)(D), whereas the maximum penalty for simple possession of the same quantity is less than one year's imprisonment, *id.* at § 844(a), and may even be treated as a non-criminal offense, *id.* at § 844a. The harsher treatment raises a host of questions. Do jurisdictions do a good job of distinguishing between supply and use offenses? For example, should the social sharing of a joint count as "distribution"? Is the cultivation of marijuana for one's own use more like possession or manufacture of the drug?

The materials in this chapter delve into these and related questions. Section A surveys the elements of marijuana supply offenses and the key legal controversies that surround the definition of those offenses. It also discusses potential legal defenses to supply charges, including defenses based on Department of Justice enforcement guidance and congressional legislation that limits the agency's funding to enforce federal marijuana laws. Section B then discusses the criminal sanctions that can be imposed for marijuana supply offenses. It discusses factors, such as the quantity of marijuana involved in an offense, that are used to determine sanctions, as well as legal controversies surrounding those factors, such as how marijuana is measured for purposes of sentencing. It also briefly reviews data on the sanctions that are typically imposed on marijuana suppliers. Finally, Section C discusses some of the civil sanctions that could be imposed on marijuana suppliers, including forfeiture, taxes, damages under the federal Racketeer Influenced

---

1. Most prohibition regimes refer to these supply activities as "trafficking." However, because "trafficking" is sometimes considered a pejorative term, the book employs the more neutral term "supply" instead.

and Corrupt Organizations (RICO) Act, and limits on suppliers' ability to protect their intellectual property.

## A. WHAT ARE MARIJUANA SUPPLY OFFENSES?

This section surveys core supply offenses and the defenses that may be raised against them. Most of the discussion in this section focuses on the actus reus of each offense—for example, whether "distribution" includes passing a joint to a friend without payment. For each offense, of course, the government must also prove that the defendant acted knowingly or intentionally (the mens rea) and that the substance involved was marijuana (the attendant circumstance). But because Chapter 3 already discussed these same elements, this section will address them only to the extent they differ, as, for example, when it discusses possession with *intent* to distribute marijuana.

### 1. Manufacture

Manufacturing is one core supply offense. But what does it mean to "manufacture" marijuana? Usually, the term is given a broad definition that includes planting, cultivating, and harvesting Cannabis plants, as well as processing plant material, e.g., to make hash oil. The CSA's approach to defining "manufacture" and related terms is representative:

> (15) The term "manufacture" means the production, preparation, propagation, compounding, or processing of a drug or other substance, either directly or indirectly or by extraction from substances of natural origin, or independently by means of chemical synthesis or by a combination of extraction and chemical synthesis, and includes any packaging or repackaging of such substance or labeling or relabeling of its container; except that such term does not include the preparation, compounding, packaging, or labeling of a drug or other substance in conformity with applicable State or local law by a practitioner as an incident to his administration or dispensing of such drug or substance in the course of his professional practice. . . .
> 
> . . .
> 
> (22) The term "production" includes the manufacture, planting, cultivation, growing, or harvesting of a controlled substance.

21 U.S.C. § 802. Under this definition, for example, someone who placed marijuana seeds between wet paper towels to encourage germination, *Missouri v. LaMaster*, 811 S.W.2d 837 (Mo. App. 1991) (applying identical state definition), and someone who turned the soil and planted seeds, *Missouri v. Netzer*, 579 S.W.2d 170 (Mo. App. 1979), could both be found guilty of manufacturing marijuana, regardless of whether the seeds or plants ever matured or were harvested.

### Notes and Questions

1. New Mexico is a rare jurisdiction that does not define manufacture to include cultivating marijuana. New Mexico's drug law was patterned on the federal CSA. However, it appears that the New Mexico legislature omitted section 802(22), which proscribes the "planting, cultivation, growing, or harvesting of a controlled substance," from its own

statute, leaving it with a narrower definition of manufacturing. Thus, in *New Mexico v. Shaulis-Powell*, 986 P.2d 463 (N.M. App. 1999), the court overturned a defendant's conviction for manufacturing marijuana, because that conviction was based solely on the defendant growing eight marijuana plants in his yard. The court explained:

> The plain meaning of "manufacture" does not include simply growing marijuana. Without more, growing marijuana does not constitute manufacture. Even if growing marijuana could be considered "production" under the statute, "production" is modified by the phrase "by extraction from substances of natural origin or independently by means of chemical synthesis[.]"

*Id.* at 468.

2. Presumably anyone who has manufactured marijuana has at some point in time also *possessed* the drug. (Recall from Chapter 2 that the definition of marijuana includes germinating seeds and plants.) So why do jurisdictions proscribe the *manufacture* of marijuana? And why do they impose harsher sanctions for this action (as discussed below in Section B)?

### a. Manufacture of Hash Oil

Apart from the planting, cultivating, and harvesting of Cannabis plants, manufacture also includes processing the plant into different consumable forms. For example, the production of hash oil is a manufacturing offense, as discussed in the following case.

### Utah v. Horsley
596 P.2d 661 (Utah 1979)

MAUGHAN, J.:

Pursuant to a search warrant, police officers on May 11, 1977, searched defendants' apartment in Logan, Utah. The officers confiscated various items including [a] cooker, substantial amounts of marijuana, small scales, and other paraphernalia. The cooker was in the "on" position and was apparently cooking a plant material inside.

At the preliminary hearing, a forensic chemist testified the plant material was marijuana, and that [the] cooker is used to remove the non-hallucinogenic elements from the raw marijuana plant, thereby producing a more concentrated and potent form of marijuana, commonly known as "hash." The process involves the addition of sulfuric acid and sodium bicarbonate at certain stages of the procedure, the goal being the extraction of the resin from the plant. The chemist testified that although certain chemical changes occur during the process, the hallucinogenic material remains essentially unchanged, but is in a more concentrated form.

Defendants assert on appeal that the . . . statute under which they were convicted . . . applies only to circumstances involving the manufacture of a controlled substance from materials which are not controlled. . . . In support of this proposition, they cite *Anheuser-Busch Brewing Association v. United States*, 207 U.S. 556 (1908), in which the Supreme Court stated that the term "manufacture" contemplates that "(t)here must be (a) transformation; a new and different article must emerge, 'having a distinctive name, character, or use.'" . . . Here, they point out, since the substance was marijuana before the cooking process and would simply have been a more potent form of marijuana thereafter, no "manufacture" has occurred and the convictions cannot stand.

We note that the following statutory definition of marijuana makes no distinction between "marijuana" and a more potent extract from the plant:

> The words "cannabis" or "marihuana" mean all parts of the plants cannabis sativa L. and cannabis indicia, (sic) whether growing or not; the seeds thereof; the resin extracted from any part of such plant; and every compound, manufacture, salt, derivative, mixture, or preparation of such plant, its seeds, or resin. . . .

. . . Thus, under the act, marijuana was both the original substance and the substance to be manufactured, although "hash" is clearly a more potent form of marijuana.

However, the key question is not whether defendants intended to manufacture a controlled substance in the usual sense of a "new and different article" as stated by the United States Supreme Court, . . . but whether defendants intended to "manufacture" a controlled substance according to the definition and intent of the legislature. [Utah law] defines "manufacture" as "the production, preparation, propagation, compounding, or processing of a controlled substance, either directly or indirectly by extraction from substances of natural origin. . . ." We believe the evidence indicates defendants intended to engage in the "processing of a controlled substance directly or indirectly by extraction from substances of natural origin" when they cooked and added chemicals to the marijuana plant in an effort to produce "hash." . . .

HALL, J. (dissenting):

I dissent for the reason that the statutory definition of marijuana makes no distinction between marijuana and "hash," or "hashish." They are simply One and the same under the statute, the possession of which constitutes a class B misdemeanor.

The statute making it unlawful to produce or manufacture a controlled substance has no application here since there was no evidence that defendant Produced or Manufactured marijuana. On the contrary, the evidence was that they simply Possessed marijuana and that they prepared it for use by eliminating some of its non-hallucinogenic parts and thus obtained a condensed form of marijuana. The expert testimony of the forensic chemist was that the chemical makeup of the substance remained unchanged and that "hash is marijuana."

It lies within the prerogative of the Legislature to classify "hash," or "hashish," as a controlled substance separate and apart from marijuana, and this Court should not infringe upon that prerogative.

## Notes and Questions

1. Although production of hash oil is typically covered by the general manufacturing bans discussed above, some states have adopted additional measures specifically aimed at the production of hash oil (and other drugs) *through chemical processes. E.g.*, Cal. Health & Safety C. § 11379(a) ("[E]very person who manufactures, compounds, converts, produces, derives, processes, or prepares, either directly or indirectly by chemical extraction or independently by means of chemical synthesis, any controlled substance . . . [including marijuana] shall be punished by imprisonment in the state prison for three, five, or seven years and by a fine not

exceeding fifty thousand dollars ($50,000).");. These targeted prohibitions carry harsher sanctions than the bans otherwise applicable to manufacturing marijuana. *Compare id.* (imposing 3-to 7-year prison term) *with* Cal. Health & Safety C. § 11358 (imposing 16- to 36-month prison term on anyone "who plants, cultivates, harvests, dries, or processes any marijuana"). Normally, the government may choose whether to charge a defendant under the general manufacturing ban, the targeted ban, *see California v. Bergen*, 82 Cal. Rptr. 3d 577 (Cal. App. 2008) (upholding prosecutor's decision to proceed under targeted ban rather than general ban), or potentially even both, see Section A.6, *infra* (discussing double jeopardy issues).

2. The harsher sanctions applicable to the production of hash oil through chemical processes reflect the added harms commonly attributed to such processes. *See Hash Oil Explosions Prompt Proposed Changes in Pot States*, N.Y. Times, Apr. 3, 2015 (reporting 30 injuries from hash oil explosions in Colorado in 2014, up threefold from the prior year). In *Bergen, supra*, the court described the chemical processes used for making hash oil and the dangers involved:

> One and a half inch round solid plastic piping is cut into 18-inch lengths. Solid caps are placed on both ends of the 18-inch tubes. A screw-off cap is placed on the top and a single hole is drilled into the top cap. Five to seven small holes are then drilled into the bottom cap and a filtering device inserted. Filters akin to coffee filters are used for this purpose.
>
> Marijuana is then loosely packed into the tube and the top cap screwed onto the tube. The tube is placed upright in a stand. A bottle of butane is inserted into the single hole in the top cap and poured slowly into the tube to allow the butane to draw the oils down through the tube. Butane is a solvent and it extracts the resin from the plant material as the butane flows from the top of the tube to the bottom. A glass dish is placed under the upright tube to collect the filtered residue as it drips through the small holes in the bottom of the tube. This resin extraction and filtering part of the process takes approximately 15 minutes. It requires another 20 minutes or so for the butane to evaporate, leaving the amber colored concentrated cannabis known colloquially as "hash oil" or "honey oil." When all the butane has safely dissipated, the "honey oil" is then poured into individual glass vials.
>
> . . .
>
> [In passing section 11379(a), the] Legislature apparently intended to punish more harshly the use of chemicals in the production of controlled substances because of the dangers posed to the public from the use of hazardous substances, such as fires, fumes or explosions. . . . These dangers include environmental damage resulting from the disposal of toxic chemicals, fire and explosions (sometimes in residential neighborhoods where the labs often are located), and increased risk to law enforcement officers who investigate these operations.

82 Cal. Rptr. 3d 577, 585 (Cal. App. 2008). The court also noted that hash oil could be produced through other, safer means, like physical extraction, thereby avoiding the need for dangerous chemicals. *Id.*

3. What other actions might count as "processing . . . by extraction from substances of natural origin"? Consider the following Problem:

**Problem 7.1**: Andy lights a marijuana joint using a butane lighter, thereby releasing THC from the dried marijuana buds inside the joint. Per *Horsley*, is Andy guilty of *manufacturing* marijuana?

Part III. Marijuana Suppliers

### b. Manufacture for Personal Use

Under the law, those who manufacture marijuana are punished more severely than those who simply possess the drug (e.g., users). But because some users like to grow their own marijuana, they may be treated like suppliers under the law. The following Problem raises the issue:

**Problem 7.2:** Delilah planted and cultivated a single marijuana plant in a corner of her garden. After a few months, she harvested the plant. She later consumed the entire harvest (a few ounces of dried bud and leaves) by herself. Is Delilah guilty of manufacturing in the eyes of the law?

Some reform regimes have relaxed prohibitions on personal cultivation, as discussed in Chapter 8. But prohibition regimes continue to treat personal cultivation no differently than cultivation for distribution to others—i.e., both are considered manufacturing and subject to the same sanctions. *E.g., United States v. Klein*, 850 F.2d 404 (8th Cir. 1988) (holding that whether defendant manufactured marijuana "for his own use rather than for purposes of distribution is irrelevant").

The following case discusses competing views of the majority rule. The case arose after Massachusetts decriminalized simple possession of one ounce or less of marijuana in 2008 but before the state legalized such possession in 2016. Decriminalization increased the disparity between the state sanction applicable to simple possession versus manufacturing of marijuana. The Justices reflected on whether manufacturing a small amount of marijuana for personal use should remain a criminal supply offense under state law.

## *Massachusetts v. Palmer*
985 N.E.2d 832 (Mass. 2013)

BOTSFORD, J.:

... On September 28, 2010, officers of the Adams police department consensually entered the defendant's residence and arrested him on active warrants. While searching for the defendant in his home, the officers observed in plain view several marijuana plants growing in a closet.[1] The cumulative weight of the marijuana found was less than one ounce.

A criminal complaint issued from the Northern Berkshire Division of the District Court Department charging the defendant with cultivation of marijuana [among other offenses]. . . .

. . . The question presented is what effect, if any, § 32L, inserted by St. 2008, c. 387, "An Act establishing a sensible State marihuana policy" (Act), has on the offense of cultivation under § 32C (a), where the amount of marijuana cultivated weighs one ounce or less. We begin with the text of the relevant statutes. Section 32C(a), provides, in pertinent part: "Any person who knowingly or intentionally manufactures, distributes,

---

1. According to the arresting officer, the closet also contained several lights, a large piece of foil, an electric timer device for the lights, a thermometer on the wall just above the plants, several packages of fertilizer, plastic bottles containing a liquid that the officer assumed was plant food or fertilizer, several glass smoking devices, empty clear plastic baggies, marijuana seeds, and a cardboard box with several prescription bottles inside, some of which had no labels.

dispenses or cultivates, or possesses with intent to manufacture, distribute, dispense or cultivate [marijuana] shall be imprisoned. . . ." [The 2008 Act] changed the status of the offense of possession of one ounce or less of marijuana from criminal to civil. . . . Section 2 of the Act, codified at § 32L, provides in relevant part:

> Notwithstanding any general or special law to the contrary, possession of one ounce or less of marihuana shall only be a civil offense, subjecting an offender who is eighteen years of age or older to a civil penalty . . . but not to any other form of criminal or civil punishment or disqualification. . . .
>
> Nothing contained herein shall be construed to repeal or modify existing laws . . . concerning the operation of motor vehicles or other actions taken while under the influence of marihuana or tetrahydrocannabinol, laws concerning the unlawful possession of prescription forms of marihuana or tetrahydrocannabinol . . . , possession of more than one ounce of marihuana or tetrahydrocannabinol, or selling, manufacturing or trafficking in marihuana or tetrahydrocannabinol. . . .

. . . The defendant argues that . . . , by definition, the cultivation of one ounce or less of marijuana means possession of that quantity. Accordingly, the argument goes, because § 32L decriminalizes possession of one ounce or less of marijuana, it also decriminalizes its cultivation in that amount. . . .

By its terms, the Act decriminalized only "possession of one ounce or less of marihuana" and correspondingly amended only § 34, the statute defining the crime of simple possession, to exempt possession of one ounce or less of marijuana from criminal status and penalties. . . . The Act did not decriminalize any other type of conduct proscribed by G.L. c. 94C, and it did not amend any other provision in c. 94C other than § 34. We adhere to our view [in *Massachusetts v. Keefner*, 961 N.E.2d 1083 (2012) (holding that Act did not decriminalize possession with intent to distribute one ounce or less of marijuana)] that the Act's specific amendment of § 34 and of no other criminal penalty provision in c. 94C—including, notably, § 32C (a)—is persuasive evidence that the Act was not intended to decriminalize any offense defined in c. 94C other than simple possession of one ounce or less of marijuana.

Moreover, the defendant offers no persuasive argument for why we should find an implied repeal of the provision in § 32C(a) proscribing cultivation when we declined to do so in relation to the provision in the very same section that proscribes possession with intent to distribute. *Keefner*. . . . Adhering to the principle that "a statute must be interpreted 'as a whole,'" we conclude that § 32L did not repeal the offense of cultivation of marijuana under § 32C(a) where the amount of marijuana cultivated is one ounce or less.[5] . . .

We address briefly the interpretation of §§ 32C(a) and 32L proposed by Justice Duffly's concurring opinion, which is different from that offered by the defendant but is also flawed. The concurrence posits that (1) the term "cultivat[ion]," as used in § 32C(a), does not include (and apparently has never included) cultivation of marijuana for "personal use," . . . ; (2) cultivation only comes within § 32C(a)'s prohibition if it is undertaken with the intent to distribute (i.e., sell) . . . ; and (3) with the passage of § 32L, cultivation of one ounce or

---

5. Finally, the practical difficulties associated in enforcing § 32L's weight-based minimum in the context of cultivation further support our conclusion that the Act did not decriminalize the cultivation of one ounce or less of marijuana. Marijuana subject to possession penalties typically is confiscated and weighed in its dried, leaf form. However, cultivation involves marijuana in the form of live plants, including stems and roots. The Act's minimum weight allowance did not provide any indication as to how live plants should be weighed to determine whether their weight exceeds the one-ounce statutory minimum.

less of marijuana for personal use "is not a crime." . . . This interpretation ignores the plain language of § 32C(a) and flies in the face of our guiding principles of statutory construction.

Section 32C(a) uses the word "cultivate" by itself. The section contains no language creating an exception for cultivation for "personal use" or indeed any exception at all. In interpreting a statute, "[w]e will not add words to a statute that the Legislature did not put there, either by inadvertent omission or by design." . . . Moreover, as the concurrence acknowledges, . . . the word "cultivate" has a plain, ordinary meaning: "To grow or tend (a plant or crop)." American Heritage Dictionary of the English Language 454 (3d ed. 1992). Our rules of statutory construction counsel that when the meaning of a word used in a statute is clear, we should interpret it in accordance with that meaning, without more. . . . As the quoted definition indicates, the word "cultivate" refers to the process of growing a plant or crop, not the purpose for which the plant or crop is grown.[7] Accordingly, we hold that the cultivation of one ounce or less of marijuana, regardless of its intended use, is a criminal offense under § 32C(a). . . .

DUFFLY, J., concurring:

. . . I write separately because I believe that § 32L did decriminalize the growing of one ounce or less of marijuana for personal use. Here, the criminal complaint alleges that the defendant grew marijuana with the intent to distribute it, and the facts alleged support probable cause to believe the defendant committed that offense. . . . [Hence,] I concur in the court's decision [to reinstate the charges against the defendant].

When read in the context of G.L. c. 94C in its entirety, it is evident that the offense of cultivation excludes the growing of marijuana when it is done only for personal use. Section 32C(a) makes it a crime to manufacture, distribute, dispense, or cultivate marijuana, or to possess marijuana with the intent to manufacture, distribute, dispense, or cultivate it. General Laws c. 94C does not define "cultivate," but the ordinary meaning of the word is "[t]o grow or tend (a plant or crop)." American Heritage Dictionary of the English Language 454 (3d ed. 1992). As used in § 32C(a), however, the word "cultivate" must be interpreted more narrowly, in light of the first three words in the phrase: manufacture, distribute, and dispense. . . .

Each of the first three terms connotes significant steps in the course of drug trafficking, and possession solely for personal use of the drugs is not included in their definitions. By statute, the term "manufacture" explicitly "does not include the preparation or compounding of a controlled substance by an individual for his own use." G.L. c. 94C, § 1. Distribution is "the facilitation of a drug transfer from seller to buyer" in furtherance of the drug trafficking business. *Commonwealth v. Jackson*, 985 N.E.2d 853 (2013). . . . And the term "dispense" means the delivery of a controlled substance to an end user by a "practitioner" who is "registered." *Id.* Just as possession for personal use is excluded from the definitions of manufacturing, distributing, and dispensing drugs, the term "cultivate" should also be read to exclude the growing of marijuana only for personal use.

---

7. There are a number of additional reasons the concurrence's interpretation of the term "cultivat[ion]" in § 32C(a) is problematic. For example, . . . [i]f "cultivat[ion]" and "possession" mean the same thing, . . . then § 32C(a)'s proscription against "cultivat[ion]," which the concurrence reads to prohibit only cultivation with intent to distribute, essentially would become superfluous. This follows because § 32C(a) expressly and separately prohibits possession with intent to distribute a controlled substance, including marijuana. It is a cardinal principle of statutory interpretation that "[n]one of the words of a statute is to be regarded as superfluous." . . .

The legislative history of § 32C(a) supports this interpretation. The Legislature enacted § 32C(a) to target those "in the drug business." ... As the Governor explained when proposing the 1980 legislation that added this statute to the General Laws, "The time has come to launch a new, more aggressive campaign against those who operate and profit from the death-dealing traffic in drugs. ... We need major changes in the way our criminal system deals with these dealers in drugs." ... Growing marijuana for personal use does not implicate such concerns. Indeed, growing marijuana for personal use arguably undermines the drug trafficking business, along with its attendant violence, ... by allowing marijuana users to obtain marijuana without supporting the drug trafficking market.

Moreover, the offense of cultivation must be considered in light of § 32L, which makes the simple possession of one ounce or less of marijuana a civil infraction. ... Section 32L, ... identifies only four categories of existing laws that shall not be "construed to [be] repeal[ed] or modif[ied]." Among the laws explicitly unaffected by the enactment of § 32L are laws concerning the "selling, manufacturing or trafficking" in marijuana. G.L. c. 94C, § 32L. ... Significantly, "cultivation" is not included among the categories not subject to repeal or modification by the enactment of § 32L. ... Although we held in [Keefner] ... that this list "cannot be construed as exhaustive," we recognized also that the passage of § 32L may have limited the reach of § 32C(a). We noted in that case that "the extent of all acts that are proscribed by the term 'distribute' under § 32C(a)" remained to be decided, despite the absence of any explicit amendment to § 32C(a). See id. ... Indeed, we have decided today that the social sharing of a decriminalized amount of marijuana does not constitute the offense of distribution. See [Massachusetts] v. Jackson. ...

In light of the enactment of § 32L, I believe it is clear that the growing of one ounce or less of marijuana for personal use is not a crime. Section § 32L was enacted as a result of the voters' adoption in 2008 of "An Act establishing a sensible State marihuana policy." St. 2008, c. 387. The goal of this initiative was to decriminalize possession of marijuana while keeping in place "other marijuana-related crimes, like sales." ... By defining the offense of cultivation to cover the growing of marijuana for personal use, the court's decision today leaves no noncriminal means by which to obtain a decriminalized amount of marijuana. I fail to see how such a policy is "sensible." ...

Treating marijuana cultivation for personal use in the same manner as simple possession is treated under § 32L, a civil infraction, is also consistent with the recent enactment of [the state's medical marijuana law,] which legalizes the medical use of marijuana by qualifying patients[. The medical marijuana law] ... recognizes the interconnection between possession, use, and cultivation of marijuana for personal use. Pursuant to [that law,] a "qualifying patient" may in certain circumstances obtain a "cultivation registration," which "shall allow the patient or the patient's personal caregiver to cultivate a limited number of plants, sufficient to maintain a 60-day supply of marijuana, and shall require cultivation and storage only in an enclosed, locked facility."

Where the language of two statutory provisions must be considered, we interpret their meaning "in a manner that, to the greatest extent possible, serves the policies underlying both." ... Interpreting the term "cultivate" in § 32C(a) to exclude growing marijuana for personal use respects both the policies underlying § 32L (decriminalizing possession of marijuana while continuing to criminalize the sale of marijuana) and § 32C(a) (targeting drug trafficking). By adopting a broader interpretation of the offense of cultivation than is necessary to resolve this case, the court's decision fails to advance these legislative goals.

## Notes and Questions

1. Why do jurisdictions treat manufacturing for one's own use as a supply offense? Does the *Palmer* majority provide a satisfactory answer? Is the problem one of proof and uncertainty about whether the defendant really is growing for her own use? Is there a way for government to reliably determine who is growing for personal use? Why did the concurrence believe there were enough facts to suggest "the defendant grew the marijuana with the intent to distribute it"? Ultimately, should manufacturing for one's own use be considered a supply offense?

2. Even if they do not explicitly exempt growing marijuana for personal use from the definition of manufacturing, some jurisdictions limit application of their manufacturing bans to cases involving a minimum number of plants. For example, Kansas proscribes the manufacture of a controlled substance, and it defines manufacture to include cultivation. But it then defines "cultivate" as "the planting or promotion of growth of *five or more* plants which contain or can produce controlled substances." Kan. Stat. Ann. 65-4101(i) (emphasis added). The limitation would, presumably, exempt some persons who cultivate for their own use from the state's ban on the manufacture of marijuana.

3. As discussed earlier, manufacturing includes actions besides cultivation. Do these other actions likewise remain manufacturing offenses when performed for one's personal use of the marijuana? Along these lines, consider the following Problem:

Problem 7.3: Benjamin has 2.5 grams of dried marijuana bud. He decides to make marijuana brownies. He does a quick Google search and finds the following recipe:

Ingredients
Vegetable oil
2.5 grams of dried marijuana bud
Brownie mix (one serving)

Directions
   Grind up the marijuana in a coffee grinder several times. Once it turns into a powder, spread it onto a frying pan. Pour the oil directly onto the powder, using the amount called for by the brownie mix. Turn the burner on low until it starts to simmer and then lower the burner to its lowest setting. Leave the burner on for 2-6 hours (the longer the better) and stir the marijuana in the oil every 30 minutes with a wooden spoon. When you are done, pour the oil mixture into a coffee filter to strain all the excess marijuana out. You should be left with a musky brown color oil without any grass, stems, or seeds in it. Use this oil to make the brownies by following the instructions on the brownie mix.

Suppose Benjamin follows the recipe. Has he thereby manufactured marijuana, in the eyes of the *Horsley* court?

4. As noted by the *Palmer* concurrence, Massachusetts' definition of "manufacture" explicitly "does not include the preparation or compounding of a controlled substance by an individual for his own use" or the "preparation, compounding, packaging, or labeling of a controlled substance . . . by a practitioner . . . or pharmacist." Mass. Gen. L. c. 94C § 1. Many other states have adopted similar exemptions. *E.g.*, *West Virginia v. Underwood*,

281 S.E.2d 491 (W. Va. 1981); *North Carolina v. Childers*, 255 S.E.2d 654 (N.C. App. 1979). The federal CSA includes one as well, but it only applies to pharmacists and other practitioners and *not* to individual users. 21 U.S.C. §802(15).

Assuming Utah had adopted an exception like that of Massachusetts, would the exception have applied to Benjamin's manufacture of marijuana brownies in **Problem 7.3**? In *Childers*, the court defined "preparation and compounding" as the "process of making something ready for use or service" and "the putting together of elements, ingredients or parts to form a whole." 255 S.E.2d at 656. The *Childers* court explained that while the provision would not exempt personal cultivation, it would exempt a person who, "being already in possession of a controlled substance, . . . makes it ready for use (i.e., rolling marijuana into cigarettes for smoking) or combines it with other ingredients for use (i.e., making the so-called 'Alice B. Toklas' brownies containing marijuana)." *Id.*

5. The Massachusetts Supreme Judicial Court has addressed the impact of the 2008 decriminalization act on other supply offenses as well. The *Jackson* and *Keefner* decisions mentioned by the *Palmer* court are discussed below.

### c. Proof of Manufacturing

What sort of evidence must the government produce to satisfy its burden of proving the defendant manufactured marijuana? It is surely enough, at least to get to a jury, if the government produces eyewitness testimony that a defendant watered and trimmed marijuana plants. But suppose that the police have no such testimony to offer. The following Problem raises such a scenario:

Problem 7.4: Following a traffic stop, the police notice three well-tended marijuana plants in the back of Benjamin's car. Benjamin is the driver and sole occupant of the car. Is there enough evidence to charge Benjamin with the *manufacture* of marijuana?

As discussed in Chapter 3, courts usually allow a jury to presume that someone like Benjamin knew of and had dominion over the marijuana, because it was found in property to which he had exclusive access. In similar fashion, courts usually also allow a jury to presume that a "person who knowingly possesses live marijuana plants intends the natural consequence that they grow." *West Virginia v. White*, 280 S.E.2d 114, 120 (W. Va. 1981). But as with possession, the second presumption breaks down when an individual's access to the marijuana plants is not exclusive. The following case discusses the issue.

### Idaho v. Vinton
718 P.2d 1270 (Idaho 1986)

MCFADDEN, J.:
Carl and Marion Vinton, husband and wife, were tried by a jury and convicted of "manufacturing" marijuana . . . On appeal, the Vintons assert that the evidence presented at trial was not sufficient for the jury to have found them guilty of growing marijuana. We hold that the evidence was not sufficient and therefore reverse the convictions.

Acting pursuant to a search warrant, law enforcement officers conducted a search of the defendants' residence and surrounding property on August 26, 1983. During the search the officers found four marijuana plants growing in containers in a corral area approximately fifty feet from the defendants' residence. They also found a plot of 56 marijuana plants growing approximately fifty yards northeast of the defendants' house. Approximately 300 yards northwest of the residence, the officers located an additional plot of 108 marijuana plants growing in a wooded area. Testimony indicated that both of these plots were found after the officers crossed fences. The testimony was confusing as to who actually owned the land where the 56 and the 108 plants were found. However, there was uncontested evidence that Mr. and Mrs. Vinton were joint owners of at least the property where the house and corral were located.

Additional evidence was presented showing that paths led from the curtilage of the defendants' house to the plots of marijuana. The officers also discovered a "bong" pipe in a wood stove in the defendants' house and another pipe in the dresser in the defendants' bedroom. In a small cabin approximately twenty-five feet from the defendants' residence, the officers found another "bong" pipe and marijuana plants being dried. . . .

The defendants base their appeal on two theories: (1) that there was no direct evidence linking the defendants to the marijuana; and (2) there was insufficient evidence to convict them of manufacturing. A review of the evidence indicates that both the defendants owned the realty where the corral was located. The two larger plots of marijuana, if not actually on the defendants' realty, were close enough to be immediately accessible. Buckets of a manure and water mixture similar to that found on many of the plants were found at the defendants' residence. Also, there were paths in the vicinity of the defendants' residence leading from the defendants' property to both of the larger plots of marijuana.

To obtain convictions of manufacturing marijuana the state had the burden of proving beyond a reasonable doubt that each of the defendants had cultivated, or had aided and abetted in cultivating, the marijuana. Testimony of the senior criminal investigator indicated that the four plants in the corral were growing in containers and had been "groomed" to be more productive. He testified that it appeared that many of the plants in the plots of 56 and 108 plants had been watered and fertilized with a horse manure mixture or compost. The officer also noted that these plants had been planted in loosely packed soil that would absorb water more readily, and that the plants were well camouflaged, yet situated to receive a lot of sunlight. Another officer testified that some plants in the group of 56 had been boxed in with poles and that the area at the base of the plants had been cleared of weeds. Still other plants in the group of 108 had small, coded tags attached to them as if to identify certain plants. The evidence was clear that the marijuana was cultivated and not wild. Viewing the evidence in light most favorable to the state, the evidence did tie the defendants as a couple to the cultivation of the marijuana.

However, the evidence suffers a glaring deficiency that demands a reversal of the convictions. That deficiency is that the evidence fails to tie the defendants as individuals in with the commission of the crime. . . . "[I]t is fundamental to our system of criminal law that guilt is individual." . . . The evidence ties the defendants collectively to the marijuana and to the place where it was discovered. However, the evidence does not connect either of them as individuals to the "cultivating or manufacturing" of that marijuana. . . . The most favorable inference that reasonably can be drawn for the state is that the husband or the wife or the couple was responsible for growing the marijuana. However, whether one was guilty and the other innocent cannot be ascertained from the evidence. We refuse to align ourselves with a "guilt by association" type of reasoning, nor to elevate passive joint ownership of land to active participation in a crime.

We readily acknowledge the perplexing problems created in joint ownership or occupancy cases, particularly where, as here, the joint owners or occupants are husband and wife. Such cases require careful police investigation before prosecution. There must be substantial evidence, either direct or circumstantial, that establishes the guilt of each defendant as an individual rather than the collective guilt of two or more persons. In some cases, each of the parties may be guilty. However, the state has the burden of proving so. . . .

Accordingly, the judgments of conviction are reversed.

## Notes and Questions

1. Is *Vinton* consistent with the doctrine of joint possession discussed in Chapter 3? In other words, would the evidence have sustained convictions for *joint* possession of marijuana? If so, should the *Vinton* court have upheld the defendants' convictions on a theory of joint *manufacture*?

2. If you were the prosecutor, how would you have handled the case? What criminal charge(s), if any, would you have brought? What other evidence would you have sought to bolster your case?

### 2. Distribute

Distribution[2] is another quintessential activity associated with supplying marijuana. But what exactly does it mean to "distribute" a drug like marijuana? The term no doubt connotes sales of the drug, as when A sells B a marijuana joint in return for $10. But what about other transfers, as when A gives B a puff of his joint, but asks for nothing in return?

As the materials below demonstrate, jurisdictions almost uniformly define "distribute" broadly to encompass *any transfer* of marijuana from one person to another, whether or not the transferor asked for (or received) anything of value in return. The CSA is representative of the dominant approach to defining distribution. 21 U.S.C. section 841(a) makes it unlawful to "distribute" marijuana. 21 U.S.C. section 802(11) defines "distribute" as "to deliver . . . a controlled substance or a listed chemical." Section 802(8) proceeds to define "deliver" to mean "the actual, constructive, or attempted transfer of a controlled substance. . . ." Under the plain terms of the CSA, then,

$$\text{distribute} = \text{deliver} = \text{transfer}$$

---

2. Some jurisdictions employ slightly different terminology (e.g., deliver, dispense, or furnish) in lieu of or in addition to "distribute." For ease of exposition, however, the book uses the term "distribute" to subsume all of these closely related terms.

Part III. Marijuana Suppliers

Not surprisingly, this definition of distribution can be applied to a broad array of factual scenarios. Consider the following Problem:

**Problem 7.5**: Camila and Delilah together buy marijuana for their mutual enjoyment. They go to a party. Camila pulls the joint from her pocket, lights it, and takes a puff. She then passes it to Delilah, who takes a puff. Delilah passes it back to Camila, and so on. Is Camila guilty of distribution? Is Delilah?

The Problem raises the question whether the law should treat *all* transfers as supply offenses, and, if not, how the law should distinguish among transfers. The following cases explore two limitations that could be applied to the definition of distribute.

### a. Commercial Purpose

One way to limit the definition of distribute would be to require a commercial purpose behind any transfer—i.e., to require the government to show that a defendant expected to receive something in return for the drug. As it stands, however, the vast majority of prohibition regimes have refused to require a commercial purpose for distribution offenses, just as they have refused to require a commercial purpose for manufacture offenses (as discussed in Section A.1.b above). *E.g., Vermont v. Francis*, 568 A.2d 389 (Vt. 1989).

The following two cases take opposite positions on this limitation.

## *Meek v. Mississippi*
806 So. 2d 236 (Miss. 2001)

SMITH, J.:

March Meek was a passenger in Delinah Chauvin's car when they were involved in a serious accident. Before entering the car, Meek had placed several items in the back seat of the vehicle. One of those items was a shaving kit. Both Chauvin and Meek were injured in the accident. Meek was unable to get out of the vehicle until help arrived.

Phillip Hemby arrived at the scene and offered to help the victims. Hemby testified that when he approached Meek's side of the car, Meek handed him a shaving kit and asked him to "get rid of this." Hemby said that he was suspicious of the contents of the shaving kit . . . [because] he could smell marijuana. Hemby testified that he immediately handed the kit back to Meek. Hemby then left to help the driver of the other vehicle.

Chauvin testified that Meek asked her if she could get out of the car because he wanted her to dispose of something. She was unable or unwilling to discard the contraband. When Hemby returned to Chauvin's car, he saw the shaving kit lying on the shoulder of the road on Meek's side of the car, approximately 12 to 15 feet from the passenger door. Hemby testified that he kicked the shaving kit into a roadside ditch to preserve the kit as evidence for law enforcement officers. Hemby later directed a highway patrolman to the shaving kit on the side of the road. The officer opened it and found what appeared to be marijuana inside. An analysis by the Mississippi Crime Laboratory revealed that the kit contained over 140 grams of marijuana.

. . .

Meek was indicted for transferring the marijuana to Hemby when he handed the shaving kit containing the marijuana through the car window following the accident. The trial court concluded that "to transfer means to pass from one hand to the other." [The jury found Meek guilty. On appeal,] Meek argues that his actions did not amount to a transfer within the meaning of the relevant statute. We disagree.

Miss. Code Ann. § 41-29-139 (Supp. 2001) provides in part:

> (a) Except as authorized by this article, it is unlawful for any person knowingly or intentionally:
>
> > (1) To sell, barter, transfer, manufacture, distribute, dispense or possess with intent to sell, barter, transfer, manufacture, distribute or dispense a controlled substance. . . .

A definition of "transfer" is not statutorily provided. However, there are two words defined in the act that aid in the understanding of what "transfer" means. Miss. Code Ann. § 41-29-105 (Supp. 2001) provides in part:

> (h) "Deliver" or "delivery" means the actual, constructive, or attempted transfer from one person to another of a controlled substance, whether or not there is an agency relationship. . . .
>
> (l) "Distribute" means to deliver other than by administering or dispensing a controlled substance.

These terms are virtually interchangeable. We have analyzed the broad language contained in these definitions as being intended "to relieve the state of the task, oftentimes difficult if not impossible, of proving the consideration paid for the contraband, its intentions being to thwart the exchange or transfer of the substance whether accompanied by consideration or not." . . . As the Court of Appeals plurality explained, the definitions indicate that "the exchange of consideration, the intent to place the contraband in commerce, and even the success of the transfer are irrelevant to a factual determination of transfer or delivery." . . .

Meek argues that his actions did not constitute a transfer because he did not intend to place the contraband in commerce nor intend to distribute the substance for economic gain. However, we have held that "distributing" a controlled substance as defined in the statute "includes transactions which are sales as well as transactions which may not be considered sales." . . . The intent of the deliver and transfer of narcotics statute is "to thwart the exchange or transfer of the substance whether accompanied by consideration or not." . . .

A transfer is a change of possession from one person to another. . . . Also, a transfer is any act by which the holder of an object delivers it to another with the intent of passing whatever rights he has in the latter. . . . The word "deliver" has been defined by this Court to be the equivalent of the word "transfer." . . . In applying the term "deliver" to the facts of this case, it is clear from this term's definition that Meek "actually, constructively, or attempted to transfer" his bag from himself to Hemby, who was immediately aware that the shaving kit contained marijuana. The shaving kit clearly passed from Meek's hands to another's, while Meek had the requisite intent to get this item out of his possession. There is no logical conclusion other than that Meek knew what was in the shaving kit, and he intended to conceal it by getting it out of his hands into the hands of another. . . .

. . . . We find that the only intent necessary . . . is that Meek, the transferor, have knowledge of the character and presence of the controlled substance and that he

Part III. Marijuana Suppliers

intentionally transfer it to another with the intent to part with possession and control. That is exactly what occurred here.

Meek also argues that because Hemby never took the marijuana but immediately handed it back to Meek, the transfer was frustrated and never occurred. We have stated that "[p]ossession, no matter how fleeting, is sufficient to sustain a conviction [for possession with intent to deliver]." . . . Likewise, the fact that the handling by Hemby was momentary should not be a factor in determining whether there was a transfer in fact.

## Notes and Questions

1. Why does the *Meek* court refuse to limit distribution (and related terms) to sale? Are you persuaded? Under the court's definition of distribution, is Hemby (the good Samaritan) *also* guilty of distribution? After all, Hemby gave the shaving kit back to Meek—i.e., transferred it—suspecting that it contained marijuana. If Hemby could be found guilty of distribution, does this suggest that the court's definition of distribution needs to be limited in some way?

2. Even if you think the defendant (Meek) was a drug supplier, was it necessary for the government to charge him with *distribution* of marijuana? Do you think the government could have convicted him of possession with the intent to distribute the marijuana instead? Had the government taken that route, would the *Meek* court have needed to decide whether distribution encompasses more than the sale of marijuana (or other drugs)? The crime of possession with intent to distribute is discussed in Section A.3 below.

---

In the next case, the court breaks rank with *Meek* and the majority of jurisdictions by holding that in order to obtain a conviction for distribution, the government must prove the defendant had a commercial purpose, at least when the crime involves a small amount of marijuana.

### *Massachusetts v. Jackson*
985 N.E.2d 853 (Mass. 2013)

DUFFLY, J.:

After police officers observed the defendant sharing what appeared to be a marijuana cigarette with two others on a park bench, they seized the cigarette and conducted a warrantless search of the defendant's person and backpack. In the backpack, they discovered a substance resembling marijuana packaged in small plastic bags, with a total weight of less than one ounce. The defendant was arrested and charged with possession of a class D substance (marijuana) with intent to distribute, G.L. c. 94C, § 32C. . . .

The defendant moved to suppress the evidence obtained from the warrantless search of his person and backpack, contending that the search violated the Fourth and Fourteenth Amendments to the United States Constitution . . . [and state law]. . . .

We conclude that the search was not a lawful search incident to arrest, because the officers had no basis to arrest the defendant before searching him. The officers' observation of the defendant and two others passing what appeared to be a marijuana cigarette back and forth did not provide probable cause to believe the defendant was committing a crime. . . .

. . .

This case turns on whether Officers . . . lawfully could have arrested the defendant after observing him share with his companions a cigarette that the officers reasonably suspected to contain marijuana. If not, their search of the defendant and his backpack cannot be justified as a search incident to a lawful arrest. The Commonwealth argues that the officers could have arrested the defendant because they had probable cause to believe that he had or was about to commit the crime of marijuana distribution. . . . This argument requires us to resolve the issue reserved in [*Massachusetts v. Keefner*, 961 N.E.2d 1083 (2012)]: whether the voters' adoption of "An Act establishing a sensible State marihuana policy" (2008 initiative) decriminalized the social sharing of one ounce or less of marijuana by modifying which acts constitute distribution. . . .

As a threshold matter, [the Act] . . . states that the decriminalization of small amounts of marijuana shall not "be construed to repeal or modify" the following four categories of existing laws: those concerning (1) the operation of motor vehicles "or other actions taken while under the influence of" marijuana, (2) unlawful possession of prescription forms of marijuana, (3) possession of more than one ounce of marijuana, and (4) the "selling, manufacturing or trafficking" in marijuana. We held in *Keefner*, . . . that this list "cannot be construed as exhaustive," and that distributing one ounce or less of marijuana remains a crime. However, we explicitly left open the possibility that the 2008 initiative modified the definition of what constitutes distribution under the distribution statute, such that the social sharing of marijuana is no longer a crime. . . .[3]

We begin with an examination of the distribution statute. Certain relevant terms are defined by the statute: "[d]istribute" means "to deliver other than by administering or dispensing a controlled substance"; "[d]eliver" means "to transfer, whether by actual or constructive transfer, a controlled substance from one person to another, whether or not there is an agency relationship." . . . "Transfer" is undefined in the statute, but its dictionary meaning is to "convey or remove from one place or one person to another; to pass or hand over from one to another, [especially] to change over the possession or control of." Black's Law Dictionary 1636 (9th ed. 2009).

In interpreting the distribution statute in situations where a defendant purchases drugs and then gives them to others, we have distinguished between "circumstances where a defendant facilitates a transfer of drugs from a seller to a buyer," which can constitute the

---

3. Indeed, we expressed doubt in . . . *Keefner*, . . . that the social sharing of marijuana constitutes the crime of distribution, in light of G.L. c. 94C, § 32L. We observed that, if the social sharing of marijuana did amount to drug distribution, the following "ironic consequence" would result:

"[T]he Commonwealth may criminally charge each person who passed the marijuana cigarette to another with distribution of marijuana or possession with intent to distribute, in violation of [G.L. c. 94C,] § 32C(a), even though such individuals could not be charged criminally with possession of marijuana, because the amount of marijuana each possessed was one ounce or less. The ironic consequence of such an interpretation would be that, as a result of the passage of G.L. c. 94C, § 32L, which was intended to decriminalize the possession of a small quantity of marijuana, individuals who share a marijuana cigarette would still be charged criminally, but the charge would now be more serious than simple possession, with a maximum sentence of two years in a house of correction rather than six months."

crime of distribution even if the defendant intends to share some of the drug with the buyer, . . . and "the passing of a drug between joint possessors who simultaneously acquire possession at the outset for their own use," which does not constitute distribution. . . . The unifying principle underlying these cases is that a defendant who gives drugs to others "distributes" those drugs whenever the defendant serves as "a link in the chain" between supplier and consumer. . . .

We have not addressed whether, by sharing a marijuana cigarette that was not jointly acquired by the person sharing it, a person acts as a link in the drug distribution chain, i.e., "facilitates a transfer of drugs from a seller to a buyer." . . . Thus, even before the enactment of [the Act], we had not determined whether the social sharing of marijuana violated the distribution statute. Such an interpretation would not have served the distribution statute's original purpose, which was to target those "in the drug business." . . . As the Governor explained to the Legislature when proposing the 1980 legislation that added the distribution statute to the General Laws, "The time has come to launch a new, more aggressive campaign against those *who operate and profit* from the death-dealing traffic in drugs. . . . We need major changes in the way our criminal system deals with *these dealers in drugs*." . . .

We now decide that the social sharing of marijuana is akin to simple possession, and does not constitute the facilitation of a drug transfer from seller to buyer that remains the hallmark of drug distribution. . . . We therefore conclude that the social sharing of marijuana does not violate the distribution statute.

Our conclusion is informed by the clear policy goals served by the passage of [the 2008 Act]: to reduce the direct and collateral consequences of possessing small amounts of marijuana, to direct law enforcement's attention to serious crime, and to save taxpayer resources previously devoted to targeting the simple possession of marijuana. . . . Significantly, "the entire statutory scheme . . . implicates police conduct in the field. Ferreting out decriminalized conduct with the same fervor associated with the pursuit of serious criminal conduct is neither desired by the public nor in accord with the plain language of the statute." . . .

As a result of the enactment of [the 2008 Act], the observation by police that an individual possesses a small amount of marijuana does not justify a warrantless search. . . .

Because Officers . . . did not have probable cause to arrest the defendant when they observed him sharing a marijuana cigarette with two others, the subsequent search of the defendant's person and backpack was not justified as a search incident to a lawful arrest. . . . [The defendant's motion to suppress the evidence is granted.]

## Notes and Questions

1. Does the *Jackson* court satisfactorily respond to the textualist reasoning of *Meek*? To what extent does the *Jackson* court's opinion rest on the passage of the 2008 Act decriminalizing simple possession of one ounce or less of marijuana? Had Massachusetts not passed the 2008 Act, would the court have reached the same conclusion that the social sharing of marijuana does not constitute the distribution of the drug? If so, would that holding still be limited to cases involving one ounce or less of marijuana?

2. Arkansas is perhaps the only state that that has, by statute, refused to treat the simple transfer of marijuana without remuneration as a distribution offense. Arkansas's

statute defines "distribute" and "deliver" as the "the actual, constructive, or attempted transfer from one (1) person to another of a controlled substance or counterfeit substance *in exchange for money or anything of value*, whether or not there is an agency relationship." Ark. Code Ann. § 5-64-101(6) (West 2016) (emphasis added).

3. Which is the better approach? Should jurisdictions narrow the definition of distribution to include only sales? Would it be too difficult for prosecutors to prove remuneration? How could they do so?

4. Even though nearly all jurisdictions label gratuitous transfers as distribution offenses, many of them punish such transfers less severely than profit motivated transfers. For example, 21 U.S.C. section 841(b)(4) provides that,

> Notwithstanding paragraph (1)(D) of this subsection [specifying punishment for supply cases involving less than 50 kg of marijuana, 50 or fewer marijuana plants, 10 kg or less of hashish, or 1 kg or less of hashish oil], any person who violates subsection (a) of this section by distributing a small amount of marihuana for no remuneration shall be treated as provided in section 844 of this title [the provision applicable to simple possession of marijuana]. . . .

This provision does not create a distinct offense—that is, distributing a small quantity of marijuana for no remuneration still constitutes a distribution offense for purposes of federal law. Rather, it mitigates the penalty that applies to such distribution, instructing courts to sentence the defendant under section 844(a) (governing misdemeanor simple possession) rather than under section 841(b) (governing felony supply).

In *United States v. Outen*, then-Judge Sonia Sotomayor explained the purpose of section 841(b)(4):

> We believe that Congress intended that § 841(b)(4) be a mitigating exception to the five-year [maximum] provision of § 841(b)(1)(D). First, as indicated by the introductory phrase of § 841(b)(4) ("Notwithstanding paragraph (1)(D) of this subsection"), distribution of a small amount of marijuana for no remuneration is an activity prohibited by § 841(a) and covered by the penalty provisions of § 841(b)(1)(D), and therefore represents an exception to an otherwise applicable penalty. Second, there is reason to consider the activity mostly contemplated by § 841(b)(4)—namely, the sharing of small amounts of marijuana in social situations—to be not just one of lesser degree than those covered by (b)(1)(D) but of a different type more akin to simple possession than to provisions intended to cover traffickers. The legislative history of this amendment suggests that Congress took exactly this view. See, e.g., Cong. Rec. 35,555 (Oct. 7, 1970) (statement of Sen. Hughes) ("[t]rafficking provisions should apply to the large distributor, rather than to the person who is only using the drug with his friends.").

286 F.3d 622, 637-38 (2d Cir. 2002).

Because the provision acts as a mitigating provision, section 841(b)(4) also functions much like an affirmative defense. This means that the defendant bears the burden of raising the issue and producing evidence in support thereof. In other words, the government need not disprove the mitigating facts—small amount and no remuneration—and if the defendant fails to make her showing, section 841(b)(1)(D) specifies the minimum sentence that is applicable. *Id.*

5. What is a small amount for purposes of section 841(b)(4)? Federal courts have declined to set hard and fast rules. The amount may depend on the context. *See, e.g., United States v. Damerville*, 27 F.3d 254 (7th Cir. 1994) (17 grams is not a small amount

*in prison*). Some states with a similar rule specify the quantity by statute. *See, e.g.*, W. Va. Code § 60A-4-402(c) (providing that person convicted of first offense of distributing 15 grams or less of marijuana without remuneration is entitled to probation in lieu of imprisonment).

6. Several states have a rule similar to section 841(b)(4). *See* Brief of Respondent Eric H. Holder, *Moncrieffe v. Holder*, 2012 WL 3803440, at 26 ("A minority of States (up to 15) treat separately—either through a lower sentencing provision/exemption similar to section 841(b)(4) or through a distinct offense—distribution of a 'small amount' of marijuana for no remuneration."). In some states, however, the rules permit remuneration up to the cost of the drug—what is known as "accommodation"—and may apply to larger quantities than allowed under federal law. For example, Virginia makes it "unlawful for any person to sell, give, distribute or possess with intent to sell, give or distribute marijuana." Va. Code. § 18.2. The statute sets the punishment according to the quantities involved, ranging from not more than 1 year in jail for offenses involving half an ounce or less to 5 to 30 years' imprisonment for offenses involving more than five pounds. *Id.* at (a)(1)-(3). The statute, however, also provides that notwithstanding the quantity involved, "[i]f such person proves that he gave, distributed or possessed with intent to give or distribute marijuana only as an accommodation to another individual and not with intent to profit thereby from any consideration received or expected nor to induce the recipient or intended recipient of the marijuana to use or become addicted to or dependent upon such marijuana, he shall be guilty of a Class 1 misdemeanor" punishable by not more than 1 year in jail. *Id.*

The court in *Stillwell v. Virginia* discusses a previous iteration of the Virginia rule and the rationale behind it:

> [In passing the Drug Control Act, [t]he General Assembly . . . concluded that the sale, possession and distribution of drugs, which in some places had reached epidemic proportions, was being carried on as a commercial enterprise and for a profit. The legislature therefore, with few authorized exceptions, made it Unlawful for Any person to manufacture, sell, give, distribute or possess with intent to manufacture, sell, give or distribute a controlled substance. And it defined marijuana as a controlled substance. It was a logical and reasonable assumption that a person who committed any of these acts was engaged in a commercial venture and for profit. Marijuana is not traded in the legitimate market place. It is an unlawful drug for which there is a large demand, and in its trafficking huge profits are reputedly made. There was therefore a rational and reasonable connection and relation between the fact of sale or distribution and the conclusion that it was with intent to profit hence the rebuttable presumption against an accommodation sale or distribution.
>
> However, the General Assembly was cognizant of the fact that in some instances a sale or distribution of a drug would be made, not by a dealer in drugs, a pusher or one who was normally engaged in the drug traffic, but by an individual citizen who was motivated by a desire to accommodate a friend, without any intent to profit or to induce or to encourage the use of drugs. Therefore, [Virginia law] . . . provides for the mitigation of punishment for those who are less culpable. And [the statute] . . . takes note of the fact that a defendant is the person with the greatest knowledge and easiest access to evidence to show that his sale or distribution was one of accommodation and not a commercial transaction, and therefore relieves the Commonwealth of what would amount to an impossible burden of affirmatively negating every exception, excuse, proviso or exemption claimed by a defendant.

... The statutory scheme behind [the Virginia statute] provides that once the guilt of the defendant has been established (a determination completely independent of the profit-accommodation distinction), a second determination of the proper punishment is to be made. This statute . . . place[s] the burden of proving the existence of an accommodation distribution (and the right to the lesser penalty) to the trier of fact on the shoulders of the defendant. In other words, the statute contains a presumption against an accommodation distribution to the extent that it is relevant to the determination of the proper degree of punishment, but only after guilt has been established. . . .

A defendant, charged with an unlawful sale of drugs, who defends on the ground that he distributed the drugs for accommodation only, is not required to establish such accommodation beyond a reasonable doubt, but only by a preponderance of the evidence. He is required to produce some evidence which satisfies the trier of the facts that his distribution was for accommodation. The presumption created by the statute retains its effect until opposing evidence (whether from the Commonwealth or the defendant) is sufficient to make a case for the jury, that is, to convince the judge that a jury could reasonably find that the defendant was an accommodation distributor. . . .

247 S.E.2d 360, 363-67 (Va. 1978).

7. *Jackson* holds that the non-commercial transfer of marijuana is not a supply offense for purposes of Massachusetts law. In *Palmer, supra,* however, the same court held that the non-commercial *cultivation* of marijuana *is* a supply offense. Can the two decisions be reconciled? (Note that Justice Duffly, the author of *Jackson*, only concurred in *Palmer*.) Does section 841(b)(4) raise a similar issue? Consider the following Problem:

Problem 7.6: Andy gave a small amount of marijuana to his friend Delilah, receiving nothing in return. Benjamin grew a small amount of marijuana for his friend Delilah, for which he expected to receive nothing in return. Camila possessed with the intent to distribute to her friend Delilah a small quantity of marijuana for no remuneration. To which of these three cases—Andy, Benjamin, and Camila—is 21 U.S.C. section 841 (b)(4) applicable? *See United States v. Campbell*, 317 F.3d 597, 603 (6th Cir. 2003); *United States v. Laakkonen*, 59 Fed. Appx. 90 (6th Cir. 2003) (unpublished). Do you think Congress meant to exclude supply offenses other than distribution from the coverage of section 841(b)(4)? If not, should courts attempt to fix apparent oversights in statutory drafting?

### b. Distribution Between Joint Possessors

Chapter 3 discussed the doctrine of joint possession, which allows the government to prove that two (or more) persons possessed the same marijuana. As the *Jackson* court briefly mentions above, some jurisdictions have held that joint possessors (like Camila and Delilah in **Problem 7.5** above) do not *distribute* a drug when they transfer it between themselves. *United States v. Swiderski* is the most notable case recognizing that transfers between joint possessors of the same drug do not constitute distribution.

## *United States v. Swiderski*
548 F.2d 445 (2d Cir. 1977)

MANSFIELD, J.:

[Walter Swiderski and his fiancée Maritza De Los Santos together bought 21 grams of a substance containing cocaine from a government informant. When later apprehended, the couple claimed they planned to share the drug between themselves. The government charged them with possession with intent to distribute the cocaine. The judge instructed the jury that

> "[I]ntent to distribute merely means that you intend at some point or later time to pass on all or some of it; it means you intend to sell it; it means you intend to give it away; you can intend to give it to a friend of yours or somebody who is close to you. If you are going to pass it on, that is to distribute under the statute."

However, after deliberating for two hours, the jury asked the judge for clarification about the meaning of distribute: "If both defendants possess the drug (i.e., one paid for it and it was found in the other's handbag) can 'intent to distribute' mean giving the drug to the other or must third parties be involved?" In reply, the trial judge made it clear over defense objections that distribution could be satisfied solely by a transfer between Swiderski and De Los Santos:

> "Well, intent to distribute merely means that you intend at some point at a later time to pass all or some of it on. It could mean a sale; it could mean that you could give it away. You could give it to a friend of yours or even to your fiancee. If you are going to do that, that is a distribution."

The jury proceeded to find the defendants guilty of possession with intent to distribute and they appealed.]

Title 21 U.S.C. § 841(a) . . . makes it unlawful to "possess with intent to . . . distribute . . . a controlled substance." . . . [and] 21 U.S.C. § 802(11) defines "distribute" as meaning "to deliver." Section 802(8) defines the term "deliver" or "delivery" as meaning "the actual, constructive, or attempted transfer of a controlled substance, whether or not there exists an agency relationship." The precise issue raised by the appellants is whether a statutory "transfer" may occur between two individuals in joint possession of a controlled substance simultaneously acquired for their own use.

In order to interpret the foregoing words of the Act it is important to understand their place in the statutory drug enforcement scheme as a whole, which draws a sharp distinction between drug offenses of a commercial nature and illicit personal use of controlled substances. . . . Section 841, which punishes the manufacture, distribution, or dispensation of controlled substances or the possession of such substances with intent to manufacture, distribute or dispense, provides for a maximum sentence of 15 years imprisonment, a fine of up to $25,000, or both, plus a special parole term of at least 3 years. In contrast, § 844(a) provides that one guilty of simple possession of a controlled substance without a prescription shall be punished by a sentence of imprisonment for not more than one year for a first offender, a fine of not more than $5,000 or both. . . .

Congress' reasoning in providing more severe penalties for commercial trafficking in and distribution of narcotics was that such conduct tends to have the dangerous, unwanted effect of drawing additional participants into the web of drug abuse. For this reason the House Report [on the CSA] equated "transactions involving others" and "distribution to others" with the harsher penalties provided by §§ 841 and 848. Where only individual possession and use is concerned, on the other hand, the Act prescribes lesser penalties and emphasizes rehabilitation of the drug abuser. Similarly, where two individuals simultaneously and jointly acquire possession of a drug for their own use, intending only to share it together, their only crime is personal drug abuse simple joint possession, without any intent to distribute the drug further. Since both acquire possession from the outset and neither intends to distribute the drug to a third person, neither serves as a link in the chain of distribution. For purposes of the Act they must therefore be treated as possessors for personal use rather than for further distribution. Their simple joint possession does not pose any of the evils which Congress sought to deter and punish through the more severe penalties provided for those engaged in a "continuing criminal enterprise" or in drug distribution.

Of course, joint possession of a drug does not preclude a finding of possession with intent to distribute to a third person in violation of § 841(a). Whether such an inference may be drawn depends upon the surrounding circumstances, including the nature of the relationship (whether it is commercial rather than personal), the quantity of the drug (whether it is too large for personal use only), the number of people involved, and statements or conduct on the part of the defendants. . . . But the mere existence of joint possession by two closely related persons here an engaged couple who later married one another is alone not enough to provide the basis for such an inference. Whatever else may be embraced within the term "transfer," a term that is not defined in the Act, we are persuaded that it was not intended to include the exchange of physical possession between two persons who jointly acquired and hold the drug for their own use. . . .

In support of its argument that the sharing of drugs between two persons who simultaneously acquire joint possession with a view to using a drug in friendly "snorts" or "blows," satisfies § 841(a)'s requirement of "intent to distribute," the government directs our attention to § 802(8) which states that a delivery may occur "whether or not there exists an agency relationship" between transferor and transferee. If an agent may be guilty of violating § 841(a) on the basis of his delivering drugs to his principal, the argument goes, joint possessors who share drugs should likewise be guilty, since each acts as the other's agent in transferring physical possession of any of the drug to the other. This contention, however, runs counter to Congress' intent, which was to distinguish between one who acts as a link in the chain of distribution and one who has already acquired possession for his own use.

The agent who delivers to his principal performs a service in increasing the distribution of narcotics. Without the agent's services the principal might never come into possession of the drug. Purchasers who simultaneously acquire a drug jointly for their own purpose, however, do not perform any service as links in the chain; they are the ultimate users. Moreover, the history of the "agency" clause militates against the government's interpretation. The clause was intended by Congress simply to insure elimination of the so-called "procuring agent defense" that had existed under the drug laws as they stood prior to the Act. Under the earlier laws, which prescribed stiff penalties for individuals involved in any sale of drugs, a defendant could escape liability as a buyer of narcotics by showing that he had purchased the drug as an agent acting upon instructions of his principal. . . .

The language of § 802(8) eliminated the "procuring agent" defense, . . . by substituting the concept of "distribution" in place of the operative concept of a "sale," a result consistent with Congress' intent to penalize severely individuals engaged in procuring drugs for others, while providing less serious penalties for those involved in personal drug abuse. Thus, under current law, the agent who delivers drugs to a principal is liable as a distributor under 21 U.S.C. § 841, while his principal, who receives the drug for personal use, is subject to a charge of simple possession under 21 U.S.C. § 844, unless it is proven directly or by inference that the user intends further to distribute the substance. We must reject the government's suggestion at oral argument that in such a case the principal would nevertheless be liable as an aider and abettor of the agent's distribution to him, since this would totally undermine the statutory scheme. Its effect would be to write out of the Act the offense of simple possession, since under such a theory every drug abuser would be liable for aiding and abetting the distribution which led to his own possession.

Applying these principles here, there was some evidence from which the jury might have inferred that appellants intended to transfer some or all of the narcotics purchased by them to a third person. . . . However, the judge's repeated instruction to the effect that an intent to distribute could be inferred from the mere giving of the drug "to a friend of yours or even to your fiancee" was error, which cannot be labelled harmless, since the jury's request indicated that its verdict might well turn on whether the passing of some or all of the drugs between the two appellants would constitute a distribution in violation of the Act. Furthermore, the Assistant United States Attorney had argued in summation that such a passing would suffice. . . .

Since the jury necessarily found all of the elements of simple possession in violation of 21 U.S.C. § 844 and rejected all of the appellants' defenses, and since we are convinced that the defendants will not be prejudiced thereby, we remand for the entry of judgment accordingly and for resentencing on this lesser-included offense [of simple possession]. . . .

## Notes and Questions

1. Many jurisdictions have recognized the so-called *Swiderski* exception to drug distribution charges. However, jurisdictions that have done so generally limit the exception to situations in which the defendants played equal roles in acquiring the drug and not merely possessing it. In light of this limitation, consider the following Problem:

Problem 7.7: Andy and his friends are regular marijuana users. After hearing about hazardous chemicals found in marijuana bought from street dealers, Andy decided to plant marijuana in his backyard. In the months that followed, Andy's friends contributed money, seeds, and labor to the care of the marijuana plants. In late summer, Andy harvested some of the marijuana, which he divided among himself and his friends. Is Andy guilty of distribution? See *Maine v. Toppan*, 425 A.2d 1336 (Me. 1981).

2. Why does the law punish distribution of drugs like marijuana? Does either the joint possession limitation recognized in *Swiderski* or the commercial purpose limitation recognized in *Jackson* undermine the purposes of this prohibition? How would you define distribution?

### 3. Possession with Intent to Distribute or to Manufacture

The third and final core supply offense is the possession of marijuana with the intent to distribute or to manufacture it. This crime has two elements which the government must satisfy:

(1) the defendant possessed marijuana
(2) with the intent to distribute or to manufacture it

The first element is the crime of simple possession studied above in Chapter 3. There is no need to discuss it further here. Suffice to say that failure to establish defendant's possession of marijuana is fatal to any charge of possession with the intent to distribute. It is the second element—intent—that distinguishes this crime from simple possession and that shall be the focus of this section. Because most charges involve possession with the intent to *distribute* (PWID) marijuana, the section focuses on that charge.

### Notes and Questions

1. Why punish PWID? The rationale is that it is difficult to catch people in the act of distributing marijuana (even though distribution is defined broadly). The transfer of the drug could take place in a fleeting, secreted moment—in a car, a parking lot, a private home, etc. But a distributor commonly will have possession of the drug for a much longer period of time before any such transfer takes place. In this way, the rationale for proscribing possession with intent to distribute is similar to the rationale for proscribing simple possession: it eases enforcement of the law.

2. Distribution has the same meaning for purposes of PWID as it does for actual distribution. In most jurisdictions, the government need only show that the defendant intended to transfer marijuana to another person. But consider the following Problem:

> Problem 7.8: Andy lives in Boston, Massachusetts. He just bought ½ ounce of marijuana. Andy put the marijuana in his glove compartment. He plans to share the marijuana with his friend Benjamin during a weekend football tailgate party. Is Andy guilty of PWID under Massachusetts law? *Compare Massachusetts v. Keefner*, 961 N.E.2d 1083 (2012) (holding that 2008 Act decriminalizing simple possession did not decriminalize PWID), *with Jackson, supra* (holding that social sharing is not distribution).

Part III. Marijuana Suppliers

### a. Proof of Intent to Distribute

As with other mens rea elements, one of the key issues that arises in PWID cases is how to prove that a defendant had the requisite intent to distribute the drug. Courts have held that the government may meet its burden by introducing a variety of circumstantial evidence, including possession of large quantities that are inconsistent with personal use, packaging that is indicative of future distribution, and possession of paraphernalia more commonly used by drug suppliers than drug users, such as scales, firearms, baggies, and large amounts of cash.

The following cases consider the sufficiency of different types and combinations of evidence introduced by the government. In the first case, *United States v. Glenn*, the government's evidence is relatively strong and straightforward; in the case that follows it, *North Carolina v. Wilkins*, the government's proof is less substantial.

## United States v. Glenn
667 F.2d 1269 (9th Cir. 1982)

FLETCHER, J.:

On June 6, 1980, Glenn was stopped by Ranger Matthew Ducasse while driving through Yosemite National Park. His driving was erratic, and his behavior after being stopped suggested that he might be under the influence of drugs.

Ducasse asked Glenn to get out of his car. He then spotted a glass jar containing hand-rolled cigarettes on the floor of the car . . . [which] proved to contain phencyclidine (PCP), a controlled substance. High levels of PCP were found in Glenn's blood and urine.

Ducasse testified that when he removed the PCP cigarettes from the car, he saw a jacket on the front seat with a plastic bag containing a leafy substance protruding from the pocket. He also testified that he saw a grey plastic tool box under the jacket, with another plastic bag containing a leafy substance protruding from it. Ducasse then seized the tool box and opened it. It contained sixteen small plastic bags of marijuana, a box of plastic sandwich bags, a 100-gram scale, a package of cigarette papers, and a map of Yosemite with several lists of numbers written on the back. Several additional bags of marijuana were found in the jacket. . . .

[The jury convicted Glenn of possession with intent to distribute the marijuana, in violation of 21 U.S.C. section 841(a)(1), among other offenses. On appeal, Glenn argued that the evidence was insufficient to prove he intended to distribute the marijuana found in his possession.]

The evidence introduced at trial showed that Glenn possessed approximately 185 grams (between five and six ounces) of marijuana. An expert witness testified that this was considerably more than a person would ordinarily possess for personal use. The marijuana was divided into small packages, as if for sale. Glenn was carrying a 100-gram scale, and a box of plastic sandwich bags suitable for packaging marijuana. In addition, the evidence showed that Glenn had several hundred dollars on his person when he was arrested, although he was unemployed; that he was arrested on payday for Yosemite employees; and that he had written on a Yosemite map several columns of figures which could have been calculations of profit.

Glenn testified . . . he bought the marijuana for his personal use, and that he had bought a large amount because the price was good. He claimed that the scale was to ensure that he had not been cheated, and that the cash came from odd jobs and a tax refund.

In reviewing the sufficiency of the evidence to support a criminal conviction, we inquire whether a rational trier of fact could have found the essential elements of the crime beyond a reasonable doubt.... We view the evidence in the light most favorable to the Government.... Applying this standard, we conclude that a rational trier of fact could have chosen to disbelieve Glenn's testimony. From the Government's evidence, a rational trier of fact could have inferred that Glenn intended to sell the marijuana in his possession....

### *North Carolina v. Wilkins*
703 S.E.2d 807 (N.C. App. 2010)

HUNTER, J.:

[Defendant Kendrick Wilkins was driving alone when he was stopped by Police Officer Bunt. When Officer Bunt] knocked on the driver's side window, defendant "kind of turned . . . away" and "refused to open" the window or the car door. Officer Bunt then opened the driver's side door, and, [after confirming defendant's identity, arrested him based on outstanding warrants.] . . .

Upon searching defendant subsequent to the arrest, Officer Bunt discovered a small plastic bag inside of defendant's pocket, which contained three smaller bags. Each of the three bags were "tied off" at the top and contained a substance Officer Bunt believed to be marijuana. The substance was later weighed and determined to be 1.89 grams of marijuana. Defendant testified that he purchased the marijuana for personal use and that typically marijuana can be bought in "nickel" or "dime" bags for $5.00 to $10.00 each.

During the pat down, Officer Bunt also found $1,264.00 in cash separated into 60 $20.00 bills, one $10.00 bill, nine $5.00 bills, and nine $1.00 bills. At trial, defendant testified that approximately $1,000.00 of the cash recovered was for a cash bond that his mother gave to him and the remaining $264.00 was from a check he had cashed. Defendant testified that he was carrying cash because he was "on the run" and if he were arrested the bail bondsman would not accept a check. Defendant was charged with [possession with intent to sell or deliver (PWISD)].

At trial, the jury was instructed on PWISD and misdemeanor possession of marijuana. The jury found defendant guilty of PWISD. . . .

Defendant's sole argument on appeal is that the trial court erred in denying his motion to dismiss the PWISD charge. We agree. . . .

"While intent [to sell or deliver] may be shown by direct evidence, it is often proven by circumstantial evidence from which it may be inferred." . . . "[T]he intent to sell or [deliver] may be inferred from (1) the packaging, labeling, and storage of the controlled substance, (2) the defendant's activities, (3) the quantity found, and (4) the presence of cash or drug paraphernalia." . . . "Although 'quantity of the controlled substance alone may suffice to support the inference of an intent to transfer, sell, or deliver,' it must be a substantial amount." . . .

In the present case, only 1.89 grams of marijuana was found on defendant's person, which alone is insufficient to prove that defendant had the intent to sell or deliver. . . .

The State points to the fact that the marijuana seized from defendant was separated into three smaller packages. Officer Bunt testified that marijuana is typically sold "in bags in different sizes." Based on his training and experience, Officer Bunt believed that each bag of marijuana found in defendant's pocket would sell for between $5.00 and $10.00 each. "The method of packaging a controlled substance, as well as the amount of the substance, may constitute evidence from which a jury can infer an intent to distribute." . . . The State has not pointed to a case, nor have we found one, where the division of such a small amount of a controlled substance constituted sufficient evidence to survive a motion to dismiss. Moreover, the 1.89 grams was divided into only three separate bags. While small bags may typically be used to package marijuana, it is just as likely that defendant was a consumer who purchased the drugs in that particular packaging from a dealer. Consequently, we hold that the separation of 1.89 grams of marijuana into three small packages, worth a total of approximately $30.00, does not raise an inference that defendant intended to sell or deliver the marijuana.

In addition to the packaging, we must also consider the fact that defendant was carrying $1,264.00 in cash. . . . Upon viewing the evidence of the packaging and the cash "cumulatively," we hold that the evidence is insufficient to support the felony charge. . . . Had defendant possessed more than 1.89 grams of marijuana, or had there been additional circumstances to consider, we may have reached a different conclusion; however, given the fact that neither the amount of marijuana nor the packaging raises an inference that defendant intended to sell the drugs, the presence of the cash as the only additional factor is insufficient to raise the inference. . . .

. . . The evidence in this case, viewed in the light most favorable to the State, indicates that defendant was a drug user, not a drug seller.

"The charge of simple possession, however, is a lesser included offense of possession with intent to sell or distribute." . . . "'When [the trier of fact] finds the facts necessary to constitute one offense, it also inescapably finds the facts necessary to constitute all lesser-included offenses of that offense.'" . . . Consequently, when the jury found defendant guilty of possession with intent to sell or deliver, it necessarily found him guilty of simple possession of a controlled substance. . . . Consequently, we vacate defendant's sentence and remand for entry of a judgment "as upon a verdict of guilty of simple possession of marijuana." . . .

## Notes and Questions

1. Was the evidence in *Wilkins* insufficient for a reasonable jury to conclude that the defendant was planning to distribute the marijuana? If so, what other evidence might the government have used to bolster its case?

2. The courts in *Wilkins* and *Glenn* both note that the way the marijuana was packaged gives rise to some permissible inferences about the defendant's intentions. But how good are these inferences? Which form of packaging is more likely to indicate that the possessor intends to distribute the drug: one bag filled with one ounce of marijuana, or eight bags each filled with ⅛ of an ounce? Why?

3. As the *Wilkins* court notes, simple possession is a lesser-included offense of PWID. Thus, a defendant who successfully challenges the sufficiency of the evidence regarding intent to distribute might still be convicted of simple possession of marijuana. But if the government fails to sustain its burden on simple possession, both the simple possession and possession with intent to distribute charges must be dismissed.

4. The possession of a large quantity of marijuana is probably the factor most commonly cited to demonstrate an intent to distribute the drug. The idea is that a defendant who possesses more than she could possibly consume herself must intend to distribute it. Indeed, possession of a sufficiently large quantity of marijuana by itself might be enough to support a jury verdict that the defendant had the requisite intent to distribute the drug. E.g., *United States v. Rodriguez*, 375 F. Supp. 589 (S.D. Tex. 1974) (holding that jury may infer an intent to distribute marijuana based solely on the large quantity involved in the case (376 pounds)).

But jurisdictions appear to disagree about how much marijuana is necessary—by itself—to support the inference of an intent to distribute. In a few jurisdictions, the threshold quantity has been set by the legislature via statute. E.g., 17A Maine Rev. Stat. Ann., § 1106.3 ("Proof that the person intentionally or knowingly possesses a scheduled drug that is in fact of a quantity . . . as provided in this subsection, gives rise to a permissible inference . . . that the person is unlawfully furnishing that scheduled drug: A. More than 2½ ounces of marijuana."). In other jurisdictions, it appears to be based on judicial decisions. E.g., *Rhode Island v. Williams*, 656 A.2d 975 (R.I. 1995) (noting that possession of 1.67 pounds of marijuana, standing alone, would not support an inference to distribute).

Is it possible to formulate a scientifically based presumption about quantities that are inconsistent with personal use? If so, what would the amount be? Consider research on consumption. On average, marijuana users consume roughly 100 grams per year. See Jonathan P. Caulkins, Beau Kilmer, and Mark A.R. Kleiman, Marijuana Legalization: What Everyone Needs to Know (Oxford University Press 2016) (hereinafter, Caulkins et al.). But consumption varies widely from person to person. For example, Beau Kilmer and his co-authors have found that the heaviest users consume roughly 39 to 57 grams per month; moderate users consume roughly 6 grams per month; and casual users consume roughly 1 gram per month. Beau Kilmer et al., *Before the Grand Opening: Measuring Washington State's Marijuana Market in the Last Year Before Legalized Commercial Sales* (RAND 2013). Considering the variability—and the fact that marijuana has a long shelf life—is it possible to make accurate assumptions about what a possessor plans to do with marijuana, based on anything less than very large quantities?

5. The government may proffer a variety of evidence to help convince the fact finder that defendants intended to distribute the drugs they possessed, but what evidence may *defendants* proffer to demonstrate that such drugs were only for their own personal use? The issue has arisen in some medical marijuana states, where defendants have sought to rebut charges of PWID by demonstrating that the quantities they possessed were consistent with the quantities they are allowed to possess for their own use under state law. For a discussion of the issue, see Stephen Mayer, Note, *Proving Personal Use: The Admissibility of Evidence Negating Intent to Distribute Marijuana*, 113 Mich. L. Rev. 1255 (2015). Mayer's Note briefly discusses the federal government's objection to the introduction of such evidence in federal cases, including its concern about inviting jury nullification (discussed more below).

### b. *Proof of* Defendant's *Intent*

In some cases, it might be plain that the defendant possessed marijuana and that *someone* intended to distribute the drug, but less clear whether the *defendant* harbored that intention. The following case raises this issue.

## *Louisiana v. Kelly*
800 So. 2d 978 (La. Ct. App. 2001)

McManus, J.:

... [A] confidential informant made a controlled drug buy from Co-Defendant, Gwendolyn Minor, at 2713 Dawson Street during which the informant purchased $20.00 worth of marijuana. The controlled buy was arranged after the confidential informant advised Detective Janell Godfrey with the Kenner Police Department that marijuana was being distributed from the address by a black female named "Gwen."

[A few days later, when the informant claimed that the 2713 Dawson Street residence had just received a large amount of marijuana, Detective Godfrey obtained a warrant to search the house.] ... In executing the search warrant, the police used a ram and made a forced entry into the residence where they found Defendant [(Anthony Kelly)], two of Defendant's brothers (James and Keithen), Co-Defendant, and Co-Defendant's juvenile son (E.M.) and young daughter.

Defendant and E.M. were found in the upstairs bathroom, where E.M. had his hands in the toilet and Defendant was frantically trying to flush the toilet. A clear plastic bag containing 21 smaller bags of marijuana was retrieved from the toilet. Additionally, three partially smoked hand-rolled marijuana cigarettes were observed in plain view in the ashtray on the living room table and a marijuana odor was detected in the home. A search of Co-Defendant's purse revealed another clear plastic bag with 21 smaller bags of marijuana, a bag of loose marijuana and EZ Wilder rolling paper which is used to package marijuana. "Dime bags," which are also used to package marijuana, were found in the bedroom of the residence.

Defendant claimed he did not live in the residence and did not know Co-Defendant was selling marijuana. However, a letter with a postage date of June 25, 1999, was found in the bedroom addressed to Defendant at that address. The defense offered a [recent] tax refund document addressed to Defendant that showed a different address of 2718 Dawson. ... Detective Godfrey testified there were men's clothes and shoes in the bedroom closet of 2713 Dawson Street. She testified the clothes and shoes were for a large size man. Defendant was described as being 6 feet tall and weighing 250 lbs. Also, in the bedroom there was a picture of Defendant and Co-Defendant together that said "Gwen, Lil Bit forever love."

Defendant and Co-Defendant were arrested and charged with possession of marijuana with intent to distribute. Defendant's two brothers, James and Keithen, and Co-Defendant's son, E.M., were arrested and charged with simple possession of marijuana. [The jury voted 10-2 to convict Defendant. He was initially sentenced to 15 years' imprisonment, but his sentence was enhanced to life imprisonment without parole under Louisiana's three strikes law.] ...

. . .

Defendant does not challenge the finding that he was in possession of marijuana. Rather, he challenges the determination that he had specific intent to distribute marijuana. Specific intent is defined as that state of mind which exists when the circumstances indicate the offender actively desired the prescribed criminal consequences as reasonably certain to result from his act or failure to act. ... The intent to distribute may be established by proving circumstances surrounding the defendant's possession which give rise to reasonable inferences of intent to distribute. . . . Factors which may give rise to a reasonable inference that defendant had the specific intent to distribute include 1) previous attempts to distribute, 2) whether the drug was in a form consistent with distribution to others, 3) the amount of the drug, 4) expert or other testimony showing the amount found in the defendant's possession to be inconsistent with personal use only, and 5) paraphernalia evidencing an intent to distribute. . . .

In the present case, the marijuana defendant was trying to flush down the toilet was packaged in 21 small colored plastic bags. These bags were identified as "dime" bags, meaning they sold on the street for $10.00 each. The total weight of the marijuana in the clear plastic bag found in the toilet was 31.7 grams. Sergeant Bruce Harrison, an expert in the use, packaging, distribution and value of street level narcotics, testified that a smaller amount of the drug—only two to three individual packages—would have been indicative of personal consumption. He explained that to purchase the 32 grams of marijuana the way it was individually packaged . . . would cost approximately $200-$210, whereas a person could buy 28 grams of marijuana in bulk for $80-$100. Thus, he concluded it would not be economical or practical to purchase that amount of marijuana, individually packaged, for personal consumption.

Drug paraphernalia, specifically "nickel" and "dime" bags used for packaging, was found in the bedroom. Loose marijuana was also found in the home. Sgt. Harrison testified that while loose marijuana alone could be consistent with personal consumption, the presence of individual packages ready for sale indicates that packaging for retail distribution has been interrupted, leaving some loose amount of the substance.

Co-Defendant testified that Defendant did not know she sold marijuana. She claimed all of the marijuana was hers and that she packaged the marijuana by herself with no help from Defendant. She testified that she kept some of the marijuana under the bathroom sink but no one knew about it. Sgt. Harrison testified that the bathroom is the most common place for people to destroy drugs when the police arrive. He explained that most suspects have a plan in place of what to do with the drugs when the police enter the house. Sgt. Harrison stated that if a person is flushing the marijuana, that person knew the marijuana was there and knew what they were going to do in the event the police actually entered the house.

The credibility of witnesses is within the sound discretion of the trier of fact, who may accept or reject, in whole or in part, the testimony of any witness. . . . It is not the function of an appellate court to assess credibility or reweigh the evidence. . . . Clearly, the jury did not believe Co-Defendant's testimony that Defendant had no knowledge that she sold marijuana and that he did not help her sell it. . . .

Admittedly, there was no evidence that Defendant had sold drugs in the past. However, there was evidence marijuana had been sold out of the residence. The evidence clearly shows Defendant had knowledge that marijuana was in the house and that he exercised enough control over the marijuana to locate it and try to destroy it when the police arrived. The existence of drug paraphernalia, the individual packaging of the marijuana Defendant was trying to destroy, and the fact the amount of the marijuana was inconsistent with personal consumption support a reasonable inference that Defendant had specific intent to distribute the marijuana. Therefore, it appears the evidence is sufficient to support defendant's conviction. . . .

Part III. Marijuana Suppliers

## Notes and Questions

1. In *Kelly*, there appears to be enough evidence to show that someone had the intent to distribute marijuana (and had been doing so). But was there enough evidence to suggest that *the defendant*, Anthony Kelly, was intending to distribute the marijuana? Is *Kelly* consistent with the decision in *Vinton* (the case of the husband and wife accused of manufacturing marijuana), excerpted above?

2. Why do you think the jury discounted co-defendant's Gwendolyn Minor's claim that she alone was distributing the marijuana?

3. Would you have charged the Defendant with PWID? Is there a different crime that might have better fit the facts of the case?

### c. Intent to Distribute the Marijuana in Possession

There is one more wrinkle to consider in PWID cases, raised by the following Problem:

**Problem 7.9:** The police searched Camila's apartment. In her bedroom they found a small jar labeled "personal stash." The jar contained about 3 grams of marijuana in usable form. In Camila's office, the police found a sensitive digital scale, about $3,000 in cash (all in small denominations), several boxes of Ziploc bags, a ledger containing a list of names under the heading "customers," a loaded handgun, and a price sheet for various grades of marijuana printed from a marijuana e-magazine. Based on these facts, do you think Camila is a drug dealer? Even so, is she guilty of possession with intent to distribute marijuana? *See United States v. Latham*, 874 F.2d 852, 862 (1st Cir. 1989).

## Notes and Questions

1. Now consider another Problem in a similar vein:

**Problem 7.10:** Benjamin lives alone in an apartment. The police search the apartment and find a silver tray with marijuana stems and seeds, a scale, pipes and bongs for smoking marijuana that contain marijuana residue, baggies used by drug dealers to package marijuana, and $345 in cash. Benjamin admitted to the police that he smoked marijuana and had, on occasion, sold it to his friends. He was charged with PWID marijuana. At trial, Benjamin gave the following testimony:

> Attorney: Benjamin, there was marijuana found in your apartment, correct?
> Benjamin: Correct.
> Attorney: In what form was that marijuana?
> Benjamin: That was the last of many a sack. I mean, it was stems and seeds. I had no more pot. I just finished smoking it, so that's why when the cops arrested me, you know, I was more than willing to go because I'm—I don't know. I didn't really think that I was going to get in that much trouble. I figured the paraphernalia would have been my problem, not stems and seeds.

> Attorney: What were you planning on doing with the stems and seeds that were found in your apartment?
>
> Benjamin: Throwing them away. I mean, there's nothing that you do with stems and seeds.

Is Benjamin guilty of PWID? *See Shumaker v. Wyoming*, 167 P.3d 11 (Wyo. 2007).

2. Chapter 3 discussed the concept of transferred intent—i.e., the notion that a defendant may be convicted of possession of marijuana based on her genuine (but mistaken) belief that she possessed another controlled substance like heroin. Should the government be allowed to proceed on a theory of transferred intent in PWID cases as well? Would the theory support a conviction in **Problem 7.9** and **Problem 7.10**? Could the government instead pursue a *different* supply-related charge in such cases?

## 4. Attempts

Jurisdictions commonly proscribe even unsuccessful attempts to commit one of the offenses discussed above. The CSA, for example, proscribes attempts and conspiracies to commit federal drug offenses:

> Any person who attempts or conspires to commit any offense defined in this subchapter shall be subject to the same penalties as those prescribed for the offense, the commission of which was the object of the attempt or conspiracy.

21 U.S.C. § 846. (Chapter 11 discusses conspiracies.)

Section 846 does not define what it means to "attempt" to commit a drug offense, so federal courts have given the crime the same common law definition that applies in most states. Under this definition, the crime of attempt includes two basic elements:

(1) the defendant must have the *specific intent* to commit one of the enumerated offenses—i.e., to possess, distribute, possess with intent to distribute, or manufacture marijuana (mens rea); and

(2) the defendant must take a substantial step in furtherance of such intent (actus reus).

While the second element focuses on the defendant's actions, it also helps to demonstrate the seriousness of the defendant's intentions. The idea is that a defendant who takes a substantial step toward commission of a crime probably desires to complete the crime and is not merely kidding around.

The following case provides a good introduction to the elements of an attempted distribution offense.

### *Lewis v. Virginia*
423 S.E.2d 371 (Va. App. 1992)

BENTON, J.:

... Kenneth W. Silvey[] was incarcerated in the James River Correctional Center serving a sentence of thirty years for felonies of rape and sodomy. Silvey testified that

Part III. Marijuana Suppliers

he obtained large quantities of money through illegal transactions with other prisoners and kept money in the correctional facility contrary to regulations. He asserted that Lewis, a prison guard, noticed his abundance of money and, in the summer of 1990, offered Silvey the opportunity to make more money by selling marijuana. Silvey stated that although he did not use drugs, he decided he would sell drugs to inmates in order to make more money. Silvey further testified that in June 1990, after his conversations with Lewis, a supervising officer initiated contact with him concerning Lewis. Silvey said that he had not informed prison officials of his contacts with Lewis at the time they approached him and that he was initially hesitant to cooperate with them. He decided to cooperate when they said "they would help [Silvey] if [he] helped them" and promised to "get [Silvey] paroled if [he] helped them." Silvey testified that he then approached Lewis and re-initiated discussions about buying marijuana.

On September 30 at 6 p.m., more than three months after Silvey said Lewis approached him, Silvey was given $150 by a corrections official in order to purchase marijuana. The money had been treated with a substance that is visible only under a fluorescent light. Silvey testified that he gave the money to Lewis while Lewis was inside his guard post and that Lewis put the money in his pocket. . . . Silvey said Lewis was to deliver the marijuana to him that same night.

. . . Lewis took his scheduled leisure break at 8 p.m. At the conclusion of his break, Lewis left the administration building and was walking toward the gate to enter the inmate compound when he was stopped, arrested, and searched. The marked money was in Lewis' pocket with $71 of Lewis' own money. Lewis' hands, the money, and the pocket in which Lewis had put the money all showed signs of the substance used to treat the $150. Lewis consented to a search of his living quarters and his vehicle. No marijuana or other illegal contraband was found on Lewis' person or among his possessions.

. . .

At trial, Lewis testified that he found the money in the desk drawer inside the guard post. He testified that he routinely left the door to the guard post open when he made rounds within the immediately adjacent inmate dormitory. He also testified that cleaning supplies were stored in one of the two rooms that comprise the guard post and that inmates were routinely allowed access to that room to get the cleaning supplies. He denied that he offered or intended to deliver marijuana to Silvey. On this evidence, Lewis was convicted of attempting to deliver marijuana to Silvey and fined $2500. . . .

"It is well established that an attempt is composed of two elements: the intention to commit the crime, and the doing of some direct act towards its consummation which is more than mere preparation but falls short of execution of the ultimate purpose." . . . The evidence must prove "an overt but ineffectual act committed in furtherance of the criminal purpose." . . .

> It is impossible to formulate a rule which will be a definite and unbending guide in determining what acts constitute preparation and what acts amount to legal attempts. "In a general way, however, it may be said that preparation consists in devising or arranging the means or measures necessary for the commission of the offense and that the attempt is the direct movement toward the commission after the preparations are made." . . .

The Commonwealth failed to prove an act done in furtherance of a delivery. No evidence proved that Lewis possessed marijuana, that Lewis made arrangements to secure marijuana, or that Lewis did any other thing connecting his possession of the money to marijuana. While it is not necessary to show that the conduct was thwarted at the instant of consummation, the evidence must prove that the preparation proceeded "far enough towards the accomplishment of the desired result to amount to the commencement of the consummation." . . .

> Preparation alone is not enough, there must be some appreciable fragment of the crime committed, it must be in such progress that it will be consummated unless interrupted by circumstances independent of the will of the attempter, and the act must not be equivocal in nature. . . .

The gravamen of the charged offense is that Lewis did some act beyond mere preparation and that the act was done in furtherance of the delivery of marijuana. Although . . . actual possession of the contraband is not required to establish the offense, the Commonwealth, in this case, proved no conduct or statement by Lewis that indicates more than mere preparation. Moreover, Lewis' conduct was at best equivocal. . . . [T]he trial judge aptly observed that the delivery of money "could also be evidence of a shakedown type fraud practiced by this guard on the inmates in which he never had any intention to deliver marijuana, but simply was getting money from them knowing that they couldn't then report him." The evidence in this record is consistent with that hypothesis. Thus, the proof concerning Lewis' conduct is equivocal and does not establish more than mere preparation.

## Notes and Questions

1. Was attempted delivery of marijuana the best choice of charge to bring against Fred Lewis? Could prosecutors have charged him with a different crime? If attempted marijuana delivery was the only charge on the horizon, what might the investigators have done differently to gather evidence that would be needed for a successful prosecution? What additional evidence might have sustained a conviction for attempted delivery of marijuana anyway?

2. Now consider the following Problem:

Problem 7.11: Delilah sold 500 grams of marijuana to Ivan, an informant working for the police. Ivan asked Delilah about purchasing an additional 10 kilograms of marijuana. Delilah agreed to try, but indicated that she doubted she could obtain more than 3 kilograms. Delilah called her previous supplier, Samuel, three times to ask whether he could come up with 10 kilograms. Each time Samuel told her he was not sure but that he would try. After the third call, the police arrested Delilah. Is she guilty of attempted distribution of marijuana? Did she go beyond mere preparation? *See United States v. Presto*, 24 M.L. 350 (Ct. Mil. App. 1987).

3. Abandonment (also called renunciation) is an affirmative defense against the crime of attempt, recognized by the federal government and about half of all of the states. *See* Daniel G. Moriarty, *Extending the Defense of Renunciation*, 62 Temp. L. Rev. 1, 3-14 (1989) (surveying law). (Defenses that apply to more crimes are discussed below in

Section A.6.) To prevail on the defense, the defendant usually must completely and voluntarily renounce his or her criminal purpose before completing the attempted crime. Model Penal Code § 5.01(4) (providing common formulation of the defense). Could the defendants in the following Problems successfully raise the defense of abandonment?

**Problem 7.12**: Revisit **Problem 7.11** above. Suppose that Delilah had met her supplier (Samuel), who indicated that he had 10 kilograms of marijuana he could sell to her. Delilah then proceeded to negotiate a firm price for the drug. She also arranged to pick it up from Samuel that evening at a nearby parking lot. A few hours later, however, Delilah called Ivan and told him: "Samuel has the marijuana and he's charging a reasonable price. But I have had a change of heart. I no longer want any part of this deal. Sorry." Did Delilah commit attempted distribution? If so, did she abandon her attempt to distribute?

**Problem 7.13**: Same facts as **Problem 7.12**, only now Samuel calls Delilah after their meeting and tells her: "We have to change our venue. If you still want the marijuana, you will have to pick it up at my sister's ranch (100 miles away) this evening." Delilah declines. She calls Ivan and tells him: "Samuel has the marijuana and he's charging a reasonable price. But he wants me to drive 100 miles to fetch it. I have had a change of heart. I no longer want any part of this deal. Sorry." Did Delilah abandon her attempt to distribute? Along these lines, consider Model Penal Code section 5.01(4).

**Problem 7.14**: Same facts as **Problem 7.12**, only now Delilah meets with Samuel and accepts delivery of the marijuana. But she then calls Ivan to tell him: "I got the marijuana. But I have had a change of heart. I no longer want to sell it to *you*. Sorry." Did Delilah abandon the attempt to distribute? Consider again Model Penal Code section 5.01(4). In any event, even if Delilah abandoned her attempt to distribute marijuana, is she now guilty of a *different* supply offense?

4. Like many state laws, 21 U.S.C. section 846 punishes an attempt to violate the CSA the same as though the crime had been successfully completed. However, a few states punish attempts less severely than successfully completed crimes. *See, e.g., Louisiana v. Callahan*, 671 So. 2d 903 (La. 1996) (holding that mandatory minimum sentence for distribution of marijuana does not apply to an attempt to distribute same, and noting that the maximum sentence for attempts under Louisiana law is half of the sentence that applies to completed offenses).

## 5. Review and Double Jeopardy Issues

**Figure 7.1** summarizes the core elements of each of the supply offenses discussed in the chapter.

Chapter 7. The Regulation of Marijuana Suppliers in Prohibition Regimes

Figure 7.1. Summary of Supply Offenses

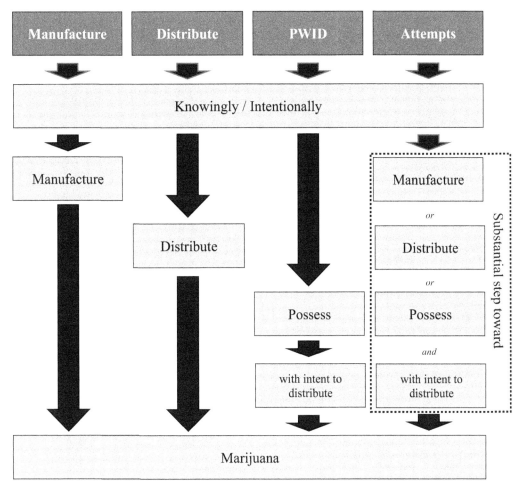

In the course of supplying marijuana, an individual may violate more than one of the prohibitions discussed above. This possibility is raised in the following Problem:

<u>Problem 7.15</u>: Andy carefully cultivated five marijuana plants. After two months, he harvested the plants and placed the trimmed buds and leaves on a drying rack to prepare them for future sale. After another month, Andy sold the marijuana (about one pound) to a buyer. Based on these facts, of which of the following crimes may Andy be convicted?

(1) Manufacturing marijuana
(2) Possession with the intent to distribute marijuana
(3) Distributing marijuana
(4) All of the above

The Double Jeopardy Clause of the United States Constitution limits the power of a single government to convict an individual for more than one crime arising out of the same

339

action or series of actions. U.S. Const. amend. V ("[N]or shall any person be subject for the same offence to be twice put in jeopardy of life or limb."). The United States Supreme Court laid down the test for determining whether multiple charges (like option (4) in **Problem 7.15**) violate double jeopardy in *Blockburger v. United States*, 284 U.S. 299 (1932). Under *Blockburger*, "where the same act or transaction constitutes a violation of two distinct statutory provisions," the defendant may be convicted of both only if each offense "requires proof of an additional fact which the other does not." *Id.* at 304.

As **Figure 7.1** shows, there is substantial—but not complete—overlap among supply offenses. Indeed, under *Blockburger*, only the offense of attempted supply would merge with any other supply offenses. That is, an individual could be convicted of manufacturing, possessing with the intent to distribute, and distributing the same marijuana, because each of those offenses has a unique element that the government is not required to prove for the others. But the individual could not be convicted of manufacturing, and possessing with the intent to distribute, and distributing the marijuana under 21 U.S.C. section 841(a) *and* attempting to commit any of those first three crimes under section 846. The government would have to choose between charging the individual with the completed offenses or charging him with an attempt (or attempts) to commit the same. *E.g., United States v. Hyska*, 29 M.J. 122 (Mil. App. 1989) (holding that the defendant's failed attempt to distribute marijuana merged with his successful distribution of the same marijuana the following day).

## Notes and Questions

1. Even though multiple convictions based on the same conduct might survive a challenge under *Blockburger*, there are several reasons why the impact on the defendant's rights will be minimal. For one thing, some courts have imposed additional limits—beyond those included in the *Blockburger* test—on the government's power to pursue multiple convictions based on the same activity. In any event, the sentencing impact of being convicted of multiple supply offenses may prove to be minimal. *United States v. Sepulveda* explains:

> Under *Blockburger* . . . a defendant can be convicted of two differently defined offenses, based on the same core of facts, so long as each offense requires an element that the other does not. . . . The offense of distribution obviously does require an element not required for the crime of possession with intent, namely, the act of distribution. It is possible—albeit unusual—to be guilty of distribution of a drug without also possessing it with intent to distribute. Someone who participates in a drug transfer—e.g., as a broker or armed guard—can be liable for distribution without ever possessing the drugs. . . . While "possession" is certainly helpful in proving distribution, it is technically not a necessary element.
> 
> But satisfying *Blockburger* has not wholly satisfied the circuit courts. Where the evidence shows only that a defendant handed over a packet of drugs, some courts have balked at the idea that Congress intended to allow a conviction both for possession with intent and for distribution. . . . Other circuits have said that conviction on both counts is permitted, but that a defendant may only be sentenced on one. . . . By contrast, this court . . . has said that "the offenses merge only where the distribution itself is the sole evidence of possession, or where possession is shown to exist only at the moment of distribution", . . . and we have also made clear that a defendant could be convicted of

both offenses, with respect to the same drug, so long as there was proof that he possessed the drug (with intent to distribute) at some point earlier than the distribution itself. . . .

It is doubtful that the game (reflected in these various distinctions drawn by the circuits) is worth the candle where both offenses are prosecuted at the same time. In most configurations, the [United States Sentencing] guidelines will assure that the sentence is the same for one or both. . . .

102 F.3d 1313, 1316-17 (1st Cir. 1996).

## 6. Defenses

This section discusses three key legal defenses that have been raised against marijuana supply charges. Although these defenses apply most commonly to supply charges, they could apply to possession charges as well, just as the defenses discussed in Chapter 3 (with the possible exception of necessity) could apply to supply charges. (Some additional defenses that are more commonly raised by defendants other than users and suppliers are discussed in Part IV.) This section also discusses the issue of jury nullification, which, while not technically a "defense," nonetheless may have the same impact on criminal prosecutions.

### a. Entrapment

#### (i) The Conventional Entrapment Defense

Because the market for drugs normally involves consenting parties, governments face challenges in detecting illicit drug transactions. To catch would-be drug suppliers, governments commonly resort to setting up controlled drug transactions. In these staged deals, government agents, including both undercover officers and confidential informants (CIs), pose as prospective drug buyers or sellers looking to make a deal. When their targets take the bait, the agents will spring the trap and make an arrest.

In their zeal to catch drug offenders, however, government agents might turn some otherwise law-abiding private citizens into criminals. The defense of entrapment is supposed to address this risk. In a nutshell, the defense excuses defendants from liability for crimes improperly instigated by government agents. The defense exists against most non-violent crimes, including drug supply and possession offenses.

To prevail on the defense of entrapment, the defendant must first show that she was improperly induced by a government agent to commit the charged crime. Inducement entails more than affording the defendant the opportunity to commit the crime. In *United States v. Evans*, 924 F.2d 714 (7th Cir. 1991), for example, the trial court refused to instruct the jury on the entrapment defense where the defendant had been caught trying to buy a large quantity of marijuana from a CI. In affirming the trial court's decision, Judge Richard Posner of the Seventh Circuit noted that

> The police did not offer [the defendant] a cent. They offered him a source of supply, in wholesale quantities, at market prices. They offered him, in other words, an opportunity to enter the drug trade (assuming improbably that he was not already in it, as the informant

suspected) on the usual terms. A person who takes advantage of an ordinary opportunity to commit criminal acts . . . is not entrapped.

*Id.* at 717. Instead, government agents must "pressure the suspect by overbearing conduct such as badgering, cajoling, importuning, or other affirmative acts. . . ." *California v. Barraza*, 591 P.2d 947, 955 (Cal. 1979) (en banc).

In the vast majority of jurisdictions, including the federal courts, the defendant must also demonstrate that he was not predisposed to commit the crime. In determining whether a defendant was predisposed, the courts consider several factors, including: "(1) the defendant's character or reputation; (2) whether the government initially suggested the criminal activity; (3) whether the defendant engaged in the criminal activity for profit; (4) whether the defendant evidenced a reluctance to commit the offense that was overcome by government persuasion; and (5) the nature of the inducement or persuasion by the government." *United States v. Pillado*, 656 F.3d 754, 765 (7th Cir. 2011). If the defendant was predisposed to commit the crime, she may not raise the entrapment defense unless the government provided "extraordinary inducement" to commit the offense. *Id.* at 765.

In a small minority of jurisdictions, however, the defendant's predisposition is irrelevant for purposes of the entrapment defense. These jurisdictions focus exclusively on the government's behavior. To establish entrapment, the defendant need only show that the government's tactics would have caused a normally law-abiding person to commit the same offense. *See Barraza, supra*.

To illustrate the competing approaches to the entrapment defense, consider the following two Problems:

**Problem 7.16**: Benjamin is a confidential informant working for the police. Benjamin saw Delilah use marijuana at a party the night before. Benjamin approaches Delilah and asks her to sell him one ounce of marijuana. Delilah initially refuses. But then Benjamin pleads with Delilah: "Please. I need it for my mom. She's got cancer, but she won't take the chemo because it makes her too sick. She's tried everything else. Doc said pot might make her less nauseous. I saw you smoking a joint last night. I don't know where else to get it." Delilah replies: "That's terrible. Look, here's a joint. It's all I have. No charge." Is Delilah guilty of distribution? If so, could she successfully assert an entrapment defense?

Per the discussion in Section A.2 above, Delilah has distributed marijuana, as that crime is defined in most jurisdictions. But based on these facts she could probably meet her burden for establishing the entrapment defense in both majority and minority jurisdictions. The fact that the government agent (Benjamin) initiated the transfer, that Delilah initially refused to accede, that Benjamin had to apply further pressure to change Delilah's mind, that Delilah only had one joint on hand, and that Delilah asked for nothing in return all suggest Delilah was not predisposed to commit the crime and had to be pressured into committing it.

**Problem 7.17**: Same facts as **Problem 7.16**, only now, Delilah has a prior conviction for distributing marijuana. Can she successfully raise an entrapment defense to distribution charges?

In this case, Delilah would have an easier time establishing entrapment in a jurisdiction following the minority approach. In such a jurisdiction, her prior conviction would be ignored for purposes of entrapment. But in a jurisdiction following the majority approach, the government could use Delilah's prior conviction to help prove that Delilah was predisposed to distribute marijuana, and thus, was not entrapped. Indeed, "[t]he authorities are unanimously agreed that even prior similar crimes which never led to convictions, let alone prior convictions themselves, are highly relevant on the subject of criminal predisposition." *Sparks v. Maryland*, 603 A.2d 1258 (Md. App. 1992). It would be a different case, however, if Delilah's prior conviction involved only the simple possession of marijuana. In *Williams v. Mississippi*, for example, the court held that evidence of a prior marijuana possession offense should not have been admitted to prove predisposition to *sell* illegal drugs. 761 So. 2d 149 (Miss. 2000).

*(ii) Entrapment by Estoppel and DOJ Enforcement Guidelines*

Many jurisdictions recognize a variation on the classic entrapment defense called *entrapment by estoppel*. Entrapment by estoppel arises when a government agent misleads a defendant into believing that his or her conduct was authorized by the government. The defense creates an exception to the normal rule that mistakes of law do not create a cognizable defense.

Since 2009, the defense of entrapment by estoppel has been asserted in a large number of marijuana prosecutions brought by the federal government. The asserted basis for the defense has included both statements made by federal officials (including President Barack Obama and Attorney General Eric Holder) suggesting that the federal government should not bother prosecuting some marijuana crimes, as well as enforcement memoranda issued by the DOJ in 2009, 2011, and 2013, suggesting to federal prosecutors that they should not expend their limited prosecutorial resources bringing legal actions against marijuana possessors (and, in the 2013 memo, suppliers) acting in compliance with state marijuana laws. (The latest memorandum is excerpted after the *United States v. Washington* decision.)

To date, however, the federal courts have uniformly held that enforcement memoranda and similar statements made by federal officials do not satisfy all of the requirements of the entrapment by estoppel defense. *United States v. Washington* is representative. It elaborates on the requirements of the defense and explains why it has been so unsuccessful.

## *United States v. Washington*
887 F. Supp. 2d 1077 (D. Mont. 2012)

CHRISTENSEN, J.:

... Defendants Jason Washington, Lisa Fleming, and Steven Sann ... are charged, along with four other co-defendants, with offenses related to the manufacture and distribution of marijuana. ... [Each of the marijuana charges carries a five-year mandatory minimum prison sentence.]

The charges allege conduct that occurred at least in part in the context of a medical marijuana dispensary established during the effective period of the Montana Medical Marijuana Act ("MMMA"). ... [The court] will assume, for purposes of deciding the pending motions to dismiss only, that the Defendants' conduct was in full compliance with the Montana Medical Marijuana Act. . . . Despite that assumption in the Defendants' favor, nearly all of their motions are denied. The Court takes this opportunity, prior to undertaking an analysis of the legal merits of each of the pending motions, to explain in general terms the reasons why it believes the law compels this outcome.

Marijuana is a prohibited Schedule I substance under the Controlled Substances Act, 21 U.S.C. § 801, et seq., a statutory classification that has been in place since 1970, and persisted throughout the time frame of the events alleged in the Indictment. Nonetheless, beginning in 2009 various officials in the executive branch of the United States government made public statements suggesting that it is the policy of the federal government to refrain from prosecuting participants in a state-authorized medical marijuana program, provided those participants acted in compliance with state law. These statements by federal officials were nebulous, equivocal, and heavily qualified. However, it is clear that no federal official has ever stated that the cultivation, sale, or use of medical marijuana is legal under federal law. Still, when taken in the aggregate, particularly through the filter of the news media, the words of federal officials were enough to convince those who were considering entry into the medical marijuana business that they could engage in that enterprise without fear of federal criminal consequences. They began cultivating and selling medical marijuana under the assumption that they could become legitimate providers under state law and not be selectively arrested and prosecuted under federal law. Regardless of the wisdom of that choice, it is a choice many Montanans have made.

That choice has now proven very costly for those providers, including the Defendants in this case, whose medical marijuana businesses have been raided by federal agents, and who are now facing federal felony marijuana distribution charges, many of which carry mandatory minimum sentences of five years or more in federal prison, notwithstanding the fact that many of these same individuals have non-existent or minimal criminal histories. While a few have been prosecuted by the federal government, thousands of Montanans continue to use medical marijuana pursuant to a state statutory scheme that was originally endorsed by 62 percent of Montana voters. Thus, there is a strongly held belief among those in the medical marijuana community that the federal government has not treated them fairly. . . .

Legal arguments are not presented and decided in a vacuum, however. Appeals to the Court's sense of fairness and equity must be tethered to an applicable legal theory, and must seek a remedy that the Court is able to provide. It is against this practical measure that the Defendants' otherwise compelling arguments ultimately come up short. The facts simply do not satisfy the elements of the various theories advanced by the Defendants. . . .

. . .

All of the pending motions to dismiss on [entrapment by] estoppel grounds rely on the common underlying principle that the federal government, having stated several times that it would not initiate federal drug prosecutions of sellers or users of medical marijuana acting in compliance with the laws of their respective states, should now be estopped from pursuing this federal prosecution in contradiction of those statements. The most prominent of the federal government's various pronouncements on the topic of medical marijuana is what has become known as the "Ogden memo."[3]

---

3. Author's note: The 2009 Ogden memorandum preceded the 2013 Cole Memorandum excerpted below.

Written by Deputy Attorney General David Ogden and issued on October 19, 2009, the Ogden memo purports to "provide[ ] clarification and guidance to federal prosecutors in States that have enacted laws authorizing the medical use of marijuana." . . . In the Ogden Memo, the Department of Justice communicated to its attorneys that certain marijuana users and providers would be a lower priority for prosecution than others. . . . "As a general matter, pursuit of [the Department's] priorities should not focus federal resources in your States on individuals whose actions are in clear and unambiguous compliance with existing state laws providing for the medical use of marijuana." . . . However, the Ogden memo also made clear that medical marijuana activity that may be authorized under state law remains illegal under federal law:

> The Department of Justice is committed to the enforcement of the Controlled Substances Act in all states. This guidance regarding resource allocation does not 'legalize' marijuana or provide a legal defense to a violation of federal law, nor is it intended to create any privileges, benefits, or rights, substantive or procedural, enforceable by any individual, party, or witness in any administrative, civil, or criminal matter. Nor does clear and unambiguous compliance with state law . . . create a legal defense to a violation of the Controlled Substances Act.

 . . . The Ogden memo did not state that medical marijuana users and providers would be exempt from prosecution. . . . "Nor does this guidance preclude investigation or prosecution, even where there is clear and unambiguous compliance with existing state laws, in particular circumstances where investigation or prosecution otherwise serves important federal interests.". . . .

. . .

. . . The [entrapment by estoppel] defense requires the accused to show that "(1) an authorized government official, empowered to render the claimed erroneous advice, (2) who has been made aware of all the relevant historical facts, (3) affirmatively told him the proscribed conduct was permissible, (4) that he relied on the false information, and (5) that his reliance was reasonable."[ *United States v. Batterjee*, 361 F.3d 1210, 1216 (9th Cir. 2004).] . . .

The Defendants assert the defense of estoppel by official misleading statement based on the Ogden memo; statements made to the press or to Congress by then-presidential-candidate Barack Obama, his campaign spokesman, his White House spokesman, and United States Attorney General Eric Holder; the characterizations of those statements in news media; . . . and statements made to at least one Defendant by Flathead Tribal Police drug investigator Arlen Auld. None of these statements justifies dismissal on a theory of estoppel by official misleading statement. . . .

. . .

Prior rulings in similar cases in this District have held that the defenses of estoppel by official misleading statement or entrapment by estoppel are not available as they relate to the Ogden memo. . . . The Ogden memo fails to satisfy most of the elements set out in *Batterjee*, but it is most obviously inconsistent with the third element, which requires a showing that an authorized official affirmatively advised the accused that proscribed conduct is permissible. Judge Molloy explained why in [*United States v. Janetski*, CR 11-37-M-DWM, Doc. No. 45 at 6 (D. Mont. Sept. 1, 2011)]:

> An entrapment by estoppel defense requires, among other things, an affirmative statement by an authorized official that the defendant's conduct was lawful under federal

law. . . . The Ogden Memo only provides a prosecution policy and in no way indicates that [defendant's] conduct was permissible under federal law. To the contrary, the Memo explains that its "guidance regarding resource allocation does not 'legalize' marijuana or provide a legal defense." Ogden Memo at 2. Moreover, the Memo explains that nothing in it precludes investigation or prosecution, "even when there is clear and unambiguous compliance with existing state law." Id. at 3. Because the Ogden Memo does not provide a statement that [defendant's] charged conduct was permissible under federal law, it cannot, as a matter of law, support an entrapment by estoppel defense.

. . .

The Defendants cannot claim to have reasonably relied on any statements made by journalists or authors of press releases. Such individuals are not "authorized government official[s], empowered to render the claimed erroneous advice" as required by *Batterjee*. . . . Moreover, when it comes to assessing the risk that one's conduct might violate federal criminal law, it is perilous and unreasonable for any person to rely on press accounts given the risk of inaccuracy and overstatement. (For example, consider these headlines: Americans for Safe Access, press release, U.S. Supreme Court: State Medical Marijuana Laws Not Preempted by Federal Law (Dec. 1, 2008) . . . ; M. Alex Johnson, DEA to Halt Medical Marijuana Raids (Feb. 27, 2009) . . . ; David Johnston and Neil A. Lewis, Obama Administration to Stop Raids on Medical Marijuana Dispensers, New York Times (March 19, 2009) . . . ; Josh Meyer and Scott Glover, Medical Marijuana Dispensaries Will No Longer be Prosecuted, U.S. Attorney General Says, Los Angeles Times (Mar. 19, 2009) . . . ; Tristan Scott, Feds Won't Arrest Medical Marijuana Patients, Suppliers in Montana, 13 Other States, Missoulian (Oct. 20, 2009). . . .) Nor are newspapers' interpretations of official statements entitled to deference; an official may be misquoted, quoted out of context, or misinterpreted. . . .

. . .

Defendants claim they relied on statements made during the 2008 presidential campaign by then-Senator Barack Obama and his campaign spokesman, as well as on statements made by President Obama's White House spokesman and Attorney General Eric Holder. . . .

. . . The Oregon Mail Tribune quoted then-presidential-candidate Senator Obama as stating: "I'm not going to be using Justice Department resources to try to circumvent state laws on this issue." . . . The San Francisco Chronicle quoted his campaign spokesman as stating: "Obama supports the rights of states and local governments to make this choice—though he believes medical marijuana should be subject to [United States Food and Drug Administration] regulation like other drugs." . . .

After President Obama took office, his White House spokesman Nick Shapiro was quoted in the Washington Times responding to DEA raids of medical marijuana collectives in California: "The President believes that federal resources should not be used to circumvent state laws, and as he continues to appoint senior leadership to fill out the ranks of the federal government, he expects them to review their policies with that in mind." . . . Cable news network MSNBC reported on its website that Attorney General Eric Holder stated at a press conference that "[w]hat the president said during the campaign . . . will be consistent with what we will be doing here in law enforcement. . . . What [Obama] said during the campaign . . . is now American policy." . . .

Defendants point to additional statements made by Attorney General Holder and other Justice Department officials to the press and Congress in the wake of the Ogden memo. For example, the Attorney General is quoted as saying:

> The policy is to go after those people who violate both federal and state law, to the extent that people do that and try to use medical marijuana laws as a shield for activity that is not designed to comport with what the intention was of the state law. . . . Those are the organizations, the people, that we will target. And that is consistent with what the president said during the campaign.

Meyer & Glover, Los Angeles Times. . . . The same article quotes another Justice Department official stating, "If you are operating a medical marijuana clinic that is actually a front, we'll come after you. . . . But if you are operating within the law, we are not going to prioritize our resources to go after them." . . . At times, Attorney General Holder clearly stated that prosecutions of people acting in compliance with state law would be deprioritized. In other instances, he made broader statements that suggested more than mere deprioritization[, for example, that] "[W]e will not use federal resources to target medical marijuana patients or their providers." . . .

These statements fail to support a defense of estoppel by official misleading for several reasons. First, the variation in the content of the statements would have put a reasonable person on notice to make further inquiries. . . . The Ogden memo was the official, written statement of the administration's policy. As already held, no reasonable person would conclude from that document that he had immunity against federal prosecution for the distribution of marijuana for medical purposes. The fifth element of the *Batterjee* test is therefore unmet.

The public statements by federal officials also fail to satisfy the second element of the *Batterjee* test. There is nothing in the record to suggest that the quoted officials had any knowledge whatsoever of the Defendants' contemplated course of action, and thus it cannot be said that any federal official was fully aware of the relevant historical facts.

Nor do the statements Defendants claim to have relied on meet the third element of *Batterjee*. The Defendants point to no incident where a government official affirmatively stated or strongly implied that distribution of medical marijuana is lawful. Instead, Defendants argue that they need not identify an authorized official's affirmative statement that the conduct in question is legal; it is sufficient, they contend, for an authorized official state merely that the conduct will not result in prosecution.

The case law is contrary to the Defendants' position. In *Raley v. Ohio*, 360 U.S. 423 (1959), four witnesses were convicted in a contempt prosecution for failure to answer certain questions before their state legislature's "Un-American Activities Commission." . . . The United States Supreme Court reversed the convictions based upon its finding that the commission had misled the witness by advising them that they had a right to rely on a privilege against self-incrimination that did not in fact exist under Ohio law. Three of the witnesses were affirmatively told by commission members that the privilege was available to them. . . . It was strongly implied to the fourth person that the privilege existed as well. . . . The Ohio Supreme Court upheld the convictions on the grounds that under Ohio's immunity statute, the protections of the privilege were not legally available to a person testifying before a legislative committee. . . . The Supreme Court reversed, holding that to do otherwise would "sanction an indefensible sort of entrapment by the State—convicting a citizen for exercising a privilege which the State had clearly told him was available to him." . . .

The Supreme Court reached a similar conclusion in *Cox v. Louisiana*, 379 U.S. 559 (1965). In that case a police chief . . . had affirmatively granted a group of demonstrators permission to protest across the street from a courthouse. . . . A demonstrator was later convicted of violating a statute that prohibited protesting "near" the courthouse. . . . The Supreme Court reversed, holding that a demonstrator, having been supplied with the police chief's "on-the-spot administrative interpretation" of the statute, "would justifiabl[y] tend to rely on this administrative interpretation of how 'near' the courthouse a particular demonstration might take place." . . . In explaining its ruling, the Court observed that the appellant had been effectively advised that a protest in that location "would not be one 'near' the courthouse within the terms of the statute." . . . As in *Raley*, the "[a]ppellant was led to believe that his [conduct] violated no statute.". . . .

In both *Raley* and *Cox*, state actors affirmatively told the defendants, or at least strongly implied, that a specific, individually contemplated course of conduct was lawful. The officials did not merely suggest they would not prosecute the defendants if they broke the law, or that their prosecution would be "deprioritized." Rather, the state actors made affirmative, "actively misleading" statements directly to the defendants that the law permitted them to assert a specific privilege or to protest in a specific place. . . .

The Ogden memo was directed to government attorneys. The Obama administration's comments concerning the Ogden memo policy were made to the press and Congress. The officials did not affirmatively tell the Defendants that their specific conduct was legal.

. . .

Arlen Auld is a drug investigator with the Flathead Tribal Police. Officer Auld testified at the hearing on these motions. He described an encounter he had with Defendant Washington and others at a medical marijuana growing site near Polson, Montana, in the fall of 2010 or 2011. Officer Auld—who at the time was a member of the Northwest Drug Task Force—received a call from a member of the High Intensity Drug Trafficking Area Task Force ("HIDTA") in Missoula asking Auld to identify the location of a growing operation. Officer Auld visited the building that housed the operation and met with Defendant Washington and several others, including Washington's attorney at the time. Officer Auld was offered an opportunity to count the plants and inspect records, and upon leaving the growing facility he indicated to Defendant Washington and the others that "everything looks okay" with respect to the operation. Officer Auld may have also reported back to the Missoula HIDTA that the operation appeared to be in compliance with state law.

Although this statement by Officer Auld is not enough to warrant dismissal of the Indictment on a theory of estoppel by official misleading, the Court nevertheless believes that Officer Auld's involvement presents a question for the jury to resolve in this case. Officer Auld was unable to recall the precise details of his visit to the growing facility, and he did not know the name of the agent who asked him to locate the facility. He was also unsure of the year in which the incident occurred. Moreover, Officer Auld testified that he has never been sworn or cross-deputized as a federal agent. But again, while these circumstances do not warrant outright dismissal of the Indictment, there are enough uncertainties with respect to Officer Auld's visit to the Polson growing facility that the Defendants are entitled to the opportunity at trial to attempt to prove estoppel by official misleading with respect to Officer Auld's statements only. Having failed to make a prima facie showing with respect to any other statements, the Defendants will not be permitted to attempt to establish estoppel by official misleading at trial based on any statements by any official other than Officer Auld. . . .

## Notes and Questions

1. What did Officer Auld mean when he said "everything looks okay"? Although the *Washington* court found statements of various federal officials insufficient as a matter of law to sustain an entrapment by estoppel defense, it gave the defendants the opportunity to persuade a jury that Officer Auld's curt statement ("everything looks okay") made them reasonably believe their conduct was legal under federal law. Do you think such a statement, standing alone, should be sufficient to establish the defense?

2. Who speaks for the federal government? Apart from the ambiguity of Officer Auld's words, reliance on *any* statement coming from him poses a separate issue, highlighted by the following Problem:

Problem 7.18: In *Washington*, suppose that Pasha had inspected the defendants' property and then proclaimed to the defendants after her visit: "Your marijuana growing and distributing operation appears perfectly legal under federal law. You may proceed to grow and distribute marijuana without violating federal law." Would Pasha's statement give rise to a cognizable entrapment by estoppel defense? Would your answer change if Pasha held any of the following jobs during her inspection (and if so, which one(s))?

(1) Licensed private attorney
(2) Deputy employed by the federal DEA's Missoula, Montana office
(3) Attorney General of the United States
(4) Vice President of the United States

3. Notwithstanding any legal deficiencies in the defendants' claim, was it fair for the federal government to prosecute them after issuing the Ogden memorandum?

---

In August 2013, after Colorado and Washington legalized recreational marijuana, the DOJ issued additional enforcement guidance (the Cole II memorandum). The new memorandum arguably provided broader and somewhat clearer assurances. Although it continued to disclaim any intention to change federal law or to create rights against prosecution, the Cole II memorandum discouraged federal prosecutors from taking enforcement actions against marijuana suppliers unless those suppliers were violating state law or implicating some delineated federal interest, such as stopping distribution to minors. The relevant portions of the Cole II memorandum are excerpted below:

### *Deputy Attorney General James M. Cole,* Guidance Regarding Marijuana Enforcement
Aug. 29, 2013

. . . The guidance set forth herein applies to all federal enforcement activity, including civil enforcement and criminal investigations and prosecutions, concerning marijuana in all states.

. . . Congress has determined that marijuana is a dangerous drug and that the illegal distribution and sale of marijuana is a serious crime that provides a significant source of revenue to large-scale criminal enterprises, gangs, and cartels. The Department of Justice is committed to enforcement of the CSA consistent with those determinations. The Department is also committed to using its limited investigative and prosecutorial resources to address the most significant threats in the most effective, consistent, and rational way. In furtherance of those objectives, as several states enacted laws relating to the use of marijuana for medical purposes, the Department in recent years has focused its efforts on certain enforcement priorities that are particularly important to the federal government:

- Preventing the distribution of marijuana to minors;
- Preventing revenue from the sale of marijuana from going to criminal enterprises, gangs, and cartels;
- Preventing the diversion of marijuana from states where it is legal under state law in some form to other states;
- Preventing state-authorized marijuana activity from being used as a cover or pretext for the trafficking of other illegal drugs or other illegal activity;
- Preventing violence and the use of firearms in the cultivation and distribution of marijuana;
- Preventing drugged driving and the exacerbation of other adverse public health consequences associated with marijuana use;
- Preventing the growing of marijuana on public lands and the attendant public safety and environmental dangers posed by marijuana production on public lands; and
- Preventing marijuana possession or use on federal property.

These priorities will continue to guide the Department's enforcement of the CSA against marijuana-related conduct. Thus, this memorandum serves as guidance to Department attorneys and law enforcement to focus their enforcement resources and efforts, including prosecution, on persons or organizations whose conduct interferes with any one or more of these priorities, regardless of state law.

Outside of these enforcement priorities, the federal government has traditionally relied on states and local law enforcement agencies to address marijuana activity through enforcement of their own narcotics laws. For example, the Department of Justice has not historically devoted resources to prosecuting individuals whose conduct is limited to possession of small amounts of marijuana for personal use on private property. Instead, the Department has left such lower-level or localized activity to state and local authorities and has stepped in to enforce the CSA only when the use, possession, cultivation, or distribution of marijuana has threatened to cause one of the harms identified above.

The enactment of state laws that endeavor to authorize marijuana production, distribution, and possession by establishing a regulatory scheme for these purposes affects this traditional joint federal-state approach to narcotics enforcement. The Department's guidance in this memorandum rests on its expectation that states and local governments that have enacted laws authorizing marijuana-related conduct will implement strong and effective regulatory and enforcement systems that will address the threat those state laws could pose to public safety, public health, and other law enforcement interests. A system adequate to that task must not only contain robust controls and procedures on paper; it must also be effective in practice. Jurisdictions that have implemented systems that provide for regulation of marijuana activity must provide the necessary resources and demonstrate the willingness to enforce their laws and regulations in a manner that ensures they do not undermine federal enforcement priorities.

In jurisdictions that have enacted laws legalizing marijuana in some form and that have also implemented strong and effective regulatory and enforcement systems to control the cultivation, distribution, sale, and possession of marijuana, conduct in compliance with those laws and regulations is less likely to threaten the federal priorities set forth above. Indeed, a robust system may affirmatively address those priorities by, for example, implementing effective measures to prevent diversion of marijuana outside of the regulated system and to other states, prohibiting access to marijuana by minors, and replacing an illicit marijuana trade that funds criminal enterprises with a tightly regulated market in which revenues are tracked and accounted for. In those circumstances, consistent with the traditional allocation of federal-state efforts in this area, enforcement of state law by state and local law enforcement and regulatory bodies should remain the primary means of addressing marijuana-related activity. If state enforcement efforts are not sufficiently robust to protect against the harms set forth above, the federal government may seek to challenge the regulatory structure itself in addition to continuing to bring individual enforcement actions, including criminal prosecutions, focused on those harms.

The Department's previous memoranda specifically addressed the exercise of prosecutorial discretion in states with laws authorizing marijuana cultivation and distribution for medical use. In those contexts, the Department advised that it likely was not an efficient use of federal resources to focus enforcement efforts on seriously ill individuals, or on their individual caregivers. In doing so, the previous guidance drew a distinction between the seriously ill and their caregivers, on the one hand, and large-scale, for-profit commercial enterprises, on the other, and advised that the latter continued to be appropriate targets for federal enforcement and prosecution. In drawing this distinction, the Department relied on the common-sense judgment that the size of a marijuana operation was a reasonable proxy for assessing whether marijuana trafficking implicates the federal enforcement priorities set forth above.

As explained above, however, both the existence of a strong and effective state regulatory system, and an operation's compliance with such a system, may allay the threat that an operation's size poses to federal enforcement interests. Accordingly, in exercising prosecutorial discretion, prosecutors should not consider the size or commercial nature of a marijuana operation alone as a proxy for assessing whether marijuana trafficking implicates the Department's enforcement priorities listed above. Rather, prosecutors should continue to review marijuana cases on a case-by-case basis and weigh all available information and evidence, including, but not limited to, whether the operation is demonstrably in compliance with a strong and effective state regulatory system. A marijuana operation's large scale or for-profit nature may be a relevant consideration for assessing the extent to which it undermines a particular federal enforcement priority. The primary question in all cases—and in all jurisdictions—should be whether the conduct at issue implicates one or more of the enforcement priorities listed above.

As with the Department's previous statements on this subject, this memorandum is intended solely as a guide to the exercise of investigative and prosecutorial discretion. This memorandum does not alter in any way the Department's authority to enforce federal law, including federal laws relating to marijuana, regardless of state law. Neither the guidance herein nor any state or local law provides a legal defense to a violation of federal law, including any civil or criminal violation of the CSA. Even in jurisdictions with strong and effective regulatory systems, evidence that particular conduct threatens federal priorities will subject that person or entity to federal enforcement action, based on the circumstances. This memorandum is not intended to, does not, and may not be relied upon to create any rights, substantive or procedural, enforceable at law by any party in any matter civil or criminal. It applies prospectively to the exercise of prosecutorial discretion in future cases and does not provide defendants or subjects of enforcement action with a basis for reconsideration of any pending civil action or criminal prosecution. Finally, nothing herein precludes investigation or prosecution, even in the absence of any one of the factors listed above, in particular circumstances where investigation and prosecution otherwise serves an important federal interest.

### Notes and Questions

1. What do you think of the enforcement priorities outlined in the Cole II memorandum? Assuming the memorandum is scrupulously followed by federal officials, do the priorities satisfactorily limit the federal government's power over the supply of marijuana?

2. Does this latest memorandum lend any further support to the entrapment by estoppel defense asserted in *Washington*? Could you imagine language that might give rise to such a defense? Along these lines, consider the following Problem:

**Problem 7.19**: The DOJ issues yet another enforcement memorandum to United States Attorneys. This memorandum states simply: "Do not prosecute anyone for possessing, manufacturing, or distributing marijuana. Period." Notwithstanding the memorandum, the U.S. Attorney for Montana, Pasha, proceeds to prosecute Andy for growing and distributing marijuana. Could Andy successfully petition a court to enforce the DOJ policy against U.S. Attorney Pasha? *See* Robert A. Mikos, *A Critical Appraisal of the Department of Justice's New Approach to Medical Marijuana*, 22 Stan. L. & Pol'y Rev. 633, 641 (2011).

3. Another, related defense is called promissory estoppel. The following variation on **Problem 7.19** illustrates a scenario in which this version of entrapment might arise:

**Problem 7.20**: Suppose U.S. Attorney Pasha had earlier told Andy: "Do not worry. Per the DOJ memorandum, my office will not prosecute you for possessing, manufacturing, or distributing marijuana." Later, Pasha changes her mind and initiates a prosecution against Andy for manufacturing and distributing marijuana. Now does Andy have a valid defense?

The *Washington* court discusses this possibility in a portion of the opinion not excerpted above:

> [Other courts] have entertained promissory estoppel theories in considering the enforceability of agreements made in criminal cases. . . . Under [the governing framework, the] promisee must show: "(1) the existence of a promise, (2) which the promisor reasonably should have expected to induce the promisee's reliance, (3) which actually induces such reliance, (4) that such reliance is reasonable, and (5) that injustice can only be

avoided by enforcement of the promise." . . . The promise must be "clear and unambiguous."

*Washington, supra*, 887 F. Supp. at 1099-1100. The court proceeded to find that the Ogden memo and public statements by federal officials were not "promises, much less clear and unambiguous ones." *Id.* at 1100. But would the statement by U.S. Attorney Pasha in **Problem 7.20** satisfy the requirements of promissory estoppel?

### b. Congressional Spending Limitations

Congress has recently sought to assert more control over the DOJ's enforcement of federal marijuana policy. Starting in late 2014, it began to restrict the DOJ's use of budgeted funds in medical marijuana states. The following case discusses the restrictions and their impact on federal criminal prosecutions brought against marijuana suppliers.

## *United States v. McIntosh*
### 833 F.3d 1163 (9th Cir. 2016)

O'SCANNLAIN, J.:

[In this consolidated appeal, a]ll Appellants have been indicted for various infractions of the Controlled Substances Act (CSA), [21 U.S.C. section 841]. They have moved to dismiss their indictments or to enjoin their prosecutions on the grounds that the Department of Justice (DOJ) is prohibited from spending funds to prosecute them.

. . .

In December 2014, Congress enacted the following rider in an omnibus appropriations bill funding the government through September 30, 2015:

> None of the funds made available in this Act to the Department of Justice may be used, with respect to the States of Alabama, Alaska, Arizona, California, Colorado, Connecticut, Delaware, District of Columbia, Florida, Hawaii, Illinois, Iowa, Kentucky, Maine, Maryland, Massachusetts, Michigan, Minnesota, Mississippi, Missouri, Montana, Nevada, New Hampshire, New Jersey, New Mexico, Oregon, Rhode Island, South Carolina, Tennessee, Utah, Vermont, Washington, and Wisconsin, to prevent such States from implementing their own State laws that authorize the use, distribution, possession, or cultivation of medical marijuana.

Consolidated and Further Continuing Appropriations Act, 2015, Pub. L. No. 113-235, § 538, 128 Stat. 2130, 2217 (2014). Various short-term measures extended the appropriations and the rider through December 22, 2015. On December 18, 2015, Congress enacted a new appropriations act, which appropriates funds through the fiscal year ending September 30, 2016, and includes essentially the same rider in § 542. Consolidated Appropriations Act, 2016, Pub. L. No. 114-113, § 542, 129 Stat. 2242, 2332-33 (2015). . . .

. . .

The parties dispute whether the government's spending money on their prosecutions violates § 542.

We focus, as we must, on the statutory text. Section 542 provides that "[n]one of the funds made available in this Act to the Department of Justice may be used, with respect to [Medical Marijuana States] to prevent any of them from implementing their own laws that authorize the use, distribution, possession, or cultivation of medical marijuana." [§ 542.] . . . Unfortunately, the rider is not a model of clarity.

. . .

"It is a 'fundamental canon of statutory construction' that, 'unless otherwise defined, words will be interpreted as taking their ordinary, contemporary, common meaning.'" . . . Thus, in order to decide whether the prosecutions of Appellants violate § 542, we must determine the plain meaning of "prevent any of [the Medical Marijuana States] from implementing their own laws that authorize the use, distribution, possession, or cultivation of medical marijuana." The pronoun "them" refers back to the Medical Marijuana States, and "their own laws" refers to the state laws of the Medical Marijuana States. And "implement" means:

> To "carry out, accomplish; *esp.*: to give practical effect to and ensure of actual fulfillment by concrete measure." *Implement, Merriam-Webster's Collegiate Dictionary* (11th ed. 2003);
>
> "To put into practical effect; carry out." *Implement, American Heritage Dictionary of the English Language* (5th ed. 2011); and
>
> "To complete, perform, carry into effect (a contract, agreement, etc.); to fulfil (an engagement or promise)." *Implement, Oxford English Dictionary*, www.oed.com.

. . . In sum, § 542 prohibits DOJ from spending money on actions that prevent the Medical Marijuana States' giving practical effect to their state laws that authorize the use, distribution, possession, or cultivation of medical marijuana.

. . .

DOJ argues that it does not prevent the Medical Marijuana States from giving practical effect to their medical marijuana laws by prosecuting private individuals, rather than taking legal action against the state. We are not persuaded.

Importantly, the "[s]tatutory language cannot be construed in a vacuum. It is [another] fundamental canon of statutory construction that the words of a statute must be read in their context and with a view to their place in the overall statutory scheme." . . . Here, we must read § 542 with a view to its place in the overall statutory scheme for marijuana regulation, namely the CSA and the State Medical Marijuana Laws. The CSA prohibits the use, distribution, possession, or cultivation of any marijuana. . . . The State Medical Marijuana Laws are those state laws that authorize the use, distribution, possession, or cultivation of medical marijuana. Thus, the CSA prohibits what the State Medical Marijuana Laws permit.

In light of the ordinary meaning of the terms of § 542 and the relationship between the relevant federal and state laws, we consider whether a superior authority, which prohibits certain conduct, can prevent a subordinate authority from implementing a rule that officially permits such conduct by punishing individuals who are engaged in the conduct officially permitted by the lower authority. We conclude that it can.

DOJ, without taking any legal action against the Medical Marijuana States, prevents them from implementing their laws that authorize the use, distribution, possession, or cultivation of medical marijuana by prosecuting individuals for use, distribution, possession, or cultivation of medical marijuana that is authorized by such laws. By officially permitting certain conduct, state law provides for non-prosecution of individuals who engage in such conduct. If the federal government prosecutes such individuals, it has prevented the state from giving practical effect to its law providing for non-prosecution of individuals who engage in the permitted conduct.

We therefore conclude that, at a minimum, § 542 prohibits DOJ from spending funds from relevant appropriations acts for the prosecution of individuals who engaged in conduct permitted by the State Medical Marijuana Laws and who fully complied with such laws.

. . .

[Some] Appellants . . . argue for a more expansive interpretation of § 542. They contend that the rider prohibits DOJ from bringing federal marijuana charges against anyone licensed or authorized under a state medical marijuana law for activity occurring within that state, including licensees who had failed to comply fully with state law.

For instance, Appellants . . . argue that "implementation of laws necessarily involves all aspects of putting the law into practical effect, including interpretation of the law, means of application and enforcement, and procedures and processes for determining the outcome of individual cases." Under this view, if the federal government prosecutes individuals who are not strictly compliant with state law, it will prevent the states from implementing the *entirety* of their laws that authorize medical marijuana by preventing them from giving practical effect to the penalties and enforcement mechanisms for engaging in unauthorized conduct. Thus, argue the . . . Appellants, the Department of Justice must refrain from prosecuting "unless a person's activities are so clearly outside the scope of a state's medical marijuana laws that reasonable debate is not possible."

To determine whether such construction is correct, we must decide whether the phrase "laws that authorize" includes not only the rules authorizing certain conduct but also the rules delineating penalties and enforcement mechanisms for engaging in unauthorized conduct. In answering that question, we consider the ordinary meaning of "laws that authorize the use, distribution, possession, or cultivation of medical marijuana." "Law" has many different meanings, including the following definitions that appear most relevant to § 542:

> "The aggregate of legislation, judicial precedents, and accepted legal principles; the body of authoritative grounds of judicial and administrative action; esp., the body of rules, standards, and principles that the courts of a particular jurisdiction apply in deciding controversies brought before them."
>
> "The set of rules or principles dealing with a specific area of a legal system [copyright law]."

*Law*, *Black's Law Dictionary* (10th ed. 2014); and:

> "1. a. The body of rules, whether proceeding from formal enactment or from custom, which a particular state or community recognizes as binding on its members or subjects. (In this sense usually *the law*.)."
>
> "One of the individual rules which constitute the 'law' (sense 1) of a state or polity. . . . The plural has often a collective sense . . . approaching sense 1."

*Law*, *Oxford English Dictionary*, www.oed.com. The relative pronoun "that" restricts "laws" to those laws authorizing the use, distribution, possession, or cultivation of medical marijuana. *See* Bryan A. Garner, *Garner's Dictionary of Legal Usage* 887-89 (3d ed. 2011). In sum, the ordinary meaning of § 542 prohibits the Department of Justice from preventing the implementation of the Medical Marijuana States' laws or sets of rules and only those rules that authorize medical marijuana use.

We also consider the context of § 542. The rider prohibits DOJ from preventing forty states, the District of Columbia, and two territories from implementing their medical marijuana laws. Not only are such laws varied in composition but they also are changing as new statutes are enacted, new regulations are promulgated, and new administrative and judicial decisions interpret such statutes and regulations. Thus, § 542 applies to a wide variety of laws that are in flux.

Given this context and the restriction of the relevant laws to those that authorize conduct, we conclude that § 542 prohibits the federal government only from preventing the implementation of those specific rules of state law that authorize the use, distribution, possession, or cultivation of medical marijuana. DOJ does not prevent the implementation of rules authorizing conduct when it prosecutes individuals who engage in conduct unauthorized under state medical marijuana laws. Individuals who do not strictly comply with all state-law conditions regarding the use, distribution, possession, and cultivation of medical marijuana have engaged in conduct that is unauthorized, and prosecuting such individuals does not violate § 542. Congress could easily have drafted § 542 to prohibit interference with laws that address medical marijuana or those that regulate medical marijuana, but it did not. Instead, it chose to proscribe preventing states from implementing laws that authorize the use, distribution, possession, and cultivation of medical marijuana.

. . .

The parties cite various pieces of legislative history to support their arguments regarding the meaning of § 542.

We cannot consider such sources. It is a fundamental principle of appropriations law that we may only consider the text of an appropriations rider, not expressions of intent in legislative history. . . .

. . .

We recognize that some members of Congress may have desired a more expansive construction of the rider, while others may have preferred a more limited interpretation. However, we must consider only the text of the rider. If Congress intends to prohibit a wider or narrower range of DOJ actions, it certainly may express such intention, hopefully with greater clarity, in the text of any future rider.

. . .

We therefore must remand to the district courts. If DOJ wishes to continue these prosecutions, Appellants are entitled to evidentiary hearings to determine whether their conduct was completely authorized by state law, by which we mean that they strictly complied with all relevant conditions imposed by state law on the use, distribution, possession, and cultivation of medical marijuana. We leave to the district courts to determine, in the first instance and in each case, the precise remedy that would be appropriate.

We note the temporal nature of the problem with these prosecutions. The government had authority to initiate criminal proceedings, and it merely lost funds to continue them. DOJ is currently prohibited from spending funds from specific appropriations acts for prosecutions of those who complied with state law. But Congress could appropriate funds for such prosecutions tomorrow. Conversely, this temporary lack of funds could become a more permanent lack of funds if Congress continues to include the same rider in future appropriations bills. In determining the appropriate remedy for any violation of § 542, the district courts should consider the temporal nature of the lack of funds along with Appellants' rights to a speedy trial under the Sixth Amendment and the Speedy Trial Act, 18 U.S.C. § 3161.[5]

## Notes and Questions

1. Do you agree with the *McIntosh* court's interpretation of section 538 (and section 542)? How would you interpret the language of Congress's budget restriction?

2. *McIntosh* indicates that the DOJ could continue to prosecute marijuana suppliers in medical marijuana states, but only if the suppliers had not "strictly complied with all relevant conditions imposed by state law." What does this proviso mean? Consider the following Problems:

**Problem 7.21**: Andy has been licensed by his state to grow up to 1,000 marijuana plants for purposes of the state's medical marijuana program. During a routine inspection, however, Andy discovers that he actually possesses 1,001 marijuana plants. Per *McIntosh*, may the DOJ charge Andy with the manufacture of 1,000 or more marijuana plants—a charge that carries a minimum sentence of ten years' imprisonment under federal law?

**Problem 7.22**: Benjamin lives in Maine. Following the *McIntosh* ruling, the state of Maine passes a new law declaring that "all marijuana is medical marijuana, and there will be no state-imposed restrictions on the use, possession, cultivation or distribution of marijuana by (and to) adults." Benjamin starts up a large marijuana shop. He quickly cultivates more than 1,000 marijuana plants, and sells the drug to any adult willing to pay his price. May the DOJ charge Benjamin with manufacture and/or distribution of marijuana?

---

5. The prior observation should also serve as a warning. To be clear, § 542 does not provide immunity from prosecution for federal marijuana offenses. The CSA prohibits the manufacture, distribution, and possession of marijuana. Anyone in any state who possesses, distributes, or manufactures marijuana for medical or recreational purposes (or attempts or conspires to do so) is committing a federal crime. The federal government can prosecute such offenses for up to five years after they occur. See 18 U.S.C. § 3282. Congress currently restricts the government from spending certain funds to prosecute certain individuals. But Congress could restore funding tomorrow, a year from now, or four years from now, and the government could then prosecute individuals who committed offenses while the government lacked funding. Moreover, a new president will be elected soon, and a new administration could shift enforcement priorities to place greater emphasis on prosecuting marijuana offenses.

Nor does any state law "legalize" possession, distribution, or manufacture of marijuana. Under the Supremacy Clause of the Constitution, state laws cannot permit what federal law prohibits. U.S. Const. art. VI, cl. 2. Thus, while the CSA remains in effect, states cannot actually authorize the manufacture, distribution, or possession of marijuana. Such activity remains prohibited by federal law.

Part III. Marijuana Suppliers

**Problem 7.23:** Camila distributes medical marijuana to qualifying patients out of a retail storefront in Little City. Her actions are legal under state law, but Little City has adopted an ordinance that prohibits the distribution of medical marijuana. Per *McIntosh*, may the DOJ charge Camila with distribution of marijuana?

**Problem 7.24:** Delilah is a qualifying patient participating in her state's medical marijuana program. After the state amended its medical marijuana law to allow the unfettered use of marijuana "in any park or other government property," Delilah lit up a marijuana joint in the following locations in her state:

(1) A national park
(2) A United States Post Office
(3) A federal courthouse

Per *McIntosh*, may the DOJ charge Delilah with simple possession of marijuana (or any other offense) for her actions in any of these locations?

### c. Jury Nullification

Even when a defendant has clearly broken the law, juries will sometimes refuse to find the defendant guilty due to a belief that the law is unjust. This phenomenon is known as jury nullification. Importantly, a jury's judgment of acquittal may not be disturbed regardless of what motivated it.

Jury nullification has a long and controversial history in the United States. It has achieved particular currency in federal prosecutions of state-sanctioned medical marijuana suppliers. Defendants facing federal marijuana supply charges have sought to play up the sympathy of juries by suggesting they broke federal law only for good reason—namely, to help seriously ill people access medicine.

Can a defendant encourage a jury to nullify the law? *United States v. Rosenthal* discusses the issue. Pursuant to an agreement with the City of Oakland, California, Ed Rosenthal openly operated a large medical marijuana cultivation facility in the City. He was indicted by the federal government for manufacturing marijuana, in violation of 21 U.S.C. section 841(a). At his federal trial, Rosenthal sought permission to lobby the jury to nullify the charges against him. In the excerpt below, Judge Charles Breyer provides a useful discussion of the power of juries to nullify the law and the limitations on defendant's ability to tap into this power.

## United States v. Rosenthal
266 F. Supp. 2d 1068 (N.D. Cal. 2003)

BREYER, J.:

... Rosenthal does not contend that the evidence was insufficient to support his conviction. Nor could he; in fact, there is overwhelming and uncontradicted evidence that he cultivated hundreds of marijuana plants for distribution to medical marijuana centers. Rather, the thrust of Rosenthal's argument is that the Court should have allowed him to present evidence and argument designed to encourage the jury to disregard the controlling law. . . .

Prior to commencement of trial, the government filed motions in limine to exclude evidence of a "medical marijuana" defense aimed at jury nullification. The government maintained that evidence of Rosenthal's motive or justification for the cultivation of marijuana could not be presented to the jury. In making this argument, the government relied on a fundamental rule of evidence, which requires that only relevant evidence be considered by the jury and that irrelevant evidence be excluded. *See* Fed. R. Evid. 402. Since the elements of the criminal offenses at issue involve only the knowing or intentional manufacturing of marijuana and not the purpose for which the marijuana was grown, the government claimed that evidence of medical purposes . . . was inadmissible.

Accordingly, the Court was required at the outset to determine whether such evidence, i.e., testimony demonstrating Rosenthal's desire to help people who suffer from serious debilitating illnesses . . . was relevant to any issue the jury had to determine in order to fairly adjudicate his guilt or innocence. If so, such evidence would be admitted; if not, it would have to be excluded because to admit it would violate the Federal Rules of Evidence and permit the jury to base its verdict on impermissible grounds.

. . . [The defense] suggested that this evidence would permit the jury to consider whether to acquit notwithstanding the facts and established law. This notion, often referred to as jury nullification, recognizes the power of the jury to refuse to apply the law as instructed by the Court. Since a jury has this power, the defense argued, it was entitled to receive evidence upon which it could choose to exercise its power.

While jury nullification is a "fact" of judicial life, the United States Supreme Court has explicitly recognized that juries have no right to nullify. *See Standefer v. United States*, 447 U.S. 10, 22 . . . (1980). As such, evidence which is otherwise inadmissible does not become admissible in order to facilitate jury nullification. Among the many reasons for discouraging such a practice is that nullification can lead to grossly unequal protection of the laws. To permit nullification in cases where a defendant has a "good" reason for his conduct when motive is not an element of the crime allows jurors to use their individualized set of beliefs as to "good" reasons to be determinative of guilt or innocence. Reasons, good or bad, are of course relevant to sentencing, but they are not accepted by courts as a basis for verdicts.

Furthermore, in light of the United States Supreme Court speaking directly on this issue of nullification, any change in the law should come from that Court, not this one. . . .

Since [the reasons] . . . offered by the defense did not support a finding that motive or state of mind was relevant to the issue of guilt or innocence, the Court concluded that the proffered evidence should not be admitted. . . . Such evidence is appropriate for consideration at sentencing. It is simply not relevant to the question of guilt or innocence. . . .

[The court discussed jury nullification again in a later portion of its opinion.]

During closing arguments, defense counsel made the following statement to the jury:

> You have an important job in front of you. I don't understate it or underestimate it at all. It's important and a difficult task that you face, but we're confident that you're up to the task. You're well-equipped to do it, however. You're well-equipped not only because of the process you've seen unfold in front of you the last couple of weeks in the course of this trial, the witnesses that you've heard testify, the exhibits that you've seen. You're well-equipped otherwise.
>
> Nobody expects you to check your common sense at the door of the courthouse and come in with some kind of a blank slate. We can't expect you to do that. And we want you

to use your life experiences to make judgments. It's unrealistic to think otherwise. You're well-equipped. Use your common sense. Use your life experiences when you judge this case.

Likewise, we don't ask you to check your common sense of justice at the courthouse door when you judge this case. That would be asking far too much. And that we do not ask. We can't ask that. It's not realistic. So use your common sense. Use your common sense of justice and judge accordingly. We have to, I think, accept that as the stream of life flows along, our sense of what is just and unjust changes. And I can only hope that there are those among you and among all of us whose conception of justice. . . .

. . . At this point, the Court interjected as follows:

Well, ladies and gentlemen, you cannot substitute your sense of justice, whatever that means, for your duty to follow the law, whether you agree with it or not. It's not your determination whether a law is just or whether a law is unjust. That can't be your task. Go ahead, [defense counsel].

. . . Defense counsel then proceeded:

Make your judgments carefully. Make your judgments considering all the tools that you bring to bear on this task. And remember that any decision you make, any decision that you make as far as the guilt or innocence is one that's going to last a very long time. This is your one opportunity to do it and get it right. And it's a crucial opportunity. Not only judge that, but as I mentioned earlier, to send a message about what you will expect and demand of the United States government when they prosecute cases like this. Send that message. You can do it. And you can acquit. . . . [W]e put our trust in your capacity to remember the evidence, and to interpret it accordingly, and to render a just result. Please do justice.

. . .

Rosenthal now argues that a new trial is required because the Court's interjection improperly "interfere[d] with [the jury's] well-recognized power" to "acquit a clearly guilty defendant due to its collective conscience." . . . In particular, Rosenthal objects to the Court's "prohibition on the jury bringing its 'sense of justice' to bear on its verdict." . . . While Rosenthal acknowledges that federal defendants are not entitled to an instruction concerning a jury's power to nullify, . . . he argues that the jury may nonetheless "act[] as a 'safety valve' for exceptional cases." . . . According to Rosenthal, the Court's instruction in this case "impermissibly divest[ed] the jury of [this] power." . . .

As an initial matter, Rosenthal's motion glosses over the distinction between a jury that "bring[s] its 'sense of justice' to bear on its verdict" and a jury whose verdict is based entirely on its "sense of justice" without regard to the Court's instructions. The Court's instruction in this case admonished the jury against "substitut[ing] its sense of justice . . . for [its] duty to follow the law." . . . As such, it was not, as Rosenthal suggests, an outright "prohibition on the jury bringing its 'sense of justice' to bear on its verdict." . . . Rather, the Court instructed the jury that it could not base its decision on its "sense of justice" as a substitute for the law and the evidence in the case.

More importantly, Rosenthal ignores the critical distinction between the power to nullify and the right to nullify. . . . [It has long been] recognized that nullification, whether proper or improper, is virtually impossible to prevent. . . . More recent cases have paid heed to the jury's role as the "conscience of the community" in the context of rulings that preserve the secrecy of jury deliberations. . . .

The sanctity of the deliberative process, however, does not give a jury license to flout the court's instructions at will. "[T]he power of juries to 'nullify' or exercise a power of lenity is just that—a power; it is by no means a right or something that a judge should encourage or permit if it is within his authority to prevent." . . . As such, the fact that juries have the power to nullify does not make the exercise of that power inherently legitimate or proper. . . .

Indeed, the same courts that have acknowledged the jury's power to nullify have also held that "trial courts have the duty to forestall or prevent such conduct . . . by firm instruction or admonition." . . . Thus a court, when made aware that a juror intends to nullify, has a duty to dismiss that juror. . . . A fortiori, it cannot be contrary to law to instruct jurors before deliberations commence that they cannot decline to follow the law merely because to do so would offend their "sense of justice." . . .

Of course, no matter how conscientiously a court may guard against the exercise of the jury's power to nullify, the court cannot divest the jury of that power altogether. "Nullification is, by definition, a violation of a juror's oath to apply the law as instructed by the court." . . . As such, the power to nullify is not a power that a court can take away from the jury by means of an instruction, because it always remains within a jury's power to ignore that very instruction. Our system therefore tolerates the possibility that the jury will disregard the law in "exceptional cases" notwithstanding the court's best efforts to prevent it. . . . Contrary to Rosenthal's suggestion, however, a court cannot make an ex ante determination of whether a case qualifies as "exceptional" and dilute its jury instructions accordingly. Rather, the court must in all cases instruct the jury to return a verdict consistent with the law; what makes a case "exceptional" is the jury's decision to disregard that instruction. The jury always retains the power to make that decision, no matter how the court instructs it.

The Court's instructions in this case were consistent with the Court's obligation to "forestall or prevent" nullification. . . . The instructions did not, however, preclude the jury from bringing its sense of justice to bear on its verdict, nor did they divest the jury of its inalienable power to nullify. As such, Rosenthal is not entitled to a new trial on this basis.

## Notes and Questions

1. *A Postscript on* Rosenthal. The jury in Rosenthal's 2003 trial unanimously voted to convict him (unanimity is required in the federal system), but several jurors later indicated they would have voted to acquit him had they known he was growing medical marijuana for the City of Oakland. *Jurors Say Key Information Withheld in Case of Pot Grower*, L.A. Times, Feb. 4, 2003. The Ninth Circuit reversed Judge Breyer's decision on other grounds and remanded for a new trial, citing juror misconduct (a juror had contacted an attorney for advice during deliberations). *United States v. Rosenthal*, 454 F.3d 943 (9th Cir. 2006). Upon retrial in 2007, a second jury, which was also kept in the dark about the motive behind Rosenthal's grow operation, likewise voted to convict him. Notably, however, following both the original (2003) and second (2007) trials, Judge Breyer elected to impose a sentence of only one day's imprisonment. Bob Egelko, *Medical Marijuana Advocate Convicted: Though Guilty Again, No Jail for Rosenthal*, S.F. Chron., May 31, 2007.

Since his trials, Rosenthal has continued to call himself the "guru of ganja" and has advocated for the repeal of marijuana prohibitions. He even has a website, https://

perma.cc/6NRU-GVR4. Rosenthal's case is discussed again in Chapter 14 below, in the context of the public authority defense, 21 U.S.C. § 885(d).

2. Do you think a defendant should have the right to ask a jury to nullify the law? Does your answer depend on your own views of the particular law being enforced? What if the defendant were being tried for a different crime, like murder, rape, or possession of child pornography?

3. Notwithstanding limitations on defendants' ability to promote nullification in the courtroom, the threat of jury nullification may have prompted federal officials to change their enforcement tactics, especially in states that have legalized marijuana for medical purposes. See Robert A. Mikos, *On the Limits of Supremacy*, 62 Vand. L. Rev. 1421, 1479 (2009) ("[I]n order to avoid sympathetic juries, the DEA has been attacking medical marijuana suppliers primarily by using civil injunctions and civil sanctions such as forfeiture, which are tactics that do not [always] require jury participation.").

## B. WHAT ARE THE CRIMINAL SANCTIONS FOR SUPPLYING MARIJUANA?

Convictions for the marijuana supply crimes just studied can trigger harsh criminal sanctions, including both long prison terms and hefty criminal fines. This section discusses in more detail the criminal sanctions that can be imposed for supplying marijuana and the factors that influence those sanctions. Section C discusses the civil sanctions and liabilities that marijuana suppliers also face under federal law.

### 1. Calculating Sentences

The federal and state governments employ similar criteria for determining the severity of criminal sanctions for marijuana supply offenses, including:

(1) the quantity of marijuana involved in the supply offense,
(2) the offender's criminal history, and
(3) any aggravating circumstances surrounding commission of the offense.

For example, 21 U.S.C. section 841(b) delineates the sentencing ranges for supply offenses under federal law:

> (1)(A) In the case of a violation of [21 U.S.C. § 841(a)] involving . . .
> (vii) 1000 kilograms or more of a mixture or substance containing a detectable amount of marijuana, or 1,000 or more marijuana plants regardless of weight . . . such person shall be sentenced to a term of imprisonment which may not be less than 10 years or more than life and if death or serious bodily injury results from the use of such substance shall be not less than 20 years or more than life, a fine not to exceed the greater of that authorized in accordance with the provisions of Title 18, or $10,000,000 if the defendant is an individual or $50,000,000 if the defendant is other than an individual, or both. If any person commits such a violation after a prior conviction for a felony drug offense has become final, such person shall be sentenced to a term of imprisonment which may not be less than 20 years and not more than life imprisonment and if death or serious bodily injury results from the use

of such substance shall be sentenced to life imprisonment, a fine not to exceed the greater of twice that authorized in accordance with the provisions of Title 18, or $20,000,000 if the defendant is an individual or $75,000,000 if the defendant is other than an individual, or both. If any person commits a violation of this subparagraph or of section 849, 859, 860, or 861 of this title after two or more prior convictions for a felony drug offense have become final, such person shall be sentenced to a mandatory term of life imprisonment without release and fined in accordance with the preceding sentence. Notwithstanding section 3583 of Title 18, any sentence under this subparagraph shall, in the absence of such a prior conviction, impose a term of supervised release of at least 5 years in addition to such term of imprisonment and shall, if there was such a prior conviction, impose a term of supervised release of at least 10 years in addition to such term of imprisonment. Notwithstanding any other provision of law, the court shall not place on probation or suspend the sentence of any person sentenced under this subparagraph. No person sentenced under this subparagraph shall be eligible for parole during the term of imprisonment imposed therein. . . .

(B) In the case of a violation of subsection (a) of this section involving . . .

(vii) 100 kilograms or more of a mixture or substance containing a detectable amount of marijuana, or 100 or more marijuana plants regardless of weight . . . such person shall be sentenced to a term of imprisonment which may not be less than 5 years and not more than 40 years and if death or serious bodily injury results from the use of such substance shall be not less than 20 years or more than life, a fine not to exceed the greater of that authorized in accordance with the provisions of Title 18, or $5,000,000 if the defendant is an individual or $25,000,000 if the defendant is other than an individual, or both. If any person commits such a violation after a prior conviction for a felony drug offense has become final, such person shall be sentenced to a term of imprisonment which may not be less than 10 years and not more than life imprisonment and if death or serious bodily injury results from the use of such substance shall be sentenced to life imprisonment, a fine not to exceed the greater of twice that authorized in accordance with the provisions of Title 18, or $8,000,000 if the defendant is an individual or $50,000,000 if the defendant is other than an individual, or both. Notwithstanding section 3583 of Title 18, any sentence imposed under this subparagraph shall, in the absence of such a prior conviction, include a term of supervised release of at least 4 years in addition to such term of imprisonment and shall, if there was such a prior conviction, include a term of supervised release of at least 8 years in addition to such term of imprisonment. Notwithstanding any other provision of law, the court shall not place on probation or suspend the sentence of any person sentenced under this subparagraph. No person sentenced under this subparagraph shall be eligible for parole during the term of imprisonment imposed therein. . . .

(C) In the case of a controlled substance in schedule I or II . . . such person shall be sentenced to a term of imprisonment of not more than 20 years and if death or serious bodily injury results from the use of such substance shall be sentenced to a term of imprisonment of not less than twenty years or more than life, a fine not to exceed the greater of that authorized in accordance with the provisions of Title 18, or $1,000,000 if the defendant is an individual or $5,000,000 if the defendant is other than an individual, or both. If any person commits such a violation after a prior conviction for a felony drug offense has become final, such person shall be sentenced to a term of imprisonment of not more than 30 years and if death or serious bodily injury results from the use of such substance shall be sentenced to life imprisonment, a fine not to exceed the greater of twice that authorized in accordance with the provisions of Title 18, or $2,000,000 if the

Part III. Marijuana Suppliers

defendant is an individual or $10,000,000 if the defendant is other than an individual, or both. Notwithstanding section 3583 of Title 18, any sentence imposing a term of imprisonment under this paragraph shall, in the absence of such a prior conviction, impose a term of supervised release of at least 3 years in addition to such term of imprisonment and shall, if there was such a prior conviction, impose a term of supervised release of at least 6 years in addition to such term of imprisonment. Notwithstanding any other provision of law, the court shall not place on probation or suspend the sentence of any person sentenced under the provisions of this subparagraph which provide for a mandatory term of imprisonment if death or serious bodily injury results, nor shall a person so sentenced be eligible for parole during the term of such a sentence.

(D) In the case of less than 50 kilograms of marihuana, except in the case of 50 or more marihuana plants regardless of weight, 10 kilograms of hashish, or one kilogram of hashish oil, such person shall, except as provided in paragraphs (4) and (5) of this subsection, be sentenced to a term of imprisonment of not more than 5 years, a fine not to exceed the greater of that authorized in accordance with the provisions of Title 18, or $250,000 if the defendant is an individual or $1,000,000 if the defendant is other than an individual, or both. If any person commits such a violation after a prior conviction for a felony drug offense has become final, such person shall be sentenced to a term of imprisonment of not more than 10 years, a fine not to exceed the greater of twice that authorized in accordance with the provisions of Title 18, or $500,000 if the defendant is an individual or $2,000,000 if the defendant is other than an individual, or both. Notwithstanding section 3583 of Title 18, any sentence imposing a term of imprisonment under this paragraph shall, in the absence of such a prior conviction, impose a term of supervised release of at least 2 years in addition to such term of imprisonment and shall, if there was such a prior conviction, impose a term of supervised release of at least 4 years in addition to such term of imprisonment. . . .

(4) Notwithstanding paragraph (1)(D) of this subsection, any person who violates subsection (a) of this section by distributing a small amount of marihuana for no remuneration shall be treated as provided in section 844 of this title. . . .

Judges use these statutory ranges as a starting point for determining a defendant's sentence under federal law. Judges then consult the United States Sentencing Guidelines (U.S.S.G.) to help further narrow the sentencing range. Although the Guidelines no longer formally bind judges, *United States v. Booker*, 543 U.S. 220 (2005) (invalidating provision of Sentencing Act making guidelines mandatory), they continue to exert a strong influence on federal sentencing practices. (For a terrific resource on the Guidelines, see Nora Demleitner et al., Sentencing Law and Policy (3d ed. 2013).)

Under the Guidelines, judges must first calculate a defendant's offense level—a number (from 1 to 43) corresponding to the seriousness of the offense(s) of conviction. U.S.S.G. section 2D1.1 (2014) provides detailed instructions for calculating the offense level for drug supply crimes, based on drug quantity and other characteristics of a defendant's offense. Judges next calculate the defendant's Criminal History Category—a number (from I to VI) reflecting a defendant's prior criminal record. Finally, judges plot the defendant's offense level and Criminal History Category on the Guidelines Sentencing Table, U.S.S.G. section 5A, to determine the defendant's Guidelines Sentencing range.

**Table 7.1** below summarizes the statutory sentencing range, Guidelines' offense level, and presumptive Guidelines sentencing range for supply offenses involving different quantities of marijuana and a criminal defendant with no criminal record (i.e., Criminal

History Category I). For example, it shows that a defendant who distributed 5 kilograms of marijuana would face a maximum sentence of 5 years' imprisonment under the CSA, and a presumptive Guidelines sentence of 10 to 16 months' imprisonment. Under both the CSA and the Guidelines, the sentences in **Table 7.1** would be increased if the defendant had a more serious criminal record or if her offense involved any of the aggravating circumstances discussed below in Section B.4.

Table 7.1. Sentencing for Marijuana Supply Offenses Under Federal Law

| Quantity (kg) | Statutory Range | U.S.S.G.* | |
| --- | --- | --- | --- |
| | | Offense Level | Guidelines Range (months) |
| ≥ 90,000 | ≥ 10 years to life | 38 | 235-293 |
| ≥ 30,000 < 90,000 | | 36 | 188-235 |
| ≥ 10,000 < 30,000 | | 34 | 151-188 |
| ≥ 3,000 < 10,000 | | 32 | 121-151 |
| ≥ 1,000 < 3,000 | | 30 | 97-121 |
| ≥ 700 < 1,000 | ≥ 5 years to 40 years | 28 | 78-97 |
| ≥ 400 < 700 | | 26 | 63-78 |
| ≥ 100 < 400 | | 24 | 51-63 |
| ≥ 80 < 100 | ≤ 20 years | 22 | 41-51 |
| ≥ 60 < 80 | | 20 | 33-41 |
| ≥ 50 < 60 | | 18 | 27-33 |
| ≥ 40 < 50 | ≤ 5 years** | | |
| ≥ 20 < 40 | | 16 | 21-27 |
| ≥ 10 < 20 | | 14 | 15-21 |
| ≥ 5 < 10 | | 12 | 10-16 |
| ≥ 2.5 < 5 | | 10 | 6-12 |
| ≥ 1 < 2.5 | | 8 | 0-6 |
| < 1 | | 6 | |

*The Statutory and Guidelines sentencing ranges in the Table apply to a defendant with no prior conviction for a felony drug offense and a Criminal History Category I.
**Section 841(b) makes further distinctions based on the type of marijuana involved in the offense and the distribution of "small amounts of marijuana for no remuneration."

## Notes and Questions

1. In cases of conflict between the Guidelines and the CSA, the statute *usually* trumps. Take, for example, the case of a defendant who manufactured 100 marijuana plants. The Guidelines would treat this as the equivalent of manufacturing 10 kilograms of dried marijuana (100 × 100 grams), resulting in a base offense level of 14 and a corresponding Guidelines sentencing range of 15 to 21 months' imprisonment (assuming no criminal history). But because 21 U.S.C. section 841(b)(1)(B)(vii) calls for a *mandatory* minimum 5 years' imprisonment for cases involving 100 or more marijuana *plants*, the sentencing judge would normally have to sentence defendant to at least 60 months' imprisonment. However, Congress has empowered federal judges to depart from the CSA's mandatory minimum sentences in extraordinary cases. See 18 U.S.C. § 3553(f) (incorporated as U.S.S.G. § 5C1.2 (2014)). Under U.S.S.G. section 5C1.2, a judge may sentence defendant below the otherwise applicable mandatory minimum "if the court finds at Sentencing, after the Government has been afforded the opportunity to make a recommendation," that

> (1) the defendant does not have more than 1 criminal history point, as determined under the sentencing guidelines;
> (2) the defendant did not use violence or credible threats of violence or possess a firearm or other dangerous weapon (or induce another participant to do so) in connection with the offense;
> (3) the offense did not result in death or serious bodily injury to any person;
> (4) the defendant was not an organizer, leader, manager, or supervisor of others in the offense, as determined under the sentencing guidelines and was not engaged in a continuing criminal enterprise, as defined in section 408 of the Controlled Substances Act; and
> (5) not later than the time of the sentencing hearing, the defendant has truthfully provided to the Government all information and evidence the defendant has concerning the offense or offenses that were part of the same course of conduct or of a common scheme or plan, but the fact that the defendant has no relevant or useful other information to provide or that the Government is already aware of the information shall not preclude a determination by the court that the defendant has complied with this requirement.

In the *Rosenthal* case discussed earlier, for example, Judge Breyer found this safety valve provision applicable. That is why he was able to sentence Ed Rosenthal to one day of imprisonment, well below the mandatory five-year minimum that normally applies to his offense of conviction—manufacturing 100 or more marijuana plants.

2. Under the Supreme Court's *Apprendi* line of jurisprudence, any factor that increases the minimum or maximum possible penalty otherwise applicable to a defendant's crime of conviction must be proven to a jury (or a judge in a bench trial) beyond a reasonable doubt. *Apprendi v. New Jersey*, 530 U.S. 466, 490 (2000) ("Other than the fact of a prior conviction, any fact that increases the penalty for a crime beyond the prescribed statutory maximum must be submitted to a jury, and proved beyond a reasonable doubt."); *Alleyne v. United States*, 133 S. Ct. 2151 (2013) (extending *Apprendi*'s holding to facts that subject a defendant to a mandatory minimum sentence). These factors include drug quantities and aggravating circumstances surrounding the offense. Nonetheless, a judge may make additional findings by a preponderance of the evidence in calculating the defendant's Guidelines sentencing range, so long as the sentence the judge

imposes does not exceed the range permitted by the jury's verdict. As the Second Circuit explained in *United States v. Thomas*:

> After *Apprendi*, drug type and quantity are elements of the offense under 21 U.S.C. §841 that must be charged in the indictment and submitted to the jury for its finding beyond a reasonable doubt. Even if a threshold drug quantity is not charged in the indictment or found by the jury, however, drug type and quantity may be used to determine the appropriate sentence so long as the sentence imposed is not greater than the maximum penalty authorized by statute for the offense charged in the indictment and found by the jury.

274 F.3d 655, 673 (2d Cir. 2001).

## 2. Measuring Quantity

Quantity obviously plays a critical role in determining a defendant's sentence. But measuring the quantity of marijuana involved in an offense has triggered a number of legal controversies, discussed in the sections below.

### a. THC Content

One controversy involves whether sentences should be based on the quantity of THC found in the marijuana, rather than the weight of the marijuana itself. As discussed in Chapter 2, not all marijuana is created alike; some strains of the drug, and even different parts of the same plant, have much higher concentrations of THC than do others. Yet the law does not explicitly take THC content into account for purposes of sentencing, any more than it does when defining marijuana. As the Second Circuit put it in *United States v. Proyect*, "a plant is a plant is a plant." 989 F.2d 84 (2d Cir. 1993) (rejecting defendant's claim that male plants should be counted differently than female plants with higher THC levels).

This can lead to some seemingly anomalous results in the sentencing of similarly situated defendants. Consider the following Problem:

Problem 7.25: Andy cultivates and harvests 10 marijuana plants. He sells 1 kilogram of dried buds to Benjamin. The buds have a THC content of 20 percent. Andy also sells 10 kilograms of stems and leaves to Camila. The stems and leaves have a THC content of 1 percent. The police separately arrest Benjamin and Camila and charge each with possession with intent to distribute marijuana. What are the sentencing ranges for each defendant under the CSA, assuming no criminal history? Do the results make sense? Should the law take THC content into consideration for purposes of sentencing? *See United States v. Baker*, 905 F.2d 1100 (7th Cir. 2010).

### b. Weight of Material That Is Not Marijuana

When determining quantities for purposes of sentencing, jurisdictions normally measure the weight of "a *mixture or substance containing* a detectable amount of marijuana," and not just the weight of the marijuana itself. 21 U.S.C. § 841(b) (emphasis added). As the U.S.S.G. explains,

> "Mixture or substance" as used in this guideline has the same meaning as in 21 U.S.C. § 841, except as expressly provided. Mixture or substance does not include materials that must be separated from the controlled substance before the controlled substance can be used. Examples of such materials include the fiberglass in a cocaine/fiberglass bonded suitcase, beeswax in a cocaine/beeswax statue, and waste water from an illicit laboratory used to manufacture a controlled substance. . . .

U.S.S.G. §2D1.1, Commentary Application Note 1.

This proviso can have a dramatic impact on sentencing in cases involving products like edibles which contain many ingredients besides marijuana. Consider the following Problem:

**Problem 7.26:** Benjamin sells Delilah 100 grams of dried marijuana buds with a THC content of 20 percent. Delilah mixes the marijuana into brownies for a party. She uses 5 boxes of brownie mix, each weighing 500 grams, to make 100 marijuana-laced brownies. The police arrest Benjamin and charge him with distributing 100 grams of marijuana. They arrest Delilah and charge her with possession with intent to distribute the marijuana laced brownies. What are the sentencing ranges for Benjamin and for Delilah under the CSA? Does your answer comport with your intuitions about the culpability and dangerousness of the two individuals?

### c. Weight of Marijuana Plants

A similar controversy arises regarding the way jurisdictions measure the weight of marijuana plants for purposes of sentencing. Under the CSA, a marijuana plant is generally considered the equivalent of 1 kilogram of usable marijuana, even though this is far more than the average yield for marijuana plants. The approach to weighing plants can lead to anomalous results, as illustrated by the following Problem.

**Problem 7.27:** Andy grows 1,000 marijuana plants. He harvests them at the end of eight weeks, yielding 30 kilograms of usable dried marijuana. Andy sells the dried marijuana to Benjamin, who plans to resell it to retail consumers. The police arrest Andy, and charge him with manufacturing 1,000 marijuana plants. They arrest Benjamin and charge him with possession with intent to distribute 30 kilograms of marijuana. What will be their sentencing ranges under the CSA? Does your answer comport with your intuitions about the culpability and dangerousness of the two individuals?

In *United States v. Osburn*, 955 F.2d 1500 (11th Cir. 1992), the defendants had been convicted of manufacturing marijuana and argued that the quantity ratio used by federal law in calculating their sentences was irrational and thus unconstitutional:

> [D]efendants proffered Dr. Mahmoud A. ElSohly as an expert in the chemistry and botany of cannabis and the production of marijuana for research purposes. Dr. ElSohly testified that he has a Drug Enforcement Administration license and has been growing marijuana under

government supervision for fifteen years. At the time of the hearing, Dr. ElSohly's program was the only one in the United States in which marijuana was grown on a significant scale under a research grant from the government. Dr. ElSohly has a three-year contract with the National Institute of Drug Abuse to produce standardized marijuana for research.

Dr. ElSohly described the three types of marijuana plants. Each variety is characterized by the length of its growth cycle: eight weeks, twelve to sixteen weeks, and twenty to twenty-four weeks. The average weight of dried marijuana leaves obtainable from the quickest maturing plants ranges from one to two ounces. The medium maturing variant yields between two and twelve ounces of marijuana, and the plant with the longest period of maturity averages between four ounces and two pounds. The biggest plant Dr. ElSohly ever grew yielded marijuana weighing approximately two pounds and was grown in an extremely congenial environment. Most of the plants grown under similarly optimum conditions produced only one pound of marijuana. Dr. ElSohly testified that he had never seen a plant weighing as much as a kilogram (2.2 pounds).

Most marijuana growers choose to cultivate the medium maturity variety because the short variety contains too little THC and the long variety takes too long to mature. Dr. ElSohly testified that a rough estimate of the weight of usable dry leaves derived from an average plant would be approximately 120 grams, or four ounces. In a two-year study conducted by Dr. ElSohly, he found that fully mature plants of the longest maturing variety yielded an average of 274 grams of marijuana.

*Id.* at 1502-03.

The *Osburn* court, however, upheld the ratios used by federal law. It noted that the "equivalency scheme reflects Congress's beliefs concerning the seriousness of the crime, *not the actual or potential weight of the plant.* . . . ." 955 F.2d at 1507 (emphasis added). The court found that Congress "could have rationally chosen" the penalty ratios in order to halt marijuana supply early in the cycle:

> If the government concentrates on eliminating the problem early in the distribution cycle, then it will be less necessary to control drug possession later when the numbers of retailers and users has multiplied. In addition, if the problem is addressed at an early stage, then it is less likely that the drug will ever reach users, and the consequent problems of drug use would be commensurately diminished. . . .

*Id.* at 1509.

By contrast, the Guidelines apply a lower ratio of 100 grams per plant, unless the actual weight of the plant is more:

> In the case of an offense involving marihuana plants, treat each plant, regardless of sex, as equivalent to 100 grams of marihuana. Provided, however, that if the actual weight of the marihuana is greater, use the actual weight of the marihuana.

U.S.S.G. § 2D1.1(c), Note E. As the Background to Section 2D explains, "[t]he decision to treat each plant as equal to 100 grams is premised on the fact that the average yield from a mature marihuana plant equals 100 grams of marihuana."

## Notes and Questions

1. Do you agree with the *Osburn* court that the weight ratios used by the CSA—even if they do not accurately measure the quantity of usable marijuana produced—could nonetheless measure the seriousness of the offense? Is there a rational reason for penalizing

the people who produce marijuana (e.g., who handle plants) more harshly than the people who distribute the drug?

2. When it originally passed the CSA, Congress did not differentiate between usable marijuana and marijuana plants, and it based sentences in both cases on the actual weight of the drug or plant(s) involved. This changed in the 1980s, with amendments to the penalty provisions of the CSA. Judge Devitt in *United States v. Fitol* provides some useful background on the legislation establishing the statutory ratio:

> Originally Section 841(b) punished the manufacture of marihuana solely by weight. In 1986, however, Congress amended the statute to enhance punishment for the growing of "100 or more marihuana plants regardless of weight." See Anti-Drug Abuse Act of 1986, Pub. L. No. 99-570, § 1003(a)(1)(C), ... codified as amended at 21 U.S.C. § 841(b)(1)(D). ... In 1988, Congress again amended the statute to provide for mandatory 5 and 10 year sentences for the growing of "100 or more" or "1,000 or more marihuana plants regardless of weight," respectively. See Anti-Drug Abuse Act of 1988, Pub. L. No. 100-690, § 6470(g)(2) & (h)(2) and § 6479, ... codified as amended at 21 U.S.C. § 841(b)(1)(A)(vii) and (b)(1)(B)(vii). ...
>
> It appears that the 1988 legislation was intended, at least in part, to curtail a debate about whether seeds and stems of marihuana were includable in determining the drug's weight under Section 841(b). ... At least one court had held that stalks of marihuana plants seized at a stage before the marihuana had been turned into a marketable product were not to be counted toward the 1,000 kilogram requirement which triggered the 10 year mandatory minimum sentence. ... Congress was apparently unhappy with this result and chose to remedy it by providing that the number of "plants regardless of weight" could also trigger the mandatory minimum sentences.
>
> The court has found no indication in the legislative history of the 1988 amendment, however, as to why this method was used instead of simply stating that stalks were to be included in determining weight. Nor has the court found any legislative material that sheds any light on what motivated the 1986 change to employing the number of plants involved in determining sentences, or what is meant by "plants" in either amendment.
>
> It seems clear, however, that by changing the determining factor from weight to number of "plants regardless of weight," Congress intended to punish growers of marihuana by the scale or potential of their operation and not just by the weight of the plants seized at a given moment. Congress must have found a defendant who is growing 100 newly planted marihuana plants to be as culpable as one who has successfully grown 100 kilograms of marihuana. ... [One court has opined:]
>
>> Weight is irrelevant, because the actual amount of usable marijuana had the plant been allowed to fully grow is unknown. The following example is illustrative of why this distinction in measures makes sense. If one is growing 500 newly planted marijuana plants, and is arrested, the plants' weight would be minimal. If, however, that same person is arrested months later when the plants are fully grown, the weight would be much greater. If defendants' argument were adopted, and weight were used as the measure, the Guidelines would reward a defendant for being arrested early in the growing cycle before his plants have matured. An interpretation of the Guidelines resulting in this situation would not be proper.
>
> [United States v. Graham, 710 F. Supp. 1290, 1291 (N.D. Cal. 1989).]

733 F. Supp. 1312, 1315 (D. Minn. 1990). Does the legislative history change your opinion of the rationality of the scheme? Is a manufacturer caught early in the grow cycle any more or less culpable than one caught later?

3. The CSA and the Guidelines also adjust sentences for quantities of other types of marijuana products, like hashish and hash oil. The CSA's treatment of those substances is covered in section 841(b), excerpted above. The Guidelines instruct courts to multiply the quantity of hashish by 5 and the quantity of hashish oil by 50 to establish the equivalent quantity of marijuana to be used for calculating a defendant's offense level. U.S.S.G. § 2D, Cmt. (8)(d) (Drug Equivalency Table). Thus, for example, a defendant who manufactured 50 marijuana plants would have the same base offense level (12) as a defendant who distributed 5 kilograms of dried marijuana buds or a defendant who distributed 1 kilogram of hashish or 100 grams of hashish oil.

#### d. What Is a "Plant"?

Figure 7.2. A Rootless Marijuana Cutting

Even though the number of plants involved in an offense plays a critical role at sentencing, statutes generally do not define the term "plant." Courts have thus been tasked with figuring out what counts as a plant for purposes of sentencing.

The issue has arisen perhaps most frequently regarding marijuana cuttings, like the one pictured in **Figure 7.2**. A cutting is a small branch with a leaf (or leaves) cut from a living marijuana plant. Because a cutting can grow its own roots if properly tended, it can be used to clone an existing marijuana plant—a useful trick if the "mother" plant has desirable characteristics. But the use of cuttings rather than seeds to produce new marijuana plants raises some thorny sentencing issues, as the following Problem illustrates:

Problem 7.28: When the police searched Delilah's house, they found 90 mature marijuana plants with fully formed root systems and another 20 rootless marijuana cuttings like the one in **Figure 7.2**. Delilah pled guilty to manufacture of marijuana. What is the sentencing range that applies to her offense under the CSA? *See United States v. Robinson*, 35 F.3d 442, 446 (9th Cir. 1994); *United States v. Eves*, 932 F.2d 856, 860 (10th Cir. 1991). *See also* U.S.S.G. § 2D1.1 Commentary Application Note 2.

#### e. Aggregating Quantities

Another issue arises when the defendant commits more than one marijuana supply offense. May the quantities involved in each separate offense be aggregated for purposes of sentencing? The following Problem illustrates the importance of the question:

Part III. Marijuana Suppliers

**Problem 7.29**: During 2013, Camila grew 49 marijuana plants in her basement. She harvested the plants and sold the dried marijuana to distributors. During 2014, Camila grew another 49 plants. She again harvested them and sold the dried marijuana to distributors. During 2015, Camila grew yet another 49 plants. The police have been observing Camila since the beginning of 2013. In 2015, when Camila is about to harvest her third crop, they arrest her and charge her with manufacturing marijuana. What is the sentencing range applicable to Camila under section 841(b)?

The court in *United States v. Retelle*, 165 F.3d 489 (6th Cir. 1999), confronted a similar problem. The defendant was convicted of manufacturing marijuana over a two-year time span. The trial court determined that she was responsible for 100 or more plants during the span and thus was subject to the mandatory minimum five-year sentence imposed by 21 U.S.C. Section 841(b)(1)(B)(vii). The appeals court disagreed, finding that the court had erred in aggregating all of the plants for sentencing purposes. It emphasized that the language of section 841(b) referred to "*a violation*" of section 841(a) (emphasis added), and thus, explicitly forbade courts from aggregating the quantities of marijuana involved in distinct *violations* for purposes of triggering mandatory minimum penalties:

> The record contains no evidence that [defendant] cultivated marijuana on a continuous basis. Rather, [defendant's] 1992 and 1993 marijuana crops were the products of distinct growing seasons separated by several months in which [defendant] apparently did not grow any plants. Despite the open-ended time frame of the indictment, the record in this case demonstrates that each year's activity was a separate offense.

165 F.3d at 492. Hence, the court refused to apply the mandatory five-year prison term required for a violation involving 100 or more plants.

By contrast, under the federal Sentencing Guidelines, courts are *supposed* to aggregate quantities involved in discrete violations of the federal drug laws. *United States v. Winston*, 37 F.3d 235, 240, 241 n.10 (6th Cir. 1994) ("When applying the guidelines to a defendant convicted of participation in multiple drug violations . . . , courts are required to aggregate the amounts of drugs for which the defendant . . . [was] responsible," while section 841(b) "requires a sentencing court to consider separate violations of § 841(a) without aggregating the amount of drugs involved"). Under this aggregation principle, what would be the Guidelines sentencing range for Camila in **Problem 7.29**, assuming she has no criminal history?

### f. Knowledge of Quantity

Even when the government clearly establishes the quantity involved in a supply offense, the question sometimes arises whether the government must also establish that the defendant knew how much marijuana she was manufacturing, distributing, etc. The issue most commonly arises in prosecutions of drug mules, namely, people who transport marijuana (and other drugs) on behalf of others. This activity is a form of supply—the mule transfers the drug from the source to another party, typically a wholesale or retail distributor. Even if the mule is caught before making the transfer, she is still liable for possession with the intent to distribute the drug. But in some cases, the mule might claim that she did not know how much marijuana she was handling.

The courts generally hold that a defendant need not know the quantity of drug involved in an offense, or, indeed, even the specific *type* of illicit drug involved, for purposes of sentencing. In *United States v. Gomez*, for example, the court explained the rule and the rationale behind it:

> In exchange for $5,000 in cash offered by two men he had met in a Miami, Florida bar, defendant Alberto Gomez agreed to drive a car from Miami to a hotel parking lot in Detroit, Michigan, and leave the car there for several hours before driving it back to Miami. According to his statement to police, Gomez knew that some kind of drug was hidden in the car, but believed the drug to be marijuana, in a small quantity, because of what the two men had told him. He did acknowledge, however, that the men had supplied him with a packet of cocaine for the purpose of helping him "stay awake" during the drive. . . .
>
> . . . [It] is well-settled that to sustain a conviction for possession with intent to distribute a controlled substance, it need not be proved that the defendant had knowledge of the particular drug involved, as long as he knew he was dealing with a controlled substance. . . .
>
> As to sentencing, it is now equally well-settled that a defendant need not know the quantity of drug involved in the offense in order to be subject to a mandatory minimum sentence based on quantity under § 841(b)(1). . . .
>
> . . . [T]hose who, acting with a deliberate anti-social purpose in mind, become involved in illegal drug transactions, assume the risk that their actions will subject them to enhanced criminal liability. . . .
>
> The imposition of greater penalties for certain classes of offenses is routinely grounded in a legislative judgment that those who commit such offenses pose an enhanced threat to society at large. In this case, it is undisputed that Gomez knew he was engaging in conduct designed to introduce some illegal substance into the stream of commerce. He was doing this at the behest of two individuals whom, he claimed, he hardly knew. Yet he lacked even the minimal consideration for the public welfare that would have caused him to determine the substance's true identity before agreeing to transport it. One who demonstrates a lack of even this minimal societal consciousness shows himself to pose an alarming menace to the public safety, because he readily allows himself to become the instrument for others' criminal designs "so long as the price is right." Accordingly, where the facts concerning the type and quantity of drug involved in such a one's conduct ultimately prove to fit within § 841(b)(1), that defendant is properly given the enhanced sentence prescribed by that statute.

905 F.2d 1513, 1514-15 (8th Cir. 1990).

## 3. Sentencing for "Fake" Marijuana

Normally the government must prove that the substance involved in the offense was actually marijuana. The proof required for satisfying this element is the same for supply offenses as it is for simple possession cases, discussed in Chapter 3. But while it is generally not a crime to possess a counterfeit drug, it is a crime to *traffic* in counterfeit substances. Indeed, in some circumstances, defendants might actually face harsher sanctions for supplying "fake" marijuana than for supplying the real thing. *Conner v. Indiana* discusses one such circumstance.

## Part III. Marijuana Suppliers

### *Conner v. Indiana*
626 N.E.2d 803 (Ind. 1993)

SHEPARD, C.J.:

If only James Conner had filled his sandwich baggies with real marijuana instead of the harmless moist plant material he sold to the police informant. To his surprise and dismay, under Indiana's drug statutes selling fake marijuana is classified as a much more serious crime than selling actual marijuana.

. . .

Deputy Ted McQuinley of the Fayette County Sheriff's Department arranged for police informant Mark Evers to purchase $1,600 worth of marijuana from Conner. During the transaction, Conner produced sixteen small plastic bags of plant material, which he conveyed to Evers in exchange for the $1,600 in cash. The State Police chemist subsequently found no traces of marijuana in the various samples of the plant material he tested. Together, the content of all the baggies weighed a total of 145.4 grams.

. . .

Ordinarily, once tests reveal even a trace of a controlled substance, the drug present determines the class of the offense. In most instances, dealing in an actual controlled substance carries a greater penalty than dealing in a fake controlled substance. For example, dealing in heroin, a schedule I drug, is a class B felony, but passing off fake heroin for the real thing is a class D felony. This statutory scheme under which sales of non-controlled substances are accorded more lenient treatment breaks down, however, when the drug in question is marijuana.

[Under Indiana law, distributing 30 grams or less of marijuana is a misdemeanor, while distributing more than 30 grams is a class D felony, carrying a maximum prison term of 3 years. Ind. Code Ann. § 35-48-4-10(b)(1)(B). However, distributing a non-controlled substance represented to be a controlled substance is a class C felony, carrying a maximum prison term of 8 years. *Id.* at § 35-48-4-4.6.] . . . Since the State's chemist did not find any traces of marijuana in the samples he tested from among the 145.4 grams of material sold to the police informant, Conner was . . . convicted of distributing a substance represented to be a controlled substance—a class C felony—for which he received a six year prison sentence. . . .

Conner's sentence was thus twice as long as the maximum penalty he would have faced had the chemist found any evidence of marijuana. Given this discrepancy in penalties, purveyors of less than pure pot presumably would be prosecuted not for peddling pot, but for either dealing or distributing any amount of oregano or other non-controlled substance found mixed-in with the demon weed. Indeed, dealing nearly ten pounds of real marijuana exposes one to less criminal liability than distributing even one gram of fake marijuana.

. . .

The legislature may, in its wisdom, define the separate crime of dealing in a substance represented to be controlled substance, and so classify that crime as to provide an appropriate penalty. Nevertheless, in light of the lesser penalties which attach to marijuana offenses, relative to other controlled substances, we conclude that the application of § 35-48-4-4.6 to Conner violates the constitutional requirement that all penalties be in proportion to the nature of the offense.

Prosecuting Conner for distributing fake marijuana exposed him to a maximum sentence of eight years in jail. The six year prison term he received was twice the maximum penalty available had he actually sold marijuana to the police informant. Such a doubling of the penalty is out of proportion to the nature of his offense.

... Accordingly, we affirm the conviction, vacate the penalty, and remand with instructions to resentence Conner up to a maximum of three years' imprisonment. ...

## Notes and Questions

1. What is the point of punishing someone who supplies "fake" illicit drugs anyway? Might such bans actually promote the black market by reducing the chance that buyers will be defrauded?

## 4. Aggravated Circumstances

In the 1980s, Congress and many states began to enhance the penalties for drug supply offenses involving aggravated circumstances, such as the distribution of marijuana *near a school*. Most of the aggravating circumstances under federal law can be found in the penalty provisions of 21 U.S.C. sections 841 and 860. Section 841 is excerpted above. Section 860 provides, in relevant part:

> (a) Penalty
> Any person who violates section 841(a)(1) of this title or section 856 of this title by distributing, possessing with intent to distribute, or manufacturing a controlled substance in or on, or within one thousand feet of, the real property comprising a public or private elementary, vocational, or secondary school or a public or private college, junior college, or university, or a playground, or housing facility owned by a public housing authority, or within 100 feet of a public or private youth center, public swimming pool, or video arcade facility, is (except as provided in subsection (b) of this section) subject to (1) twice the maximum punishment authorized by section 841(b) of this title; and (2) at least twice any term of supervised release authorized by section 841(b) of this title for a first offense. A fine up to twice that authorized by section 841(b) of this title may be imposed in addition to any term of imprisonment authorized by this subsection. Except to the extent a greater minimum sentence is otherwise provided by section 841(b) of this title, a person shall be sentenced under this subsection to a term of imprisonment of not less than one year. The mandatory minimum sentencing provisions of this paragraph shall not apply to offenses involving 5 grams or less of marihuana.
> (b) Second offenders
> Any person who violates section 841(a)(1) of this title or section 856 of this title by distributing, possessing with intent to distribute, or manufacturing a controlled substance in or on, or within one thousand feet of, the real property comprising a public or private elementary, vocational, or secondary school or a public or private college, junior college, or university, or a playground, or housing facility owned by a public housing authority, or within 100 feet of a public or private youth center, public swimming pool, or video arcade facility, after a prior conviction under subsection (a) of this section has become final is punishable (1) by the greater of (A) a term of imprisonment of not less than three years and not more than life imprisonment or (B) three times the maximum punishment

authorized by section 841(b) of this title for a first offense, and (2) at least three times any term of supervised release authorized by section 841(b) of this title for a first offense. A fine up to three times that authorized by section 841(b) of this title may be imposed in addition to any term of imprisonment authorized by this subsection. Except to the extent a greater minimum sentence is otherwise provided by section 841(b) of this title, a person shall be sentenced under this subsection to a term of imprisonment of not less than three years. Penalties for third and subsequent convictions shall be governed by section 841(b)(1)(A) of this title. . . .

(c) Employing children to distribute drugs near schools or playgrounds

Notwithstanding any other law, any person at least 21 years of age who knowingly and intentionally—

(1) employs, hires, uses, persuades, induces, entices, or coerces a person under 18 years of age to violate this section; or

(2) employs, hires, uses, persuades, induces, entices, or coerces a person under 18 years of age to assist in avoiding detection or apprehension for any offense under this section by any Federal, State, or local law enforcement official, is punishable by a term of imprisonment, a fine, or both, up to triple those authorized by section 841 of this title.

. . .

(e) Definitions

For the purposes of this section—

(1) The term "playground" means any outdoor facility (including any parking lot appurtenant thereto) intended for recreation, open to the public, and with any portion thereof containing three or more separate apparatus intended for the recreation of children including, but not limited to, sliding boards, swingsets, and teeterboards.

(2) The term "youth center" means any recreational facility and/or gymnasium (including any parking lot appurtenant thereto), intended primarily for use by persons under 18 years of age, which regularly provides athletic, civic, or cultural activities.

(3) The term "video arcade facility" means any facility, legally accessible to persons under 18 years of age, intended primarily for the use of pinball and video machines for amusement containing a minimum of ten pinball and/or video machines.

(4) The term "swimming pool" includes any parking lot appurtenant thereto.

21 U.S.C. § 860. Other, related offenses and penalty provisions are scattered throughout the federal code. *E.g.*, 18 U.S.C. § 924(c)(1) (use of a firearm during a drug supply crime). Many states have adopted similar statutory language.

In at least one crucial respect, aggravated circumstances function like the other elements of supply offenses just discussed: namely, they must be submitted to a jury (or a judge in a bench trial) and proven by the government beyond a reasonable doubt if they increase the minimum or maximum penalty to which a defendant is exposed. There is, however, one important exception to the general rule: *Apprendi* and its progeny do not require the government to prove the existence of a *prior conviction* to the jury beyond a reasonable doubt. In other words, a sentencing judge may find the existence of a prior conviction by a preponderance of the evidence, even though that fact may dramatically increase a defendant's sentence. *See United States v. Booker*, 543 U.S. 220, 244 (2005) ("Any fact (*other than a prior conviction*) which is necessary to support a sentence exceeding the maximum authorized by the facts established by a plea of guilty or a jury verdict must be admitted by the defendant or proved to a jury beyond a reasonable doubt.") (emphasis added).

## Notes and Questions

1. The federal government and the vast majority of states provide that a defendant can be punished for aggravated circumstances of which the defendant was entirely unaware. In other words, in prosecutions brought under provisions like 21 U.S.C. section 860, the government need not show that a defendant knew she was supplying marijuana in a prohibited zone. The court in *United States v. Falu*, discusses the rationale for the rule:

> The statute principally involved in this case, hereinafter referred to as the "schoolyard statute," 21 U.S.C. [§ 860(a),] was enacted in October 1984. Designed to "send a signal to drug dealers that we will not tolerate their presence near our schools," 130 Cong. Rec. S559 (daily ed. January 31, 1984) (statement of Sen. Paula Hawkins), the statute provides stiff penalties for anyone convicted of selling drugs within 1,000 feet of a public or private elementary or secondary school. A first conviction carries a term of imprisonment of up to twice that authorized for a violation of 21 U.S.C. § 841(a)(1) and a term of special parole of at least twice that authorized by section 841(b). A second offense carries a minimum sentence of three years and a maximum of life, followed by at least three times the special parole authorized by section 841(b). . . .
>
> [The court rejected the appellant's claim that the statute requires proof that he knew he was trafficking in proximity to a school.]
>
> It is true that "criminal offenses requiring no mens rea have a 'generally disfavored status,'" . . . but Congress can dispense with this requirement. The language of section [860(a)] contains no express mens rea requirement for the distance element of the offense. While "'far more than the simple omission of the appropriate phrase from the statutory definition is necessary to justify dispensing with an intent requirement,'" . . . we find that Congress has provided us with more.
>
> The purpose of the statute is clear from a reading of the legislative history. Congress sought to create a drug-free zone around schools; whether it chose to do so directly or indirectly is not particularly relevant. According to its sponsor, the provision was designed to "deter drug distribution in and around schools," including transactions which "take place in remote outdoor areas, at local hangouts, or at nearby homes or apartments," thereby helping to "eliminate outside negative influences" around schools. . . . [Another judge] has described the statute in the following terms: "It is difficult to imagine a more rational way of keeping drug traffickers out of areas where children are more likely to come into contact with them than to subject them to a risk of stiffer penalties for doing business near school property." . . . We find that a requirement that the dealer know that a sale is geographically within the prohibited area would undercut this unambiguous legislative design. . . .
>
> This construction of section [860(a)] does not criminalize otherwise innocent activity, since the statute incorporates section 841(a)(1), which already contains a mens rea requirement—one must "knowingly or intentionally . . . distribute . . . a controlled substance." . . . Anyone who violates section [860(a)] knows that distribution of narcotics is illegal, although the violator may not know that the distribution occurred within 1,000 feet of a school. . . . Although we are aware that some schools are not clearly recognizable as such from all points within the 1,000-foot radius, Congress evidently intended that dealers and their aiders and abettors bear the burden of ascertaining where schools are located and removing their operations from those areas or else face enhanced penalties.

776 F.2d 46, 48-50 (2d Cir. 1985).

2. The CSA increases the sentencing range when the defendant commits a violation "after a prior conviction for a felony drug offense has become final." 21 U.S.C. § 841(b)(A)-(D).

Part III. Marijuana Suppliers

In cases involving 1,000 kilograms or more, the sentencing range increases from 10-life to 20-life. *Id.* § 841(b)(1)(A)(vii). In cases involving 100 kilograms or more, it increases from 5-life to 10-life. In cases involving more than 50 kilograms, it increases from 0-20 years to 0-30 years. *Id.* § 841(b)(1)(B)(vii). And in cases involving 50 kilograms or less of marijuana, the range increases from 0-5 years to 0-10 years. *Id.* § 841(b)(1)(C). But what is a "felony drug offense"? Consider the following Problem:

**Problem 7.30:** Andy pled guilty to distributing more than 100 kilograms of marijuana. For purposes of sentencing, the trial court found that Andy had previously been convicted of simple possession of marijuana in violation of New Jersey law. Under New Jersey law at the time, simple possession of marijuana carried a maximum sentence of 18 months' imprisonment. Andy actually received only 3 months. What is Andy's sentencing range for the current (distribution) offense? *See* 21 U.S.C. § 802(44); *see also United States v. Campos*, 163 F. App'x 232, 233 (4th Cir. 2006) (unpublished).

### 5. What Sentences Are Actually Imposed?

The discussion above detailed the criminal sanctions that could be imposed on defendants convicted of marijuana supply offenses. But the United States Sentencing Commission has compiled data on the prison terms that are *actually* imposed under federal law. *See* United States Sentencing Commission, Quick Facts: Marijuana Trafficking Offenses (2013). For example, the Commission reports that:

- There were 6,792 offenders sentenced for marijuana trafficking in FY 2012, up from 6,056 in FY 2008.
- In FY 2012, "most offenders convicted of marijuana trafficking were male (89.6%)."
- "The average age of these offenders at sentencing was 33 years."
- "Two-thirds of marijuana traffickers had little or no prior criminal history (66.3% of these offenders were assigned to Criminal History Category I)."
- "The median base offense level in these cases was 22. This corresponds to a quantity of drugs between 132 and 176 pounds of marijuana."
- "Most marijuana trafficking offenders were sentenced to imprisonment (94.5%)."
- "The average sentence length for marijuana traffickers was 34 months."
- 80.2% received sentences of less than 5 years; 15.1% received 5-10 years; and 4.7% received 10 years or more.
- Although "[a]lmost 40 percent . . . of these offenders were convicted of a drug offense carrying a mandatory minimum penalty," "65.4% . . . were not subject to any mandatory minimum penalty at sentencing because" they either provided substantial assistance to government agents (23.4 percent) or they were eligible for relief through the statutory safety valve provision (42 percent).

## Notes and Questions

1. In light of the above data, do the criminal sanctions for marijuana supply offenses seem too harsh, too lenient, or about right?

## C. WHAT ARE THE CIVIL SANCTIONS FOR SUPPLYING MARIJUANA?

In addition to the criminal sanctions just discussed, marijuana suppliers also face a variety of civil sanctions in prohibition regimes. Some of these sanctions, like forfeiture, also apply (at least to some degree) to marijuana users, but others are reserved for marijuana suppliers. This section explores four civil sanctions in more detail. Section C.1 revisits forfeiture, a sanction first introduced in Chapter 3. It discusses the additional properties that are subject to forfeiture stemming from supply offenses, the defenses that can be raised against forfeiture, and the procedures that must be followed in forfeiture actions. Section C.2 then discusses the punitive taxes that marijuana distributors must pay in prohibition regimes. Section C.3 discusses marijuana suppliers' potential liability for damages under the federal RICO Act. Finally, Section C.4. discusses rules that appear to deny marijuana suppliers legal protection for a valuable form of intellectual property (trademark) under federal law.

### 1. Forfeiture

This section builds on the discussion of forfeiture in Chapter 3. The federal CSA has two separate provisions authorizing forfeiture of property derived from or used to commit drug supply offenses. 21 U.S.C. section 853(a) provides for forfeiture as part of a marijuana supply prosecution (criminal forfeiture), and 21 U.S.C. section 881(a) provides for forfeiture independent of any criminal prosecution (civil forfeiture). In relevant part, section 853(a) states,

> Any person convicted of a violation of this subchapter or subchapter II of this chapter punishable by imprisonment for more than one year shall forfeit to the United States, irrespective of any provision of State law—
>
> (1) any property constituting, or derived from, any proceeds the person obtained, directly or indirectly, as the result of such violation;
>
> (2) any of the person's property used, or intended to be used, in any manner or part, to commit, or to facilitate the commission of, such violation.

The text of section 881(a) is reprinted in Chapter 3, Section B.2, *supra*. (Although this discussion focuses on forfeiture under federal law, it is important to recognize that many states have adopted similar rules.)

#### a. Property Subject to Seizure

Although the language of sections 853(a) and 881(a) differs somewhat, courts have generally interpreted them to cover the same property. *E.g.*, *United States v. Littlefield*,

821 F.2d 1365 (9th Cir. 1987) ("It would frustrate the goals of judicial and prosecutorial efficiency to construe section 853 as covering only a portion of property that section 881 reaches in its entirety."). Both authorize seizure of many forms of property, such as cash, real estate, or vehicles, so long as the government demonstrates a sufficient connection between the property and a marijuana supply offense. This usually boils down to demonstrating that the property was either derived from a supply offense, or that it was used to commit or to facilitate commission of such an offense.[4] In *United States v. Smith*, for example, the court held forfeitable a tract of land on which the defendant had grown marijuana, as well as an adjacent tract of land on which the defendant had grown only corn. 966 F.2d 1045 (6th Cir. 1992). The former was forfeitable because it was used to commit defendant's manufacturing offense, and the latter was forfeitable because defendant had used the corn to "physically conceal" his marijuana plants and thus facilitate his manufacturing offense. *Id.* at 1055.

## Notes and Questions

1. If property is divisible, how much of it is subject to forfeiture? Consider the following Problem:

**Problem 7.31**: Delilah openly grows a single marijuana plant on a 5' by 5' plot on her 40-acre farm. How much of Delilah's farm is forfeitable under the CSA? See *Littlefield, supra*.

2. Can the government seek forfeiture of substitute property? Consider the following Problem:

**Problem 7.32**: Andy pled guilty in federal court to distributing 5 kilograms of marijuana. In the plea deal, Andy acknowledged receiving roughly $20,000 in return for the marijuana. Andy claimed he deposited all of his drug proceeds into a special bank account, but at the time he was charged with the drug offense, the account contained only $1,000. Andy claims that he spent the missing $19,000 on college tuition and room and board. But Andy has other assets worth more than $19,000. The government acknowledges that those assets were not connected in any way to Andy's drug offense. Nonetheless, may the government substitute them for Andy's missing drug proceeds? See 21 U.S.C. § 853(p). See also *United States v. Hall*, 434 F.3d 42, 59 (1st Cir. 2006).

---

4. In civil forfeiture actions, the test is formulated as requiring a "substantial connection between the property and the offense." 18 U.S.C. § 983(c)(3). However, as noted in the text, most courts appear to hold (or assume) that this test is identical in substance to the one that governs criminal forfeiture actions under section 853(a). See, e.g., *United States v. Herder*, 594 F.3d 352 (4th Cir. 2010).

### b. Forfeiture Procedures

What procedures must be followed when the government seeks to subject property to forfeiture? The procedures for criminal forfeiture (section 853(a)) and civil forfeiture (section 881(a)) differ, as described in the following sections.

#### (i) Criminal Forfeiture

As the name suggests, criminal forfeiture is used during a criminal prosecution. In the indictment, the government must notify the defendant that it will seek forfeiture as part of sentencing if the defendant is convicted. Fed. R. Crim. Proc. 32.2 (a). The government must then obtain a conviction of the defendant for a supply offense punishable by more than one year of imprisonment, 21 U.S.C. §853(a), which includes all of the federal supply offenses discussed above with the exception of the distribution of a small amount of marijuana for no remuneration, which is punishable by imprisonment of one year or less, 21 U.S.C. §841(b)(4).

Following a guilty plea or guilty verdict, the fact finder must then determine whether a specified piece of property is subject to forfeiture. Fed. R. Crim. Proc. 32.2(b)(1)(A), (b)(5). The government must prove the requisite connection (described above) between the property and the offense, i.e., that the property was derived from or used to commit or to facilitate the commission of the defendant's supply offense. Importantly, even though criminal forfeiture follows from a criminal prosecution, the government need only satisfy the preponderance of the evidence standard at the forfeiture hearing. E.g., *United States v. Vera*, 278 F.3d 672 (7th Cir. 2002). In other words, the government need only show that it is more likely than not that the requisite connection exists between the property in question and defendant's offense. The CSA also creates a government-friendly presumption for some types of property:

> There is a rebuttable presumption at trial that any property of a person convicted of a felony under this subchapter or subchapter II of this chapter is subject to forfeiture under this section if the United States establishes by a preponderance of the evidence that—
>
> (1) such property was acquired by such person during the period of the violation of this subchapter or subchapter II of this chapter or within a reasonable time after such period; and
>
> (2) there was no likely source for such property other than the violation of this subchapter or subchapter II of this chapter.

21 U.S.C. §853(d).

### Notes and Questions

1. Courts have held that the preponderance of evidence standard used in criminal forfeiture proceedings is consistent with *Apprendi*'s admonition that "[other than the fact of a prior conviction, any fact that increases the penalty for a crime beyond the prescribed statutory maximum must be submitted to a jury, and proved beyond a reasonable doubt." 530 U.S. at 490. The court in *Vera, supra*, explained:

> Determining the forfeitable proceeds of an offense does not come within *Apprendi*'s rule, because there is no "prescribed statutory maximum" and no risk that the defendant

has been convicted de facto of a more serious offense. Section 853(a) is open-ended; all property representing the proceeds of drug offenses is forfeitable.

278 F.3d at 673.

2. For useful background on criminal forfeiture proceedings, see Stefan D. Cassella, *Criminal Forfeiture Procedure: An Analysis of Developments in the Law Regarding the Inclusion of a Forfeiture Judgment in the Sentence Imposed in a Criminal Case*, 32 Am. J. Crim. L. 55 (2004).

*(ii) Civil Forfeiture*

In the alternative, the government can instead bring a civil forfeiture action. Because civil forfeiture involves a claim against the property itself (it is *in rem*), rather than a person (i.e., the owner), there is no need for the government to bring a criminal prosecution. (The *in rem* nature of the action is also why civil forfeiture cases are named for pieces of property.) Indeed, the government can file a civil forfeiture action even if the owner of the property has been found not guilty of a drug supply offense. *E.g., Illinois v. One 1979 Chevrolet C-20 Van*, 618 N.E.2d 1290, 1293 (Ill. App. 1993) (holding that government's civil forfeiture action following acquittal is not barred by principles of double jeopardy or collateral estoppel).

Civil forfeiture can be initiated in two ways. First, an agency such as the DEA can seize certain assets during an investigation without a court order, a process called administrative forfeiture. 19 U.S.C. § 1607 (listing the assets that may be seized through administrative forfeiture). To employ this process, the agency only needs probable cause to believe that the assets are subject to forfeiture under 21 U.S.C. section 881(a). (The concept of probable cause is discussed in Chapter 4.) After the agency has seized the property, it must notify interested parties that they have 30 days (normally) to file a claim for the property. 18 U.S.C. § 983(a)(2). If no one files a claim by that time, the government may proceed to dispose of the property—i.e., to sell it or to use it. The DEA reports that roughly 80 percent of its seizures go *uncontested*. *See* Rebecca Hausner, Note, *Adequacy of Notice Under CAFRA: Resolving Constitutional Due Process Challenges to Administrative Forfeitures*, 36 Card. L. Rev. 1917, 1938-40 (2015) (discussing statistics).

If, however, someone files a claim for the property, either the agency must return the property or the United States Attorney must commence a criminal forfeiture action (see above) or a civil *judicial* forfeiture action. 18 U.S.C. § 983(a)(3) (setting deadline of 90 days for initiation of forfeiture action following filing of claim). In the civil judicial forfeiture action, the government must satisfy the same criteria set forth above for a criminal forfeiture action. Namely, it must demonstrate, by a preponderance of the evidence, that the property was derived from a covered drug supply offense or that it was used to commit or facilitate such an offense (the latter test is rephrased as a "substantial connection between the property and the offense" in section 983(c)). However, in a civil judicial forfeiture action, the government need not demonstrate that the owner (or anyone else) has ever been convicted of a drug supply offense.

Courts have held that owners generally have a right to a jury trial regarding any factual disputes that arise in civil forfeiture actions. *E.g., United States v. One 1976 Mercedes Benz 280S, Serial No. 11602012072193*, 618 F.2d 453 (7th Cir. 1980) (holding that Seventh Amendment right to jury trial applies to civil forfeiture action). Consistent with that right, however, the judge may decide the case if there are no genuine disputes over material facts.

The following case provides a useful example of many of the issues raised in a civil forfeiture action.

### *United States v. $61,200.00 in U.S. Currency, More or Less*
805 F. Supp. 2d 682 (S.D. Iowa 2010)

JARVEY, J.:

On February 25, 2009, Iowa State Patrol Officer Jerod Clyde made a routine traffic stop of a white van traveling west on Interstate 80 in Pottawattamie County, Iowa. The van [had a] California license plate. . . . The lone occupant and driver of the vehicle was Brian Lee Szymczak, 61 years old, of Sebastopol, California. Szymczak was also the registered owner of the vehicle. When questioned as to the purpose of his travel, Szymczak told Officer Clyde that he had been in Michigan. He was traveling back to California after visiting friends and relatives. . . .

Officer Clyde smelled marijuana emitting from the vehicle. Officer Clyde questioned Szymczak if he had any marijuana in the vehicle, but Szymczak denied it. Szymczak then admitted that he had several joints but that he had a valid California prescription for marijuana. The marijuana prescription had expired one month earlier, in January 2009. Officer Clyde asked Szymczak whether he had large amounts of cash in the car, but Szymczak denied it. After reconsidering Officer Clyde's question, Szymczak stated that he had approximately $60,000 in the vehicle. To explain the large sum of money, Szymczak told Officer Clyde that he had been planning to install a safe [at his barn] in Michigan and had brought his life savings from California in anticipation of his move. However, because the ground was frozen he decided to return to California until the ground thawed. . . .

Szymczak then gave Officer Clyde consent to search the vehicle, both for the marijuana and the money. Officer Clyde found a total of $61,200 in U.S. Currency and it was located

> in three separate areas of the van. The first area was a tool bag with some wiring and just miscellaneous small tools inside there, and that was just loose, laying on the inside on the bottom of the bag.
>
> And there was two other packages of money, United States currency located—one of them was hidden inside of a Shredded Wheats box, in the bottom of a Shredded Wheats box. It was heat sealed. The bag was heat sealed, in the bottom, and there was Shredded Wheats placed on top of that, and the box was closed. That was located amongst the tools in the back of the van on the driver's side. The third bag was vacuum sealed and located on the left side on the floor of the van.

In Officer Clyde's experience, the only time he came across heat- or vacuum-sealed money was when the individual was involved in narcotics trafficking. Szymczak stated that he routinely heat-sealed multiple things in the same manner as the heat-sealed currency. The money was in the following denominations: 95–$100 bills; 144–$50 bills; 2133–$20 bills; 164–$10 bills; and 40–$5 bills. The police later took the money to an Iowa State Patrol post and a trained narcotics detection dog alerted to the odor of narcotics where the police placed the hidden money.

Szymczak explained to Officer Clyde that the $61,200 comprised his life savings. He said that did not trust banks and had buried the money at an undisclosed location on Bureau of Land Management property in California. Szymczak claimed that he had accumulated this money over the past approximately twenty-five years while working as a cable splicer in the telephone line repair business. . . .

The police subsequently found marijuana in a full search of the vehicle. Marijuana was found in multiple places including where the money had been located on the top shelf, left side of the van; in the driver's compartment, between the seats; in plastic bags; in heat-sealed bags; and in pill bottles. There was also a various assortment of drug paraphernalia found in the van, including rolling papers, lighters, and medicine bottles that contained hashish. Szymczak admitted that some of the marijuana was in bags heat-sealed in the same manner as the money. Based on the vehicle search, Szymczak pled guilty . . . to possession of a controlled substance in [state court].

Szymczak also told police that he had a rental storage unit in Michigan because he intended to move back to Michigan. When the Michigan State Police executed a search warrant on the storage unit, they found, inter alia, three hand guns; two digital scales; drug paraphernalia; and packaging materials that had marijuana residue on them. . . .

[Following defendant's guilty plea, the United States filed a complaint in rem against the cash under 21 U.S.C. section 881. The government then moved for summary judgment.]

A motion for summary judgment may be granted only if, after examining all of the evidence in the light most favorable to the nonmoving party, the court finds that no genuine issues of material fact exist as to the forfeitability of the property and that the moving party is entitled to judgment as a matter of law. . . .

The government bears the burden of proving by a preponderance of the evidence that the defendant property is subject to forfeiture. . . . Pursuant to section 881(a)(6), the following property is subject to civil forfeiture:

> All moneys, negotiable instruments, securities, or other things of value furnished or intended to be furnished by any person in exchange for a controlled substance or listed chemical in violation of this subchapter, all proceeds traceable to such an exchange. . . .

However, the government can use circumstantial evidence to demonstrate that the defendant money is substantially connected to the asserted drug-related crime. . . . It is not necessary that the government "trace the property to a specific drug transaction." . . . "Nevertheless, the quality of the circumstantial evidence . . . must be strong enough to support reasonable grounds for belief that an actual, rather than purely theoretical, connection exists between the currency in claimants' possession and the drug trade." . . .

If the government successfully meets its burden of proof, then the burden shifts to the claimant to prove that the property is not subject to forfeiture . . . , in other words, . . . ["]that he is an innocent owner by a preponderance of the evidence." . . . Here, the Court denies summary judgment because it finds there are genuine issues of material fact. . . .

. . .

The government asserts that the amount of currency and the manner of concealment supports a finding that the defendant money is connected to drug activity. . . .

A large amount of cash is "strong evidence" connecting the money to illegal drug activities. . . . The presence of money consisting of small denominations may also be demonstrative of criminal activity. . . .

How the money is concealed and packaged may further establish a connection between the money and drug activity. . . . It is common practice to mask the smell of drug-tainted money by wrapping it in a material, such as cellophane, to prevent discovery by drug-sniffing dogs. . . . Another "common ploy to mask odors such as might be detected by dog searches" is to transport the money in vacuum-sealed bags. . . . Claimants may conceal money while traveling cross-country to deter would-be thieves, but a court should determine whether the real purpose is a desire to conceal criminal activities. . . . The Court must use "a common sense view that bundling and concealment of large amounts of currency, combined with other suspicious circumstances, supports a connection between money and drug trafficking." . . . Further, a claimant must offer "competent evidence suggesting an innocent reason for packaging the currency in this unusual fashion." . . .

. . . Claimant had the money located in three areas of the van. Two heat or vacuum-sealed bags contained $36,000 and $17,000, respectively, and loose money in a cloth bag totaled $8200. The majority of the money was therefore in sealed bags and the bags were hidden in a suspicious manner. For example, one bag was at the base of a Shredded Wheats box with the bag or contents of Shredded Wheat on top of the money, while another bag was lying on the floor of the van. There is not a genuine issue of material fact that money packaged in this style is indicative of illegal activity. Neither party disputes how the money was concealed and it remains for the Court to determine whether this packaging established a substantial connection to drug trafficking.

The Court finds there are no uncontroverted facts as to the denominations of defendant currency and how the claimant concealed the defendant money. . . . The Court thus finds there is no genuine issue of material fact as to the claimant's amount of money, denominations of money, and manner of concealment, being indicative of drug activities.

. . .

The government next argues that the claimant's transportation route, from California to Michigan, supports a finding that he was engaged in criminal activity. . . .

. . . [C]ourts should consider evidence of travel between areas known for drug-trafficking activity to be a relevant factor, and California is known to be a drug source state. . . .

[B]ut the claimant states he made the trip from California to Michigan for personal reasons. Viewing the evidence in the light more favorable to the claimant, the Court concludes there is a genuine issue of material fact remaining as to whether claimant's travel was for personal or drug trafficking purposes.

. . .

The government also asserts that the presence of drugs and drug paraphernalia, as well as the alert from a trained drug detection dog, further indicates that the defendant money is connected to drug trafficking. Claimant does not refute the government's argument that these factors are, collectively, indicators of criminal activity.

. . . [T]he Court finds there is not a genuine issue of material fact that the drugs and drug paraphernalia found in the van and storage garage in Michigan indicative of the illegality of the currency's source.

. . .

Lastly, the government argues that the defendant money is substantially related to drug activity because claimant has a lack of legitimate income and he has implausible explanations as to the source of the defendant money. . . .

In response, the claimant argues that there are remaining genuine issues of material fact in dispute as to his explanations of the source of the defendant currency. Claimant argues that his "inability to provide any further documentation should not be weighed against him" because the government requested documents only as to the sources of "any" of the $61,200, not the entire amount. Claimant also contends that the government has not discredited claimant's life savings as a cable splicer for the past twenty-five years as a source for the defendant currency.

. . .

In this case, the Court views the facts in the light most favorable to claimant as to his explanations for the source of the legitimate income. The government attempts to prove by an absence of tax records and other documents, that claimant cannot attribute the defendant currency to legitimate sources of income. Claimant produced tax returns for 2006 and 2008; only two years out of the five years the government requested. Claimant asks the Court to not weigh this absence of records against him "because claimant was either unemployed and had no reportable income, or the years in question are so far removed so as to be unreasonable to expect claimant to still have said tax returns." . . . The claimant asserted that as of 2001, he had accumulated approximately $200,000 in life savings from working twenty-five years as a cable splicer. Added to the life savings are the tax returns from 2006 and 2008 that indicate he had a collective adjusted gross income of $13,880, for these two years. . . .

. . . The government has not offered evidence contradicting, as a matter of law, claimant's assertion that the bulk of the defendant currency was the product of his life savings. The government has not conclusively disproved the defendant currency did not come from claimant's life savings or the income reported for 2006 and 2008. The Court finds there is a genuine issue of material fact on the origin of the defendant currency. . . . Despite obvious credibility problems, there is evidence that this money is from his life savings. Because the Court is required to take evidence in a light most favorable to the claimant, the Court finds that claimant has established a genuine issue of material fact on whether the defendant currency is the product of his life savings or the proceeds of illegal drug activity. . . .

The government's case here is obviously strong. However, the Court finds there are genuine issues of material fact relating to the source of the defendant currency.

## Notes and Questions

1. Do you harbor any doubts about the origins of the $61,200 in currency found in Szymczak's van? Following a bench trial, the judge ruled in favor of the government, ordering forfeiture of the entire $62,100. *United States v. $61,200 in U.S. Currency, More or Less*, No. 1:09-cv-00029-JAJ-TJS (S.D. Iowa Oct. 19, 2010).

### c. Defenses to Forfeiture Actions

The following sections discuss two defenses that can be raised against some forfeiture actions.

*(i) The Eighth Amendment*

The Eighth Amendment to the United States Constitution provides that "Excessive bail shall not be required, nor excessive fines imposed, nor cruel and unusual punishments inflicted." U.S. Const. amend. VIII. Forfeiture is generally considered a "fine" for constitutional purposes. *United States v. Levesque* discusses the factors courts consider in deciding whether forfeiture constitutes an excessive fine for a marijuana supply offense.

## *United States v. Levesque*
546 F.3d 78 (1st Cir. 2008)

Lynch, C.J.:

On October 10, 2006, Levesque was stopped for speeding on I-95, in Pittsfield, Maine, by Maine State Police. Levesque's Chevrolet Avalanche had been under surveillance by federal agents after Immigration and Customs Enforcement received information that Levesque was involved in a large marijuana distribution operation. As the trooper ran Levesque's license and registration, another trooper arrived with a K-9 dog, who alerted to the bed of the pickup truck. When Levesque was asked if there was anything she wanted to say, she responded, "I'm not going to lie to you, it is in the back." "It" turned out to be ninety-four pounds of marijuana in three duffel bags.

Levesque was arrested; she admitted to having made marijuana distribution runs two to three times per week since February 2006. She stated that the marijuana was transported across the Canadian border in a secret compartment of a tractor trailer, and that she would meet the driver of the trailer in Ashland, Maine, to receive her shipments. Levesque would deliver the marijuana to locations in Massachusetts, New Jersey, Connecticut, and North Carolina, and would return to Madawaska, Maine, with large bags of cash.

On October 31, 2007, Levesque pled guilty to conspiracy to possess with intent to distribute 100 kilograms or more of marijuana, see 21 U.S.C. §§ 841(a)(1), (b)(1)(B), 846. The Information included a forfeiture allegation, pursuant to 21 U.S.C. § 853. . . .

The government moved for a preliminary order of forfeiture, asking the district court to award it a money judgment in the amount of $3,068,000.[5] To reach this figure, the government assumed, based roughly on Levesque's admissions, that Levesque had transported forty pounds of marijuana per trip and that she had made two trips per week for eighteen weeks; it added the ninety-four pounds Levesque was carrying when she was arrested, and multiplied the total, 1,534 pounds of marijuana, by a "conservative discounted price" of $2,000 per pound.

Levesque . . . urged the court to reduce the amount of her forfeiture considering her relative culpability, what she earned from her role in the conspiracy, and her ability to pay in setting the forfeiture amount. For her work as a drug runner, Levesque was paid $2,000 per trip; assuming she made two trips per week and worked for eighteen weeks, her gross pay was $72,000. She used this money to purchase the automobile she used for the drug runs and for various travel expenses. All told, Levesque estimated she made a total of $37,284.08 from her illegal activities. A single mother and high school dropout, who had

---

5. Author's note: Under Fed. R. Crim. Proc. 32.2(b)(1)(A), the government may seek a monetary judgment when a defendant lacks the substitute assets needed to cover the value of (lost) forfeitable property.

been largely unemployed since 2005, Levesque spent this money primarily on living expenses for herself and her son and on an attempt to open a beauty salon in Madawaska. As such, she claimed, "she ha[d] nothing of value left to forfeit." Levesque conceded that the court could impose a forfeiture on one conspirator for the full foreseeable proceeds of the conspiracy, . . . such that the forfeiture amount was not capped by her own personal proceeds. But she argued nonetheless that a reasonable money judgment would account for the "net proceeds [she] derived from her role in the offense, as well as [the] other mitigating factors."

The district court . . . concluded that the $3,068,000 forfeiture was not disproportionate, notwithstanding Levesque's role in the conspiracy, the amount she actually earned, or her inability to pay. . . .

The district court sentenced Levesque to twenty-three months' imprisonment on March 7, 2008, and the forfeiture order became final three days later. Levesque timely appealed . . . [arguing, inter alia, that] the imposition of the forfeiture violates the Excessive Fines Clause of the Eighth Amendment. . . .

A criminal forfeiture is unconstitutional under the Excessive Fines Clause if it is "grossly disproportional to the gravity of the defendant's offense." *United States v. Bajakajian*, 524 U.S. 321, 337 (1998). . . . To determine whether a forfeiture is grossly disproportional, a court should consider:

> (1) whether the defendant falls into the class of persons at whom the criminal statute was principally directed; (2) other penalties authorized by the legislature (or the Sentencing Commission); and (3) the harm caused by the defendant. . . .

The district court rejected Levesque's argument that the forfeiture should be decreased in light of Levesque's allegedly minor role in the conspiracy. It found that the imposition on Levesque of the full forfeiture amount, based on the foreseeable proceeds of the conspiracy, was rational under a proportionality analysis. The court thus appears to have properly concluded that a forfeiture based on vicarious but foreseeable liability, rather than on a defendant's particular role in a conspiracy, is not "grossly disproportional," in violation of the Excessive Fines Clause. . . .

In reaching this conclusion, the court also found that it was unnecessary for it to "delve into [Levesque's] personal finances" or to consider Levesque's inability to satisfy a $3,068,000 forfeiture. The court was correct to the extent that the effect of a forfeiture on a particular defendant is not pertinent under the three-part test for gross disproportionality [quoted above] . . . ; this test focuses on the relationship between the offense and the forfeiture, not the relationship between the forfeiture and the offender.

However, . . . this test is not the end of the inquiry under the Excessive Fines Clause. Beyond the three factors described [above], a court should also consider whether forfeiture would deprive the defendant of his or her livelihood. . . .

The Supreme Court has made it clear that the notion that a forfeiture should not be so great as to deprive a wrongdoer of his or her livelihood is deeply rooted in the history of the Eighth Amendment. . . .

This history . . . indicates that a court should consider a defendant's argument that a forfeiture is excessive under the Eighth Amendment when it effectively would deprive the defendant of his or her livelihood. Such ruinous monetary punishments are exactly the sort that motivated . . . the Excessive Fines Clause. This question is separate from the three-part test for gross disproportionality and may require factual findings beyond those previously made by the district court....

Although we do not define the contours of this inquiry, we note that a defendant's inability to satisfy a forfeiture at the time of conviction, in and of itself, is not at all sufficient to render a forfeiture unconstitutional, nor is it even the correct inquiry. Indeed, the purpose of imposing a forfeiture as a money judgment is to "permit[ ] the government to collect on the forfeiture order in the same way that a successful plaintiff collects a money judgment from a civil defendant. Thus, even if the defendant does not have sufficient funds to cover the forfeiture at the time of the conviction, the government may seize future assets to satisfy the order."... We acknowledge, as the district court pointed out, that even if there is "no sign" that the defendant could satisfy the forfeiture in the future, there is always a possibility that she might be fortunate enough "to legitimately come into money." And it is notable, moreover, that the Attorney General may choose to remit a forfeiture on the grounds of hardship to the defendant. [21 U.S.C. §§ 853(j) & 881(d).] ... Notwithstanding this, it is not inconceivable that a forfeiture could be so onerous as to deprive a defendant of his or her future ability to earn a living, thus implicating the historical concerns underlying the Excessive Fines Clause.

We vacate the district court's forfeiture decision and remand for further consideration consistent with this opinion.

## Notes and Questions

1. The Excessive Fines Clause applies to *civil* as well as criminal forfeiture actions. *Austin v. United States*, 509 U.S. 602, 622 (1993). In civil forfeiture actions, 18 U.S.C. section 983(g) establishes the procedures for making an Excessive Fines claim and fashions a remedy for constitutional violations:

> (1) The claimant ... may petition the court to determine whether the forfeiture was constitutionally excessive.
> (2) In making this determination, the court shall compare the forfeiture to the gravity of the offense giving rise to the forfeiture.
> (3) The claimant shall have the burden of establishing that the forfeiture is grossly disproportional by a preponderance of the evidence at a hearing conducted by the court without a jury.
> (4) If the court finds that the forfeiture is grossly disproportional to the offense it shall reduce or eliminate the forfeiture as necessary to avoid a violation of the Excessive Fines Clause of the Eighth Amendment of the Constitution.

### (ii) The Innocent Owner Defense

In civil forfeiture proceedings, the owner of property may also raise an "innocent owner" defense. To prevail on the defense, the owner must demonstrate by a preponderance of the evidence that she:

> (i) did not know of the conduct giving rise to forfeiture; or
> (ii) upon learning of the conduct giving rise to the forfeiture, did all that reasonably could be expected under the circumstances to terminate such use of the property.

18 U.S.C. § 983(d)(2)(A). For purposes of (ii), the statute lists ways that an owner could demonstrate that she "did all that reasonably could be expected," including informing law enforcement of the activity giving rise to forfeiture and revoking permission to use the property. *Id.* at § 983(d)(2)(B) (also noting that the owner is not required to take any steps that she "reasonably believes" would subject anyone to physical danger). If the individual acquired the property *after* the offense, she must demonstrate by a preponderance of the evidence that she:

> (i) was a bona fide purchaser or seller for value (including a purchaser or seller of goods or services for value); and
> (ii) did not know and was reasonably without cause to believe that the property was subject to forfeiture.

*Id.* at § 983(d)(3)(A). *See also id.* at § 983(d)(3)(B) (recognizing a narrow exception to the "for value" requirement of (i)).

Even if an owner fails to meet the requirements of the innocent owner defense, she might nonetheless prevail on the claim that forfeiture is constitutionally excessive, as the following case demonstrates.

## *von Hofe v. United States*
492 F.3d 175 (2d Cir. 2007)

WESLEY, J.:

[Harold and Kathleen von Hofe appeal the civil forfeiture of their jointly owned home, 32 Medley Lane. The von Hofes have lived in the home since 1979 and reside there now with their two sons. The home is valued at $248,000. Acting on a tip from a confidential informant, state police and the federal DEA searched the home.] Sixty-five marijuana plants, a small postage scale with marijuana residue on its pan, a jar partially filled with marijuana buds, several glass marijuana pipes, and other items commonly associated with the indoor cultivation of marijuana were discovered in the basement of the house. Neither large amounts of cash, glassine bags, nor firearms—indicia of the drug trade—were found.

. . .

[A police officer later testified that during the search, Mrs. von Hofe] admitted her husband's ownership of the marijuana plants but claimed she was not involved in the marijuana cultivation. A DEA agent testified that Mr. von Hofe admitted to owning the marijuana plants, to making marijuana available to his son and friends who smoked marijuana in the basement with him, and to bartering marijuana for household repairs. The DEA agent acknowledged that Mr. von Hofe corroborated his wife's lack of involvement in the marijuana cultivation.

[The state brought criminal charges against the couple. Mr. von Hofe pled guilty to manufacturing and distributing marijuana, and Mrs. von Hofe pled guilty to simple possession of marijuana. The federal government instituted a civil forfeiture action against 32 Medley Lane under 21 U.S.C. section 881(a)(7). Mrs. Hofe raised an innocent owner defense, which the jury rejected. The district court then rejected the von Hofes' claim that forfeiture violated the Excessive Fines Clause, and the von Hofes appealed.]

. . .

We agree with the district court that forfeiture of Harold von Hofe's one-half interest in 32 Medley Lane does not violate the Excessive Fines Clause. . . . He confessed to growing sixty-five marijuana plants in his basement for about a year, to smoking marijuana since the 1960s, and to sharing marijuana with his son and neighbors. . . . He also appears to have bartered marijuana for landscaping and roofing services with his neighbors. . . . Even though Mr. von Hofe's criminal activity involved neither violence nor threats of violence, he manufactured an illicit substance, which he contributed to the local market, thereby perpetuating the product's availability for himself, his neighbors and his son. His actions and their resulting harm, perhaps difficult to quantify in objective terms, undoubtedly frustrate society's desire to stem the use of illicit substances and the market therefor.

. . . [B]oth parties acknowledge the seriousness of manufacturing and distributing a controlled substance. . . . Congress has authorized significant penalties for such conduct; growing between fifty and one hundred marijuana plants carries a statutory maximum of a $1 million fine and twenty years imprisonment. See 21 U.S.C. § 841(b)(1)(C). . . .

. . . The statutory maximum, designed as an outer limit on the punishment available, does not necessarily reflect an individual offender's culpability or the gravity of the actual offense giving rise to forfeiture. Providing ranges of punishment with greater particularity, the Guidelines allow us to better determine proportionality and to evaluate a claimant's culpability relative to other potential violators of the federal narcotics laws. . . .

The manufacture of sixty-five marijuana plants may result in fifteen to twenty months imprisonment and a fine ranging from $4,000 to $40,000 under the Guidelines. . . .

Although forfeiture will extinguish Harold von Hofe's equity in 32 Medley Lane, the temporal and spatial extent of his criminal activity make clear that his own actions eviscerated any sanctity he might claim in his home. He made the conscious and deliberate decision to grow marijuana in his basement for approximately one year, an operation cut short only because [the police] intervened. This was neither a spur of the moment decision nor a momentary lapse of judgment. Mr. von Hofe instead expended considerable time and resources obtaining . . . marijuana seeds . . . , procuring the necessary equipment, and cultivating and cloning marijuana. . . . Mr. von Hofe's lengthy and extensive involvement in the manufacture and distribution of marijuana from his basement, the seriousness of his offenses and their relationship to his other criminal activity, allow us to easily conclude that forfeiture of his one-half interest in 32 Medley Lane is not an excessive fine.

. . .

Forfeiture of 32 Medley Lane would be severe punishment when inflicted on Mrs. von Hofe. Given her undivided one-half interest in the property, forfeiture would amount to a $124,000 fine. Not only would forfeiture extinguish her substantial equity, it would amount to an eviction, destroying her "right to maintain control over [her] home, and to be free from governmental interference, . . . a private interest of historic and continuing importance." . . . A forfeiture of this magnitude requires close consideration.

Kathleen von Hofe bears minimal blame for the criminal activity that occurred at 32 Medley Lane. The record is devoid of any evidence indicating her use of drugs or her involvement in any criminal activity whatsoever. . . . We also have no evidence to suggest Mrs. von Hofe encouraged or promoted the offensive conduct occurring at 32 Medley Lane. . . .

In saying this, we do not overlook the jury's conclusion that Mrs. von Hofe was not an innocent owner. The district court concluded that she "knowingly countenanced and allowed the illegal manufacture and distribution of a controlled substance to take place in her home." . . . Mrs. von Hofe both knew of the marijuana plants and, upon learning about their presence in the basement, did nothing to stop her husband's horticultural hobby. . . . Saying Mrs. von Hofe allowed her husband to engage in illegal activity on the property, however, must be taken in the context of the von Hofes' joint tenancy. Harold von Hofe did not need his wife's permission to use the property; joint ownership of 32 Medley Lane entitled Harold von Hofe to use of the property as if he was the sole owner. . . . It was thus Harold von Hofe's decision, almost thirty years into his marriage and as joint owner of 32 Medley Lane, to cultivate marijuana that put his wife in the present position. Mrs. von Hofe's culpability, falling at the low end of the scale, is best described as turning a blind eye to her husband's marijuana cultivation in their basement.

Serious penalties attend violations of 21 U.S.C. §§ 841 and 846, the offenses that transpired at 32 Medley Lane. Statutory penalties include a maximum $1 million fine and twenty years imprisonment, while the Guidelines allow a fine of $4,000 to $40,000 . . . , and fifteen to twenty months imprisonment. Considering these penalties on the macro level might lead one to conclude a forfeiture valued at $124,000 constitutes appropriate punishment for the cultivation of sixty-five marijuana plants. However appropriate in the abstract such a punishment may be, the present forfeiture is designed to punish Mrs. von Hofe for her complicity and awareness of the criminal conduct occurring at her home, not simply the use to which her husband put their home. Aside from the necessarily imprecise Guidelines calculation that arises in an in rem forfeiture where a claimant need not be criminally convicted, the utility of the available penalties tends to further diminish where, as here, a claimant does not have knowledge of the full extent of criminal activity occurring on the property. Given the dearth of evidence indicating the extent of any profit or gain earned from the marijuana plants, and Mrs. von Hofe's lack of knowledge that her husband sold or bartered marijuana with his friends, neither the statutory maximum nor the Guidelines maximum prove decisive in gauging the excessiveness of the forfeiture in relation to Mrs. von Hofe's culpability.

The parties offer a variety of arguments to fill this lacuna. According to the government, Mrs. von Hofe's culpability is equal to that of her husband as his coconspirator, which would allow her to be punished as such. . . . A conspiracy to violate the federal narcotics laws requires proof of an agreement. . . . Mrs. von Hofe knowledge of her husband's illegal activity cannot suffice as evidence of collusion, for "knowledge of the existence and goals of a conspiracy does not of itself make one a coconspirator." . . . Had there been evidence beyond mere knowledge to prove an agreement with Mr. von Hofe, our task would be easy. The reasonably foreseeable actions of Harold von Hofe would be attributable to his wife. . . . Without evidence indicating involvement beyond knowledge, the government finds itself characterizing Mrs. von Hofe's culpability in terms wholly unrelated to her actual conduct. . . .

On balance, forfeiture of Kathleen von Hofe's interest in 32 Medley Lane is an excessive fine. . . .

## Notes and Questions

1. Do you agree with the court's holding? Is it possible to reconcile its decision with the jury's determination that Mrs. von Hofe was both aware of her husband's manufacturing operation and "did nothing to stop her husband's horticultural hobby"? Is it enough to say that Mrs. von Hofe is off the hook because "Harold von Hofe did not need his wife's permission to use the property"?

2. Kathleen von Hofe pled guilty to misdemeanor possession of marijuana. If that is the only crime for which she could be found guilty (as the court suggests), does the CSA even

*authorize* the forfeiture of her interest in the house? *See* 21 U.S.C. § 881(a)(7) (authorizing seizure of real property "used . . . to commit, or to facilitate the commission of, a [drug crime] punishable by *more than one year's imprisonment*") (emphasis added). In any event, might the facts have supported a more serious criminal charge against Mrs. von Hofe? *See* 21 U.S.C. § 856(a) (making it a felony, punishable by up to 20 years' imprisonment and a fine of up to $500,000, to "knowingly open . . . or maintain any place . . . for the purpose of manufacturing, distributing, or using a controlled substance"). Section 856 is discussed in more detail below in Chapter 13.

3. The court focuses predominantly on Mr. von Hofe's growing of 65 marijuana plants in his basement. Would any of Mr. von Hofe's other activities, mentioned elsewhere in the opinion and noted below, have warranted forfeiture of his interest in 32 Medley Lane? Is there any other information you would need to make this determination?

(1) "smoking marijuana since the 1960s"
(2) "sharing marijuana with his son and neighbors"
(3) "barter[ing] marijuana for landscaping and roofing services with his neighbors"

4. Consider the following Problem:

**Problem 7.33:** Camila owns a house on a 100-acre lot. She resides in the house with her adult daughter, Delilah. However, Camila makes many trips for work, and is frequently away from the residence for one month at a time. After returning from her latest one-month trip, Camila noticed a few marijuana plants growing in Delilah's bedroom, along with pieces of hydroponic growing equipment (lights, etc.). Camila also knows that Delilah was previously convicted of importing large amounts of marijuana from Canada. Camila asks Delilah to remove the plants from her bedroom. The next day, Camila notices that the plants are no longer in Delilah's bedroom (though the growing equipment remains), and Camila makes no further inquiries. A day later, the police search Camila's property. They find the growing equipment in Delilah's bedroom, as well as 75 marijuana plants growing in a shed near the house and still on Camila's lot. The plants range in size from a few inches to more than four feet tall. The government commences a civil forfeiture action against Camila's entire property. Does Camila have any defense? *See United States v. Real Property in Santa Paula, California*, 763 F. Supp. 2d 1175 (C.D. Cal. 2011).

5. The Constitution, of course, guarantees legal representation to defendants in criminal cases, including criminal forfeiture actions (which are part of such cases). U.S. Const. Am. VI. The constitutional guarantee of legal representation does not extend to *civil* forfeiture actions, even ones connected to criminal cases. Nonetheless, Congress has provided for legal representation of some indigent property owners in civil forfeiture actions. In particular, it provides representation in civil forfeiture actions when owners are facing related criminal charges. 18 U.S.C. § 983(b)(a). It also provides representation when owners are not facing related criminal charges, but only if the "property subject to forfeiture is real property that is being used by the person as a primary residence. . . ." *Id.* at (b)(2).

### d. The Appeal of Civil Forfeiture

Forfeiture is intended to serve the same purposes as other types of sanctions imposed on marijuana suppliers. Among other things, it is supposed to deter and frustrate the supply of marijuana by depriving suppliers of their profits and the tools of their trade (e.g., land, grow lights, etc.). Compared to sanctions like imprisonment, however, forfeiture has some practical advantages for governments. For one thing, governments get to keep forfeited assets, enabling them to recoup some of the costs of enforcing marijuana prohibition. (The point is discussed further in Chapter 9 below.) In addition, civil forfeiture actions generally cost less than criminal prosecutions, because, among other reasons, the government normally need only satisfy the preponderance of the evidence standard rather than the more onerous beyond a reasonable doubt standard that applies in a criminal prosecution. It is thus not surprising that forfeiture has proven a favored tactic in campaigns against suppliers of illicit drugs.

Not so long ago, the federal government used civil forfeiture to crack down on some prominent medical marijuana dispensaries ostensibly operating in compliance with state medical marijuana laws. The civil forfeiture action below is one example.

## United States v. Real Property and Improvements Located at 1840 Embarcadero, Oakland, California
Northern District of California, July 9, 2012

1. This *in rem* forfeiture action is brought pursuant to Title 21, United States Code, Section 881(a)(7).

. . .

6. Defendant is the real property located at 1840 Embarcadero, Oakland, California. . . . The defendant real property is a low-rise, multi-tenant commercial building with on-site parking. The defendant real property is the business address for Patients Mutual Assistance Collective Corporation doing business as Harborside Health Center ("Harborside"), a retail marijuana store and is also the business address for ABC Security Service, Inc., ("ABC").

7. . . . Ana Chretien is the sole owner of record for the defendant real property. . . . [A] deed of trust to secure indebtedness in the amount of $1,861,000.00 and a $200,000 equity line or other receiving line of credit was recorded . . . for the benefit of Summit Bank.

8. Harborside . . . [is] believed to have a leasehold interest in the defendant real property.

. . .

11. . . . [I]n 2006 Harborside sought and obtained a permit to distribute marijuana at the defendant real property.

12. Since at least 2006 and continuing to the present, Harborside has operated a marijuana retail store engaged in the distribution of marijuana at the defendant real property.

. . .

14. ABC provides security to the parking lot that Harborside shares with ABC.

15. Ana Chretien is the President and Chief Executive Officer of ABC, and her business address is located at the defendant real property.

16. Harborside purports to be the largest retailer of marijuana on the planet, serving in excess of 100,000 customers.

17. Harborside claims that its annual gross sales revenues are in excess of $20 million.

. . .

19. According to Harborside's website, it offers for sale marijuana in various forms including "Flowers"; "Concentrates" of marijuana; "Edible" marijuana; "Topicals" containing marijuana; and Marijuana "Seeds/Clones."

20. Harborside is operating in violation of federal law.

. . .

22. Title 21, United States Code, Section 841(a) prohibits the manufacture, distribution, . . . and possession with the intent to manufacture, distribute . . . marijuana.

23. Title 21, United States Code, Section 856 makes it unlawful to rent, lease, profit from or make available for use, with or without compensation, a place for the purpose of unlawfully manufacturing, storing, distributing, or using . . . marijuana.

. . .

25. In light of the foregoing, plaintiff [United States] alleges that the defendant real property is subject to forfeiture, pursuant to [21 U.S.C. section 811(a)(7)] . . . as property which was used or intended to be used, to commit or facilitate the commission of the distribution, cultivation and possession with the intent to distribute and cultivate marijuana.

. . .

WHEREFORE, plaintiff United States of America requests that due process issue to enforce the forfeiture of the defendant real property; that notice be given to all interested parties to appear and show cause why forfeiture should not be decreed; that the Court order judgment for forfeiture of the defendant real property to the United States. . . .

## Notes and Questions

1. Although the forfeiture action above was initiated because of the actions of Harborside, who do you think stands to lose the most? Chapter 11 and 13 discusses the legal liability of third parties, such as landlords and banks, who deal with marijuana users and suppliers.

2. If you were defending the affected parties, how might you seek to challenge the forfeiture action? If you were defending Summit Bank or Ana Chretien, is there anything else you might suggest they do to avoid forfeiture?

Figure 7.3. The Real Property in Interest

3. Postscript. After nearly four years of litigation, the federal government dropped the forfeiture action against the defendant real property in May 2016. *See* Mollie Reilly, *Feds Drop Case Against Influential Medical Marijuana Dispensary*, Huffington Post, May 3, 2016, https://perma.cc/YV8F-GNJV.

Harborside continues to operate, now claiming to serve more than 200,000 medical marijuana patients. The dispensary was even the subject of a short-lived reality series ("Weed Wars") on the Discovery Channel.

### 2. Taxes

Just like other businesses, commercial marijuana suppliers are required to pay taxes on their incomes. *United States v. Sullivan*, 274 U.S. 259, 263 (1927) ("[T]he fact that a business is unlawful [is no reason to] exempt it from paying the taxes that if lawful it would have to pay."). In comparison to other (legal) businesses, however, marijuana distributors are subject to much higher tax rates for two reasons, discussed below.

#### a. Special Marijuana Taxes

Figure 7.4. Nebraska's Drug Tax Stamp

For one thing, many prohibition regimes impose special, often onerous taxes on the distribution of marijuana. (As discussed in Chapter 8, legalization regimes also impose taxes on marijuana distribution, but their taxes are usually much lower by comparison.) In Nebraska, for example, anyone possessing more than six ounces of marijuana is required to buy special drug tax stamps (pictured in **Figure 7.4**) costing $100 for every ounce possessed, even though the drug remains criminal contraband in the state. *See* Neb. Rev. Stat. § 77-4303. *See also* Nebraska Department of Revenue, Information Guide: Nebraska Marijuana and Controlled Substances Tax, July 2014, https://perma.cc/6ZUC-XP4Y (detailing Nebraska's drug tax).

Congress once imposed its own special taxes on marijuana distribution. Under the 1937 Marihuana Tax Act, marijuana distributors were required to register with the I.R.S., pay an annual occupational tax, and pay taxes on all transfers of the drug. *See Leary v. United States*, 395 U.S. 6, 14-16 (1969) (describing tax). The tax enabled Congress to curb the marijuana market at a time when the courts were narrowly interpreting its Commerce Clause authority; once the courts began to interpret Congress's regulatory powers more expansively, Congress replaced the tax with the direct prohibition imposed by the CSA.

Taxes on illicit drugs are generally designed to serve the same purpose as the criminal prohibitions discussed earlier: to quash the market for such drugs. Although few distributors actually pay them, see Faiz Siddiqui, *Nebraska Gets a Cut of Illegal Drug Revenue, in an Artful Way*, Omaha World-Herald, Apr. 6, 2014, https://perma.cc/7FG9-XQHC (reporting that Nebraska sold only $10,000 worth of stamps for all illicit drugs from 1990 to 2013), the taxes allow prohibition regimes to increase the punishment for illicit drug distribution. In Nebraska, for example, a distributor who evades the drug tax may be found guilty of felony tax evasion (*in addition* to drug distribution) and sentenced to up to five years' imprisonment and a $10,000 fine. *See* Nebraska Department of Revenue, Information Guide, *supra*.

### b. Section 280E

Apart from these special taxes, suppliers of marijuana and other drugs banned by federal law are also subject to special rules for calculating their federal income tax liability. These rules raise marijuana suppliers' effective tax rate, as compared to the rate paid by other businesses. The relevant provision of federal tax law is found in 26 U.S.C. section 280E. It provides:

> No deduction or credit shall be allowed for any amount paid or incurred during the taxable year in carrying on any trade or business if such trade or business (or the activities which comprise such trade or business) consists of trafficking in controlled substances (within the meaning of schedule I and II of the Controlled Substances Act) which is prohibited by Federal law or the law of any State in which such trade or business is conducted.

In the following excerpt, Professor Benjamin Leff explains section 280E and its impact on marijuana suppliers.

### *Benjamin M. Leff,* Tax Planning for Marijuana Dealers
#### 99 Iowa L. Rev. 523 (2014)

Generally, the Internal Revenue Code requires a business to pay a percentage of its income in tax to the federal government. In order to determine the business's taxable income, one starts with all of the money coming in to the business—its gross revenue—and then subtracts out all of the business expenses like salaries, rent, advertising, employee health insurance, state and local taxes, license fees, bookkeeping, accounting and legal services, among other things.

If the business is a retail operation, one expense will be "cost of goods sold" ("COGS"), which consists primarily of the wholesale price that the business pays its suppliers to get the goods that it sells at a retail price. Other expenses such as employee salaries, rent, equipment costs and other "ordinary and necessary business expenses" are also subtracted, and the remaining amount is the taxable income.

To illustrate, take as an example someone whose business is the retail sale of marijuana. If she paid federal income taxes like other businesses, she would perform the following calculations. Imagine that she had gross receipts of $3,000,000 and paid $2,600,000 in cost of goods sold, the wholesale cost for the marijuana she sold. She then had the following other expenses:

| | |
|---|---|
| Advertising | 5,000 |
| Legal Services | 45,000 |
| Office | 10,000 |
| Rent/Utilities | 21,000 |
| Taxes/Licenses | 9,000 |

| | |
|---|---|
| Wages/Payroll | 175,000 |
| Equipment Depreciation | 15,000 |
| Other | 20,000 |
| Total | 300,000 |

To calculate the business's taxes, she would subtract the $2,600,000 of COGS and the $300,000 of other business expenses from her gross revenue of $3,000,000 to get a taxable income of $100,000. If we apply a hypothetical 35% tax rate to that amount, her federal income taxes for the year would be $35,000 and she would take home an after-tax income of $65,000.

That is how the calculation would work if marijuana sales were taxed like other businesses in America. But marijuana sales are treated differently under the federal tax code. Instead, § 280E of the Internal Revenue Code dramatically alters the way that state-sanctioned marijuana sellers must calculate their taxes. Marijuana industry insiders believe that § 280E is the biggest impediment to the development of a legitimate marijuana industry, and could drive all legitimate sellers out of business.

Under § 280E, . . . a marijuana seller cannot deduct her expenses prior to calculating her taxable income.

The situation is not quite as dire as it initially may seem. A marijuana seller is not required to actually calculate her income tax strictly as a percentage of her gross income. The Tax Court has explained that "COGS is not a deduction within the meaning of [the tax code] but is subtracted from gross receipts in determining a taxpayer's gross income." . . . In other words, while a marijuana seller cannot deduct the ordinary and necessary expenses incurred in running her business, at least she can subtract the wholesale cost of the marijuana itself from her gross revenue before calculating how much tax she owes. Thus, § 280E disallows business deductions for marijuana sellers, but does not prevent them from subtracting COGS in arriving at taxable income.

So, because of § 280E, the tax calculation of the hypothetical marijuana seller described above would be as follows: gross revenue of $3,000,000 less COGS of $2,600,000 leaves $400,000. Instead of deducting the $300,000 of legitimate business expenses, the taxpayer would be required to calculate her tax based on the whole $400,000 of gross income. Again, at the hypothetical rate of 35%, she would owe $140,000 in tax. Her pre-tax profit, however, is still the same $100,000 it was in the original hypothetical. The effect of § 280E, then, is to turn this marijuana seller's $65,000 of after-tax profit into a $40,000 loss. She owes more in federal income tax than her entire net income for the year. Presumably, if she has a negative profit margin year after year, it will not be long before she has to shut down.

To be clear, this over-taxation of a marijuana seller's income is not simply the result of her engaging in an illegal business activity. If she were engaged in murder for hire, she would owe federal income tax on the profits she made from such activity, but would be allowed to deduct as ordinary and necessary business expenses the cost of her gun and bullets, the cost of overnight travel to and from the crime scene, any amounts she paid to employees or contractors who helped her carry out her crime, and other expenses associated with her criminal activity. Section 280E only applies to income from selling controlled substances.

Currently, state-sanctioned marijuana sellers are employing two legal strategies to minimize the impact of § 280E, but neither provides a complete solution. In 2007, the

Tax Court held that a business that both operated a marijuana dispensary and provided caregiving services to patients could bifurcate its business expenses and deduct the expenses associated with the caregiving activities even though § 280E prevented it from deducting any of the expenses associated with its dispensary operations. In effect, the Tax Court held that § 280E only applied to expenses related to the activity of selling marijuana, rather than to all expenses of any business that sold marijuana. Following this case, marijuana sellers were advised to allocate as many expenses as possible to caregiving services and deduct the expenses associated with such services fully.

In addition, because § 280E still permits a marijuana seller to subtract COGS from gross revenue prior to calculating taxable income, a marijuana seller could try to allocate as much as possible of her expenses to COGS. If a marijuana seller is vertically integrated, growing the marijuana she sells, then opportunities to shift expenses to COGS are multiplied, because cultivation costs are properly classified as costs of goods sold. So, in the hypothetical above, costs such as advertising, legal services, taxes, and wages could all be allocated between retail operations and cultivation operations using some reasonable method. Only those expenses allocated to the retail operations would be subject to § 280E. The rest would be deductible as a part of COGS.

Either of these strategies could decrease federal taxes and therefore increase profits, possibly to the point where a seller could avoid going out of business. But the primary point remains the same: § 280E dramatically increases the cost of operating a marijuana business that complies with federal tax law, much more so than any other business tax. When the cost of running a legitimate business is raised, the financial benefit of running an illegal or quasi-legal business is increased. At a certain point, the costs of legitimacy get too high, and black-market providers thrive.

## Notes and Questions

1. For a useful and accessible discussion of what counts as COGS, for purposes of 280E, see Tony Nitti, *IRS Further Limits Deductions for State-Legal Marijuana Facilities*, Forbes.com, Jan. 24, 2015, https://perma.cc/M8LH-NWX6.

2. Is there any other way for marijuana suppliers to minimize the impact of section 280E? Professor Leff has suggested that "a properly organized and operated marijuana seller could avoid the impact of § 280E by qualifying as an exempt . . . 'social welfare' organization." Leff, *supra*, at 527. For discussions of Leff's proposed workaround, see *id.* at 532-564 (detailing proposal), Philip T. Hackney, *A Response to Professor Leff's Tax Planning "Olive Branch" for Marijuana Dealers*, 99 Iowa L. Rev. Bull. 25, 26 (2014) (suggesting the proposal is "unrealistic").

3. Imposing taxes on marijuana distribution raises some thorny legal questions, as illustrated by the following Problem:

Problem 7.34: Suppose that Camila runs a medical marijuana dispensary in strict compliance with state and local law. Last year, Camila's dispensary sold $1,000,000 in marijuana. Her COGS were $600,000. Her other expenses amounted to $300,000, leaving Camila with a tidy $100,000 profit. Assume

that the federal business tax rate is 35 percent. Camila acknowledged on her federal tax return that she earned her income from the distribution of marijuana. Nevertheless, she claimed (credibly) that she would be forced to go out of business if she abided section 280E. She thus paid only $35,000 in federal taxes (35 percent of $100,000). May the IRS pursue legal action against Camila to recover the additional $105,000 it insists she owes in federal taxes, pursuant to section 280E (35 percent of $400,000)? What if she runs the state's only medical marijuana dispensary? Assuming *McIntosh* no longer applied, could the DOJ also criminally prosecute Camila under 21 U.S.C. section 841(a)? See *Dep't of Revenue of Montana v. Kurth Ranch*, 511 U.S. 767 (1994). If so, could the DOJ use the information Camila provided the IRS on her tax return to help build its criminal case against her? See *Leary v. United States*, 395 U.S. 6, 12-27 (1969).

### 3. RICO

Marijuana suppliers might also be held liable for damages under the federal Racketeer Influenced and Corrupt Organizations Act (RICO). See 18 U.S.C. § 1961 *et seq.* In a nutshell, the RICO Act makes it a crime to acquire or conduct a business through "a pattern of racketeering activity," *id.* at § 1962, which includes the "felonious manufacture, . . . buying, selling, or otherwise dealing in a controlled substance," *id.* at § 1961(1)(D). Like the CSA, the RICO Act authorizes imposition of criminal sanctions, including lengthy prison terms and forfeiture of property. *Id.* at § 1963. Unlike the CSA, however, the RICO Act also creates a civil cause of action that can be enforced by private parties. In particular, section 1964(c) provides:

> Any person injured in his business or property by reason of a violation of section 1962 of this chapter may sue therefor in any appropriate United States district court and shall recover threefold the damages he sustains and the cost of the suit, including a reasonable attorney's fee. . . .

The following excerpt explains the substance of a RICO violation and examines whether marijuana suppliers might be vulnerable to civil RICO suits.

#### Robert A. Mikos, A Critical Appraisal of the Department of Justice's New Approach to Medical Marijuana
22 Stan. L. & Pol'y Rev. 633 (2011)

The core RICO statute delineates four distinct crimes, but for present purposes, it suffices to focus on the provision that serves as the basis for most civil RICO actions: section 1962(c). To simplify somewhat, section 1962(c) makes it unlawful for a (1) person (2) to conduct (3) an enterprise (4) through a pattern of racketeering activity.

Consider how each of these elements would apply in a civil action brought against a marijuana dispensary. Suppose, for the illustration, that the dispensary is legally incorporated; that it is owned and operated by a single proprietor; and that it has been feloniously (under the CSA) distributing marijuana to several customers for at least one year.

. . .

In a RICO action, the RICO person is the defendant. It can be any "individual or entity capable of holding a legal or beneficial interest in property," [id. at § 1961(3),] though, under section 1962(c), it must be legally distinct from the RICO enterprise. For purposes of my hypothetical RICO suit, the proprietor would easily meet all of the legal requirements for being a RICO person. . . .

. . .

The enterprise named in the suit could be any "individual, partnership, corporation, association, or other legal entity, and any union or group of individuals associated in fact although not a legal entity." [Id. at § 1961(4).] In my case, the dispensary—a legal entity—could serve as the RICO enterprise.

. . .

The defendant must also conduct the affairs of the RICO enterprise. In essence, this means that the defendant must "participate in the operation or management of the enterprise." Once again, my plucky proprietor clearly satisfies this test, as she is the sole owner and employee of the dispensary.

. . .

Finally, the enterprise must commit a pattern of racketeering activity. Growing or distributing non-negligible quantities of marijuana clearly constitutes racketeering activity. Committing such crimes repeatedly over the course of a year or more also constitutes a pattern. Indeed, a pattern may involve as few as two predicate acts, as long as there is a relationship and continuity in the crimes. In essence, this means the plaintiff must show the crimes had a common purpose, participants, or modus operandi, and occurred over a substantial period of time (one year is enough) or else were likely to recur again in the future. In my hypothetical, distributing marijuana to several customers over the course of a year (or more) would easily constitute a pattern of racketeering activity.

. . .

My hypothetical marijuana dispensary has almost certainly violated section 1962(c). To be sure, the dispensary and its proprietor probably do not need to worry about *criminal* RICO liability, because only the DOJ may initiate criminal RICO prosecutions. Civil RICO liability, however, is another matter[, because section 1964(c)] creates a *private* cause of action and it empowers anyone injured by racketeering activity to recover treble damages and attorneys' fees from defendants. . . . Importantly, a civil RICO claim is viable even if a defendant is never charged with nor convicted of the predicate criminal acts. . . .

The only question remaining is whether any plaintiff could bring a RICO claim against a marijuana dispensary. Plaintiffs seeking to bring civil RICO actions must satisfy onerous standing requirements. Most importantly, for present purposes, a plaintiff must show that it (1) suffered an injury to its business or property (2) that was proximately caused by the defendant's predicate crimes.

First, a RICO plaintiff must allege injury to its business or property. This concept includes harm to any recognized property or business interest, such as the loss of plaintiff's customers. However, it excludes other sorts of injury, such as personal injury or harm to a government's sovereign interest.

Second, and more dauntingly, the plaintiff must demonstrate that her injury was directly caused by the defendant's predicate crimes. The Supreme Court has developed the proximate cause test in a series of recent cases. In *Anza v. Ideal Steel Supply Corp.*, [547 U.S. 451 (2006),] for example, the Court dismissed a civil RICO claim brought by a company against its (allegedly) tax-evading competitor. The plaintiff claimed that the defendant was able to lower its prices and poach the plaintiff's customers (the injury) by evading state taxes (the racketeering activity). Yet the Court found that the plaintiff lacked standing to pursue the RICO claim. It reasoned that the state was a more direct victim of the defendant's tax-evasion scheme. It also foresaw difficulty in ascertaining what portion of the plaintiff's injury was attributable to the defendant's alleged predicate crimes, rather than other (legitimate) reasons for the defendant's price cuts.

Similarly, in *Hemi Group, LLC v. City of New York*, [559 U.S. 1 (2010),] the Court dismissed the city's civil RICO claim against an out-of-state online cigarette vendor. The claim alleged that defendant had failed to report its cigarette sales to state authorities, as required by state law. This failure constituted mail fraud under federal law (the racketeering activity) and had allegedly cost the city millions in lost cigarette tax revenues (the injury). In particular, the city claimed it needed the sales reports to enforce the city's cigarette tax against the defendant's customers—importantly, the defendant itself was not required to pay or collect any taxes on behalf of the city. The Court, however, dismissed the claim on the ground that the city lacked RICO standing. It reasoned that the state was a more direct victim of the defendant's mail fraud. It also found that the defendant's tax-evading customers were a more direct cause of the city's injury.

The proximate cause requirement clearly limits the universe of actionable civil RICO claims. In particular, several factors could sever a defendant's legal responsibility for injuries for which it was an actual (but-for) cause: (1) the existence of other, intervening causes for the plaintiff's injury; (2) difficulty in ascertaining the amount of harm attributable to the defendant; (3) a risk of duplicative recovery against the defendant; and (4) the existence of a more direct victim to bring the claim.

. . .

Given the aforementioned requirements, it is quite possible that no plaintiff would have standing to bring a civil RICO claim against a medical marijuana dispensary. Some prospective plaintiffs would not satisfy the first part of the standing inquiry—suffering an injury to business or property. Consider, briefly, a suit that might be brought by a local government that opposes medical marijuana. Suppose, for example, that the intrepid Dispensary, Inc., operates in a socially conservative county situated in a medical marijuana state. Suppose as well, for sake of argument, that Dispensary's sale of marijuana has fueled a wave of destructive crime and reckless behavior in the county. In response, the county has been forced to increase the budget for local law enforcement.

In this scenario, the county has clearly been injured by Dispensary. But its claim would fail because the county did not suffer an injury to its *business or property*. The extra money it had to spend on law enforcement is considered a sovereign cost and is not actionable under RICO. In one case, for example, a local government in Idaho brought a civil RICO action against four companies that allegedly hired undocumented workers. The county claimed, among other things, that the influx of undocumented workers had caused it to expend additional funds on public health and law enforcement. The Ninth Circuit, however, dismissed the claim, characterizing the injury as one to the government's regulatory interests and not to its business or property.

There are, of course, plaintiffs who could allege an injury to business or property. Imagine, for example, a drug company that has lost customers to a marijuana dispensary. Marijuana has been hawked as a treatment for ailments ranging from glaucoma to cancer—ailments for which patients now spend billions on patented pharmaceuticals. Many supporters of legalized marijuana claim it outperforms standard (i.e., legal) drug treatment regimens for these and many other ailments. It seems reasonable to suppose that some patients have abandoned the drugs marketed by major pharmaceutical corporations and adopted marijuana as a course of treatment instead.

To illustrate, suppose that Pharmacology, Inc. hawks a patented medicine commonly prescribed for treating glaucoma. The medicine costs $30,000 annually. Now suppose that Dispensary, Inc. begins selling marijuana to Pharmacology's customers, touting it as an alternative glaucoma treatment. Suppose further that one hundred of Pharmacology's customers stop buying its glaucoma drug and begin using Dispensary's marijuana instead. The loss of one hundred customers and associated profits clearly constitutes an injury to Pharmacology's business or property, for purposes of RICO. Suppose as well that Dispensary is clearly the actual cause of Pharmacology's loss; in other words, but for Dispensary's marketing of marijuana, Pharmacology's former customers would have continued using its lucrative patented medicine.

Even though it might prove that Dispensary's racketeering activity actually caused it to lose $3 million in revenue (annually), Pharmacology would still face considerable difficulty satisfying the second prong of the RICO standing inquiry—showing that Dispensary is the proximate cause of that injury. In my hypothetical, one could construct a chain of causation that severs Dispensary's legal responsibility for Pharmacology's loss. For example, Dispensary could claim that Pharmacology's customers are an intervening cause of its injury. After all, they were the ones who ultimately decided to defect and use marijuana in lieu of Pharmacology's drug. And those customers might not have chosen to defect had their physicians not recommended marijuana in the first instance.

. . .

In the end, it is impossible to predict precisely how the federal courts would rule on the RICO standing question, in no small part due to the flexibility of the proximate cause inquiry.

---

In late 2015, a Colorado-licensed marijuana operation and affiliated parties were sued under the civil RICO statute. The portions of the complaint detailing plaintiffs' RICO claims are excerpted below.

## *Safe Streets Alliance v. Alternative Holistic Healing, LLC*
Second Amended Complaint, Civil Action No. 15-349 (D. Colo. Feb. 1, 2016)

10. Defendant Alternative Holistic Healing, LLC, d/b/a Rocky Mountain Organic, is a Colorado corporation that has its principal place of business at 5412 Highway 119, . . . Black Hawk, CO . . . , where it operates a recreational marijuana cultivation facility and retail shop. It operates an additional recreational marijuana cultivation facility at 6480 Pickney Road.

Part III. Marijuana Suppliers

11. Defendant Joseph R. Licata has a fifty percent interest in Alternative Holistic Healing and is one of its two members. . . .

12. Defendant Jason M. Licata has a fifty percent interest in Alternative Holistic Healing and is one of its two members. . . .

13. Defendant 6480 Pickney, LLC owns the marijuana cultivation at 6480 Pickney Road. . . . Defendant Parker Walton ("Walton") is the sole member, manager, and owner of 6480 Pickney, LLC. . . .

. . .

55. Walton is the owner and sole member and manager of 6480 Pickney, LLC, . . . and in those capacities he leased the land to Alternative Holistic Healing, LLC, which grows and sells recreational marijuana . . .

. . .

75. The . . . Defendants . . . together formed an association-in-fact enterprise for the purpose of cultivating marijuana at 6480 Pickney Road and selling it at Alternative Holistic Healing's Black Hawk store, among other places. To that end, they pooled their resources, knowledge, skills, and labor to achieve through the enterprise efficiencies in the cultivation and distribution of marijuana that none of them could have achieved individually.

76. All of the Individual Defendants and Pueblo Defendants have contractual and other relationships with each other and are collaborating together to contribute to the association-in-fact enterprise's efforts to cultivate recreational marijuana at 6480 Pickney Road and thereby engage in an ongoing pattern of racketeering activity. . . .

77. On information and belief, most decisions about how the property at 6480 Pickney Road is developed and used are made collectively by Alternative Holistic Healing, Joseph Licata, Jason Licata, 6480 Pickney, and Walton, with each having an important role in decisionmaking, operations, and management.

78. Defendants Walton and 6480 Pickney play central roles in the management and operations of the association-in-fact enterprise. Acting on behalf of the enterprise, Walton secured a water supply for growing marijuana . . . Walton also wrote the following note, which was included with Alternative Holistic Healing's county license application: "I, Parker Walton, as the sole member and manager of 6480 Pickney LLC, allow the use of RMJ (Retail Marijuana) cultivation facility on my property at 6480 Pickney Rd. /s/ Parker Walton on behalf of 6480 Pickney LLC." . . . Walton spoke at the hearing in support of [Alternative Holistic Hearing's] application [for a marijuana license], describing himself as "the owner" of 6480 Pickney Road. Also at the hearing, Joseph Licata referred to Walton as "the builder." . . .

79. Alternative Holistic Healing, Joseph Licata, and Jason Licata also have important roles managing the enterprise's affairs. Alternative Holistic Healing applied for and holds the state and local licenses that authorize cultivation of marijuana at 6480 Pickney Road. As equal owners in Alternative Holistic Healing, Joseph Licata and Jason Licata completed and signed those applications and make decisions about Alternative Holistic Healing's finances and business strategy.

. . .

83. Plaintiffs Phillis Windy Hope Reilly and Michael P. Reilly own . . . a contiguous parcel of approximately 105 acres of beautiful rolling pasture with sweeping mountain vistas that include views of Pike's Peak. Although the Reillys do not live on their land, they often visit on weekends with their children to ride horses, hike, and visit with friends in the closely-knit neighborhood. The Reillys' property includes two agricultural buildings.

84. The 6480 Pickney Road marijuana grow is west and immediately adjacent to the Reillys' property. Although Defendant 6480 Pickney owns a 40-acre parcel, the structure was built in the corner of the lot, just a few feet from the Reillys' property line. The building has marred the mountain views from the Reillys' property, thus making it less suitable for hiking and horseback riding. The building's purpose—the manufacture of illegal drugs—exacerbates this injury, for when the Reillys and their children visit the property they are reminded of the racketeering enterprise next door every time they look to the west.

85. Construction of the marijuana cultivation facility at 6480 Pickney Road was completed in the latter part of 2015, and the facility is currently being used to grow marijuana. Marijuana is an extremely odorous plant that emits a distinctive, skunk-like smell that is particularly strong when the plant is harvested. Since construction of the facility was completed, its operation has repeatedly caused a distinctive and unpleasant marijuana smell to waft onto the Reillys' property, with the smell strongest on the portion of the Reillys' property that is closest to Defendants' marijuana cultivation facility. This noxious odor makes the Reillys' property less suitable for recreational and residential purposes, interferes with the Reillys' use and enjoyment of their property, and diminishes the property's value.

. . .

89. The Individual and Pueblo Defendants' publicly disclosed drug conspiracy has also injured the value of the Reillys' property. People buy lots [in the area] because they want to keep horses or build homes in a pleasant residential area, and the Reillys' land is less suitable for those uses due to the 6480 Pickney Road marijuana grow. Furthermore, the large quantity of drugs at marijuana grows makes them targets for theft, and a prospective buyer of the Reillys' land would reasonably worry that the 6480 Pickney Road marijuana grow increases crime in the area. Prospective buyers would also object to the 6480 Pickney Road marijuana grow because it emits pungent odors, thus further interfering with the use and enjoyment of the Reillys' land. As a result, the 6480 Pickney Road marijuana grow has directly and proximately caused a decline in the market value of the Reillys' land and made it more difficult to sell at any price.

. . .

94. . . . Alternative Holistic Healing, Joseph Licata, Jason Licata, 6480 Pickney, Walton, and the Pueblo Defendants each violated [18 U.S.C. section 1962(c)].

. . .

115. The racketeering activities of [the Defendants] directly and proximately injured the Reillys' property by causing noxious smells to travel onto that property, interfering with its use and enjoyment, diminishing its market value, and making it more difficult to sell.

## Notes and Questions

1. Are you sympathetic with the plaintiffs' complaint? Have they stated a valid cause of action under section 1962(c)?

2. Even so, do these plaintiffs have *standing* to bring a civil RICO claim against the defendants? On the recommendation of the magistrate judge, the district court dismissed plaintiffs' civil RICO claims. The magistrate found that the complaint failed to provide "factual support to quantify or otherwise substantiate their inchoate concerns as to the diminution in value of their property." See *Safe Streets Alliance v. Alternative Holistic*

*Healing, LLC*, No. 15-cv-00349 (D. Colo. Feb. 8, 2016) (recommendation regarding defendants' motions to dismiss). The magistrate explained:

> Upon closer examination, the Reillys claim the following discrete injuries in their property. First, they insist that the Individual Defendants' cultivation facility "has marred the mountain views from [their] property, thus making it less suitable for hiking and horseback riding." Colorado courts have held that . . . a property owner . . . does not have a constitutionally recognized property interest in the preservation of scenic views. . . . More to the point, any adverse effect on the Reillys' scenic views constitutes an intangible harm that falls outside the scope of § 1964(c). . . .
>
> The Reillys also assert that when they and their children visit their property "they are reminded of the racketeering enterprise next door every time they look to the west" and see the cultivation facility on the adjoining property. This is best characterized as a form of emotional distress that is not recoverable through a RICO private action. . . .
>
> The Reillys aver that the Individual Defendants' actions have "directly and proximately cause[d] a decline in the market value of [their] land and made it more difficult to sell at any price," because their property is "less suitable" for keeping horses or building homes. Plaintiffs insist that prospective purchasers would "reasonably worry that the 6480 Pickney Road marijuana grow increases crime in the area" and "also object to the 6480 Pickney Road marijuana grow because it emits pungent odors." These particular allegations are based on conjecture and hardly equate to concrete financial losses. . . . More to the point, these sweeping conclusions are devoid of any factual support. Indeed, the Second Amended Complaint does not allege that the Reillys . . . have made any effort to sell their property since marijuana cultivation activities commenced at 6480 Pickney Road.
>
> . . .
>
> Finally, the Reillys insist that their property has been injured because the Individual Defendants' cultivation "operation has repeatedly caused a distinctive and unpleasant marijuana smell to waft onto the Reillys' property" which makes their land "less suitable for recreational and residential purposes [and] interferes with the Reillys' use and enjoyment of their property." While the court does not discount the very real possibility that Defendants' cultivation facility generates odors that some might find unpleasant, that allegation alone does not suggest an actual monetary loss or translate into a quantifiable financial injury.

*Id.* at 21-24.

Can you imagine any other set of facts in which these plaintiffs (or another plaintiff) would have standing to bring a civil RICO claim? *Id.* at 27 ("[T]his recommendation should not be read to preclude the possibility that some plaintiff could assert a fact-based, plausible RICO claim against a Colorado marijuana business based upon violations of the Controlled Substances Act.").

3. The plaintiffs also sought to challenge state and local marijuana regulations as preempted by federal law. The content and status of those claims are discussed in Chapter 10.

## 4. Trademark (and Other Intellectual Property)

In addition to serving as the basis for liability under the aforementioned laws, the federal marijuana ban might also preclude marijuana suppliers from seeking protection of legal rights enjoyed by other businesses. Among other things, federal law precludes marijuana suppliers from obtaining patents on marijuana products or registering (most) trademarks used with them. This means that marijuana suppliers who invest in developing new products or brands might not be able to prevent other suppliers from exploiting their innovations—i.e., from offering the same products, even under the same names.

This section discusses the limitations imposed on intellectual property protection in the marijuana industry, focusing on the issues surrounding trademarks. (Chapter 13 discusses the related limits imposed on enforcement of contract rights in the marijuana industry.) A trademark is a word, phrase, design, or symbol (or some combination thereof) that identifies the source of a good (or service) and helps to distinguish the good (or service) of one provider from that of its rivals. Think of the brand name Coca-Cola and its distinctive script or McDonald's and its famous golden arches.

The federal Lanham Act provides for the nationwide protection of trademarks that are registered with the United States Patent and Trademark Office (USPTO).[6] 15 U.S.C. § 1501 et seq. Such protection includes a cause of action for trademark infringement against unauthorized use of a mark. To register a trademark under federal law, the owner must establish:

(1) that the mark is distinctive—i.e., that it identifies the source of a given product or service, and
(2) the mark is being used in commerce—i.e., that the mark is being used on goods or services that are being sold in commerce[7]

For further background on trademark law, see United States Patent and Trademark Office, Basic Facts About Trademarks (2014), https://perma.cc/3BK4-Q6KC, and Craig Allen Nard et al., The Law of Intellectual Property (4th ed. 2014).

Can marijuana suppliers satisfy these requirements for registration? The use in commerce element has proven a substantial barrier, for reasons explained in the following decision of the Trademark Trial and Appeal Board (TTAB), an administrative board that hears appeals from USPTO refusals to register trademarks.

## *In re Morgan Brown*
119 U.S.P.Q.2d 1350 (Trademark Tr. & App. Bd. 2016)

BERGSMAN, A.T.J.:

Morgan Brown ("Applicant") seeks registration on the Principal Register of the mark HERBAL ACCESS (in standard characters) for "retail store services featuring herbs" . . . Applicant disclaimed the exclusive right to use the word "herbal."

The Trademark Examining Attorney refused registration of Applicant's mark under Sections 1 and 45 of the Trademark Act, 15 U.S.C. §§ 1051 and 1127, on the ground that the herbs offered for sale in Applicant's retail store include marijuana, a substance which cannot be lawfully distributed or dispensed under federal law.

---

6. While the book focuses on registered trademarks, it is worth noting that federal law does provide some limited protection for unregistered trademarks, and marijuana suppliers *might* enjoy more success seeking protection for unregistered marks. *See* Marsha Gentner, *Hazy Future for Federal Registration of Marijuana Marks*, 23 Westlaw Int. Prop. J. 1, 2 n.3 (2017) (noting several open questions regarding federal protection of unregistered marijuana trademarks).

7. In some instances, an intent to use the mark in commerce may suffice for registration.

We have consistently held that, to qualify for a federal service mark registration, the use of a mark in commerce must be "lawful." . . . Thus, any goods or services for which the mark is used must not be illegal under federal law. . . . [T]he fact that the provision of a product or service may be lawful within a state[2] is irrelevant to the question of federal registration when it is unlawful under federal law.

Generally, the [U.S. Patent and Trademark Office (USPTO)] presumes that an applicant's use of a mark in commerce is lawful under federal law. Thus, registration generally will not be refused based on unlawful use in commerce unless either (1) a violation of federal law is indicated by the application record or other evidence, such as when a court or a federal agency responsible for overseeing activity in which the applicant is involved, and which activity is relevant to its application, has issued a finding of noncompliance under the relevant statute or regulation, or (2) when the applicant's application-relevant activities involve a per se violation of a federal law. . . .

The Examining Attorney does not contend that a finding of noncompliance covers the case at hand and relies on an asserted per se violation of federal law by Applicant, in certain activities in which Applicant is engaged, which are encompassed by the identification of services. The Examining Attorney relied upon the evidence set forth below to support the unlawful use refusal. The evidence establishes that Applicant's retail store services include the provision of marijuana:

1. Applicant's specimen of use, submitted with his application, features two photographs of Applicant's retail establishment. One photograph includes a green cross prominently displayed on a window with a larger image of what appears to be the same green cross superimposed over the photograph. The second photograph appears to be a close-up image of the door next to the window with the green cross. The wording HERBAL ACCESS appears on the door.

2. Applicant's website (herbalaccess.com) homepage displays the following advertising text for its retail services superimposed over a picture of a marijuana plant inviting customers to "stop by" the store to "find exactly what you are looking for":

> Your Access Is Granted!
> Call or stop by today and find out why people consider our marijuana to be the best of the best!
> Now Come Check Us Out!

The webpage also includes a map showing the location of the retail establishment that includes the wording "Marijuana For The Masses."

As noted above, applicant's specimen showing use of the mark HERBAL ACCESS in connection with its retail services also includes two images of a green cross. The evidence from Jeff Duntemann's Contrapositive Diary (contrapositivediary.com), Every Joe website (everyjoe.com), Amazon.com, Patch.com, and O'Shaughnessy's online (beyondthc.com), clearly indicates that a green cross has become the symbol of the organized medical marijuana industry.

---

2. Applicant is located in the State of Washington where adults can possess 1 ounce of useable marijuana, 16 ounces of marijuana-infused product in sold form, and 72 ounces of marijuana infused product in liquid form. . . .

In addition, Applicant's website homepage encourages visitors to the page to call or stop by Applicant's retail establishment. The address and phone information, as well as the facility hours posted on the page are a further invitation to shop at applicant's establishment. The specimen and the webpage, taken together, support the conclusion that Applicant is engaged in the provision of marijuana via the retail services provided at the facility shown in the specimen and advertised on the website.

Thus, Applicant's services include the provision of an illegal substance, i.e., marijuana, in violation of the federal Controlled Substances Act (CSA).... The CSA prohibits, among other things, manufacturing, distributing, dispensing or possessing certain controlled substances, including marijuana and marijuana-based preparations. 21 U.S.C. §§ 812, 841(a)(1), 844(a). Regardless of individual state laws that may provide for legal activities involving marijuana, marijuana and its psychoactive component, THC, remain Schedule I controlled substances under federal law and are subject to the CSA's prohibitions.... In view of the foregoing, we find that there is a per se violation of the CSA and, therefore, Applicant's use of HERBAL ACCESS as evidenced by the record, includes unlawful activity under the CSA.

Applicant argues that his recitation of services is "retail store services featuring herbs" and that there is nothing illegal about herbs; but acknowledges that he "may also sell marijuana" and that such sale is "admittedly illegal under the CSA."

> The sale of herbs does not constitute a violation of the CSA. Notwithstanding this fact, the Examining Attorney issued the refusal based upon evidence that the Applicant may also sell marijuana through retail services legal in the Applicant's state although admittedly illegal under the CSA.
>
> ... [T]he issue before the Board is a critical interpretation of the scope to which a refusal to register a trademark should be applied under the CSA. In short, to affirm the Examining Attorney's refusal to register the instant trademark in connection with the lawful selling of legal herbs is akin to pronouncing that a specific class of Applicant, namely those who may also sell substances illegal under the CSA but legal in their respective states, may never be the holders of a federal trademark even if the trademark applied for is for use in connection with legal goods or services.

[Applicant's Brief.]

... This argument does not directly address or rebut the evidence that marijuana is an herb and Applicant sells marijuana. The Federal Circuit has previously rejected attempts to use generalized language in goods and services identifications in order to sidestep refusals where a particular good or services falls within the generalized identification and the evidence shows the applicant's actual usage involves the specific good or service that is the subject of the refusal....

Because the evidence that Applicant's mark is being used in connection with sales of a specific substance (marijuana) that falls within both the services identification and the prohibitions of the CSA is unrebutted, we find that Applicant's retail store services include sales of a good that is illegal under federal law, and therefore encompasses a use that is unlawful.

## Notes and Questions

1. Is there anything the Applicant in *In re Morgan Brown* could have done to improve its chances of successfully registering the HERBAL ACCESS mark, short of ceasing all sales of marijuana in its stores?

2. The TTAB refused to register the mark, HERBAL ACCESS, because the mark was being used in connection with the sale of marijuana, which remains illegal under federal law. As discussed in Section A.6.a above, however, the DOJ has issued memoranda discouraging enforcement of the federal ban. Does the agency's enforcement guidance have any relevance for trademark registration? Put another way, should the TTAB continue to bar registration on the grounds that federal law bans marijuana, given that the DOJ is declining to enforce at least parts of that ban?

In another decision, issued just months after *In re Morgan Brown*, the TTAB dismissed the DOJ enforcement guidance as irrelevant for purposes of trademark law. The decision stemmed from a company's attempt to register the mark "Powered by JUJU", for "smokeless cannabis vaporizing apparatus, namely, oral vaporizers for smoking purposes; vaporizing cannabis delivery device, namely, oral vaporizers for smoking purposes," and "Juju Joints" for "smokeless marijuana or cannabis vaporizer apparatus, namely, oral vaporizers for smokers; vaporizing marijuana or cannabis delivery device, namely, oral vaporizers for smoking purposes." *In re JJ206, LLC, DBA JUJU Joints*, 120 U.S.P.Q.2d 1568 (Trademark Tr. & App. Bd. 2016). The TTAB rejected the registration of both marks on the grounds that the Applicant's vaporizers were designed for use in consuming marijuana, making them unlawful drug paraphernalia under the CSA. 21 U.S.C. § 863(a) (2016) (making it "unlawful . . . to sell or offer for sale drug paraphernalia"); *id*. at § 863(d) (defining drug paraphernalia to include, inter alia, "equipment . . . of any kind which is primarily intended or designed for use in manufacturing, compounding, converting, concealing, producing, processing, preparing, injecting, ingesting, inhaling, or otherwise introducing into the human body a controlled substance, possession of which is unlawful . . .").

Applicant had argued that "because the jurisdictions where it does business 'comply with federal directives such as the Cole Memo,' its goods should be considered lawful." 120 U.S.P.Q.2d 1568. However, the TTAB dismissed the argument, reasoning that

> the [Cole] memorandum does not and cannot override the CSA, and in fact, explicitly underscores that 'marijuana is a dangerous drug and that the illegal distribution and sale of marijuana is a serious crime.' We cannot simply disregard the requirement of lawful use or intended lawful use in commerce under the Trademark Act, or Congress's determination as to what uses are illegal, regardless of the alleged business or consumer consequences of denying registration, and regardless of any analogies between marijuana and other goods that do not violate the CSA. In conclusion, because Applicant's identified goods constitute illegal drug paraphernalia under the CSA, Applicant's use and intended use of the applied-for marks on these goods is unlawful, and cannot serve as the basis for federal registration.

*Id.* Do you agree? As discussed in A.6.b, Congress has gotten into the enforcement quagmire, by arguably stripping the DOJ of funding to enforce the federal ban in some cases. Is Congress's spending legislation more relevant for TTAB's analysis? In other words, should the congressional spending limitation change the TTAB's decision? Why, why not?

3. Did the TTAB err in finding that the sale of JUJU's marijuana paraphernalia is illegal under *federal* law? Section 863 of the CSA includes a seldom noticed provision, stipulating that the federal ban on drug paraphernalia "shall not apply to . . . any person authorized by local, State, or Federal law to manufacture, possess, or distribute such

items. . . ." 21 U.S.C. § 863(f)(1). Does Section 863(f)(1) legalize the sale of marijuana paraphernalia under federal law and thereby enable the registration of trademarks used on such paraphernalia? In a subsequent non-precedential decision, the TTAB rejected the argument as applied to a company that sought to register the mark "ULTRA TRIMMER" for use on a device that processes marijuana. *In re Ultra Trimmer*, LLC, 2016 WL 7385764 (Trademark Tr. & App. Bd. 2016) (unpublished). In so doing, the TTAB noted that "there is no evidence in the record that Applicant has received a license or other manifestation of authorization from any local, State, or Federal governmental authority to manufacture, possess, or distribute drug paraphernalia that would otherwise be illegal under the CSA, and that Applicant thus has not shown that its goods are exempted from illegality under § 863(f)(1) of the CSA."

In light of *In re Ultra Trimmer*, consider the following Problem:

**Problem 7.35**: Camilla owns and operates a state-licensed marijuana supplier that complies with all State regulations.[8] The State recently passed legislation providing that "State law explicitly authorizes licensed marijuana suppliers to produce and distribute marijuana paraphernalia, including equipment of any kind which is primarily intended or designed for use in manufacturing, processing, ingesting, inhaling, or otherwise introducing into the human body, marijuana." Camilla has developed a vaporizer apparatus she calls "RaRa Roaches." Camilla has already sold several thousand units to consumers who visit her retail shop and to dozens of other licensed marijuana suppliers located throughout the State. She has recently applied for federal trademark registration for "RaRa Roaches" for use on a "smokeless marijuana or cannabis vaporizer apparatus." What result? Should the USPTO approve the mark? Why, why not?

4. States also provide trademark protection, and state licensed marijuana suppliers might have more luck registering their marks with the states, even if they are unable to do so with the USPTO. Sam Kamin & Viva R. Moffat, *Trademark Laundering, Useless Patents, and Other IP Challenges for the Marijuana Industry*, 73 Wash. & Lee L. Rev. 217, 256-59 (2016) (reporting that Colorado had already registered more than 200 trademarks including the word "marijuana" or something similar). However, the protection afforded by state trademark registration is more limited than that afforded by federal registration. *Id.* at 258-59 (discussing limitations). And not all states (even ones that have legalized marijuana) necessarily allow the registration of trademarks used on marijuana products. *See* Alison Malsbury, *California Cannabis Trademarks are a No-Go*, Canna Law Blog, Nov. 2, 2016, http://www.cannalawblog.com/california-cannabis-trademarks-are-a-no-go/ (explaining that California "has been steadfast in refusing to register marks used on cannabis").

5. Even for supporters of legalization, is the lack of federal (and possibly even state) trademark protection necessarily a bad thing? For example, might it curb advertising by

---

8. State licensing and regulation of commercial marijuana suppliers are discussed in depth in Chapter 8.

the legal marijuana industry, see Sean K. Clancy, Note, *Branded Bud or Generic Ganja? Trademarks for Marijuana in Washington*, 18 Lewis & Clark L. Rev. 1063, 1074-75 (2014), or prevent the industry from consolidating, see Robert A. Mikos, *State Taxation of Marijuana Distribution and Other Federal Crimes*, 2010 U. Chi. Legal Forum 222, 257-58? As discussed in Chapter 9, many policymakers are wary of advertising and consolidation in the marijuana industry.

CHAPTER 8

# The Regulation of Marijuana Suppliers in Legalization Regimes

A growing number of people are allowed by their states to possess and to use marijuana, but how are those users supposed to obtain the drug? To supply the demands of lawful users, *most* states have carved out exceptions to their otherwise strict prohibitions on the production and distribution of marijuana. In particular, these states now permit

(1) users to produce marijuana for their own personal consumption (personal supply), and/or
(2) private businesses to produce marijuana and sell it to users (commercial supply).

This chapter examines these and other possible sources of supply and the regulations that states have adopted to govern them. Section A begins by exploring personal supply. It discusses which users states allow to cultivate and even distribute marijuana and the limits states impose on those users' supply-related activities, such as prohibitions on producing marijuana collectively. Next, Section B explores the commercial supply of marijuana. It examines the licensing framework states use to determine who may produce and distribute marijuana commercially. It then explores the regulations states impose on these licensees, including, for example, restrictions on the advertisements they may run, and the special civil disciplinary processes states use to enforce these regulations. Section C briefly considers a third possible source of supply—government-owned and -operated marijuana stores. Finally, Section D concludes by examining the different combinations of personal and commercial supply that states have approved and what happens when a state fails to authorize *any* method of supplying lawful users.

## A. PERSONAL SUPPLY

Several reform states permit at least some lawful users to cultivate marijuana for their own consumption, and a few states even permit them to transfer the drug to other lawful users. The materials below discuss the laws governing users qua suppliers in legalization regimes.

### 1. May Users Cultivate Their Own Marijuana?

Problem 8.1: Andy satisfies all of the criteria required to possess and use marijuana under state law. May he also possess and cultivate marijuana plants for his own consumption?

Part III. Marijuana Suppliers

Reform states have taken three basic approaches regarding which, if any, lawful users may cultivate marijuana for their own consumption: (1) some allow all users to cultivate; (2) some allow only a subset of users to cultivate; and (2) some do not allow any users to cultivate. **Figure 8.1** displays the percentage of states following each approach as of the end of 2016, under medical marijuana, recreational marijuana, or CBD laws.

Figure 8.1. State Approaches to Personal Cultivation (2016)*

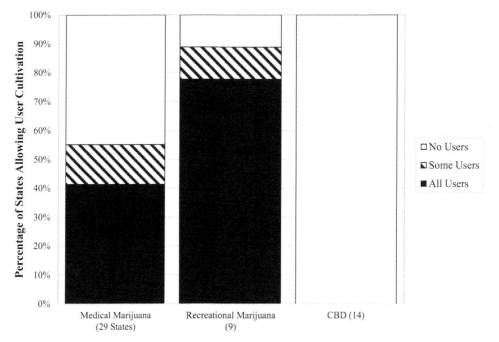

States following the first approach permit all lawful users to possess and cultivate marijuana plants for their own consumption. (To be eligible, of course, these individuals must meet the criteria for lawful use and possession, discussed in Chapter 4.) Colorado's Amendment 64 serves as a representative example of this approach. It provides, in relevant part,

> (3) Notwithstanding any other provision of law, the following acts are not unlawful and shall not be an offense under Colorado law or the law of any locality within Colorado . . . for persons twenty-one years of age or older:
>
> (a) Possessing, using, displaying, purchasing, or transporting marijuana accessories or one ounce or less of marijuana.
>
> (b) Possessing, *growing, processing*, or transporting no more than six marijuana plants, with three or fewer being mature, flowering plants, and possession of the marijuana produced by the plants on the premises where the plants were grown, provided that the growing takes place in an enclosed, locked space, is not conducted openly or publicly, and is not made available for sale.

---

*A total of 43 states are represented in **Figure 8.1**. All nine of the states in the recreational marijuana column also appear in the medical marijuana column, but they may have different rules for recreational and medical marijuana, as discussed in the text.

(c) Transfer of one ounce or less of marijuana without remuneration to a person who is twenty-one years of age or older.

. . .

Colo. Const. art. XVIII, § 16 (2016) (emphasis added). *See also*, *e.g.*, Massachusetts Question 4, § 7 (2016). Colorado's medical marijuana law similarly provides that "it shall be an exception from the state's criminal laws for any patient or primary caregiver in lawful possession of a registry identification card to engage or assist in the medical use of marijuana." Colo. Const. art. XVIII, § 14(2)(b) (2016). Crucially, the law defines "medical *use*" to mean the "acquisition, possession, *production*, use, or transportation of marijuana." *Id.* at § 14(1)(b) (emphases added). A large majority of recreational marijuana states and slightly less than half of medical marijuana states, but no CBD states, follow this first approach.

States following the second approach permit only a subset of lawful users to cultivate their own marijuana. In some jurisdictions, this permission extends to either medical users or recreational users, but not to both. For example, Washington state allows only its medical users to cultivate their own marijuana, Wash. Rev. Code Ann. § 69.51A.040 (2016), whereas Washington, D.C., allows only its recreational users to do so, D.C. Code § 48-904.01(a)(1)(C) (2016).[1] In other states, permission is granted only to users—medical and/or recreational—who have limited access to another source of supply (usually a state-licensed commercial supplier). For example, under Nevada's medical marijuana law, a qualifying patient is allowed to cultivate marijuana only if:

(a) All the medical marijuana dispensaries in the county of residence of the person who holds the registry identification card close or are unable to supply the quantity or strain of marijuana necessary for the medical use of the person to treat his or her specific medical condition;

(b) Because of illness or lack of transportation, the person who holds the registry identification card is unable reasonably to travel to a medical marijuana dispensary; or

(c) No medical marijuana dispensary was operating within 25 miles of the residence of the person who holds the registry identification card at the time the person first applied for his or her registry identification card.

Nev. Rev. Stat. Ann. § 453A.200(6) (2016). In similar fashion, under Nevada's recreational marijuana law, adult users are permitted to cultivate their own marijuana only if they live more than 25 miles from a licensed retail marijuana store. Nevada Question 2, §§ 6(2), 14(a)(1) (2016). Only a handful of states with medical or recreational marijuana laws follow the limited personal cultivation approach.

States following the third approach do not authorize *any* users to cultivate marijuana for their own consumption. In these states, cultivation remains subject to criminal bans on drug manufacturing, bans that—as discussed in Chapter 7—generally do not differentiate between personal cultivation and cultivation for distribution to others. For example, Arkansas's 2016 medical marijuana law expressly states that it "[a]uthorizes the growing of marijuana at a dispensary or cultivation facility that is properly licensed with the state" but "[d]oes not authorize a qualifying patient, designated caregiver, or other person to

---

1. Of course, most medical marijuana users could cultivate marijuana under a law that permits all adults to do so; but some medical marijuana users, including minors, would not be allowed to do so.

grow marijuana." Arkansas Medical Marijuana Amendment Act of 2016 (Issue 6), §§ 21(1)-(2).

## Notes and Questions

1. As discussed in Chapter 7, prohibitions on manufacturing marijuana cover a wide range of activities besides cultivating marijuana plants. *See, e.g.*, 21 U.S.C. § 802(15) ("The term 'manufacture' means the production, preparation, propagation, compounding, or processing of a drug. . . ."). Do states that allow users to grow their own marijuana also allow them to engage in other manufacturing activities? Consider the following Problem:

Problem 8.2: Benjamin is 35 years old and lives in Colorado. He grows a single marijuana plant in his basement. Benjamin later inserts the trimmed and dried buds of his plant into a plastic tube and pours butane in the tube to create a concentrated THC resin called "hash oil." (The process for making hash oil is described in more detail in Chapter 7.) Does the language of Amendment 64 quoted above permit Benjamin's manufacture of hash oil?

2. Some states require users to obtain formal authorization before cultivating their own marijuana. *E.g.*, Or. Rev. Stat. 475B.420 (2016) (describing registration system for personal production of medical marijuana); New Mexico Department of Health, Personal Production License Application, https://perma.cc/7PTT-8QYM. The process is similar to the patient registration process used by many medical marijuana states and the licensing process for commercial suppliers discussed in Section B.1 below.

3. As shown by **Figure 8.1**, to date, states have been more receptive to personal cultivation when it is intended for recreational (or other adult) use as opposed to medical use (including CBD). Can you think of reasons for distinguishing among the uses to which marijuana will be put when designing laws to govern personal production of the drug?

## 2. What Limits Are Imposed on User Cultivation?

Every state that allows some or all users to cultivate marijuana also imposes limits on such cultivation. For one thing, every state limits the number of marijuana plants that a lawful user may possess at any point in time. (Chapter 4 discussed similar limits that states impose on the quantity of *usable marijuana* individuals may possess.) The plant limits vary across states, but most jurisdictions set the limit between 4 and 12 plants. *E.g.*, Colo. Const. art. XVIII, § 16(3)(b) (2016) (6 plants total). Some states impose separate limits for mature and immature plants and seedlings. For example, Colorado's Amendment 64, excerpted above, allows adults to possess "no more than six marijuana plants, with three or fewer being mature, flowering plants." *Id.* In some medical marijuana states, however, these numerical limits are merely presumptive; in other words, qualifying patients may be allowed to possess and cultivate more plants if necessary to supply their medical needs. *E.g.*, Colo. Const. art. XVIII, § 14(4)(b) (2016). *See also* Chapter 4 (discussing similar exceptions to limits on possession of *usable* marijuana in medical marijuana states).

In addition to limiting the number of marijuana plants users may possess, many states also limit where marijuana plants may be grown. Michigan's medical marijuana law, for example, requires that "marihuana plants [must be] kept in an enclosed, locked facility." Mich. Comp. Laws Ann. § 333.26424(a) (2016). It furthers defines "[e]nclosed, locked facility" as

> a closet, room, or other comparable, stationary, and fully enclosed area equipped with secured locks or other functioning security devices that permit access only by a registered primary caregiver or registered qualifying patient. Marihuana plants grown outdoors are considered to be in an enclosed, locked facility if they are not visible to the unaided eye from an adjacent property when viewed by an individual at ground level or from a permanent structure and are grown within a stationary structure that is enclosed on all sides, except for the base, by chain-link fencing, wooden slats, or a similar material that prevents access by the general public and that is anchored, attached, or affixed to the ground; located on land that is owned, leased, or rented by either the registered qualifying patient or a person designated through the departmental registration process as the primary caregiver for the registered qualifying patient or patients for whom the marihuana plants are grown; and equipped with functioning locks or other security devices that restrict access to only the registered qualifying patient or the registered primary caregiver who owns, leases, or rents the property on which the structure is located. Enclosed, locked facility includes a motor vehicle if both of the following conditions are met:
>
> (1) The vehicle is being used temporarily to transport living marihuana plants from 1 location to another with the intent to permanently retain those plants at the second location.
>
> (2) An individual is not inside the vehicle unless he or she is either the registered qualifying patient to whom the living marihuana plants belong or the individual designated through the departmental registration process as the primary caregiver for the registered qualifying patient.

*Id.* at § 333.26423(d).

## Notes and Questions

1. As noted in the text, some states make separate allowances for mature and immature marijuana plants. But what is the difference between a mature and an immature marijuana plant? *See, e.g.*, Or. Rev. Stat. Ann. § 475B.015(11) (West 2016) ("'Immature marijuana plant' means a marijuana plant that is not flowering."); Vt. Stat. Ann. tit. 18, § 4472(7) (2016) ("'Immature marijuana plant' means a female marijuana plant that has not flowered and which does not have buds that may be observed by visual examination.").

2. Unlike much of the marijuana that is produced and sold by commercial suppliers, the marijuana that is produced by users is generally not subject to state and local marijuana taxes, giving users who personally cultivate a potentially large tax break vis-à-vis commercial suppliers. Marijuana taxes are discussed further in Section B.2.e below and in Chapter 9.

## 3. May Users Grow Collectively?

Problem 8.3: Andy, Benjamin, and Camila are all qualified patients under the state's medical marijuana law. Each of them separately has been growing 6 marijuana plants to meet their needs—the maximum allowed by state law. The three patients have been struggling to care for their plants, so one day, Camila proposes that they pool their efforts and cultivate their 18 plants in one collective garden. Under Camila's proposal, each of them would take shifts tending the plants in the garden—e.g., watering them, trimming their buds and leaves, etc. May they do so without violating state law?

The majority of states that allow users to cultivate their own marijuana do not allow them to cultivate marijuana collectively. *E.g.*, Me. Rev. Stat. tit. 22, § 2423-A (2016) ("Collectives are prohibited under this chapter."); *Michigan v. Blysma*, 825 N.W.2d 543, 548 (Mich. 2012) ("[T]he MMMA does not explicitly provide for collective growing operations. . . ."). The main problem is that each member of a collective could be held responsible for—i.e., in possession of—all of the plants grown by the entire collective, which would thereby likely (though not necessarily) put each of them in violation of the numerical plant limits discussed above. *Id.* at 551-52 (finding that defendant had exceeded Michigan's plant limits by assisting several other qualifying patients in growing more than 86 marijuana plants).

At least a few states, however, do explicitly authorize users to cultivate collectively.[2] California has the most extensive experience with collective cultivation. Although its original medical marijuana law (the CUA) did not allow collective cultivation, *California v. Urziceanu*, 33 Cal. Rptr. 3d 859 (Cal. App. 3d 2005), the state legislature passed a law—the Medical Marijuana Program Act (MMP)—in 2003 stipulating that "[q]ualified patients . . . and the designated primary caregivers of qualified patients . . . , who associate within the State of California in order *collectively or cooperatively* to cultivate marijuana for medical purposes, shall not solely on the basis of that fact be subject to state criminal sanctions." Cal. Health & Safety C. § 11362.775 (emphasis added).

In the following case, the court opines on what it means to "collectively or cooperatively" cultivate marijuana. The case stemmed from the prosecution of William Colvin on drug charges related to his operation of a pair of medical marijuana dispensaries, called Hollywood Holistic, in Los Angeles. At his trial, he invoked section 11362.775 as a defense.

### *California v. Colvin*
137 Cal. Rptr. 856 (Cal. App. 2d 2012)

ALDRICH, J.:

As of March 2009, Holistic had 1,500 patients or members, although that number grew to over 5,000 by the time of trial. Approximately 14 members, including Colvin,

---

2. Relatedly, some states permit designated caregivers to cultivate marijuana on behalf of more than one patient, an operation that could resemble a collective. Caregivers are discussed in Section A.5 below.

grow marijuana, and Holistic reimburses growers for expenditures, such as fertilizer, hydroponic equipment, and lighting for indoor growing. Some growers are in Los Angeles County, but others are in Humboldt County. Those who grow marijuana drop it off at Holistic for other members to buy. Holistic also grows marijuana onsite. . . . None of the marijuana Holistic distributes is from a source other than a collective member.

If a person comes in with a prescription for medical marijuana, he or she is first left in "primary holding" while someone looks him or her up online or calls his or her doctor to make sure he or she is "legal." The person's identification is checked. Once that process is completed, the person is let in and fills out a membership application and patient information sheet. The person is then given a prescription number that Holistic uses to identify him or her and to track when his or her prescription expires. He or she also signs a registry so that Holistic has a record of his or her medical problem. Finally, the person is given his or her medicine, which is "legally tagged" and put in a stapled bag. Every time the person returns, the visit is registered in a computer program. Patients are allowed no more than one ounce of marijuana in one day, and, to minimize the chance of crime, each Holistic establishment has no more than two to three pounds of marijuana at any time. People who come to Holistic for the first time might pay for the marijuana, but returning members pay a "charter fee," determined each quarter based on the person's needs, that is used to grow marijuana for the person.

. . .

[The Attorney General claims that] section 11362.775 does not condone "a large-scale, wholesale-retail marijuana network" like Holistic, which has approximately 5,000 members. The Attorney General argues that a collective or cooperative cultivation "must entail some united action or participation among all those involved, as distinct from merely a supplier-consumer relationship." There must be, the Attorney General suggests, "some modicum of collaboration" in which qualified patients and caregivers "'come together'" in "some way."

Nothing on the face of the statute or in its legislative history supports this interpretation. . . .

On the face of the statute, to be entitled to a defense under section 11362.775, a defendant must, first, be either a qualified patient, person with a valid identification card or a designated primary caregiver. Second, the defendant must associate with like persons to collectively or cooperatively cultivate marijuana. . . . There is no dispute as to the first requirement, namely, that Colvin was a qualified patient. The trial court made a finding he was a qualified patient, and the Attorney General does not challenge that finding. There does not even appear to be a dispute that Holistic is comprised of other qualified patients, persons with valid identification cards or designated primary caregivers. . . .

The dispute concerns what it means to "collectively or cooperatively" cultivate medical marijuana. The MMPA's legislative history tells us little about section 11362.775 or what it means to associate to "collectively or cooperatively . . . cultivate [medical] marijuana.". . .

But, in general, cooperatives are organizations that provide services for use primarily by their members. (Gurnick, Consumer Cooperatives: What They Are and How They Work (July/Aug. 1985, 8 L.A. Lawyer No. 5, p. 23).) "Entities such as production, service, purchasing, and marketing cooperatives engage on a cooperative basis in producing or procuring goods, services or supplies for members and patrons and promoting use of their members' products and services." (*Ibid.*) Cooperatives perform functions its individual members could not do alone as effectively and conduct business for the mutual benefit of members. (*Id.* at pp. 23, 24.)

The evidence here was Holistic obtained its business licenses, was a nonprofit corporation, and was in the process of complying with then applicable ordinances. The trial court thus found that Holistic was a "legitimate" dispensary, which implies that the court believed Holistic was complying with the appropriate laws.

The Attorney General does not argue otherwise, instead maintaining that a medical marijuana cooperative seeking the protections of section 11362.775 must establish that some number of its members participate in the process in some way. The Attorney General does not specify how many members must participate or in what way or ways they must do so, except to imply that Holistic, with its 5,000 members and 14 growers, is simply too big to allow any "meaningful" participation in the cooperative process; hence, it cannot be a "cooperative" or a "collective" in the way section 11362.775 intended. But this interpretation of section 11362.775 would impose on medical marijuana cooperatives requirements not imposed on other cooperatives. A grocery cooperative, for example, may have members who grow and sell the food and run a store out of which the cooperative's products are sold. But not everyone who pays a fee to become a member participates in the cooperative other than to shop at it.

. . .

Holistic complied with other guidelines[ regarding marijuana collectives, including those promulgated by the Attorney General. Attorney General Edmund G. Brown, Jr., *Guidelines for the Security and Non-Diversion of Marijuana Grown for Medical Use* (2008), https://perma.cc/5RMA-P7UX]. Holistic, for example, is a nonprofit registered with the City of Los Angeles in 2007, and Colvin took steps to comply with applicable ordinances (Guidelines, §IV(A)(1), (2) & (B)(1), (2) at pp. 8, 9 [advising cooperatives to incorporate under the Corp. Code or Food & Agr. Code and to obtain applicable business licenses and permits]); Holistic requires members to fill out membership forms, assigns each member a number to track prescription expiration, and keeps a record of members' medical problems and each time a member returns (*id.*, §IV(B)(3) at p. 9 [potential members should complete a written membership application, their status should be verified, membership records should be maintained, and expiration of prescriptions should be tracked]); all money Holistic receives from members goes back into the cooperative (*id.*, §IV(B)(5) at p. 10 ["[a]ny monetary reimbursement that members provide to the collective or cooperative should only be an amount necessary to cover overhead costs and operating expenses"]); Holistic bases membership fees on the cost to cover the member's needs (*id.*, §IV(B)(6) at p. 10 [marijuana may be allocated based on fees that are reasonably calculated to cover overhead costs and operating expenses]); . . . and Holistic employs security measures, namely, it keeps new applicants in a "primary holding" area and verifies their information before admitting them and has no more than two to three pounds of marijuana on the premises at any given time (*id.*, §IV(B)(8) at p. 11 [collectives and cooperatives should take security measures to protect patients and surrounding neighborhoods]). Thus, to the extent these guidelines have any weight, they contemplate cooperatives like Holistic.

Taken to its logical conclusion, an effect of imposing the Attorney General's suggested requirement likely would be to limit drastically the size of medical marijuana establishments. It may be that the Legislature, in trying to implement voters' wishes, envisioned small community or neighborhood marijuana gardens. That may be good policy. But nothing on the face of section 11362.775, or in the inherent nature of a cooperative or collective, requires some unspecified number of members to engage in unspecified "united action or participation" to qualify for the protection of section 11362.775. . . .

## Notes and Questions

1. Postscript on section 11362.775. Legislation passed in 2015 will eventually replace section 11362.775 collectives with licensed commercial suppliers. The Medical Cannabis Regulation and Safety Act of 2015 provides, in relevant part,

> [Section 11362.775] shall remain in effect only until one year after the Bureau of Medical Marijuana Regulation posts a notice on its Internet Web site that the licensing authorities have commenced issuing licenses pursuant to the Medical Marijuana Regulation and Safety Act . . . , and is repealed upon issuance of licenses.

2015 Cal. Legis. Serv. Ch. 689 (A.B. 266), § 6(b) (West). Nonetheless, section 11362.775 remains in effect in California for the time being, and California's lengthy experience applying that section could provide lessons for other states also considering collective cultivation.

2. Do you think the *Colvin* court reaches the correct result under section 11362.775? Is Holistic's business model what the California legislature had in mind when it passed the MMPA? Is it what you think of when you imagine qualified patients and their caregivers "associat[ing] . . . in order collectively or cooperatively to cultivate marijuana for medical purposes"?

3. California requires collectives to operate on a non-profit basis. *See California v. Jackson*, 148 Cal. Rptr. 3d 375, 384 (Cal. App. 4th 2012) (holding that "a collective or cooperative protected by the MMPA must be a nonprofit enterprise") (discussing Cal. Health & Safety Code section 11362.765 (stipulating that "nothing in this section shall authorize . . . any individual or group to cultivate or distribute marijuana for profit")). But what does it mean to operate on a non-profit basis?

In 2008, California's Attorney General issued non-binding guidance on the operation of marijuana collectives. Portions of the guidance were quoted by the *Colvin* court, *supra*. Regarding the finances of collectives, the guidance states that

> Marijuana grown at a collective or cooperative for medical purposes may be:
>
> a) Provided free to qualified patients and primary caregivers who are members of the collective or cooperative;
> b) Provided in exchange for services rendered to the entity;
> c) Allocated based on fees that are reasonably calculated to cover overhead costs and operating expenses; or
> d) Any combination of the above.

*Guidelines for the Security and Non-Diversion of Marijuana Grown for Medical Use, supra*. One California court has further elaborated on the factors that help establish whether a collective has operated on a non-profit basis:

> Plainly, in determining whether a collective or cooperative is a nonprofit enterprise, its establishment as such under [California Corporations Code Section 12201[3]] and any financial records of the enterprise will be relevant, including in particular any processes or procedures by which the enterprise makes itself accountable to its membership. An operator's testimony as to the nonprofit nature of the enterprise is of course also relevant. However, by the same token the absence of fairly complete financial records and any accountability to members will also be relevant, especially when combined with a large number of members and evidence of a high volume of business. In the latter circumstance a trier of fact could reasonably conclude that, notwithstanding an operator's testimony, a large membership, high volume enterprise was in fact operated for profit.

*Jackson*, 148 Cal. Rptr. 3d at 384-85. Some states similarly require commercial suppliers to operate on a non-profit basis. *See* Section B.1.c below.

4. Even though formal establishment as a cooperative corporation may help to demonstrate that a collective satisfies the non-profit requirement of section 11362.775, the California courts have declined to impose any formalities on the organization of collectives. As one court has explained,

> The collective cultivation provision set forth in section 11362.775 refers to qualified patients who associate to collectively or cooperatively cultivate marijuana. . . . [N]either the statute itself, nor case law, has specified any size or formality requirements for the proper creation of the cooperative endeavor. . . .
>
> Further, permitting application of the defense to informal collective cultivation activity is consistent with the overall statutory goal of ensuring that qualified persons have access to marijuana for medical use.

*California v. Orlosky*, 182 Cal. Rptr. 3d 561, 572-73 (Cal. App. 4th 2015).

5. Washington state has also expressly authorized the formation of patient collectives. Its medical marijuana law provides:

> (1) Qualifying patients or designated providers may form a cooperative and share responsibility for acquiring and supplying the resources needed to produce and process marijuana only for the medical use of members of the cooperative. No more than four

---

3. Author's note: The referenced section states that

> [a cooperative] corporation may be formed under this part for any lawful purpose provided that it shall be organized and shall conduct its business primarily for the mutual benefit of its members as patrons of the corporation. The earnings, savings, or benefits of the corporation shall be used for the general welfare of the members or shall be proportionately and equitably distributed to some or all of its members or its patrons, based upon their patronage . . . of the corporation, in the form of cash, property, evidences of indebtedness, capital credits, memberships, or services.
>
> Such corporations are democratically controlled and are not organized to make a profit for themselves, as such, or for their members, as such, but primarily for their members as patrons.

Cal. Corp. Code § 12201 (2016).

qualifying patients or designated providers may become members of a cooperative under this section and all members must hold valid recognition cards. . . .

(2) Qualifying patients and designated providers who wish to form a cooperative must register the location with the state liquor and cannabis board and this is the only location where cooperative members may grow or process marijuana. This registration must include the names of all participating members and copies of each participant's recognition card. Only qualifying patients or designated providers registered with the state liquor and cannabis board in association with the location may participate in growing or receive useable marijuana or marijuana-infused products grown at that location.

(3) No cooperative may be located in any of the following areas:

    (a) Within one mile of a marijuana retailer;

    (b) Within the smaller of either:

        (i) One thousand feet of the perimeter of the grounds of any elementary or secondary school, playground, recreation center or facility, child care center, public park, public transit center, library, or any game arcade that admission to which is not restricted to persons aged twenty-one years or older; or

        (ii) The area restricted by ordinance, if the cooperative is located in a city, county, or town that has passed an ordinance . . . ; or

    (c) Where prohibited by a city, town, or county zoning provision.

. . .

. . .

(6) Qualifying patients or designated providers who participate in a cooperative under this section:

    (a) May grow up to the total amount of plants for which each participating member is authorized on their recognition cards, up to a maximum of sixty plants. . . .

    (b) May only participate in one cooperative;

    (c) May only grow plants in the cooperative and if he or she grows plants in the cooperative may not grow plants elsewhere;

    (d) Must provide assistance in growing plants. A monetary contribution or donation is not to be considered assistance under this section. Participants must provide nonmonetary resources and labor in order to participate; and

    (e) May not sell, donate, or otherwise provide marijuana, marijuana concentrates, useable marijuana, or marijuana-infused products to a person who is not participating under this section.

(7) The location of the cooperative must be the domicile of one of the participants. . . . A copy of each participant's recognition card must be kept at the location at all times.

(8) The state liquor and cannabis board may adopt rules to implement this section including:

    (a) Any security requirements necessary to ensure the safety of the cooperative and to reduce the risk of diversion from the cooperative;

    (b) A seed to sale traceability model that is similar to the seed to sale traceability model used by licensees that will allow the state liquor and cannabis board to track all marijuana grown in a cooperative.

(9) The state liquor and cannabis board or law enforcement may inspect a cooperative registered under this section to ensure members are in compliance with this section. . . .

Wash. Rev. Code Ann. § 69.51A.250 (2016). What are the key differences between the rules governing collective cultivation in California (per *Colvin*) and those governing collective cultivation in Washington state? Which state's approach do you favor and why?

6. Recall the discussion of the *Swiderski* defense from Chapter 7. In jurisdictions that recognize the defense, the transfer of a drug between joint possessors is not considered "distribution" for purposes of criminal drug trafficking prohibitions. Could the members of a collective successfully assert this defense, at least against a charge of distributing marijuana to each other, in violation of 21 U.S.C. section 841? Would the members of a collective operated pursuant to Washington's regulations stand a better chance of asserting the defense, as compared to the members of a collective operated pursuant to California's section 11362.775 (e.g., the defendant in *Colvin*)?

### 4. May Lawful Users Distribute Marijuana to Other Lawful Users?

<u>Problem 8.4</u>: Camila is a qualified patient who grows six marijuana plants, the maximum allowed by her state medical marijuana law. Camila recently harvested one of her plants, and in so doing, realized that she has more usable marijuana than required to satisfy her own needs (though still within the limits permitted by state law). By contrast, Camila's friend Delilah, another qualified patient, has harvested less than she needs (and that state law allows) from her marijuana plants. May Camila give Delilah some of her excess marijuana?

Personal cultivation is primarily designed to satisfy the demand of the individual cultivator. But some states allow users to transfer (i.e., to *distribute*) marijuana to other lawful users. Colorado's Amendment 64, for example, permits an adult to "[t]ransfer . . . one ounce or less of marijuana without remuneration to a person who is twenty-one years of age or older." Colo. Const. art. XVIII, § 16(3)(c) (2016). *See also, e.g.*, Ariz. Rev. Stat. § 36-2811 (2016) (providing that a qualifying patient is not subject to penalty for "providing marijuana to a registered qualifying patient or a registered designated caregiver . . . if nothing of value is transferred in return and the person giving the marijuana does not knowingly cause the recipient to possess more than the allowable amount of marijuana").

As the quoted statutes suggest, states commonly impose two limits on user-to-user distribution. First, states limit the quantity of marijuana that users may distribute. Typically this means that one user may transfer no more than either she (the transferor) or the second user (the transferee) is allowed to possess. *E.g.*, Colo. Const. art. XVIII, § 16(3)(c) (one ounce); Ariz. Rev. Stat. § 36-2811 (permitting transfer, so long as transferor does not thereby exceed possession limits). Second, states also commonly limit the compensation the transferor may receive in return for the marijuana. Indeed, it appears that most—if not all—states bar users from receiving *anything* in return for their marijuana—i.e., they may only gift the drug to the transferee. *E.g., id.*

Many reform states, however, bar outright the transfer of marijuana among users, even without compensation. For example, Washington's medical marijuana law provides that "[i]t is unlawful for a person to knowingly or intentionally . . . sell, donate, or otherwise supply marijuana produced by the qualifying patient to another person." Rev. Code Wash. Ann. 69.51A240(1)(e) (2016). In the following case, the court confronts the issue as to whether the Michigan Medical Marijuana Act (MMMA) permits qualified patients to transfer marijuana to other patients.

## *Michigan v. McQueen*
828 N.W.2d 644 (Mich. 2013)

Young, C.J.:

Defendants Brandon McQueen and Matthew Taylor own and operate C.A., LLC (hereinafter CA), . . . a members-only medical marijuana dispensary located in Isabella County. McQueen is both a registered qualifying patient and a registered primary caregiver within the meaning of the MMMA, while Taylor is a registered primary caregiver. Their stated purpose in operating CA is to "assist in the administration of [a] member patient's medical use" of marijuana.

CA requires every member to be either a registered qualifying patient or registered primary caregiver. . . . CA's basic membership fee of $5 a month allows a member to access CA's services. For an additional fee, a member can rent one or more lockers to store up to 2.5 ounces of marijuana [(the maximum allowed by the MMMA)] and make that marijuana available to other CA members to purchase. The member sets the sale price of his marijuana, and defendants retain a percentage of that price (about 20 percent) as a service fee. Defendants and their employees retain access at all times to the rented lockers, although the member may remove his marijuana from the lockers during business hours if he no longer wishes to make it available for sale.

All CA members may purchase marijuana from other members' lockers. A member who wishes to purchase marijuana for himself (or, if the member is a registered primary caregiver, for his patient) must show his unexpired . . . qualifying patient or primary caregiver registry identification card when entering CA. A representative of CA—either one of the individual defendants or an employee—will then take the member to the display room, where a variety of strains are available for purchase. The member makes a selection, and the CA representative measures and weighs the marijuana, packages it, seals it, and records the transaction.

. . . In July 2010, the Isabella County Prosecuting Attorney . . . filed a complaint in the Isabella Circuit Court, alleging that defendants' business constitutes a public nuisance because it does not comply with the MMMA. The complaint sought . . . a permanent injunction.

. . .

At the time this action was brought, MCL 600.3801 stated that "[a]ny building . . . used for the *unlawful* manufacture, transporting, sale, keeping for sale, bartering, or furnishing of any controlled substance as defined in [MCL 333.7104] . . . is declared a nuisance. . . ." Marijuana is a controlled substance as defined in MCL 333.7104. However, because "[t]he medical use of marihuana is allowed under state law to the extent that it is carried out in accordance with [the MMMA]," the MMMA controls whether defendants' business constitutes a public nuisance.

. . .

. . . [T]he MMMA does not explicitly provide for businesses that dispense marijuana to patients. Nevertheless, defendants claim that § 3(e) of the MMMA allows their business to facilitate patient-to-patient sales of marijuana. . . .

. . . § 7(a) of the MMMA provides that "[t]he medical use of marihuana is allowed under state law to the extent that it is carried out in accordance with the provisions of [the MMMA]." The MMMA specifically defines "medical use" in § 3(e) as

> the acquisition, possession, cultivation, manufacture, use, internal possession, delivery, transfer, or transportation of marihuana or paraphernalia relating to the administration of marihuana to treat or alleviate a registered qualifying patient's debilitating medical condition or symptoms associated with the debilitating medical condition.

[MCL 333.26423(e).] At issue in this case is whether the sale of marijuana is an activity that falls within this definition of "medical use." The definition specifically incorporates nine activities relating to marijuana as "medical use," but it does not expressly use the word "sale." Because of this omission, plaintiff argues . . . that the sale of marijuana falls outside the statutory definition of "medical use":

> [T]he sale of marijuana is not equivalent to the delivery or transfer of marijuana. The delivery or transfer of marijuana is only one component of the sale of marijuana—the sale of marijuana consists of the delivery or transfer *plus* the receipt of compensation. The "medical use" of marijuana, as defined by the MMMA, allows for the "delivery" and "transfer" of marijuana, but not the "sale" of marijuana. MCL 333.26423(e). We may not ignore, or view as inadvertent, the omission of the term "sale" from the definition of the "medical use" of marijuana.

Defendants claim that the Court of Appeals erred by excluding sales from the definition of "medical use."

In determining whether a sale constitutes "medical use," we first look to how the MMMA defines the term "medical use." In particular, the definition of "medical use" contains the word "transfer" as one of nine activities encompassing "medical use." The MMMA, however, does not itself define "transfer" or any of the other eight activities encompassing "medical use." Because undefined terms "shall be construed and understood according to the common and approved usage of the language," it is appropriate to consult dictionary definitions of terms used in the MMMA.

A transfer is "[a]ny mode of disposing of or parting with an asset or an interest in an asset, including a gift, *the payment of money*, release, lease, or creation of a lien or other encumbrance." Similarly, a sale is "[t]he *transfer* of property or title for a price." Given these definitions, to state that a transfer does not encompass a sale is to ignore what a transfer encompasses. That a sale has an *additional* characteristic, distinguishing it from other types of transfers, does not make it any less a transfer, nor does that additional characteristic require that the definition of "medical use" separately delineate the term "sale" in order for a sale to be considered a medical use.

. . .

Therefore, we hold that the definition of "medical use" in § 3(e) of the MMMA includes the sale of marijuana. . . . Nevertheless, this definition of "medical use" only forms the beginning of our inquiry. Section 7(a) of the act requires *any* medical use of marijuana to occur "in accordance with the provisions of [the MMMA]." That limitation requires this

Court to look beyond the definition of "medical use" to determine whether defendants' business operates "in accordance with the provisions of [the MMMA]." . . .

. . .

Section 4(a) of the MMMA grants a "qualifying patient who has been issued and possesses a registry identification card" immunity from arrest, prosecution, or penalty "for the medical use of marihuana in accordance with this act. . . ." Similarly, § 4(b) grants the same immunity from arrest, prosecution, or penalty to "[a] primary caregiver who has been issued and possesses a registry identification card . . . for assisting a qualifying patient to whom he or she is connected through the . . . registration process with the medical use of marihuana in accordance with this act. . . ."

Furthermore, § 4(d) creates a presumption of medical use, which informs how § 4 immunity can be asserted or negated:

> There shall be a presumption that a qualifying patient or primary caregiver is engaged in the medical use of marihuana in accordance with this act if the qualifying patient or primary caregiver:
>
> (1) is in possession of a registry identification card; and
> (2) is in possession of an amount of marihuana that does not exceed the amount allowed under this act. *The presumption may be rebutted* by evidence that conduct related to marihuana *was not for the purpose of alleviating the qualifying patient's debilitating medical condition or symptoms associated with the debilitating medical condition*, in accordance with this act.

[MCL 333.26424(d) (emphasis added).] Because § 4(d) creates a presumption of medical use and then states how that presumption may be rebutted, we conclude that a rebutted presumption of medical use renders immunity under § 4 of the MMMA inapplicable.

The text of § 4(d) establishes that the MMMA intends to allow "a qualifying patient or primary caregiver" to be immune from arrest, prosecution, or penalty *only* if conduct related to marijuana is "for the purpose of alleviating *the* qualifying patient's debilitating medical condition" or its symptoms. Section 4 creates a *personal* right and protection for a registered qualifying patient's medical use of marijuana, but that right is limited to medical use that has the purpose of alleviating that patient's *own* debilitating medical condition or symptoms. If the medical use of marijuana is for some *other* purpose—even to alleviate the medical condition or symptoms of *a different registered qualifying patient*—then the presumption of immunity attendant to the "medical use" of marijuana has been rebutted.

The dissent claims that the presumption of immunity attendant to the "medical use" of marijuana applies when a qualifying patient transfers marijuana to another qualifying patient. However, the dissent's construction is not consistent with the statutory language that the people of Michigan actually adopted. The presumption that "a qualifying patient" is engaged in the medical use of marijuana under § 4(d) is rebutted when marijuana-related conduct is "not for the purpose of alleviating *the* qualifying patient's debilitating medical condition. . . ." Contrary to the dissent's conclusion that § 4(d) only requires "one of the two qualified patients involved in the transfer of marijuana [to] have a debilitating medical condition that the transfer of marijuana purports to alleviate," the definite article in § 4(d) refers to the qualifying patient who is asserting § 4 immunity, not to *any* qualifying patient involved in a transaction. While the introductory language of § 4(d) refers to "a" qualifying patient, that indefinite article simply means that any qualifying patient may claim §4(d) immunity, as long as the marijuana-related conduct is related to alleviating "the" patient's medical condition.

Thus, §4 immunity does not extend to a registered qualifying patient who transfers marijuana to another registered qualifying patient for the transferee's use because the transferor is not engaging in conduct related to marijuana for the purpose of relieving *the transferor's own* condition or symptoms. Similarly, §4 immunity does not extend to a registered primary caregiver who transfers marijuana for any purpose other than to alleviate the condition or symptoms of a specific patient *with whom the caregiver is connected through the . . . registration process.*

Defendants' business facilitates patient-to-patient sales, presumably to benefit the transferee patient's debilitating medical condition or symptoms. However, those transfers do not qualify for §4 immunity because they encompass marijuana-related conduct that is not for the purpose of alleviating the *transferor's* debilitating medical condition or its symptoms. Because the defendants' "medical use" of marijuana does not comply with the immunity provisions of §§4(a), 4(b), and 4(d), defendants cannot claim that §4 insulates them from a public nuisance claim.

. . .

. . . Because the business model of defendants' dispensary relies entirely on transactions that do not comply with the MMMA, defendants are operating their business in "[a] building . . . used for the unlawful . . . keeping for sale . . . or furnishing of any controlled substance," and plaintiff is entitled to an injunction enjoining the continuing operation of the business because it is a public nuisance.

Cavanagh, J. (dissenting):

As the majority explains, defendants' activity falls under the definition of "medical use" of marijuana set forth in §3(e) of the act. . . . However, the majority erroneously concludes that *only* the qualified patient who receives marijuana is entitled to assert §4 immunity in light of its interpretation of §4(d)(2). . . .

. . . It is true that, in order for the §4(d) presumption to apply, the marijuana-related conduct at issue must be for the purpose of alleviating the medical condition or symptoms of the qualified patient who in fact suffers from a debilitating medical condition. However, when a qualified patient transfers marijuana to another qualified patient, the transferor is also engaged in marijuana-related conduct for the purpose of alleviating the medical condition of the qualified patient who is also involved in the transfer and is suffering from a debilitating medical condition. The marijuana-related conduct is the transfer of marijuana, which is expressly included in the definition of "medical use" of marijuana. MCL 333.26423(e). Thus, the reference in §4(d)(2) to "the" qualifying patient simply requires that one of the two qualified patients involved in the transfer of marijuana have a debilitating medical condition that the transfer of marijuana is intended to alleviate.

. . .

The majority characterizes its holding as creating "asymmetric" immunity under §4 because it permits a qualified patient who receives marijuana to assert immunity, but a qualified patient who transfers marijuana is not entitled to the same protection. . . . Thus, under the majority's holding, a qualified patient's right to receive marijuana is effectively extinguished because a patient-to-patient transfer of marijuana can never occur lawfully for both qualifying patients. I cannot conclude from the plain meaning of the language of the MMMA that the electorate intended to afford a person a right only to foreclose any real possibility that the person may benefit from that right. Furthermore, the majority's view is inconsistent with the purpose of the MMMA—to promote the "health and welfare of [Michigan] citizens"—because qualified patients who are in need of marijuana for medical use, yet do not have the ability to either cultivate marijuana or find a trustworthy primary caregiver, are, for all practical purposes, deprived of an additional route to obtain marijuana for that use—another qualified patient's transfer. MCL 333.26422(c).

## Notes and Questions

1. Do you agree more with the majority or the dissent in *McQueen*? As the majority acknowledges, the MMMA explicitly authorizes the transfer of marijuana. Under the majority's interpretation of the statute, what sort of transfers are permitted?

2. Michigan has addressed supply issues in a somewhat obtuse fashion, by defining "medical *use*" to include not only "use" and activities directly related thereto (e.g., "possession"), but also supply activities, like "cultivation," "manufacture," "delivery," and "transfer." Several other states have followed a similar path. *E.g.*, Or. Rev. Stat. Ann. § 475B.410(17) (2016) ("'Medical use of marijuana' means the *production, processing*, possession, *delivery* or administration of marijuana. . . .") (emphasis added); 21 R.I. Gen. Laws Ann. § 21-28.6-3 (15)(2016)("'Medical use' means the acquisition, possession, *cultivation, manufacture*, use, *delivery, transfer*, or transportation of marijuana. . . ."). Lumping these activities together represents a break from historical practice, in which states generally defined and regulated each of these activities separately. See Chapters 3 and 7. Why do you think some states have defined "medical *use*" to encompass both use and supply? Should states separately address the legality of each of the distinct activities involved in their medical marijuana programs? How would states do so?

3. Violating the limitations imposed on transfers could expose the transferor to criminal liability. In *Arizona v. Matlock*, for example, the court held that a qualifying patient could be criminally prosecuted for distributing marijuana, based on his act of transferring three marijuana plants to another qualifying patient in return for a $75 "donation." 350 P.3d 835 (Ariz. App. 2d 2015). The court found the protections of Ariz. Rev. Stat. § 36-2811(B)(3) governed only transfers *for no remuneration* and thus did not apply to the defendant's case. 350 P.3d at 840.

## 5. May Anyone Assist Patients with the Cultivation and Handling of Marijuana?

Problem 8.5: Delilah is a qualifying patient under her state's medical marijuana law. The law allows patients like Delilah to cultivate marijuana for their own medical needs, but Delilah is too ill to grow marijuana plants on her own. She has hired Camila to help her with basic tasks, like cooking, cleaning, and running errands. May Camila also handle Delilah's marijuana—e.g., fetch her a joint—or even grow the drug on her behalf?

All medical marijuana states permit designated caregivers (alternatively called designated providers or primary caregivers) to assist qualified patients with their medical use of marijuana, including activities like handling usable marijuana or even cultivating marijuana plants (at least when patients themselves are allowed to cultivate). For example, California's Compassionate Use Act provides:

> Section 11357, relating to the possession of marijuana, and Section 11358, relating to the cultivation of marijuana, shall not apply to a patient, or to a patient's *primary caregiver*, who possesses or cultivates marijuana for the personal medical purposes of the patient upon the written or oral recommendation or approval of a physician.

Cal. Health & Safety Code § 11362.5(d) (2016) (emphasis added). Caregiver laws are designed to address the needs of patients who, like Delilah in **Problem 8.5** above, may be "unable to act on their own behalf." *California v. Mentch*, 195 P.3d 1061, 1069 (Cal. 2008).

But states have also adopted sundry regulations governing caregivers, including who may serve in this capacity, how many patients each caregiver may serve, and what caregivers may be compensated for their services. Colorado's medical marijuana law provides one, illustrative example:

> A. A patient who designates a primary care-giver for him or herself cannot also be a primary care-giver to another patient.
>
> B. A cultivating or transporting caregiver shall be listed as a primary caregiver for no more than five patients in the medical marijuana registry at any given time unless a waiver . . . has been granted for exceptional circumstances.
>
> . . .
>
> D. A primary care-giver if asked by law enforcement shall provide a list of registry identification numbers for each patient. If a waiver has been granted for a cultivating or transporting caregiver to serve more than five patients, this will be noted on the department record of cultivating and transporting care-givers and will be available for verification to law enforcement upon inquiry to the department.
>
> E. A primary care-giver shall have his/her primary registration card available on his/her person at all times when in possession of marijuana and produce it at the request of law enforcement. . . .
>
> F. A patient may only have one primary care-giver at a time.
>
> G. A designated primary care-giver shall not delegate the responsibility of provision of medical marijuana for a patient to another person.
>
> H. A primary care-giver shall not join together with another primary care-giver for the purpose of growing marijuana. Any marijuana grows by a care-giver shall be physically separate from grows by other primary care-givers and licensed growers or medical marijuana centers, and a primary care-giver shall not grow marijuana for another primary care-giver. If two or more care-givers reside in the same household and each grows marijuana for their registered patients, the marijuana grows must be maintained in such a way that the plants and/or ounces grown and or maintained by each primary care-giver are separately identified from any other primary care-givers plants and/or ounces.
>
> I. A primary care-giver shall not establish a business to permit patients to congregate and smoke or otherwise consume medical marijuana.
>
> J. A primary care-giver shall not:
>
>> 1. Engage in the medical use of marijuana in a way that endangers the health and well-being of a person;

2. Engage in the medical use of marijuana in plain view of or in a place open to the general public;

3. Undertake any task while under the influence of medical marijuana, when doing so would constitute negligence or professional malpractice;

4. Possess medical marijuana or otherwise engage in the use of medical marijuana in or on the grounds of a school or in a school bus except when the possession or use occurs in accordance with a school district board policy . . . ;

. . .

7. Provide medical marijuana if the patient does not have a debilitating medical condition as diagnosed by the person's physician in the course of a bona fide physician-patient relationship and for which the physician has recommended the use of medical marijuana.

K. A primary care-giver may charge a patient no more than the cost of cultivating or purchasing the medical marijuana, and may also charge for care-giver services. Such care-giver charges shall be appropriate for the care-giver services rendered and reflect market rates for similar care-giver services and not costs associated with procuring the marijuana.

L. A primary care-giver shall have significant responsibility for managing the well-being of a patient with a debilitating condition.

5 Colo. Code Regs. § 1006-2:9. The materials in the following sections discuss such regulations and the issues that arise under them.

### a. Who May Serve as a Caregiver?

Problem 8.6: Return to the facts of **Problem 8.5**, *supra*. Suppose that Delilah asked Camila to grow marijuana on her behalf, but Camila declined: "I just don't know the first thing about growing marijuana. But I have a friend, Andy, who might be able to help you. He knows all about growing marijuana—he's been doing it for 30 years." Delilah contacts Andy. Andy says he would be willing to provide Delilah with the marijuana she needs and even to advise her on how best to use it; but he would not do anything else for her. Would Andy be eligible to serve as Delilah's caregiver?

One way states regulate caregivers is by restricting who may serve in this capacity. In particular, states commonly require caregivers to register with a state agency (similar to the way patients must register in many states), *e.g.*, 410 Ill. Comp. Stat. Ann. 130/25(b) ("A *registered* designated caregiver is not subject to arrest. . . .") (emphasis added), to be of a minimum age, *e.g.*, *id.* at 130/10(i) (must be at least 21 years old), and even to have a clean criminal record, *e.g.*, *id.* (must not have been convicted of "an excluded offense"). In most states, someone like Andy in **Problem 8.6**, who does no more than supply a patient with marijuana, may serve as a designated caregiver, provided, of course, that he meets the other criteria just mentioned.

In a few states, however, designated caregivers must perform other services for patients as well. California's CUA is illustrative. It defines a caregiver as someone "who has *consistently assumed responsibility for the housing, health, or safety of that person.*" Cal. Health & Safety Code § 11362.5 (2016) (emphasis added).[4] *See also, e.g.,* 5 Colo. Code Regs. § 1006-2:9(L) (excerpted above). In the following case, the court discusses this relationship requirement under California law.

## *California v. Mentch*
195 P.3d 1061 (Cal. 2008)

WERDEGAR, J.:

[In 2003, Roger Mentch was arrested and charged with the cultivation of marijuana and possession with the intent to distribute marijuana following a search of his house that uncovered "several elaborate marijuana growing set ups," including "82 marijuana plants in the flowering or budding stage, 57 'clone' marijuana plants, 48 marijuana plants in the growing or vegetative stage, and three 'mother' plants."

During the search, Mentch stated that he had a recommendation to use medical marijuana and that he also sold marijuana to five other medical marijuana patients. At trial, Mentch asserted a caregiver defense under Cal. Health & Safety Code § 11362.5. To that end, he called to the stand two of the patients for whom he claimed to serve as a caregiver.]

Leland Besson testified that he had known Mentch for two years. In June 2003, Besson was on disability and had a medical marijuana recommendation for a bad back, neck, and joints. . . . For about one year before Mentch was arrested, Besson purchased his marijuana exclusively from Mentch, who knew about Besson's medical marijuana recommendation. Mentch supplied medical marijuana through his business, the Hemporium. Besson gave Mentch $150 to $200 in cash every month for one and one-half ounces of marijuana, the amount Besson usually consumed in a month.

Laura Eldridge testified she had known Mentch for about three years. In June 2003, she was working as a caretaker for Besson, cooking and cleaning for him, driving him to the grocery store, and driving him to medical appointments and to pick up his medications. Eldridge also drove Besson to Mentch's house to get him his marijuana. The only time Besson saw Mentch was when Eldridge took him to Mentch's house to get marijuana.

At the time, Eldridge herself had a medical marijuana recommendation for migraine headaches and posttraumatic stress disorder. . . . Eldridge obtained marijuana exclusively from Mentch for approximately one and one-half years before his arrest. Mentch provided the marijuana through his medical marijuana business, the Hemporium. Eldridge obtained the marijuana from Mentch every month, paying him $200 to $250 in cash for one ounce and $25 in cash for one-eighth of an ounce if she needed more.

Eldridge was at Mentch's house getting her daughter ready for school on the morning of Mentch's arrest. At the time, she and Mentch were not living together but were seeing each other romantically, and Eldridge had stayed over at Mentch's house the night before the search warrant was served.

---

4. Although the CUA itself does not impose any other eligibility criteria on caregivers, the MMP imposes some additional requirements that apply for purposes of the special legal protections afforded only by the MMP (discussed in Chapter 4). Cal. Health & Safety Code § 11362.7 (2016) (specifying, for example, that a caregiver normally must be at least 18 years old).

[Mentch testified that he] opened the Hemporium, a caregiving and consultancy business, in March 2003. The purpose of the Hemporium was to give people safe access to medical marijuana. Mentch regularly provided marijuana to five other individuals, including Besson [and] Eldridge. . . . Sometimes he did not charge them. All five individuals had valid medical marijuana recommendations. . . .

Mentch provided marijuana to Besson about once every month and to Eldridge about once or twice every month. On average, they each gave him $150 to $200 for an ounce and a half of marijuana a month. Mentch considered his marijuana "high-grade" and provided it to Besson and Eldridge for less than street value. He used the money they paid him to pay for "nutrients, utilities, part of the rent." Mentch did not profit from his sales of marijuana, and sometimes he did not even recover his costs of growing it. Mentch counseled his patients/customers about the best strains of marijuana to grow for their ailments and the cleanest way to use the marijuana. He took a "couple of them" to medical appointments on a "sporadic" basis.

Although Mentch asked all five patients to come to court and testify on his behalf, only Besson and Eldridge showed up. He did not subpoena the others because one of them was out of state, another did not want to be involved because his father was an attorney, and the third did not want to testify.

. . .

. . . [T]he jury convicted Mentch of both cultivation and possession for sale. . . . The trial court suspended imposition of sentence and imposed three years' probation.

. . .

Section 11362.5, subdivision (d) provides: "Section 11357, relating to the possession of marijuana, and Section 11358, relating to the cultivation of marijuana, shall not apply to a patient, or to a patient's primary caregiver, who possesses or cultivates marijuana for the personal medical purposes of the patient upon the written or oral recommendation or approval of a physician." In turn, section 11362.5, subdivision (e) defines "primary caregiver" as "the individual designated by the person exempted under this section who has consistently assumed responsibility for the housing, health, or safety of that person."

This statutory definition has two parts: (1) a primary caregiver must have been designated as such by the medicinal marijuana patient; and (2) he or she must be a person "who has consistently assumed responsibility for the housing, health, or safety of" the patient. . . . [T]o qualify for exemption under this subdivision, a person must satisfy both halves—the "designee" clause and the "responsibility" clause. . . .

Three aspects of the structure of the responsibility clause are noteworthy. From these aspects, as we shall explain, we conclude a defendant asserting primary caregiver status must prove at a minimum that he or she (1) consistently provided caregiving, (2) independent of any assistance in taking medical marijuana, (3) at or before the time he or she assumed responsibility for assisting with medical marijuana.

First, the text requires that the primary caregiver have "consistently" assumed responsibility for the patient's care. "Consistently" suggests an ongoing relationship marked by regular and repeated actions over time. . . . "A person purchasing marijuana for medicinal purposes cannot simply designate seriatim, and on an ad hoc basis, drug dealers on street corners and sales centers such as the Cannabis Buyers' Club as the patient's 'primary caregiver.'["] . . . One must consistently—"with persistent uniformity" (3 Oxford English Dict. (2d ed. 1989) p. 773) or "in a persistent or even manner" (Webster's 3d New

Internat. Dict. (2002) p. 484)—have assumed responsibility for a patient's housing, health, or safety, or some combination of the three.

Second, the definition of a primary caregiver is written using a past participle—"has consistently assumed." . . . This reinforces the inference arising from the use of the word "consistently" that primary caregiver status requires an existing, established relationship. In some situations, the formation of a bona fide caregiving relationship and the onset of assistance in taking medical marijuana may be contemporaneous, as with a cancer patient entering chemotherapy who has a recommendation for medical marijuana use and has a live-in or home-visit nurse to assist with all aspects of his or her health care, including marijuana consumption. . . . Even in this scenario, however, the caregiving relationship will arise at or before the onset of assistance in the administration of marijuana. What is not permitted is for an individual to establish an after-the-fact caregiving relationship in an effort to thereby immunize from prosecution previous cultivation or possession for sale. . . .

Third, from these two aspects of the text, as well as logic, we draw a further inference: a primary caregiver must establish he or she satisfies the responsibility clause based on evidence independent of the administration of medical marijuana. Under the Act, a primary caregiver relationship is a necessary antecedent, a predicate for being permitted under state law to possess or cultivate medical marijuana. The possession or cultivation of marijuana for medical purposes cannot serve as the basis for making lawful the possession or cultivation of marijuana for medical purposes; to conclude otherwise would rest the primary caregiver defense on an entirely circular footing.

. . .

The trial court accurately assessed the law when, . . . in denying Mentch's motion for a judgment of acquittal . . . , [it stated that]: "There has to be something more to be a caregiver than simply providing marijuana. Otherwise, there would be no reason to have the definition of a caregiver, because anybody who would be providing marijuana and related services would qualify as a caregiver[,] therefore giving them a defense to the very activity that's otherwise illegal, and I don't think that makes any sense in terms of statutory construction, nor do I think it was intended by the people or the Legislature."

Mentch himself highlights the dog-chasing-its-tail absurdity of allowing the administration of medical marijuana to patients to form the basis for authorizing the administration of medical marijuana to patients in his attempts to distinguish this case from . . . [others, which,] he argues, involved only casual or occasional provision of medical marijuana; here, in contrast, he "consistently" provided medical marijuana, "consistently" allowed his patients to cultivate medical marijuana at his house, and was his five patients' "exclusive source" for medical marijuana. The essence of this argument is that the occasional provision of marijuana to someone is illegal, but the frequent provision of marijuana to that same person may be lawful. The vice in the approach of the [supply operations at issue in other cases] . . . therefore evidently was not that they provided marijuana to their customers; it was that they did not do it enough.

Nothing in the text or in the supporting ballot arguments suggests this is what the voters intended. The words the statute uses—housing, health, safety—imply a caretaking relationship directed at the core survival needs of a seriously ill patient, not just one single pharmaceutical need. The ballot arguments in support suggest a patient is generally personally responsible for noncommercially supplying his or her own marijuana: "Proposition 215 allows patients to cultivate their own marijuana simply because federal laws prevent the sale of marijuana, and a state initiative cannot overrule those laws." (Ballot Pamp., Gen. Elec. (Nov. 5, 1996) argument in favor of Prop. 215, p. 60.) But as the focus is on the "seriously and terminally ill" (*ibid.*), logically the Act must offer some alternative for those unable to act in their own behalf; accordingly, the Act allows "'primary caregiver[s]' the same authority to act on behalf of those too ill or bedridden to do so." To exercise that authority, however, one must be a "primary"—principal, lead, central—"caregiver"—one responsible for rendering assistance in the provision of daily life necessities—for a qualifying seriously or terminally ill patient.

We note in passing that some other states in adopting their own medical marijuana compassionate use acts have adopted substantially different and manifestly broader language in defining their primary caregiver exceptions. In New Mexico, for example, a primary caregiver is "a resident of New Mexico who is at least eighteen years of age and who has been designated by the patient's practitioner as being necessary to take responsibility for managing the well-being of a qualified patient with respect to the medical use of cannabis." (N.M. Stat. § 26-2B-3, par. F. . . . ) Had the drafters of the Act intended the broad understanding of "primary caregiver" that Mentch urges, they might well have been expected to select similar language. They did not.[8]

We have no doubt our interpretation of the statute will pose no obstacle for those bona fide primary caregivers whose ministrations to their patients the Act was actually intended to shield from prosecution. The spouse or domestic partner caring for his or her ailing companion, the child caring for his or her ailing parent, the hospice nurse caring for his or her ailing patient—each can point to the many ways in which they, medical marijuana aside, attend to and assume responsibility for the core survival needs of their dependents. The Act allows them, insofar as state criminal law is concerned, to add the provision of marijuana, where medically recommended or approved, as one more arrow in their caregiving quiver. It simply does not provide similar protection where the provision of marijuana is itself the substance of the relationship.

. . .

We turn to the merits of Mentch's request for a primary caregiver instruction in light of the evidence he adduced and the evidence he sought to adduce.

. . .

Mentch relies on three strands of evidence: his alleged provision of shelter to one patient, his taking of other patients to medical appointments, and his ongoing provision of both marijuana and marijuana advice and counseling to all his patients. Even crediting this evidence, as we must for purposes of deciding whether he was entitled to an instruction, we discern a series of interrelated shortcomings. Some of Mentch's caregiving was independent of providing marijuana, but was not provided at or before the time he began providing marijuana. Some of it may have been at or before the time he began providing marijuana, but was not consistent. And some of it was consistent, but was not independent of providing marijuana. But none of the evidence demonstrated satisfaction

---

8. More generally, we note that in the 12 states to have adopted compassionate use acts, all such states' acts include a primary caregiver exception or its equivalent, and virtually all include some mechanism for limiting primary caregiver status so the exception does not swallow the rule. Most rely on either mandatory state registries . . . or confine each caregiver to a set number of patients . . . or both. . . .

A minority . . . have instead adopted California's approach of limiting the caregiver exception by using a higher standard for the nature of the relationship and responsibility assumed. . . .

of each of the three aspects of the responsibility clause we have identified; none of it was sufficient to raise a reasonable doubt as to whether Mentch had provided his patients consistent caregiving, independent of providing them marijuana, at or before the time he began providing them marijuana.

First, Mentch argues Eldridge moved in shortly before the June 6, 2003 search. Unfortunately for Mentch's argument, the record directly contradicts this assertion. Eldridge testified she lived elsewhere at the time, and Mentch did not testify to the contrary. Even if the record supported it, however, the argument would not address the lack of any evidence of a primary caregiving relationship during the preceding year and a half during which Mentch was, by his own admission, selling Eldridge marijuana; it would not retroactively bless Mentch's prior cultivation of marijuana and sale of marijuana to her.

Second, Mentch testified he took "a couple" patients to medical appointments "sporadically." A sporadic assumption of responsibility is the antithesis of a consistent assumption of responsibility; it cannot satisfy the responsibility clause.

Third, Mentch otherwise relied almost exclusively on the provision of medical marijuana to establish a primary caregiving relationship. But the evidence must establish an assumption of responsibility independent of the provision of medical marijuana. This shortcoming is also intertwined with Mentch's problems showing a consistent assumption of responsibility: what "caregiving" was consistent consisted only of providing marijuana, while what caregiving was independent of providing marijuana was not consistent.

There is a final overarching problem with the evidence. Mentch testified to providing marijuana to five patients and also to occasionally growing too much and providing the excess to marijuana clubs. But where, as here, Mentch was charged with single counts of possession and cultivation, primary caregiver status would provide Mentch a defense only if it extended to all the marijuana he possessed or cultivated. Consider, for example, a defendant who testified that he (1) grew marijuana, (2) gave half to his critically ill daughter, a qualified patient for whom he was the designated primary caregiver and by whom he was reimbursed for growing expenses, and (3) sold the other half on the street. However much the primary caregiver defense might protect his actions toward his daughter, it would have no bearing on his case because a portion of his distribution of marijuana for money would be unprotected from state prosecution. Similarly, Mentch's testimony that he "sporadically" took "a couple" of the five patients to medical appointments, and his assertion (unsupported by the record) that he provided Eldridge shelter, would, even if believed, do nothing to insulate from prosecution his cultivation of and sale of marijuana to those for whom he did not provide shelter or nonmarijuana-based health care. . . . Nor would it protect him from prosecution for cultivating marijuana and providing it to cannabis clubs. . . .

## Notes and Questions

1. The events of *Mentch* took place in 2003, just before the passage of the MMP, which, as discussed above, permits patients and caregivers to collectively cultivate marijuana. Would the defendant in *Mentch* have been entitled to assert a collective cultivation defense, had the MMP been in effect at the time of his offense? Why, why not?

2. Courts in other states with laws similar to California's CUA have reached a similar conclusion, namely, that "the act of supplying marijuana for medical use, by itself, is

insufficient to . . . qualify a person doing so as a 'primary care-giver.'" *Colorado v. Clendenin*, 232 P.3d 210, 214 (Colo. App. 2009) (reviewing caselaw). But should states require caregivers to do more than just provide marijuana to qualifying patients? Are the people who are capable of providing other services—e.g., nurses, home health aides, family members—necessarily well suited to helping patients to use or even grow marijuana? Conversely, are the people who are proficient at using or growing marijuana necessarily well suited to housing, feeding, bathing, or otherwise caring for qualifying patients?

### b. What Limits Are Imposed on Caregivers?

In addition to limiting who may serve as a caregiver, states also impose other limitations on the activities of caregivers.

#### (i) Number of Patients

Many states limit the number of patients that a caregiver may serve. **Figure 8.2** displays the numerical limits imposed by 29 medical marijuana states as of 2016:

Figure 8.2. Limits on the Number of Patients Caregivers May Serve*

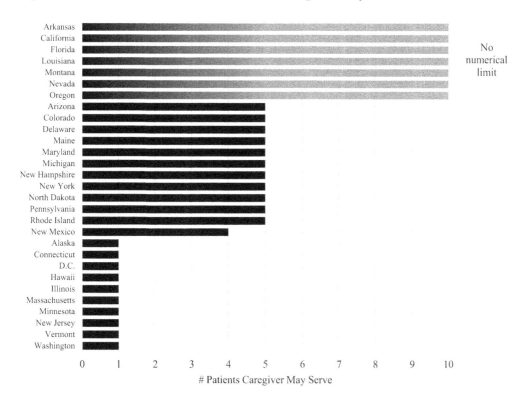

*For a useful summary of patient limits (among other matters) enacted prior to September 2016, see Marijuana Policy Project, *Key Aspects of State and D.C. Medical Marijuana Laws*, https://www.mpp.org/issues/medical-marijuana/state-by-state-medical-marijuana-laws/key-aspects-of-state-and-d-c-medical-marijuana-laws/.

Like the eligibility restriction discussed in *Mentch, supra*, the limits imposed on the number of patients caregivers appear designed to "avoid[] large-scale commercial marijuana production." *Montana Cannabis Indus. Ass'n v. Montana*, 368 P.3d 1131, 1147 (Mont. 2016), (upholding three-patient limit as "reasonably related" to this end), *superceded by statute*, 2016 Montana Medical Marijuana Act (I-182) (repealing three-patient limit).

But the wording of these limits has sometimes sparked confusion. In the following case, the court confronts a since-revised statutory requirement that an individual may be a designated provider "to only one patient at any one time."

## *Washington v. Shupe*
289 P.3d 741 (Wash. App. 2012)

SWEENEY, J.:

This appeal follows a successful prosecution for delivery, possession with intent to deliver, and manufacture of marijuana. The defendant freely admitted that he possessed, delivered, and manufactured marijuana and he claimed to do so under authority of Washington's Medical Use of Marijuana Act. . . .

Scott Shupe, along with others, owned and operated a medical marijuana dispensary called "Change[," located in Spokane, Washington.]

Mr. Shupe asserts that he is an authorized medical marijuana provider. In particular, he urges that he is a "designated provider" and a "designated provider to only one patient at any one time." RCW 69.51A.010(1)(d). . . .

Mr. Shupe reads the phrase "only one patient at any one time" to mean that he cannot physically give marijuana to more than one person at a time. In other words, Mr. Shupe reads the phrase to cover one transaction at a time. The State urges that "only one patient at any one time" means that Mr. Shupe could be a marijuana provider to only one person at a time. . . . This would mean that Mr. Shupe could not keep records showing that he was the provider for 1,280 people. Instead, he would have to be the provider for one patient—period. . . .

. . .

Mr. Shupe's interpretation of this pivotal phrase is supported by the definition of the word "at." While the term "designated provider" seems to imply an ongoing relationship, the word "at" gives a sense of immediacy. "At" links the language of the first part of the phrase to the second part. "At" is defined as: "used as a function word to indicate presence in, on, or near: . . . used as a function word to indicate age or position in time. . . .

Applying this definition of "at" here, the words "any one time" take on a sense of immediacy, making it, for us, more likely that the phrase could refer to a transaction rather than a relationship. This reading of the word "at" does not appear to encompass the continuous nature of the term "designated provider." The phrase "provider to only one patient at any one time" is at war with itself; it is ambiguous.

But if "only one patient at any one time" is ambiguous, we must accept the interpretation urged by Mr. Shupe. . . . The legislature's expressed intent here is helpful:

> Intent—2007 c 371: "The legislature intends to clarify the law on medical marijuana so that the lawful use of this substance is not impaired and medical practitioners are able to

exercise their best professional judgment in the delivery of medical treatment, qualifying patients may fully participate in the medical use of marijuana, and designated providers may assist patients in the manner provided by this act without fear of state criminal prosecution. This act is also intended to provide clarification to law enforcement and to all participants in the judicial system."

RCW 69.51A.005; see RCW 69.51A.010.

. . .

. . . Given these goals, the proper interpretation of "to only one patient at any one time" is an interpretation that allows the greatest number of qualified patients to receive the medical marijuana treatment that they need. In other words, "only one patient at any one time" means one transaction after another so that each patient gets individual care.

Mr. Shupe testified that he served only one medical marijuana patient at a time. He never delivered marijuana to an individual who did not have documentation. Change took copies of each patient's medical marijuana patient documentation to keep for its records. Concerned about the "only one patient at any one time," receipts from Change show the time to the minute as to when each patient was served. The State presented nothing to rebut that Mr. Shupe served one patient at a time, under this interpretation of the statute.

## Notes and Questions

1. Do you agree with the court that the statutory language—"at any one time"—is ambiguous? Does the phrase do any work, given the court's interpretation of it? In any event, how does the limitation apply to *manufacturing* offenses? Consider the following Problem:

Problem 8.7: Under state law, a caregiver is allowed to assist in the "medical use of marijuana," which is defined to include the "cultivation of up to 6 marijuana plants" and the "possession and transfer of any usable marijuana produced therefrom." State law limits each caregiver to serving "only one patient at any one time." Camila has been growing 600 marijuana plants in one large undivided warehouse for her patients. She has been careful to transfer the dried leaves and buds to each patient separately, only one at a time. Nonetheless, the police have charged her with *manufacturing* marijuana. May she assert a caregiver defense, per *Shupe*?

2. *Postscript.* In 2011, though too late to apply to *Shupe*, Washington modified its regulations to require that a designated provider "has not served as a designated provider to more than one qualifying patient *within a fifteen-day period.*" Wash. Rev. Code Ann. § 69.51A.040 (2016) (emphasis added). What do you think of this amendment? Does it satisfactorily clarify the limitation imposed on caregivers?

3. Should states limit the number of patients that one caregiver may serve? Does it depend on what other requirements states impose on caregivers? If you favor a numerical limit, what limit would you impose?

*(ii) Compensation*

Many states that allow caregivers to supply marijuana to patients limit the compensation caregivers may receive. The regulations run the gamut.

At least one state has attempted to bar its caregivers from receiving *any* compensation for their services. In 2011, Montana lawmakers amended the state's medical marijuana law to forbid caregivers from "accept[ing] anything of value, including monetary remuneration, for any services or products provided to a registered [patient]." Mont. Legis. 419 Sec. 5(6)(a) (2011). Montana's ban on compensation, however, was later invalidated by the Montana Supreme Court in *Montana Cannabis Indus. Ass'n v. Montana, supra*, a decision excerpted and discussed in Chapter 9.

Some states allow caregivers to recoup only their out-of-pocket expenses. For example, the relevant provision of Arizona law stipulates that a designated caregiver

> may receive reimbursement for actual costs incurred in assisting a registered qualifying patient's medical use of marijuana if the registered designated caregiver is connected to the registered qualifying patient through the department's registration process. The designated caregiver *may not be paid any fee or compensation for his service as a caregiver.* . . .

Ariz. Rev. Stat. Ann. § 36-2801(e) (2016) (emphasis added).

Lastly, some states allow caregivers to recoup any out-of-pocket expenses incurred for supplying marijuana and standard wages for any other services they provide to patients. In Colorado, for example,

> A primary care-giver may charge a patient no more than the cost of cultivating or purchasing the medical marijuana, and may also charge for care-giver services. Such care-giver charges shall be appropriate for the care-giver services rendered and reflect market rates for similar care-giver services and *not costs associated with procuring the marijuana*.

5 Colo. Code Regs. § 1006-2:9 (K) (emphasis added). *See also* Cal. Health & Safety Code § 11362.765 (2016) (instructing that a caregiver may receive "compensation for actual expenses, including reasonable compensation incurred for services provided to an eligible qualified patient . . . or for payment for out-of-pocket expenses incurred in providing those services, or both").

## Notes and Questions

1. What explains the variation in compensation rules? Does it track the variation in state eligibility requirements for caregivers—and in particular, whether such caregivers must perform services besides supplying marijuana to patients? Is a limit on compensation necessary if a state also imposes other limits on caregivers, like those discussed above?

## 6. What Legal Protections Do Users and Caregivers Enjoy as Suppliers?

The legal protections users enjoy regarding their marijuana-supply activities (i.e., cultivating or distributing marijuana) are the same as the ones they enjoy regarding their possession and use of marijuana. Those protections are discussed at length in Chapter 4. To a large extent, caregivers stand in the shoes of and enjoy the same legal protections as the patients they serve. But it may prove more difficult for caregivers to successfully invoke those protections.

For one thing, a caregiver must establish not only that she met all of the eligibility criteria set forth above, but also that her patient(s) satisfied the patient-focused criteria discussed in Chapter 4. The following Problem poses the question of what happens if a caregiver's patient does not, in fact, qualify for the protections afforded by state law:

Problem 8.8: Camila has known Andy for about three years. During that time, she has provided him with various caregiving services—cooking, cleaning, running errands, and so on. Six months ago, Camila took Andy to the doctor. After the appointment, Andy told Camila that his doctor had just diagnosed him with Crohn's disease and had recommended marijuana as a promising treatment. Andy told Camila that he could not afford to buy marijuana at a dispensary, and that he has no place to grow it himself. Camila knew how to grow marijuana, so she offered to serve as Andy's designated caregiver. She started growing six marijuana plants in her basement on his behalf. The police later discovered the plants and charged Camila with manufacturing marijuana. Camila has asserted a defense under the state's medical marijuana law, which allows a caregiver to grow up to six plants on behalf of a qualifying patient. However, it turns out that Andy is *not* a qualifying patient. He simply made up the qualifying diagnosis and physician's recommendation to get Camila to provide him with cheap marijuana. May Camila nonetheless assert a caregiver defense to the manufacturing charges?

The Michigan Supreme Court opined on this scenario in *Michigan v. Hartwick*, a case discussed in depth in Chapter 4:

> A primary caregiver has the burden of establishing the elements of [the affirmative defense] for each patient to whom the primary caregiver is alleged to have unlawfully provided marijuana. In this context, a primary caregiver who provides marijuana to a putative patient plainly assumes the risk that the patient does not actually meet the elements of [the defense] or that the patient may not cooperate in a subsequent prosecution of the primary caregiver, regardless what that person may have otherwise told the primary caregiver.

870 N.W.2d 37, 58-59 (Mich. 2015).

*Hartwick* suggests that a caregiver must verify that someone who claims to be a qualifying patient is, in fact, a qualifying patient, or else risk criminal liability for supplying marijuana to someone who—like Andy in **Problem 8.8**—is not allowed to possess the drug. Though the rule may seem harsh, the task of verifying eligibility should be easy in those states that have a registration process designed for this very purpose. But how is a caregiver to verify someone's qualifications in the minority of states that do not require patients to register? The question is raised in the following Problem:

Problem 8.9: Same facts as **Problem 8.8** above. This time, however, Andy's physician really did diagnose him with Crohn's disease and did recommend marijuana to him. At her trial, Camila has even introduced a signed, written statement from the physician attesting to the timely diagnosis and recommendation. Unfortunately for Camila, however, the prosecution has introduced its own evidence, demonstrating conclusively that the physician's diagnosis was flawed: Andy does not, in fact, have Crohn's disease, or any other qualifying condition. May Camila nonetheless assert a caregiver defense to the manufacturing charges? See *Washington v. Constantine*, 330 P.3d 226, 233 (Wash. App. 2014).

Establishing that a patient satisfied the eligibility criteria imposed by state law could prove even more difficult if a patient refuses to cooperate with the caregiver's defense. Indeed, in *Mentch*, discussed above, the court noted that only two out of the five patients for whom the defendant claimed to have served as caregiver responded to his request to testify at his trial. The *Hartwick* court suggests that there may be little a caregiver can do to compel such testimony:

> Because "[p]ossession, manufacture, and delivery of marijuana remain punishable offenses under Michigan law," . . . a caregiver-defendant's patient might be unwilling to testify to the patient's marijuana-related activities due to fear of criminal prosecution. This would present a significant barrier to the caregiver's ability to establish a defense under [the medical marijuana law]. And because a witness cannot be compelled to give testimony that the witness reasonably believes could be used against him or her in a criminal prosecution, a patient's justified refusal to cooperate might prove fatal to the primary caregiver's [affirmative] defense. . . . While this may seem a harsh consequence, this Court has no power to alter the statutory language.

*Hartwick*, supra, at 59 n.78.

Caregivers (and their patients) may also face a challenge in demonstrating that they complied with limits imposed on their joint possession and cultivation of marijuana. Under Maine law, for example, "[t]he *total* number of mature marijuana plants per qualifying patient, whether cultivated by the patient *or by a primary caregiver*, may not exceed 6." Me. Rev. Stat. tit. 22, §2423-A(B)(2016) (emphases added).

**Problem 8.10**: Camila serves as the caregiver for Andy, who is a bona fide qualifying patient. State law permits a patient and a caregiver to cultivate up to six plants combined. For the past few years, Camila has been growing three marijuana plants on Andy's behalf. A few months ago, however, Andy complained that he was not getting enough marijuana to meet his needs. In response, and unbeknownst to Andy, Camila started growing three more plants. At the same time, and unbeknownst to Camila, Andy started growing three plants on his own. Is Camila potentially liable for exceeding the state's six-plant limit? Is Andy? What if one (or both) of them was aware of what the other was doing?

## B. COMMERCIAL SUPPLY

A growing number of states authorize businesses to produce and sell marijuana to users (medical or otherwise). Commercial suppliers take many forms across the states, owing to the variety of approaches states have adopted to regulate them. As discussed below, they may be big or small, vertically integrated or not, for-profit or non-profit, and so on. And they go by nearly as many names, e.g., Registered Organizations in New York, Alternative Care Centers in New Jersey, and Retail Marijuana Stores in Colorado. But commercial suppliers all share some traits in common that help distinguish them from the typical personal supplier discussed in the prior section: They are comparatively large, more formal enterprises that produce and distribute marijuana for money. (Some personal suppliers might share some of these same characteristics—think of the large patient collectives in California discussed in Section A.3 above—and thus might also be considered commercial suppliers.)

Figure 8.3. The Inside of a Licensed Retail Marijuana Store in Colorado

**Figure 8.4** shows the percentage of states that have formally authorized some form of commercial supply under the three main types of marijuana reforms.

Figure 8.4. States Allowing Commercial Suppliers

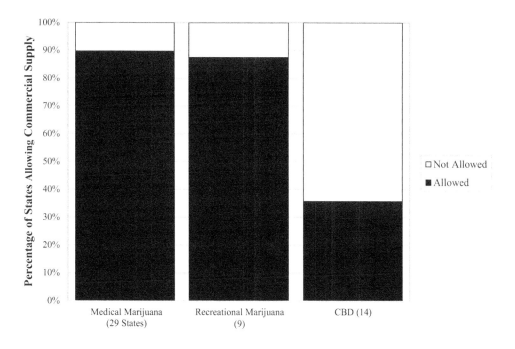

443

Part III. Marijuana Suppliers

The sections below explore how legalization states regulate the commercial supply of marijuana. Section B.1 begins by discussing the licensing requirement all states impose on commercial suppliers. The licensing requirement not only helps states identify who may produce and distribute marijuana commercially, it also serves as the foundation for state regulation of the commercial marijuana industry. Section B.2 discusses such regulation, including some of the key restrictions and obligations imposed on commercial licensees. Lastly, Section B.3 discusses the special disciplinary procedures states use to enforce licensing regulations.

### 1. Who Is Allowed to Produce and Sell Marijuana Commercially?

All states require commercial suppliers to get a formal license to produce and/or distribute marijuana. For example, Washington's I-502 provides that the "production, possession, delivery, distribution, and sale of marijuana . . . by a *validly licensed marijuana producer*, shall not be a criminal or civil offense under Washington state law." Wash. Rev. Code Ann. § 69.50.325 (2016) (emphasis added). *See also, e.g.*, N.J. Admin. Code § 8:64-7.6(a) ("No person shall operate an alternative treatment center without a Department-issued permit."); N.Y. Comp. Codes R. & Regs. tit. 10, § 1004.5 (a) ("No person or entity shall produce, grow or sell medical marihuana . . . unless it has complied with [state regulations] and *is registered* by the department.") (emphasis added). The license constitutes the state's permission to engage in activities that the state otherwise forbids, such as the production or distribution of marijuana.

Figure 8.5. A Retail Marijuana License Issued by Colorado

### Notes and Questions

1. Although the textbook focuses on the licensing of marijuana businesses, it is worth noting that states also commonly require employees of those businesses to get a separate occupational license to handle marijuana. *E.g.*, 12 Colo. Code Reg. 233 ("Any person who possesses, cultivates, manufactures, tests, dispenses, sells, serves, transports or delivers Retail Marijuana or Retail Marijuana Product as permitted by privileges granted under a Retail Marijuana Establishment license must have a valid Occupational License.").

2. In almost every state, licensing is handled by a state authority. However, commercial suppliers may also be required to get a license from a local authority as well. While this

chapter focuses on state licensing regulations, Chapter 10 discusses the authority of local governments to impose their own regulations on state-licensed marijuana businesses.

### a. The Number of Licenses

Many states limit the number of licenses they offer.[5] Some states impose specific numerical caps on licenses. For example, Illinois caps the number of medical marijuana cultivation licenses at 22, whereas New York permits no more than five. See 410 Ill. Comp. Stat. Ann. 130/85; N.Y. Pub. Health Law § 3365 (McKinney) (2016). Some states do not set specific numerical limits, but instead use other criteria to determine how many licenses to award. For example, upon expiration of a temporary numerical cap, Maryland's medical marijuana commission is instructed to issue as many licenses as necessary to satisfy patient demand "in an affordable, accessible, secure, and efficient manner." Md. Code Ann. Health-Gen. § 13-3306(2) (2016) (criteria to be used after June 1, 2018).

By contrast, a few states offer an unlimited number of licenses. Colorado, for example, does not limit the number of licenses the state itself will issue (though it does allow localities to restrict their number or even ban them, as discussed in Chapter 10). Indeed, as of December 2016, Colorado had already issued almost 800 medical marijuana cultivation licenses—and was still accepting new applications. See Marijuana Enforcement Division, *Licenses*, https://www.colorado.gov/pacific/enforcement/licensees-marijuana-enforcement-division.

## Notes and Questions

1. Numerical limits arguably help foster concentration of the local marijuana industry—i.e., the degree to which a few firms control a large share of the market. (Whether limits actually foster concentration depends on whether the limits are set *artificially* low, i.e., lower than the number of suppliers that would exist in an unregulated market.) The benefits and drawbacks of concentration and other characteristics of the marijuana industry are discussed in Chapter 9.

2. Many states also impose substantial licensing fees, which might also foster concentration in the marijuana industry. In New York, for example, a Registered Organization (i.e., a medical marijuana dispensary) license costs $210,000 annually. N.Y. Comp. Codes R. & Regs. tit. 10, §§ 1004.6-1004.7 (2016). Colorado charges fees for licenses, but they are more modest in comparison. For example, Colorado's application fee for a new medical marijuana dispensary with optional cultivation license starts at $9,000, with an annual renewal fee set at $2,300. See Colorado Marijuana Enforcement Division, *Fee Table* (July 2016), https://perma.cc/9AYZ-4UWP (summarizing fees).

3. A few states are attempting to promote industry *fragmentation* by limiting the size of individual licensees' operations. California's 2016 Proposition 64, for example, prohibits the issuance of large cultivation licenses for the first five years of the initiative, 10 Cal. Bus. & Prof. Code Section 26061, ostensibly "to ensure[] the nonmedical marijuana industry in California will be built around small and medium sized businesses," Proposition 64, § 2(J).

---

[5]. For a list of limits across the states, see Jeremy M. Vaida, *The Altered State of American Drug Taxes*, 68 Tax Law. 761, 773 n.75 (2015).

Part III. Marijuana Suppliers

### b. Who Can Get a License?

Not everyone can get a license, even in states that do not limit their number. All states impose some eligibility criteria on licensees, and states that limit their number also adopt criteria by which to award them in case there are more eligible applicants than available licenses (as is often the case).

To apply for a license, interested parties must complete a form that runs anywhere from 7 pages (in New York) to 70 pages (in New Jersey), not including any additional documentation that may be required. The application form typically solicits information about the candidate's eligibility and suitability for a license, including the good moral character, residency, location, and finances of the applicant or its owners/managers (in the case of a corporation). Follow the links below to check out the license application forms for a sampling of states:

- Colorado Retail Marijuana Business License Application, https://perma.cc/9GDB-T24G
- New Jersey Alternative Care Center Permitting Request Form, https://perma.cc/YG6R-3NJ3
- New York Medical Marijuana Program, Application for Registration as a Registered Organization, https://perma.cc/ZY5V-DNDB

State licensing authorities review these applications to verify applicant eligibility, and, in states that limit the number of licenses, decide who among the eligible applicants will receive one of the scarce licenses. The process used by the state of New York is illustrative. In 2015, New York received 43 completed applications for its five Registered Organization licenses. The state's licensing authority (the Department of Health) then reviewed these applications, scoring each one based on criteria enumerated in the state's medical marijuana law, including the following factors:

(1) the applicant will be able to manufacture approved medical marihuana products, each with a consistent cannabinoid profile (the concentration of total tetrahydrocannabinol (THC) and total cannabidiol (CBD) will define the brand) and each able to pass the required quality control testing;

(2) the applicant will produce sufficient quantities of approved medical marihuana products as necessary to meet the needs of certified patients;

(3) the applicant will be able to maintain effective control against diversion of marihuana and medical marihuana products;

(4) the applicant will be able to comply with all applicable state and local laws and regulations;

(5) the applicant is ready, willing and able to properly carry on the activities set forth in this [law];

(6) the applicant possesses or has the right to use sufficient real property, buildings and equipment to properly carry on the activity described in its operating plan;

(7) it is in the public interest that such registration be granted;

(8) the number of registered organizations in an area will be adequate or excessive to reasonably serve the area, including whether there is sufficient geographic distribution across the state;

(9) the moral character and competence of board members, officers, managers, owners, partners, principal stakeholders, directors, and members of the applicant's organization;

(10) the applicant has entered into a labor peace agreement with a bona-fide labor organization . . . that is actively engaged in representing or attempting to represent the applicant's employees; and

(11) evaluation of the applicant's proposed operating plan and suitability of the proposed manufacturing and dispensing facilities, including but not limited to the suitability of the location and architectural and engineering design of the proposed facilities. Department approval of the applicant's operating plan and architectural and engineering design of the proposed facilities shall be required for issuance of a registration.

N.Y. Comp. Codes R. & Regs. tit. 10, § 1004.6(b) (2016). The scores awarded by the Department ranged from 45.09 to 97.12 (out of 100). The Department ultimately awarded licenses to the applicants with the top five scores. *See* New York State Medical Marijuana Program, Evaluation Criteria, https://perma.cc/VRZ9-JQT4 (describing process).

The sections that follow elaborate on some of the more common licensing criteria employed by the states.

## Notes and Questions

1. Licenses are limited in duration and typically must be renewed every one to two years. *E.g.*, 1 Colo. Code Reg. 252 (one year for most licenses); Wash. Admin. Code § 314-55-075-079 (2016) (one year); Md. Code Regs. 10.62.08.10(A) (2016) (two years); N.Y. Comp. Codes R. & Regs. tit. 10, § 3365(4) (2016) (same).

### c. The Role of Criminal History

All states take criminal history into consideration in awarding licenses, often couched as part of a good moral character requirement. But states take many different positions regarding the sorts of criminal convictions that will disqualify applicants. The following regulations illustrate the different positions.

**California**

Under California's recreational marijuana law (Proposition 64), the state licensing authority may deny an application for a state commercial marijuana license if

> (4) The applicant . . . has been convicted of an offense that is substantially related to the qualifications, functions, or duties of the business or profession for which the application is made, except that if the licensing authority determines that the applicant or licensee is otherwise suitable to be issued a license, and granting the license would not compromise public safety, the licensing authority shall conduct a thorough review of the nature of the crime, conviction, circumstances, and evidence of rehabilitation of the applicant, and shall evaluate the suitability of the applicant or licensee to be issued a license based on the evidence found through the review. In determining which offenses are substantially related to the qualifications, functions, or duties of the business or profession for which the application is made, the licensing authority shall include, but not be limited to, the following:
> (A) A violent felony conviction . . .
> (B) A serious felony conviction, as specified in subdivision (c) of Section 1192.7 of the Penal Code.[6]

---

6. Author's note: The referenced provision defines "serious felony" to include a laundry list of particularly violent crimes, such as murder, rape, and grand theft involving a firearm.

(C) A felony conviction involving fraud, deceit, or embezzlement.

(D) A felony conviction for hiring, employing, or using a minor in transporting, carrying, selling, giving away, preparing for sale, or peddling, any controlled substance to a minor; or selling, offering to sell, furnishing, offering to furnish, administering, or giving any controlled substance to a minor.

(E) A felony conviction for drug trafficking [involving large quantities of heroin, cocaine base, or cocaine].

(5) Except as provided in subparagraphs (D) and (E) of paragraph (4) . . . , a prior conviction, where the sentence, including any term of probation, incarceration, or supervised release, is completed, for possession of, possession for sale, sale, manufacture, transportation, or cultivation of a controlled substance is not considered substantially related, and shall not be the sole ground for denial of a license. Conviction for any controlled substance felony subsequent to licensure shall be grounds for revocation of a license or denial of the renewal of a license.

. . .

Cal. Bus. & Prof. Code § 26057(b) (2016).

**Colorado**

For purposes of its retail (i.e., recreational) licenses, Colorado stipulates that a license "shall not be issued to or held by . . . an individual whose criminal history indicates that he or she is not of good moral character after considering the factors in [Colo. Rev. Stat. 24-5-101(2)]." Colo. Rev. Stat. Ann. § 12-43.4-306(b) (2016). The referenced provision explains that

> Whenever any state or local agency is required to make a finding that an applicant for a license . . . is a person of good moral character as a condition to the issuance thereof, the fact that such applicant has, at some time prior thereto, been convicted of a felony or other offense involving moral turpitude, and pertinent circumstances connected with such conviction, shall be given consideration in determining whether, in fact, the applicant is a person of good moral character at the time of the application. The intent of this section is to expand employment opportunities for persons who, notwithstanding that fact of conviction of an offense, have been rehabilitated and are ready to accept the responsibilities of a law-abiding and productive member of society.

Colo. Rev. Stat. Ann. § 24-5-101(2).

Colorado uses a somewhat different standard for the award of medical marijuana licenses. As with retail licenses, Colorado stipulates that a medical license "shall not be issued to or held by . . . a person whose criminal history indicates that he or she is not of good moral character." Colo. Rev. Stat. § 12-43.3-307(b). However, the medical marijuana licensing provision does not specifically reference Section 24-5-101(2). It does, however, instruct that the bar categorically applies to

> (I) A person who has discharged a sentence for a conviction of a felony in the five years immediately preceding his or her application date; or
>
> (II) A person who has discharged a sentence for a conviction of a felony pursuant to any state or federal law regarding the possession, distribution, manufacturing, cultivation, or use of a controlled substance in the ten years immediately preceding his or her application date or five years from May 28, 2013, whichever is longer; except that the licensing authority may grant a license to a person if the person has a state felony conviction based on possession or use of marijuana or marijuana concentrate that would not be a felony if the person were convicted of the offense on the date he or she applied for licensure. . . .

Id. at § 12-43.3-307(h).

## New Jersey

New Jersey's medical marijuana law provides that

> A person who has been convicted of a crime involving any controlled dangerous substance . . . except [simple possession of 50 grams or less of marijuana or five grams or less of hashish] . . . shall not be issued a permit to operate as an alternative treatment center or be a director, officer, or employee of an alternative treatment center, unless such conviction occurred after the effective date of this act and was for a violation of federal law relating to possession or sale of marijuana for conduct that is authorized under this act.

N.J. Stat. Ann. § 24:6I-7(c) (2016). However, the statute also makes an exception for employees who have "affirmatively demonstrated to the [licensing] commissioner clear and convincing evidence of rehabilitation." N.J. Stat. Ann. § 24:6I-7 (2016) (also listing the factors the commissioner shall consider in determining whether the employee has been rehabilitated).

## New York

New York has a good moral character requirement for Registered Organizations, but its medical marijuana law does not specifically define what that requirement entails. The medical marijuana statute does, however, require applicants to provide information regarding *some* types of criminal convictions, including

> whether such person or any such business has been convicted of a felony or had a registration or license suspended or revoked in any administrative or judicial proceeding. In addition, any managers who may come in contact with or handle medical marihuana, including medical marihuana products, shall be subject to a fingerprinting process as part of a criminal history background check. . . .

N.Y. Comp. Codes R. & Regs. tit. 10, § 1004.5(b)(6)(ii) (2016).

## Washington

Under Washington law, the state's licensing authority—the Liquor and Cannabis Board (LCB)—may consider "any prior criminal conduct of the applicant" in determining whether to grant a license. Wash. Rev. Code Ann. § 69.50.331(1)(b) (2016). The LCB has developed a unique point-based system for grading criminal history:

Table 8.1. Washington's Point-Based Criminal History Scoring System*

| Description | Time period during which points will be assigned | Points assigned |
| --- | --- | --- |
| Felony conviction | 10 years | 12 points |
| Gross misdemeanor conviction | 3 years | 5 points |
| Misdemeanor conviction | 3 years | 4 points |
| Currently under federal or state supervision for a felony conviction | n/a | 8 points |
| Nondisclosure of any of the above | n/a | 4 points each |

*Wash. Admin. Code 314-55-040.

Part III. Marijuana Suppliers

Under this system, the LCB "may not issue a marijuana license to anyone who has accumulated eight or more points." Wash. Admin. Code 314-55-040. However, the LCB considers this to be a "discretionary threshold" and has "recommended that the following exceptions to this standard be applied":

> (a) Prior to initial license application, two federal or state misdemeanor convictions for the possession only of marijuana within the previous three years may not be applicable to the criminal history points accumulated. All criminal history must be reported on the personal/criminal history form.
> (i) Regardless of applicability, failure to disclose full criminal history will result in point accumulation;
> (ii) State misdemeanor possession convictions accrued after December 6, 2013, exceeding the allowable amounts of marijuana, usable marijuana, and marijuana-infused products . . . shall count toward criminal history point accumulation.
> (b) Prior to initial license application, any single state or federal conviction for the growing, possession, or sale of marijuana will be considered for mitigation on an individual basis. Mitigation will be considered based on the quantity of product involved and other circumstances surrounding the conviction.

Id.

## Notes and Questions

1. What are the key differences regarding the treatment of criminal history in the licensing statutes excerpted above? Consider the following Problem:

Problem 8.11: In 2012, Camila pled guilty to the use of the proceeds of unlawful activity, a felony money laundering violation under 18 U.S.C. § 1957. (The elements of the offense are discussed in Chapter 11.) Her plea deal arose from the following facts. For several years prior, Camila helped to manage a collective in California that supplied marijuana to roughly 1,000 members, all of whom were qualifying patients under state law. Camila deposited all of the funds received by the collective from the sale of marijuana. Although the collective complied with all state marijuana laws, the federal government indicted Camila and her co-workers for the distribution of marijuana, in violation of 21 U.S.C. section 841. However, to help Camila avoid the harsh mandatory minimum sentence that would have applied under section 841, the federal Assistant United States Attorney offered Camila a plea deal to the section 1957 charge. Camila accepted the deal and the section 841 charge was dropped. Camila was sentenced by the court to two years supervised released, with no prison time. She has no other criminal history. Camila wants to apply for a commercial marijuana license in California, Colorado, New Jersey, New York, or Washington. Would she meet the good moral character requirement in any of those states, and in Colorado, would she meet the requirements under both the state's retail marijuana law and its medical marijuana law?

2. Should a licensing authority consider criminal history when awarding licenses? If so, what sort of criminal convictions should be disqualifying?

### d. The Role of Residency

Many states require licensees to be residents of the state (or to be firms incorporated in the state). For example, Washington's rules stipulate that the LCB shall not issue a commercial marijuana license to

> (ii) A person doing business as a sole proprietor who has not lawfully *resided in the state for at least six months* prior to applying to receive a license;
>
> (iii) A partnership, employee cooperative, association, nonprofit corporation, or corporation unless formed *under the laws of this state*, and unless all of the members thereof are qualified to obtain a license as provided in this section. . . .

Wash. Rev. Code Ann. § 69.50.331(1)(c) (2016) (emphases added). California's 2016 Proposition 64 establishes perhaps the most onerous residency requirements to date, declaring that

> (a) No licensing authority shall issue or renew a license to any person that cannot demonstrate continuous California residency from or before January 1, 2015. In the case of an applicant or licensee that is an entity, the entity shall not be considered a resident if any person controlling the entity cannot demonstrate continuous California residency from and before January 1, 2015.
>
> (b) Subdivision (a) shall cease to be operable on December 31, 2019 unless reenacted prior thereto by the Legislature.

Cal. Bus. & Prof. Code § 26054.1 (2016).

Notably, Colorado relaxed its residency requirement in 2016, to enable "Colorado retail marijuana businesses . . . to have ready access to capital from investors in states outside of Colorado." 2016 Colo. Legis. Serv. Ch. 293 (S.B. 16-040). Notwithstanding the change, however, Colorado still imposes some discriminatory limits on the ability of nonresidents to participate in its marijuana industry. Under the rules adopted by the state in 2016,

> (3)(a) A retail marijuana business may be comprised of an unlimited number of direct beneficial interest owners that have been residents of Colorado for at least one year prior to the date of the application.
>
> (b) On and after January 1, 2017, a retail marijuana business that is comprised of one or more direct beneficial interest owners who have not been Colorado residents for at least one year prior to application shall have at least one officer who has been a Colorado resident for at least one year prior to application and all officers with day-to-day operational control over the business must be Colorado residents for at least one year prior to application. A retail marijuana business under this paragraph (b) is limited to no more than fifteen direct beneficial interest owners, including all parent and subsidiary entities, all of whom are natural persons.
>
> . . .
>
> (5) (a) A person who intends to apply as a direct beneficial interest owner and is not a Colorado resident for at least one year prior to the date of application shall first submit a request to the state licensing authority for a finding of suitability as a direct beneficial

interest owner. The person shall receive a finding of suitability prior to submitting an application to the state licensing authority to be a direct beneficial interest owner. . . .

Colo. Rev. Stat. Ann. § 12-43.4-306.5 (2016).

## Notes and Questions

1. Who qualifies as a resident of a state? The following Problem raises the issue:

<u>Problem 8.12</u>: Benjamin has lived in Wyoming his entire life, but for the past two years he has been enrolled as a student at the University of Colorado, Boulder, Leeds School of Business. Benjamin resided on campus for the nine months of each school year, but he spent summers interning at businesses in other states. Benjamin just graduated with his MBA, and he sorely wants to get into the marijuana business in Colorado. At this time, does he qualify as a resident of Colorado? *See* 1 Colo. Code Regs. § 212-2.232 (providing criteria for determining whether an individual is a "resident" for purposes of marijuana licensing). *See also* Office of the Registrar, University of Colorado Boulder, *Residency Guidelines,* at www.colorado.edu/registrar/students/state-residency/guidelines (providing guidelines for determining eligibility for in-state tuition).

2. For reasons discussed in Chapter 6, residency requirements for marijuana users and suppliers are constitutionally suspect. But is there any difference—for constitutional purposes—between a ban (even a temporary one) on all non-resident participation, like California's, and a limit on non-resident participation, like Colorado's?

### e. *Other Criteria*

#### (i) *Non-profit Status*

Several medical marijuana states require or encourage licensees to operate as non-profits.[7] For example, Arizona's medical marijuana law provides that

> A registered nonprofit medical marijuana dispensary shall be operated on a not-for-profit basis. The bylaws of a registered nonprofit medical marijuana dispensary shall contain such provisions relative to the disposition of revenues and receipts to establish and maintain its nonprofit character. A registered nonprofit medical marijuana dispensary need not be recognized as tax-exempt by the internal revenue service. . . .

Ariz. Rev. Stat. § 36-2806 (A) (2016). *See also, e.g.,* N.J. Stat. Ann. 24:6I-7(a) (2016) (reserving first six state licenses for non-profits). *But see, e.g.,* N.Y. Pub. Health Law § 3364 (McKinney) (2016) ("A registered organization shall be a for-profit business entity

---

7. Vaida, *The Altered State, supra,* at 773 n.76, has a useful list of non-profit requirements in marijuana licensing.

or not-for-profit corporation organized for the purpose of acquiring, possessing, manufacturing, selling, delivering, transporting, distributing or dispensing marihuana for certified medical use.").

## Notes and Questions

1. Section A.3 above discussed some of the peculiar limits imposed on non-profit collectives under California law. More generally, however, what does it mean to be a non-profit? Notwithstanding the name, a non-profit *can* make money. The term "non-profit" simply describes the charitable purposes that are served by an organization, including what it does with any money it earns. The Draft Restatement of Law of Charitable Nonprofit Organizations Section 1.01 (2016) provides a useful definition of non-profit (qua "charity"):

> (a) A charity is a legal entity with exclusively charitable purposes, established for the benefit of indefinite beneficiaries, and prohibited from providing impermissible private benefit.
> (b) Charitable purposes include:
> (1) the relief of poverty;
> (2) the advancement of knowledge or education;
> (3) the advancement of religion;
> (4) the promotion of health;
> (5) governmental or municipal purposes; and
> (6) other purposes that are beneficial to the community.
> (c) A purpose is not charitable if it is unlawful, its performance requires the commission of criminal or tortious activity, or it is otherwise contrary to fundamental public policy.

Do you think medical marijuana dispensaries satisfy the draft Restatement's definition of charity?

2. Many non-profits seek to be recognized as such by the federal Internal Revenue Service, in order to gain tax-exempt status under federal law, 26 U.S.C. section 501(c). The IRS has determined, however, that a marijuana distributor—even one that operates on a non-profit basis—cannot qualify as a non-profit organization under section 501(c), because its activity "violates federal law" and thereby "furthers a substantial non-exempt purpose." *See* Internal Revenue Service, *Final Determination Regarding Tax Exempt Status*, No. 201224036 (June 2012), https://perma.cc/DKU6-X4ZH. This is why many states (including Arizona) do not require medical marijuana licensees to be recognized as 501(c) organizations. *See also, e.g.,* N.J. Stat. Ann. 24:6I-7(a)(2016) ("Applicants for authorization as nonprofit alternative treatment centers shall be subject to all applicable State laws governing nonprofit entities, but *need not be recognized as a 501(c)(3) organization by the federal Internal Revenue Service*.") (emphasis added).

### (ii) Geography

Many states also consider the geographic location of applicants in the award of licenses, ostensibly to ensure that users throughout the state have adequate access to marijuana. New York's medical marijuana law quoted above, for example, instructs the state's licensing authority to consider whether "the number of registered organizations in an area will be adequate or excessive to reasonably serve the area, including whether there is sufficient geographic distribution across the state." N.Y. Comp. Codes R. & Regs. tit. 10, § 1004.6(b)(8) (2016). *See also, e.g.*, N.J. Stat. Ann. § 24:6I-7 (2016) ("The department shall seek to ensure the availability of a sufficient number of alternative treatment centers throughout the State, pursuant to need, including at least two each in the northern, central, and southern regions of the State."); 35 Pa. Stat. Ann. § 10231.603 (2016) ("The department shall establish a minimum of three regions within this Commonwealth for the purpose of granting permits to grower/processors and dispensaries" and "shall approve permits for grower/processors and dispensaries in a manner which will provide an adequate amount of medical marijuana to patients and caregivers in all areas of this Commonwealth.").

**Notes and Questions**

1. Maryland's medical marijuana law also appears to require its licensing authority (the Commission) to consider race in awarding marijuana licenses. The relevant provision states that the Commission shall "[a]ctively seek to achieve racial, ethnic, and geographic diversity when licensing medical cannabis growers." Md. Code Ann., Health-Gen. § 13-3306(9)(i) (2016). The constitutionality of Maryland's law and other measures designed to boost minority participation in the marijuana industry is discussed in Chapter 9.

2. Licenses are valuable assets, especially when the state limits their number. Do states permit the transfer of licenses? The rules vary by state. Some states allow transfers, provided the transferee meets all license eligibility criteria, the licensing authority approves of the transfer, and the parties pay a transfer fee. For example, Maryland's medical marijuana law provides:

> A. No interest of 5 percent or more of a license issued pursuant to this chapter shall be assignable or transferable unless:
> (1) The Commission has received notice of the intent of the owner of the interest . . . to transfer or assign an interest in a license to another party;
> (2) The transferee has had forwarded the criminal history record information and audited financial statement to the Commission of the transferee;
> (3) The Commission does not object to the transfer or assignment within 45 days of its receipt of notice; and
> (4) The transferee has paid the required fee [of $7,000].
> B. The Commission may deny transfer of an interest in a license for any proposed transferee if the:
> (1) Criminal history record information or the background investigation demonstrate an absence of good moral character; or
> (2) Payment of taxes due in any jurisdiction is in arrears.

Md. Code Regs. 10.62.08.08 (2016). *See also, e.g.*, N.J. Admin. Code § 8:64-7.5(b) (2016) ("An ATC permit is not assignable or transferable without Department approval. . . ."); *id.* at § 8.64-7.10(a)(4) ("The fee for the transfer of ownership of a permit is $20,000."). However, a few states appear to forbid outright the transfer of a license, even to another eligible party. *E.g.*, N.Y. Comp. Codes R. & Regs. tit. 10, § 1004.8(b) (2016) ("Registrations are not transferable or assignable, including, without limitation, to another registered organization.").

3. Ultimately, what sort of criteria should states use to award licenses? What effects do different criteria have on the demographics, structure, and conduct of the marijuana industry? Chapter 9 revisits this question especially as it pertains to minority participation in the marijuana industry.

## 2. What Regulations Do States Impose on Commercial Licensees?

The permission granted to licensees comes with strings attached. The states have adopted comprehensive regulations to govern licensees, both restricting what licensees are permitted to do and also obliging them to perform certain duties on behalf of the state. Colorado, for example, has passed more than 200 pages of regulations to govern just its *retail* marijuana licensees. 1 Colo. Code Reg. 212-2, et seq. Among many other things, this Retail Marijuana Code (RMC) limits what licensees may produce and sell, and requires them to test and label their wares, track their inventory, and collect taxes on behalf of the state. The entire RMC as of July 2016 can be found https://perma.cc/4F6H-6EM3. Key regulations found in the RMC and in laws adopted by other states are discussed in the sections below.

### a. Vertical Integration

Can marijuana producers also sell their wares at retail (i.e., to users), and, conversely, can marijuana retailers also produce their own goods for sale? The answer to these questions helps determine the degree to which the marijuana industry is *vertically integrated*—i.e., the degree to which the same firms both produce and distribute marijuana. States have taken three basic approaches to vertical integration, as evidenced by both the types of licenses they choose to offer and the restrictions they impose (if any) on owning more than one type.

First, many states *forbid* vertical integration. These states require a different license to cultivate (or process) and to distribute the drug. Furthermore, these states also forbid an enterprise from holding both types of licenses. For example, Washington state issues producer licenses, processor licenses, and retailer licenses, and it stipulates that "[n]either a licensed marijuana producer nor a licensed marijuana processor shall have a direct or indirect financial interest in a licensed marijuana retailer." Wash. Rev. Code Ann. § 69.50.328 (2016).

A second set of states *permits* vertical integration. These states might issue separate licenses for production and distribution of marijuana, but they allow a single entity to hold both types of licenses. For example, Maryland issues separate licenses for growing, processing, and dispensing marijuana, but it allows a single firm to hold both a growing license and a dispensing license. Md. Code Regs. 10.62.14.01 (2016).

Third and finally, a few states *require* at least a degree of vertical integration. For example, New York issues only one type of commercial license under its medical marijuana law, and it expects the holders of such a license (called Registered Organizations) to manufacture the marijuana they sell to qualifying patients. N.Y. Pub. Health § 3364 (2016) (authorizing Registered Organizations to manufacture marijuana and to distribute to qualifying patients, but not to other Registered Organizations). Colorado requires a degree of vertical integration, at least among its medical marijuana licensees. The state offers four basic types of medical marijuana licenses: Medical Marijuana Center (i.e., distributor), Medical Marijuana Infused Product Manufacturer (i.e., processor), Medical Marijuana Optional Premises Cultivation, and Medical Marijuana Testing Facility. *See* Marijuana Enforcement Division, *Business License Applicant Criteria-Medical Marijuana*, https://perma.cc/P5SS-TAEM (describing each type of license). But under the state's so-called 70/30 rule, a licensed Medical Marijuana Center is required to obtain an "Optional" Premises Cultivation License and to produce at least 70 percent of the marijuana that it sells. Colo. Rev. Stat. 12-43.3-402(4). For a short time, the state applied a similar rule to its retail (i.e., recreational) marijuana industry, but that rule expired in 2014. *See* John Hudak, *Colorado's Rollout of Legal Marijuana is Succeeding: A Report on the State's Implementation of Legalization*, 65 Case W. Res. L. Rev. 649, 679-81 (2015) (discussing history of Colorado's 70/30 rule).

## Notes and Questions

1. In a similar fashion, states can influence the *segmentation* of the marijuana market—i.e., the degree to which the same firms will serve both medical and recreational users. For example, Colorado maintains a separate licensing system for recreational and medical marijuana suppliers. The recreational (i.e., retail) licenses parallel those for medical marijuana suppliers and include licenses for Retail Marijuana Store, Retail Marijuana Product Manufacturing, Retail Marijuana Cultivation, and Retail Marijuana Testing Facility. *See* Marijuana Enforcement Division, *Business License Applicant Criteria—Retail Marijuana*, https://perma.cc/2VFL-36V7 (describing each type of license). It should be noted, however, that Colorado allows licensees to hold both types of licenses, as long as they physically separate their retail and medical operations or else serve only adult customers. Colo. Rev. Stat. Ann. § 12-43.4-104 (2016). In comparison, Washington has adopted a single licensing system to serve both the medical and the recreational markets, although it offers a special "medical marijuana endorsement" that grants some licensees additional privileges to encourage them to meet the special needs of medical users. *See* Cannabis Patient Protection Act, 2015 Wash. Legis. Serv. Ch. 70 (SSSB 5052).

### b. Product Testing, Labeling, and Packaging

States are increasingly requiring licensees to test their products and specifying the way they must label and package those products. Colorado's RMC illustrates the detailed rules that licensees must abide. The relevant provisions of the RMC are excerpted and discussed in the sections below.

#### (i) Testing

R 1501 – Retail Marijuana Testing Program – Contaminant Testing

A. Contaminant Testing Required. Until a Retail Marijuana Cultivation Facility's or a Retail Marijuana Product Manufacturing Facility's cultivation or production process has been validated under this rule, it shall not wholesale, transfer, or process into a Retail Marijuana Concentrate or Retail Marijuana Product any Retail Marijuana, Retail Marijuana Concentrate or Retail Marijuana Product unless Samples from the Harvest Batch or Production Batch from which that Retail Marijuana, Retail Marijuana Concentrate or Retail

Marijuana Product was derived was tested by a Retail Marijuana Testing Facility for contaminants and passed all contaminant tests required by paragraph C of this rule.

B. Validation of Process – Contaminant Testing

1. Retail Marijuana. A Retail Marijuana Cultivation Facility's cultivation process shall be deemed valid regarding Contaminants if every Harvest Batch that it produced during at least a six week period but no longer than a 12 week period passed all contaminant tests required by paragraph C of this rule. This must include at least 6 Test Batches that contain Samples from entirely different Harvest Batches.

2. Retail Marijuana Concentrate or Retail Marijuana Product. A Retail Marijuana Cultivation Facility's or a Retail Marijuana Products Manufacturing Facility's production process shall be deemed valid regarding contaminants if every Production Batch that it produced during at least a four week period but no longer than an eight week period passed all contaminant tests required by paragraph C of this rule. This must include at least four Test Batches that contain Samples from entirely different Production Batches.

3. Process Validation is Effective for One Year. Once a Retail Marijuana Cultivation Facility or Retail Marijuana Products Manufacturing Facility has successfully obtained process validation for contaminants, the process validation shall be effective for one year from the date of the last passing test required to satisfy the process validation requirements.

C. Required Contaminant Tests

1. Microbial Contaminant Testing. Each Harvest Batch of Retail Marijuana and Production Batch of Water- or Food-Based Retail Marijuana Concentrate and Retail Marijuana Product must be tested for microbial contamination by a Retail Marijuana Testing Facility. The microbial contamination test must include, but need not be limited to, testing to determine the presence of and amounts present of Salmonella sp., Escherichia coli., and total yeast and mold.

2. Mold and Mildew Contaminant Testing. Each Harvest Batch of Retail Marijuana and Production Batch of Retail Marijuana Concentrate and Retail Marijuana Product must be visually inspected, in addition to other required mold testing, by a Retail Marijuana Testing Facility for toxic amounts of mold and mildew contamination.

3. Filth Contaminant Testing. Each Harvest Batch of Retail Marijuana must be visually inspected by a Retail Marijuana Testing Facility for toxic amounts of filth.

4. Residual Solvent Contaminant Testing. Each Production Batch of Solvent-Based Retail Marijuana Concentrate produced by a Retail Marijuana Products Manufacturing Facility must be tested by a Retail Marijuana Testing Facility for residual solvent contamination. The residual solvent contamination test must include, but need not be limited to, testing to determine the presence of, and amounts present of, butane, heptanes, benzene*, toluene*, hexane*, and xylenes*. * Note: These solvents are not approved for use. Testing is required for these solvents due to their possible presence in the solvents approved for use. . . .

. . .

R 1503 – Retail Marijuana Testing Program – Potency Testing

A. Potency Testing – General

1. Test Batches. A Test Batch submitted for potency testing may only be comprised of Samples that are of the same strain of Retail Marijuana or from the same Production Batch of Retail Marijuana Concentrate or Retail Marijuana Product.

2. Cannabinoid Profile. A potency test conducted pursuant to this rule must at least determine the level of concentration of THC, THCA, CBD, CBDA and CBN.

B. Potency Testing for Retail Marijuana.

Part III. Marijuana Suppliers

> 1. Initial Potency Testing. A Retail Marijuana Cultivation Facility must have potency tests conducted by a Retail Marijuana Testing Facility on four Harvest Batches, created a minimum of one week apart, for each strain of Retail Marijuana that it cultivates.
> 
>> a. The first potency test must be conducted on each strain prior to the Retail Marijuana Cultivation Facility wholesaling, transferring or processing into a Retail Marijuana Concentrate any Retail Marijuana of that strain.
> 
> . . .
> 
> D. Potency Testing for Retail Marijuana Product
> 
>> 1. Potency Testing Required for non-Edible Retail Marijuana Product. A Retail Marijuana Products Manufacturing Facility shall have potency tests conducted by a Retail Marijuana Testing Facility on every Production Batch of Retail Marijuana Product that is not Edible Retail Marijuana Product that it produces prior to transferring or wholesaling any of the non-Edible Retail Marijuana Product from that Production Batch.
>> 
>> 1.5 Potency Testing Required for Edible Retail Marijuana Product. A Retail Marijuana Products Manufacturing Facility shall have potency tests conducted by a Retail Marijuana Testing Facility on every Production Batch of each type of Edible Retail Marijuana Product that it produces prior to transferring or wholesaling any of the Edible Retail Marijuana Product from that Production Batch, . . .
>> 
>> 2. Required Tests. Potency tests conducted on Retail Marijuana Product must determine the level of concentration of the required cannabinoids and whether or not THC is homogeneously distributed throughout the product.
> 
> . . .

1 Colo. Code Reg. 212-2.1501 & .1503 (2016).[8]

## Notes and Comments

1. What is the purpose of the different testing requirements imposed by Colorado? In other words, what does Colorado require testing for and why?

2. What happens if a product fails the tests? Under Colorado law, a licensee must quarantine any batch of product that fails testing and either destroy it or submit it for re-testing. *Id.* at 212-2.1507. The failure to test or to quarantine are potentially serious violations that could result in the revocation of a license. *Id.* at 212-2.1501(G) & 1507(D). The discipline of licensees is discussed below in Section B.3.

### *(ii) Labeling and Packaging*

The following Colorado rules apply to the packaging and labeling of retail marijuana products, including edibles:

> R 604 – Retail Marijuana Products Manufacturing Facility: Health and Safety Regulations
> 
> . . .
> 
> C.5. Product Safety.
> 
> . . .
> 
>> 2. The size of a Standardized Serving Of Marijuana shall be no more than 10mg of active THC. A Retail Marijuana Products Manufacturing Facility that manufactures

---

8. For examples of other state testing requirements, *see, e.g.*, Md. Code Regs. 10.62.15.05 (2016); N.J. Admin. Code § 8:64-13.4(3) (2016); and N.Y. Comp. Codes R. & Regs. tit. 10, § 1004.14 (2016).

Edible Retail Marijuana Product shall determine the total number of Standardized Servings Of Marijuana for each product that it manufactures. No individual Edible Retail Marijuana Product unit for sale shall contain more than 100 milligrams of active THC.
. . .

4. Each single Standardized Serving Of Marijuana shall be marked, stamped, or otherwise imprinted with the Universal Symbol directly on at least one side of the Edible Retail Marijuana Product in a manner to cause the Universal Symbol to be distinguishable and easily recognizable. . . .

Figure 8.6. Colorado's Universal Symbol for Marijuana

5. Notwithstanding the requirement of subparagraph (C.5)(4), an Edible Retail Marijuana Product shall contain no more than 10 mg of active THC per Child-Resistant package and the Retail Marijuana Products Manufacturing Facility must ensure that the product [is packaged within a Child-Resistant Container] when:

    a. The Edible Retail Marijuana Product is of the type that is impracticable to mark, stamp, or otherwise imprint with the Universal Symbol directly on the product in a manner to cause the Universal Symbol to be distinguishable and easily recognizable; or

    b. The Edible Retail Marijuana Product is of the type that is impracticable to clearly demark each Standardized Serving Of Marijuana or to make each Standardized Serving Of Marijuana easily separable.

6. The following categories of Edible Retail Marijuana Product are considered to be per se practicable to mark with the Universal Symbol:

    a. Chocolate
    b. Soft confections
    c. Hard confections or lozenges
    d. Consolidated baked goods (e.g. cookie, brownie, cupcake, granola bar)
    e. Pressed pills and capsules

7. The following categories of Edible Retail Marijuana Product are considered to be per se impracticable to mark with the Universal Symbol:

    a. Liquids
    b. Loose bulk goods (e.g. granola, cereals, popcorn)
    c. Powders

. . .

9. Multiple-Serving Edible Retail Marijuana Product.

    a. A Retail Marijuana Products Manufacturing Facility must ensure that each single Standardized Serving Of Marijuana of a Multiple-Serving Edible Retail Marijuana Product is physically demarked in a way that enables a reasonable person to intuitively determine how much of the product constitutes a single serving of active THC.

    b. Each demarked Standardized Serving Of Marijuana must be easily separable in order to allow an average person 21 years of age and over to physically separate, with minimal effort, individual servings of the product.

Part III. Marijuana Suppliers

        c. Each single Standardized Serving Of Marijuana contained in a Multiple-Serving Edible Retail Marijuana Product shall be marked, stamped, or otherwise imprinted with the Universal Symbol directly on the product in a manner to cause the Universal Symbol to be distinguishable and easily recognizable. The Universal Symbol marking shall comply with the requirements of subparagraph (C.5)(4) of this rule. . . .
    10. Remanufactured Products Prohibited. A Retail Marijuana Product Manufacturing Facility shall not utilize a commercially manufactured food product as its Edible Retail Marijuana Product. The following exceptions to this prohibition apply:
        a. A food product that was commercially manufactured specifically for use by the Retail Marijuana Product Manufacturing Facility Licensee to infuse with marijuana shall be allowed. The Licensee shall have a written agreement with the commercial food product manufacturer that declares the food product's exclusive use by the Retail Marijuana Product Manufacturing Facility.
        b. Commercially manufactured food products may be used as ingredients in a Retail Marijuana Product Manufacturing Facility's Edible Retail Marijuana product so long as: (1) they are used in a way that renders them unrecognizable as the commercial food product in the final Edible Retail Marijuana Product, and (2) the Retail Marijuana Product Manufacturing Facility does not state or advertise to the consumer that the final Edible Retail Marijuana Product contains the commercially manufactured food product.

R 1006 – Packaging and Labeling of Retail Marijuana Product by a Retail Marijuana Store

. . .

A. Packaging Requirements for a Retail Marijuana Store.
    1 . . . [A] Retail Marijuana Store shall not purchase, take possession of, or sell Retail Marijuana Product that does not comply with rules R 604 and R 1004 [concerning the wholesale packaging of marijuana products].
    2. A Retail Marijuana Store must ensure that each Edible Retail Marijuana Product placed within a Container for sale to a consumer pursuant to this rule must also be placed in an Opaque Exit Package at the point of sale to the consumer.
    3. A Retail Marijuana Store must ensure that each Retail Marijuana Product that is not an Edible Retail Marijuana Product is placed within a Container prior to sale to a consumer. If the Container is not Child-Resistant, the Retail Marijuana Store must place the Container within an Exit Package that is Child-Resistant.
B. Labeling of Retail Marijuana Product by a Retail Marijuana Store. Every Retail Marijuana Store must ensure that a label(s) is affixed to every Exit Package at the time of sale to a consumer that includes all of the information required by this rule. If an Exit Package is not required pursuant to paragraph (A)(3) of this rule, and the Retail Marijuana Store elects not to provide one, then the Retail Marijuana Store must ensure the labels required by this rule are affixed to each Container.
    1. Required Information.
        a. The license number of the Retail Marijuana Store that sold the Retail Marijuana Product to the consumer;
        b. The Identity Statement and Standardized Graphic Symbol of the Retail Marijuana Store that sold the Retail Marijuana Product to the consumer. A Licensee may elect to have its Identity Statement also serve as its Standardized Graphic Symbol for purposes of complying with this rule. The Licensee shall maintain a record of its Identity Statement and Standardized Graphic Symbol and make such information available to the State Licensing Authority upon request;
        c. The date of sale to the consumer;
        d. The following warning statements;

i. "There may be health risks associated with the consumption of this product."

...

iii. "This product was produced without regulatory oversight for health, safety, or efficacy."

iv. "The intoxicating effects of this product may be delayed by two or more hours."

v. "There may be additional health risks associated with the consumption of this product for women who are pregnant, breastfeeding, or planning on becoming pregnant."

vi. "Do not drive a motor vehicle or operate heavy machinery while using marijuana."

e. The Universal Symbol, which must be located on the front of the Container or Exit Package as appropriate and no smaller than ½ of an inch by ½ of an inch, and the following statement which must be labeled directly below the Universal Symbol: "Contains Marijuana. Keep out of the reach of children."

1 Colo. Code Reg. 212-2.604 & .1006 (2016).[9]

## Notes and Questions

1. Consider the following Problem involving application of Colorado's labeling and packaging rules:

**Problem 8.13**: Take a look at the marijuana-infused chocolate bar pictured in **Figure 8.7** at right. Suppose that each square contained 10 mg of THC. Does it comply with the requirements of Rule 604 quoted above?

2. Labeling and packaging rules like those excerpted above are generally intended to protect the public safety. But do they actually work? Consider the Universal Symbol pictured in **Figure 8.6** above and imprinted on the chocolate bar pictured in **Figure 8.7**. Does the Symbol put people on notice that the product they are about to consume contains marijuana? Is a consumer likely to think each square of that chocolate bar is a full serving? If this were a regular (i.e., not marijuana-infused) chocolate bar, how many squares would you eat? For one reporter's tale of unwittingly eating an entire marijuana-infused chocolate bar, see Maureen Dowd, *Don't Harsh Our Mellow, Dude*, N.Y. Times, June 3, 2014.

Figure 8.7. A Marijuana Infused Chocolate Bar

---

9. For examples of other states' labeling and packaging requirements, *see, e.g.*, Md. Code Regs. 10.62.29.02 (2016); N.J. Admin. Code § 8:64-10.6(b)-(e) (2016); and N.Y. Comp. Codes R. & Regs. tit. 10, § 1004.12(h) (2016).

3. Instead of imposing labeling and packaging requirements, some states bar commercial licensees from producing or distributing certain types of marijuana products altogether, including edibles and smokable marijuana. *E.g.*, N.Y. Comp. Codes R. & Regs. tit. 10, § 1004.11(g)(4)-(5) (2016) ("Smoking is not an approved route of administration. . . . [A]pproved medical marihuana products may not be incorporated into edible food products by the registered organization [i.e., a medical marijuana dispensary], unless approved by the commissioner."). For further discussion of restrictions imposed on the types of marijuana that may be possessed and sold, see Chapter 4.

4. The RMC has a separate, similar set of rules that govern the labeling and packaging of loose marijuana—e.g., dried buds and leaves. 1 Colo. Code Reg. 212-2.1005.5 (2016).

### c. Sales

Licensed distributors, of course, may only sell to people who are themselves allowed to possess the drug—i.e., qualifying patients in medical marijuana regimes or all adults in recreational regimes. To help prevent diversion to unapproved users, states generally limit the size of permissible retail transactions and require licensees to verify the eligibility of buyers to make purchases. For example, the RMC provides,

R 402 – Retail Marijuana Sales: General Limitations or Prohibited Acts

A. Sales to Persons Under 21 Years. Licensees are prohibited from selling, giving, or distributing Retail Marijuana or Retail Marijuana Product to persons under 21 years of age.

B. Age Verification. Prior to initiating the sale of Retail Marijuana or Retail Marijuana Product, a Licensee must verify that the purchaser has a valid government-issued photo identification showing that the purchaser is 21 years of age or older.

C. Quantity Limitations On Sales.
. . .
3. A Retail Marijuana Store and its employees are prohibited from selling more than one ounce of Retail Marijuana flower or its equivalent in Retail Marijuana Concentrate or Retail Marijuana Product during a sales transaction to a consumer. Except that non-edible, non-psychoactive Retail Marijuana Products including ointments, lotions, balms, and other non-transdermal topical products are exempt from the one-ounce quantity limitation on sales.

    a. One ounce of Retail Marijuana flower shall be equivalent to eight grams of Retail Marijuana Concentrate.

    b. One ounce of Retail Marijuana flower shall be equivalent to 80 ten milligram servings of THC in Retail Marijuana Product.

D. Licensees May Refuse Sales. Nothing in these rules prohibits a Licensee from refusing to sell Retail Marijuana or Retail Marijuana Product to a customer.

E. Sales over the Internet. A Licensee is prohibited from selling Retail Marijuana or Retail Marijuana Product over the internet. All sales and transfers of possession of Retail Marijuana and Retail Marijuana Product must occur within the Retail Marijuana Store's Licensed Premises.

F. Purchases Only Within Restricted Access Area. A customer must be physically present within the Restricted Access Area of the Retail Marijuana Store's Licensed Premises to purchase Retail Marijuana or Retail Marijuana Product.
. . .

H. Prohibited Items. A Retail Marijuana Store is prohibited from selling or giving away any consumable product that is not a Retail Marijuana Product including, but not limited to, cigarettes or tobacco products, alcohol beverages, and food products or non-alcohol beverages that are not Retail Marijuana Product.

I. Free Product Prohibited. A Retail Marijuana Store may not give away Retail Marijuana or Retail Marijuana Product to a consumer for any reason.

J. Nicotine or Alcohol Prohibited. A Retail Marijuana Store is prohibited from selling Retail Marijuana or Retail Marijuana Product that contain nicotine or alcohol, if the sale of the alcohol would require a license pursuant to Articles 46 or 47 of Title 12, C.R.S.

K. Consumption Prohibited. A Licensee shall not permit the consumption of marijuana or marijuana product on the Licensed Premises.

1 Colo. Code Reg. 212-2.402 (2016).

## Notes and Questions

1. The following Problems test the application of the RMC sales regulations:

**Problem 8.14:** Andy is only 17 years old, but he looks like his older brother Benjamin, who is 22 years old. Andy goes to a state-licensed retail marijuana store wearing his high school letter jacket, and he shows the clerk Benjamin's driver's license. The clerk takes a quick look at the license and then at Andy, and he proceeds to sell Andy one ounce of marijuana (the cheapest the store offers, per Andy's request). Has the store violated Colorado's Rule 402? Does it have a defense? See 1 Colo. Code Reg. 212-2.404.

**Problem 8.15:** Benjamin is 22 years old. He goes to a state-licensed retail marijuana store, shows the clerk his driver's license, and the clerk sells him one ounce of marijuana. Benjamin leaves the store, but he returns an hour later. He shows the same clerk his driver's license. The clerk shrugs and proceeds to sell Benjamin another one ounce of marijuana. Has the store violated Rule 402? What if Benjamin visits the store three more times that day, purchasing one ounce of marijuana on each occassion?

2. New York's medical marijuana law includes a unique provision (for marijuana laws), giving the state Department of Health the power to set the retail prices charged by Registered Organizations for marijuana. The Department's regulations provide that the price shall reflect "the cost to manufacture, market and distribute approved medical marijuana products plus a reasonable profit." N.Y. Comp. Codes R. & Regs. tit. 10, § 1004.15 (a)(2). The regulations also provide that the Department shall seek the input of licensees in making its pricing determinations. *Id.* at § 1004.15(c). Can you think of other products for which states set the prices? Are price restrictions wise? Are they workable?

Part III. Marijuana Suppliers

### *d. Advertising*

States also restrict advertising by commercial licensees. The RMC includes several common and a few not-so-common restrictions:

R 1102 – Advertising General Requirement: No Deceptive, False or Misleading Statements

A Retail Marijuana Establishment shall not engage in Advertising that is deceptive, false, or misleading. A Retail Marijuana Establishment shall not make any deceptive, false, or misleading assertions or statements on any product, any sign, or any document provided to a consumer.

R 1104 – Advertising: Television
. . .
B. Television Advertising. A Retail Marijuana Establishment shall not utilize television Advertising unless the Retail Marijuana Establishment has reliable evidence that no more than 30 percent of the audience for the program on which the Advertising is to air is reasonably expected to be under the age of 21.

R 1105 – Advertising: Radio
. . .
B. Radio Advertising. A Retail Marijuana Establishment shall not engage in radio Advertising unless the Retail Marijuana Establishment has reliable evidence that no more than 30 percent of the audience for the program on which the Advertising is to air is reasonably expected to be under the age of 21.

R 1106 – Advertising: Print Media
A Retail Marijuana Establishment shall not engage in Advertising in a print publication unless the Retail Marijuana Establishment has reliable evidence that no more than 30 percent of the publication's readership is reasonably expected to be under the age of 21.

R 1107 – Advertising: Internet
A Retail Marijuana Establishment shall not engage in Advertising via the internet unless the Retail Marijuana Establishment has reliable evidence that no more than 30 percent of the audience for the internet web site is reasonably expected to be under the age of 21. . . .

R 1108 – Advertising: Targeting Out-of-State Persons Prohibited.
A Retail Marijuana Establishment shall not engage in Advertising that specifically targets Persons located outside the state of Colorado.

R 1111 – Signage and Advertising: Outdoor Advertising
. . .
B. Outdoor Advertising Generally Prohibited. Except as otherwise provided in this rule, it shall be unlawful for any Retail Marijuana Establishment to engage in Advertising that is visible to members of the public from any street, sidewalk, park or other public place, including Advertising utilizing any of the following media: any billboard or other outdoor general Advertising device; any sign mounted on a vehicle, any hand-held or other portable sign; or any handbill, leaflet or flier directly handed to any person in a public place, left upon a motor vehicle, or posted upon any public or private property without the consent of the property owner.
C. Exception. The prohibitions set forth in this rule shall not apply to any fixed sign that is located on the same zone lot as a Retail Marijuana Establishment and that exists solely for the purpose of identifying the location of the Retail Marijuana Establishment and otherwise complies with any applicable local ordinances.

R 1112 – Signage and Advertising: No Content That Targets Minors

A Retail Marijuana Establishment shall not include in any form of Advertising or signage any content that specifically targets individuals under the age of 21, including but not limited to cartoon characters or similar images.

R 1113 – Advertising: Advertising via Marketing Directed Toward Location-Based Devices

A Retail Marijuana Establishment shall not engage in Advertising via marketing directed towards location-based devices, including but not limited to cellular phones, unless the marketing is a mobile device application installed on the device by the owner of the device who is 21 year of age or older and includes a permanent and easy opt-out feature.

R 1114 – Pop-Up Advertising

A Retail Marijuana Establishment shall not utilize unsolicited pop-up Advertising on the internet.

R 1115 – Advertising: Event Sponsorship

A Retail Marijuana Establishment may sponsor a charitable, sports, or similar event, but a Retail Marijuana Establishment shall not engage in Advertising at, or in connection with, such an event unless the Retail Marijuana Establishment has reliable evidence that no more than 30 percent of the audience at the event and/or viewing Advertising in connection with the event is reasonably expected to be under the age of 21.

1 Colo. Code Reg. 212-2.1102, .1104-08, & .1111-15 (2016).

## Notes and Questions

1. Many of the excerpted regulations are designed to limit the exposure of minors to marijuana advertising. The regulations are modeled on voluntary guidelines that have been adopted by associations of alcoholic beverages producers. *E.g.*, 1 Colo. Code Reg. 212-2.1104 (2016) (Basis and Purpose). For example, the Beer Institute advises member brewers not to place advertisements in print media, on television or radio, or in digital media, unless "at least 71.6% of the audience is expected to be adults of legal drinking age." Advertising and Marketing Code § 3(c)(i) (June 2015), http://www.beer-institute.org/assets/uploads/general-upload/2015-Beer-Ad-Code-Brochure.pdf.

2. Consider the following Problem:

**Problem 8.16:** Delilah is the owner of a licensed Retail Marijuana Store in Small Town, Colorado. Seventy-five percent of the population of Small Town is 21 years old or older. In early December, Delilah runs a small advertisement for her store in the local paper. The ad has a picture of Santa Claus stuffing marijuana into a stocking with the name "Mrs. Claus" on it. Does the ad violate the Colorado rules? *Cf.* Beer Institute Advertising and Marketing Code, *supra*, at § 3(b).

3. At least one state had, until recently, banned advertising outright. A provision of Montana's medical marijuana law, which was repealed by initiative in 2016, barred qualifying patients and caregivers from advertising "marijuana or marijuana-related products in any medium, including electronic media." Mont. Stat. 50-46-341 (2016). The constitutionality of bans and lesser restrictions on advertising is discussed in Chapter 9.

Part III. Marijuana Suppliers

## *e. Reporting*

All states require licensees to collect and report information on their operations to state licensing authorities. The information helps licensing authorities to monitor compliance with regulations like those discussed above. The data collection and reporting requirements imposed by Colorado's RMC are perhaps the most extensive in the country, calling for the tracking of all marijuana from seed to sale (among other things). Some of the state's more notable requirements are excerpted here:

R 306 - Video Surveillance

A. Minimum Requirements. The following video surveillance requirements shall apply to all Retail Marijuana Establishments.

    1. Prior to exercising the privileges of a Retail Marijuana Establishment, an Applicant must install a fully operational video surveillance and camera recording system. . . .

. . .

    3. Video surveillance records and recordings must be made available upon request to the [Marijuana Enforcement] Division, the relevant local jurisdiction, or any other state or local law enforcement agency for a purpose authorized by the Retail Code or for any other state or local law enforcement purpose.

    4. Video surveillance records and recordings of point-of-sale areas shall be held in confidence by all employees and representatives of the Division, except that the Division may provide such records and recordings to the relevant local jurisdiction, or any other state or local law enforcement agency for a purpose authorized by the Retail Code or for any other state or local law enforcement purpose

. . .

C. Placement of Cameras and Required Camera Coverage

    1. Camera coverage is required for all Limited Access Areas, point-of-sale areas, security rooms, all points of ingress and egress to Limited Access Areas, all areas where Retail Marijuana or Retail Marijuana Product is displayed for sale, and all points of ingress and egress to the exterior of the Licensed Premises.

    2. Camera placement shall be capable of identifying activity occurring within 20 feet of all points of ingress and egress and shall allow for the clear and certain identification of any individual and activities on the Licensed Premises.

. . .

E. Video Recording and Retention Requirements

    1. All camera views of all Limited Access Areas must be continuously recorded 24 hours a day. . . .

    2. All surveillance recordings must be kept for a minimum of 40 days and be in a format that can be easily accessed for viewing. . . .

R 309 − Retail Marijuana Establishments: Inventory Tracking Solution

A. Inventory Tracking System Required. A Retail Marijuana Establishment is required to use the Inventory Tracking System as the primary inventory tracking system of record. A Retail Marijuana Establishment must have an Inventory Tracking System account activated and functional prior to operating or exercising any privileges of a license. . . .

. . .

D. RFID Tags Required

    1. Authorized Tags Required and Costs. Licensees are required to use RFID tags issued by a Division-approved vendor that is authorized to provision RFID tags for the

Inventory Tracking System. Each licensee is responsible for the cost of all RFID tags and any associated vendor fees.

2. Use of RFID Tags Required. A Licensee is responsible to ensure its inventories are properly tagged where the Inventory Tracking System requires RFID tag use. A Retail Marijuana Establishment must ensure it has an adequate supply of RFID tags to properly tag Retail Marijuana and Retail Marijuana Product as required by the Inventory Tracking System.

R 405 – Retail Marijuana Store: Inventory Tracking System

A. Minimum Tracking Requirement. A Retail Marijuana Store must use Inventory Tracking System to ensure its inventories are identified and tracked from the point they are transferred from a Retail Marijuana Cultivation Facility or Retail Marijuana Products Manufacturing Facility through the point of sale, given to a Retail Marijuana Testing Facility, or otherwise disposed of. . . .

Figure 8.8. RFID Tags on Marijuana Plants

1. A Retail Marijuana Store is prohibited from accepting any Retail Marijuana or Retail Marijuana Product from a Retail Marijuana Cultivation Facility or Retail Marijuana Products Manufacturing Facility without receiving a valid transport manifest generated from the Inventory Tracking System.

2. A Retail Marijuana Store must immediately input all Retail Marijuana and Retail Marijuana Product delivered to the Licensed Premises, accounting for all RFID tags, into the Inventory Tracking System at the time of delivery from a Retail Marijuana Cultivation Facility or Retail Marijuana Products Manufacturing Facility. All delivered Retail Marijuana must be weighed and the scale used shall be tested and approved in accordance with measurement standards. . . .

3. A Retail Marijuana Store must reconcile transactions from their point of sale processes and on-hand inventory to the Inventory Tracking System at the close of business each day.

1 Colo. Code Reg. 2-212, 306, .309, & .405 (2016).

## Notes and Questions

1. Colorado's Inventory Tracking System alone has collected detailed data on more than 20,000 participants in the marijuana industry and more than 5,000,000 marijuana plants. See Metrc, https://perma.cc/9G8F-EB6B. States like Colorado purport to make their data confidential, but as discussed in Chapter 14, state assurances as to confidentiality might not bind the *federal* government.

2. In a similar fashion, states require licensees to collect and remit state and local taxes imposed on marijuana sales and to maintain detailed records of transactions to help ensure compliance with tax laws. *E.g.*, 1 Colo. Code Reg. 221-2.902. Marijuana taxes are discussed in more detail in Chapter 9.

Part III. Marijuana Suppliers

## 3. How Are Licensees Disciplined?

Licensing authorities are empowered to investigate the conduct of licensees and to sanction licensees found to be in violation of their regulations. The sections below explore the distinct rules governing this disciplinary process.

### a. *Investigations*

Licensing authorities have been given broad powers to enforce the licensing regulations discussed in Sections B.1 and B.2 above. The following provisions of Colorado's RMC provide a sampling of the powers wielded by the state's Marijuana Enforcement Division (MED):

> R 1201 — Duties of Employees of the State Licensing Authority
>
> . . .
>
> B. Duties of Division Investigators. The State Licensing Authority, the Department's Senior Director of Enforcement, the Director, and Division investigators shall have all the powers of any peace officer to:
>
> 1. Investigate violations or suspected violations of the Retail Code and any rules promulgated pursuant to it. Make arrests, with or without warrant, for any violation of the Retail Code, any rules promulgated pursuant to it, Article 18 of Title 18, C.R.S. [the state Uniform Controlled Substances Act], any other laws or regulations pertaining to Retail Marijuana in this state, or any criminal law of this state, if, during an officer's exercise of powers or performance of duties pursuant to the Retail Code, probable cause exists that a crime related to such laws has been or is being committed;
>
> 2. Serve all warrants, summonses, subpoenas, administrative citations, notices or other processes relating to the enforcement of laws regulating Retail Marijuana and Retail Marijuana Product;
>
> . . .
>
> 4. Inspect, examine, or investigate any premises where the Licensee's Retail Marijuana or Retail Marijuana Product are grown, stored, cultivated, manufactured, tested, distributed, or sold, and any books and records in any way connected with any licensed or unlicensed activity;
>
> 5. Require any Licensee, upon demand, to permit an inspection of Licensed Premises during business hours or at any time of apparent operation, marijuana equipment, and marijuana accessories, or books and records; and, to permit the testing of or examination of Retail Marijuana or Retail Marijuana Product;
>
> 6. Require Applicants to submit complete and current applications and fees and other information the Division deems necessary to make licensing decisions and approve material changes made by the Applicant or Licensee;
>
> 7. Conduct investigations into the character, criminal history, and all other relevant factors related to suitability of all Licensees and Applicants for Retail Marijuana licenses and such other Persons with a direct or indirect interest in an Applicant or Licensee, as the State Licensing Authority may require; and
>
> 8. Exercise any other power or duty authorized by law.
>
> . . .
>
> R 1202 — Requirement for Inspections and Investigations, Searches, Administrative Holds, Voluntary Surrenders and Such Additional Activities as May Become Necessary from Time to Time

A. Applicants and Licensees Shall Cooperate with Division Employees

1. Applicants and Licensees must cooperate with employees of the Division who are conducting inspections or investigations relevant to the enforcement of laws and regulations related to the Retail Code.

. . .

1 Colo. Code Reg. 2-212.1201-.1202 (2016).

Among other things, Rule 1202 gives the MED the power to conduct warrantless inspections of the records and facilities of commercial licensees. Colorado is hardly unique in this regard. Many states have granted their licensing authorities broad power to search and inspect licensees. For example, Maryland's medical marijuana law cautions that by merely applying for a marijuana license, the licensee "irrevocably gives the Commission consent to conduct all inspections necessary to ensure compliance with State law and regulations." Md. Code Regs. 10.62.33.02 (2016). The law proceeds to describe the Commission's inspection authority:

A. The Commission may conduct announced and unannounced inspections of the facilities of licensed growers, licensed processors, licensed dispensaries, and independent testing laboratories subject to the Commission's regulation, mission, and function, to determine compliance with statute and regulations.

B. Failure by a licensed grower, licensed processor, licensed dispensary or registered independent testing laboratory to provide the Commission with immediate access to any part of a premises, requested material, information, or agent as part of an inspection may result in the imposition of a civil fine, suspension of license, or revocation of license.

C. During an inspection, the Commission may:

(1) Review and make copies of all records;

(2) Enter any place, including a vehicle, in which medical cannabis is held, dispensed, sold, produced, tested, delivered, transported, manufactured or otherwise disposed of;

(3) Inspect all equipment, raw and processed material, containers and labeling, and all things therein;

(4) Inventory any medical cannabis;

. . .

(6) Question personnel present at the location and any agent of the licensee.

*Id.* at 10.62.33.04. *See also, e.g.,* N.J. Admin. Code § 8:64-13.3 (2016) (similar).

## Notes and Questions

1. Do warrantless inspections violate the Fourth Amendment? As discussed in Chapter 4, law enforcement normally needs probable cause to conduct the search of an individual. When it comes to businesses in "closely regulated" industries, however, less suspicion (and no warrant) is required. The United States Supreme Court has explained the rationale behind relaxing the suspicion and warrant requirements for the search of such businesses:

Because the owner or operator of commercial premises in a "closely regulated" industry has a reduced expectation of privacy, the warrant and probable-cause requirements, which fulfill the traditional Fourth Amendment standard of reasonableness for a government search, . . . have lessened application in this context. Rather, we conclude that, as in other situations of "special need," see *New Jersey v. T.L.O.*, [469 U.S. 325, 353, (1985)] (opinion concurring in judgment), where the privacy interests of the owner are weakened and the government interests in regulating particular businesses are concomitantly heightened, a warrantless inspection of commercial premises may well be reasonable within the meaning of the Fourth Amendment.

*New York v. Burger*, 482 U.S. 691, 702 (1987).

Nonetheless, the *Burger* Court also imposed some limitations on this exception to the warrant and probable cause requirements:

> . . . [W]arrantless inspection, . . . even in the context of a pervasively regulated business, will be deemed to be reasonable only so long as three criteria are met. First, there must be a "substantial" government interest that informs the regulatory scheme pursuant to which the inspection is made. . . .
>
> Second, the warrantless inspections must be "necessary to further [the] regulatory scheme." *Donovan v. Dewey*, [452 U.S. 594, 600 (1981)]. For example, in *Dewey* we recognized that forcing mine inspectors to obtain a warrant before every inspection might alert mine owners or operators to the impending inspection, thereby frustrating the purposes of the Mine Safety and Health Act—to detect and thus to deter safety and health violations. *Id.*, at 603. . . .
>
> Finally, "the statute's inspection program, in terms of the certainty and regularity of its application, [must] provid[e] a constitutionally adequate substitute for a warrant." *Ibid.* In other words, the regulatory statute must perform the two basic functions of a warrant: it must advise the owner of the commercial premises that the search is being made pursuant to the law and has a properly defined scope, and it must limit the discretion of the inspecting officers. . . . To perform this first function, the statute must be "sufficiently comprehensive and defined that the owner of commercial property cannot help but be aware that his property will be subject to periodic inspections undertaken for specific purposes." *Donovan v. Dewey*, 452 U.S., at 600. . . . In addition, in defining how a statute limits the discretion of the inspectors, we have observed that it must be "carefully limited in time, place, and scope." *United States v. Biswell*, [406 U.S. 311, 315 (1972)].

*Burger*, 482 U.S. at 702-03. Applying this test, the *Burger* Court proceeded to uphold the warrantless search of an automobile junkyard, pursuant to a New York statute that required all vehicle dismantlers to be registered and to produce business records upon the request of law enforcement. *Id.* at 703-04.

Analogizing to the facts of *Burger*, the few courts that have addressed the issue have likewise held that the warrantless inspection of marijuana businesses passes constitutional scrutiny. In one case, a Montana court rejected a preemptive Fourth Amendment challenge to a Montana law that authorized "unannounced inspection of registered premises" where providers cultivate and manufacture marijuana. Mont. Code Ann. § 50-46-329 (2015). (The inspection provision was repealed by the 2016 Montana Medical Marijuana Act (I-182).) The court explained:

> . . . In *Burger*, the U.S. Supreme court upheld a New York statute that authorized spontaneous, unannounced inspections of automobile junkyards by law enforcement officers and for the purpose of discovering criminal activities as well as violations of the regulatory statute.
>
> This Court is persuaded by the analysis in *Burger*. There can be little doubt that medical marijuana is a closely regulated activity in Montana. Indeed, it is against these restrictions that [Plaintiff] MCIA has brought its complaint.[10] The fact remains that the possession and use of marijuana remains a crime under federal law and, with the narrow exceptions created by the Montana Marijuana Act, under Montana law. Likewise, in *Burger*, the

---

10. Author's note: Plaintiff MCIA challenged several other restrictions imposed by the state, including a ban on the compensation of providers. The Montana Supreme Court's discussion of those challenges is excerpted in Chapter 9.

Supreme Court noted that criminal behavior, specifically auto theft, often was intertwined with auto junkyards.

Further, the Court in *Burger* noted that the statutory scheme put junkyard operators on notice that they were subject to unannounced searches and who was authorized to conduct the inspections. . . . Section 329 of the Montana provides the same notice and information to providers. It should be noted that such inspections may only be conducted "during normal business hours." § 50-46-329(3)(a), MCA. The *Burger* Court found these types of provisions to be a constitutionally adequate substitute for a warrant. *Id.* Inspections under § 329 conducted by law enforcement officials to uncover and use evidence of criminal behavior, provisions to which [Plaintiff MCIA] objects, were permitted by the Court in *Burger*. Further, the Montana statutes allow the provider to define the registered premises subject to inspection: "the location at which a provider or marijuana-infused products provider has indicated the person will cultivate or manufacture marijuana for a registered cardholder." § 50-46-302(13), MCA. By carefully defining his registered premises, the provider can address concerns that the inspection might be too broad or intrusive.

In summary, the Court can find no principled distinction between the unannounced inspections allowed in *Burger* and the unannounced inspections authorized under Montana's medical marijuana law.

*Montana Cannabis Industry Ass'n v. Montana*, No. DDV-2011-518 (Dist. Ct. Lewis and Clark Cty., 2015), *aff'd by Montana Cannabis Indus. Ass'n v. Montana*, 368 P.3d 1131 (Mont. 2016).

In a second case, a court rejected a similar challenge to a local ordinance that required medical marijuana collectives to keep records of all patients to whom they provide marijuana, and to make those records available to the Los Angeles Police Department upon demand:

> [T]he Ordinance does not violate any right to privacy. To the extent the respondents *as collectives* are asserting their own privacy rights, we find no issue with either the recordkeeping or disclosure requirements of the Ordinance given the heavily regulated area in which the collectives operate. Whether analyzed as creating an unreasonable expectation of privacy or an invasion of a reasonable expectation of privacy justified by a legitimate competing state interest, such entities are subject to greater privacy intrusions than would be allowed in the context of individuals or more ordinary businesses. Insofar as collectives are asserting the privacy rights of their *individual* members or, in the case of [some of the parties], asserting their own *individual* privacy rights, we also find no invasion of privacy, based largely on similar analysis. . . .
>
> Both the federal and state courts have long recognized that "closely regulated" businesses have a reduced expectation of privacy that relaxes the probable cause and warrant requirements ordinarily required for law enforcement searches. . . . This is so, at least in part, because of the strong government interest in regulating such businesses or industries. . . .
>
> Ordinary pharmacies dispensing traditional prescription drugs are closely regulated businesses. . . . Consequently, they are required to maintain records of the type described by the Ordinance and present them to "'authorized officers of the law'" without a warrant. . . . We see no reason to accord marijuana collectives greater privacy with respect to the information at issue here. Marijuana collectives are engaged in the distribution of a substance, illegal under state law except as a basis for the prosecution of specified offenses under the specified conditions set forth in the CUA and the MMPA. Furthermore, marijuana is a schedule I controlled substance still *entirely illegal* under federal law. . . .

The record below supports a finding that a number of so-called medical marijuana collectives are collectives in name only: rather than distribute marijuana to collective members for medical purposes, they instead sell marijuana to third parties for profit. The record also shows that the Los Angeles Police Department is forced to expend scarce resources to combat this criminal activity. Under these circumstances, it would be entirely irrational to accord marijuana collectives—as entities—greater privacy rights than pharmacies involved in the distribution and use of traditional prescription drugs. We find that any expectation of privacy by a collective in the limited, and nonintimate, information sought by the Ordinance to be unreasonable. Alternatively, and based on the same facts described above, we find any invasion of a reasonable expectation of privacy to be justified by a legitimate and competing state interest.

*420 Caregivers, LLC v. City of Los Angeles*, 163 Cal. Rptr. 3d 17 (Cal. App. 2d 2012).

2. Should governments be allowed to inspect and search licensed marijuana suppliers without a warrant or even probable cause to believe that the licensee is violating the law? Why, why not?

3. Based on the foregoing cases, consider the constitutionality of the inspection scheme described in the following Problem:

**Problem 8.17:** California's Proposition 64, passed in 2016, allows adults to cultivate no more than six marijuana plants within a private residence. The initiative bars localities from completely prohibiting such personal cultivation, but it does allow them to "reasonably regulate" it. Cal. Health & Safety Code § 11362.2 (2016). Suppose that the City of Los Angeles, California, adopts a regulation requiring all personal cultivators to register with the City for a nominal fee. The regulation also stipulates that all registered personal cultivation sites are subject to inspection by law enforcement during normal business hours. Does the requirement pass muster under *Burger*? Is it even authorized by Proposition 64?

### b. Disciplinary Process

Beyond investigation, licensing laws also specify the procedures that licensing authorities must use to demonstrate and ultimately sanction licensing violations. The RMC illustrates the steps involved in the disciplinary process:

R 1301 – Disciplinary Process: Non-Summary Suspensions
A. How a Disciplinary Action is Initiated
  1. If the State Licensing Authority, on its own initiative or based on a complaint, has reasonable cause to believe that a Licensee has violated the Retail Code, any rule promulgated pursuant to it, or any of its orders, the State Licensing Authority shall issue and serve upon the Licensee an Order to Show Cause (administrative citation) as to why its license should not be suspended, revoked, restricted, fined, or subject to other disciplinary sanction.
  2. The Order to Show Cause shall identify the statute, rule, regulation, or order allegedly violated, and the facts alleged to constitute the violation. The order shall also provide an advisement that the license could be suspended, revoked, restricted, fined, or

subject to other disciplinary sanction should the charges contained in the notice be sustained upon final hearing.

B. Disciplinary Hearings. Disciplinary hearings will be conducted in accordance with Rule.

R 1304 – Administrative Hearings

A. General Procedures

1. Hearing Location. Hearings will generally be conducted by the Department of Revenue, Hearings Division. Unless the hearing officer orders a change of location based on good cause, as described in this rule, hearings generally will be conducted at a location in the greater Denver metropolitan area to be determined by the hearing officer. Under unusual circumstances where justice, judicial economy and convenience of the parties would be served, hearings may be held in other locations in the state of Colorado.

2. Scope of Hearing Rules. This rule shall be construed to promote the just and efficient determination of all matters presented.

3. Right to Legal Counsel. Any Denied Applicant or Respondent has a right to legal counsel throughout all processes described in rules associated with the denial of an application and disciplinary action. Such counsel shall be provided solely at the Denied Applicant's or Respondent's expense.

B. Requesting a Hearing

1. A Denied Applicant that has been served with a Notice of Denial may request a hearing within 60 days of the service of the Notice of Denial by making a written request for a hearing. . . .

2. A Denied Applicant that timely requests a hearing following issuance of a Notice of Denial shall be served with a Notice of Grounds for Denial, and shall be entitled to a hearing regarding the matters addressed therein.

3. A Respondent that has been served with an Order to Show Cause shall be entitled to a hearing regarding the matters addressed therein.

C. When a Responsive Pleading is Required

1. A Respondent shall file a written answer with the Hearings Division and the Division within 30 days after the date of mailing of any administrative notice or Order to Show Cause. . . . If a Respondent fails to file a required answer, the Hearing Officer, upon motion, may enter a default against that Person. . . .

2. A Denied Applicant shall file a written answer with the Hearings Division and the Division within 30 days after the date of mailing of any administrative notice or Notice of Grounds for Denial. . . . If a Denied Applicant fails to file a required answer, the hearing officer, upon motion, may enter a default against that Person. . . .

D. Hearing Notices

. . .

2. Notice of Hearing. The Hearings Division shall notify the Division and Denied Applicant or Respondent of the date, place, time and nature of the hearing regarding denial of the license application or whether discipline should be imposed against the Respondent's license at least 30 days prior to the date of such hearing, unless otherwise agreed to by both parties. . . .

. . .

F. Conduct of Hearings

. . .

2. The hearing officer may allow a hearing, or any portion of the hearing, to be conducted in real time by telephone or other electronic means. . . .

3. The hearing officer shall administer oaths to all witnesses at hearing. The hearing officer may question any witness.

Part III. Marijuana Suppliers

. . .
    5. Court Rules.
        a. To the extent practicable, the Colorado Rules of Evidence apply. . . . A hearing officer has discretion to consider evidence not admissible under such rules, including but not limited to hearsay evidence. . . .
        b. To the extent practicable, the Colorado Rules of Civil Procedure apply.
    6. Exhibits.
. . .
    7. The hearing officer may proceed with the hearing or enter default judgment if any party fails to appear at hearing after proper notice.

G. Post Hearing. After considering all the evidence, the hearing officer shall determine whether the proponent of the order has proven its case by a preponderance of the evidence, and shall make written findings of evidentiary fact, ultimate conclusions of fact, conclusions of law, and a recommendation. These written findings shall constitute an Initial Decision subject to review by the State Licensing Authority pursuant to the Colorado Administrative Procedure Act and as set forth in Rule R 1306 – Administrative Hearing Appeals/Exceptions to Initial Decision.

R 1305 – Administrative Subpoenas
. . .
B. Hearing Officer May Issue Subpoenas
    1. A party or its counsel may request the hearing officer to issue subpoenas to secure the presence of witnesses or documents necessary for the hearing or a deposition, if one is allowed.
. . .
D. Subpoena Enforcement
. . .
    2. A hearing officer may quash a subpoena if he or she finds on the record that compliance would be unduly burdensome or impracticable, unreasonably expensive, or is unnecessary.

R 1306 – Administrative Hearing Appeals/Exceptions to Initial Decision
A. Exception(s) Process. Any party may appeal an Initial Decision to the State Licensing Authority pursuant to the Colorado Administrative Procedure Act by filing written exception(s) within 30 days after the date of mailing of the Initial Decision to the Denied Applicant or Respondent and the Division. The written exception(s) shall include a statement giving the basis and grounds for the exception(s). Any party who fails to properly file written exception(s) within the time provided in these rules shall be deemed to have waived the right to an appeal. . . .
. . .
    D. No Oral Argument Allowed. Requests for oral argument will not be considered.

1 Colo. Code Reg. 2-212.1301 & .1304-05 (2016).

## Notes and Questions

1. How does the civil administrative process described above differ from the judicial process employed in criminal prosecutions? Does the administrative process adequately safeguard the interests of licensees?

2. Colorado has established a separate procedure for "summary suspension," which applies when the MED "has reasonable grounds to believe and finds that a Licensee has

been guilty of a deliberate and willful violation of any applicable law or regulation or that the public health, safety, or welfare imperatively requires emergency action." *Id.* at 2-212.1302. In these cases, the MED can issue a "Summary Suspension Order" to immediately block the licensee's operations. The licensee can then request an expedited hearing at which to contest the suspension. *Id.*

3. Other states employ similar procedures for the sanctioning of marijuana licensees. *See, e.g.*, Md. Code Reg. 10.62.34.01 *et seq.* (detailing disciplinary process); Wash. Admin. Code §§ 314-55-505–515 (same).

### c. Licensing Sanctions

State licensing laws provide a variety of sanctions for violations of licensing regulations. The sanctions are intended to correspond to the severity of violations and can range anywhere from a simple warning to revocation of the license and disbarment from holding another license for a period of years. (Some violations may also constitute criminal offenses, which must be prosecuted in the criminal justice system.) The following excerpt details the grading of licensing violations under the RMC:

> R 1307 – Penalties
>
> A. Penalty Schedule. The State Licensing Authority will make determinations regarding the type of penalty to impose based on the severity of the violation in the following categories:
>
> 1. License Violations Affecting Public Safety. This category of violation is the most severe and may include, but is not limited to, Retail Marijuana sales to persons under the age of 21 years, consuming marijuana on the Licensed Premises, Retail Marijuana sales in excess of the relevant transaction limit, permitting the diversion of Retail Marijuana outside the regulated distribution system, possessing Retail Marijuana or Retail Marijuana Product obtained from outside the regulated distribution system or from an unauthorized source, making misstatements or omissions in the Inventory Tracking System, failing to continuously escort a visitor in a Limited Access Area, violations related to co-located Medical Marijuana Centers and Retail Marijuana Businesses, failure to maintain books and records to fully account for all transactions of the business, Advertising violations directly targeting minors, or packaging or labeling violations that directly impact consumer safety. Violations of this nature generally have an immediate impact on the health, safety, and welfare of the public at large. The range of penalties for this category of violation may include license suspension, a fine per individual violation, a fine in lieu of suspension of up to $100,000, and/or license revocation depending on the mitigating and aggravating circumstances. Sanctions may also include restrictions on the license.
>
> 2. License Violations. This category of violation is more severe than a license infraction but generally does not have an immediate impact on the health, safety and welfare of the public at large. License violations may include but are not limited to, Advertising and/or marketing violations, packaging or labeling violations that do not directly impact consumer safety, failure to maintain minimum security requirements, failure to keep and maintain adequate business books and records, or minor or clerical errors in the inventory tracking procedures. The range of penalties for this category of violation may include a written warning, license suspension, a fine per individual violation, a fine in lieu of suspension of up to $50,000, and/or license revocation depending on

the mitigating and aggravating circumstances. Sanctions may also include restrictions on the license.

3. License Infractions. This category of violation is the least severe and may include, but is not limited to, failure to display required badges, unauthorized modifications of the Licensed Premises of a minor nature, or failure to notify the State Licensing Authority of a minor change in ownership. The range of penalties for this category of violation may include a verbal or written warning, license suspension, a fine per individual violation, and/or a fine in lieu of suspension of up to $10,000 depending on the mitigating and aggravating circumstances. Sanctions may also include restrictions on the license.

B. Other Factors

1. The State Licensing Authority may take into consideration any aggravating and mitigating factors surrounding the violation which could impact the type or severity of penalty imposed.

2. The penalty structure is a framework providing guidance as to the range of violations, suspension description, fines, and mitigating and aggravating factors. The circumstances surrounding any penalty imposed will be determined on a case-by-case basis.

. . .

C. Mitigating and Aggravating Factors. The State Licensing Authority may consider mitigating and aggravating factors when considering the imposition of a penalty. These factors may include, but are not limited to:

1. Any prior violations that the Licensee has admitted to or was found to have engaged in.

2. Action taken by the Licensee to prevent the violation (e.g., training provided to employees).

3. Licensee's past history of success or failure with compliance checks.

4. Corrective action(s) taken by the Licensee related to the current violation or prior violations.

5. Willfulness and deliberateness of the violation.

6. Likelihood of reoccurrence of the violation.

7. Circumstances surrounding the violation, which may include, but are not limited to:
    a. Prior notification letter to the Licensee that an underage compliance check would be forthcoming.
    b. The dress or appearance of an underage operative used during an underage compliance check (e.g., the operative was wearing a high school letter jacket).

8. Owner or manager is the violator or has directed an employee or other individual to violate the law.

9. Participation in state-approved educational programs related to the operation of a Retail Marijuana Establishment.

R 1303 – Suspension Process: Regular or Summary Suspensions

. . .

B. Prohibited Activity During Active Suspension

1. Unless otherwise ordered by the State Licensing Authority, during any period of active license suspension the Licensee shall not permit the selling, serving, giving away, distribution, manufacture, sampling, acquisition, purchase, transfer, or transport of Retail Marijuana or Retail Marijuana Product on the Licensed Premises, nor allow customers to enter the Licensed Premises.

2. Unless otherwise ordered by the State Licensing Authority, during any period of suspension the Licensee may continue to possess, maintain, cultivate or harvest Retail Marijuana or Retail Marijuana Product on the Licensed Premises. The Licensee must fully

account for all such Retail Marijuana and Retail Marijuana Product in the Inventory Tracking System. . . .

1 Colo. Code Reg. 2-212, .1301 & .1304 (2016).

## Notes and Questions

1. Compare the sanctions authorized for different offenses under the Colorado RMC. From the perspective of a licensee, what is the difference between a license suspension (say, for six months), a fine in lieu of suspension (say, for $50,000), and a revocation of the license?

2. Do the sanctions authorized by the RMC seem proportionate to the gravity of the offenses that trigger them? Are they adequate to deter violations of licensing regulations? Along these lines, consider the following Problem:

Problem 8.18: Return to the facts of **Problem 8.14** (underage purchase) and **Problem 8.16** (advertising) above. Assuming that the MED has found a violation in each case (and ignoring mitigating or aggravating factors), what would be the sanction under the RMC in each case? What sanction should apply?

3. Some states provide more detailed guidance regarding the sanctions to be imposed for specific licensing offenses. Consider Washington state's licensing enforcement system. Like Colorado, Washington sorts licensing offenses into a few discrete categories, called Groups. Wash. Admin. Code § 314-55-515. For each Group, however, Washington provides a detailed table of the specific recommended sanction for each of several specific types of violations, including repeat violations of the same type. *Id.* at §§ 314-55-520–537 (providing sanctioning tables for Groups 1-5). (Like Colorado, Washington allows its licensing authority to deviate from these recommendations based on aggravating or mitigating factors. *Id.* at § 314-55-515(5). **Table 8.2** reprints the guidance provided for just a sample of Group 1 violations against public safety, the most serious violations under Washington law:

Table 8.2. Recommended Sanction for Sample of Group 1 Violations in Washington

| Violation Type | 1st Violation | 2d Viol in 3 years | 3d Viol in 3 years | 4th Viol in 3 years |
|---|---|---|---|---|
| Sale to minor | 10-day suspension or $2,500 fine (if mitigating circumstances) | 30-day suspension | Cancellation of license | NA |
| Allowing minor in store | $1,000 fine | $1,000 fine | $1,000 fine | $1,000 fine |

Part III. Marijuana Suppliers

| Violation Type | 1st Violation | 2d Viol in 3 years | 3d Viol in 3 years | 4th Viol in 3 years |
|---|---|---|---|---|
| Purchased marijuana from unauthorized source | Cancellation of license | NA | NA | NA |
| Sale in excess of transaction limits | 10-day suspension or $2,500 fine (if mitigating circumstances) | 30-day suspension | Cancellation of license | NA |
| Opening or consuming marijuana in store | $1,000 fine | $1,000 fine | $1,000 fine | $1,000 fine |

Should licensing authorities have more discretion to determine the sanction (as in Colorado) or less discretion (as in Washington)? Why?

4. What sanctions has the Colorado MED actually imposed? The MED issues an annual report to the state legislature, summarizing its enforcement actions against licensees during the prior year. In calendar year 2015, the MED suspended 17 medical and retail establishment licenses owned by 4 businesses. All of those licenses were eventually revoked, following disciplinary processes that lasted three to six months. In total, the MED also levied nearly $700,000 in fines against an additional 30 businesses holding 66 establishment licenses. The fines imposed on individual businesses ranged from $5,000 to $150,000. See Marijuana Enforcement Division, *Report to the General Assembly Re: Fines, Suspensions and Revocations*, Jan. 15, 2016, https://perma.cc/8N4U-LYE5. The McAllister Law Office has compiled additional details on many of these enforcement actions. It reports that the most common violations pursued by the MED involved tracking and recordkeeping requirements, video monitoring requirements, and underage compliance checks. See McAllister Law Office, P.C., *Summary of MED Disciplinary Actions for 2015*, https://www.newcannabisventures.com/wp-content/uploads/McAllister-Summary-of-Colorado-MED-Disciplinary-Actions-for-2015.pdf. For a similar discussion of enforcement actions taken by Washington state against its marijuana licensees, see Northwest High Intensity Drug Trafficking Area, *Washington State Marijuana Impact Report* 48-53 (2016), https://perma.cc/MQN7-VA8D.

## C. GOVERNMENT SUPPLY

A large majority of reform states now authorize either personal supply, commercial supply, or some combination of the two (more on that below). But there is one more option states could consider: *government* supply. Under this third option, the state itself would produce and/or distribute marijuana directly, similar to the way some states now distribute alcohol through state-owned- and operated- liquor stores. The key difference between government supply and commercial supply is that in the former model, the licensee is a *state* actor rather than a *private* one.

As of 2016, no state has yet participated directly in the cultivation or distribution of marijuana (at least outside the context of federally approved research trials).[11] The reluctance is due to concerns over the liability of state employees, the possible loss of federal grant funding, and federal preemption. (Those concerns are discussed in Chapter 14.)

Nonetheless, at least one *local* government is giving the government-supply model a try. In 2013, the City of North Bonneville, Washington, created a Public Development Authority (PDA) to control "the retail sales of marijuana products" in its county. City of North Bonneville, Ordinance Number 1028, Nov. 8, 2013, https://perma.cc/LL6J-BCYF. The PDA subsequently applied for and received a Marijuana Retailer license from the state of Washington, and in March 2015, it opened the Cannabis Corner, which claims to be the "first government-owned and operated marijuana retailer in the country." The Cannabis Corner, *Welcome!*, http://thecannabiscorner.org/?age-verified=676e23c6a9.

## Notes and Questions

1. For more details on the creation of the North Bonneville PDA, see Bill Kilby, *The Story Behind America's First Government-Run Weed Shop*, Vice (Mar. 12, 2015), http://www.vice.com/read/the-story-behind-americas-first-government-run-weed-shop-311. For more background on Washington law governing the creation and operation of public corporations like the North Bonneville PDA, see *Mount Spokane Skiing Corp. v. Spokane Cnty.*, 936 P.2d 1148 (1997) (upholding creation of PDA to operate a local ski slope); Municipal Research and Services Center, *Public Corporations/Public Development Authorities* (PDA) (2016), https://perma.cc/U3W8-PJDQ; and Jay Reich et al., *Public Development Authorities* (2003), https://perma.cc/RVS9-HGLX.

2. Louisiana has recently authorized two public universities (Louisiana State University and Southern University) to produce marijuana for the state's nascent medical marijuana program—thus priming itself to become the first state government to supply marijuana directly to users outside of research trials. LSU has drafted a proposal for the establishment and operation of a cultivation and distribution facility. *See* LSU AgCenter, *Project Concept for the Alison Neustrom Act* (undated), https://perma.cc/92JX-NMZM. Chapter 14 discusses the concerns such a proposal would raise under the Drug Free Schools and Communities Act of 1989. If neither LSU nor Southern University follow through, the state would license private commercial suppliers instead.

---

11. As noted in Chapter 5, the University of Mississippi currently supplies the marijuana that is used in federally approved research trials.

Part III. Marijuana Suppliers

## D. SUMMARY

To summarize, most reform states have authorized two basic means to supply the demands of consumers: personal and commercial. The two are not mutually exclusive, and many states have authorized both. It is also important to note, however, that at present, at least eight CBD states have not explicitly authorized anyone to supply marijuana to individuals who are allowed by state law to possess and use the drug.

Including CBD states that have not yet authorized any source of supply, but ignoring yet-to-be implemented government sources of supply, reform states have pursued five distinct approaches toward supplying legal marijuana:

(1) Personal only: Under state law, the only way for users to obtain marijuana lawfully is to produce it themselves (or with the help of a caregiver);
(2) Commercial only: Under state law, the only way for users to obtain marijuana lawfully is to buy it from a licensed commercial supplier;
(3) Commercial preferred: Under state law, users may buy marijuana from a licensed commercial supplier, but only some may produce it themselves;
(4) Mixed: Under state law, users may choose to buy from a licensed commercial supplier, produce it themselves, or both; or
(5) None: Under state law, users have no lawful way to obtain marijuana

**Figure 8.9** shows the the popularity of each approach under state medical, recreational, and CBD laws:

Figure 8.9. State Approaches to Supply (2016)

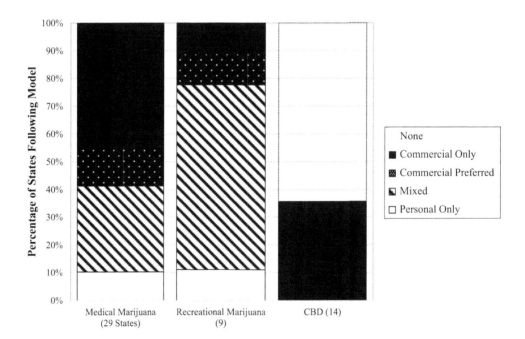

## Notes and Questions

1. How is someone who is allowed to possess and use marijuana supposed to obtain the drug in the first instance if the state has not authorized anyone to produce or distribute it (as in some CBD states)? The following Problem raises the issue:

**Problem 8.19:** State law bans the possession, use, manufacture, and distribution of marijuana, which it defines to include CBD. Recently, the state authorized qualifying patients to *possess and use* CBD; however, it has not yet authorized anyone to manufacture or distribute the drug. Andy is a qualifying patient who wants to use CBD. What options does he have to obtain the drug? What are the legal risks involved with each option?

2. A similar issue arises even in states that authorize users to produce their own marijuana, as the following Problem illustrates:

**Problem 8.20:** State law bans the possession, use, manufacture, and distribution of marijuana. The state has just legalized the possession, use, and manufacture of marijuana by qualifying patients to treat their own qualifying medical conditions. Andy is a qualifying patient who wants to use marijuana. Even though state law allows him to cultivate marijuana plants (i.e., it is a personal supply state), is there any legal way for him to *acquire* the plants (or germinating seeds) in the first instance? See Colorado v. Clendenin, 232 P.3d 210, 217 (Colo. App. 2009) (Loeb, J., concurring) ("[T]the reality that a qualifying patient . . . must somehow engage in an initial transaction to acquire the marijuana from some other person who is not protected from criminal prosecution. . . ."); *People ex rel. Lungren v. Peron*, 70 Cal. Rptr. 2d 20, 32 (Ct. App. 1997) (Kline, J., concurring) ("[A] person cannot . . . cultivate marijuana without first obtaining seeds, and the majority does not suggest how this may legally be accomplished.").

3. The mix of supply models depicted by **Figure 8.9** is far from static. Individual jurisdictions have shifted approaches to supply over time, and the overall popularity of each of the approaches outlined above has shifted (considerably) over time as well—both arguably in response to changing federal enforcement policies, as discussed in Chapter 10.

# CHAPTER 9

# Policy Toward Marijuana Suppliers

Chapter 5 identified two broad objectives animating marijuana policy:

(1) to curb harmful uses of marijuana while enabling beneficial ones (however such uses might be defined), and
(2) to do so at the lowest cost to the public fisc and individual rights and liberties.

The chapter also examined how well the different laws governing marijuana users serve those objectives.

In a similar fashion, this chapter examines how well the laws governing *marijuana suppliers* serve the same objectives. Do the strict prohibitions on manufacture and distribution surveyed in Chapter 7 curb marijuana use? Do the regulatory reforms surveyed in Chapter 8 provide adequate supply for approved uses of marijuana without also furnishing unapproved ones? What is the fiscal impact of state reforms? Have reforms lessened the racial disparities that have arisen under prohibitions, or have they simply recreated those disparities in a new setting?

This chapter explores these and related questions. In so doing, it does not aim to persuade the reader that any particular approach to regulating the supply of marijuana is necessarily superior to any other. Rather, this chapter is designed to enable the reader to better understand the benefits and drawbacks of the regulatory options now being debated and tested by policymakers, and thus, to make more informed judgments about the wisdom and feasibility of each.[1]

## A. HOW DOES THE REGULATION OF SUPPLY IMPACT USE?

Regulations directed at suppliers are designed in large part to curb the use of marijuana—either all use, as in prohibition regimes, or just those uses that a jurisdiction considers harmful, such as recreational use by minors. Section A.1 explores how prohibitions directed at suppliers are supposed to curb consumption by users. It also discusses the likely impact these prohibitions have on consumption. Section A.2 shifts the focus to legalization regimes. It examines how these regimes have sought to enable suppliers to

---

1. The reader, of course, may wish to explore these issues further. There is an already large and ever-growing body of literature analyzing marijuana policy. This chapter references and excerpts some of that literature. For readers interested in a more thorough introduction to the policy issues surrounding marijuana, I highly recommend Jonathan Caulkins et al., Marijuana Legalization: What Everyone Needs to Know (Oxford Univ. Press 2016), portions of which are excerpted in this chapter.

furnish beneficial uses of marijuana, while simultaneously preventing them from supplying ones the regimes still consider harmful.

## 1. Supply Prohibitions and Marijuana Consumption

### a. Prohibition, Prices, and Consumption

Supply prohibitions affect consumption primarily by raising the price that suppliers charge for marijuana. In a nutshell, prohibitions impose various costs on suppliers (detailed below). Suppliers, in turn, seek to pass these costs on to users in the prices they charge for marijuana. As long as users are responsive to prices—i.e., as long as demand for marijuana is elastic (a topic discussed in Chapter 5), users will purchase less marijuana when the prices charged by suppliers go up.

To simplify somewhat, the costs incurred by market suppliers under prohibition fall into one of three broad categories:

(1) risk premiums;
(2) avoidance costs; and
(3) third-party costs

The pargaraphs below elaborate upon each of these costs, but for a more detailed discussion of them, see Peter Reuter & Mark A.R. Kleiman, *Risks and Prices: An Economic Analysis of Drug Enforcement*, 7 Crime & Justice 289 (1986).

The first type of cost stems from the legal risks suppliers face for manufacturing and distributing marijuana. Marijuana suppliers demand a risk premium for shouldering this risk, the same way that other occupations demand extra compensation (e.g., hazard pay) for bearing risks (like working in a dangerous part of the world). The size of the risk premium depends on the expected legal sanction for producing or distributing marijuana, e.g., the probability that a supplier will be caught and punished multiplied by the magnitude of the sanction that would be imposed. The higher this expected sanction is, the larger will be the risk premium added to a supplier's price.

The second type of cost stems from the tactics suppliers employ to avoid the aforementioned legal risks. Some of these tactics involve expenditures on goods or services, as, for example, when a supplier pays someone to install a hidden storage compartment in a car to conceal marijuana shipments from law enforcement. Other tactics entail engaging in relatively inefficient business practices, for example, growing marijuana plants indoors, using expensive artificial lighting, rather than outdoors, which is cheaper but also more apt to be detected. To be sure, incurring these avoidance costs should reduce the legal risks associated with manufacturing and distributing marijuana. But because no avoidance tactic is foolproof—i.e., the expected legal sanction for manufacturing and distributing marijuana is never *zero*, the prices suppliers charge for marijuana will commonly reflect a mix of both avoidance costs and risk premiums.

The final type of cost arises from prohibitions that are directed at third parties who might as a result refuse to deal with marijuana suppliers or else charge a premium for doing business with them. (All of these third-party prohibitions are discussed in more detail in Chapters 11-13.) For example, federal law prohibits financial institutions from providing banking services to marijuana suppliers. Among other things, this means that marijuana suppliers (even state-licensed ones) generally cannot utilize electronic payment systems and must instead conduct all of their transactions in cash—a less convenient and more dangerous alternative.

Even if banks and other third parties are willing to flout such prohibitions, they will generally charge a premium for shouldering the legal risks involved for so doing—just like marijuana suppliers charge a premium to their customers for flouting prohibitions on the manufacture and distribution of marijuana. For example, an investor who loans money to a marijuana supplier may demand an above-market rate of interest on the loan to compensate for the fact that the loan agreement may prove unenforceable in court (as discussed in Chapter 13).

These costs accumulate throughout the supply chain. That is, marijuana growers, wholesalers, and retailers each incur these costs and add them to the price they charge for marijuana. All of these costs add up and ultimately raise the price paid by consumers.

The supply and demand curves introduced in Chapter 5 helps to illustrate the impact supply prohibitions have on price and consumption. **Figure 9.1** again depicts a purely hypothetical market for marijuana. To focus attention on supply, however, only a single demand curve is pictured; it is identical to the prohibition demand curve from **Figure 5.3** in Chapter 5. As before, demand is assumed to be elastic, meaning that less marijuana will be purchased by users the higher the price that is charged by suppliers.

Figure 9.1. Hypothetical Supply and Demand Curves for Marijuana

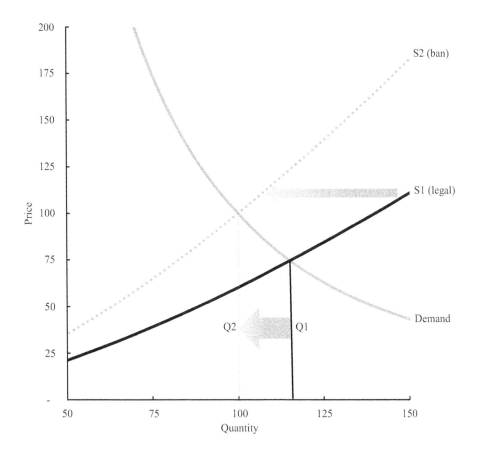

485

Unlike **Figure 5.3**, which included only one supply curve, **Figure 9.1** includes two possible supply curves (S1 and S2). These curves depict the total quantity of marijuana (x-axis) that all suppliers in society would *sell* at different market prices (y-axis) under two different legal regimes: S1 models a regime in which the production and distribution of marijuana are legal and unregulated—i.e., there are no legal restrictions or sanctions imposed on these activities; and S2 models a regime in which the production and distribution of marijuana (among other activities) are *prohibited*, and there is an expected legal sanction (S * p) associated with violating these prohibitions. The graph places S2 above S1, reflecting the theory that prohibitions impose costs on suppliers and suppliers seek to pass those costs on to consumers in the prices they charge for marijuana.

The point at which each supply curve intersects the demand curve indicates the total quantity of marijuana that is consumed under each legal regime. In **Figure 9.1**, the total quantity consumed is less under prohibition (Q2) than under legalization (Q1), suggesting that regulations directed at marijuana suppliers can suppress marijuana use.

## Notes and Questions

1. The *price elasticity of supply* is the technical phrase economists use to describe how much the supply of marijuana changes in response to changes in the price of the drug. It is calculated as *(% change in quantity supplied)/(% change in price)*. The slope of the supply curve in **Figure 9.1** reflects a hypothetical price elasticity of 0.67. In other words, the supply of marijuana would increase about 6.7 percent in response to a 10 percent increase in the price of the drug. This suggests that suppliers demand a relatively large increase in compensation for increasing their production or distribution and hence, their exposure to the costs discussed in the text above. The precise figure used here is largely conjecture—even less is known about the price elasticity of supply for marijuana than is known about the price elasticity of demand. Nonetheless, the reader can easily posit supply curves with other characteristics and explore the policy ramifications thereof.

2. Supply regulations can affect marijuana use in other ways as well, i.e., not just by raising the market price of the drug. Most notably, prohibitions and other regulations on supply restrict the availability of marijuana. As discussed in Chapter 5, this adds to the *effective* price borne by consumers, e.g., because it forces consumers to spend more time and effort searching for suppliers. For an interesting study examining the relationship between marijuana consumption and proximity to medical marijuana dispensaries, see Bridget Freisthler & Paul J. Gruenewald, *Examining the Relationship Between the Physical Availability of Medical Marijuana and Marijuana Use Across Fifty California Cities*, 143 Drug and Alcohol Dependence 244, 248 (2014) (finding positive relationship between proximity to medical marijuana dispensaries and/or delivery services and marijuana use).

### b. The Magnitude of Prohibition's Impact on Price and Consumption

The prohibitions discussed in Chapters 7 and 11-13 arguably impose substantial costs on marijuana suppliers. But just how big of an impact do these prohibitions have on the price and consumption of marijuana? One way to answer that question is by estimating what the price of marijuana would be in an unregulated market—a task undertaken in the following excerpt.

## *Jonathan Caulkins, Beau Kilmer, and Mark A.R. Kleiman,* **Marijuana Legalization: What Everyone Needs to Know**
(Oxford University Press 2016)

Since no industrialized nation in the modern era has yet implemented large-scale commercial production nationally, there are no solid historical analogies one can draw on to estimate what production costs or prices would be under those conditions. Instead, one has to work through the numbers, the same way a farmer would when considering the possibility of growing any other new crop.

Thinking about the problem that way suggests that legalization might dramatically reduce production costs in the long run. The size of the potential decline is not widely appreciated.

Herbal marijuana is just dried plant material. A joint has about as much of that plant material as a teabag. Yet the marijuana in a joint currently costs ten to one hundred times as much as a comparable amount of tea sold as a box of teabags in a supermarket. That is primarily because prohibition has forced producers to operate in inefficient ways, not because of any intrinsic difficulties with growing the cannabis plant.

. . .

Sinsemilla prices in the United States have already fallen as policies have liberalized in California, prices have fallen (on an inflation-adjusted basis) from well over five thousand dollars per pound to the producer (what is called the "farm gate price") in the mid-to late 1990s to roughly two thousand per pound in 2010. Since then pound prices have been falling by roughly 10-15 percent a year retail prices have also fallen, but not as quickly.

Those prices are still greatly inflated by the fact that marijuana growing is illegal (or, in California, quasi-legal). The United Nations reports that wholesale prices of commercial grade marijuana in Mexico are just $80 per pound, and prices of $30-$50 per pound are reported anecdotally. Granted, that is typically an inferior product with perhaps one-third the THC of California-grown Sinsemilla, but the price per unit of THC is still just one-tenth that of the California product at wholesale.

Another sign of the effects of prohibition is that the price of that pound jumps from $80 to $400 on the US side of the border. And wholesale prices within the United States increase by an additional roughly $400 per pound per thousand miles as one moves north and east, e.g., to $800 per pound in cities one thousand miles from the border. Needless to say, trucking Mexican cucumbers costs much less. (As this was written, the USDA was quoting the truckload prices for transporting Mexican produce to northern US cities that worked out to almost exactly 4 cents per pound per thousand miles, or one ten-thousandth the cost gradient of marijuana under the prohibition.)

The key question is how cheaply professional farmers in the United States could produce THC after legalization, when the threat of enforcement is even lower than it is now in Mexico.

Agricultural experiments show that outdoor farming can achieve yields of two to three thousand pounds of (dry) usable marijuana per acre per year, with roughly six hundred pounds of that being flowers and the rest leaves and the other lower-qualities material that could be used to produce extracts.

In the United States marijuana is often grown from transplanted cuttings rather than seeds. Production costs for transplanted crops, such as cherry tomatoes and asparagus, are generally in the range of $5,000-$20,000 per acre. This suggests production costs for outdoor growing might be under $20 per pound for the flowers ($10,000 per acre divided by six hundred pounds per acre). The two thousand or so additional pounds of lower quality material might in total contain nearly as much THC suitable for extraction as for the six hundred pounds of flowers, with the lower potency being offset by the greater mass. So, on a "bud-equivalent" basis the cost per pound might fall further, perhaps to around $10, as compared to the current figure of more than $1,000.

. . .

Under conditions of illegality, marijuana processing—manicuring, drying, curing, resin production, etc.—is as burdensome as growing. However, legalization, and the consequent mechanization, could change this dramatically; tobacco costs less than a dollar a pound to receive, grade, stem, and cure.

So in the long run, after the industry has had time to mature, achieve economies of scale, and figure out ways to mechanize steps that are now done by hand, we could see production costs under national legalization as low as $10 or $20 per pound of flowers, or the equivalent of that in terms of THC content. . . .

Production costs anywhere near these figures could upend the traditional industry structure. Since a competitive market tends to drive prices down toward costs, the effect on patterns of use could be profound. The typical marijuana user who consumes once a week and so uses about an ounce a year isn't spending enough even at today's prices for price to matter much. But the heavy daily users who dominate consumption now spend a few thousand dollars per year each. In the long run, after national legalization, it might cost as little as $25 to produce that amount of intoxicant.

Legal marijuana could become far and away the cheapest intoxicant on a per-hour basis. At current supermarket beer prices, getting drunk costs something like $5-$10—call it a dollar or two per drunken hour. The price of marijuana intoxication today is roughly comparable. But unless regulators impose very heavy taxes or prices floors, commercial legalization at the national level might allow a user to buy an hour's marijuana intoxication for dimes rather than dollars. It's hard to imagine that such a dramatic price drop wouldn't affect patterns of use. (A market in very cheap generic marijuana could co-exist with a higher-priced market for artisanal products.)

## Notes and Questions

1. Are you convinced by Caulkins et al.'s analysis and estimates? If prohibition has increased the price of marijuana by 20 to 100 times what it would be in a laissez-faire market, why does the drug remain so popular? After all, roughly 20 million people were regularly using marijuana even before states started relaxing their own prohibitions. Does the excerpt suggest an answer?

2. What are the implications of Caulkins et al.'s analysis for marijuana policy? In particular, are supply prohibitions an effective means of curbing marijuana use? Could prohibition regimes inflate the price of marijuana any more than they already have? *See* Reuter & Kleiman, *Risks and Prices, supra*, at 291 (concluding that the size and fragmented nature of the marijuana market make it difficult for governments to increase supplier costs any further).

3. Ultimately, how much of an impact would full legalization have on marijuana use?

## 2. Legalized Supply and Marijuana Use

Although many states have repealed their own strict prohibitions on marijuana supply activities, none of them has yet sought to (or even could) create the laissez faire marijuana market that Caulkins et al. posit in the excerpt above. Indeed, the manufacture and distribution of marijuana remain heavily regulated activities, even in states that have legalized them. Further, like the prohibitions discussed above, these regulations impose costs on suppliers that are ultimately passed down to consumers in the form of higher prices for marijuana.

In legalization regimes, however, the goal of supply regulations is not to curb marijuana use indiscriminately. After all, for reasons discussed in Chapter 5, these regimes do not disapprove of all marijuana use. Instead, the regulations they have adopted are designed to prevent suppliers from furnishing uses of marijuana these regimes still consider to be *harmful*, including:

(1) use for non-medical purposes (in medical marijuana states)
(2) non-medical use by minors (all states)
(3) use that impairs safety, such as use before driving (all states)
(4) use by addicts (all states)

So how well do these regulations perform? Alas, the jury is still out—and it may be out for some time to come. As one prominent group of scholars has soberingly remarked, "[t]here are now enough contradictory published findings that advocates on any side can weave whatever story they wish to tell." Caulkins et al., What Everyone Needs to Know, *supra*, at 212. At least part of the reason for the contradictory findings stems from the fact that regulations vary considerably from state to state, as discussed in Chapter 8, making it very difficult to draw valid comparisons across jurisdictions. See, *e.g.*, Rosalie L. Pacula et al., *Assessing the Effects of Medical Marijuana Laws on Marijuana Use; The Devil is in the Details*, 34 J. Policy Analysis & Management 7 (2015) (suggesting that failures to account for differences in state laws could explain why studies reach different conclusions regarding the impact marijuana reforms have had on use and other policy outcomes).

Because making broad brush comparisons between legalization and prohibition can be misleading, this section focuses on the potential impact of four discrete measures reform states have adopted: (1) marijuana taxes; (2) product packaging and labeling requirements; (3) marijuana advertising restrictions; and (4) regulations affecting the structure of the marijuana industry.

### a. Marijuana Taxes

Imposing a tax on marijuana is commonly touted as way to boost government revenues, as discussed in Section B.1 below. But a tax can also serve a *regulatory* function. In particular, a tax can be used to increase the effective price of marijuana and thereby to curb use of the drug. See Robert A. Mikos, *State Taxation of Marijuana Distribution and Other Federal Crimes*, 2010 U. Chi. Legal Forum 222, 226-27 (noting that a tax could "force marijuana users to internalize some of the societal costs of drug use: the accidents, crimes, and emergency-room visits that (arguably) stem from marijuana use" but that are not otherwise reflected in the price of the drug).

Part III. Marijuana Suppliers

Table 9.1: Comparison of Marijuana Taxes Across Three States in 2016*

| | Colorado | | Washington | | California | |
|---|---|---|---|---|---|---|
| | Medical | Recreational | Medical | Recreational | Medical | Recreational |
| **Nominal Tax Rate (%)** | | | | | | |
| @ Wholesale** | NA | 15% | NA | NA | $9.25/oz. | $9.25 |
| @ Retail*** | 2.9% | 12.9% | 37% | 43.5% | 15% | 22.5% |
| **Tax Paid ($)****** | | | | | | |
| @ Wholesale | NA | $15 | NA | NA | $9.25 | $9.25 |
| @ Retail | $5.80 | $27.30 | $74.00 | $87.00 | $31.39 | $47.08 |
| Total Tax Paid | $5.80 | $42.30 | $74.00 | $87.00 | $40.64 | $56.33 |
| Net Price to Consumer | $205.80 | $242.30 | $274.00 | $287.00 | $240.64 | $256.33 |
| **Effective Tax Rate** | **2.9%** | **21.1%** | **37.0%** | **43.5%** | **20.3%** | **28.2%** |

\* Sources: Colorado Department of Revenue, Marijuana Taxes—File, https://perma.cc/KN6N-SMUV; Washington State Department of Revenue, Taxes due on marijuana, http://dor.wa.gov/Content/FindTaxesAndRates/marijuana/Default.aspx; California State Board of Equalization, Tax Guide for Medical Cannabis Businesses, https://perma.cc/4PEE-ED22 (also detailing taxes imposed on recreational marijuana).
\*\* Washington state does impose a business and occupation (B&O) tax on the gross revenue of all businesses, including marijuana producers and distributors. But because the tax rate is generally low (less than 0.5 percent), it is excluded here.
\*\*\* The retail tax rate includes special taxes imposed on marijuana distribution (if any) as well as the state sales tax (if applicable).
\*\*\*\* The Tax Paid is calculated using a wholesale price of $100 per ounce for bud and a retail markup of $100 on top of the wholesale price and any wholesale taxes paid. Colorado uses an "average market rate" to calculate its wholesale (excise) tax. In 2016, the rate was about $92 per ounce for bud. To enable comparisons, however, I used the same wholesale price across all jurisdictions ($100).

All jurisdictions that have authorized commercial supply of marijuana impose taxes on commercial marijuana transactions. **Table 9.1** details the taxes imposed by three prominent legalization regimes.

The table illustrates the different ways that states tax marijuana. For example, Colorado and California tax marijuana at both the wholesale and retail level, whereas Washington state taxes marijuana only at the retail level. The table also highlights variations in the effective tax rates both across and within states (not even accounting for local taxes).[2] In Colorado, a medical marijuana user pays only a 2.9 percent effective tax on her purchase, whereas the recreational marijuana user pays a 21.1 percent effective tax for the same bud. The latter rate is still lower than the one paid by a medical user in Washington (37.0 percent) and lower still than the rate paid by a recreational user in that state (43.5 percent).

## Notes and Questions

1. For helpful surveys of state marijuana taxes, see Joseph Henchman & Morgan Scarboro, Tax Foundation, *Marijuana Legalization and Taxes: Lessons for Other States from Colorado and Washington*, May 12, 2016, https://taxfoundation.org/marijuana-taxes-lessons-colorado-washington/; Jeremy M. Vaida, *The Altered State of American Drug Taxes*, 68 Tax Law. 761 (2015).

*(i) Designing a Tax*

To discourage only *harmful* use of the drug, a marijuana tax ideally would be tailored for the use to which it would be put. But is there any realistic way to design a tax to correspond to the harm imposed by the drug's use? The report below addresses this question by considering *what*, exactly a jurisdiction might tax (i.e., the *tax base*). The report was prepared by a notable group of researchers at the behest of the Vermont legislature, which was considering a proposal to legalize recreational marijuana.

## *Jonathan P. Caulkins et al.*, Considering Marijuana Legalization: Insights for Vermont and Other Jurisdictions
(RAND 2015)

### SIMPLE WEIGHT BASE

Vermont and the federal government tax cigarettes and many other tobacco products by weight, and [a proposal] would have taxed marijuana at $50 per ounce [in Vermont]. . . .

A weight base is easier to set up and to administer than a potency base but harder than a price base, especially because moisture must be accounted for. . . . However, taxing based on weight creates an incentive to pack the most intoxicating material into each gram, which could be dangerous. Only an extremely low rate, like the low federal per-

---

2. The effective tax rate is the sum of all of the taxes paid on one ounce of bud at the wholesale and retail levels, divided by the sum of the wholesale price of the same bud (here, assumed to be $100) and the retail markup (again, $100).

gallon tax on beer, tames the incentive. . . . A weight base, incidentally, pushes industry away from mass production, toward organic, artisanal, and other high-value-added products. That is because luxurious or fancy products do not bear more tax.

### PRICE (AD VALOREM) BASE

Vermont taxes chewing tobacco and certain other noncigarette tobacco products ad valorem, literally, according to value, at 92 percent of wholesale price. Vermont taxes liquor with an ad valorem retail excise tax; that is in addition to a 6-percent sales tax and monopoly profits.

In Colorado, voters approved two ad valorem taxes on marijuana . . . : A 10-percent tax on retailers . . . [and] a 15-percent tax on producers . . . Across the nation, many localities have enacted price-based taxes on medical marijuana.

If consumers pay more for powerful products, taxing price is a little like taxing potency. But high price might not always mean high potency. Price could also be high because consumers like the blend of cannabinoids or the look, smell, feel, and taste of the product; because of marketing factors, such as branding, and convenience and ambience of retail location; or for other reasons.

A price-based tax has some advantages. First, an ad valorem base is simple; it does not require indexing or equipment. Weight or potency bases would take more time to set up. Second, a price base tempers regressivity. Taxes on prices of products other than luxuries tend to be regressive: They take a higher percentage of income from poor people than from rich people. Price-based taxes tend to favor low-priced products and could therefore benefit scrimping purchasers, who might tend to be relatively poor.

But an ad valorem tax has disadvantages. The most serious one is that an ad valorem tax base amplifies changes in pretax prices automatically. Here is why that is a problem: At first, as the legal industry struggles to gear up, supply cannot meet demand, so pretax prices could be abnormally high early on. (That is what happened in Colorado and Washington.) A price-based tax amplifies those high pretax prices and makes early after-tax prices much too high. So bootleggers benefit. . . .

But as time goes on, as legal operators learn and become efficient, and as they expand and achieve economies of scale, their costs can drop dramatically. If they pass cost savings on to consumers, pretax prices decline, and a price-based tax automatically declines with them. As after-tax prices drop, the dangers of youth use, abuse, and leakage to other states grow. So a price base then can lead to taxes that are too low, which could be a problem for a maturing marijuana industry.

Another problem with a price base is that taxpayers might manipulate or game it. Two ploys available with a price base are bundling marijuana with other products and related-party (and intracompany) transfers. Bundled sales charge one (undifferentiated) price for two items with different tax rates. The tax problem arises if taxable marijuana is given away, or bundled, with excise-tax-free purchases. So where the consumer buys an untaxed pipe or pays an untaxed cover charge and gets free marijuana, a price-based tax would be hard to calculate. Vermont already has detailed antibundling rules for some taxes . . . , and a price tax base for marijuana could require more. But antibundling rules do not prevent disputes about valuations and thresholds. There is a way to protect a price-based tax from bundling: by allowing marijuana sellers to sell only marijuana. Then there is nothing with which to bundle.

Phony transfer prices turn up between related parties, who can charge one another any price they want. Naturally enough, the price they want is the one that results in the least tax. So a price-based tax depends on the existence of a real price—normally, on an arm's-length sale between unrelated parties.

. . .

The problem arises when [a] cultivation facility does not sell marijuana to anyone and transfers it only to itself. That is standard in Colorado, where, most of the time, marijuana is not "sold or transferred" before retail. That is because Colorado once required all marijuana businesses to be vertically integrated. Vertical integration means that only one company handles marijuana from farm to market—all the way from seedling to retail sale, with no sellers in between. Vertically integrated companies still dominate the market in Colorado—with no sale from a producer to a manufacturer or retailer. So there is no market-based or arm's-length price to tax at 15 percent. There is no sale of any kind, not even a related-party sale, just an intracompany transfer.

So Colorado had to alter tactics and tax not a price, but "fifteen percent of the average market rate" (AMR) of a producer's marijuana. . . . That rate is supposed to reflect the value of marijuana as it leaves the producer's hands. . . . The Colorado Department of Revenue (CDOR) is in charge of finding that AMR. For 2014, it found the AMR of bud, the potent flower of the plant, to be $1,876 per pound, so it imposed on bud a tax of $281.40 per pound. . . .

. . .

A potential final drawback of an ad valorem tax might be the perception that it is excessive. In Europe, for instance, various tobacco taxes often combine to take more than 80 percent of the after-tax price that consumers pay. . . . Stating that high a burden as a percentage of pretax price would show a rate of more than 400 percent.

. . .

### ACTUAL TETRAHYDROCANNABINOL POTENCY BASE

There are precedents for taxing alcohol as a function of potency (e.g., federal tax on liquor depends on alcohol content[]). . . . We are not aware of any jurisdiction that has levied a THC tax on marijuana. . . .

To clarify, a THC base might work this way: Say 10 g of marijuana were tested and determined to contain 12 percent THC content by weight. Then the THC potency base would be 1.2 g.

A THC base, or potency base, could correlate with intoxication better than any other base. Thus, taxing actual THC or potency has an important policy advantage if it can be made to work, but it does pose some important implementation challenges. We consider a THC or potency base for two very different marijuana products: concentrates and raw, usable marijuana.

#### Tetrahydrocannabinol Base for Concentrates

We can tax distilled spirits based on alcohol content because they are homogeneous liquids that can be stirred and mixed thoroughly, so one needs to extract and test only one sample taken from any corner of a well-mixed vat. Marijuana concentrates, such as oil, wax, or shatter (wax hardened to a glasslike state), are products made from raw marijuana and used in various forms, such as edibles (cookies, cooking oil), electronic-joint cartridges, tinctures, sublinguals, and dabs (an intensely powerful vapor material). Raw marijuana made into concentrates is something like wine distilled into brandy, an intoxicant made stronger. But concentrates are not simply stronger marijuana: Concentration changes the form of the intoxicant. The production of concentrates could involve a stage when material is homogeneous enough for replicable testing, but resources will need to be devoted to develop and validate testing procedures.

### Tetrahydrocannabinol Base for Plant Matter

Raw, usable marijuana—that is, dry plant matter—is far from homogeneous. Indeed, THC content can vary from bud to bud within a single plant, and powerful trichomes make material even from a single bud heterogeneous. Thus, the threshold issue for a potency tax base is whether it can provide replicable, auditable results, close enough for the government work of honest taxation. If the tax base can be gamed, some taxpayers will try to beat it, and the state will try to stop them—all at a cost, possibly a significant cost. To be clear, potency testing is already at work, informing and even warning consumers about products they are buying. For consumers, ballpark numbers are helpful and usually adequate. For taxation, though, ballpark numbers are problematic.

. . .

Setting up the world's first tax-worthy THC-testing regime would require significant planning and resources. . . .

At first, the cost of testing might be passed on to consumers, to the benefit of the black market. As the legal market takes market share, the black market will become less worrisome. When the black market is so marginalized that the legal market can bear high prices, the cost of testing could be more acceptable. Time is the friend of a potency base. Regulators might implement a particular potency base once they have time to set up a workable system. . . . In the meantime, tax could be imposed on some other base.

## Notes and Questions

1. Could you design a tax that curbs any of the harmful uses of marijuana listed at the start of Section A.2—and *only* those uses? How would you do so? What tax base would you employ? What tax rate would you impose?

2. As **Table 9.1** demonstrates, states commonly exempt *medical* users from paying at least part of the tax they impose on marijuana. Should medical marijuana be exempt from state taxation? Pat Oglesby has provided a thoughtful analysis of the question in an addendum to the report excerpted above (to which he contributed). On the one hand, he writes, "[m]edicine is usually tax-exempt" and "the public should assist—or at least not burden—sick people financially." Pat Oglesby, *Supplemental Thoughts About Revenue from Marijuana in Vermont*, Jan. 16, 2015, https://perma.cc/NJ5M-L5VJ. On the other hand, "marijuana is strange medicine," and some buyers could exploit a medical exemption to evade taxes imposed on recreational marijuana. *Id.* Ultimately, he suggests that "tax relief for medical users may turn out to be unnecessary" because "[e]ven paying full tax, medical users may be better off after legalization than they are now." *Id.* What do you think? Should medical marijuana be exempt from most or even all state taxes?

3. What impact do price changes have on the efficacy of a tax designed to regulate consumption? The following Problem raises the issue:

<u>Problem 9.1</u>: Revisit **Table 9.1** above. What would be the net (total) price paid by a consumer and the effective tax rate in each jurisdiction if the wholesale price of recreational marijuana dropped from $100 per ounce to $10 per ounce and the retailer charged a similar markup (i.e., 100 percent of wholesale price, or $10), in addition to any wholesale tax the retailer had to pay? Under this scenario, which state would have the lowest and highest tax rates on recreational marijuana? Would the taxes imposed by any of these jurisdictions have much of an impact on consumption (harmful or not)?

*(ii) Evasion*

Even if a jurisdiction could design some ideal tax on marijuana, it would still need to confront the threat of tax evasion. Suppliers have an obvious incentive to avoid the costs imposed by taxes. A supplier who does so gains a potentially sizable competitive advantage vis-à-vis her tax-paying rivals. The supplier could exploit this cost-advantage by expanding her profit margins or by poaching customers from those higher-cost rivals.

The following excerpt from the textbook author assesses the likelihood of evasion and the options states have to combat it.

## *Robert A. Mikos*, **State Taxation of Marijuana Distribution and Other Federal Crimes**
U. Chi. Legal Forum 222 (2010)

The tax rate helps determine the tax gap—the bigger the tax, the bigger the incentive to evade—but it is only half of the story. Apart from the tax rate, a distributor deciding whether to pay or evade must also consider the expected sanction for evasion. If the expected sanction exceeds the tax burden, a distributor would opt to pay the tax and there would be no tax gap problem. . . . [F]or example, a distributor would pay [a $70 per ounce marijuana] tax if (but *only if*) the expected sanction for evasion exceeds $70. . . .

The expected legal sanction for tax evasion is a function of the probability of detection (p) and the gross sanction (S) imposed on violators who are detected. In theory, the state government could manipulate either variable (p or S) to achieve optimal deterrence whereby p * S > T [where T is the cost of the tax]. In practice, however, the government's ability to achieve optimal deterrence by imposing legal sanctions is constrained [in two ways]. . . .

### 1. DETECTION.

The state's ability to deter tax evasion rests, in large part, on its powers of observation—namely, its ability to detect evasion. But detecting tax evasion is easier said than done. Among other things, it requires knowing the identity (location, and so on) of firms that sell marijuana and how much they sell. Without this information, the government cannot discern which firms have satisfied their tax obligations. . . .

Since the government cannot monitor taxable activity directly—and since it cannot necessarily trust taxpayers' self-reports—it must rely upon knowledgeable and preferably disinterested third parties (for example, employers) to report taxable activity. The government commonly relies upon third-party reporting to obtain the information it needs to enforce tax codes. The federal Internal Revenue Service, for example, requires employers to submit periodic reports detailing employees' wages (the W-2). These reports greatly enhance the ability of resource-constrained agencies to enforce taxes. Empirical studies have shown, for example, that targeted audits—that is, ones based on leads generated by third party reports—uncover nearly twenty times more evaded tax (in dollar terms), on average, than do random audits. Indeed, the tax compliance literature has demonstrated just how important observing taxable activity is to curbing tax evasion. In general, tax gaps shrink the more information government receives concerning taxable activity. Consider federal income taxes. The IRS estimates on average that 16 percent of federal income taxes go unpaid, but the gap varies considerably by source of income. In particular, the gap is estimated to be much larger for income sources the IRS cannot easily monitor, such as farm income (72 percent gap), self-employment income (52 percent), and income from royalties and rents (51 percent)—the IRS cannot rely upon third parties to report such income. By contrast, the gap is estimated to be smaller for income the IRS can observe through third party reporting: the gap is only 1 percent for salary income (reported on W-2s) and 4 percent for dividend income (reported on form 1099).

. . .

Given how crucial monitoring is for enforcing other taxes, it seems reasonable to suppose [a state] would likewise need to monitor marijuana distribution in order to deter evasion of [any] marijuana tax. In particular, [a state] would need to observe 1) who sells marijuana and 2) how much is sold. . . . Holding all else constant, the more complete are [a state's] data on these two matters, the smaller the marijuana tax gap will be.

This begs the question: is there any way for [a state] to reliably monitor marijuana distribution? . . . [A] licensing system for the distribution and production of marijuana that would (arguably) enhance tax monitoring. Under this system, distributors would need a state-issued license to distribute marijuana legally. As a condition of holding such license, distributors would be required to maintain business records detailing sales (among other things) and periodically submit such records to the state's licensing authority (also its taxing authority). Producers would be subject to similar licensing, recordkeeping, and reporting requirements. States commonly employ such licensing systems to assist collection of other vice taxes.

A licensing system could bolster evasion detection in two main ways. First, [a state] could use the system to limit the number of firms distributing marijuana, and hence, the number of firms the state would need to monitor. By limiting the number of distribution licenses, [a state] would ensure that its "administrative resources [would] not be swamped by the necessity of overseeing thousands of extremely minor operations."[57] Second, by compelling licensees to reports sales (among other things), the system

---

57. Jim Leitzel, Regulating Vice [162 (Cambridge 2008)].

would help generate the data the state needs to review tax compliance—for example, a licensee's sales records could be used to estimate its tax base.

To be sure, the licensing system is not a panacea. For one thing, the system could be circumvented. Consumers could bypass commercial distributors altogether and grow their own supplies. After all, compared to tobacco, marijuana is relatively easy to cultivate and process—it costs roughly $100 to get started and for the horticulturally challenged, there are even numerous "idiot's guide"-type books to show the way. And [a state] could not feasibly license or tax home-grown marijuana, any more than it could license or tax home-grown tomatoes. Alternatively, consumers could patronize black market (unlicensed) distributors. By evading the tax, such distributors could offer consumers a steep price discount. One illustrative survey of New York cigarette smokers found that 37 percent admitted to buying cigarettes from non-taxed sources. Of course, most consumers would presumably opt for the safety and convenience of licensed marijuana distributors. But even those licensed distributors could evade taxes by under-reporting sales. The third-parties best situated to detect tax evasion—customers—are highly unlikely to report it, since they usually gain by it (via lower prices). To be sure, rival distributors, suppliers, and undercover buyers could catch and report some evasion, keeping most licensees tolerably honest. In other words, the licensing system should help, but it is hardly foolproof; some portion of marijuana tax evasion would undoubtedly escape detection.

## 2. SANCTIONS.

In theory, even if [a state] cannot observe marijuana distribution reliably and detect all instances of evasion, it could still achieve optimal deterrence by imposing harsh sanctions on the tax evaders it does apprehend. To illustrate, to compensate for a very low probability of detection (say, $p = 10$ percent), [a state] could impose a sanction multiplier ($T/p$), to boost expected sanctions to the level needed to deter evasion ($p * (T/p) = T$). In this case, where $p = 10$ percent, sanctions would need to be 1,000 percent of the tax originally due. In fact, economists generally prefer this option—namely, a high sanction paired with a low rate of detection—because it is cheaper to impose more severe sanctions (especially monetary sanctions) than it is to catch more criminals.

As it stands, however, the sanctions for tax evasion are too low to compensate even for small gaps in detection. In California, [for example,] the sanction for intentionally evading taxes is only 125 percent of the original tax burden (plus interest), that is, 1.25T. The same is true in most jurisdictions; in fact, legal scholars have frequently called attention to the low level of sanctions imposed for tax evasion. In our example above, where p equals 10 percent, the expected legal sanction a distributor would face per dollar of tax evaded in California is only about a dime ($0.125)—not nearly enough to deter risk-neutral distributors from evading.

Assuming its capacity to detect evasion is limited, as I have already shown, [a state] would need to raise its sanctions—perhaps dramatically—in order to curb evasion. Such a strategy, however, is fraught with shortcomings. First, adopting substantial sanctions multipliers might not be politically feasible. It seems politicians do not want to appear as though they are empowering tax enforcement agencies (even for the greater good). And as a legal matter, the Eighth Amendment and like-minded provisions found in state constitutions could bar imposition of the sort of draconian fines that might be needed to deter tax evasion. What is more, a substantial sanction multiplier is more likely to be deemed "punitive" for purposes of constitutional analysis, a determination that could raise the cost of imposing the sanction and collecting the tax, thereby detracting from its appeal.

Second, even assuming high sanction multipliers could be adopted, the government's ability to impose them is constrained. Perhaps most importantly, offender wealth establishes a de facto ceiling on the maximal financial sanction. To the extent it exceeds offender wealth, a monetary fine contributes nothing to deterrence. And there is no reason to assume that marijuana distributors who evade taxes could necessarily afford to pay fines several times larger than the taxes evaded. . . . Thus, despite the sound theoretical argument suggesting that high sanctions should deter evasion, empirical studies generally have failed to demonstrate that raising sanctions actually deters evasion. . . .

## Notes and Questions

1. The excerpt suggests that states need to closely monitor taxable activity to ensure compliance with taxes. Chapter 8 discussed the extensive monitoring and reporting requirements certain states have imposed on marijuana suppliers, including requirements that licensed cultivators, processors, and retailers track every gram of marijuana from seed to sale using RFID tags and other technology. Do these requirements effectively deter evasion of marijuana taxes and other regulations? *Compare* Caulkins et al., *Considering Marijuana Legalization*, supra, at 87 (suggesting that concerns over evasion "might be moot if tracking of product were as bulletproof as Colorado and Washington would like to make it. . . . However, it is far from clear when, if ever, tracking will meet that promise. Video surveillance, for instance, requires more eyes on monitors than states might be able reasonably to afford.") *with* John Hudak, *Colorado's Rollout of Legal Marijuana Is Succeeding: A Report on the State's Implementation of Legalization*, 65 Case W. Res. L. Rev. 649, 661 (2015) (noting that Colorado's "tracking system is technologically advanced, comprehensive, and serves as the backbone for the regulatory regime's enforcement activities").

2. What is the highest tax rate that a jurisdiction could impose on marijuana without triggering rampant evasion? *Cf.* Caulkins et al., What Everyone Needs to Know, at 148 (estimating feasible tax rates under national legalization). Would this maximum tax rate be sufficient to combat the harms (however defined) that stem from marijuana use?

3. Consider the following Problem:

**Problem 9.2:** Suppose you live in Town A. Town A has imposed a tax on soda everywhere it is sold in town. The tax is $1 per 12 ounce serving (assume the pre-tax price of the beverage is $2). Town B is just down the road, about 10 miles from Town A. Town B imposes no tax on soda. Would you drive to Town B to obtain soda without paying the tax? (Substitute your favorite, comparably priced beverage if soda does not appeal to you.) If not, how high would the tax need to be before you would consider taking this step to evade it?

### b. Product Packaging and Labeling Requirements

Some marijuana products have raised unique concerns because of their association with harmful use. Marijuana edibles are a case in point. Since 2012, the consumption of edibles has been linked to a handful of deaths and injuries in legalization states. These incidents prompted Colorado to adopt regulations regarding the potency, packaging, and labeling of edibles (discussed in Chapter 8).

The story of one tragic death is chronicled in the following report:

> In March 2014, the Colorado Department of Public Health and Environment (CDPHE) learned of the death of a man aged 19 years after consuming an edible marijuana product. . . . The decedent's friend, aged 23 years, had purchased marijuana cookies and provided one to the decedent. A police report indicated that initially the decedent ate only a single piece of his cookie, as directed by the sales clerk. Approximately 30–60 minutes later, not feeling any effects, he consumed the remainder of the cookie. During the next 2 hours, he reportedly exhibited erratic speech and hostile behaviors. Approximately 3.5 hours after initial ingestion, and 2.5 hours after consuming the remainder of the cookie, he jumped off a fourth floor balcony and died from trauma. The autopsy, performed 29 hours after time of death, found marijuana intoxication as a chief contributing factor. Quantitative toxicologic analyses for drugs of abuse, synthetic cannabinoid, and cathinones ("bath salts") were performed on chest cavity blood by gas chromatography and mass spectrometry. The only confirmed findings were cannabinoids (7.2 ng/mL delta-9 tetrahydrocannabinol [THC] and 49 ng/mL delta-9 carboxy-THC, an inactive marijuana metabolite). The legal whole blood limit of delta-9 THC for driving a vehicle in Colorado is 5.0 ng/mL. This was the first reported death in Colorado linked to marijuana consumption without evidence of polysubstance use since the state approved recreational use of marijuana in 2012.
> 
> According to the police report, the decedent had been marijuana-naïve, with no known history of alcohol abuse, illicit drug use, or mental illness. In addition to listing inactive ingredients, the cookie label described the psychoactive ingredients as "65 mg THC/6.5 servings (THC, tetrahydrocannabinol, the principal psychoactive agent in cannabis)." The label also noted, "This marijuana product has not been tested for contaminants or potency." According to the police report, the sales clerk had instructed the buyer and decedent to divide each cookie into sixths, each piece containing approximately 10 mg of THC, the serving size, and to ingest one serving at a time. The police report did not indicate whether the sales clerk provided specific instructions for how long to wait between ingesting each serving.
> 
> This case illustrates a potential danger associated with recreational edible marijuana use. . . . An estimated 45% of Colorado's marijuana sales involve edible marijuana, including THC-infused food, drink, and pills. . . .
> 
> Systemic THC levels and psychoactive effects after ingestion are highly variable because of differences in bioavailability, rate of gastrointestinal absorption, and metabolic first-pass effect whereby an orally administered drug is partially metabolized (principally in the liver) before reaching systemic distribution. . . . Because absorption is slower, the onset of effects is delayed (with mean peak plasma concentration at 1–2 hours after ingestion, in contrast with 5–10 minutes to peak plasma concentrations if smoked), and duration of intoxication is longer when THC is ingested compared with when it is smoked. . . . Whereas a single-serving recreational edible marijuana dose in Colorado was set at 10 mg of THC, multiple-dose recreational edible products, often containing 100 mg of THC, were available during March 2014. . . . The marijuana store where the implicated cookies had been purchased voluntarily gave all 67 remaining cookies of the same brand to the Denver Police Department. Testing confirmed that the THC levels in the items were within

required limits. Because of the delayed effects of THC-infused edibles, multiple servings might be consumed in close succession before experiencing the "high" from the initial serving, as reportedly occurred in this case. Consuming a large dose of THC can result in a higher THC concentration, greater intoxication, and an increased risk for adverse psychological effects.

. . . Although the decedent in this case was advised against eating multiple servings at one time, he reportedly consumed all five of the remaining servings of the THC-infused cookie within 30-60 minutes after the first serving, suggesting a need for improved public health messaging to reduce the risk for overconsumption of THC.

Jessica B. Hancock-Allen et al., *Notes from the Field: Death Following Ingestion of an Edible Marijuana Product—Colorado, March 2014*, 64 Morbidity and Mortality Weekly 771-772 (July 24, 2015).

## Notes and Questions

1. Why, exactly, do marijuana edibles seem more dangerous than other forms of marijuana? Does it stem from their potency? The latency of their effects? The novelty of them? Do any other marijuana products raise similar concerns?

2. Colorado's rules governing the packaging and labeling of edibles have changed since the incident occurred and since the report excerpted above was published. In light of the details in the report, however, are Colorado's latest rules, surveyed in chapter 8, enough to prevent the harms associated with the consumption of marijuana edibles? Would you revise Colorado's packaging and labeling requirements in any way?

3. To a large extent, labeling requirements are designed to inform consumers how to consume marijuana edibles safely. But not everyone necessarily reads the labels on marijuana packages before consuming the drug. Is there any other way for states to educate consumers? In 2015, Colorado launched a $5.7 million media campaign (Good to Know) designed to educate consumers about how to use marijuana safely. The campaign website can be found at http://goodtoknowcolorado.com/. Are such educational campaigns effective? For a discussion of the efficacy of media campaigns more generally, see Chapter 5.

4. A few medical marijuana states have banned commercial licensees from producing or distributing marijuana edibles. See Chapter 8. Is a ban feasible, given the popularity of edibles? The report above notes, for example, that edibles account for 45 percent of Colorado marijuana sales. Even if a state bans commercial licensees from distributing marijuana edibles, could it prevent users from making their own? Do homemade edibles pose the same risks as commercially produced edibles? Why, why not?

5. Are marijuana producers and distributors potentially liable in tort for supplying marijuana products (edibles or otherwise) that cause harm to consumers? See Julie A. Steinberg, *Pot Product Liability Suits Coming*, Product Safety & Liability Reporting, Nov. 2, 2016 (discussing two product liability suits that have been brought against marijuana suppliers, including one stemming from the incident described in the report excerpted above). Could products liablity help curb the dangers associated with marijuana edibles? How, exactly?

6. What else could states like Colorado do to address the potential harms posed by marijuana edibles? For further discussion of the policy options noted above and others,

see Robert J. MacCoun & Michelle M. Mello, *Half-Baked—The Retail Promotion of Marijuana Edibles*, 372 N. Eng. J. Med. 989, 989-91 (2015).

7. How frequently do tragedies like the one discussed in the report occur? Are states like Colorado potentially overreacting? *See* Josiah M. Hesse, *Why Are People Going to the Emergency Room for Weed?*, The Cannabist, Jan. 14, 2016, http://www.thecannabist.co/2016/01/14/pot-emergency-room-marijuana-er/42939/.

### c. Marijuana Advertising Restrictions

As discussed in Chapter 8, a large and growing number of legalization states have authorized the commercial supply of marijuana. One of the chief concerns raised by this move is that the commercial marijuana industry will seek to promote consumption of the drug (and hence its sales), even when such consumption is not in the best interests of society. Of particular concern is the possibility that the marijuana industry might promote use by minors and addicts to boost its sales—a questionable tactic that has been employed by similar industries in the past.

To address this concern, states have attempted to restrict some forms of marijuana advertising. Those restrictions are detailed in Chapter 8. But are these restrictions enforceable—i.e., are they constitutional? And is there any other way for states to prevent the marijuana industry from promoting harmful uses? The materials below address these questions.

### (i) Do Advertising Restrictions Violate the First Amendment?

Chapter 8 surveyed the advertising restrictions that many states impose on commercial marijuana suppliers. Do these restrictions run afoul of the free speech rights of those suppliers?

The Constitution provides some limited protections for commercial speech, including commercial advertising. The constitutionality of restrictions imposed on such speech is judged under the test set forth in *Central Hudson Gas & Electric Corp. v. Public Services Commission*:

> At the outset, we must determine whether the expression is protected by the First Amendment. For commercial speech to come within that provision, it at least must concern lawful activity and not be misleading. Next, we ask whether the asserted governmental interest is substantial. If both inquiries yield positive answers, we must determine whether the regulation directly advances the governmental interest asserted, and whether it is not more extensive than is necessary to serve that interest.

447 U.S. 557, 566 (1980).

The following excerpt considers whether marijuana advertising concerns "lawful activity," for purposes of *Central Hudson*, and if so, whether states nonetheless may have the power to restrain such speech.

### Alex Kreit, What Will Federal Marijuana Reform Look Like?
65 Case W. Res. L. Rev. 689 (2015)

Federal marijuana prohibition may not be able to block state legalization laws, effectively ceding all regulatory decisions to states that decide to legalize. Federal prohibition does, however, allow for a complete ban on marijuana advertising because there is no First Amendment right to advertise the sale of an illegal good. . . .

If federal law were to formally recognize state legalization . . . , advertising bans would be on very shaky ground. The framework for addressing commercial advertising restrictions dates back to the Supreme Court's 1980 *Central Hudson* decision. [*Cen. Hudson Gas & Elec. Corp. v. Pub. Serv. Comm'n of N.Y.*, 447 U.S. 557 (1980).] Under *Central Hudson*, the government can ban advertising that is deceptive or that is "related to illegal activity." Non-misleading advertisements for legal goods can only be prohibited if the government is able to (1) claim a substantial interest in restricting the speech, (2) demonstrate that its restriction directly and materially advances its interest, and (3) show that the restriction is narrowly tailored to that interest. . . .

Government restrictions on vice advertisements under *Central Hudson* typically fail the requirements that the restriction would actually advance the government's interest and that there aren't narrower, non-speech restrictive alternatives. This can be true even where advertisements appear to target an audience that cannot legally buy the product being advertised. A recent Fourth Circuit decision overturning a Virginia ban on advertising alcohol in college student newspapers is instructive. The ads could not be restricted on the theory that they involve illegal activity because "alcohol advertisements—even those that reach a partially underage audience—concern the lawful activity of alcohol consumption." [*Educ. Media Co. at Va. Tech, Inc. v. Insley*, 731 F.3d 291, 299 (4th Cir. 2013).] Though the court granted that the government has a substantial interest in combatting underage drinking, it concluded that the ban was not narrowly tailored because "roughly 60% of the Collegiate Times's readership is age 21 or older and the Cavalier Daily reaches approximately 10,000 students, nearly 64% of whom are age 21 or older." *Central Hudson* leaves room for some limits on advertisements on legal goods, of course. A ban on alcohol advertisements in high school newspapers would likely withstand a First Amendment challenge. But marijuana prohibitionists' concerns that legalization might mean having to allow a great deal of marijuana advertising are not misplaced.

Of course, there might be creative ways to directly limit some marijuana advertising in the absence of federal prohibition. The federal government could attempt to devise a legal hook for advertising limits by enacting a prohibition that it does not intend to enforce—for example, criminalizing the use of marijuana while licensing its manufacture and sale and allowing its possession. In theory, this may allow for bans on marijuana advertising that promoted use. Or if the federal government legalized only the intrastate sale of marijuana, it could try banning advertisements that crossed state lines. Unless the Supreme Court were to reassess its view of the commercial speech doctrine, however, it may be impossible to put any significant restrictions on marijuana advertising in the absence of federal marijuana prohibition.

For this reason, First Amendment concerns may lead prohibitionists to view appropriations restrictions as the most acceptable method for reconciling federal and state marijuana laws. Forbidding the executive to spend money interfering with state marijuana reforms would leave federal marijuana prohibition untouched, thereby almost certainly permitting bans on advertising. An affirmative defense based on compliance with state marijuana laws or a state waiver policy might also leave room for advertising bans, though this is less certain. If the federal government continued to ban marijuana sales with an affirmative defense, it is hard to predict whether the activity would still be considered illegal under *Central Hudson*. . . .

## Notes and Questions

1. Professor Kreit suggests that the constitutionality of state advertising restrictions may hinge on whether marijuana remains illegal under *federal* law. *See also Montana Cannabis Indus. Ass'n v. Montana*, 368 P.3d 1131, 1150 (Mont. 2016) ("[A]n activity that is not permitted by federal law—even if permitted by state law—is not a 'lawful activity' within the meaning of *Central Hudson's* first factor."). Do you agree? Does it seem odd to say that a *state* may restrict free speech concerning an activity it considers lawful, simply because the *federal* government considers that same activity unlawful? A similar issue arises under state contract law and state anti-discrimination laws, which are both discussed in Chapter 13.

2. Now consider the following Problems:

Problem 9.3: Delilah runs a marijuana tourism business based in Colorado. Her business helps adults from other states travel to Colorado to purchase and use marijuana there. Delilah wants to post an advertisement on a Nebraska roadway sign. The [FG4]advertisement she has in mind declares, "Get a Rocky Mountain High!," and it provides Delilah's business information. However, Nebraska law forbids the possession and use of marijuana, and Nebraska has also recently banned all advertising for marijuana tourism. Could Delilah challenge *Nebraska's* advertising ban on First Amendment grounds? *See New England Accessories Trade Ass'n, Inc. v. City of Nashua*, 679 F.2d 1, 3-4 (1st Cir. 1982). *See also* Judy Endejan, *Can Puff the Magic Dragon Lawfully Advertise His Wares?*, 31 Comm. Lawyer 1 (Summer 2015) (discussing constitutionality of analogous restrictions on advertising).

Problem 9.4: As discussed in Chapter 8, many states impose restrictions on marijuana advertising that fall short of outright bans. Colorado's Retail Marijuana Code, for example, stipulates that marijuana licensees shall not engage in advertising

(1) "that is deceptive, false, or misleading"
(2) on television or radio unless the licensee "has reliable evidence that no more than 30 percent of the audience for the program on which the Advertising is to air is reasonably expected to be under the age of 21"
(3) in print unless the licensee "has reliable evidence that no more than 30 percent of the publication's readership is reasonably expected to be under the age of 21"
(4) on the internet unless the licensee "has reliable evidence that no more than 30 percent of the audience for the internet web site is reasonably expected to be under the age of 21"
(5) "that specifically targets Persons located outside the state of Colorado"

(6) that is "visible to members of the public from any street, sidewalk, park or other public place, including . . . any billboard . . . ; any sign mounted on a vehicle, any hand-held or other portable sign; or any handbill, leaflet or flier directly handed to any person in a public place, left upon a motor vehicle, or posted upon any public or private property without the consent of the property owner," except that a licensee may post a sign at its establishment "solely for the purpose of identifying the location" of the establishment

(7) that includes "cartoon characters or similar images" that specifically target individuals under the age of 21

1 Colo. Code Reg. 212-2.1102, .1104-08, & .1111-15 (2016). Assuming for the sake of argument that all of the affected advertising concerns "lawful activity," would any of these restrictions pass muster under the *Central Hudson* test?

3. What role should federal enforcement practices play in the first part of the *Central Hudson* test (i.e., determining whether marijuana advertising concerns lawful activity)? What does Kreit say? Do you agree? Should it matter, for First Amendment purposes, whether a ban on advertised activity is being enforced?

4. To date, the courts have had relatively few occasions on which to opine on the constitutionality of laws, like Colorado's, that restrict advertising by the licensed marijuana industry. For example, one notable challenge to Colorado's advertising restrictions, brought by the magazine High Times, was dismissed for lack of standing. *Trans-High Corp. v. Colorado*, No. 14-CV-00370-MSK, 2014 WL 585367, at *3 (D. Colo. Feb. 14, 2014) (unpublished). Nonetheless, the courts have issued numerous decisions regarding the constitutionality of other laws that restrict commercial and political speech about marijuana. For a small sampling, see *Morse v. Frederick*, 551 U.S. 393 (2007) (holding that a high school student had no First Amendment right to display a banner reading "BONG HITS 4 JESUS" at a school approved event); *Ridley v. Mass. Bay Transp. Auth.*, 390 F.3d 65 (1st Cir. 2004) (holding that non-profit group seeking marijuana law reforms had right to buy advertising space on public transportation); *Conant v. Walters*, 309 F.3d 629 (9th Cir. 2002) (holding that physicians have a right to discuss the benefits of marijuana use with their patients) (*Conant* is excerpted in Chapter 12); *Gerlich v. Leath*, 152 F. Supp. 3d 1152 (S.D. Iowa 2016) (holding that student chapter of NORML had a right to include university mascot and logo on its promotional materials).

*(ii) Alternatives to Restricting Advertising*

Given doubts surrounding the constitutionality of government-imposed restrictions on marijuana advertising, it is worthwhile to consider whether policymakers have any other options to curb the marijuana industry's promotional activities. The following report discusses some possibilities.

### *Blue Ribbon Commission on Marijuana Policy*, Pathways Report: Policy Options for Regulating Marijuana in California
(July 22, 2015)

There are several available policy tools to limit advertising and marketing. The first, and perhaps most effective policy tool is shaping the industry's structure itself, specifically, creating an industry structure that works to limit the size and scale of any one actor. Without very large actors in the industry, few, if any, will have the resources for broadcast media advertising. This type of indirect limit on advertising rests on the government's ability to license and regulate the industry. While a trade association may band together to advertise, its resources would likely be more limited than what a single large corporation could deploy.

A second approach is to limit in-store sales and marketing to only those retail locations or dispensaries where adults aged 21 and over can enter, and . . . to limit what other non-cannabis products can be sold in these establishments so that adults enter with the sole purpose of purchasing cannabis. These choices can have the effect of preventing youth exposure to in-store advertising, and likewise that adults who were not intending to buy marijuana would not initiate a purchase due to point-of-sale marketing tactics.

The third tool is to adopt actual limits to advertising through legislation that meets constitutional standards. Because the federal government regulates broadcast media such as TV and radio, and because the Controlled Substances Act specifically bars advertising of a Schedule I controlled substance, marijuana advertising would not have federal constitutional protection. State constitutional protections might apply to some mediums of advertising (perhaps not those explicitly regulated by the federal government) and some types of restrictions, for example, those aimed at limiting exposure to youth. Whether and how state constitutional protections for this form of advertising would affect the ability of state and local government to regulate it in certain media requires further analysis.

The fourth policy tool is the denial of tax deductions for business advertising. Under section 280E of current income tax law, taxpayers cannot deduct the expenses of cannabis advertising on their federal returns. Similarly, individual taxpayers cannot now deduct those expenses on their California returns. There is no federal or state Constitutional right to deduct advertising or marketing expenses for any business, cannabis related or not. To be sure, denying state tax deductions would not eliminate advertising, but that approach would make it somewhat more costly. . . .

A different but related approach is to limit the overall extent and types of marketing to adults, and in particular, to regulate sales practices that draw in new users (bundled sales for discount with other products, free offers with purchases of other products, etc.) or that may encourage regular or habitual use of marijuana (bulk discounts, coupons, loyalty points, etc.).

## Notes and Questions

1. To get around First Amendment concerns, the BRC report suggests regulating advertising indirectly by denying marijuana businesses—and presumably *only* marijuana businesses—tax deductions for advertising expenses. For an elaboration on the proposal, see Pat Oglesby, *How Bob Dole Got America Addicted to Marijuana Taxes*, Brookings, Dec. 18, 2015, https://www.brookings.edu/blog/fixgov/2015/12/18/how-bob-dole-got-america-addicted-to-marijuana-taxes/. Would such a tax plan really avoid the constitutional concerns discussed in Section A.2.c.i above? How would the plan need to be structured? For example, could a state deny deductions only for the advertising expenditures of the marijuana industry, or would it have to deny those deductions for other industries (or other expenditures by the marijuana industry) as well?

2. Is it a foregone conclusion that the marijuana industry will seek to promote use by minors and addicts? As discussed in Chapter 8, the alcohol industry has issued voluntary guidelines designed to discourage members from promoting underage alcohol consumption. Voluntary limits on advertising presumably avoid the constitutional concerns raised by government-imposed advertising restrictions. But could the marijuana industry be trusted to restrain itself from promoting harmful uses? Does it have the incentive and ability to do so? Why, why not?

3. Colorado has adopted a number of restrictions aimed specifically at preventing minors from being exposed to marijuana advertising. But is there anyone else states should be worried about when it comes to marijuana advertising? Consider the following:

> For any newly legalized substance, most of the new users will be casual users. But most of the increased volume will reflect increased use by people who use frequently. The volume of drug consumption doesn't depend very strongly on the total number of users; what's crucial is the number of heavy users. one eight-joint-a-day smoke . . . is more important to the marijuana industry—legal or illegal—than fifty people who smoke a joint a week.
>
> . . .
>
> That has a frightening implication: if we create a licit commercial industry to grow and sell marijuana, the resulting businesses will have a strong financial incentive to create and sustain frequent and intensive consumption patterns, because the heaviest users consume so much of the product. So we should expect the industry's product design, pricing, and marketing to be devoted to creating as much heavy use as possible.

Caulkins et al., What Everyone Needs to Know, *supra*, at 112-13. Do any of the advertising restrictions discussed in Chapter 8 or any of the tactics proposed by the Pathways Report above prevent suppliers from targeting *this* group of harmful users (i.e., heavy users)? Are there any other regulations or policy interventions directed at suppliers that might curb sales to heavy users (e.g., transaction limits)?

4. Marijuana stores pose an added challenge for regulators seeking to limit promotional activity. The visibility of these stores itself might catch the interest of consumers. For this reason, many state and local governments restrict the location and signage of marijuana stores, for example, barring stores from locating in school zones and limiting the size of any signage posted outside of retail shops. *See, e.g.*, Rev. Code Wash. Ann. 69.50.357(4) (2016) ("Licensed marijuana retailers may not display any signage outside of the licensed premises, other than two signs identifying the retail outlet by the license's business or trade name. Each sign must be no larger than one thousand six hundred square inches, be permanently affixed to a building or other structure, and be posted not less than one thousand feet from any elementary school, secondary school, or playground.").

Canada has gone one step further. Under its Marijuana for Medical Purposes Regulations (MMPR), promulgated in 2014, the country has seemingly banned marijuana storefronts altogether, and instead requires qualifying medical marijuana patients to purchase their marijuana *through the mail* from licensed commercial suppliers. See 2014 Marijuana for Medical Purposes Regulations, Section 122 (Canada) ("In filling an order . . . , a licensed producer must not transfer physical possession of the dried marihuana to the client . . . *other than by shipping it to that person*.") (emphasis added), http://www.laws-lois.justice.gc.ca/eng/regulations/SOR-2013-119/20140331/P1TT3xt3.html. Would eliminating marijuana storefronts help to curb harmful use? Would Canada's direct mail approach even be feasible in the United States, as long as federal prohibition remains on the books (it is the *United States* Postal Service, after all)?

5. Background on the Pathways Report. The Blue Ribbon Commission was formed by prominent policymakers, academics, and advocates to help steer California's marijuana policy. The Pathways Report excerpted above was the culmination of the work of Committee. Many of its recommendations were incorporated into California's Proposition 64, which voters approved in in the fall 2016 election.

### d. Regulations Affecting Industry Structure

Apart from regulating certain industry practices (e.g., advertising) directly, the states have also sought to regulate those practices indirectly by shaping the structure of the marijuana industry. The idea is that certain industry characteristics, for example, the degree to which the industry is concentrated (i.e., a few firms control a large share of the market), may be more conducive to the states' regulatory goals, including the goal of limiting harmful use of marijuana.

The following sections examine ways the states have regulated industry structure—including outright bans on commercial supply—and the potential for those regulations to foster the states' regulatory goals.

#### (i) Banning Commercial Supply

Given that many of the concerns regulations seek to address stem from the creation of a commercial marijuana industry, it begs the question whether states should authorize commercial supply in the first instance. After all, as discussed in Chapter 8, a few medical marijuana states and at least one recreational marijuana jurisdiction (D.C.) have not yet done so, and instead expect qualifying patients or recreational users to cultivate marijuana on their own (or with the help of a caregiver).

But does personal supply meet the needs of lawful users? In one case reversing the conviction of a marijuana cooperative founder on charges of selling marijuana to the cooperative's members, a California appellate court opined that "[i]t would be cruel for those whose need for medical marijuana is the most dire to require that they devote their limited strength and efforts to the actual cultivation of the marijuana, and then wait months for it to grow so they can use it." *California v. Baniani*, 176 Cal. Rptr. 3d 764, 776 (Cal. App. 4th 2014).

In the following case, the Montana Supreme Court finds that some restrictions imposed by legalization regimes on marijuana commerce may be irrational. The case involves a due process challenge to portions of the 2011 Montana Medical Marijuana Act, which limits designated caregivers (called providers under Montana law) to serving no more than three patients and also bars them from accepting any compensation for their services.

### *Montana Cannabis Indus. Ass'n v. Montana*
368 P.3d 1131 (Mont. 2016)

BAKER, J.:

[The 2011 Montana Medical Marijuana Act (Act)] repealed the 2004 Medical Marijuana Act (2004 Act)—which was established by voter initiative (I-148)—and replaced it with a new statutory framework. The Act contains multiple provisions that limit both the

Part III. Marijuana Suppliers

eligibility of patients to qualify for its protections and the activities of medical professionals and providers of marijuana for medical purposes.

. . .

. . . [T]he Act was enacted in response to the Legislature's concern about a number of abuses that occurred following passage of the 2004 Act. As we noted in [an earlier case], the 2011 Act was passed "in response to a drastic increase of caregivers and medical marijuana users." . . . The goal of the Act, according to its sponsor, was "to repeal a system that is obviously broken, cleanse the system out, and then restore the laws of the State of Montana in a fashion that will recognize the intent of the Montana voters in 2004." . . .

. . .

. . . The careful regulation of access to an otherwise illegal substance for limited use by persons for whom there is little or no other effective alternative serves a legitimate state objective.

Having determined that the Act serves a legitimate objective, we proceed to consider whether the statutes are reasonably related to achieving that objective. . . . A statute that is unreasonable, arbitrary, or capricious and bears no reasonable relationship to a permissible government interest offends due process.

. . .

. . . The Act accomplishes its commercial restraint through two primary mechanisms: a three-patient limit for providers of marijuana products and a restriction against remuneration to providers. Section 50-46-308, MCA, provides:

(3)
  (a)
    (i) A provider or marijuana-infused products provider may assist a maximum of three registered cardholders.
    . . .

(4) A provider or marijuana-infused products provider may accept reimbursement from a cardholder only for the provider's application or renewal fee for a registry identification card issued under this section.

. . .

(6) A provider or marijuana-infused products provider may not:
  (a) accept anything of value, including monetary remuneration, for any services or products provided to a registered cardholder;
  (b) buy or sell mature marijuana plants, seedlings, cuttings, clones, usable marijuana, or marijuana-infused products.

. . .

*Three-Patient Limit: § 50-46-308(3), MCA.*

The three-patient limit is rational so long as it is not a capricious or arbitrary means of accomplishing the Act's legitimate purpose. . . . [T]he Act was passed "in response to a drastic increase of caregivers and medical marijuana users." Because of this concern, one of the Act's explicit purposes is to "allow individuals to assist a limited number of registered cardholders with the cultivation and manufacture of marijuana or marijuana-infused products." . . .

The Legislature determined that placing a limit on the number of registered cardholders a provider may assist serves the objectives of keeping marijuana away from large-scale manufacturing operations, making it less appealing to major traffickers. This relates directly to the federal government's goals of preventing marijuana sales revenue from going to criminal enterprises and of keeping state-authorized marijuana activity from being used as a cover for other drug trafficking. . . . The Legislature conceivably could have fixed a different number. But in the face of marijuana's outright prohibition under federal law, and the U.S. government's avowed intention to investigate and prosecute marijuana offenses where it finds "an important federal interest," Cole Memorandum . . . , it is not irrational for the Legislature to put mechanisms in place to limit its commercial profitability. Whether a limit of just three patients is the best or the most effective means of achieving the State's legitimate purpose is not for the Court to judge. . . .

Because the three-patient limit is reasonably related to the legitimate governmental concern of affording a means of treatment while avoiding large-scale commercial marijuana production, we hold that the [court] erred in concluding that the three-patient limit fails rational basis scrutiny. . . .

### REMUNERATION RESTRICTIONS: § 50-46-308(4), (6)(A), (B), MCA

. . .

Legislative history indicates that the purpose of imposing restrictions against financial compensation of providers was to "keep the money out" of the marijuana business—presumably, to meet the federal government's objectives of preventing large-scale marijuana production operations that could serve as a front for other illegal drug trafficking and could funnel revenues to cartels, gangs, and criminal enterprises. While this is a legitimate objective, we must be able to ascertain a rational relationship between a complete prohibition against financial compensation and the objectives the Legislature sought to achieve. . . . We conclude that the remuneration restrictions fail this inquiry.

We first observe that the Act does not prohibit physicians from being compensated for their services or expenses when they examine a patient and provide written certification for the patient's medical use of marijuana products. In addition, the State has not cited, and the Court has not found, any other service or product sanctioned by state law that the Legislature has mandated be provided for free. Although the State argues that the remuneration restrictions do effectively "keep the money out," the restrictions are at odds with the Legislature's stated purpose of allowing the limited possession and use of marijuana by persons with debilitating medical conditions in order to alleviate their symptoms. . . . More, the restriction is contrary to the purpose of keeping marijuana revenues out of the hands of criminals because it drives the business of medical marijuana to the black market. The Act allows marijuana to be used medically with approval by a physician. The complete prohibition against compensation is invidious because medical marijuana, even when approved by a physician, would have no commercially available source of supply.

. . .

Accordingly, we conclude that the absolute prohibition against remuneration is not reasonable "when balanced against the purpose of the [L]egislature in enacting the [Act]." We uphold the [court's] permanent injunction against the remuneration restrictions, . . . and declare that those provisions are invalid as violative of the equal protection and due process clauses of the Montana Constitution.

RICE, J., dissenting:

I concur with the Court's Opinion on all issues except for the remuneration provision. . . .

Part III. Marijuana Suppliers

. . .

Given that marijuana is illegal under federal law, and that the State's interest may be "any possible purpose of which the court can conceive," . . . it requires a particularly uncreative judge indeed to be unable to articulate a legitimate state interest that justifies the remuneration provision. Further, against this first backdrop of federal illegality, there is a second backdrop: the abuses of the drug and of the access provided to it under the I-148 initiative. In response to this chaos . . . , the Legislature chose to decisively restrict, limit and constrain all aspects of marijuana availability, and to impose heavy regulation by passing the Act. . . . The Act, in its entirety, is a clear constriction of access in response to the abuses under prior law. The Legislature specifically sought to impose new, heavy regulations upon the illegal drug, particularly by "eliminating commercial access," as the State's brief states. This is a legitimate purpose, given the concerns created by commercial access to medical marijuana, such as the need to police, license, and tax commercial goods. The Legislature may well have believed that eliminating commercial access alleviated these concerns, as it has with other home products. See § 16-3-201(2), MCA (exempting from regulation the manufacture of beer not intended for sale).

The Court counters that the remuneration provision will likely drive the business of medical marijuana back to the black market. . . . Perhaps so, but the proper inquiry does not permit the Court to entertain such policy speculations, and, in fact, as properly applied, mandates the Court do just the opposite: speculation and presumption is required in favor of upholding the provision. . . . Employing such a presumption here, the remuneration provision certainly seems likely to eliminate commercial access and alleviate the State's concerns for purposes of due process analysis. . . .

## Notes and Questions

1. *Postscript on the Montana restrictions.* Both of the limits reviewed by the *MCIA* court above were repealed by the 2016 Montana Medical Marijuana Initiative (I-182).

2. Are limits on the number of patients caregivers may serve and/or bans on remuneration for marijuana suppliers irrational? Can you think of "any other service or product sanctioned by state law" that a legislature has "mandated be provided for free"? What about bans on remuneration for blood or bodily organs? Do those bans suggest it could be rational for states to require that marijuana be provided for free? Or does the *MCIA* court suggest that bans on remuneration for blood and organs are irrational? *Cf.* Nicola Lacetera et al., *Economic Rewards to Motivate Blood Donations*, 340 Science 927, 927-28 (2013) (arguing that bans on remuneration for blood are misguided and that providing some types of economic incentives for "donating" blood could boost blood supplies).

3. What sort of restrictions could governments impose on the supply of marijuana, if a court were to find that citizens have a *fundamental* right to use the drug? As discussed in Chapter 6, government regulations that burden fundamental rights are subject to strict scrutiny, which is a far more demanding test than the rational basis test applied by the *MCIA* court and even more demanding than the intermediate scrutiny called for by *Central Hudson, supra*. Of course, no court has yet found a fundamental right to use marijuana under the United States Constitution. *See* Chapter 4. But the Canadian courts have recognized something akin to a fundamental right to use marijuana for medical purposes under the Canadian Charter of Rights and Freedoms. *Id.* And one Canadian court

has seemingly held that qualifying patients must be allowed to cultivate their own marijuana in order to vindicate that right. *See Allard et al. v. Her Majesty the Queen in Right of Canada*, 2016 FC 236. The *Allard* court invalidated government regulations that had required medical marijuana patients to buy marijuana from nationally licensed commercial suppliers. The court found that those suppliers did not offer enough strains of marijuana—and at low enough prices—to meet the needs of some patients. *Id.*[3]

4. Whether or not it adequately supplies beneficial uses, does the personal supply model necessarily prevent marijuana from being supplied for harmful ones? Among other things, can states successfully enforce restrictions on personal suppliers like those discussed in Chapter 8, including limits on the number of plants they may cultivate and on selling marijuana to other users (lawful or not)? Consider the task facing the state of Oregon. It has more than *17,000* separate grow sites registered by medical marijuana patients or their caregivers. Oregon Medical Marijuana Program, Statistical Snapshot, Oct. 2016, https://perma.cc/X69D-ZDTA. Not all patients, of course, are disposed to breaking state law; but is there any way for a state to ensure that most of them will abide state regulations? For studies analyzing the effects of personal supply on marijuana use, *see, e.g.,* Robert J. MacCoun, *The Paths Not (Yet) Taken: Lower Risk Alternatives to Full-Market Legalization of Cannabis* 47, in Something's in the Air: Race, Crime, and the Legalization of Marijuana (Katherine Tate et al. eds., 2013) ("The available evidence does not suggest that decriminalized home cultivation leads to increases in the prevalence of use."); Pacula et al., *Assessing the Effects, supra,* at 29 (reporting that medical marijuana states "that allow dispensaries face a greater risk of increased recreational use," but finding "inconsistent evidence regarding the effect of home cultivation allowances" on such use). *But see* D. Mark Anderson et al., *Medical Marijuana Laws and Teen Marijuana Use*, 17 Am. L. & Econ. Rev. 495 (2015) (finding no correlation between medical marijuana laws and teenage marijuana use).

5. Comparisons are often made between marijuana and alcohol and the regulations governing the two substances. So how do states regulate the production of alcoholic beverages by consumers? The answer varies considerably based on the type of alcoholic beverage being produced. Since 1978, federal law has permitted consumers to brew their own beer, and since 2013, *all* states have followed suit by permitting home brewing. American Homebrewers Association, Statutes, https://perma.cc/WN3A-MDE3 (summarizing and discussing state and federal laws). However, the federal government continues to ban home distilling of spirits. *See* Alcohol and Tobacco Tax and Trade Bureau, *Home Distilling*, https://perma.cc/WBG5-DKFN (describing federal laws governing home distilling). And it appears that *no* state has yet legalized home distillation of spirits. *See* Home Distiller's Association, *Laws by State*, https://perma.cc/XY4G-Z2MW (surveying home distilling laws of all 50 states).

Do the laws governing home brewing and/or home distilling provide any guidance as to what states should do regarding the personal cultivation of marijuana? In particular, is the personal cultivation of marijuana more like the home brewing of beer or the home distilling of spirits? What about the personal manufacture of marijuana-based products, like hash oil?

---

3. In the interest of disclosure, the textbook author served as an expert witness for the Canadian government in the case.

6. What do you think? Should jurisdictions authorize personal supply, commercial supply, or both?

### *(ii) Licensing Rules Restricting Industry Concentration*

Some states that have authorized a commercial marijuana industry have nonetheless sought to limit the concentration of that industry. They have done so either by offering an unlimited number of licenses (as Colorado has done) or by capping the size of any licensee (as California plans to do). Professor Mark Kleiman has explained the rationale behind these efforts to limit the concentration of marijuana industry:

> . . . [I]t might well be desirable to limit the production of each participant to prevent the domination of production by one or a few firms, as happens with mass-market beer, cigarettes, and breakfast cereals. Economies of scale might make it difficult for "craft" producers to compete with "mass-market" producers, perhaps limiting the variety of products available and stifling innovation. If early regulatory decisions push the market in the direction of concentration, those effects may prove to be enduring.
>
> There are many reasons why state interests might be better served by an array including small-and medium-sized producers rather than one or a few giants. A competitive industry might be more responsive to customers. Large firms might be more likely to attract federal enforcement attention. Moreover, larger firms might be more capable than smaller ones of carrying out expensive marketing campaigns (with potentially unfortunate effects on drug abuse and sales to minors) and lobbying efforts (limiting the state's capacity to effectively tax and regulate the cannabis industry). On the other hand, a more concentrated market might prove easier to regulate.
>
> Of course limiting production has disadvantages as well as advantages. It will impose costs on producers, consumers, and regulators, and it might lead to attempts at evasion and the need for enforcement. It could also leave more room for wholly illegal production, partially frustrating the goals of shrinking the illicit market, protecting public health, and generating tax revenue. . . .

Mark Kleiman, Alternative Bases for Limiting Cannabis Production, BOTEC Analysis Corp., I-502 Project #430-5e (June 28, 2013).

## Notes and Questions

1. Why is a fragmented industry less likely "to carry[] out expensive marketing campaigns" as compared to a concentrated industry? What are the other benefits Kleiman attributes to fragmenting the marijuana industry?

2. Is there a case to be made *for* industry concentration? Consider the following argument:

> The obvious benefit [of limiting the number of licenses] is that fewer licensees imply fewer companies and sites to monitor and inspect. The more subtle benefit is that artificially restricting the number of licenses can make those licenses valuable. . . . Businesses with millions in annual revenues flowing from scarce licenses are less likely to be tempted by the opportunity to make money illegally than are holders of licenses that are easy to obtain and provide only meager profits to those who follow the rules.

Jonathan P. Caulkins et al., *High Tax States: Options for Gleaning Revenue from Legal Cannabis*, 91 Or. L. Rev. 1041, 1052 (2013). Ultimately, which do you think would better serve a state's regulatory goals—a fragmented marijuana industry or a concentrated marijuana industry? To what extent does your answer depend on how you frame (or prioritize) those goals?

3. In the long run, can states prevent consolidation of the marijuana industry? Consider the fate of the beer industry. Immediately following the repeal of alcohol Prohibition, the beer industry was fragmented. In 1947, for example, the top five brewers controlled only nineteen percent of the beer market. *See* Kenneth Elzinga & Anthony Swisher, *The Supreme Court and Beer Mergers: From Pabst/Blatz to the DOJ-FTC Merger Guidelines*, 26 Rev. Ind. Org. 245, 246 (2005). Over the ensuing decades, however, the industry became increasingly concentrated. Indeed, by 2015, just four firms controlled almost ninety percent of the nation's beer market. *See* Bart Watson, *Brewery Consolidation is Not Inevitable*, Brewers Association, Jan. 28, 2015, https://www.brewers association.org/insights/brewery-consolidation/. Is the marijuana industry destined to follow the same path toward consolidation? What factors might facilitate or impede concentration of the marijuana industry? *See* Mikos, *State Taxation, supra*, at 252-54 (discussing the factors that have faciliated consolidation of other vice industries and the prospects for consolidation of the marijuana industry).

4. A similar issue concerns the segmentation of the marijuana market—in other words, the extent to which the same firms supply both medical and recreational users of the drug. The Pathways Report excerpted earlier discusses three options states have for segmenting (or not) the two markets and the reasoning behind each option:

> *1) Unitary System: All policy choices completely merge the two markets into one and treat them the same.*
>
> This has the advantage that state and local governments have to establish only one—rather than two—legal systems, while they also work to limit the illicit market. Legal actors in the market can reach the entire market of both recreational and medical users, which would help them offset the costs of compliance with regulations and better compete against the illicit market. A possible drawback is the potential for medical patients to now pay additional excise taxes, although this could be offset if there is a comparable drop in prices, such that the after-tax price before and after is similar to what it is now without an excise tax.
>
> Another drawback to a unitary system is the potential for the larger recreational market to drown out the development and marketing of products with medical and therapeutic benefits. That could be offset with strategies outside the marijuana marketplace: 1) investments in scientific research into the medical benefits and limits of marijuana for a variety of medical conditions, age groups, etc. and 2) education and dissemination of information to doctors about those medical benefits and limits so they can make better informed recommendations to patients that match the labeling requirements for all cannabis products (product type, chemical content, dosage, etc.) leaving the customer to only need assistance in the retail store to find that type of product, without further medical advice needed in the retail store.
>
> *2) Completely Separate Systems: All policy choices to maintain complete separation of medical and adult use from seed to sale.*
>
> This model ensures that those patients with valid medical needs receive different, specialized products and services. The issue of 18-21 year olds with valid medical need would be addressed; they would pick up their medicine at the same retailers with adults 21

and over that also have medical need. This model does risk increasing the costs both for regulators and for cultivators and retailers because they could only work on one side of the industry or the other. If the medical products are subject to stronger testing requirements, and have a more limited market size and customer base to spread their fixed costs, those products may well become more expensive—potentially much more expensive—because of the underlying business costs, even if the tax rate is lower than recreational. In this case, some medical users would likely turn to the adult use retailers anyway, which will still have tested and labeled products for basic consumer safety needs, potentially leaving the medical retailers with even fewer customers.

*3) Hybrid System(s): Some policy choices merged and some separated.*

Starting with a unitary system where all functions are merged, perhaps the first accommodation of a separate function would be how to provide medical marijuana to patients with valid medical needs between the ages of 18-21. Consideration should be given as to whether stricter controls for access to medical cards would be needed for 18-21 year olds than current policy. The reality is that these young adults, who are not minors, can currently access marijuana through either the medical or illicit market.

Policymakers could also mix and match additional functions, with a dizzying number of combinations. For example, the same regulatory agency could oversee both systems (the FDA regulates certain aspects of both food and drug regulation), and cultivators could grow cannabis for either market. Retailers could be the same, but the employees who sell could be differently trained and licensed within the same retail facility.

Policymakers could merge almost all the functions to achieve the greatest efficiency but tax patients with serious medical needs at a lower rate than recreational users or offer them subsidized or reduced prices at the point of retail sale. This avoids the risk of a small separate medical system with higher operating costs passed on as higher prices to patients, despite a lower tax for patients.

But it creates a new problem—incentivizing adults to still get medical marijuana cards. To combat the problem of adults abusing the medical system, the state could establish stronger requirements to obtain a medical card, which would impose a burden on doctors and legitimate patients. Yet another option is to waive taxes or offer subsidized prices to patients with both a valid medical marijuana card and on Medi-Cal, ensuring that subsidies are going only to those with financial need.

These questions have to be asked: Does the benefit of a lower tax for patients justify the burden to patients and doctors posed by stricter requirements for medical cards in order to keep recreational users out of the less taxed medical marijuana system? Or, in an effort to avoid that burden on patients and doctors, is the benefit of a lower tax for everyone applied equally worth the reduction in tax revenue? Could a smaller medical industry provide competitive prices for unique products and services relative to the legal adult-use market, regardless of tax? What other unique issues face patients who need medicine, as compared to other adult users who choose marijuana for recreational purposes?

These policy decisions need to be made and their impacts monitored, with flexibility built in to the new rules so that they can be adjusted in response to lessons learned. California can also learn from lessons in Washington and Colorado, with the former integrating medical and adult use, and the latter maintaining separate systems.

Blue Ribbon Commission on Marijuana Policy, *Pathways Report, supra,* at 34-35.

Which approach to segmentation do you favor, and why? Is one supplier necessarily right for all consumers? In the long run, can a state sustain a segmented market, any more than it can sustain a fragmented one? As the BRC Pathways Report briefly notes, Washington state consolidated its recreational and medical markets in 2015. *See* Cannabis Patient Protection Act, 2015 Wash. Legis. Serv. Ch. 70 (SSSB 5052). In a nutshell,

Washington folded the medical marijuana market into the more heavily regulated recreational marijuana market (though it continues to offer some licensees a special "medical marijuana endorsement," as noted in Chapter 8). Are other states that legalize both medical and recreational marijuana bound to follow Washington's path? Why, why not?

### *(iii) Government-Owned and -Operated Marijuana Suppliers*

Although no state as yet has assumed direct ownership and operation of a marijuana manufacturing or distribution business, the idea is not so farfetched. Indeed, as discussed in Chapter 8, Louisiana has authorized two state universities to supply marijuana for the state's medical marijuana program, and the City of North Bonneville, Washington, has created a public development authority to own and operate a state-licensed retail marijuana store. Putting aside the preemption, grant funding, and legal liability questions these efforts raise (questions discussed in Chapters 10 and 14), would direct government control of the marijuana industry assuage some of the problems attributed to a commercial marijuana industry? The following excerpt discusses the potential benefits and costs of the government supply model.

### *Jonathan P. Caulkins et al.*, Considering Marijuana Legalization: Insights for Vermont and Other Jurisdictions (cont'd)
(RAND 2015)

... [A]fter repeal of federal alcohol prohibition in 1933, some states chose to move beyond mere licensing and regulation to directly own and operate parts of the supply chain in order to limit the influence of for-profit businesses.... It was a partial—not a pure—government monopoly because none of the states produced its own alcohol, but, in many places, the state was the only wholesale distributor or the retail shops were state-run....

Given the wealth of research suggesting that alcohol monopolies are better for public health than less regulated options . . . , we focus special attention on this particular supply alternative. . . .

Direct government control of the supply chain would offer at least four categories of potentially beneficial effects. . . .

#### POTENTIAL BENEFIT 1: CONTROL OF DIVERSION

If the state itself operates the production and distribution chain, limiting diversion could become somewhat easier. It could transform diversion from a regulatory violation by an independent private company to theft or unlawful sale by a supervised government employee. Also, unless the regulatory system is extremely efficient, distributing licenses for legal production to private entities might help provide cover for illegal production, in somewhat the way owning a cash-based business can provide cover for a money-laundering operation. Minimizing diversion from private production is possible, but it could require more effort, partially offsetting legalization's anticipated benefit of eliminating the government's costs of enforcing a prohibition.

## POTENTIAL BENEFIT 2: REVERSIBILITY

If monopoly proves the best method of legalization, it will be easy to retain monopoly if Vermont adopts that method from the beginning. If Colorado- and Washington-style commercial legalization proves to be a better choice for Vermont, it will be relatively easy to switch from monopoly to private commerce. But, if Vermont adopts commercial legalization from the beginning and later realizes that it prefers another supply architecture, change might be more difficult. Commercial interests, at that point vested, would presumably oppose any proposal to take away their profits. Because it is more readily reversible in light of information yet to be obtained, monopoly is a more adaptable method of legalizing than private commerce.

## POTENTIAL BENEFIT 3: AVOIDING ADVERTISING AND PRODUCT INNOVATION

Private companies in the United States can advertise; their First Amendment protections of commercial free speech are very strong. . . . However, if a government monopoly controlled supply, firms would have no incentive to spend their money promoting consumption of the government's product, even if they technically retained that right. So placing the entire distribution system in the government's hands sidesteps concerns about commercial advertising.

Government monopoly of just the retail stores would achieve a bit of this benefit; the government could directly control signage and point-of-sale displays, as opposed to merely issuing constitutionally questionable regulations of those practices. However, if the government stores sold name-brand merchandise produced by private companies, then those companies would continue to have an interest in promoting their brands.

The government could also outsource production but sell only a generic commodity with no branding or other labeling that identified the producer. In theory, that might limit producers' incentive to advertise as much as government operation of production would.

. . .

## POTENTIAL BENEFIT 4: PREVENTING A PRICE COLLAPSE

We expect that in the medium to long run, a free-market industry would innovate in ways that drive down production costs, and competitive pressures would force companies to pass along those savings to consumers in the form of lower prices. For most consumer goods, lower prices are a cause for celebration, but, if consumers are vulnerable to overindulging, low prices might be problematic. For example, some view innovation that has led to very low prices for soda pop, junk food, and candy to be a curse, not a blessing, for the American public.

The typical response of economists is that low production costs remain a blessing even if one prefers moderately high prices because one can always use taxes to prop prices up to whatever level is deemed socially optimal. . . .

Propping up prices with high taxes always works in the classroom, and usually works in the real world, but there are two caveats. The first is that, if the industry gets too powerful, it could lobby successfully for lower taxes. Arguably, that applies to alcohol, federal taxes for which have not been adjusted for inflation since 1991 and so have fallen enormously in real terms. The second catch is that, if taxes are too high, they invite evasion.

A government monopoly will not solve this problem completely. If the prices are too high either in government stores or in private stores subject to large taxes, then that might induce black-market production. However, a government monopoly might be able to sustain a higher retail price because it would be easier to detect and suppress illegal activity if legitimate production were a government monopoly. Then any production outside of the identified government facilities would necessarily be illegal, whereas, if tax-evading activity could hide amid legal private production, it might be hard for enforcement agents to ascertain quickly whether a particular production site or a particular shipment in transit is legal or illegal.

### POTENTIAL COST AND ITS POSSIBLE IRRELEVANCE

One of the usual arguments against government monopolies is that they are inefficient and unimaginative. Oddly, inefficiency might not be a serious problem with regard to marijuana production. Freed from the obligation to produce discreetly, marijuana-production costs might be quite low in the long run. So if the government wastefully produces at double the cost of an efficient free-market enterprise, that deadweight loss to society might not be all that large in absolute terms. . . .

## Notes and Questions

1. What do you think of government ownership and control of the marijuana industry? Would government ownership and control ameliorate the problems associated with a private marijuana industry? In any event, could a state controlled industry compete with the black market or with private suppliers from other states?

2. Could a state with an already established private marijuana industry assume monopoly control over all (or even part) of the industry? Would such a move be politically feasible? What other costs might be entailed?

3. Are there any other ways to align the incentives of commercial suppliers with the interests of society? Would requiring commercial suppliers to operate on a non-profit basis help? As discussed in Chapter 8, some states already require commercial suppliers to do this.

4. Ultimately, how much (if at all) do you think harmful use will increase under the different approaches states have pursued toward regulating the supply of marijuana? Might any of these approaches be *too* restrictive? After all, reform states do not want to curb *all* use of marijuana. How can a state best balance the competing goals of ensuring access for beneficial uses of marijuana and denying access for harmful ones?

## B. REGULATORY COSTS

This section shifts the focus to the costs of prohibition and its alternatives. It compares not only the fiscal impacts of competing regulatory approaches, but also their effects on equality under the law—mirroring Chapter 5's discussion of policies towards marijuana users.

Part III. Marijuana Suppliers

## 1. Fiscal Costs

For two reasons, regulating legalized marijuana is commonly thought to be more budget-friendly than prohibiting marijuana outright. The textbook author has explained:

> [For one thing, legalizing and then taxing marijuana] is supposed to generate substantial revenues for cash-strapped state governments. State governments already derive substantial revenues from vice taxes imposed on alcohol and tobacco products. Tobacco taxes generated more than $16.1 billion for state governments in 2008, and alcohol taxes contributed another $5.3 billion to state coffers. Some estimates suggest that imposing a tax on marijuana sales could dramatically increase state vice tax revenues. The California Board of Equalization (BOE), for example, suggests that legalizing and taxing marijuana [under Proposition 19] would generate $1.382 billion in new revenue for California alone—more than the state now generates from alcohol and cigarette taxes combined ($327 million and $1.04 billion, respectively).
>
> In a related vein, imposing a marijuana tax in lieu of criminal sanctions (like imprisonment) could also save states millions (if not billions) of dollars they currently spend on enforcing marijuana prohibition. The basic idea is that it is cheaper to impose taxes on drug distributors than it is to imprison them. For one thing, prisons cost upwards of $65,000 per bed to construct; a tax, by contrast, has no comparable start-up capital expenses. A prison also costs exorbitant sums to operate—roughly $40,000 per bed annually. To be sure, a tax costs something to enforce; the state must process tax filings, audit taxpayers, prosecute evaders, and so on. But on balance, the costs of administering a tax system are going to be less (possibly far less) than the costs of administering a criminal justice system. Many constitutional guarantees that drive up the cost of enforcing law—such as the right to a government-supplied attorney—apply only to criminal proceedings; and the burden of proof in establishing criminal liability (beyond a reasonable doubt) is much more onerous for government agents to satisfy than is the burden of proof in establishing tax liability (preponderance of the evidence).
>
> The marginal cost-savings of replacing prohibition with a tax could be substantial. One estimate suggests that American governments (state and federal combined) spend $10 billion annually enforcing the marijuana prohibition. California alone is thought to spend roughly $156 million per year on law enforcement directed at marijuana prohibition. Some of that would need to be re-deployed to collect marijuana taxes: for example, to process filings, and to detect, prosecute, and punish tax evaders. And California would still need to police other restrictions on marijuana, such as the continuing prohibition on sales to minors. The BOE has not yet projected these expenses, but California currently spends $36 million annually to enforce the state's tax on cigarettes. Assuming the state would need to spend a comparable sum enforcing the marijuana tax and related restrictions, the marginal cost savings of imposing a tax in lieu of criminal sanctions would be around $120 million.
>
> It is this financial motive—the prospect of generating new revenue and shedding expensive criminal-justice costs—that has recently propelled marijuana law reform into the national spotlight. . . .

Mikos, *State Taxation, supra*, at 226-29.

In the years since the quoted passage was written, several states have legalized recreational marijuana. The experience of those early adopters might shed some light on the comparative fiscal costs of prohibition and legalization. To that end, **Figure 9.2** displays an estimate of the revenues and expenditures attributable to marijuana regulation under Colorado's Amendment 64 (the dark bars) in fiscal year 2014-2015. It also displays an estimate of what Colorado's revenues and expenditures would have been in that same fiscal year had the state continued to prohibit marijuana (the white bars).

Figure 9.2. Estimated Revenues and Expenditures Under Prohibition and Legalization in Colorado, FY 2014-15 (in millions)*

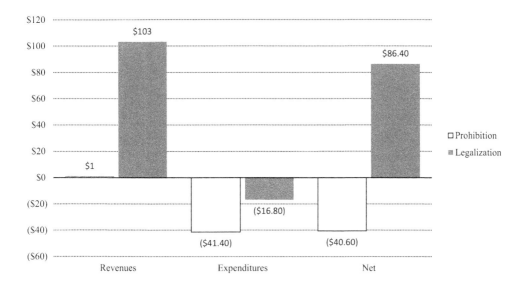

In that year, that state spent an estimated $16.8 million enforcing its nascent licensing system and remaining criminal prohibitions, e.g., distributing without a license. The same year, the state collected $103.2 million in revenue from marijuana taxes, licensing fees, and licensing fines. On balance, the state *netted* $86.4 million from marijuana under legalization. No one knows for certain how much Colorado would have spent had it continued to prohibit marijuana—indeed, even historical data concerning spending on marijuana prohibition can be hard to estimate. However, a study of prior expenditures

---

* The income under legalization ($103 million) includes taxes, licensing fees, and licensing fines collected by the state for FY 2014-2015 (i.e., the figure does not include local taxes and fees). Marijuana Enforcement Division, Report to the Joint Budget Committee and House and Senate Finance Committees of the Colorado General Assembly, Apr. 1, 2016, https://perma.cc/DV6F-V9RE. Income under prohibition ($0.8 million) includes the value of forfeited assets and fines collected. It is necessarily a (rough) estimate, based on an analysis finding that jurisdictions recoup about 2 percent of what they spend enforcing drug prohibitions through fines and seizures. See Jeffrey Miron & Katherine Waldock, *The Budgetary Impact of Ending Drug Prohibition* 4 tbl. 2 (Cato Inst. 2010). The expenditures under prohibition (adjusted to $41.4 for inflation) represent the costs of apprehending, prosecuting, and punishing marijuana offenders (including both users and suppliers). They are, again, necessarily only (rough) estimates, based on Christopher Stiffler, *Amendment 64 Would Produce $60 Million in New Revenue and Savings for Colorado*, Aug. 16, 2012, https://perma.cc/3PVZ-4YLK. The expenditures under legalization include the MED's enforcement expenditures for FY 2014-2015, totaling $8.6 million, MED, Report, *supra*, plus a rough estimate of the money spent by other agencies to enforce marijuana crimes ($8.2 million). The latter figure was calculated using the prohibition expenditures figure noted above, discounted by the reduction in the criminal marijuana caseload since Amendment 64 was passed—a reduction of about 80 percent from 2010 to 2014. See Jon Gettman, *Marijuana Arrests in Colorado After the Passage of Amendment 64* (undated), https://perma.cc/SPV3-9D9A.

estimates that Colorado would have spent $41.4 million (inflation adjusted) on enforcing marijuana prohibition that year. It might have recouped roughly $800,000 of that from fines and seizures. On balance, then, the state would have spent $40.6 million more than it recouped. The difference in the net fiscal costs associated with the two regimes is thus about $127 million. (The footnote to **Figure 9.2** includes additional explanations and sources used to calculate these figures.)

## Notes and Questions

1. Are there any other costs that should be included in a fiscal analysis of marijuana policy? Doctor Kevin Sabet, the head of Smart Approaches to Marijuana, suggests that analyses like the one outlined above leave out an important category of costs and are thus misleading. He explains:

> The social costs of marijuana production and use will far exceed what state and local governments collect as actual tax revenue. We've been down this road with alcohol. . . . Society gains about $15 to $20 billion a year from the taxes imposed on alcohol, while it loses over $200 billion a year in healthcare, criminal justice, and other costs directly related to alcohol use and abuse. That's a ratio of 10 to 1 . . . of costs to revenue.

Kevin A. Sabet, Reefer Sanity: Seven Great Myths About Marijuana 124 (Beaufort 2015). Sabet's argument rests on the notion that the harms of marijuana use will necessarily increase following legalization. Do you agree? If so, what is the likely magnitude of these additional marijuana-related harms? Is one billion dollars (i.e., 10 times Colorado's annual marijuana tax revenues) a reasonable estimate? Even if the harms of *marijuana* use increase, might the harms associated with the use other substances—including alcohol—fall? *See* Chapter 5 (discussing debates over whether marijuana and alcohol/tobacco are substitutes or complements). In any event, what about the *benefits* of marijuana use? Should those be included in any fiscal analyses? Is there any way to measure them?

2. Colorado's marijuana tax revenues continue to grow, along with sales of the drug. In FY 2015-2016, the state collected $156.7 million in marijuana taxes and licensing fees, an increase of more than 50 percent from the prior year (reported in **Figure 9.2** above). Are Colorado's revenue figures representative—i.e., could other legalization states expect to collect a similar figure? Are they sustainable? In particular, what do you think will happen to Colorado's marijuana tax revenues as more states legalize recreational marijuana? As discussed in Chapter 10, a large portion of Colorado's tax receipts appear to come from sales to non-residents.

3. Marijuana taxes are designed to serve two distinct purposes: (1) curb harmful uses, as discussed in Section A.2.a, *supra*; and (2) raise revenues. Might these purposes sometimes conflict? In other words, does the tax rate that best curbs harmful use also necessarily maximize revenues? If not, what are the ramifications for marijuana law and policy?

### 2. Liberty Costs

Prohibition regimes exact the heaviest toll on personal liberty, especially when it comes to marijuana supply activities. In prohibition regimes, individuals who manufacture or distribute marijuana are subjected to particularly harsh sanctions—including long periods of imprisonment. Furthermore, the burdens imposed by supply prohibitions—just like the burdens imposed by use prohibitions, see Chapter 5—may be borne disproportionately by minorities, raising distinct equal justice concerns. *See* Gettman, *Marijuana Arrests*, *supra* (reporting that blacks were 2.5 times more likely than whites to be arrested for marijuana possession and 6.9 times more likely to be arrested for marijuana distribution in Colorado in 2010—two years before passage of Amendment 64).

While legalization has reduced the number of people charged with marijuana offenses and thus the collective toll on personal liberty, it has not yet reduced disparities in the distribution of the remaining burden. Disparities in arrest rates for marijuana supply offenses—like those for possession offenses discussed in Chapter 5—persist in the wake of reforms. In a report prepared for the Drug Policy Alliance, for example, Professor Jonathan Gettman concluded that "[r]acial disparities in Colorado marijuana arrests persist and have not substantially changed after the passage of Amendment 64. While the number of arrests for marijuana offenses dropped dramatically in 2014, they are still characterized by higher arrest rates for black people than for white people." *Id.* (reporting that blacks were 2.1 times more likely than whites to be arrested for marijuana possession and 5.7 times more likely to be arrested for marijuana distribution in Colorado in 2013—the year following passage of Amendment 64).

Perhaps just as importantly, legalization regimes may be re-creating those same inequalities in the distribution of the new economic *opportunities* created by legalization. As one commentator has pessimistically quipped, "American racisim does not go away—it evolves." Christian Davenport, *The "Chronic" and Coercion*, in Something's in the Air, *supra*, at 148. So how have minorities fared in the new state-licensed marijuana industry? And what can states do to enable minority participation in that industry? The materials below explore these questions.

*(i) Minority Participation in the Legal Marijuana Industry*

The following report discusses the rate of minority ownership of state-licensed marijuana suppliers.

## Amanda Chicago Lewis, How Black People Are Being Shut Out of America's Weed Boom
Buzzfeed (Mar. 16, 2016)

For most jobs, experience will help you get ahead. In the marijuana industry, it's not that simple. Yes, investors and state governments are eager to hire and license people with expertise in how to cultivate, cure, trim, and process cannabis. But it can't be someone who got caught. Which for the most part means it can't be someone who is black.

Even though research shows people of all races are about equally likely to have broken the law by growing, smoking, or selling marijuana, black people are much more likely to have been arrested for it. Black people are much more likely to have ended up with a criminal record because of it. And every state that has legalized medical or recreational marijuana bans people with drug felonies from working at, owning, investing in, or sitting on the board of a cannabis business. After having borne the brunt of the "war on drugs," black Americans are now largely missing out on the economic opportunities created by legalization.

. . .

Nobody keeps official statistics on race and cannabis business ownership. But based on more than 150 interviews with dispensary owners, industry insiders, and salespeople who interact with a lot of pot shops, it appears that fewer than three dozen of the 3,200 to 3,600 storefront marijuana dispensaries in the United States are owned by black people—about 1%.

At this rare and decisive moment in American history, state governments are literally handing control of a multibillion-dollar industry to a chosen few, creating wealth overnight. The pot trade has long been open to anyone with some seeds and some hustle, so there are more than enough cannabis experts out there to form a truly diverse industry—if only the laws weren't systematically preventing thousands of qualified black people from participating.

Even without a criminal record, black people looking to get involved in legal weed face major obstacles. Sarah Cross, the chief operating officer of Green Rush Consulting, estimated that it takes at least a quarter of a million dollars to start a legal marijuana business. After centuries of systemic discrimination in housing, employment, and education, black Americans are far less likely to have or be able to raise that kind of money. Small business loans are out of the question, because banks are insured by federal agencies, and the federal government still considers cannabis illegal.

Legalizing marijuana sounds revolutionary, but with every day that passes, the same class of rich white men that control all other industries are tightening their grip on this one, snatching up licenses and real estate and preparing for a windfall. First-mover advantage, they call it. That means that anyone who doesn't make the risky leap to violate federal law and get involved now will miss out, forever. In a few years, when the land grab is over, the cannabis industry may become just another example in America's never-ending cycle of racially motivated economic injustices.

## Notes and Questions

1. Are you surprised the rate of minority participation in the licensed marijuana industry? According to Lewis, why are so few marijuana licenses held by minority-owned enterprises? Can you think of any other reasons for the low rate of participation? *See* Tracy Jarrett, *Six Reasons African Americans Aren't Breaking into Cannabis Industry*, NBC News, Apr. 19, 2016, http://www.nbcnews.com/news/nbcblk/6-reasons-african-americans-cant-break-cannabis-industry-n344486.

### (ii) How Can States Boost Minority Participation in the Legal Marijuana Industry?

At least one state (Maryland) has taken a very direct approach to increasing minority participation in its licensed marijuana industry. As described in Chapter 8, Maryland's medical marijuana law is supposed to give racial and ethnic minorities some preference in the award of the state's commercial marijuana licenses. But do such preferences violate the Equal Protection Clause of the Constitution? U.S. Const. Am. XIV, § 1 ("No state shall . . . deny to any person within its jurisdiction the equal protection of the law."). In the following letter, written in response to the inquiry of a state legislator, the state Attorney General's Office opines on the constitutionality of Maryland's efforts to boost minority participation in the marijuana industry.

## The Attorney General of Maryland, Office of Counsel to the General Assembly, Letter to Delegate Chris West, March 13, 2015

Dear Delegate West:

You have asked for advice concerning the validity of certain provisions of the Natalie M. LaPrade Medical Marijuana Commission Law[, and s]pecifically, . . . whether these provisions are unconstitutional. . . .

Health—General Article, § 13-3309(a)(9)(i) provides that, in licensing growers of medical marijuana, the Medical Marijuana Commission ("the Commission") shall:

> 1. Actively seek to achieve racial, ethnic, and geographic diversity when licensing medical marijuana growers; and
> 2. Encourage applicants who qualify as a minority business enterprise. . . .

Health—General Article, § 13-3310(c), which relates to the licensing of dispensaries, provides that the Commission shall:

> (2) Actively seek to achieve racial, ethnic, and geographic diversity when licensing dispensaries.

. . . [T]he Attorney General [has previously] advised "that these provisions be implemented consistent with the provisions of the United States Constitution as described in *Richmond v. J.A. Croson Co.*, 488 U.S. 469 (1989) and *Fisher v. University of Texas at Austin*, 133 S. Ct. 2411 (2013)." . . . It is well-established that a race-conscious affirmative action program is subject to strict scrutiny and will be upheld by the courts only if it is narrowly tailored to achieve a compelling public purpose. . . . The *Croson* case held that a governmental entity has a compelling interest in remedying identified past and present race discrimination. *Id.* at 492, 509, For this interest to be compelling, the government must be able to identify discrimination in the relevant market in which the entity is a participant. *Id.* at 501-504. In addition, there must be a "strong basis in evidence" of that discrimination at the time the program is established. *Id.* at 500, 510. In the context of government contracting, which was the subject of *Croson*, this requires a study showing a "significant statistical disparity" between the availability of qualified, willing, and able minority subcontractors and the utilization of such subcontractors by the governmental entity or its prime contractors. *HB Roue Co., Inc. v. Tippett*, 615 F.3d 233, 241 (4th Cir. 2010). The *Fisher* case, for our purposes, confirms that the test set out in *Croson* still stands, and that a Court will closely scrutinize a government's justification of a race-conscious program and its evidence in support of that program.

The provisions of *Croson* and *Fisher* apply to ethnicity in the same way as race. They do not, however, apply to geographically conscious programs. Thus, the law should be read to have full force to the extent that it requires the Commission to seek geographic diversity to the extent possible. Moreover, it is not unconstitutional to encourage businesses of any type, including . . . minority business enterprise[s] . . . , to apply to participate in any type of government program. Constitutional limits, however, would prevent the Commission from conducting race- or ethnicity conscious licensing in the absence of a disparity study showing past discrimination in similar programs. I am aware of no study that would cover grower or dispensary licensees, or even licensing in general. . . . As a result, the efforts of the Commission to seek racial and ethnic diversity among growers and dispensaries would have to be limited to broad publicity given to the availability of the licenses and encouragement of those from various groups.

. . .

Sincerely,
Kathryn M. Rowe
Assistant Attorney General

## Notes and Questions

1. Do you agree with the Attorney General's analysis? Do racial and ethnic preferences in the award of marijuana licenses necessarily violate the Equal Protection Clause? Does the Lewis report excerpted above adequately demonstrate discrimination in the marijuana market and thereby provide Maryland with a compelling interest for considering race in the award of its medical marijuana licenses?

2. Postscript. In response to the letter, the Chair of the Commission issued a statement that reads, in relevant part:

> When drafting the original law for issuing licenses to grow, process, and dispense medicinal cannabis in the State of Maryland, the Commission initially took every step possible to include racial diversity as a weighted component of the regulations . . . because of a strong belief that minority inclusion is of paramount importance to this new industry. . . . Based on the Attorney General's opinion to Delegate Chris West concerning this issue, the Commission found it necessary to remove the provisions from the final regulations.
>
> . . .
>
> [The Commission] followed strict regulations and guidelines defined at the beginning of the application process as required by law, to ensure a fair and objective selection process [for the award of licenses]. The Commission enlisted Towson University's Regional Economic Studies Institute ("RESI") to conduct the evaluation of applicants through a double-blinded process. Due to the Attorney General's opinion . . . , there were no requirements to disclose race on the application. In addition, all identifying information such as individual, entity, investor, and employee names were redacted. The Commissioners voted only on coded and redacted RESI applications.
>
> We all know that this process was extremely competitive. The Commission received 145 Grower applications, but could only grant up to 15 Grower pre-approvals because of statutory limitations implemented by the legislature.

A Letter from the Chairman of the Maryland Medical Cannabis Commission, at https://perma.cc/4YXP-526N. Even if the Attorney General's opinion regarding the constitutionality of racial and ethnic preferences is correct, was the Commission precluded from gathering data on the racial and ethnic composition of license applicants, as the Chair seems to suggest? If so, how is a state to determine whether there has been racial or ethnic discrimination that might justify remedial preferences in the first place?

3. The Attorney General's letter suggests that the Maryland licensing Commission could still *encourage* minority business owners to apply for licenses. Is encouragement by itself likely to boost minority participation rates? Do states like Maryland have any other, race neutral options by which to increase minority participation in the marijuana

industry? Along these lines, consider the novel approach taken by Oakland California, as described in following Problem:

**Problem 9.5**: In 2016, the City of Oakland, California, adopted the Dispensary Equity Permit Program, under which the City will award at least 50 percent of its marijuana business licenses to applicants who meet the following criteria:

A. Criteria. Applicant must have at least one member who meets all of the following criteria:

1. Be an Oakland resident who:

a. Resides for at least two (2) years prior to the date of application in Oakland Police Department Beats 26Y, 30X, 30Y, 31Z, 32Y, and 34X; or those individuals who, within the last ten (10) years, have been previously incarcerated for a marijuana-related offense as a result of a conviction arising out of Oakland, California;

b. Maintains not less than a fifty percent (50%) ownership in the Dispensary applicant entity, partnership, limited liability corporation, collective, corporation, worker cooperative or other recognized ownership entity; and

2. Prior marijuana or cannabis conviction shall not be a bar to equity ownership.

Oakland Mun. Code 5.80.045 (2016). Is the Dispensary Equity Permit Program constitutional? *See generally* Brian T. Fitzpatrick, *Can Michigan Universities Use Proxies for Race After the Ban on Racial Preferences?*, 133 Mich. J. Race & L. 277 (2007).

4. Ultimately, how should governments regulate the supply of marijuana? What policy objectives would you prioritize? Which of the many regulations discussed above and in Chapters 7 and 8 would you favor and why?

CHAPTER 10

# Authority over Marijuana Suppliers

Just like the laws governing marijuana possession and use, the laws governing marijuana production and distribution raise a host of fascinating questions about the power of different government actors to shape marijuana policy. Chapter 6 provided an introduction to how power is spread across *levels* of government (federal, state, and local) and different *branches* within those levels (legislative, executive, and judicial). This chapter builds on that discussion by exploring a series of questions of special relevance to the regulation of marijuana suppliers.

The questions addressed in the chapter include: Can the President stop enforcing the federal marijuana ban? Are licensing laws or any other state supply regulations preempted by the federal CSA? May local governments ban the production and distribution of marijuana, even when those activities are permitted by state law? Finally, who *should* control policy toward marijuana suppliers?

## A. CAN THE PRESIDENT STOP ENFORCING THE FEDERAL MARIJUANA BAN?

Chapter 6 discussed the executive branch's power to re-schedule marijuana under the CSA. In addition to that formal power, the executive branch also exerts some de facto power over federal marijuana policy by controlling how federal law is enforced.

The Department of Justice's marijuana enforcement guidelines discussed in Chapter 7 are one prominent example of how the executive branch has used enforcement discretion to help shape federal policy. Even though Congress's marijuana ban remains on the books, the DOJ's enforcement policy has arguably narrowed the scope of that ban by discouraging federal prosecutors from pursuing legal action against certain individuals who have plainly violated federal law.

But the executive branch's use of enforcement discretion to re-shape the content of federal policy has generated controversy. One of the primary objections is that by refusing to enforce the law the executive branch is, in practical effect, amending the law, and is thereby usurping Congress's legislative powers. The following article discusses this objection.

## *Sam Kamin*, Prosecutorial Discretion in the Context of Immigration and Marijuana Law Reform: The Search for a Limiting Principle
___ Ohio St. Crim. L. Rev. ___ (2016)

[I]n the enforcement of both federal marijuana law and immigration policy, the Obama administration has quite publicly promulgated a policy of limited and selective enforcement of federal law. Unable or unwilling to change federal policy in these areas through legislation, the Obama administration has, controversially, sought to use its enforcement discretion to achieve policy outcomes. Marijuana and immigration, then, serve as tests of the permissible power of the executive to set federal policy through the selective enforcement of the law as written rather than through legislative enactment.

. . .

[W]e can imagine two extreme views of prosecutorial discretion, both of which are untenable. On the one hand, the power to invalidate completely a criminal statute by refusing categorically to enforce a valid law is clearly beyond the authority of a prosecutor. Such a policy would be a clear usurpation of the legislative prerogative, tantamount to allowing a prosecutor to substitute her own views regarding the wisdom of criminal laws for those of a duly elected legislative body. On the other hand, the conception that prosecutorial discretion should or even could be completely legislated away is a fallacy; for better or for worse and in a world of limited resources, any sensible criminal justice system will always rely in part on the wisdom and judgment of those charged with enforcing the laws.

The trick, of course, lies in determining exactly how far toward one of these extremes executive policy may stray in practice. . . .

. . .

Under the Take Care Clause, the federal executive [] is charged with taking care that the laws of the United States are faithfully executed. . . . [H]owever, . . . the Take Care Clause has never been read as requiring the executive branch to carry out every federal law, in every context, precisely as written. Rather, the size and scope of the federal government and enormity of the tasks with which it is charged necessarily require the federal executive to use discretion, including the discretion not to act, in carrying out its constitutional obligation. The Take Care Clause forms a limit on this discretion, preventing administrative lawlessness in the form of overreaching or inaction. . . .

The Supreme Court's principal modern case on the limits of the federal executive's authority not to act is set forth in *Heckler v. Chaney*[, 470 U.S. 821 (1985)]. There the Court considered the challenge brought by a number of condemned inmates against the Food and Drug Administration (FDA). Respondents argued that the states' proposed use of certain drugs to put [them] to death violated a federal statute the FDA was charged with enforcing and that the agency should takes steps to prevent the states from doing so. The Court disagreed, holding that while many exercises of executive agency discretion are reviewable under the APA, the presumption in favor of review could be overcome if the "agency action is committed to agency discretion by law."

> [A]n agency decision not to enforce often involves a complicated balancing of a number of factors which are peculiarly within its expertise. Thus, the agency must not only assess whether a violation has occurred, but whether agency resources are best spent on this violation or another, whether the agency is likely to succeed if it acts, whether the particular enforcement action requested best fits the agency's overall policies, and, indeed, whether the agency has enough resources to undertake the action at all. An agency

generally cannot act against each technical violation of the statute it is charged with enforcing. The agency is far better equipped than the courts to deal with the many variables involved in the proper ordering of its priorities. Similar concerns animate the principles of administrative law that courts generally will defer to an agency's construction of the statute it is charged with implementing, and to the procedures it adopts for implementing that statute.

Applying these principles to the case at bar, the Court concluded that the decision not to bring an enforcement action is similar in structure to a decision of a federal prosecutor not to bring a case, a decision generally deemed to be completely insulated from judicial review. Thus, although it seemed clear that the states were in fact planning to use execution drugs in a method not permitted under federal law, the Supreme Court insulated from review the agency's decision to do nothing about it.

In upholding agency inaction, the *Chaney* Court described the Take Care Clause as a shield in the hands of the executive as much as a sword in the hands of the public. Because it is the executive that is charged with executing the laws it is not for private litigants—or courts—to second guess those decisions without good cause. The assignment of the power to enforce laws to the executive branch, the Court reasoned, is often reason enough for Courts to be wary of reviewing those decisions.

Although the Supreme Court has not given us many interpretations of the Take Care Clause, we can draw certain conclusions regarding the permissible scope of agency discretion not to act from *Chaney* and elsewhere. For example, these cases tell us that deference to agency discretion is at its strongest when the agency chooses not to act rather than when it affirmatively chooses to act: "[W]hen an agency refuses to act, it generally does not exercise its coercive power over an individual's liberty or property rights, and thus does not infringe upon areas that courts often are called upon to protect." [*Chaney, supra*, at 832.] The decision to act—to remove an individual from the country, say, or to prosecute an individual for violating federal marijuana laws—has significantly more consequence than the decision to do nothing. The harms associated with inaction, by contrast, are diffuse and difficult for a court to evaluate.

It also seems clear that Congress may limit the exercise of agency discretion through legislation. That is, if Congress feels so strongly about the way law it is passing is to be enforced, the Take Care Clause provides no obstacle to Congress specifying exactly how the law is to be enforced. So, for example, in *Dunlop v. Bachowski*, [421 U.S. 560 (1975),] the Supreme Court concluded that a statute mandating that the Secretary of labor "shall" investigate union election complaints and "shall" bring a civil action if probable cause to believe that a violation has occurred was sufficiently directive to overcome the presumption against judicial review. The *Chaney* Court found no such language or intent present, however, in the language of the FDA's charge; the decision not to bring an enforcement action against the state was deemed to be the sort of run-of-the-mill enforcement discretion generally beyond the reach of courts to evaluate.

In addition, the executive is more likely to have its act of prosecutorial discretion left undisturbed by courts when it engages in case-by-case adjudication rather than making blanket policy pronouncements. That is, a policy setting forth criteria to be used in determining whether or not prosecution will be initiated in a particular case is entitled to far greater deference than an announcement that no cases will be prosecuted or that only certain ones will.

. . .

Thus, the Take Care Clause provides more of a framework than a rule. It both provides that the executive the authority to implement the laws and sets limits on the way the executive does so.

. . .

In the context of federal marijuana law enforcement, it seems clear that the Obama administration's guidance to prosecutors regarding the allocation of scarce resources is nothing more than an exercise of prosecutorial discretion. Through these memos the Obama administration has not announced that it will no longer be prosecuting any marijuana conduct in the states. Rather, it has set forth criteria to help local federal prosecutors determine when they should, and should not, bring marijuana prosecutions. The eight policy outcomes outlined by the administration to guide agency discretion—keeping marijuana distribution from being a front for the distribution of other drugs, keeping marijuana from the hands of children, making sure that it is not trafficked from one state to another, and so on—are exactly the kinds of specific, fact-intensive criteria that prosecutors are used to evaluating in determining whether to initiate prosecutions.

Perhaps more fundamentally, [the DOJ guidelines] did not purport to, and do not operate to, make legal that which Congress, in its wisdom, has chosen to criminalize; rather, they reiterate the fact that marijuana remains illegal throughout the country. This is not a distinction without a difference; the decision not to prosecute those in clear and unambiguous compliance with robust state laws regulating marijuana simply does not do the same work as legalizing that conduct. As has been well-documented, notwithstanding the federal government's prosecutorial forbearance in those states creating robust marijuana regulations, the continuing marijuana prohibition has profound negative effects on those who use marijuana and those who participate in the emerging marijuana industry. So, for example, for the consumer there is the risk of losing one's employment, parental rights, or eligibility for federal benefits. For a business, the risks are less personal but no less substantial. The federal prohibition on all marijuana activity means that marijuana businesses are unable to gain reliable access to banking services. Federal legal protections are almost wholly unavailable to marijuana businesses: a federal bankruptcy court has held that marijuana businesses cannot benefit from federal bankruptcy protection because they come to the court with unclean hands; intellectual property protections—principally trademark and copyright—will be either practically or legally impossible for marijuana businesses to obtain; even finding a lawyer willing to represent a marijuana business in federal court may prove increasingly difficult.

All of these consequences are unaltered by the Obama administration's criminal enforcement memos. Thus, it is simply incorrect to claim, as some have, that the effect of the Obama administration's de-emphasis of marijuana law enforcement in some states has the effect of writing marijuana out of the Controlled Substances Act. Rather, the Administration has removed but one consequence of marijuana's continued prohibition—the threat of criminal or civil enforcement action. Marijuana possession, production, and sale all remain illegal, with significant potential consequences for those violating federal law, whether they are ever charged with a crime or not.

What is more, there has been little Congressional objection to the policy of limited enforcement of marijuana laws. Quite the contrary: rather than taking action to require the executive to enforce the laws more stringently, Congress has done almost exactly the opposite. By passing the Farr-Rohrbacher amendment as part of the Omnibus Spending Bill of 2015, Congress prohibited the Justice Department from expending any funds to "prevent" 23 states "from implementing their own" medical marijuana laws. While the exact meaning of this enactment is the subject of current litigation, it seems clear that majorities of both houses of Congress prefer less marijuana law enforcement in the states to more. Congress' endorsement of the Second Cole Memo makes it considerably harder to view that document as a usurpation of Congress' authority.

## Notes and Questions

1. Does the DOJ's non-enforcement policy usurp Congress's legislative authority? Should the President have the power to refuse to enforce (or only selectively enforce) a law on the books? Does your answer depend on the specific law at issue? Imagine, for example, the DOJ refusing to vigorously enforce laws governing campaign finance, political corruption, immigration, banking, firearms, etc. Would relaxed enforcement of any of these laws give you pause?

2. Does the CSA allow the DOJ to commit itself to non-enforcement without violating the separation of powers principles outlined above? Section 873(a) of the statute states, in relevant part:

> The Attorney General shall cooperate with local, State, tribal, and Federal agencies concerning traffic in controlled substances and suppressing the abuse of controlled substances. To this end, he is authorized to . . . notwithstanding any other provision of law, enter into contractual agreements with State, tribal, and local law enforcement agencies to provide for cooperative enforcement and regulatory activities under this chapter.

21 U.S.C. § 873(a). Professor Mark Kleiman has suggested that this provision empowers the Attorney General to enter into "a cooperative agreement binding the state and its localities to vigorous enforcement against exports in return for federal acquiescence in intra-state sales regulated and taxed under state law . . ." Mark A.R. Kleiman, *Cooperative Enforcement Agreements and Policy Waivers: New Options for Federal Accommodation to State-Level Cannabis Legalization*, 6 J. Drug Pol'y Analysis 41 (2013). Do you agree? Would there be any limits to the DOJ's substantive authority under such agreements?

3. Suppose the political winds change and Congress now wants the executive branch to crack down on marijuana. Is there any way for Congress to push the executive branch to enforce a law (like the marijuana ban) more aggressively? *See* Daniel C. Richman, *Federal Criminal Law, Congressional Delegation, and Enforcement Discretion*, 46 U.C.L.A. L. Rev. 757 (1999) (describing means by which Congress might influence the executive's enforcement decisions). Could Congress even impose a duty on United States Attorneys to prosecute known marijuana violations to the full extent of the law? Some state legislatures have tried this tactic for another crime, domestic violence, because they object to the low rate at which prosecutors were filing domestic abuse charges. *See* Angela Corsilles, Note, *No-Drop Policies in the Prosecution of Domestic Violence Cases: Guarantee to Action or Dangerous Solution?*, 63 Ford. L. Rev. 853 (1994). Could Congress impose a similar mandatory prosecution policy for marijuana cases? If so, what would such a policy look like? Is such a policy even feasible?

4. What is the practical significance of the DOJ's enforcement guidelines? Professor Kamin suggests several reasons why the "decision not to prosecute . . . does not do the

Part III. Marijuana Suppliers

same work as legalizing" marijuana. Kamin, *supra*. *See also* Robert A. Mikos, *A Critical Appraisal of the Department of Justice's New Approach to Medical Marijuana*, 22 Stanford L. & Pol'y Review 633, 634 (2011) ("[T]he [DOJ's non-enforcement policy (NEP)] represents at most a very modest change in federal policy. . . . [The reason is that] the NEP does not repeal the federal ban on marijuana—marijuana technically remains illegal under federal law and that ban triggers a host of civil sanctions on top of the criminal sanctions controlled by the DOJ.").

Notwithstanding its limitations, however, the DOJ's enforcement policy may have significantly altered the way that states regulate the supply of marijuana. Before the policy was first announced in 2009, few medical marijuana states had expressly authorized the commercial supply of marijuana, arguably due to concerns that the federal government could shut down any large-scale commercial suppliers. *See* Robert A. Mikos, *Expert Report in Allard v. Her Majesty the Queen in Right of Canada* (Oct. 2014). After the policy was announced, however, a growing number of medical marijuana states began to authorize commercial supply, even to the exclusion of personal supply—which is less vulnerable to federal enforcement. *Id.* **Figure 10.1** shows the number of medical marijuana states adopting each of the supply models discussed in Chapter 8, from 1996 to 2016. (For a full description of the models, see Chapter 8.)

Figure 10.1. Trends in Supply Models in Medical Marijuana States*

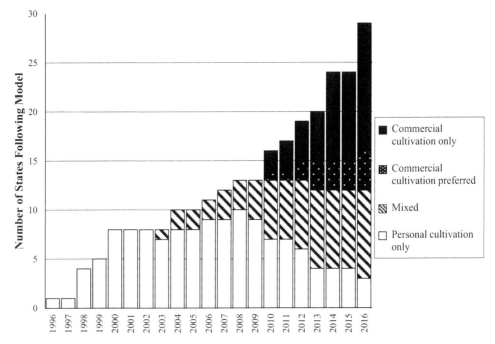

---

* The chart is an update of one included by the textbook author in the Expert Report, *supra*.

5. Ultimately, how much authority does the executive branch have to re-shape federal marijuana policy? Do you think the executive branch could achieve your optimal policy (or something close to it), on its own, i.e., without congressional action?

## B. ARE STATE LICENSING LAWS AND SIMILAR REGULATIONS PREEMPTED BY THE FEDERAL CSA?

Even though the DOJ is—for the time being at least—not pursuing legal action against most state-licensed marijuana suppliers, that has not stopped *other* parties from seeking to challenge state reforms as preempted. But does the federal CSA preempt state regulations of the marijuana market? Section 1 provides a quick primer on preemption and the preemptive language of the CSA. Section 2 then explores the most noteworthy preemption challenge brought to date: the suit filed by Nebraska and Oklahoma against Colorado seeking to block the implementation of Colorado's Amendment 64.

### 1. An Introduction to Preemption

#### *Robert A. Mikos*, Preemption Under the Controlled Substances Act
16 J. Health Care L. & Pol'y 5 (2013)

The issue of preemption arises anytime Congress and the states pass laws that govern the same activity. The Constitution, of course, makes federal law the Supreme law of the land, meaning that Congress can normally preempt (i.e., void) state laws if it so desires. The key in every preemption case is thus divining Congress's preemptive intent.[25]

The best indication of Congress's preemptive intent comes from express statutory language addressing the preemption issue. As the Supreme Court has explained, when Congress speaks directly to preemption, "'there is no need to infer congressional intent to preempt state laws from the substantive provisions' of the legislation."[26]

When Congress neglects to address preemption, courts will nonetheless infer that Congress intended to preempt state law in two situations. First, the courts infer that state law is preempted when Congress passes a "framework of regulation 'so pervasive ... that Congress left no room for the States to supplement it' or where there is a 'federal interest ... so dominant that the federal system will be assumed to preclude enforcement of state laws on the same subject.'"[28] This is called field preemption.

Second, the courts find state law preempted when it conflicts with federal law. Conflicts come in two basic varieties: direct conflicts and obstacles conflicts. The narrower of the two, a direct (or impossibility) conflict arises when it is physically impossible to

---

25. *E.g., Retail Clerks v. Schermerhorn*, 375 U.S. 96, 103 (1963) (noting that Congressional intent is the "ultimate touch-stone" for determining whether state laws are preempted).
26. *Cipollone v. Liggett Group, Inc.*, 505 U.S. 504, 517 (1992) (internal citations omitted).
28. *Arizona v. United States*, 132 S. Ct. 2492, 2501 (2012) (internal citations omitted).

comply with both state and federal law. This would happen, say, if state law orders [someone] to distribute marijuana . . . , because it would be impossible for this person to fulfill his obligation under state law and simultaneously heed the federal ban on distributing marijuana.

The broader type of conflict, called an obstacle (or impediment) conflict, arises anytime state law "stands as an obstacle to the accomplishment and execution of the full purposes and objectives of Congress."[31] This would happen, say, if state law barred employers from discriminating against individuals who participate in the state's medical marijuana program. This particular state law does not require employers to violate federal law; i.e., it does not pose a direct conflict, because federal law does not require employers to terminate known drug users. Yet the law would still arguably undermine one of Congress's goals—that of combating drug abuse—because it would protect marijuana users from adverse employment sanctions, sanctions that might otherwise deter their drug use.[1]

. . .

The CSA includes an express statement of Congress's intent to preempt (or not) state drug laws. Section 903 of the CSA provides:

> No provision of this subchapter shall be construed as indicating an intent on the part of the Congress to occupy the field in which that provision operates, including criminal penalties, to the exclusion of any State law on the same subject matter which would otherwise be within the authority of the State, unless there is a positive conflict between that provision of this subchapter and that State law so that the two cannot consistently stand together.[47]

Section 903 is clear in at least one important respect: it rejects any inference that Congress wanted to preempt the field of drug regulation. Field preemption is Congress's nuclear option. It makes federal law the exclusive law governing a particular subject. But Congress had—and continues to have—strong reasons for not assuming sole responsibility for drug control. Most importantly, the states have far greater law enforcement capacity than does the federal government. The states, for example, handle a very high volume of drug cases every year . . . , far more than does the federal government. . . . Notwithstanding their relatively permissive approach to medical marijuana, the states have adopted laws that generally mimic the substance of the CSA. . . . If Congress wanted to kick the states out of this field altogether, it would likely need to hire thousands more federal law enforcement agents, confirm more federal judges, and build more federal prisons to replace the work now done by their state counterparts.

Congress instead chose to preempt state law only to the extent that it "positive[ly] conflicts" with a provision of the CSA governing "the same subject matter," such that "the two cannot consistently stand together." What did Congress mean by this language? In particular, what sort of conflicts did Congress have in mind to preempt?

---

31. *Hines v. Davidowitz*, 312 U.S. 52, 67 (1941).
1. Author's note: Chapter 13 analyzes whether state anti-discrimination laws are preempted by the CSA to the extent they protect medical marijuana users from employment or housing sanctions.
47. 21 U.S.C. §903 (2011).

Unfortunately, there is very little known legislative history concerning the precise meaning of Section 903.[55] The . . . provision apparently garnered little attention during congressional hearings concerning comprehensive drug law reforms.

Prior to the adoption of state medical marijuana reforms, the courts had remarkably few occasions on which to ponder Congress's preemptive designs. The issue did arise in a handful of early cases brought by defendants in state criminal proceedings. The defendants in those cases challenged state drug laws as preempted because those laws imposed harsher sanctions than those prescribed by the federal CSA. In other words, the defendants claimed that the CSA established a ceiling on penalties for drug-related crimes. These preemption challenges were uniformly rebuffed and the courts spent very little time discussing the issue.

But the rapid proliferation of state marijuana law reforms has occasioned the need for the courts to make more in-depth inquiries into Congress's preemptive intent under the CSA. Courts have been confronted by a growing docket of suits claiming that state reforms are preempted by the CSA.

## 2. The State Suit Against Amendment 64

As noted in the excerpt above, state marijuana regulations have been challenged as preempted in an ever-growing number of cases. The Complaint excerpted below remains the most prominent of these preemption challenges to date. It was filed by two neighboring states seeking to block the implementation of Colorado's regulations governing the commercial supply of marijuana. (The status of the case is discussed more in the notes that follow the Complaint.)

### *States of Nebraska and Oklahoma v. State of Colorado*, Complaint
No. 220144, Original, in the Supreme Court of the United States (2014)

3. In our constitutional system, the federal government has preeminent authority to regulate interstate and foreign commerce, including commerce involving legal and illegal trafficking in drugs such as marijuana. . . .

4. The nation's anti-drug laws reflect a well established—and carefully considered and constructed—balance of national law enforcement, foreign relations, and societal priorities. Congress has assigned to the United States Department of Justice ("DOJ") and the United States Drug Enforcement Administration ("DEA"), along with numerous other federal agencies, the task of enforcing and administering these anti-drug laws and treaty obligations. In administering these laws, the federal agencies balance the complex—and often competing—objectives that animate federal drug law and policy. Although states may exercise their police power in a manner which has an effect on drug policy and trafficking, a state may *not* establish its own policy that is directly counter to federal policy against trafficking in controlled substances or establish a state-sanctioned system for possession, production, licensing, and distribution of drugs in a manner which interferes with the federal drug laws that prohibit possession, use, manufacture, cultivation, and/or

---

55. The few statements on the record simply reiterate the language that became Section 903. See H.R. Rep. No. 91-1444, pt. 1, at 29, 60 (1970).

distribution of certain drugs, including marijuana. *See* 21 U.S.C. § 903. The Constitution and the federal anti-drug laws do not permit the development of a patchwork of state and local pro-drug policies and licensed distribution schemes throughout the country which conflict with federal laws.

5. Despite the preeminent federal authority and responsibility over controlled substances including marijuana, . . . the State of Colorado recently enacted and is now implementing Amendment 64, a sweeping set of provisions which are designed to permit "Personal use of marijuana" and the "Lawful operation of marijuana-related facilities," and further to require the "Regulation of marijuana" provided that "Such regulations shall not prohibit the operation of marijuana establishments, either expressly or through regulations that make their operation unreasonably impractical." *See* [Colo. Const.]. Article XVIII, Section 16.(3), Section 16.(4) and Section 16.(5).

6. Amendment 64 and its resultant statutes and regulations are devoid of safeguards to ensure marijuana cultivated and sold in Colorado is not trafficked to other states, including Plaintiff States.

7. In passing and enforcing Amendment 64, the State of Colorado has created a dangerous gap in the federal drug control system enacted by the United States Congress. Marijuana flows from this gap into neighboring states, undermining Plaintiff States' own marijuana bans, draining their treasuries, and placing stress on their criminal justice systems.

### Federal Authority and Law Governing Controlled Substances and Other Drugs

8. The Supremacy Clause of the Constitution mandates that "[t]his Constitution, and the Laws of the United States which shall be made in Pursuance thereof . . . shall be the supreme Law of the Land . . . any Thing in the Constitution or Laws of any State to the Contrary notwithstanding." U.S. Const., Art. VI, cl. 2.

9. The Constitution affords the federal government the power to "regulate Commerce with foreign Nations, and among the several States, and with the Indian Tribes." U.S. Const., Art. I § 8, cl. 3. The Constitution further affords the federal government the power "[t]o make all Laws which shall be necessary and proper for carrying into Execution" its authority to "regulate Commerce." U.S. Const., Art. I § 8, cl. 18. As such, the federal government has broad authority to regulate the status of drugs within the boundaries of the United States.

10. The U.S. Congress has exercised its authority to do so. The [Controlled Substances Act] (CSA)], enacted in 1970 as part of the Comprehensive Drug Abuse Prevention and Control Act, 84 Stat. 1242-84, is a lengthy and detailed statute creating a comprehensive framework for regulating the production, distribution, and possession of five classes of "controlled substances." The CSA places various plants, drugs, and chemicals (such as narcotics, stimulants, depressants, hallucinogens, and anabolic steroids) into one of these five classes, called "Schedules," based on the substance's medical use, potential for abuse, and safety or dependence liability. 21 U.S.C. §§ 811-812. Each Schedule is associated with a distinct set of controls regarding the manufacture, distribution, and use of the substances listed therein. §§ 821-830. The CSA and its implementing regulations set forth strict requirements regarding registration, labeling and packaging, production quotas, drug security, and recordkeeping. *Id.* . . .

11. In adopting the CSA, Congress stated its particular concern with the need to prevent the diversion of drugs from legitimate to illicit channels. H. R. Rep. No. 91-1444, pt. 2, p. 22 (1970).

12. Marijuana was classified by Congress as a Schedule I drug. 21 U.S.C. §812(c). Marijuana is therefore subject to the *most* severe restrictions contained within the CSA. Schedule I drugs are categorized as such because of their high potential for abuse, lack of any accepted medical use, and absence of any accepted safe use in medically supervised treatment. 21 U.S.C. §812(b)(1).

13. While the statute provided for the periodic updating of the five schedules, Congress itself made the initial classifications. It identified 42 opiates, 22 opium derivatives, and 17 hallucinogenic substances as Schedule I drugs. . . . Congressional intent is clear: by classifying marijuana as a Schedule I drug, as opposed to listing it on a lesser schedule, Congress *mandated* that the manufacture, distribution, or possession of marijuana be a criminal offense, with the sole exception being the use of the drug as part of a United States Food and Drug Administration pre-approved research study. 21 U.S.C. §§ 823(f), 841(a)(1), 844(a).

14. The Schedule I classification of marijuana was merely one of many essential parts of a larger regulation of economic activity, in which the regulatory scheme would be undercut unless the *intrastate* activity identified by Congress were regulated as well as the interstate and international activity. Congress specifically included marijuana intended for intrastate consumption in the CSA because it recognized the likelihood that high demand in the interstate market would significantly attract such marijuana. See, e.g., 21 U.S.C. § 801(3)-(6).

15. The diversion of marijuana from Colorado contradicts the clear Congressional intent, frustrates the federal interest in eliminating commercial transactions in the interstate controlled-substances market, and is particularly burdensome for neighboring states like Plaintiff States where law enforcement agencies and the citizens have endured the substantial expansion of Colorado marijuana.

16. Although various factors contribute to the ultimate sentence received, the simple possession of marijuana generally constitutes a misdemeanor offense with a maximum penalty of up to one year imprisonment and a minimum fine of $1,000. 21 U.S.C. § 844(a). Conversely, the cultivation, manufacture, or distribution of marijuana, or the possession of marijuana with the intent to distribute, is subject to significantly more severe penalties. Such conduct generally constitutes a felony with a maximum penalty of up to five-years' imprisonment and a fine of up to $250,000. 21 U.S.C. § 841(b).

17. It also is unlawful to conspire to violate the CSA, 21 U.S.C. § 846; to knowingly open, lease, rent, use, or maintain property for the purpose of manufacturing, storing, or distributing controlled substances, 21 U.S.C. § 856(a)(1); and to manage or control a building, room, or enclosure and knowingly make it available for the purpose of manufacturing, storing, distributing, or using controlled substances, 21 U.S.C. § 856(a)(2). Federal law further criminalizes aiding and abetting another in committing a federal crime, conspiring to commit a federal crime, assisting in the commission of a federal crime, concealing knowledge of a felony from the United States, and laundering the proceeds of CSA offenses. 18 U.S.C. §§ 2-4, 371, 1956.[2]

---

2. Author's note: Chapter 11 discusses aiding and abetting, conspiracy, and money laundering offenses; Chapter 13 discusses the property related offenses created by 21 U.S.C. § 856.

18. Furthermore, the CSA provides for plenary seizure and forfeiture as "contraband" of "[a]ll controlled substances in schedule I or II that are possessed, transferred, sold, or offered for sale in violation of the provisions of [the CSA]." 21 U.S.C. § 881(f). The CSA further provides that "[a]ll species of plants from which controlled substances in schedules I and II may be derived which have been planted or cultivated in violation of [the CSA] . . . may be seized and summarily forfeited to the United States. 21 U.S.C. § 881(g). By virtue of these provisions, state and local law-enforcement officers have regularly exercised the power to seize marijuana, marijuana products, and marijuana plants found in their jurisdictions for summary forfeiture to the United States by delivery to Special Agents of the DEA or the Federal Bureau of Investigation.

19. Admittedly, by enacting the CSA, Congress did not intend to preempt the entire field of drug enforcement. Under 21 U.S.C. § 903, the CSA shall not "be construed" to "occupy the field" in which the CSA operates "to the exclusion of any [s]tate law on the same subject matter which would otherwise be within" the state's authority. Rather, Section 903 provides that state laws are preempted only when "a positive conflict" exists between a provision of the CSA and a state law "so that the two cannot consistently stand together." *Id.*

20. Given the directly contradictory provisions in Colorado Amendment 64 and the CSA, a "positive conflict" clearly exists and "the two cannot consistently stand together."

21. Colorado Amendment 64 obstructs a number of the specific goals which Congress sought to achieve with the CSA. By permitting, and in some cases requiring, the cultivation, manufacture, packaging for distribution, and distribution of marijuana, Amendment 64 undercuts Congressional edicts, including the Congressional finding that such distribution has a "substantial and detrimental effect on the health and general welfare of the American people," 21 U.S.C. § 801(2); that although local drug trafficking may itself not be "an integral part" of the interstate flow of drugs, it nonetheless has "a substantial and direct effect upon interstate commerce," § 801(3); and that "*[f]ederal control of the intrastate incidents*" of drug trafficking "*is essential to the effective control of the interstate incidents of drug trafficking.*" § 801(6)) (emphasis added).

22. Colorado state and local officials who are now required by Amendment 64 to support the establishment and maintenance of a commercialized marijuana industry in Colorado are violating the CSA. The scheme enacted by Colorado for retail marijuana is contrary and obstructive to the CSA. . . . The retail marijuana laws embed state and local government actors with private actors in a state-sanctioned and state-supervised industry which is intended to, and does, cultivate, package, and distribute marijuana for commercial and private possession and use in violation of the CSA (and therefore in direct contravention of clearly stated Congressional intent). It does so without the required oversight and control by the DOJ (and DEA) that is *required* by the CSA—and regulations adopted pursuant to the CSA—for the manufacture, distribution, labeling, monitoring, and use of drugs and drug infused products which are listed on lesser Schedules. . . .

### Colorado's Amendment 64

31. Amendment 64 was passed as a ballot initiative in Colorado . . . on November 6, 2012[,] . . . resulting in its adoption as an amendment to Article XVIII of the Colorado Constitution. . . .

32. Section 1 of Article XVIII includes among its "purposes and findings" that "In the interest of the efficient use of law enforcement resources, enhancing revenue for public

purposes, and individual freedom, the people of the state of Colorado find and declare that the use of marijuana should be legal for persons twenty-one years of age or older and taxed in a manner similar to alcohol." Section 1 further includes a finding and declaration "that marijuana should be regulated in a manner similar to alcohol" to the effect that: (1) selling, distributing, or transferring marijuana to individuals of twenty-one years of age or older is legal; (2) "taxpaying business people" will be permitted to conduct sales of marijuana; and (3) marijuana offered for sale must be labeled according to state regulations and are subject to additional state regulations.

### Section 4 of Amendment 64

33. Section 4 of Amendment 64 is entitled "LAWFUL OPERATION OF MARIJUANA-RELATED FACILITIES." It provides that *"Notwithstanding any other provision of law"* certain acts "are not unlawful and shall not be an offense under Colorado law or the law of any locality within Colorado or be a basis for seizure or forfeiture of assets under Colorado law for persons twenty-one years of age or older." Amendment 64, Section 4 (emphasis added). The acts which Section 4 deems lawful notwithstanding any other provision of law—including the CSA—are:

- "Manufacture, possession, or purchase of marijuana accessories or the sale of marijuana accessories to a person who is twenty-one years of age or older";
- "Possessing, displaying, or transporting marijuana or marijuana products; purchase of marijuana from a marijuana cultivation facility; purchase of marijuana or marijuana products from a marijuana product manufacturing facility; or sale of marijuana or marijuana products to consumers, if the person conducting the activities described in this paragraph has obtained a current, valid license to operate a retail marijuana store or is acting in his or her capacity as an owner, employee or agent of a licensed retail marijuana store";
- "Cultivating, harvesting, processing, packaging, transporting, displaying, or possessing marijuana; delivery or transfer of marijuana to a marijuana testing facility; selling marijuana to a marijuana cultivation facility, a marijuana product manufacturing facility, or a retail marijuana store; or the purchase of marijuana from a marijuana cultivation facility, if the person conducting the activities described in this paragraph has obtained a current, valid license to operate a marijuana cultivation facility or is acting in his or her capacity as an owner, employee, or agent of a licensed marijuana cultivation facility";
- "Packaging, processing, transporting, manufacturing, displaying, or possessing marijuana or marijuana products; delivery or transfer of marijuana or marijuana products to a marijuana testing facility; selling marijuana or marijuana products to a retail marijuana store or a marijuana product manufacturing facility; the purchase of marijuana from a marijuana cultivation facility; or the purchase of marijuana or marijuana products from a marijuana product manufacturing facility, if the person conducting the activities described in this paragraph has obtained a current, valid license to operate a marijuana product manufacturing facility or is acting in his or her capacity as an owner, employee, or agent of a licensed marijuana product manufacturing facility";
- "Possessing, cultivating, processing, repackaging, storing, transporting, displaying, transferring or delivering marijuana or marijuana products if the person has

obtained a current, valid license to operate a marijuana testing facility or is acting in his or her capacity as an owner, employee, or agent of a licensed marijuana testing facility"; and
- "Leasing or otherwise allowing the use of property owned, occupied or controlled by any person, corporation or other entity for any of the activities conducted lawfully in accordance with . . . this subsection."

34. Section 4 of Amendment 64 permits and enables the operation of marijuana-cultivation facilities, marijuana- and marijuana-products-manufacturing facilities, licensed marijuana-testing facilities, licensed retail establishments to sell marijuana; the transportation, distribution, advertising, packaging and sales in support of these licensed operations; leasing, renting, and maintaining property for the purpose of such trafficking; and/or aiding and abetting another to do so.

### Section 5 of Amendment 64

Section 5 of Amendment 64 is entitled "REGULATION OF MARIJUANA." It provides, among other things, that "Not later than July 1, 2013, the [Department of Revenue] shall adopt regulations necessary for implementation of this section. Such regulations *shall not prohibit the operation of marijuana establishments*, either expressly or through regulations that make their operation unreasonably impracticable." Amendment 64, Section 5 (emphasis added). The regulations that Section 5 mandates, despite their express conflict with the CSA and the treaty obligations of the United States "shall" include, among others, the following:

- "Procedures for the issuance, renewal, suspension, and revocation of a license to operate a marijuana establishment . . .";
- "A schedule of application, licensing and renewal fees . . .";
- "Qualifications for licensure . . .";
- "Security requirements for marijuana establishments";
- "Labeling requirements for marijuana and marijuana products sold or distributed by a marijuana establishment"; and
- "Health and safety regulations and standards for the manufacture of marijuana products and the cultivation of marijuana."

35. Section 5 of Amendment 64 prohibits state regulations which would ban commercial marijuana establishments of the type permitted and enabled by Section 4, requires the issuance by state employees of licenses to operate marijuana establishments, requires regulation by state employees of advertising in support of marijuana sales, and requires state employees to develop health and safety regulations and standards for the manufacture of marijuana products.

### Colorado Legislation Implementing Amendment 64

36. In order to fully implement Colorado Amendment 64, the Colorado General Assembly adopted several bills during the 2013 legislative session. . . .

37. Colorado House Bill 13-1317, among other things, provided for a state marijuana enforcement division and gives the division the authority to regulate medical marijuana and retail marijuana. The law also created a regulatory framework for retail marijuana. The law

further requires the state licensing authority to promulgate rules as required by Amendment 64, and authorizes the state licensing authority to promulgate other rules *intended to support the commercialization of marijuana cultivation, distribution, and sale under state auspices* with the assistance of the department of public health and environment. 2013 CO H.B. 1317.

38. Colorado Senate Bill 13-283, as passed, implements certain provisions of Amendment 64. Among its provisions, the bill: (1) requires recommendations to the General Assembly regarding criminal laws which need to be revised to ensure statutory compatibility with Amendment 64; (2) designates a relatively small number of specified locations where marijuana may *not* be consumed; (3) allows retail marijuana stores to deduct certain business expenses from their state income taxes that are prohibited by federal tax law; and (4) authorizes Colorado to designate state agencies to carry out other duties under the bill. 2013 CO S.B. 283.

### Colorado Retail Marijuana Rules

39. Amendment 64 and the implementing legislation (particularly, House Bill 13-1317) required that the State Licensing Authority, the Executive Director of the Colorado Department of Revenue, promulgate certain rules on or before July 1, 2013.

40. To comply with these requirements, the State Licensing Authority adopted emergency rules governing "Retail Marijuana" in the State of Colorado. These rules became effective on October 15, 2013 as The Permanent Rules Related to the Colorado Retail Marijuana Code ("the Permanent Rules"). Pursuant to the Permanent Rules, retail marijuana dispensaries and establishments were permitted to commence operations on January 1, 2014. . . .

### Unconstitutionality of Colorado Amendment 64 and Its Implementing Statutes and Regulations

41. Because Amendment 64, in both its stated purpose and necessary operation, conflicts with the federal government's carefully crafted balance of competing objectives in the enforcement of federal drug control laws, its passage already has resulted in detrimental impacts on Plaintiff States.

42. Amendment 64 directly conflicts with federal law and undermines express federal priorities in the area of drug control and enforcement, and regulates and enables the retail and other use of marijuana in the United States. Colorado's adoption of a law that enables and supports the commercialization of marijuana cultivation, distribution, and sale under state auspices with the assistance of the Colorado Department of Public Health and Environment undermines the national enforcement regime set forth in the CSA and reflected in the long-standing and well-established federal controlled-substances enforcement policy and practice as it relates to marijuana, including the federal government's prioritization of enforcement against Schedule I drugs. . . . Because Amendment 64 attempts to set state-specific drug regulation and use policy, it legislates in an area constitutionally reserved to the federal government, conflicts with the federal drug-control laws and federal drug-control policy, . . . and obstructs the accomplishment and execution of the full purposes and objectives of Congress—and is therefore preempted.

43. The State of Colorado's pursuit of a policy to promote widespread possession and use and the commercial cultivation, distribution, marketing, and sales of marijuana, and

ignoring every objective embodied in the federal drug control and regulation system (including the federal government's prioritization of the interdiction of Schedule I drugs including marijuana), directly conflicts with and otherwise stands as an obstacle to the mandate of Congress that *all* possession and use of Schedule I drugs, including marijuana, *be prohibited.* . . .

44. Amendment 64 stands in direct opposition to the CSA, the regulatory scheme of which is designed to foster the beneficial and lawful use of those medications on Schedules II-V, to prevent their misuse, and to *prohibit entirely* the possession or use of marijuana, as one of the controlled substances listed in Schedule I, anywhere in the United States, except as a part of a strictly controlled research project. . . . Such interference with federal priorities, driven by a state-determined policy as to how possession and use of a controlled substance should be regulated, constitutes a violation of the Supremacy Clause.

45. Amendment 64 conflicts with and otherwise stands as an obstacle to the full purposes and objectives of Congress . . . in creating a uniform and singular federal policy and regulatory scheme for interstate or intrastate possession and use of controlled substances, a scheme which expressly includes marijuana, and its regulatory scheme for registration, inventory control, advertising, and packaging for drugs intended for human consumption.

46. Colorado's permission and enabling in direct contravention of these prohibitions also conflicts with and otherwise stands as an obstacle to the full purposes and objectives of Congress in creating a comprehensive system of penalties for individuals who are unlawfully in possession of, or using, marijuana in the United States in violation of the CSA's scheme for interstate or intrastate possession and use of controlled substances, or who are aiding and abetting another to do so, and for registration, inventory control, advertising, and/or packaging for drugs intended for human consumption.

47. The Permanent Rules, promulgated by the Colorado Department of Revenue as described above, lack safeguards to prevent the interstate transfer of marijuana sold by retail dispensaries within Colorado.

48. The Permanent Rules permit persons over the age of twenty-one years of age who do not possess evidence of Colorado residency to purchase up to one quarter ounce of marijuana in a single sales transaction. *See* Permanent Rules, R 402. A person over the age of twenty-one years of age who does possess evidence of Colorado residency may purchase up to one ounce of marijuana in a single sales transaction. *See id.*

49. The Permanent Rules are devoid of any requirement that marijuana purchased at a retail dispensary be consumed, in its entirety, at the point of purchase.

50. The Permanent Rules are further devoid of any prohibition on multiple purchases of marijuana from the same retail dispensary in a brief period of time, nor do the Permanent Rules prohibit a single person from making multiple purchases of marijuana from separate retail dispensaries in even a single day.

51. The Permanent Rules provide for tracking of marijuana inventory by a Retail Marijuana Store "to ensure its inventories are identified and tracked from the point they are transferred from a Retail Marijuana Cultivation Facility or Retail Marijuana Products Manufacturing Facility through the point of sale, given to a Retail Marijuana Testing Facility, or otherwise disposed of." *See* Permanent Rules, R 405. However, the Permanent Rules are devoid of any requirement that marijuana be tracked after the point of sale.

52. The Permanent Rules are further devoid of any requirement that a purchaser of marijuana from a Retail Marijuana Store be subjected to a criminal background check. Thus, the Permanent Rules lack any safeguard to prevent criminal enterprises, gangs, and cartels from acquiring marijuana inventory directly from Retail Marijuana Stores.

53. Due to the foregoing, the Permanent Rules lack safeguards to prevent the retail sale of marijuana either to persons intending to transport marijuana to other states or to persons engaged in a criminal enterprise.

**Detrimental Impact of Amendment 64 on the Plaintiff States**

54. By reason of the foregoing, the State of Colorado's actions have caused and will continue to cause substantial and irreparable harm to the Plaintiff States for which Plaintiff States have no adequate remedy except by this action.

55. Since the implementation of Amendment 64 in Colorado, Plaintiff States have dealt with a significant influx of Colorado-sourced marijuana.

56. The detrimental economic impacts of Colorado Amendment 64 on the Plaintiff States, especially in regard to the increased costs for the apprehension, incarceration, and prosecution of suspected and convicted felons, are substantial.

57. Plaintiff States' law enforcement encounters marijuana on a regular basis as part of day-to-day duties and will continue to do so. These types of encounters arise, among other circumstances, when Plaintiff States' law-enforcement officers make routine stops of individuals who possess marijuana purchased in Colorado which, at the time of purchase, complied with Amendment 64. . . .

58. The result of increased Colorado-sourced marijuana being trafficked in Plaintiff States due to the passage and implementation of Colorado Amendment 64 has been the diversion of a significant amount of the personnel time, budget, and resources of the Plaintiff States' law enforcement, judicial system, and penal system resources to counteract the increased trafficking and transportation of Colorado-sourced marijuana.

59. Plaintiff States have incurred significant costs associated with the increased level of incarceration of suspected and convicted felons on charges related to Colorado-sourced marijuana include housing, food, health care, transfer to-and-from court, counseling, clothing, and maintenance.

60. The increased costs to Plaintiff States' law enforcement include the costs associated with the arrest, impoundment of vehicles, seizure of contraband and suspected contraband, transfer of prisoners, and appearance of law enforcement personnel in court for arraignment, trial, and/or sentencing (including the overtime costs associated with appearing in court and/or obtaining replacement law-enforcement personnel for the court-appearing officers).

61. Plaintiff States are suffering a direct and significant detrimental impact—namely the diversion of limited manpower and resources to arrest and process suspected and convicted felons involved in the increased illegal marijuana trafficking or transportation.

62. Colorado Amendment 64 harms Plaintiff States' law enforcement, judicial, and penal system personnel in their individual and official capacities in the performance of their jobs and the accomplishment of their professional goals and objectives as a result of the greater burdens it places and the diversion of resources it necessitates.

63. Accordingly, Plaintiff States have suffered direct and significant harm arising from the increased presence of Colorado-sourced marijuana in violation of the CSA.

64. Unless restrained by this Court, Colorado sourced marijuana undoubtedly will continue to flow into and through Plaintiff States in violation of the Controlled Substances Act and thus compromise federal laws and treaty obligations.

. . .

Part III. Marijuana Suppliers

WHEREFORE, the Plaintiff States pray that the State of Colorado:

1. Be subject to a declaratory judgment stating that Sections 16(4) and (5) of Article XVIII of the Colorado Constitution are preempted by federal law, and therefore unconstitutional and unenforceable under the Supremacy Clause, Article VI of the U.S. Constitution;

2. Be enjoined from any and all application and implementation of Sections 16(4) and (5) of Article XVIII of the Colorado Constitution;

3. Be enjoined from any and all application and implementation of statutes or regulations promulgated pursuant to Sections 16(4) and (5) of Article XVIII of the Colorado Constitution; and

4. Be ordered to pay the Plaintiff States' costs and expenses associated with this legal action, including attorneys' fees.

Respectfully submitted,

JON BRUNING
Nebraska Attorney General
DAVID D. COOKSON
Chief Deputy Attorney General
KATHERINE J. SPOHN
Deputy Attorney General
RYAN S. POST
Assistant Attorney General
*Counsel of Record*
. . .
*Attorneys for Plaintiff*
*State of Nebraska*

E. SCOTT PRUITT
Oklahoma Attorney General
PATRICK R. WYRICK
Solicitor General
OKLAHOMA ATTORNEY
GENERAL'S OFFICE
. . .
*Attorneys for Plaintiff*
*State of Oklahoma*

## Notes and Questions

1. The Complaint makes several claims regarding Colorado's responsibility for the actions of the state's marijuana industry:

- "By *permitting*, and in some cases *requiring*, the cultivation, manufacture, packaging-for distribution, and distribution of marijuana, Amendment 64 undercuts Congressional edicts."
- "Colorado state and local officials who are now *required* by Amendment 64 to *support* the establishment and maintenance of a commercialized marijuana industry in Colorado are violating the CSA."
- "The retail marijuana laws *embed* state and local government actors with private actors in a state-*sanctioned* and state-*supervised* industry which is intended to, and does, cultivate, package, and distribute marijuana. . . ."
- "Amendment 64 *permits* and *enables* the operation of marijuana-cultivation facilities, marijuana- and marijuana-products-manufacturing facilities, licensed marijuana-testing facilities, licensed retail establishments to sell marijuana. . . ."
- "The State of Colorado [has pursued] . . . a policy to *promote* widespread possession and use and the commercial cultivation, distribution, marketing, and sales of marijuana."

- "[T]he State of Colorado's actions have *caused* and will continue to *cause* substantial and irreparable harm to the Plaintiff States."

In their Supplemental Brief, Nebraska and Oklahoma make some additional, even more colorful claims:

- "The State of Colorado *authorizes*, *oversees*, *protects*, and *profits* from a sprawling $100-million-per-month marijuana growing, processing, and retailing organization that exported thousands of pounds of marijuana to some 36 States in 2014. If this entity were based south of our border, the federal government would prosecute it as a drug cartel."[3]
- "Colorado has *created* a massive criminal enterprise whose sole purpose is to *authorize* and *facilitate* the manufacture, distribution, sale, and use of marijuana. It has granted a property interest in federal contraband and, like any well-run cartel, it *protects* its distributers' operations."
- "Colorado has also *facilitated* purchase of marijuana by residents of neighboring states by issuing licenses to an unusually high number of marijuana retailers perched on Colorado's borders."
- "Given all this, to deny that Colorado is responsible for the harms its marijuana is causing in neighboring States is like saying that a tavern keeper cannot be held responsible for the drunk who kills a family with his car even though he knowingly sold the drunk ten beers in two hours. The actions of third-party interstate traffickers are in no way 'independent' of Colorado's marijuana regime."

*States of Nebraska and Oklahoma v. State of Colorado, Plaintiff's Supplemental Brief,* 2016 WL 74964 (emphasis added).

Do the Complaint and Supplemental Brief accurately and fairly characterize the actions that Colorado has taken to implement Amendment 64? In particular, has Colorado *promoted* the production and distribution of marijuana by adopting its Retail Marijuana Code and similar regulations? Along these lines, consider the following excerpt from the textbook author:

> [A]n examination of its purposes suggests Congress [at most] likely wanted to preempt only those state regulations that promote rather than restrict marijuana-related activities. Regulations that promote are those that reduce the cost of engaging in marijuana-related activities. Examples include cash subsidies for the purchase of marijuana and bans on private discrimination against marijuana users. Regulations that restrict marijuana-related activities are those that increase the cost, however minimally, of engaging in those activities. Examples include licensing requirements for marijuana vendors, taxes imposed on marijuana sales, and registration requirements for medical marijuana users. . . . [B]oth types of regulation could be preempted by Congress, but there are strong reasons to believe that Congress only wanted to preempt regulations that promote marijuana.
>
> Regulations that promote marijuana-related activities are preempted because they undermine one of the chief objectives of the CSA—curbing the consumption of marijuana. By definition, such regulations reduce the cost of using, growing, or distributing marijuana,

---

3. Author's note: Chapter 14 discusses whether state officials could be held criminally liable under the CSA, as the Supplemental Brief appears to suggest.

thereby stimulating more of these activities. For example, a state marijuana subsidy would reduce the market price of marijuana, resulting in greater consumption of the drug. . . .

By contrast, regulations that restrict the marijuana market are not preempted, because they help to advance Congress's objective of curbing marijuana consumption, at least to some extent. Consider, for example, a state excise tax on all marijuana sales. This tax would be passed on to marijuana consumers, helping to boost the price of the drug. In turn, higher prices should suppress demand for the drug. Indeed, that is a key assumption behind federal drug enforcement policy.

It is even easier to see why Congress does not want to preempt these regulations once we consider what would happen if it did preempt them. Preemption would have the very perverse effect of relaxing—not tightening—state controls on marijuana. In other words, it would widen the gap between state and federal drug policy. Consider state marijuana licensing programs. Many states want to limit marijuana distribution (medical or otherwise) to a set of state-licensed distributors, in effect, to create a state-licensed oligopoly. Among other things, this licensing regime is designed to help the states collect excise taxes from vendors and prevent unlawful sales to minors. The licensing process enables states to screen out vendors they deem more likely to break state law, and it also enables states to keep a close eye on the operations of licensees. But if the licensing scheme is blocked by a court, it will be considerably more difficult for the states to collect taxes from or enforce other regulatory restrictions against marijuana vendors. Congress may want the states to do more, but given how limited its own enforcement resources are, it seems unlikely to refuse whatever drug control assistance the states might volunteer, no matter how meager.

It is telling that the DOJ itself has not sued to block state regulations of the medical marijuana market in the past. Indeed, in a twist of irony, the claim that state medical marijuana regulations are preempted by federal law has been championed instead by segments of the medical marijuana industry—hardly a group that shares common goal with Congress. In one suit, for example, a medical marijuana dispensary in California convinced a state court that a local licensing requirement was preempted by federal law. It did not do so because it supported the federal ban, but because it wanted to operate free and clear of the local government's interference—the local government had ordered the dispensary to close because it failed to comply with the licensing ordinance. Again, it seems safe to say that the court erred in that case, for Congress would clearly prefer to have some state-imposed restrictions on marijuana distribution than none at all.

Mikos, *Preemption, supra,* at 17-21. In light of this analysis, do you think Colorado's regulations *promote* the production and distribution of marijuana, in the legally relevant sense? Would Congress necessarily want to preempt those regulations (or others like them)?

2. Even if they are accurate, do all of the claims quoted in the previous Note state a valid preemption cause of action? To be more specific, could Congress stop Colorado from "*permitting*" the production and distribution of marijuana—at least for purposes of Colorado law? Chapter 6 discussed the anti-commandeering rule and the limits it imposes on Congress's preemptive authority. The article excerpted above provides a framework for identifying which state laws are preemptable and which are not:

[A]lthough Congress has the power to preempt state laws that regulate marijuana, it has no authority to preempt state laws that merely legalize the drug. For present purposes, regulation entails state interference with marijuana-related activities (possession, distribution, etc.). Examples include prohibitions against selling marijuana to minors, requirements that marijuana vendors obtain special business licenses, and bans on employment discrimination against medical marijuana users. . . . [R]egulations such as these either restrict or promote marijuana-related activities. Legalization, by contrast, entails a laissez faire approach in which the state allows some marijuana-related activity to occur free of state regulation. Examples include repeal of state criminal bans against the possession of marijuana for medical purposes and repeal of state licensing sanctions against physicians who recommend the drug to patients. When a state legalizes marijuana, it simply chooses to leave marijuana-related activities to the vagaries of private market forces and federal regulation.

Pursuant to the Supremacy Clause, Congress may preempt any state regulation of marijuana-related activity. It could circumscribe or eliminate altogether state regulation of private activity. When it preempts state regulations, Congress merely removes state interference—i.e., it forces the state to do nothing.

Under the Supreme Court's anti-commandeering rule, however, Congress may not likewise preempt state legalization of marijuana-related activity. In a nutshell, the anti-commandeering rule says that Congress may not force the states to "enact or administer a federal regulatory program." This means that Congress could not force the states to enact a marijuana ban. Neither, logically, could it force the states to keep bans already enacted but no longer wanted. To put it another way, Congress may not "preempt" state legalization, because doing so forces states to keep pre-existing marijuana bans—bans that Congress could not force the states to adopt in the first instance. (Congress may, of course, continue to enforce its own criminal prohibitions, notwithstanding state legalization, but that is only for purposes of federal proceedings.)

Nonetheless, some courts, officials, and commentators have failed to heed the distinction between regulating and legalizing marijuana. They have suggested that state laws that merely allow residents to use marijuana free of state-imposed constraints have been preempted by the CSA. In 1994, for example, Governor Pete Wilson of California refused to sign legislation that legalized medical marijuana under state law, arguing that the measure "would be preempted by the federal controlled substances law [which] prohibits the use of marijuana for medical purposes." More recently, eight former heads of the Drug Enforcement Administration (DEA) implored the DOJ to pursue legal action to nullify Colorado's and Washington's recreational marijuana legalization measures.

The obstacle preemption rule has arguably fueled these claims that state legalization has been preempted by the CSA. After all, it is easy to see how state legalization threatens to undermine congressional objectives. Congress has long depended upon the states to wage its war on marijuana. Among other things, the states have historically handled nearly ninety-nine percent of all marijuana related arrests. The DEA simply cannot pick up the slack if a state legalizes marijuana or stops enforcing a state ban; the federal government would need to increase its own efforts nearly one-hundred fold just to maintain the same enforcement rate. There is little doubt, then, that marijuana use will increase following state legalization. Nonetheless, the anti-commandeering rule does not allow Congress to force states to suppress the drug. Because the broad language of obstacle preemption does not incorporate this important constraint on Congress's preemptive power, the obstacle preemption test has led courts and government agents astray.

Mikos, *Preemption*, supra, at 15-17. *See also* Erwin Chemerinsky et al., *Cooperative Federalism and Marijuana Regulation*, 62 U.C.L.A. L. Rev. 74, 111-12 (2015) ("It is true that removal of state sanctions and assistance would make the federal enforcement of its own laws more difficult in that the federal government would lose an enforcement partner. But that loss of state assistance cannot constitute an obstacle for purposes of the federal preemption analysis.").

3. Moving from the general to the more specific, consider whether the particular regulations discussed in each of the following Problems is preempted:

**Problem 10.1:** Under State law, only state-licensed firms are allowed to produce and distribute marijuana. Without a license, the production and distribution of marijuana remain criminal offenses under State law. Is the State licensing system preempted by federal law? *See Joe Hemp's First Hemp Bank v. City of Oakland*, No. C 15-05053 WHA, 2016 WL 375082, at *2-4 (N.D. Cal. Feb. 1, 2016).

**Problem 10.2:** Under State law, only state-licensed firms are allowed to distribute marijuana. Furthermore, State law requires that all of the marijuana that licensees offer for sale first be tested by an independent laboratory for harmful contaminants. The distribution of untested marijuana remains a criminal offense under State law. Is the State testing requirement preempted? Does it matter how the testing requirement can be satisfied by licensees? *See Joe Hemp's First Hemp Bank, supra.*

**Problem 10.3:** Under State law, only state-licensed firms are allowed to distribute marijuana. Furthermore, State law requires licensees to pay a 25 percent tax on all sales of marijuana. Failure to pay the tax is a criminal offense. Is the State marijuana tax preempted? *See No Over Taxation v. Hickenlooper*, Dismissal of Action Pursuant to C.R.C.P. 12(b)(5) (Dist. Ct. Denver, 2016).

4. Are there any other state regulations discussed in Chapter 7 or 8 (e.g., state trademark protection) that might prove vulnerable to a preemption challenge? Chapter 14 discusses the particularly complex issues regarding whether states may own and operate marijuana producers and distributors.

5. What happens if a state law impedes one congressional goal—but furthers another? The following Problem raises this issue:

**Problem 10.4:** Suppose researchers have convincingly demonstrated that following the implementation of Colorado's Amendment 64, (a) adult use of marijuana *increased* by 20 percent; but (b) marijuana use by minors (18 years and younger) *decreased* by 10 percent. In light of these findings, would Congress want to preempt Amendment 64 (assuming it could do so)?

6. Is there anything states can do to prevent the federal government from preempting their marijuana reforms? *See generally* Robert A. Mikos, *Making Preemption Less Palatable: State Poison Pill Legislation*, 85 Geo. Wash. L. Rev. 1 (2017) (suggesting that states could insulate their reforms by making them inseverable from other state drug laws that Congress plainly favors).

7. *Postscript.* Nebraska and Oklahoma made the unusual move of filing their lawsuit directly in the United States Supreme Court, citing the Court's original jurisdiction. U.S. Const. art III, § 2 ("In all cases affecting ambassadors, other public ministers and consuls, and those in which a state shall be party, the Supreme Court shall have original jurisdiction."); 28 U.S.C. § 1251 (a) ("The Supreme Court shall have original and exclusive jurisdiction of all controversies between two or more States."). The Court, however, deems its original jurisdiction to be discretionary, and in March 2016, it declined to hear the case, without expressing any opinion on the merits of the suit. *Nebraska v. Colorado*, 136 S. Ct. 1034 (2016). Nebraska and Oklahoma have since attempted to join a nearly identical preemption suit brought by other parties (discussed in the next note). For a useful introduction to the Supreme Court's original jurisdiction, see Stephen Wermiel, *SCOTUS for Law Students: Original Cases*, http://www.scotusblog.com/2014/10/scotus-for-law-students-original-cases/.

8. *Who is allowed to challenge state laws under the CSA?* In February 2015, while the Nebraska and Oklahoma suit was still pending, private landowners, a public interest group, and several state and local officials filed two nearly identical lawsuits in the United States District Court for the District of Colorado. Both suits challenged Amendment 64 as preempted, using the same reasoning as the Nebraska and Oklahoma suit excerpted above. In early 2016, however, the district court dismissed both lawsuits on the grounds that the federal CSA did not authorize non-federal plaintiffs—i.e., plaintiffs other than the federal government itself—to initiate preemption challenges to state law. *Smith v. Hickenlooper*, 164 F. Supp. 3d 1286, 1289-190 (D. Colo. 2016); *Safe Streets Alliance v. Alternative Holistic Healing, LLC*, No. 1:15-cv-00349-REB-CBS, 2016 WL 223815 (D. Colo. Jan. 19, 2016). The suits have been consolidated and are currently on appeal before the Tenth Circuit. *See Order Granting Motion to Consolidate Appeals, Smith v. Hickenlooper*, No. 16-01095 (10th Cir. Apr. 1, 2016).[4] Nebraska and Oklahoma have also filed a motion seeking to intervene in the case. Who do you think should have the ability to challenge state marijuana laws as preempted?

9. The Supreme Court occasionally asks the DOJ—and in particular, the Solicitor General of the United States—to weigh in on cases of particular import to the federal government, even when the federal government itself is not a named party in the case. Indeed, the Supreme Court asked the Solicitor General for its opinion on whether or not the Court should agree to hear Nebraska and Oklahoma's suit against Colorado. The Solicitor General subsequently wrote a lengthy brief urging the Court to decline to hear the suit. *See* Brief for the United States as Amicus Curiae, *Nebraska v. Colorado*, 136 S. Ct. 1034 (2016) (No. 144, Orig.).

> **Problem 10.5:** Now suppose, counterfactually, that the Supreme Court had instead agreed to hear Nebraska and Oklahoma's suit. Furthermore, suppose that the Solicitor General generally agreed with the plaintiff states' suit on the

---

4. In the interest of disclosure, the textbook author drafted an amicus brief in the case. Amicus Curiae Brief of Law Professors in Support of Respondent State of Colorado and Affirmance, *Safe Streets Alliance, et al. v. Hickenlooper* and *Smith v. Hickenlooper* (Aug. 15, 2016).

merits—i.e., that the CSA preempts Colorado's Amendment 64. Would the Solicitor General have been barred from submitting another amicus brief to the Court, urging it to rule for the plaintiff states? In particular, would such a filing violate the terms of recent spending legislation, in which Congress has prohibited the DOJ from using budgeted funds "to prevent [states] from implementing their own State laws that authorize the use, distribution, possession, or cultivation of medical marijuana"? (The spending restriction and the *McIntosh* court's interpretion thereof is discussed in more detail in Chapter 7.)

## C. MAY LOCAL GOVERNMENTS BAN STATE-APPROVED PRODUCTION AND DISTRIBUTION OF MARIJUANA?

Within the fifty states, there are thousands more local governments, including more than 3,000 counties and 15,000 municipalities. *See* Paul Diller, *Intrastate Preemption*, 87 B.U. L. Rev. 1113, 1114 (2007). Many of these local governments have sought to put their own stamp on marijuana policy by regulating the possession, use, production, and distribution of the drug. Chapter 6 discussed local authority to regulate possession and use. This section discusses the metes and bounds of local authority to regulate the production and distribution of marijuana, especially when those activities are permitted by state law.

### 1. Introduction to Local Authority

Like federalism, localism is a means of decentralizing government power. Localism is governed by rules that are similar—though not identical—to those governing federalism. The following excerpt provides a brief primer on localism, highlighting the power that states wield over local governments located therein. The excerpt also surveys how states have chosen to excerise that authority, and in particular, the extent to which states tolerate local regulation of marijuana suppliers.

### *Robert A. Mikos*, Marijuana Localism
65 Case W. Res. L. Rev. 719 (2015)

#### WHAT STATES COULD DO

It is up to the states to decide whether or not to allow local governments to regulate marijuana sales. In other words, states do not necessarily have to tolerate local resistance to decisions made by statewide majorities. The states can prevent local governments from exercising authority over marijuana sales in two basic ways.

First, states can withhold regulatory authority from local governments. Local governments are creatures of the state and derive all of their regulatory authority from the state. In other words, the states decide what powers local governments shall exercise. It follows that the states could withhold the power to regulate marijuana from local governments. Without the grant of authority from the state, local governments would be powerless to regulate the drug.

This is a distinguishing feature of localism and one of the primary ways it differs from federalism. Unlike localities, the states are not creatures of [another government—the national government], and they do not require the national government's blessing to pass legislation. The states are presumed to have authority to regulate for the health, safety, and morals of the population, with the exception of a few narrow instances under which the Constitution deprives them of authority. The states are, of course, entitled to limit their powers via their own constitutions; but the important point here is that the national Constitution does not impose such constraints, at least in ways that are relevant here.

. . .

Second, states can also preempt local legislation. That is, even if a local government has express or implied authority to regulate marijuana, the state may still veto any local regulations adopted pursuant to this authority. Intrastate preemption follows the same basic rules as federal-state preemption. Local law is preempted when it conflicts with state law, with or without any express statement of the legislature's preemptive intentions.

. . .

. . . Local bans on marijuana sales are clearly preemptable, and private actors subject to those bans have every incentive to challenge the assertion of local authority. Local legalization of marijuana could prove more durable against an intra-state preemption challenge. But it is not clear there is any state law analog to the federal anticommandeering rule that would protect local communities from being forced to criminalize sales of marijuana. In other words, states might command local governments to ban marijuana [or to enforce a state ban], even though Congress could not command states to do the same. . . .

In sum, marijuana localism is on precarious legal footing. States have the power to determine the precise role, if any, local governments will play in the marijuana policy domain. To be sure, this choice may be more or less constrained, depending on the rules of state constitutional law, but it is one the states are clearly empowered to make.

## WHAT STATES HAVE DONE

Twenty-three states have legalized marijuana for some purposes under state law. As of the November 2014 election, at least twenty-one of those states have also legalized some form of retail distribution of marijuana. But they have split regarding whether to allow local communities to ban retail distribution.

Seven states have authorized local governments to ban retail marijuana shops that are otherwise legal under state law.[196] Five of these states have done so expressly via statute or ballot initiative. For example, Amendment 64 specifies that "[a] locality may prohibit the operation of marijuana cultivation facilities, marijuana product manufacturing facilities, marijuana testing facilities, or retail marijuana stores through the enactment of an ordinance or through an initiated or referred measure." [Colo. Const. art. XVIII, § 16(5)(f).] In the two other states, state laws failed to address the localism question,

---

196. The states include Alaska, California, Colorado, Montana, Nevada, Vermont, and Washington.

but key state authorities have found local bans to be consistent with state law. In California, the state supreme court upheld a local ban on medical marijuana dispensaries against a preemption challenge brought under the state's long-standing medical marijuana law. It reasoned that state law "merely exempts" medical marijuana dispensaries from "prohibitions that would otherwise apply under state law. . . . [It] does not thereby mandate that local governments authorize, allow, or accommodate the existence of such facilities." [*City of Riverside v. Inland Empire Patients Health and Wellness Ctr., Inc.*] Similarly, in Washington, the state attorney general opined that local governments could ban retail marijuana shops, reasoning that the state's law legalizing and regulating marijuana distribution did not "amount to entitling one to engage in such businesses regardless of local law."

Four states have denied local governments the power to ban retail marijuana shops.[202] Three states have rejected the local option expressly via statute or ballot initiative. In Oregon, for example, Measure 91 expressly provides that the essential portions of the measure are "designed to operate uniformly throughout the state, shall be paramount and superior to and shall fully replace and supersede any and all municipal charter enactments or local ordinances inconsistent with it. Such charters and ordinances hereby are repealed." [Or. Ballot Meas. 91, §58 (2014).] Massachusetts' medical marijuana law is silent regarding local authority over marijuana dispensaries. However, the state's attorney general has invoked the law to block local communities from banning medical marijuana dispensaries outright. She noted that state law is intended to give qualifying patients "reasonable access" to medical marijuana dispensaries, and to serve that end, it requires dispensaries to be "reasonably dispersed throughout the Commonwealth." The attorney general reasoned that "This legislative purpose could not be served if a municipality could prohibit treatment centers within its borders, for if one municipality could do so, we see no principled basis on which every other municipality could not do the same."

Notwithstanding their firm rejection of local authority to ban marijuana shops, all of these states do allow local authorities to enact some reasonable regulations to govern them. For example, Measure 91 permits localities to adopt "reasonable time, place and manner regulations of the nuisance aspects of establishments that sell marijuana" but only if "the city or county makes specific findings that the establishment would cause adverse effects to occur."

In the remaining ten states that permit retail distribution of marijuana, the status of local power to ban marijuana shops remains unsettled because no statute expressly addresses the issue and no high court or other high-level state official has yet opined on the question.

## Notes and Questions

1. Short of banning marijuana supply activities outright, local governments have also imposed sundry restrictions on those activities, e.g., limiting the location, hours, signage, etc., of commercial marijuana suppliers. For surveys of the local regulations, *see* Jeremy Nemeth & Eric Ross, *Planning for Marijuana: The Cannabis Conundrum*, J. Am. Plan.

---

202. The states include Arizona, Delaware, Massachusetts, and Oregon.

Assoc. 6 (Aug. 2014); Patricia E. Salkin, *Medical Marijuana*, in 3 Am. Law Zoning § 18:53:10 (5th ed.); Patricia E. Salkin & Zachary Kansler, *Medical Marijuana Meets Zoning: Can You Grow, Sell, and Smoke That Here?*, 62 Planning & Envtl L. 3 (Aug. 2010).

## 2. Why Have Courts Reached Different Conclusions Regarding Local Authority to Regulate Marijuana Supply?

As noted in the excerpt above, some state reforms fail to expressly address the power of local governments, leaving it to the courts (and sometimes other government actors) to decide whether localities may ban supply activities permitted by state law. The following excerpts illustrate the different conclusions that courts have reached on this question.

### a. The View that Local Bans Are Permitted

### City of Riverside v. Inland Empire Patients Health & Wellness Ctr., Inc.
300 P.3d 494 (Cal. 2013)

BAXTER, J.:

The issue in this case is whether California's medical marijuana statutes preempt a local ban on facilities that distribute medical marijuana. We conclude they do not.

. . . California statutes, the Compassionate Use Act of 1996 (CUA[)] . . . and the more recent Medical Marijuana Program (MMP[)] . . . , have removed certain state law obstacles from the ability of qualified patients to obtain and use marijuana for legitimate medical purposes. Among other things, these statutes exempt the "collective[ ] or cooperative[ ] cultiva[tion]" of medical marijuana by qualified patients and their designated caregivers from prosecution or abatement under specified state criminal and nuisance laws that would otherwise prohibit those activities. (§ 11362.775.)

The California Constitution recognizes the authority of cities and counties to make and enforce, within their borders, "all local, police, sanitary, and other ordinances and regulations not in conflict with general laws." (Cal. Const., art. XI, § 7.) This inherent local police power includes broad authority to determine, for purposes of the public health, safety, and welfare, the appropriate uses of land within a local jurisdiction's borders, and preemption by state law is not lightly presumed.

In the exercise of its inherent land use power, the City of Riverside (City) has declared, by zoning ordinances, that a "[m]edical marijuana dispensary"—"[a] facility where marijuana is made available for medical purposes in accordance with" the CUA . . .—is a prohibited use of land within the city and may be abated as a public nuisance. . . . The City's ordinance also bans, and declares a nuisance, any use that is prohibited by federal or state law.

Invoking these provisions, the City brought a nuisance action against a facility operated by defendants [seeking an injunction] . . . against the distribution of marijuana from the facility. . . . Defendants insist the local ban is in conflict with, and thus preempted by, those state statutes.

. . . [W]e disagree. We have consistently maintained that the CUA and the MMP are but incremental steps toward freer access to medical marijuana, and the scope of these statutes is limited and circumscribed. They merely declare that the conduct they describe cannot lead to arrest or conviction, or be abated as a nuisance, as violations of enumerated provisions of the Health and Safety Code. Nothing in the CUA or the MMP expressly or impliedly limits the inherent authority of a local jurisdiction, by its own ordinances, to regulate the use of its land, including the authority to provide that facilities for the distribution of medical marijuana will not be permitted to operate within its borders. . . .

. . .

When they adopted the CUA in 1996, the voters declared their intent "[t]o ensure that seriously ill Californians have the right to obtain and use marijuana for medical purposes" upon a physician's recommendation (§ 11362.5, subd. (b)(1)(A)), "[t]o ensure that patients and their primary caregivers who obtain and use marijuana for medical purposes upon the recommendation of a physician are not subject to criminal prosecution or sanction" (*id.*, subd. (b)(1)(B)), and "[t]o encourage the federal and state governments to implement a plan to provide for the safe and affordable distribution of marijuana to all patients in medical need" of the substance (*id.*, subd. (b)(1)(C)).

But the operative steps the electorate took toward these goals were modest. In its substantive provisions, the CUA simply declares that (1) no physician may be punished or denied any right or privilege under state law for recommending medical marijuana to a patient (§ 11362.5, subd. (c)), and (2) two specific state statutes prohibiting the possession and cultivation of marijuana, sections 11357 and 11358 respectively, "shall not apply" to a patient, or the patient's designated primary caregiver, who possesses or cultivates marijuana for the patient's personal medical use upon a physician's recommendation or approval (§ 11362.5, subd. (d)).

When it later adopted the MMP, the Legislature declared this statute was intended, among other things, to "[c]larify the scope of the application of the [CUA] and facilitate the prompt identification of qualified [medical marijuana] patients and their designated primary caregivers" in order to protect them from unnecessary arrest and prosecution for marijuana offenses, to "[p]romote uniform and consistent application of the [CUA] among the counties within the state," and to "[e]nhance the access of patients and caregivers to medical marijuana through collective, cooperative cultivation projects" (Stats. 2003, ch. 875, § 1, subd. (b), pp. 6422, 6423).

Again, however, the steps the MMP took in pursuit of these objectives were limited and specific. The MMP established a program for issuance of medical marijuana identification cards to those qualified patients and designated primary caregivers who wish to carry them, and required responsible county agencies to cooperate in this program. . . . It provided that the holder of an identification card shall not be subject to arrest for possession, transportation, delivery, or cultivation of medical marijuana, within the amounts specified by the statute, except upon reasonable cause to believe the card is false or invalid or the holder is in violation of statute. . . .

The MMP further specified that certain persons, including (1) a qualified patient, or the holder of a valid identification card, who possesses or transports marijuana for personal medical use, or (2) a designated primary caregiver who transports, processes, administers, delivers, or gives away, in amounts no greater than those specified by statute, marijuana for medical purposes to or for a qualified patient or valid cardholder "shall not be subject, on that sole basis, to criminal liability" under section 11357 (possession of marijuana), 11358 (cultivation of marijuana), 11359 (possession of marijuana for sale), 11360 (sale, transportation, importation, or furnishing of marijuana), 11366 (maintaining place for purpose of unlawfully selling, furnishing, or using controlled substance), 11366.5 (knowingly providing place for purpose of unlawfully manufacturing, storing, or distributing controlled substance), or 11570 (place used for unlawful selling, furnishing, storing, or manufacturing of controlled substance as nuisance). (§ 11362.765, subd. (a).)

Finally, as indicated above, the MMP declared that "[q]ualified patients, persons with valid identification cards, and the designated primary caregivers of [such persons], who associate within the State of California in order collectively or cooperatively to cultivate marijuana for medical purposes, shall not solely on the basis of that fact be subject to state criminal sanctions." . . . (§ 11362.775. . . .) . . .

. . .

### 1. NO EXPRESS PREEMPTION.

. . . [T]he plain language of the CUA and the MMP is limited in scope. It grants specified persons and groups, when engaged in specified conduct, immunity from prosecution under specified state criminal and nuisance laws pertaining to marijuana. . . . The CUA makes no mention of medical marijuana cooperatives, collectives, or dispensaries. It merely provides that state laws against the possession and cultivation of marijuana shall not apply to a qualified patient, or the patient's designated primary caregiver, who possesses or cultivates marijuana for the patient's personal medical use upon a physician's recommendation.

Though the CUA broadly states an aim to "ensure" a "right" of seriously ill persons to "obtain and use" medical marijuana as recommended by a physician (§ 11362.5, subd. (b)(1)(A)), the initiative statute's actual objectives, as presented to the voters, were "modest" . . . , and its substantive provisions created no "broad right to use [medical] marijuana without hindrance or inconvenience." . . . There is no basis to conclude that the CUA expressly preempts local ordinances prohibiting, as a nuisance, the use of property to cooperatively or collectively cultivate and distribute medical marijuana.

The MMP, unlike the CUA, does address, among other things, the collective or cooperative cultivation and distribution of medical marijuana. But the MMP is framed in similarly narrow and modest terms. As pertinent here, it specifies only that qualified patients, identification card holders, and their designated primary caregivers are exempt from prosecution and conviction under enumerated state antimarijuana laws "solely" on the ground that such persons are engaged in the cooperative or collective cultivation, transportation, and distribution of medical marijuana among themselves. (§ 11362.775.)

The MMP's language no more creates a "broad right" of access to medical marijuana "without hindrance or inconvenience" . . . than do the words of the CUA. No provision of the MMP explicitly guarantees the availability of locations where such activities may occur, restricts the broad authority traditionally possessed by local jurisdictions to regulate zoning and land use planning within their borders, or requires local zoning and licensing laws to accommodate the cooperative or collective cultivation and distribution of medical marijuana. Hence, there is no ground to conclude that Riverside's ordinance is expressly preempted by the MMP.

### 2. NO IMPLIED PREEMPTION.

The considerations discussed above also largely preclude any determination that the CUA or the MMP impliedly preempts Riverside's effort to "de-zone" facilities that dispense

Part III. Marijuana Suppliers

medical marijuana. . . . The CUA and the MMP "decriminalize," for state purposes, specified activities pertaining to medical marijuana, and also provide that the state's antidrug nuisance statute cannot be used to abate or enjoin these activities. On the other hand, the Riverside ordinance finds, for local purposes, that the use of property for certain of those activities does constitutes a local nuisance.

. . .

The presumption against preemption is additionally supported by the existence of significant local interests that may vary from jurisdiction to jurisdiction. Amici curiae League of California Cities et al. point out that "California's 482 cities and 58 counties are diverse in size, population, and use." As these amici curiae observe, while several California cities and counties allow medical marijuana facilities, it may not be reasonable to expect every community to do so.

For example, these amici curiae point out, "[s]ome communities are predominantly residential and do not have sufficient commercial or industrial space to accommodate" facilities that distribute medical marijuana. Moreover, these facilities deal in a substance which, except for legitimate medical use by a qualified patient under a physician's authorization, is illegal under both federal and state law to possess, use, furnish, or cultivate, yet is widely desired, bought, sold, cultivated, and employed as a recreational drug. Thus, facilities that dispense medical marijuana may pose a danger of increased crime, congestion, blight, and drug abuse, and the extent of this danger may vary widely from community to community.

Thus, while some counties and cities might consider themselves well suited to accommodating medical marijuana dispensaries, conditions in other communities might lead to the reasonable decision that such facilities within their borders, even if carefully sited, well managed, and closely monitored, would present unacceptable local risks and burdens. . . . Under these circumstances, we cannot lightly assume the voters or the Legislature intended to impose a "one size fits all" policy, whereby each and every one of California's diverse counties and cities must allow the use of local land for such purposes.

. . .

. . . The CUA and the MMP create no all-encompassing scheme for the control and regulation of marijuana for medicinal use. These statutes, both carefully worded, do no more than exempt certain conduct by certain persons from certain state criminal and nuisance laws against the possession, cultivation, transportation, distribution, manufacture, and storage of marijuana.

The gravamen of defendants' argument throughout is that the MMP "authorizes" the existence of facilities for the collective or cooperative cultivation and distribution of medical marijuana, and that a local ordinance prohibiting such facilities thus cannot be tolerated. . . .

. . .

[W]e have made clear that a state law does not "authorize" activities, to the exclusion of local bans, simply by exempting those activities from otherwise applicable state prohibitions. . . .

. . .

. . . [H]ere, the MMP merely exempts the cooperative or collective cultivation and distribution of medical marijuana by and to qualified patients and their designated caregivers from prohibitions that would otherwise apply under state law. The state statute does not thereby mandate that local governments authorize, allow, or accommodate the existence of such facilities.

Defendants emphasize that among the stated purposes of the MMP, as originally enacted, are to "[p]romote uniform and consistent application of the [CUA] among the counties of the state" and to "[e]nhance the access of patients and caregivers to medical marijuana through collective, cooperative cultivation projects." . . . Hence, they insist, the encouragement of medical marijuana dispensaries, under section 11362.775, is a matter of statewide concern, requiring the uniform allowance of such facilities throughout California, and leaving no room for their exclusion by individual local jurisdictions.

We disagree. . . . [T]hough the Legislature stated it intended the MMP to "promote" uniform application of the CUA and to "enhance" access to medical marijuana through collective cultivation, the MMP itself adopts but limited means of addressing these ideals. Aside from requiring local cooperation in the voluntary medical marijuana patient identification card program, the MMP's substantive provisions simply remove specified state-law sanctions from certain marijuana activities, including the cooperative or collective cultivation of medical marijuana by qualified patients and their designated caregivers. . . . The MMP has never expressed or implied any actual limitation on local land use or police power regulation of facilities used for the cultivation and distribution of marijuana. We cannot employ the Legislature's expansive declaration of aims to stretch the MMP's effect beyond a reasonable construction of its substantive provisions.

. . .

Finally, defendants urge that by exempting the collective or cooperative cultivation of medical marijuana by qualified patients and their designated caregivers from treatment as a nuisance under the state's drug abatement laws (§ 11362.775; see § 11570 et seq.), the MMP bars local jurisdictions from adopting and enforcing ordinances that treat these very same activities as nuisances subject to abatement. But for the reasons set forth at length above, we disagree. Nuisance law is not defined exclusively by what the state makes subject to, or exempt from, its own nuisance statutes. Unless exercised in clear conflict with general law, a city's or county's inherent, constitutionally recognized power to determine the appropriate use of land within its borders (Cal. Const., art. XI, § 7) allows it to define nuisances for local purposes, and to seek abatement of such nuisances. . . .

No such conflict exists here. In section 11362.775, the MMP merely removes state law criminal and nuisance sanctions from the conduct described therein. By this means, the MMP has signaled that the state declines to regard the described acts as nuisances or criminal violations, and that the state's enforcement mechanisms will thus not be available against these acts. Accordingly, localities in California are left free to accommodate such conduct, if they choose, free of state interference. As we have explained, however, the MMP's limited provisions neither expressly nor impliedly restrict or preempt the authority of individual local jurisdictions to choose otherwise for local reasons, and to prohibit collective or cooperative medical marijuana activities within their own borders. A local jurisdiction may do so by declaring such conduct on local land to be a nuisance, and by providing means for its abatement.

We thus conclude that neither the CUA nor the MMP expressly or impliedly preempts the authority of California cities and counties, under their traditional land use and police powers, to allow, restrict, limit, or entirely exclude facilities that distribute medical marijuana, and to enforce such policies by nuisance actions. Accordingly, we reject defendants' challenge to Riverside's [medical marijuana dispensary] ordinances.

## Notes and Questions

1. Do you agree with the *Riverside* court's conclusion regarding the preemptive effect of California law? Is a local ban on marijuana dispensaries consistent with the purposes behind the CUA and the MMP? Would your answer change if *each* of California's 58 counties had enacted a similar ban on collective cultivation? Does anything in the *Riverside* court's decision prevent this from happening?

2. *Riverside* held that local governments have the power to ban marijuana dispensaries. But do local governments also have the power to ban personal cultivation of marijuana? At least one California court has held that they do. In *Maral v. City of Live Oak*, 164 Cal. Rptr. 3d 804 (Cal. App. 3d 2013), the court upheld a local ban on personal cultivation of medical marijuana, citing *Riverside* and reasoning that "there is no right— and certainly no constitutional right—to cultivate medical marijuana." *Id.* at 811. But is the holding of *Maral* consistent with *California v. Kelly*, 222 P.3d 186 (Cal. 2010)? As discussed in Chapter 6, the *Kelly* court found that the limits imposed on personal possession and cultivation by the MMP "conflict with—and thereby substantially restrict—the CUA's guarantee that a qualified patient may possess and cultivate *any amount of marijuana reasonably necessary for his or her current medical condition*" and therefore "improperly amend[] the CUA in violation of the California Constitution." *Id.* at 209-10.

3. *Postscript.* The *Riverside* court noted that "nothing prevents future efforts by the Legislature, or by the People, to adopt a different approach." 300 P.3d at 513. It appears the 2015 Medical Cannabis Regulation and Safety Act preserves local authority over medical marijuana dispensaries. Cal. Bus. & Prof. Code § 19316 (2016). *See also Safe Life Caregivers v. City of Los Angeles*, 197 Cal. Rptr. 3d 524, 535 (Cal. App. 2d 2016) (finding MCRSA does not preempt local regulation). Likewise, California's 2016 Proposition 64 appears to allow local governments to regulate recreational marijuana shops, although it denies them authority to ban user cultivation outright. Cal. Health & Safety Code § 11362.2 (2016).

### b. The View that Local Bans Are Preempted

Breaking with *Riverside*, the Michigan Supreme Court has found that local ordinances banning personal supply of marijuana are preempted by the Michigan Medical Marijuana Act (MMMA), which permits such supply and which (like the CUA discussed in *Riverside*) does not expressly address local authority.[5]

### Ter Beek v. City of Wyoming
846 N.W.2d 531 (Mich. 2014)

McCormack, J.:

The Michigan Medical Marihuana Act (MMMA) . . . , affords certain protections under state law for the medical use of marijuana in the state of Michigan. Among

---

5. In the interest of disclosure, the textbook author wrote an amicus brief in the case arguing that the MMMA was not preempted by the federal CSA. *See Brief Amici Curiae of the Cato Institute, the Drug Policy Alliance, and Law Enforcement Against Prohibition, Ter Beek v. City of Wyoming*, 2013 WL 5499999 (Mich.).

them is §4(a) of the MMMA, which immunizes registered qualifying patients from ["arrest, prosecution, or penalty in any manner . . . for the medical use of marihuana in accordance with this act." MCL 333.26424(a). Under the MMMA, medical use includes "the acquisition, possession, *cultivation, manufacture*, use, internal possession, delivery, transfer, or transportation of marihuana." MCL 333.26423(f) (emphasis added)]. . . . At issue here is the relationship between this immunity . . . and a local zoning ordinance adopted by the city of Wyoming which prohibits and subjects to civil sanction any land "[u]ses that are contrary to federal law." City of Wyoming Code of Ordinances, § 90-66.

. . .

. . . Under the city code, violations of the Ordinance constitute municipal civil infractions punishable by "civil sanctions, including, without limitation, fines, damages, expenses and costs," City of Wyoming Code of Ordinances, § 1-27(a) to (b), and are also subject to injunctive relief, City of Wyoming Code of Ordinances, § 1-27(g).

Plaintiff, John Ter Beek, lives in the City and is a qualifying patient under the MMMA who possesses a state-issued registry identification card. Upon the City's adoption of the Ordinance, Ter Beek filed the instant lawsuit. . . . Ter Beek alleges that he wishes to grow, possess, and use medical marijuana in his home in accordance with the MMMA. The Ordinance, however, by its incorporation of the CSA's federal prohibition of marijuana, prohibits and penalizes such conduct. This, Ter Beek contends, impermissibly contravenes § 4(a) of the MMMA. . . . Accordingly, Ter Beek seeks a declaratory judgment that the Ordinance is preempted by the MMMA and a corresponding injunction prohibiting the City from enforcing the Ordinance against him for the medical use of marijuana in compliance with the MMMA.

. . .

Under the Michigan Constitution, the City's "power to adopt resolutions and ordinances relating to its municipal concerns" is "subject to the constitution and the law." Const. 1963, art. 7, § 22. As this Court has previously noted, "[w]hile prescribing broad powers, this provision specifically provides that ordinances are subject to the laws of this state, i.e., statutes." [*AFSCME v. Detroit*, 662 N.W.2d 695 (Mich. 2003).] The City, therefore, "is precluded from enacting an ordinance if . . . the ordinance is in direct conflict with the state statutory scheme, or . . . if the state statutory scheme preempts the ordinance by occupying the field of regulation which the municipality seeks to enter, to the exclusion of the ordinance, even where there is no direct conflict between the two schemes of regulation." [*Michigan v. Llewellyn*, 257 N.W.2d 902 (Mich. 1977) (footnotes omitted)] A direct conflict exists when "the ordinance permits what the statute prohibits or the ordinance prohibits what the statute permits." *Id.* . . . Here, the Ordinance directly conflicts with the MMMA by permitting what the MMMA expressly prohibits—the imposition of a "penalty in any manner" on a registered qualifying patient whose medical use of marijuana falls within the scope of § 4(a)'s immunity.

. . . [E]njoining a registered qualifying patient from engaging in MMMA-compliant conduct unambiguously falls within the scope of penalties prohibited by § 4(a)[,] . . . a prohibition which expressly includes "civil penalt[ies]." . . . Under the Ordinance, individuals are subject to civil punishment for engaging in the medical use of marijuana in accordance with the MMMA; by the plain terms of § 4(a), the manner of that punishment—be it requiring the payment of a monetary sanction, or denying the ability to engage in MMMA-compliant conduct—is not material to the MMMA's immunity from it. . . .

. . .

The City . . . points to *Riverside v. Inland Empire Patients Health & Wellness Ctr., Inc.* . . . in support of its position. . . . *Riverside*, however, is beside the point. At issue there was whether a local zoning ordinance prohibiting medical marijuana dispensaries within city limits was preempted by California's Compassionate Use Act (CUA) and Medical Marijuana Program Act (MMP). The California Supreme Court concluded that there was no preemption, as the CUA and MMP offered only a limited immunity from sanction under certain specified state criminal and nuisance statutes, thereby "signal[ing] that the *state* declines to regard the described acts as nuisances or criminal violations, and that the *state's* enforcement mechanisms will thus not be available against these acts." *Id.* at 762, 156 Cal. Rptr. 3d 409, 300 P.3d 494. As such, these "limited provisions" were found to "neither expressly or impliedly restrict or preempt the authority of individual local jurisdictions to choose otherwise for local reasons, and to prohibit collective or cooperative medical marijuana activities within their own borders." *Id.* The scope of § 4(a)'s immunity, however, is not similarly circumscribed; in prohibiting certain individuals from being "subject to . . . penalty in any manner," § 4(a) draws no distinction between state and local laws or penalties. We thus do not find *Riverside*'s reasoning instructive.

## Notes and Questions

1. Is the MMMA distinguishable from the CUA and MMP discussed in *Riverside*? Why, why not? If not, which court's analysis of the preemptive effect of state law do you find more persuasive?

2. In *Ter Beek*, the City also claimed that MMMA section 4(a) was preempted by the federal CSA—an argument that, if successful, would have enabled the City to enforce its ordinance. However, in a portion of its decision not excerpted above, the *Ter Beek* court rejected the federal preemption claim, finding that

> there is no "positive conflict" between the CSA and § 4(a) of the MMMA such that the two "cannot consistently stand together," 21 USC § 903: it is not impossible to comply with both the CSA's federal prohibition of marijuana and § 4(a)'s limited state-law immunity for certain medical marijuana use, and § 4(a) does not stand as an obstacle to the accomplishment and execution of the full purposes and objectives of the CSA.

846 N.W.2d at 541. Is it possible to reconcile this holding with the court's finding (noted above) that the City Ordinance "directly conflicts with the MMMA by permitting what the MMMA expressly prohibits"? *Id.*

## D. WHO *SHOULD* REGULATE THE SUPPLY OF MARIJUANA?

Sections B and C examined the current metes and bounds of state and local authority to regulate marijuana supply activities. This section asks the related *normative* question: What power *should* each of these levels of government wield over the supply of marijuana?

The following excerpt—another portion of the textbook author's article excerpted earlier—examines the normative theory of localism and the arguments both for and against local control of marijuana supply. Although the article focuses on *localism*, its analysis arguably applies to marijuana federalism as well, given that the case for local control and the case for state control rest on similar considerations. *See, e.g.*, Richard Briffault, *"What About the 'Ism'?" Normative and Formal Concerns in Contemporary Federalism*, 47 Vand. L. Rev. 1303, 1305 (1994) ("[T]he values said to be advanced by federalism are not distinctively associated with the states. Many of these values . . . may be served better by local governments than by states.").

### *Robert A. Mikos*, Marijuana Localism (cont'd)
65 Case W. Res. L. Rev. 719 (2015)

. . . [The] economic theory of localism . . . strives to maximize total satisfaction with government policy. To that end, it asks which level of government, state or local, would maximize the combined utility of all residents of the state. Maximizing preference satisfaction is not, of course, the only—or, indeed, even necessarily a good—rationale for localism, but it is one of the most commonly invoked rationales for local control. . . .

Localism's net impact on preference satisfaction depends on the strength of two competing considerations. On the one hand, localism could potentially boost preference satisfaction if local communities in the same state disagree about policy. Each state is comprised of a large number of local communities. When some of those communities disagree with the way the state would handle an issue, localism enables them to pursue the policy their own majorities would prefer. By giving communities the opportunity to opt out of a state policy that some find disagreeable, localism should satisfy a larger number of state residents overall.

. . .

On the other hand, localism could potentially diminish satisfaction with government policy if some residents care about what happens outside their home communities. For a variety of reasons, people commonly do care about what is going on in other communities. For example, those happenings might harm them physically—think of lung disease caused by pollution emanating from a neighboring town's factory—as well as psychologically—think of the disgust felt upon hearing of ISIS beheadings halfway across the globe.

. . .

When people care about what happens elsewhere, localism will not necessarily increase total satisfaction in the state and could even diminish it. This is because localism requires surrendering a degree of control over activities occurring elsewhere.

. . .

Ultimately, the problem is that local communities have no incentive to consider the costs and benefits of local activity that are borne by outsiders. This means that the interests of local communities and the interests of the entire state do not necessarily coincide, and we cannot trust local communities to regulate activities in a way that will maximize the total satisfaction of the entire state. In particular, when local activity imposes costs on outsiders, local authorities will allow or produce too much of it. . . . And when local activity instead confers benefits on outsiders, local authorities will allow or produce too little of it.

. . . The normative case for localism thus hinges on the strength of two competing considerations: (1) the degree to which local communities disagree about how to regulate a given activity, and (2) the degree to which local communities absorb the full costs and benefits of the regulated activity. Ceteris paribus, the stronger is the former consideration, the stronger will be the case for local control. Conversely, the stronger is the latter consideration, the stronger will be the case for state control. . . .

. . .

## [THE CASE FOR MARIJUANA LOCALISM]

It seems safe to posit that communities disagree about how to regulate marijuana sales. The best evidence stems from the fact that local communities have adopted starkly different policies toward marijuana stores. In Colorado, for example, 165 municipalities have voted to ban retail marijuana stores, but another fifty-three municipalities have voted to permit them.[6] Marijuana stores garnered as little as 21 percent support and as much as 65 percent support in the most recent round of local referenda. Even among Colorado communities that allow marijuana stores, there is some differentiation in policy. For example, only half of the fifty-three municipalities that permit retail marijuana shops have chosen to levy special local taxes on marijuana sales. And to varying degrees communities in Colorado and elsewhere restrict the number, location, size, and hours of operation of locally permitted marijuana stores.

The passage of different policies arguably reflects the distinctive beliefs, priorities, and conditions of local communities. To simplify somewhat, communities that have banned marijuana dispensaries fear the stores fuel marijuana consumption and all the harms they attribute to it, and that they also attract "crime, congestion, blight, and drug abuse" to surrounding neighborhoods. Communities that allow dispensaries might share some of these concerns, but they prefer less-draconian means to address them, for example, keeping stores away from areas frequented by children. Communities that allow marijuana stores also see an upside to them. The stores provide medicine for seriously-ill patients, recreation for consenting adults, tax revenues for cash-strapped local governments, or jobs for local workers.

. . .

Given these disagreements, localism theory suggests that more people might be satisfied if their local government rather than the state (or national) government controlled marijuana sales policy. The results of . . . statewide elections could even help estimate the magnitude of the preference-satisfaction gains to be had from marijuana localism. . . .

Consider . . . the . . . vote on Colorado's Amendment 64. In the 2012 election, 1,383,140 Coloradoans voted for Amendment 64 and were presumably satisfied with the outcome; another 1,116,894 Coloradoans voted against Amendment 64 and were presumably dissatisfied with the outcome. In total, a net 266,246 more Coloradoans preferred the new state policy (legalization) over the old one (prohibition). But the county-by-county vote suggests that even more people would have been satisfied by localism. [I]n thirty of Colorado's sixty-four counties . . . , the total number of "no" votes (215,973) exceeded the total number of "yes" votes (181,369) by 34,604. This suggests that a net of 34,604

---

6. Author's note: For more up-to-date figures on the number of Colorado communities allowing retail marijuana stores, *see* Colorado Marijuana Enforcement Division, *Local Authorities Allowing Retail Marijuana Facilities*, at https://perma.cc/64TH-CHBS (updated Aug. 15, 2016).

Coloradoans [(about 1.4 percent of all voters)] might have been happier under localism. While the results on Amendment 64 might be indicative only of Colorado circa 2012, the county-by-county votes on marijuana ballot measures in other states tell a very similar story. . . .

In theory, of course, the number of people who benefit from localism would be even larger and the case for localism correspondingly stronger if some dissatisfied residents relocated to communities espousing more like-minded preferences toward marijuana regulation. After all, estimating the number of people who benefit from localism using only the votes they cast in an election fails to count anyone who benefits from localism by voting with their feet instead. Nonetheless, I suspect few people actually change residences solely on account of local marijuana sales policy. For most people, marijuana is not an important enough issue to justify incurring the costs of permanent relocation, especially when, as I suggest below, they can easily take advantage of neighboring community's laws without relocating there.

. . .

### [THE CASE AGAINST MARIJUANA LOCALISM]

Localism could potentially reduce overall satisfaction with government policy if people care about the marijuana policies adopted by other communities. . . . [T]here are at least two reasons people will mind what other communities do. Marijuana users can smuggle marijuana in from neighboring communities (marijuana smuggling), and marijuana users can travel out to neighboring communities to consume the drug (marijuana tourism). Both marijuana smuggling and marijuana tourism threaten to undermine the efficacy of many local controls and thus satisfaction with marijuana localism among a large segment of the population.

#### 1. Marijuana Smuggling

In a world of divergent local marijuana policies, marijuana smuggling could undermine all but the most lenient of them. All marijuana regulations impose costs on the drug. . . . The problem for governments is that marijuana consumers have strong incentives to avoid these costs, and the availability of cheaper marijuana in neighboring jurisdictions—especially nearby local jurisdictions—gives them an easy means by which to do so.

For reasons both legal and practical, smuggling marijuana between local communities is easy. To begin, local residents have a constitutional "right to travel and to take advantage of the legal entitlements of neighboring jurisdictions."[67] . . .

Thus, a community may not bar its residents from buying marijuana somewhere else, even if it chooses to ban marijuana inside its own borders. For example, if Aurora, Colorado, prohibits retail marijuana sales, it may not stop its residents from buying the drug next door in Denver, where sales are legal.

The United States Constitution would allow local governments to bar the importation and possession of "noxious" goods in its borders, but it appears that no state has yet

---

67. Seth F. Kreimer, *The Law of Choice and Choice of Law: Abortion, the Right to Travel, and Extraterritorial Regulation in American Federalism*, 67 N.Y.U. L. Rev. 451, 462 (1992).

Part III.  Marijuana Suppliers

actually empowered a local community to ban the simple possession or even importation of marijuana bought legally elsewhere in the state. In any event, even if a state did allow localities to ban possession and transportation of marijuana purchased in another community, residents would face little practical difficulty buying marijuana elsewhere and bringing it back home. The costs of making the trip to another community would be negligible as legal marijuana stores may sit just feet outside the resident's [home] jurisdiction. Moreover, the marijuana could be easily concealed for the trip home, meaning the resident would face little risk of being caught by local police in possession of marijuana from another jurisdiction. The resident could further limit this risk and the size of the sanction she would face by limiting the quantities she smuggles, which is only a minimal inconvenience, considering that even heavy users consume less than two grams daily. And in the unlikely event she is caught with a small quantity of marijuana (say, twenty-eight grams or less), the resident would, at worst, likely face only simple possession charges. For all of these reasons, the expected sanction for smuggling marijuana across local communities is likely to be extremely low.

Indeed, marijuana is commonly smuggled through less porous borders and across longer distances than those separating communities in the same state. Much of the marijuana consumed in the United States is smuggled all the way from Mexico, and states like Nebraska and Oklahoma claim they have "dealt with a significant influx of Colorado-source marijuana" since the state legalized commercial sales of the drug. Though it is wise to take such claims with a grain of salt, the Colorado Department of Revenue itself estimates that out-of-state residents bought between eight and ten *tons* of marijuana legally in Colorado in 2014, and it reports that out-of-staters comprised nearly one-half of the roughly 2,500 customers served by a Denver marijuana store in the course of a single week. . . .

For local communities and possibly even for states and nations, it is just not feasible to prevent cheap marijuana from being smuggled across their borders. In their suit against Colorado, for example, Nebraska and Oklahoma claim they have had to invest substantial new resources in their unsuccessful attempt to stem the tide of marijuana flowing in from Colorado:

> The result of increased Colorado-sourced marijuana being trafficked in Plaintiff States due to the passage and implementation of Colorado Amendment 64 has been the diversion of a significant amount of the personnel time, budget, and resources of the Plaintiff States' law enforcement, judicial system, and penal system resources to counteract the increased trafficking and transportation of Colorado-sourced marijuana.

Not surprisingly, Nebraska and Oklahoma would probably prefer that Colorado shut off the water at the spigot instead—recall that a *single* marijuana store in Denver serves *thousands* of customers every *week*. But that preferred strategy is simply unavailable to local communities and even states and nations when the source of a drug lay outside their borders.

Marijuana smuggling threatens to undermine the policy objectives of local communities and hence their satisfaction with localism. For one thing, smuggling could undermine the efforts of some communities to curb consumption of marijuana and all of the harms those communities attribute (rightly or wrongly) to such consumption, including intellectual and motivational impairment, heart attacks, psychoses, traffic accidents, and moral corruption, to name a few. . . . [O]ne goal of local regulation is to raise the price of marijuana and thereby reduce its consumption among residents. But if local regulations can be evaded by shopping at a marijuana store located in the town next door, those local regulations will not work as intended. And if local marijuana regulations do not actually work as intended, marijuana localism will not boost preference satisfaction in communities that adopt the regulations and might even diminish satisfaction.

To be sure, local communities could attempt to achieve some of their policy objectives by means other than controlling the supply of marijuana. For example, a community could establish more sobriety checkpoints to combat driving under the influence. But many communities would not deem such measures to be perfect substitutes for source controls. For one thing, as noted above, they might believe that controlling marijuana at its source is a cheaper or more effective strategy compared to combatting harmful behaviors associated with use of the drug. In addition, harm-reduction measures like sobriety checkpoints will not necessarily address all of the harms local residents attribute to marijuana use; think of accidents that take place in the home or the moral corruption some people believe inheres in the use of substances like marijuana.

Local communities that ban the sale of marijuana might have more luck deflecting the "crime, congestion, blight, and drug abuse" they associate with dispensaries onto other communities. But as discussed in more detail below, that does not represent a gain to *society*.

In addition to undermining efforts to combat consumption, marijuana smuggling could also undermine efforts to collect local taxes on the drug. Enthusiasm for marijuana legalization has been fueled at least in part by the promise of new tax revenues from sales of legal marijuana. Many states have already imposed their own taxes on the drug, but local jurisdictions are now trying to get in on the act. Twenty-seven of the fifty-three municipalities that have legalized marijuana sales in Colorado have levied local add-on taxes on sales of marijuana. For example, Denver imposes an 8.25% tax on retail marijuana sales on top of Colorado's 12.90% tax (for a combined rate of 21.15%). Now suppose that Aurora decides to legalize commercial marijuana sales. But to capture some of *Denver's* marijuana business, suppose Aurora decides not to impose its own local tax on the drug. Since a portion of the state sales tax would be returned to Aurora anyway, the city would not necessarily need to impose an additional local tax to help fill its coffers. It would hardly be surprising if some Denverites now made the short trip *to Aurora* to buy marijuana. In so doing they could evade Denver's comparatively steep local tax and save a tidy sum in the process (marijuana costs roughly $200-400 an ounce). Indeed, in a recent report Professor Jonathan Caulkins and his co-authors conclude that "the idea that individual states can function as separate policy laboratories is optimistic." [Jonathan P. Caulkins, et al., *Considering Marijuana Legalization: Insights for Vermont and Other Jurisdictions* (RAND 2015).] They warn that the budgetary impacts of legalizing marijuana in one state (Vermont) "are highly uncertain and depend very much on what neighboring states do about their own marijuana policies." Indeed, they suggest that "it might only take one of the lower 48 states breaking ranks and charging low marijuana taxes to challenge tax collections in the other states." . . . At the very least, the threat of smuggling likely imposes a ceiling on the effective tax rate that any local community can realistically expect to collect on marijuana.

Ultimately, the problem with marijuana localism is that marijuana sold legally in one community imposes costs on other communities, and the point-of-sale community will not necessarily consider these costs when deciding how to regulate marijuana distribution. Nebraska and Oklahoma have emphasized the smuggling concerns in their suit against Colorado: "[m]arijuana flows from [the legal gap created by Amendment 64] into neighboring states, undermining Plaintiff States' own marijuana bans, draining their treasuries, and placing stress on their criminal justice systems." . . . In light of concerns over smuggling, there is no reason to expect that local communities will necessarily adopt marijuana policies that boost *societal* welfare.

## 2. Marijuana Tourism

A related problem confronting local communities stems from marijuana tourism. Marijuana tourism occurs when residents travel to a neighboring locality not only to *buy* marijuana but also to *consume* it there as well. As noted above, residents have a constitutional right to travel to other jurisdictions "to take advantage of the legal entitlements" thereof, including, presumably, the right to consume marijuana to the same extent as locals.

For the reasons discussed above, it is easy for residents to travel to neighboring communities to *buy* marijuana. It is clear that marijuana dispensaries do a brisk business with nonlocal residents. In addition to dispensaries, other businesses have sprouted up to cater to the marijuana tourism industry. For example, one tour bus operator is offering regular $400 round-trip service from Dallas, Texas, to one of Denver's marijuana shops.

Marijuana tourism threatens to impose costs on both home and destination jurisdictions. For home jurisdictions, marijuana tourism could create the same problems caused by marijuana smuggling even if residents never smuggle the drug back home. The psychoactive chemical found in marijuana (THC) can impair cognitive functioning for hours, some even claim *weeks*, after use. Hence, it is possible that marijuana could impair driving, learning, productivity, and so on in one community long after it was consumed somewhere else. For example, a Colorado Springs resident might legally consume marijuana at a club in Denver, then drive seventy miles back home and strike a pedestrian in Colorado Springs. The harm to Colorado Springs is the same regardless of where the consumption occurred.

Even long after the acute effects of marijuana wear off, users might experience latent harms caused by long-term chronic use of the drug. Under the right circumstances, these latent harms could cause concerns in outside communities. For example, suppose a young Colorado Springs resident goes on regular weekend marijuana binges in Denver; now suppose she takes no physical risks while there, but after several months of heavy use, she suffers permanent neurological damage. As a result, she might need medical care, special tutoring, and other social services—all paid for by her domicile (Colorado Springs) rather than by her weekend destination (Denver).

More controversially, the use of marijuana by local residents in neighboring communities could also cause moral harms back home. Some people object to drug use by others for religious or other moral reasons. To them, drug use constitutes a sinful indulgence, a debasement of the soul (to paraphrase James Q. Wilson). They feel morally indignant when other people use drugs, whether or not such drug use causes them, or anyone else, *physical* injury. Even readers who do not share this worldview might empathize a bit by thinking of the grief or anger felt when hearing about racial bigotry, animal cruelty, greed, or other behaviors that occur elsewhere. To be sure, the law says that locals have no right to regulate their residents extra-territorially. And that may be a good rule from a normative perspective. But like many constitutional rules, it is not a rule designed to maximize preference satisfaction. It suggests that we should ignore some preferences (like my preference that you not use marijuana in your town), not satisfy them.

. . .

Marijuana tourism could also undermine the interests of tourist destinations, notwithstanding the business it generates for them. Call this the "crashing the party problem." For one thing, marijuana tourism enables outsiders to enjoy many of the benefits that tourist destinations generate without paying the full costs of those benefits. Marijuana destinations like Denver are supplying a drug that has medical value, recreational value, or both to nonresidents. To illustrate, suppose that Colorado Springs bans marijuana shops and Denver allows them; suppose as well that some Colorado Springs residents enjoy using marijuana and make the short trek to Denver to buy and consume the drug. In this case, local activity in Denver is conferring an external benefit on the community of Colorado Springs. Denver cannot easily charge outsiders for this benefit. Neither can it recoup the costs those outsiders inflict while in Denver. For example, after consuming marijuana, those Colorado Springs residents might cause accidents, brawls, and other disorderly conduct that harms the citizens of Denver. In fact, it seems reasonable to suppose that outsiders will create more problems than locals because (1) their connection to the local community is weaker, so they feel less inhibited while there; (2) their lack of familiarity with the local environment may make them more prone to accidents; (3) they have to travel farther than residents to consume marijuana, so they might drive longer distances under the influence of marijuana; (4) they may be more inclined to overindulge since they have limited access back home; and (5) on average, tourists may be less experienced with marijuana use and thus more susceptible to—or simply less aware of—its psychoactive effects.

Legal and economic forces arguably prevent tourist destinations from satisfactorily addressing the burdens imposed by outsiders. As discussed, tourist destinations may not deny outsiders the legal privileges they confer upon their own residents. In other words, once a community allows its own residents to buy and consume marijuana it must allow non-residents to do so on the same terms. . . .

. . .

Neither can tourist destinations easily recoup the costs that nonresidents might impose on them. Destinations like Denver do, of course, generate tax revenues from marijuana tourism. But it is difficult for any destination to charge nonresidents a sufficiently high Pigouvian tax to fully compensate for the unique costs they impose. . . .

The residents of communities that legalize marijuana might be aggrieved for a second reason as well. They cannot travel and enjoy easy access to marijuana in other communities that prohibit sales of drug. In other words, they cannot take their home communities' privileges into neighboring communities and must abide by their disagreeable laws. Not surprisingly, these residents do not want to be denied access to a drug that gives them joy, medical relief, or both. Thus, while they might be pleased if their local community permits the distribution of marijuana, they might be *even happier* if the entire state (or nation) were to do the same. In other words, marijuana localism will not *necessarily* improve their well-being vis-a-vis federalism or nationalism because they too are not necessarily indifferent to how their neighbors regulate the drug.

In sum, the desirability of marijuana localism hinges on empirical claims about the extent to which local communities disagree about marijuana policy and the extent to which local governments can address the concerns that matter to their residents. On the one hand, local majorities clearly disagree about how best to regulate marijuana sales. Localism would thus appear to boost satisfaction in communities that would disagree with the way their state would regulate such sales. But the appeal of localism may prove illusory. The mobility of marijuana and of its users undermines the efficacy of any local controls. In other words, localism will not necessarily give people what they really want—like a reduction in marijuana consumption or an increase in tax revenues or an increase in access to the drug. It is thus not safe to assume that local majorities have something to gain from localism, or that statewide majorities have nothing to lose by acceding to it.

## Notes and Questions

1. Do you think marijuana smuggling and marijuana tourism threaten to significantly undermine satisfaction with local (and possibly even state) marijuana supply policies?

2. Do you think preference satisfaction should be the main criteria on which power over marijuana is allocated? Are there any other criteria you would consider in deciding who should be allowed to regulate marijuana? For example, might state and local governments serve as useful testing grounds for experimenting with new marijuana policies? *E.g.*, Jonathan Caulkins et al., Marijuana Legalization: What Everyone Needs to Know 119-20 (Oxford University Press 2016) (lauding benefits of state experimentation).

3. If you think that local governments should have power over marijuana suppliers, how far down would you be willing to go? In other words, would you allow counties to regulate marijuana supply? How about cities within counties? Or districts within cities? Or blocks within districts? Or individual parcels of land within blocks? How do you decide where power should ultimately rest?

4. Conversely, if you think that local governments should *not* have power over marijuana suppliers, would you say the same of *state* governments? After all, the concerns the excerpted article raised about marijuana localism are similar to the concerns that Nebraska and Oklahoma raise about marijuana federalism—e.g., that marijuana flows from Colorado "into neighboring states, undermining [their] own marijuana bans, draining their treasuries, and placing stress on their criminal justice systems." If states should not have power over marijuana suppliers, should it be left to the national government? Or perhaps even some international forum?

5. Is there any empirical evidence on "the extent to which local governments can address the concerns that matter to their residents"? In another section of the article not excerpted above, the textbook author compared marijuana localism to alcohol localism and examined the social science research on the effects of local control over alcohol distribution:

> The experience with alcohol localism provides a sobering lesson. It appears that counties have encountered many of the problems that I predicted could plague local marijuana controls. Wet counties have probably undermined the controls imposed by dry counties, or dry counties have displaced their harms onto wet counties, or both. If alcohol localism has failed to meet expectations, why would we expect marijuana localism to fare any better?

Mikos, *Marijuana Localism*, *supra*, at 761. Can you think of any other case studies that might shed light on the desirability of marijuana localism?

6. Ultimately, how would you allocate power over marijuana suppliers? Is there a desirable role for each level of government to play in shaping law and policy toward suppliers? What sorts of activities would you allow federal, state, and local governments to regulate (and perhaps even to ban)?

# PART IV

# THIRD PARTIES

# CHAPTER 11

# The Regulation of Third Parties

Many people interact with marijuana users and suppliers on a regular basis. Physicians recommend marijuana to their patients; landlords rent property to tenants who grow and sell the drug; employers hire workers who use marijuana; police officers seize marijuana from—and may be asked to return marijuana to—users; and so on. As suggested in Chapter 1, third parties like these have been drawn into the ambit of marijuana law and policy, even if they do not use or supply the drug themselves.

The field's treatment of such third parties raises a host of law, policy, and authority questions distinct from those surrounding users and suppliers. This chapter begins to explore these questions. It discusses a handful of key regulations that apply to a broad range of third parties (and to users and suppliers as well), including aiding and abetting, conspiracy, and money laundering offenses created by prohibition regimes. The next three chapters (12-14) examine the application of these broad prohibitions—as well as more targeted regulations—to specific groups of third parties, including professionals, businesses, and government employees, and the policy and authority issues surrounding the regulation of such groups.

The chapter proceeds as follows. Section A discusses the liability of third parties for aiding and abetting the use and supply offenses discussed in earlier chapters. Section B discusses liability for conspiracy to commit those same offenses. Finally, Section C discusses liability for engaging in transactions involving the proceeds of marijuana offenses.

## A. AIDING AND ABETTING

Statutes like 18 U.S.C. section 2(a) make it a crime to aid and abet the commission of another crime, including any of the sundry crimes surveyed in Chapters 3-4 and 7-8. To illustrate, suppose that Andy offers his friend, Pasha, some helpful advice on how to grow marijuana, in the hope that Pasha will share some of her harvest in gratitude. On these facts, Andy could not be found guilty of manufacturing marijuana himself, at least if he played no part in cultivating Pasha's plants. But Andy could still be found guilty of aiding and abetting Pasha's manufacture of marijuana because of the assistance he provided Pasha and, just as importantly, his reasons for helping her.

So what does it mean, exactly, to aid and abet a crime? The offense usually entails four basic elements:

(1) a crime was committed (the attendant circumstance), and
(2) the defendant encouraged or assisted the commission of the crime (actus reus), and

(3) the defendant had knowledge of the crime (mens rea), and
(4) the defendant desired to help the crime succeed (mens rea)

*E.g.*, M.P.C. § 2.06; *United States v. Zafiro*, 945 F.2d 881, 887 (7th Cir. 1991) (discussing elements).

As for the first element, the government need only prove that a crime was committed. It need not *convict* anyone of that crime. In the illustration above, for example, the government could charge Andy with aiding and abetting Pasha's manufacture of marijuana without necessarily charging (or convicting) Pasha with a manufacturing offense; it would just need to demonstrate that she manufactured marijuana.

Regarding the second element, "[i]t is often said that any amount of influence or aid suffices, no matter how slight." Sanford H. Kadish, *Complicity, Cause and Blame: A Study in the Interpretation of Doctrine*, 73 Calif. L. Rev. 323, 361-62 (1985). It should come as no surprise, then, that defendants have been convicted of aiding and abetting marijuana crimes for, among other things, merely driving a seller to meet up with a buyer, *South Dakota v. Caylor*, 434 N.W.2d 582 (S.D. 1989), introducing a buyer to a seller, *Robichaud v. Virginia*, 199 S.E.2d 508 (1973), or vouching for the quality of a seller's marijuana, *Washington v. Wilson*, 631 P.2d 362 (Wash. 1981) (en banc). Importantly, the government need not show that the encouragement or assistance actually *caused* the crime, in other words, that the crime would not have occurred without the defendant's encouragement or assistance. *See* Kadish, *Complicity*, *supra*, at 357. In the illustration above, for example, the government could convict Andy of aiding and abetting Pasha's manufacture of marijuana, even if Pasha would have grown the marijuana without any help from Andy.

Aiding and abetting also includes two related mens rea elements (the third and fourth elements above), both of which pose more daunting proof challenges for prosecutors. First, the government must show that the defendant knew that a crime was being (or would be) committed. In the illustration, it is clear that Andy knows that Pasha is planning to grow marijuana, because his advice to her is specifically tailored for that purpose. But if Andy and Pasha had merely discussed gardening in general and Andy remained unaware of Pasha's plan to grow marijuana, he would not be guilty of aiding and abetting, even if his advice did in fact help Pasha grow marijuana plants successfully.

The fourth and final element is often the most difficult to comprehend and to establish beyond a reasonable doubt. Usually the government must show that the defendant wanted her actions to help the crime succeed. *See* John F. Decker, *The Mental State Requirement for Accomplice Liability in American Criminal Law*, 60 S.C. L. Rev. 237 (2008) (surveying state law). In the original illustration above, Andy's desire to help Pasha succeed is fairly obvious because he hoped that Pasha might share some of her crop with him. However, the government does not necessarily need direct evidence to demonstrate a defendant's intentions. Imagine, for example, that Pasha mentioned to Andy one day that Pasha wanted to grow marijuana, and Andy simply replied "Cannabis plants need a lot of light and fresh air." While hardly a smoking gun, Andy's statement in context might be enough for a jury to find he intended to help Pasha manufacture marijuana. *Cf. North Carolina v. Thomas*, 309 S.E.2d 564 (Ct. App. N.C. 1983) (upholding conviction for aiding and abetting the distribution of marijuana, based on defendant's statement to buyers that her friend, from whom they had just bought LSD, also had some marijuana).

The following case explores the limits of aiding and abetting liability for marijuana crimes.

## *Washington v. Gladstone*
474 P.2d 274 (Wash. 1970) (en banc)

HALE, J.:

A jury found defendant Bruce Gladstone guilty of aiding and abetting one Robert Kent in the unlawful sale of marijuana. . . . He appeals . . . contending that the evidence as a matter of law was insufficient to sustain a verdict of guilty. His point, we think, is well taken.

. . .

Gladstone's guilt as an aider and abettor in this case rests solely on evidence of a conversation between him and one Douglas MacArthur Thompson concerning the possible purchase of marijuana from one Robert Kent. There is no other evidence to connect the accused with Kent who ultimately sold some marijuana to Thompson.

When asked by Thompson—an agent of the police—where marijuana could be bought, the defendant did no more than name Kent as an individual who might be willing to sell some and draw a sketch of his location. There was no evidence whatever that the defendant had any association, understanding, agreement or arrangement, direct or indirect, tacit or express with Kent to aid or persuade him in any way in the sale of marijuana.

The conversation between defendant and Thompson occurred at defendant's residence. . . .

. . . Thompson asked Gladstone if he would sell him some marijuana. Describing this incident, Thompson testified as follows:

> Well, I asked—at the time Gladstone told me that he was—he did not have enough marijuana on hand to sell me any, but he did know an individual who had quite a sufficient quantity and that was very willing to sell and he named the individual as Robert Kent, or Bob Kent as he put it, and he gave me directions to the residence and he—due to the directions I asked him if, you know, if he could draw me a map and he did.

When Thompson said he asked Gladstone to draw the map for him, he added, "I'm not sure whether he did give me the exact address or not, he told me where the residence was." He said that Gladstone then with pencil and paper sketched the location of Kent's place of residence. Thompson had no prior knowledge of where Kent lived, and did not know if he might have marijuana or that he had ever possessed it.

[Thompson then went to Kent's residence and bought marijuana.] . . . Kent was subsequently arrested and convicted of selling Thompson approximately 8 ounces of marijuana—the very sale which defendant here was convicted of aiding and abetting.

That ended the prosecution's case. Even if it were accorded all favorable inferences, there appears at this point a gap in the evidence which we feel as a matter of law is fatal to the prosecution's cause. Neither on direct examination nor under cross-examination did Thompson testify that he knew of any prior conduct, arrangements or communications between Gladstone and Kent from which it could be even remotely inferred that the defendant had any understanding, agreement, purpose, intention or design to participate or engage in or aid or abet any sale of marijuana by Kent. Other than to obtain a simple map from Gladstone and to say that Gladstone told him Kent might have some marijuana available, Thompson did not even establish that Kent and the defendant were acquainted with each other. Testimony of the brief conversation and Gladstone's very crude drawing consisting of 8 penciled lines indicating where Kent lived constitute the whole proof of the aiding and abetting presented.

. . . Thus, at the close of its case in chief, the state had failed to show any connection or association whatever between Gladstone and Kent or even that they knew each other. . . .

Defendant's proof did not aid the state's case either. . . .

Gladstone took the stand and testified that he had been a student at the University of Puget Sound in Tacoma for 2 years and that he did not know the police informant, Douglas MacArthur Thompson, personally but had seen him on campus. Prior to the evening of April 10, 1967, he said, Thompson had never been in his home. As to Kent, the party whom he was accused of aiding and abetting, he said he had seen him between classes having coffee at the student union building, and perhaps had been in his company about 10 times altogether. He knew where Kent lived because once en route home in his car he had given Kent a lift from the student union building to the latter's house. On this singular occasion, Gladstone did not get out of the car. He said that he did not know that Kent used marijuana or kept it for sale to other people.

Describing the incidents of April 10, 1967, when Thompson came to his door, Gladstone's version of the event differed somewhat from Thompson's. He testified that Thompson asked him to sell him some pot and Gladstone said, "No," and:

A. Then he asked me if I knew Rob Kent and I said yes.
Q. What did you tell him?
A. I said yes, I knew Rob Kent, and he asked me if I knew where Rob Kent lived and I said that I didn't know the address, nor did I know the street upon which he lived, but I told him that I could direct him there.
Q. And did he ask you to direct him?
A. Yes, I started to explain how to get there and he asked me if I would draw him a map.
Q. And did you do so?
A. Yes, I did.

. . . After that brief conversation, Thompson said, "Thank you," and left. Gladstone testified that he did not counsel, encourage, hire, command, induce or otherwise procure Robert Kent to make a sale of marijuana to Douglas Thompson—or do anything that would be their legal equivalent. Thus, the state at the close of its case had not established prima facie that Gladstone, as charged, aided and abetted Kent in the sale of marijuana, and its position did not improve with the defendant's case.

If all reasonable inferences favorable to the state are accorded the evidence, it does not, in our opinion, establish the commission of the crime charged. That vital element—a nexus between the accused and the party whom he is charged with aiding and abetting in the commission of a crime—is missing. The record contains no evidence whatever that Gladstone had any communication by word, gesture or sign, before or after he drew the map, from which it could be inferred that he counseled, encouraged, hired, commanded, induced or procured Kent to sell marijuana to Douglas Thompson as charged, or took any steps to further the commission of the crime charged. He was not charged with aiding and abetting Thompson in the purchase of marijuana, but with Kent's sale of it.

. . .

... Although an aider and abettor need not be physically present at the commission of the crime to be held guilty as a principal, his conviction depends on proof that he did something in association or connection with the principal to accomplish the crime. . . .

. . .

It would be a dangerous precedent indeed to hold that mere communications to the effect that another might or probably would commit a criminal offense amount to an aiding and abetting of the offense should it ultimately be committed.

There being no evidence whatever that the defendant ever communicated to Kent the idea that he would in any way aid him in the sale of any marijuana, or said anything to Kent to encourage or induce him or direct him to do so, or counseled Kent in the sale of marijuana, or did anything more than describe Kent to another person as an individual who might sell some marijuana, or would derive any benefit, consideration or reward from such a sale, there was no proof of an aiding and abetting, and the conviction should, therefore, be reversed as a matter of law. . . .

## Notes and Questions

1. Why does the *Gladstone* court say that there must be a "connection or association" between the defendant accomplice and the principal? In so doing, does the court conflate aiding and abetting with the separate crime of conspiracy (discussed below)? See *Gladstone*, 474 P.2d at 280 (Hamilton, J., dissenting) ("It is not necessary to sustain a charge of aiding, abetting or counseling a crime that there be proof of a conspiratorial relationship or confederacy between the actual perpetrator of the primary crime and the one charged as an aider or abettor. Criminal conspiracy, in which concert of purpose becomes a salient element, is a separate substantive offense.").

2. Did the state charge Gladstone with the wrong crime? Would the court have upheld a conviction for aiding and abetting *Thompson's possession* of marijuana, as opposed to Kent's sale thereof? *Cf. Michigan v. Doemer*, 192 N.W.2d 330 (1971) (recognizing that one can aid and abet the possession of marijuana).

3. Now consider the following Problems:

Problem 11.1: Andy visits the The Dude Ranch Marijuana Dispensary in Boulder, Colorado, and subsequently writes the following review on Leafly.com, a website that (among other things) publishes locations and reviews of marijuana dispensaries around the United States: "I just visited The Dude Ranch for the first time. They have an AMAZING selection and top notch customer service! The bud tender who helped me was knowledgeable and made me feel really comfortable. I HIGHLY recommend this dispensary to anyone and everyone!" Suppose Camila, who has never met Andy, reads this review and decides to visit The Dude Ranch, where she purchases one ounce of marijuana. Is Andy guilty of aiding and abetting Camila's possession of marijuana under federal law? Is Andy guilty of aiding and abetting The Dude Ranch's sale to Camila? Is Leafly.com liable?

Problem 11.2: Same facts as **Problem 11.1**. Could Andy be found guilty of aiding and abetting the distribution of marijuana, based solely on The Dude Ranch's sale *to him* (Andy)? *See* M.P.C. § 2.06(6). *See also United States v. Hill*, 25 M.J. 411, 413 (Ct. Mil. App., 1988).

Problem 11.3: Now suppose that when Andy visited The Dude Ranch in **Problem 11.1**, he also saw a promotional sign stating that: "Refer a friend and get 10% off your reefer!" After leaving the store, Andy emails his friend Delilah, using the same text he later posts in his Leafly.com review. Delilah replies, "Wow, this place sounds great. I'll give them a shot." Andy then tells Delilah "be sure to tell them I sent you!" Delilah visits The Dude Ranch and buys one ounce of marijuana, telling them "Andy recommended I try you guys." Is Andy guilty of aiding and abetting The Dude Ranch's sale to Delilah?

Problem 11.4: Benjamin owns and operates The Dude Ranch Marijuana Dispensary in Boulder. Lately, business has been flagging, so Benjamin asks his friend Edgar for help in distributing some advertising leaflets around town. The leaflets state "Get a 10% discount on your first visit!" Edgar agrees. He distributes hundreds of leaflets around town, encouraging everyone he meets to visit The Dude Ranch. The next day, some teens to whom Edgar had given leaflets visit The Dude Ranch, and Benjamin waves a handgun at them, warning them never to visit his shop again: "You're not supposed to be in here, get out!" he yells at them. Soon thereafter, federal officials raid The Dude Ranch and charge Benjamin with a violation of 21 U.S.C. section 924(c), which makes it a crime punishable by a minimum five years' imprisonment to use or carry a firearm during a drug trafficking crime, or to possess a firearm in furtherance of such crime. Could Edgar be charged with aiding and abetting a violation of section 924(c)? What if Edgar had seen Benjamin carrying the firearm in his shop when he went to pick up the leaflets? What if Edgar had pleaded with Benjamin to "get rid of that gun" before he distributed the leaflets? *See Rosemund v. United States*, 134 S. Ct. 1240, 1250 (2014).

4. The punishment for aiding and abetting a given offense is typically the same as the punishment for committing the offense directly. In other words, laws generally do not distinguish between the principal who commits the crime and her accomplice. *E.g.*, M.P.C. § 2.06(1)-(2) ("A person is guilty of an offense if it is committed by his own conduct or by the conduct of another person . . . when . . . he is an accomplice of such other person in the commission of the offense."); 18 U.S.C. § 2(a) ("Whoever commits an offense against the United States or aids, abets, counsels, commands, induces, or procures its commission, is punishable as a principal.").

## B. CONSPIRACY

Individuals may also fall under the purview of marijuana laws by conspiring to commit any of the offenses discussed in Chapters 3-4 and 7-8. An individual completes the conspiracy offense when she enters into an agreement with one or more other persons to commit a drug offense—i.e., to possess, manufacture, distribute, etc., marijuana. 21 U.S.C. § 846 ("Any person who attempts or conspires to commit any offense defined [in the CSA] is punishable by imprisonment or fine or both which may not exceed the maximum punishment prescribed for the offense, the commission of which was the object of the attempt or conspiracy."). The government need not show that the conspirators actually accomplished their objective, or even that they took any action in furtherance thereof. *E.g., United States v. Shabani*, 513 U.S. 10 (1994) ("[T]o establish a violation of 21 U.S.C. § 846, the Government need not prove the commission of any overt acts in furtherance of the conspiracy."). It is thus commonly remarked that the agreement to commit a crime is the essence of a conspiracy. The agreement also "serves to distinguish conspiracy from aiding and abetting which, although often based on agreement, does not require proof of that fact. . . ." *Iannelli v. United States*, 420 U.S. 770, 778, n.10 (1975).

To illustrate, suppose that while watching a TV news program about pesticides found in store-bought marijuana, Camila turns to Delilah and says "We should totally grow our own pot. It would be safer. Want to do it?" and Delilah replies "Sure!" On these facts alone, Camila and Delilah could be convicted of a *conspiracy* to manufacture marijuana, even though neither could (yet) be convicted of manufacturing marijuana, or even attempting to manufacture marijuana, or of aiding and abetting the other person to do so.

An agreement, for purposes of conspiracy, requires a meeting of the minds. Put another way, the alleged conspirators must share a common purpose to commit a crime. Importantly, the conspirators need not agree on all of the details of the enterprise, only its "essential nature." *Blumenthal v. United States*, 332 U.S. 539, 557 (1947). What is more, "[t]he agreement need not be shown to have been explicit. It can instead be inferred from the facts and circumstances of the case." *Iannelli*, 420 U.S. at 777 n.10.

The government, of course, must also prove that the defendant was aware of and voluntarily joined the agreement. *E.g., United States v. Valdez*, 453 F.3d 252 (5th Cir. 2006). In very simple cases, like the illustration above, there may be no doubt that a defendant was a party to the agreement. But in more complicated cases involving more than two parties, it may be more difficult for the government to demonstrate that all of the parties were necessarily part of the same conspiracy, even if the government has no difficulty establishing the existence of an agreement between *some* of them. Nonetheless, for these purposes, it is important to recognize that a defendant's connection to a conspiracy need only be "slight." As one court has noted, "a defendant need not know all of his coconspirators, comprehend the reach of the conspiracy, participate in all the enterprises of the conspiracy, or have joined the conspiracy from its inception." *United States v. Burgos*, 94 F.3d 849, 861 (4th Cir. 1996).

The following case examines the sufficiency of the government's proof regarding the existence of (and defendant's participation in) a conspiracy to manufacture and distribute marijuana.

## Massachusetts v. Camerano
677 N.E.2d 678 (Ct. App. Mass. 1997)

KASS, J.:

In order to convict Antonio Camerano, the defendant, of conspiracy to possess marihuana with intent to distribute it (G.L. c. 94C, § 40), the Commonwealth was bound to prove that Camerano had agreed with his tenant, Robert Howell, to cultivate, cure, process, and sell marihuana. . . .

After trial in the District Court, a jury of six returned a verdict of guilty. Camerano has appealed . . . on the ground that it was error not to have granted his motion for a required finding of not guilty. We decide that the Commonwealth's evidence, viewed in the light most favorable to the prosecution, did not establish participation by the defendant in an agreement and combination to accomplish a criminal purpose. . . .

On September 13, 1993, [officers in a drug task force] . . . engaged in fly-over surveillance by helicopter of Spencer and parts of West Boylston. After forty-five minutes in the air, they spotted a green-colored, roofless structure in which vegetation was growing. The structure was in a clearing at the end of a 200-foot unpaved driveway running off Redemption Rock Trail in Sterling. As soon as they returned to base, some of the officers . . . obtained a warrant to search the open structure, as well as a house, a house trailer, and a utility trailer that were in the clearing.

What the search party found was the residence of the defendant and his wife; some sixty feet behind it, the roofless structure that had attracted their interest; some one hundred feet behind that, a house trailer; and another one hundred feet behind the house trailer, a blue utility trailer. The Camerano property was in a pine woods. There were no neighbors within one hundred yards.

Such was the strength of the aroma wafting from the green structure that the search party officers, who had developed educated noses for marihuana, sniffed it at a distance of sixty feet. Sylvia Camerano, the defendant's wife, [who was charged as a codefendant but acquitted by the jury,] was home when the police arrived and denied knowledge of what was going on in the green enclosure. Also present when the police made their raid was Robert Howell, a tenant of the Cameranos. For $200 a month, Howell had arranged to rent land on which he pitched his house trailer and on which, some time after the initial rental arrangement, he built his garden enclosure. A plastic water line ran on the ground from an outside tap on the Cameranos' house to Howell's trailer. A curled up hose lay outside that trailer.

One member of the search party, Michael Tartini, a Spencer police officer, described Howell as sitting by his trailer, nursing a can of beer, when the police came on the scene. To Tartini's announcement that he had a search warrant, Howell responded, "Go ahead and search. I knew you were coming hours ago." The other government witness, Robert Burke, a police detective from the town of Clinton, testified that Howell emerged from his trailer as the search party moved in and that he was walking toward a white Cadillac when he, Burke, intercepted him. He described Howell as denying any knowledge of marihuana and saying, when told that the police had a search warrant, "[G]o ahead. You won't find nothing."

Howell's garden enclosure was not a conventional greenhouse. The structure was twenty-eight feet wide, thirty feet long, and about eighteen feet high. The sides were of plywood nailed on a frame of two-by-fours and two-by-sixes. As noted, the structure was open to the sky. It had no windows and its single door was padlocked. That padlock the police pried off. Inside, they found 107 marihuana plants, twelve to fifteen feet high. Howell later said the marihuana plants were his. Buried behind Howell's trailer, the police found five pounds of dried, cut, and packaged marihuana. In the trailer they found a food processor with marihuana residue, two scales, a box of gallon-sized zip-lock bags, and a small amount of cut and dried marihuana. The utility trailer belonged to Gary Pomerlow, a friend of Camerano, for whom Camerano occasionally repaired trucks. Camerano had allowed Pomerlow to store the utility trailer on the Camerano property. Pomerlow had introduced Camerano to Howell. In the utility trailer, the police found a suitcase stuffed with eight pounds of marihuana, cut, dried, and packaged in approximately one-pound bags.

The task force searched the Camerano house thoroughly and turned up no drugs or drug paraphernalia, no key to the padlock of the green structure, nor anything else connected to drug use or distribution.

> Conspiracy seldom occurs in a fishbowl; rather, the conspirators take pains to act secretively. Direct evidence of a conspiracy, therefore, is rarely available and, typically, the government must rely on circumstantial evidence. . . . The inferences that a jury may permissibly draw from the circumstantial evidence do not need to be inescapable; they need only be reasonable. . . . "The acts of different persons who are shown to have known each other, or to have been in communication with each other, directed towards the accomplishment of the same object, especially if by the same means or in the same manner, may be satisfactory proof of a conspiracy." . . .

No evidence, as we read it, permitted the jury to find, beyond a reasonable doubt, that Camerano had agreed with Howell to a marihuana growing and selling project. Nothing suggests that Camerano, when he rented to Howell, intended that Howell would raise marihuana or was aware of Howell's plans so to do. Howell built the growing enclosure after he had arranged to move his trailer onto the Cameranos' property for a rent of $200 per month. Intent is a requisite mental state for conspiracy, not mere knowledge or acquiescence. . . .

Here, the prosecution is quite right in pointing out that the jurors need not have believed Camerano when he testified that he did not know what marihuana smelled like and thought Howell was growing tomatoes and flowers in the enclosure. Disbelief, however, does not prove the contrary proposition, that Camerano *did* know Howell was growing marihuana. . . . The jury were entitled to infer that the very nature of the locked structure announced to Camerano that something unlawful was going on inside it. That leaves the government with having proved no more than awareness that Howell was growing contraband, not having proved beyond a reasonable doubt an agreement to further that undertaking. . . . [I]ndependent evidence of an agreement is lacking, and there is only evidence of presence and, it may be inferred, awareness. There is no evidence that $200 per month was an untoward rent for parking a trailer, nor that Howell had used water in an amount that was unusual and had reflected itself in a higher than normal water bill received by Camerano. No key to the enclosure was found on Camerano's person or in his house, which the police had searched thoroughly. Nothing in the evidence suggested that Camerano used marihuana or would in some other manner share in the success, such as it might be, of Howell's operation. Even Camerano's presence was limited; he was away each working day at his job as a security guard. Awareness may translate to acquiescence but not to "affirmative acquiescence." . . .

As to certain activities, the Legislature has enacted statutes that make it a crime to have knowledge of criminal conduct and to suffer that conduct to continue. . . . [But n]o statute makes criminal knowing presence where marihuana is grown or awareness that it is being grown, processed, stored, or sold. An agreement to participate in the illicit enterprise might be inferred from evidence such as conversations, writings, unusual rent, unusual water consumption, activity suggesting concurrence with the enterprise, or possession or constructive possession of the contraband. No evidence of that sort is present and the motion for a required finding of not guilty should have been allowed.

. . .

The judgment is reversed, the verdict is set aside, and a finding of not guilty shall be entered on behalf of the defendant.

LAURENCE, J., dissenting:

Camerano's motions for a required finding of not guilty were properly denied. Viewing the evidence in the light most favorable to the prosecution, a rational jury could have found, beyond a reasonable doubt, the essential element of unlawful, though tacit, agreement or combination on Camerano's part. The majority appears to concede that a jury could find from the circumstances proved by the Commonwealth—especially the bizarrely and suspiciously constructed and padlocked "garden enclosure" and the pungent, hovering aroma of the growing marihuana—that Camerano, a trained security guard, was unmistakably aware of Howell's cultivation of an illegal marihuana crop a few feet from his house.

The Commonwealth's proof, however, went beyond the mere demonstration of Camerano's knowledge of the illegal activity and continued association with its perpetrator. The evidence was sufficient to allow the jury, informed by their common sense and life experience, to infer Camerano's eventual willing participation in Howell's criminal enterprise from his conduct, most particularly the facts that (1) Camerano continued to permit Howell to cultivate and presumably harvest the illicit crop despite his power to evict Howell, who appears at most to have been a tenant at will, if not a mere licensee; (2) Camerano continued to allow Howell to use his water, the only available supply, which Camerano either knew or had to have known was being used to grow the contents of the "enclosure"; and (3) Camerano continued willingly to accept monthly rental money from Howell who, on this record, had no other source of income than from his acknowledged drug activities.

These facts entitled the jury rationally to conclude that Camerano did not just manifest acquiescent consent to the continuation of Howell's illegal business, but in fact facilitated the business's operations. It is irrelevant that Camerano may not have had complete knowledge of the scope and details of those operations. . . . Against this background, the majority has overlooked the teachings of our seminal conspiracy case, *Commonwealth v. Beneficial Fin. Co.*, . . . 275 N.E.2d 33 (1971), . . . as to proving conspiratorial combination or agreement:

> "Although the need for concerted action or active participation requires actual commitment to the conspiratorial plan, . . . it is not necessary that one play an active

role in the actual execution of the object of the conspiracy. The language in [an earlier] case . . . that one 'must do something in furtherance of [the conspiracy]' we construe to mean simply that one must be shown to have at least communicated to other conspirators his willingness to join in the conspiracy. The very fact that one gives his affirmative acquiescence to the object of a conspiracy may in many cases be doing 'something in furtherance of it.' *A particular defendant's participation in a conspiracy may be proved where his approval of the plan stimulates the activities of others to carry out the conspiracy, even though his participation does not involve an overt act.* . . . *In this context, the line that separates mere knowledge of the fact that a conspiracy exists from participation in the conspiracy is often vague and uncertain. It is within the province of the jury to determine from the evidence whether a particular defendant had crossed that line"* (emphasis added).

Under those guidelines, the judge properly denied Camerano's motion for a required finding at the close of the Commonwealth's case, because the evidence permitted the jury to find from Camerano's conduct that he had gone from passive onlooker to conspiratorial, if unspoken, participant.[1]

## Notes and Questions

1. Do you agree with the court's holding? Was the evidence sufficient to demonstrate that Camerano conspired with Howell to supply marijuana? If not, what additional proof would you require for the government to make its case?

2. Consider the following Problems:

**Problem 11.5**: Camila runs a small gardening supply company. Andy, who is 23 years old, dropped by Camila's shop one day and asked her whether she carried a particular piece of hydroponic growing equipment—one that is commonly used by indoor marijuana grow operations. Camila told Andy that she could order the equipment for him. Andy said that he would have to use cash to pay for the equipment. He showed her $5,000 cash he had brought in a Ziploc bag, all in small bills, and promised Camila that he would have even more "after my first harvest comes in, about 3 months from now." Andy also told Camila that he did not want to sign any contract or let anyone know that he was the one ordering the equipment. Camila agreed to these terms, but in return she charged Andy a premium for the equipment—$20,000, which was roughly twice the going market price. Andy gave her the $5,000 as a down payment. Camila ordered the equipment and Andy picked it up. Andy was later arrested for manufacturing marijuana; his operation had used the

---

1. The additional element of intent to distribute could properly have been inferred from the fact that some thirty-nine pounds of marihuana were confiscated on Camerano's property, an amount inconsistent with personal use. . . .

hydroponic equipment to grow more than 100 marijuana plants. Based on these facts, could Camila be convicted of conspiracy to manufacture marijuana? Of aiding and abetting the manufacture of marijuana? *Cf. United States v. Morse*, 851 F.2d 1317 (11th Cir. 1988).

**Problem 11.6:** Andy and Benjamin met and agreed to sell 10 kilograms of Colorado-grown marijuana to a buyer in Nebraska. Benjamin would buy the marijuana by making repeated trips to several Denver area licensed marijuana shops. Andy would then rent a car and drive from Denver to Omaha to make the delivery and to retrieve their payment. To that end, Andy approached Delilah, who worked at Rental Car Co. Andy told Delilah that he needed to rent a "plain car, for about 12 hours, off the books" so that Andy's name could not be connected to the car. In return, Andy promised to give Delilah one ounce of marijuana. Delilah agreed to the arrangement. Could Delilah be convicted of conspiracy to distribute 10 kilograms of marijuana? Of aiding and abetting such distribution? *Cf. United States v. Umagat*, 998 F.2d 770 (9th Cir. 1993).

**Problem 11.7:** Marijuana, Inc. is a state-licensed marijuana cultivator and retail distributor. Last year, Marijuana, Inc. grew 1,000 marijuana plants and sold more than 100 kilograms of marijuana products from its single building. Since its inception, Marijuana, Inc. has employed the following eight people. Which of these employees could be found guilty of conspiracy to manufacture and distribute marijuana?

   (1) Andy, an agronomist who cultivates Marijuana, Inc.'s marijuana plants from seed to harvest.
   (2) Benjamin, a budtender who helps customers choose from among Marijuana, Inc.'s marijuana product offerings.
   (3) Camila, a chemist who produces hash oil from Marijuana, Inc.'s marijuana plants.
   (4) Gina, a security guard who checks the IDs of customers who walk in the door and also patrols the firm's premises.
   (5) Hank, the handyman who built Marijuana, Inc.'s irrigation, ventilation, and drying system and who maintains all of the equipment used to grow and process the firm's marijuana plants.
   (6) Ivan, an unpaid intern who makes coffee for Marijuana, Inc.'s employees.
   (7) Tina, a trimmer who cuts the buds and leaves from all of Marijuana, Inc.'s marijuana plants and prepares them for sale or further processing.
   (8) Pasha, the President of Marijuana, Inc., who manages all of the firm's operations.

3. Do all agreements to commit a drug crime establish a conspiracy? The following Problems explore this question:

Problem 11.8: Benjamin runs The Dude Ranch Marijuana Dispensary in Boulder, Colorado. Andy is a marijuana user and regular customer of The Dude Ranch. He stops by the shop one day, sees that the store is offering Sour Diesel for $500 an ounce, and asks Benjamin "Would you take $475 for the Sour Diesel?" Benjamin agrees. Has Andy conspired with Benjamin to distribute marijuana? See *United States v. Colon*, 549 F.3d 565, 567-71 (7th Cir. 2008).

Problem 11.9: Camila is approached by Ivan, who, unbeknownst to her, is a government informant. Ivan suggests that they go into business together making and selling hash oil. After some haggling over the terms of their arrangement (e.g., their respective contributions, profit sharing, etc.), Camila agrees and even memorializes their contract in writing. That evening, Ivan shows the agreement to the police. Is Camila guilty of conspiracy to manufacture marijuana? See *United States v. Paret-Ruiz*, 567 F.3d 1, 6 (1st Cir. 2009).

4. The sanction for conspiracy is ostensibly the same as the sanction imposed for the crime that was its object. *E.g.*, 21 U.S.C. § 846. Nonetheless, a conspiracy conviction can substantially increase a defendant's sentence. In large part, this is because a defendant may be held liable for the actions of her co-conspirators. In drug conspiracies, this means that a defendant may be sanctioned for (among other things) quantities of marijuana possessed, manufactured, or distributed by her co-conspirators. *E.g.*, U.S.S.G. § 1.3(a)(B) (instructing that a defendant's Guidelines range should be calculated based on actions of co-conspirators that were "within the scope of the jointly undertaken criminal activity, . . . in furtherance of that criminal activity, and . . . reasonably foreseeable in connection with that criminal activity"); *United States v. Pizarro*, 772 F.3d 284, 292-993 (1st Cir. 2014) (noting that for purposes of the CSA, the total quantity of drugs handled by the conspiracy determines the defendant's maximum sentence, but only the quantity foreseeable to the defendant may be used to trigger a mandatory minimum sentence). In light of this rule, consider what sentences would apply to the defendants in the following Problem:

Problem 11.10: Andy, Benjamin, and Camila meet and agree to "grow and sell marijuana." Andy and Benjamin will grow and process the plants, while Camila will handle all retail sales. Andy and Benjamin know that manufacturing marijuana can trigger harsh mandatory minimum sentences, so during the initial meeting they insist that each of them grow less than 50 plants. To keep things quiet, they also agree that they will operate separately and communicate only when necessary. After the initial meeting, Andy and Benjamin go to their separate farms and start growing marijuana plants. Each begins by planting 100 marijuana seeds—each knows that most seeds typically fail to germinate. A few weeks later, Camila stops by Andy's farm to check on his progress. Andy tells her that his seeds are doing better than expected: "I have 60 small plants growing well." Camila then checks on Benjamin, who has not communicated with Andy since their original meeting. Benjamin tells Camila that his seeds are doing "about as expected. I've got about 45 plants sprouting, though a few of them probably won't make it." The next day, DEA agents raid both Andy's and Benjamin's farm. What is the statutory sentencing range that would apply to each of the three participants?

5. A defendant's sentence may be enhanced under conspiracy law even if she is not held accountable for the actions of her co-conspirators. The following Problem illustrates:

**Problem 11.11**: On January 1, Camila sold 50 kilograms of marijuana. On June 1, she sold another 50 kilograms of marijuana. The government then prosecutes her for two separate counts of marijuana distribution under 21 U.S.C. section 841. What is Camila's sentencing range? Now suppose instead that on January 1 Camila had entered into a conspiracy to sell 100 kilograms of marijuana. However, the government arrests her before she gets a chance to sell anything. The government prosecutes Camila for conspiracy to distribute marijuana. It does not try to hold her accountable for the actions of any of her co-conspirators. What is Camila's sentencing range? Do the results make sense? *Cf. United States v. Pruitt*, 156 F.3d 638, 644 (6th Cir. 1998).

6. A defendant may be convicted of both conspiracy and the crimes that were its object. In other words, a conspiracy charge does not merge with the underlying offenses committed pursuant to it. *Pinkerton v. United States*, 328 U.S. 640, 643 (1946) (holding that "the commission of the substantive offense and a conspiracy to commit it are separate and distinct offenses," and "the plea of double jeopardy is no defense to a conviction for both offenses"). However, for reasons discussed in Chapter 7, the addition of a conspiracy conviction will not necessarily increase defendant's net sentence (at least outside of the scenarios discussed in the prior notes).

## C. FINANCIAL CRIMES

Growing and distributing marijuana can be potentially lucrative activities. To dampen the financial incentives to engage in these (and other) crimes, the federal government and many states have banned certain transactions involving the proceeds of illegal activity. The most relevant and illustrative regulations of this sort are found in 18 U.S.C. sections

1956 and 1957. (Chapter 13 discusses additional financial regulations that are targeted specifically at banks.)

Section 1956 provides, in relevant part:

(a)

(1) Whoever, knowing that the property involved in a financial transaction represents the proceeds of some form of unlawful activity, conducts or attempts to conduct such a financial transaction which in fact involves the proceeds of specified unlawful activity—

(A)

(i) with the intent to promote the carrying on of specified unlawful activity; or

(ii) with intent to engage in [tax evasion] . . . ; or

(B) knowing that the transaction is designed in whole or in part—

(i) to conceal or disguise the nature, the location, the source, the ownership, or the control of the proceeds of specified unlawful activity; or

(ii) to avoid a transaction reporting requirement under State or Federal law,

shall be sentenced to a fine of not more than $500,000 or twice the value of the property involved in the transaction, whichever is greater, or imprisonment for not more than twenty years, or both. . . .

(2) Whoever transports, transmits, or transfers, or attempts to transport, transmit, or transfer a monetary instrument or funds from a place in the United States to or through a place outside the United States or to a place in the United States from or through a place outside the United States—

(A) with the intent to promote the carrying on of specified unlawful activity; or

(B) knowing that the monetary instrument or funds involved in the transportation, transmission, or transfer represent the proceeds of some form of unlawful activity and knowing that such transportation, transmission, or transfer is designed in whole or in part—

(i) to conceal or disguise the nature, the location, the source, the ownership, or the control of the proceeds of specified unlawful activity; or

(ii) to avoid a transaction reporting requirement under State or Federal law,

shall be sentenced to a fine of not more than $500,000 or twice the value of the monetary instrument or funds involved in the transportation, transmission, or transfer, whichever is greater, or imprisonment for not more than twenty years, or both. . . .

(3) Whoever, with the intent—

(A) to promote the carrying on of specified unlawful activity;

(B) to conceal or disguise the nature, location, source, ownership, or control of property believed to be the proceeds of specified unlawful activity; or

(C) to avoid a transaction reporting requirement under State or Federal law,

conducts or attempts to conduct a financial transaction involving property represented to be the proceeds of specified unlawful activity, or property used to conduct or facilitate specified unlawful activity, shall be fined under this title or imprisoned for not more than 20 years, or both. . . .

. . .

(c) As used in this section—

(1) the term "knowing that the property involved in a financial transaction represents the proceeds of some form of unlawful activity" means that the person knew the property involved in the transaction represented proceeds from some form, though not

necessarily which form, of activity that constitutes a felony under State, Federal, or foreign law . . .

(2) the term "conducts" includes initiating, concluding, or participating in initiating, or concluding a transaction;

(3) the term "transaction" includes a purchase, sale, loan, pledge, gift, transfer, delivery, or other disposition, and with respect to a financial institution includes a deposit, withdrawal, transfer between accounts, exchange of currency, loan, extension of credit, purchase or sale of any stock, bond, certificate of deposit, or other monetary instrument, use of a safe deposit box, or any other payment, transfer, or delivery by, through, or to a financial institution, by whatever means effected;

(4) the term "financial transaction" means (A) a transaction which in any way or degree affects interstate or foreign commerce (i) involving the movement of funds by wire or other means or (ii) involving one or more monetary instruments, or (iii) involving the transfer of title to any real property, vehicle, vessel, or aircraft, or (B) a transaction involving the use of a financial institution which is engaged in, or the activities of which affect, interstate or foreign commerce in any way or degree;

(5) the term "monetary instruments" means (i) coin or currency of the United States or of any other country, travelers' checks, personal checks, bank checks, and money orders, or (ii) investment securities or negotiable instruments, in bearer form or otherwise in such form that title thereto passes upon delivery;

. . .

(7) the term "specified unlawful activity" means . . . [inter alia felonious manufacture, importation, receiving, concealment, buying, selling, or otherwise dealing in a controlled substance or listed chemical (as defined in section 102 of the Controlled Substances Act), punishable under any law of the United States, incorporated by reference from 18 U.S.C. § 1961(1)].

Section 1957 provides, in relevant part:

(a) Whoever . . . knowingly engages or attempts to engage in a monetary transaction in criminally derived property of a value greater than $10,000 and is derived from specified unlawful activity, shall be punished as provided in subsection (b).

(b)

(1) Except as provided in paragraph (2), the punishment for an offense under this section is a fine under title 18, United States Code, or imprisonment for not more than ten years or both. . . .

(2) The court may impose an alternate fine to that imposable under paragraph (1) of not more than twice the amount of the criminally derived property involved in the transaction.

(c) In a prosecution for an offense under this section, the Government is not required to prove the defendant knew that the offense from which the criminally derived property was derived was specified unlawful activity.

. . .

(f) As used in this section—

(1) the term "monetary transaction" means the deposit, withdrawal, transfer, or exchange, in or affecting interstate or foreign commerce, of funds or a monetary instrument . . . by, through, or to a financial institution . . . , including any transaction that would be a financial transaction under section 1956(c)(4)(B) of this title, but such term does not include any transaction necessary to preserve a person's right to representation as guaranteed by the sixth amendment to the Constitution;

(2) the term "criminally derived property" means any property constituting, or derived from, proceeds obtained from a criminal offense; and

(3) the terms "specified unlawful activity" and "proceeds" shall have the meaning given those terms in section 1956 of this title.

These two statutes create several distinct financial crimes. To simplify the discussion, the following sections focus on the core money laundering offense established by section 1956(a)(1)(B)(i) and the use of criminal proceeds offense established by section 1957.

## 1. Money Laundering

Money laundering typically describes a transaction used to make the proceeds of some illegal activity—like the distribution of marijuana—appear legitimate, i.e., clean, and thus easier to use. Importantly, the core money laundering offense created by section 1956(a)(1)(B)(i) applies not only to the individual who committed the illegal activity in the first instance—i.e., the one who generated the proceeds, but also to other individuals who are involved in the transaction.

Under section 1956, the core money laundering offense includes four basic elements. In particular, the government must show that the defendant:

(1) conducted a financial transaction (§ 1956(a)(1)),
(2) involving the proceeds of specified unlawful activity (§ 1956(a)(1)),
(3) knowing that the transaction involved such proceeds (§ 1956(a)(1)), and
(4) knowing that the transaction was designed to conceal the nature, location, source, or control of such proceeds (§ 1956(a)(1)(B)(i)).

To illustrate, suppose that Andy is a car dealer who knows that Delilah distributes marijuana for a living. Delilah visits Andy's car dealership. She offers to buy a used car from Andy for $10,000 cash, all of it in small bills and reeking of the odor of marijuana. Her offer is $1,000 above Andy's asking price. But Delilah insists that the car be put in someone else's name: "Use anybody's name. I don't care. It just can't be mine." Andy agrees to Delilah's terms. He sells Delilah the car for the $10,000 in cash, and puts the title to the car in the name of Andy's sister. On these facts, both Delilah and Andy could be convicted of money laundering under section 1956(a)(1)(B)(i).

Let us explore each of the four elements of the offense, beginning with the definition of a "financial transaction." Section 1956(c) provides two relevant definitions, both of which must be met. Section 1956(c)(3) defines "transaction" broadly to include "a purchase, sale, loan, pledge, gift, transfer, delivery, or other disposition, and with respect to a financial institution includes a deposit, withdrawal, transfer between accounts, exchange of currency, loan, extension of credit, purchase or sale of any stock, bond, certificate of deposit, or other monetary instrument, use of a safe deposit box, or any other payment, transfer, or delivery by, through, or to a financial institution, by whatever means effected . . ." As this definition makes clear, a transaction need not involve a bank or other financial institution. Indeed, courts have found that delivering the proceeds of a drug sale to the seller, *United States v. Dimeck*, 24 F.3d 1239 (10th Cir. 1994), giving the proceeds of a marijuana sale to a lawyer for safekeeping, *United States v. Reed*, 77 F.3d 139 (6th Cir. 1996), and using those proceeds to buy a car, *United States v. Cruz*, 993 F.2d 164 (8th Cir. 1993), all constitute transactions for purposes of section 1956.

So is there any limit to what constitutes a "transaction" under section 1956(c)(3)? The following Problem explores the question:

**Problem 11.12:** Delilah has $500 cash on hand from her marijuana sales. She carries the money to her backyard and buries it deep underground. Has Delilah engaged in a "transaction" for purposes of section 1956? *See United States v. Puig-Infante*, 19 F.3d 929, 938 (5th Cir. 1994) ("[Section 1956] makes plain that for something (not involving a financial institution or its facilities) to be a transaction, it must be a 'disposition.' 'Disposition' most commonly means 'a placing elsewhere, a giving over to the care or possession of another.'"). What if Delilah had given the cash to a neighbor to hold for her for a few moments while she tied her shoes on her way to her backyard?

The first element also includes a jurisdictional component. Namely, section 1956(c)(4) defines the requisite "financial transaction" as one that

> (A) . . . in any way or degree affects interstate or foreign commerce (i) involving the movement of funds by wire or other means or (ii) involving one or more monetary instruments, or (iii) involving the transfer of title to any real property, vehicle, vessel, or aircraft, or
>
> (B) . . . involv[es] the use of a financial institution which is engaged in, or the activities of which affect, interstate or foreign commerce in any way or degree . . .

18 U.S.C. § 1956(c)(4). This definition is jurisdictional in the sense that it is designed to limit the reach of the federal money laundering statute to those transactions that fall squarely within Congress's Commerce Clause authority, i.e., its substantive jurisdiction. As a practical matter, however, the additional criteria imposed by section 1956(c)(4) are not especially limiting. As one court has acknowledged, "the 'in or affecting interstate commerce' requirement has been broadly read," meaning "that a 'minimal effect' on interstate commerce is sufficient to establish federal jurisdiction." *United States v. Kelley*, 929 F.2d 582, 586 (10th Cir. 1991) (finding criteria met where defendant used proceeds of illegal activity to purchase a car manufactured in another state from an automobile dealership that, in turn, used the sale proceeds to buy other vehicles from out of state).

For the second element, the government must show that the transaction involved the *proceeds of unlawful activity*. Again, this phrase has been interpreted quite broadly. It includes any assets received from crime, including, per section 1956(c)(7), the marijuana offenses discussed in Chapters 3 and 7. However, consider the following Problem, which tests the outer limits of the meaning of *proceeds*.

**Problem 11.13:** Benjamin is a casual marijuana user. He calls his supplier, Delilah, to arrange for the purchase of one ounce of marijuana for $500. Per their arrangement, Delilah places the marijuana in Benjamin's locker at the local gym. Benjamin, in turn, wire transfers $500 from his bank account to a bank account under a fictitious name controlled by Delilah. Does Benjamin's

transfer of funds involve the *proceeds* of marijuana distribution? *See United States v. Harris*, 666 F.3d 905, 909-10 (5th Cir. 2012).

The third and fourth elements describe the mens rea necessary to commit the money laundering offense. The sections below discuss these two remaining elements in more detail.

### a. Knowledge (and Willful Ignorance)

To begin, the defendant must *know* that the transaction involves the proceeds of unlawful activity. For these purposes, the defendant need not know the exact crime that generated the proceeds, only that they came from *some* unlawful activity. Under section 1956, knowledge has the same meaning as it does for other crimes. It includes actual knowledge, a concept discussed in detail in Chapter 3. But it may also include willful ignorance of the facts, as the following case discusses.

### United States v. Campbell
977 F.2d 854 (4th Cir. 1992)

ERVIN, J.:

The United States appeals from the district court's grant of Ellen Campbell's motion for judgment of acquittal on charges of [inter alia] money laundering, 18 U.S.C. § 1956(a)(1)(B)(i). . . . Campbell had been convicted of the charges by a jury in the Western District of North Carolina. We reverse the judgment of acquittal, but affirm the district court's conditional grant of a new trial, and, accordingly, we remand the case for further proceedings.

. . . In the summer of 1989, Ellen Campbell was a licensed real estate agent working at Lake Norman Realty in Mooresville, North Carolina. During the same period, Mark Lawing was a drug dealer in Kannapolis, North Carolina. Lawing decided to buy a house on Lake Norman. He obtained Campbell's business card from Lake Norman Realty's Mooresville office, called Campbell, and scheduled an appointment to look at houses.

Over the course of about five weeks, Lawing met with Campbell approximately once a week and looked at a total of ten to twelve houses. Lawing and Campbell also had numerous phone conversations. Lawing represented himself to Campbell as the owner of a legitimate business, L & N Autocraft, which purportedly performed automobile customizing services. When meeting with Campbell, Lawing would travel in either a red Porsche he owned or a gold Porsche owned by a fellow drug dealer, Randy Sweatt, who would usually accompany Lawing. During the trips to look at houses, which occurred during normal business hours, Lawing would bring his cellular phone and would often consume food and beer with Sweatt. At one point, Lawing brought a briefcase containing $20,000 in cash, showing the money to Campbell to demonstrate his ability to purchase a house.

Lawing eventually settled upon a house listed for $191,000 and owned by Edward and Nancy Guy Fortier. The listing with the Fortiers had been secured by Sara Fox, another real estate agent with Lake Norman Realty. After negotiations, Lawing and the Fortiers agreed on a price of $182,500, and entered into a written contract. Lawing was unable to secure a loan and decided to ask the Fortiers to accept $60,000 under the table in cash and to lower the contract price to $122,500.[1] Lawing contacted Campbell and informed her of this proposal. Campbell relayed the proposal to Fox, who forwarded the offer to the Fortiers. The Fortiers agreed, and Fox had the Fortiers execute a new listing agreement which lowered the sales price and increased the commission percentage (in order to protect the realtors' profits on the sale).

Thereafter Lawing met the Fortiers, Fox and Campbell in the Mooresville sales office with $60,000 in cash. The money was wrapped in small bundles and carried in a brown paper grocery bag. The money was counted, and a new contract was executed reflecting a sales price of $122,500. Lawing tipped both Fox and Campbell with "a couple of hundred dollars." . . .

William Austin, the closing attorney, prepared closing documents, including HUD-1 and 1099-S forms, reflecting a sales price of $122,500, based on the information provided by Campbell. Campbell, Fox, Austin, Lawing, Lawing's parents and the Fortiers were all present at the closing. The closing documents were signed, all reflecting a sales price of $122,500.

Campbell was indicted [for, inter alia,] . . . money laundering, in violation of 18 U.S.C. § 1956(a)(1)(B)(i). . . . She was tried and convicted by a jury. . . . After the verdict, the district court granted Campbell's motion for judgment of acquittal. . . . The Government appeals.

. . .

In reviewing a district court's grant of a post-verdict acquittal, this court must decide "whether, viewing the evidence in the light most favorable to the government, *any* rational trier of facts could have found the defendant guilty beyond a reasonable doubt." . . . Because the question is a matter of law, we review the issue *de novo* and need accord no deference to the district court's determination that the evidence is insufficient. . . .

The money laundering statute under which Campbell was charged applies to any person who:

> knowing that the property involved in a financial transaction represents the proceeds of some form of unlawful activity, conducts or attempts to conduct such a financial transaction which in fact involves the proceeds of specified unlawful activity . . . knowing that the transaction is designed in whole or in part . . . to conceal or disguise the nature, the location, the source, the ownership, or the control of the proceeds of specified unlawful activity. . . .

18 U.S.C. § 1956(a)(1). The district court found, and Campbell does not dispute, that there was adequate evidence for the jury to find that Campbell conducted a financial transaction which in fact involved the proceeds of Lawing's illegal drug activities. The central issue in contention is whether there was sufficient evidence for the jury to find that Campbell possessed the knowledge that: (1) Lawing's funds were the proceeds of illegal activity, and (2) the transaction was designed to disguise the nature of those proceeds.

In assessing Campbell's culpability, it must be noted that the statute requires actual subjective knowledge. Campbell cannot be convicted on what she objectively should have

---

[1]. Lawing's explanation to Campbell of this unorthodox arrangement was that the lower purchase price would allow Lawing's parents to qualify for a mortgage. Lawing would then make the mortgage payments on his parent's behalf. Lawing justified the secrecy of the arrangement by explaining that his parents had to remain unaware of the $60,000 payment because the only way he could induce their involvement was to convince them he was getting an excellent bargain on the real estate.

known. However, this requirement is softened somewhat by the doctrine of willful blindness. In this case, the jury was instructed that:

> The element of knowledge may be satisfied by inferences drawn from proof that a defendant deliberately closed her eyes to what would otherwise have been obvious to her. A finding beyond a reasonable doubt of a conscious purpose to avoid enlightenment would permit an inference of knowledge. Stated another way, a defendant's knowledge of a fact may be inferred upon willful blindness to the existence of a fact.
>
> It is entirely up to you as to whether you find any deliberate closing of the eyes and inferences to be drawn from any evidence. A showing of negligence is not sufficient to support a finding of willfulness or knowledge.
>
> I caution you that the willful blindness charge does not authorize you to find that the defendant acted knowingly because she should have known what was occurring when the property at 763 Sundown Road was being sold, or that in the exercise of hindsight she should have known what was occurring or because she was negligent in failing to recognize what was occurring or even because she was reckless or foolish in failing to recognize what was occurring. Instead, the Government must prove beyond a reasonable doubt that the defendant purposely and deliberately contrived to avoid learning all of the facts.

. . . Neither party disputes the adequacy of these instructions on willful blindness or their applicability to this case.

As outlined above, a money laundering conviction under section 1956(a)(1)(B)(i) requires proof of the defendant's knowledge of two separate facts: (1) that the funds involved in the transaction were the proceeds of illegal activity; and (2) that the transaction was designed to conceal the nature of the proceeds. In its opinion supporting the entry of the judgment of acquittal, the district court erred in interpreting the elements of the offense. After correctly reciting the elements of the statute, the court stated, "in a prosecution against a party other than the drug dealer," the Government must show "*a purpose of concealment*" and "knowledge of the drug dealer's activities." . . . This assertion misstates the Government's burden. The Government need not prove that the defendant had the *purpose* of concealing the proceeds of illegal activity. Instead, as the plain language of the statute suggests, the Government must only show that the defendant possessed the *knowledge* that the transaction was designed to conceal illegal proceeds.

This distinction is critical in cases such as the present one, in which the defendant is a person other than the individual who is the source of the tainted money. It is clear from the record that Campbell herself did not act with the purpose of concealing drug proceeds. Her motive, without question, was to close the real estate deal and collect the resulting commission, without regard to the source of the money or the effect of the transaction in concealing a portion of the purchase price. However, Campbell's motivations are irrelevant. Under the terms of the statute, the relevant question is not Campbell's purpose, but rather her knowledge of Lawing's purpose.[4]

---

4. We have no difficulty in finding that *Lawing*'s purpose satisfied the statutory requirement that the transaction be "designed in whole or in part . . . to conceal or disguise the nature, the location, the source, the ownership, or the control of the proceeds of specified unlawful activity. . . ." 18 U.S.C. § 1956(a)(1)(B). The omission of $60,000 from all documentation regarding the sales price of the property clearly satisfies this standard—concealing both the nature and the location of Lawing's illegally derived funds. . . . Accordingly, we need not address the Government's alternative argument that Lawing concealed ownership of the funds by placing title to the Lake Norman property in the name of his parents.

The sufficiency of evidence regarding Campbell's knowledge of Lawing's purpose depends on whether Campbell was aware of Lawing's status as a drug dealer. Assuming for the moment that Campbell knew that Lawing's funds were derived from illegal activity, then the under the table transfer of $60,000 in cash would have been sufficient, by itself, to allow the jury to find that Campbell knew, or was willfully blind to the fact, that the transaction was designed for an illicit purpose. . . . Only if Campbell was oblivious to the illicit nature of Lawing's funds could she credibly argue that she believed Lawing's explanation of the under the table transfer of cash and was unaware of the money laundering potential of the transaction. In short, the fraudulent nature of the transaction itself provides a sufficient basis from which a jury could infer Campbell's knowledge of the transaction's purpose, if, as assumed above, Campbell also knew of the illegal source of Lawing's money. As a result, we find that, in this case, the knowledge components of the money laundering statute collapse into a single inquiry: Did Campbell know that Lawing's funds were derived from an illegal source?

The Government emphasizes that the district court misstated the Government's burden on this point as well, by holding that the Government must show Campbell's "knowledge of the drug dealer's activities." . . . As the text of the statute indicates, the Government need only show knowledge that the funds represented "the proceeds of some form of unlawful activity." 18 U.S.C. § 1956(a)(1); see also 18 U.S.C. § 1956(c)(1) (money laundering provision requires "that the person knew the property involved in the transaction represented proceeds from some form, though not necessarily which form, of [specified unlawful] activity"). Practically, this distinction makes little difference. All of the Government's evidence was designed to show that Campbell knew that Lawing was a drug dealer. There is no indication that the jury could have believed that Lawing was involved in some form of criminal activity other than drug dealing. As a result, the district court's misstatement on this point is of little consequence.

The evidence pointing to Campbell's knowledge of Lawing's illegal activities is not overwhelming. . . .

However, the district court . . . downplayed evidence that we find to be highly relevant. Sara Fox, the listing broker, testified at trial that Campbell had stated prior to the sale that the funds "may have been drug money." . . .

In addition, the Government presented extensive evidence regarding Lawing's lifestyle. This evidence showed that Lawing and his companion both drove new Porsches, and that Lawing carried a cellular phone, flashed vast amounts of cash, and was able to be away from his purportedly legitimate business for long stretches of time during normal working hours. The district court conceded that this evidence "is not wholly [sic] irrelevant" to Campbell's knowledge of Lawing's true occupation, . . . but noted that Lawing's lifestyle was not inconsistent with that of many of the other inhabitants of the affluent Lake Norman area who were not drug dealers. . . . Again, we find that the district court has drawn inferences from the evidence which, while possibly well-founded, are not the only inferences that can be drawn. It should have been left to the jury to decide whether or not the Government's evidence of Lawing's lifestyle was sufficient to negate the credibility of Campbell's assertion that she believed Lawing to be a legitimate businessman.

We find that the evidence of Lawing's lifestyle, the testimony concerning Campbell's statement that the money "might have been drug money," and the fraudulent nature of the transaction in which Campbell was asked to participate were sufficient to create a question for the jury concerning whether Campbell "deliberately closed her eyes to what would otherwise have been obvious to her." As a result, we find that a reasonable jury could have found that Campbell was willfully blind to the fact that Lawing was a drug dealer and the fact that the purchase of the Lake Norman property was intended, at least in part, to conceal the proceeds of Lawing's drug selling operation. Accordingly, we reverse the judgment of acquittal on the money laundering charge.

## Notes and Questions

1. Did Campbell actually know that the cash Lawing used to buy the house came from specified unlawful activity? According to the court, what evidence allowed the jury to conclude that she knew Lawing's cash came from specified unlawful activity?

2. Is Campbell guilty of aiding and abetting Lawing's drug business as well? How does the mens rea for the section 1956 offense compare to the mens rea for aiding and abetting (discussed *supra*)?

3. Could the Fortiers (the sellers of the house) also have been convicted of a violation of section 1956? Why, why not?

### b. Designed to Conceal

Lastly, the defendant must also know that the transaction was designed to conceal the nature, location, source, or control of proceeds. This, of course, means that the government must prove that the transaction was, in fact, designed to conceal one of these things. The following case discusses this additional mens rea element.

### United States v. Corchado-Peralta
318 F.3d 255 (1st Cir. 2003)

BOUDIN, J.:

Between 1987 and 1996, Ubaldo Rivera Colon ("Colon") smuggled over 150 kilograms of cocaine into Puerto Rico, yielding some $4 million in profits, which he then laundered through a variety of investments and purchases. Colon was indicted on drug, bank fraud, and conspiracy charges and, based on a plea agreement, was sentenced in June 2002 to over 20 years in prison. This case concerns not Colon but three peripheral figures, including his wife.

Colon's wife, Elena Corchado Peralta ("Corchado"), and two associates, Basilio Rivera Rodriguez ("Rivera") and Oscar Trinidad Rodriguez ("Trinidad") were indicted and tried together on one count of conspiring with Colon to launder money. 18 U.S.C. §§ 1956(a)(1)(B) and (h). Corchado was also indicted on one count of bank fraud. 18 U.S.C. § 1344 (2000). During their eight-day trial, Colon provided extensive testimony about his money laundering methods, which included a variety of transactions (purchases, investments, and loans) involving the defendants.

All three defendants were convicted on the charges against them. Corchado received a 27-month sentence, Rivera, 57 months, and Trinidad, 63 months. All three defendants appealed, each arguing that the evidence was not sufficient to support conviction. Trinidad and Rivera raise other issues as well and we address their claims in a companion opinion. Corchado appeals alone, but it is helpful to begin by outlining the criminal offense that was the principal charge against all of them.

The money laundering statute, 18 U.S.C. § 1956 (2000), among other things makes it criminal for anyone, "knowing that the property involved in a financial transaction represents the proceeds of some form of unlawful activity" to "conduct . . . such a financial transaction which in fact involves the proceeds of specified unlawful activity"—

> (A)(i) with the intent to promote the carrying on of specified unlawful activity; or
> . . .
> (B) knowing that the transaction is designed in whole or in part—
> (i) to conceal or disguise the nature, the location, the source, the ownership or the control of the proceeds of specified unlawful activity;

*Id.* § 1956(a)(1).

The three defendants in this case were charged under subsection (B)(i), based on knowledge of "design[ ]", and not under (A)(i), based on an "intent to promote." In each instance, there is no doubt that the defendant did engage in one or more financial transactions involving Colon's drug proceeds. The issue turns, rather, on state of mind elements. Pertinently, as to Corchado, she disputes knowing either that the "property" represented proceeds of drug dealing or that "the transaction" was "designed . . . to conceal or disguise. . . ." The evidence, taken most favorably to the government, *United States v. Gomez*, 255 F.3d 31, 35 (1st Cir. 2001), showed the following.

Elena Corchado Peralta met Colon sometime in the early 1990s and they were married in 1994. Corchado, then about 25 years old, was a student when they met and later worked part-time in her mother's jewelry store. She has a college degree in business administration and some training in accounting. Colon testified that he held himself out as a successful legitimate businessman throughout their relationship and that his wife knew about neither his drug smuggling nor his own money laundering activities.

Corchado performed many transactions involving Colon's drug proceeds. These transactions fell into two broad categories—expenditures and deposits. On the expenditure side, Colon directed Corchado to write and endorse checks to purchase a cornucopia of expensive cars, boats, real estate, and personal services. Colon maintained that his wife thought that the money was derived from legitimate businesses.

The purchases themselves were extensive and expensive, affording the couple a fancy lifestyle. For example, Corchado purchased a BMW, a Mercedes Benz, and a Porsche for the couple. At another time, she made a single monthly payment to American Express of $18,384 for interior decorating purchases. And on another day, she signed three checks totaling $350,000 that were used to purchase land for one of Colon's businesses. In total, Corchado signed the majority of 253 checks, representing many hundreds of thousands of dollars of purchases.

With respect to deposits, Corchado's main responsibility was to deposit $6,000 checks on a monthly basis into one of Colon's accounts. Colon testified that he had made a $700,000 loan to an associate using his drug profits with the understanding that the associate was to pay him back over the course of many months so as to dissociate Colon from the illegal proceeds. Under the terms of the arrangement, the checks came from legitimate businesses, and Colon testified that his wife was not aware of the circumstances underlying the monthly payments. At trial, the government also presented evidence showing that on one occasion Corchado wired $40,000 to a Florida company at Colon's request.

Tax records signed by Corchado showed that she knew that her husband's reported income from his legitimate businesses was far less than the money she was handling. For example, the joint tax return that Corchado signed for 1995 listed a total amount of claimed income of only $12,390. The government presented evidence showing that the couple's total reported income between 1992 and 1997 was only approximately $150,000. Corchado did not testify at trial.

We begin with the first knowledge requirement—namely, that Corchado was aware, at the time of the transactions she conducted, that the money she was handling, at least much of the time, was derived from drug dealings.[2] Corchado argues, correctly, that there is no direct evidence of her knowledge (say, by an admission by her or testimony from Colon that he told her about his business). Indeed, he testified repeatedly that she was unaware of his drug business; that in response to a question from her he had denied doing anything unlawful; that he never allowed her to attend meetings involving his drug business; and that he stopped distributing drugs when they were married.

Needless to say, the jury did not have to accept Colon's exculpatory testimony. It was clearly self-interested since Corchado was his wife and mother of their two children. But here, at least, the jury's disbelief could not count for much in the way of affirmative proof. . . . Rather, whether there was knowledge of drug dealing, or so much awareness that ignorance was willful blindness, turns in this case on the same circumstantial evidence.

What the evidence shows is that Corchado knew that the family expenditures were huge, that reported income was a fraction of what was being spent and that legitimate sources were not so obvious as to banish all thoughts of possible illegal origin—as demonstrated by Colon's testimony that Corchado once raised the issue. Interviewed by an FBI agent, Corchado told him that her husband had been involved in the cattle business and, more recently, in real estate development but that none of the businesses had employees and that Colon had worked mainly out of his house. And, as the government fairly points out, Corchado was herself well educated and involved in the family bookkeeping.

This might seem to some a modest basis for concluding—beyond a reasonable doubt— that Corchado knew that her husband's income was badly tainted. But the issue turns on judgments about relationships within families and about inferences that might be drawn in the community from certain patterns of working and spending. Further, it is enough to know that the proceeds came from "some form, though not necessarily which form," of felony under state or federal law. 18 U.S.C. § 1956(c)(1). The jury's judgment on this factual issue cannot be called irrational.

The other knowledge requirement is harder for the government. Here, the statute requires, somewhat confusingly, that Corchado have known that "the transaction" was "designed," at least in part, "to conceal or disguise the nature, the location, the source, the

---

2. Formally, the charge is "conspiracy," under subsection (h) to violate subsection (a)(1)(B)(i); but the "agreement" requirement is undisputed: many, if not all, of the transactions were performed at Colon's request or with his consent. Thus, the open issue is Corchado's state of mind.

ownership or the control of the proceeds." 18 U.S.C. § 1956(a)(1)(B)(i). We will assume that it would be enough if Corchado herself undertook a transaction for her husband, knowing that her husband had such a design to conceal or disguise the proceeds, or if she undertook a transaction on her own having such a design herself. Other variations might exist, but these two seem the foremost possibilities.

It may help to treat separately the purchases on the one hand and the check deposits (and in one case a transfer) on the other. Any purchase of goods or services, whether by cash or by check, has a potential to conceal or disguise proceeds simply because it transforms them from money into objects or dissipates them in the performance of the services. But if this were enough, every expenditure of proceeds known to be tainted would itself be unlawful. Instead, the statute requires that someone—the instigator or spender—must have an intent to disguise or conceal and the spender must share or know of that intent. . . .

Here, the government showed that from their marriage onward Corchado wrote most of the checks used by the couple to purchase expensive items (*e.g.*, several high-priced cars) and pay off credit card bills and that some of these payments were very large (one credit card bill exceeded $18,000). And, for reasons already given, it is assumed that the jury permissibly found that Corchado knew that some of the money she was spending was criminally derived. Finally, the government stresses that she must have known that Colon was bringing in and spending far more than he reported on his income tax returns. Is this enough for the jury to infer a specific intent to conceal or disguise and impute the intent itself, or knowledge of it, to Corchado?

In this case, nothing about the purchases, or their manner, points toward concealment or disguise beyond the fact that virtually *all expenditures* transform cash into something else. Here, the purchased assets were not readily concealable (*e.g.*, diamonds) nor peculiarly concealed (*e.g.*, buried in the garden) nor acquired in someone else's name nor spirited away to a foreign repository (*e.g.*, a Swiss bank deposit box).[3] Indicia of this kind have been stressed in cases upholding money laundering charges and their absence noted in cases coming out the other way. . . .

To hold that a jury may convict on this evidence—that Corchado spent her husband's money knowing that the money was tainted—is to make it unlawful wherever a wife spends any of her husband's money, knowing or believing him to be a criminal. That the purchases here were lavish or numerous hardly distinguishes this case from one in which a thief's wife buys a jar of baby food; if anything, Corchado's more flamboyant purchases were less likely than the baby food to disguise or conceal. Perhaps a hard-nosed Congress might be willing to adopt such a statute, *compare* 18 U.S.C. § 1957 (2000), but it did not do so here.

Less need be said about the deposit and transfer side. So far as we can tell, Corchado mostly did no more than make large regular deposits in an account given to her by her husband; there was no inference of concealment or disguise. As for the single transfer she made to another person at her husband's request, nothing suspicious about the circumstances is cited to us, let alone anything that would suggest knowledge on Corchado's part that the transfer was meant to conceal or disguise proceeds—as opposed to merely paying

---

3. The evidence indicated that the family apartment had been purchased by Colon and his mother but was held in her name; but there is nothing extraordinary about that.

off a debt, making an investment, or conducting some other transaction incident to a business, lawful or otherwise.

## Notes and Questions

1. Why does the court find that Corchado knew the funds involved in her transactions came from illicit activity—i.e., that the government had satisfied the first mens rea element? Given its finding that Corchado knew of the illicit source of the funds, why does the court find that the second mens rea element—i.e., that she knew the transactions were designed to conceal something—was not met? Do you agree? Do you think these transactions may have been designed to conceal something besides the *existence* of the illicit funds?

2. What sort of evidence might be used to establish an intent to conceal (and knowledge thereof)? In *United States v. Garcia-Emanuel*, 14 F.3d 1469, 1475-76 (8th Cir. 1998), the court listed several types of evidence the government had used in prior cases to establish an intent to conceal, including: "statements by a defendant probative of intent to conceal; unusual secrecy surrounding the transaction; structuring the transaction in a way to avoid attention; depositing illegal profits in the bank account of a legitimate business; highly irregular features of the transaction; using third parties to conceal the real owner; a series of unusual financial moves cumulating in the transaction; or expert testimony on practices of criminals." The following Problem explores the sufficiency of the evidence used to demonstrate an intent to conceal:

Problem 11.14: Andy has $25,000 in cash proceeds from selling marijuana. He gives the money to his wife, Delilah, who knows that the money came from drug dealing. Delilah uses the cash to buy a truck and horse trailer, title to which she puts in her own name. Are these facts sufficient to establish an intent to conceal? See *Garcia-Emanuel, supra.*

3. The sanctions for money laundering offenses can be steep, including up to 20 years' imprisonment and a fine equal to the greater of $10,000 or the value of the property involved in the transaction. 18 U.S.C. §§ 1956(a) & 1956(b)(1). Money laundering does not merge with the crimes that generated the proceeds used in the transaction, so a defendant may be convicted of both those crimes and money laundering.

## 2. Use of Criminal Proceeds

It is commonly said that spending criminal proceeds for one's immediate benefit does not constitute money *laundering. Corchado-Peralta*, 318 F.3d at 259. Even so, there is a crime for that too. 18 U.S.C. section 1957 bars the *use* of the proceeds of unlawful activity. Under section 1957, the government must show that the defendant:

(1) engaged in a monetary transaction,
(2) involving more than $10,000 derived from specified unlawful activity, and
(3) knowing that the funds were criminally derived.

Let us briefly review these elements, which are similar—but not identical to—the elements of a section 1956 offense. First, the defendant must engage in a *monetary* transaction, which is defined somewhat more narrowly than a *financial* transaction. Importantly, a monetary transaction includes only a deposit, withdrawal, or transfer made through a financial institution. However, for these purposes, a financial institution is defined to include not only banks but many other entities as well, including jewelry stores, pawn shops, and car dealers.

Second, the transaction must involve a minimum threshold of funds—$10,000—derived from specified unlawful activity. The latter requirement is the same as section 1956—i.e., the funds must must constitute the proceeds of unlawful activity. However, the former requirement is unique to section 1957: the government must show that a minimum amount ($10,000) in tainted funds were involved in the transaction. To meet this requirement, the government is allowed to aggregate related transactions, such as multiple bank deposits involving criminal proceeds. But the minimum can pose a challenge for the government when a defendant intermingles both tainted and untainted funds, as in the following Problem:

**Problem 11.15:** In late 2016, Delilah bought a car with $14,000 in cash. She was subsequently charged with a violation of section 1957 based on this transaction. The government introduced evidence that Delilah sold marijuana and that her marijuana operation generated more than $20,000 in cash income from 2014 to 2016. Delilah introduced evidence that she earned about $10,000 in cash income from odd jobs and waitressing over the same time period. Is there enough evidence to convict Delilah under section 1957? *See United States v. Shafer,* 608 F.3d 1056, 1067 (8th Cir. 2010).

The third element (knowledge) under section 1957 is identical to the third element under section 1956. In other words, the government need only show that the defendant knew—or was willfully blind to the fact that—the funds came from some unlawful activity.

## Notes and Questions

1. Do the proceeds of illegal activity ever become clean? For example, will the use of income earned today from marijuana distribution ever fall outside of the purview of section 1957? Does the statute of limitations provide an answer? *See* 18 U.S.C. § 3282(a) (establishing five-year statute of limitations for federal crimes). Why, why not? Consider the following Problem:

**Problem 11.16:** Andy made a small fortune from operating a state-licensed marijuana shop in 2013. At the end of 2013, Andy closed his shop and buried the $100,000 in profits (all in cash) he had made from the operation in his backyard. Fast-forward to 2018. In January, a new Congress passes legislation

that repeals the federal prohibition on the distribution of marijuana. Immediately thereafter, Andy digs up the cash from his backyard, takes it to his bank, and deposits it in his account. Could Andy be convicted under section 1957 for this deposit? Why, why not?

2. Violations of section 1957 are punished somewhat less severely than violations of section 1956. The applicable sanctions include a term of imprisonment of up to 10 years and/or a fine of up to twice the value of the property involved in the transaction. 18 U.S.C. § 1957(b).

CHAPTER 12

# The Law, Policy, and Authority Issues Confronting Professionals

Physicians and attorneys play a special role in marijuana law and policy. In particular, states have relied on these professionals to help ensure compliance with their marijuana reforms. For example, physicians help identify which patients are eligible to use marijuana for medical purposes, and attorneys help marijuana suppliers comply with the complicated licensing and regulatory systems states have constructed.

At the same time, however, the federal government's continuing prohibition on marijuana use and supply complicates the work of these professionals. The federal prohibition exposes these professionals to potential legal sanctions and may thereby curb their willingness to perform the roles that states have designed for them.

This chapter examines key issues surrounding the regulation of both groups of professionals. Section A focuses on physicians: Section A.1 examines whether physicians may be sanctioned by the federal government for recommending marijuana to patients; Section A.2 discusses what physicians must do in order to recommend marijuana under state law; Section A.3 asks whether state and federal policies have made it too difficult for physicians to recommend marijuana to their patients; and, finally, Section A.4 asks whether those policies have instead made it too *easy* for physicians to do so. Section B then shifts to questions surrounding attorneys. Section B.1 asks what services attorneys may provide to marijuana clients under state professional rules of conduct; Section B.2 asks whether such rules permit attorneys to use or supply marijuana themselves; and, finally, Section B.3 asks whether attorneys may be punished by federal courts for providing legal services to clients who they know are violating federal law.

## A. PHYSICIANS

Given popular beliefs about marijuana's medical benefits, it should come as no surprise that physicians are commonly asked about the drug by some patients. How do governments regulate physicians' responses to such inquiries? May physicians be sanctioned for discussing marijuana with their patients? What if they recommend the drug? Do regulations ensure that patients can get a recommendation when one is warranted—and not otherwise? The materials below explore these questions.

## 1. May Physicians Be Sanctioned for Recommending Marijuana?

As discussed in Chapter 4, patients in every medical marijuana state must obtain a physician's recommendation in order to obtain the benefits provided by state reforms. But in the early days of state reforms, the federal government sought to discourage physicians from providing such recommendations. Just months after California voters approved Proposition 215, the federal Drug Enforcement Administration (DEA) announced that it would sanction any physician who recommended marijuana to a patient. Office of National Drug Control Pol'y, Administration Response to the Passage of Arizona Proposition 200 and California Proposition 215, 62 Fed. Reg. 6164-01 (Feb. 11, 1997). In particular, the agency threatened to revoke an offending physician's registration under the federal Controlled Substances Act (CSA). See Drug Enforcement Administration, Practioner's Manual 18 (2006), https://perma.cc/58HJ-FKPP. Physicians need such registration in order to write prescriptions for a broad range of controlled substances (e.g., Xanax, Percocet, etc.). Though physicians may practice medicine without the DEA registration, the loss of it can substantially impair their business.

After the DEA policy was announced, several physicians filed lawsuits challenging it. In the following case, one court enjoins enforcement of the policy on the grounds that it violates the free speech rights of physicians under the First Amendment. The opinion explains why the court found that physicians are constitutionally entitled to recommend marijuana to their patients, but it also recognizes that there are limits to the protection afforded physicians by the First Amendment.

### *Conant v. Walters*
309 F.3d 629 (9th Cir. 2002)

SCHROEDER, C.J.:

This is an appeal from a permanent injunction . . . [preventing] the federal government from either revoking a physician's license to prescribe controlled substances or conducting an investigation of a physician that might lead to such revocation, where the basis for the government's action is solely the physician's professional "recommendation" of the use of medical marijuana. . . .

. . .

The federal government promulgated its policy in 1996 in response to initiatives passed in both Arizona and California decriminalizing the use of marijuana for limited medical purposes and immunizing physicians from prosecution under state law for the "recommendation or approval" of using marijuana for medical purposes. See Cal. Health & Safety Code § 11362.5. The federal policy declared that a doctor's "action of recommending or prescribing Schedule I controlled substances is not consistent with the 'public interest' (as that phrase is used in the federal Controlled Substances Act)" and that such action would lead to revocation of the physician's registration to prescribe controlled substances. [Author's note: 21 U.S.C. section 823(f) authorizes the Attorney General to deny or revoke a physician's registration under the CSA if it would be "inconsistent with the public interest."] The policy relies on the definition of "public interest" contained in 21 U.S.C. § 823(f), which provides:

> In determining the public interest, the following factors shall be considered: (1) The recommendation of the appropriate State licensing board or professional disciplinary

authority. (2) The applicant's experience in dispensing, or conducting research with respect to controlled substances. (3) The applicant's conviction record under Federal or State laws relating to the manufacture, distribution, or dispensing of controlled substances. (4) Compliance with applicable State, Federal, or local laws relating to controlled substances. (5) Such other conduct which may threaten the public health and safety.

. . .

Plaintiffs [include, inter alia,] physicians licensed to practice in California who treat patients with serious illnesses. . . . Plaintiffs filed this action in early 1997 to enjoin enforcement of the government policy insofar as it threatened to punish physicians for communicating with their patients about the medical use of marijuana. . . .

[The district court entered a preliminary injunction in April, 1997. It subsequently made the order permanent, enjoining the federal government from:]

> (i) revoking any physician class member's DEA registration merely because the doctor makes a recommendation for the use of medical marijuana based on a sincere medical judgment and (ii) from initiating any investigation solely on that ground. The injunction should apply whether or not the doctor anticipates that the patient will, in turn, use his or her recommendation to obtain marijuana in violation of federal law.

In explaining [its] reasons for entering the injunction, [the court] pointed out that there was substantial agreement between the parties as to what doctors could and could not do under the federal law. . . . The government agreed with plaintiffs that revocation of a license was not authorized where a doctor merely discussed the pros and cons of marijuana use. . . . The court went on to observe that the plaintiffs agreed with the government that a doctor who actually prescribes or dispenses marijuana violates federal law. The fundamental disagreement between the parties concerned the extent to which the federal government could regulate doctor-patient communications without interfering with First Amendment interests. . . . This appeal followed.

. . .

The dispute in the district court in this case focused on the government's policy of investigating doctors or initiating proceedings against doctors only because they "recommend" the use of marijuana. While the government urged that such recommendations lead to illegal use, the district court concluded that there are many legitimate responses to a recommendation of marijuana by a doctor to a patient. . . . For example, the doctor could seek to place the patient in a federally approved, experimental marijuana-therapy program. . . . Alternatively, the patient upon receiving the recommendation could petition the government to change the law. . . . By chilling doctors' ability to recommend marijuana to a patient, the district court held that the prohibition compromises a patient's meaningful participation in public discourse. . . . The district court stated:

> Petitioning Congress or federal agencies for redress of a grievance or a change in policy is a time-honored tradition. In the marketplace of ideas, few questions are more deserving of free-speech protection than whether regulations affecting health and welfare are sound public policy. In the debate, perhaps the status quo will (and should) endure. But patients and physicians are certainly entitled to urge their view. To hold that physicians are barred from communicating to patients sincere medical judgments would disable patients from understanding their own situations well enough to participate in the debate. As the government concedes, . . . many patients depend upon discussions with their physicians as their primary or only source of sound medical information. Without open communication

with their physicians, patients would fall silent and appear uninformed. The ability of patients to participate meaningfully in the public discourse would be compromised.

On appeal, the government first argues that the "recommendation" that the injunction may protect is analogous to a "prescription" of a controlled substance, which federal law clearly bars. We believe this characterizes the injunction as sweeping more broadly than it was intended or than as properly interpreted. If, in making the recommendation, the physician intends for the patient to use it as the means for obtaining marijuana, as a prescription is used as a means for a patient to obtain a controlled substance, then a physician would be guilty of aiding and abetting the violation of federal law. That, the injunction is intended to avoid. . . .

. . .

As [the district court] noted in the preliminary injunction order, conviction of aiding and abetting requires proof that the defendant "associate[d] himself with the venture, that he participate[d] in it as something that he wishe[d] to bring about, that he [sought] by his actions to make it succeed." . . . The district court also noted that conspiracy requires that a defendant make "an agreement to accomplish an illegal objective and [that he] knows of the illegal objective and intends to help accomplish it." . . .

The government on appeal stresses that the permanent injunction applies "whether or not the doctor anticipates that the patient will, in turn, use his or her recommendation to obtain marijuana in violation of federal law," and suggests that the injunction thus protects criminal conduct. A doctor's anticipation of patient conduct, however, does not translate into aiding and abetting, or conspiracy. A doctor would aid and abet by acting with the specific intent to provide a patient with the means to acquire marijuana. . . . Similarly, a conspiracy would require that a doctor have knowledge that a patient intends to acquire marijuana, agree to help the patient acquire marijuana, and intend to help the patient acquire marijuana. . . . Holding doctors responsible for whatever conduct the doctor could anticipate a patient *might* engage in after leaving the doctor's office is simply beyond the scope of either conspiracy or aiding and abetting.

The government also focuses on the injunction's bar against "investigating" on the basis of speech protected by the First Amendment and points to the broad discretion enjoyed by executive agencies in investigating suspected criminal misconduct. . . .

. . . [W]e interpret this portion of the permanent injunction to mean only that the government may not initiate an investigation of a physician solely on the basis of a recommendation of marijuana within a bona fide doctor-patient relationship, unless the government in good faith believes that it has substantial evidence of criminal conduct. Because a doctor's recommendation does not itself constitute illegal conduct, the portion of the injunction barring investigations solely on that basis does not interfere with the federal government's ability to enforce its laws.

The government policy does, however, strike at core First Amendment interests of doctors and patients. An integral component of the practice of medicine is the communication between a doctor and a patient. Physicians must be able to speak frankly and openly to patients. That need has been recognized by the courts through the application of the common law doctor-patient privilege. . . .

The doctor-patient privilege reflects "the imperative need for confidence and trust" inherent in the doctor-patient relationship and recognizes that "a physician must know all that a patient can articulate in order to identify and to treat disease; barriers to full disclosure would impair diagnosis and treatment." *Trammel v. United States*, 445 U.S. 40, 51 . . . (1980). The Supreme Court has recognized that physician speech is entitled to First Amendment protection because of the significance of the doctor-patient relationship. . . .

. . .

Being a member of a regulated profession does not, as the government suggests, result in a surrender of First Amendment rights. . . . To the contrary, professional speech may be entitled to "the strongest protection our Constitution has to offer." . . . Even commercial speech by professionals is entitled to First Amendment protection. . . . Attorneys have rights to speak freely subject only to the government regulating with "narrow specificity." . . .

In its most recent pronouncement on regulating speech about controlled substances, *Thompson v. Western States Medical Ctr.*, 535 U.S. 357 . . . (2002), the Supreme Court found that provisions in the Food and Drug Modernization Act of 1997 that restricted physicians and pharmacists from advertising compounding drugs violated the First Amendment. . . . The Court refused to make the "questionable assumption that doctors would prescribe unnecessary medications" and rejected the government's argument that "people would make bad decisions if given truthful information about compounded drugs." . . . The federal government argues in this case that a doctor-patient discussion about marijuana might lead the patient to make a bad decision, essentially asking us to accept the same assumption rejected by the Court in *Thompson*. . . . We will not do so. Instead, we take note of the Supreme Court's admonition in *Thompson*: "If the First Amendment means anything, it means that regulating speech must be a last—not first—resort. Yet here it seems to have been the first strategy the Government thought to try." *Id.*

The government's policy in this case seeks to punish physicians on the basis of the content of doctor-patient communications. Only doctor-patient conversations that include discussions of the medical use of marijuana trigger the policy. Moreover, the policy does not merely prohibit the discussion of marijuana; it condemns expression of a particular viewpoint, i.e., that medical marijuana would likely help a specific patient. Such condemnation of particular views is especially troubling in the First Amendment context. "When the government targets not subject matter but particular views taken by speakers on a subject, the violation of the First Amendment is all the more blatant." . . . Indeed, even content-based restrictions on speech are "presumptively invalid." . . .

. . .

The government seeks to justify its policy by claiming that a doctor's "recommendation" of marijuana may encourage illegal conduct by the patient, which is not unlike the argument made before, and rejected by, the Supreme Court in a recent First Amendment case. *See Ashcroft v. Free Speech Coalition*, 535 U.S. 234 . . . (2002). In *Free Speech Coalition*, the government defended the Child Pornography Prosecution Act of 1996 by arguing that, although virtual child pornography does not harm children in the production process, it threatens them in "other, less direct, ways." . . . For example, the government argued pedophiles might use such virtual images to encourage children to participate in sexual activity. . . . The Supreme Court rejected such justifications, holding that the potential harms were too attenuated from the proscribed speech. "Without a significantly stronger, more direct connection, the Government may not prohibit speech on the ground that it may encourage . . . illegal conduct." . . . The government's argument in this case mirrors the argument rejected in *Free Speech Coalition*.

...

Our decision is consistent with principles of federalism that have left states as the primary regulators of professional conduct. . . .

For all of the foregoing reasons, we affirm the district court's order entering a permanent injunction.

KOZINSKI, J., concurring:

I am pleased to join Chief Judge Schroeder's opinion. I write only to explain that for me the fulcrum of this dispute is not the First Amendment right of the doctors. That right certainly exists and its impairment justifies the district court's injunction for the reasons well explained by Chief Judge Schroeder. But the doctors' interest in giving advice about the medical use of marijuana is somewhat remote and impersonal; they will derive no direct *benefit* from giving this advice, other than the satisfaction of doing their jobs well. At the same time, the *burden* of the federal policy the district court enjoined falls directly and personally on the doctors: By speaking candidly to their patients about the potential benefits of medical marijuana, they risk losing their license to write prescriptions, which would prevent them from functioning as doctors. In other words, they may destroy their careers and lose their livelihoods.[1]

This disparity between benefits and burdens matters because it makes doctors peculiarly vulnerable to intimidation; with little to gain and much to lose, only the most foolish or committed of doctors will defy the federal government's policy and continue to give patients candid advice about the medical uses of marijuana.[2] Those immediately and

---

1. Dr. Neil M. Flynn, Professor at the University of California at Davis School of Medicine, offers one perspective:

> AIDS medicine is my profession and my passion. I have dedicated myself to this disease since 1983 when I opened the Clinic at U.C. Davis. Thus, I am deeply concerned about civil and criminal sanctions that loom over me. . . . If I lost my Schedule II license, my ability to provide care for people with AIDS—80% of my patients—would be severely compromised. I write 30–50 narcotic prescriptions per month for my seriously ill patients. I would no longer be able to do so if my DEA license were revoked.

2. As Alice Pasetta Mead explained in her expert report:

> [P]hysicians are particularly easily deterred by the threat of governmental investigation and/or sanction from engaging in conduct that is entirely lawful and medically appropriate. . . . [A] physician's practice is particularly dependent upon the physician's maintaining a reputation of unimpeachable integrity. A physician's career can be effectively destroyed merely by the fact that a governmental body has investigated his or her practice. . . .

The federal government's policy had precisely this effect before it was enjoined by the district court. Dr. Milton N. Estes, Associate Clinical Professor in the Department of Obstetrics, Gynecology and Reproductive Medicine at the University of California–San Francisco (UCSF), reports:

> As a result of the government's public threats, I do not feel comfortable even discussing the subject of medical marijuana with my patients. I feel vulnerable to federal sanctions that could strip me of my license to prescribe the treatments my patients depend upon, or even land me behind bars. . . . Because of these fears, the discourse about medical marijuana has all but ceased at my medical office. . . . My patients bear the brunt of this loss in communication. . . .

directly affected by the federal government's policy are the patients, who will be denied information crucial to their well-being, and the State of California, whose policy of exempting certain patients from the sweep of its drug laws will be thwarted. In my view, it is the vindication of these latter interests—those of the patients and of the state—that primarily justifies the district court's highly unusual exercise of discretion in enjoining the federal defendants from even investigating possible violations of the federal criminal laws.

## Notes and Questions

1. Not all speech is protected by the First Amendment. *See* Eugene Volokh, *Crime-Facilitating Speech*, 57 Stan. L. Rev. 1095 (2005) (surveying doctrine). The *Conant* court implicitly recognizes that crime facilitating speech, including physician speech that aids and abets a patient's possession of marijuana, is not protected by the First Amendment. The court just found that recommending marijuana, by itself, does not aid and abet the possession of marijuana. But the court suggests that *prescribing* marijuana *would* be unlawful—and thus unprotected—speech. In pertinent part, it notes that "[i]f in making the recommendation, the physician intends for the patient to use it as the means for obtaining marijuana, *as a prescription is used as a means for a patient to obtain a controlled substance*, then a physician would be guilty of aiding and abetting the violation of federal law." 309 F.3d at 635 (emphasis added).

Medical marijuana states have all designed their laws around this distinction. In particular, every medical marijuana state asks physicians only to recommend—rather than to prescribe—marijuana.[1] "By carefully circumscribing the task that physicians must perform, the states . . . prevented the federal government from squeezing one of the most important chokepoints in state medical marijuana programs." *See* Robert A. Mikos, *On the Limits of Supremacy: Medical Marijuana and the States' Overlooked Power to Legalize Federal Crime*, 62 Vand. L. Rev. 1421, 1467 (2009).

But is there a meaningful difference between prescribing marijuana and recommending the drug? A second court adjudicating an identical challenge to the DEA policy rejected the distinction drawn by *Conant*. Instead, it held that a physician's recommendation is indistinguishable from a prescription and thus provides the government with adequate justification for revoking a physician's registration. *Pearson v. McCaffrey*, 139 F. Supp. 2d 113 (D.D.C. 2001). The *Pearson* court explained:

> [I]n some states, such as California, the term "recommend" has a special significance under the law because patients are able to take a recommendation for medicinal marijuana to a buyers' club to receive the drug. In these situations, a recommendation is analogous to a prescription. . . .

---

1. The states arguably learned from previous failed experiments with medical marijuana reforms. In particular, more than a decade before California voters approved Proposition 215, several states had already legalized possession of marijuana pursuant to a physician's prescription. *E.g.*, Va. Code Ann. §18.2-251.1 (West) ("No person shall be prosecuted . . . for the possession of marijuana or tetrahydrocannabinol when that possession occurs *pursuant to a valid prescription* issued by a medical doctor in the course of his professional practice for treatment of cancer or glaucoma.") (emphasis added) (legislation passed in 1979). However, physicians in these states were apparently unwilling to prescribe marijuana at least in part because of concerns over federal sanctions.

*Id.* at 120-121. The court reasoned that because "there are no First Amendment protections for speech that is used 'as an integral part of conduct in violation of a valid criminal statute'[,] . . . the First Amendment does not prohibit the federal government from taking action against physicians whose prescription or recommendation of medicinal marijuana violates the CSA." *Id.* at 121.

Why did the *Conant* and *Pearson* courts reach such different conclusions regarding the meaning and significance of a recommendation? Which court's conclusion is more persuasive? Is it "willfully ignorant to say that a physician who recommends medical marijuana to a patient does not intend that the patient will use that recommendation as a means to obtain medical marijuana"? Nicole Santamaria, Note, *Medical Marijuana Legislation in Florida: The Recommendation vs. Prescription Distinction for Healthcare Providers*, 45 Stetson L. Rev. 537, 558 (2016).

2. A post-script on *Conant*. Although it is not formally bound by *Conant* outside of the states making up the Ninth Circuit, the DEA has abided the decision nationwide and no longer threatens to revoke a physician's registration merely for recommending marijuana. Nonetheless, it is important to note that the protection afforded by the *Conant* decision is not without limits. The following Problems test those limits. In which of them could the physician be sanctioned notwithstanding *Conant*?

**Problem 12.1**: After thoroughly examining her patient, Dr. Delilah diagnoses him with chronic pain, which is a qualifying condition under the state's medical marijuana law. Dr. Delilah tells the patient, orally, that his medical condition "might benefit from the use of marijuana." Under the state's medical marijuana law, an oral recommendation suffices to establish a patient's eligibility to possess and use marijuana for medical purposes. The patient proceeds to acquire a small amount of marijuana, within the quantity restrictions imposed by state law.

**Problem 12.2**: Same facts as **Problem 12.1**, only now, suppose that chronic pain is *not* a qualifying condition under the state's medical marijuana law.

**Problem 12.3**: Same facts as **Problem 12.1**. This time, however, Dr. Delilah also tells her patient orally "You should start by using about ⅛ of an ounce, daily. Pick a strain with a high THC content. Smoking or vaping the drug would be best for your condition. If ⅛ of an ounce doesn't work, then start upping the dose." *See* California Medical Association Legal Counsel, *The Compassionate Use Act of 1996*, CMA On-Call #1315 at 17 (Jan. 2004) ("A physician should avoid . . . [o]ffering a specific patient *individualized* advice concerning appropriate dosage timing, amount, and route of administration."). Is the guidance provided by the CMA overly cautious?

**Problem 12.4**: Same facts as **Problem 12.1**. This time, however, the patient asks "Where can I find marijuana?" Dr. Delilah responds, "There's a medical dispensary at the corner of Main and First Avenue. I've heard good things

about them." The patient proceeds to the dispensary, where he acquires a small amount of marijuana. CMA On-Call #1315 at 17 ("A physician should avoid ... [d]escribing to a patient how the patient may obtain cannabis, for example, by giving the name and address of a cannabis distributor."). Again, is the guidance provided by the CMA overly cautious?

Problem 12.5: Same facts as **Problem 12.1**. This time, however, the state requires recommendations to be memorialized in writing. The patient tells Dr. Delilah (accurately) that "I need a written recommendation from you to acquire and use the drug legally under state law." On a sheet of office stationary, Dr. Delilah writes: "I have diagnosed patient with chronic pain. His condition might benefit from the use of marijuana." Dr. Delilah gives the letter to the patient, who submits it to the state health department as part of his registration application. After he receives his medical marijuana identification card, the patient acquires a small amount of marijuana from a state-licensed medical marijuana dispensary. See Conant v. McCaffrey, 2000 WL 1281174, at *16 (N.D. Cal. 2000) (not reported), aff'd sub nom. Conant v. Walters, 309 F.3d 629 (9th Cir. 2002).

Problem 12.6: Same facts as **Problem 12.5**, only now, the state requires physicians to submit a written recommendation and related forms directly to the state's health department in order for a patient to register to use medical marijuana. Dr. Delilah completes and submits the forms and recommendation directly to the state agency. (For an example of such a form, see Reviewing Physician Written Certification Form for Qualifying Patients Under 18 Years of Age, https://perma.cc/U4MW-L3AQ.) A few weeks later, the patient receives his medical marijuana identification card in the mail, and he proceeds to acquire a small amount of marijuana from a state-licensed medical marijuana dispensary.

3. The Veterans Health Administration (VHA) is a federal agency that runs one of the largest health care systems in the country, serving nearly 9 million veterans. United States Dep't of Veterans Affairs, Veterans Health Administration, About VHA, https://perma.cc/FT7H-CZ5G. The VHA has adopted a policy that forbids its physicians from recommending marijuana to their patients. Veterans Health Administration, Access to Clinical Programs for Veterans Participating in State-Approved Marijuana Programs, VHA Directive 2011-004 (Jan. 31, 2011) ("It is VHA policy to prohibit VA providers from completing forms seeking recommendations or opinions regarding a Veteran's participation in a State marijuana program."). Is this policy constitutional under Conant? Is it distinguishable from the policy the DEA adopted toward private physicians? Cf. Rust v. Sullivan, 500 U.S. 173 (1991) (upholding ban on using federal grant funds to advocate for or counsel patients on abortion).

Whether or not the policy violates the First Amendment, Congress has recently forbidden the VHA from using its budgeted funds to enforce it. See Patricia Kime, *VA Docs to be Able to Recommend Marijuana in Some States*, Military Times, May 19, 2016, https://perma.cc/J7U3-FBLM (describing policy). As discussed in Chapter 7, Congress adopted similar language that forbids the DOJ from spending budgeted funds to block the implementation of state medical marijuana laws.

4. Does the DEA policy enjoined by *Conant* also exceed the agency's *statutory* authority under the CSA? After *Conant* was decided, the Supreme Court invalidated a similar policy that had been adopted by the Attorney General, one that threatened to revoke the DEA registration of physicians who prescribed drugs to assist a patient in committing suicide—a practice permitted by Oregon law but opposed by the United States Attorney General. *Gonzales v. Oregon*, 546 U.S. 243 (2006). In relevant part, the Attorney General's policy declared that "[A]ssisting suicide is not a 'legitimate medical practice,' and that prescribing . . . federally controlled substances to assist suicide violates the Controlled Substances Act." *Id.* at 254. In invalidating the policy, the Court reasoned that "the CSA's prescription requirement does not authorize the Attorney General to bar dispensing controlled substances for assisted suicide in the face of a state medical regime permitting such conduct." *Id.* at 274-275. Does *Gonzales v. Oregon* preclude the DEA from revoking a physician's registration for recommending marijuana? Might it also preclude revocation when a physician *prescribes* marijuana—i.e., might it provide even broader protection for physicians than does *Conant*?

## 2. What Must Physicians Do to Make Valid Recommendations?

In legalization regimes, physicians play a critical role in policing access to medical marijuana and the special legal perks accorded medical marijuana users. In particular, physicians determine both whether a patient has a qualifying condition and whether marijuana might benefit that patient's condition. As discussed in Chapter 4, the diagnosis and recommendation are both required for patients to participate in state medical marijuana programs.

The states have adopted a body of regulations to ensure that physicians are willing to play this role and to ensure they do so scrupulously. A sample of illustrative state regulations is reprinted here. The Federation of State Medical Boards has also issued Model Guidelines for the Recommendation of Marijuana in Patient Care (Apr. 2016).

**California:**

California's Proposition 215 (Compassionate Use Act) grants legal protections to physicians who recommended marijuana, although it does not impose any particular requirements on those physicians. It simply states that "[n]otwithstanding any other provision of law: no physician in this state shall be punished, or denied any right or privilege, for having recommended marijuana to a patient for medical purposes." Cal. Health & Safety Code § 11362.5(c).

In response to concerns over physicians providing sham recommendations, the California state legislature imposed additional requirements on physicians. The most recent legislation, the Medical Cannabis Regulation and Safety Act (MCRSA) of 2015, provides, in relevant part:

2525. (a) It is unlawful for a physician and surgeon who recommends cannabis to a patient for a medical purpose to accept, solicit, or offer any form of remuneration from or to a [licensed medical marijuana facility] . . . if the physician and surgeon or his or her immediate family have a financial interest in that facility.

(b) For the purposes of this section, "financial interest" shall have the same meaning as in Section 650.01[. Under Section 650.01, financial interest "includes, but is not limited to, any type of ownership interest, debt, loan, lease, compensation, remuneration, discount, rebate, refund, dividend, distribution, subsidy, or other form of direct or indirect payment, whether in money or otherwise, between a [physician] and a person or entity to whom the [physician] refers a person for a good or service. . . . A financial interest also exists if there is an indirect financial relationship between a [physician] and the referral recipient including, but not limited to, an arrangement whereby a licensee has an ownership interest in an entity that leases property to the referral recipient. . . ."]

(c) A violation of this section shall be a misdemeanor punishable by up to one year in county jail and a fine of up to five thousand dollars ($5,000) or by civil penalties of up to five thousand dollars ($5,000) and shall constitute unprofessional conduct.

. . .

2525.2. An individual who possesses a license in good standing to practice medicine or osteopathy issued by the Medical Board of California or the Osteopathic Medical Board of California shall not recommend medical cannabis to a patient, unless that person is the patient's attending physician[, defined as "an individual who possesses a license in good standing to practice medicine or osteopathy issued by the Medical Board of California or the Osteopathic Medical Board of California and who has taken responsibility for an aspect of the medical care, treatment, diagnosis, counseling, or referral of a patient and who has conducted a medical examination of that patient before recording in the patient's medical record the physician's assessment of whether the patient has a serious medical condition and whether the medical use of marijuana is appropriate." Cal. Health & Safety Code § 11362.7.]

2525.3. Recommending medical cannabis to a patient for a medical purpose without an appropriate prior examination and a medical indication constitutes unprofessional conduct.

2525.4. It is unprofessional conduct for any attending physician recommending medical cannabis to be employed by, or enter into any other agreement with, any person or entity dispensing medical cannabis.

2525.5. (a) A person shall not distribute any form of advertising for physician recommendations for medical cannabis in California unless the advertisement bears the following notice to consumers:

> NOTICE TO CONSUMERS: The Compassionate Use Act of 1996 ensures that seriously ill Californians have the right to obtain and use cannabis for medical purposes where medical use is deemed appropriate and has been recommended by a physician who has determined that the person's health would benefit from the use of medical cannabis. Recommendations must come from an attending physician as defined in Section 11362.7 of the Health and Safety Code. Cannabis is a Schedule I drug according to the federal Controlled Substances Act. Activity related to cannabis use is subject to federal prosecution, regardless of the protections provided by state law.

(b) Advertising for attending physician recommendations for medical cannabis shall meet all of the requirements in Section 651 [prohibiting, inter alia, false, fraudulent, or misleading health claims]. Price advertising shall not be fraudulent, deceitful, or misleading, including statements or advertisements of bait, discounts, premiums, gifts, or statements of a similar nature.

Cal. Bus. & Prof. Code §§ 2525-2525.5 (2016).

**Colorado:**

Colorado too has expanded upon its regulations of relevant physician practices over the years. As of 2016, Colorado law provides the following legal protections for physicians:

> It shall be an exception from the state's criminal laws for any physician to:
>
> (I) Advise a patient whom the physician has diagnosed as having a debilitating medical condition, about the risks and benefits of medical use of marijuana or that he or she might benefit from the medical use of marijuana, provided that such advice is based upon the physician's contemporaneous assessment of the patient's medical history and current medical condition and a bona fide physician-patient relationship; or
>
> (II) Provide a patient with written documentation, based upon the physician's contemporaneous assessment of the patient's medical history and current medical condition and a bona fide physician-patient relationship, stating that the patient has a debilitating medical condition and might benefit from the medical use of marijuana.
>
> No physician shall be denied any rights or privileges for the acts authorized by this subsection.

Colo. Const. art. xviii, § 14(c).

Colorado laws also imposes the following restrictions and obligations on physicians:

> A physician who certifies a debilitating medical condition for an applicant to the medical marijuana program shall comply with all of the following requirements:
>
> (a) The physician shall have a valid and active license to practice medicine, which license is in good standing.
>
> (b) After a physician, who has a bona fide physician-patient relationship with the patient applying for the medical marijuana program, determines, for the purposes of making a recommendation, that the patient has a debilitating medical condition and that the patient may benefit from the use of medical marijuana, the physician shall certify to the state health agency that the patient has a debilitating medical condition and that the patient may benefit from the use of medical marijuana. If the physician certifies that the patient would benefit from the use of medical marijuana based on a chronic or debilitating disease or medical condition, the physician shall specify the chronic or debilitating disease or medical condition and, if known, the cause or source of the chronic or debilitating disease or medical condition.
>
> (c) The physician shall maintain a record-keeping system for all patients for whom the physician has recommended the medical use of marijuana. . . .
>
> (d) A physician shall not:
>
> (I) Accept, solicit, or offer any form of pecuniary remuneration from or to a primary caregiver, distributor, or any other provider of medical marijuana;
>
> (II) Offer a discount or any other thing of value to a patient who uses or agrees to use a particular primary caregiver, distributor, or other provider of medical marijuana to procure medical marijuana;

(III) Examine a patient for purposes of diagnosing a debilitating medical condition at a location where medical marijuana is sold or distributed; or

(IV) Hold an economic interest in an enterprise that provides or distributes medical marijuana if the physician certifies the debilitating medical condition of a patient for participation in the medical marijuana program.

Colo. Rev. Stat. § 25-1.5-106(5).

**Massachusetts:**

Massachusetts 2012 Humanitarian Medical Use of Marijuana Act provides that:

A physician, and other health care professionals under a physician's supervision, shall not be penalized under Massachusetts law, in any manner, or denied any right or privilege, for:

(a) Advising a qualifying patient about the risks and benefits of medical use of marijuana; or

(b) Providing a qualifying patient with written certification, based upon a full assessment of the qualifying patient's medical history and condition, that the medical use of marijuana may benefit a particular qualifying patient.

Mass. Gen. Laws ch. 94C App., § 1-3 (2012).

Regulations promulgated to implement the Act further define the obligations of physicians who recommend marijuana to their patients:

(A) A physician who wishes to issue a written certification for a qualifying patient shall have at least one established place of practice in Massachusetts and shall hold:

(1) An active full license, with no prescribing restriction, to practice medicine in Massachusetts; and

(2) A Massachusetts Controlled Substances Registration from the Department [of Public Health].

(B) To register as a certifying physician, a physician shall submit, in a form and manner determined by the Department, the physician's:

(1) Full name and business address;

(2) License number issued by the Massachusetts Board of Registration in Medicine;

(3) Massachusetts Controlled Substances Registration number; and

(4) Any other information required by the Department.

(C) Once registered by the Department, a certifying physician will retain indefinitely a registration to certify a debilitating medical condition for a qualifying patient unless:

(1) The physician's license to practice medicine in Massachusetts is suspended, revoked, or restricted with regard to prescribing, or the physician has voluntarily agreed not to practice medicine in Massachusetts;

(2) The physician's Massachusetts Controlled Substances Registration is suspended or revoked;

(3) The physician has fraudulently issued a written certification of a debilitating medical condition;

(4) The physician has certified a qualifying patient for a debilitating medical condition . . . without appropriate completion of continuing professional development credits pursuant to [section 725.010(A)]; or

(5) The physician surrenders his or her registration.

(D) After registering, a certifying physician is responsible for notifying the Department, in a form and manner determined by the Department, within five business days after any changes to the physician's information.

105 C.M.R. § 725.005.

(A) A certifying physician issuing a written certification . . . must have completed a minimum of 2.0 Category 1 continuing professional development credits . . . Such program must explain the proper use of marijuana, including side effects, dosage, and contraindications, including with psychotropic drugs, as well as on substance abuse recognition, diagnosis, and treatment related to marijuana.

(B) A certifying physician issuing a written certification shall comply with generally accepted standards of medical practice. . . .

. . .

(D) A certifying physician may issue a written certification only for a qualifying patient with whom the physician has a *bona fide* physician-patient relationship. [Bona Fide Physician-patient Relationship means a relationship between a certifying physician, acting in the usual course of his or her professional practice, and a patient in which the physician has conducted a clinical visit, completed and documented a full assessment of the patient's medical history and current medical condition, has explained the potential benefits and risks of marijuana use, and has a role in the ongoing care and treatment of the patient. § 725.004.]

(E) Before issuing a written certification, a certifying physician must utilize the Massachusetts Prescription Monitoring Program, unless otherwise specified by the Department, to review the qualifying patient's prescription history.

. . .

(G) An initial written certification submitted before a clinical visit is prohibited. A renewal written certification may be submitted after a clinical visit or a telephonic consultation, however a clinical visit must occur no less than once per year.

. . .

. . .

(K) A certifying physician, and such physician's co-worker, employee, or immediate family member, shall not:

(1) Have ever directly or indirectly accepted or solicited from, or offered to an [Registered Marijuana Dispensary (RMD)], a board member or executive of an RMD, any RMD personnel, or any other person associated with an RMD, or a personal caregiver, anything of value;

(2) Offer a discount or any other thing of value to a qualifying patient based on the patient's agreement or decision to use a particular personal caregiver or RMD;

(3) Examine or counsel a patient, or issue a written certification, at an RMD;

(4) Have a direct or indirect financial interest in an RMD; or

(5) Directly or indirectly benefit from a patient obtaining a written certification, which shall not prohibit the physician from charging an appropriate fee for the clinical visit.

(L) A certifying physician shall not issue a written certification for himself or herself or for his or her immediate family members.

*Id.* at § 725.010.

## Notes and Questions

1. What are the main differences in the regulations excerpted above? Along these lines, consider the following Problems:

Problem 12.7: Same facts as **Problem 12.5**. Dr. Delilah is licensed by the state to practice medicine. This time, however, suppose that Dr. Delilah conducted

only a cursory (one-minute) examination of the patient, whom she has never seen before. She calls herself "The Pot Doc," and her advertisements say "Come in for your medical marijuana evaluation. Only $40! If you don't get your medical marijuana card, the visit is free!" Her patient proceeds to acquire a small amount of marijuana. Has Dr. Delilah violated any of the regulations excerpted above? Even so, could she assert a defense under *Conant*? *Cf. Revocation of Registration*, 67 Fed. Reg. 78015-03 (Dec. 20, 2002).

**Problem 12.8**: Andy suffers from several debilitating medical conditions that cause him significant abdominal and bladder pain and nausea. When his primary care physician refused to recommend marijuana for his condition, Andy mailed a packet of materials to Dr. Delilah, who is licensed by the state to practice medicine. The packet contained Andy's own written statement of his medical history and letters from his primary care physician describing his medical condition in detail. Based solely on the written materials that Andy sent her, Dr. Delilah signed a statement concluding that Andy "has a qualifying condition and might benefit from the medical use of marijuana" as part of Andy's application to register under the state's medical marijuana law. Has Dr. Delilah violated any of the regulations excerpted above? Even so, could she assert a defense under *Conant*? See *Oregon v. Miles*, 104 P.3d 604 (Or. App. 2005).

2. State regulations normally shield physicians from civil and criminal sanctions imposed under *state* law, but could they also shield physicians from sanctions that might be imposed under *federal* law? Does *United States v. McIntosh*, 833 F.3d 1163 (9th Cir. 2016), provide an answer? For a discussion of *McIntosh*, see Chapter 7.

3. Many states bar physicians from having a financial interest or contractual relationship with a marijuana supplier. See Cal. Bus. & Prof. Code § 2525.4; Colo. Rev. Stat. § 25-1.5-106(5)(d)(I); 105 C.M.R. § 725.010(K)(1). See also Kay Lazar & Shelley Murphy, *DEA Targets Doctors Linked to Medical Marijuana*, Boston Globe (Jun. 6, 2014) (reporting that the DEA has also warned physicians that having a financial interest in a medical marijuana dispensary could jeopardize their DEA registration). Such prohibitions are not unique to marijuana; many states likewise bar physicians from referring patients to health care providers (e.g., testing laboratories) in which they have a financial interest. *E.g.*, Cal. Bus. & Prof. Code § 650.01. These rules are designed to eliminate the conflict of interest that arises when a physician benefits financially from a patient's use of marijuana (or other services).

4. A few states, including New York, also require physicians to complete special training on the medical use of marijuana before recommending the drug to their patients. *E.g.*, 10 C.R.R.-N.Y. § 1004.1(a) (2016) ("No practitioner shall be authorized to issue a patient certification . . . unless the practitioner . . . has completed a four hour course approved by the commissioner as set forth in subdivision (b) . . ."): *id.* at (b) ("The commissioner shall approve at least one, if not more, courses for practitioners seeking to become registered, which shall be four hours in duration. The educational content of such course shall include: the pharmacology of marihuana; contraindications; side effects; adverse

reactions; overdose prevention; drug interactions; dosing; routes of administration; risks and benefits; warnings and precautions; abuse and dependence; and such other components as determined by the commissioner.").

5. Physicians who flout requirements imposed by state law could lose the legal protections that states provide against civil and criminal sanctions. For one thing, physicians could have their medical licenses suspended or revoked by state medical boards. See In Medical Marijuana States, 'Pot Doctors' Push Boundaries, Associated Press, Nov. 28, 2015, http://www.bigstory.ap.org/article/57cd21046c874c9e8a75cd2340082ac6/medical-marijuana-states-pot-doctors-push-boundaries (discussing disciplinary actions against physicians). In addition, physicians could be prosecuted for crimes related to their violations. *E.g.*, N.Y. Penal Law § 179.10 (McKinney) (2016) (providing that a physician "is guilty of criminal diversion of medical marihuana in the first degree," a class E felony, "when he or she . . . issues a [recommendation] with knowledge of reasonable grounds to know that (i) the recipient has no medical need for it, or (ii) it is for a purpose other than to treat a [qualifying condition]"); *Colorado v. Montante*, 351 P.3d 530 (Col. Ct. App. 2015) (affirming physician's conviction for attempt to influence a public servant; physician had issued false diagnosis to help patient register as medical marijuana patient); *Michigan v. Butler-Jackson*, 862 N.W.2d 423 (Mich. App. 2014), *judgment vacated in part, appeal denied in part on other grounds*, 880 N.W.2d 544 (Mich. 2016) (affirming physician's conviction for falsification of records; physician sold blank medical marijuana recommendations for $250).

### 3. Are Physicians Willing and Able to Recommend Marijuana?

Problem 12.9: Put yourself in the shoes of a physician you know well. Would you recommend marijuana to a patient who suffers from a state-designated qualifying condition? Why, why not?

Notwithstanding the *Conant* decision above enjoining DEA policy (and the DEA's abandonment of that policy), many physicians remain reluctant to recommend marijuana to their patients. In one survey, for example, only 9 percent of Minnesota physicians planned to recommend marijuana to their patients following the launch of the state's medical marijuana program (another 17 percent of the 500 physicians surveyed were as yet undecided). Riham Feshir, *Survey: Minnesota Doctors Taking Wait-and-See Approach to Medical Marijuana*, Minnesota Public Radio News, June 3, 2015. Even in states with more mature medical marijuana programs, only a minority of physicians report having ever recommended the drug to a patient. For example, in a survey of 520 family practitioners in Colorado, conducted more than a decade after the passage of Colorado's original medical marijuana law, only 31 percent reported having ever recommended marijuana to a patient. Elin Kondrad & Alfred Reid, *Colorado Family Physicians' Attitudes Toward Medical Marijuana*, 26 J. Am. Bd. Fam. Med. 52, 55-57 (2013). The apparent reluctance to recommend marijuana has raised concerns that some patients who would benefit from marijuana (at least in the eyes of state lawmakers) might not be able to secure the physician's recommendation they need to possess and use the drug under state law.

Why are some physicians reluctant to recommend marijuana? Apart from the legal risks and burdens discussed above, one possibility is that many physicians are not yet

Figure 12.1. Physician Recommendation History and Attitudes Toward Marijuana*

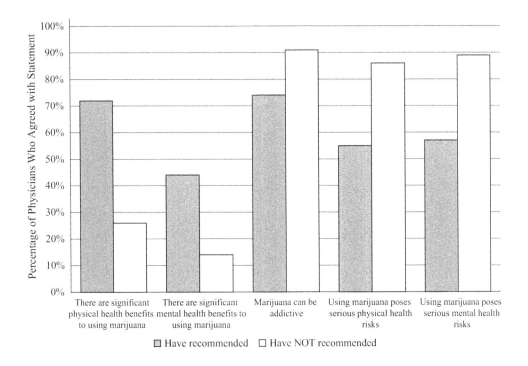

convinced that marijuana might benefit their patients—the conclusion they usually need to reach in order to recommend the drug. The survey of Colorado family physicians noted above, for example, found large and statistically significant differences between the attitudes of physicians who had recommended marijuana to patients and those who had not. Kondrad & Reid, *supra*. **Figure 12.1** compares the attitudes of both groups on five seemingly relevant issues.

Another, related possibility is that physicians do not have enough information to recommend marijuana. *See* Shefali Luthra, *Doctors Face Medical Marijuana Knowledge Gap*, CNN.com, Aug. 23, 2016, https://perma.cc/DWW6-X6WQ. Physicians have a variety of well-known resources they can consult to determine whether *other* drugs might benefit a patient. The Physicians Desk Reference Manual (PDR), for example, includes a wealth of information on all prescription drugs that have been approved by the Food and Drug Administration (FDA). *See* Physicians' Desk Reference (70th ed. 2016). Marijuana, of course, has not yet been approved by the FDA, and thus does not appear in the PDR. As yet, physicians appear to have no comparable resource to which they can turn for marijuana, though one can find a handful of desk references on Amazon.com and similar sites. The lack of such resources might make it difficult for physicians to conclusively determine whether marijuana might benefit a particular patient's condition.

---

*Source: Kondrad & Reid, *Colorado Family Physicians' Attitudes*, supra, at 58, tbl 2.

## Notes and Questions

1. Chapter 5 discussed public media campaigns designed to change popular attitudes toward marijuana, e.g., to make the drug seem more dangerous or less cool. In similar fashion, could state lawmakers attempt to change *physician's* attitudes toward marijuana, e.g., to make the drug seem more beneficial or less harmful? Should lawmakers even try to do this? Why, why not? Would you impose any limits on such a campaign?

2. To bring physicians up to speed with the latest research, some states have organized continuing medical education (CME) courses on medical marijuana. *See supra*, Section A.2. A few states also compile treatment resources for physicians, including summaries of research studies on the use of marijuana to treat various conditions. *E.g.*, Minnesota Department of Health, Medical Cannabis Clinical Information Resources, https://perma.cc/ZDG7-ZYFT. Are such programs likely to increase the number of physicians recommending marijuana?

3. Do physicians have an obligation to recommend marijuana when doing so is warranted by state law? Consider the following Problem:

Problem 12.10: Benjamin is a police officer who has suffered from Post-Traumatic Stress Disorder (PTSD) for several years. On his most recent visit to see his regular physician, Dr. Delilah, Benjamin expressed frustration that none of the treatments she has previously recommended to him—including therapy and drugs like Prozac—have improved his condition. Benjamin lives (and Dr. Delilah practices) in a medical marijuana state that recently added PTSD to its list of qualifying conditions. Benjamin asks Dr. Delilah whether marijuana might be a good option for him, but she tells him: "No. I won't recommend it to you or to anybody else. Pot is a wicked drug." Has Dr. Delilah broken any law or regulation by refusing to recommend marijuana? *See, e.g.*, 745 Ill. Comp. Stat. Ann. 70/6; Wash. Rev. Code Ann. § 69.51A.060. In any event, could Benjamin go to another physician to ask for a marijuana recommendation? *See* Connecticut Department of Consumer Protection, Qualifying Patient FAQs, https://perma.cc/B3PX-YYNR.

4. Ultimately, what portion of the patients who you believe might benefit from the medical use of marijuana are able to get a physician's recommendation? If fewer than all, what, if anything, should states do about it?

### 4. Are Some Physicians Too Willing to Recommend Marijuana?

The flip side of the concern just discussed is that some physicians may be *too willing* to recommend marijuana. The states want physicians to serve as faithful gatekeepers, i.e., to recommend marijuana only to those individuals for whom the drug might provide some medical benefits. But some physicians have engaged in questionable recommendation practices. In California, for example, some medical marijuana clinics purportedly will provide a recommendation to just about anyone willing to pay a fee. *E.g.*, Daniela Drake, *I Got a Weed License in Minutes*, The Daily Beast (June 25, 2014). **Figure 12.2** depicts a medical marijuana clinic in Los Angeles, California. The proliferation of such clinics has even led one commentator to conclude that "it's a cinch to get a marijuana 'recommendation' in California." Steve Lopez, *A Visit to the Medical Marijuana Doctor*, L.A. Times, Oct. 28, 2009).

Figure 12.2. A Medical Marijuana Clinic in Los Angeles, California

The 2015 MCRSA excerpted above was designed in part to combat fraudulent recommendations. But even states that impose regulations and requirements on physicians have detected potential problems with physician recommendation practices. The Colorado State Auditor conducted an audit of the state's medical marijuana program in 2013. Its report, excerpted below, raises several red flags concerning oversight of physician recommendations.

## *Colorado Office of The State Auditor,* Medical Marijuana Regulatory System, Part II (June 2013)

We evaluated the effectiveness of Public Health's oversight of physician recommendations by reviewing the physician certification form and analyzing aggregate, non-personally-identifiable data from Public Health showing the number of Registry patients per physician. We also reviewed studies published about physician characteristics and attitudes relevant to the medical marijuana industry and conducted research on physicians advertising medical marijuana–related services in Colorado. We did not review completed physician certification forms or other application materials submitted by individuals because of [confidentiality restrictions imposed by Colorado law].

Overall, we found evidence suggesting that some physicians are making inappropriate recommendations for medical marijuana or have improper relationships with medical marijuana businesses and are, therefore, helping nonqualifying individuals to gain access to medical marijuana. . . .

**Number of recommendations per physician.** We found that a majority of patients on the Registry were recommended by a small group of physicians who have more medical marijuana patients than appears reasonable. It is not clear exactly how many patients per physician would be too many to allow for a bona fide physician-patient relationship in each case for the purposes of recommending marijuana for medical use. . . . However, a 2005 survey of national physician, patient, and practice characteristics . . . found that U.S. physicians have an average of 2,300 patients each.

Part IV. Third Parties

Figure 12.3. Top Fifty Physicians Recommending Marijuana in Colorado, October 2012*

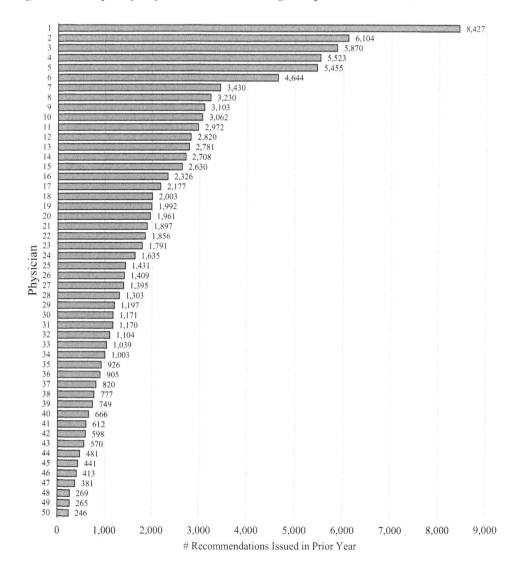

Using this average physician patient load as a benchmark, we analyzed data provided by Public Health to determine how many physicians recommended more than 2,300 patients for the Registry. As of October 2012, a total of 903 physicians had recommended medical marijuana for the roughly 108,000 patients holding valid red cards [i.e.,

---

* Source: Adapted from Colorado Office of the State Auditor, *Medical Marijuana Regulatory System, Part II, supra*, at 24.

medical marijuana registration cards]. Because red cards are valid for 1 year, each of these recommendations would have been made in the year prior to October 2012. We found that 60 percent of these recommendations came from 16 physicians. These 16 physicians had recommended medical marijuana in the preceding year to more patients than the average U.S. physician annual caseload of 2,300 patients. One physician had more than 8,400 recommendations. . . .

. . .

Public Health has had concerns regarding physicians who recommend medical marijuana for large numbers of patients. In January 2011, Public Health identified five physicians as possibly making inappropriate recommendations for medical marijuana and referred those physicians to the Medical Board for investigation. In those cases, the five physicians had each recommended medical marijuana for more than 1,200 individuals in the previous 7-month period and were collectively responsible for more than 22 percent of all recommendations over that period. As a result of Public Health's referrals, the Medical Board found there was reasonable cause to believe that violations of the Medical Practice Act had occurred in four of the five cases that warranted further investigation by the Medical Board. Public Health reported that in one of the four cases, the physician's license was suspended and in another case, there was a "letter of agreement" with the physician that, among other provisions, prohibited the physician from making further medical marijuana recommendations. For the remaining three of the five cases referred to the Medical Board, Public Health reported knowing that all three physicians are still in good standing with the Medical Board but not whether the Medical Board had completed its investigations of these three physicians.

**Physician advertising.** We conducted a basic Internet search and identified 12 websites for Colorado physicians advertising their services for performing evaluations that could result in a recommendation to use medical marijuana. Claims made by these physicians' websites indicated that not all of these medical evaluations would be genuine or objective. . . .

- **Convenience for easy access to marijuana.** All websites we reviewed made claims about the convenient services they provide for getting access to medical marijuana. For example, a number of websites advertised sameday service, where patients can leave the physician's office with all the paperwork they need to be able to purchase marijuana, and other websites advertised night and weekend hours and the availability of walk-in assistance. The claims of convenience for gaining easy access to marijuana suggest that these physicians may not be primarily interested in providing an objective evaluation of the patient's medical condition. For example, one website claimed: "Our company's core business is getting patients registered with the state medical marijuana program by referring patients to intelligent and open minded doctors specializing in medical marijuana."
- **High plant counts.** Three websites we reviewed advertised the availability of getting a recommendation for a higher-than-standard marijuana plant count. In two cases, the website indicated that a higher plant count was available for an additional fee. The third website advertised that it had "highest edible counts," a reference to the physicians being willing to recommend the higher plant counts that are required

to produce edible (i.e., food- and drink-based) marijuana products. While the Constitution allows for higher-than-standard plant counts when "medically necessary to address the patient's medical condition" [art. XVIII, sec. 14(4)(b)], physicians with websites stating that they would be willing to recommend higher plant counts may not be determining the medical necessity for those higher plant counts.

- **Medical records not necessary.** Five websites we reviewed indicated that medical records were not necessary for the medical marijuana evaluation. For example, one website claimed: "No prior medical records are necessary. Our doctors are qualified to provide you with the original diagnosis with or without medical history. If you don't have medical history, that is not a problem." Section 25-1.5-106(2)(a), C.R.S., which defines a bona fide physician-patient relationship, specifies that the physician must complete a full assessment of the patient's medical history and current medical condition before the patient applies for a red card. Physicians who advertise that individuals do not need to bring medical records may not be completing a full assessment of the individual's medical history before recommending medical marijuana for the individual.

- **Refunds and guarantees.** One website advertised the availability of a refund of all the processing fees and half of the medical evaluation fee if the physician finds the patient does not have a qualifying medical condition. Another website guaranteed that the paperwork would be accepted by Public Health. Physicians who guarantee such results may not be conducting objective evaluations of the individual's medical condition.

- **On-site physicians and possible financial ties with dispensaries.** Three websites advertised the availability of on-site physicians where medical marijuana is sold. Section 25-1.5-106(5)(d)(III), C.R.S., prohibits physicians from examining a patient for the purposes of diagnosing a debilitating medical condition at a location where medical marijuana is sold or distributed. We also found three websites that offered discounts or incentives for using certain dispensaries. As previously stated, Section 25-1.5-106(5)(d), C.R.S., prohibits physicians from soliciting or offering any form of monetary payment from or to a medical marijuana provider, or offering a discount or any other thing of value to a patient who uses or agrees to use a particular medical marijuana provider.

Because we could not access personally identifiable Registry data, we could not conduct further audit work to determine the extent to which any of the physicians we found to be advertising had made recommendations for patients currently on the Registry.

**Percentage of patients reporting severe pain.** Data released monthly by Public Health shows that the percentage of individuals on the Registry reporting severe pain as their only qualifying condition has increased sharply in recent years. Specifically, . . . the percentage of patients claiming severe pain as a qualifying condition increased from 87 percent in January 2009 to 94 percent in January 2013. At the same time, the percentage of all other qualifying medical conditions claimed by patients decreased. As a result, these data show that in January 2009 at least 30 percent of Registry patients reported severe pain as their only qualifying medical condition (87 percent with severe pain minus the 57 percent with all other qualifying medical conditions), whereas in January 2013, at least 59 percent of Registry patients reported severe pain as their only qualifying medical condition (94 percent with severe pain minus the 35 percent with all other qualifying medical conditions).

. . .

The high percentage of patients reporting severe pain as a qualifying medical condition has raised concerns about the diagnosis. For example, staff reported that in 2010 when the percentage of patients reporting severe pain as a qualifying condition crossed the 90 percent threshold, they received a legislative inquiry. As a result, they added a question to the physician certification form asking physicians to identify the cause or source of the severe pain, if known.

It is important to note that because we could not access personally identifiable information from the Registry, we were unable to analyze trends in medical conditions reported by patients, such as whether patients reporting only severe pain were more likely to have been referred by a physician with a higher than reasonable patient count or one that includes questionable claims in his or her advertising.

**Extremely high plant counts.** We analyzed a subset of data provided by Public Health showing aggregated data for patients with caregivers and found evidence that some patients have had what appear to be higher than reasonable plant counts recommended for them by their physicians. For example, in one case, the physician had recommended 501 plants for the patient, and in another case, the physician had recommended 75 ounces of useable marijuana for the patient. Although an increased plant and ounce count over the standard six plants and 2 ounces may be appropriate for a patient who is consuming marijuana through edibles or tinctures (as opposed to smoking), a dispensary owner we spoke to during the audit reported that no patient should need more than 25 plants to make his or her edible or tincture products. We also heard anecdotal evidence from law enforcement officials and the dispensary owner about physicians who routinely mark patients down for increased plant and ounce counts, regardless of the patient's need for an increased count.

**Anecdotal data.** We identified two studies with anecdotal evidence suggesting that not all patients on the Registry have a legitimate, qualifying medical condition. For example, a 2013 study of Colorado family physicians published in The Journal of the American Board of Family Medicine reported that a significant number of physicians surveyed believe that medical marijuana is being used predominantly by people who are well but want legal protection for recreational marijuana use. The study also found that the physicians in the study who had recommended medical marijuana for their patients reported severe pain as a qualifying condition in 76 percent of cases, compared to the 87 to 94 percent reported in the Registry population overall. These results led the researchers to conclude, "The gulf between physicians who are providing medical marijuana recommendations as a substantial portion of their practice and primary care providers who are far more likely to have a continuity relationship with a patient suggests that a continuity relationship influences provider behavior related to medical marijuana and may lead to a more judicious recommendation of medical marijuana."

## Notes and Questions

1. Are you troubled by the Colorado Auditor's report? How serious are the problems it identifies with Colorado's medical marijuana program?

2. The Colorado Auditor also made several recommendations to address the problems it identified. *Id.* at 33-36. In response, in 2015 the Colorado Department of Public Health and Environment adopted a new policy to boost supervision of physician recommendations. In relevant part, the new policy provides:

> . . . This policy outlines the criteria that the department [of Public Health] will use to refer recommending physicians to the Colorado Department of Regulatory Agencies (DORA) Medical Board, as the state entity with the investigative authority and expertise to evaluate physician conduct and take licensing actions as deemed appropriate.
>
> . . .
>
> A. Referral to Colorado Department of Regulatory Agencies {DORA}. The department will identify physicians for referral using the following procedure:
>
> 1. Physician Certifications
>
> The department will conduct a statistical review of physician recommendations to determine if there is reasonable cause to refer a physician to the Colorado Medical Board based upon the following factors:
>
> a) Physician caseload as determined by the number of patients for whom medical marijuana is recommended. A high caseload is calculated as 3,521 or more patient recommendations in one year for a general practitioner. This reflects the recommendation of patients equal to or greater than the national average of patient visits per year for a generalist physician as reported by the Centers for Disease Control and Prevention. . . .
>
> b) The plant and ounce recommendations by the physician. Physician certification forms with a plant count recommendation above the constitutional standard six plants and two ounces will be referred to DORA for review:
>
> (a) Physicians recommending increased plant counts for more than 30% of their caseload may be recommended for referral.
>
> (b) The physician's area of specialty will be taken into consideration when considering the appropriateness of a higher rate of increased plant/ounce count recommendations.
>
> c) Age demographics of the patient caseload. According to the CDC, older adults have a significantly higher prevalence of chronic conditions than younger adults. . . . Physicians for whom more than one-third of the patient caseload is under the age of 30 may be recommended for referral.
>
> 2. Other Circumstances
>
> The Department will also refer physicians to the Medical Board for whom there is evidence of potential violation of the constitution, statutes, Board of Health regulations or any violation of the Colorado Medical Practice Act. . . . These referrals may include:
>
> a) Patient safety concerns given the physician's training in a field which raises questions as to his/her ability to competently evaluate and treat minor patients and those who have clinical conditions not in the physician's prescribed area of specialty/expertise;
>
> b) Potential substandard care of patients by physicians making patient recommendations for the use of medical marijuana; or
>
> c) Other information known or received by CDPHE that may constitute a violation of the Medical Practice Act. . . .

B. Department sanctions. Once the referral is received, DORA will review the documentation and conduct an investigation as deemed appropriate. If sufficient evidence is found, DORA may provide information to the Office of the Attorney General pursuant to board policy for criminal investigation and may impose disciplinary action. . . .

If provided with sufficient evidence from DORA or the Office of the Attorney General or some other credible source the Department will revoke a physician's authority to authorize Medical Marijuana. . . .

Colorado Medical Marijuana Registry, *Medical Marijuana Policy Number* 2015-01_001 (Apr. 2, 2015). Do the policy changes adopted by the Department adequately address the issues raised in the Colorado Auditor's report? If not, what other steps should the Department take?

3. The Colorado policy calls for closer scrutiny of physicians who make a large number of recommendations in a year. What do you think of this tactic? Is the suspicion around these physicians warranted? If so, what number of recommendations should trigger closer scrutiny? *Compare* Colorado Medical Marijuana Registry, *Medical Marijuana Policy*, *supra* (calling for investigation of physicians who make 3,521 or more recommendations in a year) *with* Mont. Code Ann. § 50-46-303(10)(a) (West) (calling for investigation of physicians who make 25 or more recommendations in a year).

4. Between 2009-2015, the Colorado Medical Board sanctioned a total of six physicians for inappropriately recommending marijuana. *In Medical Marijuana States, "Pot Doctors" Push Boundaries*, Associated Press, Nov. 28, 2015, http://www.bigstory.ap.org/article/57cd21046c874c9e8a75cd2340082ac6/medical-marijuana-states-pot-doctors-push-boundaries. The Board suspended the licenses of four additional physicians in July 2016 because they had recommended excessive plant counts for their patients. John Ingold, *Four Colorado Doctors Suspended over Medical Marijuana Recommendations*, Denver Post, July 19, 2016, http://www.denverpost.com/2016/07/19/four-colorado-doctors-suspended-over-medical-marijuana-recommendations/.

5. Other states have reported similar statistics concerning the distribution of physician recommendations. In Oregon, for example, 1,722 physicians recommended marijuana to a total of 73,619 patients in 2015. However, 22 of those physicians (roughly 1 percent of the group) accounted for more than 75 percent of all recommendations (55,217 of the total). *See* Oregon Health Authority, Oregon Medical Marijuana Program Statistical Snapshot 6 (Apr. 2016), https://perma.cc/JT3B-93GS.

6. How do states police prescriptions for other controlled substances? To combat abuse of prescription drugs, nearly every state has implemented a Prescription Drug Monitoring Program (PDMP). For a description of these programs, see National Alliance for Model State Drug Laws, *2015 Annual Review of Prescription Monitoring Programs* (Sept. 2015), https://perma.cc/D8ZE-EYBY. PDMPs track prescriptions for controlled substances from the time when they are issued by physicians to the time when they are filled by pharmacists. State officials then use the data to detect potential prescription drug mills, among other things. At least one federal agency has suggested that PDMPs are "among the most promising state-level interventions to improve opioid prescribing, inform clinical practice, and protect patients at risk." Center for Disease Control, Prescription Drug Monitoring Programs (PDMPs), https://perma.cc/822Q-PJR6.

State medical marijuana registries collect similar data that could be used to identify marijuana recommendation mills. The Colorado Auditor, for example, used registry data to complete its report. But how do states without medical marijuana registries monitor physician recommendation practices? See Lisa Leff, *Number of California's Medical Pot Smokers is Unknown*, Monterey Herald News, March 24, 2012, https://perma.cc/PN9C-U3GZ. Should all states require registration in order to improve their monitoring of physician recommendation practices?

## B. ATTORNEYS

As discussed in Chapter 1, there is strong demand for attorneys to help clients navigate the complicated rules governing the use and supply of marijuana. But what legal services may attorneys perform in this field? Does an attorney who negotiates a lease on behalf of a state-licensed marijuana supplier violate state rules of professional conduct? What if the attorney uses marijuana herself? Regardless, can the attorney be disciplined by a federal court? The following materials address these and related questions.

### 1. What Services May Attorneys Provide to Marijuana Users and Suppliers?

In addition to regulations that apply to the general population, attorneys are also subject to rules of professional conduct that govern the legal profession. All states have adopted some version of the American Bar Association's ("ABA") Model Rules of Professional Conduct. Geoffrey C. Hazard et al., The Law of Lawyering § 1.01 (4th ed. 2015). "Most federal courts have adopted disciplinary rules based on the applicable rules in the state in which they sit," *id.*, though they sometimes make exceptions (as discussed in Section B.3 below). Attorneys who flout these rules risk sanctions, including censure or even disbarment from the practice of law.

Rule 1.2(d) is particularly relevant to attorneys working in the field of marijuana law:

> A lawyer shall not counsel a client to engage, or assist a client, in conduct that the lawyer knows is criminal or fraudulent, but a lawyer may discuss the legal consequences of any proposed course of conduct with a client and may counsel or assist a client to make a good faith effort to determine the validity, scope, meaning or application of the law.

Model Rules of Professional Conduct Rule 1.2(d) (2012). The ABA has also promulgated comments concerning the meaning and application of Rule 1.2:

> [9] Paragraph (d) prohibits a lawyer from knowingly counseling or assisting a client to commit a crime or fraud. This prohibition, however, does not preclude the lawyer from giving an honest opinion about the actual consequences that appear likely to result from a client's conduct. Nor does the fact that a client uses advice in a course of action that is criminal or fraudulent of itself make a lawyer a party to the course of action. There is a critical distinction between presenting an analysis of legal aspects of questionable conduct and recommending the means by which a crime or fraud might be committed with impunity.
>
> [10] When the client's course of action has already begun and is continuing, the lawyer's responsibility is especially delicate. The lawyer is required to avoid assisting the client, for

example, by drafting or delivering documents that the lawyer knows are fraudulent or by suggesting how the wrongdoing might be concealed. A lawyer may not continue assisting a client in conduct that the lawyer originally supposed was legally proper but then discovers is criminal or fraudulent. The lawyer must, therefore, withdraw from the representation of the client in the matter. . . .

. . .

[12] . . . Paragraph (d) does not preclude undertaking a criminal defense incident to a general retainer for legal services to a lawful enterprise. The last clause of paragraph (d) recognizes that determining the validity or interpretation of a statute or regulation may require a course of action involving disobedience of the statute or regulation or of the interpretation placed upon it by governmental authorities.

*Id.* at Cmt. 1.2.

Interestingly, jurisdictions with similar laws have come to quite different conclusions about the implications of Rule 1.2(d) for attorneys who work in this field. The sections below examine the two competing positions states have taken regarding the services that attorneys may provide to marijuana users and suppliers. Both sections draw on ethics opinions issued by state disciplinary boards. While these opinions are not strictly binding, they are considered highly persuasive authority.

### a. The Restrictive Interpretation of Rule 1.2

## Ohio Supreme Court, Board of Professional Conduct, Ethical Implications for Lawyers under Ohio's Medical Marijuana Law
Opinion 2016-6 (Aug. 5, 2016)

The conflict between the Ohio and federal marijuana laws complicates the application of the Rules of Professional Conduct for Ohio lawyers. While Ohio law permits certain conduct by its citizens and grants immunity from prosecution for certain state crimes for the cultivation, processing, sale, and use of medical marijuana, the same conduct constitutes a federal crime, despite instructions to U.S. attorneys from the current administration to not vigorously enforce the law and therefore implicates Prof. Cond. R. 1.2 for lawyers with clients seeking to engage in activities permissible under state law.

. . .

A lawyer cannot assist a client who engages or seeks to engage in conduct the lawyer knows to be illegal. Prof. Cond. R. 1.2(d). . . . Prof. Cond. R. 1.2(d) embodies a lawyer's important role in promoting compliance with the law by providing legal advice and assistance in structuring clients' conduct in accordance with the law. The rule underscores an essential role of lawyers in preventing clients from engaging in conduct that is criminal in nature or when the legality of the proposed conduct is unclear. . . .

Prof. Cond. R. 1.2(d) does not distinguish between illegal client conduct that will, or will not, be enforced by the federal government. The first inquiry of a lawyer is whether the legal services to be provided can be construed as assisting the client in conduct that is a violation of either state or federal law. If the answer is in the affirmative under either law, Prof. Cond. R. 1.2(d) precludes the lawyer from providing those legal services to the client.

Under Prof. Cond. R. 1.2(d), a lawyer cannot deliver legal services to assist a client in the establishment and operation of a state regulated marijuana enterprise that is illegal under federal law. The types of legal services that cannot be provided under the rule include, but are not limited to, the completion and filing of marijuana license applications, negotiations with regulated individuals and businesses, representation of clients before state regulatory boards responsible for the regulation of medical marijuana, the drafting and negotiating of contracts with vendors for resources or supplies, the drafting of lease agreements for property to be used in the cultivation, processing, or sale of medical marijuana, commercial paper, tax, zoning, corporate entity formation, and statutory agent services. . . . Similarly, a lawyer cannot represent a property owner, lessor, supplier or business in transactions with a marijuana regulated entity, if the lawyer knows the transferred property, facilities, goods or supplies will be used to engage in conduct that is illegal under federal law. Even though the completion of any of these services or transactions may be permissible under Ohio law, and a lawyer's assistance can facilitate their completion, the lawyer ultimately would be assisting the client in engaging in conduct that the lawyer knows to be illegal under federal law.

However, Prof. Cond. R. 1.2(d) does not foreclose certain advice and counsel to a client seeking to participate in the Ohio medical marijuana industry. Prof. Cond. R. 1.2(d) also provides:

> A lawyer may discuss the legal consequences of any proposed course of conduct with a client and may counsel or assist a client in making a good faith effort to determine the validity, scope, meaning, or application of the law.

This portion of the rule permits a lawyer to explain to the client the conflict that currently exists between state and federal law, the consequences of engaging in conduct that is permissible under Ohio law but contrary to federal law, and the likelihood of federal enforcement given the policies of the current administration. A lawyer may counsel and advise a client regarding the scope and general requirements of the Ohio medical marijuana law, the meaning of its provisions, and how the law would be applied to a client's proposed conduct. A lawyer also can advise a client concerning good faith arguments regarding the validity of the federal or state law and its application to the client's proposed conduct.

In addition to the permissible range of advice permitted under Prof. Cond. R. 1.2(d), the rule does not preclude a lawyer from representing a client charged with violating the state medical marijuana law, representing a professional license holder before state licensing boards, representing an employee in a wrongful discharge action due to medical marijuana use, or aiding a government client in the implementation and administration of the state's regulated licensing program. With regard to the latter, lawyers assisting a government client at the state or local level in the establishment, operation, or implementation of the state medical marijuana regulatory system are not advising or assisting the client in conduct that directly violates federal law. The state or a local government is not directly involved in the sale, processing, or dispensing of medical marijuana prohibited by federal law, even though it is arguably enabling the conduct through the issuance of licenses and the maintenance of its regulatory system.

For these reasons, the Board concludes that a lawyer violates Prof. Cond. R. 1.2(d) when he or she transitions from advising a client regarding the consequences of conduct under federal and state law to counseling or assisting the client to engage in conduct the lawyer knows is prohibited under federal law. . . . Unless and until federal law is amended to authorize the use, production, and distribution of medical marijuana, a lawyer only may advise a client as to the legality of conduct either permitted under state law or prohibited under federal law and explain the scope and application of state and federal law to the client's proposed conduct. However, the lawyer cannot provide the types of legal services necessary for a client to establish and operate a medical marijuana enterprise or to transact with medical marijuana businesses. . . .

. . . The Supreme Court may amend the Rules of Professional Conduct to address this conflict. Several jurisdictions have reached similar conclusions to those contained in this opinion and have amended, or are considering amending Rule 1.2 or the comments to that rule. . . .

## Notes and Questions

1. Do you agree with the Ohio Board's interpretation of Rule 1.2(d)? Why, why not? Does the opinion provide clear guidance concerning the services that attorneys may and may not perform for clients? Consider the following Problems:

**Problem 12.11:** Andy is an attorney who is licensed to practice in a recreational marijuana state. Camila tells Andy that she wants to launch a retail marijuana store. Under the state's marijuana law, Camila must first apply for a retail marijuana license from the state. Camila has no legal training. She asks Andy for help in completing the license application, which is 13 pages long and includes many questions for which legal training would be helpful. See, e.g., https://perma.cc/FHX3-KM7U (Colorado retail marijuana license application). If Andy completes the application on behalf of Camila, would he be in violation of Rule 1.2(d) under Ohio's interpretation of the Rule? Suppose Camila completes the application herself, but she asks Andy for help in deciphering the meaning of certain questions on the application (e.g., "Has any interest or share in the profits of the sale of Marijuana been pledged or hypothecated as security for a debt or deposited as a security for the performance of an act or to secure the performance of a contract?"). Can Andy answer Camila's pointed questions under the Ohio opinion?

**Problem 12.12:** Same facts as **Problem 12.11**. Suppose that Andy declined to help Camila. Nonetheless, Camila completed the license application entirely by herself. About a month later, however, Camila received a notice in the mail informing her that her application had been denied by the state licensing agency. Camila asks Andy to help her appeal the state's decision. If Andy helps Camila, would he be in violation of Rule 1.2(d) in Ohio?

**Problem 12.13:** Same facts as **Problem 12.12**. Now suppose that the state granted Camila her license. She launched her retail marijuana shop six months ago. However, after Camila's store failed a recent inspection, the state's licensing agency fined her $10,000. Camila has requested a hearing before the

agency to contest the inspection and fine. She asks Andy to represent her at the hearing. Can he do so under Ohio's opinion? What if Camila asks Andy to help bring her shop into compliance with state regulations, in order to avoid future fines; may Andy help her with this task? Now suppose that the federal DEA hears about Camila's compliance problems. They quickly charge her with distributing marijuana in violation of 21 U.S.C. section 841. Camila asks Andy to represent her in the criminal prosecution. If Andy does so, would he be in violation of Rule 1.2(d)?

2. As the Ohio Board opinion notes, several states that have reached similar conclusions regarding the application of existing Rule 1.2(d) have amended their Rules to expressly permit attorneys to serve clients who they know are violating federal marijuana laws. Indeed, just months after the Ohio Board issued its opinion, the Ohio Supreme Court added the following language to Rule 1.2(d), which expressly allows an attorney to:

> (2) . . . counsel or assist a client regarding conduct expressly permitted under [Ohio's medical marijuana laws]. In these circumstances, the lawyer shall advise the client regarding related federal law.

Ohio Rules of Prof. Conduct Rule 1.2 (adopted Sept. 20, 2016). *See also* Illinois Rules of Prof. Conduct Rule 1.2 (similar); Connecticut Rules of Prof. Conduct Rule 1.2(d)(3) (2015) (similar); Hawai'i Rules of Prof. Conduct Rule 1.2 (similar) (2014); Oregon Rules of Prof. Conduct Rule 1.2 (similar) (2015).

Rather than changing the language of Rule 1.2(d), a few other states have instead added new comments to their Rules to achieve a similar result. For example, after the Colorado Bar Association Ethics Committee concluded that attorneys were not allowed to perform some services for clients in the marijuana industry, see *The Extent to Which Lawyers May Represent Clients Regarding Marijuana-Related Activities*, 42 Colo. Law. 19 (Dec. 2013), the Colorado Supreme Court approved a new comment to Rule 1.2(d) to permit such services. In particular, Comment 14 to the Colorado Rules now provides:

> A lawyer may counsel a client regarding the validity, scope, and meaning of Colorado constitution [provisions regarding medical and recreational marijuana] and may assist a client in conduct that the lawyer reasonably believes is permitted by these constitutional provisions and the statutes, regulations, orders, and other state or local provisions implementing them. In these circumstances, the lawyer shall also advise the client regarding related federal law and policy.

Colorado Rules of Prof. Conduct Rule 1.2, cmt. 14 (2014). *See also* Nevada Rules of Prof. Conduct Rule 1.2, cmt. 1 (2014) (similar).

3. Like other contractors, attorneys may have difficulty collecting from clients in the marijuana industry if those clients have had (or might later have) their assets seized by the federal government. For a discussion of forfeiture sanctions applicable to marijuana users and suppliers, see Chapters 3 and 7. Importantly, the government may seize assets even when the client needs them to pay attorney's fees in a criminal case. See *Caplin &*

*Drysdale, Chartered v. United States*, 491 U.S. 617 (1989) (rejecting claim brought in drug forfeiture case that forfeiture violated Sixth Amendment and Due Process Clauses).

### b. The Permissive Interpretation of Rule 1.2

Now consider the opinion of the New York State Bar Association, which has reached a different conclusion regarding the application of existing Rule 1.2(d).

## New York State Bar Association Committee on Professional Ethics, Counseling Clients in Illegal Conduct; Medical Marijuana Law
### Opinion 1024 (Sept. 29, 2014)

1. In July 2014, New York, following the lead of 22 other states, adopted the Compassionate Care Act ("CCA") 1, a law permitting the use of medical marijuana in tightly controlled circumstances. The CCA regulates the cultivation, distribution, prescription and use of marijuana for medical purposes. . . .

2. At the same time, federal criminal law forbids the possession, distribution, sale or use of marijuana, and the federal law provides no exception for medical uses. . . . [H]owever, the U.S. Department of Justice has adopted and published formal guidance restricting federal enforcement of the federal marijuana prohibition when individuals and entities act in accordance with state regulation of medical marijuana.

. . .

3. Under these unusual circumstances, do the New York Rules of Professional Conduct ("Rules") permit a lawyer to provide legal advice and assistance to doctors, patients, public officials, hospital administrators, and others engaged in the cultivation, distribution, prescribing, dispensing, regulation, possession, or use of marijuana for medical purposes to help them act in compliance with state regulation regarding medical marijuana and consistently with federal enforcement policy?

. . .

4. Lawyers may advise clients about the lawfulness of their proposed conduct and assist them in complying with the law, but lawyers may not knowingly assist clients in illegal conduct. [Rule 1.2(d).] . . . As this Committee has observed, if a client proposes to engage in conduct that is illegal, "then it would be unethical for an attorney to recommend the action or assist the client in carrying it out." . . .

5. This ethical restriction reflects lawyers' fundamental role in the administration of justice, which is to promote compliance with the law by providing legal advice and assistance in structuring clients' conduct in accordance with the law. . . . Ideally, lawyers will not only attempt to prevent clients from engaging in knowing illegalities but also discourage clients from conduct of doubtful legality:

> The most effective realization of the law's aims often takes place in the attorney's office, . . . where the lawyer's quiet counsel takes the place of public force. Contrary to popular belief, the compliance with the law thus brought about is not generally lip-serving and narrow, for by reminding him of its long-run costs the lawyer often deters his client from a course of conduct technically permissible under existing law, though inconsistent with its underlying spirit and purpose. . . .

> The reasons that justify and even require partisan advocacy in the trial of a cause do not grant any license to the lawyer to participate as legal adviser in a line of conduct that is immoral, unfair, or of doubtful legality.

Am. Bar Ass'n & Ass'n of Am. Law Sch., Professional Responsibility Report of the Joint Conference, 44 A.B.A. J. 1159, 1161 (1958). The public importance of lawyers' role in promoting clients' legal compliance is reflected in the attorney-client privilege, which protects the confidentiality that is traditionally considered essential in order for lawyers to serve this role effectively. . . .

6. It is counter-intuitive to suppose that the lawyer's fundamental role might ever be served by assisting clients in violating a law that the lawyer knows to be valid and enforceable. But the question presented by the state's medical marijuana law is highly unusual if not unique: Although participating in the production, delivery or use of medical marijuana violates federal criminal law as written, the federal government has publicly announced that it is limiting its enforcement of this law, and has acted accordingly, insofar as individuals act consistently with state laws that legalize and extensively regulate medical marijuana. Both the state law and the publicly announced federal enforcement policy presuppose that individuals and entities will comply with new and intricate state regulatory law and, thus, presuppose that lawyers will provide legal advice and assistance to an array of public and private actors and institutions to promote their compliance with state law and current federal policy. Under these unusual circumstances, for the reasons discussed below, the Committee concludes that Rule 1.2(d) does not forbid lawyers from providing the necessary advice and assistance.

. . .

12. Lawyers might provide a range of assistance to clients seeking to comply with the CCA and to act consistently with federal law enforcement policy. Among the potential clients are public officials and agencies including the Health Department that have responsibility for implementing the law, health care providers and other entities that may apply to be selected or eventually be selected as Registered Organizations authorized to manufacture and dispense medical marijuana, physicians seeking to prescribe medical marijuana, and patients with severely debilitating or life-threatening conditions seeking to obtain medical marijuana. Any or all of these potential clients may seek legal assistance not only so that they may be advised how to comply with the state law and avoid running afoul of federal enforcement policy but also for affirmative legal assistance. The Health Department may seek lawyers' help in establishing internal procedures to conduct the registrations and other activities contemplated by the law. Entities may seek assistance in applying to become Registered Organizations as well as in understanding and complying with employment, tax and other requirements of the law. Physicians may seek help in understanding the severe restrictions on the issuance of prescriptions for medical marijuana and in navigating the procedural requirements for effectively issuing such prescriptions.

13. Leaving aside the federal law, the above-described legal assistance would be entirely consistent with lawyers' conventional role in helping clients comply with the law. Indeed, it seems fair to say that state law would not only permit but affirmatively expect lawyers to provide such assistance. In general, it is assumed that lawyers, by virtue of their expertise and ethical expectations, have a necessary role in ensuring the public's compliance with the law. "As our society becomes one in which rights and responsibilities

are increasingly defined in legal terms, access to legal services has become of critical importance." Rule 6.1, Cmt. [1]. This is especially true with regard to complex, technical regulatory schemes such as the one established by the CCA, and where, as in the case of the CCA, noncompliance can result in criminal prosecution.

14. However, the federal law cannot easily be left aside. The question of whether lawyers may serve their traditional role is complicated by the federal law. Assuming, as we do for purposes of this opinion, that the federal marijuana prohibition remains valid and enforceable notwithstanding state medical marijuana law, then individuals and entities seeking to dispense, prescribe or use medical marijuana, or to assist others in doing so, pursuant to the CCA would potentially be violating federal narcotics law as principals or accessories; in that event, the legal assistance sought from lawyers might involve assistance in conduct that the lawyer knows to be illegal.

. . .

15. Several other bar association ethics committees have confronted this problem but reached different conclusions under their counterparts to Rule 1.2(d). . . .

. . .

21. As Rule 1.2(d) makes clear, although a lawyer may not encourage a client to violate the law or assist a client in doing so, a lawyer may advise a client about the reach of the law. . . . Thus, a lawyer may give advice about whether undertaking to manufacture, transport, sell, prescribe or use marijuana in accordance with the CCA's regulatory scheme would violate federal narcotics law. If the lawyer were to conclude competently and in good faith that the federal law was inapplicable or invalid, the lawyer could so advise the client and would not be subject to discipline even if the lawyer's advice later proved incorrect. . . .

22. Further, Rule 1.2(d) forbids a lawyer from assisting a client in conduct only if the lawyer knows the conduct is illegal or fraudulent. If the lawyer believes that conduct is unlawful but there is some support for an argument that the conduct is legal, the lawyer may provide legal assistance under the Rules (but is not obligated to do so). . . .

23. The difficult question arises if the lawyer knows that the client's proposed conduct, although consistent with state law, would violate valid and enforceable federal law. Ordinarily, in that event, while the lawyer could advise the client about the reach of the federal law and how to conform to the federal law, the lawyer could not properly encourage or assist the client in conduct that violates the federal law. That would ordinarily be true even if the federal law, although applicable to the client's proposed conduct, was not rigorously enforced and the lawyer anticipated that the law would not be enforced in the client's situation. . . . But the situation is different where the state executive branch determines to implement the state legislation by authorizing and regulating medical marijuana, consistent with current, published federal executive-branch enforcement policy, and the federal government does not take effective measures to prevent the implementation of the state law. In that event, the question under Rule 1.2(d) is whether a lawyer may assist in conduct under the state medical marijuana law that the lawyer knows would violate federal narcotics law that is on the books but deliberately unenforced as a matter of federal executive discretion.

24. . . . We do not believe that by adopting Rule 1.2(d), our state judiciary meant to declare a position on this debate or meant to preclude lawyers from counseling or assisting conduct that is legal under state law. Rule 1.2(d) was based on an ABA model and there is no indication that anyone—not the ABA, not the state bar, and not the state court

itself—specifically considered whether lawyers may serve in their traditional role in this sort of unusual legal situation. We assume for purposes of this Opinion that state courts will themselves serve in their traditional role: As issues of interpretation arise in litigation under the CCA, state courts will be available to issue interpretive rulings and take other judicial action that has the practical effect of assisting in the implementation of the CCA. Serving this role will not undermine state judicial integrity. Similarly, we do not believe that it derogates from public respect for the law and lawyers, or otherwise undermines the objectives of the professional conduct rules, for lawyers as "officers of the court" to serve in their traditional role as well, if they so choose. . . .

25. We conclude that the New York Rules of Professional Conduct permit lawyers to give legal assistance regarding the CCA that goes beyond a mere discussion of the legality of the client's proposed conduct. In general, state professional conduct rules should be interpreted to promote state law, not to impede its effective implementation. . . . [A] state medical-marijuana law establishing a complex regulatory scheme depends on lawyers for its success. Implicitly, the state law authorizes lawyers to provide traditional legal services to clients seeking to act in accordance with the state law. Further, and crucially, in this situation the federal enforcement policy also depends on the availability of lawyers to establish and promote compliance with the "strong and effective regulatory and enforcement systems" that are said to justify federal forbearance from enforcement of narcotics laws that are technically applicable. The contemplated legal work is not designed to escape law enforcement by avoiding detection. . . . Lawyers would assist clients who participate openly and subject to a state regulatory structure that the federal government allows to function as a matter of discretion. Nothing in the history and tradition of the profession, in court opinions, or elsewhere, suggests that Rule 1.2(d) was intended to prevent lawyers in a situation like this from providing assistance that is necessary to implement state law and to effectuate current federal policy. If federal enforcement were to change materially, this Opinion might need to be reconsidered.

. . .

26. In light of current federal enforcement policy, the New York Rules of Professional Conduct permit a lawyer to assist a client in conduct designed to comply with state medical marijuana law, notwithstanding that federal narcotics law prohibits the delivery, sale, possession and use of marijuana and makes no exception for medical marijuana.

## Notes and Questions

1. Which interpretation of existing Rule 1.2 (Ohio's or New York's) do you find more persuasive and why?

2. How do the Ohio and New York interpretations differ in terms of the services each allows attorneys to perform? To make the question more concrete, re-examine **Problems 12.11-12.13** above. Would New York permit Andy (the attorney) to perform any services that Ohio (prior to its amendment of Rule 1.2) would not?

3. What is the relevance of DOJ enforcement guidance for the application of Rule 1.2? In particular, suppose that the DOJ disavowed its enforcement guidance. (For present purposes, ignore any spending restrictions Congress has imposed on the agency.) Would the shift narrow the range of services attorneys could perform for clients in New York or Ohio? Now suppose the DOJ disavowed the guidance but acknowledged that it still would

not prosecute marijuana suppliers because it lacked the resources needed to do so. Same result? Should either stated enforcement policy or enforcement practice matter for purposes of the Rules?

4. Is there any practical difference between existing Rule 1.2 as interpreted by New York and the amended version of Rule 1.2 adopted by states like Ohio (*see supra*)?

5. What impact do legal services have on compliance with marijuana laws? One of the purposes behind Rule 1.2 is to prevent attorneys from lending a "legitimizing or facilitating hand" to clients whom they know are violating the law. Hazard et al., *The Law of Lawyering, supra*, at §6.02. But do attorneys who advise marijuana users and suppliers help increase violations of *federal* marijuana laws? In other words, are clients more likely to buy, sell, use, or grow marijuana if they are able to obtain legal services?

Conversely, do attorneys help reduce violations of *state* marijuana laws? In other words, are clients more likely to comply with state regulations surrounding the possession, use, production, or distribution of marijuana if they are able to obtain legal services? *Cf.* Colorado Bar Association Ethics Committee, *The Extent to Which* . . . , *supra* ("Public policy considerations favor lawyers providing the full range of legal advice . . . so that their clients may comply with Colorado's marijuana use laws. '[I]t too often is overlooked that the lawyer and the law office are indispensable parts of our administration of justice. Law-abiding people can go nowhere else to learn the ever changing and constantly multiplying rules by which they must behave and to obtain redress for their wrongs.' *Hickman v. Taylor*, 329 U.S. 495, 514 (1947) (Jackson, J., concurring).").

## 2. May Attorneys Use or Supply Marijuana?

Rule 1.2(d) applies when an attorney provides services to a client she knows is violating federal law. But what if an attorney uses or supplies marijuana herself? A different Rule arguably governs such conduct:

> It is professional misconduct for a lawyer to:
> . . .
> (b) commit a criminal act that reflects adversely on the lawyer's honesty, trustworthiness or fitness as a lawyer in other respects . . .
> . . .

Model Rules of Professional Conduct Rule 8.4 (2012). The Comments to Rule 8.4 provide, in relevant part:

> [2] Many kinds of illegal conduct reflect adversely on fitness to practice law, such as offenses involving fraud and the offense of willful failure to file an income tax return. However, some kinds of offenses carry no such implication. Traditionally, the distinction was drawn in terms of offenses involving "moral turpitude." That concept can be construed to include offenses concerning some matters of personal morality, such as adultery and comparable offenses, that have no specific connection to fitness for the practice of law. Although a lawyer is personally answerable to the entire criminal law, a lawyer should be professionally answerable only for offenses that indicate lack of those characteristics relevant to law practice. Offenses involving violence, dishonesty, breach of trust, or serious interference with the administration of justice are in that category. A pattern of repeated offenses, even ones of minor significance when considered separately, can indicate indifference to legal obligation.
> . . .

[7] Lawyers holding public office assume legal responsibilities going beyond those of other citizens. A lawyer's abuse of public office can suggest an inability to fulfill the professional role of lawyers. The same is true of abuse of positions of private trust such as trustee, executor, administrator, guardian, agent and officer, director or manager of a corporation or other organization.

*Id.* at Cmt. 8.4.

Though fewer states have addressed the application of Rule 8.4, those that have again appear to disagree about whether the Rule bars attorneys from using and/or supplying marijuana. Some state disciplinary bodies suggest that these activities are sanctionable under Rule 8.4. For example, the Ohio Board opinion excerpted above warned that:

> Under current federal law, an Ohio lawyer's use of medical marijuana, even obtained through a state regulated prescription, constitutes an illegal act and subjects a lawyer to possible prosecution under federal law. Such activity may implicate [*inter alia* Rule 8.4(b)]. . . .
> 
> Whether the illegal act "reflects adversely on the lawyer's honesty or trustworthiness" under Prof. Cond. R. 8.4(b) only can be determined on a case-by-case basis. A lawyer is "answerable to the entire criminal law," but is only "professionally answerable" to those offenses that demonstrate a lack of honesty or trustworthiness. . . . For example, a single violation of the CSA by a lawyer using medical marijuana would not, by itself, demonstrate the requisite lack of honesty or trustworthiness to constitute a violation of Prof. Cond. R. 8.4(b). Other misconduct related to the illegal act, such as lying to federal investigators or obtaining a prescription for medical marijuana for purposes of resale or providing it to a minor, would need to be present to trigger a violation of Prof. Cond. R. 8.4(b). A nexus must be established between the commission of an illegal act and the lawyer's lack of honesty or trustworthiness. . . . Similarly, multiple violations of federal law would likely constitute "a pattern of repeated offenses" indicating an "indifference to legal obligations" and constitute a violation of the rule. Prof. Cond. R. 8.4(b), cmt. [3].
> 
> . . .
> 
> Similar to the issue of personal marijuana use, a lawyer's personal ownership or other participation in an Ohio medical marijuana enterprise violates federal law. Consequently, under circumstances similar to those previously discussed in relation to personal marijuana use, a lawyer's ownership of a medical marijuana enterprise may implicate Prof. Cond. R. 8.4(b). . . . Likewise, participating in a medical marijuana enterprise as an employee or personally investing or lending money to a medical marijuana enterprise, subjects the lawyer to the same criminal and professional liabilities as having an ownership interest in a medical marijuana enterprise.

Ohio Board of Professional Conduct, Opinion 2016-6, *supra*. *See also* State Bar Ass'n of North Dakota Ethics Committee, Op. No. 14-02 (2014) (advising that attorney's use of marijuana for medical purposes in compliance with Minnesota law would still constitute crime and sanctionable under Rule 8.4, given federal and North Dakota prohibitions on drug). (The North Dakota decision may now be moot, as the state's voters legalized medical marijuana in the fall 2016 election.)

In contrast, some states take a more permissive approach under Rule 8.4. For example, prior to the passage of Amendment 64, the Colorado Bar Association Ethics Committee issued the following opinion regarding an attorney's use and personal cultivation of medical marijuana:

The Committee concludes . . . that a Colorado lawyer's violation of federal criminal law prohibiting the cultivation, possession, and use of marijuana where the lawyer's cultivation, possession, or use is for a medical purpose permitted under Colorado law does not necessarily violate Colo. RPC 8.4(b). The Committee reads Colo. RPC 8.4(b) as requiring a nexus between the violation of law and the lawyer's honesty, trustworthiness, or fitness as a lawyer in other respects. . . .

Colorado has come to its own conclusion about the difficult and sensitive question of whether marijuana should be available to relieve severe pain and suffering. . . . [E]ven if a lawyer's cultivation, possession, or use of medical marijuana to treat a properly diagnosed debilitating medical condition under Colorado law may constitute a federal crime, the Committee does not see a nexus between the lawyer's conduct and his or her "honesty" or "trustworthiness," within the meaning of Colo. RPC 8.4(b), provided that the lawyer complies with the requirements of Colorado law permitting and regulating his or her medical use of marijuana. The Committee also does not see a nexus between the lawyer's conduct and his or her "fitness as a lawyer in other respects," provided that (a) again, the lawyer complies with the requirements of Colorado law permitting his or her medical use of marijuana, and (b) in addition, the lawyer satisfies his or her obligation under Colo. RPC 1.1 to provide competent representation. . . .

Colorado Bar Association Ethics Committee, *Formal Opinion 124—A Lawyer's Medical Use of Marijuana*, Adopted, 41 Colo. Law. 28 (July 2012).

## Notes and Questions

1. What do you think? Is it professional misconduct for an attorney to violate federal law? Does your answer depend on the type of offense committed? *E.g.*, Hazard et al., *The Law of Lawyering, supra*, at § 69.02 ("A code of professional discipline should deter and punish conduct that is of special significance to the *profession*, but it should not concern itself with 'ordinary' misconduct at all. If a lawyer engages in such other misconduct, the lawyer can be punished and the conduct deterred through other legal processes . . ."); Sam Kamin & Eli Wald, *Marijuana Lawyers: Outlaws or Crusaders?*, 91 Or. L. Rev. 869, 915-17 (2013) (arguing that Rule 8.4 should distinguish between less serious, private crimes, like possession of marijuana, and more serious, public crimes, like distribution of marijuana). Along these lines, consider the following Problems:

Problem 12.14: Andy is a licensed attorney. Which of the activities listed below would be sanctionable under either Ohio's or Colorado's interpretation of Rule 8.4? Which, if any, should be sanctioned?

(1) Andy uses marijuana for medical purposes, in compliance with state (but not federal) law

(2) Andy uses marijuana for recreational purposes, in compliance with state (but not federal) law

(3) Andy uses marijuana for medical purposes, in violation of both state and federal law

(4) Andy uses marijuana for recreational purposes, in violation of both state and federal law

(5) Andy grows marijuana for his own personal use, in compliance with state (but not federal) law
(6) Andy shares a joint with a friend for no remuneration. The social sharing of marijuana is a civil infraction under state law and a felony under federal law

**Problem 12.15**: Andy, a licensed attorney, recently represented Camila, a state-licensed marijuana supplier, in a criminal prosecution brought by the federal government. Andy successfully motioned to have the charges against Camila dismissed on the basis of *United States v. McIntosh* (discussed in Chapter 7). Following the conclusion of Camila's case, Andy sent Camila the bill for his services ($25,000 total). Camila gave Andy a bag containing $25,000 cash, all small bills reeking of marijuana. She told him "Thank you for your help. I wouldn't be able to pay my bills without my marijuana shop." Andy takes the cash and deposits it into his bank account. Is Andy guilty of a violation of 18 U.S.C. sections 1956 or 1957? (These provisions are discussed in Chapter 11.) If so, could he be sanctioned under Rule 8.4?

2. Some conduct might implicate both Rule 1.2 and Rule 8.4. The following Problem raises this possibility:

**Problem 12.16**: Andy is a licensed attorney. He recently helped Camila, a state-licensed marijuana supplier, negotiate a lease for her marijuana storefront. At present, Camila is Andy's only client. He is hoping Camila will hire him to represent her in other legal matters. Is Andy sanctionable under Rule 1.2? Even if not, is Andy sanctionable under Rule 8.4 for aiding and abetting Camila's distribution of marijuana? *See* New York State Bar Association Committee on Professional Ethics, *supra*, at n.8.

### 3. Can Federal Courts Punish Attorneys for Assisting Marijuana Users and Suppliers?

Although the regulation of attorneys has been traditionally handled by the states, federal courts too play a role in this domain. Professor Geoffrey Hazard and his co-authors explain:

> Federal courts and other federal agencies have a role to play in the regulation of lawyers, but it is a distinctly secondary one, as befits a federalist legal and political system that favors local control over local governance issues.[56] Thus, although every federal court has rules

---

[56]. There are many reasons for the strong federal deference to the state systems of lawyer regulation. Historically, admission to the practice of law was a state-by-state system. Deference to the rights of states to control the practice of law was an important principle of federalism. Also, federal courts do not possess the personnel needed properly to establish a primary system for regulating lawyers. Often, federal courts defer to the local state admissions process and await state results on lawyer discipline matters, even though such a difference is not required. The primary reason for the requirement of local bar admission for federal court admission is that a contrary result would slowly but certainly erode the state-by-state systems of regulations for lawyers. Lawyers admitted to deferral courts could travel from state to state and practice law in those stats under the guise of federal court practice. . . .

governing admission to its bar, all such rules include a threshold requirement of admission to practice in the state courts, almost always the state courts of the state in which the federal court sits. Moreover, although federal courts possess both statutory and inherent power to discipline lawyers in connection with pending litigation, federal courts generally borrow heavily from the states in which they sit for more detailed and more comprehensive codes of conduct. Indeed, most federal district courts have by local rule either formally incorporated the applicable state code of conduct or made direct reference to the Model Rules of Professional Conduct.

Hazard et al., *The Law of Lawyering, supra*, at § 1.17.

However, as Hazard et al. note, "some federal courts have rejected the applicable state rule in particular settings and fashioned a federal common law rule. These departures from intrastate uniformity can cause serious problems for litigating lawyers, whether they cross state lines to practice or not." *Id.* Indeed, the federal district court in Colorado recently rejected the Colorado Supreme Court's Rule 1.2 comment 14 (*see supra*), i.e., the comment permitting attorneys to knowingly assist marijuana users and suppliers. The relevant provision of the local federal rules for the District of Colorado thus provides:

> STANDARDS OF PROFESSIONAL CONDUCT
>
> (a) Standards of Professional Conduct. Except as provided by Subdivision (b) . . . the Colorado Rules of Professional Conduct (Colo. RPC) are adopted as standards of professional responsibility for the United States District Court and the United States Bankruptcy Court for the District of Colorado.
>
> (b) Exceptions. The following provisions of the Colorado Rules of Professional Conduct (Colo. RPC) are excluded from the standards of professional responsibility for the United States District Court and the United States Bankruptcy Court for the District of Colorado:
>
> . . .
>
> > (2) Colo. RPC 1.2(d), Comment [14] (counseling and assisting client regarding Colorado Constitution art. XVIII, §§ 14 and 16 and related statutes, regulations, or orders, and other state or local provisions implementing them), except that a lawyer may advise a client regarding the validity, scope, and meaning of Colorado Constitution art. XVIII, §§ 14 and 16 and the statutes, regulations, orders, and other state or local provisions implementing them, and, in these circumstances, the lawyer shall also advise the client regarding related federal law and policy;
>
> . . .

District Ct. Colorado Local Atty Rule 2.

The federal court's rejection of Colorado's rule has raised questions about whether attorneys who practice before the federal district court of Colorado must refrain from providing the services that Colorado (like Ohio) found professionally questionable under unamended Rule 1.2. The following excerpt discusses the ramifications of the federal court decision.

## Eli Wald et al., Representing Clients in the Marijuana Industry: Navigating State and Federal Rules
44 Colo. Law. 61 (2015)

The Colorado Supreme Court's adoption of Comment 14 and the [United States District Court's (USDC's)] subsequent rejection of Comment 14 have created an uncertain playing field for Colorado lawyers admitted to practice in the USDC who wish to represent clients in Amendment 64 matters. Specifically, these lawyers face two challenges. First, which jurisdiction's rules of professional conduct apply to their representation of clients in the marijuana industry—the Colo. [Rules of Professional Conduct (RPC)], which permit assisting such clients, or the USDC Local Attorney Rules, which prohibit assistance? Second, if the USDC Local Attorney Rules apply, what is the scope of permitted advice regarding related federal law and policy as opposed to (the at least negatively implied) prohibited assistance? . . .

### RECONCILING COLO. RPC 8.5, USDC LOCAL ATTORNEY RULE 8.5, AND THE USDC'S INHERENT POWER

Consider the following examples: Suppose Colorado is sued in USDC by sheriffs from Colorado and neighboring states arguing that Amendment 64 puts an undue economic burden on other states. Attorney A is admitted in the USDC and enters an appearance on behalf of Colorado in the matter. Has Attorney A violated the USDC Local Attorney Rules by representing Colorado?

Attorney B represents Client X, a marijuana dispensary owner, negotiating a commercial real estate lease. Attorney B is admitted in the USDC and represents Client Y in an unrelated litigation matter pending before the USDC. Has Attorney B violated the USDC Local Attorney Rules by representing Client X?

. . .

Colo. RPC 8.5(b), adopted by the USDC, provides choice of law provisions that instruct the court as to what law to apply. Rule 8.5(b)(1) states:

> [F]or conduct in connection with a matter pending before a tribunal, the rules of the jurisdiction in which the tribunal sits [apply], unless the rules of the tribunal provide otherwise.

Rule 8.5(b)(2) adds:

> [F]or any other conduct, the rules of the jurisdiction in which the lawyer's conduct occurred, or, if the predominant effect of the conduct is in a different jurisdiction, the rules of that jurisdiction shall be applied to the conduct. A lawyer shall not be subject to discipline if the lawyer's conduct conforms to the rules of a jurisdiction in which the lawyer reasonably believes the predominant effect of the lawyer's conduct will occur.

Because Attorney A is representing Colorado in a matter pending before the USDC, Rule 8.5(b)(1) means that the USDC would apply its Local Attorney Rule 2(b) to determine whether Attorney A committed misconduct. Attorney B's representation, however, presents a more complicated choice of law question because the representation of Client X is not before the USDC.

On the one hand, a plain reading of Colo. RPC 8.5 suggests that where the representation of clients in the marijuana industry is not "in connection with a matter pending before" the USDC, the USDC must apply, per Rule 8.5(b)(2), "the rules of the jurisdiction in which the lawyer's conduct occurred," namely the Colo. RPC. Here, because Attorney B's conduct—the representation of Client X—is not pending before the USDC, the Colo. RPC that permit the representation would apply. Colo. RPC 8.5(b)(2) does not allow a court to discipline an attorney if the attorney's conduct conforms to the rules of the jurisdiction in which the attorney reasonably believed the predominant effect of the conduct would occur, therefore the USDC would apply the Colo. RPC (and Attorney B would not face discipline).

. . .

On the other hand, the USDC might decide to exercise its inherent power to apply its Local Attorney Rules, Colo. RPC 8.5 notwithstanding, finding that any other construction would deny its ability to discipline lawyers admitted to its bar and force it to apply Colo. RPC 1.2 Comment 14, which it explicitly rejected. The USDC has the power to discipline or disbar attorneys admitted to practice before it. Nothing in the Local Rules negates or diminishes the USDC's inherent power to discipline attorneys who are members of its bar. This disciplinary and contempt power is "far-reaching and potentially drastic." Thus, while contemplating what rules the USDC will apply, it is incumbent on attorneys practicing before it to recognize that the court may invoke its inherent power to apply its Local Rule 2(b), ostensibly even to attorney conduct in matters not pending before it.[21] Here, if the USDC were to invoke its inherent power to disregard its own Rule 8.5(b)(2), Attorney B's representation of Client X would be subject to Local Rule 2(b) although the representation of Client X was not before the tribunal and was unrelated to its representation of Client Y before the court.

. . .

## SEMANTICS OR SUBSTANCE? DISCUSS V. ASSIST/COUNSEL V. ADVISE

Colorado lawyers who fear discipline by the USDC must confront a second quandary: What is the scope of permitted advising under the Local Attorney Rules as opposed to prohibited assisting? . . . The USDC rejected Comment 14 to the extent that it permitted an attorney to assist a client regarding Amendment 64, but accepted that an attorney could advise his or her client regarding Amendment 64 and related federal law and policy. Further, the USDC has adopted Colo. RPC 1.2(d), which states that while a "lawyer shall not counsel a client to engage, or assist a client, in conduct that the lawyer knows is criminal," a lawyer

> may discuss the legal consequences of any proposed course of conduct with a client and may counsel or assist a client to make a good faith effort to determine the validity, scope, meaning or application of the law.

This requires an analysis of the difference between three categories of attorney conduct: (1) discuss, (2) counsel and assist, and (3) advise.

### Discussing

Colo. RPC 1.2(d), adopted by the USDC, states in relevant part that a lawyer "may discuss the legal consequences of any proposed course of conduct with a client." Thus, a lawyer may discuss and explain to a client the legal consequences of any conduct given Amendment 64, the CSA, and related bodies of law. Comment 9 clarifies that, in discussing the law with a client, a lawyer is not precluded "from giving an honest opinion about the actual consequences that appear likely to result from a client's conduct." It adds that

---

21. Richardson, "Demystifying the Federal Law of Attorney Ethics," 29 U Georgia L. Rev. 137, 149-50, n.45 (Fall 1994) (citing *In re Sanchez-Ferrer*, 620 F. Supp. 951 (D.P.R. 1983) (disbarring lawyer from bar of federal court for conduct committed in state court)).

"[t]here is a critical distinction between presenting an analysis of legal aspects of questionable conduct," which is permitted under the Rule, "and recommending the means by which a crime or fraud might be committed with impunity," which is prohibited.

### Assisting and Counseling

While a Colorado lawyer is always permitted to discuss the consequences of a proposed Amendment 64 conduct with a client under the Local Attorney Rules, an attorney must not assist or counsel a client to engage in violating the CSA given the USDC's rejection of Comment 14. What attorney conduct amounts to prohibited assisting and counseling? Comment 10 to Colo. RPC 1.2 offers guidance in drawing the line, noting that

> [t]he lawyer is required to avoid assisting the client, for example, by drafting or delivering documents that the lawyer knows are fraudulent or by suggesting how the wrongdoing might be concealed.

By analogy, a lawyer prohibited from assisting Amendment 64 client conduct under Local Rule 2(b)(2) would be prohibited from drafting or delivering documents that the lawyer knows will be used to violate the CSA, such as drafting a lease or an employment agreement on behalf of a marijuana dispensary owner.

. . .

[Author's note: The Colorado Bar Association Ethics Commission took the position later espoused by the Ohio Board—i.e., that Rule 1.2(d) restricts the services that attorneys may provide to marijuana suppliers. 42 The Colorado Lawyer 19, *supra* (detailing Opinion 125).] Opinion 125's analysis does not quite resolve our first example. The Opinion states that a lawyer can always represent a client accused of a crime, but it bases its conclusion on the fact that the client's conduct in question is past conduct. Attorney A, in contrast, has been retained by Colorado to represent it regarding ongoing conduct. We believe, however, that Attorney A has likely not violated the USDC's Local Rules for two related reasons. First, the court's Local Rules allow a lawyer to "counsel or assist a client to make a good faith effort to determine the validity, scope, meaning or application of the law." Because in our example the sheriffs are challenging the validity and application of Amendment 64, it seems likely that that court will not find Attorney R's representation of Colorado to violate its Local Rules.

. . .

Second, disciplining Attorney A for agreeing to represent Colorado in our example defies common sense because such discipline would deprive Colorado of representation in the case. But what about Colorado lawyers who generally agree to represent Amendment 64 clients before the USDC in matters involving ongoing—as opposed to past—client conduct? While such lawyers might argue that the representations constitute "a good faith effort to determine the validity, scope, meaning or application of the law," and might construe *In re Arenas* to suggest that the USDC would not refer them to discipline, such lawyers do risk a determination that their representations constitute prohibited assistance under the court's Local Rules.

Next, what about lawyers who represent Amendment 64 clients in matters not before the court, like Attorney B? Withdrawn Opinion 125 is once again helpful in construing Local Rule 2(b). [Among other things, it concludes that attorneys may not draft or negotiate contracts for state-licensed marijuana suppliers.] . . .

Accordingly, because negotiating a commercial real estate lease for Client X constitutes prohibited assistance under USDC's Local Rule 2(b), if the court were to invoke its inherent power and attempt to discipline Attorney B for conduct not pending before it, Attorney B might be found to have violated Rule 2(b). Notably, however, the Restatement (Third) of the Law Governing Lawyers § 94 defines "assistance" differently than withdrawn Opinion 125. Assisting a client under the Restatement means to, with the intent of facilitating or encouraging the client's action, as opposed to mere knowledge, provide professional services such as "preparing documents, drafting correspondence, negotiating with a non-client, or contacting a governmental agency." That is, drafting and preparing documents on behalf of a client only amounts to assisting if a lawyer acts with intent to help the client, as opposed to mere knowledge of the client's criminal conduct. Contrary to Colo. RPC 1.2 Comment 10 and withdrawn Ethics Opinion 125, a Colorado lawyer facing USDC discipline for drafting documents for an Amendment 64 client may argue that her conduct does not constitute prohibited assistance because she lacked the intent to help the client.

Here, Attorney B may argue that even if the USDC invokes its inherent power and attempts to impose discipline for conduct not before it, Attorney B has not violated Local Rule 2(b) unless it can be established that Attorney B had the intent to help Client Y. In any event, recall that as explained above, when the representation of Amendment 64 clients is not before it, the USDC might interpret its choice of law Rule 8.5(b)(2) to require it to apply the Colo. RPC, including Comment 14, in which case it will likely find no misconduct on Attorney B's part.

## Advising

Local Attorney Rule 2(b)(2) appears to introduce a new hybrid category—advise. Recall that the Local Rule states in relevant part that a lawyer "may advise a client" regarding the validity, scope, and meaning of Amendment 64 and its implementing laws, and must "advise the client regarding related federal law and policy." Thus, arguably, a Colorado lawyer may do more than merely discuss the legal consequences with an Amendment 64 client, but less than assist or counsel that client.

Once again, the Colo. RPC Comment and withdrawn Ethics Opinion 125 provide guidance in delineating the meaning of this new category of conduct. Comment [9] notes in relevant part that

> [t]here is a critical distinction between presenting an analysis of legal aspects of questionable conduct *and recommending the means* by which a crime or fraud might be committed with impunity. (Emphasis added.)

"Recommending the means" is prohibited by Comment 9 because it, unlike Local Rule 2(b)(2), had only two categories of attorney conduct to construe—discussing and assisting—and recommending appeared to go above and beyond discussing. The USDC, however, may conclude that recommending is an example of permitted advising because while more than discussing, it is sufficiently less than assisting.

Opinion 125 provided two additional examples of advising.

First, it explained:

> The CSA provides that "no civil or criminal liability shall be imposed by virtue of this subchapter upon . . . any duly authorized officer of any State . . . who shall be lawfully

engaged in the enforcement of any law or municipal ordinance relating to controlled substances." 21 U.S.C. § 885(d). Some courts have interpreted this section to provide civil and criminal immunity for state law enforcement officers enforcing valid state marijuana laws.

Importantly, added the Opinion,

> state officials carrying out their responsibilities under Colorado's marijuana laws are not engaging in criminal activity. Relying on these cases, the Committee believes that government lawyers *advising* these officials do not violate Colo. RPC 1.2(d) when they work to help their clients enforce, interpret, or apply marijuana laws. (Emphasis added.)

Second, Opinion 125 noted that

> in the family law context, a lawyer may advise a client about the consequences of using marijuana before, during, or after exercising parental rights or parenting time without violating the Rules.

Thus, it appears that permissible advising under Local Attorney Rule 2(b)(2) creates a third hybrid category of attorney conduct, in addition to discussing and assisting, pursuant to which a Colorado lawyer may do more than discuss the consequences of a proposed course of conduct with an Amendment 64 client without reaching the prohibited assisting, for example, by recommending a course of conduct based on the permitted discussion.

## CONCLUSION

The USDC's rejection of Comment 14 introduces uncertainty into the practice of law for Colorado lawyers admitted to practice before the USDC. Specifically, while we believe that the court's choice of law rule requires it to apply the Colorado Rules to attorney conduct not pending before it, lawyers admitted to practice before the USDC face the possibility that the court may exercise jurisdiction to discipline them for representing Amendment 64 clients in matters pending before it and even regarding representations not before it. In doing so, it might apply its Local Attorney Rules, which reject Comment 14. Moreover, Colorado lawyers also face uncertainty as to the scope of permitted advising under the Local Attorney Rules, as well as the scope of prohibited assisting.

## Notes and Questions

1. What do you think of Wald et al.'s interpretation of the local rule? Do you think the federal court would ever follow through and actually sanction an attorney for representing "Amendment 64 clients in matters pending before it and even representations not before it?"

2. Could Congress bar the federal courts from disciplining attorneys who comply with state professional rules, in the same way Congress has barred the DOJ from prosecuting marijuana users and suppliers who comply with state law? *Cf.* Hazard et al., *The Law of Lawyering, supra,* at § 1.07 ("Congress is the courts' co-equal partner in regulating the practice of law, and may replace court regulations with regulations of its own. It should not be thought, however, that the power of Congress is so broad as to oust the federal courts of all inherent power. . . .")

3. Ultimately, what services should attorneys be allowed to provide marijuana users and suppliers, as long as the federal marijuana prohibition remains on the books?

# CHAPTER 13

# The Law, Policy, and Authority Issues Confronting Businesses

Many businesses do business with marijuana users and suppliers. For example, landlords lease property used for marijuana storefronts; contractors build irrigation and ventilation systems used to grow marijuana; and banks handle cash generated by marijuana sales. Even firms that have no ties to the marijuana industry often employ people who use marijuana.

But transacting with marijuana users and suppliers raises a host of thorny issues: Will courts enforce contracts between marijuana suppliers and other businesses? If those contracts are not enforceable in court, how can businesses protect their reliance interests? Do some types of contracts expose businesses to legal sanctions? For example, could a landlord be criminally prosecuted for leasing property for a marijuana storefront? Can banks handle the proceeds of marijuana sales? May employers terminate employees for using marijuana? Who decides these questions?

This chapter addresses the key law, policy, and authority issues confronting businesses[1] that deal with marijuana users and suppliers. It proceeds as follows. Section A examines whether courts will enforce contracts with marijuana suppliers and the impact on businesses if their contracts are not enforceable in court. Section B discusses the special rules governing landlords. It examines the scope of the federal prohibition against renting property to drug users and suppliers and the tension between the federal prohibition and state laws requiring accommodation of tenants who use medical marijuana pursuant to state law. Section C then explores the rules governing employers. It surveys state employment discrimination protections for medical marijuana users and examines whether these protections are preempted by the federal CSA. Finally, Section D examines the rules governing banks and the limits on the marijuana industry's access to banking services.

## A. CONTRACTING PARTIES, GENERALLY

### 1. Will Courts Enforce Contracts with Marijuana Suppliers?

Problem 13.1: Ivan is an investor who loaned $500,000 to Oma. Oma is the owner of The Dude Ranch, a state-licensed medical marijuana dispensary.

---

1. Although the chapter refers to businesses, the topics covered herein apply to many individuals as well.

Pursuant to the terms of the loan agreement, Oma was supposed to use the funds "to grow and sell marijuana through The Dude Ranch, to the extent permitted by state law." In return, Oma would pay Ivan 12 percent interest annually over 30 years, with the principal due at the end of the loan term. However, Oma instead used the $500,000 to buy a house for herself. She has refused to pay Ivan any of the interest due on the loan, and she has refused to refund any of the loan principal. Ivan has sued Oma in state court for breach of contract. Will the court enforce the contract? If so, what remedy will it award?

Typically, if one party fails to live up to its end of a bargain, the aggrieved party can sue for breach of contract. Such suits are normally governed by state law, though they may be brought in federal court when jurisdictional requirements are met. If the court finds that one party has breached the contract, it will usually order that party to pay monetary damages equivalent to the profit the aggrieved party expected to reap from the contract; in exceptional cases, the court might instead order the breaching party to perform per the terms of the contract. (For elaboration on the finer points of contract law, see E. Allan Farnsworth, Contracts (4th ed. 2004).)

If Oma in **Problem 13.1** had promised to grow and sell, say, apples, the court would not hesitate to enforce her financial obligations to Ivan. But because her contract instead involves *marijuana*—the growing and selling of which are banned by federal law—the court might balk. It is well-settled law that a court may refuse to enforce a contract that is against public policy. The late Professor Farnsworth has explained the twin rationales behind the rule. In particular, a court may see its refusal to enforce "as an appropriate sanction to discourage undesirable conduct," or "it may regard enforcement of the promise as an inappropriate use of the judicial process. . . ." *Id.* at § 5.01. The doctrine, however, is qualified. As Farnsworth notes, "[e]nforcement should not be refused unless the potential benefit in deterring misconduct or avoiding an inappropriate use of the judicial process outweighs the factors favoring enforcement," including "the public interest in protecting the justified expectations of the parties" and whether the breaching party would be unjustly enriched if enforcement is denied. *Id.*

Courts have disagreed about whether contracts with marijuana suppliers are unenforceable as against public policy. The two cases excerpted below stake out conflicting positions on the issue. In the first case, on which the facts of **Problem 13.1** are loosely based, a state court finds an investor's loan agreement with a medical marijuana dispensary void as against public policy, citing the federal government's ongoing prohibition on marijuana.

## *Hammer v. Today's Health Care II, Co.*

Nos. CV2011-051310 & -051311 (Super. Ct. Maricopa Cty., Ariz., Apr. 17, 2012)

McVey, J.:

1. On or about August 12, 2010, each of the Plaintiffs entered into separate loan agreements with Defendant, Today's Health Care II, a Nevada corporation ("THC").

2. Each Plaintiff loaned THC $250,000 for the stated purpose of financing a "retail medical marijuana sales and growth center." Each loan was memorialized by a loan agreement and a promissory note (the "loan documents").

3. These loan documents required THC to pay Plaintiffs interest at the rate of 12% per annum on the 12th day of each month.

4. The agreement provided that in the event of a default, THC had five (5) days within which to cure its default.

5. If THC failed to cure its default within five (5) days, Plaintiffs were entitled to repayment of the principal loan amount at a default interest rate of 21%, plus any costs and attorneys' fees associated with enforcement and collection.

6. THC failed to timely pay interest on the loans by March 12, 2011.

7. As of March 17, 2011, THC defaulted on its obligations under the loan obligation.

. . .

[Plaintiffs sued for breach of contract and both parties filed motions for summary judgment.]

The sole legal issue presented by both [motions] is whether the loan documents are enforceable, or whether they are void and unenforceable due to illegality. As mentioned, both loan agreements specifically provide as follows:

> "Borrower shall use the loan proceeds for a retail medical marijuana sales and grow center."

The retail medical marijuana sales and grow center was located in Colorado. Colorado, like Arizona, has adopted a scheme by which patients may obtain amounts of marijuana for medicinal purposes with a prescription from a physician. However, the United States' Controlled Substances Act ("CSA") makes it illegal to manufacture, distribute, or dispense or possess with intent to manufacture, distribute, or dispense a controlled substance. 21 U.S.C.A. §841. The United States still categorizes marijuana as a Schedule I, controlled substance. . . . It is unlawful to knowingly open, lease, rent, use or maintain property for the manufacturing, storing, or distribution of controlled substances. 21 U.S.C.A. §856. Finally, under Federal Law, it is unlawful to aid and abet the commission of a Federal crime. 18 U.S.C.A. §2.

In *Gonzales* [v. *Raich*, 545 U.S. 1 (2005)], the U.S. Supreme Court addressed the conflict between Federal Law, which continues to outlaw the possession and distribution of marijuana, and state medical marijuana laws. In that case, the Supreme Court held that prohibition of such sales of marijuana is properly within Congress' authority under Art. I, Sec. 8 of the United States Constitution (The Commerce Clause). Thus, dispensation of marijuana, even for medicinal purposes, remains illegal—state law notwithstanding.

An agreement is unenforceable if the acts to be performed would be illegal or would violate public policy. . . .

Plaintiffs argue the promissory notes are still enforceable despite the recitation of an illegal purpose in the Loan Agreement, because the promissory notes can be enforced without any proof of an illegal purpose. However, a contract which in itself is not unlawful either in what it promises or in the consideration for the promise may nevertheless be rendered void as against public policy as part of a general scheme to bring about an unlawful result. . . .

The explicitly stated purpose of these loan agreements was to finance the sale and distribution of marijuana. This was in clear violation of the laws of the United States. As such, this contract is void and unenforceable. This Court recognizes the harsh result of this ruling. Although Plaintiffs did not plead any equitable right to recovery such as unjust enrichment, or restitution, this Court considered whether such relief may be available to these Plaintiffs. Equitable relief is not available when recovery at law is forbidden because the contract is void as against public policy. . . . The rule is that a contract whose formation or performance is illegal is, subject to several exceptions, void and unenforceable. But this is not all, for one who enters into such a contract is not only denied enforcement of his bargain, he is also denied restitution for any benefits he has conferred under the contract. . . .

This Court finds that there are no genuine issues of material fact and that THC is entitled to judgment as a matter of law. . . .

## Notes and Questions

1. Purely as a matter of *contract* law, should a *state* court refuse to enforce a contract because it goes against a *federal* policy that is not shared by the state? *See* Robert A. Mikos, *Are Contracts with Marijuana Dealers Enforceable?*, Marijuana Law, Policy & Reform Blog, Jan. 15, 2014, https://perma.cc/3QY3-KBS2 ("[I]t's not clear the agreement [in *Hammer*] is against a *relevant* public policy. After all, both Arizona and Colorado have legalized medical marijuana, and it's not obvious . . . why their policy interests should be passed over in favor of Congress's, at least as a matter of contract law."). *See also* Luke Scheuer, *Are "Legal" Marijuana Contracts "Illegal"?*, 16 U.C. Davis Bus. L.J. 31, 33 (2015) ("Since contract law is a product of state law, it can be argued that nothing is 'illegal' for purposes of upholding public policy in states which have legalized marijuana.").

2. In a similar vein, should a court consider neighboring states' policies in deciding whether or not to enforce a contract? The following Problem raises the issue:

**Problem 13.2:** Andy and Benjamin live in Colorado. They have agreed to buy a large quantity of marijuana in Colorado and then resell the drug to adults in Nebraska, where possession and distribution remain criminal offenses. Pursuant to the agreement, Andy buys small quantities of marijuana (the maximum permitted) from several state-licensed stores in Colorado, using his own money. He then gives the drugs to Benjamin, who crosses into Nebraska, where he sells it all for a tidy profit. When Benjamin returns to Colorado, however, he refuses to share any of the profit with Andy or to refund any of the money Andy used to buy the marijuana in the first instance. Andy sues Benjamin for breach of contract in a Colorado court. Should the court enforce the contract?

3. Does the *Hammer* court give adequate attention to factors that might weigh in favor of enforcement, such as unjust enrichment of the medical marijuana dispensary? *See* Farnsworth, *supra*, at § 5.01. In other words, are all contracts that undermine the federal marijuana ban necessarily unenforceable? *See* Scheuer, *Are "Legal" Marijuana Contracts "Illegal"?*, *supra*, at 57 ("[A] mere violation of the law should not automatically cause a contract to be voided absent a strong public policy supporting the violated law."). Consider the following Problem:

**Problem 13.3:** The Dude Ranch is a state-licensed retail marijuana distributor. The Dude Ranch has entered into the following three contracts:

(1) The Dude Ranch will pay Andy, a state-licensed marijuana producer, $10,000 for one kilogram (1 kg) of marijuana.

(2) The Dude Ranch will pay Benjamin, a builder, $10,000 to install glass cabinets it will use to display marijuana products on its sales floor.

(3) The Dude Ranch will pay Camila, who runs a snow plowing business, a fixed price of $10,000 to plow the parking lot, delivery ramp, and sidewalk surrounding The Dude Ranch's store for one year.

Under *Hammer*, are any of these contracts enforceable in a court of law?

4. Colorado is a rare (and perhaps the only) state to have addressed the public policy exception in legislation. To implement Amendment 64—and to respond to at least one state court decision that found (for reasons similar to the ones cited by *Hammer*) marijuana contracts unenforceable as against public policy, *see Haeberle v. Lowden*, 2012 WL 7149098 (Colo. Dist. Ct.), Colorado passed legislation in 2013 providing that: "It is the public policy of the state of Colorado that a contract is not void or voidable as against public policy if it pertains to lawful activities authorized by [Amendment 64 and Colorado's medical marijuana law]." Colo. Rev. Stat. Ann. § 13-22-601 (West 2016). What is the likely effect of this provision? For example, what impact, if any, would it have on the resolution of *Hammer* or **Problems 13.1-13.3**?

---

In the next case, a federal court rejects *Hammer* and finds that a marijuana supplier's contract with an insurance company is enforceable, notwithstanding the federal marijuana ban.

## *Green Earth Wellness Ctr., LLC v. Atain Specialty Ins. Co.*
### 163 F. Supp. 3d 821 (D. Colo. 2016)

KRIEGER, C.J.:

Green Earth operates a retail medical marijuana business and an adjacent growing facility in Colorado Springs, Colorado. In April 2012, Green Earth sought commercial insurance for its business from Atain. Atain issued Green Earth a Commercial Property and General Liability Insurance Policy (hereinafter "the Policy") that became effective June 29, 2012.

A few days earlier, on June 23, 2012, a wildfire started in Waldo Canyon outside of Colorado Springs. Over the course of several days, the fire advanced towards the city. The fire did not directly affect Green Earth's business, but Green Earth contends that smoke and ash from the fire overwhelmed it[|]s ventilation system, eventually intruding into the growing operation and causing damage to Green Earth's Colorado plants.

In November 2012, Green Earth made a claim under the Policy for the smoke and ash damage. . . . [When Atain denied its claim, Green Earth commenced this suit for breach of contract. In response, Atain argued, inter alia, that the Policy expressly excluded coverage for contraband or was otherwise void as against public policy.]

. . .

[The Policy expressly excludes coverage for "Contraband, or property in the course of illegal transportation or trade."] The Policy does not define the term "Contraband," so the Court turns to the common and ordinary meaning of that term: "goods or merchandise whose importation, exportation, or possession is forbidden." Merriam-Webster Collegiate Dictionary (10th ed.). The Court accepts Atain's observation that the possession of marijuana for distribution purposes continues to constitute a federal crime under

21 U.S.C. §§ 841(a)(1) and (b)(1)(D). But, as the parties are well-aware, the nominal federal prohibition against possession of marijuana conceals a far more nuanced (and perhaps even erratic) expression of federal Policy. The Court will not attempt to explain nor summarize the conflicting signals that the federal government has given regarding marijuana regulation and enforcement since 2009. It is sufficient to recognize that as early as 2009, and again mere weeks before Atain formally denied Green Earth's claim from the Waldo Canyon fire, federal authorities had made public statements that reflected an ambivalence towards enforcement of the Controlled Substances Act in circumstances where a person or entity's possession and distribution of marijuana was consistent with well-regulated state law. Other than pointing to federal criminal statutes, Attain offers no evidence that the application of existing federal public policy statements would be expected to result in criminal enforcement against Green Earth for possession or distribution of medical marijuana, nor does Atain assert that Green Earth's operations were somehow in violation of Colorado law. In short, the Policy's "Contraband" exclusion is rendered ambiguous by the difference between the federal government's *de jure* and *de facto* public policies regarding state-regulated medical marijuana.

. . .

More fundamentally, it is undisputed that, before entering into the contract of insurance, Atain knew that Green Earth was operating a medical marijuana business. It is also undisputed that Atain knew—or very well should have known—that federal law nominally prohibited such a business. Notwithstanding that knowledge, Atain nevertheless elected to issue a policy to Green Earth, and that policy unambiguously extended coverage for Green Earth's inventory of saleable marijuana. Nothing in the record ever indicates that Atain sought to disclaim coverage for Green Earth's inventory, much less that Atain ever informed Green Earth of its position that such inventory was not insurable. In such circumstances, the Court finds that the record suggests that the parties shared a mutual intention that the Policy would insure Green Earths' marijuana inventory and that the "Contraband" exclusion would not apply to it.

Under these circumstances, the Court finds that the "Contraband" exclusion is ambiguous such that Atain is not entitled to summary judgment on Green Earth's claim for breach of contract arising from Atain's refusal to pay for harvested plants damaged by the Waldo Canyon fire.

This leaves Atain's "public Policy" requests. Atain "asks for some direction and assurances from this Court" as to how it should proceed. It "asks the Court to rule on" a specific question: "Whether, in light of [federal and state law], it is legal for Atain to pay for damage to marijuana plants and products, and if so, whether the Court can order Atain to pay for these damages."

These requests present problems. First, the Court does not and cannot give "assurances" to a party about the legality of engaging in particular conduct, nor does the Court intend to offer any particular opinion as to "whether . . . it is legal for Atain to pay for damages to marijuana plants and products." The Court assumes that Atain obtained legal opinions and assurances on these points from its own counsel before ever embarking on the business of insuring medical marijuana operations.[8] Nor does the Court provide

---

8. As noted, before it ever entered into the Policy, Atain knew of the nature of Green Earth's business and the peculiar legal concerns attendant to doing business in this sphere. Atain chose to insure Green Earth's

"direction" to parties as to how they should proceed. The Court's function here is purely adjudicatory—applying Colorado law. Green Earth alleges that Atain made contractual promises, then breached them. With regard to such claim, the Court merely interprets and applies the terms of the Policy, and where there is a material factual dispute, directs that matter be set for trial. Any judgment issued by this Court will be recompense to Green Earth based on Atain's failure to honor its contractual promises, not an instruction to Atain to "pay for damages to marijuana plants and products."

The unarticulated sub-text to this argument appears to be a request that the Court declare the Policy unenforceable as against public policy. . . .

For the reasons discussed above, and particularly in light of several additional years evidencing a continued erosion of any clear and consistent federal public policy in this area, this Court declines . . . Atain's indirect invitation to declare the Policy void on public policy grounds. Atain, having entered into the Policy of its own will, knowingly and intelligently, is obligated to comply with its terms or pay damages for having breached it.

Thus, the Court finds that Green Earth's breach of contract claim with regard to the approximately $40,000 claim made by Green Earth for damage to harvested marijuana buds and flowers damaged in the Waldo Canyon fire must be tried. . . .

## Notes and Questions

1. Why do the *Hammer* and *Green Earth* courts reach such different conclusions about the enforceability of contracts with marijuana suppliers? Are the cases distinguishable on the facts? If not, which court's analysis of contract doctrine is more persuasive?

2. Should courts consider enforcement practices in deciding whether a contract is against public policy? Do enforcement practices provide reliable information about the content of public policy in a jurisdiction?

3. Would the *Green Earth* court enforce the contract in **Problem 13.2** above?

4. Even if contracts are not void as against public policy, is enforcement potentially *preempted* by the federal CSA? In a blog post, the textbook author has explained the preemption concern:

> Even if the [*Hammer*] court erred as a matter of contract law . . . there might be a sounder basis on which to bar enforcement of these agreements: preemption. The investors in [the] case were asking the state to help them violate federal law. Whether or not this offends contracts principles, it likely offends the Supremacy Clause. . . . Congress has the constitutional authority to block all state interference with the private market, including, in a case like this, a state's intervention in a contract dispute between two private parties.

---

inventory, without taking any apparent precautions to carefully delineate what types of inventory would and would not be covered. Atain's newfound concerns that writing such a Policy might somehow be unlawful thus ring particularly hollow and its request for an advisory opinion appears somewhat disingenuous.

Indeed, were the Court to be compelled to find that Atain promises were void as against public Policy, the Court would be inclined to permit Green Earth to amend its pleadings to replace any claims sounding in breach of contract with a claim that Green Earth's payment of premiums for an illusory promise of insurance operated to unjustly enrich Atain. Moreover, given that Green Earth relied upon Atain's apparent promise of coverage by not seeking out alternative coverage, the Court would be inclined when exercising its equitable powers over such a claim to measure Green Earth's loss via expectation damages—that is, to award damages to Green Earth that would reflect what Green Earth would have expected to receive had Atain honored the coverage it promised. . . .

> To be sure, . . . Congress might not want to preempt enforcement of all contracts involving the marijuana industry. But it's unlikely to tolerate enforcement of at least some types of contracts.

Mikos, *Are Contracts with Marijuana Dealers Enforceable?*, *supra*. Would enforcement of any of the contracts in *Hammer*, *Green Earth*, or **Problems 13.1-13.3** above be preempted by federal law? Why, why not? How does preemption doctrine differ from contract's public policy doctrine?

### 2. What Are the Consequences If Contracts Are Unenforceable?

Contracts are an everyday part of nearly all industries. What is likely to happen if courts refuse to enforce contracts with the marijuana industry? The following excerpt suggests some dire possibilities.

### *Luke Scheuer*, Are "Legal" Marijuana Contracts "Illegal"?
16 U.C. Davis Bus. L.J. 31 (2015)

. . . The ability to form contracts is integral to long term planning and relationship building for businesses and helps promote their stability. "[A] contract enables parties to project exchange into the future and to tailor their affairs according to their individual needs and interests. . . ." Contracts do not simply enforce long term relationships; without contracts many relationships between marijuana business stakeholders will break down and many types of transactions simply will not happen. Marijuana companies form contracts with suppliers, employees, customers, service providers, and investors, among others. All these stakeholders depend on the enforceability of their agreements to make deals that depend on non-simultaneous exchange. For example, consider a situation where a business pays a farmer in advance for a product and the farmer fails to deliver without any legal consequences. Businesses would no longer form this sort of relationship, which would cut down on the success of these businesses and hurt the economy. If you cannot depend on contracts, then the only agreements you can rely on are ones where no executory action must take place, such as contracts in which each side completes their end of the bargain at the same time. When both parties are performing at the same time, there is no need to rely upon the other side's future ability or willingness to perform. But even these contracts will present problems if a court will not enforce them. . . .

. . .

States have articulated many reasons for legalizing marijuana. These include combating crimes that come from ceding a profitable industry to cartels, creating a new source of tax revenue, failure of the war on drugs, disproportionate impact of criminalization on minorities, unnecessarily high incarceration rates, and, of course, compassionate care for sick people who would potentially benefit from the pain mitigating effects of the drug. . . .

Enforceable marijuana contracts can help further many of these policy goals by promoting the industry. A more successful marijuana industry should produce more taxes and jobs, for instance. Further supporting the special interest behind enforcement is the fact that a well-regulated industry, with the ability to enforce agreements is more likely to produce and sell products in a responsible manner compared to an industry operating without the benefit of contracts. . . . On the flip side, if the marijuana industry is legalized, but forced into a legal grey zone, it will be more likely to produce fewer public benefits and more public harms by skirting laws such as the ban on selling marijuana to minors.

. . . If marijuana businesses cannot rely upon contracts, they will be forced even further into the world of illegal businesses. If they cannot get legitimate loans, they may borrow money from cartels or other criminal and dangerous parties. These lenders will not rely upon enforceability of their contracts in court, but will rely on threats of violence instead. These parties could also exercise power over the business. This will make these businesses less reputable and less attractive as an operation for the non-criminal elements that need to be joining it if it is to grow into a responsible and productive member of the business community. It could also lead to more dangerous marijuana being sold on the market or consumers being overcharged when they are sold a product that is mislabeled. . . .

. . .

Marijuana businesses are not cheap to start up. . . . In order to finance this operation, many businesses will need a loan. . . . But . . . [i]f lenders cannot depend on their loan agreements, they will stop lending. . . .

. . . Shutting this industry out of the debt market could adversely affect the public. Lenders bring discipline and impose caution on borrowers. Since lenders get paid a fixed rate of return they generally do not benefit from risky business decisions. These risky business decisions could produce massive returns for equity holders, but could also bankrupt a company. Lenders, in the loan agreements, typically require that borrowers take certain precautions to protect the value of the business. These precautions include maintaining adequate insurance, instituting a compliance system, or providing personal guarantees from the equity holders or third parties. By denying marijuana companies the ability to access this market, the discipline and restraint imposed by lenders will also be lost. This can cause the industry to take risks that could end up harming both the industry's long-term growth and reputation but also the public. Aside from the risks of marijuana businesses turning towards criminal elements for financing (such as cartels) briefly discussed above, marijuana companies may simply decide to forgo proper financing and instead cut corners to save money and by doing so avoid hiring better quality employees, consulting lawyers and accountants, skipping safety tests etc., all steps that should improve customer safety. . . .

. . .

Most commercial sales of marijuana will be a cash-for-product transaction in which the consideration is simultaneously exchanged. In this case, little trust is required between the parties because you immediately receive something you pay for in cash. If you walk into a 7-11 and buy a bag of Cheetos with cash, you have what you wanted while the store has what they wanted. In such situations, the fact that contracts cannot be enforced will have few consequences. But of course, even these relatively straightforward forward contracts pose problems if the contracts cannot be enforced.

One issue will be whether the implied warranties included in all U.C.C. contracts (unless excluded by the seller) apply. Normally, when a seller knows that a buyer is buying a good for a particular purpose, it is implied into the agreement that the good sold is fit for that purpose. If consumers buy marijuana, it should be implied into the sale agreement that the marijuana will, in fact, get the user high, especially if the buyer is relying on the seller's skill or judgment. If a seller sold oregano under the guise of marijuana, the buyer would naturally want to return the product and get their money back. By making marijuana contracts unenforceable, courts will be hurting consumers by taking away legal protections given to them in other areas of the law. It also opens the door to unscrupulous businesses to exploit the court's unwillingness to enforce their agreement. Essentially the lack of contract enforceability gives marijuana businesses an incentive to act in a shady underhanded manner because of the lack of consequences. While the marijuana business could suffer reputational harm, in a fast growing and rapidly developing industry like marijuana's, a business' reputation may not be easily ascertainable by the public and is certainly less dependable than a contract. While it is true that consumers who purchase marijuana illegally already lacked the right to enforce their agreement, with marijuana's legalization, marijuana is becoming more mainstream and states should seek to promote marijuana business professionalism so as to better protect the public than when it was sold illegally.

In addition, not all commercial sales can be completed simultaneously. In some cases, especially where large purchases are made, payment is often made prior to delivery or vice versa.

## Notes and Questions

1. What are the likely benefits and harms if courts refuse to enforce contracts with the marijuana industry? Do the former outweigh the latter? In other words, should courts enforce contracts with the marijuana industry?

2. If courts refuse to enforce contracts, is there anything the marijuana industry or its contracting partners could do to protect their expectation interests? In footnote 8, the *Green Earth* court suggested that a claim for breach of contract could simply be relabeled as one for unjust enrichment in order to circumvent the void for public policy doctrine. *But see* Farnsworth, Contracts, *supra,* at § 5.9 ("Courts generally do not grant restitution under agreements that are unenforceable on grounds of public policy.").

The textbook author has examined other alternatives to contract law:

> Without the state's help in enforcing their bargains, the state-legalized marijuana industry will face higher costs of doing business compared to other industries. After all, contracting parties are more likely to engage in opportunistic behavior (e.g., refusing to repay a loan) when their partners have no legal recourse.
>
> But the unavailability of legal remedies isn't the "final nail in the coffin" of the marijuana industry because there are viable, albeit second-best alternatives to contract law. Indeed, black markets can flourish without lawful contracts (think Silk Road), and even lawful businesses sometimes prefer cheaper non-legal solutions to expensive legal ones.
>
> . . .
>
> One, obvious solution is to limit the universe of contracting partners, namely, to persons who are known and can be trusted. Indeed, reputation plays a pivotal role in some industries (think Amazon, EBay, and their illicit cousin Silk Road). A good reputation is a valuable asset, one that vendors won't sacrifice too readily (particularly when they hope to remain in the industry). For example, if a marijuana dealer . . . thought it might need future financing, it would be less likely to walk away from $500,000 in obligations to its current lenders. Firms can even take this idea to the next level and integrate. Indeed, Colorado has required vertical integration of marijuana growers and sellers. Such

integration creates its own problems, but a dealer which grows its own stock now at least doesn't have to worry about enforcing deals with third-party suppliers.

A second strategy involves taking various forms of self-protection against breach. Think of a security deposit paid to a landlord. The deposit reduces the risk to the landlord that the tenant will just walk away from the lease. The payment of such a deposit should help marijuana dealers secure leases. And as long as tenants remain in possession of the property under lease, they have their own ways of protecting themselves against breach by landlords.

See Robert A. Mikos, *Alternatives to Contract Law in the Marijuana Industry*, Marijuana Law, Policy, & Reform Blog, Jan. 23, 2014, https://perma.cc/5SKK-J6WJ. What do you think? Do the suggested tactics provide a workable alternative to judicial enforcement of contracts?

Can you think of any other ways for parties to protect their interests in this field? Consider the following Problem:

**Problem 13.4:** Suppose you are an attorney and your client, Ivan, is considering making a loan to a state-licensed medical marijuana dispensary. Ivan thinks the dispensary's business prospects are very good, but he is worried about the legal risks associated with the loan. How would you advise Ivan? If Ivan decides to make the loan, what would you recommend he do to minimize those legal risks?

## B. LANDLORDS

Certain types of contracts with marijuana users and suppliers are subject to additional regulations. Leases are one of them. Indeed, in some states, leases with marijuana users and suppliers are subject to two seemingly contradictory rules: a provision of the federal CSA that bars landlords from allowing tenants to use rental property for purposes of consuming, manufacturing, or distributing marijuana, and state laws that—to varying degrees—appear to bar landlords from discriminating against some such tenants. The following sections discuss both regulations and the tension between them.

### 1. May Landlords Rent Property to Tenants Who Use or Supply Marijuana on It?

In 1986, Congress added a new provision to the CSA which bars individuals from using—or allowing others to use—property for purposes of consuming, manufacturing, or distributing illicit drugs. In relevant part, section 856 of the CSA, commonly known as the "crack house statute," declares:

> (a) Unlawful acts
> Except as authorized by this subchapter, it shall be unlawful to—
> (1) knowingly open, lease, rent, use, or maintain any place, whether permanently or temporarily, for the purpose of manufacturing, distributing, or using any controlled substance;

(2) manage or control any place, whether permanently or temporarily, either as an owner, lessee, agent, employee, occupant, or mortgagee, and knowingly and intentionally rent, lease, profit from, or make available for use, with or without compensation, the place for the purpose of unlawfully manufacturing, storing, distributing, or using a controlled substance.

(b) Criminal penalties

Any person who violates subsection (a) of this section shall be sentenced to a term of imprisonment of not more than 20 years or a fine of not more than $500,000, or both, or a fine of $2,000,000 for a person other than an individual.

. . .

(d) Civil penalties

(1) Any person who violates subsection (a) of this section shall be subject to a civil penalty of not more than the greater of

(A) $250,000; or

(B) 2 times the gross receipts, either known or estimated, that were derived from each violation that is attributable to the person.

. . .

(e) Declaratory and injunctive remedies

Any person who violates subsection (a) of this section shall be subject to declaratory and injunctive remedies as set forth in section 843(f) of this title.

21 U.S.C. § 856.

Section 856 creates two distinct offenses, but we will focus on the one aimed at landlords who do not themselves use or supply marijuana—section 856(a)(2). In a criminal prosecution under section 856(a)(2), the government must establish beyond a reasonable doubt that the defendant:

(1) managed or controlled a place that she
(2) rented or otherwise made available to another person who
(3) she knew would use it for purposes of consuming, manufacturing, or distributing marijuana (or other drugs)

The first two elements are straightforward and describe something akin to a landlord-tenant relationship (although the statute is not confined to such). For ease of exposition I will refer to the defendant as the landlord. The third element is somewhat trickier. Under section 856(a)(2) the government need not demonstrate that the landlord herself intended that the property be used to consume, manufacture, or distribute drugs; rather, "the purpose in issue is that of the person renting or otherwise using the place"—i.e., the tenant's. *United States v. Chen*, 913 F.2d 183, 191 (5th Cir. 1990). The landlord need only be aware of the tenant's purpose or willfully blind to it. *Id.* The third element is thus similar to the mens rea requirement for federal money laundering offenses, discussed in Chapter 11 Section C.1.d.

## Notes and Questions

1. What does it mean to use a place "for the purpose of" consuming, manufacturing, or distributing marijuana? The following Problems test the outer limits of the statute:

**Problem 13.5:** Terrence is interested in renting a house from Lana. When they meet to discuss the terms of the lease, Terrence asks Lana about her

smoking policy: "Do you allow your tenants to smoke? I'll be up front with you. Every once in a while, I like to smoke a joint just to relax. There's nowhere else I can do it. Are you okay with that?" Lana replied: "Tenants and their guests may smoke in the house, but if they do, they have to pay a special cleaning fee of $250." At the end of their meeting, Terrence and Lana sign a one-year lease agreement. Terrence moves into the house and, on occasion, smokes a marijuana joint inside. Is Lana guilty of a violation of section 856(a)(2)? *United States v. Gilbert*, 496 F. Supp. 2d 1001, 1011 (N.D. Iowa 2007).

**Problem 13.6:** Lana rents prime retail space in a strip mall to The Dude Ranch, a state-licensed medical marijuana dispensary and alternative care center. The Dude Ranch uses roughly half of the property as a medical marijuana storefront; the other half it uses to provide a variety of alternative medicine practices—acupuncture, meditation, etc.—to consumers. Is Lana guilty of a violation of section 856(a)(2)? *Compare United States v. Tamez*, 941 F.2d 770, 774 (9th Cir. 1991), *with Gilbert, supra*, 496 F. Supp. 2d at 1011.

2. How does the offense created by section 856(a)(2) differ (if at all) from the aiding and abetting offense discussed in Chapter 11? For example, is Lana in **Problem 13.6** guilty of aiding and abetting The Dude Ranch's sale of marijuana?

3. In the first 15 years following California's passage of Proposition 215, section 856(a)(2) was a key tool used by the Department of Justice (DOJ) to combat the medical marijuana industry. In several states, federal agents sent letters to landlords who were renting property to medical marijuana dispensaries (often in school zones), warning the landlords to terminate their tenants' illegal activities or else risk forfeiting the rental property (among other sanctions). *E.g.*, Drug Enforcement Admin., Enforcement Notices Sent to Marijuana Storefronts in Western Washington Operating Within School Zones, Aug. 23, 2012, https://perma.cc/UQ55-SVQU; Brett Wolf, *U.S. Targets Landlords in Fight Against Medical Pot*, Reuters.com, June 14, 2012, https://perma.cc/E8CS-6GDH. The following letter is representative:

> To Whom It May Concern:
> The Drug Enforcement Administration has determined that there may be a marijuana enterprise operating under the name [REDACTED] at the real property located at [REDACTED]. In addition, it appears that [REDACTED] is within 1,000 feet of an educational facility or other prohibited area. It is our understanding that you may own or have the property of the marijuana enterprise under your management or control, or that you own and/or operate the marijuana enterprise itself.
> Please be advised that distributing, possessing with intent to distribute, or manufacturing controlled substances, or aiding and abetting such an offense violates federal law. Doing any of these activities in close proximity to an educational facility or playground, subjects the persons involved to enhanced penalties pursuant to Title 21, United States Code, Section 860.

Part IV. Third Parties

> This letter serves as notice to you that, under United States law, the sale and distribution of marijuana is illegal and subject to criminal prosecution and civil enforcement actions. Property involved in such operations, including real property, is subject to seizure by, and forfeiture to the United States. Specifically, Title 21, United States Code, Section 856(a) provides in relevant part:
>
>> [I]t shall be unlawful to . . . knowingly and intentionally rent, lease, profit from, or make available for use, with or without compensation, the place for the purpose of unlawfully manufacturing, storing, distributing or using a controlled substance.
>
> Section 881(a) of Title 21 provides in relevant part:
>
>> The following shall be subject to forfeiture to the United States and no property right shall exist in them: . . . [a]ll real property, including any right, title, and interest (including any leasehold interest) in the whole of any lot or tract of land and any appurtenances or improvements, which is used, or intended to be used, in any manner or part, to commit, or to facilitate the commission of, a violation of this sub-chapter . . .
>
> United States law takes precedence over state law and applies regardless of the particular uses for which an enterprise is distributing marijuana. Accordingly, it is not a criminal defense or a defense to the forfeiture of property that an enterprise is providing "medical" marijuana. Even under these circumstances, an owner of real property with knowledge or reason to know of illegal marijuana distribution occurring on real property that he/she owns or controls may have the interest in that property forfeited to the government without compensation.
>
> Your prompt attention to this matter is strongly advised. Please take the necessary steps to discontinue the sale and/or distribution of marijuana at the above-referenced location within 30 days of this letter. If you have questions, you may wish to obtain legal counsel. If your counsel has questions, he/she may contact the U.S. Attorney's Office for The Western District of Washington.
>
> Sincerely,
> Matthew G. Barnes
> Special Agent in Charge
> Seattle Field Division

Matthew G. Barnes, Drug Enforcement Administration, Illegal Marijuana Enterprise at [REDACTED] within School Zone or Other Prohibited Area, Apr. 29, 2013, https://perma.cc/W87V-9BG6.

Even though the DOJ is no longer threatening to use section 856 against landlords, a private creditor has recently used the provision to block a landlord/debtor from obtaining the protections of federal bankruptcy law. *See In re Rent-Rite Super Kegs W. Ltd.*, 484 B.R. 799, 807 (Bankr. D. Colo. 2012). In the case, the landlord/debtor had borrowed $1.8 million from the creditor, using the debtor's Denver warehouse as collateral. The landlord/debtor subsequently rented the warehouse to a state-licensed marijuana producer, in violation of section 856. When the landlord/debtor later filed for Chapter 11 bankruptcy, the creditor objected, claiming that the landlord/debtor's misconduct foreclosed the relief it sought, such as an automatic stay of credit payments. The bankruptcy court agreed, holding that:

> [E]ven if the Debtor is never charged or prosecuted under the CSA, it is conducting operations in the normal course of its business that violate federal criminal law. . . . Unless

and until Congress changes that law, the Debtor's operations constitute a continuing criminal violation of the CSA and a federal court cannot be asked to enforce the protections of the Bankruptcy Code in aid of a Debtor whose activities constitute a continuing federal crime.

*Id.* at 805 (dismissing landlord/debtor's Chapter 11 petition).

4. Many states have adopted provisions similar to section 856. *See Validity and Construction of State Statutes Criminalizing the Act of Permitting Real Property to be Used in Connection with Illegal Drug Activities*, 24 A.L.R.5th 428 (1994). Following the adoption of marijuana reforms, some states have expressly shielded landlords from state criminal liability for renting property to tenants who use or supply marijuana in compliance with state law. *E.g.*, Colo. Const. art. XVIII, § 16(4) ("Notwithstanding any other provision of law, the following acts are not unlawful and shall not be an offense under Colorado law or be a basis for seizure or forfeiture of assets under Colorado law for persons twenty-one years of age or older: . . . (f) Leasing or otherwise allowing the use of property owned, occupied or controlled by any person, corporation or other entity for any of the activities conducted lawfully in accordance with [Colorado law]."). Is it necessary for states to do so? In other words, would landlords still be liable under state law for renting property to marijuana users or suppliers without such shields?

## 2. Can Landlords Ever Be Sanctioned for *Refusing* to Rent to Marijuana Users?

Under federal law, in circumstances just discussed, a landlord may be sanctioned for renting property to someone she knows will use it for consuming marijuana. But could a landlord ever be sanctioned for *refusing* to rent to a marijuana user? In other words, do reform states shield marijuana users from housing discrimination?[2]

Most reform states appear to bar landlords from discriminating against lawful marijuana users based solely on their *status as users*. Put differently, landlords may not refuse to rent to or evict someone just because she uses marijuana *somewhere*. For example, Arizona's medical marijuana law provides that:

> No school or landlord may refuse to enroll or lease to and may not otherwise penalize a person *solely for his status as a [registered medical marijuana] cardholder*, unless failing to do so would cause the school or landlord to lose a monetary or licensing related benefit under federal law or regulations.

Ariz. Rev. Stat. Ann. § 36-2813(A) (West 2016) (emphasis added). *See also* Conn. Gen. Stat. Ann. § 21a-408p(2) (West 2016) (similar); Del. Code Ann. tit. 16, § 4905A(a)(1) (West 2016) (similar).

---

2. Federal anti-discrimination laws are addressed in notes 3-4, *infra*, and in Chapter 14 (discussing bans on discrimination in public housing). Suffice to say that federal law generally does not shield marijuana users from discrimination based on their status as such.

At the same time, a few of these states expressly permit landlords to bar tenants from *using* marijuana *on the rental property*. Montana's medical marijuana law, for example, makes clear that it does not require "a landlord to allow a tenant who is a registered cardholder, provider, or marijuana-infused products provider to cultivate or manufacture marijuana or to allow a registered cardholder to use marijuana" on the rental premises. Mont. Code Ann. § 50-46-320(4) (West 2016). *See also, e.g.*, Colo. Const. art. XVIII, § 16(d) (2016) ("Nothing in this section shall prohibit a person, employer, school, hospital, detention facility, corporation or any other entity who occupies, owns or controls a property from prohibiting or otherwise regulating the possession, consumption, use, display, transfer, distribution, sale, transportation, or growing of marijuana on or in that property.").

In contrast, a handful of states arguably require landlords to accommodate at least *some* marijuana use on rental property. Maryland's medical marijuana law is illustrative. While it does not require landlords to accommodate marijuana *smoking* on rental property, the Maryland statute does require them to accommodate marijuana *vaporizing*:

> (a) This subtitle may not be construed to authorize any individual to engage in . . . the following:
> . . .
> (5) Except as provided in subsection (b) of this section, smoking marijuana or cannabis on a private property that:
> (i)
> 1. Is rented from a landlord; and
> 2. Is subject to a policy that prohibits the smoking of marijuana or cannabis on the property; or
> (ii) Is subject to a policy that prohibits the smoking of marijuana or cannabis on the property of an attached dwelling adopted by one of the following entities:
> 1. The board of directors of the council of unit owners of a condominium regime; or
> 2. The governing body of a homeowners association.
> (b) The provisions of subsection (a)(5) of this section do not apply to vaporizing cannabis.

Md. Code Ann., Health-Gen. § 13-3314 (West 2016). Other states make a similar distinction between smoking marijuana and consuming it in other forms. *E.g.*, Me. Rev. Stat. tit. 22, § 2423-E (West 2016) ("This subsection does not prohibit a restriction on the administration or cultivation of marijuana on premises *when that administration or cultivation would be inconsistent with the general use of the premises*. A landlord or business owner *may prohibit the smoking* of marijuana for medical purposes on the premises of the landlord or business *if the landlord or business owner prohibits all smoking* on the premises and posts notice to that effect on the premises.") (emphases added); Haw. Rev. Stat. § 521-39 (West 2016) (similar); 410 Ill. Comp. Stat. Ann. 130/40(a)(1) (West 2016); N.H. Rev. Stat. Ann. § 126-X:3(I) (West 2016) (similar).

## Notes and Questions

1. Do laws that prohibit discrimination against medical marijuana users suggest that landlords must accommodate a tenant's use of marijuana on the rental property? After

all, what purpose would be served by a law that requires landlords to rent to medical marijuana users but not to accommodate their use on rental property?

2. In a similar vein, does a state law that expressly authorizes a landlord to ban smoking of marijuana—but does not mention other modes of consumption—implicitly forbid the landlord from banning other modes of consumption? If the statutes above seem unclear, how would you redraft them to more clearly delineate the rights and obligations of landlords?

3. Even if state law does not require a landlord to accommodate a tenant's use of marijuana, may a landlord necessarily evict a tenant for using marijuana on rental property? *See, e.g.*, Tschetter, Hamrick, Sulzer, *Marijuana—You've Got Questions, We've Got Answers*, 15 Landlord News (Feb. 2014), https://perma.cc/7DG4-UPFP (discussing landlord rights under Colorado law and advising landlords to clearly address marijuana use and cultivation in lease documents).

4. Is it possible to reconcile the state laws discussed above with 21 U.S.C. section 856(a)(2)? In other words, are state laws preempted by federal law? The following Problems raise the issue:

**Problem 13.7**: Lana discovers that a prospective tenant, Terrence, is a registered medical marijuana patient. Lana is a staunch opponent of the state's medical marijuana program and for that reason does not want to rent to Terrence. However, state law bars landlords from refusing to lease property to a person solely because he/she is a registered medical marijuana patient. If Lana refuses to rent to Terrence and he sues her for violating the state nondiscrimination law, may Lana raise a preemption defense? *See* Robert A. Mikos, *Preemption Under the Controlled Substances Act*, 16 J. Health Care L. & Pol'y 5, 32-33 (2013).

**Problem 13.8**: Lana has rented a small house to Terrence. A few months into the lease, Lana discovers that Terrence has been growing 75 marijuana plants throughout the house. Lana seeks to evict Terrence, citing the lease agreement's "Crime Free Addendum," which stipulates that a tenant "shall not engage in any criminal activity" on the rental property. In response to the notice of eviction, Terrence invokes a provision of the state's medical marijuana law that provides that "a landlord may not sanction a tenant solely for engaging in conduct permitted by the state medical marijuana law." Lana acknowledges that Terrence's marijuana cultivation comports with state law. Could Lana nonetheless challenge the state non-discrimination law as preempted? *See Forest City Residential Management, Inc. ex rel. Plymouth Square Ltd. Dividend Housing Ass'n v. Beasley*, 71 F. Supp. 3d 715 (E.D. Mich. 2014); Mikos, *Preemption, supra*, at 32-33

5. Should landlords be required to lease property to marijuana users? Only medical users or all users? Should landlords also be required to accommodate marijuana use on

rental property? What about the cultivation or distribution of marijuana? Should landlords ever be required to accommodate those activities?

## C. EMPLOYERS

Businesses in the United States commonly require their employees to undergo drug testing. *E.g.*, Scott Macdonald et al., *Testing for Cannabis in the Work-Place: A Review of the Evidence*, 105 Addiction 408, 409 (2010) ("In the United States, 80 percent of the top Fortune 1000 companies have some type of drug testing programme."). Not infrequently, workplace drug testing reveals that an employee has been using marijuana. *Id.* at 408 ("Recent 2007 US figures indicate that 2.34% of 6.6 million tests were positive for cannabis, compared to 0.58% for cocaine and 0.44% for amphetamines.").

Federal law neither requires employers to accommodate marijuana use by employees,[3] nor does it—outside of narrow circumstances—require them to discharge employees who use marijuana.[4] But in states where the employee's use is legal under state law, do employers have any obligation to accommodate such use? And if so, are state laws preempted by federal law? The following sections address these questions.

### 1. Are Employers Ever Required to Accommodate an Employee's Marijuana Use?

Some states have explicitly addressed employment issues in their marijuana reforms. A few of them specifically require employers to accommodate an employee's medical use of marijuana. Section 1.a discusses the metes and bounds of this duty. Other states, however, have not explicitly addressed the employment issues raised by their marijuana reforms. In these states, a duty to accommodate marijuana use—if it exists at all—is only implied by state marijuana reforms or by pre-existing anti-discrimination laws. Section 1.b examines whether such laws create an implied cause of action for employees who have been discharged because they use marijuana pursuant to state law.

#### a. *Express Duty to Accommodate*

Several states have now expressly addressed employment issues in their marijuana laws. A handful of them impose a duty on employers to accommodate employee marijuana use outside of the workplace. Arizona's medical marijuana law is representative:

---

3. For example, the Americans with Disabilities Act (ADA) specifies that "a qualified individual with a disability shall not include any employee or applicant who is currently engaged in the illegal use of drugs, when the covered entity acts on the basis of such use." 42 U.S.C. § 12114.

4. As noted by the *Ross* dissent excerpted below, federal law would at most seem to prohibit federal contractors and grantors from allowing their employees to use drugs *at the workplace*. 41 U.S.C. § 8101 (2016) (Federal Drug Free Workplace Act) (defining a drug free workplace, for purposes of federal contractor conditions, as "a site of an entity . . . (B) at which employees of the entity are prohibited from engaging in the unlawful manufacture, distribution, dispensation, possession, or use of a controlled substance. . . .").

B. Unless a failure to do so would cause an employer to lose a monetary or licensing related benefit under federal law or regulations, an employer may not discriminate against a person in hiring, termination or imposing any term or condition of employment or otherwise penalize a person based upon either:
    1. The person's status as a cardholder.
    2. A registered qualifying patient's positive drug test for marijuana components or metabolites, unless the patient used, possessed or was impaired by marijuana on the premises of the place of employment or during the hours of employment.

Ariz. Rev. Stat. Ann. § 36-2813(B) (West 2016). *See also* Conn. Gen. Stat. Ann. § 21a-408p (West 2016) (similar); Del. Code Ann. tit. 16, § 4905A (West 2016) (similar); 410 Ill. Comp. Stat. Ann. 130/40 (West 2016) (similar); Me. Rev. Stat. tit. 22, § 2423-E(2) (2016).

Pennsylvania has adopted more extensive regulations regarding employment of medical marijuana users. It imposes a duty to accommodate marijuana use, but it also recognizes several limitations on that duty. In relevant part, Pennsylvania's 2016 Medical Marijuana Act provides:

(1) No employer may discharge, threaten, refuse to hire or otherwise discriminate or retaliate against an employee regarding an employee's compensation, terms, conditions, location or privileges solely on the basis of such employee's status as an individual who is certified to use medical marijuana.

(2) Nothing in this act shall require an employer to make any accommodation of the use of medical marijuana on the property or premises of any place of employment. This act shall in no way limit an employer's ability to discipline an employee for being under the influence of medical marijuana in the workplace or for working while under the influence of medical marijuana when the employee's conduct falls below the standard of care normally accepted for that position.

(3) Nothing in this act shall require an employer to commit any act that would put the employer or any person acting on its behalf in violation of Federal law.

35 Pa. Stat. Ann. § 10231.2103 (West 2016).

(2) A patient may not perform any employment duties at heights or in confined spaces, including, but not limited to, mining while under the influence of medical marijuana.

(3) A patient may be prohibited by an employer from performing any task which the employer deems life-threatening, to either the employee or any of the employees of the employer, while under the influence of medical marijuana. The prohibition shall not be deemed an adverse employment decision even if the prohibition results in financial harm for the patient.

(4) A patient may be prohibited by an employer from performing any duty which could result in a public health or safety risk while under the influence of medical marijuana. The prohibition shall not be deemed an adverse employment decision even if the prohibition results in financial harm for the patient.

35 Pa. Stat. Ann. § 10231.510 (West 2016).

## Notes and Questions

1. No state appears to require employers to accommodate marijuana use *at the workplace*. But what does it mean to use marijuana at the workplace? An Oregon court

confronted this question under a state law that provided "[n]othing in [Oregon's Medical Marijuana Law] requires . . . (2) An employer to accommodate the medical use of marijuana in the workplace." Or. Rev. Stat. Ann. § 475B.413 (West 2016). In the case, an employer fired an employee after a drug test revealed that the employee had used marijuana at some time in the previous two to three weeks. *Washburn v. Columbia Forest Prods., Inc.*, 104 P.3d 609 (Or. App. 2005), *rev'd. Washburn v. Columbia Forest Prods., Inc.*, 134 P.3d 161 (2006). The employer relied on a company policy that barred employees from "[r]eport[ing] for work with the presence of [a] controlled substance, intoxicant, or illegal drug in their system." The employee sued under an Oregon law that bars employment discrimination against individuals with disabilities, claiming the law required the employer to accommodate his medical use of marijuana outside of the workplace. In response, the employer argued that the employee had technically "used" marijuana at the workplace because he still had traces of the drug in his system when he showed up for work. The court disagreed. After quoting a provision of Oregon law that defines medical use of marijuana as "the production, possession, delivery, or administration of marijuana," the court found:

> The somewhat closer question is whether, by having evidence of marijuana consumption in his urine, plaintiff "possessed" marijuana in the workplace. No form of the word "possess" is defined in [Oregon law]. However, we have previously rejected the contention that a person who has evidence of a controlled substance in his or her bloodstream "possesses" that substance for purposes of a prosecution for possession of a controlled substance. . . . *State v. Daline*, 175 Or. App. 625, 632, 30 P.3d 426 (2001) (holding that, because dominion and control are central to "possession," once a person consumes a controlled substance and the substance enters bodily fluids, the person no longer possesses the substance). We perceive no reason why the view of the meaning of the term "possession" that we applied with respect to [Oregon criminal law] should not apply here as well. Accordingly, plaintiff did not engage in "possession" of marijuana in the workplace when he reported to work with evidence of marijuana consumption in his urine.

104 P.3d at 615. The decision was overturned on other grounds by the Oregon Supreme Court. 134 P.3d at 479 (finding that employee was not disabled for purposes of Oregon law). What if Oregon followed the minority rule—discussed in Chapter 4—that defines simple possession to include the presence of a drug in one's body? Would the *Washburn* court have reached a different conclusion about whether the employee had used marijuana are the workplace?

2. Even if they require employers to accommodate medical marijuana use off of the job, most reform states do not require employers to cover the costs of medical marijuana—even when an employee uses it to treat a workplace related injury. *See, e.g.*, 410 Ill. Comp. Stat. Ann. 130/40(d) (West 2016) ("(d) Nothing in this Act may be construed to require a government medical assistance program, employer, property and casualty insurer, or private health insurer to reimburse a person for costs associated with the medical use of cannabis."); Or. Rev. Stat. Ann. § 475B.413 (West 2016) (similar). *But see Lewis v. Am. Gen. Media*, 355 P.3d 850 (N.M. Ct. App. 2015) (holding that employer is responsible for cost of medical marijuana used to treat work-related injury).

3. Many professional football players have expressed support for allowing players to use marijuana to treat the pain associated with sports-related injuries. But even if other

employers are required to accommodate the medical marijuana use of employees, are National Football League (NFL) teams required to do so? Not necessarily. The existing Collective Bargaining Agreement (CBA) between the League and its players "prohibit[s] Players from the illegal use, possession, or distribution of drugs, including but not limited to cocaine; marijuana; opiates and opioids." National Football League, Policy and Program on Substances of Abuse 1, n.1 (2015), https://perma.cc/CY6T-NDX9. The CBA provides for drug testing and sanctions—including fines and suspensions—for players who test positive for marijuana use. However, the NFL and the players' union are considering relaxing the restrictions on medical marijuana use in their next CBA. See Ian Rapaport, *Several NFL Owners, Execs, Eyeing Marijuana Discipline Changes*, NFL.com, Nov. 13, 2016, https://perma.cc/L2CT-Z72J.

### b. Implied Duty to Accommodate

In states that have not expressly imposed a duty to accommodate employee marijuana use, the question has arisen whether such a duty may nonetheless be implied by state medical marijuana laws and/or general state anti-discrimination laws. Nearly all courts to have addressed the issue have answered "no." The following case—one of the first on point—discusses the arguments on both sides of the question.

### *Ross v. RagingWire Telecommunications, Inc.*
174 P.3d 200 (Cal. 2008)

WERDEGAR, J.:

Plaintiff Gary Ross suffers from strain and muscle spasms in his back as a result of injuries he sustained while serving in the United States Air Force. Because of his condition, plaintiff is a qualified individual with a disability under the [California Fair Employment and Housing Act (FEHA)]. . . . In September 1999, after failing to obtain relief from pain through other medications, plaintiff began to use marijuana on his physician's recommendation pursuant to the Compassionate Use Act.

On September 10, 2001, defendant RagingWire Telecommunications, Inc., offered plaintiff a job as lead systems administrator. Defendant required plaintiff to take a drug test. Before taking the test, plaintiff gave the clinic that would administer the test a copy of his physician's recommendation for marijuana. Plaintiff took the test on September 14 and began work on September 17. Later that week, the clinic informed plaintiff by telephone that he had tested positive for tetrahydrocannabinol (THC), a chemical found in marijuana. On September 20, defendant informed plaintiff he was being suspended as a result of the drug test. Plaintiff gave defendant a copy of his physician's recommendation for marijuana and explained to defendant's human resources director that he used marijuana for medical purposes to relieve his chronic back pain. . . . On September 21, defendant's board of directors met to discuss the matter and, on September 25, defendant's chief executive officer informed plaintiff that he was being fired because of his marijuana use.

Plaintiff's disability and use of marijuana to treat pain, he alleges, do not affect his ability to do the essential functions of the job for which defendant hired him. Plaintiff has worked in the same field since he began to use marijuana and has performed satisfactorily, without complaints about his job performance.

Based on these allegations, plaintiff alleges defendant violated the FEHA by discharging him because of, and by failing to make reasonable accommodation for, his disability.... [The trial court dismissed Plaintiff's complaint and the Plaintiff appealed.] ...

. . .

The FEHA declares and implements the state's public policy against discrimination in employment.... The particular section of the FEHA under which plaintiff attempts to state a claim, Government Code section 12940, provides that "[i]t shall be an unlawful employment practice . . . [¶] (a) For an employer, because of the . . . physical disability [or] medical condition . . . of any person, to refuse to hire or employ the person . . . or to bar or to discharge the person from employment . . ." An employer may discharge or refuse to hire a person who, because of a disability or medical condition, "is unable to perform his or her essential duties even with reasonable accommodations." . . . The FEHA thus inferentially requires employers in their hiring decisions to take into account the feasibility of making reasonable accommodations.

Plaintiff, seeking to bring himself within the FEHA, alleges he has a physical disability in that he "suffers from a lower back strain and muscle spasms in his back. . . ." He uses marijuana to treat the resulting pain. Marijuana use, however, brings plaintiff into conflict with defendant's employment policies, which apparently deny employment to persons who test positive for illegal drugs. By denying him employment and failing to make reasonable accommodation, plaintiff alleges, defendant has violated the FEHA. . . . [Plaintiff] is asking defendant to accommodate his use of marijuana at home by waiving its policy requiring a negative drug test of new employees. "Just as it would violate the FEHA to fire an employee who uses insulin or Zoloft," plaintiff argues, "it violates [the] statute to terminate an employee who uses a medicine deemed legal by the California electorate upon the recommendation of his physician." In this way, plaintiff reasons, "the [FEHA] works together with the Compassionate Use Act . . . to provide a remedy to [him]."

Plaintiff's position might have merit if the Compassionate Use Act gave marijuana the same status as any legal prescription drug. But the act's effect is not so broad. . . . Nothing in the text or history of the Compassionate Use Act suggests the voters intended the measure to address the respective rights and obligations of employers and employees.

The FEHA does not require employers to accommodate the use of illegal drugs. The point is perhaps too obvious to have generated appellate litigation, but we recognized it implicitly in [*Loder v. City of Glendale*, 927 P.2d 1200 (Cal. 1997).] . . . In reaching [the conclusion that an employer may require an employee to undergo a drug test], we relied on a regulation adopted under the authority of the FEHA . . . that permits an employer to condition an offer of employment on the results of a medical examination. . . . We held that such an examination may include drug testing and, in so holding, necessarily recognized that employers may deny employment to persons who test positive for illegal drugs. . . . We determined the employer's interest was legitimate "[i]n light of the well-documented problems that are associated with the abuse of drugs and alcohol by employees—increased absenteeism, diminished productivity, greater health costs, increased safety problems and potential liability to third parties, and more frequent turnover. . . ." . . .

The Compassionate Use Act (Health & Saf. Code, § 11362.5) does not eliminate marijuana's potential for abuse or the employer's legitimate interest in whether an employee uses the drug. Marijuana . . . remains illegal under federal law because of its "high potential for abuse," its lack of any "currently accepted medical use in treatment in the United States," and its "lack of accepted safety for use . . . under medical supervision." . . . Although California's voters had no power to change federal law, certainly they were free to disagree with Congress's assessment of marijuana, and they also were free to view the possibility of beneficial medical use as a sufficient basis for exempting from criminal liability under state law patients whose physicians recommend the drug. The logic of this position, however, did not compel the voters to take the additional step of requiring employers to accommodate marijuana use by their employees. The voters were entitled to change the criminal law without also speaking to employment law.

The operative provisions of the Compassionate Use Act (Health & Saf. Code, § 11362.5) do not speak to employment law. Except in their treatment of physicians, who are protected not only from "punish[ment]" but also from being "denied any right or privilege . . . for having recommended marijuana" (id., subd. (c)), the act's operative provisions speak exclusively to the criminal law. . . .

Neither is employment law mentioned in the findings and declarations (Health & Saf. Code, § 11362.5, subd. (b)(1)(A)-(C) & (2)) that precede the Compassionate Use Act's operative provisions. In those introductory provisions, the voters declared their intent "[t]o ensure that seriously ill Californians have the right to obtain and use marijuana for medical purposes" under the conditions stated in the act (id., subd. (b)(1)(A)), to ensure that medical users of marijuana and their primary caregivers "are not subject to criminal prosecution or sanction" (id., subd. (b)(1)(B)), and "[t]o encourage the federal and state governments to implement a plan to provide for the safe and affordable distribution of marijuana" (id., subd. (b)(1)(C)). In a final introductory provision, the voters declared that "[n]othing in this section [i.e., the Compassionate Use Act] shall be construed to supersede legislation prohibiting persons from engaging in conduct that endangers others, nor to condone the diversion of marijuana for nonmedical purposes." (Id., subd. (b)(2).)

Plaintiff would read the first of these findings and declarations . . . as if it created a broad right to use marijuana without hindrance or inconvenience, enforceable against private parties such as employers. . . . Not to require employers to accommodate marijuana use, plaintiff contends, "would eviscerate the right promised to the seriously ill by the California electorate." To the contrary, the only "right" to obtain and use marijuana created by the Compassionate Use Act is the right of "a patient, or . . . a patient's primary caregiver, [to] possess[ ] or cultivate[ ] marijuana for the personal medical purposes of the patient upon the written or oral recommendation or approval of a physician" without thereby becoming subject to punishment under sections 11357 and 11358 of the Health and Safety Code. (Id., § 11362.5, subd. (d).) An employer's refusal to accommodate an employee's use of marijuana does not affect, let alone eviscerate, the immunity to criminal liability provided in the act. . . .

. . .

Finally, plaintiff contends that legislation enacted after the Compassionate Use Act (Health & Saf. Code, § 11362.5) requires employers to accommodate employees' use of medical marijuana at home. Plaintiff attempts to find such a rule in Health and Safety Code section 11362.785, subdivision (a) (added by Stats. 2003, ch. 875, § 2), which took effect more than two years after defendant terminated plaintiff's employment. The statute provides as follows: "Nothing in this article shall require any accommodation of any medical use of marijuana on the property or premises of any place of employment or during the hours of employment or on the property or premises of any jail, correctional facility, or other type of penal institution in which prisoners reside or persons under arrest are detained." (Health & Saf. Code, § 11362.785, subd. (a).) Plaintiff would read this language as if it articulated express exceptions to a general requirement of accommodation that appears only implicitly. Plaintiff's interpretation might be plausible if the failure to infer a requirement of accommodation would render the statute meaningless, but such is not the case. Even without inferring a requirement of accommodation, the statute can be given literal effect as negating any expectation that the immunity to criminal liability for possessing marijuana granted in the Compassionate Use Act gives medical users a civilly enforceable right to possess the drug at work or in custody.

In any event, given the controversy that would inevitably have attended a legislative proposal to require employers to accommodate marijuana use, we do not believe that Health and Safety Code section 11362.785, subdivision (a), can reasonably be understood as adopting such a requirement silently and without debate.

. . .

We thus conclude that plaintiff cannot state a cause of action under the FEHA based on defendant's refusal to accommodate his use of marijuana.

. . .

KENNARD, J. [, dissenting from the majority's decision regarding FEHA]:

Under this state's Compassionate Use Act of 1996[,] doctor-recommended marijuana use as a medical treatment is "not subject to criminal prosecution or sanction." (Health & Saf. Code, § 11362.5, subd. (b)(1)(B).) In a decision conspicuously lacking in compassion, however, the majority holds that an employer may fire an employee for such marijuana use, even when it occurs during off-duty hours, does not affect the employee's job performance, does not impair the employer's legitimate business interests, and provides the only effective relief for the employee's chronic pain and muscle spasms. I disagree.

. . .

Courts must construe statutes to effectuate the purpose of the law. . . . [T]he purpose of the Compassionate Use Act is to allow California residents to use marijuana, when a doctor recommends it, to treat medical conditions, including chronic pain, without being subject "to criminal prosecution *or sanction.*" (Health & Saf. Code, § 11362.5, subd. (b)(1)(B), italics added.) The majority's construction defeats, rather than effectuates, that purpose. The majority renders illusory the law's promise that responsible use of marijuana as a medical treatment will be free of sanction. The majority allows employers to impose the sanction of job termination on those employees who use marijuana under the statute's provisions. The majority's decision leaves many Californians with serious illnesses just two options: continue receiving the benefits of marijuana use "in the treatment of cancer, anorexia, AIDS, chronic pain, spasticity, glaucoma, arthritis, migraine, or [ ] other illness" (Health & Saf. Code, § 11362.5, subd. (b)(1)(A)) and become unemployed, giving up what may be their only source of income, or continue in their employment, discontinue marijuana treatment, and try to endure their chronic pain or other condition for which marijuana may provide the only relief. Surely this cruel choice is not what California voters intended when they enacted the state Compassionate Use Act.

Nor is this cruel choice something that the FEHA permits. One of the FEHA's stated purposes is "to protect and safeguard the right and opportunity of all persons to seek, obtain, and hold employment without discrimination or abridgement on account of . . . physical disability . . . [or] medical condition. . . ." (Gov. Code, § 12920.) The FEHA recognizes that "the practice of denying employment opportunity . . . [on account of physical disability or medical condition] deprives the state of the fullest utilization of its capacities for development and advancement, and substantially and adversely affects the interest of employees, employers, and the public in general." (*Ibid.*) Under the FEHA, it is an unlawful employment practice "[f]or an employer . . . to fail to make reasonable accommodation for the known physical or mental disability of an applicant or employee" (*id.*, § 12940, subd. (m)) or "to fail to engage in a timely, good faith, interactive process with [an] employee or applicant to determine effective reasonable accommodations" (*id.*, § 12940, subd. (n)). The FEHA directs that its provisions are to be construed liberally to accomplish each of its purposes. (*Id.*, § 12993, subd. (a).)

. . .

Nothing in the text of the FEHA or in California decisional law supports the proposition that a requested accommodation can never be deemed reasonable if it involves off-duty conduct by the employee away from the jobsite that is criminal under federal law, even though that same conduct is expressly protected from criminal sanction under state law. Rather, under the FEHA, determining whether an employee-proposed accommodation is reasonable requires consideration of its benefits to the employee (including its effectiveness in meeting the employee's disability-related needs and enabling the employee to competently perform the essential job functions), the burdens it would impose on the employer and other employees, and the availability of suitable and effective alternative forms of accommodation. . . .

The FEHA does not require an employer to make any accommodation that the employer can demonstrate would impose an "undue hardship" on the operation of its business. (Gov. Code, § 12940, subd. (m).) The FEHA defines an "[u]ndue hardship" as "an action requiring significant difficulty or expense, when considered in light of the following factors: [¶] (1) The nature and cost of the accommodation needed. [¶] (2) The overall financial resources of the facilities involved in the provision of the reasonable accommodations, the number of persons employed at the facility, and the effect on expenses and resources or the impact otherwise of these accommodations upon the operation of the facility. [¶] (3) The overall financial resources of the covered entity, the overall size of the business of a covered entity with respect to the number of employees, and the number, type, and location of its facilities. [¶] (4) The type of operations, including the composition, structure, and functions of the workforce of the entity. [¶] (5) The geographic separateness, administrative, or fiscal relationship of the facility or facilities." (*id.*, § 12926, subd. (s).)

Here, plaintiff's complaint alleges in substance that marijuana use is essential to provide him relief from the chronic pain and muscle spasms of his disabling back condition, that more conventional medications have not provided similar relief, and that effective treatment is necessary for him to work productively. RagingWire has not argued that plaintiff's requested accommodation would interfere with the rights or interests of its other employees. Accordingly, the reasonableness of the proposed accommodation of allowing plaintiff to use marijuana at home, as an exception to RagingWire's normal drug-screening policies, turns on *how it would affect RagingWire's legitimate interests as an employer* and, more specifically, whether it would impose an "undue hardship"— defined as "an action requiring significant difficulty or expense"—on the operation of the RagingWire's business. . . . To establish that plaintiff's proposed accommodation was unreasonable, therefore, RagingWire must show that, because marijuana possession is illegal under federal law, an employee's off-duty and offsite use of marijuana would adversely affect its business operations.

RagingWire cites the state Drug-Free Workplace Act of 1990 (Gov. Code, § 8350 et seq.) as demonstrating that employers are not required to tolerate marijuana use by their employees. Under that legislation, persons or organizations that provide property or services to any state agency are required to certify that they will "provide a drug-free workplace" (*id.*, § 8355), which is defined as "a site . . . at which employees of the entity are prohibited from engaging in the unlawful manufacture, distribution, dispensation, possession, or use of a controlled substance" (*id.*, § 8351, subd. (a)). The term "controlled substance" is defined to include any substance, like marijuana, listed in schedule I of the federal Controlled Substances Act (21 U.S.C. § 812). (Gov. Code, § 8351, subd. (c).) Under federal law, federal grant recipients are subject to a similar drug-free workplace requirement. (41 U.S.C. § 702.)

RagingWire argues that, under these state and federal laws, tolerating plaintiff's doctor-approved marijuana use would jeopardize its ability to contract with state agencies or to obtain federal grants. Both the state and federal drug-free workplace laws are concerned only with conduct *at the jobsite*, however. RagingWire argues that an employee who ingested marijuana at home but remained under its influence at work might be viewed as "using" marijuana at work. But plaintiff has not sought an accommodation that would allow him to possess or be under the influence of marijuana at work. The drug-free workplace laws are not concerned with employees' possession or use of drugs like marijuana away from the jobsite, and nothing in those laws would prevent an employer that knowingly accepted an employee's use of marijuana as a medical treatment at the employee's home from obtaining drug-free workplace certification.

. . .

The majority appears to rely in part on [*Loder v. City of Glendale*]. There, the City of Glendale had adopted a drug testing program under which all job applicants who had conditionally been offered employment and all existing employees who had been approved for promotion to new positions were required to undergo urinalysis testing for a variety of illegal drugs. . . . If the test revealed "the presence of drugs *for which the applicant* [had] *no legitimate medical explanation*, the applicant [was] disqualified for hiring or promotion . . ." [*Id.* (italics added.)] . . .

In *Loder*, a majority of this court acknowledged that an employer has a legitimate interest in determining whether job applicants and employees are *abusing* drugs, because drug *abuse* is commonly associated with increased absenteeism, diminished productivity, greater health costs, increased safety problems, potential liability to third parties, and more frequent turnover. . . . "[A]n employer generally need not resort to suspicionless drug testing to determine whether a *current employee* is likely to be absent from work or less productive or effective as a result of current drug or alcohol abuse: an employer can observe the employee at work, evaluate his or her work product and safety record, and check employment records to determine whether the employee has been excessively absent or late." [*Id.* (italics added).] . . . For a *job applicant*, however, "an employer has not had a similar opportunity to observe the applicant over a period of time" and "reasonably may lack total confidence in the reliability of information supplied by a former employer or other references." [*Id.*] . . .

A necessary implication of this reasoning is that *in the absence of a legitimate medical explanation*, test results showing a job applicant's drug use are generally a sufficient basis to deny employment. . . . Another necessary implication of *Loder's* reasoning is that the likely impacts on the employer's business operations—in the form of increased absenteeism, diminished productivity, greater health costs, increased safety problems, potential liability to third parties, and more frequent turnover—provide the appropriate yardstick for measuring the employer's legitimate interests in this context.

*Loder* is not directly relevant here because plaintiff is not challenging RagingWire's right to conduct preemployment drug testing, and because the program at issue in *Loder* sought to detect the presence of drugs "for which the applicant [had] no legitimate medical explanation". . . . By contrast, plaintiff uses marijuana as a doctor-recommended treatment under the state Compassionate Use Act for a disabling physical condition. No evidence before this court establishes that use of a controlled substance under a doctor's recommendation poses the same risks of excessive absences and diminished productivity that a majority of this court relied on in *Loder* to uphold a drug testing program.

Considered strictly in terms of its physical effects relevant to employee productivity and safety, and not its legal status, marijuana does not differ significantly from many prescription drugs—for example, hydrocodone (Vicodin), hydromorphone (Dilaudid), oxycodone (OxyContin), methylphenidate (Ritalin), methadone (Dolophine), and diazepam (Valium)—that may affect cognitive functioning and have a potential for abuse. The medical use of any such drug poses some risks of absenteeism and impaired productivity. Indeed, many nonprescription medications taken for the common cold, seasonal allergies, and similar minor afflictions frequently have side effects, such as drowsiness or dizziness, that may impair productivity. The majority does not deny that the FEHA may require an employer to accommodate a disabled employee's doctor-approved medical use of other substances that potentially could impair job performance.

I conclude, for these reasons, that plaintiff's complaint states a cause of action for disability discrimination under California's FEHA.

## Notes and Questions

1. As a matter of statutory interpretation, which opinion do you find more persuasive—the majority or the dissent? Do you agree with the dissent that the language of the CUA—shielding qualified patients from "criminal prosecution *or sanction*"—was intended to shield qualified patients from employment sanctions? If so, would it shield qualifying patients from other private sanctions as well?

2. As a matter of policy, *should* employers be required to accommodate their employees' state-approved marijuana use off of the job? Why would employers want to limit such use in the first instance? Does marijuana use contribute to work-related accidents? *See*

Macdonald, *Testing for Cannabis, supra,* at 411 ("Numerous research studies have either compared injury/accident rates among workers who test positive for cannabis versus those who test negative, or compared injury/accident rates among workers who self-report drug use versus those who do not. Findings from these studies are mixed, with some studies showing a significant relationship and others failing to do so."). Is there any way for employers to address these safety concerns, other than by adopting a blanket non-use policy? *See* Stacy A. Hickox, *Drug Testing of Medical Marijuana Users in the Workplace: An Inaccurate Test of Impairment,* 29 Hofstra Lab. & Emp. L.J. 273, 274 (2012) ("[E]mployers should rely on evidence of actual impairment of the applicant or employee rather than a drug screen. With individualized assessment of impairment, employers can still promote safety and productivity in the workplace, while giving medical marijuana users an opportunity to continue working productively.").

3. *Ross* and similar cases involve the application of state medical marijuana laws and/or state laws prohibiting discrimination based on disability, like California's FEHA. But some state laws bar discrimination against employees based on *any* lawful activities outside the workplace. *E.g.,* Colo. Rev. Stat. Section 24-34-402.5(1) (2016) ("It shall be a discriminatory or unfair employment practice for an employer to terminate the employment of any employee due to that employee's engaging in any lawful activity off the premises of the employer during nonworking hours."). Do these broader state anti-discrimination laws impose a duty to accommodate state-approved recreational marijuana use "off the premises of the employer during nonworking hours"? *See Coats v. Dish Network, LLC,* 350 P.3d 849, 853 (Colo. 2015) (finding that "because employee's marijuana use was unlawful under federal law, it does not fall within section 24-34-402.5's protection for 'lawful' activities").

## 2. Is a State-Imposed Duty to Accommodate Marijuana Use Preempted by Federal Law?

Even if a state imposes a duty to accommodate marijuana use, could an employer nonetheless defend against an employment suit based on the grounds that the state duty is preempted by federal law? The Oregon Supreme Court court confronted this question in *Emerald Steel Fabricators, Inc. v. Bureau of Labor and Industries,* 230 P.3d 518 (Or. 2010). The facts of the case are similar to those of *Ross, supra.*

In *Emerald Steel,* the plaintiff/employee was discharged from his job at a steel products manufacturer when he informed the company that he was using marijuana to treat a medical condition, pursuant to Oregon's medical marijuana law. Plaintiff then sued the company under a state law that requires employers to accommodate drug use that is "authorized under the Controlled Substances Act or under other provisions of state or federal law." Or. Rev. Stat. Ann. § 659A.122(2) (West 2016). The *Emerald Steel* court held that:

> The Oregon Medical Marijuana Act affirmatively authorizes the use of medical marijuana, in addition to exempting its use from state criminal liability. Specifically, ORS 475.306(1) provides that "[a] person who possesses a registry identification card * * * may engage in * * * the medical use of marijuana" subject to certain restrictions. ORS 475.302(10), in turn, defines a registry identification card as "a document * * * that identifies a person authorized to engage in the medical use of marijuana." . . .

But the court then held that Oregon law is preempted by the federal CSA to the extent it "authorizes" the medical use of marijuana. The portion of the court's opinion addressing the preemption issue is excerpted below.

## *Emerald Steel Fabricators, Inc. v. Bureau of Labor and Industries*
230 P.3d 518 (Or. 2010)

KISTLER, J.:

The Court has applied the physical impossibility prong [of preemption] narrowly. . . . For example, in *Barnett Bank v. Nelson*, 517 U.S. 25 [] (1996), the question was whether "a federal statute that permits national banks to sell insurance in small towns pre-empts a state statute that forbids them to do so." . . . Although the two statutes were logically inconsistent, the Court held that it was not physically impossible to comply with both. . . . A national bank could simply refrain from selling insurance. . . .

Under that reasoning, it is not physically impossible to comply with both the Oregon Medical Marijuana Act and the federal Controlled Substances Act. To be sure, the two laws are logically inconsistent; state law authorizes what federal law prohibits. However, a person can comply with both laws by refraining from any use of marijuana, in much the same way that a national bank could comply with state and federal law in *Barnett Bank* by simply refraining from selling insurance.

Because the "physical impossibility" prong of implied preemption is "vanishingly narrow," Caleb Nelson, *Preemption*, 86 Va. L. Rev. 225, 228 (2000), the Court's decisions typically have turned on the second prong of implied preemption analysis—whether state law "stands as an obstacle to the accomplishment and execution of the full purposes and objectives of Congress." . . . In *Barnett Bank*, for example, the Court stated, as a self-evident proposition, that a state law that prohibited national banks from selling insurance when federal law permitted them to do so would stand as an obstacle to the full accomplishment of Congress's purpose, but it then added "unless, of course, that federal purpose is to grant [national] bank[s] only a very *limited* permission, that is, permission to sell insurance *to the extent that state law also grants permission to do so*." . . . Having considered the text and history of the federal statute and finding no basis for implying such a limited permission, the Court held that the state statute was preempted.

The Court has reached the same conclusion when, as in this case, state law permits what federal law prohibits. *Michigan Canners & Freezers Association v. Agricultural Marketing and Bargaining Bd.*, 467 U.S. 461 [] (1984). In *Michigan Canners*, federal law prohibited food producers' associations from interfering with an individual food producer's decision whether to bring that individual's products to the market on his or her own or to sell them through the association. . . . [H]owever, Michigan law permitted food producers' associations to apply to a state board for authority to act as the exclusive bargaining agent for all producers of a particular commodity. . . . When the state board gave a producer's association that authority, all producers of a commodity had to adhere to the terms of the contracts that the association negotiated with food processors, even when the producer had declined to join the association. . . .

. . . The Court went on to conclude . . . that "because the Michigan Act authorizes producers' associations to engage in conduct that the federal Act forbids, it 'stands as an obstacle to the accomplishment and execution of the full purposes and objectives of Congress.'" . . .

The preemption issue in this case is similar to the issue in *Michigan Canners* and *Barnett Bank*. In this case, ORS 475.306(1) affirmatively authorizes the use of medical marijuana. The Controlled Substances Act, however, prohibits the use of marijuana without regard to whether it is used for medicinal purposes. As the Supreme Court has recognized, by classifying marijuana as a Schedule 1 drug, Congress has expressed its judgment that marijuana has no recognized medical use. *See* [*Gonzales v. Raich*, 545 U.S. 1, 14 (2005)]. Congress did not intend to enact a limited prohibition on the use of marijuana—*i.e.*, to prohibit the use of marijuana unless states chose to authorize its use for medical purposes. . . . Rather, Congress imposed a blanket federal prohibition on the use of marijuana without regard to state permission to use marijuana for medical purposes. . . .

Affirmatively authorizing a use that federal law prohibits stands as an obstacle to the implementation and execution of the full purposes and objectives of the Controlled Substances Act. . . . To be sure, state law does not prevent the federal government from enforcing its marijuana laws against medical marijuana users in Oregon if the federal government chooses to do so. But the state law at issue in *Michigan Canners* did not prevent the federal government from seeking injunctive and other relief to enforce the federal prohibition in that case. Rather, state law stood as an obstacle to the enforcement of federal law in *Michigan Canners* because state law affirmatively authorized the very conduct that federal law prohibited, as it does in this case.

To the extent that ORS 475.306(1) affirmatively authorizes the use of medical marijuana, federal law preempts that subsection, leaving it "without effect." . . . Because ORS 475.306(1) was not enforceable when employer discharged employee, no enforceable state law . . . authorized employee's use of marijuana. . . .

[The court proceeded to distinguish an Opinion of the State Attorney General, relied on by the plaintiff, which concluded that the parts of Oregon's Medical Marijuana Act that exempt marijuana use from state criminal sanctions were not preempted by the federal CSA.] . . . In concluding that those exemptions from state criminal liability were valid, the Attorney General relied on a line of federal cases holding that "Congress cannot compel the States to enact or enforce a federal regulatory program." *See Printz v. United States*, 521 U.S. 898, 935 [] (1997) (so stating); *New York v. United States*, 505 U.S. 144, 162 [] (1992) (stating that "the Constitution has never been understood to confer upon Congress the ability to require the States to govern according to Congress's instructions"). The Attorney General concluded that Oregon was free, as a matter of state law, to exempt medical marijuana use from criminal liability because Congress lacks the authority to require Oregon to prohibit that use.

The Attorney General's opinion has no bearing on the issue presented in this case. . . .

. . . [T]he validity of the exemptions and the validity of the authorization turn on different constitutional principles. The Attorney General reasoned that the exemptions from criminal liability are valid because "Congress cannot compel the States to enact or enforce a federal regulatory program"—a restriction that derives from Congress's limited authority under the federal constitution. . . .

By contrast, there is no dispute that Congress has the authority under the Supremacy Clause to preempt state laws that affirmatively authorize the use of medical marijuana. Whether Congress has exercised that authority turns on congressional intent: that is, did Congress intend to preempt the state law? . . . More specifically, the constitutional question in this case is whether, under the doctrine of implied preemption, a state law authorizing the use of medical marijuana "stands as an obstacle to the accomplishment and execution of the full purposes and objectives of Congress." . . .

. . . [T]he dissent would hold that a state law stands as an obstacle to the execution and accomplishment of the full purposes of a federal law (and is thus preempted) if the state law purports to override federal law either by giving permission to violate the federal law or by preventing the federal government from enforcing its laws. We do not disagree that such a law would be an obstacle. But it does not follow that anything less is not an obstacle. Specifically, we disagree with the dissent's view that a state law that specifically authorizes conduct that a federal law expressly forbids does not pose an obstacle to the full accomplishment of the purposes of the federal law and is not preempted.

If Congress chose to prohibit anyone under the age of 21 from driving, states could not authorize anyone over the age of 16 to drive and give them a license to do so. The state law would stand as an obstacle to the accomplishment of the full purposes and objectives of Congress (keeping everyone under the age of 21 off the road) and would be preempted. Or, to use a different example, if federal law prohibited all sale and possession of alcohol, a state law licensing the sale of alcohol and authorizing its use would stand as an obstacle to the full accomplishment of Congress's purposes. ORS 475.306(1) is no different. To the extent that ORS 475.306(1) authorizes persons holding medical marijuana licenses to engage in conduct that the Controlled Substances Act explicitly prohibits, it poses the same obstacle to the full accomplishment of Congress's purposes (preventing all use of marijuana, including medical uses).

. . .

Another thread runs through the dissent. It reasons that, as a practical matter, authorizing medical marijuana use is no different from exempting that use from criminal liability. It concludes that, if exempting medical marijuana use from criminal liability is not an obstacle to the accomplishment of the purposes of the Controlled Substances Act and is thus not preempted, then neither is a state law authorizing medical marijuana use. The difficulty with the dissent's reasoning is its premise. It presumes that a law exempting medical marijuana use from liability is valid because it is not preempted. As the Attorney General's opinion explained, however, Congress lacks the authority to compel a state to criminalize conduct, no matter how explicitly it directs a state to do so. When, however, a state affirmatively authorizes conduct, Congress has the authority to preempt that law and did so here. The dissent's reasoning fails to distinguish those two analytically separate constitutional principles.

WALTERS, J., dissenting:

. . .

The majority seems to accept that the Oregon Medical Marijuana Act does not bar the federal government from enforcing the Controlled Substances Act. The majority acknowledges that "state law does not prevent the federal government from enforcing its marijuana laws against medical marijuana users in Oregon if the federal government chooses to do so." . . . The majority also seems to accept, as a result, that provisions of the Oregon Medical Marijuana Act that exempt persons from state criminal liability do not pose an obstacle to the Controlled Substances Act. However, in the majority's view, one subsection of the Oregon Medical Marijuana Act, ORS 475.306(1), presents an obstacle to the

Controlled Substances Act and does so solely because it includes words of authorization. . . .

. . .

The Oregon Medical Marijuana Act contains a number of subsections that use words of authorization. Those subsections are interwoven with the subsections of the act that except and exempt medical marijuana users from criminal liability. For instance, ORS 475.309, which the majority cites as a provision that excepts persons who use medical marijuana from state criminal liability, . . . provides that a person engaged in or assisting in the medical use of marijuana "is *excepted* from the criminal laws of the state" *if* certain conditions, including holding a "*registry identification card*," are satisfied. (Emphases added.) ORS 475.302(10) defines "registry identification card" as follows:

> "a document issued by the department that identifies a person *authorized* to engage in the medical use of marijuana and the person's designated primary caregiver, if any."

(Emphasis added.)

Consider also ORS 475.306(1), the section of the act that the majority finds offending. That subsection references both ORS 475.309, the exception section, and the registry identification card necessary to that exception. ORS 475.306(1) provides:

> "A person who possesses a *registry identification card* issued *pursuant to ORS 475.309* may engage in, and a designated primary caregiver of such person may assist in, the medical use of marijuana only as justified to mitigate the symptoms or effects of the person's debilitating medical condition."

(Emphasis added.) Reading those three provisions together, it is clear that ORS 475.306(1) serves as a *limitation* on the use of medical marijuana that the registry identification card and ORS 475.309 together permit. Under ORS 475.306(1), a person who possesses a registry identification card issued pursuant to ORS 475.309 may engage in the use the card permits "*only* as justified to mitigate the symptoms or effects of the person's debilitating medical condition." (Emphasis added.)

ORS 475.319, another section of the act that the majority cites as creating an exemption from criminal liability, also depends on words of permission for its operation. . . . ORS 475.319 creates an affirmative defense to a criminal charge of possession of marijuana, but only for persons who possess marijuana "in amounts *permitted* under ORS 475.320." (Emphasis added.) ORS 475.320(1)(a) provides: "A *registry identification cardholder* * * * *may possess* up to six mature marijuana plants and 24 ounces of usable marijuana." (Emphasis added.)

The words of authorization used in ORS 475.306(1) are no different from the words of authorization that are used in other sections of the act and that are necessary to effectuate ORS 475.309 and ORS 475.319 and the exceptions to and exemptions from criminal liability that they create. Those words of authorization do not grant permission that would not exist if those words were eliminated or replaced with words of exception or exclusion. Even if it did not use words of permission, the Oregon Medical Marijuana Act would permit, for purposes of Oregon law, the conduct that it does not punish. Furthermore, the statutory sections that provide that citizens may, for state law purposes, engage in the conduct that the state will not punish have no effect on the Controlled Substances Act that is greater than the effect of the sections that declare that the state will not punish that conduct.

Because neither the Oregon Medical Marijuana Act nor any subsection thereof gives permission to violate the Controlled Substances Act or affects its enforcement, the Oregon act does not pose an obstacle to the federal act necessitating a finding of implied preemption. . . .

. . . [T]he majority relies on two United States Supreme Court cases for the proposition that state law that permits what federal law prohibits is impliedly preempted. . . . The majority then concludes that, "[t]o the extent that ORS 475.306(1) affirmatively authorizes the use of medical marijuana, federal law preempts that subsection, leaving it 'without effect.'" . . . I disagree with the majority's analysis. . . .

. . .

In the first of the two cases on which the majority relies, *Barnett Bank v. Nelson*, . . . a federal statute explicitly granted national banks the unlimited power to sell insurance in small towns. A state statute forbade and impaired the exercise of that power, and the court held that it was preempted. . . .

*Michigan Canners* . . . , the second case on which the majority relies, concerned a conflict between the federal Agricultural Fair Practices Act, which protects the rights of producers of agricultural goods to remain independent and to bring their products to market on their own without being required to sell those products through an association, and a Michigan statute. . . . The Michigan statute at issue prevented the exercise of the right conferred by the act by precluding an agricultural producer "from marketing his goods himself" and "impos[ed] on the producer the same incidents of association membership with which Congress was concerned * * *." . . . The Court held that under those circumstances, the state statute was preempted.

Neither *Barnett* nor *Michigan Canners* stands for the proposition that a state statute that permits conduct that the federal government punishes is preempted. In those cases, the federal statutes did not punish conduct; they created powers or rights. The Court therefore struck down state statutes that forbade, impaired or prevented exercise of those powers or rights. Because the Controlled Substances Act does not create a federal power or right and the Oregon Medical Marijuana Act does not forbid, impair, or prevent the exercise of a federal power or right, *Barnett* and *Michigan Canners* are inapposite. . . .

. . .

The majority does not contend . . . that ORS 475.306(1) or the Oregon Medical Marijuana Act as a whole precludes enforcement of the Controlled Substances Act or has any other demonstrated effect on its "accomplishment and execution." The only obstacles to the federal act that the majority identifies are Oregon's differing policy choice and the lack of respect that it signifies. . . .

As an example of the way it believes the Supremacy Clause to operate, the majority posits that, if Congress were to pass a law prohibiting persons under the age of 21 from driving, a state law authorizing persons over the age of 16 to drive and giving them a license to do so would be preempted.[7] . . . The majority would be correct *if* Congress had authority to make such a law and *if* Congress expressly preempted state laws allowing

---

7. As I read the majority opinion, a state law providing that Oregon would not punish drivers between the ages of 16 and 21, as opposed to permitting those persons to drive, *would* withstand a Supremacy Clause challenge.

persons under the age of 21 to drive or indicated an intent to occupy the field. However, without such statement of Congressional intent, implied preemption does not necessarily follow. As a sovereign state, Oregon has authority to license its drivers and to choose its own age requirements. If Oregon set at 16 years the minimum age for its drivers then, the Oregon driver licenses it issued would give 16-year-olds only state permission to drive. The Oregon law would not be preempted, but neither would it protect 16-year-olds from federal prosecution and liability.

. . .

. . . The majority states that it does not decide "whether the legislature, if it chose to do so and worded Oregon's disability law differently, could require employers to reasonably accommodate otherwise qualified disabled employees who use medical marijuana to treat their disabilities." . . . Indeed, different words could be used for that purpose. For instance, the legislature could state expressly in ORS chapter 659A that disabled persons who would be entitled to the affirmative defense set forth in ORS 475.319 (a provision the majority does not find preempted) are not disqualified from the protections of the Oregon Disability Act, including the requirement of reasonable accommodation. Or, to be even more careful, the legislature could state, in chapter 659A, the conditions that a medical marijuana user must meet to be entitled to the protections of the Oregon Disability Act without any reference to the Oregon Medical Marijuana Act. If the legislature took either of those actions, reasonable accommodation would not be tied to the provision of the Oregon Medical Marijuana Act that the majority finds to be of "no effect."

Although such changes could secure the right of reasonable accommodation for disabled persons who use medical marijuana in compliance with Oregon law, the changes would not eliminate the questions that the majority's analysis raises about the validity of other provisions of the Oregon Medical Marijuana Act that use words of authorization or about the reach of Oregon's legislative authority. If the majority decision simply represents a formalistic view of the Supremacy Clause that permits Oregon to make its own choices about what conduct to punish (and thereby to permit) as long as it phrases its choices carefully, perhaps my concern is overstated. But as I cannot imagine that Congress would be concerned with the phrasing, rather than the effect, of state law, I not only think that the majority is wrong, I fear that it wrongly limits the legislative authority of this state. . . .

## Notes and Questions

1. The majority repeatedly states that Oregon law is preempted because it *authorizes* conduct that is forbidden by federal law. But does the majority ever define what it means by authorize? The dissent suggests there is no meaningful difference between authorizing conduct and exempting conduct from sanction. Do you agree? Is the language of authorization helpful in deciding cases? Along these lines consider the following Problem:

<u>Problem 13.9</u>: Federal law provides that "It is a federal crime for anyone under the age of 21 to operate a motor vehicle on the road." States A and B have adopted the following laws concerning driver age:

> State A: "Anyone 16 years or older is authorized to operate a motor vehicle on the road. It is a state crime for anyone else to operate a motor vehicle on the road."

State B: "It is a state crime for anyone under the age of 16 to operate a motor vehicle on the road."

Is either state law preempted by the federal law? Is there any legally meaningful difference between them?

2. **Problem 13.09** is obviously based on the hypothetical posed by the majority and discussed by the dissent. But does their hypothetical resemble the employment law at issue in *Emerald Steel*? Consider this variation:

Problem 13.10: Federal law provides that "It is a federal crime for anyone under the age of 21 to operate a motor vehicle on the road." States A, B, and C have adopted the following laws concerning driver age:

State A: "Anyone 16 years or older is authorized to operate a motor vehicle on the road. It is a state crime for anyone else to operate a motor vehicle on the road."
State B: "It is a state crime for anyone under the age of 16 to operate a motor vehicle on the road."
State C: "Private schools that provide drivers' education courses may not discriminate against students on the basis of age."

Which of the three laws is most like the law that was challenged in *Emerald Steel*? Why? Is there any meaningful difference among these laws, at least for purposes of preemption?

3. Does Congress even have the power to preempt the employment law at issue in *Emerald Steel*? The textbook author has explained why the court's decision comports with the anti-commandeering rule (discussed in Chapters 6 and 10), even if it does not necessarily reflect Congress's intentions:

> Congress may not preempt the exemptions [from state-imposed legal sanctions that are] at the core of state medical marijuana laws. The exemptions merely restore the proverbial state of nature. To be sure, marijuana use has increased following passage of these laws, but the increase is not a result of anything the states have done. Rather, it is a result of what the states stopped doing: punishing medical use of the drug. Arguments that the CSA already does preempt—or that Congress even could preempt—state exemptions are mistaken. Properly understood, this is commandeering, not preemption. . . .
> . . .
> State laws purporting to shield patients, caregivers, suppliers, and physicians from sanctions imposed by private persons or groups are on weaker footing. Some states, for example, bar private hospitals and clinics from taking adverse action (such as denying privileges) against any physician who recommends marijuana to a patient. Some states also bar landlords from terminating the lease of any qualified patient, caregiver, or supplier for possessing, using, or growing marijuana on rental property in accordance with state law. Such protection is not, of course, found in the state of nature, where employers and landlords are free to punish marijuana use as they deem fit. To illustrate, suppose landlord L terminates tenant T's lease because T, a qualified patient, is growing marijuana on the rental property. To assert state protection from eviction, T would need to initiate a lawsuit against L. The lawsuit would be heard, and any remedy would be enforced by a state agent.

The involvement of state agents would constitute a clear departure from the state of nature and would thus be preemptable.

Robert A. Mikos, *On the Limits of Supremacy: Medical Marijuana and the States' Overlooked Power to Legalize Federal Crime*, 62 Vand. L. Rev. 1421, 1455-56 (2009).

4. Even if Congress has the power to preempt state laws shielding marijuana users from private sanctions, there is still the question whether Congress intended to exercise this power. The Supreme Court has repeatedly intoned that congressional intent is the "ultimate touchstone" in preemption analysis. *Retail Clerks Int'l Ass'n v. Schermerhorn*, 375 U.S. 96, 103 (1963). Did the Congress that enacted the CSA intend to preempt state law to the extent it requires employers to accommodate some drug use that is forbidden under the CSA? Does either the majority or dissent satisfactorily address that question? Why would Congress want to preempt a such a state law anyway? Even if the law removed one potential deterrent against drug use, see MacDonald, *Testing for Cannabis*, *supra*, at 410, do you think Congress necessarily wanted to leave people who use illicit drugs to the mercy of their employers? In other words, does Congress necessarily place the goal of deterring illicit drug use above all other possible goals?

5. The majority argues that generic implied preemption rules govern the case, notwithstanding the express preemption language of 21 U.S.C. section 903. However, the textbook author suggests that the language of section 903 calls for a narrower preemption test:

> Regulations directly promoting marijuana activities are plainly preempted because they immediately impact congressional drug control goals. Indeed, one could argue that such laws invariably make it impossible to comply with both state and federal law—a type of conflict Congress undoubtedly sought to prevent [under the CSA].
>
> By contrast, regulations that only indirectly promote marijuana are not preempted because Congress expressly spared them. This choice is evident from the language of Section 903[, the express preemption clause of the CSA]. In particular, Section 903 provides that a state law is preempted only to the extent that it "positive[ly] conflict[s]" with a provision of the CSA governing the *"same subject matter,"* "so that the two cannot consistently stand together." The highlighted language suggests Congress did not want to preempt all state laws that impacted drug behavior but only those laws that did so in a way the CSA directly addresses, i.e., only when state law regulates a specific subject, say, the landlord-tenant relationship, that is also regulated by the CSA.
>
> It is easy to see why Congress might want to spare state regulations that only indirectly promote marijuana-related activities. Although these laws might undermine somewhat Congress's objective of curbing marijuana consumption, subjecting them to preemption challenges could prove enormously burdensome for the courts and for state and local officials. After all, countless state laws, including many wholly unrelated to the drug law field, could promote drug use at the margin. Suppose, for example, that a city imposes a special assessment to widen and abate congestion on a public road that happens to be connected to a popular marijuana dispensary. One could argue that this expenditure of public funds would undermine Congress's goal of combatting marijuana distribution; among other things, the road improvement would likely make it easier for residents to shop at the dispensary. And any disgruntled payers of the special assessment would likely have standing (in state court, if not federal) to challenge the roadway program as preempted. But it seems hard to imagine that Congress would want the CSA to be used as a sword against state laws having only tangential relevance to drug abuse. After all, preemption lawsuits could wreak havoc on the administration of mundane state and local government

programs. As the Supreme Court has observed, it arguably "frustrates rather than effectuates legislative intent simplistically to assume that whatever furthers the statute's primary objective must be the law, given that '"no legislation pursues its purposes at all costs."'

Unfortunately, . . . some courts and commentators have failed to heed this distinction. For example, the Oregon Supreme Court has held that a state law barring employment discrimination against medical marijuana users is preempted because it conflicts with congressional objectives. The problem here is not the court's capacity for applying obstacle preemption, for it is surely correct that extending employment discrimination to cover drug use would impair at least one congressional objective. . . . Rather, the problem is the court's assumption that obstacle preemption applies to this case despite Congress's express statutory language disavowing such intent. In their dogged application of broad implied conflict preemption principles, courts have simply paid no attention to the "same subject matter" limiting language of Section 903.

Robert A. Mikos, *Preemption Under the Controlled Substances Act*, 16 J. Health Care L. & Pol'y 5, 22-23 (2013). What do you think? What weight—if any—should courts give the "same subject matter" language of section 903?

## D. BANKS

Nearly all businesses use banking services—to deposit cash, process payments, provide credit, and so on. But providing these services to firms that manufacture and/or distribute marijuana carries legal risks and compliance costs for financial institutions. The following sections discuss those risks and costs and the power of different government actors to mitigate them.

### 1. May Banks Do Business with the Marijuana Industry?

Handling the proceeds of *any* illicit activity triggers a host of federal regulations directed at the financial industry. In the following excerpt, Professor Julie Hill surveys the federal regulations that impede access to banking services for the marijuana industry.

#### *Julie Andersen Hill*, Banks, Marijuana, and Federalism
65 Case W. Res. L. Rev. 597 (2015)

The United States has a dual banking system: banks can choose a federal charter issued by the Office of the Comptroller of the Currency or a state charter from a state banking regulator. Likewise, credit unions can generally choose a federal charter from the National Credit Union Administration (NCUA) or a state charter from a state credit union regulator. Indeed, the federalism represented by the dual banking system has been described as "competitive" because regulators compete to charter institutions. In general, national financial institutions must follow a set of federal laws while state institutions must follow state law. If the dual banking system were truly dichotomous (federal law only regulated national institutions and state law only regulated state institutions), the answer for marijuana banking would be clear: state-chartered institutions in states where marijuana is legal would be free to provide banking services to marijuana-related entities.

But state and federal financial institution regulators do not "operate in distinct spheres." . . .

. . .

. . . [F]ederal control [over the banking system] is pervasive. As an initial matter, federal and state financial institutions, like other businesses and individuals, must comply with lawfully enacted federal criminal laws. In addition, through federal deposit insurance, federal holding company regulation, and federally administered payment systems, federal financial regulators have significant oversight of state-chartered banks and credit unions. This federal oversight currently leaves little room for marijuana banking.

### A. FEDERAL CONTROLLED SUBSTANCES ACT

The federal Controlled Substances Act prohibits manufacturing, distributing, or dispensing marijuana. Federal law also criminalizes conduct beyond directly handling marijuana. It is illegal to aid and abet the manufacture, distribution, or dispensing of marijuana. It is illegal to conspire to manufacture, distribute, or dispense marijuana. . . .

It is not hard to imagine how a financial institution and its employees could run afoul of these laws by providing banking services to a marijuana dispensary. Suppose a marijuana entrepreneur in Colorado comes to a financial institution and forthrightly explains her proposed business. Her business needs a small inventory loan, a checking account, and credit card payment processing services. By providing the loan and placing the proceeds in the checking account, the institution would be conspiring to distribute marijuana. By facilitating customers' credit card payments, the institution would be aiding and abetting the distribution of marijuana. . . .

. . .

. . . Even if the federal government does not prosecute financial institutions directly, institutions risk losing money as a result of criminal and civil forfeiture laws allowing federal officials to seize marijuana-related property, including bank accounts.

### B. FEDERAL ANTI-MONEY LAUNDERING STATUTES

Federal law, however, expects financial institutions to do more than merely avoid assisting those who manufacture, distribute, or dispense marijuana. Financial institutions must discover illegal activity, report it to federal officials, and prevent wrongdoers from accessing the banking system.

The Money Laundering Control Act makes individuals and entities subject to criminal liability for money laundering. There are several ways to commit the offense of money laundering, but two are especially relevant to financial institutions considering marijuana banking. First, a financial institution commits money laundering by conducting a financial transaction involving the proceeds of a known "specified unlawful activity" while "knowing that the transaction is designed in whole or in part to conceal or disguise the nature, the location, the source, the ownership or the control of the proceeds of specified unlawful activity or to avoid a transaction reporting requirement under State or Federal law."[63] Second, a financial institution commits money laundering if it "knowingly engages or

---

63. [18 U.S.C.] § 1956(a)(1)(B).

attempts to engage in a monetary transaction in criminally derived property of a value greater than $10,000."[64] . . .

Press reports suggest that because financial institutions are well aware of the anti-money laundering laws, some marijuana businesses attempt to gain access to banking services by disguising the nature of their business. . . .

Of course, these surreptitious businesses may be subject to money laundering charges themselves. Moreover, it is far from clear that such measures result in long-term access to the banking system; banking law does not allow financial institutions to simply take customer assertions at face value.

Under the Bank Secrecy Act and the USA PATRIOT Act, financial institutions must maintain robust programs designed to prevent money laundering. Every financial institution must implement a customer identification program to make reasonable efforts to "verify the identity of any person seeking to open an account."[73] . . .

Verifying the identity of the customer is only the beginning. Federal regulators expect institutions to undertake sufficient due diligence on each customer to adequately assess the risk associated with that customer. For "higher-risk" accounts (like accounts belonging to "cash-intensive businesses"), financial institutions must know the purpose of each account, the source of funds in the account, and the customer's primary trade area.

Armed with information about the normal business of each customer, financial institutions are then tasked with identifying suspicious transactions. The Bank Secrecy Act requires that financial institutions report illegal and suspicious activities to the federal Financial Crimes Enforcement Network (FinCEN). Institutions must file currency transaction reports for any transaction that involves more than $10,000 in cash.[78] Financial institutions must also provide suspicious activity reports for transactions involving "at least $5,000 in funds or other assets" if the bank knows, suspects, or has reason to suspect the following:

> (i) The transaction involves funds derived from illegal activities or is intended or conducted in order to hide or disguise funds or assets derived from illegal activities (including, without limitation, the ownership, nature, source, location, or control of such funds or assets) as part of a plan to violate or evade any Federal law or regulation or to avoid any transaction reporting requirement under Federal law or regulation;
> [ . . . ][79]

Recent FinCEN guidance makes it clear that virtually every transaction conducted by a state-legal marijuana business "involve[s] funds derived from illegal activities" as described in the Bank Secrecy Act regulations.[80] Thus, banks must prepare suspicious activity reports for most marijuana-related business transactions.

Run-of-the-mill marijuana-related transactions warrant only "Marijuana Limited" suspicious activity reports. These reports identify the parties involved, state that "the filing

---

64. *Id.* § 1957(a). [Author's note: Sections 1956-57 are examined in more detail in Chapter 11.]
73. [31 U.S.C.] § 5318(l); C.F.R. § 1020.220 (2014).
78. 31 U.S.C. § 5313(a) (2012); 31 C.F.R. § 1010.311 (2014).
79. 31 C.F.R. § 1020.320(a)(2).
80. [Department of the Treasury Financial Crimes Enforcement Network, BSA Expectations Regarding Marijuana-Related Businesses, FIN-2014-G001, Feb. 14, 2014, at https://perma.cc/9YD7-ZP5V.]

institution is filing the [report] solely because the subject is engaged in a marijuana-related business," and represent that "no additional suspicious activity has been identified."

However, FinCEN expects financial institutions to conduct due diligence to determine whether the marijuana-related transactions implicate any of the Department of Justice's Controlled Substances Act enforcement priorities or state law. If an institution discovers transactions that might violate those priorities or state law, the institution must file a "Marijuana Priority" suspicious activity report. Recognizing that "a financial institution filing a [report] on a marijuana-related business may not always be well positioned to determine whether the business implicates one of the [Department of Justice] priorities or violates state law," FinCEN provides a long, but not exhaustive, list of "red flags" that could indicate improper conduct.

Among those red flags are the following:

- The business is unable to demonstrate that its revenue is derived exclusively from the sale of marijuana in compliance with state law, as opposed to revenue derived from (i) the sale of other illicit drugs, (ii) the sale of marijuana not in compliance with state law, or (iii) other illegal activity.
- A customer seeks to conceal or disguise involvement in marijuana-related business activity. For example, the customer may be using a business with a non-descript name (e.g., a "consulting," "holding," or "management" company) that purports to engage in commercial activity unrelated to marijuana, but is depositing cash that smells like marijuana.

Finally, a financial institution must provide a "marijuana termination" suspicious activity report when the institution determines "it necessary to terminate a relationship with a marijuana-related business in order to maintain an effective anti-money laundering compliance program." When an institution learns that a terminated "marijuana-related business seeks to move to a second financial institution," FinCEN encourages the first institution to voluntarily alert the second institution of its concerns.

FinCEN has authority to seek substantial civil money penalties from financial institutions and individuals who violate the Bank Secrecy Act. Such fines often reach well into the millions of dollars. Federal officials also have an even bigger hammer: criminal prosecution.

> For example, a person, including a bank employee, willfully violating the BSA or its implementing regulations is subject to a criminal fine of up to $250,000 or five years in prison, or both. A person who commits such a violation while violating another U.S. law, or engaging in a pattern of criminal activity, is subject to a fine of up to $500,000 or ten years in prison, or both.[92]

Institutions face criminal money penalties of "not less than 2 times the amount of the transaction, but not more than $1,000,000."[93]

In connection with the FinCEN guidance, the Department of Justice issued guidance regarding marijuana-related financial crimes.[94] The Department reiterated its previous

---

92. [Fed. Fin. Inst. Examination Council, Bank Secrecy Act/Anti-Money Laundering Examination Manual 14 (2010).]
93. 31 U.S.C. § 5322(d).
94. [Deputy Attorney General James M. Cole, Guidance Regarding Marijuana Related Financial Crimes, Feb. 14, 2014, at https://perma.cc/6KYW-G9Y2.]

enforcement priorities, including preventing the sale of marijuana to minors and preventing the sale of marijuana in states where it is illegal under state law. The new guidance stated that enforcement of marijuana-related financial crimes "should be subject to the same consideration and prioritization." Thus, "if a financial institution or individual offers services to a marijuana-related business whose activities do not implicate any of the eight priority factors, prosecution for [money-laundering] offenses may not be appropriate." The guidance also warns that financial institutions could face prosecution if their due diligence efforts fall short.

> For example, if a financial institution or individual provides banking services to a marijuana-related business knowing that the business is diverting marijuana from a state where marijuana sales are regulated to ones where such sales are illegal under state law, or is being used by a criminal organization to conduct financial transactions for its criminal goals, such as the concealment of funds derived from other illegal activity or the use of marijuana proceeds to support other illegal activity, prosecution for violations of 18 U.S.C. §§ 1956, 1957, 1960 or the BSA might be appropriate. Similarly, if the financial institution or individual is willfully blind to such activity by, for example, failing to conduct appropriate due diligence of the customers' activities, such prosecution might be appropriate.

Like previous guidance, the memorandum further warns that the Department of Justice is not bound by the enforcement priorities and can choose to investigate and prosecute anyone violating the money laundering laws.

. . .

## C. FEDERAL DEPOSIT AND SHARE INSURANCE

The next tool of federal control in the banking system is the ubiquitous nature of federal deposit and share insurance. The vast majority of financial institutions, whether federal- or state-chartered, are federally insured. The Banking Act of 1933 created the Federal Deposit Insurance Corporation and required that all national banks obtain FDIC insurance. All states subsequently required that their state banks obtain FDIC insurance. The story is much the same for credit unions. In 1970, Congress created the National Credit Union Share Insurance Fund to insure the shares (essentially the deposits) of federal- and state-chartered credit unions. Federal credit unions must be insured by the NCUA. Most states also require federal insurance for state-chartered credit unions, but a few states still allow their credit unions to purchase alternative private share insurance.

With the benefit of federal insurance comes the burden of federal regulation. In order to retain the federal insurance, financial institutions must comply with FDIC or NCUA restrictions. To ensure state-chartered banks and credit unions comply with federal regulations, the FDIC and NCUA conduct regular examinations.

Under the laws governing federal deposit and share insurance, financial institutions and related individuals face significant civil penalties for Bank Secrecy Act violations. FDIC and NCUA examinations scrutinize financial institution compliance with the Act. The federal insurers can bring civil money penalty actions for Bank Secrecy Act violations. Federal insurers can also impose the "death penalty"—revocation of deposit insurance—effectively forcing the closure of any institution that is required to have federal insurance. Finally, insured financial institution employees who violate money laundering laws or the Bank Secrecy Act face regulatory suspension or prohibition from the banking industry.

. . .

## D. FEDERAL RESERVE REGULATION OF MEMBER BANKS

Just as state-chartered financial institutions subject themselves to federal regulation by using federal deposit or share insurance, state banks subject themselves to federal regulation if they choose to become members of the Federal Reserve System. All state-chartered banks (but not credit unions) are eligible to apply for Federal Reserve membership. In order to become a member of the Federal Reserve System, a state-chartered bank must make an application and must purchase stock in its regional Federal Reserve Bank. There are currently 850 state member banks.

Once a state bank becomes a member of the Federal Reserve, it must comply with federal laws governing member banks and regulations established by the Federal Reserve. A Federal Reserve member bank must "at all times conduct its business and exercise its powers with due regard to safety and soundness." In order to meet this safety and soundness requirement, a member bank must monitor "[c]ompliance with applicable laws and regulations."

The Federal Reserve regularly examines state member banks. Among other things, the examination evaluates a bank's risk management practices and compliance with the Bank Secrecy Act. The Federal Reserve's Commercial Bank Examination Manual instructs examiners to evaluate each state member bank's operations to ensure that the bank does not provide deposit or loan services to illegal enterprises. The Manual explains that a bank "should perform its due diligence by adequately and reasonably ascertaining and documenting that the funds of its . . . customers were derived from legitimate means." It further explains that "if accounts at U.S. banking entities are used for illegal purposes, the entities could be exposed to reputational risk and risk of financial loss as a result of asset seizures and forfeitures." In addition, banks are warned that loans should only be provided "for legitimate purposes" and that loan collateral "derived from illegal activities . . . is subject to forfeiture through the seizure of assets by a government agency."

Unsurprisingly, the Federal Reserve's Commercial Bank Manual does not specifically address customer activities that are illegal under federal law but allowed under state law. Yet it is clear that the Federal Reserve, under its duty to enforce the Bank Secrecy Act and regulate member bank risk, has ample authority to impose civil penalties on state member banks that do business with the marijuana industry.

. . .

## F. FEDERAL PAYMENT SYSTEMS ADMINISTRATION

The federal government also wields significant control over payment systems. The Federal Reserve provides four important payment services: (1) a centralized check collection system, (2) the Automated Clearinghouse (ACH) network for processing batched electronic smalldollar payments, (3) the Fedwire system for larger electronic payments, and (4) coin and currency services.

Financial institutions use each of these systems to provide customers payment services. The Monetary Control Act of 1980 requires that the Federal Reserve offer payment system services to all "depository institutions," regardless of whether the institution is a member of the Federal Reserve System. Thus, the Federal Reserve currently provides services to banks and credit unions alike. By establishing regulations and policies governing access to its payment systems, the Federal Reserve has the ability to impact practices at all financial institutions using these systems.

Accessing the Federal Reserve's payment systems is not administratively difficult. It requires only a resolution from the financial institution's board of directions and the completion of forms designating individuals authorized to initiate transactions and identifying the types of services wanted. Under normal circumstances, once a financial institution receives a charter, the Federal Reserve grants the institution a "master account" and access to payment services. This process makes sense because the prospective financial institution has already been vetted by the chartering authority, and usually by the deposit or share insurer as well.

Of course, nothing prevents the Federal Reserve from adjusting the terms and conditions for use of the Federal Reserve's payment systems. It is possible that future terms and conditions could cut off access to financial institutions that provide services to the marijuana industry.

## 2. *Should* Banks Be Allowed to Do Business with the Marijuana Industry?

**Problem 13.11**: You are a lobbyist working for the financial industry. You are scheduled to meet with a key policymaker to discuss marijuana banking. Your client wants you to convince the policymaker that financial institutions should be allowed to provide traditional banking services to the marijuana industry. In the past, the policymaker has been receptive to the entreaties of the financial industry. However, the policymaker also opposes the legalization of marijuana. How do you make your case to the policymaker?

The Problem raises a key policy question: *Should* banks be allowed to do business with the marijuana industry? In another portion of her Article excerpted above, Professor Hill identifies several problems that could arise from denying the industry access to banking services:

> Lack of banking services stands as a formidable barrier to growth of the state-legal marijuana industry. Without access to banking services, marijuana businesses must conduct transactions in cash and spend an inordinate amount of time and resources on cash management. From vaults, to cameras, to security personnel, to finding suppliers that accept cash payment, managing cash can quickly become a logistical and security nightmare. In Colorado, the controller of one recreational marijuana retailer described cash management as "a full-time job." Stories abound concerning marijuana retailers attempting to surreptitiously drive large quantities of concealed cash across town just to pay tax bills.
>
> At the same time, lack of banking services equates to a lack of capital for the marijuana industry. Banks are the traditional backbone of small business financing, but banks will not lend to marijuana-related businesses. The state-legal marijuana industry must instead "rely on short-term loans from individuals, usually with higher interest rates." Even if a marijuana-related business finds financing, there is still the problem of not having a bank account. As a marijuana retailer hoping to finance the one-million-dollar purchase of a new building explains, "What do you say? . . . I want it in cash, guys?"

The banking problem also raises hurdles for states seeking to allow but regulate marijuana use. Notwithstanding the security efforts of marijuana businesses themselves, the combination of marijuana and cash raises local law enforcement concerns. Even federal officials recognize the "public safety" concern caused by "[s]ubstantial amounts of cash, just kind of lying around with no place for it to be appropriately deposited." So far media reports of successful robberies and related violence are limited but chilling.

Perhaps more importantly from a public policy standpoint, when marijuana-related businesses are outside the banking system, those businesses are harder to tax and regulate. Colorado and Washington allow recreational marijuana use but regulate marijuana similarly to alcohol. They prohibit the sale of marijuana to minors, require that businesses be registered, and take other regulatory measures designed to keep the marijuana industry separate from other illegal drugs. Both states plan to fund the monitoring and registration of growers, distributors, retailers, and medical users by taxing the marijuana industry itself. But cash businesses have opportunities and incentives to underreport taxes. Without anticipated tax revenues, states could potentially have trouble funding their regulatory structures. Cash businesses may also be more likely to funnel earnings to illicit activities. Finally, tax authorities (including federal tax authorities) prefer to be paid by check, credit card, or electronic deposit, rather than with bags of cash smelling of weed.

In short, it is unsurprising that banking has been described as "the most urgent issue facing the legal cannabis industry today."

Hill, *Banks, Marijuana, and Federalism, supra,* at 600-03.

## Notes and Questions

1. To what extent are the concerns identified by Hill shared by people who do not support marijuana legalization, or even people who do not work in the marijuana industry? For example, do you think Hill's argument would convince the policymaker in **Problem 13.11** to permit marijuana banking?

2. As Hill notes, access to banking services would reduce the marijuana industry's reliance on cash transactions and thereby mitigate some of compliance concerns raised by cash-only businesses. But could banks potentially help boost compliance with state laws in another way as well? The textbook author explains:

> [I]f banks DO end up serving marijuana businesses, it might give a boost to state and federal efforts to police the marijuana industry. In particular, banks could help government officials determine whether the marijuana industry is violating state law and/or engaging in behavior that would justify federal legal action under those 2013 DOJ enforcement guidelines (e.g., selling to minors).
>
> Here's how. Federal law requires banks to monitor and report on the financial transactions of their clients. Under federal law, for example, banks are required to file "Suspicious Activity Reports" anytime they know, suspect, or have reason to suspect a client is engaging in a financial transaction involving proceeds of illegal activity. The government then uses these SARs to investigate and prosecute federal crimes committed by the clients.
>
> Importantly, the bulk of the [2014 FinCen guidance] is actually devoted to reaffirming and clarifying the duty of banks to file SARs on clients engaged in the marijuana industry. It makes abundantly clear that a "financial institution that decides to provide financial services to a marijuana-related business *would be required to file suspicious activity reports* ('SARs') . . . if, consistent with FinCEN regulations, the financial institution knows, suspects,

or has reason to suspect that a transaction conducted or attempted by, at, or through the financial institution . . . involves funds derived from illegal activity." (emphasis added)

To be sure, the reporting requirement could simply overwhelm government agents, since *every* transaction involving a marijuana business might trigger a new report. Indeed, federal agents are already deluged with SARs; in 2009, for example, banks submitted more than 700,000 SARs (banks in Colorado and Washington submitted more than 17,000 SARs), far too many for the government to investigate them all.

But the new Treasury guidance instructs banks to distinguish between good and bad marijuana businesses. Namely, if a bank believes a marijuana business is abiding state law and avoiding activities the federal government considers objectionable (e.g., selling across state lines), the bank may file an abbreviated SAR, simply by writing "MARIJUANA LIMITED" in the notations section of the report. But if the bank believes the business is flouting state law or engaging in one of those objectionable activities, it is supposed to file more detailed SAR, writing "MARIJUANA PRIORITY" in the notations section and explaining why the bank believes the business deserves closer scrutiny.

The information provided on these SARs could greatly enhance the efforts of federal and state enforcement agencies to police the marijuana industry. Banks won't necessarily have perfect information about their clients, but they will often possess information that government agencies cannot realistically gather on their own. Indeed, . . . governments commonly use private parties to gather information they need to enforce their regulations; e.g., without the W-2s filed by employers, the IRS would struggle (mightily) to collect individual income taxes. And requiring banks to further distinguish between law-abiding and law-shirking marijuana business greatly enhances the utility of this information for government agencies.

Knowing that banks will share information with the federal government could have a powerful deterrent effect on marijuana businesses. These businesses need bank services—try operating any business without a checking account, for example. But if they misbehave, banks will shun them, or worse yet, report their misbehavior to the feds. To be sure, some misbehaving businesses will simply avoid the banks altogether. But those businesses will be put at a serious competitive disadvantage vis a vis their more law abiding rivals.

In sum, *if* the guidance works (a big if), marijuana businesses will get access to banking services; banks will expand their market; and government agencies will get a new watchdog to help police the marijuana industry.

Robert A. Mikos, *Using Banks to Police the Marijuana Industry*, Marijuana Law, Policy & Reform Blog, Feb. 18, 2014, at https://perma.cc/PS38-9KH8. Would the addition of a "new watchdog to help police the marijuana industry" help convince policymakers to enable marijuana banking?

### 3. Who Ultimately Decides the Marijuana Banking Question?

<u>Problem 13.12</u>: You are an attorney advising the financial industry, which wants to be allowed to do business with the marijuana industry. Your client has a skilled lobbyist who is ready to make the financial industry's case to policymakers. However, the financial industry has asked you to help identify key policymakers who could mitigate the legal risks and compliance costs

associated with marijuana banking. They have already identified a handful of policymakers they believe could help them, including:

(1) the Directors of various state Departments of Banking and Finance
(2) the Director of the Financial Crimes Enforcement Network (FinCEN)
(3) the Deputy Attorney General of the United States
(4) the Chair of the Federal Reserve
(5) the Chair of the Senate Finance Committee.

What power does each of these policymakers wield over access to banking services for the marijuana industry? Can you think of any other policymakers who could make marijuana banking a reality?

The materials above identified possible reasons for allowing financial institutions to provide services to the marijuana industry. But who has the ability to increase access to those services? Agencies in the executive branch and some states have attempted to soften or circumvent the obstacles to marijuana banking posed by federal law. Professor Hill discusses these attempts, and, in so doing, highlights some key limitations on the authority of these government actors.

### *Julie Andersen Hill*, Banks, Marijuana, and Federalism (cont'd)
65 Case W. Res. L. Rev. 597 (2015)

Notwithstanding the clarity of federal criminal law and the pervasiveness of federal banking regulation, both the federal and state governments are experimenting with measures to facilitate marijuana banking. . . .

### . . . FEDERAL GUIDANCE

. . .

Recognizing their limited enforcement resources, the Department of Justice and FinCEN issued guidance addressing marijuana banking. As previously explained, the FinCEN guidance describes when financial institutions should file "Marijuana Limited," "Marijuana Priority," and "Marijuana Termination" suspicious activity reports. According to FinCEN, the guidance was intended to "enhance the availability of financial services for, and the financial transparency of, marijuana-related businesses." The Department of Justice guidance explains its marijuana enforcement priorities and suggests that banks may not face criminal prosecution if they only service state-legal marijuana businesses.

Financial institutions' response to the guidance was tepid. According to Don Childears, president and CEO of the Colorado Bankers Association, the guidance did little to facilitate marijuana industry banking. "At best, [it] amounts to 'Serve these customers at your own risk' and it emphasizes all those risks." The American Bankers Association agreed: "[The] guidance . . . doesn't alter the underlying challenge for banks . . . As it stands, possession or distribution of marijuana violates federal law, and banks that provide support for those activities face the risk of prosecution and assorted sanctions."

Still, FinCEN was quick to declare the guidance a success in opening the doors for marijuana banking. In August 2014, FinCEN Director Jennifer Shasky Calvery revealed that FinCEN had received 502 "Marijuana Limited" reports. She also announced that based on the reports, "there are currently 105 individual financial institutions from states in more than one third of the country engaged in banking relationships with marijuana-related businesses." Thus she concluded that "from our perspective the guidance is having the intended effect. It is facilitating access to financial services, while ensuring that this activity is transparent and the funds are going into regulated financial institutions responsible for implementing appropriate [anti-money laundering] safeguards."

But those who believe that the FinCEN and Department of Justice guidance entirely solves the marijuana-banking problem are wrong. First, the marijuana industry continues to report difficulty in securing access to banking services. Even if every "Marijuana Priority" report involved a separate marijuana business, the 502 reports cover far less than the state-legal marijuana industry. There are more than 502 state-licensed marijuana businesses in Colorado alone. Second, it is far from clear that most financial institutions feel comfortable offering services to the marijuana industry. There are more than 13,000 banks and credit unions. The 105 institutions that have filed "Marijuana Priority" reports are a small drop in the bucket when considering the larger banking industry. Since the FinCEN guidance, some of the largest banks, including Bank of America and Wells Fargo, have reiterated their position: they do not offer services to the marijuana industry. . . . FinCEN's report data show that since the guidance, "[j]ust over 475 [reports] filed to date reflect 'Marijuana Termination.'" This suggests financial institutions may actually be choosing to end relationships with state-legal marijuana businesses.

It is not hard to see why financial institutions are still skittish. Marijuana is still illegal under federal law. The FinCEN and Department of Justice guidance does not change that. Any bank or credit union providing services could face criminal prosecution at any time. Even if financial institutions were willing to rely on public statements about enforcement priorities, the Department of Justice's assurance to banks is quite weak. It promises only that it "may not" prosecute financial institutions who provide financial services to state-legal marijuana businesses. Actual enforcement practices could change anytime—with or without warning.

Furthermore, the federal guidance seems to set the bar for financial institution compliance quite high. When comparing compliance costs with the profits available from the growing but still small marijuana industry, banking the industry may not make economic sense. The paperwork associated with anti-money laundering reporting may be enough to dissuade some institutions from banking some marijuana businesses. And then there is the problem of confirming that none of the institution's customers deal with marijuana in a way that implicates the Department of Justice's enforcement priorities. . . .

Finally, the Department of Justice and FinCEN are only two of the many federal authorities with regulatory oversight of financial institutions. Even if a financial institution felt confident that it could rely on Department of Justice and FinCEN guidance and that it could implement a robust (but economic) compliance program, the FDIC, NCUA, or Federal Reserve might determine that the institution was not effectively managing its risk and take civil enforcement action.

. . .

### . . . STATE-CHARTERED FINANCIAL COOPERATIVES

When the federal guidance failed to alleviate the marijuana banking problems, Colorado tried to take matters into its own hands. In 2014 Colorado passed legislation allowing licensed marijuana businesses to form financial services cooperatives. These "cannabis credit co-ops" are empowered to provide financial services, including deposit services and loans, to marijuana-related businesses.[213] Entities eligible for co-op membership include "licensed marijuana businesses, industrial hemp businesses, and entities that provide goods or services to licensed marijuana businesses and that provide documentation to the co-op of an inability to get comparable services from a bank or credit union."[214]

Although Colorado cannabis credit co-ops do not need to secure federal deposit insurance . . . the co-ops are still dependent upon federal banking regulators. To be granted a charter, each co-op must "provide the Commissioner written evidence of approval by the Federal Reserve System Board of Governors for access by the co-op to the Federal Reserve System in connection with the proposed depository activities of the co-op."[217]

By requiring that any cannabis credit co-op get "approval . . . for access . . . to the Federal Reserve System," the Colorado legislature was trying to ensure that any co-op would have access to the payment services provided by the Federal Reserve. After all, lack of access to payment systems was the primary banking problem lawmakers hoped the cannabis credit co-ops would alleviate. Unless the Federal Reserve granted access to its payment systems, the co-ops would not be able to effectively meet the marijuana industry's banking needs.

Is the Federal Reserve likely to grant cannabis credit co-ops access to any of the Fed's payment services? . . .

One potential problem is that, by design, cannabis credit co-ops are not banks or credit unions. Under the Monetary Control Act of 1980, the Federal Reserve must provide services to "nonmember depository institutions" at the same price as it does to members of the Federal Reserve. "Depository institution" is defined to include all federally insured financial institutions. "Depository institution" also includes banks, mutual savings banks, savings banks, credit unions, and savings associations that are eligible to apply for federal deposit or share insurance. The cannabis credit co-op does not fit into any of those categories. According to Colorado law, a cannabis credit coop cannot be federally insured. Furthermore, a cannabis credit co-op is not a bank or credit union and cannot use "bank" or "credit union" in its name. Thus, the co-ops are not the type of financial institution to which Congress expected the Federal Reserve to regularly provide payment services.

. . .

If the Federal Reserve provided payment services to a cannabis credit co-op, the Federal Reserve and its employees would be engaging in money laundering. They might also be conspiring to manufacture and distribute marijuana [or] aiding and abetting the manufacture and distribution of marijuana. . . . Even if many policymakers at the Federal Reserve were convinced of the necessity of marijuana banking, it is difficult to imagine the Federal Reserve openly defying federal drug law.

But federal hurdles are not the only impediments to the creation of cannabis credit co-ops. First, a group of marijuana businesses must decide to form a co-op. Given the legal uncertainty, private actors may be unwilling to invest in start-up plans for a co-op. So far, Colorado has not received any applications. . . . Second, Colorado must develop an

---

213. [Colo. Rev. Stat. Ann.] § 11-33-107. . . .
214. *Id.* § 11-33-106(2)(a). . . .
217. *Id.* § 11-33-104(4)(a).

administrative structure for regulating co-ops—a process that could take several years. According to Chris Myklebust, Colorado's Commissioner of the Division of Financial Services, "[r]ule-making wouldn't occur until after access to the federal system was granted and an application [was] approved by [the Colorado Commissioner]." As part of the approval process, Colorado regulatory authorities would "convene a stakeholder group, including all trade associations representing banks and credit unions, to identify conflicts that may exist" between the cannabis credit co-op law and other state law. Banking trade associations may be hostile to coops, particularly if co-ops can bank customers who are off limits to traditional financial institutions. Regulators may not grant any coop charters "until the general assembly resolves all of the identified state law conflicts."

Finally, even if Colorado authorities issue a cannabis credit co-op charter, it is not clear that the co-op could operate consistent with Colorado law. Under Colorado law, the co-op must "comply with all applicable requirements of federal law, including . . . [t]he federal 'Bank Secrecy Act.'" Yet, elsewhere, the Colorado statute requires a co-op to disclose to its members that "[f]ederal law does not authorize financial institutions, including marijuana financial services cooperatives, to accept proceeds from activity that is illegal under federal law, such as that from licensed marijuana businesses." If a cannabis credit co-op must comply with federal law and cannot accept deposits from state-legal marijuana businesses, it will likely be of little use to the marijuana industry.

. . .

Department of Justice and FinCEN guidance failed to adequately address marijuana banking. Colorado's cannabis credit co-op legislation will also fail to provide banking for the marijuana industry. These failed attempts show that for banking services to become widely available to the marijuana industry, Congress must act. . . .

## . . . CONGRESSIONAL ACTION

Congress could facilitate banking services for the marijuana industry by legalizing or decriminalizing marijuana. . . . From a banking perspective, the key is that marijuana-related entities must have the capacity to operate without running afoul of state or federal law. If marijuana businesses cannot operate without violating federal and state law, and banks must follow the law, then banks will not be able to provide services to marijuana businesses.

Another option for congressional action is legislation aimed narrowly at the marijuana banking problem. Rather than adjust the legality of marijuana, Congress could excuse banks from complying with the law. Proposals in this vein range from expansive to narrow.

On the expansive end of the spectrum is a 2013 bill introduced by Representative Ed Perlmutter from Colorado—the Marijuana Business Access to Banking Act. Under the bill, "[a] depository institution that provides financial services to a marijuana-related legitimate business, and the officers, directors, and employees of that depository institution, shall be immune from Federal criminal prosecution or investigation for providing those services." Additionally, federal banking regulators could not "terminate or limit deposit insurance" or "prohibit, penalize or otherwise discourage a depository institution from providing financial services to a marijuana-related legitimate business." The bill, however, has not been reported out of committee and seems unlikely to gain traction. . . .

Other proposed federal marijuana banking legislation is narrower. In July 2014, as part of the financial services appropriations bill, the House of Representatives passed a provision introduced by Representative Denny Heck from Washington. The provision would prohibit funds appropriated by the bill from being used

> to penalize a financial institution solely because the institution provides financial services to an entity that is a manufacturer, producer, or a person that participates in any business or organized activity that involves handling marijuana or marijuana products and engages in such activity pursuant to a law established by a State or a unit of local government.

. . . Even if enacted, the provision is insufficient to open doors to marijuana banking. Federal financial institution regulators generally do not rely on congressional appropriations for funding. The FDIC, NCUA, and Federal Reserve are all funded by assessments on regulated institutions and investment income. . . .

## Notes and Questions

1. The state-licensed marijuana industry has been built by firms that are willing to flout federal law. Indeed, thousands of firms are now manufacturing and distributing marijuana notwithstanding the fact that doing so violates federal law and exposes them to harsh sanctions. The financial industry, by contrast, appears to be quite skittish about flouting federal law. Why aren't more financial institutions lining up to provide banking services to the marijuana industry?

2. Postscript I. FinCEN reports that the number of financial institutions doing business with the marijuana industry has increased nearly six-fold in the two years since it issued its guidance, from 51 institutions in March 2014 to 301 institutions in March 2016. *See* Kristena Hansen & Gene Johnson, *Banking Woes Easing for Some Legal Pot Businesses*, The Associated Press, Apr. 20, 2016. *See also* Alison Jimenez & Steven Kemmerling, *New Marijuana Banking SAR Data Has International Implications*, Nov. 3, 2015 (reporting that 6,931 marijuana-related SARs had been filed with FinCEN between February 14, 2014 and July 31, 2015, and that 266 depository institutions had open accounts with marijuana businesses as of July 2015), http://securitiesanalytics.com/bank_marijuana_sar_fincen; Alison Jimenez & Steven Kemmerling, *Who Is Filing Suspicious Activity Reports on the Marijuana Industry? New Data May Surprise You*, Apr. 13, 2015 (reporting additional data), http://securitiesanalytics.com/marijuana_SARs. Does the increase alter your assessment of the impact of FinCen guidance on access to banking services?

3. Postscript II. As of the end of 2016, it appears that no cannabis credit co-ops are doing business in Colorado. In November 2014, Colorado issued a state charter to a credit union (Fourth Corner Credit Union) whose membership specifically includes marijuana businesses. However, in July 2015, the Federal Reserve denied the credit union's application for a master account, and thus, access to the critical payment systems it superintends. Fourth Corner subsequently sued the Federal Reserve, but a federal district court rejected its request for an injunction ordering the Federal Reserve to grant the master account. As the court explained, "[t]he problem . . . is that the Credit Union is asking the Court to exercise its equitable authority to issue a mandatory injunction. But courts cannot use equitable powers to issue an order that would facilitate criminal activity." *Fourth Corner Credit Union v. Federal Reserve Bank of Kansas City*, 154 F. Supp. 3d 1185, 1188 (D. Colo. 2016). The Fourth Corner Credit Union has yet to open for business. *See* http://www.thefourthcornercreditunion.com/.

4. Ohio's 2016 medical marijuana law calls for the creation of a novel closed loop payment system:

> (A) The director of commerce may . . . adopt rules that establish a closed-loop payment processing system under which the state creates accounts to be used only by registered patients and caregivers at licensed dispensaries as well as by all license holders under this chapter. The system may include record-keeping and accounting functions that identify all parties involved in those transactions.

Ohio Rev. Code Ann. § 3796.031 (West 2016). The system is designed to reduce reliance on cash transactions and the compliance problems associated with them. *Id.* For commentary and further details on the proposal, see Robert McVay, *Ohio's Proposal for a Marijuana Banking Fix*, Canna Law Blog, Aug. 19, 2016, http://www.cannalawblog.com/ohios-proposal-for-a-marijuana-banking-fix/. Does Ohio's system address the banking needs of the marijuana industry? Could you imagine any other system that might do so, given the constraints presently imposed by federal law?

# CHAPTER 14

# The Law, Policy, and Authority Issues Confronting Government Officials

State officials have been caught in the crossfire of marijuana law and policy. While the federal government continues to criminalize the possession, manufacture, and distribution of marijuana, state lawmakers have ordered state officials to implement more permissive policies toward the same activities.

Marijuana reforms thus raise challenging questions concerning the rights and duties of state officials. Could state officials be prosecuted under the federal CSA for implementing state reforms? Could they be held civilly liable if they *refuse* to implement such reforms? May state officials prevent federal law enforcement agents from obtaining sensitive information the states gather from marijuana users and suppliers? Will state agencies lose federal funding by pursuing a softer approach toward marijuana?

This chapter addresses each of these questions in turn.

## A. COULD STATE OFFICIALS BE CRIMINALLY PROSECUTED UNDER THE FEDERAL CSA?

In the course of performing their duties, state employees may on occasion violate the literal terms of the federal Controlled Substances Act. The following Problem illustrates:

Problem 14.1: Pasha is a police officer working for the City. As part of an undercover sting operation, Pasha approaches Delilah, a suspected retail drug dealer. Pasha offers to sell Delilah 1 kilogram of marijuana for $7,000. Delilah says "Show me the goods and I'll consider it." That night, Pasha takes 1 kilogram of marijuana from the police evidence locker and drives to a pre-arranged location. Pasha hands the marijuana to Delilah, who, upon inspecting it, gives Pasha $7,000 cash. At that point, Francisco, an FBI agent who has been surreptitiously monitoring Delilah, bursts out of the bushes and arrests Pasha for distribution of marijuana and Delilah for possession with intent to distribute marijuana. Could Pasha be tried, convicted, and punished under 21 U.S.C. section 841?

In the Problem, Pasha appears to have "distributed" marijuana when she gave the drug to Delilah. After all, as discussed in Chapter 7, the offense of distribution entails no more than the *transfer* of a drug. Nonetheless, it is absurd to think that Pasha could be punished for her actions. Indeed, a special provision of the CSA would appear to immunize Pasha from punishment in these circumstances. In particular, 21 U.S.C. section 885(d) expressly immunizes state officials who violate the CSA while enforcing their own drug laws. It states:

> [N]o civil or criminal liability shall be imposed by virtue of this subchapter upon any duly authorized Federal officer lawfully engaged in the enforcement of this subchapter, or upon any duly authorized officer of any State, territory, political subdivision thereof, the District of Columbia, or any possession of the United States, who shall be lawfully engaged in the enforcement of any law or municipal ordinance relating to controlled substances.

*Id.*[1]

The original purpose of section 885(d) seems readily apparent. As one court has explained,

> [Section 885(d)] protects accepted law enforcement tactics such as sting or reverse-sting operations in which officers handle and transfer drugs, the transfer of suspected drugs to DEA laboratory agents for analysis, or to a clerk of court in the course of presenting evidence at trial, none of which could give rise to prosecution under [21 U.S.C.] § 841.

*United States v. Cortes-Caban*, 691 F.3d 1, 20-21 (1st Cir. 2012). But could section 885(d) be applied to other scenarios? The following sections discuss possible applications stemming from the implementation of state marijuana reforms.

## 1. ... For Growing and Selling Marijuana?

Following the repeal of the Eighteenth Amendment and its state law equivalents, many states created state-run monopolies to control the retail distribution of alcohol. In these states, only state-owned and -operated liquor stores could sell many forms of alcohol. Some states continue to operate state liquor stores, like the one depicted in **Figure 14.1**.

Could a state follow a similar path and assume ownership and control of the marijuana industry following a repeal of marijuana prohibition? Congress, of course, has not yet repealed its ban on marijuana—the equivalent of the Eighteenth Amendment for alcohol.

---

1. At least a few states have adopted similar provisions to shield their agents from liability under state drug laws. *See, e.g.*, Cal. Health & Safety Code § 11704(b) (West 2016) ("A law enforcement officer or agency, the state, or a person acting at the direction of a law enforcement officer or agency or the state is not liable [under the Drug Dealer Liability Act] for participating in the marketing of illegal controlled substances, if the participation is in furtherance of an official investigation."); S.D. Codified Laws § 34-20B-91 (West 2016) ("No liability shall be imposed by virtue of [the South Dakota Controlled Substances Act] upon any duly authorized local, state, or federal officer engaged in the enforcement of this chapter, or who shall be engaged in the enforcement of any law or municipal ordinance relating to controlled drugs and substances."); W. Va. Code Ann. § 60A-5-506(c) (West 2016) ("No liability is imposed by [the West Virginia Uniform Controlled Substances Act] upon any authorized state, county, or municipal officer, engaged in the lawful performance of his duties."). Even without explicit statutory immunity, however, it appears that "every American jurisdiction" has recognized a "public authority defense," which would excuse the otherwise criminal actions of a government agent acting in her official capacity. Elizabeth E. Joh, *Breaking the Law to Enforce It: Undercover Police Participation in Crime*, 62 Stan. L. Rev. 155, 169 (2009).

Chapter 14. The Law, Policy, and Authority Issues Confronting Government Officials

Figure 14.1. A State Operated Liquor Store in New Hampshire

Nonetheless, might section 885(d) enable state employees to manufacture and/or distribute marijuana? The following Problem raises the issue:

<u>Problem 14.2</u>: City passes an ordinance providing: "We designate Delilah as an official of the City. In that capacity, Delilah is hereby authorized to supply marijuana to the City's qualified medical marijuana patients." Pursuant to the ordinance, Delilah starts growing and distributing marijuana to the City's medical marijuana patient population. Soon thereafter, she is arrested by federal law enforcement agents and charged with violating 21 U.S.C. section 841. Can Delilah raise a defense under section 885(d)?

*United States v. Rosenthal* confronts the question raised by the Problem.[2]

## *United States v. Rosenthal*
266 F. Supp. 2d 1068 (N.D. Cal. 2003)

BREYER, C.J.:

On January 31, 2003, a jury convicted defendant Edward Rosenthal of violating the federal Controlled Substances Act. [The jury found, inter alia, that Rosenthal had manufactured marijuana in violation of 21 U.S.C. section 841.] . . . The charges arose out of Rosenthal's operation of an indoor marijuana-growing facility in Oakland, California. Now pending before the Court is Rosenthal's motion for a new trial. . . .

### BACKGROUND

Federal law prohibits the manufacture, distribution or sale of marijuana for any purpose. See 21 U.S.C. § 841. . . . In 1996, California voters enacted the "Compassionate Use Act," also known as Proposition 215. Proposition 215 makes it legal under California

---

2. Another portion of the *Rosenthal* decision concerning jury nullification is discussed in Chapter 7.

699

law for seriously ill patients and their primary caregivers to possess and cultivate marijuana for use by the seriously ill patient if the patient's physician recommends such treatment. To be precise, it exempts a seriously ill patient, or the patient's primary caregiver, from prosecution under California Health and Safety Code section 11357, relating to the possession of marijuana, and section 11358, relating to the cultivation of marijuana. *See* Cal. Health & Safety Code § 11362.5(d). It does not make it legal under California law for persons other than a seriously ill patient or his caregiver to possess or cultivate marijuana. . . .

In July 1998, the City of Oakland passed . . . Chapter 8.42. The expressed purpose of Chapter 8.42 was to "ensure safe and affordable medical cannabis pursuant to the Compassionate Use Act of 1996," and to "provide immunity to medical cannabis provider associations pursuant to Section 885(d) of Title 21 of the United States Code." That section provides that "no criminal or civil liability shall be imposed" under the Controlled Substances Act "upon any duly authorized officer of any State, territory or political subdivision thereof . . . who shall be lawfully engaged in the enforcement of any law or municipal ordinance relating to controlled substances." In an attempt to create immunity from liability under federal law for suppliers of medical marijuana, Chapter 8.42 provided that the City could designate a medical cannabis provider association and its employees and agents as officers of the City of Oakland to the extent they were "enforcing" the purpose of the Ordinance to provide safe medical cannabis to seriously ill patients. Chapter 8.42, § 3.

Following the passage of Chapter 8.42, Oakland designated the Oakland Cannabis Buyers Cooperative ("OCBC") to distribute marijuana in accordance with the new ordinance. At the time of the OCBC's designation, a federal court order was issued barring the OCBC from cultivating or distributing marijuana in violation of federal law. . . .

Two weeks after the designation, this Court ruled in the OCBC lawsuit that notwithstanding Chapter 8.42, 21 U.S.C. § 885(d) does not immunize from federal liability the OCBC's manufacture and distribution of marijuana. . . . The day after the Court issued this ruling, Jeffrey Jones, the OCBC's Executive Director, gave Rosenthal a letter stating that while Rosenthal "is acting within the scope of [his] duties as an agent of the [OCBC], [he is] deemed a duly authorized 'officer of the City of Oakland' and as such [is] immune from civil and criminal liability under Section 885(d) of the federal Controlled Substances Act." All of the conduct for which Mr. Rosenthal was convicted occurred after Jones purported to make Rosenthal an agent of the OCBC.

## PROCEDURAL HISTORY

In February 2002, the federal government indicted Rosenthal for growing marijuana indoors at 1419 Mandela Parkway in Oakland, California, during the period October 2001 through February 2002. . . .

[Rosenthal moved to dismiss the indictment on several grounds, including official immunity.] He argued that the City of Oakland had made him a city official for the purpose of cultivating marijuana for distribution to medical marijuana clubs and therefore he was immune from prosecution pursuant to section 885(d) of the Controlled Substances Act. . . .

[The court denied Rosenthal's pre-trial motion to dismiss, finding section 885(d) inapplicable to his actions. When Rosenthal filed a post-conviction motion for a new trial, the court found it necessary to further explain its ruling regarding 885(d).]

Discussion

... Rosenthal's conduct does not fall within the language of the immunity statute and is contrary to the expressed purpose of the Controlled Substances Act.

First, as the Court noted in its September 3, 1998 Order in the OCBC lawsuit, for an official to be "lawfully engaged" in the enforcement of a law relating to controlled substances, and therefore entitled to immunity, the law which the municipal official is "enforcing" must itself be consistent with federal law. Chapter 8.42, to the extent it provides for the cultivation and distribution of medical marijuana, is not lawful under federal or state law.[3]

Second, Section 885(d) applies to the "enforcement" of a law related to controlled substances. Rosenthal argues that by cultivating marijuana for medical use he was "enforcing" Chapter 8.42. Chapter 8.42 itself states that a City-designated medical cannabis provider shall "enforce" the purpose of the Chapter to ensure that seriously ill Californians have access to marijuana. To "enforce," however, generally means "to compel someone to do something or not to do something." ... Thus, as used in Section 885(d), to "enforce" a law related to a controlled substance means to compel compliance with the law. Rosenthal's conduct cannot reasonably be construed as "enforcing" Chapter 8.42, assuming the Chapter is a law related to controlled substances. At best, Rosenthal was implementing or facilitating the purpose of the statute; he was not compelling anyone to do or not to do anything.

Moreover, Rosenthal's interpretation of Section 885(d) directly contradicts the purpose of the Controlled Substances Act. As the Supreme Court has held, the Act "reflects a determination that marijuana has no medical benefits worthy of an exception (outside the confines of a Government-approved research project)." *United States v. Oakland Cannabis Buyers' Cooperative*, 532 U.S. 483, 491 (2001). ... To hold that Section 885(d) applies to the cultivation of marijuana for a medical cannabis club would conflict with the stated purpose of the Controlled Substances Act. "[L]awfully engaged" in "enforcing a law related to controlled substances" must mean engaged in enforcing, that is, compelling compliance with, a law related to controlled substances which is consistent ... or at least not inconsistent ... with the Controlled Substances Act. Section 885(d) cannot reasonably be read to cover acting pursuant to a law which itself is in conflict with the Act. ...

## Notes and Questions

1. On appeal, the Ninth Circuit endorsed two of the limitations Judge Breyer imposed on section 885(d) immunity. First, the court held that to be "lawfully engaged in the enforcement of any law or municipal ordinance relating to controlled substances," the defendant must compel someone to do something. Second, the court held that defendant's actions also must be consistent with the underlying purposes of the CSA. See *United States v. Rosenthal*, 454 F.3d 943 (9th Cir. 2006).

---

3. Author's note: At the time of the decision, California law had not yet explicitly authorized cooperatives to supply marijuana to qualified patients.

What do you think of the two limitations? As for the first, did Pasha, the unlucky Oakland police officer from **Problem 14.2** above, compel anyone to do anything in the course of her sting operation? If not, would Pasha be entitled to assert section 885(d) immunity under the reasoning of *Rosenthal*?

As for the second limitation, why, exactly, must the defendant's actions be consistent with the purposes of the CSA? If a defendant is "lawfully engaged in the enforcement of any law or municipal ordinance relating to controlled substances," why does it matter whether that ordinance is consistent with those purposes? After all, when interpreting statutes, courts are generally supposed to follow the explicit text of a statute, as opposed to the statute's purposes. *See, e.g., Exxon Mobil Corp. v. Allapattah Servs., Inc.*, 545 U.S. 546, 569 (2005) ("As we have repeatedly held, the authoritative statement is the statutory text, not the legislative history or any other extrinsic material. Extrinsic materials have a role in statutory interpretation only to the extent they shed a reliable light on the enacting Legislature's understanding of otherwise ambiguous terms.").

Judge Breyer proffered a textual argument for conditioning immunity on a finding that the defendant's actions were consistent with the CSA's purposes:

> [F]or an official to be 'lawfully engaged' in the enforcement of a law relating to controlled substances, and therefore entitled to immunity, the law which the municipal official is 'enforcing' must itself be consistent with federal law. Chapter 8.42, to the extent it provides for the cultivation and distribution of medical marijuana, is not lawful under federal or state law.

*Rosenthal*, 266 F. Supp. 2d at 1078 (emphasis added). *See also* Robert A. Mikos, *On the Limits of Supremacy*, 62 Vand. L. Rev. 1421, 1458-60 (2009) ("[G]ranting state police (or other state officials) immunity under section 885(d) for distributing or manufacturing marijuana would render the express preemption language of section 903 meaningless. . . . Clearly, a state law ordering state agents to cultivate and distribute marijuana to private citizens creates a 'positive conflict' with federal law. The law would therefore be preempted and unenforceable, and a state agent cannot be immune from federal prosecution under section 885(d) for enforcing an unenforceable state statute."). What do you think?

2. Postscript on *Rosenthal* sentencing. Although Judge Breyer rejected Ed Rosenthal's invocation of section 885(d) immunity, he nonetheless took Rosenthal's good faith belief that Oakland had immunized his operation from federal criminal liability into account at sentencing. Judge Breyer ultimately imposed a sentence of only one day's imprisonment. Under the sentencing provisions of the CSA, discussed in Chapter 7, Rosenthal had initially faced a *mandatory minimum* five-year prison term for his manufacturing offenses. However, Judge Breyer found that a safety valve provision spared Rosenthal from the mandatory term. He also found that the 27-33 month prison term otherwise required by the (then-mandatory) federal Sentencing Guidelines was inapplicable, due to the extraordinary nature of Rosenthal's case:

> This is not an ordinary drug case. In July 1998, two years before the defendant committed the offenses for which he was convicted, the City of Oakland passed . . . Chapter 8.42. . . . The City's theory was that a designated association would be immune from federal criminal liability pursuant to section 885(d) because by cultivating and distributing medical marijuana it would be acting as an official enforcing a municipal law related to controlled substances.

Shortly after the City passed the Ordinance it designated the Oakland Cannabis Buyers' Cooperative ("OCBC") to "enforce" the Ordinance. The OCBC in turn designated the defendant as its agent for purposes of what the City characterized as "enforcement" of the Ordinance, that is, cultivation of marijuana in accordance with the Ordinance. During pretrial proceedings the defendant testified that during the period at issue in this case he understood that he was cultivating marijuana pursuant to the Ordinance and therefore that under section 885(d) he was immune from federal criminal liability.

Prior to trial the Court concluded that despite the Ordinance, section 885(d) did not immunize the defendant's conduct from federal liability. Although the City of Oakland's purported designation of the defendant as a City official for the purpose of cultivating marijuana was not a legal defense to the charges in this case, it is a factor that takes this case well outside the "heartland" of narcotics cases. The Controlled Substances Act has been in effect since the 1970's, yet the Court is unaware of a single case in which a city—through a lawfully enacted ordinance—encouraged a defendant to manufacture a controlled substance and publicly represented—again through the ordinance—that notwithstanding federal law's prohibition of such conduct, the defendant would be shielded from liability under federal law. That is precisely what happened here. These unusual—indeed, unprecedented—circumstances warrant a downward departure.

The Court finds that the defendant honestly believed he was acting as a City official in accordance with state and local law, and therefore that his cultivation of marijuana was not a violation of federal law. The Court's finding is based on all the evidence in this case, including the evidence presented before and after the trial, and, in particular, on the defendant's testimony during the pre-trial evidentiary hearing. The Court finds the defendant's testimony to be credible on this issue.

The Court also finds that the defendant's belief—while erroneous—was reasonable because of the actions of the Oakland City Council in enacting the Ordinance. A reading of the Ordinance by the public, not by lawyers, would lead a reasonable person to believe, albeit erroneously, that his conduct would be immunized from federal prosecution.

The Court rejects the government's assertion that the defendant did not have a good faith belief in the legality of his conduct. The surprising evidence, discovered after trial, that the City of Oakland's attorney actually advised the City Council that the Ordinance would not shield violators of federal law from prosecution calls into question the City Council's belief in the efficacy of its Ordinance. There is no evidence, however, that the defendant was aware of the City attorney's advice or that he was made aware of this Court's ruling in September 1998 that the Ordinance did not confer immunity. Again, the Court finds the defendant's testimony on this issue credible.

Moreover, the defendant's good faith belief that he was acting as an Oakland City official and was therefore immune from liability is corroborated by the openness of his conduct. He did not hide the fact that he was cultivating marijuana. He had the Oakland Fire Department inspect [his grow site] on two occasions and an Oakland City Council member also visited the site. He also told several City Council members of his intention to cultivate marijuana in accordance with Oakland's proposed plan. There is no evidence that any of these people ever advised the defendant that notwithstanding Oakland's Ordinance he could be imprisoned for his conduct.

*United States v. Rosenthal*, 266 F. Supp. 2d 1091 (N.D. Cal. 2003) (*Rosenthal II*).

3. Putting aside the doctrinal question, *should* states be allowed to own and operate marijuana production and retail outlets? For further discussion of the policy arguments both for and against government ownership and control of the marijuana industry, see Chapter 9.

## 2. ... for Returning Marijuana?

**Problem 14.3** raises a more common scenario in which section 885(d) has been invoked:

> **Problem 14.3:** During a consensual search, State Police Officer Pasha finds a baggie containing one ounce of marijuana in Delilah's backpack. Pasha immediately seizes the baggie. However, Delilah shows Pasha her medical marijuana registration card. After examining the card, Pasha concludes that Delilah's possession comports with the state's medical marijuana law. Delilah then asks Pasha to return her marijuana. State law requires police to immediately return any marijuana seized from individuals who are allowed to possess it under state law. If Pasha fulfills her duty and gives Delilah the marijuana, would section 885(d) immunize her from liability under 21 U.S.C. section 841?

At least a handful of states do, in fact, specifically require law enforcement agents to return any marijuana they have wrongfully seized from private citizens. For example, New Mexico's medical marijuana law provides that

> Any property interest that is possessed, owned or used in connection with the medical use of cannabis, or acts incidental to such use, shall not be harmed, neglected, injured or destroyed while in the possession of state or local law enforcement officials. Any such property interest shall not be forfeited under any state or local law providing for the forfeiture of property except as provided in the Forfeiture Act. Cannabis, paraphernalia or other property seized from a qualified patient or primary caregiver in connection with the claimed medical use of cannabis shall be returned immediately upon the determination by a court or prosecutor that the qualified patient or primary caregiver is entitled to the protections of the provisions of the Lynn and Erin Compassionate Use Act, as may be evidenced by a failure to actively investigate the case, a decision not to prosecute, the dismissal of charges or acquittal.

N.M. Stat. Ann. § 26-2B-4(G) (2011). *See also* Colo. Const. art. XVIII, § 14(e) (same); 15 Maine Rev. Stat. Ann. § 5821-A (West 2016) (similar). And even states without a law specifically requiring the return of marijuana may find such a duty implied by statutes calling for the return of seized property more generally. *E.g., The City of Garden Grove v. Kha*, 157 Cal. App. 4th 355 (Cal. App. 2007) (holding that statute requiring police to return "controlled substances . . . [that] were lawfully possessed" by a defendant applies to medical marijuana).

But authorities disagree about whether such a duty to return seized marijuana is pre-empted by the CSA. In large part, the debate turns on whether section 885(d) would immunize a state agent from federal criminal charges stemming from the act of returning seized marijuana to a private citizen. Several authorities have found that section 885(d) would apply and would thereby defuse any conflict between state and federal law. *See Arizona v. Okun*, 296 P.3d 998, 1002 (Ariz. App. 2013) (finding section 885(d) applicable); *The City of Garden Grove*, 157 Cal. App. 4th at 388 (same); *Oregon v. Kama*, 39 P.3d 866, 868 (Or. App. 2002) (same). By contrast, other authorities have found that any duty to return seized marijuana is preempted and unenforceable, notwithstanding section 885(d). *See Colorado v. Crouse*, ___ P.3d ___, ___ (Colo. 2017) (finding section 885(d) inapplicable); *Oregon v. Ehrensing*, 296 P.3d 1279, 1286 (Or. App. 2013) (same); Op. Or. Att'y Gen., No. OP-2012-1 (Jan. 19, 2012) (same); Op. Mich. Att'y Gen., No. 7262 (Nov. 10, 2011) (same).

The two excerpts below elaborate on the competing views. The first excerpt argues that section 885(d) would not immunize a state official who returns seized marijuana and that any state-imposed duty to do so is therefore preempted.

## *Office of the Attorney General, State of Michigan*
Opinion No. 7262, Nov. 10, 2011

[State Representative Kevin Cotter has] asked whether a law enforcement officer who arrests a patient or primary caregiver registered under the Michigan Medical Marihuana Act (MMMA or Act) . . . must return marihuana found in the possession of the patient or primary caregiver upon his or her release from custody. . . .

. . .

. . . [T]he MMMA specifically prohibits the forfeiture of marihuana possessed in connection with the medical use of marihuana. Section 4(h) of the Act provides:

> Any marihuana, marihuana paraphernalia, or licit property that is possessed, owned, or used in connection with the medical use of marihuana, as allowed under this act, or acts incidental to such use, *shall not be* seized or *forfeited*. [MCL 333.26424(h); emphasis added.]

The term "forfeited" is not defined in the Act. An undefined statutory term must be accorded its plain and ordinary meaning. . . . The word "forfeit" has a well-understood meaning in the law. It means "[t]o lose, or lose the right to, by some error, fault, offense, or crime." Black's Law Dictionary (6th ed.), p 650. Thus, as used in section 4(h), "forfeited" means the permanent loss of marihuana or related property as a consequence of having done something improper.

According section 4(h) its plain meaning, and reading it in conjunction with section 7(e), MCL 333.26427(e), which renders conflicting state statutes subject to the MMMA, section 4(h) prohibits the forced or involuntary surrender of marihuana if the person in possession is a registered patient or caregiver in complete compliance with all other provisions of the MMMA. Therefore, if a registered patient or caregiver's marihuana is confiscated by law enforcement during the course of an arrest, if the person's registration card is valid and the possession complies with the MMMA, the officer must return the marihuana to the patient or caregiver upon release from custody.

But this does not conclude the analysis because . . . federal law prohibits the manufacture, distribution, or possession of marihuana. . . .

. . .

Section 4(h) of the MMMA, forbidding forfeiture of marihuana, directly conflicts with the CSA's prohibition against possession or distribution of marihuana because it is impossible for a law enforcement officer to comply with both federal and state law.

. . . If a law enforcement officer returns marihuana to a patient or caregiver as required by section 4(h), the officer is distributing or aiding and abetting the distribution or possession of marihuana by the patient or caregiver in violation of the CSA. Thus, a Michigan law enforcement officer cannot simultaneously comply with the federal prohibition against distribution or aiding and abetting the distribution or possession of marihuana and the state prohibition against forfeiture of marihuana. In other words, it is "impossible" for state law enforcement officers to comply with their state-law duty not to forfeit medical marihuana, and their federal-law duty not to distribute or aid in the distribution of marihuana. Under these circumstances, the unavoidable conclusion is that section 4(h) of the MMMA is preempted by the CSA to the extent it requires law enforcement officers to return marihuana to registered patients or caregivers. As a result, law enforcement officers are not required to return marihuana to a patient or caregiver.

By returning marihuana to a registered patient or caregiver, a law enforcement officer is exposing himself or herself to potential criminal and civil penalties under the CSA for the distribution of marihuana or for aiding or abetting the possession or distribution of marihuana. Section 841(a) of the CSA applies to "any person," which, courts have presumed, covers government employees as well as private citizens. While section 885(d) of the CSA, 21 USC 885(d), confers immunity on state law enforcement officers who violate its provisions while "lawfully engaged in the enforcement of any law . . . relating to controlled substances," returning marihuana to a registered patient or caregiver under the MMMA could not be considered lawful "enforcement" of a law related to controlled substances. "Enforcement" in this context means the prosecution of unlawful possession or distribution of controlled substances. See *United States v Rosenthal*, 266 F. Supp. 2d 1068, 1078-79 (N.D. Cal. 2003), *aff'd in part, reversed in part*, 445 F.3d 1239, opinion amended and superseded on denial of rehearing 454 F.3d 943 (2006). Otherwise, a state could contradict the fundamental purpose of the CSA and immunize any state officials who participate in the competing state regime. . . . Moreover, the state officers' conduct would remain "unlawful" in any event because immunity does not decriminalize the underlying conduct, it only provides protection from prosecution or other penalty.

The people of this State, even in the exercise of their constitutional right to initiate legislation, cannot require law enforcement officers to violate federal law by mandating the return of marihuana to registered patients or caregivers. . . .

It is my opinion, therefore, that section 4(h) of the Michigan Medical Marihuana Act, MCL 333.26424(h), which prohibits the forfeiture of marihuana possessed for medical use, directly conflicts with and is thus preempted by, the federal Controlled Substances Act, 21 U.S.C. 801 *et seq.*, to the extent section 4(h) requires a law enforcement officer to return marihuana to a registered patient or primary caregiver upon release from custody.

---

In the next case, the court finds that section 885(d) would immunize local police and that a court order requiring police to return marijuana is enforceable.

## *The City of Garden Grove v. Kha*
157 Cal. App. 4th 355 (Cal. App. 2007)

BEDSWORTH, J.:

During a traffic stop, Garden Grove police seized about a third of an ounce of marijuana from real party in interest Felix Kha. However, because Kha had a doctor's approval to use marijuana for medical reasons, the prosecutor dismissed the drug charge he was facing. The trial court then granted Kha's motion for return of property and ordered the Garden Grove Police Department to give him back his marijuana. . . .

...

The City of Garden Grove (the City) petitions for a writ of mandate and/or prohibition directing the trial court to vacate its order and enter a new one denying Kha's motion for return of property. The City sees itself "caught in the middle of a conflict between state and federal law"—a position with which we can certainly sympathize—on the issue of medical marijuana and does not want to be perceived as facilitating a breach of federal law by returning Kha's marijuana to him. . . . [Inter alia, the City] maintains that to the extent state law authorizes or mandates the return of Kha's marijuana, it is preempted by federal law.

...

These restrictions are consistent with the goals of the CSA. Irrespective of Congress' prohibition against marijuana possession, "[i]t is unreasonable to believe that use of medical marijuana by [qualified users under the CUA] for [the] limited purpose [of medical treatment] will create a significant drug problem" (*Conant v. McCaffrey* (N.D. Cal. 1997) 172 F.R.D. 681, 694, fn. 5, *affd. in Conant v. Walters*, [309 F.3d 629 (9th Cir. 2002)], so as to undermine the stated objectives of the CSA. . . .

It is even more unreasonable to believe returning marijuana to qualified patients who have had it seized by local police will hinder the federal government's enforcement efforts. Practically speaking, this subset of medical marijuana users is too small to make a measurable impact on the war on drugs. Not only are their numbers meager, persons seeking the return of their medical marijuana are not entitled to possess the drug in such quantities as would make them likely candidates for federal prosecution. (See *Conant v. Walters*, *supra*, 309 F.3d at p. 646, fn. 10 (conc. opn. of Kozinski, J.) [noting federal prosecutors typically pursue marijuana charges only in cases involving the cultivation of over 500 indoor plants or 1,000 outdoor plants, or the possession of more than 1,000 pounds of the drug].) Upholding the return of Kha's 8.1 grams of marijuana would simply not constitute a real or meaningful threat to the federal drug enforcement effort. This is not a case in which preemption is necessary to the federal scheme.

...

We share Justice O'Connor's viewpoint in this regard. Since Kha's possession of marijuana is legal under state law, we do not believe the trial court's order interferes with, or is preempted by, federal law. Admittedly, there is tension between state and federal drug policy on the issue of medicinal marijuana. It is quite clear California has chosen a policy that is at odds with the federal government's. But the important point for purposes of this case is that state law does not interfere with the federal government's prerogative to criminalize marijuana. As a general rule, it is still illegal to possess marijuana under federal law, and nothing in this opinion should be construed as suggesting otherwise. In fact, our holding with respect to the preemption issue presented in this case is very narrow. All we are saying is that federal supremacy principles do not prohibit the return of marijuana to a qualified user whose possession of the drug is legally sanctioned under state law.

...

. . . [City and amici] fear the Garden Grove police would be violating federal law by returning Kha's marijuana to him. . . . [City argues that the police would be aiding and abetting violations of the CSA, but] amici go a step further . . . and argue the police would be in direct violation of federal law were they to comply with the trial court's order. They point out that distribution of a controlled substance is generally prohibited under 21 U.S.C. § 841(a)(1), but that section does not apply to persons who regularly handle controlled substances in the course of their professional duties. For example, in *United States v. Feingold* (9th Cir. 2006) 454 F.3d 1001, 1008, the court held that 21 U.S.C. §841(a)(1) could only be applied to a doctor if, in distributing a controlled substance, he intended "to act as a pusher rather than a medical professional." . . .

By analogy, it would stand to reason that the only way a police officer could be found in violation of 21 U.S.C. §841(a)(1) for distributing a controlled substance is if he or she intended to act as a drug peddler rather than a law enforcement official. In this case, it is quite obvious the police do not want to give Kha his marijuana back at all, let alone have him use it for illicit purposes. They are acting under the compulsion of a lawful court order. Therefore, we cannot see how anyone could regard compliance with this order a violation of 21 U.S.C. §841(a)(1).

Assuming someone could, it seems to us clear the police would be entitled to immunity under 21 U.S.C. §885(d). . . . [T]hat statute provides immunity to law enforcement personnel who are responsible for handling controlled substances as part of their official duties. . . . From a legal standpoint, that should alleviate any fears the Garden Grove police have about returning Kha's marijuana to him. As a practical matter, moreover, it seems exceedingly unlikely that federal prosecutors would ever attempt to haul a local constable into federal court for complying with a state judicial order calling for the return of a qualified patient's medical marijuana. We are not aware of a single instance in which this has ever occurred. We are confident, had there been such a phenomenon, it would have been brought to our attention.

. . .

Mindful as we are of the general supremacy of federal law, we are unable to discern any justification for the City or its police department to disregard the trial court's order to return Kha's marijuana. The order is fully consistent with state law respecting the possession of medical marijuana, and for all the reasons discussed, we do not believe the federal drug laws supersede or preempt Kha's right to the return of his property. That right has its origins in the CUA and MMP, but it is grounded, at bottom, on fairness principles embodied in the due process clause. Those principles require the return of Kha's property.

## Notes and Questions

1. Compare the Michigan Attorney General and California court interpretations of section 885(d). Which is more persuasive? Does the *City of Garden Grove* court accurately interpret section 885(d) when it suggests that the provision immunizes agents "for handling controlled substances as part of their official duties"? Does this interpretation square with the limitations noted by *Rosenthal, supra*? Consider this (fanciful) Problem:

**Problem 14.4**: The state has passed a law making it part of the official duty of the state and local police to produce and sell marijuana to anyone 18 years or older. Pursuant to the new law, Pasha, a state police officer, produces and then sells 1 kilogram of marijuana to Benjamin, who is 18 years old and from out of state. If Pasha is prosecuted by the federal government for this act, can she assert immunity under section 885(d)?

2. The *City of Garden Grove* court also suggests that a police officer who returns seized marijuana to its original owner does not thereby "distribute" the drug, because she lacks the intent "'to act as a drug pusher.'" Does the court accurately define the mens rea element for distribution under 21 U.S.C. section 841? *See* Chapter 7.

3. No state agent has ever been prosecuted by the federal government merely for returning seized marijuana to its original owner. Indeed, the *City of Garden Grove* court suggested in a portion of its opinion not excerpted above that "the City and its police officers really have nothing to lose by returning Kha's marijuana to him." 157 Cal. App. 4th at 369. If that is true, do state officials even have standing to challenge the state duty as preempted? *Id.* at 365-71 (discussing standing issues under state law). For a discussion of standing issues surrounding other preemption challenges to state supply regulations, see Chapter 10.

4. Does barring state officials from returning marijuana constitute prohibited commandeering? The textbook author discusses the possibility:

> On the one hand, by returning marijuana state agents would seem to take positive action that violates the CSA—namely, distributing marijuana. As defined under the CSA, distribution simply means to transfer drugs from one person to another; no money need be exchanged. Hence, at first glance, it would seem that laws requiring state agents to return marijuana to qualified patients are preempted because they require state agents to violate the CSA—this clearly poses a positive conflict with the CSA.
>
> On the other hand, returning seized marijuana to its original possessor merely restores the state of nature. The quantity of marijuana in existence and the identity of the possessor are no different than had the state government never seized the drugs. Viewed this way, preemption of these state laws would compel state action and not merely block it: state agents who have seized marijuana would now be obliged to store it, destroy it, or transfer it to federal authorities. . . . [T]his is an obligation Congress may not impose . . .

Mikos, *On the Limits*, *supra*, at 1459-60. What do you think? To test your intuitions, consider the following Problem:

**Problem 14.5**: Police Officer Pasha has seized one ounce of marijuana from a private citizen, Camila. In plain sight of Camila, Pasha places the marijuana on the hood of her patrol car. After questioning Camila, Pasha determines that Camila is allowed to possess the marijuana under state law. Camila then asks Pasha to return her marijuana. Pasha considers two options:

(1) Grab the marijuana off the hood and physically hand it back to Camila, or
(2) Allow Camila to retrieve it from the car hood herself

Is there any meaningful difference between these two options? Does option (1) constitute a crime? Does option (2)? Could Congress somehow preempt option (2)? If not, is there any reason to treat option (1) any differently from (2)?

5. Could state officials be criminally prosecuted for implementing any of the other regulatory reforms surveyed in Chapters 4 and 8? As noted in Chapter 10, the states of Nebraska and Oklahoma have accused Colorado officials of "authoriz[ing],

oversee[ing], protect[ing], and profit[ing] from a sprawling $100-million-per-month marijuana growing, processing, and retailing organization that . . . [i]f . . . based south of our border, the federal government would prosecute . . . as a drug cartel." *States of Nebraska and Oklahoma v. State of Colorado, Plaintiff's Supplemental Brief*, 2016 WL 74964. Is the Colorado Marijuana Enforcement Division (MED) akin to a drug cartel? Could it be prosecuted as such?

## B. COULD STATE OFFICIALS BE HELD CIVILLY LIABLE?

The flip side of the issue just discussed is whether state officials can be held civilly liable if they violate state law, at least when federal law does not require them to do so. The following Problem raises the issue:

**Problem 14.6:** Pasha is a police officer in a state that has legalized medical marijuana. She stops Delilah for a traffic violation. As Pasha approaches Delilah's car, she detects the odor of marijuana emanating from inside. Delilah refuses to consent to a search, but Pasha searches the car anyway and finds six live potted marijuana plants in the trunk. Pasha seizes the plants, which she later deposits in a windowless evidence room. Pasha arrests Delilah for the manufacture of marijuana. A few weeks later, Delilah convinces a judge to dismiss the charges on the grounds that her actions comported with the state's medical marijuana law. When Delilah asks about her plants, however, Pasha tells her "They all died." Could Delilah pursue legal action against Pasha? If so, what remedy could she obtain?

Consider, first, Delilah's options under federal law. Congress has created a cause of action for the deprivation of rights created under *federal* law:

> Every person who, under color of any statute, ordinance, regulation, custom, or usage, of any State or Territory or the District of Columbia, subjects, or causes to be subjected, any citizen of the United States or other person within the jurisdiction thereof to the deprivation of any rights, privileges, or immunities secured by the Constitution and laws, shall be liable to the party injured in an action at law, suit in equity, or other proper proceeding for redress. . . .

42 U.S.C. § 1983. For more background on section 1983, see Karen M. Blum & Kathryn R. Urbonya, Section 1983 Litigation, Federal Judicial Center (1998), available at https://perma.cc/PV2X-RWH7

It is highly doubtful that Delilah in **Problem 14.6** could state a claim under section 1983 *for the destruction* of her marijuana. Although the Due Process Clause of the Fourteenth Amendment protects against deprivations of property, federal law as yet recognizes no property interest in marijuana. *E.g., Little v. Gore*, 148 F. Supp. 3d 936, 955 (S.D. Cal. 2015) ("[T]here is no protected property interest [in marijuana] for purposes of the Fourteenth Amendment."); *Brown v. Ely*, 14 P.3d 257, 261 (Alaska 2000) ("[V]iolating rights recognized in *Ravin* [*v. Alaska*] does not generate a cause of action under § 1983."). *But see The City of Garden Grove v. Kha*, 157 Cal. App. 4th at 388 (suggesting that a qualified patient has a federal due process interest in seized marijuana). Nonetheless, Delilah might be able to state a claim for deprivation of other federal rights. For example, Delilah could try to convince a court that Pasha violated her federal constitutional right against unreasonable searches and seizures. (For a more in-depth discussion of search and seizure, see Chapter 4.)

But even if a plaintiff like Delilah could state a claim under section 1983, she might run into another obstacle: police officers and other government officials have qualified immunity from suits for monetary damages. The Supreme Court has explained that "government officials performing discretionary functions, generally are shielded from liability for civil damages insofar as their conduct does not violate clearly established statutory or constitutional rights of which a reasonable person would have known." *Harlow v. Fitzgerald*, 457 U.S. 800, 818 (1982). *See also Sinclair v. City of Grandview*, 973 F. Supp. 2d 1234 (E.D. Wash. 2013) (discussing qualified immunity in section 1983 suit against police officers in connection with search of medical marijuana patient's home).

Even when no relief is available under section 1983, however, comparable state statutes might give individuals a cause of action against state officials who deprive them of unique rights created by state law, including state marijuana reforms. For more background on state causes of action, see Friesen, State Constitutional Law: Litigating Individual Rights, Claims, and Defenses (4th ed. 2006).

In such a suit, of course, a plaintiff would need to demonstrate that the official indeed violated state law. This may prove more challenging than first appears, depending on the nuances of state law. In some states, for example, a claim like Delilah's in **Problem 14.6** based on the destruction (or neglect) of marijuana plants would be dismissed because "a law enforcement agency has no responsibility to maintain *live marijuana plants* lawfully seized." Or. Rev. Stat. Ann. § 475B.490.2 (West 2016) (emphasis added).

Like section 1983, state laws also typically grant qualified immunity to state officials. *See* Friesen, State Constitutional Law, *supra*, at § 6.04 (discussing immunity under state law). At least one state has even adopted a special immunity provision to shield state officials from lawsuits stemming from the enforcement of the state's medical marijuana laws. N.J. Stat. Ann. § 24:6I-15 (West 2016) ("In addition to any immunity or defense provided by law, the State and any employee or agent of the State shall not be held liable for any actions taken in accordance with [the New Jersey Compassionate Use Medical Marijuana Act] or for any deleterious outcomes from the medical use of marijuana by any registered qualifying patient.").

The opinions in the following case provide some insights into litigation stemming from the deprivation of rights created by state marijuana reforms.

## *County of Butte v. Superior Court*
175 Cal. App. 4th 729 (Cal. App. 2009)

RAYE, J.:

Real party in interest David Williams is a qualified medical marijuana patient who uses marijuana upon the recommendation of his physician. Williams belonged to a seven-member collective of medical marijuana patients who agreed to contribute comparable amounts of money, property, and labor to the collective cultivation of marijuana; each then would receive an approximately equal share of the marijuana produced. The marijuana was grown at Williams's home.

In September of 2005 a Butte County Sheriff's deputy came to Williams's home without a warrant. Williams produced copies of medical marijuana recommendations for himself and the other members of the collective. The deputy ordered Williams, under threat of arrest and prosecution, to destroy all but 12 of the 41 medical marijuana plants. Williams complied.

. . .

Williams alleged that Hancock's action was undertaken pursuant to the county's policy to allow qualified patients to grow marijuana collectively only if each member actively participates in the actual cultivation of the marijuana by planting, watering, pruning, or harvesting the marijuana.

[Williams brought suit, alleging various state law violations by defendants Butte County, the Butte County Sheriff's office, and the deputy involved (collectively, County).]

. . .

In its demurrer, County argued that if Williams believed he was lawfully cultivating all 41 marijuana plants, his only option under the law was to refuse to remove the plants and to prove the legality of the patient collective in criminal court. Instead, County contends, Williams is attempting to convert the limited defense provided to him under the Act into an affirmative right, allowing him to challenge Hancock's actions and seek civil damages.

. . .

We disagree with County's assertion that the Constitution and laws of the state do not provide Williams any relief at law. . . .

. . .

Article I, section 13 of the California Constitution guarantees individuals the right to be secure in their persons, houses, papers, and effects, free from unreasonable searches and seizures.

. . .

Here the deputy, without a warrant, ordered Williams to destroy marijuana plants. Lacking a warrant, an officer must possess """facts as would lead a man of ordinary caution or prudence to believe, and conscientiously entertain a strong suspicion of the guilt of the accused."""" [*California v. Mower*, 49 P.3d 1067 (Cal. 2002).] Any consideration of probable cause must include the officer's consideration of the individual's status as a qualified medical marijuana patient. [*Id.*]

. . .

. . . Williams seeks an adjudication as to whether the deputy had probable cause to order Williams to destroy his property, or whether a lack of probable cause led to a violation of his constitutional rights.

. . .

. . . Williams's claim does not implicate employment law, property law, or any other discrete branch of the law. Instead, Williams posits causes of action based on his constitutional right to due process, a right growing out of the administration of criminal law, the very subject of the [Compassionate Use] Act.

Nor do we see floodgates opening and lawsuits flooding our burdened court system as a result of Williams's suit. Instead, we see an opportunity for an individual to request the same constitutional guarantee of due process available to all individuals, no matter what their status, under the state Constitution. The fact that this case involves medical marijuana and a qualified medical marijuana patient does not change these fundamental constitutional rights or an individual's right to assert them.

Our dissenting colleague asserts that under federal law "marijuana is just as illegal as cocaine, and therefore is contraband per se." Thus, marijuana cannot be lawfully possessed, not even by desperately ill patients who obtain permission to use marijuana for medical purposes; such permission will be useful in a criminal prosecution but is worthless in resisting warrantless intrusions and seizures by law enforcement. This anomalous result, which would surely shock the sensibilities of the voters who approved the initiative measure, is compelled, according to the dissent, because federal law reigns supreme. We disagree.

We have acknowledged that the Act has no effect on marijuana arrests and prosecutions or searches and seizures under federal law. The many authorities cited by the dissent on contraband per se all involve property characterized as such under the laws of the seizing jurisdiction. The Act presents the unusual circumstance of a state law that, under limited circumstances, permits the possession of a substance deemed to be contraband under federal law. There are no decisions holding that federal law renders the Act unconstitutional or otherwise unenforceable. Here, the deputy was acting under color of California law, not federal law. Accordingly, the propriety of his conduct is measured by California law. The numerous federal authorities cited by the dissent are without application in the present appeal.

. . .

MORRISON, J., dissenting:

. . . [P]eace officers swear to uphold the constitution and laws of both California and the United States. . . . Imposing civil liability for an officer who complies with federal law will lead to further confusion surrounding medical marijuana. Judges take the same oath, and the courts should not encourage illegal acts.

. . .

In this case the CUA is not raised as a shield against criminal charges; it is used as a sword in an attempt to impose civil liability against a peace officer. Allowing this suit to proceed exceeds the proper scope of the CUA, frustrates federal law, requires California courts to validate illegal conduct and needlessly complicates the work of law enforcement. Therefore, I would issue a peremptory writ of mandate.

. . .

The CUA states that one of its purposes is "[t]o ensure that seriously ill Californians have the right to obtain and use" medical marijuana. (Health & Saf. Code, § 11362.5, subd. (b)(1)(A).) While this language can be read broadly to create a protected property interest in marijuana, such interest would be of no effect in light of federal law. And the California Supreme Court has read this language narrowly, holding that the limited "'right' to obtain and use marijuana created by the [CUA] is the right" to avoid criminal sanctions. [*Ross v. RagingWire Telecommunications, Inc.*, 174 P.3d 200 (Cal. 2008).] The CUA did not and could not vest a person with a true "right" to possess marijuana in derogation of the CSA as interpreted in *Raich*. The CUA merely created "a narrow exception to the criminal law." . . .

. . .

Under the supreme law of the land, marijuana is just as illegal as cocaine, and therefore is contraband per se: "The following shall be subject to forfeiture to the United States and no property right shall exist in them: (1) All controlled substances which have been manufactured, distributed, dispensed, or acquired in violation of this subchapter. [¶] . . . [¶] (8) All controlled substances which have been possessed in violation of this subchapter." (21 U.S.C.A. § 881(a).) In part the CSA defines what may be subject to forfeiture, but it also declares that "no property right shall exist" in, among other things, specified substances including marijuana. Federal law is supreme, making marijuana contraband per se even in California.

. . .

Under settled common law principles, there can be no tort liability for the destruction of contraband per se.

Nor does the seizure and destruction of contraband per se offend due process principles. Due process protects *lawful* property interests: "'There can be no forfeiture of property without notice to the owner and a hearing at which he can be heard, except in a few cases of necessity, i.e., *property kept in violation of law which is incapable of lawful use.*'" [*California v. One 1941 Chevrolet Coupe*, 231 P.2d 832 (Cal. 1951) (italics added).] . . .

. . .

Had Deputy Hancock been accompanied by a federal agent who ordered the destruction, no suit would lie. . . . And Deputy Hancock had no legal duty to refrain from seizing and destroying all of the plants. Nothing in the complaint suggests his direction to Williams to destroy the plants was unreasonable *apart from* Williams' view that he had the right to grow marijuana. So, how has Deputy Hancock subjected himself and his department to possible liability? . . .

Compensating Williams for the purported value of the destroyed marijuana would assure growers of marijuana that the courts of California will protect their crops. This obstructs the federal policy adopted by Congress in the CSA as interpreted and upheld by the United States Supreme Court in [*Gonzales v.*] *Raich*.

Medical marijuana users under the CUA do have some administrative protection for their marijuana. The California Attorney General, the "chief law officer of the State" (Cal. Const., art. V, § 13), has issued a bulletin that "recommends that state and local law enforcement officers not arrest individuals or seize marijuana under federal law when the officer determines from the facts available that the cultivation, possession, or transportation is permitted under California's medical marijuana laws." (Cal. Dept. of Justice, *Guidelines for the Security and Non-Diversion of Marijuana Grown for Medical Use* (Aug. 2008) p. 4.) This is a sensible position, and presumably local law enforcement agencies will adopt appropriate policies and training programs. But it is only in benign forbearance that medical marijuana users are protected. They do not have any "right" to sue to protect their marijuana until federal law is changed.

## Notes and Questions

1. Should states or state officials pay damages for searches, seizures, arrests, prosecutions, or other actions that violate marijuana reforms? Are damages suits a good way to

vindicate the rights created by state marijuana laws? Is there another way to ensure that state officials respect the rights created by state law?

2. The dissent suggests that the court may not order defendants to compensate plaintiff for destroying his marijuana because doing so would obstruct federal drug policy. Do you agree? Along these lines, consider the following Problem:

**Problem 14.7**: Andy grows 41 marijuana plants in a barn behind his house—the maximum he is allowed to do so pursuant to the state's medical marijuana law. One night, Benjamin sneaks into the barn and steals all of Andy's marijuana plants. Andy reports the theft to the police, and the police identify Benjamin as the culprit from video surveillance. The plants are never found, but the local district attorney charges Benjamin with theft, which the state defines as "the unlawful taking of the personal property of another." In his defense, Benjamin claims that marijuana is not "property" and that the state theft statute is preempted by the CSA to the extent it recognizes a property interest in marijuana. Is the case distinguishable from *County of Butte*? What result? *Cf. California v. Dillon*, 668 P.2d 697, 705 n.5 (1983).

3. In *County of Butte*, the plaintiff sued the county and county sheriff's office, in addition to the officer who ordered him to destroy his marijuana plants. Under federal law, local governments can be sued, but only for actions of local officials that stem from local policy. *Monell v. Dep't of Soc. Servs. of City of N.Y.*, 436 U.S. 658, 690 (1978) ("Local governing bodies . . . can be sued directly under § 1983 for monetary, declaratory, or injunctive relief where . . . the action that is alleged to be unconstitutional implements or executes a policy statement, ordinance, regulation, or decision officially adopted and promulgated by that body's officers."). However, these local governments—unlike their officials—cannot claim qualified immunity. *Owen v. City of Indep., Mo.*, 445 U.S. 622, 657 (1980) (holding that "municipalities have no immunity from damages liability flowing from their constitutional violations"). By contrast, "neither a State nor its officials acting in their official capacities are 'persons' under § 1983." *Will v. Mich. Dep't of State Police*, 491 U.S. 58, 71 (1989). And state governments—unlike local governments—do enjoy immunity from suits for monetary damages.

4. Marijuana users and suppliers are not the only parties who might pursue civil rights claims stemming from state marijuana reforms. For example, *in Denney v. Drug Enf. Admin.*, 508 F. Supp. 2d 815 (E.D. Cal. 2007), a physician sued federal and state agencies and officials, based on an alleged violation of his First Amendment rights protected by *Conant v. Walters* (a case discussed in Chapter 12). In particular, the physician claimed that the defendants had investigated his medical practice "as an act of retaliation for his speech concerning medical marijuana." *Id.* at 828. The court initially allowed the First Amendment claim to proceed, *id.* at 837, but it subsequently granted the defendants' motion for summary judgment, *Denney v. Drug Enf. Admin.*, No. CIV.S06-1711LKKGGH, 2008 WL 1808289, at *10 (E.D. Cal. Apr. 22, 2008), *aff'd sub nom.* Denney v. Drug Enf't Agency, 348 F. App'x 327 (9th Cir. 2009).

## C. CAN STATE OFFICIALS STOP THE FEDERAL GOVERNMENT FROM ACCESSING INFORMATION THEY COLLECT ABOUT MARIJUANA USERS/SUPPLIERS?

Through patient registration, commercial licensing, and similar requirements, the states are collecting troves of detailed information about marijuana users and suppliers. Since 2013, for example, the system Colorado uses to monitor marijuana licensees has tracked more than 20,000 participants and more than 5,000,000 marijuana plants. *See* Metrc, https://perma.cc/9G8F-EB6B. (Chapter 8 provides more details concerning Colorado's efforts to monitor the marijuana industry.)

The states gather this information to enforce their own marijuana regulations, but the same data could also be used to enforce federal law, as the following Problem illustrates:

Problem 14.8: Delilah is the Director of the Marijuana Enforcement Division (MED) in a state that has legalized recreational marijuana. All firms that are licensed to manufacture and distribute marijuana must submit regular reports to the MED. Among other things, the reports must track the number of marijuana plants the licensee cultivates and/or the quantity of marijuana product the licensee sells. Under state law, these reports are considered "strictly confidential" and may be accessed only by the MED, and then only for purposes of monitoring the licensee's compliance with state marijuana regulations. Until recently, the DOJ has tolerated the state's booming marijuana industry. Following a recent presidential election, however, the agency announced that it had had a change of heart and would begin to crack down on the state-licensed marijuana industry. To that end, the local United States Attorney has launched a criminal investigation into marijuana licensees. In the course of the investigation, the Attorney General of the United States has subpoenaed Delilah, demanding "All information, records, reports, etc. in the possession of the state MED concerning the manufacture and/or distribution of marijuana by state licensees." Does Delilah have to hand over such information to the federal government?

In the following case, the court addresses the question posed by **Problem 14.8**.

### *United States v. Michigan Department of Community Health*
2011 WL 2412602 (W.D. Mich. 2011)

Brenneman, M.J.:

The United States seeks to enforce a federal administrative subpoena issued on June 4, 2010 to the Michigan Department of Community Health (MDCH) requesting certain documents in possession of that department regarding seven specified individuals. Originally the subpoena sought the following information:

> Pursuant to an investigation of violations of 21 U.S.C. 801 et seq., you are to provide copies of any and all documents, records, applications, payment method of any application

for Medical Marijuana Patient Cards and Medical Marijuana Caregiver cards and copies of front and back of any cards located for the following: [names redacted in the public court record].

... At the hearing on this motion and in its supplemental brief the United States clarified that the subpoena has been narrowed and only seeks copies of patient and caregiver registration cards, or applications given the effect of such cards, for seven named individuals in connection with its investigation. A registration card contains a person's name, a random identification number, an address, date of birth, and expiration date. An application also identifies the certifying doctor. ... Respondent has resisted complying with the subpoena due to a conflict arising from the passage of the Michigan Medical Marijuana Act ("MMMA"), MCL § 333.26421 *et seq.*

The federal statute authorizing the issuance of this administrative subpoena, 21 U.S.C. § 876, provides in pertinent part as follows:

> (a) Authorization of use by Attorney General
>
> In any investigation relating to his functions under this subchapter with respect to controlled substances, listed chemicals, tableting machines, or encapsulating machines, the Attorney General may subpena witnesses, compel the attendance and testimony of witnesses, and require the production of any records (including books, papers, documents, and other tangible things which constitute or contain evidence) which the Attorney General finds relevant or material to the investigation. The attendance of witnesses and the production of records may be required from any place in any State or in any territory or other place subject to the jurisdiction of the United States at any designated place of hearing; except that a witness shall not be required to appear at any hearing more than 500 miles distant from the place where he was served with a subpena. Witnesses summoned under this section shall be paid the same fees and mileage that are paid witnesses in the courts of the United States.
>
> * * *
>
> (c) Enforcement
>
> In the case of contumacy by or refusal to obey a subpena issued to any person, the Attorney General may invoke the aid of any court of the United States within the jurisdiction of which the investigation is carried on or of which the subpenaed person is an inhabitant, or in which he carries on business or may be found, to compel compliance with the subpena. The court may issue an order requiring the subpenaed person to appear before the Attorney General to produce records, if so ordered, or to give testimony touching the matter under investigation. Any failure to obey the order of the court may be punished by the court as a contempt thereof. All process in any such case may be served in any judicial district in which such person may be found.

21 U.S.C. § 876(a), (c).

Section 876 was enacted over 40 years ago, in 1970, as part of the Federal Controlled Substances Act, 21 U.S.C. § 801 *et seq.* ...

...

When it enacted the MMMA, the Michigan Legislature adopted a course different from that followed by the federal government and the majority of other states. ...

...

In *United States v. Hicks*, 722 F. Supp. 2d 829 (E.D. Mich. 2010), the court summarized Michigan's statutory regulation of medical marijuana:

> As codified, the MMMA allows a "qualifying patient" who has been issued a "registry identification card" to possess up to 2.5 ounces of marijuana for medical purposes.

§ 333.26424(a). A qualifying patient is "a person who has been diagnosed by a physician as having a debilitating medical condition." § 333.26423(h). *See also* § 333.26423(a) (enumerating qualifying "debilitating medical conditions"). A qualifying patient may designate one primary caregiver "to assist with [the] patient's medical use of marihuana," who must also obtain a registry identification card to legally possess marijuana. §§ 333.26423(g), 333.26424(b). A qualifying patient, or his or her registered primary caregiver, may also cultivate up to 12 marijuana plants for that patient's care. § 333.26424(a). A primary caregiver may be registered for up to five qualifying patients, and he or she may possess up to 2.5 ounces of marijuana and 12 cultivated marijuana plants for each qualifying patient. 333.26424(b), 333.26426(d).

*Hicks*, 722 F. Supp. 2d at 832.

In creating the registry related to the issuance of the identification cards, the MMMA provided that certain information would be kept confidential:

> (1) Applications and supporting information submitted by qualifying patients, including information regarding their primary caregivers and physicians, are confidential.
>
> (2) The department shall maintain a confidential list of the persons to whom the department has issued registry identification cards. Individual names and other identifying information on the list is confidential and is exempt from disclosure under the freedom of information act, 1976 PA 442, MCL 15.231 to 15.246.
>
> (3) The department shall verify to law enforcement personnel whether a registry identification card is valid, without disclosing more information than is reasonably necessary to verify the authenticity of the registry identification card.
>
> (4) A person, including an employee or official of the department or another state agency or local unit of government, who discloses confidential information in violation of this act is guilty of a misdemeanor, punishable by imprisonment for not more than 6 months, or a fine of not more than $1,000.00, or both. Notwithstanding this provision, department employees may notify law enforcement about falsified or fraudulent information submitted to the department.

M.C.L. § 333.26426(h).

It is this last provision that has caused respondent to hesitate. The MDCH's reluctance to produce the requested documents because of this provision eventually prompted the United States to file the present petition seeking a federal court order to enforce the federal subpoena. In its response to the petition, the MDCH stated that it "will comply with a valid order from this Court" requiring it to comply with the subpoena, but wants this court's order "to make clear" that its employees and agents "will be immunized from liability for providing information that is confidential" under a state statute. . . .

. . .

When Michigan adopted the MMMA with its confidentiality provisions, it, of course, only changed *Michigan* law. The very text of the MMMA recognizes that "federal law currently prohibits any use of marijuana" (MCL § 333.26422(c)). Thus, anyone who is not deluding himself or trying to push an agenda knows that the confidentiality provisions are only binding on the State of Michigan and its agents, not the federal government and its agencies. . . .

. . .

"[I]t must be emphasized that a district court's role in the enforcement of an administrative subpoena is a limited one." *United States v. Markwood*, 48 F.3d 969, 976 (6th Cir. 1995). "Following Supreme Court precedent on the enforcement of administrative subpoenas, this circuit has held that a subpoena is properly enforced if 1) it satisfies the terms of its authorizing statute, 2) the documents requested were relevant to the [agency's] investigation, 3) the information sought is not already in the [agency's] possession, and 4) enforcing the subpoena will not constitute an abuse of the court's process." *Doe v. United States*, 253 F.3d 256, 265 (6th Cir. 2001). The agency has the burden to satisfy the first three prongs of the test, while the respondent has the burden of establishing an abuse of court process under the fourth prong. . . .

. . .

The subpoena was issued pursuant to § 876 as part of an ongoing investigation of possible violations of the Controlled Substances Act by a very limited number of specified individuals in the Lansing, Michigan area. . . . This is an appropriate purpose authorized by § 876. Courts have held that "[a] subpoena issued under 21 U.S.C. § 876 is not restricted for use solely in enforcing the regulatory provisions of the Controlled Substances Act[]" [but may also be used in criminal investigations.] . . .

. . .

. . . As a state law authorizing the use of medical marijuana, the MMMA cannot negate, nullify or supersede the federal Controlled Substances Act, which criminalized the possession and distribution of marijuana throughout the entire country long before Michigan passed its law. "It is a seminal principle of our law 'that the constitution and the laws made in pursuance thereof are supreme; that they control the constitution and laws of the respective States, and cannot be controlled by them.'" *Hancock v. Train*, 426 U.S. 167, 178 (1976), quoting *McCulloch v. Maryland*, 17 U.S. 316, 426 (1819). . . .

. . .

The Michigan Legislature . . . cannot create a statutory obstacle to the federal government's enforcement of federal law regulating this controlled substance. The MMMA's confidentiality provision 'stands as an obstacle to the accomplishment and execution of the full purposes and objectives of Congress,' by preventing the federal government from using a proper federal subpoena to obtain records which involve a controlled substance, the use of which is prohibited by federal law, i.e., marijuana and marijuana plants. The MMMA's confidentiality provision must be and is nullified to the extent it conflicts with the federal law by preventing the federal government's exercise of its subpoena power under § 876. . . .

. . .

The question of an administrative subpoena's relevance should be construed broadly. . . . The court defers to the agency's appraisal of relevancy, which must be accepted so long as it is not obviously wrong. . . .

Here, the subpoena was issued as part of an investigation for violations of the Controlled Substances Act. The DEA is a federal law enforcement agency. It is charged with, among other things, investigating the possession, manufacture and disposition of marijuana, a controlled substance, which are violations of federal law. The documents sought here include cards identifying persons who are presumably involved in possessing and distributing marijuana contrary to federal law. The subpoena clearly seeks documents relevant to the investigation, the conduct of which is a lawful function of the DEA.

. . .

. . . Respondent has neither claimed nor demonstrated any abuse of the court's process or bad faith in the issuing of this subpoena, nor is any apparent. It is the responsibility of the DEA to enforce 21 U.S.C. § 801 *et seq.*, and even if the Attorney General of the United States has adopted a policy of not prosecuting persons who are *bona fide* medical marijuana users and providers as far as the MMMA is concerned, it certainly falls within the scope of the DEA's responsibility, and authority, to determine, among other things, whether those claiming the benefits of the medical marijuana statute are doing so legitimately and should enjoy the Attorney General's largess. Only the truly naive or the disingenuous would try to argue that the MMMA will not be abused by others seeking a cover for illicitly using or distributing marijuana. Those who are legitimate users or providers of marijuana under the MMMA and their supporters should be concerned that if the federal government cannot satisfy itself that the medical marijuana shield, which it is voluntarily choosing to recognize, is not also sheltering non-medical marijuana traffickers, this Administration or the next may simply pull the plug and prosecute anyone using or distributing marijuana, which it unquestionably may do under existing federal law. . . .

. . .

Petitioner has met its burden of satisfying the first three prongs of the *Doe* test for enforcing an administrative subpoena, while the respondent has not established the fourth prong. Accordingly, the "Petition to enforce Drug Enforcement Administration Subpoena" . . . will be granted. . . . The subpoena shall be complied with forthwith. . . .

## Notes and Questions

1. Are you troubled by the federal subpoena of the state's medical marijuana registry? Is there any other legal defense the MDCH could have raised to challenge the subpoena? The textbook author has suggested a possibility, based on the Supreme Court's anti-commandeering doctrine discussed in Chapter 6:

> It should come as no surprise that the states do not always want to share their data with the federal government. For one thing, doing so increases the cost to the states of gathering the information in the first instance. Citizens already have an incentive to evade state regulations and avoid detection by state regulators. This makes the task of gathering information about regulated activity enormously expensive. Commandeering states' secrets adds to that expense by giving citizens an additional incentive to conceal their activity from state regulators: doing so may dramatically reduce the chances that federal regulators will catch them. All governments rely extensively on their citizens for information. To replace or restore this vital source of information, the states would need to hire more agents, employ more technology, or make deeper concessions to encourage private reporting.
>
> The commandeering of states' secrets also has political costs. In many cases, it forces state officials to help advance federal policies they or their constituents deem objectionable. In addition, when the federal government orders a state official to provide information about violations of an unpopular federal law, there is also a real danger that citizens will denounce the state official for being complicit in federal law enforcement. They will label him a "snitch" and not merely a "stooge." For example, when a citizen is discovered and prosecuted by the federal government using information she submitted to her state in the course of applying for her medical marijuana distribution license, she may blame the state official who disclosed the information (especially if that official had earlier vouchsafed her confidentiality).
>
> Despite these costs and protests by the states, . . . lower courts have almost invariably upheld [federal demands for information gathered by states], brushing aside any comparison to constitutionally prohibited commandeering on two grounds.

First, some lower courts have simply presumed that providing information about violations of federal law does not amount to assisting in the administration or enforcement of federal law. These courts have made a categorical distinction between demands for information about federally regulated activity and demands for other types of administrative services. The latter are subject to the anti-commandeering rule, but the former, somehow, are not.

Second, some courts have suggested that demands for information simply do not raise the same constitutional concerns that animated the Court's rulings in *New York v. United States* and *Printz v. United States*. In those cases, the Court emphasized the economic and political costs commandeering imposes on the states—namely, the burden they bear in administering federal programs and the political responsibility they shoulder if those programs prove unpopular with constituents. In essence, the lower courts have concluded that forcing states to share information either imposes no burden (since the states already have the information on hand), or imposes a trivial burden that is minimal as compared to the federal government's interest in the information. As a result of these rulings, federal authorities may now seize and use to enforce federal law almost any information gathered by state governments.

. . . [T]he prevailing assessment of the constitutionality and resulting harms of secrets commandeering [is misguided]. . . . [T]he commandeering of states' secrets should be deemed constitutionally prohibited. . . . [T]he distinction between demands for information and demands for other types of enforcement services has no obvious basis. As a descriptive matter, this distinction fails to account for the bulk of what law enforcement agents actually do—gather and report information about regulated activity. As a matter of precedent, it contradicts the very holding of the *Printz* decision, which invalidated provisions of the Brady Act requiring state officials to do no more than search state databases. As a matter of history, it ignores the fact that most methods now employed to commandeer states' secrets were unknown to the Framers and emerged only in the last several decades. Most fundamentally, the distinction allows the federal government to transform state law enforcement officials into the unwitting tools of federal law enforcement—the very harm the anti-commandeering rule is designed to prevent.

Mikos, *Can the States Keep Secrets From the Federal Government?*, 161 U. Penn. L. Rev. 103, 106-08 (2012). What do you think? Does a federal demand for information a state has gathered about private citizens compel the state to help enforce federal law?

2. Federal subpoenas for similar information have also been challenged—sometimes successfully—on other, rights-based grounds. *See Oregon Prescription Drug Monitoring Program v. U.S. Drug Enf't Admin.*, 998 F. Supp. 2d 957, 967 (D. Or. 2014) (quashing DEA subpoena of Oregon prescription drug records on Fourth Amendment grounds); *In re Grand Jury Subpoena for THCF Medical Clinic Records*, 504 F. Supp. 2d 1085, 1090 (E.D. Wash. 2007) (quashing federal subpoena of state medical marijuana records on reasonableness grounds). *See also* Mikos, *Can the States Keep Secrets, supra*, at 144-53 (analyzing additional defenses). Now consider the following Problem:

**Problem 14.9:** Andy has a state license to produce marijuana. In return for the license, which exempts Andy from the state's criminal prohibition on the manufacture of marijuana, Andy submits monthly reports to the state's Marijuana Enforcement Division (MED), detailing the number of marijuana plants he has under cultivation, the number he harvested in the past month, and the quantity of raw and processed marijuana he sold to state-licensed distributors in the past month. Benjamin has a state license to distribute marijuana. In return for the license, which exempts him from the state's criminal prohibition on the distribution of marijuana, Benjamin submits monthly reports to the MED, detailing his current inventory, the quantity of marijuana he purchased from licensed producers in the past month, and the quantity of marijuana he sold at retail in the past month. Under state law, the information provided by Andy and Benjamin to the MED is considered "strictly confidential." However, the DEA has subpoenaed the information from the MED. Following in the footsteps of *MDCH*, a court has refused to quash the DEA subpoena. Does the Constitution limit how the DEA uses the information that Andy and/or Benjamin have provided? For example, could the DEA use the information Andy provided in a criminal prosecution against Andy? How about a criminal prosecution against *Benjamin*? See Mikos, *Can the States Keep Secrets, supra*, at 150-53 (discussing limits imposed on the privilege against self-incrimination and other relevant doctrines).

## D. COULD STATE AGENCIES LOSE FEDERAL FUNDING BECAUSE OF STATE REFORMS?

Chapter 13 discussed whether states have the power to require private parties—like landlords and employers—to accommodate marijuana use. A related question addressed here is whether state officials can accommodate such use themselves, for example, by allowing students to use marijuana on public school property.

For reasons discussed in Chapters 6 and 10, Congress may not simply force the states to punish marijuana users and suppliers. *See* Chapters 6 and 10. Notwithstanding the anticommandeering rule, however, Congress may try to *persuade* the states to do so. The most common way Congress does so is by offering the states federal grants in return for the states adopting federally scripted policies—a practice called conditional spending.

The Supreme Court has approved of federal conditional spending, subject to a few limitations. Most notably, conditions on federal grants must be stated unambiguously, and the financial inducement offered to the states must not be so powerful as to practically compel their acceptance of the conditions. *See Nat'l Fed'n of Indep. Bus. v. Sebelius*, 132 S. Ct. 2566, 2604-05 (2012).

Has Congress threatened to withhold federal funds from states that accommodate marijuana users or suppliers? In other words, do state marijuana reforms jeopardize the receipt of any federal grant funds? In the past, members of Congress proposed legislation that would explicitly withhold federal law enforcement grants from states that legalized medical marijuana, but such measures have never been passed. *See* Mikos, *On the Limits, supra*, at 1462 (discussing past proposals). Nonetheless, Congress has passed more generic drug-free statutes that could restrain the states' ability to accommodate marijuana use in schools and public housing. The following sections discuss these statutes.

# Chapter 14. The Law, Policy, and Authority Issues Confronting Government Officials

## 1. Schools

### a. Higher Education

The federal government provides substantial financial support for institutions of higher education. In the 2013 academic year alone, for example, Congress spent more than $75 billion on student financial aid and research at the nation's colleges and universities. *See* The Pew Charitable Trusts, *Federal and State Funding of Higher Education*, June 11, 2015, http://www.pewtrusts.org/en/research-and-analysis/issue-briefs/2015/06/federal-and-state-funding-of-higher-education. The same year, these federal funds accounted for 16 percent of the budgets of public colleges and universities (on average). *Id.*

The funds provided by Congress come with strings attached. Most relevantly, for present purposes, ever since it passed the Drug Free Schools and Communities Act of 1989, Congress has required federally supported colleges and universities to prohibit the use of illicit drugs on school property:

> (a) . . . Notwithstanding any other provision of law, no institution of higher education shall be eligible to receive funds or any other form of financial assistance under any Federal program, including participation in any federally funded or guaranteed student loan program, unless the institution certifies to the Secretary that the institution has adopted and has implemented a program to prevent the use of illicit drugs and the abuse of alcohol by students and employees that, at a minimum, includes—
>
> (1) the annual distribution to each student and employee of—
>
> (A) standards of conduct that clearly prohibit, at a minimum, the unlawful possession, use, or distribution of illicit drugs and alcohol by students and employees on the institution's property or as part of any of the institution's activities;
>
> (B) a description of the applicable legal sanctions under local, State, or Federal law for the unlawful possession or distribution of illicit drugs and alcohol;
>
> (C) a description of the health-risks associated with the use of illicit drugs and the abuse of alcohol;
>
> (D) a description of any drug or alcohol counseling, treatment, or rehabilitation or re-entry programs that are available to employees or students; and
>
> (E) a clear statement that the institution will impose sanctions on students and employees (consistent with local, State, and Federal law), and a description of those sanctions, up to and including expulsion or termination of employment and referral for prosecution, for violations of the standards of conduct required by subparagraph (A); and
>
> (2) a biennial review by the institution of the institution's program to—
>
> (A) determine the program's effectiveness and implement changes to the program if the changes are needed;
>
> (B) determine the number of drug and alcohol-related violations and fatalities that—
>
>> (i) occur on the institution's campus (as defined in section 1092(f)(6) of this title), or as part of any of the institution's activities; and
>>
>> (ii) are reported to campus officials;
>
> (C) determine the number and type of sanctions described in paragraph (1)(E) that are imposed by the institution as a result of drug and alcohol-related violations and fatalities on the institution's campus or as part of any of the institution's activities; and

(D) ensure that the sanctions required by paragraph (1)(E) are consistently enforced.

20 U.S.C. § 1011i (2016).

Largely because of section 1011i, colleges and universities have uniformly refused to accommodate the use of marijuana on school property, even when such use is permitted by state law. The official policy of Tufts University in Medford, Massachusetts, is representative:

> Although students, staff, and faculty who legally obtain a medical marijuana "registration card" from the Massachusetts Department of Public Health are allowed to possess and consume certain quantities of marijuana, doing so is not permitted on Tufts University property or at university-sponsored events (either on or off campus).
>
> Marijuana is classified as a Schedule I drug according to the Controlled Substances Act. Thus, the use, possession, cultivation, or sale of marijuana violates federal policy. Federal grants are subject to university compliance with the Drug Free Communities and Schools Act, and the Drug Free Workplace Act. The university is also subject to the Controlled Substances Act. This prohibits the university from allowing any form of marijuana use on campus.
>
> The university will accommodate legally recognized Massachusetts medical marijuana users. Students who obtain a registration card from the Massachusetts Department of Public Health may submit a letter to the Dean of Student Affairs requesting to be released from their university housing and dining contract. In such situations students will be released from their contracts with no financial penalty. Any payments made to the university for dining services or housing facilities will be returned to the student in proportion to the remainder of their time on a university meal plan or in university residence halls.
>
> . . .
>
> Why is Tufts prohibited from allowing medical marijuana use on campus despite state law that makes it legal?
>
> First, the law allows exemptions for schools and employers. On these grounds alone, Tufts is not required to allow medical use. Secondly, the Drug Free Schools and Communities Act amendments of 1989 (amendments to the Higher Education Act) tie large portions of university funding to a drug-free environment. For example, according to 20 USC § 1011i institutions of higher education will lose federal funding for financial aid if they allow the use of illicit drugs on campus. Marijuana is considered an illicit drug (Schedule I according to the Controlled Substances Act).

Tufts University Medical Marijuana Policy, https://perma.cc/NS4H-ZTMV. Other schools in reform states have adopted similar policies. *See, e.g.*, Colorado College, Colorado College Policy on Marijuana, Dec. 13, 2012, https://perma.cc/73UR-59CC (similar).

## Notes and Questions

1. Tufts suggests a possible compromise. Namely, the school offers to release any registered medical marijuana patient from policies that would otherwise require them to reside and dine on campus. Does the compromise adequately address the needs of students who are medical marijuana users? Does it comport with section 1011i? In other words, could the federal government deny a school like Tufts federal grant funds for providing marijuana users special exemptions from school policies?

2. Chapter 8 noted that two public universities, Louisiana State University (LSU) and Southern University, plan to produce and distribute all of the marijuana destined for qualifying patients under Louisiana's new medical marijuana law. If these schools follow through and manufacture and distribute marijuana, could they lose all of their federal funding, per section 1011i? Would the revocation of *all* federal higher education funding amount to unconstitutional coercion, per *Nat'l Fed'n of Indep. Bus. v. Sebelius, supra*?

### b. Primary Schools (K-12)

Congress also provides substantial financial support to primary schools. No federal statute explicitly requires *primary* schools to ban their students from using illicit drugs. The terms of the Drug Free Schools and Communities Act of 1989 excerpted above apply only to "institution[s] of higher education." When Congress passed the 1989 Act, it likely never occurred to federal lawmakers that a K-12 school might permit students to use marijuana on school property. Nonetheless, state policymakers remain worried that *other* federal statutes might require them to bar marijuana use on primary school property—or else lose their federal funding.

The Colorado Legislative Council sounded alarms when it analyzed a proposal (later adopted) that would require primary schools to accommodate medical marijuana use on school grounds.

## *Colorado Legislative Council,* Student Medical Marijuana Use at School
Fiscal Note HB16-1373, Apr. 7, 2016

This bill requires that every school district adopt a policy that authorizes a student's parent or medical professional to assist students holding a valid recommendation for medical marijuana to possess the medicine on school property.

. . .

Both the [Colorado Department of Education] and local education providers are recipients of U.S. Department of Agriculture (USDA) and U.S. Department of Education (ED) grants and sub-grants. ED funding is typically Title I money in support of schools in high poverty areas. For the current school year, ED grant funding in Colorado is about $432.5 million. USDA funding is typically in support of school lunch programs, which provide free or reduced price meals to low income students, and other school nutrition programs. Current USDA funding in Colorado is about $194.3 million. Federal grants are subject to federal regulations implementing drug-free workplace requirements. Noncompliance with this provision can result in the loss of federal funding. Both the courts and other federal agencies have declined to provide an exception for the use of medical marijuana in drug-free zones in their interpretation of federal law.

Consistent with these drug-free workplace requirements, grantees and sub-grantees must make a "good faith effort" to maintain a drug-free workplace as a condition of the grant award. A drug-free workplace includes any location where the performance of work is done in connection with a specific award, which includes school buildings that administer ED and USDA grant programs. Federal agencies have discretion in determining whether a grantee or sub-grantee is in violation of the drug-free workplace requirements, and has a range of options to compel compliance.

After receiving notice, violations can ultimately result in the suspension of grant payments and the termination of awards; however, this fiscal note assumes that withholding federal funds is the last and most extreme action the federal government can take, and that any conflict between state laws and federal rules can be addressed without forfeit of federal grants and other distributions.

. . .

## Notes and Questions

1. The concern about the loss of federal funds may help explain why so few states have so far explicitly required K-12 schools to accommodate medical marijuana use. As discussed in Chapter 4, as of 2016, only three states—Colorado, Maine, and New Jersey—appear to require schools to accommodate marijuana use by students on school grounds.

But is the risk of losing federal funding exaggerated or even unfounded? In other words, do you think that the federal Department of Education (DOE) would—or even could—deny federal funding to a K-12 school, simply because it allowed students to use marijuana for medical purposes on school grounds? Consider the Federal Drug Free Workplace Act, one of the statutes cited by the Colorado Legislative Council, *supra*. The Act, which was briefly discussed in Chapter 13, provides in relevant part:

> A person other than an individual shall not receive a grant from a Federal agency unless the person agrees to provide a drug-free workplace. . . .

41 U.S.C.A. § 8103(a) (West 2016). The statute defines "drug free workplace" as

> a site of an entity—
>
> (A) for the performance of work done in connection with a specific . . . grant . . . and
> (B) at which *employees* of the entity are prohibited from engaging in the unlawful manufacture, distribution, dispensation, possession, or use of a controlled substance. . . .

41 U.S.C. § 8101 (emphasis added). Could the statute be interpreted to bar schools from allowing their *students* to use marijuana on school property? Even so, does the statute state that condition *unambiguously*? Pennhurst State School and Hospital v. Halderman, 451 U.S. 1, 17 (1981) ("[I]f Congress intends to impose a condition on the grant of federal moneys, it must do so unambiguously.").

2. Consider the following Problem:

> **Problem 14.10**: Suppose that federal spending legislation clearly and unambiguously requires K-12 schools to ban all marijuana possession and use on campus in order to receive federal grant funding. Could a state require K-12 schools to accommodate marijuana possession and use and thus to forego federal financial support? Or would such a state requirement be preempted?

3. To minimize the financial risks spawned by marijuana reforms, some states explicitly exempt schools and other federal grant recipients and contractors from requirements

of state marijuana laws that would cause them to lose federal grant funds or contracts. *E.g.*, Colo. Rev. Stat. Ann. § 22-1-119.3 (West 2016) (exempting schools from accommodating marijuana use on school grounds if the school district would lose federal funding as a result); 410 Ill. Comp. Stat. Ann. 130/40 (a)(1) (West 2016) ("No school, employer, or landlord may refuse to enroll or lease to, or otherwise penalize, a person solely for his or her status as a registered qualifying patient or a registered designated caregiver, unless failing to do so would put the school, employer, or landlord in violation of federal law or unless failing to do so would cause it to lose a monetary or licensing-related benefit under federal law or rules. . . ."). Do such exemptions provide adequate protections for the interests of lawful marijuana users? Do they provide adequate guidance to federal grant recipients and contractors concerning their rights and responsibilities under state law?

## 2. Public Housing

Chapter 13 discussed the rights and duties of private landlords. Per that discussion, some states now require private landlords to accommodate tenants' state-approved marijuana use on rental property. This section discusses whether states could require Public Housing Authorities (PHAs)[4] to do the same.

Although they are administered by state and local governments, PHAs—like public schools—receive substantial funding from the federal government. In return for this funding, PHAs must comply with federal regulations governing the rights and responsibilities of the PHAs and their tenants. Most relevant to our discussion, those federal regulations require every PHA to utilize leases that

> provide that any criminal activity that threatens the health, safety, or right to peaceful enjoyment of the premises by other tenants or *any drug-related criminal activity on or off such premises*, engaged in by a public housing tenant, any member of the tenant's household, or any guest or other person under the tenant's control, shall be cause for termination of tenancy . . .

42 U.S.C. § 1437d(l)(6) (2016) (emphasis added).

Notwithstanding the lease term, could states require PHAs to accommodate marijuana use in public housing? The General Counsel of the Department of Housing and Urban Development (HUD) addresses the question in the following memorandum.

### *Helen R. Kanovsky*, Medical Use of Marijuana and Reasonable Accommodation in Federal Public and Assisted Housing
General Counsel, U.S. Dep't of Housing and Urban Development, Jan. 20, 2011

The Office of Fair Housing and Equal Opportunity (FHEO) requested our opinion as to whether Public Housing Agencies (PHAs) and owners of other federally assisted housing may grant current or prospective residents a reasonable accommodation under federal or state nondiscrimination laws for the use of medical marijuana. . . .

---

4. For present purposes, the book defines PHAs to include anyone who provides government subsidized housing.

Part IV. Third Parties

. . .

Section 576(b) of [the Quality Housing and Work and Responsibility Act of 1998 (QHWRA)] addresses admission standards related to current illegal drug use for all public housing and other federally assisted housing. Pursuant to that section, PHAs or owners

> shall establish standards that prohibit admission to the program or admission to federally assisted housing for any household with a member—(A) who the public housing agency or owner determines is illegally using a controlled substance; or (B) with respect to whom the public housing agency or owner determines that it has reasonable cause to believe that such household member's illegal use (or pattern of illegal use) of a controlled substance . . . may interfere with the health, safety, or right to peaceful enjoyment of the premises by other residents.

42 U.S.C. § 13661(b)(1).

QHWRA therefore requires PHAs and owners to deny admission to those households with a member who the PHA or owner determines is, at the time of consideration for admission, illegally using a "controlled substance" as that term is defined by the CSA. . . .

In contrast, under QHWRA's termination standards, PHAs and owners have the discretion to evict, or refrain from evicting, a current tenant who the PHA or owner determines is illegally using a controlled substance. PHAs or owners must establish standards or lease provisions that

> allow the agency or owner (as applicable) to terminate the tenancy or assistance for any household with a member—(1) who the public housing agency or owner determines is illegally using a controlled substance; or (2) whose illegal use (or pattern of illegal use) of a controlled substance . . . is determined by the public housing agency or owner to interfere with the health, safety, or right to peaceful enjoyment of the premises by other residents.

42 U.S.C. § 13662(a).

Thus, while PHAs and owners may elect to terminate occupancy based on illegal drug use, they are not required to evict current tenants for such use. . . . Further, PHAs and owners may not establish lease provisions or policies that affirmatively permit occupancy by medical marijuana users because doing so would divest PHAs and owners of the very discretion which Congress intended for them to exercise. . . .

. . .

### III. FEDERAL NONDISCRIMINATION LAWS DO NOT REQUIRE PHAS AND OWNERS TO ALLOW MARIJUANA USE AS A REASONABLE ACCOMMODATION FOR DISABILITIES.

A. Under Section 504 of the [Americans with Disabilities Act (ADA)], current illegal drug users, including medical marijuana users, are excluded from the definition of "individual with a disability" when the provider acts on the basis of the illegal drug use.

An individual must be disabled to be entitled to a reasonable accommodation. Although medical marijuana users may meet this standard because of the underlying medical conditions for which they use or seek to use marijuana, Section 504 and the ADA categorically exempt current illegal drug users from their definitions of "disability" when the covered entity acts on the basis of such use[. 29 U.S.C. § 705(20)(C)(i).]

. . .

A housing provider is acting on the basis of current drug use when, for example, the provider evicts a tenant for violating the provider's drug-free policies. In that context, the tenant, even if suffering from a serious impairment such as cancer or multiple sclerosis, would not be "disabled" under the ADA or Section 504 for purposes of filing a claim under those laws challenging the eviction as disability discrimination. . . . A tenant who has a disabling impairment and is a current illegal drug user could, however, bring a claim under the ADA or Section 504 for disability discrimination where the housing provider evicted the tenant because the tenant asked to have grab bars installed in the shower. In that case, the provider would not have acted on the basis of the illegal drug use, but because the tenant requested grab bars.

. . .

Thus, persons seeking an accommodation to use medical marijuana are not "individuals with a disability" under Section 504 and the ADA and therefore do not qualify for reasonable accommodations that would allow for such use. Furthermore, because requests to use medical marijuana prospectively are tantamount to requests to become a "current illegal drug user," PHAs are prohibited from granting such requests. . . .

**B. Though otherwise disabled medical marijuana users are not excluded from the Fair Housing Act's definition of "handicap," accommodations allowing for the use of medical marijuana in public housing or other federally assisted housing are not reasonable.**

. . . Unlike the language in Section 504 and the ADA, [the Fair Housing Act's (FHA) definition of "handicap"] does not categorically exclude individuals from protection. . . . Rather, it prevents a current illegal drug user or addict from asserting that the drug use or addiction is itself the basis for claiming that he or she is disabled under the Act. [42 U.S.C. § 3602(h).] . . .

Under the Fair Housing Act and other civil rights statutes protecting persons with disabilities, an accommodation may be denied as not reasonable if either: 1) granting the accommodation would require a *fundamental alteration in the nature* of the housing provider's operations; or 2) the requested accommodation imposes an *undue financial and administrative burden* on the housing provider. . . .

Accommodations that allow the use of medical marijuana would sanction violations of federal criminal law and thus constitute a fundamental alteration in the nature of the housing operation. Indeed, allowing such an accommodation would thwart a central programmatic goal of providing a safe living environment free from illegal drug use. Since the inception of the public housing program in 1937, Congress and HUD have consistently maintained that one of the primary concerns of public housing and other assisted housing programs is to provide "decent, safe, and sanitary dwellings for families of low income." Unite States Housing Act of 1937, Pub. L. No. 75-412, 50 Stat. 888 (1937). . . . Congress has made it clear that providing drug-free housing is integral to the government's responsibility in this regard: "[T]he Federal Government has a duty to provide public and other federally assisted low-income housing that is decent, safe, and *free from illegal drugs*." 42 U.S.C. § 11901(1) (emphasis added). Toward this end, Congress specifically vested PHAs and owners with the authority to take action against illegal drug use, including the use of medical marijuana. Illegal drug use renders the user ineligible for admission to public or other assisted housing, conflicts with drug-free standards that PHAs and others are required to establish for current tenants, and would violate a user-tenant's lease obligation to refrain from engaging in any drug-related criminal activity on or off the premises.

Although PHAs and owners are not charged with enforcing federal criminal laws, requiring them to condone violations of those laws would undermine a PHA or owner's operations. . . . Because they would require that PHAs and owners condone illegal drug use and would undermine the long-standing programmatic goal of providing a safe living environment free from illegal drug use, accommodations allowing marijuana-related activity constitute a fundamental alteration in the nature of the PHA or owner's operations and are therefore not reasonable.

. . .

### IV. IN THE UNLIKELY EVENT THAT STATE ANTIDISCRIMINATION LAWS ARE CONSTRUED SO AS TO REQUIRE PHAS AND OWNERS TO PERMIT MEDICAL MARIJUANA USE AS A REASONABLE ACCOMMODATION, THOSE LAWS WOULD BE SUBJECT TO PREEMPTED BY FEDERAL LAW.

Because PHAs and owners are also bound by the laws of the state in which they operate, medical marijuana users might attempt to avail themselves of the reasonable accommodation provisions found in state nondiscrimination laws. . . .

If a state nondiscrimination law were construed to require accommodations allowing for the use of medical marijuana, such an interpretation would be subject to preemption by the federal laws governing drug use in public housing and other federally assisted housing, and by the CSA. . . . A state law that would require accommodation of medical marijuana use "positively conflicts" with the CSA because it would mandate the very conduct the CSA proscribes. See 21 U.S.C. §903; 21 U.S.C. §841(a)(1); 844(a) (criminalizing marijuana-related conduct). . . .

Although federal laws governing public housing and federally assisted housing do not expressly state an intention to preempt state law, a state law interpreted to require accommodation of medical marijuana use would nonetheless be subject to preemption under the doctrine of implied conflict preemption. Implied conflict preemption arises where "compliance with both federal and state regulations is a physical impossibility," or where state law "stands as an obstacle to the accomplishment and execution of the full purposes and objectives of Congress." *Gade v. Nat'l Solid Wastes Mgmt.*, 505 U.S. 88, 98 (1992) (internal citations and quotations omitted). State nondiscrimination laws requiring accommodation of medical marijuana use would be subject to preemption by federal laws governing drug use in public housing and other federally assisted housing because: 1) by requiring an accommodation when federal admissions standards mandate the exclusion of the applicant, they would render compliance with federal law impossible; and 2) by requiring an accommodation that divests PHAs and owners of the discretion to evict provided by QHWRA and HUD regulations, they would stand as an obstacle to the accomplishment and execution of federal law objectives. *See supra*. . . .

### V. CONCLUSION

In sum, PHAs and owners may not grant reasonable accommodations that would allow tenants to grow, use, otherwise possess, or distribute medical marijuana, even if in doing so tenants are complying with state laws authorizing medical marijuana-related conduct.

Further, PHAs and owners must deny *admission* to those applicant households with individuals who are, at the time of consideration for admission, using medical marijuana. . . .

We note, however, that PHAs and owners have statutorily-authorized discretion with respect to evicting or refraining from evicting *current residents* on account of their use of medical marijuana. . . . If a PHA or owner desires to allow a resident who is currently using medical marijuana to remain as an occupant, the PHA owner may do so as an exercise of that discretion, but not as a reasonable accommodation. HUD regulations provide factors that PHAs and owners may consider when determining how to exercise their discretion to terminate tenancies because of current illegal drug use. *See* 24 C.F.R. §§ 996.4(l)(5)(vii)(B) (factors for PHAs); 5.852 (factors for PHAs and owners operating other assisted housing programs).

## Notes and Questions

1. The HUD Memorandum suggests that while a PHA is *required* to bar admission of new tenants whom it knows are using marijuana, it is *not necessarily required* to evict current tenants whom it knows are using marijuana. HUD Memorandum, *supra*, at 3. *See also* Benjamin T. Metcalf, Dep'ty Ass't Sec. for Multifamily Housing Programs, HT, Use of Marijuana in Multifamily Assisted Properties, Dec. 29, 2014 (noting distinction); Sandra B. Henriquez, Ass't Sec. for Public and Indian Housing, Medical Marijuana Use in Public Housing and Housing Choice Voucher Programs, Feb. 10, 2011 (same). What is the rationale for distinguishing between prospective and current tenants?

2. In a similar vein, the HUD Memorandum advises that while PHAs may not grant accommodations for the medical use of marijuana in public housing, they are not necessarily required to evict tenants who use marijuana in public housing. HUD Memorandum, *supra*, at 10 ("If a PHA or owner desires to allow a resident who is currently using medical marijuana to remain as an occupant, the PHA or owner may do so as an exercise of [statutorily granted] discretion, but not as a reasonable accommodation."). Is there any meaningful difference between (A) granting a tenant a reasonable accommodation to use marijuana, and (B) declining to evict the same tenant for using marijuana? Consider the following Problem:

Problem 14.11: Terrence has been a tenant of the PHA for 25 years. For the past 10 years, he has been using marijuana in his apartment pursuant to the state's medical marijuana law. Even though the PHA has known of Terrence's marijuana use for several years, it has never sought to evict him. (It has, however, issued him several notices warning him that his marijuana use is in violation of his lease terms.) Three months ago, however, the state appointed Delilah as the new Director of the PHA. Delilah has taken a hard-line stance against drug use in public housing. As soon as she heard of Terrence's marijuana use, she immediately initiated proceedings to evict him from his PHA apartment. Terrence does not want to be evicted, but he also does not want to stop using marijuana in his apartment. Does the PHA's earlier forbearance bar it from seeking to evict Terrence now?

3. If eviction is left to the discretion of the PHA, what factors may the PHA consider in deciding whether or not to evict a current tenant based on the tenant's marijuana use? The federal regulations referred to in the HUD Memorandum provide, in pertinent part:

> In a manner consistent with . . . policies, procedures and practices [designed to appropriately evict any public housing residents who engage in certain activity detrimental to the public housing community], the PHA may consider all circumstances relevant to a particular case such as the seriousness of the offending action, the extent of participation by the leaseholder in the offending action, the effects that the eviction would have on family members not involved in the offending activity and the extent to which the leaseholder has shown personal responsibility and has taken all reasonable steps to prevent or mitigate the offending action.

24 C.F.R. § 966.4(l)(5)(vii)(B). Applying this provision, do you think the PSA in **Problem 14.11** would have a valid reason *not* to evict Terrence, assuming he would continue to use marijuana on the premises?

4. As noted, the HUD Memorandum declares that states may not require PHAs to accommodate the use of marijuana in public housing. HUD Memorandum, *supra*, at 10. *See also Forest City Residential Mgmt., Inc. ex rel. Plymouth Square Ltd. Dividend Hous. Ass'n v. Beasley*, 71 F. Supp. 3d 715, 730 (E.D. Mich. 2014) ("[T]o require [the PHA] to grant [the tenant] a reasonable accommodation to use marijuana would be to require [the PHA] to violate federal law. Such a requirement would fundamentally alter the nature of [the PHA's] operation by thwarting Congress's mission to provide drug-free federally assisted housing."); *Assenberg v. Anacortes Hous. Auth.*, No. C05-1836RSL, 2006 WL 1515603, at *4 (W.D. Wash.) (unreported), *aff'd*, 268 F. App'x 643 (9th Cir. 2008) (unreported) ("[T]o the extent that the state law legalizes marijuana use and prohibits the forfeiture of public housing, it conflicts with the CSA and the federal statutes and regulations that criminalize marijuana use and prohibit illegal drug use in public housing."). In light of the HUD Memorandum and the cases just cited, could a state impose *any* limits on a PHA's discretion to evict a tenant for using marijuana in public housing?

**Problem 14.12**: Terrence has been a tenant of the federally subsidized local Public Housing Authority (PHA) for the past 25 years. During a routine maintenance call a few months ago, the PHA observed a single marijuana plant growing in the bathtub of Terrence's PHA apartment. On the basis of this observation, the PHA initiated court proceedings to evict Terrence, citing a provision of his lease stipulating that each tenant shall "assure that no tenant, member of the tenant's household, or guest engages in any drug-related criminal activity on or off the premises." In response, Terrence cites a provision of state housing law that authorizes a court to order eviction from public housing only when it finds that a tenant's breach is "substantial." Terrence also claims that his breach was not substantial. He notes, for example, that he is a registered medical marijuana patient and that he has strictly complied with the state's medical marijuana law. Assuming the court agrees that Terrence's breach of the PHA's no-drug policy was not substantial,

may the court refuse to order his eviction? *See Hosford v. Chateau Foghorn LP*, 145 A.3d 616, 630 (Md. Ct. Sp. App. 2016).

5. Chapter 13 discussed 21 U.S.C. section 856, which bars landlords from knowingly allowing tenants to use rental property for purposes of consuming, manufacturing, or distributing drugs. Section 856 would (presumably) apply to PHAs, and not just private landlords.[5] The following Problem examines how the restrictions imposed by section 856 compare to those imposed by the federal public housing regulations discussed above:

<u>Problem 14.13</u>: Terrence and his adult daughter, Camila, share an apartment as tenants of the federally subsidized local Public Housing Authority (PHA). Last month, PHA public safety officers caught Camila smoking a marijuana joint outdoors in the courtyard of the apartment. The PHA initiated court proceedings to evict both Camila *and* Terrence, citing a provision of the lease stipulating that each tenant shall "assure that no tenant, member of the tenant's household, or guest engages in any drug-related criminal activity on or off the premises." *See* 24 C.F.R. § 966.4 (describing obligatory lease term). Terrence, however, has claimed that he was entirely unaware of Camila's marijuana use. Taking Terrence's assertion at face value, could he be convicted under 21 U.S.C. section 856? Regardless, could he be evicted from the apartment? *See Dep't of Hous. & Urban Dev. v. Rucker*, 535 U.S. 125, 136 (2002).

6. *Should* PHAs evict/deny admission to tenants who use marijuana in public housing? Always? Never? Sometimes? If sometimes, under what circumstances would eviction or denial of admission be appropriate?

---

5. Even though section 856 might thereby impose a burden on state officials, it does not violate the anti-commandeering rule because it imposes the same burden on private landlords—i.e., the statute is generally applicable. *E.g., Printz v. United States*, 521 U.S. 898, 932 n.17 (1997) (acknowledging that generally applicable statutes do not offend the anti-commandeering rule).

# Table of Cases

*Principal cases are italicized.*

*Alaska v. Crocker, 162,* 166, 170, 177
Allard v. Her Majesty the Queen in Right of Can., 511
Alleyne v. United States, 366
Alliance for Cannabis Therapeutics v. Drug Enf't Admin., 276
Americans for Safe Access v. Drug Enf't Admin., 276
Andreade v. Texas, 76
Apprendi v. New Jersey, 366, 376, 381
Arizona v. Cheatham, 187
Arizona v. Fields, 128, 187
Arizona v. Liwski, 187
Arizona v. Matlock, 429
Arizona v. Okun, 704
Arizona v. Sisco, 177
Assenberg v. Anacortes Hous. Auth., 732
Austin v. United States, 389

Baker; United States v., 367
Birchfield v. North Dakota, 156
Blockburger v. United States, 340
Blumenthal v. United States, 577
Booker; United States v., 364, 376
Bouie v. City of Columbia, 51
Brown v. Ely, 710
Buntion v. Texas, 76
Burgos; United States v., 577
*Butte, County of, v. Superior Court, 711,* 715

California v. Baniani, 507
California v. Barraza, 342
California v. Bergen, 307
California v. Brooks, 122
*California v. Colvin, 418,* 421, 424
California v. Dillon, 715
California v. Fisher, 178
California v. Galambos, 189
California v. Hughes, 122
California v. Jackson, 421, 422
California v. Jones, 114
California v. Kelly, 126, 294, 558
California v. Leal, 121, 122
California v. Lent, 121
*California v. Mentch, 430,* 432, 436, 438, 442
California v. Moret, 122
California v. Mower, 177, 178, 187, 188
California v. Mulcrevy, 131
California v. Orlosky, 422
California v. Rigo, 115
*California v. Spark, 106,* 110
California v. Strasburg, 178
California v. Tilehkooh, 123
California v. Trippet, 128, 159
California v. Urziceanu, 418
California v. Windus, 116, 127
*California v. Young, 157,* 159, 160
Campbell; United States v. (317 F.3d 597 (6th Cir. 2005)), 323
*Campbell; United States v. (977 F.2d 854 (4th Cir. 1992)), 589*
Campos; United States v., 378
Caplin & Drysdale, Chartered v. United States, 630-631
Central Hudson Gas & Elec. Corp. v. Public Servs. Comm'n, 501, 504, 510
Chen; United States v., 656
City of. *See name of city*
Coats v. Dish Network, LLC, 672
Colon; United States v., 583
Colorado v. Clendenin, 437, 481
Colorado v. Crouse, 705
Colorado v. Montante, 616
Colorado v. Watkins, 120, 122
Conant v. McCaffrey, 609
*Conant v. Walters, 504, 602,* 607, 608, 609, 610, 615, 616, 715
Conner v. Indiana, 373, 374
*Corchado-Peralta; United States v., 593,* 597
Cortes-Caban; United States v., 698

735

Cronan v. Georgia, 27
Cruz; United States v., 587

Damerville; United States v., 321
*Davis; United States v.,* 146, 149
Denney v. Drug Enf't Agency (348 F. App'x 327 (9th Cir. 2009)), 715
Denney v. Drug Enf't Admin. (508 F. Supp. 2d 815 (E.D. Cal. 2007)), 715
Denney v. Drug Enf't Admin. (2008 WL 1808289 (E.D. Cal. Apr. 22, 2008)), 715
Department of Hous. & Urban Dev. v. Rucker, 733
Department of Revenue of Mont. v. Kurth Ranch, 400
Dimeck; United States v., 587
Dobson v. McClennen, 154
Durham; United States v., 75

*Emerald Steel Fabricators, Inc. v. Bureau of Labor & Industries,* 672, 673, 679
*Ervin v. Virginia,* 38, 47, 48
Evans; United States v., 341
Eves; United States v., 371
Exxon Mobil Corp. v. Allapattah Servs., Inc., 702

Falu; United States v., 377
Feezel; People v., 150
Fitol; United States v., 370
Florida v. Eckroth, 62, 76
*Folk v. Maryland,* 72, 74
Forest City Residential Mgmt., Inc. ex rel. Plymouth Square Ltd. Dividend Hous. Ass'n v. Beasley, 661, 732
420 Caregivers, LLC v. City of L.A., 472
Fourth Corner Credit Union v. Federal Reserve Bank of Kan. City, 694

Garcia-Emanuel; United States v., 597
*Garden Grove, City of, v. Kha,* 160, 704, 706, 708, 709, 710
Gerlich v. Leath, 504
Gilbert; United States v., 657
Gimble v. State, 63
*Glenn; United States v.,* 328, 330
Gomez; United States v., 373
Gonzales v. Oregon, 610
Gonzales v. Raich, 254, 265, 266, 272, 275, 277-278, 300
Grand Jury Subpoena for THCF Med. Clinic Records, In re, 721
*Green Earth Wellness Center, LLC v. Atain Specialty Insurance Co.,* 649, 651, 652, 654

Haeberle v. Lowden, 649
Hall; United States v., 380
*Hammer v. Today's Health Care II, Co.,* 646, 648-649, 651, 652
Harlow v. Fitzgerald, 711
Harris; United States v., 589
Hemp Indus. Ass'n v. Drug Enf't Agency, 26, 27
Herder; United States v., 380
Hickman v. Taylor, 635
Hill; United States v., 576
Holland; United States v., 36
*Honneus; United States v.,* 28, 29
Hosford v. Chateau Foghorn LP, 733
Hyska; United States v., 340

Iannelli v. United States, 577
*Idaho v. Vinton,* 313, 315, 334
*Illinois v. McPeak,* 155, 156
Illinois v. One 1979 Chevrolet C-20 Van, 382
Illinois v. Park, 75
Illinois v. Schmalz, 72
*Iowa v. Bash,* 60, 62
*Iowa v. Cashen,* 66, 68, 69, 71, 74
*Iowa v. Heinrichs,* 52, 54
*Iowa v. Henderson,* 38, 69, 71

JJ206, LLC, DBA JUJU Joints, In re, 410
Joe Hemp's First Hemp Bank v. City of Oakland, 548
*Joslin v. Fourteenth District Judge,* 298, 300

Kansas v. Cooper, 289
Kelley; United States v., 588
*Kennewick, City of, v. Day,* 37, 85
Kentucky v. Adkins, 83
Kentucky v. Harrelson, 25
Klein; United States v., 308

Laakkonen; United States v., 323
Latham; United States v., 334
Leary v. United States, 396, 400
*Levesque; United States v.,* 387
Lewis v. American Gen. Media, 664
*Lewis v. Virginia,* 335
Little v. Gore, 710
Littlefield; United States v., 379-380
Lopez; United States v., 265
Louisiana v. Callahan, 338
*Louisiana v. Kelly,* 332, 334
Love v. Georgia, 245
Lucas v. State, 76
Lungren, People ex rel., v. Peron, 481

Maine v. Toppan, 326
Mapp v. Ohio, 162
Maral v. City of Live Oak, 558

*Massachusetts v. Camerano*, 578
Massachusetts v. Canning, 177
*Massachusetts v. Cruz*, 168, 170, 171
Massachusetts v. Harvard, 62
*Massachusetts v. Jackson*, 313, *318*, 320, 323, 327
Massachusetts v. Keefner, 313, 327
Massachusetts v. MacDonald, 75
Massachusetts v. Overmyer, 171, 172
*Massachusetts v. Palmer*, *308*, 312, 313, 323
McFadden v. United States, 38, 48, 51
McIntosh; United States v., 353, 357, 358, 400, 550, 615, 638
*Meek v. Mississippi*, *316*, 318, 320
Michigan v. Blysma, 418
Michigan v. Brown, 178
Michigan v. Butler-Jackson, 616
Michigan v. Carruthers, 131-132, 133
Michigan v. Doemer, 575
Michigan v. Feezel, 150
*Michigan v. Hartwick*, 118, 129, *180*, 187, 293, 294, 441, 442
Michigan v. Jones, 119
Michigan v. Kolanek, 115, 116
Michigan v. Koon, 154
Michigan v. McQueen, *425*, 429
Michigan v. Nicholson, 118
*Michigan Department of Community Health; United States v.*, 716, 722
Minnesota v. Siirila, 47
*Missouri v. Bell*, *45*, 46, 47
Missouri v. LaMaster, 304
Missouri v. Netzer, 304
*Missouri v. Paul*, 48, 51
Moncrieffe v. Holder, 322
Monell v. Department of Soc. Servs. of City of N.Y., 715
Montana v. Burwell, 75
Montana v. Nelson, 120, 121, 122
Montana v. Stoner, 115
*Montana Cannabis Industry Ass'n v. Montana (368 P.3d 1131 (Mont. 2016))*, 438, 440, 471, 503, *507*, 510
Montana Cannabis Indus. Ass'n v. Montana (No. DDV-2011-518 (Dist. Ct. Lewis and Clark County 2015)), 471
*Montgomery, Arizona ex rel., v. Harris*, 150, 154
Moreau v. State, 62
*Morgan Brown, In re*, *407*, 409, 410
Morse v. Frederick, 504
Morse; United States v., 582
Mount Spokane Skiing Corp. v. Spokane Cnty., 479

National Fed'n of Indep. Bus. v. Sebelius, 722, 725
National Org. for Reform of Marijuana Laws (NORML) v. Drug Enf't Admin., 274-275

Neal, Illinois ex rel., v. Ryan, 95, 96
Nebraska v. Colorado, 549
*Nebraska & Oklahoma, States of, v. State of Colorado (No. 220144 (U.S. 2014))*, *535*
Nebraska & Okla., States of, v. State of Colo. (2016 WL 74964 (U.S. 2016)), 545, 710
New England Accessories Trade Ass'n, Inc. v. City of Nashua, 503
*New Hampshire Hemp Council, Inc. v. Marshall*, 22, 25, 26, 29
New Mexico v. Hodge, 65
New Mexico v. McCoy, 65
New Mexico v. Shaulis-Powell, 305
New York v. Burger, 470, 472
*New York v. Jackson*, *134*, 139
New York v. Van Vorst, 38
Niles, City of, v. Howard, 297
No Over Taxation v. Hickenlooper, 548
North Carolina v. Childers, 313
North Carolina v. Harris, 64, 68
*North Carolina v. Mitchell*, *89*, 91
North Carolina v. Thomas, 572
*North Carolina v. Wilkins*, *328*, 329, 330
*North Charleston, City of, v. Harper*, *295*
North Dakota v. Peterson, 27
Noy v. Alaska, 189, 226

*Oakland Cannabis Buyers' Cooperative; United States v.*, 80, 82, 272
Ohio v. Dempsey, 47
*One Clipper Bow Ketch NISKU; United States v.*, *93*, 95
One 1976 Mercedes Benz 280S, Serial No. 11602012072193, 382
Oregon v. Beck, 144
Oregon v. Berringer, 287
Oregon v. Ehrensing, 705
*Oregon v. Fries*, *57*, 61, 62
Oregon v. Kama, 704
Oregon v. Luster, 116
Oregon v. Miles, 189, 615
*Oregon v. Smalley*, *166*, 170
Oregon Prescription Drug Monitoring Program v. U.S. Drug Enf't Admin., 721
Osburn; United States v., 368-369
Outen; United States v., 321
Owen v. City of Indep., Mo., 715

Paret-Ruiz; United States v., 583
Pearson v. McCaffrey, 607, 608
Pennhurst State Sch. & Hosp. v. Halderman, 726
*Pennsylvania v. Hutchins*, *144*, 149
Pickard; United States v., 270
Pillado; United States v., 342

Pinkerton v. United States, 584
Pizarro; United States v., 583
Powell v. State, 63
Presto; United States v., 337
Printz v. United States, 283, 733
Proyect; United States v., 367
Pruitt; United States v., 584
Puig-Infante; United States v., 588

R. v. Caine, 226
R. v. Malmo-Levine, 226
R. v. Parker, 271
R. v. Smith, 271
Raich v. Gonzales (Raich II), 266, 270, 271, 272
Randall; United States v., 77, 80
Ravin v. Alaska, 163, 223, 226, 271
Real Property & Improvements Located at 1840 Embarcadero, Oakland, California; United States v., 394
Real Prop. in Santa Paula, Cal.; United States v., 393
Reed; United States v., 587
Reed-Kaliher v. Hoggatt, 120, 122
Regan v. Wyoming, 54, 57
Rent-Rite Super Kegs W. Ltd., In re, 658
Retail Clerks Int'l Ass'n v. Schermerhorn, 680
Retelle; United States v., 372
Rhode Island v. Williams, 331
Richardson v. Georgia, 144
Ridley v. Massachusetts Bay Transp. Auth., 504
Riverside, City of, v. Inland Empire Patients Health & Wellness Center, Inc., 553, 558, 560
R.L.H., In re, 64, 65, 66
Robichaud v. Virginia, 572
Robinson; United States v., 371
Rodriguez; United States v., 331
Rose v. Martin, 293-294
Rosemund v. United States, 576
Rosenthal; United States v. (454 F.3d 943 (9th Cir. 2006)), 361, 701
Rosenthal; United States v. (266 F. Supp. 2d 1068 (N.D. Cal. 2003)), 358, 361 366, 699, 702, 706, 708
Rosenthal; United States v. (266 F. Supp. 2d 1091 (N.D. Cal. 2003)) (Rosenthal II), 703
Ross v. RagingWire Telecommunications, Inc., 662, 665, 672
Ruggles v. Yagong, 299, 300
Rust v. Sullivan, 609

Saenz v. Roe, 283
Safe Life Caregivers v. City of L.A., 558
Safe Sts. Alliance v. Alternative Holistic Healing, LLC (No. 15-cv-00349 (D. Colo. Feb. 8, 2016)), 405-406

Safe Streets Alliance v. Alternative Holistic Healing, LLC, second amended complaint, 403
Safe Sts. Alliance v. Alternative Holistic Healing, LLC (No. 1:15-cv-00349-REB-CBS, 2016 WL 223815 (D. Colo. Jan. 19, 2016)), 549
Safe Sts. Alliance v. Hickenlooper, 549
Sepulveda; United States v., 340-341
Shabani; United States v., 577
Shafer; United States v., 598
Shumaker v. Wyoming, 335
Sinclair v. City of Grandview, 711
$61,200.00 in U.S. Currency, More or Less; United States v. (805 F. Supp. 2d 682 (S.D. Iowa 2010)), 383
$61,200.00 in U.S. Currency, More or Less; United States v. (No. 1:09-cv-00029-JAJ-TJS (S.D. Iowa Oct. 19, 2010)), 386
Smith v. Hickenlooper (164 F. Supp. 3d 1286 (D. Colo. 2016))), 549
Smith v. Hickenlooper (No. 16-01095 (10th Cir. Apr. 1, 2016)), 549
Smith; United States v., 380
South Dakota v. Caylor, 572
South Dakota v. Schroeder, 66
Sparks v. Maryland, 343
Stillwell v. Virginia, 322
Sullivan; United States v., 396
Swiderski; United States v., 324, 326, 327, 424

Tamez; United States v., 657
Teemer; United States v., 83-84
Ter Beek v. City of Wyoming, 558, 560
Thomas; United States v., 367
Trans-High Corp. v. Colorado, 504
Turner v. Arkansas, 63

Ultra Trimmer, In re, 411
Umagat; United States v., 582
United States v. See name of opposing party
Utah v. Horsley, 305, 307, 312

Valdez; United States v., 577
Vera; United States v., 381-382
Vermont v. Francis, 316
von Hofe v. United States, 390

Washburn v. Columbia Forest Prods., Inc., 664
Washington v. Cleppe, 37, 85
Washington v. Constantine, 105, 442
Washington v. Dalton, 105
Washington v. Diana, 189
Washington v. Fry, 101, 172, 177, 187
Washington v. Gladstone, 573, 575
Washington v. Kurtz, 189
Washington v. Olson, 162

Washington v. Otis, 114
*Washington v. Shepherd, 111*, 113, 114
*Washington v. Shupe, 438,* 439
Washington v. Weiss, 38
Washington v. Wilson, 572
*Washington; United States v., 343,* 349, 352-353
Webb v. Georgia, 143

West Virginia v. Underwood, 312-313
West Virginia v. White, 313
Will v. Michigan Dep't of State Police, 715
Williams v. Mississippi, 343
Winston; United States v., 372

Zafiro; United States v., 572

# Index

Abandonment, as defense to attempt, 337-338
Accommodation. *See* Employers; Landlords; Public housing
ACLU. *See* American Civil Liberties Union (ACLU)
ADA. *See* Americans with Disabilities Act (ADA)
Administrative forfeiture. *See* Forfeiture
Advertising
   expenses, denying tax deductions for, 505
   restrictions on, 464-466
      alternatives to, 504-507
      constitutionality of, 501-505
   trademarks, effect on, 411-412
Affirmative defenses. *See* Defenses
Age requirements
   alcoholic beverages, 124
   caregivers, 431
   medical marijuana laws, 119-120
   recreational marijuana laws, 124
Aggravated circumstances. *See* Sanctions, criminal
Agriculture departments, research by, 25
Aiding and abetting
   applicability to marijuana crimes, 572-575
   elements of offense, 571-572
   generally, 57, 62, 537, 571-576, 657
   punishment for, 576
AIDS/HIV, research on use for, 206-207
Alabama
   Carly's law (CBD law), 99, 123-124, 131
Alaska
   caregivers, 437
   necessity defense, 189
   physician recommendation, 111
   privacy right, 223-226, 271
   quantity limits, 126-127
   searches, 162-166
Alcoholic beverages
   age requirements, 124
   exemption from CSA, 213, 272
   personal production of, 511
American Civil Liberties Union (ACLU), 229, 246, 248-249

Americans with Disabilities Act (ADA)
   illegal use of drugs, and, 662
   qualified individual with disability, 662
Analogue Act, 30-31. *See* Controlled Substance Analogue Enforcement Act of 1986
Anderson, D. Mark, 242
Anti-commandeering doctrine, 278-283, 546-547, 679, 720-721, 722, 733
Anti-discrimination laws. *See* Employers; Housing; Landlords; Public housing
Arizona
   caregivers, 437, 440
   contract law, 646-648
   DUI laws, 144, 149-154
   employment law, 662-663
   housing law, 659
   legal protections, 161, 187
   licensing, 452
   probationers, 120
   quantity limits, 128
   return of seized marijuana, 704
   schools, accommodation by, 659
   searches, 177
   transfers between users, 424, 429
Arkansas
   ballot initiatives, 293-294
   caregivers, 437
   control, 63
   cultivation by user or caregiver, 415-416
   distribution, defined, 320-321
Arrests for marijuana-related offenses,
   racial disparities in, 248-249, 521
   statistics, 5, 37, 246-247, 248-249, 521
Assisted housing. *See* Public housing
Assisted suicide, 610
Ataxia, research on use for, 207
Attempts
   abandonment defense, 337-338
   elements of, 335-337
Attitudes toward marijuana
   high school seniors, 233, 236
   law, effect on, 235-236
   media campaigns, effect on, 233-235
   research on, 236

741

Attorney General
  enforcement memoranda and other statements by, 343, 349-352
  scheduling authority, 272-277
Attorneys
  effect on client compliance with law, 635
  ethical implications of advising marijuana users and suppliers, 15, 626-635
  federal court and agency regulation of, 626, 638-644
  forfeiture actions
    attorney's fees, and seizure of client assets, 630-631
    civil forfeiture actions, representation in, 393
    indigent property owners, representation for, 393
  MRPC Rule 1.2, 15, 626-635
    permissive interpretation, 631-635
    restrictive interpretation, 627-631
  MRPC Rule 8.4, 635-638
  payment for services, 638
  use or supply of marijuana by, 626, 635-638
Authority
  federal government
    anti-commandeering rule as constraint on. *See* Anti-commandeering doctrine
    Congress, enumerated powers, 253-266
    DEA, scheduling authority, 272-277
    Due process as constraint on, 266-271, 283
    FDA, role of, 274-277
    President, enforcement powers, 527-533
  local government
    preemption of local law. *See* Preemption, by state law
    regulation of supply, 550-568
    regulation of use and possession, 295-300
  state government
    ballot initiatives, 291-295
    discrimination against non-residents, 283-288, 451-452
    extra-territorial application of laws, 288-290
    preemption of state law. *See* Preemption, by federal law

Ballot initiatives, 291-295
Banks and banking
  authority over, 689-695
  closed-loop payment processing system, 695
  credit unions, 694
  policy issues surrounding, 687-689
  regulation of services to marijuana industry, 681-687
  suspicious activity reports (SARs), 694
  use of, to police marijuana industry, 688-689

Bankruptcy, 658-659
Beer, *See also* Alcoholic beverages
  Beer Institute Advertising and Marketing Code, 465
  home brewing, regulation of, 511
  prohibition, market after, 513
Benefits of marijuana. *See* Use of marijuana, benefits of
Blake, David, 140
Blue Ribbon Commission on Marijuana Policy, 504-505, 507, 513-514

California
  abuse of laws, 294
  ballot initiatives, 291-294
  Blue Ribbon Commission on Marijuana Policy, role of, 507
  caregivers, 430-436
  civil rights violations, cause of action for, 698, 711-715
  Compassionate Use Act (CUA), 80, 99, 106-110, 116, 121-122, 126, 131, 160, 177-178, 187-188, 196, 254-265, 294, 430-436, 553-558, 560, 602, 610, 665-671, 699-701
  Dispensary Equity Permit Program in Oakland, 15, 525
  employers, 665-671
  Fair Employment and Housing Act, 665-671
  forms of marijuana, restrictions on, 131
  hash oil, production of, 306-307
  industrial hemp, 25
  landlords, 657
  local authority in, 553-558
  Medical Cannabis Regulation and Safety Act of 2015, 421, 558, 611-612, 619
  Medical Marijuana Program Act (MMP), 106, 126-127, 159-160, 188, 294, 418-421, 432, 436, 560
  necessity defense, 189
  physicians
    conflicts of interest, regulation of, 615
    discipline of, 602, 610
    legal protections provided to, 610
    recommendations by, 105-106, 110, 114, 608-612, 619
    requirements imposed on, 610-612
  probationers and parolees, restrictions on use by, 121
  Proposition 215. *See* Compassionate Use Act (CUA), *this heading*
  Proposition 64, 64, 99, 141, 445, 447-448, 451, 472, 507, 558
  prosecution, user immunity from, 187-188
  public consumption, 141
  qualifying conditions, 105-106, 116

quantity, limits on, 126-127, 294, 472
registration, 117, 626
residency requirements, 451
return of seized marijuana, 704, 706-709
searches, 177-178, 187-188
supply by
  caregiver, 106-110, 430
  collective or cooperative, 412-422, 424, 436, 443
  commercial firms
    generally, 507
    industry structure, regulation of, 512
    licensing, 445, 447-448, 451
    policing of, 471-472
  designated state officials, 699-701
  user, 106-110, 430
taxes, 490, 491
trademarks, 411
transportation of marijuana, 157-160
Canada
  Charter of Rights and Freedoms, 271, 510
  direct-mail approach, 506-507
  harm principle, 226
  Marijuana for Medical Purposes Regulation, 506
  medical purposes, right to use for, 510-511
  storefronts, ban on, 506
Cancer chemotherapy, research on use for alleviating symptoms of, 207-208
Cannabidiol (CBD). *See also* Cannabinoids; Cannabis; Marijuana; Synthetic cannabinoids; THC
  effects of, 219
  included in definition of marijuana, 27
  generally, 9, 18
  regulation of
    possession and use, 123-124, 131
    supply, 443, 480
Cannabimimetic agents, 31
Cannabinoids, 17, 200-201. *See also* Cannabidiol; Cannabis; Marijuana; Synthetic cannabinoids; THC
Cannabis. *See also* Cannabidiol; Cannabinoids; Marijuana; Synthetic cannabinoids; THC
  plant
    botany of, 20
    counting, for purposes of sentencing, 368-370
    drugs produced from, 18-20
    genetics, 18
    parts excluded from definition of marijuana, 21-22, 26
    photograph, 18
  taxonomy
    indica, 18, 27-29
    ruderalis, 18, 27
    sativa, 18

Caregivers, 111-113, 430
  compensation, regulation of, 440, 507-510
  cultivation and handling by, 418, 429-442
  legal protections for, 440-442
  limitations on activities of, 437-440
  number of patients allowed to serve, regulation of, 437-439, 507-510
  qualifications required of, 431-437
Caulkins, Jonathan P., et al., 219-222, 246, 331, 512-513, 515-517, 483, 487-489, 491-494, 506
Chronic pain, as qualifying condition, 105
Civil forfeiture. *See* Forfeiture
Civil rights violations, cause of action for, 710-715
Closed-loop payment processing system. *See* Banks and banking
Cochrane Collaboration, reviews of medical research, 205-209
Collective cultivation, 418-424. *See also* Manufacture
Colleges and universities
  federal grant funds, conditions on, 723-725
  Higher Education Act, 724
  participation in production of
    industrial hemp, 25
    marijuana for use in research projects, 25, 201, 479
    marijuana for use by qualified patients, 479, 515, 725
  policies toward use on school property, 142, 723-724
Colorado
  advertising, regulation of, 464-465, 503-506
  Amendment 64, 99, 124, 133-134, 140-141, 277, 282, 295, 414, 416, 424, 518-519, 521, 533, 535-550, 636, 639-644, 649
  arrests in, 521
  attorneys
    professional conduct rules governing, 630, 636-637, 639-644
    use and cultivation of marijuana by, 636-637
  caregivers, 430-432, 436-437, 440
  contract law, 649-651
  credit unions, 694
  DUI law, 150
  edibles, 458-461, 499-500
  educational campaigns, 234-235, 500
  employment law, 672
  fiscal impact, comparing legalization vs. prohibition, 518-520
  inventory tracking, 466-469, 716
  labeling and packaging rules, 458-462
  landlords, 659-661

Colorado (cont'd)
    local authority, 295, 551
    medical use, defined, 415
    physicians
        conflicts of interest, regulation of, 615
        discipline of, 624-625
        legal protections provided to, 612
        recommendations by, 616, 619-625
        requirements imposed on, 612-613, 624-625
    preemption. See Preemption, by federal laws
    probationers, use by, 120
    public consumption, 133-134, 140-141
    qualifying conditions, 204-205, 241
    quantity limits, 127-128, 416-417
    registration, 117, 240-241, 625
    residency requirements, 284-287, 451-452
    Retail Marijuana Code (RMC), 5, 10, 14, 456-469, 472-477, 503-504, 545
    return of seized marijuana, 704-705
    sales regulations, 462-463
    schools, use in, 725-727
    supply by
        commercial firms
            discipline of, 472-478
            generally, 4, 443-444
            industry structure, 455-456
            licensing, 445-448, 451-452, 455-456, 458, 475-478, 512, 520, 629
        user
            cultivation, 414, 416-417
            transfer between, 424
    taxes, 467, 490-491, 518-519, 548
    testing, 456-458
    trademarks, 411
    video surveillance, 466-467
Commandeering. See Anti-commandeering doctrine
Commerce Clause, 254-266, 396
Commercial supply, 413, 443-480. See also Government supply; Personal supply
    advertising. See Advertising
    bans on, 507-512. See also Distribute; Manufacture; Possession with Intent to Distribute
    industry structure, regulations affecting
        concentration of, 445, 512-515
        segmentation, 456
        vertical integration, 455-456
    inventory tracking. See Inventory tracking
    legalization of, 443-444, 480-481
    labeling and packaging. See Labeling and Packaging.
    licensing. See Licensing testing. See Testing.
Conditional spending, 722, 726
Confidential informants, 341-342

Confidentiality rules, medical marijuana states, 118
Connecticut
    attorneys, 630
    caregivers, 437
    employment law, 663
    landlords, 659
    physician recommendations, 618
    prisoners, use by, 120
    registration of qualifying patient, 116
    schools, use in, 133, 141
Consolidation in marijuana industry. See Commercial supply, industry structure
Conspiracy
    elements of, 577
    generally, 57, 62, 335, 571, 575
    limits on, 583
    non-merger with underlying offenses, 584
    proof of, 578-582
    sanction for, 583-584
Consumption of marijuana. See Use of marijuana
Continuing medical education (CME) courses, 618
Contract law
    alternatives to contract, 652-655
    breach of contract, 646, 654
    employment; See Employers
    enforcement
        preemption of, 651-652
        public policy exception to, 645-652
    leases. See Landlords
    purpose behind, 654
Control. See also Possession
    duration of control, 62-63
    exclusive access, 63-66
    generally, 36, 54-57
    non-exclusive access, 66-72
    ownership and, 57-62
    proof of control, 63-74
Controlled Substance Analogue Enforcement Act of 1986 (Analogue Act), 30-31
Controlled Substances Act (CSA), *passim*
    aggravated circumstances, 375-378
    alcoholic beverages, exemption of, 213, 272
    attempts, 335, 338
    conspiracy, 335, 577, 583
    distribute, defined, 315
    distribution of small amount for no remuneration, 321
    drug paraphernalia, 410-411
    forfeiture, 92, 379-381
    immunity for state officials, 697-710
    knowledge, 51
    landlords, 655-658, 733

manufacture, defined, 304, 416
marijuana, defined, 21, 27
quantity. *See* Quantity
physician registration, 602-607
possession, defined, 35
preemption under. *See* Preemption, by federal
scheduling. *See* Scheduling
sentencing. *See* Sanctions
synthetic THC, 30
THC, 26-27
tobacco, exemption of, 213, 272
Copyright, 406, 530
Counterfeit drug, 373
Crack house statute, 655-658, 733. *See also* Landlords; Public housing
Credit unions, 694. *See also* Banks and banking
Crime and marijuana use, correlation between, 219
Criminal forfeiture. *See* Forfeiture
Criminal history
  licensing, role in, 447-451
  medical marijuana, eligibility to use, and, 120-123
Cultivation. *See* Collective cultivation; Commercial supply; Manufacture; Personal supply

DEA. *See* Drug Enforcement Administration (DEA)
Debilitating medical condition. *See* Qualifying conditions
Decriminalization
  local authority to pursue, 297-300
  sanctions under, 96-97
Defenses
  attempts, 337-338
  congressional spending limitations (Rohrabacher-Farr Amendment), 353-358
  entrapment. *See* Entrapment
  forfeiture actions, in. *See* Forfeiture
  innocent possession, 83-84
  medical marijuana states, in, 179-188
  mistakes
    of fact, 158
    of law, 158, 343
  necessity, 77-82, 189-194
  *Swiderski* defense, 323-327, 424
  unwitting possession, 84-87
Definitions
  deliver, 315
  distribute, 315-327, 339, 698
  manufacture, 304, 416
  marijuana, 17-20, 21-31
  plant, 371

possession, 35-76
production, 304
Delaware
  caregivers, 437
  employment law, 663
  landlords, 659
  qualifying conditions, 291
  schools, use in, 142
Deliver, 315. *See also* Distribute
Delta-9-tetrahydrocannabinol (THC). *See* THC
Demand for marijuana. *See* Use of marijuana
Dementia, research on use for, 208
Denning, Brannon, 284-287
Department of Health and Human Services (HHS)
  delegation of authority, 274
  Food and Drug Administration (FDA), role of in scheduling decisions, 274-277
  positions regarding
    benefits of use, 196-203
    harms of use, 214-222
  recommendation regarding marijuana scheduling, 6, 196, 197-200, 202, 214-218
Department of Housing and Urban Development (HUD), 727-733
Department of Justice (DOJ)
  enforcement guidance, 5, 10, 77, 303, 410, 527
    Cole memorandum, 344, 349-352, 410, 531
    effect of, 532
  entrapment and, 343-353
  MRPC Rule 1.2, relevance to, 634-635
  Ogden memorandum, 343-348, 349, 353
  Take Care Clause and, 527-533
  restrictions on use of funds by, 353-358
Designated caregivers. *See* Caregivers
Designated providers. *See* Caregivers
Designer drugs, 31. *See also* Synthetic cannabinoids
Deterrence theory, 227, 230, 236
Direct democracy. *See* Ballot initiatives
Discrimination
  by employers, 662-672
  by landlords, 659-662
  race based
    in arrests, 248-249, 521
    in licensing, 520-525
  residency based, 119-120, 283-288, 451-452
Dispensary. *See* Commercial supply
Dispense. *See* Distribute
Distribute. *See also* Commercial supply
  attempted distribution, 335-337
  between users, 5, 320-322, 424-429

745

Distribute (cont'd)
  commercial purpose, 316-323
  defined, 315-327, 339, 698
  joint possessors, liability for transfers
      between, 323-327, 424
  mens rea, 709
District of Columbia, 119, 124-125, 507
  ballot initiatives, 291
  caregivers, 437
  quantity limits, 127
  supply by
    commercial firms, 507
    user, 415
DOJ. See Department of Justice (DOJ)
Double jeopardy, 339-341
Driving under the influence (DUI), 9,
      143-156, 247
  DUI-impaired, 143-149, 242
  DUI-marijuana vs. DUI-alcohol, 241-242
  DUI-per se, 143, 149-156, 242, 244-245
    blood or urine test, 156
    metabolites, application to, 150-154
    proof of presence of marijuana, 154-156
  harms of, 241-245
  measures to combat harms, 245
  THC and, 242, 244
Drug cartels, 350, 710
Drug Enforcement Administration (DEA)
  enforcement capacity, 282-283
  physicians, regulation of, 9, 602-610
  positions regarding
    benefits of use, 196-203
    harms of use, 214-222
  scheduling authority, 272-277
  scheduling decisions, 214-218, 222, 251,
      274-275
Drug Free Schools and Communities
      Act of 1989, 479, 723-724, 725
Drug free workplace, defined, 726. See also
      Employers
Drug paraphernalia, 410-411
Drug Policy Alliance, 18-20
Drug testing
  drivers, 156
  employees, 92, 662-672
  positive drug test, and possession, 64-66
Due process, 10, 51, 266-271, 283, 510, 710
DUI. See Driving under the influence

Edibles, 19, 48, 75. See also Use of marijuana
  harms from, 499-501
  labeling and packaging requirements. See
      Labeling and packaging requirements
  measurement for purposes of
      sentencing, 368
Eighteenth Amendment, 698

Eighth Amendment, 387-389
Employers
  accommodation of employee use
    express duty, 662-665
    implied duty, 665-672
  drug testing of employees, 92, 662-672
  federal contracts and grants, 662, 726-727
  NFL teams, 664-665
  preemption of state-imposed duty to
      accommodate use, 672-681
Entrapment
  conventional entrapment, 341-343
  by estoppel, 343-353
  inducement, 341
  predisposition, 342-343
  promissory estoppel, 352-353
Epilepsy, research on use for, 208
Equal Protection Clause, 248, 522-524
Estoppel. See Entrapment
Eviction. See also Landlords; Public housing
  public housing, 731, 732, 733
  rental property, 661
Excessive fine. See Eighth Amendment;
      Forfeiture
Extraterritorial application of state law,
      289-290

Fagan, Jeffrey, 247
Fake marijuana, sentencing for, 373-375
Farnsworth, E. Allan, 646
FDA. See Food and Drug
      Administration (FDA)
Federal Drug Free Workplace Act, 662,
      726-727
Federal government authority. See Authority,
      federal government
Federal grants
  amount of, in higher education, 723
  conditions on, 722-723
  employers, 662, 726-727
  potential loss of, because of state reforms,
      722-733
  public housing, 726-727
Federal Rules of Criminal Procedure,
      381, 387
Federalism. See Authority, federal government;
      Authority, state government
Federation of State Medical Boards, 610
Financial aid, 723. See also Federal grants;
      Higher Education Act
Financial crimes. See Money laundering
Financial Crimes Enforcement Network
      (FinCEN), 690, 694
Financial industry. See Banks and banking
FinCEN. See Financial Crimes Enforcement
      Network (FinCEN)

Finlaw, Jack, 140
Firearms, 350, 531
  possession of, 37, 83, 122, 177, 265, 328
  use during drug crime, 376, 576
First Amendment, 9, 266, 501-502, 602-609, 715
Fiscal impact
  enforcement costs, 245-247, 518-520
  revenues, 518-520
Fleeting possession, 62-63. *See also* Possession
Florida
  caregivers, 437
  criminal sanctions, 88
Food and Drug Administration (FDA). *See* Department of Health and Human Services (HHS)
Forfeiture
  administrative, 382
  civil
    advantages of, 394-396
    possession offenses, 92-96
    procedure used in, 382-386
    supply offenses, 379-380
  criminal, 379-382
  defenses to
    Eighth Amendment, 386-389
    innocent owner, 389-393
  judicial, 382
  legal representation and, 393, 630-631
  medical marijuana dispensaries, use against, 394-396
  property subject to, 92-96, 379-381,
  state forfeiture, as compared to federal, 95-96
Fourth Amendment, 161-177, 469-470. *See also* Searches; Seized property
Furnish. *See* Distribute

Gateway hypothesis, 219-221
Geller, Amanda, 247
Geographic preferences, 15
Georgia
  DUI laws, 143, 156, 245
Gettman, Jonathan, 521
Government officials, 697-733. *See also* Public housing; Schools; State officials
Government supply. *See also* Commercial supply; Personal supply
  benefits and costs of, 515-517
  criminal liability of state employees, 698-704
  generally, 478-479
Grants. *See* Federal grants
Gratuitous transfers, 318-320, 320-323

Growing marijuana. *See* Collective cultivation; Commercial supply; Manufacture; Personal supply

Harm principle, 223-226, 251
Harms of marijuana. *See* Use of marijuana, harms of
Hash oil
  manufacture of, 305-307, 416
  measurement of, 371
Hawaii
  attorneys, 630
  caregivers, 437
  landlords, 660
  local authority, 299-300
Hazard, Geoffrey, 638-639
Hemp. *See* Industrial hemp
HHS. *See* Department of Health and Human Services (HHS)
Higher education. *See* Colleges and universities
Higher Education Act, 724
Hill, Julie Andersen, 681-688, 690-694
HIV/AIDS, research on use for, 206-207
Holder, Eric, 343
Husak, Douglas, 210-213

Idaho, 313-315, 402
Illinois
  attorneys, 630
  caregivers, 431, 437
  decriminalization in, 96
  DUI law, 154-155
  employment law, 663-664, 727
  felony drug offenders, use by, 121
  forfeiture, 95-96
  landlords, 660, 727
  licensing, 445
  physician recommendations, 618
  qualifying conditions, 291
  schools, 727
Incarceration for marijuana offenses, 5, 97, 378. *See also* Sanctions
Indiana, 373-375
Industrial hemp, 18, 21-22, 22-27
Industrial Hemp Farming Act of 2015, 25
Inspections, warrantless, 469-470
Intellectual property. *See* Copyright; Patents; Trademarks
Inventory tracking, 466-468, 719
Iowa
  CBD law, 131
  knowledge, 38, 52-53
  possession, 60-61, 66-71
  synthetic cannabinoids, 52-53

Joint possession, 72-74. *See also Swiderski* defense
Jury nullification, 358-362, 699
Jury trial in civil forfeiture actions, 382

Kamin, Sam, 411, 528-532
Kansas
  manufacture, 312
  possession, prohibition on, 288-289
Kentucky
  industrial hemp, 25
  innocent possession defense, 83
Kilmer, Beau, 229, 331
Kleiman, Mark, 512, 531
Knowledge. *See also* Possession
  generally, 36-37
  notice, and, 51-54
  presumptions, 45-47
  proof of, 38-45
  regarding
    law, 51-54
    quantity, 47
    substance, 47-51
  willful ignorance, 589-593
Kreimer, Seth F., 289-290
Kreit, Alex, 201-202, 214, 501-504

Labeling and packaging, 458-462, 499-501
Landlords, 655-662
  liability for
    evicting tenant for use on rental property, 660-661
    refusing to rent based on tenant's status as medical marijuana patient, 659-662
    renting to tenant who uses or supplies marijuana on rental property, 655-659
  preemption of state laws by federal law, 661
  public housing, 733
Lanham Act, 407
Law school courses, 6
Lawyers. *See* Attorneys
Leafly.com, 18, 19, 575-576
Leases, 655. *See also* Landlords
  generally, 655
  public housing, terms of, 727, 733
Leff, Benjamin M., 397-399
Legalization
  defined, 8, 10
  effects on
    price, 487-488
    use, 239-241, 487-488
  fiscal costs, 246-247, 518-520
  history of, 4
  liberty costs, 249-251, 520-524
  public opinion toward, 204
  varieties of, 4, 99-100

Lewis, Amanda Chicago, 521-522
Licensing
  as a requirement for supplying marijuana, 444-446
  criteria for awarding licenses
    criminal history, 447-451
    generally, 446-447
    geography, 453-455
    non-profit status, 422, 452-453
    race, 454, 520-525
    residency, 451-452
  cross-ownership of licenses, 455-456
  discipline of licensees
    investigations, 468-472
    procedures, 472-475
    sanctions, 475-478
  fees, 445
  local role in. *See* Authority, local government
  number of licenses, 445, 512-515
  regulation of licensees. *See* Commercial supply
  transfer of licenses, 454
LLEP. *See* Lowest law enforcement priority (LLEP)
Local authority. *See* Authority, local government
Local regulations. *See* Authority, local government
Localism. *See* Authority, local government
Louisiana
  attempts, 338
  caregivers, 437
  Louisiana State University, proposal to produce marijuana at, 479, 515, 725
  possession with intent, 332-334
  Southern University, proposal to produce marijuana at, 479, 515, 725
Lowest law enforcement priority (LLEP), 299-300

MacCoun, Robert, 227, 230
Maine
  caregivers, 437, 442
  collective cultivation, 418
  employers, 663
  intent to distribute, 331
  joint possessors, distribution between, 326
  landlords, 660
  return of marijuana, 704
  schools, 141, 726
Mandatory minimum sentences. *See* Sanctions
Manufacture. *See also* Collective cultivation; Commercial supply; Government supply; Personal supply
  defined, 304, 416

designated state official, by 698-703
for personal use
   prohibition regimes, 99, 308-313
   legalization regimes, 414-416
generally, 304-315
hash oil, production of, 305-307
local authority over. See Authority, local government
proof of, 313-315
Marihuana Tax Act of 1937, 396
Marijuana. See also Cannabidiol; Cannabinoids; Cannabis; Synthetic cannabinoids; THC
   alternative names for, 17
   benefits of. See Use of marijuana, benefits of
   definition
      absorbed into body, 27
      burned residue, 27
      CBD, 27
      generally, 17-31
      industrial hemp, 25-27
      synthetic cannabinoids, 29-31
      THC content and, 22-25, 27
   harms of. See Use of marijuana, harms of
   proof that substance is, 75-76
Marijuana tourism. See Tourism.
Maryland
   caregivers, 437
   commercial supply
      discipline, 475
      generally, 455, 469, 475
      inspections, 469
      licensing, 445, 447, 454, 522
      minority participation in, 454, 522-524
      transfer of licenses, 454
      vertical integration, 455
   entrapment, 343
   labeling and packaging, 461
   landlords, 660
   testing requirements, 458
Massachusetts
   caregivers, 437
   conspiracy, 578-581
   decriminalization, scope of, 308-313, 320, 327
   distribution, commercial purpose, 318-320
   Humanitarian Medical Use of Marijuana Act, 613
   marijuana, definition of, 21
   Massachusetts Marijuana Legalization Initiative (Question 4), 125, 141
   personal supply, 308-312, 318-323, 415
   physicians
      recommendations by, 613-614
      requirements imposed on 613-615

quantity limits, 126
searches, 168-171
Mayer, Stephen, 331
McCaffrey, Barry, 235
Media campaigns, 233-235
Medical benefits. See Use of marijuana, benefits of
Medical marijuana laws
   affirmative defenses, 178-188
   benefits of marijuana use. See Use of marijuana, benefits of
   CBD laws, as compared to, 124
   caregivers. See Caregivers
   criminal history, limits on use by those with, 120-123
   diversion, 240
   forms of marijuana, restrictions on, 131-133
   harms of marijuana use. See Use of marijuana, harms of
   history of, 4, 100
   immunity, 179-188
   landlords. See Landlords
   limits imposed by, generally, 125-126
   medical purpose, 129-130
   minors, use by, 119-120
   necessity defense and, 189-194
   physician recommendations. See Physician recommendations
   physicians. See Physicians
   public housing, 727-733
   qualifying conditions. See Qualifying conditions
   qualifying patients. See Qualifying patients
   quantity limits, 126-128
   reciprocity, 119
   recommendation of physician. See Physician recommendations
   recreational marijuana states, continuing relevance in 125
   registration. See Registration
   residency, 119
   Rohrabacher-Farr Amendment, 353-358
   schools, use in. See Schools
   supply, approaches to, 413-414, 443, 507, 532. See also Commercial supply; Personal supply
   taxes, exemptions from, 490, 494
Mens rea. See Distribute, commercial purpose; Knowledge; Money laundering; Possession; Possession with intent to distribute (PWID); Strict liability
Mexico, 271
Michigan
   affirmative defense, 179-187
   aiding and abetting, 575
   ballot initiative, 293
   caregivers, 429, 437, 441, 442
   collective cultivation, 418

749

Michigan (cont'd)
  DUI laws, 149-150, 154
  forms of marijuana, restrictions on, 131-133
  immunity, 179-187
  local authority, 298-299, 558-560
  manufacture by users, 417
  medical purpose, 129-133
  Michigan Medical Marijuana Act (MMMA), 115-116, 118-119, 125-126, 149-154, 178-188, 417-418, 424-429
  minors, use by, 120
  personal supply, 417
  physician
    diagnosis, 116
    recommendation by, 114-115
    requirements imposed on, 616
  quantity limits, 125-126
  registration, 116, 118, 716-720
  residency requirements, 119
  return of marijuana, 705-706
  transfer between users, 424-429
Mikos, Robert A., 229-230, 236-239, 278-283, 400-403, 495-498, 518, 533-535, 545-546, 550-552, 561-568, 651-652, 654-655, 679-681, 688-689, 709, 720-721
Mill, John Stuart, 223, 226, 251
Minnesota
  caregivers, 437
  continuing medical education (CME) courses, 618
  physician recommendations, 616
  prisoners, use by, 120
  residency requirement, 119
Minors
  advertising and, 464-466, 511
  attitudes toward marijuana, 232-233
  bans on distribution to, 462-463
  medical marijuana, requirements for use by, 120
  use by, trends, 233
Mississippi
  distribution, 316-318
  entrapment, 343
  University of Mississippi, as exclusive supplier of marijuana for use in federally approved research studies, 201, 479
Missouri, 48, 51
Mistakes of fact, 48-51, 158
Mistakes of law, 51-54, 158, 343
Mixture or substance containing marijuana, 367-368
Model Guidelines for the Recommendation of Marijuana in Patient Care, 610

Model Penal Code
  aiding and abetting, 572, 576
  attempt, renunciation of, 338
Model Rules of Professional Conduct (MRPC)
  Rule 1.2
    amendments to, 15, 626-627
    permissive interpretation, 631-635
    restrictive interpretation, 627-631
  Rule 8.4, 635-636
Money laundering
  elements of, 587
    designed to conceal, 593-597
    knowledge, 589-593
    proceeds of unlawful activity, 597
  sanctions for, 597
  statutory provisions, 585-587
Montana
  advertising, 465
  caregivers, 437, 438, 440, 507-510
  commercial supply, 470-471
  landlords, 660
  physician recommendations, 625
  possession based on positive drug test, 64-65
  probationers, use by, 120-121
  qualifying conditions, 204
  registration, 115

Nabilone, 31. *See also* Synthetic cannabinoids
National Alliance for Model State Drug Laws, 625
National Cannabis Bar Association, 6
National Football League (NFL), 664-665
National Highway Safety Administration, 242
National Institute on Drug Abuse, 30, 274
National Youth Anti-Drug Media Campaign, 233-234
Nebraska
  drug tax, 396-397
  preemption suit challenging Colorado regulations, 535-545, 549, 568, 709-710
Necessity defense, 77-82, 189-194
Nevada
  attorneys, 630
  caregivers, 437
  DUI laws, 149-150
  personal supply, 415
New Hampshire
  caregivers, 437
  industrial hemp, 22-25
  landlords, 660
New Jersey
  caregivers, 437

commercial supply
  generally, 443-444
  inspections, 469
  licensing, 446, 449, 452-454
 labeling and packaging, 461
 qualifying conditions, 101
 schools, 141-142, 726
 state officials, immunity for enforcement of laws, 711
New Mexico
 caregivers, 437
 employment laws, 664
 manufacture
  defined, 304-305
  user, by, 416
 possession based on positive drug test, 65
 return of marijuana, 704
New York
 attorneys, 631-634, 638
 caregivers, 437
 commercial supply
  generally, 443-444, 455, 463
  licensing, 445-447, 449, 452-454
  vertical integration, 455
 Compassionate Care Act, 631-634
 forms of marijuana, restrictions on, 131, 462
 labeling and packaging, 461
 physicians
  discipline of, 616
  training regarding marijuana, 615-616
 pricing, restrictions on, 463
 public consumption, 134-139
 quantity limits, 126
 stop and frisk, efficacy of, 247
 testing, 458
NFL. See National Football League (NFL)
Nguyen, Holly, 229
Non-profit, defined, 453
North Carolina
 aiding and abetting, 572
 intent to distribute, proof of, 329-330
 knowledge, 68-69
 manufacture, 313
 possession
  generally, 68-69
  positive drug test and, 63-64
  punishment, 88-91
North Dakota
 attorneys, use by, 636
 caregivers, 437

Obama, Barack, 343
Odor of marijuana. See Smell of marijuana
Office of National Drug Control Policy (ONDCP), 97-98, 233-234
Oglesby, Pat, 494

Ohio
 attorneys, 627-630, 636
 closed-loop payment processing system, 695
 local authority, 297
Oklahoma
 preemption suit challenging Colorado regulations, 535-545, 549, 568, 709-710
Oregon
 attorneys, 630
 caregivers, 437
 DUI laws, 144
 employment law, 663-664, 672-678
 manufacture by user, 416, 511
 necessity defense, 189
 physician recommendations, 116, 615, 625
 quantity limits, 126-127
 residency requirements, 287-288
 return of marijuana, 704-705, 711
 searches, 166, 170
Original jurisdiction, 549

Packaging requirements. See Labeling and packaging
Pacula, Rosalie, 240
Pain. See Chronic pain, as qualifying condition; Qualifying conditions
Paraphernalia. See Drug paraphernalia
Patents, 406-407
Pathways Report (Blue Ribbon Commission on Marijuana Policy), 504-505, 507, 513-514
PDMPs. See Prescription Drug Monitoring Programs (PDMPs)
Penalties. See Sanctions
Pennsylvania
 caregivers, 437
 DUI laws, 144
 employment law, 663
 licensing, 454
Personal cultivation. See Personal supply
Personal supply. See also Commercial supply; Government supply
 in legalization regimes
  caregivers, assistance with, 429-442, 507-512
  collective cultivation, 418-424
  distribution between users, 424-429
  manufacture by users, 413-417, 481, 511
  use, effect on, 511
 in prohibition regimes
  distribution between users, 320-322
  manufacture by users, 308-312
Physician authorization. See Physician recommendations

751

Physician certification. *See* Physician recommendations
Physician recommendations
   DEA registration and, 602-607
   First Amendment protections for, 602-610
   prescriptions, as compared to, 8-9, 607-608
   requirements for making, 110-116, 610-616
   statistics concerning who recommends, 616-626
Physicians, 601-626
   attitudes toward marijuana, 617
   discipline of, 624-626
   recommendation to use marijuana. *See* Physician recommendations
   right to refuse to recommend, 618
   training of, 615-616
Physicians Desk Reference Manual (PDR), 617
Possession
   arrests for, statistics, 246-247
   as proxy for use, 36-37
   defenses
      fleeting possession, 62-63
      innocent possession, 83-84
      necessity, 77-82
      unwitting possession, 84-87
   elements of, 35-36
      control. *See* Control
      knowledge. *See* Knowledge
      marijuana. *See* Marijuana
   positive drug test, and, 63-65
   quantity required for conviction, 47, 76
   sanctions for. *See* Sentencing
   strict liability for, 37, 46, 84
Possession with intent to distribute (PWID). *See also* Distribute; Possession
   elements of, 327
   proof of intent, 327-335
   simple possession as lesser-included offense, 330
Post-traumatic stress disorder (PTSD), research on treatment for, 209
Preemption, by federal law. *See also* Authority, state government
   Amendment 64, suits challenging, 535-550
   anti-commandeering rule, and. *See* Anti-commandeering doctrine
   cause of action, 549
   confidentiality provisions, 716-720
   contract law, 651-652
   employment laws, 672-681
   generally, 533-535
   landlord-tenant laws, 661
   return of marijuana, 709
Preemption, by state law. *See also* Authority, local government
   bans on supply, 553-560
   decriminalization. *See* Decriminalization
   generally, 550-553
   increased penalties, 295-297
   lowest law enforcement priority. *See* Lowest law enforcement priority
Prescription Drug Monitoring Programs (PDMPs), 625
Price of marijuana. *See also* Use of Marijuana
   law's impact on, 484-488
   price elasticity of demand, 230-231
Primary caregivers. *See* Caregivers
Probable cause. *See* Searches
Processing. *See* Commercial Supply; Manufacture
Product-liability suits, 500
Production. *See* Manufacture
Professional athletes, rules governing, 664-665
Professionals
   attorneys. *See* Attorneys
   physicians. *See* Physicians
Prohibition laws
   aiding and abetting. *See* Aiding and abetting
   civil RICO. *See* Civil RICO
   conspiracy. *See* Conspiracy
   cultivation. *See* Manufacture
   distribution. *See* Distribute
   driving under the influence. *See* Driving under the influence
   fiscal impact of, 245-246, 518-520
   forfeiture. *See* Forfeiture
   manufacture. *See* Manufacture
   money laundering. *See* Money laundering
   possession. *See* Possession
   prices, impact on, 486-489
   racial disparities in enforcement of, 248-249
   sentencing under. *See* Sanctions
   taxes, 396-400
   trademarks. *See* Trademarks
PTSD. *See* Post-traumatic stress disorder (PTSD)
Public authority defense, 697-710. *See also* State officials
Public housing
   accommodation of medical marijuana in, 727-733
   denying admission to tenant for using marijuana, 731, 733
   evicting tenant for using marijuana, 731-733
   lease terms in federally funded housing, 727, 733

Public use, 35, 133-134, 140-141, 249-250
PWID. *See* Possession with intent to distribute (PWID)

Qualified immunity
  local governments and, 715
  police officers and government officials, 711
Qualifying conditions
  approaches to defining, 101-110
  diagnosis and, 101, 610-614
  exhaustion requirement, 105
  survey of, 204
Qualifying patients, 100-123
Quantity
  hashish and hash oil, 371
  knowledge of, 372-373
  limits imposed on possession of, 126-128
  measuring, 367-373
  plants, 268-271
  sentencing, impact on, 367-371
  "small amount", defined, 321-322
  THC and, 367
  usable quantity, defined, 47, 76

Racial disparities in
  legalization regimes, 520-525
  prohibition regimes, 248-249
Racketeer Influenced and Corrupt Organizations Act (RICO)
  civil cause of action, 400-406
  damages, 400-406
  standing, 405-406
Radio-frequency identification (RFID), 466-467
Rational basis test, 270, 510
Reasonable accommodation. *See* Employers; Landlords; Public housing
Reciprocity, medical marijuana states, 119
Recommendation of physician. *See* Physician recommendations
Recreational benefits. See Use of marijuana, benefits of
Recreational marijuana laws
  age requirements, 124-125
  college campuses, use on, 142
  fiscal impact of, 245-247, 518-520
  history of, 4, 100
  public use. *See* Public use
  quantity limits, 127
  racial disparities and, 520-525
  searches, 162-166
  supply, approaches to, 413-414, 443, 480, 507, 532. *See also* Commercial supply; Government supply; Personal supply
  taxes. *See* Taxes
Reefer madness, 219

Registration
  confidentiality of registries, 716-721
  effect on diversion, 239-240
  requirements in medical marijuana states, 116-118
  sample registry card, 117
Renunciation of attempt, 337-338
Re-scheduling. *See* Scheduling
Research on marijuana. *See also* Use of marijuana, benefits of; Use of marijuana, harms of
  barriers to, 200-202
  higher education institutions, 201, 479, 723
  industrial hemp, 25
Residency requirements, 119, 283-288, 451-452
Restatement of Law of Charitable Nonprofit Organizations (draft), 453
Returning marijuana, state official criminal liability for, 704-710
Reuter, Peter, 227, 229
RFID. *See* Radio-frequency identification (RFID)
Rhode Island
  caregivers, 437
  felony drug offenders, use by, 121
  intent to distribute, 331
  registration, 117
Rohrabacher-Farr Amendment, 353-358
Rosen, Mark D., 289, 290
Roth, Andrea, 242, 243-245

Sabet, Kevin, 520
Sale of marijuana. *See* Commercial supply; Distribute
Sanctions
  actual vs. authorized, 97-98, 378-379
  civil
    civil RICO, liability under, 400-406
    employment, loss of, 92
    forfeiture of assets, 92-96, 379-381
    licensing sanctions, 475-478
    public benefits, loss of, 92
    public housing, termination of lease, 92, 727-733
    student aid, denial of, 92, 98
    taxes, 396-400
    trademarks, 406-410
  criminal
    money laundering, 597
    possession offenses, 87-92
    supply offenses
      aggravated circumstances, 375-378
      distribution of small quantity for no remuneration, 321-323
      mandatory minimum sentences, 366, 702

753

Sanctions (cont'd)
   quantity, 367-373
   summary, 365
  decriminalization, sanctions under, 96-97
  expected legal sanctions, 227, 229
SARs. *See* Suspicious activity reports (SARs)
Scheduling under CSA. *See also* Authority, federal government; Department of Health and Human Services (HHS); Drug Enforcement Administration
  authority, 272-274
  criteria, 196-202, 214, 275
  decisions, 214-218, 222, 251, 274-275
Scheuer, Luke, 652-654
Schools, 723-727
  high school seniors' attitudes toward marijuana, 233, 236
  higher education. *See* Colleges and universities
  primary schools (K-12), use of medical marijuana in, 725-727
  zoning of commercial supply, 657-658
Searches
  probable cause, background, 161-162
  probable cause in
   decriminalization states, 166-172
   medical marijuana states, 172-178
   prohibition states, 161
   recreational marijuana states, 162-166
Section 1983. *See* Civil rights violations, cause of action for
Seized property, return of, 704-710
Self-incrimination, privilege against, 722
Sentencing. *See* Sanctions
Sentencing Guidelines. *See* United States Sentencing Guidelines (USSG)
Serious medical condition. *See* Qualifying condition
Simple possession. *See* Possession
Single Convention on Narcotic Drugs, 274
Sinsemilla, 18
Smart Approaches to Marijuana, 520
Smell of marijuana
  estimating quantity based on, 171
  probable cause and, 171-172
Smuggling, 563-566, 568
Social norms, shifts in, 236, 238
South Carolina, 295-297
South Dakota
  aiding and abetting, 572
  liability of state officials enforcing drug laws, 698
  marijuana, definition of, 27, 66, 290
Speech, protection of. *See* First Amendment

State officials
  civil liability for deprivation of rights, 710-715
  criminal liability under CSA
   generally, 545
   immunity from, 698-710
   for manufacturing and selling marijuana, 698-704
   for returning marijuana, 704-710
  federal demands for information collected by, 716-722
State-operated liquor stores, 698-699. *See also* Government supply
Statute of limitations, federal crimes, 598
Stevens, Ronald, 37
Strict liability, 37, 46, 84, 85-87
Strict scrutiny, 270, 510
Subpoenas, 716-720
Supremacy Clause, 229-230, 235, 236-238, 260, 278-283, 535-544, 546-547, 679-680, 709. *See also* Authority, federal government
Suspicious activity reports (SARs), 694
*Swiderski* defense, 323-327, 424. *See also* Joint possession
Synthetic cannabinoids. *See also* Cannabinoids; Cannabidiol; Cannabis; Marijuana; THC
  K2/Spice, 29
  medical use, approval for, 31, 202
   dronabinol (Marinol), 202
   nabilone (Cesamet), 202
Synthetic D9-THC, 30-31
Synthetic Drug Abuse Prevention Act of 2012 (Synthetic Act), 31
Synthetic marijuana. *See* Synthetic cannabinoids

Take Care Clause, 528-531
Taxes
  evasion of, 495-498
  exemptions for
   medical marijuana, 494
   personal cultivation, 417
  legalization regimes, in
   tax base, 489-495
   tax rates, survey of, 490-491
   tax revenue, 518-520
  prohibition regimes, in
   deductions (Section 280E), 397-399
   drug tax stamps, 396-397
   duty to pay taxes on income from crime, 396-397
   Marihuana Tax Act of 1937, 396
  purposes behind, 489
Tenants. *See* Landlords
Tennessee, 160

Testing, 456-458
Tetrahydrocannabinol (THC). *See* THC
Texas, 76
THC. *See also* Cannabinoids; Cannabidiol; Cannabis; Marijuana; Synthetic cannabinoids
  as controlled substance, 26
  benefits of. *See* Use of marijuana, benefits of
  definition of marijuana, relevance to, 21-27
  driving under influence, 150-154, 242, 244. *See also* Driving under influence
  generally, 17-18, 21
  harms of, 218. *See also* Use of marijuana, harms of
  potency trends, 218
  sentencing, role in, 367
Tobacco, exemption from CSA, 213, 272
Tourette's Syndrome, research on use for, 209
Tourism, 284-287, 464-465, 503, 566-568
Trademark Trial and Appeal Board (TTAB), 407-411
Trademarks
  defined, 406-407
  effect on industry concentration, 411-412
  federal registration
    denial of, 407-412
    requirements for
      distinctiveness, 407
      use in commerce, 407-409
  state trademark protection, 411
Traffic accidents, 241. *See also* Driving under influence
Trafficking. *See* Commercial supply; Distribute; Manufacture; Possession with intent to distribute
Transaction costs, influence on use, 231-232
Transfer. *See* Distribute
Transferred intent, 335
Travel rights, 283-290
Treaty obligations, 274-275
TTAB. *See* Trademark Trial and Appeal Board (TTAB)

Uniform Controlled Substances Act, 37
United States Patent and Trademark Office (USPTO), 407, 411
United States Sentencing Commission, 378
United States Sentencing Guidelines (USSG)
  conspiracy, sentencing for, 583
  generally, 364-366
  quantity, measurement of, 367-369, 371-372
  safety valve provision, 702
Universal symbol for marijuana, 459, 461
Universities. *See* Colleges and universities
Unwitting possession defense, 84-87
Usable marijuana, 47, 76, 370

Use of marijuana
  benefits of
    medical benefits. *See also* Qualifying conditions
      DEA's position on, 196-203, 209
      reviews of studies, 206-209
      states' positions on, 203-209
    recreational benefits, 210-213
  demand curves, 227-229, 485-486
  harms of
    comparative safety, 222
    crime, relationship to, 219
    driving harms, 241-245. *See also* Driving under the influence
    gateway hypothesis, 219-221
    generally, 213-222
    potency and, 218
    reviews of studies, 206
    role in policymaking, 222-226
  influences on
    advertising, 501-507
    attitudes toward marijuana, 232-236
    legal sanctions, 227-230, 484-488
    media campaigns, 233-235
    price of marijuana, 230-231, 484-488
    registration, 239-240
    taxes, 489-499
    transaction costs, 231-232
  methods of
    inhalation, 18-20
    oral. *See* Edibles
    sublingual, 19
    topical, 20
  public, 35, 133-134, 140-141. *See also* Public use
  statistics on, 214-215, 233
USPTO. *See* United States Patent and Trademark Office (USPTO)
USSG. *See* United States Sentencing Guidelines (USSG)
Utah
  hash oil, manufacture of, 305-306
  synthetic cannabinoids, 30

Vaporizers, 48, 75, 410-411, 660
Vermont, 143, 417, 437, 491, 515
Veterans Health Administration (VHA), 609-610
VHA. *See* Veterans Health Administration (VHA)
Virginia
  aiding and abetting, 572
  attempted distribution, 335-337
  distribution of small amount without remuneration, 322-323
  presumption of knowledge, 47

Vitiello, Michael, 291-293, 294
Void and unenforceable agreements. *See* Contract law

Wald, Eli, et al., 639-644
Warrantless inspections, 469-470
Washington
  aiding and abetting, 572-575
  Cannabis Patient Protection Act, 514
  caregivers, 111-113, 437-439
  collective cultivation, 422-424
  exhaustion requirement, 105
  knowledge, 37
  necessity defense, 189-193
  physician recommendations, 111-114, 618
  probationers, use by, 120
  qualifying conditions, 101-105, 172, 204
  quantity limits, 127
  searches, 172-177
  supply by
    commercial firms
      consolidation of recreational and medical markets, 514-515
      discipline, 475, 477-478
      enforcement actions, 478
      generally, 444, 455, 456
      licensing, 447, 449-451, 456
      vertical integration, 455
    local government, 479, 515
    users
      cultivation by, 415
      transfer between, 424-425
  taxes, 490-491
  unwitting possession, 85-87
Washington, D.C. *See* District of Columbia
Weight of marijuana. *See* Quantity, measuring
West Virginia, 312, 322, 698
Whitebread, Charles, 37
Workplace drug testing. *See* Drug testing; Employers
Wyoming, 54-57, 335